Advances in
Meat
Research

Meat and Poultry
Microbiology

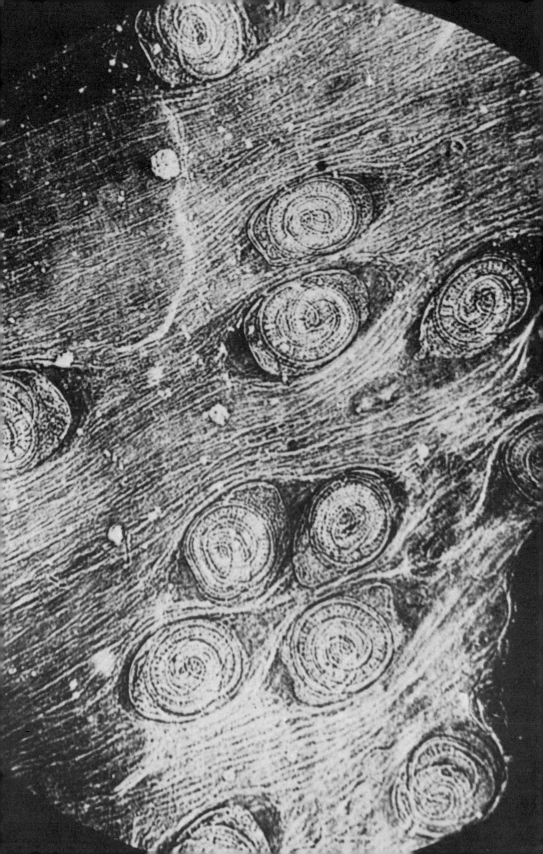

Advances in Meat Research

Meat and Poultry Microbiology

Edited by

A. M. Pearson
T. R. Dutson

Department of Food Science and
Human Nutrition
Michigan State University
East Lansing, Michigan

MACMILLAN
PUBLISHERS

Published in the United Kingdom by
MACMILLAN PUBLISHERS LTD
(Journals Division) 1986
Distributed by Globe Book Services Ltd
Brunel Road, Houndmills
Basingstoke, Hants RG21 2XS, England

British Library Cataloguing in Publication Data
Pearson, A.M.
    Advances in meat research : meat and
    poultry microbiology-
    1. Meat—Microbiology
    I. Title   II. Dutson, T. R.
    664'.9'001576   QR117

    ISBN 0-333-42887-0

Printed in the United States of America

Contents

Contributors

J. N. BACUS. (123)[1] MicroSure, Inc., 1925 Lone Star Drive, Dallas, Texas 75212

FRANK L. BRYAN.[2] (241) Department of Health and Human Services, Centers for Disease Control, Atlanta, Georgia 30333

F. F. BUSTA.[3] (165) Department of Food Science and Nutrition, University of Minnesota, 1334 Eckles Avenue, St. Paul, Minnesota 55108

DEAN O. CLIVER. (379) Food Research Institute, World Health Organization Collaborating Centre of Food Virology, and Department of Bacteriology, University of Wisconsin—Madison, Madison, Wisconsin 53706

J. P. DUBEY. (311) Animal Parasitology Institute, ARS, USDA, Beltsville, Maryland 20705

JAMES B. EVANS. (231) Department of Microbiology, North Carolina State University, Raleigh, North Carolina 27695

R. FAYER. (311) Animal Parasitology Institute, ARS, USDA, Beltsville, Maryland 20705

PEGGY M. FOEGEDING. (165) Department of Food Science, North Carolina State University, 339 Schaub Hall, Box 7624, Raleigh, North Carolina 27695-7624

---

[1]Numeral in parentheses indicates the page on which the author's contribution begins.
[2]*Present address*: Food Safety Consultation and Training, 2022 LaVista Circle, Tucker, GA 30084.
[3]*Present address*: Food Science & Human Nutrition Department, University of Florida, 359 Food Science Building, Gainesville, FL 32611.

DAMIEN A. GABIS. (209) Silliker Laboratories, Inc., 1304 Halsted Street, Chicago Heights, Illinois 60411

C. O. GILL. (49) Meat Industry Research Institute of New Zealand (Inc.), P.O. Box 617, Hamilton, New Zealand

F. H. GRAU. (1) CSIRO Division of Food Research, Meat Research Laboratory, P.O. Box 12, Cannon Hill, Queensland, Australia

A. A. KRAFT. (191) Department of Food Technology, Iowa State University, Ames, Iowa 50011

K. D. MURRELL. (311) Animal Parasitology Institute, ARS, USDA, Beltsville, Maryland 20705

C. F. NIVEN, Jr. (397) 2100 Belford Drive, Walnut Creek, California 94598

JAMES J. PESTKA. (277) Department of Food Science & Human Nutrition, Michigan State University, East Lansing, Michigan 48824

JOHN H. SILLIKER. (209) Silliker Laboratories of California, Inc., 1139 E. Dominguez, Suite I, Carson, California 90746

R. B. TOMPKIN. (89) Beatrice Companies, Inc., 1919 Swift Drive, Oak Brook, Illinois 60521

Preface

Fresh meat and poultry not only provide ideal media for the growth of spoilage microorganisms but they are frequently involved in foodborne illnesses. The role of meat and poultry products in the transmission of pathogenic microorganisms to human beings has been better elucidated in recent years, leading to improved methods for controlling their growth on these important foods. Consequently, the present volume is devoted to providing the most up-to-date information on the microbiology of these products to researchers in universities, governmental agencies, and industry in order to minimize both meat spoilage and the illnesses transmitted to human beings.

Topics covered include the whole gamut of microorganisms found on meat and poultry products, with emphasis on their sources and methods for controlling their growth. In view of the importance of certain groups of microorganisms, they have received special emphasis, i.e., sporeforming bacteria, salmonellae, psychrotrophs, and staphylococci. Chapters are also devoted to parasitic organisms, miscellaneous pathogenic bacteria, fungi and mycotoxins, and to viruses in meat and poultry products.

Two other important topics discussed are the microbiology of ready-to-eat and fermented meat and poultry products. These two chapters not only cover the best method of controlling growth of microorganisms in processed products, but in the latter case demonstrate how certain species of microorganisms can be utilized to produce special products that are relatively shelf stable. The use of desirable microorganisms as an aid to preservation is an interesting and virtually untouched area

for future research. This brings us to the last chapter, which emphasizes perspectives for future research that can be useful in improving
the shelf life and in preventing meat and poultry food-borne illnesses.

A. M. Pearson
T. R. Dutson

1

Microbial Ecology of Meat and Poultry

F.H. Grau[1]*F.H. Grau*[1]

INTRODUCTION

Meat animals may be regarded as a source of edible tissue sandwiched between two regions that are heavily contaminated with microorganisms. These two regions are the external layer of skin, hair, wool or feathers and the internal intestinal tract and its contents. The first aim of the abattoir is to harvest the edible tissue (meat) from between these highly contaminated layers with as little contamination as possible. Second, care is needed to ensure that contamination of dressed carcasses and edible offals from sources within the abattoir itself is kept to a minimum. Subsequent procedures for the handling of meat through chilling, freezing, cooking, packaging, and distribution to the consumer are aimed at reducing or preventing increases in the microbial content that may occur either by growth or by further contamination. The only time that the growth of particular organisms is encouraged is when it is desired to manufacture a fermented product (e.g., salami).

The relative importance of the wide variety of microorganisms that may contaminate meat during its production is dependent on the type of microorganism and the subsequent treatment of the meat.

[1]CSIRO Division of Food Research, Meat Research Laboratory, P.O. Box 12, Cannon Hill, Queensland, Australia.
[1]CSIRO Division of Food Research, Meat Research Laboratory, P.O. Box 12, Cannon Hill, Queensland, Australia.

Advances in Meat Research, Volume 2
Copyright 1986 by AVI Publishing Co.
All rights of reproduction in any form reserved
ISBN 0-87055-498-0

GENERAL BACKGROUND

Classification of Microorganisms

Viruses are noncellular entities composed of nucleic acid, either deoxyribonucleic or ribonucleic, wrapped in a protein coat. They are obligate parasites having to grow within an appropriate host cell (Chapter 12). Viruses are not considered further here.

Bacteria are typically unicellular, lack a nuclear membrane, reproduce predominantly by binary fission, and are spherical, rodlike or spiral in shape. Gram-positive bacteria have a single-layered thick cell wall. They retain crystal violet during the gram stain reaction and appear deep purple-violet in color when examined after this procedure. Gram-negative bacteria have a triple-layered thinner cell wall, lose crystal violet during the gram stain reaction, and when conterstained with safranine appear red. Molds and yeasts have a nuclear membrane and internally are structurally more complex than are bacteria. Molds are generally filamentous and yeasts generally unicellular. Of these three categories of microorganisms, bacteria have received the most attention as contaminants of meat.

Microorganisms can also be classified or grouped, by their temperature and water requirements for growth, and by their metabolic response to oxygen.

Temperature Requirements

Psychrotrophic microorganisms are able to grow at normal refrigeration temperatures (Eddy 1960). Psychrotrophic pseudomonads are able to grow down to $-3°C$ (Barnes 1976), and some psychrotrophic molds down to about $-5°$ to $-7°C$ (Barnes 1976; Gill and Lowry 1982). The temperature for optimum growth of psychrotrophs is at or above 20°C, but many psychrotrophs will not grow at 35°–37°C. Psychrophiles are also able to grow at refrigeration temperatures but have an optimum temperature for growth at 15°C or less and a maximum temperature for growth at about 20°C (Morita 1975). The microorganisms that grow on chilled meat appear to be psychrotrophs and not psychrophiles. Mesophilic microorganisms are not able to sustain growth below about 5°–7°C and grow optimally at 30°–40°C. Thermophiles have even higher minimum and optimum temperatures for growth, often failing to grow below about 35°–40°C and being able to grow up to 80°C and above. Facultative thermophiles, or thermotrophs, have minimum and optimum growth temperatures that fall between those for mesophiles and thermophiles (Mossel 1977). The distinction between these groups is not sharp since there is a gradual merging of the minimum, optimum, and maximum temperatures for growth of different microorganisms.

Water Requirements

Microorganisms cannot grow without water. The water requirements for microbial growth are best specified in terms of water activity (Scott, 1957, 1962). Water activity (a_w) is the chemical potential of the water in a food or solution relative to that of pure water at the same temperature and pressure. The a_w of a food is thus equal to p/p_0, where p and p_0 are the water vapor pressures of the food and of pure water, respectively, at the same temperature. Thus pure water has an a_w of 1.00. Freezing point, boiling point, equilibrium relative humidity, osmotic pressure and a_w are all related to the colligative properties of the number of molecules and ions in solution.

As aqueous solutions are cooled below 0°C, pure ice will form at the freezing point and the solutes remain in the liquid phase. The ice and the liquid phase are in equilibrium and both have the same vapor pressure. The vapor pressure of the ice depends only on the temperature of the ice. The ratio vapor pressure of pure ice at the freezing point to that of pure water at the same temperature is the a_w. Lean beef has an a_w of 0.993 and will begin to freeze at about −0.8°C. As the temperature of frozen meat decreases the remaining unfrozen solution will have a lower a_w.Thus, at −5°C the unfrozen liquid in meat will have an a_w of 0.953 (vapor pressure of ice at −5° ÷ vapor pressure of water at −5°C). For an organism to be able to grow on frozen meat at −5°C, the organism will have to be able to grow not only at −5°C but also at an a_w of 0.953. Similarly, at −10°C, the organism would need to be able to grow at an a_w of 0.907 (Scott 1962). Such a combination of temperature and water activity must be sufficient to prevent microbial growth since microbial growth does not occur in frozen foods below about −10°C.

The most rapid growth of many microorganisms, including pathogenic bacteria, is at an a_w in the range 0.995–0.980. The approximate minimum values of a_w allowing growth of some microorganisms when other growth conditions are at or near the optimum are given in Table 1.1. A more detailed list is given by Troller and Christian (1978). Halophilic bacteria require sodium ions and often need substantial amounts of sodium chloride for growth. The optimum sodium chloride concentrations for the growth of some halophiles corresponds to an a_w of 0.80 to 0.85 (Scott 1962; Christian 1980). Halophilic bacteria are common in the cover brine used in the manufacture of Wiltshire-style bacon (Gardiner 1982) and halophilic *Vibrio* spp. can cause spoilage of bacon (Gardiner 1980–1981). The term osmophilic is usually applied to yeasts that are able to grow in high concentrations of sugars. Pitt (1975) defined xerophilic fungi as those yeasts and molds able to grow at a_w values below 0.85, thus including osmophilic yeasts in his definition.

As the water activity of meat decreases, either by drying (e.g., during chilling of carcasses and the production of fermented sausages) or by the

TABLE 1.1. Approximate Minimal a_w for Growth of Some Microorganisms Found on Meats

Organism	a_w	Reference
Bacteria		
Pseudomonas fluorescens	0.97	Wodzinski and Frazier (1960)
Enterobacter aerogenes	0.95	Wodzinski and Frazier (1961A)
Escherichia coli	0.95	Burcik (1950)
Salmonella spp.	0.95	Christian and Scott (1953)
Lactobacillus brevis	0.95	Lanigan (1963)
Clostridium perfringens	0.95	Troller and Christian (1978)
Clostridium botulinum A	0.95	Troller and Christian (1978)
Clostridium botulinum B	0.94	Troller and Christian (1978)
Brochothrix thermosphacta	0.94	Brownlie (1966)
Lactobacillus viridescens	0.94	Wodzinski and Frazier (1961B)
Pediococcus cerevisiae	0.94	Lanigan (1963)
Lactobacillus plantarum	0.93	Lanigan (1963)
Micrococci	0.75–0.94	Christian and Waltho (1962)
Staphylococcus aureus	0.86	Scott (1953)
Vibrio costicolus	0.86	Troller and Christian (1978)
Yeasts		
Trichosporon pullulans	0.89	Scott (1957)
Candida spp.	0.88–0.90	Bem and Leistner (1970)
Debaryomyces spp.	0.87	Bem and Leistner (1970)
Molds		
Mucor sp.	0.93	Leistner and Rödel (1975)
Rhizopus sp.	0.93	Leistner and Rödel (1975)
Cladosporium cladosporoides	0.86–0.92	Gill and Lowry (1982)
Penicillium spp.	0.79–0.83	Pitt (1975)

addition of salt, the growth of gram-negative nonhalophilic bacteria is repressed first. Gram-positive lactic acid bacteria and micrococci then tend to be the principle flora capable of fastest growth. For example, the addition of 2 to 3% sodium chloride to fresh meat (a_w, 0.98–0.975) is sufficient to reduce the growth rate of pseudomonads but still allow rapid growth of lactobacilli. Under conditions of even lower a_w, for example, below about 0.93, micrococci, yeasts, and molds tend to dominate the flora (e.g., on the surface of dried sausages).

Oxygen Requirements

Aerobic microorganisms (e.g., pseudomonads) couple the oxidation of a substrate to the reduction of oxygen by means of a respiratory chain containing cytochromes. The flow of electrons through the respiratory chain to oxygen results in the formation of adenosine triphosphate (ATP) from adenosine diphosphate (ADP) and phosphate. ATP provides energy for growth and metabolic processes. Some aerobic organisms are also able to synthesize a modified respiratory chain that is able to use nitrate (or nitrite) instead of oxygen as the terminal electron acceptor. Micro-aerophilic organisms are aerobes which grow best at oxygen concentrations less than that found in air [e.g., *Campylobacter jejuni (coli)*]. The concentration of oxygen in air may be bacteriostatic or bacteriocidal for such organisms.

Obligately anaerobic organisms are not able to synthesize the components of an oxygen (or nitrate)-linked respiratory chain. Such organisms obtain energy for growth by fermentation in which a variety of organic compounds, carbon dioxide, hydrogen, and sulfur compounds are involved in oxidation-reduction reactions. The yield of ATP, and therefore of cells, per mole of substrate metabolized is less than that obtained by aerobes. Many anaerobes cannot tolerate oxygen and are killed by exposure to air. Such strict anaerobes lack both catalase and superoxide dismutase activity needed to metabolize potentially lethal hydrogen peroxide and the superoxide radical O_2^- formed by the oxidation of electron carriers such as reduced flavins, quinones, and iron-sulfur proteins by oxygen. The mere absence of oxygen is often not sufficient to ensure growth of many strict anaerobes. A low redox potential is also needed (e.g., for *Bacteroides* spp.).

Facultative anaerobes (e.g., Enterobacteriaceae) are able to grow aerobically using a respiratory chain coupled to oxygen, and anaerobically using fermentation reactions for the generation of energy.

Importance of Microorganisms

Microorganisms on meat are important for three reasons: (1) some organisms may be pathogenic (able to produce disease in man); (2) some may cause spoilage of meat; and (3) some may be used as indicator organisms.

Food Poisoning. The principal pathogenic organisms of concern on meats are those able to cause food poisoning. Food poisoning is caused by two different mechanisms. In food-borne infections, the organisms are ingested with the food and grow in the intestinal tract causing diarrhea, vomiting, nausea and/or abdominal pain. Members of the genus *Salmonella, Yersinia entercolitica, Clostridium perfringens*, and *C. jejuni (coli)* all cause infective food poisoning. While growth of these organisms is usually necessary to produce sufficient viable cells to form an infective dose, it is unlikely that this applies to *C. jejuni* on meats. An infective dose of *C. jejuni* can be only a few hundred cells (Robinson 1981). Growth of *C. jejuni* requires a temperature between 32° and 45°C (Skirrow and Benjamin 1980; Doyle and Roman 1981), and an atmosphere higher in carbon dioxide and lower in oxygen than occurs in air, i.e., it is microaerophilic (Doyle 1981). In the second type of food poisoning, the microorganisms grow in the food and excrete a toxin which causes intoxication when the food is ingested (e.g., *Cl. botulinum, Staphylococcus aureus, Bacillus cereus*). The lower limit of temperature for growth of nonproteolytic type B and the aquatic type E *Cl. botulinum* is 3°–4°C. *Yersinia enterocolitica* is able to grow at refrigeration temperatures, and incubation temperatures of 4°C are used in its isolation. The other food-poisoning bacteria are either mesophilic or facultative thermophiles and do not grow below about 7°C.

Spoilage.   Spoilage of chilled, raw meats in air is caused mainly by the growth and metabolic activities of psychrotrophic aerobic organisms such as pseudomonads, moraxellas, and altermonads. When raw meats are vacuum-packaged, the principle microflora that develops during chilled storage consists of lactic acid bacteria together with a varying population of *Brocothrix thermosphacta,* psychrotrophic Enterobacteriaceae, *Aeromonas* spp. and *Altermonas* spp. The extent of the population of these latter groups of organisms on vacuum-packaged meat is dependent on the pH of the tissue, oxygen permeability of the packaging film, and temperature of storage. All of these organisms can play some role in the deterioration of vacuum-packed fresh meat.

On cooked cured meats, lactic acid bacteria, *Br. thermosphacta,* micrococci, yeasts, and molds can cause spoilage.

Indicator Organisms.   Frequently estimates of the numbers of aerobic mesophiles, Enterobacterieaceae, coliforms, fecal coliforms, and *Escherichia coli* are made on carcasses at slaughter. These counts can be regarded as counts of indicator organisms.

The number of mesophiles on carcasses is usually taken as an indicator of the degree of care taken in sanitation during slaughter and dressing (Johnston and Elliot 1976; Roberts *et al.* 1980) even though very few of the organisms will actually grow on meat. Because of differences in the processes of slaughtering and dressing of the animal species used for meat, the significance of the mesophilic count will not be the same for all meats. In the production of pig and poultry carcasses, the skin is not removed so that the number of organisms on the skin is a reflection of the destruction of organisms by scalding (and singeing) and of recontamination in the abattoir. On sheep and cattle carcasses, the number of mesophiles is a consequence of contamination of a surface which was sterile before removal of the skin or viscera. The number of mesophiles detected on carcasses will vary with the temperature of incubation used during their enumeration. Incubation temperatures of $35°–37°C$ give somewhat lower counts than are found at $20°–30°C$ (Barnes 1976; Ingram and Roberts 1976; Roberts *et al.* 1980), but the high temperatures have the advantage in that the estimate is obtained more quickly.

In general, procedures in slaughtering which reduce the mesophilic count on carcasses would be expected to reduce the count of psychrotrophs. For instance, scalding reduces the numbers of both mesophiles and psychrotrophs on poultry skin (Notermans *et al.* 1977). However, during later stages of poultry processing the count of mesophiles on the carcass appears to bear little relationship to the psychrotrophic count. In the stages after evisceration, when there may be no significant increase in mesophiles, considerable increases in psychrotrophs occur. While there was no significant difference in the mean count of mesophiles on carcasses produced at two abattoirs, the mean counts of psychrotrophs differed by more than 100-fold (Notermans *et al.* 1977).

The count of psychrotrophs also varies in relation to the count of meso- philes for carcasses of other animal species. For example, psychrotrophs have been found to range from 32% to less than 0.03% of the count of mesophiles (20°C) obtained from one site on sheep carcasses at one abat- toir over a 2-week period (F.H. Grau unpublished). Nevertheless, on aver- age there is a correlation between the counts of mesophiles and psy- chrotrophs for cattle and sheep carcasses. When pooled samples of five sites from each of 63 sheep carcasses were examined over a 3-month peri- od, the correlation coefficient between counts of meophiles and psy- chrotrophs was 0.50 (F.H. Grau unpublished). While this is not a high correlation, it is statistically significant. The ratio of psychrotrophs to mesophiles on beef carcasses is lower in summer and in warmer climates since this ratio shows a negative correlation with ambient temperature (Empey and Scott 1939). For instance, the mean count of psychrotrophs expressed as a percentage of the mean count of mesophiles on sheep car- casses is 2.7 to 10% in the United Kingdom (Roberts 1980; Roberts *et al.* 1980), 0.3 to 4.7% in New Zealand in spring-summer (Newton *et al.* 1978), and about 0.2% in Southeastern Queensland (Australia) in spring-summer (F. H. Grau, unpublished). The count of mesophiles can be a useful, al- though necessarily crude, indicator of psychrotrophic contamination on beef and sheep carcasses at the completion of slaughter and dressing. A better indicator of the keeping quality of meat which is to be stored under aerobic, chilled conditions is a direct count of psychrotrophs.

In general, the majority of aerobic mesophiles that contaminate car- casses do not originate from the intestinal tract but from the outer sur- faces of the animals and from equipment in the abattoir. There may be little significant change in the count of mesophiles as a result of eviscera- tion but contamination with organisms from the intestinal tract can occur (Grau 1979; Gerats *et al.* 1981). There appears to be no clear relationship between the count of mesophiles on carcasses and the numbers of Entero- bacteriaceae, coliforms or fecal streptococci (Roberts *et al.* 1980). Thus, the count of mesophiles does not appear to be a particularly good indicator of possible contamination of the carcass with organisms, including patho- gens, which may have arisen from the intestinal tract.

Counts of Enterobacteriaceae, coliforms, fecal coliforms, and *E. coli* have been used as indicators of contamination of carcasses with organisms associated with intestinal tract contents. The detection of such organisms on carcasses does not a priori indicate direct contamination from the intes- tinal tract during slaughter since these organisms, along with salmonel- lae, are frequently found on the outside surfaces of animals (Hess and Lott 1970; Smith and Grau 1973; Notermans *et al.* 1977; Grau 1979; McBride *et al.* 1980). Although there is usually not a very large difference between counts of Enterbacteriaceae, coliforms, and *E.coli* obtained from intestinal tract contents (Dickinson and Mocquot, 1961; Grau 1979), Enterobac- teriaceae on the outside surfaces of animals are often 100- to 1000-fold more numerous than *E.coli* (Notermans *et al.* 1977; Grau 1979). Both the

Enterobacteriaceae and coliform groups contain nonenteric organisms, and care is needed in interpreting their presence on carcasses as indicators of contamination with organisms derived from the intestinal tract. For instance, up to one-half the Enterobacteriaceae detected by Mead et al. (1982) on chicken carcasses after evisceration were psychrotrophic and appeared to be derived from processing equipment. On chilled meats, Enterobacteriaceae and coliforms are even less reliable as indicators because of growth of psychrotrophic members of these groups (Eddy and Kitchell 1959; Hechelmann et al. 1974; Cox et al. 1975; Patterson and Gibbs 1977, 1978A; Grau 1979; Mead et al. 1982).

The presence of *E. coli* on carcasses implies that other organisms of fecal origin, including salmonellae, *may* be present, not that they *will* be present. There is no absolute count of *E. coli* on carcasses that implies salmonella or other pathogen will be present. Obviously, many animals will have *E. coli* within their intestinal tract but no salmonellae. Salmonellae have been isolated from samples taken from carcasses in which the *E. coli* count ranged from 0.1 to 1800 per cm² (Grau, 1979) and the count of Enterobacteriaceae ranged from less than 20 to more than 1000 per cm² (Gerats et al. 1981). Nevertheless, with these reservations, *E. coli* (and Enterobacteriaceae) can be useful in the definition of the stages of slaughtering and dressing responsible for contamination, and the sites on carcasses most likely to be contaminated with salmonellae.

POULTRY

Development of the Microflora of the Live Bird

Freshly laid eggs rarely contain microorganisms, but salmonellae, from either the ovaries or oviduct, can occasionally infect the egg during its formation. However, the egg is more commonly infected through the egg shell after laying. Salmonellae from fecal material can contaminate the outside of the egg as it passes through the cloaca, and as the egg rests in the nesting material. Penetration of the shell by salmonellae, and other bacteria, occurs when the shell is wet and when a drop in temperature causes the air sac in the egg to contract and draw moisture and bacteria through the shell (Board 1969; Elliot and Hobbs 1980). Shell contamination is reduced by providing clean nesting material, by frequent collection of eggs, and by prompt fumigation of eggs (Bryan 1980).

The chick, on hatching from a noninfected egg, will be microbiologically sterile, but will immediately begin to acquire microflora from the outside of its own shell, other egg shells, and from fluff, fecal material, dust, and air in the hatchery. The chick will also ingest microorganisms when feeding and drinking.

Microflora of the Intestinal Tract. Within 1 day the intestinal tract of the chick contains a large population of fecal streptococci, Enterobacteriaceae, and clostridia (Lev and Briggs 1956A,B; Smith 1965; Mead and Adams 1975; Barnes *et al.* 1978). However, this is not a stable population. As the chick grows the microflora changes so that different parts of the intestine become populated by a microflora characteristic of that region.

Initially there are, in the contents of the crop, up to 10^7–10^8 fecal streptococci and coliforms per gram (Lev and Briggs 1956B; Smith 1965). Within 24 hours after the chick has access to feed, a developing population of lactobacilli is found both in the lumen and attached to the epithelium of the crop; by the time the bird is 3 days old, lactobacilli become the predominant flora (Smith 1965; Fuller 1973). The numbers of fecal streptococci and coliforms decline significantly and these organisms become only a minor component of the flora. The lactobacilli of the crop presumably play a role in regulating the type of microorganisms that flow through to the lower intestine. In poultry, since feed is held in the crop before it reaches the acidic environment of the gizzard, some mechanism is required to prevent excessive growth of undesirable microorganisms. The lactobacilli adhering to the wall of the crop provide a large inoculum to ensure that they are the predominant flora growing on the food in the crop, maintaining the contents at about pH 4. Removal of this resident flora of lactobacilli (e.g., by penicillin) allows coliforms to grow to large numbers (10^8 per gram) in the crop (Fuller 1973).

During the first day of the chick's life, the small intestine can harbor 10^8–10^9 coliforms and fecal streptococci per gram (Lev and Briggs 1956B; Smith 1965). However, after 2 days, the numbers of these organisms decrease and lactobacilli appear in increasing numbers. Within a week, lactobacilli are the most numerous of the flora in the small intestine being present at up to 10^7 per gram while there are only about 10^4 or less per gram of fecal streptococci and coliforms (Barnes *et al.* 1972, 1978). The flora of the small intestine is composed predominantly of facultative anaerobes. Strictly anaerobic organisms form, at most, 10–40% of the flora (Salanitro *et al.* 1978). Clostridia are present in only small numbers (Smith 1965; Barnes *et al.* 1972).

The initial flora of the cecum is also formed of large numbers (10^{10} per gram) of coliforms and fecal streptococci, followed by lactobacilli which grow in the cecum reaching 10^9–10^{10} per gram by about the fourth day (Mead and Adams 1975). The numbers of coliforms and fecal streptococci then decline. After the first 4 days, strictly anaerobic nonsporing bacteria become the predominant flora and remain dominant for the life of the bird. From about 1 week of age, the numbers of lactobacilli, fecal streptococci, and coliforms fluctuate from about 10^5 to 10^8 per gram, while the total count is about 10^{10}–10^{11} per gram (Salanitro *et al.* 1974A,B, 1978; Mead and Adams 1975; Barnes *et al.* 1978). Although clostridia may be present at up to 10^8 per gram, the numbers of *Cl. perfringens* are usually less than 10^5 per gram (Smith 1965; Barnes and Impey 1970; Barnes *et al.* 1972).

TABLE 1.2. Detection of *Campylobacter jejuni* (*coli*) from the Lower Intestinal Tract of Poultry

Country	Animal	No.	Positive (%)	Reference
Australia	Chicken	327	41	Shanker *et al.* (1982)
Canada	Chicken	210	24	Prescott and Bruin-Mosch (1981)
Canada	Duck	94	88	Prescott and Bruin-Mosch (1981)
Netherlands	Chicken	217	29	Goren and de Jong (1980)
Sweden	Chicken	150	16	Svedhem and Kaijser (1981)
U.K.	Chicken	34	91	Ribeiro (1978)
U.K.	Chicken	50	72	Simmonds and Gibbs (1979)
United States	Chicken	46	83	Grant *et al.* (1980)
United States	Turkey	600	100	Luechtefeld and Wang (1981)
United States	Turkey	50	46	Acuff *et al.* (1982)

Campylobacter jejuni(coli) are routinely found in the lower intestinal tract of poultry (Table 1.2) and frequently can be present at up to 10^7 per gram of feces (Grant *et al.* 1980).

Salmonellae in the Intestinal Tract. During the first 1–2 days of life, young chicks are very easily infected with salmonellae, and as a result can shed more than 10^8 salmonellae per gram of feces. Thereafter, resistance to salmonella infection increases with age (Bierer 1960; Sadler *et al.* 1969). As they become older, even infected chickens excrete fewer salmonella cells, and fewer chickens shed detectable salmonellae. However, some antibiotics permitted as feed additives (e.g., nitrovin) can increase and extend the carrier rate (Smith and Tucker 1975). Furthermore, salmonellae can be found in cecal contents when there appears to be no fecal excretion of salmonellae (Brownell *et al.* 1969; Fanelli *et al.* 1971; Lafont *et al.* 1983).

It has long been considered that the growth of pathogens is inhibited by the normal intestinal flora, and that this explains the acquisition of resistance to pathogens with increasing age. Bergeim (1940) considered that the concentration of undissociated volatile fatty acids is important in affecting growth of *E.coli* in the lower intestine. Later the susceptibility of mice to salmonella infection was shown to be increased (infective dose reduced from 10^6 to about 10^1 salmonella cells) by a single dose of streptomycin which destroyed most of the obligately anaerobic bacteria in the lower intestine (Bohnhoff *et al.* 1954; Meynell 1955; Bohnhoff and Miller 1962; Miller and Bohnhoff 1963). Elimination of the normal anaerobic flora causes the redox potential and the pH of cecal and colonic contents to rise and the concentration of volatile fatty acids to fall (Meynell 1963; Bohnhoff *et al.* 1964B). Under such conditions salmonellae grow faster both *in vivo* (Meynell and Subbaiah 1963) and *in vitro* (Meynell 1963). On the other hand, the concentration of volatile fatty acids (40–80 mM) found in the contents of the lower intestinal tract of normal mice is sufficient to prevent, or severely inhibit, the anaerobic growth of salmonellae if the pH is 6.0 or lower (Bohnhoff *et al.* 1964A). Mice, which have been made susceptible to salmonellae by treatment with streptomycin, can have their resistance to salmonella infection increased by a protective dose of intestinal microorganisms provided the protective dose is given prior (6–48 hr) to the challenge. Suspensions of fecal material from normal mice, anaerobic enrichments of fecal material or of cecal contents (best), or cultures of *Bacteroides* spp. provide protection (Miller and Bohnhoff 1963; Bohnhoff *et al.* 1964A). However, these treatments do not completely restore the level of resistance to that found in mice not previously treated with streptomycin.

In 1- to 2-day-old chicks, salmonellae can grow to 10^6 per gram in the crop and 10^8 per gram in cecal contents. However, if a mixture of intestinal and crop contents of normal adult birds are given per os 1 day before the salmonellae, the chicks are protected from infection, and salmonella growth in the crop and cecum is severely repressed (Nurmi and Rantala 1973). Even though the use of intestinal tract material from adults gives considerable protection, it is not absolute. Inoculation of germ-free chicks with 100 salmonella cells per bird results in salmonellae being shed at 10^9–10^{10} per gram of feces for at least 3 weeks (Lafont *et al.* 1983). While most chicks receiving intestinal flora before the salmonella challenge do not shed salmonellae in the feces, a few birds can shed up to 10^7 per gram of feces for short times. Furthermore, salmonellae can be present at about 10^5 per gram in cecal contents even though salmonellae do not appear in the feces. In addition, in chicks from which no salmonellae can be detected in the feces, the establishment of subclinical coccidiosis can lead to more than 10^6 salmonellae per gram being shed in the feces for at least 2 weeks (Lafont *et al.* 1983).

Since the use of intestinal tract material or feces is not really practicable and runs the risk of introducing pathogenic microorganisms into flocks, attempts have been made to prepare cultures that may be effective. Intestinal tract contents and fecal material that are cultured anaerobically, but not aerobically, give protection from salmonella infection (Rantala and Nurmi 1973; Snoeyenbos *et al.* 1978). Establishment of monocultures of the strict anaerobes *Bacteroides* sp. and of *Bifidobacterium* sp. in newly hatched chicks is insufficient to protect the chicks (Barnes *et al.* 1979A). Homofermentative or heterofermentative lactobacilli (isolated from the ceca) alone, or in mixtures of 3 or 4 strains, or with bacteroides, bifidobacteria or eubacteria strains also appear not to be able to protect young chicks from salmonella infection (Barnes *et al.* 1980).

In newly hatched chicks, the cecal contents have a pH of about 6.7 and a volatile fatty acid concentration of about 12 mM (Barnes *et al.* 1979A). This will not prevent or limit salmonella growth. As the chick becomes older, the pH falls and the acid concentration increases in the cecum until, by about 7 days of age, the combination is sufficient to prevent the growth of salmonella. The aim of dosing young chicks with intestinal flora from adults is to speed up the development of a high concentration of volatile acids, a low pH, and a low redox potential in the cecum and colon. In addition, some of the intestinal flora may occupy attachment sites on the epithelium of the intestinal tract and prevent salmonella from adhering (Soerjadi *et al.* 1981). A combination of microorganisms may, therefore, be required to protect chicks from salmonella infections.

Pivnick and Nurmi (1982) provide a full review of this "Nurmi Concept" of diminishing infection of poultry by salmonellae, together with a discussion of four field trials with commercial flocks.

Intensive rearing of poultry where many thousands of birds are kept together favors the spread of salmonellae. In this situation, control of salmonella infection involves elimination of salmonella carriers in the breeding stock, fumigation of eggs, hygiene in the incubator and hatchery, prevention of salmonella contamination of feed and water, and, in the future, may involve the "Nurmi Concept." Meat and fish meals are usually incorporated into the feed. Although the temperatures used in the production of meat and fish meal are sufficient to destroy salmonellae, such meals are frequently contaminated (see Chapter 7).

Staphylococcus aureus.   While staphylococci are usually not detected in the throat or cloaca of 1-day-old chicks, at between 2 and 8 weeks of age these organisms can be found frequently at these sites (Kusch and Götze 1976). *Staphylococcus aureus* is also present on the body surfaces and in the nasal cavities of poultry at 2 weeks of age (Devriese *et al.* 1975). About 10^5 cells of *S. aureus* can be obtained from whole body rinses. The number of *S. aureus* both on body surfaces and in nasal cavities increases with age. *Staphylococcus aureus* is absent from, or present in only small numbers in the intestinal tract (Devriese *et al.* 1975; Notermans *et al.* 1982).

Mesophiles and Psychrotrophs on Poultry.   Most of the mesophilic flora that resides permanently on the skin of chickens appears to be micrococci (Thomas and McMeekin 1980). However, the skin, feathers, and feet will also be contaminated with microorganisms from environmental sources such as litter and feces. Used litter contains 10^{10}–10^{11} aerobic mesophiles, 10^8 psychrotrophs, and 10^6 *E. coli* per gram (Barnes 1960; Schefferle 1965; Mead *et al.* 1982). Enterobacteriaceae and *E. coli* can be found at counts of 10^4 to 10^6 per gram of skin (Notermans *et al.* 1977; Mead *et al.* 1982) and the outside of birds can often be contaminated with salmonellae (Mead 1976; McBride *et al.* 1980). Clostridia are also found on the feet and feathers, frequently at counts of more than 10^3 per gram of feathers (Mead and Impey 1970). Psychrotrophs (mainly moraxella-acinetobacter) are carried principally on the feathers (Barnes *et al.* 1979B), but are also found on the skin. On the skin the psychrotrophs are present at less than 0.1% of the numbers of the mesophiles (Notermans *et al.* 1977; Lahellec and Colin 1979; Thomas and McMeekin 1980). Since the body temperature of poultry (42°C) is well above the optimum growth temperature of most psychrotrophs, it is not surprising that these organisms are rarely found in the intestinal tract (Barnes *et al.* 1979B).

Transport from Farm to Slaughter

Birds are usually starved for a few hours before slaughter to reduce the volume of intestinal contents and thus fecal contamination of carcasses during processing (Mead 1982). However, stress caused by transport, crowding, and exposure to inclement weather can increase the volume of both cecal contents and feces excreted. Cages with solid floors used during transportation enable birds to sit in accumulated droppings. On the other hand, cages with perforated floors allow birds at higher levels to contaminate birds at lower levels. Since cages become contaminated with fecal material, they need to be thoroughly cleaned and disinfected before being reused to avoid cross-contamination of other flocks (Bryan 1980).

Slaughter and Processing

Birds are shackled by their legs to a conveyor, and are stunned, bled, scalded, defeathered, washed, eviscerated, washed, and chilled in cold water or in air. Throughout these operations there is ample opportunity for cross-contamination between birds, flocks, and equipment (Bryan 1980; Mead 1982). High rates of through-put make it difficult to prevent the spread of contamination. Salmonellae are frequently found on equipment and tools during processing (Galton et al. 1955; Bryan et al. 1968; Morris and Wells 1970). Defeathering and evisceration are the two stages which are most responsible for major bacterial contamination of the edible parts of the carcass.

During shackling, microorganisms are transferred into the surrounding air as the birds struggle (Kotula and Kinner 1964; Zottola et al. 1970; Patterson 1973). The shackles themselves may be heavily contaminated with S. aureus (Gibbs et al. 1978B). An additional source of contamination is associated with feces which are sometimes shed during electrical stunning.

Scalding. Feathers are loosened by scalding, normally in water, at either 50°–52°C or about 60°C. The lower temperatures are used primarily in the production of chilled carcasses and the higher temperatures, which result in damage of the outer cuticle (Barnes et al. 1979B), in the production of frozen poultry. During scalding, microorganisms are washed from the bird into the scald water; some microorganisms on the feathers and skin are destroyed as well.

The survival of microorganisms that enter the scald water varies with the organism, and the temperature and pH of the water. Psychrotrophs are relatively easily destroyed in the water even at the lower scald temperatures (Notermans and Kampelmacher 1975), but spores are little affected. Clostridium perfringens can be found in scald water at 53°–63°C (Mead and Impey 1970; Mulder and Dorresteijn 1977). Predictably the survival of Enterobacteriaceae, salmonellae, and aerobic mesophiles is higher at the lower scald temperatures (Büchli *et al.* 1966; Notermans and Kampelmacher 1975; Mulder and Dorresteijn 1977; Humphrey *et al.* 1981) and cross-contamination with salmonellae is therefore more likely. During use, scald water at 52°C can contain over 10^7 mesophiles and 10^4 coliforms per milliliter (Humphrey *et al.* 1981). However, even at 60°C more than 10^4 mesophiles and 10^2 Enterobacteriaceae per milliliter can be found (Mulder and Veerkamp 1974). Even when the scald temperature is 58°–62°C, cross-contamination is possible (Mulder *et al.* 1978). During scalding, dissociation of ammonium urate from feces causes the pH of scald water to fall rapidly from 8.4 and to remain at about 6.0 (Humphrey 1981). This latter pH is close to the optimum for salmonella survival ($D_{52°C}$ value of 34.5 minutes for one strain of *S. typhimurium*). The death rate of salmonellae is increased($D_{52°C}$, 1.25 min.) by adjusting the pH of the water to 9.0 (Humphrey *et al.* 1981).

Most of the psychrotrophs on the skin are destroyed even at low scald temperatures (Lahellec *et al.* 1972; Notermans and Kampelmacher 1975; Notermans *et al.* 1977; Barnes *et al.* 1979B). While *S. aureus,* salmonellae, *E. coli,* Enterobacteriaceae, and mesophiles are also reduced on the carcass skin by scalding (Mead 1976; Notermans *et al.* 1977; Gibbs *et al.* 1978B), the extent of the reduction is dependent on temperature. At a scald temperature of 61°C, reductions of more than 1000-fold can be obtained, whereas at scald temperatures of 53° to 55.5°C the counts are reduced by 10- to 100-fold (Notermans *et al.* 1977). Organisms attached to chicken skin do not show a logarithmic death rate (Notermans and Kampelmacher 1975). A proportion of the organisms die at a rapid rate initially but the remainder survive for considerable periods. Presumably these survivors are protected by being embedded in the tissue, or in a fatty (nonpolar) environment.

Defeathering.   During defeathering there can be considerable spread of microorganisms from carcass to carcass and from the defeathering equipment itself (Bryan 1980; Mead 1982). Aerosols are generated and feathers are scattered (Kotula and Kinner 1964; Patterson 1973).

Studies with indicator organisms (van Schothorst *et al.* 1972; Mulder *et al.* 1978) show that microbes from one bird can cross-contaminate large numbers of other birds. The warm, moist conditions under which processing operates are conducive to microbial growth. Furthermore, the flails and fingers of the defeathering machines are difficult to clean (Notermans and Kampelmacher 1983). Microorganisms can persist in cracks and other imperfections even after vigorous cleaning. Up to 10^6 *S. aureus* per cm^2 can be found on the rubber fingers of the defeathering machines and treatment with 100 ppm chlorine for 30 min may reduce this count by only about tenfold (Gibbs *et al.* 1978B). *Staphylococcus aureus* from the defeathering machines can be transferred onto the skin, resulting in a higher count of *S. aureus* and in the appearance of phage types on the carcasses that are only rarely found on the live bird but found in high numbers on the rubber fingers of the defeathering machines (Gibbs *et al.* 1978B). Notermans *et al.* (1982) observed that, when a single flock was slaughtered at two abattoirs, the numbers of *S. aureus* on the skin increased from about 10 to 10^4–10^5 per gram during defeathering, with the phage types on the carcasses differing between the two abattoirs and corresponding to the types indigenous to each plant.

The numbers of both aerobic mesophiles (Walker and Ayres 1956, 1959) and psychrotrophs on poultry skin can increase during defeathering (Lahellec *et al.* 1972; Notermans *et al.* 1977; Lahellec and Colin 1979; Thomas and McMeekin 1980) as can the numbers of Enterobacteriaceae and *E. coli* (van Schothorst *et al.* 1972; Notermans *et al.* 1977). Salmonellae are frequently isolated from carcasses after defeathering and from the defeathering machines (Bryan *et al.* 1968; Morris and Wells 1970; Mead 1976). During defeathering microorganisms can become attached to the tissue surface and gain access to channels and crevices in the skin (Thomas and McMeekin 1980; Bryan 1980; Mead 1982) thus resisting removal by later treatments.

Evisceration.   Evisceration offers many opportunities for contamination with organisms from the intestines. Bacteria are transferred from carcass to carcass by knives, eviscerating implements, and the hands of workers. While aerobic mesophiles on the carcass usually do not increase significantly during evisceration (Mulder and Veerkamp 1974; Notermans *et al.* 1977, 1980), the numbers of Enterobacteriaceae and the frequency of contamination with salmonellae often increase (Morris and Wells 1970; van Schothorst *et al.* 1972; Mulder and Veerkamp 1974; Notermans *et al.* 1980). Significant contamination with *S. aureus* can occur even though *S. aureus* is not detected in the intestinal tract. This contamination comes from sources other than the bird, and the contaminating strains appear to be indigenous to the plant (Notermans *et al.* 1982).

Washing.   Washing of carcasses removes organic matter and some of the contaminating microorganisms. Washing after defeathering, and during and after evisceration, reduces the count of aerobic mesophiles, coliforms, and Enterobacteriaceae and decreases the incidence of salmonellae on carcasses (Morris and Wells 1970; van Schothorst *et al.* 1972; Mulder and Veerkamp 1974; May 1974; Notermans *et al.* 1980). Washing is important in reducing both the amount of loose organic material and the microbial load entering water-immersion chilling systems.

The reduction in microbial numbers due to washing does not often exceed about tenfold (Bryan 1980; Mead 1982), the remainder of the contaminants being firmly attached (Notermans and Kampelmacher 1983). During scalding (58°C) and defeathering most of the rough and folded epidermis is removed and the underlying dermal layer of the skin is exposed (Thomas and McMeekin 1980). Although smoother than the epidermal surface, the exposed dermal layer is still deeply channelled and creviced. Microorganisms occur both in a superficial fluid layer and inside the deep channels in the skin. Microorganisms in the superficially located film are probably more readily removed by cleaning and washing than are those lodged in channels and crevices.

Chilling.   Carcasses are rapidly chilled either in air or cold water to prevent microbial growth. More commonly, chilling is by water immersion. In the slush-ice static system, carcasses are held for 4 to 24 hr and during this time psychrotrophic organisms can grow on the carcasses and in the water (Barnes and Shrimpton 1968). Faster rates of chilling are obtained with continuous-immersion, mechanical systems (Furnish 1974). During such treatments microorganisms are removed from carcass surfaces because of agitation in the cooling medium and can therefore be transferred to other carcasses. In addition, the bacterial count can rise during production if there is insufficient water replenishment, or if the water temperature is too high. Nevertheless, under well-controlled chilling conditions there is a reduction in the number of mesophiles and coliforms on carcasses (Thomas *et al.* 1974; Mead 1982).

Microflora of the Chilled Carcass

At the end of chilling, the microflora of poultry carcasses will reflect the microflora initially on or in the live bird modified at various stages of the slaughter and dressing process by the addition and removal of microorganisms from the carcass, and the transfer of microorganisms from one carcass to another and from one flock to another. The number of microorganisms detected on the finished carcasses will vary with both the site sampled and the method of sampling. When skin samples are excised from the chilled carcasses and macerated, the microflora found is composed of approximately 10^3–10^5 aerobic mesophiles per cm^2, 10^1–10^3 psychrotrophs per cm^2, 10^3–10^4 Enterobacteriaceae per cm^2, 10^1–10^3 *E. coli* per cm^2, less than 10^2 *Cl. perfringens* per cm^2, and up to 10^3 *S. aureus* per cm^2 (Mead and Impey 1970; Barnes 1976; Notermans *et al.* 1977, 1982; Gibbs *et al.* 1978A,B; Thomas and McMeekin 1980; Mead *et al.* 1982). Of 139 poultry strains of *S. aureus* examined by Harvey *et al.* (1982), 35 (25%) produced enterotoxin, mainly enterotoxin D. Salmonellae are frequently detected on poultry carcasses (Bryan 1980), usually at numbers of less than 30 cells per carcass when determined by whole carcass rinses (Campbell *et al.* 1983). *Campylobacter jejuni (coli)* is also frequently detected (Table 1.3). For one group of 10 chicken carcasses, Shanker *et al.* (1982) found from carcass rinses a mean count of 8.6×10^4 campylobacter cells per carcass with a range of 1.2×10^4 to 4.8×10^6.

Although the processing of live birds into carcasses causes a significant reduction in the number of microorganisms on the skin (from about 10^5 to 10^7 mesophiles per cm^2 to 10^3–$10^5/cm^2$), there are also subtle changes in the composition of the microflora. For instance, micrococci, the predomi-

TABLE 1.3. Detection of *Campylobacter jejuni* (*coli*) on Poultry Meat

Animal	Where sampled	No.	Positive (%)	Reference
Chicken	Abattoir	40	45	Shanker *et al.* (1982)
Chicken	Abattoir	50	72	Simmonds and Gibbs (1979)
Turkey	Retail	12	92	Simmonds and Gibbs (1979)
Turkey	Abattoir	83	34	Luechtefeld and Wang (1981)
Chicken	Retail	165	1.8	Smith and Muldoon (1974)
Chicken	Retail	100	58	Park *et al.* (1981)
Chicken	Retail	82	22	Norberg (1981)

nant aerobic mesophiles on the skin of unprocessed chickens, become replaced by a more heterogeneous mesophilic population largely composed of gram-negative organisms (Thomas and McMeekin 1980). During processing, the initial psychrotrophic population of moraxella-acinetobacter types also changes to a more heterogeneous flora with an increase in the percentage of pseudomonads (Lahellec *et al.* 1972). The final ratio of types of psychrotrophic microorganisms varies with the processing plant but differs from that on the live bird (Lahellec and Colin 1979). After processing, many of the Enterobacteriaceae on chicken carcasses may be psychrotrophic, although these organisms are not readily detected in or on the live bird (Mead *et al.* 1982). Sometimes the same types of *S. aureus* are found on the live bird and on the carcasses (Kusch and Götze 1976; Gibbs *et al.* 1978B); at other times different phage types appear on the carcasses (Gibbs *et al.* 1978B; Notermans *et al.* 1982).

HOGS

Microflora of the Intestinal Tract

During the first day of life the pH of the stomach contents of the pig is in the range 5.3–5.9, and rapid growth of *E. coli, Cl. perfringens,* and streptococci leads to the flow of large numbers of these organisms through the small and large intestine (Smith 1965). After 1 day, as the pH of the stomach contents falls, the numbers of these bacteria decrease and lactobacilli grow and become the dominant flora of the stomach and small intestine. In the large intestine, *E. coli, Cl. perfringens,* and streptococci form the initial major flora but with time are largely replaced by strict anaerobes. In about the first 3 days of life the principal flora in the feces are *E. coli* (10^{10} per gram), *Cl. perfringens* (10^8 per gram), streptococci (10^9 per gram), and lactobacilli (10^8 per gram) (Smith 1961). Nonsporing anaerobes thereafter appear in large numbers (10^{10} per gram) and the numbers of *E. coli,* streptococci and, particularly, *Cl. perfringens* shed in the feces decrease. As occurs with other animal species, the development of an adult-type flora in the intestinal tract presumably protects against growth in, and true infection of, the intestinal tract by salmonellae. Very young pigs are more susceptible than older pigs to salmonella infections (Kampelmacher *et al.* 1969).

The number of *Cl. perfringens* in the feces is increased if pigs are starved and then refed (Smith 1961). During the first day of refeeding, when large quantities of food are consumed, the count of *Cl. perfringens* in the feces increases up to 10^6-fold. With continuation of feeding the count of *Cl. perfringens* falls to its normal low level. About 6 hr after feeding, material bactericidal to *Cl. perfringens* appears in the small intestine and persists in the starved animal for up to at least 24 hr (Fuller and Moore 1967). The principal components of this bactericidal material are linoleic and arachidonic acids, lysolecithin, and phospholipid. The first 3 components are derived from hydrolysis of biliary lecithin in the small intestine when the rate of passage of digesta from the stomach is reduced. Since most of the products of lipolysis are absorbed anterior to the cecum, material inhibitory to *Cl. perfringens* is absent from the lower intestinal tract. Thus, during normal feeding of pigs, there will be periods of the day when the contents of the small intestine will be inhibitory to *Cl. perfringens,* and this may play a role in controlling the population of this organism in the intestinal tract. After an enforced starvation, the large consumption of feed on re-feeding (Smith 1961) presumably delays the period before inhibitory material appears in the small intestine and allows greater growth of *Cl. perfringens.*

Salmonella.   Clinical salmonellosis is often associated with the host-adapted serotype, *S. cholerae-suis* (Gibson 1969). For instance, in the U.K. between 1958 and 1967 this serotype was responsible for 83%, and *S. typhimurium* for only 8%, of incidents of salmonellosis in pigs (Sojka and Field 1970). Subsequently, control measures have led to a marked decrease in infections caused by *S. cholerae-suis* (Linton 1979). After clinical signs of salmonellosis disappear, apparently healthy pigs can continue to excrete salmonellae sporadically in feces for a considerable time. For instance, Gitter and Kidd (1967) noted that *S. typhimurium* was excreted for up to 6 months. In pigs which have never had clinically recognizable salmonellosis, a wide variety of salmonella serotypes is often shed in feces and it is such pigs that are the source of most salmonellae entering the abattoir.

The incidence of salmonellae in pigs on the farm is extremely variable and can be high. Leistner *et al.* (1961) found 2 of 75 fecal samples from 23 farms positive for salmonellae; Kampelmacher *et al.* (1963) detected salmonellae in 71 (7.5%) fecal samples from 953 individual pigs; Williams and Newell (1967) isolated salmonellae only once from 491 rectal swabs at one farm; Haddock (1970) found salmonellae in 68 (18%) of 370 rectal swabs from 63 pigs on one farm. Many pigs excrete salmonellae only intermittently. In some cases the salmonellae in the feces may simply be transient and have survived passage through the stomach and intestine.

Salmonella-contaminated feeds provide a common route for the introduction and maintenance of salmonellae in herds of swine. Reduction in the salmonella content of feed has long been known to reduce the extent of salmonella excretion on farms. Edel *et al.* (1967) examined the salmonella status of 9- to 10-week-old pigs, which were initially free of salmonellae, when the pigs were reared either on commercial meal or on the same meal commercially pelleted. Pelleting reduced the count of Enterobacteriaceae in the meal by about 300-fold. From 160 pigs raised on the pelleted meal for about 6 months only 1 of 6047 fecal samples contained salmonellae. In a group of pigs fed the unpelleted meal as a mash, salmonellae began to appear frequently in the feces after 8 weeks of feeding. By 10 weeks, 114 of 117 fecal samples contained salmonellae. Similarly, when salmonella-contaminated fish meal was fed as a mash at a pig-fattening unit (Lee *et al.* 1972), salmonellae were detected in 58 of 256 cecal samples at slaughter, but in only 1 of 60 when no fish meal was fed.

Although the numbers of salmonellae in dry feed may be low, growth of salmonella can take place when the feed is wetted. Linton *et al.* (1970) found substantial growth of salmonellae when dry and contaminated feed was made into a mash and held at 20°C. Salmonella excretion by pigs was only transient when freshly prepared mash was fed. However, when the mash was held at 20°C for 24 hr before feeding, salmonellae excretion lasted at least 37 days. The holding of bulk liquid feed, and the presence of residual feed in troughs and pipelines can allow salmonella growth and increase both the rate of infection and duration of fecal excretion (Linton 1979).

Even when salmonellae are eliminated from feed, a salmonella infection can be maintained by persistent excretion of salmonellae by symptomless animals. Ghosh (1972) found in a pig-breeding farm that breeding sows and boars frequently shed salmonellae (present in 62% of 577 feces samples) and movement of stock around the farms aided the spread of infection. After structural changes to the farm, disinfection of pens, introduction of feed pelleted at high temperature, and restocking with salmonella-free animals, the incidence of salmonellae in fecal samples from pigs throughout the farm fell from 53 to 0.5%.

Transport to and Holding at Slaughter

During the transport of pigs from farm to abattoirs, salmonellae shed in feces can contaminate the transport vehicle (Williams and Newell 1968) and the pens in which the animals are held awaiting slaughter (Leistner *et al.* 1961; Williams and Newell 1968; Timoney 1970). Thus, cross-contamination of the skin, feet, and intestinal tract can occur.

Some workers have found that transport and its associated stress apparently increase the ease with which salmonellae can be detected in feces. When 566 pigs were slaughtered at an abattoir 3–10 hr after leaving farms, salmonellae were detected in 13.1% of fecal samples compared with only 8.1% of samples taken on the farm (Kampelmacher *et al.* 1963). On the other hand, when 387 pigs were slaughtered on the farm, there was no significant difference in the detection rate of salmonellae from fecal samples taken before or after slaughter. Williams and Newell (1968, 1970), when examining pigs raised on salmonella-contaminated feed, were unable to detect excretion of salmonellae when rectal swabs were obtained on the farm, but frequently detected salmonellae on rectal swabs taken after transport or after arrival at the abattoir for slaughter. On the other hand, Tsai *et al.* (1971) found no evidence that transport stress increased excretion of salmonellae. However, they did find salmonellae in the cecal and colon contents of pigs in which salmonellae were not detected when multiple samples of feces were taken before slaughter.

Holding of pigs for long times in lairages while awaiting slaughter markedly increases the number of animals with salmonellae in their intestinal tract (McDonagh and Smith 1958; Leistner *et al.* 1961; Hansen *et al.* 1964). Since 1966, slaughterhouse regulations in the U.K. have forbidden the holding of pigs in lairages for longer than 72 hr, which should help to reduce the incidence of salmonellae infection.

Slaughtering and Processing

The process of pig slaughter and the preparation of carcasses bear some semblance to that used for poultry. In both, the outside surfaces of the animal are scalded prior to cleaning of the skin. The major differences are that the rate of processing of pigs through the slaughtering line is slower than it is for poultry, the abdomen is opened for removal of the viscera, and the split carcasses are chilled in air. After stunning, pigs are bled, scalded, dehaired, singed, scraped to remove charred material, washed, eviscerated, split along the backbone, washed, and chilled. Salmonellae are frequently found on the dehairing and scraping machinery, hand scrapers, and other equipment used during the slaughtering process (Galton *et al.* 1954; McDonagh and Smith 1968; Kampelmacher *et al.* 1961; Shotts *et al.* 1961). Although scalding and singeing are the major processes causing a reduction in the bacterial count on pig carcasses, the processes of dehairing, scraping, and evisceration are responsible for increasing the bacterial load.

The skin of pigs sampled at the bleeding stage of the slaughtering process carries about: 10^6–10^7 per cm^2 of aerobic mesophiles, 10^3–10^4 per cm^2, Enterobacteriaceae, 10^2–10^3 per cm^2 spores of *Bacillus* spp., 10^2 or less per cm^2, *Clostridium* spp., and 10^4 per cm^2, psychrotrophs (Dockerty *et al.* 1970; Prost and Libelt 1972; Snijders and Gerats 1976; Gerats *et al.* 1981; Scholefield *et al.* 1981). The skin may also be contaminated with salmonellae acquired on the farm, in transport, or in lairages before slaughter. Kampelmacher *et al.* (1963) found salmonellae on skin samples of 17.5% of 1200 pigs examined at 6 abattoirs.

Fecal material contains from 10^4 to 10^9 (mean about 10^7) Enterobac-

TABLE 1.4. Detection of *Campylobacter jejuni* (*coli*) from the Lower Intestinal Tract of Pigs

Country	No.	Positive (%)	Reference
Canada	208	1	Prescott and Bruin-Mosch (1981)
Netherlands	300	60.7	Oosterom (1980)
Sweden	138	95	Svedhem and Kaijser (1981)
United States	38	87	Stern (1981)

teriaceae, about 10^5 of aerobic sporeformers, but only a few hundred psychrotrophic bacteria per gram (Dickinson and Mocquot 1961; Hess and Lott 1970). Frequently the lower intestinal tract contains *C. jejuni (coli)* (Table 1.4) and salmonellae. The incidence of salmonella varies widely and, when animals are slaughtered soon after leaving the farm, is mostly determined by the conditions under which pigs are reared. For instance, Ghosh (1972) found a 32% incidence of salmonellae in the intestinal tract of 1053 pigs from one farm,but only a 6% incidence at the same abattoir from 586 pigs from other farms.

Scalding and Dehairing.   Pigs are scalded to loosen the attachment of the hair to the skin. The operation is carried out in tanks of hot water, in spray tunnels, or in steam.

Use of the tank-scalding system leads to the accumulation of soil, feces, and blood. However, most of the associated microorganisms are destroyed in the scald water. Survivors are predominantly spores of bacilli together with smaller numbers of clostridia (Prost and Libelt 1972). Snijders (1975) showed that the number of viable bacteria in the scald water during use varied between 10^2 and 10^4 per milliliter and was reduced as the temperature rose (range 59° to 63°C) and as the pH of the scald water increased. Gram-negative organisms were found in scald water only when the vat temperature was less than 60°C. Salmonellae can apparently survive in the sediment from scalding tanks since Kampelmacher *et al.* (1961) detected salmonellae in 6% of sediment samples.

The microbial count of the water used in spray-tunnel systems was not found to be significantly less than that in the scald-tank system since some of the water was recirculated and because it was difficult to clean the spray nozzles adequately (Snijders 1975).

One of the problems associated with the use of tank scalding is the potential for invasion by organisms via the stick wound or through the mouth. Viable organisms which gain access by these routes infect the vascular system and the lungs (Roberts 1980). Scalding in steam rather than in tanks of water is reported to reduce the frequency with which bacteria can be detected in the aorta (Roberts 1980).

During the process of scalding and dehairing there are substantial decreases on the skin in the numbers of mesophiles, psychrotrophs, *Bacillus* spp., *Clostridium* spp., and Enterobacteriaceae, and a reduction in the incidence of salmonellae (Kampelmacher *et al.* 1963; Dockerty *et al.* 1970; Prost and Libelt 1972; Snijders and Gerats 1976; Gerats *et al.* 1981; Scholefield *et al.* 1981). The reduction in mesophilic count increases as the scald temperature increases from 54° to 60°C (Dockerty *et al.* 1970). Snijders and Gerats (1976) found that, after scalding, the mesophilic count on the skin decreased from 10^6 per cm^2 to 2×10^3 per cm^2, and the count of Enterobacteriaceae decreased from about 4×10^3 per cm^2 to less than 70 per cm^2, but, after dehairing, these counts had increased again to about 10^5 per cm^2 and 700 per cm^2, respectively. Pig carcasses are recontaminated with fecal and other material in dehairing machines. Both Galton *et al.* (1954) and Kampelmacher *et al.* (1961) showed that both dehairing machines and hand scrapers used in dehairing are frequently contaminated with and, because they are often inadequately cleaned, disseminate salmonellae. Bacterial recontamination of carcasses can be reduced if the water used in the dehairing machines to remove dislodged hair and debris is hot (Snijders and Gerats 1976).

Singeing, Scraping, and Washing.   After scalding and dehairing, carcasses are further cleaned by singeing to burn remaining hair, by scraping manually or by machine to remove charred material, and by washing. Singeing destroys microorganisms on surfaces exposed to the heat. However, heat treatment over all surfaces of the carcass is uneven, and organisms in deeper layers of the surface tissue are protected. Scalding at 60°–63°C destroys some of the epithelial layer and organisms may gain access to exposed subepithelial tissue during dehairing. When salmonellae were rubbed on the skin of pig carcasses which then were singed in an oven (1200°–1400°C) for 15–30 sec, salmonellae were not detected in skin scrapings but were found in 39 of 44 pieces of excised skin (Kampelmacher *et al.* 1961).

There is wide variation in the reported reduction in mesophile numbers caused by singeing. Some of the variations may reflect different sampling sites on the carcass and some the difference in the skin temperature achieved during the singe. For example, Dockerty *et al.* (1970) observed only about a two-fold reduction in mesophiles during singeing, and provided some evidence that destruction of organisms varies with the site sampled. After singeing there were 10^4–10^5 mesophiles per cm^2 on the skin. On the other hand, Snijders and Gerats (1976) and Gerats *et al.* (1981) obtained a much greater reduction of both mesophiles and *Enterobacteriaceae*. In their studies the mesophilic count fell from about 10^5 per cm^2 to a mean count of less than 300 per cm^2, and Enterobacteriaceae were not detected after singeing.

In a number of plants examined by Dockerty *et al.* (1970) mesophilic counts did not change significantly during manual scraping, and were only slightly reduced by washing. However, Snijders and Gerats (1976) and Gerats *et al.* (1981) found considerable increases in mesophiles and Enterobacteriaceae after scraping. These increases varied widely between plants and were often greater on the first pigs treated. Mesophilic counts increased from a mean of less than 300 per cm^2 to 10^3–10^5 per cm^2 depending on the abattoir. In one abattoir, the Enterobacteriaceae count increased from less than 20 per cm^2 to a mean of 300 per cm^2 on the first pigs treated. These increases were traced to inadequate cleaning of scraping and polishing machines in which residual hair and epidermal tissue provided opportunity for bacterial growth. The machines then transferred the organisms to the skin of carcasses. On occasion, salmonellae can also be isolated from these machines (Kampelmacher et al. 1961).

Evisceration.   Contamination at this stage of processing is influenced by the care taken in removal of viscera. During opening of the carcass and removal of the abdominal contents, any puncture of the intestinal tract or escape of material from the rectum will result in contamination of the carcass and facilitate cross-contamination of other carcasses via hands and knives. Usually, little change in the mesophilic count is associated with evisceration and it is detectable only on carcasses which have a low count before evisceration (Dockerty et al. 1970; Gerats et al. 1981). Gerats et al. (1981) observed a correlation between care in the evisceration procedure and the extent of contamination of the carcass with Enterobacteriaceae. They also observed that where counts of Enterobacteriaceae were high, contamination with salmonellae was also more likely. When samples contained less than 20 Enterobacteriaceae per cm^2, the incidence of salmonella was about 9%, but the incidence rose to 55% when the Enterobacteriaceae count was greater than 10^3 per cm^2. Salmonella contamination was also found to increase during evisceration by Galton et al. (1954) and Shotts et al. (1961).

Salmonellae can be present not only in the intestinal tract but also in mesenteric and portal lymph nodes. They are often present in lymph nodes when they are undetectable in intestinal contents. The incidence of salmonellae reported in mesenteric lymph nodes is varied: 32% (Cortesi and Catellani 1982), 14–18% (Kampelmacher et al. 1961, 1963; Chung and Frost 1969; Moo et al. 1980), 6% (McCaughey et al. 1973), 3–6% (PHLS et al. 1972), and 2.4% (Nottingham et al. 1972). Kampelmacher et al. (1961, 1963) also found salmonellae in 6–7% of portal lymph nodes from over 3600 pigs examined. Incision of lymph nodes during veterinary inspection can result in contamination of meat if the inspector handles other meat or parts of the carcass. Cortesi and Catellani (1982) noted that, after slicing of mesenteric lymph nodes of pigs with sterile knives, salmonellae could be detected on 17.3% of the knives. Similarly, salmonellae were detected on 5% of knives used during inspection and incision of lymph nodes in the Netherlands (Kampelmacher et al. 1969).

Campylobacters can be isolated from gall bladders and associated bile ducts, and, frequently, from the surfaces of livers at evisceration (Rosef 1981). Incision of the bile ducts during postmortem examination may aid in the spread of these organisms to the liver.

Microflora of the Pig Carcass before Chilling

The number of microorganisms on the carcass at completion of the slaughtering process is the net result of the reduction in the microbial flora of the skin during scalding and singeing and of recontamination during dehairing, scraping, evisceration, and other stages of handling. Not surprisingly, there is a large variation in the counts of organisms reported.

There are significant differences in the counts of mesophilic organisms obtained between abattoirs, between carcasses, and between sites sampled on the carcass. The mean count on carcasses produced at one abattoir was 10^4 per cm^2 and, at another abattoir, 10^5 per cm^2 (Dockerty *et al.* 1970). Roberts *et al.* (1980) found that the mean counts on carcasses produced at 5 abattoirs ranged from 10^2 to 10^4 per cm^2. Although the mean mesophilic count on pig's cheeks was 7×10^2, the count ranged from less than 4×10^1 to $4 \times 10^4/cm^2$ on different carcasses (Ingram and Roberts 1976). Significant differences in counts between carcass sites have been observed by Dockerty *et al.* (1980), Roberts *et al.* (1980), and Scholefield *et al.* (1981). Mean counts obtained from different sites on the carcass can vary by up to 100-fold. Furthermore, the sites with the highest and lowest counts differ in different abattoirs.

The numbers, or presence, of other groups of bacteria found on pig carcasses also show considerable variability. There are significant differences in the counts of psychrotrophs and Enterobacteriaceae between abattoirs (Roberts *et al.* 1980). Contamination with psychrotrophic organisms can vary between 1 and 10% of the mesophilic count and can range from less than 100 to almost 10^4 per cm^2 (Ingram and Roberts 1976; Scholefield *et al.* 1981). *Clostridium perfringens* were found on 66% of swabs from pork carcasses with counts of up to 200/100 cm^2 (Smart *et al.* 1979). Salmonellae have been detected on carcasses at varying rates: 40–50% (Galton *et al.* 1954; Shotts *et al.* 1961), 12.5% (Williams and Newell 1968), and 5% (Timoney 1970). Over a 6-week period in one abattoir, the incidence of salmonellae varied from no salmonellae detected on 200 carcasses, to salmonellae being detected on 28 of 60 carcasses (Biemuller *et al.* 1973). In another abattoir, salmonellae were isolated from 11 of 200 carcasses examined in one 2-year period, and not at all from 230 carcasses examined in the following 2-year period (Roberts 1976). Campylobacters (mainly *C. coli*) can also be found on pig carcasses and pork meat (Table 1.5).

CATTLE AND SHEEP

Microflora of the Intestinal Tract

The distinctive feature of ruminants is the modification of the stomach into an organ of four compartments: rumen, reticulum, omasum, and

TABLE 1.5. Detection of *Campylobacter jejuni (coli)* on Red Meats

Animal	Where sampled	No. sampled	Positive (%)	Reference
Calf	Abattoir	90	18	Gill and Harris (1982)
Cattle	Abattoir	58	2	Stern (1981)
Sheep	Abattoir	59	24	Stern (1981)
Pig	Abattoir	58	38	Stern (1981)
Pork/beef/lamb	Abattoir	1236	4[a]	Turnbull and Rose (1982)
Pork/beef/lamb	Retail	4933	1	Turnbull and Rose (1982)

[a] 32 of 49 positive samples were from pork. Isolates from pork were *C. coli;* most of the isolates from beef and lamb were *C. jejuni* biotype 1.

abomasum. The abomasum is the true stomach where gastric juice is excreted and the pH of digesta is lowered to around pH 2. In the rumino-reticulum, food is converted by anaerobic microbial fermentation into volatile fatty acids and microbial protein to meet, respectively, the energy and nitrogen needs of the animals.

At birth, the digestive tract of sheep and cattle is physiologically that of a nonruminant and, at this time, the abomasum is the largest of the four compartments. Within the first day, large numbers of *E. coli, Cl. perfringens,* and streptococci are found in the contents of the rumen, abomasum, cecum, and the rest of the intestinal tract (Ziolecki and Briggs 1961; Smith 1965). Lactobacilli are next to appear and from about 2 to 12 days they are present in high numbers in the rumen and small intestine. The initial high counts (10^6–10^8 per gram) of *E. coli* in the rumen begin to decrease after about 1 week and by 3 weeks fall to about 10^3 per gram. When animals are about 2 days old, bacteroides are found in large numbers (10^8–10^9 per gram) in the cecum. In the first few days of life, 10^7–10^8 *Cl. perfringens* per gram are shed in the feces. Thereafter, the number of *Cl. perfringens* in the feces declines so that by about 2 weeks only about 10^4 or less per gram appear in the feces (Smith 1961). The number of *E. coli* in feces remain at about 10^9 per gram for about 2 weeks, and then decline to around 10^6 per gram by the time lambs and calves are about 3 months of age.

In the meantime considerable changes are taking place in the rumino-reticulum. Between 2 and 6 weeks of age this organ grows rapidly so that it becomes considerably larger than the abomasum. By about 3 months, the relative mass of each compartment of the stomach is about that in the adult animal. Dry feed elicits an early increase in size and development of the rumen (Warner and Flatt 1965). In the functional rumen, there is a very diverse flora of about 10^{10} anaerobic bacteria and 10^6 protozoa per milliliter of rumen fluid. However the flora is not static, changing even diurnally in response to the intake of feed.

Salmonella.   In well-fed adult sheep or cattle, neither salmonellae nor *E. coli* are able to survive in the rumen (Brownlie and Grau 1967; Grau *et al.* 1969). A single dose of 10^7 to 10^8 salmonellae, introduced directly into the rumen, is rapidly eliminated from that organ at a rate faster than expected from simple wash-out. Salmonellae are shed in the feces in only low numbers and for only a few days. The concentration of volatile fatty acids and the pH in the rumen liquor of the well-fed animal inhibit growth of *E. coli* and salmonellae (Wolin 1966; Chambers and Lysons 1979). If the concentration of the volatile fatty acids is lowered and the pH raised in the rumen liquor by reduction of feed intake or by starvation, then both *E. coli* and salmonellae can grow (Brownlie and Grau 1967; Grau *et al.* 1969). The time at which growth of salmonellae occurs after withdrawal of food from the animal varies from 18 to 54 hr, depending on the composition of the last feed. In the starved animal, growth in the rumen fluid soon ceases, presumably because of limitation of growth substrates for both *E. coli* and salmonellae. On subsequent feeding of the animal, there is another period (6–12 hr) of rapid growth for *E. coli* and salmonellae when fermentation in the rumen is abnormal and considerable amounts of nonvolatile acids (lactate and succinate) are produced. It appears that during this period of abnormal fermentation sufficient substrates for growth of *E. coli* and salmonellae are provided, but that the volatile fatty acid concentration is insufficient to prevent growth. Subsequently, the concentration of volatile fatty acids increases and, on continued feeding of the animal, both *E. coli* and salmonellae are eliminated from the rumen. Thus, the physiological status of the rumen plays a role in amplifying or reducing the numbers of ingested salmonellae and *E. coli* that flow into the lower intestinal tract.

While a single inoculum of 10^7 to 10^8 salmonellae into the rumen of well-fed animals can be rapidly eliminated from both rumen liquor and feces, an inoculation of only 300 to 400 salmonella cells at the time of refeeding after starvation can result in up to about 10^6 salmonellae per gram being shed in the feces for about 1 week and continuing to be shed in lower numbers for at least 5 weeks. Similarly, the numbers of *E. coli* in feces appear to be influenced by the effect feeding and starvation has on *E. coli* growth in the rumen. In well-fed animals, where there are no detectable *E. coli* in the rumen, only about 10^4 per gram are shed in the feces. After a starvation and refeeding cycle, when *E. coli* are growing in the rumen, the numbers of *E. coli* in the feces increase up to 10^9 per gram and remain high for a few days before returning to about 10^4 per gram after *E. coli* have disappeared from the rumen.

Salmonellae may enter the host tissue from the alimentary tract. Hall *et al.* (1978) found that *S. dublin* inoculated into the rumen of cows could be isolated in high numbers from the walls of the distal ileum, cecum, and colon and from the lymph nodes draining these areas. Similarly, Samuel *et al.* (1980A, 1981) provided evidence that a wide variety of salmonella serotypes invade through the lower intestinal tract rather than through the gastric complex. Lymph nodes were examined from 128 adult cattle which had been starved and intermittently fed during a holding period of at least 4 days in a salmonella-contaminated environment. Salmonellae were detected in 52–54% of the jejunal and cecal lymph nodes, in 39% of colonic lymph nodes, but in only 2–4% of ruminal and abomasal lymph nodes. Other lymph nodes and tissue samples were also examined in 28 of these animals (Samuel *et al.* 1980A), and, in these, salmonellae were detected in the tonsils and retropharyngeal lymph nodes of only one animal, in the gall bladder of one animal, and not at all from the duodenal, hepatic, or other lymph nodes and not from the spleen. The percentage of the 128 animals in which salmonellae were found in the intestinal tract contents was as follows: rumen, 46%, ileum, 31%, cecum, 53%, and rectum, 57%. Thus, while about as many cattle contained salmonellae in the anterior region of the digestive tract as in the posterior region, salmonellae were more commonly found in the lymph nodes associated with the lower digestive tract. Furthermore, the pattern of infection in lymph nodes and tissue suggested that, in these apparently healthy cattle, there was no significant spread beyond the mesenteric lymph nodes. As has been shown experimentally in the mouse (Carter and Collins 1974; Carter *et al.* 1975), salmonellae spreading systematically from the mesenteric lymph nodes would be expected to localize in the liver and spleen.

Sheep and other animals can also become infected by salmonellae via an intranasal route (Tannock and Smith 1971A,B). Sheep are more susceptible to an intranasal than an oral inoculum of salmonellae. Continuous inoculation of the alimentary tract may result from swallowing organisms shed from the upper respiratory tract.

Young ruminant animals are more susceptible to salmonellae than are older animals, presumably because neither the rumen nor lower intestinal tract have developed an adult-type microflora. For instance, 2-day-old calves given 10^4–10^6 cells of *S. typhimurium* shed more salmonellae in their feces and for a longer time than did 14- to 21-day-old calves (Robinson and Loken 1968). Furthermore, salmonellae were detected in lymph nodes from the younger calves more frequently than in those from the older calves. The older calves had been fed milk and hay for 10–17 days before inoculation and, compared to 2-day-old calves, would by this time have developed a microflora in both rumen and lower intestinal tract that was more like that of the normal adult (Smith 1961, 1965; Ziolecki and Briggs 1961).

Outbreaks of clinical salmonellosis on farms, although sporadic, tend to show seasonal patterns. In the U.K., bovine salmonellosis and abortion caused by *S. dublin* and fecal isolations of this serotype are highest toward the end of summer and in autumn (Hughes *et al.* 1971; Hinton 1975). Although bovine salmonellosis is normally low in winter-spring, a high incidence of fecal isolations can occur during winter when animals are housed (Heard *et al.* 1972). In New Zealand, outbreaks of clinical bovine salmonellosis caused by *S. typhimurium* are highest in spring and early summer (Salisbury 1958) and salmonellosis in sheep in summer-autumn (Salisbury 1958; Robinson and Royal 1971). The season of high incidence of salmonellosis in sheep is associated with movement and congregation of animals (e.g., for shearing and dipping) and high stocking densities. In winter-spring, it was shown that 1–2% of sheep sampled excreted salmonellae and this rose to 10% in summer (Robinson and Royal 1971).

The overall incidence of detectable salmonella in the feces of animals on the farm is usually low. In the U.K., salmonellae were found in only about 0.5% of about 5400 samples from calves (Anderson *et al.* 1961; PHLS 1965); in the Netherlands, in 0.7% of 6837 samples from 1360 calves (Edel and Kampelmacher 1971); in New Zealand, in 0.9% of 2868 calves (Robinson 1966); in the United States, in 1.3% of 1196 cattle (Galton *et al.* 1954).

Microflora of Hide and Fleece

During the raising of sheep and cattle, the fleece and hide acquire a large population of microorganisms. Some of this population will include the normal flora of the skin (e.g., micrococci, staphylococci, and yeasts) together with microorganisms derived from soil, pasture, and feces (Ingram and Simonsen 1980). Factors such as moisture and substrates available for microbial growth and contamination acquired from external sources are responsible for the considerable variation in microbial population between animals and between sites on the animal. On wet hides microbial growth causes about a tenfold increase in count (Empey and Scott 1939). Contamination of livestock on pasture under wet muddy conditions differs from that of animals from dry, dusty fields (Ingram and Simonsen 1980). The hide or fleece may also become heavily contaminated with fecal material particularly under feed-lot conditions (Anon. 1978), thus giving surface contamination with a larger proportion of organisms from the intestinal tract.

The proportion of the microbial population in surface soils which is psychrotrophic varies with ambient and soil temperatures so that there are both seasonal and geographical differences in the incidence of these types. Psychrotrophs are present at their highest level in winter. They are less prominent in the soils of tropical and subtropical regions than in those of more temperate zones. Similarly, the number of psychrotrophs on the hide and fleece varies with ambient temperature, season, and climate (Empey and Scott 1939; Newton *et al.* 1978).

Transport from Farm to Slaughter

During transport from farm to slaughter, cattle and sheep can be exposed to fecal, and therefore salmonella, contamination in the transport vehicles, in sale-pens, and in abattoir holding-pens (Grau *et al.* 1968).

The incidence of salmonellae in fecal samples from cattle at slaughter can be about tenfold greater than on the farm (Galton *et al.* 1954). Anderson *et al.* (1961) showed that the longer calves are held in collecting centers awaiting slaughter, the greater the incidence of salmonellae in fecal samples. When calves were held 2–5 days, salmonellae were found in

35.6% of fecal samples but were detected in only 0.6% of samples from calves held only a few hours. The proportion of cattle with salmonellae in their rumen contents also increases with time from farm to slaughter (Grau *et al.* 1968). In addition to the effect of time between farm and slaughter, the feeding regime during holding also influences the salmonella status. For cattle slaughtered after holding for 3–7 days, those which were fed once during this period were 3 to 4 times more likely to have salmonellae in their feces and rumen contents than animals which were not fed (Grau *et al.* 1968).

Salmonella contamination of sheep can also increase significantly during the period between leaving the farm and slaughter. When sheep from which no salmonellae could be detected were held in abattoir pens, salmonellae were found on the fleece within 1 day, even though there was less than one salmonella cell per gram of soil in the pens (Grau and Smith 1974). Salmonellae were first shed in the feces after holding for 2–3 days. Both the percentage of infected sheep and the number of salmonellae per gram of feces then increased rapidly. Such increased shedding of salmonellae causes a substantial increase in salmonella contamination in the environment through which other groups of animals have to pass on their way to slaughter.

If cattle and sheep are killed within about 48 hr of their last feed on the farm, then there is a reduced opportunity for ingested salmonellae to grow in the rumen and appear in the feces. Beyond this period, salmonellae can grow in the rumen, flow through to the lower intestine in increased numbers, and be shed in large numbers in the feces. Intermittent feeding between farm and slaughter not only increases the chance of ingesting salmonellae but also stimulates growth of salmonellae in the rumen.

Slaughter and Dressing

In contrast to the procedure used for poultry and pig carcasses, the slaughter and dressing of cattle and sheep involves removal of the skin and does not incorporate a scalding treatment. Cattle and sheep are stunned and bled; the head, hocks, and skin are removed; the carcass is eviscerated and, in the case of cattle, the carcasses split along the backbone. After washing, the carcasses are chilled.

In the cradle system of dressing, the carcass, after removal of the head, is held on a cradle in a horizontal position. The hocks are removed, a considerable portion of the hide is freed from the carcass, and the abdomen and thorax opened, before the carcass is hoisted to an overhead rail for evisceration and final removal of the hide. In the chain system, the carcass remains suspended from an overhead rail from bleeding through to dispatch to the chiller.

The main problem of hygiene is the removal of the hocks, hide or fleece, and viscera with as little contamination as possible of the exposed sterile tissue of the carcass and of the edible offal meats, such as the liver and kidney. The hide, or fleece, and intestinal tract contain an enormous population of microorganisms, and the mesenteric lymph nodes of some animals may contain salmonellae (Table 1.6).

Hide and fleece can carry (per gram or cm^2), 10^6–10^8 aerobic mesophiles, 10^4–10^6 psychrotrophs, 10^3–10^6 Enterobacteriaceae, 10^1–10^5 *E. coli*, 10^5–10^6 bacillus spores, and 10^3 or more yeasts and molds (Empey and Scott 1939; Hess and Lott 1970; Mulder 1978; Grau 1979). Salmonellae may also be present. Salmonellae have been detected on the hide and fleece of more than one-half of 200 animals examined at slaughter (Smith and Grau 1973) and at counts of up to 400 per cm^2 (Grau and Smith 1974). Patterson and Gibbs (1978B) found up to 4×10^6 *S. dublin* per gram of cattle hair. A large number and variety of microorganisms is also carried onto the slaughter floor on the hooves of the animals, and this population may also include salmonellae (Hess and Lott 1970; Patterson and Gibbs 1978B).

At slaughter, rumen contents may contain per gram, 10^6–10^8 aerobic mesophiles, 10^2–10^5 psychrotrophs, and 10^3–10^7 Enterobacteriaceae and *E. coli* (Empey and Scott 1939; Grau 1979). Feces contain per gram, 10^8–10^9 aerobic mesophiles, 10^2–10^5 psychrotrophs, and 10^6–10^9 of Enterobacteriaceae and *E. coli* (Empey and Scott 1939; Hess and Lott 1970; Howe *et al.* 1978; Grau 1979). In addition, feces may contain up to 10^6 *Cl. perfringens* spores per gram (Smith 1961), as well as salmonellae (Table 1.6) and campylobacters (Table 1.7).

Stunning and Bleeding.   Cattle are sometimes stunned by a captive bolt pistol, which pierces the forehead part of the skull, and may be pithed by forcing a rod through the cranium and into the spinal column. Mackey and Derrick (1979) showed that when about 10^8 to 10^{11} cells of genetically marked organisms contaminated the captive bolt, pithing rod, or sticking knife, the marker organisms could be recovered in low numbers from internal tissue. Bacteria from the captive bolt could be detected in the spleen but not in muscle. If cattle were pithed, the marker organisms were found in both spleen and muscle. Damage to a greater number of blood vessels as a result of pithing presumably increases the number of organisms that can gain access to the blood supply. Bacteria from the sticking knife used to bleed sheep could be recovered from heart, lung, spleen, liver, and kidneys, but only rarely from muscle.

During this stage of the slaughter process, the esophagus is cleared from its surrounding tissue and usually tied to reduce leakage of rumen contents, which can contaminate the neck and pleural region of the carcass. Salmonellae have been isolated from instruments used in this operation (Smeltzer *et al.* 1979).

Removal of Hide and Fleece.   After the hocks are removed, the separation of the skin from the carcass is begun with incisions along the inside of the legs, along the abdomen and sternum, and around the anus. Knives

TABLE 1.6. Salmonella Contamination of Animals at Slaughter

| Country | Animal | | Samples positive (%) | | | | | | Reference |
		Rumen	Feces	MLN[a]	HLN[a]	Liver	Gall bladder	Spleen	
Australia	Cattle	45							Grau and Brownlie (1965)
	Cattle	18	10.1						Daleel and Frost (1967)
	Cattle			19					Moo et al. (1980)
England	Calves		1.1	1.25	2.2	1.25	0.6		Nazer and Osborne (1976)
The Netherlands	Cattle			0.3					Guinée et al. (1964)
	Calves		4.9	2.6	3.1	0.7	6.4	1.2	Guinée et al. (1964)
New Zealand	Cattle		9.4	7.2		2.2		1.6	Nottingham and Urselmann (1961)
	Calves		6.3	3.5		4.3		7.6	Nottingham and Urselmann (1961)
	Calves		4.2	2.1		1.6		2.9	Nottingham et al. (1972)
	Sheep	<0.1	1.7	4				0	Kane (1979)
Northern Ireland	Cattle		7.8						McCaughey et al. (1971)
Saudi Arabia	Sheep/goats		4.7	14.7			4.8	0.8	Nabbut and Al-Nakhli (1982)
United States	Cattle	3	12						Galton et al. (1954)
	Cattle		1.5						Childers et al. (1973)

[a] MLN, mesenteric lymph node; HLN, hepatic lymph node.

TABLE 1.7. Detection of *Campylobacter jejuni* (*coli*) from the Lower Intestinal Tract of Sheep, Goats, and Cattle

Country	Animal	No. sampled	Positive (%)	Reference
Canada	Calf/cattle	202	2.5	Prescott and Bruin-Mosch (1981)
New Zealand	Calf	50	48	Gill and Harris (1982)
New Zealand	Cattle	65	0	Gill and Harris (1982)
Netherlands	Cattle	400	2.8	Oosterom *et al.* (1982)
Sweden	Cattle	90	19	Svedhem and Kaijser (1981)
United States	Cattle	31	0	Stern (1981)
United States	Cattle	78	64	Doyle and Roman (1982)
Canada	Lamb/sheep	110	13.6	Prescott and Bruin-Mosch (1981)
Canada	Goat	72	2.7	Prescott and Bruin-Mosch (1981)
New Zealand	Lamb	42	2.4	Gill and Harris (1982)
New Zealand	Sheep	71	14.1	Gill and Harris (1982)
United States	Sheep	214	16.8	Smibert (1965)
United States	Sheep	15	73	Stern (1981)

are used to free a considerable proportion of the skin before the rest of the skin is pulled away from the carcass.

Most of the bacterial contamination of the carcass is acquired during the removal of the skin. The first incision through the heavily contaminated skin carries microorganisms onto the underlying carcass tissue. Wool and hair that may be cut by this incision can fall onto the exposed tissue. As the knife is used to free the skin from the tissue, organisms are wiped from the knife onto the carcass. Bacterial populations on the tissue are highest in the region below the initial incision through the skin, and lowest in the regions furthest removed from the incision (Empey and Scott 1939; Kelly *et al.* 1980). Further contamination of the carcass can occur from the hide or fleece folding over and contacting the exposed tissue and from contact with the hands of workers. During removal of the skin and feet, salmonellae can be transferred from the hooves, fleece, and hide to the carcass (Grau and Smith 1974; Grau 1979; Stolle 1981).

The hands of workmen handling the skin and hocks become heavily contaminated (Empey and Scott 1939; Hess and Lott 1970). Sterile knives used in incising the skin and removing hocks can acquire on the blades about 10^7 aerobic mesophiles, 10^5 bacillus spores and psychrotrophs, and 10^3 Enterobacteriaceae (Empey and Scott 1939; Hess and Lott 1970). Salmonellae are detected more frequently on the hands, knives, steels, and aprons of workers involved in operations up to the removal of the hide than on those used by workers after the hide is removed (Peel and Simmonds 1978; Smeltzer *et al.* 1979, 1980A,B; Stolle 1981).

Although water at 82°C is provided in most abattoirs for decontamination of knives, hock cutters, and other equipment, decontamination is often not achieved because the time of immersion in the hot water is usually too short to destroy vegetative cells (e.g., salmonellae). To eliminate salmonellae from contaminated equipment, an immersion time of about 10 seconds in water at 82°C is required (Peel and Simmonds 1978).

However, since steels and scabbards are also often contaminated with salmonellae, unless steels are also frequently decontaminated and scabbards kept clean, knives can readily be inoculated with salmonellae from these sources (Smeltzer et al. 1980A).

Evisceration.   During evisceration there is an increase in contamination of the carcass with salmonellae and Enterobacteriaceae without any significant increase in the numbers of mesophilic organisms (Grau 1979). While any puncture of the intestinal tract and spillage of its contents can lead to a massive contamination of carcasses, this is not common. During removal of the viscera, some leakage of rumen fluid occasionally occurs, and this may contaminate the carcass and offals. However, most of the contamination of carcasses with microorganisms from the intestinal tract seems to occur without obvious spillage. The operations involved in freeing the anal-sphincter and rectal end of the intestine constitute a major source of E. coli and salmonella contamination of sheep and cattle carcasses (Grau 1979). Normally, the rectal end of the intestine is freed from its attachments during skin removal. Sometimes with sheep, however, the anal-sphincter-rectal region is freed only after the skin is removed and as part of the process of viscera removal. Most of the contamination of sheep carcasses with E. coli and salmonellae occurs at the time when the anal sphincter-rectum is freed whether this takes place as part of the operation of removing the viscera, or as part of skin removal. The perianal region of cattle carcasses, immediately after the tissue is exposed, is often heavily contaminated with E. coli and salmonellae (Grau 1979). In an attempt to reduce contamination of the abdominal cavity, the rectal end of the intestine is often enclosed in a plastic bag before it is allowed to fall into the abdomen.

From Table 1.6, it can be seen that the gall bladder, and hepatic and mesenteric lymph nodes may be infected with salmonellae. At times there can be more than 5000 salmonella cells per gram in mesenteric lymph nodes (Samuel et al. 1980A). Frequently, campylobacters can also be found in bile (Bryner et al. 1972). During incision of hepatic and mesenteric lymph nodes and bile ducts as part of veterinary inspection, these organisms may contaminate the knives and so may be spread to offal meats (Samuel et al. 1980B; Smeltzer and Thomas 1981). Usually only a small percentage of livers are internally infected with salmonellae (Table 1.6), but surface contamination can occur during evisceration and during inspection. For instance, Samuel et al. (1980B) detected salmonella only once in the internal tissue of livers, but found salmonellae on the surfaces of 16 of 50 livers immediately on removal from the carcass, and on 41 after inspection. Contamination during evisceration was presumably due to direct contact with material from the digestive tract and to indirect contact via the knife and hands of the eviscerator. The surface of the viscera table, and the knives and hands of the inspectors have been shown to be frequently contaminated with salmonellae (Samuel et al. 1980B; Smeltzer and Thomas 1981). The increased surface contamination of livers after inspection was probably derived from these sources. Because palpation is used to detect lesions, livers are handled considerably during inspection.

Washing. Carcasses are washed to remove blood, bone-dust, hair, and soil. The effectiveness of washing varies with the time spent in washing, the volume, pressure and temperature of the water, and the design of the spray device (Bailey 1971; Sheridan 1982). While washing removes some microorganisms, often the reduction in bacterial numbers on carcasses is small. Patterson (1968, 1972), Bailey (1971), and Marshall *et al.* (1977) found that washing gave only a small reduction in count (usually two- to threefold). On the other hand, Sheridan (1982) obtained a mean reduction of 60-fold.

Washing tends to redistribute organisms. Sometimes the count will be reduced at one site on the carcass but remain unchanged or may even increase at another site. For instance, when sheep carcasses were washed with water at 50°C, the numbers of aerobic mesophiles on the hind legs were reduced tenfold, but on the brisket, neck, and rump the reduction was only two- to sixfold. On the middle of the back,there was no significant change in count (L. E. Brownlie and F. H. Grau, unpublished). Similarly, Kelly *et al.* (1981) found that there was a three- to tenfold reduction in count on ventral surfaces but no reduction on the back of washed lamb carcasses.

Efforts have been made to increase the effectiveness of washing in reducing the microbial population on carcasses by including chlorine or organic acids in the wash water, or by raising the temperature of the water.

The effect of the incorporation of chlorine on reducing microbial contamination appears to be variable and small. Anderson *et al.* (1977A) found no significant difference between water only and water containing 200–250 mg chlorine per liter. Patterson (1968) obtained a two- to threefold reduction in microbial count with 20 mg chlorine per liter; Kelly *et al.* (1981), a fivefold reduction with 30 mg chlorine per liter and a ninefold reduction with 450 mg chlorine per liter; Marshall *et al.* (1977), a four- to fivefold reduction with 200–250 mg chlorine per liter. It seems that low concentrations of chlorine (20–30 mg/l) give a small reduction in bacterial contamination and this reduction is not markedly increased with increasing chlorine concentration (Kelly *et al.* 1981).

When sprayed on beef tissue, both acetic and lactic acids reduce the microbial population (Anderson *et al.* 1977A,B; Snijders *et al.* 1979; Dezeure-Wallays and van Hoof 1980). However the effectiveness of the treatment varies not only with the concentration of the acid but also the region of the carcass treated. When 0.75 to 1% lactic acid is sprayed on beef carcasses, the reduction in count can vary between 3- and 100-fold over different sites on the carcass. Acid treatment at the concentrations needed to give a worthwhile reduction in count causes an initial discoloration of the carcass (Snijders *et al.* 1979; Dezeure-Wallays and van Hoof 1980). During chilled storage, the discoloration becomes less marked. Even though acetic and lactic acids are natural constituents of meats, the addition of these acids to fresh meats is normally prohibited.

There are several problems in the use of water of high temperatures for washing carcasses, apart from the increased cost. Hot water can cause an initial discoloration of the carcass, but after chilling carcasses regain their normal appearance (Smith and Graham 1978). If a spray system is used, there is a considerable drop in temperature before the water contacts the carcass. The temperature of water delivered at 90°C can fall to 63°C at impact on a carcass at a distance of 25 cm (Bailey 1971) and considerable amounts of water vapor can escape into the slaughter area (Patterson 1970). On contact with the carcass the water will cool rapidly, and this cooler water running down the carcass will form a heat-sink and reduce the effectiveness of heat transfer to the surface tissue. For hot water to be effective, all surfaces should be contacted by the hot water. The percentage destruction of organisms on, or in, the surface tissue will depend on the temperature of the water and its time of contact (Smith and Graham 1978) and on how deeply the organisms are embedded in the surface.

Patterson (1970) obtained a five- to eightfold reduction in aerobic mesophiles on cattle carcasses with water heated to 80°–96°C, while water at 80°C or less did not decrease the count on sheep carcasses (Patterson 1968). Bailey (1971) found only small differences in the counts of mesophiles on sheep carcasses washed with water at 15° or at 90°C (impact temperature of 63°C). However, the numbers of psychrotrophs were about tenfold lower on carcasses treated with hot water. Sheridan (1982) found no difference in the effectiveness of water at 40°–50°C and at 85°–90°C in reducing the count of mesophiles. However, both treatments gave a 36- to 60-fold reduction in the microbial count. On the other hand, a statistically significant effect of temperature was observed by Kelly *et al.* (1981) when carcasses were washed with water at impact temperatures of 10°, 37°, 65°, and 80°C. On the outside surfaces of lamb carcasses, a mean reduction in mesophiles of about tenfold was achieved when water with an impact temperature of 80°C was used. In contrast, on the diaphragm area of carcasses, water at 80°C had little effect on microbial count (Kelly *et al.* 1982). Even on the outer surfaces of carcasses, where hot water gave significant reductions in the mesophilic count, the numbers of pseudomonads and *Br. thermosphacta* were not significantly reduced. Why these organisms were apparently less sensitive to removal or destruction than aerobic mesophiles is not clear.

While hot water has the potential to reduce both mesophiles and psychrotrophs on carcasses, it is evident that the reductions obtained by spray-washing with hot water are variable and often relatively small. Presumably there are difficulties in obtaining a sufficiently long contact time of the hot water over all areas of the carcass. Immersion of naturally contaminated sheep carcasses in water at 80°C for 10 sec results in reductions of at least 10- to 100-fold in coliforms, and of 20- to 60-fold in aerobic mesophiles on both outer and body cavity surfaces (Smith and Graham 1978). When carcasses are sprayed for 10 seconds with water at approximately 90°C (impact temperature of 80°C) in a cabinet designed to reduce heat and water vapor loss and to provide a spray pattern covering all the outer surfaces of sheep carcasses, reductions of 300-fold in coliforms and aerobic mesophiles can be obtained on the outer surfaces of naturally contaminated carcasses (Graham *et al.* 1978).

Microflora of Cattle and Sheep Carcasses

At the completion of slaughter, dressing, and washing, cattle and sheep carcasses will have on their surfaces about 10^3 to 10^5 aerobic mesophiles per cm^2, the count varying with site and animal species (Ingram and Roberts 1976). The number of psychrotrophs varies between 0.1 and 10% of the mesophiles. While there are usually less than 10 Enterobacteriaceae or *E. coli* cells per cm^2, the number again depends on site and animal species (Ingram and Roberts 1976; Howe *et al.* 1976; Grau 1979). *Clostridium perfringens* can frequently be found in small numbers on sheep and cattle carcasses (Smart *et al.* 1979). The rate of detection of salmonellae varies considerably and is strongly influenced by the pre-slaughter treatment of the animals. While occasionally all carcasses in a group can be contaminated with salmonellae (Grau and Smith 1974), contamination rates are normally considerably less than this: 12–35.6% (Ingram and Simonsen 1980), 1.9% (Nazer and Osborne 1976), and less than 1% (Childers *et al.* 1973; Roberts 1976). *Campylobacter jejuni* (*coli*) may also be found on sheep and cattle carcasses (Table 1.5).

REFERENCES

ACUFF, G. R., VANDERZANT, C., GARDNER, F. A. and GOLAN, F. A. 1982. Examination of turkey eggs, poults and brooder house facilities for *Campylobacter jejuni*. J. Food Prot. *45*, 1279.

ANDERSON, E. S., GALBRAITH, N. S. and TAYLOR, C. E. D. 1961. An outbreak of human infection due to *Salmonella typhimurium* phage-type 20a associated with infection in calves. Lancet *1*, 854.

ANDERSON, M. E., MARSHALL, R. T., STRINGER, W. C. and NAUMANN, H. D. 1977A. Combined and individual effects of washing and sanitizing on bacterial counts of meat. A model system. J. Food Prot. *40*, 688.

ANDERSON, M. E., MARSHALL, R. T., STRINGER, W. C. and NAUMANN, H. D. 1977B. Efficacies of three sanitizers under six conditions of application to surfaces of beef. J. Food Sci. *42*, 326.

ANON. 1978. Canadian industry takes stand on bacteriological standards. Nat. Provis. 4th Feb., p. 8.

BAILEY, C. 1971. Spray washing of lamb carcasses. Proc. 17th Europ. Mtg. Meat Res. Workers, Bristol, England, p. 175.

BARNES, E. M. 1960. The sources of the different psychrophilic spoilage organisms on chilled eviscerated poultry. Proc. 10th Intnat. Congr. Refrig., Copenhagen 3, 97.
BARNES, E. M. 1976. Microbiological problems of poultry at refrigerator temperatures. A review. J. Sci. Food Agric. 27, 777.
BARNES, E. M. and IMPEY, C. S. 1970. The isolation and properties of the predominant anaerobic bacteria in the caeca of chickens and turkeys. Brit. Poult. Sci. 11, 467.
BARNES, E. M. and SHRIMPTON, D. H. 1968. The effect of processing and marketing procedures on the bacteriological condition and shelf life of eviscerated turkeys. Brit. Poult. Sci. 9, 243.
BARNES, E. M., MEAD, G. C., BARNUM, D. A. and HARRY, E. G. 1972. The intestinal flora of the chicken in the period 2 to 6 weeks of age, with particular reference to the anaerobic bacteria. Brit. Poult. Sci. 13, 311.
BARNES, E. M., MEAD, G. C., IMPEY, C. S. and ADAMS, B. W. 1978. The effect of dietary bacitracin on the incidence of Streptococcus faecalis sub-species liquefaciens and related streptococci in the intestines of young chicks. Brit. Poult. Sci. 19, 713.
BARNES, E. M., IMPEY, C. S. and STEVENS, B. J. H. 1979A. Factors affecting the incidence and anti-salmonella activity of the anaerobic caecal flora of the young chick. J. Hyg. 82, 263.
BARNES, E. M., MEAD, G. C., IMPEY, C. S. and ADAMS, B. W. 1979B. Spoilage organisms of refrigerated poultry meat. In Cold Tolerant Microbes in Spoilage and the Environment. p. 101. Academic Press, NY.
BARNES, E. M., IMPEY, C. S. and COOPER, D. M. 1980. Competitive exclusion of salmonellas from the newly hatched chick. Vet. Rec. 106, 61.
BEM, Z. and LEISTNER, L. 1970. Die Wasseraktivitätstoleranz der bei Pökelfleischwaren vorkommenden Hefen. Fleischwirtschaft 50, 492.
BERGEIM, O. 1940. Toxicity of intestinal volatile fatty acids for yeast and Esch. coli. J. Infect. Dis. 66, 222.
BIEMULLER, G. W., CARPENTER, J. A. and REYNOLDS, A. E. 1973. Reduction of bacteria on pork carcasses. J. Food Sci. 38, 261.
BIERER, B. W. 1960. Effect of age factor on mortality in Salmonella typhimurium infection in turkey poults. J. Am. Vet. Med. Assoc. 137, 657.
BOARD, R. G. 1969. The microbiology of the hen's egg. Advan. Appl. Microbiol. 11, 245.
BOHNHOFF, M. and MILLER, C. P. 1962. Enhanced susceptibility to Salmonella infection in streptomycin-treated mice. J. Infect. Dis. 111, 117.
BOHNHOFF, M., DRAKE, B. L. and MILLER, C. P. 1954. Effect of streptomycin on susceptibility of intestinal tract to experimental salmonella infection. Proc. Soc. Exp. Biol. Med. 86, 132.
BOHNHOFF, M., MILLER, C. P. and MARTIN, W. R. 1964A. Resistance of the mouse's intestinal tract to experimental salmonella infection. I. Factors which interfere with the initiation of infection by oral inoculation. J. Exp. Med. 120, 805.
BOHNHOFF, M., MILLER, C. P. and MARTIN, W. R. 1964B. Resistance of the mouse's intestinal tract to experimental salmonella infection. II. Factors responsible for its loss following streptomycin treatment. J. Exp. Med. 120, 817.
BROWNELL, J. R., SADLER, W. W. and FANELLI, M. J. 1969. Factors influencing the intestinal infection of chickens with Salmonella typhimurium. Avian Dis. 13, 804.
BROWNLIE, L. E. 1966. Effect of some environmental factors on psychrophilic microbacteria. J. Appl. Bacteriol. 29, 447.
BROWNLIE, L. E. and GRAU, F. H. 1967. Effect of food intake on growth and survival of salmonellas and Escherichia coli in the bovine rumen. J. Gen. Microbiol. 46, 125.
BRYAN, F. L. 1980. Poultry and poultry meat products. In Microbial Ecology of Foods. Vol. 2, p. 410. Academic Press, NY.

BRYAN, F. L., AYRES, J. C. and KRAFT, A. A.   1968.   Contributory sources of salmonellae on turkey products. Am. J. Epidemiol. *87*, 578.
BRYNER, J. H., O'BRIEN, P. A., ESTES, P. C. and FOLEY, J. W.   1972.   Studies of vibrios from gallbladder of market sheep and cattle. Am. J. Vet. Res. *33*, 1439.
BÜCHLI, K., VON SCHOTHORST, M. and KAMPELMACHER, E. H.   1966.   Untersuchungen über die hygienische Beschaffenheit von mit Wasser resp. Luft gekühltem Schlachtgeflügel. Arch. Lebensmittelhyg. *17*, 97.
BURCIK, E.   1950.   Uber die Beziehungen zwishen Hydratur und Wachstum bei Bacterien und Hefen. Arch. Mikrobiol. *15*, 203.
CAMPBELL, D. F., JOHNSTON, R. W., CAMPBELL, G. S., McCLAIN, D. and MACALUCO, J. F.   1983.   The microbiology of raw, eviscerated chickens: A ten year comparison. Poult. Sci. *62*, 437.
CARTER, P. B. and COLLINS, F. M.   1974.   The route of enteric infection in normal mice. J. Exp. Med. *139*, 1189.
CARTER, P. B., WOOLCOCK, J. B. and COLLINS, F. M.   1975.   Involvement of the upper respiratory tract in orally induced salmonellosis in mice. J. Infect. Dis. *131*, 570.
CHAMBERS, P. G. and LYSONS, R. J.   1979.   The inhibitory effect of bovine rumen fluid on *Salmonella typhimurium*. Res. Vet. Sci. *26*, 273.
CHILDERS, A. B., KEAHEY, E. E. and VINCENT, P. G.   1973.   Sources of salmonellae contamination of meat following approved livestock slaughtering procedures. II. J. Milk Food Technol. *36*, 635.
CHRISTIAN, J. H. B.   1980.   Reduced water activity. *In* Microbial Ecology of Foods. Vol. 1, p. 70. Academic Press, NY.
CHRISTIAN, J. H. B. and SCOTT, W. J.   1953.   Water relations of salmonellae at 30°C. Austral. J. Biol. Sci. *6*, 565.
CHRISTIAN, J. H. B. and WALTHO, J. A.   1962.   The water relations of staphylococci and micrococci. J. Appl. Bacteriol. *25*, 399.
CHUNG, G. T. and FROST, A. J.   1969.   The occurrence of salmonellae in slaughtered pigs. Austral. Vet. J. *45*, 350.
CORTESI, M. L. and CATELLANI, G.   1982.   The inspection of pig mesenteric lymph nodes: A possible source of salmonella diffusion. Proc. 28th Europ. Mtg. Meat Res. Workers, Madrid, Spain, p. 285.
COX, N. A., MERCURI, A. J., JUVEN, B. J. and THOMPSON, J. E.   1975.   *Enterobacteriaceae* at various stages of poultry chilling. J. Food Sci. *40*, 44.
DALEEL, E. E. and FROST, A. J.   1967.   The isolation of salmonella from cattle at Brisbane abattoirs. Austral. Vet. J. *43*, 203.
DEVRIESE, L. A., DEVOS, A. H. and VAN DAMME, L. R.   1975.   Quantitative aspects of *Staphylococcus aureus* flora of poultry. Poult. Sci. *54*, 95.
DEZEURE-WALLAYS, BR. and VAN HOOF, J.   1980.   Effect of lactic acid sprays on beef carcass contamination. Proc. 26th Europ. Mtg. Meat Res. Workers, Colorado Springs, CO., p. 316.
DICKINSON, A. B. and MOCQUOT, G.   1961.   Studies on the bacterial flora of the alimentary tract of pigs. I. *Enterobacteriaceae* and other gram-negative bacteria. J. Appl. Bacteriol. *24*, 252.
DOCKERTY, T. R., OCKERMAN, H. W., CAHILL, V. R., KUNKLE, L. E. and WEISER, H. H.   1970.   Microbial level of pork skin as affected by the dressing process. J. Anim. Sci. *30*, 884.
DOYLE, M. P.   1981.   *Campylobacter fetus* subsp. *jejuni*: An old pathogen of new concern. J. Food Prot. *44*, 480.
DOYLE, M. P. and ROMAN, D. J.   1981.   Growth and survival of *Campylobacter fetus* subsp. *jejuni* as a function of temperature and pH. J. Food Prot. *44*, 596.
DOYLE, M. P. and ROMAN, D. J.   1982.   Prevalence and survival of *Campylobacter jejuni* in unpasteurized milk. Appl. Environ. Microbiol. *44*, 1154.
EDEL, W. and KAMPELMACHER, E. H.   1971.   Salmonella infection in fattening calves at the farm. Zentralbl. Veterinaermed., Reihe *B18*, 617.

EDEL, W., GUINÉE, P. A. M., VAN SCHOTHORST, M. and KAMPELMACHER, E. H. 1967. Salmonella infections in pigs fattened with pellets and unpelleted meal. Zentralbl. Veterinaermed., Reihe *B14*, 393.

EDDY, B. P. 1960. The use and meaning of the term "psychrophilic." J. Appl. Bacteriol. *23*, 189.

EDDY, B. P. and KITCHELL, A. G. 1959. Cold-tolerant fermentative gram-negative organisms from meat and other sources. J. Appl. Bacteriol. *22*, 57.

ELLIOT, R. P. and HOBBS, B. C. 1980. Eggs and egg products. *In* Microbial Ecology of Foods. Vol. 2, p. 521. Academic Press, NY.

EMPEY, W. A. and SCOTT, W. J. 1939. Investigations on chilled beef. Part 1. - Microbial contamination acquired in the meatworks. Bulletin No. 126, Council for Scientific and Industrial Research, Australia.

FANELLI, M. J., SADLER, W. W., FRANTI, C. E. and BROWNELL, J. R. 1971. Localization of salmonellae within the intestinal tract of chickens. Avian Dis. *15*, 366.

FULLER, R. 1973. Ecological studies on the lactobacillus flora associated with the crop epithelium of the fowl. J. Appl. Bacteriol. *36*, 131.

FULLER, R. and MOORE, J. H. 1967. The inhibition of the growth of *Clostridium welchii* by lipids isolated from the contents of the small intestine of the pig. J. Gen. Microbiol. *46*, 23.

FURNISH, K., JR. 1974. Chilling poultry meat 4. An equipment suppliers viewpoint. Poult. Sci. *53*, 1286.

GALTON, M. M., SMITH, W. V., McELRATH, H. B. and HARDY, A. B. 1954. Salmonella in swine, cattle and the environment of abattoirs. J. Infect. Dis. *95*, 236.

GALTON, M. M., MACKEL, D. C., LEWIS, A. L., HAIRE, W. C. and HARDY, A. V. 1955. Salmonellosis in poultry and poultry processing plants in Florida. Am. J. Vet. Res. *16*, 132.

GARDINER, G. A. 1980–81. Identification and ecology of salt requiring *Vibrio* associated with cured meats. Meat Sci. *5*, 71.

GARDNER, G. A. 1982. Microbiology of processing: Bacon and ham. *In* Meat Microbiology. p. 129. Applied Science Publishers Ltd., London.

GERATS, G. E., SNIJDERS, J. M. A. and VAN LOGTESTIJN, J. G. 1981. Slaughter techniques and bacterial contamination of pig carcasses. Proc. 27th Europ. Mtg. Meat Res. Workers, Vienna, Austria, p. 198.

GHOSH, A. C. 1972. An epidemiological study of the incidence of salmonellas in pigs. J. Hyg. *70*, 151.

GIBBS, P. A., PATTERSON, J. T. and HARVEY, J. 1978A. Biochemical characteristics and enterotoxigenicity of *Staphylococcus aureus* strains isolated from poultry. J. Appl. Bacteriol. *44*, 57.

GIBBS, P. A., PATTERSON, J. T. and THOMPSON, J. K. 1978B. The distribution of *Staphylococcus aureus* in a poultry processing plant. J. Appl. Bacteriol. *44*, 401.

GIBSON, E. A. 1969. Salmonella infection in pigs. Brit. Vet. J. *125*, 431.

GILL, C. O. and HARRIS, L. M. 1982. Contamination of red-meat carcasses by *Campylobacter fetus* subsp. *jejuni*. Appl. Environ. Microbiol. *43*, 977.

GILL, C. O. and LOWRY, P. D. 1982. Growth at sub-zero temperatures of black spot fungi from meat. J. Appl. Bacteriol. *52*, 245.

GITTER, M. and KIDD, A. R. M. 1967. Isolation of *Salmonella typhimurium* from carrier pigs. Vet. Rec. *81*, 358.

GOREN, E. and DE JONG, W. A. 1980. *Campylobacter fetus* subspecies *jejuni* in chickens. Tijdschr. Diergeneesk. *105*, 724.

GRAHAM, A., EUSTACE, I. J. and POWELL, V. H. 1978. Surface decontamination—A new processing unit for improved hygiene on carcass meat. Proc. 24th Europ. Mtg. Meat Res. Workers, Kulmbach, West Germany, *B8*, 1.

GRANT, I. H., RICHARDSON, N. J. and BOKKENHEUSER, V. D. 1980. Broiler chickens as potential source of *Campylobacter* infections in humans. J. Clin. Microbiol. *11*, 508.

GRAU, F. 1979. Fresh meats: Bacterial association. Arch. Lebensmittelhyg. *30*, 81.

GRAU, F. H. and BROWNLIE, L. E. 1965. Occurrence of salmonellas in the bovine rumen. Austral. Vet. J. *41*, 321.

GRAU, F. H. and SMITH, M. G. 1974. Salmonella contamination of sheep and mutton carcasses related to pre-slaughter holding conditions. J. Appl. Bacteriol. *37*, 111.

GRAU, F. H., BROWNLIE, L. E. and ROBERTS, E. A. 1968. Effect of some pre-slaughter treatments on the *Salmonella* population in the bovine rumen and faeces. J. Appl. Bacteriol. *31*, 157.

GRAU, F. H., BROWNLIE, L. E. and SMITH, M. G. 1969. Effects of food intake on numbers of salmonellae and *Escherichia coli* in rumen and faeces of sheep. J. Appl. Bacteriol. *32*, 112.

GUINÉE, P. A. M., KAMPELMACHER, E. H., VAN KEULEN, A. and HOFSTRA, K. 1964. Salmonellae in healthy cows and calves in the Netherlands. Zentralbl. Veterinaermed., Reihe *B11*, 728.

HALL, G. A., JONES, P. W. and AITKEN, M. M. 1978. The pathogenesis of experimental intra-ruminal infections of cows with *Salmonella dublin*. J. Comp. Pathol. *88*, 409.

HADDOCK, R. L. 1970. Asymptomatic salmonellosis in a swine herd. Am. J. Publ. Health *60*, 2345.

HANSEN, R., ROGERS, R., ENGE, S. and JACOBS, N. J. 1964. Incidence of *Salmonella* in the hog colon as affected by handling practices prior to slaughter. J. Am. Vet. Med. Assoc. *145*, 139.

HARVEY, J., PATTERSON, J. T. and GIBBS, P. A. 1982. Enterotoxigenicity of *Staphylococcus aureus* strains isolated from poultry: Raw poultry carcasses as a potential food-poisoning hazard. J. Appl. Bacteriol. *52*, 251.

HEARD, T. W., JENNETT, N. E. and LINTON, A. H. 1972. Changing patterns of salmonella excretion in various cattle populations. Vet. Rec. *90*, 359.

HECHELMANN, H., BEM, Z., UCHIDA, K. and LEISTNER, L. 1974. Occurrence of the tribe *Klebsielleae* in refrigerated meat and meat products. Proc. 20th Europ. Mtg. Meat Res. Workers, Dublin, Ireland, p. 240.

HESS, E. and LOTT, G. 1970. Kontamination des Fleisches während und nach der Schlachtung. Fleischwirtschaft *50*, 47.

HINTON, M. 1975. *Salmonella dublin* abortion in cattle: Incidence and epidemiology. Brit. Vet. J. *131*, 94.

HOWE, K., LINTON, A. H. and OSBORNE, A. D. 1976. An investigation of calf carcass contamination by *Escherichia coli* from the gut contents at slaughter. J. Appl. Bacteriol. *41*, 37.

HUGHES, L. E., GIBSON, E. A., ROBERTS, H. E., DAVIES, E. T., DAVIES, G. and SOJKA, W. J. 1971. Bovine salmonellosis in England and Wales. Brit. Vet. J. *127*, 225.

HUMPHREY, T. J. 1981. The effects of pH and levels of organic matter on the death rates of salmonellas in chicken scald-tank water. J. Appl. Bacteriol. *51*, 27.

HUMPHREY, T. J., LANNING, D. G. and BERESFORD, D. 1981. The effect of pH adjustment on the microbiology of chicken scald-tank water with particular reference to the death rate of salmonellas. J. Appl. Bacteriol. *51*, 517.

INGRAM, M. and ROBERTS, T. A. 1976. The microbiology of the red meat carcass and the slaughterhouse. Roy. Soc. Health J. *96*, 270.

INGRAM, M. and SIMONSEN, B. 1980. Meat and meat products. *In* Microbial Ecology of Foods. Vol. 2, p. 333. Academic Press, NY.

JOHNSTON, R. W. and ELLIOTT, R. P. 1976. Meat and poultry products. *In* Compendium of Methods for the Microbiological Examination of Foods. p. 540. American Public Health Association, Inc., Washington, DC.

KAMPELMACHER, E. H., GUINÉE, P. A. M., HOFSTRA, K. and VAN KEULEN, A. 1961. Studies on salmonella in slaughter-houses. Zentralbl. Veterinaermed., Reihe *8*, 1025.

KAMPELMACHER, E. H., GUINÉE, P. A. M., HOFSTRA, K. and VAN KEULEN, A. 1963. Further studies on salmonella in slaughterhouses and in normal slaughter pigs. Zentralbl. Veterinaemed., Reihe *B10*, 1.

KAMPELMACHER, E. H., EDEL, W., GUINÉE, P. A. M. and VAN NOORLE JANSEN, L. M. 1969. Experimental salmonella infections in pigs. Zentralbl. Veterinaermed., Reihe *B16*, 717.

KANE, D. W. 1979. The prevalence of salmonella infection in sheep at slaughter. New Z. Vet. J. *27*, 110.

KELLY, C. A., LYNCH, B. and McLOUGHLIN, A. J. 1980. The microbiological quality of Irish lamb carcasses. Irish J. Food Sci. Technol. *4*, 125.

KELLY, C. A., DEMPSTER, J. R. and McLOUGHLIN, A. J. 1981. The effect of temperature, pressure and chlorine concentration of spray washing water on numbers of bacteria on lamb carcasses. J. Appl. Bacteriol. *51*, 415.

KELLY, C. A., LYNCH, B. and McLOUGHLIN, A. J. 1982. The effect of spray washing on the development of bacterial numbers and storage life of lamb carcasses. J. Appl. Bacteriol. *53*, 335.

KOTULA, A. W. and KINNER, J. A. 1964. Airborne micro-organisms in broiler processing plants. Appl. Microbiol. *12*, 179.

KUSCH, D. and GÖTZE, U. 1976. Die Ursachen der Staphylokokken-kontamination bei der Gerwinnung von Brathähnchen. Fleischwirtshaft *56*, 707.

LAFONT, J. P., BRÉE, A., NACIRI, M., YVORÉ, P., GUILLOT, J. F. and CHASLUS-DANCLA, E. 1983. Experimental study of some factors limiting 'competitive exclusion' of salmonella in chickens. Res. Vet. Sci. *34*, 16.

LAHELLEC, C. and COLIN, P. 1979. Bacterial flora of poultry: Changes due to variations in ecological conditions during processing and storage. Arch. Lebensmittelhyg. *30*, 95.

LAHELLEC, C., MEURIER, C. and CATSARAS, M. 1972. La flore psychrotrophe des carcasses de volailles. I. Evolution aux différents postes d'une chaîne d'abbatage. Ann. Rech. Vet. *3*, 421.

LANIGAN, G. W. 1963. Silage bacteriology 1. Water activity and temperature relationships of silage strains of *Lactobacillus plantarum*, *Lactobacillus brevis*, and *Pediococcus cerevisiae*. Austral. J. Biol. Sci. *16*, 606.

LEE, J. A., GHOSH, A. C., MANN, P. G. and TEE, G. H. 1972. Salmonellas on pig farms and in abattoirs. J. Hyg. *70*, 141.

LEISTNER, L. and RÖDEL, W. 1975. The significance of water activity for microorganisms in meats. *In* Water Relations of Foods. p. 309. Academic Press, NY.

LEISTNER, L., JOHANTGES, J., DEIBEL, R. H. and NIVEN, C. F., Jr. 1961. The occurrence and significance of salmonellae in meat animals and animal by-product feeds. Proc. 13th Res. Conf., p. 9. American Meat Institute Foundation, Chicago, IL.

LEV, M. and BRIGGS, C. A. E. 1956A. The gut flora of the chick. I. The flora of newly hatched chicks. J. Appl. Bacteriol. *19*, 36.

LEV, M. and BRIGGS, C. A. E. 1956B. The gut flora of the chick. II. The establishment of the flora. J. Appl. Bacteriol. *19*, 224.

LINTON, A. H. 1979. Salmonellosis in pigs. Brit. Vet. J. *135*, 109.

LINTON, A. H., JENNETT, N. E. and HEARD, T. W. 1970. Multiplication of salmonella in liquid feed and its influence on the duration of excretion in pigs. Res. Vet. Sci. *11*, 452.

LUECHTEFELD, N. W. and WANG, W-L. L. 1981. *Campylobacter fetus* subsp. *jejuni* in a turkey processing plant. J. Clin. Microbiol. *13*, 266.

McBRIDE, G. B., SKURA, B. J., YADA, R. Y. and BOWMER, E. J. 1980. Relationship between incidence of *Salmonella* contamination among pre-scalded, eviscerated and post-chilled chickens in a poultry processing plant. J. Food Prot. *43*, 538.

McCAUGHEY, W. J., McCLELLAND, T. G. and HANNA, J. 1971. Some observations on *Salmonella dublin* infection in clinically healthy beef cattle. Brit. Vet. J. *127*, 549.

McCAUGHEY, W. J., McCLELLAND, T. G. and RODDY, R. M.   1973.   Salmonella isolations in pigs. Vet. Rec. *92*, 191.

McDONAGH, V. P. and SMITH, H. G.   1958.   The significance of the abattoir in salmonella infection in Bradford. J. Hyg. *56*, 271.

MACKEY, B. M. and DERRICK, C. M.   1979.   Contamination of the deep tissues of carcasses by bacteria present on the slaughter instruments or in the gut. J. Appl. Bacteriol. *46*, 355.

MAY, K. N.   1974.   Chilling poultry meat. 3. Changes in microbial numbers during final washing and chilling of commercially slaughtered broilers. Poult. Sci. *53*, 1282.

MARSHALL, R. T., ANDERSON, M. E., NAUMANN, H. D. and STRINGER, W. C.   1977.   Experiments in sanitizing beef with sodium hypochlorite. J. Food Prot. *40*, 246.

MEAD, G. C.   1976.   Microbiology of the poultry carcass and processing plant. Roy. Soc. Health J. *96*, 164.

MEAD, G. C.   1982.   Microbiology of poultry and game birds. *In* Meat Microbiology. p. 67. Applied Science Publishers Ltd., Barking, Essex, England.

MEAD, G. C. and ADAMS, B. W.   1975.   Some observations on the caecal microflora of the chick during the first 2 weeks of life. Brit. Poult. Sci. *16*, 169.

MEAD, G. C. and IMPEY, C. S.   1970.   The distribution of clostridia in poultry processing plants. Brit. Poult. Sci. *11*, 407.

MEAD, G. C., ADAMS, B. W. and HAQUE, Z.   1982.   Studies on the incidence, origin and spoilage potential of psychrotrophic Enterobacteriaceae occurring on processed poultry. Fleischwirtschaft *62*, 1140.

MEYNELL, G. G.   1955.   Some factors affecting the resistance of mice to oral infection by *Salmonella typhimurium*. Proc. R. Soc. Med. *48*, 916.

MEYNELL, G. G.   1963.   Antibacterial mechanisms of the mouse gut II: The role of Eh and volatile fatty acids in the normal gut. Brit. J. Exp. Pathol. *44*, 209.

MEYNELL, G. G. and SUBBAIAH, T. V.   1963.   Antibacterial mechanisms of the mouse gut I. Kinetics of infection by *Salmonella typhimurium* in normal and streptomycin-treated mice studied with abortive transductants. Brit. J. Exp. Pathol. *44*, 197.

MILLER, C. P. and BOHNHOFF, M.   1963.   Changes in the mouse's enteric microflora associated with enhanced susceptibility to *Salmonella* infection following streptomycin treatment. J. Infect. Dis. *113*, 59.

MOO, D., O'BOYLE, D., MATHERS, W. and FROST, A. J.   1980.   The isolation of salmonella from jejunal and caecal lymph nodes of slaughtered animals. Austral. Vet. J. *56*, 181.

MORITA, R. Y.   1975.   Psychrophilic bacteria. Bact. Rev. *39*, 144.

MORRIS, G. K. and WELLS, J. G.   1970.   *Salmonella* contamination in a poultry-processing plant. Appl. Microbiol. *19*, 795.

MOSSEL, D. A. A.   1977.   Microbiology of Foods. Revised Ed. University of Utrecht, Utrecht, The Netherlands.

MULDER, S. J.   1978.   *Microbacterium thermosphacta*: Spoilage indicator of beef. Proc. 24th Europ. Mtg. Meat Res. Workers, Kulmbach, West Germany, *B4*, 1.

MULDER, R. W. A. W. and DORRESTEIJN, L. W. J.   1977.   Hygiene beim Brühen von Schlachtgeflügel. Fleischwirtshaft *57*, 2220.

MULDER, R. W. A. W. and VEERKAMP, C. H.   1974.   Improvements in poultry slaughterhouse hygiene as a result of cleaning before cooling. Poult. Sci. *53*, 1690.

MULDER, R. W. A. W., DORRESTEIJN, L. W. J. and VAN DER BROEK, J.   1978.   Cross-contamination during the scalding and plucking of broilers. Brit. Poult. Sci. *19*, 61.

NABBUT, N. H. and AL-NAKHLI, H. M.   1982.   Incidence of salmonellae in lymph nodes, spleens and feces of sheep and goats slaughtered in the Riyadh public abattoir. J. Food Prot. *45*, 1314.

NAZER, A. H. K. and OSBORNE, A. D.   1976.   Salmonella infection and contamination of veal calves: A slaughterhouse survey. Brit. Vet. J. *132*, 192.

NEWTON, K. G., HARRISON, J. C. L. and WAUTERS, A. M.   1978.   Sources of psychrotrophic bacteria on meat at the abattoir. J. Appl. Bacteriol. *45*, 75.

NORBERG, P.   1981.   Enteropathogenic bacteria in frozen chicken. Appl. Environ. Microbiol. *42*, 32.

NOTERMANS, S. and KAMPELMACHER, E. H.   1975.   Heat destruction of some bacterial strains attached to broiler skin. Brit. Poult. Sci. *16*, 351.

NOTERMANS, S. and KAMPELMACHER, E. H.   1983.   Attachment of bacteria in meat processing. Fleischwirtschaft *63*, 72.

NOTERMANS, S., VAN LEUSDEN, F. M. and VAN SCHOTHORST, M.   1977.   Suitability of different bacterial groups for determining faecal contamination during post scalding stages in the processing of broiler chickens. J. Appl. Bacteriol. *43*, 383.

NOTERMANS, S., TERBIJHE, R. J. and VAN SCHOTHORST, M.   1980.   Removing faecal contamination of broilers by spray-cleaning during evisceration. Brit. Poult. Sci. *21*, 115.

NOTERMANS, S., DUFRENNE, J. and VAN LEEUWEN, W. J.   1982.   Contamination of broiler chickens by *Staphylococcus aureus* during processing; incidence and origin. J. Appl. Bacteriol. *52*, 275.

NOTTINGHAM, P. M. and URSELMANN, A. J.   1961.   Salmonella infection in calves and other animals. New Z. J. Agric. Res. *4*, 449.

NOTTINGHAM, P. M., PENNEY, N. and WYBORN, R.   1972.   Salmonella infection in calves and other animals. III. Further studies with calves and pigs. New Z. J. Agric. Res. *15*, 279.

NURMI, E. and RANTALA, M.   1973.   New aspects of *Salmonella* infection in broiler production. Nature (London) *241*, 210.

OOSTEROM, J.   1980.   The presence of *Campylobacter fetus* subspecies *jejuni* in normal slaughtered pigs. Tijdschr. Diergeneesk. *105*, 49.

OOSTEROM, J., ENGELS, G. B., PETERS, R. and POT, R.   1982.   *Campylobacter jejuni* in cattle and raw milk in The Netherlands. J. Food Prot. *45*, 1212.

PARK, C. E., STANKIEWICZ, Z. K., LOVETT, J. and HUNT, J.   1981.   Incidence of *Campylobacter jejuni* in fresh eviscerated whole market chickens. Canad. J. Microbiol. *27*, 841.

PATTERSON, J. T.   1968.   Hygiene in meat processing plants. 3. Methods of reducing carcase contamination. North. Ireland Minist. Agric. Rec. Agric. Res. *17*, 7.

PATTERSON, J. T.   1970.   Hygiene in meat processing plants. 4. Hot-water washing of carcases. North. Ireland Minist. Agric. Rec. Agric. Res. *18*, 85.

PATTERSON, J. T.   1972.   Hygiene in meat processing plants. 5. The effect of different methods of washing, drying and cooling on subsequent microbial changes in sheep carcases. North. Ireland Minist. Agric. Rec. Agric. Res. *20*, 7.

PATTERSON, J. T.   1973.   Airborne microorganisms in poultry processing plants. Brit. Poult. Sci. *14*, 161.

PATTERSON, J. T. and GIBBS, P. A.   1977.   Incidence and spoilage potential of isolates from vacuum-packaged meat of high pH value. J. Appl. Bacteriol. *43*, 25.

PATTERSON, J. T. and GIBBS, P. A.   1978A.   Some microbiological considerations applying to the conditioning, ageing and vacuum packaging of lamb. J. Food Technol. *13*, 1.

PATTERSON, J. T. and GIBBS, P. A.   1978B.   Sources and properties of some organisms isolated in two abattoirs. Meat Sci. *2*, 263.

PEEL, B. and SIMMONS, G. C.   1978.   Factors in the spread of salmonellae in meatworks with special reference to contamination of knives. Austral. Vet. J. *54*, 106.

PITT, J. I.   1975.   Xerophilic fungi and the spoilage of foods of plant origin. *In* Water Relations of Foods. p. 273. Academic Press, NY.

PIVNICK, H. and NURMI, E.   1982.   The Nurmi concept and its role in the control of salmonellae in poultry. *In* Developments in Food Microbiology—1. p. 41. Applied Science Publishers Ltd., Essex, England.

PRESCOTT, J. F. and BRUIN-MOSCH, C. W.   1981.   Carriage of *Campylobacter jejuni* in healthy and diarrheic animals. Am. J. Vet. Res. *42*, 164.

PROST, E. and LIBELT, K.   1972.   Variabilität der bakteriellen Kontamination der Schlachttierkörper und des Brühwassers bei der Schlachtung von Schweinen. Fleischwirtschaft *52*, 867.

PUBLIC HEALTH LABORATORY SERVICE AND VETERINARY LABORATORY SERVICES.   1965.   Salmonellae in cattle and their feeding stuffs, and the relation to human infection. J. Hyg. *63*, 223.

PUBLIC HEALTH LABORATORY SERVICE WORKING GROUP, SKOVGAARD, N. and NIELSEN, B. B.   1972.   Salmonellas in pigs and animal feeding stuffs in England and Wales and in Denmark. J. Hyg. *70*, 127.

RANTALA, M. and NURMI, E.   1973.   Prevention of the growth of *Salmonella infantis* in chicks by the flora of the alimentary tract of chickens. Brit. Poult. Sci. *14*, 627.

RIBEIRO, C. D.   1978.   Campylobacter enteritis. Lancet *ii*, 270.

ROBERTS, T. A.   1976.   Microbiological guidelines for meat. Proc. 22nd Europ. Mtg. Meat Res. Workers, Malmö, Sweden, L0, 1.

ROBERTS, T. A.   1980.   Contamination of meat. The effects of slaughter practices on the bacteriology of the red meat carcass. Roy. Soc. Health J. *100*, 3.

ROBERTS, T. A., MACFIE, H. J. H. and HUDSON, W. R.   1980.   The effect of incubation temperature and site of sampling on assessment of the numbers of bacteria on red meat carcasses at commercial abattoirs. J. Hyg. *85*, 371.

ROBINSON, D. A.   1981.   Infective dose of *Campylobacter jejuni* in milk. Brit. Med. J. *282*, 1584.

ROBINSON, R. A.   1966.   Field and experimental epidemiology of salmonella infection in calves. Proc. New Z. Soc. Anim. Prod. *26*, 134.

ROBINSON, R. A. and LOKEN, K. I.   1968.   Age susceptibility and excretion of *Salmonella typhimurium* in calves. J. Hyg. *66*, 207.

ROBINSON, R. A. and ROYAL, W. A.   1971.   Field epizootiology of salmonella infection in sheep. New Z. J. Agric. Res. *14*, 442.

ROSEF, O.   1981.   Isolation of *Campylobacter fetus* subsp. *jejuni* from the gallbladder of normal slaughter pigs, using an enrichment procedure. Acta Vet. Scand. *22*, 149.

SADLER, W. W., BROWNELL, J. R. and FANELLI, M. J.   1969.   Influence of age and inoculum level on shed pattern of *Salmonella typhimurium* in chickens. Avian Dis. *13*, 793.

SALANITRO, J. P., BLAKE, I. G. and MUIRHEAD, P. A.   1974A.   Studies on the cecal microflora of commercial broiler chickens. Appl. Microbiol. *28*, 439.

SALANITRO, J. P., FAIRCHILDS, I. G. and ZGORNICKI, Y. D.   1974B.   Isolation, culture characteristics, and identification of anaerobic bacteria from the chicken cecum. Appl. Microbiol. *27*, 678.

SALANITRO, J. P., BLAKE, I. G., MUIRHEAD, P. A., MAGLIO, M. and GOODMAN, J. R.   1978.   Bacteria isolated from the duodenum, ileum, and cecum of young chicks. Appl. Environ. Microbiol. *35*, 782.

SALISBURY, R. M.   1958.   Salmonella infections in animals and birds in New Zealand. New Z. Vet. J. *6*, 76.

SAMUEL, J. L., O'BOYLE, D. A., MATHERS, W. J. and FROST, A. J.   1979.   Isolation of salmonella from mesenteric lymph nodes of healthy cattle at slaughter. Res. Vet. Sci. *28*, 238.

SAMUEL, J. L., O'BOYLE, D. A., MATHERS, W. J. and FROST, A. J.   1980A.   Distribution of *Salmonella* in the carcasses of normal cattle at slaughter. Res. Vet. Sci. *28*, 368.

SAMUEL, J. L., O'BOYLE, D. A., MATHERS, W. J. and FROST, A. J.   1980B.   The contamination with salmonella of bovine livers in an abattoir. Austral. Vet. J. *56*, 526.

SAMUEL, J. L., ECCLES, J. A. and FRANCIS, J.   1981.   Salmonella in the intestinal tract and associated lymph nodes of sheep and cattle. J. Hyg. *87*, 225.

SCHEFFERLE, H. E.   1965.   The microbiology of built up poultry litter. J. Appl. Bacteriol. *28*, 403.

SCHOLEFIELD, J., MENON, T. G. and LAM, C. W.   1981.   Psychrotroph contamination of pig carcasses. Proc. 27th Europ. Mtg. Meat Res. Workers, Vienna, Austria, p. 621.

SCOTT, W. J.   1953.   Water relations of *Staphylococcus aureus* at 30°C. Austral. J. Biol. Sci. *6*, 549.

SCOTT, W. J.   1957.   Water relations of food spoilage organisms. Advan. Food Res. *7*, 83.

SCOTT, W. J.   1962.   Available water and microbial growth. Proc. Low Temp. Microbiol. Symp., 1961, p. 89. Campbell Soup Co., Camden, NJ.

SHANKER, S., ROSENFIELD, J. A., DAVEY, G. R. and SORRELL, T. C.   1982. *Campylobacter jejuni*: Incidence in processed broilers and biotype distribution in human and broiler isolates. Appl. Environ. Microbiol. *43*, 1219.

SHERIDAN, J. J.   1982.   Problems associated with commercial lamb washing in Ireland. Meat Sci. *6*, 211.

SHOTTS, E. B., MARTIN, W. T. and GALTON, M. M.   1961.   Further studies on salmonella in human and animal foods and in the environment of processing plants. Proc. U.S. Livestock Sanit. Assoc., 65th Ann. Mtg., p. 309.

SIMMONS, N. A. and GIBBS, F. J.   1979.   *Campylobacter* spp. in oven-ready poultry. J. Infect. *1*, 159.

SKIRROW, M. B. and BENJAMIN, J.   1980.   '1001' Campylobacters: Cultural characteristics of intestinal campylobacters from man and animals. J. Hyg. *85*, 427.

SMART, J. L., ROBERTS, T. A., STRINGER, M. F. and SHAH, N.   1979.   The incidence and serotypes of *Clostridium perfringens* on beef, pork and lamb carcasses. J. Appl. Bacteriol. *46*, 377.

SMELTZER, T. and THOMAS, R.   1981.   Transfer of salmonellae to meat and offal by knives. Austral. Vet. J. *57*, 433.

SMELTZER, T. I., PEEL, B. and COLLINS, G.   1979.   The role of equipment that has direct contact with the carcase in the spread of salmonella in a beef abattoir. Austral. Vet. J. *55*, 275.

SMELTZER, T., THOMAS, R. and COLLINS, G.   1980A.   The role of equipment having accidental or indirect contact with the carcase in the spread of *Salmonella* in an abattoir. Austral. Vet. J. *56*, 14.

SMELTZER, T., THOMAS, R. and COLLINS, G.   1980B.   Salmonellae on posts, handrails and hands in a beef abattoir. Austral. Vet. J. *56*, 184.

SMIBERT, R. M.   1965.   *Vibrio fetus* var *intestinalis* isolated from fecal and intestinal contents of clinically normal sheep: Isolation of microaerophilic vibrios. Am. J. Vet. Res. *26*, 315.

SMITH, H. W.   1961.   The development of the bacterial flora of the faeces of animal and man: The changes that occur during ageing. J. Appl. Bacteriol. *24*, 235.

SMITH, H. W.   1965.   The development of the flora of the alimentary tract in young animals. J. Pathol. Bacteriol. *90*, 495.

SMITH, H. W. and TUCKER, J. F.   1975.   The effect of feeding diets containing permitted antibiotics on the faecal excretion of *Salmonella typhimurium* by experimentally infected chickens. J. Hyg. *75*, 293.

SMITH, M. G. and GRAHAM, A.   1978.   Destruction of *Escherichia coli* and salmonellae on mutton carcasses by treatment with hot water. Meat Sci. *2*, 119.

SMITH, M. G. and GRAU, F. H.   1973.   Occurrence of salmonellas on the hides and fleeces of cattle and sheep at slaughter. Austral. Vet. J. *49*, 219.

SMITH, M. V. and MULDOON, P. J.   1974.   *Campylobacter fetus* subspecies *jejuni* (*Vibrio fetus*) from commercially processed poultry. Appl. Microbiol. *27*, 995.

SNIJDERS, J. M. A.   1975.   Hygiene bei der Schlachtung von Schweinen. I. Das Brühen der Schlachtschweine. Fleischwirtschaft *55*, 836.

46   F. H. GRAU

SNIJDERS, J. M. A. and GERATS, G. E.   1976.   Hygeine bei der Schlachtung von
    Schweinen. IV. Bakteriologische Beschaffenheit der Schlachttierkörper während
    verschiedener Schlachtphasen. Fleischwirtschaft 56, 717.
SNIJDERS, J. M. A., SCHOENMAKERS, M. J. G., GERATS, G. E. and DE PIJPER, F.
    W. 1979. Dekontamination schlachtwarmer Rinderkörper mit organischen
    Säuren. Fleischwirtschaft 59, 656.
SNOEYENBOS, G. H., WEINACK, O. M. and SMYSER, C. F.   1978.   Protecting
    chicks and poults from salmonellae by oral administration of "normal" gut micro-
    flora. Avian Dis. 22, 273.
SOERJADI, A. S., STEHAN, S. M., SNOEYENBOS, G. H., WEINACK, O. M. and
    SMYSER, C. F. 1981. Some measurements of protection against paratyphoid
    salmonella and Escherichia coli by competitive exclusion in chickens. Avian Dis.
    25, 706.
SOJKA, W. J. and FIELD, H. I.   1970.   Salmonellosis in England and Wales 1958–
    1967. Vet. Bull. 40, 515.
STERN, N. J.   1981.   Recovery rate of Campylobacter fetus ssp. jejuni on eviscerated
    pork, lamb, and beef carcasses. J. Food Sci. 46, 1292.
STOLLE, A.   1981.   Spreading of salmonellas during cattle slaughtering. J. Appl. Bac-
    teriol. 50, 239.
SVEDHEM, A. and KAIJSER, B.   1981.   Isolation of Campylobacter jejuni from do-
    mestic animals and pets: Probable origin of human infection. J. Infect. 3, 37.
TANNOCK, G. W. and SMITH, J. M. B.   1971A.   A Salmonella carrier state involving
    the upper respiratory tract of mice. J. Infect. Dis. 123, 502.
TANNOCK, G. W. and SMITH, J. M. B.   1971B.   A Salmonella carrier state of sheep
    following intranasal inoculation. Res. Vet. Sci. 12, 371.
THOMAS, C. J. and McMEEKIN, T. A.   1980.   Contamination of broiler carcass skin
    during commercial processing procedures: An electron microscopic study. Appl.
    Environ. Microbiol. 40, 133.
THOMSON, J. E., WHITEHEAD, W. K. and MERCURI, A. J.   1974.   Chilling poultry
    meat 2. Chilling poultry meat—A literature review. Poult. Sci. 53, 1268.
TIMONEY, J.   1970.   Salmonellae in Irish pigs at slaughter. Irish Vet. J. 24, 141.
TROLLER, J. A. and CHRISTIAN, J. H. B.   1978.   Water Activity and Food. Academic
    Press, NY.
TSAI, R. Y. T., GOEPFERT, J. M., CASSENS, R. G. and BRISKEY, E. J.   1971.   A
    comparison of salmonella excretion by stress-susceptible and stress-resistant pigs.
    J. Food Sci. 36, 889.
TURNBULL, P. C. B. and ROSE, P.   1982.   Campylobacter jejuni and salmonella in
    raw red meats. J. Hyg. 88, 29.
VAN SCHOTHORST, M., NOTERMANS, S. and KAMPELMACHER, E. H.   1972.
    Einige hygienische aspekte der Geflügelschlachtung. Fleischwirtschaft 52, 749.
WALKER, H. W. and AYRES, J. C.   1956.   Incidence and kinds of micro-organisms
    associated with commercially dressed poultry. Appl. Microbiol. 4, 345.
WALKER, H. W. and AYRES, J. C.   1959.   Microorganisms associated with commer-
    cially processed turkeys. Poult. Sci. 38, 1351.
WARNER, R. G. and FLATT, W. P.   1965.   Anatomical development of the ruminant
    stomach. In Physiology of Digestion in the Ruminant. p. 24. Butterworth Inc.,
    Washington, DC.
WILLIAMS, L. P. and NEWELL, K. W.   1967.   Patterns of salmonella excretion in
    market swine. Am. J. Publ. Health 57, 466.
WILLIAMS, L. P. and NEWELL, K. W.   1968.   Sources of salmonellae in market
    swine. J. Hyg. 66, 281.
WILLIAMS, L. P. and NEWELL, K. W.   1970.   Salmonella excretion in joy-riding pigs.
    Am. J. Publ. Health 60, 926.
WODZINSKI, R. J. and FRAZIER, W. C.   1960.   Moisture requirements of bacteria I.
    Influence of temperature and pH on requirements of Pseudomonas fluorescens. J.
    Bacteriol. 79, 572.

WODZINSKI, R. J. and FRAZIER, W. C.   1961A.   Moisture requirements of bacteria II. Influence of temperature, pH, and malate concentration on requirements of *Aerobacter aerogenes*. J. Bacteriol. *81*, 353.
WODZINSKI, R. J. and FRAZIER, W. C.   1961B.   Moisture requirements of bacteria V. Influence of temperature and decreased partial pressure of oxygen on requirements of three species of bacteria. J. Bacteriol. *81*, 409.
WOLIN, M. J.   1966.   Volatile fatty acids and the inhibition of *Escherichia coli*. Bacteriol. Proc., p. 18.
ZIOLECKI, A. and BRIGGS, C. A. E.   1961.   The microflora of the rumen of the young calf: II. Source, nature and development. J. Appl. Bacteriol. *24*, 148.
ZOTTOLA, E. A., SCHMELTZ, D. L. and JEZESKI, J. J.   1970.   Isolation of salmonellae and other airborne microorganisms in turkey processing plants. J. Milk Food Technol. *33*, 395.

The Control of Microbial Spoilage in Fresh Meats

C.O. Gill[1]

INTRODUCTION

Fresh meats present a rich medium for the support of microbial growth and will ultimately be rendered unacceptable to consumers as a consequence of such growth unless the meat is frozen to temperatures too low for growth to occur. However, it is possible at higher temperatures to alter the rate of spoilage development by modifying the storage conditions, and thus the environment to which the bacteria are exposed. The effectiveness of any particular set of storage conditions can only be fully appreciated if the reactions of the microbial population to them are understood. Variations of storage conditions can alter not only the rate of growth of the

[1]Meat Industry Research Institute of New Zealand (Inc.), P.O. Box 617, Hamilton, New Zealand.

Advances in Meat Research, Volume 2
Copyright 1986 by AVI Publishing Co.
All rights of reproduction in any form reserved
ISBN 0-87055-498-0

spoilage flora but also its composition, and the form of spoilage that develops is dependent upon the flora composition. It is, therefore, the purpose of this chapter to consider meat as an ecological niche for microbial growth with the objective of explaining spoilage development and control in terms of microbial ecology.

SPOILAGE—A DEFINITION

Some authors have had difficulty in deciding what is meant by the term spoilage. This is not surprising as the word is generally used in a subjective sense to signify that the writer would be loath to consume the food in question, although in reports of experimentation the criteria for spoilage are usually clearly evident without being precisely defined. It has been contended that spoilage mechanisms cannot be properly understood without a sound definition of the term (Jay 1972). This is not really a practical problem but rather one of logic and communication. Part of the problem seems to arise from spoilage being thought of as a single, particular, objective state. In fact, spoilage describes the subjective evaluation of a multiplicity of conditions. Because the term is subjective it is not always possible to usefully equate "spoilage" and "nonacceptability" as the question arises of not acceptable to whom. The term spoilage will therefore be used in this chapter to signify *any single symptom or group of symptoms of overt microbial activity, manifest by changes in meat odor, flavor, or appearance*, without considering whether any particular consumers would find these changes objectionable, although some almost certainly would.

GROWTH OF BACTERIA ON MEAT

The Substrate

Meat comprises various proportions of muscle, fat, and connective tissue. Fat and connective tissue are very different than muscle, and under most circumstances spoilage of muscle tissue is the critical factor determining meat storage life.

Muscle tissue composition changes after death with the development of rigor. The quantities of the bulk materials, protein, and fat, do not alter during rigor development. Neither are they substrates for microbial attack before the development of spoilage (Dainty et al. 1975; Gill and Newton 1980a). Instead, bacteria grow on meat at the expense of some low molecular weight soluble components. The concentrations of several of these microbial nutrients alter considerably during the development of rigor (Table 2.1), with the major changes resulting from the degradation of reserve glycogen via glycolysis. Most of the glycogen is converted to lactic

TABLE 2.1. Concentrations of the Main Low Molecular Weight Soluble Components of Beef Before and After Completion of Rigor

Substance	Concentration (mg/gm)	
	Prerigor	Postrigor
Creatine phosphate	3.0	—
Creatine	4.5	6.5
Adenosine triphosphate	3.0	—
Inosine monophosphate	0.2	3.0
Glycogen	10.0	1.0
Glucose	0.5	0.1
Glucose 6-phosphate	1.0	0.2
Lactic acid	1.0	9.0
Amino acids	2.0	3.5
Dipeptides (carnosine, anserine)	3.0	3.0
pH	7.2	5.5

acid, the accumulation of which causes the muscle pH to fall. Glycolysis finally ceases when deamination of adenosine monophosphate has removed this substance which is an essential cofactor for activity of some glycolytic enzymes. There is, therefore, usually residual glycogen in the postrigor muscle, which normally has an ultimate pH between 5.8 and 5.5 (Bendall 1973). Glycolytic intermediates, notably glucose 6-phosphate, are present in low concentration as is glucose itself (Fischer and Augustini 1977). Glucose is not a glycolytic intermediate and the process by which it is formed from glycogen remains speculative (Bendall 1973). Several studies have found the glucose concentration in beef to be around 100 μg/g of tissue, but other meats are reported to have concentrations up to 1 mg/g (Fischer and Augustini 1977; Gill 1976). However, glucose concentrations of several hundred micrograms per gram have recently been reported for beef (Farber and Idziak 1982) so it is possible that environmental factors may cause glucose levels in meat from any species to vary as widely as the reported interspecific variation. Since glucose concentration can be a prime determinant of the time of spoilage onset in meat, further work on its formation in muscle tissue would seem necessary.

Site of Microbial Activity

It has been claimed that deep muscle tissue harbors an "intrinsic" flora derived from the gut via the blood or lymphatic systems (Ingram and Dainty 1971), but it is now clear that deep tissue from animals killed under reasonably hygienic conditions is generally sterile (Gill 1979). Surface bacteria do not penetrate into muscle tissue until high bacterial numbers have been attained and overt spoilage has developed. Penetration is delayed because bacterial proteolytic activity is required and proteolytic enzymes are produced only in the late logarithmic phase of growth (Gill and Penney 1977). Spoilage of meat is, therefore, a surface phenomenon unless comminution or mechanical tenderizing have destroyed the tissue integrity and spread bacteria from the surface throughout the meat.

Spoilage Bacteria

In developed countries, most meat is at least kept cool and the bulk of it is refrigerated. Spoilage is, therefore, caused predominantly by organisms capable of growth at refrigeration temperatures, <5°C. Such spoilage organisms are all psychrotrophs, that is, they are capable of growth at temperatures close to zero but do not show the low optimum growth temperature of psychrophiles (Eddy 1960).

The relative abilities of different organisms to render meat unappetizing to consumers are important for any consideration of spoilage. Visible effects, if they occur, will be very obvious to a consumer. All organisms can eventually form visible colonies or slime, but this requires very large numbers to be present. However, if H_2S is formed it will combine with muscle pigments to form sulfmyoglobin which is seen as green discoloration (Nicol et al. 1970). In addition, H_2S and organic sulfides have highly offensive odors and are organoleptically detectable in very low concentrations. Organisms capable of producing substantial quantities of these substances are therefore regarded as having a high spoilage potential (Herbert and Shewan 1976). Other organisms that can produce relatively large quantities of other volatile organic compounds, such as amines, esters, and acetoin, are also regarded as being of high spoilage potential (McMeekin 1981).

The development of spoilage will vary depending on which groups or species of bacteria are dominant in the flora. Some of the groups commonly referred to are very broad and the organisms within them of greatest importance for spoilage have been more precisely defined (Gillespie 1981; Hitchener et al. 1982; Molin and Ternstrom 1982; Shaw and Latty 1982; Vanderzant et al. 1982). However, elaborating on the identities of organisms within these groups would complicate a general discussion of control of spoilage without necessarily conferring commensurate benefits. These groups will therefore be referred to as single entities although it must be borne in mind that each embraces a range of organisms with wide quantitative variations in characteristics ascribed to the group as a whole.

The Onset of Spoilage

All bacteria grow at the expense of the low molecular weight soluble components of meat (Gill and Newton 1978). The concentration of these substrates, and the order in which they are attacked by different groups (Table 2.2), can affect the course of spoilage. Other environmental factors,

TABLE 2.2. Order of Utilization of Individual Low Molecular Weight Components of Meat for Bacterial Growth[a]

Substrate	Pseudomonas	Aerobic growth		Brochothrix thermosphacta	Alteromonas putrifaciens
		Acinetobacter	Enterobacter		
Glucose	1	—	1	1	1
Glucose 6-phosphate	—	—	2	—	—
Amino acids	2	1	3	2 (glutamate only)	1 and 2 (serine, cysteine)
Lactate	3	2	4	—	3

	Anaerobic growth		Brochothrix thermosphacta	Alteromonas putrefaciens
	Lactobacillus	Enterobacter		
Glucose	1	1	1	1
Glucose 6-phosphate	—	2	—	—
Amino acids	2 (arginine only)	—	—	1 (serine, cysteine)

[a] Data from Gill and Newton 1977; Newton and Gill 1978A.

such as the presence or absence of oxygen, can drastically alter the flora composition. Spoilage by each of the major groups will therefore be considered separately.

Pseudomonas. These strict aerobes are the most important organisms in the aerobic spoilage of meat. The pseudomonads preferentially utilize glucose (Jacoby 1964). While using this substrate they do not produce malodorous compounds. However, when glucose is exhausted they attack amino acids with malodorous sulfides, esters, acids, etc., being formed as by-products (Miller *et al.* 1973A,B; Thomas and McMeekin 1981; Pittard *et al.* 1982). The odors of such by-products are usually the first symptom of chill temperature spoilage. Pseudomonads growing on the muscle surface will consume glucose until, as their numbers increase, the rate of diffusion of glucose from the underlying tissue becomes inadequate to meet the bacterial demand. Glucose concentration gradients will then develop with reduced glucose concentrations at the surface. Finally, the surface concentration falls to zero and the pseudomonads start to utilize amino acids (Gill 1976). This usually occurs when the bacterial cell density exceeds 10^8 cells per cm^2 (Fig. 2.1). When bacterial numbers approach 10^9 per cm^2, slime becomes visible on the meat surface. When glucose concentrations are about 1 mg/g or even greater, appearance of visible slime and off-odors are likely to be nearly contemporaneous. Growth of the aerobic flora ceases with bacterial numbers in excess of 10^9 per cm^2, apparently be-

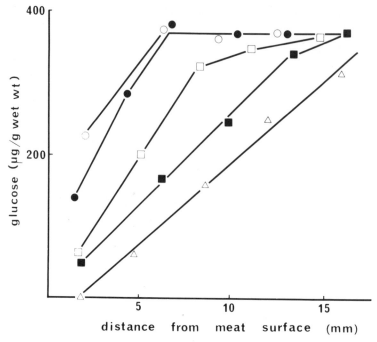

FIG. 2.1.   Concentration gradients of glucose in meat with a *Pseudomonas* sp. on the surface at viable counts per cm^2 of 2.7×10^7 (○); 6.3×10^7 (●); 3.2×10^8 (□); 1.1×10^9 (■); and 2.8×10^9 (△).
From Gill (1976).

cause the rate of diffusion of oxygen into the bacterial slime is not sufficient to support further growth (Gill and Newton 1977).

Acinetobacter/Moraxella.   These strict aerobes commonly form a significant portion of any aerobic spoilage flora on meat. They are unable to utilize hexoses (Juni 1978) and utilize amino acids preferentially while growing on meat (Gill and Newton 1977). Unlike the pseudomonads, they do not seem to readily produce malodorous by-products from amino acid degradation and therefore have only low spoilage potential (Lerke *et al.* 1965). Pure cultures of some strains have been described as imparting "fishy" odors to meat (Barnes 1976), but any direct effects of this group are usually minor and subordinate to the spoilage activities of pseudomonads. However, when organisms of the *Acinetobacter/Moraxella* group are the major components of a flora approaching its maximum density, it is possible that they enhance the spoilage activities of the pseudomonads and *Alteromonas putrefaciens* by restricting the oxygen available to these latter organisms. When oxygen limits growth, pseudomonads may attack amino acids even when glucose is present

(Newton and Rigg 1979) and they probably degrade amino acids less efficiently with a concommitant increased rate of by-product formation. As conditons become anaerobic, *A. putrefaciens* will generate H_2S with deleterious effects on the appearance as well as the odor of meat.

Alteromonas putrefaciens.   This facultative anaerobe was previously misassigned to the genus *Pseudomonas* as *P. putrefaciens* (Lee *et al.* 1977). Under aerobic conditions its spoilage behavior is very similar to that of the pseudomonads although, unlike the latter organisms, it utilizes the amino acids cysteine and serine even when glucose is abundant (Gill and Newton 1979). It is possible that offensive products of amino acid degradation are not elaborated during aerobic growth when glucose is simultaneously metabolized, but it is certainly capable of producing organic sulfides in relatively large quantities, and, under anaerobic conditions, hydrogen sulfide (Freeman *et al.* 1976; Herbert and Shewan 1976). It is, therefore, a very potent spoilage organism both aerobically and anaerobically. If conditions allow its growth, this species can be the major determinant of spoilage onset even though it may not be numerically dominant in the spoilage flora.

Brochothrix thermosphacta.   This gram-positive facultative anaerobe can occur in floras of meat stored in air and in vacuum packages, but it is of greater importance in the latter. Glucose is the only substantial component of meat that supports its growth (Grau 1979). Acetic acid and acetoin are major products of its aerobic glucose metabolism and, in addition, isovaleric and isobutyric acids are produced by metabolism of leucine and valine, respectively. The high spoilage potential of *B. thermosphacta* is due to the production of these odiferous compounds (Dainty and Hibbard 1980). The major end product of its anaerobic metabolism is lactic acid, only small amounts of volatile acids being formed (Davidson *et al.* 1968). The organism should therefore have a rather low spoilage potential under strictly anaerobic conditions. It probably contributes most to spoilage of vacuum-packaged meat when oxygen is available in quantities that allow formation of some end products of aerobic metabolism.

Lactobacillus.   These anaerobic, aerotolerant organisms usually dominate the flora of meat stored anaerobically. Glucose and arginine are the only substrates in meat utilized for growth. Maximum cell densities are therefore determined by the availability of substrates for fermentation and maximum numbers do not greatly exceed 10^8 per cm^2 (Newton and Gill 1978A; Egan and Shay 1982). Volatile fatty acids are produced from valine and leucine (Nakae and Elliott 1965). These acids accumulate relatively slowly, but ultimately spoil meat by imparting "dairy" or "cheesy" odors and flavors (Dainty 1981). Spoilage becomes apparent only long after maximum numbers have been attained (Newton and Gill 1978A), so adjusting conditions to favor development of a *Lactobacillus*-dominated flora of low spoilage potential greatly extends the shelf life of chilled meat.

Enterobacteriaceae. This group includes a wide range of facultatively anaerobic organisms, including potential pathogens. There are, therefore, likely to be exceptions to any generalization about this group, but any such exceptions do not seem to be of great importance for meat spoilage. The relative paucity of reports dealing with spoilage of fresh meats by organisms of this group reflects the minor contribution they usually make to aerobic spoilage floras.

Enterobacteriaceae preferentially utilize glucose, and some at least can also take up glucose 6-phosphate (Winkler 1971). Metabolism of these substances produces strong catabolite repression of the enzymes of amino acid degradation (Paigen and Williams 1970). Only when these carbohydrates are exhausted are amino acids attacked (Gill and Newton 1977). As with the pseudomonads, organic sulfides can be produced from amino acids and many strains can release H_2S, although not in the quantities produced by *A. putrefaciens* (McMeekin and Patterson 1975; Patterson and Gibbs 1977, 1978). In addition, amino acids can be decarboxylated to give malodorous amines (Eskin *et al.* 1971). Organisms of this group therefore have a high spoilage potential and can be important in spoilage if conditions favor their growth.

INTERACTIONS BETWEEN MICROORGANISMS

The contribution that any group of organisms makes to spoilage will depend, in part, upon their relative numbers in a spoilage flora. In aerobic floras there appear to be no significant interactions between species until maximum numbers are approached (Table 2.3). At that time some species sequester the limited available oxygen at the expense of competitors (Gill and Newton 1977). In anaerobic floras, competition for glucose can produce similar effects when maximum numbers are approached (Newton and Gill 1978A). In addition, lactobacilli produce antimicrobial agents that inhibit competitors (Upreti and Hinsdill 1975; Raccach and Baker 1978), but even in this case numbers must be relatively high (Fig. 2.2) before such effects become apparent (Roth and Clark 1975; Newton and Gill 1978A). For most of the time that floras are growing, organisms are indifferent to the presence of competitors.

Under these circumstances, dominance is primarily determined by the relative rates of growth of competing organisms, the fastest-growing species ultimately predominating. The relative growth rates of the various groups will, of course, be affected by the storage conditions. To prolong the shelf life of meat it is, therefore, desirable not only to retard the total growth of all bacteria, but to adjust conditions to produce a greater selec-

TABLE 2.3. Effect of a Second Species at Maximum Cell Density on the Aerobic Growth of Bacteria on Meat at 10°C[a]

Test species	Pure culture		Mixed culture		
	Generation time of test species (hr)	Maximum cell density of test species (No. per cm^2)	Competing species at maximum cell density	Generation time of test species (hr)	Maximum cell density of test species (No. per cm^2)
Enterobacter	3.5	1.8×10^9	Pseudomonas	10.4	6.2×10^7
			B. thermosphacta	6.0	7.6×10^8
B. thermosphacta	3.4	1.2×10^9	Pseudomonas	7.2	7.1×10^7
			Enterobacter	9.1	2.7×10^7
Pseudomonas	3.0	3.4×10^9	Enterobacter	3.2	1.1×10^9
			B. thermosphacta	3.2	1.6×10^9

[a] Data from Gill and Newton 1977.

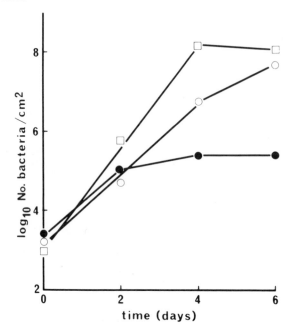

FIG. 2.2. Inhibition of competing species by *Lactobacillus* during anaerobic growth at 10°C of cultures inoculated onto sterile meat slices. Growth of *Enterobacter* in pure culture (○) and of *Enterobacter* (●) and *Lactobacillus* (□) in mixed culture. In the mixed culture, *Enterobacter* was inhibited when *Lactobacillus* numbers approached 10^6 per cm^2, inhibition apparently being due to antimicrobial agents produced by the latter species.
From Newton and Gill (1978A).

tive retardation of otherwise fast-growing organisms of high spoilage potential.

THE INITIAL FLORA

The initial floras of animal carcasses are derived mainly from soil and fecal organisms present on the hides. The large majority of these organisms are gram-positive mesophiles, e.g., *Micrococcus, Staphylococcus,* and *Bacillus.* Only a small fraction are gram-negative psychrotrophs originating from soil, water, and vegetation. Butchering of carcasses adds further to the microbial load as bacteria are transferred to meat surfaces from tools, work surfaces, and hands. However, the majority of such contaminants are still gram-positive mesophiles. Meat from mammalian carcasses butchered under hygienic conditions is normally contaminated by an initial flora of 10^3 to 10^4 bacteria per cm^2 of which less than 10%, and often only 1%, are capable of growth at chiller temperatures (West *et al.* 1972; Newton *et al.* 1978).

The proportions of mesophiles to psychrotrophs in the initial floras of poultry carcasses are similar to the proportions on meat of mammalian origin although the psychrotrophic contaminants on poultry are derived from a somewhat different source. Poultry carcasses are subject to immersion washing and spin chilling. The water used in these processes carries a psychrotrophic population which contaminates the poultry carcasses with about 10^3 psychrotrophs per cm^2 (Barnes 1976; Notermans *et al.* 1977). The initial psychrotrophic flora is therefore generally present in greater absolute numbers on poultry than on other meats, and poultry psychrotrophic floras are likely to be less variable than those on other meats as they will be composed predominantely of species capable of good growth in chilled, agitated wash waters.

Only those bacteria initially present on meat will be able to contribute to the spoilage flora. The relative and absolute numbers at which different spoilage species are initially present can influence the composition of the final spoilage flora. Relatively high initial numbers of a slow-growing species can offset any growth-rate advantage of species present in relatively small numbers. In addition, if absolute initial numbers of spoilage types are high, the number of generations elapsing before spoilage becomes evident are reduced so that there is less opportunity for a growth-rate advantage to be expressed. This latter effect seems to account for the typical differences between final chill temperature spoilage floras from red meats and poultry (Table 2.4). Poultry is generally contaminated with high initial numbers of psychrotrophs and although the *Acinetobacter/ Moraxella* group are overgrown by pseudomands on both types of meat the higher absolute numbers of the *Acinetobacter/Moraxella* group initially present on poultry ensures these organisms are still present in significant numbers when growth of the spoilage flora has ceased.

MEAT COMPOSITION AND EARLY SPOILAGE

DFD Meat

It has long been known that meat in the condition described as "dark, firm, dry (DFD)" with a characteristically high ultimate pH (>6.0) is prone to early spoilage. This was explained by postulating faster growth of the spoilage flora at the elevated pH (Tarrant 1976). However, this explanation is untenable as growth rates of pseudomonads are unaffected by pH in the range that occurs in meat (Gill and Newton 1982).

In mammals, DFD meat is obtained from animals that have been subject to stress or exhaustive exercise before slaughter. These factors can cause the muscle glycogen reserve to be reduced to less than one-half the

TABLE 2.4. Flora Development on Beef and Chicken Leg Muscle Stored at 2°C, Both with a pH < 6.0

Substrate	Time (days)	Cell density[c]	Flora composition (%)				
			Pseudomonas	Acinetobacter/ Moraxella	B. thermosphacta	Flavobacteria	Others
Beef[a]	0	1×10^3	1	11	13	—	75[e]
	7	2×10^5	56	40	2	—	2
	12	6×10^7	99	—	—	—	1
	17	4×10^9	97	2	1	—	—
Chicken[b]	0	4.2×10^3	29	26	—	32	13
	8	7.3×10^4	29[d]	53	—	12	4[f]
	12	4.7×10^6	65	28	—	2	6[f]
	16	9.2×10^8	79	17	—	0	4[f]

[a] Data from Gill and Newton, 1982.
[b] Data from McMeekin, 1977.
[c] Cell density of beef in No. per cm², and of chicken in No. per gram.
[d] Group III and IV Pseudomonas (21% at day 0) replaced by group I and II types.
[e] Mainly Micrococcus and Staphylococcus.
[f] Alteromonas putrefaciens.

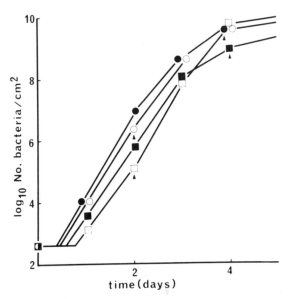

FIG. 2.3.   Growth of a fluorescent *Pseudomonas* at 10°C on meat slices of different pH and glucose contents. (○) pH 6.3, glucose absent; (●) pH 6.3, glucose 100
μg/g (wet weight); (□) pH 5.6, glucose absent; (■) pH 5.85, glucose 112 μg/g
(wet weight); (▲) spoilage odors detected.
From Newton and Gill (1978B).

normal level. After death, the remaining glycogen is still degraded via
glycolysis, but this process ceases when all glycogen has been consumed.
The pH remains high because less lactic acid than normal can be formed
from the available glycogen. In addition, no glucose at all may be present
(Bendall 1973). It is the absence of glucose that is responsible for early
aerobic spoilage of DFD meat (Newton and Gill 1978). In the absence of
glucose the psudomonads attack amino acids from the earliest stage of
growth. Spoilage will therefore become apparent when the flora has
reached a density sufficient for offensive by-products to be produced in
amounts detectable by the senses. This occurs when the cell density exceeds 10^6 per cm^2 (Fig. 2.3).

The DFD condition appears to be the normal state for poultry leg muscle
(Barnes and Impey 1968; Lea *et al.* 1969). The lactic acid content is less
than one-half that of breast muscle, giving an ultimate pH between 6.4
and 6.7. There are no published data on the glucose content of poultry leg
muscle, but since the total carbohydrate content is less than 20% of that in
breast muscle it is likely that glucose is absent.

Fat Tissue

Meat is composed of adipose and connective tissues as well as muscle
tissue. From the viewpoint of microbial growth, surfaces covered by a

fascia of connective tissue have the same characteristics as the underlying tissue. However, adipose tissue is very different from muscle. The insoluble fat, which is the major component of adipose tissue, must be emulsified and degraded before it can be effectively utilized by microorganisms. Thus, triglyceride is not the substrate for microbial growth on adipose tissue. Instead, low molecular weight soluble components, (glucose and amino acids) provided by the serum from damaged blood vessels are utilized. Unlike muscle tissue, the lactic acid concentration at adipose tissue surfaces is low, so the pH of fat cover remains near neutrality; glycolytic intermediates are absent, and nutrients are not readily replenished by diffusion from the underlying tissue. Bacteria will grow on moist fat surfaces at the same rate as on muscle tissue, but they tend to form discrete colonies rather than a continuous slime layer. Glucose is exhausted in the region of colonies when bacterial numbers exceed 10^6 per cm^2 and spoilage then develops at this early stage of growth as for DFD meat (Gill and Newton 1980A).

Early spoilage of fat does not seem to be a problem in commercial storage of meat as drying of uncovered fat surfaces during chilling prevents bacterial growth while fat surfaces of packaged meat are usually bathed in drip and so have the same spoilage qualities as the muscle tissue. Early spoilage of fat is more common in the domestic refrigerator, as fat surfaces can be kept moist by repeated ingress of warm moist air. Such early spoilage can probably be prevented by wrapping meat in plastic film to spread a layer of drip over all fat surfaces.

Variety Meats

It has generally been thought that rapid spoilage of edible organ meats is an unavoidable consequence of some intrinsic characteristic of these tissues. The anticipated chill temperature storage life of variety meats is only 2 to 3 days (Patterson and Gibbs 1979). Consideration of the tissue composition of liver in relation to the spoilage process suggests no obvious reason for early spoilage to occur, and study of liver spoilage under controlled conditions has shown that this tissue can in fact be stored for the same length of time as muscle before microbial spoilage becomes evident (Gill and De Lacy 1982). The short storage life attributed to liver appears to be a consequence of the commercial practice of bulk packaging warm livers before chilling or freezing. This usually results in the organs remaining at temperatures above 10°C for periods that may exceed 24 hr. The extensive growth of both mesophilic and psychrotrophic organisms during this period of warm storage is the cause of early spoilage (Gill and Penney 1984).

Bulk packaging of warm livers not only accelerates spoilage but also greatly increases health risks. The warm, anaerobic environment provided by bulk packs favors growth of mesophilic enterobacteria (Gill and Newton 1980B), a group including both potentially and frankly pathogenic species, and may allow growth of other pathogens, such as *Leptospira,* that can infect organs without causing clinical symptoms (Ho and Blackmore 1979).

There are few published data on edible organs other than liver, but most variety meats are commonly bulk packed while warm and so would be subject to the same temperature abuse as livers. The poor keeping qualities attributed to these meats would seem to be the result of consistent gross mishandling of products of low commercial value. If properly treated by cooling soon after removal from the carcass, there is no reason why variety meats should not have an extensive chill-temperature shelf life.

SPOILAGE CONTROL BY ADDITION OF GLUCOSE

As the glucose content of meat largely determines the cell density reached before spoilage onset, it would seem possible to extend the period of innocuous bacterial growth by increasing the glucose available to the aerobic flora. In the case of DFD meat this strategy is effective since adding glucose at a level of 100 µg/g to meat previously devoid of glucose will increase the shelf life to that of normal meat (Newton and Gill 1978B). It is, however, doubtful whether any substantial extension of shelf life can be achieved by adding glucose to meat that already has a normal content in excess of 100 µg/g.

Shelef (1975) observed liver spoilage by lactobacilli and concluded, erroneously, that these relatively benign organisms had developed in response to the high carbohydrate content on the tissue. In fact, the storage conditions employed had produced an anaerobic environment, which accounts for the dominance of anaerobic organisms (Gill and De Lacy 1982). However, addition of glucose to meat at concentrations of 2% or more by weight did suppress odor and slime formation (Shelef 1977). This occurred because excess glucose is converted extracellularly by pseudomonads to gluconic and oxogluconic acids (Whiting *et al.* 1976; Mitchell and Dawes 1982), and accumulation of these metabolites inhibits growth of the pseudomonads, delaying the appearance of slime (Shelef 1977; Barua and Shelef 1980). Off-odors were not formed because amino acid utilization is suppressed by glucose (Jacoby 1964).

Although the addition of large amounts of glucose delays the more obvious symptoms of spoilage, it is doubtful whether it could be of any practical value because of adverse flavor effects. Glucose at 2% in meat would be unacceptable to many, while the presence of substantial concentrations of the acid derivatives might be unacceptable to most consumers. However, routine treatment of carcasses and cuts with much smaller amounts of glucose could be used to prevent the early spoilage of any undetected DFD muscle during aerobic chiller storage.

Addition of glucose to meat that will be vacuum-packaged is positively deleterious. The presence of glucose does not prevent early spoilage by greening of DFD meat as H_2S production by *A. putrefaciens,* the spoilage organisms responsible, is not inhibited by glucose. If anything, addition of glucose to vacuum-packaged DFD meat stimulates growth of this organism. The growth of *B. thermosphacta* in high pH meat will also be favored by added glucose. Addition of glucose to normal pH meat will only increase the final cell density of the *Lactobacillus* flora and so accelerate the accumulation of volatile acids (Newton and Gill 1980). However, it may be advantageous to add glucose on opening vacuum packages to display the meat; as this would replace the glucose exhausted by the anaerobic flora and so delay the onset of aerobic spoilage by pseudomonads.

SPOILAGE CONTROL BY REDUCTION OF pH

Some strains of most groups of gram-negative psychrotrophs contaminating meat are inhibited by the pH of normal meat (Fig. 2.4). *Alteromonas putrefaciens* is particularly sensitive, no strains being capable of growth at chiller temperatures below pH 6.0. Strains of *Pseudomonas* are notably insensitive to the normal meat pH (Gill and Newton 1982). Reducing the pH of DFD meat to normal values has no effect upon the growth rate of pseudomonads (see Fig. 2.3), and therefore does not prevent early spoilage (Newton and Gill 1978B). Although many more organisms can initiate growth on meat of high pH, an elevated pH does not seem to result in any significant change in the composition of red meat spoilage floras (Gill and Newton 1982). However, comparison of floras on chicken leg and breast muscle (Fig. 2.5) shows that strains of the *Acineto-bacter/Moraxella* group are likely to be of greater quantitative importance in the flora of the high-pH leg muscle. In addition, *A. putrifaciens* can occur in the leg muscle flora but is unable to grow on breast muscle (Barnes and Impey 1968; McMeekin 1975, 1977).

Although the pH of meat is of little significance in delaying the onset of aerobic spoilage, it is of considerable importance for anaerobic spoilage. When the pH is greater than 6.0, growth of *A. putrefaciens* will be accompanied by H_2S production and resultant greening of meat if the numbers of this organism approach 10^6 per cm^2. This can reduce by one-half the normal shelf life of vacuum-packaged meat (Taylor and Shaw 1977). A high pH will also allow anaerobic growth of *B. thermosphacta;* this organism can grow in air at the normal pH of meat but will not grow anaerobically on meat below pH 5.8 (Campbell *et al.* 1979; Grau 1980). The anaerobic growth of some psychrotrophic species of Enterobacteriaceae, including the cold-tolerant pathogen *Yersinia enterocolitica* and common spoilage species, is similarly affected by the pH and lactic acid concentration of normal meat (Grau 1981).

Early spoilage of vacuum-packaged meat by pH-sensitive organisms may be prevented by treating meat with small quantities of citric acid buffer. A few milliliters of citrate buffer, pH 4.8, are added to packs before

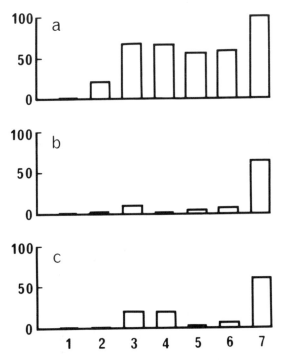

FIG. 2.4.   Percentage of bacterial strains unable to initiate growth on nutrient agar with the pH adjusted by addition of lactic acid: (a) pH 5.5, 2°C; (b) pH 6.0, 2°C; (c) pH 5.5, 25°C. (1) *Pseudomonas*; (2) Enterobacteriaceae; (3) *Moraxella*; (4) *Aeromonas*; (5) *Acinetobacter*; (6) *Flavobacterium*; (7) *Alteromonas*.
From Gill and Newton (1982).

the vacuum is drawn. A lower pH cannot be used as below pH 4.5 protein denaturation occurs resulting in brown discoloration of meat. When the vacuum is drawn, close approximation of the plastic film to the meat spreads the buffer as a thin film over the meat surface. The reduced surface pH inhibits growth of the organisms of high spoilage potential but does not affect growth of lactobacilli. Although the surface pH returns to that of the bulk meat as the buffer is absorbed, the substantial *Lactobacillus* population which has developed by that time continues to inhibit growth of the organisms causing early spoilage (Newton and Gill 1980). High-pH beef is usually excluded from vacuum packaging but the routine addition of a suitable buffer to vacuum packages would be useful in preventing early spoilage of meat of marginally high pH that was inadvertantly packaged. Such treatment may be essential to reliably obtain shelf lives in excess of 8 weeks with vacuum packaged lamb cuts since sheepmeats tend to have ultimate pH values above 5.8 and spoil as a result of growth of *B. thermosphacta* (Newton *et al.* 1977; Shaw *et al.* 1980).

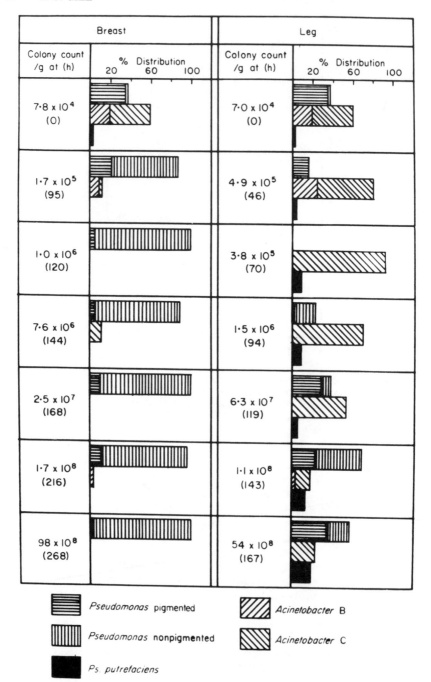

Pseudomonas pigmented

Pseudomonas nonpigmented

Ps. putrefaciens

Acinetobacter B

Acinetobacter C

TREATMENT WITH ORGANIC ACID

The objective of the buffer treatment discussed above is to produce a transient drop in surface pH, but treatment of meat with buffered solutions of organic acid has been proposed, on rather different grounds, as a general method for extending shelf life. Many organic acids have bacteriocidal or bacteriostatic properties. The lactic acid in meat is itself inhibitory to some groups of organisms (Gill and Newton 1982; Grau 1980, 1981) but the most effective acids are the short-chain length n-fatty acids, such as acetic (Goepfert and Hicks 1969). These acids are biologically active only in the undissociated form. The degree of dissociation increases with increasing pH, so there is a very marked increase in biological activity with decreasing pH. Organic acids are generally ineffective against meat spoilage organisms above pH 6.0 (Gill and Newton 1982).

It has been suggested that carcasses be sprayed with hot solutions of acetic acid with the objective of killing a substantial fraction of the contaminating flora, particularly pathogenic organisms. Logarithmic decreases in population number approaching 3 have been observed with this technique (Eustace 1981). Residual acid need not affect odor or flavor as it evaporates during holding on the cooling floor. The efficacy of this treatment for extending aerobic shelf life would depend upon reduction of the numbers of psychrotrophic pseudomonads. This could differ from the overall reduction of bacterial numbers, but some substantial effect could still be anticipated. A major extension of the storage life of vacuum-packaged lamb is claimed for the technique (Eustace et al. 1980). This improvement is ascribed to reduction of initial flora numbers, but in this case reduction of the surface pH is probably equally important as the pH of some lamb muscles tends to be high. Certainly, the results indicate that an important effect of acid treatment is in the prevention of greening, presumably by inhibiting growth of A. putrefaciens.

OTHER TREATMENTS FOR REDUCING INITIAL CONTAMINATION

Chlorination of wash water and hot-water washing have both been examined as methods for reducing initial contamination. Substantial claims have been made for chlorination (Emswiler et al. 1976; Marshall et al. 1977) but later work suggested that there had been considerable overestimation of the reduction in numbers achieved. Although there is a real decline in numbers after chlorination, this reduction is apparently too

FIG. 2.5.   Changes in the distribution of organisms during storage at 1°C of minced chicken breast and leg muscle.
From Barnes and Impey (1968).

small to have significant effect upon the shelf life (Stevenson *et al.* 1978; Kelly *et al.* 1981).

Hot water treatment appears to be more successful, provided the surface reaches a high enough temperature for a sufficient period to pasteurize the surface. Raising the surface temperature to 60°C for 10 sec can give a 3 log reduction in microbial counts and although there is initial surface discoloration, acceptable color is regained after cooling. Surface heating to this degree is readily obtained by immersion in hot water, but use of immersion tanks is aesthetically displeasing. Washing with hot water sprays can be employed, but greater control is necessary to ensure the required degree of surface heating (Smith and Graham 1978; Graham *et al.* 1978). The objective of these studies was reduction of contamination by pathogens and there appears to be no published data on shelf life extension, but some such extension would be expected. Surface pasteurization does not appear to have been attempted with poultry, although it might offer a method of reducing the perennial problem of widespread contamination of poultry carcasses by enteric pathogens.

SURFACE DRYING

All microorganisms require water for growth. The availability of liquid water to microorganisms is modified by the presence of solutes as any dissolved material will depress the water vapor pressure. The availability of water in a system is commonly expressed as the water activity (a_w), the ratio of the equilibrium aqueous vapor pressure of the solution to that of pure water at the same temperature (Scott 1957). The nature of the solute determining a_w is not without effect as microorganisms can tolerate a greater reduction of a_w in solutions of glycerol or other polyols than in solutions of sugars or electrolytes (Brown 1976). Such specific solute effects are, however, largely irrelevant to consideration of the effects of reduction of a_w in fresh meats, as the same solutes of quantitative importance are always present.

Meat spoilage bacteria do not generally exhibit any marked xerotolerance, being unable to grow when the a_w is below 0.95 (Leistner *et al.* 1981). Yeasts and molds are more xerotolerant with the most common spoilage species being capable of growth below a_w 0.90 (Lowry and Gill 1983A,B). The a_w of muscle tissue is about 0.99, which imposes no restraint on growth of any of the spoilage organisms. Microbial growth on unfrozen meat will only be affected by water activity if storage conditions produce some desiccation of the surfaces where microbes will grow.

Such surface desiccation, far from being uncommon, normally occurs during cooling of carcasses. This process was thoroughly investigated by Scott and his co-workers. Water evaporates from the warm carcass reducing the a_w of the surface layers to below that required for bacterial growth.

The rate and degree of water loss is greatest at muscle surfaces overlying the thickest areas of tissue where cooling is slowest, although the reduction in a_w is greatest in connective tissue overlying fat. Wide differences between a_w values for surfaces arise because of the complex dynamic situation where the effects of evaporation on a_w are countered by migration of water toward and of solutes away from the drying surface (Scott and Vickery 1939; Hicks et al. 1955).

After the carcass has cooled the surface tissues will tend to rehydrate, although fat surfaces will remain dry in the absence of humid conditions. Adjustment of atmospheric humidity and air speed can, however, maintain the drying process and continue to inhibit bacterial growth. Chilled meat held under such conditions will develop a surface flora of molds. The weight loss associated with extended holding under drying conditions would be regarded as unacceptable today, but before World War II shipment of chilled beef from Australia and New Zealand to Britain relied in part upon such drying to inhibit microbial spoilage during the voyage of 8 to 10 weeks (Law and Vere-Jones 1955).

With uncontrolled ambient conditions, the surface desiccation associated with cooling will usually ensure a lag of about 24 hr before any growth commences (Hicks et al. 1955; Nottingham and Wyborn 1975). Desiccation will even delay for several hours microbial growth on carcasses held at body temperature (Wilhelm et al. 1982). This delay is particularly valuable as meat cannot be chilled soon after slaughter without toughening (Locker et al. 1975). Slow cooling, which would allow rapid bacterial growth in the absence of drying, is therefore essential unless carcasses are subject to electrical stimulation which accelerates the rigor process and so allows early chilling without irreversible toughening (Chrystall and Devine 1983).

If surface desiccation is prevented by an impervious cover bacterial numbers increase rapidly (Table 2.5). The effect is greater the earlier the impervious covering is applied (Scott and Vickery 1939). Bacterial proliferation can also proceed at any carcass sites where evaporation is limited because of poor air circulation or rapid cooling of thin areas of tissue, e.g., the abdominal wall of entire lamb carcasses. Above average bacterial numbers at such sites after cooling are frequently observed. Loss of the transient microbial stability due to the absence of surface drying is also a problem that arises with meat that is boned and packaged while still warm (Nottingham 1982).

Inhibition of microbial growth by surface drying can also inhibit microbial growth on poultry carcasses that are air chilled or stored unwrapped. However, other differences in processing may eliminate the expected extension of shelf life that can in principle be obtained by chilling in air rather than in water (Mead 1982). Surface drying does not appear to be of the same practical importance for poultry as for larger animals, although there are some poultry processing and storage systems that use the effect to advantage. A notable example is the greater shelf life of uneviscerated

TABLE 2.5. Effect on Bacterial Numbers of Retarding Desiccation at the Surfaces of Cooling Beef Carcasses[a]

Carcass storage time (hr)	Uncovered surfaces	No. bacteria per cm^2		
		Covered surfaces; time covered (hr)		
		0–5	0–10	0–24
0	1.0×10^3	1.0×10^3	1.0×10^3	1.0×10^3
10	3.9×10^2	2.1×10^3	1.5×10^4	1.5×10^4
24	4.8×10^2	2.1×10^3	3.6×10^4	2.8×10^5
72	2.7×10^2	6.7×10^4	1.7×10^5	1.7×10^7

[a] Desiccation was prevented by placing water impermeable coverings over portions of the carcasses' surfaces. Data from Scott and Vickery, 1939.

(New York dressed) poultry carcasses where the moist body cavity is not available for growth of spoilage organisms (Barnes and Impey 1975).

TEMPERATURE

Growth Rates and Temperature

Storage of meat at low temperatures will retard the growth of all bacteria and thus extend the shelf life. However, the extent to which growth rates decrease with decreasing temperature varies between species and strains of organisms (Table 2.6).

Besides the differential effects of temperature on growth rates of different organisms, the flora composition is also affected by increasing temperature as growth initiation by an increasing proportion of the initial contaminants on meat is permitted. This occurs for two reasons. Increasing the temperature above the minimum for growth of mesophiles will

TABLE 2.6. Variation of Generation Times of Psychrotrophic Spoilage Bacteria with Temperature for Growth of Pure Cultures on Meat[a]

	Generation time (hr)							
	Aerobic (°C)				Anaerobic (°C)			
	2	5	10	15	2	5	10	15
Pseudomonas								
Non-fluorescent	7.6	5.1	2.8	2.0	—	—	—	—
Fluorescent	8.2	5.4	3.0	2.0	—	—	—	—
Acinetobacter	15.6	8.9	5.2	3.1	—	—	—	—
Enterobacter	11.1	7.8	3.5	2.4	55.7	23.2	8.5	5.4
Brochothrix thermosphacta	12.0	7.3	3.4	2.8	32.8	20.1	9.7	6.8
Lactobacillus	—	—	—	—	8.4	6.5	4.6	3.8

[a] Data from Gill and Newton 1977; Newton and Gill 1978A.

obviously allow these organisms to commence growth. In addition, psychrotrophs that find the conditions of pH and/or lactic acid concentration in meat inhibitory at low temperatures will be able to grow as the temperature rises (see Fig. 2.4) (Gill and Newton 1980B). The synergistic effects of two or more marginal growth conditions, which do not inhibit growth when applied singly but do so in combination, are well documented (Ingram and Mackey 1976). Preservation of many nonsterile foods depends upon such synergistic effects (Leistner 1978).

In the case of aerobic floras, the pseudomonads maintain a growth rate advantage over competing psychrotrophs and mesophiles at temperatures up to at least 20°C (Barnes 1976; Gill and Newton 1980B). That the pseudomonads form a smaller portion of the final spoilage flora at room than at chiller temperatures is to be expected from their relatively low numbers in the initial flora. However, it is only when temperatures are closer to the optimum for mesophilic growth and approach the maximum for growth of the psychrotrophic pseudomonads (about 30°C) that these latter organisms relinquish their dominance of the spoilage flora, being displaced largely by mesophilic strains of *Acinetobacter* and the Enterobacteriaceae (Table 2.7). Even then, the pseudomonads are still present in significant numbers (Gill and Newton 1980B). The ability to initiate growth comparatively rapidly at low temperatures may also be a factor in spoilage flora dominance by pseudomonads, but data on this point are lacking.

With anaerobic storage, psychrotrophic lactobacilli have an increasing growth rate advantage over competing psychrotrophs as temperatures decrease below 20°C (Newton and Gill 1978A). At 20°C the anaerobic flora is dominated by Enterobacteriaceae with both mesophilic and psychrotrophic types being present in similar proportions (Table 2.7). This dominance by Enterobacteriaceae is a result of their greater numbers in the

TABLE 2.7. Percentage Composition of Initial and Final Bacterial Floras Developing on Beef Stored at Warm Temperatures[a]

	Initial flora	Final aerobic flora (°C)		Final anaerobic flora (°C)	
		20	30	20	30
Pseudomonas	1	60	19	—	—
Acinetobacter	9	11	44	—	—
Moraxella	30	10	1	—	—
Micrococcus	52	8	—	—	—
Enterobacteriaceae	4	5	36	80	5
Lactobacillus	—[b]	—	—	20	33
Clostridium	—	—	—	—	62
Brochothrix thermosphacta	4	5	—	—	—
Others	—	1	—	—	—
Total psychrotrophs	10	68	37	50	1

[a] Data from Gill and Newton 1980b.
[b] Not present in sample of 100 colonies.

initial flora rather than indication of an advantage in growth rate over the lactobacilli. The Enterobacteriaceae can probably predominate at higher temperatures also, but mesophilic lactobacilli appear to become of increasing importance. At temperatures of 30°C and above *Clostridium perfringens* can predominate, provided it was present in the initial flora (Gill and Newton 1980B).

Holding meat at room temperatures is clearly to be avoided because of the possibility of growth of pathogenic organisms. If meat is not packaged, the flora will at least be largely dominated by innocuous saprophytic organisms whose spoilage activities can give warning of possible health risks. In comparison, the environment provided by vacuum-packaged meat at warm room temperatures is highly favorable for growth of potentially pathogenic Enterobacteriaceae and clostridia, which could reach hazardous numbers while total numbers were still comparatively low and without any signs of spoilage. For this reason it would seem that special care should be taken to avoid vacuum-packaged meat being held for any significant period without refrigeration.

Minimum Growth Temperatures

Bacteria. Spoilage by bacteria will not occur if storage temperatures are below the minimum for bacterial growth. Psychrotrophic bacteria are certainly capable of growth below 0° (Larkin and Stokes 1968) and there are several reports of bacterial growth on meat at −5°C or below (Michener and Elliott 1964). There is, however, reason to doubt that bacterial spoilage can occur at the latter temperature. Much of the data on low-temperature growth were obtained under conditions giving no guarantee of strict temperature control. Because of the long periods of observation necessary to detect any increase in numbers when growth rates are very slow, the possibility of upward fluctuations of temperature cannot be discounted (Michener and Elliott 1964). A further consideration is the effect of freezing on water activity (a_w).

When freezing occurs, the a_w of any medium becomes the same as that of ice of the same temperature. Meat starts to freeze between −1 and −2°C. Only a small fraction of the water in meat is frozen at −2°C, but the ice fraction increases rapidly with decreasing temperature, forming 75% of the total water at −5°C. There is little further increase at lower temperatures. Even at temperatures where the frozen water fraction is small, because of increased solute concentrations in the remaining liquid, the free water will have the same a_w as ice (Fennema *et al.* 1973).

The bacteria responsible for meat spoilage are not notably xerotolerant, having a_w minima at optimum temperatures between 0.98 and 0.96 (Prior 1978; Leistner *et al.* 1981). These a_w levels are attained in meat between −2° and −4°C (Table 2.8). Freezing will therefore subject these bacteria to water stress at temperatures close to their minima for growth. The synergistic effects of the two factors probably ensures that spoilage bacteria do not usually grow on frozen meat, although some strains could possibly

TABLE 2.8. Water Activity (a_w) of
Meat at Various Freezing
Temperatures[a]

Temperature (°C)	Fresh meat
25	0.993
unchanged	
0	
−1	
−2	0.981
−3	0.971
−4	0.962
−5	0.953
−10	0.907
−15	0.864
−20	0.823

[a] Data from Rodel and Krispien, 1977.

grow at temperatures below −2°C if the meat was supercooled instead of frozen.

Supercooling of meat occurs readily if temperatures do not fall more than 2° or 3°C below the freezing point (Fennema *et al.* 1973). With such inefficient freezing growth of bacteria might occur at temperatures down to −5°C, but freezer inadequacies are more likely to produce temperature cycling than hold steady temperatures a degree or two below the freezing point of meat. The practical minimum growth temperature for meat spoilage bacteria is therefore probably −2°C.

Fungi. At temperatures above the freezing point of meat, spoilage by the relatively rapid growth of bacteria usually precludes spoilage by the slower growing yeasts and molds. Meat is therefore spoiled by fungi only when it is held under conditions that inhibit bacterial growth. Yeast are generally thought to be of little importance for meat spoilage, but mold growth still causes considerable loss. It is usually considered that mold spoilage is the result of growth of these organisms on frozen meat when bacterial growth is inhibited by the low storage temperature. Minimum growth temperatures for molds of −10° to −12°C, or even −18°C, are commonly assumed (Ingram and Mackey 1976; Liestner *et al.* 1981; Gracey 1981).

Recent studies have shown that the abilities of molds to grow on frozen meat have been rather exaggerated (Table 2.9). Most meat-spoilage molds are moderately xerotolerant and have intrinsic minimum growth temperatures on unfrozen media of about −5°C or above. Only one species, *Thamnidium elegans,* is able to grow at lower temperatures on supercooled media. Although growth rate data indicate an intrinsic minimum

TABLE 2.9. Limiting Conditions for Growth of Meat Spoilage Molds.[a]

Mold	Spoilage produced	Minimum temperature (°C)	Minimum a_w	Growth on frozen media
Cladosporium herbarum	Black spot	−5.5	0.88	+
Cladosporium cladosporoides	Black spot	−5.0	0.88	+
Penicillium hirsutum	Black spot	−5.0	0.92	+
Chrysosporium pannorum	White spot	−5.0	0.92	+
Thamnidium elegans	Whiskers	−10.0[b]	0.94	−
Acremonium sp.	White spot	−2.0	0.88	
Pencillium corylophilum	Blue-green mold	−2.0	0.88	−
Mucor racemosus	Whiskers	−1.0	0.94	−

[a] Data from Gill and Lowry 1982; Lowry and Gill 1984A.
[b] Calculated minimum temperature for growth on supercooled medium.

growth temperature for this organism of −10°C, it is unable to grow below −5°C on frozen media because of its low xerotolerance. It therefore seems that −5°C is the practical minimum temperature for growth of molds on meat (Gill and Lowry 1982; Lowry and Gill 1984A).

At −5°C molds grow very slowly. When poultry or meat is held at this temperature for long periods, a flora of psychrotrophic yeasts develops, reaching maximum numbers of about 10^6 per cm^2 after 4 months. The yeasts grow as discreet, ultimately visible, colonies on the dry environment provided by the frozen meat surface at −5°C. Visible mold colonies do not appear until about the eighth month of storage (Schmidt-Lorenz and Gutschmidt 1969; Lowry and Gill 1984B).

It can be concluded that mold spoilage will develop on frozen meat only if it is held for prolonged periods at 2° or 3°C below its freezing point. If the meat surface reaches higher temperatures, mold spoilage can occur if surface drying inhibits bacterial growth. The latter circumstances are likely to be the usual conditions leading to mold spoilage during supposed frozen storage. Yeasts would seem to be the organisms best able to grow on meat that remains frozen at the surface. Growth of yeasts does not seem to impart undesirable odors or flavors to the meat, and the pin-head colonies formed at freezing temperatures might easily be overlooked, particularly on fat surfaces (Winger and Lowry 1983). However, if the meat is then exposed to higher temperatures the preformed yeast colonies would rapidly increase in size to give more visible spoilage. Visible spoilage may be further enhanced by deposition of heme pigments resulting in the appearances of brown spots on fat surfaces (Egan and Shay 1977), although it is not clear whether the species growing at freezing temperatures are identical with "brown spot" organisms. Yeasts are not usually considered to be of any real significance for meat spoilage, but it appears that in some restricted circumstances they may preempt spoilage by either bacteria or molds.

STORAGE IN MODIFIED ATMOSPHERES

Since it became obvious that vacuum packaging of meat could give a much extended shelf life at chiller temperatures there have been many studies of bacterial growth and spoilage in both vacuum and modified atmosphere packages. The objective of such studies has usually been to determine a potential practical shelf life for vacuum-packaged meat. The studies have therefore been much concerned with the initial packaging conditions, but less so with the conditions that develop in packages during storage. In consequence, results and conclusions have been somewhat variable because all the data necessary for understanding and relating the course of flora development in individual cases have not been available. There are, however, two main factors affecting flora development in sealed packages, anaerobiosis and CO_2 inhibition of portions of the flora. Most fungi are strictly aerobic and many are highly susceptible to inhibition by CO_2 (Tabak and Cooke 1968), so modified atmospheres are inimicable to their development and preclude spoilage by these fungi.

Anaerobiosis

If all oxygen is excluded from the package there can be no growth of the strictly aerobic bacteria, *Pseudomonas* and *Acinetobacter/Moraxella* (Clark and Burki 1972). If the meat pH is below 5.8 anaerobic growth of *B. thermosphacta* will not be possible (Grau 1980) and growth of *A. putrefaciens* will also be prevented. The only groups of organisms capable of growth at chill temperatures will be the Enterobacteriaceae and lactobacilli. However, growth of some strains of psychrotrophic enterobacteria on meat of normal pH is also prevented by strictly anaerobic conditions (Grau 1981), and it is possible that these findings are of wide application to organisms of this group. Even if anaerobic growth of enterobacteria is possible, at temperatures approaching zero the growth rate advantage of the lactobacilli is so great as to completely exclude the psychrotrophic Enterobacteriaceae from meat spoilage floras (Newton and Gill 1978A). A strictly anaerobic environment for chilled meat of normal pH will therefore ensure development of a flora of lactobacilli with a greatly extended shelf life for the meat.

CO_2 Inhibition

It has long been recognized that CO_2 can inhibit the growth of some microorganisms. This has been ascribed to the effect on pH of CO_2 solution in the medium but there is no doubt that CO_2 exerts direct effects upon microbial metabolism (Coyne 1933). The nature of these effects remains somewhat speculative. CO_2 is soluble in water and forms carbonic acid in aqueous solution. It can dissolve in and pass freely across biological membranes and it is a substrate for or product of a number of enzymatic reactions. Its possible modes of action therefore include: alteration of intracellular pH with consequent effects on intracellular enzyme activities and substrate transport (Wolfe 1980), inhibition of decarboxylating enzymes by a mass action effect (King and Nagel 1975), dissolution in and expansion of cell membranes with consequent disruption of membrane functions (Sears and Eisenberg 1961; Enfors and Molin 1978), and inhibition of nondecarboxylating enzymes by action at nonpolar sites (Ransom et al. 1960; White 1974). Recent work indicates that the two latter mechanisms are those most likely to be operating in the case of meat-spoilage bacteria as the early stages of substrate utilization appear to be the sites of inhibitory activity by CO_2 (Tan and Gill 1982).

Whatever the mode of action, the salient points of CO_2 inhibition with respect to meat spoilage floras are as follows. First, all organisms are not equally susceptible (Table 2.10); the pseudomonads are particularly sensitive to CO_2 while the lactobacilli are largely unaffected (Sutherland et al. 1977; Enfors and Molin 1980). Second, the pattern of CO_2 inhibition is dependent upon the growth medium (Fig. 2.6); growth of P. fluorescens decreases linearly with increasing CO_2 concentration in minimal medium but in rich media, such as that provided by meat, there is an initial large decrease in growth rate with CO_2 concentrations up to 20% of atmospheric pressure, but relatively little increased inhibition with further increases in CO_2 concentration. Third, the degree of inhibition by any concentration of CO_2 in solution is enhanced by decreasing temperature. Finally, exposure of susceptible organisms to CO_2 before growth is initiated prolongs the lag phase (King and Nagel 1967; Clark and Lentz 1969; Gill and Tan 1979, 1980).

When pseudomonads growing on chilled meat are exposed to 20% CO_2 in the atmosphere, the growth rate is reduced by about 30%. Further increases in CO_2 give no further significant reduction. Under aerobic con-

TABLE 2.10. Growth Rates of Spoilage Bacteria on High pH, Dark, Firm, Dry (DFD) Meat at 3°C in Air and in Air–20% CO_2 Atmosphere[a]

| | Generation time (Gt) (hr^{-1}) | | |
Organism	Air	20° CO_2	Ratio of Gt in air and CO_2 to Gt in air
Pseudomonas			
Nonfluorescent	7.1	8.5	1.20
Fluorescent	7.8	10.0	1.28
Acinetobacter	9.6	12.4	1.29
Y. enterocolitica	11.5	14.7	1.28
A. putrefaciens	9.1	13.6	1.49
Enterobacter	10.8	10.8	1.00
B. thermosphacta	12.1	12.1	1.00

[a] Data from Gill and Tan 1980.

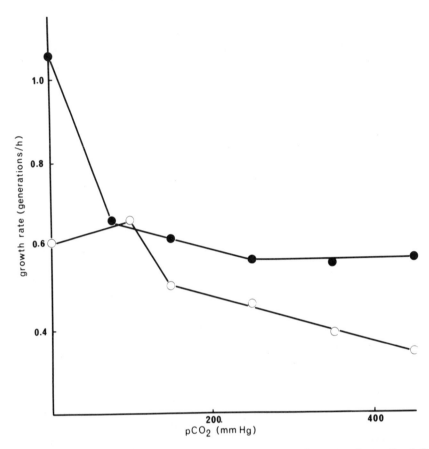

FIG. 2.6.   Effect of CO_2 concentration in solution on the rate of growth of *P. fluorescens* at 30°C in simple (○) or complex (●) medium.
From Gill and Tan (1979).

ditions CO_2 can therefore extend the shelf life of meat by 30% once growth has started. If CO_2 is applied while the spoilage organisms are still in the stationary phase, the increase in shelf life is extended to 50% (Clark and Lentz 1969; Gill and Tan 1980). This lag phase increase may not be attainable with poultry because of contamination of carcasses with already-growing psychrotrophs from the chilling water (Sanders and Soo 1978).

The Vacuum Package

With vacuum packaging, meat is sealed in plastic bags of low gas permeability after drawing a vacuum in excess of 700 mm Hg. The enclosed muscle tissue is still respiring and will convert the remaining oxygen to carbon dioxide. Although respiration rates of muscle fall exponentially with time, a minimum value is finally reached and indefinitely maintained (Bendall and Taylor 1972).

The vacuum package therefore contains an atmosphere composed mainly of nitrogen and CO_2. The presence of residual oxygen will presumably depend upon the equilibrium between the rate at which the gas diffuses into the package and the rate at which it is consumed by the meat. Any facultative or aerobic bacteria present would also consume oxygen although the initial bacterial mass would be too small for bacterial respiration to contribute significantly to oxygen consumption. If maximal respiration by meat fell below the rate of diffusion through the film, oxygen within the package would increase, while in the absence of permeation all oxygen would be consumed. For a steady concentration of oxygen to be maintained, the rate of oxygen consumption would seemingly have to be limited by the partial pressure of oxygen in the package atmosphere.

Measurements of oxygen concentrations with vacuum packages have usually yielded a figure of about 1% (Gardner et al. 1967; Sutherland et al. 1977; Shaw et al. 1980; Seideman et al. 1980). An atmosphere of 1% oxygen is more than sufficient to allow rapid growth of aerobic organisms (Clark and Burki 1972; Wells 1974; Enfors et al. 1979), so it is possible that the measured oxygen concentrations offer little information as to the actual conditions within the package. There are considerable technical difficulties in efficient removal of uncontaminated gas samples from packages with very little head space. Moreover, the head space atmosphere may derive largely from gas trapped in film folds that restrict its contact with the meat surface. As oxygen is a minor component of the package atmosphere maintained by a dynamic equilibrium, the measured concentration in partially isolated pockets may have little relevance to the concentration obtaining at the meat/film interface. Even future measurement of gross interfacial conditions could be misleading as it is likely that some oxygen concentration gradient will exist between the inner film and meat surface despite their close contact. The oxygen concentrations to which bacteria within packages are exposed cannot, therefore, be deduced from existing data.

However, some permeation of oxygen occurs through all commercial films in current use and normal microbial behavior would suggest the fullest exploitation of any areas of elevated oxygen concentration by oxygen-utilizing species. That this is the case is suggested by the observation of differences in the floras developing at fat and lean surfaces of vacuum-packaged meat, although pH differences may also play a part in allowing greater proliferation of oxygen-utilizing species on fat surfaces (Grau 1983).

Factors other than oxygen deprivation would seem necessary to fully explain the shelf life extension obtained when meat is packaged in film of moderately low oxygen permeability. Two such factors that have been identified are inhibition by CO_2 and the antimicrobial activities of lactobacilli. Although it has been suggested that storage life extension is mainly due to the inhibitory effects of CO_2, the degree of growth rate reduction due to CO_2 alone could not account for the observed inhibition of aerobic organisms if significant amounts of oxygen were available within packages.

The inhibitory effects against pseudomonads and other gram-negative organisms of antimicrobial agents produced by a flora of lactobacilli are well documented (Raccach and Baker 1978; Dubois et al. 1979). Antimicrobial activities of lactobacilli might also explain the failure of Enterobacteriaceae to increase in numbers during prolonged storage of vacuum-packaged meat. Such an increase would otherwise be expected as the Enterobacteriaceae can ferment substrates, such as glucose 6-phosphate, that are present in meat but not utilized by the lactobacilli (Newton and Gill 1978A). The most important function of CO_2 for extending shelf life in vacuum packages may therefore be to impose an extended lag phase on the pseudomonads and so allow development of a population of lactobacilli to a point where subsequent growth of pseudomonads is severely restricted by the synergistic effects of CO_2, low oxygen tension, and antimicrobial agents.

Although it is possible to obtain a substantial extension of shelf life without rigorous exclusion of all oxygen, the maximum shelf life is obtained if strictly anaerobic conditions are employed. That anaerobiosis is the critical factor for maximizing the shelf life of packaged meats is demonstrated by the decreasing shelf life of meat when it is packaged in films of increasing oxygen permeability (Newton and Rigg 1979; Vanderzant et al. 1982). Both the growth rates and final counts of Pseudomonas species increase with increasing oxygen permeability of films (Table 2.11). Spoilage occurs when pseudomonad numbers reach 10^6 per cm^2, possibly because catabolite repression by glucose is relieved during growth under oxygen-limited conditions (Newton and Rigg 1979). The longest shelf life is achieved when an oxygen scavenging system is incorporated into the packaging as there is then die-off rather than growth of organisms requir-

TABLE 2.11. Effect of Oxygen Permeability of Packaging Film on Growth of Pseudomonads and Storage Life of Vacuum-Packaged Beef Held at 0°C[a]

Film permeability (ml O_2/m^2/24 hr/atm at 25°C and 100% RH)	Storage life (weeks)	Pseudomonas numbers at spoilage (No. per cm^2)
0	>15	0^b
190	>15	7×10^{4b}
290	11–15	5×10^5
532	6–9	2×10^6
818	4–6	1×10^6
920	2–4	7×10^5

[a] Data from Newton and Rigg 1979.
[b] Numbers at 15 weeks; no putrefactive spoilage.

ing oxygen (Newton and Rigg 1979). As a bonus, undesirable color changes due to metmyoglobin formation at the surface are also prevented by oxygen-free packaging (O'Keefe and Hood 1981).

Gas Flushing

Gas flushing with various mixtures of oxygen, nitrogen, and CO_2 has been advocated, mainly with the objective of improving the color of packaged meat. In general, any substantial amount of oxygen improves the initial color but markedly reduces the shelf life by allowing growth of aerobic organisms and/or *B. thermosphacta* (Silliker *et al.* 1976; Newton *et al.* 1977; Christopher *et al.* 1979). Flushing with either nitrogen or CO_2 alone has also been examined with the objective of producing anaerobic conditions from the start of packaged storage. Some early results were confused by the use of industrial gases containing up to 1% oxygen (O'Keefe and Hood 1981). With oxygen-free gases, flushing with nitrogen or nitrogen–CO_2 mixtures gives results similar to those obtained with good vacuum packaging. However, it has been claimed that an atmosphere of CO_2 alone can give a further extension of shelf life by reducing the growth rate of the flora of lactobacilli (Blickstad *et al.* 1981). This is quite possible as the multiple biological effects of CO_2 would seem to ensure that with high enough concentrations of the gas all organisms will be adversely affected, although hyperbaric concentrations are necessary to inhibit very resistant species (Enfors and Molin 1980). The claimed effect of CO_2 at atmospheric or higher pressures on lactobacilli would seem to merit further investigation.

Carbon Monoxide

Use of carbon monoxide has been suggested as a method of overcoming the color deterioration that occurs with packaged meats (El-Badawi *et al.* 1964; Lanier *et al.* 1978). The use of this gas is unattractive because of its highly poisonous nature, but it has apparently been used with commercial success for preservation of vegetables (Mermelstein 1977) and the small quantities likely to be consumed if it were used with meat do not seem to be a significant health hazard (Stupfel and Bouly 1970).

Carbon monoxide is poisonous for mammals because of its greater affinity than oxygen for hemoglobin, but it can also inactivate other hemoproteins such as the cytochrome oxidase (cytochrome a/a^3) and cytochrome c of the eukaryote electron transport system (Goldsmith and Landaw 1968). It reacts similarly with some bacterial cytochromes, including cytochrome oxidases (Lemberg and Barrett 1973). Most bacterial cytochrome systems have very different components to the eukaryote system: branched systems with more than one cytochrome oxidase are common, and the individual components are induced under different circumstances

(Haddock and Jones 1977). Despite this, some inhibitory effect of CO, at least on bacteria growing aerobically, can be anticipated.

There appears to have been only one study on the effect of CO on meat spoilage, which employed samples inoculated with a mixed culture of aerobic spoilage organisms. A greatly increased lag phase and a reduced ultimate growth rate were observed, these effects increasing with increasing CO concentration up to at least 5% (Clarke *et al.* 1976). The effect of CO upon a naturally occurring flora has not been studied, but use of low concentrations of this gas might be of value in some circumstances and its use would seem to merit further investigation.

CONCLUSIONS

As spoilage is a function of microbial activity, the effect of storage conditions on the time taken for spoilage to develop, and the form in which spoilage becomes manifest, must ultimately be understood in terms of the physiologies of the individual bacterial species that can contribute to spoilage floras. If all species in the wide range of organisms that contaminate meat had to be considered this approach would require an impossible wealth of data, but fortunately the organisms of major importance in meat spoilage can be reduced to a few groups and only those characteristics relevant to spoilage need be considered for each group. It is therefore now possible to make generally valid statements about the effects of individual parameters on the course of spoilage. These broad statements will doubtless be refined by future studies on the activities of individual species within the larger groups of spoilage organisms.

Even with current knowledge it should be possible, with appropriate processing, packaging, and storage temperatures, to extend the shelf life of any chilled meat to 12 weeks, although the specific treatments required to achieve this would have to be defined for each type of product. At present, many published studies start with a "practical" process, often with some critical factors poorly defined or ignored, and attempt to make deductions regarding microbial behavior and the general usefulness of the process from such incomplete data. It is not surprising that reports of this type can yield contradictory results and erroneous explanations of microbial behavior. It is to be hoped that the growing understanding of the microbial ecology of meat spoilage will in the future allow the design of more effective and reproducible systems for the extended storage of fresh meats.

REFERENCES

BARNES, E. M. 1976. Microbiological problems of poultry at refrigerator temperatures. A review. J. Sci. Food. Agr. *27,* 777.
BARNES, E. M. and IMPEY, C. S. 1968. Psychrophilic spoilage bacteria of poultry. J. Appl. Bacteriol. *31,* 97.

BARNES, E. M. and IMPEY, C. S.   1975.   The shelf-life of uneviscerated and eviscerated chicken carcasses stored at 10°C and 4°C. Brit. Poult. Sci. *16*, 319.

BARUA, M. and SHELEF, L. A.   1980.   Growth suppression of pseudomonads by glucose utilization. J. Food Sci. *45*, 349.

BENDALL, J. R.   1973.   Post mortem changes in muscle. *In* Structure and Function of Muscle. 2nd ed. Vol. 2, pp. 243–309. G. H. Bourne (Editor). Academic Press, New York.

BENDALL, J. R. and TAYLOR, A. A.   1972.   Consumption of oxygen by the muscles of beef animals and related species. II. Consumption of oxygen by post-rigor muscle J. Sci. Food Agr. *23*, 707.

BLICKSTAD, E., ENFORS, S. O. and MOLIN, G.   1981.   Effect of hyperbaric carbon dioxide pressure on the microbial flora of pork stored at 4 or 14°C. J. Appl. Bacteriol. *50*, 493.

BROWN, A. D.   1976.   Microbial water stress. Bacteriol. Rev. *40*, 803.

CAMPBELL, R. J., EGAN, A. F., GRAU, F. H. and SKAY, B. J.   1979.   The growth of *Microbacterium thermosphactum* on beef. J. Appl. Bacteriol. *47*, 505.

CHRISTOPHER, F. M., SEIDEMAN, S. C., CARPENTER, Z. L., SMITH, G. C. and VANDERZANT, C.   1979.   Microbiology of beef packaged in various gas atmospheres. J. Food Prot. *42*, 240.

CHRYSTALL, B. B. and DEVINE, C. E.   1985.   Electrical stimulation: Its early development in New Zealand. pp. 73–119. *In* Advances in Meat Research. Vol. 1. A. M. Pearson and T. R. Dutson (Editors). AVI. Publishing Co., Westport, Connecticut.

CLARK, D. S. and BURKI, T.   1972.   Oxygen requirements of strains of *Pseudomonas* and *Achromobacter.* Canad. J. Microbiol. *18*, 321.

CLARK, D. S. and LENTZ, C. P.   1969.   The effect of carbon dioxide on the growth of slime-producing bacteria on fresh beef. Canad. Instit. Food Sci. Technol. J. *2*, 72.

CLARK, D. S., LENTZ, C. P. and ROTH, L. A.   1976.   Use of carbon monoxide for extending shelf-life of prepackaged fresh beef. Canad. Instit. Food Sci. Technol. J. *9*, 114.

COYNE, F. P.   1933.   The effect of carbon dioxide on bacterial growth. Proc. Royal Soc. London *B113*, 196.

DAINTY, R. H.   1981.   Volatile fatty acids detected in vacuum-packaged beef during storage at chill temperatures. Proc. 27th European Mtg. Meat Res. Workers, Vienna. p. 688.

DAINTY, R. H. and HIBBARD, C. M.   1980.   Aerobic metabolism of *Brochothrix thermosphacta* growing on meat surfaces and in laboratory media. J. Appl. Bacteriol. *48*, 387.

DAINTY, R. H., SHAW, B. G., DE BOER, K. A. and SCHEPS, E. S. J.   1975.   Protein changes caused by bacterial growth on beef. J. Appl. Bacteriol. *39*, 73.

DAVIDSON, C. M., MOBBS, P. and STUBBS, J. M.   1968.   Some morphological and physiological properties of *Microbacterium thermosphactum.* J. Appl. Bacteriol. *31*, 551.

DUBOIS, G., BEAUMIER, H. and CHARBONNEAU, R.   1979.   Inhibition of bacteria isolated from ground meat by Streptococcaceae and Lactobacillaceae. J. Food Sci. *44*, 1649.

EDDY, B. P.   1960.   The use and meaning of the term 'psychrophilic'. J. Appl. Bacteriol. *23*, 189.

EGAN, A. F. and SHAY, B. J.   1977.   Brown spot. Ann. Rpt., CSIRO Meat Res. Lab. Cannon Hill, Australia, p. 26.

EGAN, A. F. and SHAY, B. J.   1982.   Significance of lactobacilli and film permeability in the spoilage of vacuum-packaged beef. J. Food Sci. *47*, 1119.

EL-BADAWI, A. A., CAIN, R. F., SAMUELS, C. E. and ANGLEMEIER, A. F.   1964.   Color and pigment stability of packaged refrigerated beef. Food Technol. *18*, 753.

EMSWILER, B. S., KOTULA, A. W. and ROUGH, D. K.   1976.   Bactericidal effectiveness of three chlorine sources used in beef carcass washing. J. Anim. Sci. *42*, 1445.

ENFORS, S-O. and MOLIN, G. 1978. Studies on the mechanism of the inhibition of spore germination by inert gases and carbon dioxide. *In* "Spores VII." pp. 80–84. G. Chambliss and J. C. Vary (Editors). Amer. Soc. for Microbiol., Washington D.C.

ENFORS, S-O. and MOLIN, G. 1980. Effect of high concentrations of carbon dioxide on growth rate of *Pseudomonas fragi, Bacillus cereus* and *Streptococcus cremonis*. J. Appl. Bacteriol. *48*, 409.

ENFORS, S-O., MOLIN, G. and TERNSTROM, A. 1979. Effect of packaging and carbon dioxide, nitrogen or air on the microbial flora of pork stored at 4°C. J. Appl. Bacteriol. *47*, 197.

ESKIN, N. A. M., HENDERSON, H. M. and TOWNSEND, A. J. 1971. Microbiological deterioration of proteins and protein foods. *In* Biochemistry of Foods. pp. 183–217. Academic Press, New York.

EUSTACE, I. J. 1981. Control of bacterial contamination of meat during processing. Food Technol. Austral. *33*, 28.

EUSTACE, I. J., BILL, B. A., GIBBONS, R. A. and POWELL, V. H. 1980. Vacuum packaged lamb carcasses: Extension of storage life by treatment with acetic acid solution prior to packaging. CSIRO Meat Res. Lab. Rpt. 8/80. Brisbane, Australia.

FARBER, J. M. and IDZIAK, E. S. 1982. Detection of glucose oxidation products in chilled fresh beef undergoing spoilage. Appl. Environ. Microbiol. *44*, 521.

FENNEMA, O. R., POWRIE, W. D. and MARTH, E. H. 1973. Supercooling and freezing of food myosystems. *In* Low-Temperature Preservation of Foods and Living Matter. pp. 294–302. Marcel Dekker, New York.

FISCHER, K. and AUGUSTINI, C. 1977. Stadien der postmortalen Glykogenolyse bei unterschiedlichen pH—Werten in Schweinefleisch. Fleischwirtschaft *57*, 1191.

FREEMAN, L. R., SILVERMAN, G. J., ANGELINI, P., MERRITT, C., JR and ESSELEN, W. B. 1976. Volatiles produced by microorganisms isolated from refrigerated chicken at spoilage. Appl. Environ. Microbiol. *32*, 222.

GARDNER, G. A., CARSON, A. W. and PATTON, J. 1967. Bacteriology of prepacked pork with reference to the gas composition within the pack. J. Appl. Bacteriol. *30*, 321.

GILL, C. O. 1976. Substrate limitation of bacterial growth at meat surfaces. J. Appl. Bacteriol. *41*, 401.

GILL, C. O. 1979. Intrinsic bacteria in meat. J. Appl. Bacteriol. *47*, 367.

GILL, C. O. and DE LACY, K. M. 1982. Microbial spoilage of whole sheep livers. Appl. Environ. Microbiol. *43*, 1262.

GILL, C. O. and LOWRY, P. D. 1982. Growth at sub-zero temperatures of black spot fungi from meat. J. Appl. Bacteriol. *52*, 245.

GILL, C. O. and NEWTON, K. G. 1977. The development of aerobic spoilage flora on meat stored at chill temperatures. J. Appl. Bacteriol. *43*, 189.

GILL, C. O. and NEWTON, K. G. 1978. The ecology of bacterial spoilage of fresh meat at chill temperatures. Meat Sci. *2*, 207.

GILL, C. O. and NEWTON, K. G. 1979. Spoilage of vacuum-packaged dark, firm, dry meat at chill temperatures. Appl. Environ. Microbiol. *37*, 362.

GILL, C. O. and NEWTON, K. G. 1980A. Development of bacterial spoilage at adipose tissue surfaces of fresh meat. Appl. Environ. Microbiol. *39*, 1076.

GILL, C. O. and NEWTON, K. G. 1980B. Growth of bacteria on meat at room temperatures. J. Appl. Bacteriol. *49*, 315.

GILL, C. O. and NEWTON, K. G. 1982. Effect of lactic acid concentration on growth on meat of Gram-negative psychrotrophs from a meat works. Appl. Environ. Microbiol. *43*, 284.

GILL, C. O. and PENNEY, N. 1977. Penetration of bacteria into meat. Appl. Environ. Microbiol. *33*, 1284.

GILL, C. O. and PENNEY, N. 1984. The shelf life of sheep livers packed in closed tubs. Meat Sci. *11*, 73.

GILL, C. O. and TAN, K. H. 1979. Effect of carbon dioxide on growth of *Pseudomonas fluorescens*. Appl. Environment. Microbiol. *38*, 237.

GILL, C. O. and TAN, K. H.   1980.   Effect of carbon dioxide on meat spoilage bacteria. Appl. Environ. Microbiol. *39*, 317.

GILLESPIE, N. C.   1981.   A numerical taxanomic study of *Pseudomonas*-like bacteria isolated from fish in southeastern Queensland and their association with spoilage. J. Appl. Bacteriol. *50*, 29.

GOEPFERT, J. M. and HICKS, R.   1969.   Effect of volatile fatty acids on *Salmonella typimurium*. J. Bacteriol. *97*, 956.

GOLDSMITH, J. R. and LANDAW, S. A.   1968.   Carbon monoxide and human health. Science *162*, 1352.

GOLL, D. E., ARAKAWA, N., STROMER, M. H., BUSCH, W. A. and ROBSON, R. M.   1970.   Chemistry of muscle proteins as a food. *In* The Physiology and Biochemistry of Muscle as a Food. Vol. 2. pp. 755–800. E. J. Briskey, R. G. Cassens, and B. B. Marsh. (Editors). University of Wisconsin Press, Madison.

GRACEY, J. F.   1981.   Moulds. *In* Thornton's Meat Hygiene. pp. 195–196. Balliere Tindall, London.

GRAHAM, A., CAIN, B. P. and EUSTACE, I. J.   1978.   An enclosed hot water spray cabinet for improved hygiene of carcass meat. CSIRO Meat Res. Lab. Rpt. 11/78. Brisbane, Australia.

GRAU, F. H.   1979.   Nutritional requirements of *Microbacterium thermosphactum*. Appl. Environ. Microbiol. *38*, 818.

GRAU, F. H.   1980.   Inhibition of the anaerobic growth of *Brochothrix thermosphacta* by lactic acid. Appl. Environ. Microbiol. *40*, 433.

GRAU, F. H.   1981.   Role of pH, lactate and anaerobiosis in controlling the growth of some fermentative Gram-negative bacteria on beef. Appl. Environ. Microbiol. *42*, 1043.

GRAU, F. H.   1983.   Microbial growth on fat and lean surfaces of vacuum-packaged chilled beef. J. Food Sci. *48*, 326.

HADDOCK, B. A. and JONES, C. W.   1977.   Bacterial respiration. Bacteriol. Rev. *41*, 47.

HERBERT, R. A. and SHEWAN, J. M.   1976.   Roles played by bacterial and autolytic enzymes in the production of volatile sulfides in spoiling North Sea cod (*Gadhus morhua*). J. Sci. Food Agr. *27*, 89.

HICKS, E. W., SCOTT, W. J. and VICKERY, J. R.   1955.   Influence of water in surface tissues on storage of meat. Bul. Internat. Instit. Refrig. Annexe *1955-1*, 72.

HITCHENER, B. J., EGAN, A. F. and ROBERS, P. J.   1982.   Characteristics of lactic acid bacteria isolated from vacuum-packaged beef. J. Appl. Bacteriol. *52*, 31.

HO, H. F. and BLACKMORE, D. K.   1979.   Effect of chilling and freezing on survival of *Leptospira interrogans* serovar *pomona* in naturally infected pig kidneys. New Z. Vet. J. *27*, 121.

INGRAM, M. and DAINTY, R. H.   1971.   Changes caused by microbes in spoilage of meats. J. Appl. Bacteriol. *34*, 21.

INGRAM, M. and MACKEY, B. M.   1976.   Inactivation by cold. *In* Inhibition and Inactivation of Vegetative Microbes. pp. 111–151. F. A. Skinner and W. B. Hugo (Editors). Academic Press, New York.

JACOBY, G. A.   1964.   The induction and repression of amino acid oxidation in *Pseudomonas fluorescens*. Biochem. J. *92*, 1.

JAY, J. M.   1972.   Mechanism and detection of microbial spoilage in meats at low temperatures: A status report. J. Milk Food Technol. *35*, 467.

JUNI, E.   1978.   Genetics and physiology of *Acinetobacter*. Ann. Rev. Microbiol. *32*, 349.

KELLY, C. A., DEMPSTER, J. F. and MCLOUGHLIN, A. J.   1981.   The effect of temperature, pressure and chlorine concentration of spray washing water on numbers of bacteria on lamb carcasses. J. Appl. Bacteriol. *51*, 415.

KING, A. D., JR. and NAGEL, C. W.   1967.   Growth inhibition of a *Pseudomonas* by carbon dioxide. J. Food Sci. *32*, 575.

KING, A. D., JR. and NAGEL, C. W.   1975.   The influence of carbon dioxide upon the metabolism of *Pseudomonas aeruginosa*. J. Food Sci. *40*, 362.

LANIER, T. C., CARPENTER, J. A., TOLEDO, R. T. and REAGAN, J. O.   1978. Metmyoglobin reduction in beef systems as affected by aerobic, anaerobic and carbon monoxide-containing environments. J. Food Sci. *43*, 1788.

LARKIN, J. M. and STOKES, J. L.   1968.   Growth of psychrophilic microorganisms at sub-zero temperatures. Canad. J. Microbiol. *14*, 97.

LAW, N. H. and VERE-JONES, N. W.   1955.   Shipment of chilled beef. N.Z. Dept. of Sci. Indus. Res. Bull. 118. Wellington, New Zealand.

LEA, C. H., PARR, L. J. and JACKSON, H. F.   1969.   Chemical and organoleptic changes in poultry meat resulting from the growth of psychrophilic spoilage bacteria at 1°C. 3. Glutamine, glutathione, tyrosine, ammonia, lactic acid, creatine, carbohydrate, heme pigment and hydrogen sulfide. Brit. Poult. Sci. *10*, 229.

LEE, J. V., GIBSON, D. M. and SHEWAN, J. M.   1977.   A numerical taxonomic study of some *Pseudomonas*-like marine bacteria. J. Gen. Microbiol. *98*, 439.

LEISTNER, L.   1978.   Hurdle effect and energy saving. *In* Food Quality and Nutrition. pp. 553–557. W. K. Downey (Editor). Applied Science Publishers, London.

LEISTNER, L., RODEL, W. and KRISPIEN, K.   1981.   Microbiology of meat and meat products in high- and intermediate-moisture ranges. *In* Water Activity: Influences on Food Quality. pp. 855–916. L. B. Rockland and G. F. Stewart (Editors). Academic Press, New York.

LEMBERG, R. and BARRETT, J.   1973.   Bacterial cytochromes and cytochrome oxidases. *In* Cytochromes. pp. 217–326. Academic Press, New York.

LERKE, P., ADAMS, R. and FARBER, L.   1965.   Bacteriology of spoilage of fish muscle III. Characterization of spoilers. Appl. Microbiol. *13*, 625.

LOCKER, R. H., DAVEY, C. L., NOTTINGHAM, P. M., HAUGHEY, D. P. and LAW, N. H.   1975.   New concepts in meat processing. Advan. Food Res. *21*, 157.

LOWRY, P. D. and GILL, C. O.   1984A.   Temperature and water activity minima for growth of spoilage molds from meat. J. Appl. Bacteriol. *56*, 193.

LOWRY, P. D. and GILL, C. O.   1984B.   The development of a yeast microflora on frozen lamb stored at −5°C. J. Food Prot. *47*, 309.

McMEEKIN, T. A.   1975.   Spoilage association of chicken breast muscle. Appl. Microbiol. *29*, 44.

McMEEKIN, T. A.   1977.   Spoilage association of chicken leg muscle. Appl. Environ. Microbiol. *33*, 1244.

McMEEKIN, T. A.   1981.   Microbial spoilage of meats. *In* Developments in Food Microbiology. Vol. 1, pp. 1–40. R. Davies (Editor). Applied Science Publishers, London.

McMEEKIN, T. A. and PATTERSON, J. T.   1975.   Characterization of hydrogen sulfide-producing bacteria isolated from meat and poultry plants. Appl. Microbiol. *29*, 165.

MARSHALL, R. J., ANDERSON, M. E., NAUMANN, H. D. and STRINGER, W. C.   1977.   Experiments in sanitizing beef with sodium hypochlorite. J. Food Prot. *40*, 246.

MEAD, G. C.   1982.   Microbiology of poultry and game birds. *In* Meat Microbiology. pp. 67–101. M. H. Brown (Editor). Applied Science Publishers, London.

MERMELSTEIN, N. H.   1977.   Success or failure? How the food technology industrial achievement award winners have faired over the years. Food Technol. *31*(7), 36.

MICHENER, H. D. and ELLIOTT, R. P.   1964.   Minimum growth temperatures for food-poisoning, fecal indicator and psychrophilic microorganisms. Advan. Food Res. *13*, 349.

MILLER, A., III, SCANLAN, R. A., LEE, J. S. and LIBBEY, L. M.   1973A.   Volatile compounds produced in sterile fish muscle (*Sebastes melanops*) by *Pseudomonas putrefaciens*, *Pseudomonas fluorescens* and *Achromobacter* species. Appl. Microbiol. *26*, 18.

MILLER, A., III, SCANLAN, R. A., LEE, J. S., LIBBEY, L. M. and MORGAN, M. E. 1973B. Volatile compounds produced in sterile fish muscle (*Sebastes melanops*) by *Pseudomonas perolens*. Appl. Microbiol. *25*, 257.

MITCHELL, C. G. and DAWES, E. A. 1982. The role of oxygen in the regulation of glucose metabolism, transport and the tricarboxylic acid cycle in *Pseudomonas aeruginosa*. J. Gen. Microbiol. *128*, 49.

MOLIN, G. and TERNSTROM, A. 1982. Numerical taxonomy of psychrotrophic pseudomonads. J. Gen. Microbiol. *128*, 1249.

NAKAE, T. and ELLIOTT, J. A. 1965. Production of volatile fatty acids by some lactic acid bacteria II. Selective formation of volatile fatty acids by degradation of amino acids. J. Dairy Sci. *48*, 293.

NEWTON, K. G. and GILL, C. O. 1978A. The development of the anaerobic spoilage flora of meat stored at chill temperatures. J. Appl. Bacteriol. *44*, 91.

NEWTON, K. G. and GILL, C. O. 1978B. Storage quality of dark, firm, dry meat. Appl. Environ. Microbiol. *36*, 375.

NEWTON, K. G. and GILL, C. O. · 1980. Control of spoilage in vacuum packaged dark, firm, dry (DFD) meat. J. Food Technol. *15*, 227.

NEWTON, K. G. and RIGG, W. J. 1979. The effect of film permeability on the storage life and microbiology of vacuum-packaged meat. J. Appl. Bacteriol. *47*, 433.

NEWTON, K. G., HARRISON, J. C. L. and SMITH, K. M. 1977. The effect of storage in various gaseous atmospheres on the microflora of lamb chops held at −1°C. J. Appl. Bacteriol. *43*, 53.

NEWTON, K. G., HARRISON, J. C. L. and WAUTERS, A. M. 1978. Sources of psychrotrophic bacteria on meat at the abattoir. J. Appl. Bacteriol. *45*, 75.

NICOL, D. J., SHAW, M. K. and LEDWARD, D. A. 1970. Hydrogen sulfide production by bacteria and sulfmyoglobin formation in prepackaged chilled beef. Appl. Microbiol. *19*, 937.

NOTERMANS, S., VAN LEUSDEN, F. M. and VAN SCHOTHORST, M. 1977. Suitability of different bacterial groups for determining faecal contamination during post scalding stages in the processing of broiler chickens. J. Appl. Bacteriol. *43*, 383.

NOTTINGHAM, P. M. 1982. Microbiology of carcass meats. *In* Meat Microbiology. pp. 13–65. M. H. Brown (Editor). Applied Science Publishers, London.

NOTTINGHAM, P. M. and WYBORN, R. 1975. Microbiology of beef processing II. Chilling and aging. New Z. J. Agric. Res. *18*, 23.

O'KEEFE, M. and HOOD, D. E. 1981. Anoxic storage of fresh beef. 1. Nitrogen and carbon dioxide storage atmospheres. Meat Sci. *5*, 27.

PAIGEN, K. and WILLIAMS, B. 1970. Catabolite repression and other control mechanisms in carbohydrate utilization. Advan. Microb. Physiol. *4*, 251.

PATTERSON, J. T. and GIBBS, P. A. 1977. Incidence and spoilage potential of isolates from vacuum-packaged meat of high pH value. J. Appl. Bacteriol. *43*, 25.

PATTERSON, J. T. and GIBBS, P. A. 1978. Sources and properties of some organisms isolated in two abattoirs. Meat Sci. *2*, 263.

PATTERSON, J. T. and GIBBS, P. A. 1979. Vacuum packaging of bovine edible offals. Meat Sci. *3*, 209.

PITTARD, B. T., FREEMAN, L. R., LATER, D. W. and LEE, M. L. 1982. Identification of volatile organic compounds produced by fluorescent pseudomonads on chicken breast muscle. Appl. Environment Microbiol. *43*, 1504.

PRIOR, B. A. 1978. The effect of water activity on the growth and respiration of *Pseudomonas fluorescens*. J. Appl. Bacteriol. *44*, 97.

RACCACH, M. and BAKER, R. C. 1978. Lactic acid bacteria as an antispoilage and safety factor in cooked, mechanically deboned poultry meat. J. Food Prot. *41*, 703.

RANSOM, S. L., WALKER, D. A. and CLARKE, I. D. 1960. Effects of carbon dioxide on mitochondrial enzymes from *Ricinus*. Biochem. J. *76*, 216.

RODEL, W. and KRISPIEN, K. 1977. Der Einflus von kuhl-und Gefriertemperaturen auf die Wasseraktivitat (a_w-Wert) von Fleisch und Fleischerzeugnissen. Fleischwirtschaft *57*, 1863.

ROTH, L. A. and CLARK, D. S.   1975.   Effects of lactobacilli and carbon dioxide on the growth of *Microbacterium thermosphactum* on fresh beef. Canad. J. Microbiol. *21*, 629.

SANDERS, E. H. and SOO, H-M.   1978.   Increasing shelf life by carbon dioxide treatment and low temperature storage of bulk pack fresh chickens packaged in nylon/surlyn film. J. Food Sci. *43*, 1519.

SCHMIDT-LORENZ, W. and GUTSCHMIDT, J.   1969.   Mikrobielle und sensoriche Veranderungen gefrorener Brathahnchen und Poularden bei Lagerung im Temperaturbereich von $-2.5°C$ bis $-10°C$. Fleischwirtschaft *49*, 1033.

SCOTT, W. J.   1957.   Water relations of food spoilage microorganisms. Advan. Food Res. *7*, 84.

SCOTT, W. J. and VICKERY, J. R.   1939.   Investigations on chilled beef II. Cooling and storage in the meat works. Council Sci. Ind. Res. Bul. No. 129, Melbourne, Australia.

SEARS, D. F. and EISENBERG, R. M.   1961.   A model representing a physiological role of CO_2 at the cell membrane. J. Gen. Physiol. *44*, 869.

SEIDEMAN, S. C., VANDERZANT, C., SMITH, G. C., DILL, C. W. and CARPENTER, Z. L.   1980.   Appearance of beef, pork and lamb stored in vacuum or modified gas atmospheres. J. Food Protect. *43*, 252.

SHAW, B. G. and LATTY, J. B.   1982.   A numerical taxonomy study of *Pseudomonas* strains from spoiled meat. J. Appl. Bacteriol. *52*, 219.

SHAW, B. G., HARDING, C. D. and TAYLOR, A. A.   1980.   The microbiology and storage stability of vacuum packed lamb. J. Food Technol. *15*, 397.

SHELEF, L. A.   1975.   Microbial spoilage of fresh refrigerated beef liver. J. Appl. Bacteriol. *39*, 273.

SHELEF, L. A.   1977.   Effect of glucose on the bacterial spoilage of beef. J. Food Sci. *42*, 1172.

SILLIKER, J. H., WOODRUFF, R. E., LUGG, J. R., WOLFE, S. K. and BROWN, W. D.   1976.   Preservation of refrigerated meats with controlled atmospheres: Treatment and post-treatment effects of carbon dioxide on pork and beef. Meat Sci. *1*, 195.

SMITH, M. G. and GRAHAM, A.   1978.   Destruction of *Escherichia coli* and Salmonellae on mutton carcasses by treatment with hot water. Meat Sci. *2*, 119.

STEVENSON, K. E., MERKEL, R. A. and LEE, H. C.   1978.   Effects of chilling rate, carcass fatness and chlorine spray on microbiological quality and case-life of beef. J. Food Sci. *43*, 849.

STUPFEL, M. and BOULEY, G.   1970.   Physiological and biochemical effects on rats and mice exposed to small concentrations of carbon monoxide for long periods. Ann. N.Y. Acad. Sci. *174*, 342.

SUTHERLAND, J. P., PATTERSON, J. T., GIBBS, P. A. and MURRAY, J. G.   1977.   The effect of several gaseous environments on the multiplication of organisms isolated from vacuum-packaged beef. J. Food Technol. *12*, 249.

TABAK, H. H. and COOKE, W. B.   1968.   The effects of gaseous environments on the growth and metabolism of fungi. Botan. Rev. *34*, 126.

TAN, K. H. and GILL, C. O.   1982.   The physiological basis of CO_2 inhibition of a meat spoilage bacterium, *Pseudomonas fluorescens*. Meat Sci. *7*, 9.

TARRANT, P. V.   1976.   The occurrence of dark-cutting beef. Proc. 22nd Europ. Mtg. Meat Research Workers, Malmo, *1*, B8.

TAYLOR, A. A. and SHAW, B. G.   1977.   The effect of meat pH and packaging permeability on putrefaction and greening in vacuum packed beef. J. Food Technol. *12*, 515.

THOMAS, C. J. and McMEEKIN, T. A.   1981.   Production of off odours by isolates from poultry skin with particular reference to volatile sulfides. J. Appl. Bacteriol. *51*, 529.

UPRETI, G. C. and HINSDILL, R. D.   1975.   Production and mode of action of lactocin 27: Bacteriocin from a homofermentative *Lactobacillus*. Antimicrob. Agents Chemother. *7*, 139.

VANDERZANT, C., HANNA, M. O., EHLERS, J. G., SAVELL, J. W., SMITH, G. C., GRIFFIN, D. B., TERRELL, R. N., LIND, K. D. and GALLOWAY, D. E. 1982.   Centralized packaging of beef loin steaks with different oxygen-barrier films. Microbiological Characteristics. J. Food Sci. *47*, 1070.

WELLS, J. M.   1974.   Growth of *Erwina caratovora, E. atroseptica* and *Pseudomonas fluorescens* in low oxygen and high carbon dioxide atmospheres. Phytopathology *64*, 1012.

WEST, R. L., BERRY, B. W., SMITH, G. C., CARPENTER, Z. L. and HOKE, K. E. 1972.   Microbial studies in a beef distribution centre. J. Anim. Sci. *35*, 209.

WHITE, D. C.   1974.   Anaesthetic and enzyme interactions. *In* Molecular Mechanisms in General Anaesthesia. M. J. Halsey, R. A. Millar and J. A. Sutton (Editors). pp. 209–221. Churchill Livingstone, Edinburgh.

WHITING, P. H., MIDGLEY, M. and DAWES, E. A.   1976.   The role of glucose limitation in the regulation of the transport of glucose, gluconate and 2-oxogluconate, and of glucose metabolism in *Pseudomonas aeruginosa*. J. Gen. Microbiol. *92*, 304.

WILHELM, K. E., MARSH, B. B. and LOCHNER, J. V.   1982.   High temperature tenderizing of beef sides: Bacterial considerations. Appl. Environ. Microbiol. *44*, 1244.

WINGER, R. J. and LOWRY, P. D.   1983.   Sensory evaluation of lamb after growth of yeasts at $-5°C$. J. Food Sci. *48*, 1883.

WINKLER, H. H.   1971.   Kinetics of endogenous induction of the hexose-6-phosphate transport system of *Escherichia coli*. J. Bacteriol. *107*, 74.

WOLFE, S. K.   1980.   Use of CO and CO_2-enriched atmospheres for meats, fish and produce. Food Technol. *43*(3), 55.

3

Microbiology of Ready-to-Eat Meat and Poultry Products

R. B. Tompkin[1]

INTRODUCTION

Ready-to-eat meat and poultry products evolved from the necessity to preserve fresh meat for future consumption. They are now purchased because they offer flavor appeal, convenience, nutritional value, and variety to the diet at a price that is competitive with fresh meats and poultry. Today's products reflect many of the changes in processing procedures that have been attempted over the years to achieve preservation. If the literature is examined, it will be apparent that the microbiology of these products parallels the various stages of process and product development. A general introduction to some of the changes that have occurred will help provide a basis for understanding the microbiology of the products that are now available.

Initially, meats were dried for long-term storage. At some point in time it was learned that adding salt to meat would preserve the meat and retain more of the original characteristics of fresh meat (i.e., moistness and tenderness). It also must have become evident that the salt from certain locations produced superior products due to the contaminant, saltpeter or so-

[1]Beatrice Companies, Inc., 1919 Swift Drive, Oak Brook, IL 60521.

Advances in Meat Research, Volume 2
Copyright 1986 by AVI Publishing Co.
All rights of reproduction in any form reserved
ISBN 0-87055-498-0

dium nitrate in the salt. It was not until the turn of this century that the conversion of nitrate to nitrite was found to be necessary for the curing reaction to occur. This knowledge permitted new options for the curing of meat. Since the mid-1920s meats have been cured through the addition of nitrate, nitrate and nitrite, or nitrite alone. The microbiology of meat and poultry products is influenced by selection of the curing agent and the processing method used to apply it. In some countries the level of nitrite and nitrate are controlled by their being premixed with specified levels of salt. This premix is given the term "curing salt." Throughout this chapter the term "salt" will be used for sodium chloride. "Cure" or "curing agent" will be used only when nitrite and/or nitrate are added. A curing brine will mean an aqueous solution containing salt and curing agent. Although emphasis will be given to salt and curing agent, other additives may be present (e.g., sugar, phosphate) but will not be mentioned.

When dry curing primal cuts, the effect of adding salt to the surface of meat is simply another means to accomplish dehydration. Dehydration occurs as a result of moisture being drawn from meat that is packed in salt. In addition, as the salt penetrates the meat, the water activity within the primal meat cut is reduced.

At about the time mechanical refrigeration became increasingly available in commercial processing plants, methods were developed for introducing the salt, curing agents, and other additives (e.g., sugar) into the meat. These methods made it possible to produce primal meat products more rapidly, at lower cost, and having characteristics even closer to those of fresh meat in moistness and tenderness. An early method consisted of vat curing which involved immersing the meat in a solution containing salt and nitrate. It was next learned that by injecting a solution of the salt and nitrate into the meat, the subsequent time the meat had to be held in vats could be reduced. Initially, injection was via the arterial system but later equipment became available for injecting the solution directly into the muscle tissues. After injection by either method, the meat was placed into vats to which was added a cover pickle consisting of a solution of salt and cure. This step was necessary to achieve the necessary distribution of salt and curing agent throughout the meat. Periodically, the meat was overhauled or transferred to fresh vats to facilitate a more uniform distribution of salt and curing agent throughout the meat. During the vat-curing process, microbial growth occurred in the curing brine solution which, under normal circumstances, was considered favorable or, at least, acceptable. Used, mature curing brine solutions were inoculated into fresh curing brine solutions to facilitate the development of a favorable microbial flora. Occasionally, certain defects resulted from microbial growth which materially reduced the quality of the product, if not the loss of the product. A considerable portion of the literature in the United States up to the mid-1950s dealt with such problems. The process of vat curing was performed at refrigeration temperatures, often in the basement of the plant or curing cellar. Following the curing process, the products were then distributed and sold either as fresh cured hams or hams which received some degree of heating. The length of time these perishable products would keep before spoiling depended upon a variety of factors with water activity being only one among the list. In the case of pork, hams were sold as fresh cured, smoked, fully cooked, or baked depending upon the degree of heat that was applied. Over the past 20 years it has become increasingly difficult to purchase fresh cured hams or smoked hams at the retail level. They have been replaced by fully cooked and, to a lesser extent, baked hams. Also, vat curing of pork is no longer practiced on a large scale. In the case of beef, both fresh cured and cooked corned beef continue to be available and vat curing is still commonly used as a step in the process.

Within the past 20 years immersing injected meat in a cover pickle has ceased to be necessary for producing most fully cooked cured meats. This was accomplished by improvements in the equipment for injecting the brine curing solution and the use of an additive (e.g., sodium erythorbate) to accelerate the chemical reactions involved in cure color development. This knowledge led to significant changes in the processing of primal cuts such as ham. Fresh brine curing solutions are now commonly used each day for injection. This latter change eliminated the microbiological problems associated with curing brines. Microbial growth in curing brines is no longer an issue in most plants.

The latest innovation to be adopted on a large commercial scale is to massage or tumble the meat after injection. Among the benefits of massaging or tumbling are further improved control of moisture, salt and cure throughout the meat; improved binding of the meat particles; and increased yields following cooking. The next major change could involve the production of processed meat and poultry products from prerigor or hot-processed meats.

In the case of ready-to-eat comminuted products, the processing changes have been less dramatic. One reason is that the problem of obtaining uniform distribution of salt and curing agent throughout the product is considerably reduced. It is comparatively easy to distribute salt and cure throughout the comminuted meat before it is stuffed or filled into a mold for cooking. The major changes in processing comminuted cooked products have involved improved control of the processing conditions and the development of specialized equipment for increasing production rates and volumes. The addition of curing accelerators with nitrite significantly reduced the production times for sausage products as it did for primal cuts. In addition, the development of vacuum packaging during the 1950s had a profound impact on the microbiological stability of refrigerated luncheon meats and similar products. Additional information on the historical development of the processed meats industry can be found in the National Provisioner (Anon. 1952, 1981).

The foregoing changes in processing procedures have led to a variety of processes being used commercially today. Instead of entirely leaving behind the older slower processes, it is more likely one will encounter various combinations of the old and new processes being used throughout the industry. Products produced on a large scale for wide distribution will most likely be produced using the more recently developed processes and equipment. This situation leads to differences throughout the industry in the microbial content of similar products during their processing and, to some extent, in the finished ready-to-eat products. For this reason, the older microbiological literature continues to have some value but, more often than not, it is not pertinent to today's processes and products. At present, there is no single text which can be used to guide the North American microbiologist through the maze of products that currently exist in the marketplace.

The microbiology of ready-to-eat meat and poultry products can best be discussed if the products are grouped according to common processing procedures and product characteristics. The emphasis in this chapter will be placed upon ready-to-eat products produced in the United States. Products produced in Canada are, for all practical purposes, very similar to those produced in the United States. Differences which do exist primarily reflect differences in the regulations between the two countries. Other recently published texts provide additional information on similar products produced elsewhere in the world (ICMSF 1980; Gardner 1982, 1983).

In certain instances, the microbiology of processed meat and poultry products differ from their counterparts produced in Europe. In North America, large-scale, rapid processing procedures have evolved which provide reasonably priced products with sufficient keeping quality to withstand long-distance shipment and complex distribution systems. This is particularly true for many noncanned perishable cooked meats which must be of acceptable quality for up to 2 months to be commercially viable. This keeping quality can be easily achieved with products that are cooked in the package in which they are sold (e.g., braunschweiger chubs cooked in impermeable casings), but is more difficult if the products must be removed from the container in which they are cooked and then repackaged for the market (e.g., frankfurters, sliced ham, and luncheon meats). It is in these latter products that the impact of the warmer season of the year takes its toll. Even though all factors seemingly remain under control within the processing environment, the same products are prone to more rapid microbiological spoilage in the warmer season.

To fully understand the microbiology of meat and poultry products produced in the United States, the regulations controlling their production and labeling must be considered. Table 3.1 lists the maximum moisture: protein ratios permitted for a variety of products. These values must be met before the products can be released for sale. In certain products these values influence the subsequent microbiological stability. In others the values control the amount of moisture and texture (dryness) of the product. The USDA regulations also specify certain minimum processing requirements for some, but not all, of the ready-to-eat meat and poultry

TABLE 3.1. USDA Moisture-to-Protein Ratio Requirements for Meat Products[a]

Product	Maximum moisture to one part protein
Jerky, Pemmican	0.75
Pepperoni	1.6
Chorizo in lard, canned	$1.8 + pH \leq 5.5$
Dry sausage (e.g., hard salami)	1.9
Tasajo	2.1
Parma ham	2.03 + 4.0% salt
Kippered beef	2.03
Dried meat (chipped beef, dried beef, sliced dried beef)	2.04
Roast beef, parboiled and steam roasted (canned)	2.25
Summer sausage	2.25
Corned beef, canned imported	2.28
Genoa salami	2.3
Air-dried sausage (raw, cured pork sausage in casing)	2.7
Summer sausage, shelf stable	$3.1 + pH \leq 5.0$
Tropic cure pork (shelf stable)	$3.25 + \geq 6.0\%$ salt
Thuringer (semi-dry sausage)	3.7
Brown and serve sausage	3.7
Mortadella (canned and heated to 65.6°C)	3.85
Meat broth	135

[a] USDA (1973), deHoll and deHoll (1983), Hibbert (1983).

products. Examples of the minimum processing requirements which have direct impact on the microbiological content of these products are listed in Table 3.2.

As in any set of regulations, there are those which could be questioned in light of current knowledge. Of concern to microbiologists is the rationale for the minimum temperatures required for heating different meat and poultry products. If 58.3°C is necessary to destroy trichinae in cured pork products and 62.8°C, or its equivalent at a lower temperature for a longer time, is necessary to destroy salmonellae in noncured meat (e.g., roast beef), then what is the intent of the temperatures imposed during the processing of the other products listed in Tables 3.3 and 3.4? The 71.1°C requirement for cooked noncured poultry products has some of its origins in microbiological control. It is based upon research which demonstrated that heating poultry rolls to an internal temperature of 71.1°C assures the destruction of enterococci. At the time the research was conducted, enterococci were considered a cause of food-borne illness (Wilkinson et al. 1965). This temperature requirement is now being retained by the USDA to assure the products appear fully cooked to consumers. In another example, after filling cooked headcheese ingredients into raw animal casings, the filled product must then be reheated to an internal temperature of 68.3°C. The intent of this requirement is to assure the destruction of salmonellae which could be present on the casings. This hazard is particularly present when fresh casings (e.g., pork stomachs) are removed from the kill floor, washed, and used shortly thereafter for headcheese production in the same plant. It would seem that if 62.8°C is adequate to assure salmonellae

TABLE 3.2. Examples of Minimum USDA Processing Requirements Influencing the Microbial Content of Ready-to-Eat Products

Processing requirement	Intended/effect
1. Midshift clean-up in rooms where cooked products are handled. Alternatively, develop data showing the processing equipment is microbiologically under control.	Generally improved sanitary quality and safety of product
2. Midshift clean-up of equipment surfaces contacting raw product when the processing area exceeds 10°C.	Generally improved sanitary quality of product
3. Cooked roast beef must be heated to an internal temperature of 62.8°C or its equivalent at a lower temperature for a longer time.	Assure destruction of salmonellae
4. Cured, nondried ready-to-eat products containing pork must be heated to ≥58.3°C.	Assure destruction of trichinae
5. Separation of raw from cooked product.	Prevent cross-contamination of enteric pathogens from raw to cooked

destruction in roast beef, then 62.8°C also should be adequate for head-cheese. The intent of the remaining temperature requirements in Tables 3.3 and 3.4 would appear to have their basis in assuring product quality characteristics of texture and appearance rather than for microbial control.

The thermal process is among the most important factors controlling the microbial content and stability of finished products. The current minimum internal temperatures required by the USDA evolved over the years in response to contemporary needs. Could new research data be developed which would provide a more uniform approach to establishing temperature requirements based upon the desired intent? In terms of microbiological control, the only products which consider both processing temperature and time are perishable roast beef, shelf-stable products heated

TABLE 3.3. Minimum Internal Temperatures Required by USDA for Perishable Cooked Uncured Products[a]

Cooked uncured product	Minimum internal temperature (°C)
Baked loaves	71.1
Baked pork cuts	76.7
Cooked poultry products	71.1
Pinkelwurst	66.7
Roast beef	62.8[b]

[a] Angelotti (1978) and deHoll and deHoll (1983).
[b] Or its equivalent at a lower temperature for a specified time.

TABLE 3.4. Minimum Internal Temperatures Required by USDA for Perishable Cooked Cured Products[a]

Cured product	Minimum internal temperature (°C)
Cured pork products for trichinae destruction (does not qualify as "cooked")	58.3
Ham, cooked (includes "tender smoked")	60.0
Corned beef, cooked	62.8[b]
Ham and other cured and/or smoked products	
Fully cooked	64.4
Completely cooked	65.6–71.1
Canned, perishable cured	
Hams, luncheon meat, mortadella, etc.	65.6
Poultry products	68.3
Headcheese in natural casings	65.6
Poultry products, cooked	68.3
Ham, baked	76.7

[a] deHoll and deHoll (1983) and USDA (1983).
[b] Or its equivalent at a lower temperature for a specified time.

in hermetically sealed containers, and trichinae control requirements for certain products containing pork. To what extent could the current minimum internal temperature requirements for other products be modified to permit equivalent thermal processes at lower temperatures for longer times? Would the application of P values (Shapton et al. 1971) provide a basis for arriving at alternative thermal processes?

The reader should be aware that the minimum internal temperatures required by the USDA do not assure microbiological stability of perishable products. Numerous instances could be cited where a properly refrigerated product has undergone unusually rapid microbiological spoilage even though the minimum USDA requirements had been met. Commercial establishments continue to be reminded through product losses that they must employ thermal processes which meet not only the USDA requirements but also control the microbial population in their specific products. Different companies and even different plants within a company have different requirements for the keeping quality of their perishable ready-to-eat products. Also, each plant is somewhat unique in that the microbial population of its products before heating can differ from other plants or, for that matter, from day to day. Another major factor influencing microbial stability is that the method of heating and the uniformity of the thermal process will differ among plants. These differences make it impossible to provide a listing of processing temperatures that are necessary for assuring maximum stability of commercially produced perishable ready-to-eat products.

The USDA has made limited use of brine values [% brine = (% salt/% salt + % water) × 100] as a measure of microbiological stability and safety. In those instances where brine values have been established (Table 3.5) their intent has been to assure microbial control. For example, per-

TABLE 3.5. USDA Brine Requirements for Meat

Product	Percentage brine
Beef brisket (canned shelf stable)	≥ 5.5
Loaf (perishable canned cured luncheon or meat loaf)	≥ 3.5
Loaf (as above but with cereal, starch, or other extenders)	≥ 6.1
Bacon (canned, then pasteurized for shelf stability)	≥ 7.0
Bacon or bacon crumble (prefried and then canned):	
1. Moisture ÷ salt × protein index of 0.400 or less	
2. Brine concentration (moisture ÷ salt) of 9.0 or less	
Products (e.g., bacon, pepperoni) which are normally cured but do not contain nitrite or nitrate	≥ 10.0

ishable canned cured luncheon or meat loaf must have a brine level of 3.5% or greater. If cereal, starch, or other extenders are added, the product must have a brine level of 6.0% or greater. The higher brine requirement was based upon two factors. First, it was apparently believed that cereal, starch, and other extenders could serve as a source of botulinal spores or otherwise influence the microbiological safety of these products if they were temperature abused. Second, it was believed at the time that *Clostridium botulinum* could not germinate, grow, and produce toxin if the product had a brine level greater than 6.0% (Tompkin 1983A). It is now known that botulinal growth can occur at brine levels greater than 6.0%. Furthermore, it is also now evident that certain extenders could improve the safety of these products because they contain acid-producing spore formers which upon temperature abuse cause the pH of the product to decrease to levels which are inhibitory to botulinal outgrowth. There has been periodic commercial interest in producing perishable canned cured meats with extenders. However, the high brine requirement results in products which are too salty for consumer acceptance. Hence, they are virtually nonexistent in the U.S. market. A reevaluation of the high brine requirement is needed.

The minimum brine level of 10% was established to prevent the growth of *C. botulinum* in products (e.g., bacon) which are normally cured but are prepared without the addition of nitrite or nitrate. The rationale behind this regulation was outlined by Houston (1979). Alternative to the use of 10% or higher brine the product may be processed to F_0 of 3 or more, acidified to pH 4.6 or below, or dried to a water activity of 0.92 or below. If the brine or alternative requirements are not met, the products must be labeled with precautionary statements (uncured, no nitrite or nitrate added, not preserved—keep refrigerated below 40°F at all times).

Canned shelf-stable bacon can be produced by several methods. In the case of bacon which is filled into the can and given a heat treatment, the brine level must be equal to or greater than 7.0% (Table 3.5). Two other criteria which the USDA has established for canned prefried bacon which is not given a subsequent heat treatment are also listed in Table 3.5. The formula for calculating brine concentration is unique as it is used here by the USDA for prefried canned bacon. The rationale for requiring that canned shelf-stable beef brisket must have a brine level of 5.5% or greater undoubtedly has its origins in microbiological control, but its significance is unknown to this writer.

A unique feature of the USDA regulations has been the mechanism of label approval. Each company has had to submit to the USDA a copy of the proposed label for each new product. This requirement at times has provided an opportunity for USDA microbiologists to comment upon the microbiological safety of a proposed product, process, or container. This system has had some influence on the microbiology of existing products. Instances could be cited where certain products have been prevented from entering the marketplace and others where extensive microbiological data were required before approval. Although there have been differences of opinion over the years between the industry and USDA, the overall impact on the microbiological safety of USDA inspected products has been favorable for both consumers and industry.

Two major issues developed over the past 15 years which relate to the microbiological safety and stability of ready-to-eat meat and poultry products. During the 1970s the use of nitrate and nitrite was reevaluated in terms of the potential for nitrosamine formation in cured meats. Both voluntary and mandated changes were made in the usage levels of nitrate and nitrite in cured meats produced in the United States and other countries. Additional research and changes may be forthcoming in response to the review by the National Research Council (1981, 1982). The second major issue concerns the level of salt in ready-to-eat meat and poultry products. There is an abundance of research showing that the level of salt influences the microbiological stability and safety of these products. Despite this prior experience, the 1980s will show an intensified research interest in the preservation value of salt, salt replacements, and the risk-benefit associated with reduced salt or sodium content of ready-to-eat meat and poultry products. A review by Sofos (1983) provides an introduction to previous research on this topic.

RAW SALTED CURED MEATS

General Processing Procedures and Product Characteristics

Traditionally, the primary meat preserved for long-term storage has been pork. The procedures for producing shelf-stable dry cured meats were developed in Europe where regional variations in processing resulted in products having different characteristics. Immigrants entering the New World brought with them the formulations and processing methods for

producing products like those of their original homeland. With the passage
of time, variations were added by the North American settlers. Some of the
variations resulted from mixing technologies from the different countries.
Other variations resulted from changes in processing methods, equipment,
raw materials, and marketing conditions. As changes have occurred in the
products, the selection of terms for use in labeling has become somewhat
unclear. For example, prosciutto may be the Italian word for ham, but in
the United States, the terms Italian ham, prosciutto, and prosciutto ham
are all used to imply an Italian-style ham.

The dry cured hams of continental Europe (Bayonne ham–France, Parma ham–Italy, Westphalian ham–Germany) continue to be produced in a
traditional manner and have retained their original organoleptic qualities. Each of these hams are sliced thinly and eaten without further cooking. The only shelf-stable dry cured ham produced in any large quantity in
the United States is the country-style ham. Country-style hams are processed to assure the destruction of trichinae. This is a necessary safeguard
for those ethnic groups who might eat the hams without prior cooking.
Technically, country-style hams are ready-to-eat but, traditionally, they
are cooked before being eaten.

In the past, dry cured meats were prepared following slaughtering during the cooler months of the year and the meat preserved for later use.
This is still the case for much of the country-style ham production. The
process of dry curing consists of coating the surface of the meat with salt
and cure, stacking the meat in a pile, and holding at cool temperatures
until the salt and curing agents penetrate and moisture is expressed from
the meat. The meat is usually restacked one or more times with fresh salt
and cure after an initial period of storage. Dry curing requires comparatively lengthy holding periods until the salt has equilibrated throughout the meat. This is an expensive and time-consuming process. Some
producers have modified the dry curing process by incorporating injection
procedures to reduce the equilibration time. Once the salt content has
reached a sufficiently high level ($\geq 4.0\%$) throughout the ham, the hams
are processed according to the type of product that is desired. Some are
subjected to a cold smoking process with the temperature of the smokehouse not exceeding 37.8°C. They are then transferred to ambient temperatures for a period of months up to a year or more for drying and aging
to develop the desired texture and flavor. The products may be given a
coating of spices (e.g., pepper) just prior to release from the plant.

As one might expect, the most common cause of spoilage of dry cured
meats is due to microbial growth within the interior of the product before
adequate salt penetration has occurred. This is particularly true if the
hams are not sufficiently cold at the time they are packed in salt and cure.
Spoilage can also occur if the meat is moved to warmer temperatures for
smoking and drying before the salt content has reached preservative levels. The microbiological stability of finished dry cured meats is due to their
low water activity, the presence of nitrite, either added directly or result-

ing from conversion of nitrate by certain desirable microorganisms, and smoke having been applied between the salting and drying processes. The hard, dry outer surface of the skin and meat serves as a barrier of protection. The temperature employed for smoking must be sufficiently low to retain the raw texture of the meat and not inactivate the inherent enzymes involved in flavor development during aging. Accordingly, microbial destruction which might occur during the smoking process would be due to the antimicrobial properties of the smoke and further dehydration at the surface of the meat.

Prior to cooking as whole hams, country-style hams are soaked in water to remove some of the excess salt and the skin is removed. After the hams are baked, they should be considered perishable. Country-style hams and bacon are also sold as vacuum-packaged raw sliced products. These items are typically sold as perishable products at refrigeration temperatures.

The second most popular dry cured ham produced in North America is the Italian-style ham. These hams are processed generally as outlined above except that spices are added with the salt and curing agent, the hams are soaked in water to remove excess salt before heating, and smoke is never applied during the period of warm holding. They are commonly marketed at refrigeration temperatures as whole pieces or vacuum-packaged portions or slices. These dry cured hams are eaten only as thin slices without prior cooking.

Dried beef for slicing into shelf-stable product can be prepared from whole beef hams or as a sectioned and formed product. Dry curing of whole beef hams can be employed but other methods of processing are more likely to be used today and, therefore, will not be further discussed in this section.

It is normal for extensive microbial growth to occur during the initial stages of processing the foregoing products. None of the products receive a sufficient thermal process to destroy all the natural flora that develops during processing. This may be a positive feature for preventing the development of high levels of enterotoxigenic *Staphylococcus aureus*. The dry cured hams produced commercially in North America have a favorable record of safety. The major cause of spoilage of finished dry cured products is due to yeast and mold growth during storage in conditions of high humidity.

Research

The recent research on the products in this category has dealt primarily with (1) factors influencing the organoleptic quality of the products (Lillard and Ayres 1969), (2) the microbial flora that develops during processing (Bartholomew and Blumer 1980), (3) control of undesirable microbial growth (e.g., mold) during the curing and aging process (Draughon et al. 1981; Kemp et al. 1981 1983), (4) the potential production of mycotoxins on these products during storage (Ayres *et al.* 1974), and (5) the production of botulinal toxin during the salt equilibration process (Lücke *et al.* 1982). The references cited serve as examples of each research problem. They also will provide background information and an entrance to the literature on each topic.

PERISHABLE COOKED UNCURED PRODUCTS

General Processing Procedures and Product Characteristics

With the exception of the loin section, the majority of pork receives some further processing before being offered for sale. Within the category of perishable cooked pork products, there are only a few which are not cured with nitrite or nitrate. These include cooked sausage patties and links, barbecued pork, roast beef, hamburger patties, meat for TV dinners and meat pies, meat loaf, roast pork, paté, poultry rolls and roasts, fried chicken, Italian beef, cooked, boned poultry meat, and bratwurst.

A relatively small number of cooked uncured beef or pork products is produced on a large scale. The production of cooked ready-to-eat poultry items has been increasing in both quantity and variety. The minimum internal temperatures required by the USDA for products in this category are listed in Table 3.3.

The USDA prohibits the sale of perishable canned noncured meat or poultry products in rigid hermetically sealed containers (i.e., glass jars or cans). This policy only applies to products produced in federally inspected establishments. Cooked perishable soups, stews, patés, and meat or poultry salads, for example, cannot be packed in glass jars or cans. Such products can be packed in rigid containers only if the products are high acid (pH 4.6 or lower) or if they are given a thermal process sufficient to assure the destruction of *C. botulinum*. In the latter case they are no longer perishable but for marketing purposes the products could appear in the refrigerated display cases of retail outlets. The intent of this policy is to reduce the risk that someone will assume the product is shelf stable and mistakenly place the product at room temperature for storage or sale.

There has been virtually no recently published research on the microbial spoilage of these products. One reason may be because many of these products are distributed frozen. The emergence of refrigerated vacuum-packaged cooked uncured poultry products presents unique problems for attaining a suitable shelf life. Generally, the brine content of cooked poultry products is lower than that of red meat products. As a result, they have a shorter shelf life than their red meat counterparts. One solution being applied to these products is to cook the products in the package in which they are sold.

Research

Recently published research on the products in this category has dealt primarily with the destruction or control of food-borne pathogens. Examples include: (1) Microbial destruction during the cooking of ground beef (Buck et al. 1975; Kotula et al. 1977; Stern and Kotula 1982; Craven and Blankenship 1983; Koidis and Doyle 1983; Gill and Harris 1984). (2) Destroying salmonellae and preventing of recontamination during the production of roast beef in USDA inspected establishments (Thompson et al. 1979B; Blankenship et al. 1980; AMI 1984). (3) The control of salmonellae during the production and serving of barbecued meats and poultry products (Todd and Pivnick 1973; Todd et al. 1974). (4) The control of C. perfringens and other pathogens during the preparation of cooked beef and poultry products (Bryan and McKinley 1974; Sundberg and Carlin 1978; Willardsen et al. 1978; Thompson et al. 1979A; Craven et al. 1981; Smith et al. 1981).

PERISHABLE COOKED CURED PRODUCTS

General Processing Procedures and Product Characteristics

The majority of the products in this category (Table 3.6) are derived from pork or blends of pork and beef. There is a large number of poultry products which has been developed to compete with products derived from red meats. The poultry products often share the same general characteristics as traditional pork products such as ham, franks, and bologna. From a microbiological viewpoint, they differ in having a lower brine content and a higher pH. This can result in the poultry products undergoing more rapid spoilage. The production of cooked cured beef is limited to a few items such as pastrami, corned beef, frankfurters (all beef), and Kosher products.

The products in this category are all fully cooked and ready-to-eat; however, it is common for many of them to be heated before serving. Bacon is not fully cooked but since it is a major commodity it deserves comment. Even though bacon is heated to an internal temperature of only about 53.3°C, bacon shares many characteristics of the ready-to-eat products in this category. Vacuum-packaged bacon has a shelf life that is comparable to many fully cooked perishable cured meats. Likewise, it is the same microbial flora which causes eventual spoilage.

These products all receive a heat treatment at some step in their processing. The degree of heating is, however, highly dependent upon the product. The minimum internal temperatures required by the USDA are listed in Table 3.4. For some of the products, the temperatures attained in commercial processes will considerably exceed the values listed. For exam-

TABLE 3.6. Perishable Cooked Cured Products

Emulsified
  Franks, bologna, liver sausage, luncheon meats, loaves
Coarse ground or chopped
  Thuringer, mordatella
Sectioned and formed meats
  Ham, dried beef (ca. 10% brine)
Primal cuts
  Corned beef, pastrami, ham, Canadian bacon, smoked
  poultry
Jellied meats
  Headcheese, souse, blood, and tongue

---

ple, bologna would normally be cooked to an internal temperature in excess of 65.6°C to assure destruction of potential spoilage organisms as well as to satisfy the minimum requirement of 64.4°C for a fully cooked product.

The processing procedures used to produce cooked cured meats involve three general schemes (Table 3.7). The major factors which determine the microbial content of these products as they are ready for shipping from the producing plant are outlined. The following factors influence the type of microorganisms that multiply in these products and the rate at which spoilage occurs:

1. Product characteristics
   a. Brine content or water activity
   b. Type and level of fermentable carbohydrate
   c. pH; type and level of acidulants
   d. Level of smoke, liquid or natural
   e. Phosphate content
   f. Level of residual nitrite
   g. Hot oil dipping or flaming to brown the surface
   h. Spices, condiments applied to product surface after heating
2. Packaging
   a. Product temperature during packaging and palletizing
   b. Degree of vacuumization and leaker formation
   c. Rate of oxygen transmission through packaging materials
3. Microbial
   a. Types and levels of microorganisms surviving the heating process
   b. Types and levels of microorganisms contaminating the product between heating process and packaging

These products seldom have been involved in food-borne illness, the notable exception being ham. There appears to have been an increase in outbreaks of staphylococcal food poisoning following the introduction of the modern ham, which replaced the traditional country-style ham. The lower brine content of the modern ham appears to have made it even more favorable for the growth of *S. aureus*. Historically, the outbreaks have involved contamination after the ham was cooked in a home, church,

TABLE 3.7. The Influence of Processing on the Microbial Content of Perishable Cooked Cured Meat and Poultry Products

Type of product	General processing steps	Major factors influencing microbial content of finished products
Emulsified, coarse ground or chopped, section and formed	a. Meats reduced to proper size and mixed with ingredients b. Section and formed meats may be massaged. c. Mixture filled into casings or molds to obtain desired shape d. Products heated in smokehouses or hot water e. Products chilled f. Product removed from casing or mold; some are sold with the casings still on g. Packaging as slices, chunks, or whole pieces	1. Rework having high levels of heat-resistant bacteria 2. Time-temperature of heating inadequate to destroy flora in meat mixture 3. Contamination and/or growth during steps (e–g)
Primal cuts, smoked poultry	a. Bones may be removed b. Meats injected with or immersed in brine solutions containing other additives c. Meats cooked on racks or while hanging from sticks, smoke is often applied d. Products chilled e. Stockinette or other material may be removed f. Packaging as slices, large portions, or whole pieces	1. Excessive contamination or growth during deboning and applying the brine solution 2. Same as (2), above 3. Contamination and/or growth during (d–f)
Jellied meats	a. Meats water-cooked; meat and broth is then separated b. Cooked meat is cut to desired size c. Cooked meat mixed with proper portion of broth containing other ingredients d. Mixture cooled then filled into molds; if filled into natural casings, then reheated e. Product chilled in molds or casings f. Product removed from molds g. Packaging	1. Contamination and/or growth during steps (b–g) 2. Allowing mixture to become too cool so nonspore formers are not killed as mixture is filled into molds (step d) 3. Not reheating product in natural casings to sufficiently high internal temperature

restaurant, or similar setting. Holding the cooked ham at room temperature permits staphylococcal growth and enterotoxin formation.

In other parts of the world certain perishable sausage products are produced and marketed for short periods of time (days) at ambient temperature. This practice does not exist in the United States. State and local regulations require that all perishable meat and poultry products be held at 7.2°C or less. It is also common in certain countries to offer for sale raw sausages which are intended to be consumed without cooking by the consumer. Teawurst and mettwurst are two such products that are produced domestically in United States. These are smoked, spreadable sausages which can be prepared with raw certified pork to assure trichinae destruction. Many, however, are heated to ≥58.3°C as an alternative method for trichinae control, to extend the shelf life of the products, and to permit wider distribution.

An as yet unanswered question is why *C. perfringens* is of little or no consequence as a cause of food-borne illness from ham and other large cured meat products (e.g., corned beef) while it is a major cause of illness from roast beef and turkey which are not cured. It is tempting to attribute this to the presence or absence of nitrite, but it could also be largely due to differences in salt or brine content.

Research

There has been a continuing research interest in perishable cooked cured meat and poultry products. Despite the economic importance of these products, published research on these products is approaching a standstill in North America. The majority of current information must be derived from research in other countries. The most active research topic has concerned nitrite as an inhibitor of microbial growth. The majority of this research has been reviewed by Tompkin (1983A). Factors that can influence the antibotulinal efficacy of nitrite in perishable cooked cured meat and poultry products include the following (Tompkin 1983A): (1) pH of the product during abuse; (2) brine level; (3) residual nitrite upon abuse and the rate of depletion during abuse; (4) level of viable botulinal spores and vegetative cells at the time of abuse; (5) temperature of abuse; (6) level of ascorbate or isoascorbate; (7) level of "available" iron in the product; (8) type of meat and other formulation ingredients; (9) the thermal process applied to the product; (10) the growth of competitive flora; (11) the growth of nitrite-depleting bacteria; (12) the level and type of phosphate; and (13) combined effects of the above factors. Additional information includes research by Woods and Wood (1982) who reported that the addition of sodium nitrite to cell suspensions of *Clostridium botulinum* led to an accumulation of pyruvic acid. This suggested that nitrite inhibits the phosphoroclastic system of *C. botulinum*. Vahabzadeh *et al.* (1983) reported carbon monoxide to be an ineffective replacement of nitrite for inhibition of *C. botulinum* in pork. Nitric oxide was inhibitory but this could be attributed to the formation of analytically detectable nitrite in the meat. Adding ferric chloride or myoglobin decreased the antibotulinal efficacy of nitrite. Adding EDTA or denatured nitrosylated myoglobin increased the efficacy of nitrite. The decreased efficacy of nitrite when iron compounds were added appeared to be due to a reduction in residual nitrite levels in the product rather than serving as a nutrient to stimulate botulinal growth. Vahabzadeh *et al.* (1983) concluded that the anti-botulinal effect of nitrite and related compounds is probably due to the inhibition of iron-containing enzymes within the botulinal cell rather than the complexing of iron as a nutrient in the product.

Hauschild (1982) summarized a large number of botulinal test packs prepared in various meat products. From the data, estimates were developed of the relative degree of risk associated with botulism. The degree of risk was found to differ for the various products. Bacon was considered a low risk product, whereas turkey roll was a high risk product. The degree of risk could also differ among products of the same type due to differences in their brine concentration. He concluded that major across-the-board reductions in nitrite should not be attempted but that selective reductions in nitrite could be safely made provided the basic levels of brine, carbohydrate, and erythorbate were not altered.

It has become increasingly clear that it is the level of analytically detectable residual nitrite that influences microbial inhibition. The rate at which residual nitrite disappears in cured meats can be influenced by many factors. One which is being examined more closely is the presence of nitrite-depleting bacteria. Collins-Thompson and Rodriguez Lopez (1982) and Dodds and Collins-Thompson (1984) have demonstrated that the lactic acid bacteria, particularly homofermentative lactobacilli, possess this capability. Among the bacteria tested, the old nemesis of the meat packing industry, *L. viridescens,* was among the more active species. The depletion of nitrite was attributed to enzymatic activity (i.e., nitrite reductase) rather than solely due to lowering the pH of the medium. Collins-Thompson *et al.* (1982) found *Enterobacter* and *Serratia* species isolated from bologna to be capable of utilizing nitrite. These species, however, develop late in the spoilage cycle. They concluded that the delay in their growth on vacuum-packaged bologna was related to glucose concentration which influences the growth of antibiotic-producing lactics.

The fate of pathogens inoculated onto ready-to-eat cured meats has been examined by Stiles *et al.* (1979) and Stiles and Ng (1979A, B) and were not included in the review by Tompkin (1983A). Their data showed that *Clostridium perfringens* was incapable of growing on sliced ham, chopped ham, or bologna at abusive holding temperatures (i.e., 21° or 30°C). During storage at lower temperatures (i.e., 4° or 10°C), *C. perfringens* decreased to nondetectable levels. *Bacillus cereus, Escherichia coli, Salmonella typhimurium,* and *Staphylococcus aureus* could grow on sliced ham, chopped ham, and bologna at abusive temperatures (21° or 30°C) under certain circumstances. Growth was influenced by the age of the product (i.e., level of indigenous flora) at the time of contamination and whether sufficient acid was produced by the indigenous flora to inhibit the contaminants. Acid production was likely influenced by the level of fermentable carbohydrate in the products. Under conventional refrigeration (4°C), S. typhimurium survived well in all three products.

There have been numerous reports on the microbiological quality of ready-to-eat luncheon meats. Several recently published reports can serve as examples and provide an entrance into this literature (Surkiewicz et al. 1976, 1977; Oblinger and Kennedy 1980; Tiwari and Kadis 1981; Tompkin 1983B). Generally, the surveys substantiate that these products are perishable at the normal temperatures of storage used for perishable foods. The debated question is when will the microbial population reach a sufficiently high level to cause consumer rejection of the products. At normal refrigeration temperatures, this is often sometime after the population has reached its maximum level. The level of $D(-)$-lactate recently has been proposed as an index of spoilage for these products (Schneider et al. 1983). The use of microbiological criteria for assessing the quality and safety of foods, including meat and poultry products, is currently being reviewed by the National Academy of Sciences at the request of the USDA, FDA and NMF. Their report, which is soon to be published, should influence the future application of microbiological criteria in the United States. In addition, a revised second edition of ICMSF (1974) which recommends sampling plans and criteria for meat and poultry products in international trade should soon be available. A revised edition of the Compendium of Methods for the Microbiological Examination of Food (APHA 1984) has been published. Included in the text are methods recommended for the examination of meat and poultry products. The methods actually used by the USDA for routine monitoring and analysis of ready-to-eat meat and poultry products appear in the Microbiology Laboratory Guidebook (1975).

It would be appropriate to review the more recent research on how to delay microbial growth and extend the keeping quality of ready-to-eat cured meats. This research falls into three areas: the effect of product composition, processing temperature, and packaging.

Two reports have recently been published which show how these factors can affect the rate of spoilage of liver sausage. In addition, the effect these factors have on C. botulinum in liver sausage has been studied.

Chyr et al. (1980) found the most important factors influencing the shelf life of liver sausage were the degree of cooking and the level of nitrite. A marginal thermal process (i.e., 63°–68°C) led to the survival and eventual growth of enterococci as the predominant flora over a 4- to 16-week period at 7°C. The time at which substantial population increases occurred in the product was prolonged by increasing the level of sodium nitrite (0, 50, 100, 150 ppm). In the absence of nitrite, a perfumy odor developed and was associated with the growth of enterococci. The level of enterococci surviving in the product decreased with an increase in the processing temperature (63°, 68°, 74°C). Product prepared from good quality raw materials, with 156 ppm sodium nitrite, and processed to 68°C had a shelf life in excess of 16 weeks at 5°C. Further investigation by Chyr *et al.* (1981) of cured liver sausage, which spoiled at 5°–7°C, led to the identification of the enterococcus as *Streptococcus faecalis*. In addition to *S. faecalis*, the spoilage flora of the liver sausage prepared without nitrite included *Pediococcus pentosaceus*. The pediococcus isolate was less heat resistant than the enterococcus. The pediococcus isolate survived 65°C for 5 minutes with 10^8 cells per milliliter of broth but not with 10^3 cells per milliliter. The enterococcus survived 65°C for 5 minutes or 60°C for 60 minutes with only 10^3 cells per milliliter. A survey of the industry found that liver sausage was commonly being cooked to an internal temperature of 65°C.

Hauschild *et al.* (1982) assessed the relative risk of botulism from temperature-abused liver sausage. They reported that at moderate brine levels (3.8–4.2%), nitrite levels in the range of 0 to 100 ppm had little or no effect on toxinogenesis. At 150 ppm there was a higher level of protection. In liver sausage with a higher brine level (5.44%), the effect of nitrite was increased so that an appreciable delay in toxicity occurred with 50 and 100 ppm nitrite. Product having low levels of toxin often appeared acceptable. Holding the product at 8°C until there was a nearly complete loss of nitrite did not diminish the inhibitory effect of the initial nitrite. It was reported that with an increased processing temperature and/or prolonged time of processing, the inhibitory effect of the nitrite was reduced. Another possible explanation, however, could be offered for this observation. Perhaps the milder thermal process permitted the survival of a competitive flora which prevented toxigenesis. As the thermal process was increased, the competitive flora could have been controlled so that the more heat-resistant *C. botulinum* could dominate and permit toxigenesis. Hauschild and Hilsheimer (1983) examined 138 samples of liver sausage from retail outlets in Canada. Their results led them to estimate the most probable number of botulinal spores as being 0.15 spores per kilogram in the product tested. The estimate for total *C. botulinum* was 0.24 per kilogram. At the 99% confidence level the values were 0.02–0.53 and 0.05–0.69 per kilogram, respectively, for the samples.

Zeuthen (1980) investigated the effect of the pH of meat on the rate of microbial growth on sliced ham. Fresh pork was selected on the basis of pH and separated into two groups: low pH meat (5.5–5.7) and high pH meat (6.3–6.5). The hams were boned and pumped with a pickle solution containing sodium tripolyphosphate prior to processing as canned hams. After cooking and chilling, the canned hams were opened, sliced, vacuum packaged, and then placed at 5°C. The ham prepared with the lower pH meat had a pH of about 6.0 and a residual nitrite level of 38 ppm after processing. The ham prepared with the higher pH meat had a pH of 6.35 and a residual nitrite level of 90 ppm. Both products had a brine level of approximately 4.0%. During the 7 to 8 weeks storage at 5°C, the rate of microbial growth was considerably slower in the sliced ham prepared from the lower pH meat.

Nielsen and Zeuthen (1983) examined the use of glucose and two phosphate additives in bologna. During vacuum-packaged storage at 2°C, lactic acid bacteria grew faster in bologna containing glucose and no phosphate. Growth in the five other combinations of glucose and phosphate was the same. The growth of *Brochothrix thermosphacta* and *Serratia liquefaciens* was slowest in bologna having a lower pH of 5.93 due to the addition of a blend of three phosphates. Their growth rate in the control product (pH 6.4) and bologna containing sodium tripolyphosphate (pH 6.4) was the same.

Perishable cooked cured meats are most commonly packaged under vacuum. Attempts have been made to develop alternative forms of packaging which provide equal or longer keeping quality. One approach which has been considered is to package the products under various gas atmospheres. To be successful, the packaging system must at least assure the dominance of a lactic acid-producing flora comparable to that which occurs in the vacuum package. This is the least repugnant flora which could be tolerated if microbial growth must eventually occur. Among the more recent attempts to evaluate the potential use of gas atmosphere control is the work of Blickstad and Molin (1983). Smoked pork loin and frankfurters were packaged under vacuum, nitrogen gas, and carbon dioxide prior to storage at 4°C. They found the total aerobic plate count of the smoked pork loin to reach 10^7 per gram after 37 days in vacuum, 43 days in nitrogen, and 49 days in carbon dioxide. Even more encouraging results were obtained with frankfurters. The total aerobic plate count of the frankfurters reached 10^7 per gram after 77 days in vacuum. Growth stopped at 10^4 per gram after 98 days in nitrogen and at 10^2 per gram after 48 days in carbon dioxide.

The work of Nielsen (1983) can serve as a recent example of research on the effect of packaging on microbial spoilage. It was demonstrated that the temperature of storage (2°, 5°, and 10°C) and gas permeability of four different packaging films interact to influence the type of microbial growth in vacuum-packed sliced bologna. In this test a surprisingly short shelf life was observed for vacuum-packaged bologna stored at 2°C. The levels of total aerobic bacteria increased from 10^2 or below to greater than 10^7 per gram within 15 days of storage at 2°C regardless of the packaging film. The bacteria which dominated in all the packaging materials and temperatures throughout the first 15 days was *Brochothrix thermosphacta*. In another study (Lee *et al.* 1984) the shelf life of sliced cooked cured meat loaf packaged under vacuum or with a nitrogen backfill was compared. This product also had a short shelf life at refrigeration temperatures. The times at which the microbial counts reached approximately 10^8 per gram were related to the temperature of storage (i.e., 7 days at 7°C, 21 days at 3°C, and 28 days at 0°C). This short shelf life probably reflects the high initial microbial levels at the time of packaging (i.e., lactobacilli counts were 10^5–10^6 per gram). The lactics eventually became the dominant spoilage organisms during storage over the 49-day holding period.

Within the past 10 years there has been an increasing variety and quantity of cooked cured sausages marketed in the United States as small chubs of less than 1 pound in size. These products are very similar to the heavily smoked semidry summer sausages which have been traditionally marketed by processors in Wisconsin as being shelf stable. The majority of these products are either fermented or acidified. To reduce weight loss and maintain organoleptic quality during shipping and storage, many of these products are being packaged in moisture- and oxygen-impermeable films (Galloway 1982; Gehrke 1982). An increasing number of these products are being marketed at ambient temperatures. To do so, the products must meet the USDA requirements of a moisture to protein ratio of 3.1:1 and a pH of 5.0 or less (Hibbert 1983). Despite this regulation, commercial spoilage due to the growth of yeast and/or lactobacilli can occur during prolonged storage at ambient temperatures. The desire to move selected sausage products from perishable to shelf-stable status can be desirable and could increase (Leistner et al. 1981). Tändler and Rödel (1983A, B) have reviewed the manufacture and packaging of these products for marketing at ambient temperatures. The sausages could be placed into two categories. They recommended that uncooked dry sausages should have a moisture content of less than 22% or a_w values of 0.82 or below. Cooked sausages should be cooked to an internal temperature of 70°C and dried to a water activity of 0.85 or below. Although these sausages may have been fermented or acidified, pH was not included as a controlling factor in their recommendations for assuring long-term stability. Information also has been published on the spoilage associated with nonfermented, nonacidified luncheon meat chubs which were cooked in a plastic casing having low oxygen permeability and stored at 25°C. In this case, the chubs were not subjected to additional packaging (Bell and Gill 1982; Bell and DeLacy 1982, 1983; Bell 1983).

The normal spoilage flora of properly refrigerated vacuum-packaged perishable cooked cured meat products consists primarily of lactics. Four reports provide basic information concerning the significance of lactics in these products (Niven 1952; Allen and Foster 1960; Kempton and Bobier 1970; Mol et al. 1971). Additional or newer information could be cited which would introduce other aspects important to the spoilage of these products. The four cited papers, however, clearly identify the problem of lactic spoilage and include recommendations toward controlling the lactics and improving keeping quality.

There has been increasing interest in Brochothrix thermosphacta as a spoilage organism associated with processed meat products. Among the reasons for this interest is that perishable cooked cured meats develop off-odors and flavors in a shorter time period when B. thermosphacta becomes the major cause of spoilage. Egan et al (1980) determined the rate of organoleptic spoilage of sliced cooked corned beef packaged in a film of high oxygen permeability and stored at 5°C. An off-aroma was detected when the B. thermosphacta population reached 10^8 per gram. Off-flavor was detected 2 to 3 days later. Homofermentative lactobacilli caused spoilage more slowly. No off-aroma was detected even though the population had been at a level of 10^8 for 21 days. It was at this time, however, that an off-flavor became evident. Heterofermentative lactobacilli yielded results between those observed for *B. thermosphacta* and the homofermentative lactobacilli. Stanley *et al.* (1981) identified the major volatile compounds produced by *B. thermosphacta* which were responsible for off-aroma as acetoin and diacetyl.

There have been many reports of competitive inhibition of *B. thermosphacta* by other spoilage organisms growing on meats. Collins-Thompson and Rodriguez Lopez (1982) reported this inhibition to be species dependent. The growth of *B. thermosphacta* was restricted when grown on sliced vacuum-packaged bologna in the presence of *Lactobacillus brevis* or *L. plantarum* but not in the presence of *L. viridescens* or *Leuconostoc mesenteroides*. The inhibitory species caused the pH of the bologna to drop to pH 5.3 within 2 weeks at 5°C. The noninhibitory strains dropped the pH of the bologna to only 5.5 within 4 weeks. The authors suggested that the inhibitory strains produced specific antibiotic substances other than hydrogen peroxide or lactic acid. The data of Grau (1980), however, appear convincing that the inhibition is dependent upon the concentration of undissociated lactic acid and the degree of anaerobiosis existing at the site of growth.

Among the various forms of spoilage which have been noted in perishable vacuum-packed cured meats is the development of putrefactive spoilage with a dominance in off-odor from hydrogen sulfide or methane thiol. This form of spoilage has been attributed to *Vibrio, Proteus,* and *Enterobacter-Hafnia* species (Gardner 1979). The formation of a cabbage odor in vacuum-packaged bacon during the warmer months of the year has been found to be due to the formation of methane thiol by *Proteus inconstans* (Gardner and Patterson 1975).

An organism which continues to cause isolated but major spoilage losses is *Lactobacillus viridescens*. Several properties contribute to make this spoilage organism noteworthy. It is the major cause of greening in cured meats; being heterofermentative, it can cause swelling of perishable canned or vacuum-packaged cured meats; and it is able to grow at normally acceptable refrigeration temperatures, yet has unusual heat resistance. While it may be possible to isolate these bacteria from the environment of processed meats plants, the control of these bacteria lies primarily in the judicious control of the cooked product which is reworked into succeeding lots of the same type of meat. Of primary concern is to prevent recycling these bacteria through successive lots and providing the opportunity for a buildup of an increasing population of increasing heat resistance to the point where the thermal process is no longer adequate to cope with the population levels. The heat resistance of these bacteria has been reported by Niven *et al.* (1954), Iwata *et al.* (1965), Gardner (1967), Vrchlabsky and Leistner (1971) and Milbourne (1983). Unpublished research by Shaparis and Christiansen (1976) has shown D values in minced ham to be $D_{63} = 30.5$; $D_{65.5} = 12.5$–15; $D_{68} = 5.5$–6.5; and $D_{71} = 1$–2 minutes.

PERISHABLE CANNED CURED PRODUCTS

General Processing Procedures and Product Characteristics

These products include canned hams, luncheon meat, and ham patties prepared from pork. The production of perishable cured beef or poultry products in rigid metal containers is negligible or nonexistent. The pork products differ mainly in whether the cans are filled with whole muscles, section and formed meat, or comminuted meat. Ham patties are prepared from ground meat which is formed into patties and then filled into the can.

Although the products differ in their appearance, perishable canned cured pork products are similar in that their final brine content will normally exceed 3.0%. The level of nitrite is commonly targeted for an input level of 156 ppm. The products may differ in their fermentable carbohydrate content according to the characteristics desired by the producer. Domestically produced cured pork products must be processed to a minimum internal temperature of 65.6°C. Imported perishable canned cured products containing pork (e.g., canned hams) must have been processed to a minimum internal temperature of 68.9°C to assure the destruction of certain viruses that are of concern for animal disease control (e.g., foot-and-mouth disease). The USDA requires that perishable canned cured poultry products be processed to 68.3°C. Refrigerated storage is recommended to be below 4.4°C but may be as high as 7.2°C and still comply with local and state regulations governing the storage and display of potentially hazardous foods. This limit may be higher in Europe where the upper limit has been recommended to be 10°C.

These products are microbiologically stable at storage temperatures below 4.4°C. They show no loss in product quality or stability during storage periods of 1 year or more. Their microbiological stability can be attributed to the combined effect of a moderate brine content, the use of nitrite, a thermal process which destroys or injures the potential psychrotrophic spoilage flora, and storage at refrigeration temperatures. Commercial experience has shown that failure to control any one of the four factors can lead to a microbiologically unstable product. In addition, an abnormally high microbial level of certain psychrotrophic bacteria in the product before heating can lead to surviving bacteria and an unstable product.

The earlier literature within the United States mentions enterococci as being a major cause of spoilage of perishable canned cured meats. Experience over the past 20 years has seldom found this to be the case. This might be due to the changes occurring in the process of curing the meat prior to canning. The method of curing has been changed from vat curing to the more rapid process of injection curing. This offers less opportunity for microbial growth to occur during the curing process prior to canning. One predominant cause of spoilage in recent years has involved *Lactobacillus viridescens*. The products have consisted of comminuted or ground meats which offer the opportunity for mixing in a portion of rework from previously cooked product. The process of recycling rework into future production lots can lead to the selection of more heat-resistant strains of *L. viridescens*. Eventually sufficiently high levels can be reached in the raw meat blends so that the thermal process is no longer adequate to assure their destruction. Being psychrotrophic in nature, the surviving organisms eventually multiply in the products, typically beginning in the center of the product which receives the least thermal process. Spoilage is characterized by the product developing a sour taste and the container losing its vacuum or eventually swelling.

Another cause of microbial spoilage at commercial refrigeration temperatures is *Clostridum putrefaciens*. This, fortunately, is of rare occurrence. The factors which limit its occurrence are still unclear although it appears that products having abnormally low brine levels (e.g., below 3%) are more prone to spoilage from *C. putrefaciens*. This raises questions about the microbial stability of perishable canned cured meats if the salt levels are reduced to satisfy the concerns of some over hypertension.

Occasionally nonmicrobial defects occur in these products. Cans which appear to have lost their vacuum can result from overfilling or entrapping air in the bottom of the can as the meat is placed into the can. Black spots developing at the surface of the meat can result from chemical reactions between the salts of the meat and the metal container. This is particularly noticeable when the anode in the can lid is defective. Black discoloration also can be induced in canned cured meats by low levels of copper (Board and Ihsan-ul-Haque 1965).

Research

The recently published research on perishable canned cured meats has consisted of: (1) The role of nitrite and other factors in botulinal inhibition of temperature abused product (Tompkin 1983A). (2) Examining whether a trend exists toward lower brine levels in commercially produced products and assessing the potential impact this trend may have on microbiological stability and safety (Johnston and Krumm 1980). It is of interest that products imported from Europe have higher average brine levels (3.7–3.8%) than domestically produced products (3.2–3.6%).

SHELF-STABLE CANNED CURED PRODUCTS

General Processing Procedures and Product Characteristics

These products fall into four categories on the basis of the procedures used to achieve shelf stability: (1) Products processed to $F_0 \geq 2.78$: viennas, corned beef, franks, and spreads. (2) Products processed to $F_0 = 0.1–0.7$: luncheon meat and canned hams (≤ 3 lb). (3) Products controlled by water activity: sausages covered with hot lard or oil, sliced dried beef in jars, and prefried bacon and bacon bits. (4) Products controlled by pH: vinegar pickled sausages and pigs feet. Products in the first category are given a thermal process which is typical of low acid canned foods. That is, they are thermally processed to assure the destruction of *Clostridium botulinum* and achieve commercial sterility.

The second category consists of canned luncheon meat which is normally of 12 ounces in size and canned hams up to 3 pounds in size. These products are given a thermal process which may be in the range of $F_0 = 0.1$ to 0.7. Shelf stability is also dependent upon the addition of sodium chloride, sodium nitrite, and a thermal injury to an indigenous low level of spores. Since the thermal process does not assure the destruction of all mesophilic spores, these products may not comply with the definition of commercial sterility as set forth by the Food and Drug Administration (Randolph 1979). Theoretically, it should be possible to recover viable but nonproliferating *C. botulinum* from these products.

The third category is comprised of those products which rely upon water activity for shelf stability. These products may be characterized as having a high brine content due to the removal of moisture during processing.

The USDA requires that sausages for canning with hot oil or lard must have a water activity of 0.92 or below to assure the control of *C. botulinum* or a moisture:protein ratio of 1.8:1 and a pH of ≤ 5.5. There are no water activity requirements for sliced dried beef or bacon. The only USDA control for sliced dried beef is that it must meet the moisture:protein ratio (2.04 : 1) required of dried meat. Experience has shown that sliced dried beef is shelf stable if packaged under vacuum, as in a glass jar, with a brine content of 16% or above or a water activity of 0.86 or below. Microbial spoilage resulting from the growth of micrococci can occur if the product is packaged under poor vacuum, the brine values are below 16%, and if sufficient residual nitrate is present to serve as an electron acceptor. The various methods for producing sliced dried beef have been recently discussed (Bischoff 1984).

Several processes can be used to produce shelf-stable bacon. The two most commonly used include (1) cooking bacon, then filling into the container and relying upon a sufficiently high brine content for stability, and

(2) heating the bacon in the container to an internal temperature of 68.9°C to destroy nonspore formers and relying upon a moderate brine level to control spore formers. In the first process, the USDA has established two criteria. One states that the bacon must have a moisture divided by salt times protein index of 0.400 or less. In the other, the brine concentration (moisture divided by salt) must be 9.0 or less. The term, brine concentration, as used here, must not be confused with the use of the term brine which appears elsewhere in this chapter. Aside from the USDA requirements, experience has shown that prefried bacon having a water activity of 0.86 or below is microbiologically shelf stable as long as the container is vacuumized and leakers do not develop. A factor which enters into the production of these products is whether the products are sold on the basis of the number of slices or the weight of the product. There is no economic incentive to exceed the 0.86 water activity level when the products are sold by the slice, but there is an economic incentive to exceed that level when sold on a weight basis. This is one example of many which could be cited among the ready-to-eat products where economic considerations influence microbiological stability.

The shelf stability of pH-controlled product is due to these products having a low pH, the use of acetic acid for pH adjustment, control of fermentable carbohydrate, and packaging in an airtight container (Niven 1952). Spoilage, when it occurs, consists of the growth of lactics or, if the container has not been properly sealed, the growth of mold.

Research

Published research on shelf-stable canned cured products during the past 20 years has involved the following questions: (1) The role of nitrite in the stability of canned cured pork given less than a botulinal cook ($F_0 \geq 2.78$) (Tompkin 1983A). (2) Evaluation of the USDA and the U.S. military criteria for the stability of canned prefried bacon (Silverman *et al.* 1983).

SHELF-STABLE CANNED UNCURED PRODUCTS

General Processing Procedures and Product Characteristics

The following examples of the products in this category are shelf stable as opposed to perishable: (1) products processed to $F_0 \geq 2.78$: roast beef with gravy, beef stew, goulash, chili con carne, tamales, whole chicken, and spaghetti with meat balls. (2) Products having pH ≤ 4.6: sloppy joe and spaghetti sauce with meat. Shelf stability is achieved by two methods. In the first method the products are thermally processed in hermetically sealed containers to an F_0 of 2.78 or greater with a value of $F_0 = 6.0$ being typical. The microbiological safety and stability of these products is the same as exists with low acid canned foods which contain no meat.

The second method of processing involves a milder thermal process and the control of pH to 4.6 or below to achieve shelf stability. The meat composition in these products consists of small particle size to quickly achieve the desired pH throughout the product. The microbiological safety and stability of these products compares with high acid canned foods which contain no meat.

Canned uncured meat and poultry products have a favorable record of microbiological safety and stability. The fact that meat was present in the products has had no bearing in those few instances when problems have occurred.

Research

These products have been successfully produced on a commercial basis for years. Unique problems have not arisen which have required research to be performed. The microbiological research that has been performed has involved potentially new methods of thermal processing. Aside from research on irradiation, this research has been performed by commercial laboratories and has not been published.

DRIED MEATS

General Processing Procedures and Product Characteristics

Drying is the oldest method of preserving meat for future use. Today, commercially dried meats in North America are marketed as snack foods or for use as ingredients with other foods (e.g., dehydrated or freeze-dried cooked meat or poultry products). They are jerky, beer sticks, tasajo, pemmican, dehydrated meat or poultry, and freeze-dried meat or poultry. Two products are produced in quantity in the United States as ready-to-eat products. Jerky consists of thin strips of salted and cured beef which can be prepared from primal cuts, section and formed, or coarsely ground beef. The meat may have been smoked before air or oven drying. The time-temperature of heating and drying must be controlled to assure that microbial growth does not occur during the drying process. Environmental contamination also must be controlled to avoid cross-contamination from the raw meat to the cooked product.

Beer sticks are short thin sausages which are produced from chopped or ground meat. The meat is mixed with salt, curing agent, and spices, stuffed into edible casings, and then heated and dried to achieve shelf stability.

The USDA has established moisture:protein ratio requirements for certain dried meats: jerky 0.75:1, tasajo 2.0:1, kippered beef 2.03:1, dried beef 2.04:1 (Table 3.1). Storage conditions must prevent moisture uptake or high humidities, which will encourage spoilage due to mold growth.

Research

There has been no recently published research on these products. There have been four published reports of food-borne illness involving dried meats in the United States during the past 20 years. On two occasions beef jerky was implicated as the cause of salmonellosis (CDC 1967). More recently an Armenian uncooked dried beef product, basturma, was implicated in an outbreak of salmonellosis (Anon. 1982; Johnston 1983). Home prepared venison jerky was responsible for an outbreak of botulism due to *C. botulinum* type F (Midura *et al.* 1972).

SUMMARY

This chapter is intended to serve two purposes. First, it should provide some understanding of the microbiology of meat and poultry products as they are currently produced in the United States. A brief historical review of changes in processing procedures offers a perspective of current products relative to the existing technical literature. The USDA regulations are then discussed in terms of their impact on microbiological content and stability. The products are then grouped on the basis of processing procedure, perishability, and the addition of curing agent. The factors influencing the microbial content of the products within each group are discussed. The second purpose of the chapter has been to identify topics of current research within each group of products. The references have been selected to provide a guide to the literature for each topic.

REFERENCES

ALLEN, J. R. and FOSTER, E. M. 1960. Spoilage of vacuum-packed sliced processed meats during refrigerated storage. Food Res. *25*, 19.
AMI. 1984. Precooked, fresh and cured cooked beef. Good Manufacturing Practices. No. 1. American Meat Institute, Washington, DC.
ANGELOTTI, R. 1978. Cooking requirements for cooked beef and roast beef. Fed. Reg. *43*, 30791.
ANON. 1952. The Significant Sixty. A Historical Report on the Progress and Development of the Meat Packing Industry, 1891–1951. Section 2. The National Provisioner, Chicago, IL.
ANON. 1981. Meat for the Multitudes. Volume 2. The National Provisioner, Chicago, IL.
ANON. 1982. USDA announces recall of chili and dried beef. Meat Industry *28*(12), 67.

APHA. 1984. Compendium of Methods for the Microbiological Examination of Foods. M. L. Speck (Editor). American Public Health Association, Washington, DC.

AYRES, J. C., LEISTNER, L., SUTIC, M., KOEHLER, P. E., WU, M. T., HALLS, N. A., STRZELECKI, E. and ESCHER, F. 1974. Mold growth and mycotoxin production on aged hams and sausages. Proc. 4th Intern. Congr. Food Sci. Technol. *3*, 218.

BARTHOLOMEW, D. T. and BLUMER, T. N. 1980. Inhibition of *Staphylococcus* by lactic acid bacteria in country-style hams. J. Food Sci. *45*, 420.

BELL, R. G. 1983. The effect of variation of thermal processing on the microbial spoilage of chub-packed luncheon meat. J. Appl. Bacteriol. *54*, 249.

BELL, R. G. and GILL, C. O. 1982. Microbial spoilage of luncheon meat prepared in an impermeable plastic casing. J. Appl. Bacteriol. *53*, 97.

BELL, R. G. and DELACY, K. M. 1982. The role of oxygen in the microbial spoilage of luncheon meat cooked in a plastic casing. J. Appl. Bacteriol. *53*, 407.

BELL, R. G. and DELACY, K. M. 1983. A note on the microbial spoilage of undercooked chub-packed luncheon meat. J. Appl. Bacteriol. *54*, 131.

BISCHOFF, J. 1984. Making dried beef. Is it a lost art? Meat Ind. *30(3)*, 23.

BLANKENSHIP, L. C., DAVIS, C. E. and MAGNER, G. J. 1980. Cooking methods for elimination of *Salmonella typhimurium* experimental contaminant from rare dry-roasted beef roasts. J. Food Sci. *45*, 270.

BLICKSTAD, E. and MOLIN, G. 1983. The microbial flora of smoked pork loin and frankfurter sausage stored in different gas atmospheres at 4°C. J. Appl. Bacteriol. *54*, 45.

BOARD, P. W. and IHSAN-UL-HAQUE. 1965. Discoloration of canned cured meats caused by copper. Food Technol. *19(11)*, 117.

BRYAN, F. L. and McKINLEY, T. W. 1974. Prevention of foodborne illness by time–temperature control of thawing, cooking, chilling, and reheating turkeys in school lunch kitchens. J. Milk Food Technol. *37*, 420.

BUCK, C. E., MONTGOMERY, D. and PRATT, D. B. 1975. The effect of cooking on the quantity of *Escherichia coli* in ground beef. Research in the Life Sciences, Univ. of Maine at Orono *23(2)*, 1.

CENTER FOR DISEASE CONTROL. 1967. Salmonella Surveillance Report No. 67. National Communicable Disease Center, Athens, GA.

CHYR, C. Y., WALKER, H. W. and SEBRANEK, J. G. 1980. Influence of raw ingredients, nitrite levels, and cooking temperatures on the microbiological quality of braunschweiger. J. Food Sci. *45*, 1732.

CHYR, C. Y., WALKER, H. W. and SEBRANEK, J. G. 1981. Bacteria associated with spoilage of braunschweiger. J. Food Sci. *46*, 468.

COLLINS-THOMPSON, D. L. and RODRIGUEZ LOPEZ, G. 1982. Control of *Brochothrix thermosphacta* by *Lactobacillus* species in vacuum packed bologna. Canad. Inst. Food Sci. Technol. J. *15*, 307.

COLLINS-THOMPSON, D. L., WOOD, D. and JONES, M. 1982. Factors controlling the growth of gram-negative bacteria in vacuum-packed bologna. J. Food Prot. *45*, 305.

CRAVEN, S. E. and BLANKENSHIP, L. C. 1983. Increased heat resistance of salmonellae in beef with added soy proteins. J. Food Prot. *46*, 380.

CRAVEN, S. E., BLANKENSHIP, L. C. and McDONEL, J. L. 1981. Relationship of sporulation, enterotoxin formation, and spoilage during growth of *Clostridium perfringens* type A in cooked chicken. Appl. Environ. Microbiol. *41*, 1184.

deHOLL, J. C. and deHOLL, J. F. 1983. Encyclopedia of Labeling Meat and Poultry Products. 6th Edition. Meat Plant Magazine, St. Louis, MO.

DODDS, K. L. and COLLINS-THOMPSON, D. L. 1984. Incidence of nitrite-depleting lactic acid bacteria in cured meats and in meat starter cultures. J. Food Prot. *47*, 7.

DRAUGHON, F. A., MELTON, C. C. and MAXEDON, D. 1981. Microbial profiles of country-cured hams aged in stockinettes, barrier bags, and paraffin wax. Appl. Environ. Micrbiol. *41*, 1078.

EGAN, A. F., FORD, A. L., and SHAY, B. J. 1980. A comparison of *Microbacterium*

118   R. B. TOMPKIN

thermosphactum and lactobacilli as spoilage organisms of vacuum-packaged sliced luncheon meats. J. Food Sci. *46*, 1745.

GALLOWAY, D. E.   1982.   Packaging processed meats to provide for extended shelf life. Natl. Provis. *186(6)*, 40.

GARDNER, G. A.   1967.   Discoloration in cooked ham. Proc. Biochem. *2*(3), 49.

GARDNER, G. A.   1979.   Sulfide spoilage in vacuum-packed bacon. J. Appl. Bacteriol. *47*(3), iii.

GARDNER, G. A.   1982.   Microbiology of processing: Bacon and ham. In Meat Microbiology. p. 129. M. H. Brown (Editor). Applied Science Publishers Ltd., NY.

GARDNER, G. A.   1983.   Microbial spoilage of cured meats. In Food Microbiology: Advances and Prospects. p. 179. T. A. Roberts and F. A. Skinner (Editors). Academic Press, NY.

GARDNER, G. A. and PATTERSON, R. L. S.   1975.   A *Proteus inconstans* which produces "cabbage odour" in the spoilage of vacuum-packed sliced bacon. J. Appl. Bacteriol. *39*, 263.

GEHRKE, W. H.   1982.   Packaging procedures and materials. Meat Processing *21*(6), 54.

GILL, C. O. and HARRIS, L. M.   1984.   Hamburgers and broiler chickens as potential sources of human *Campylobacter* enteritis. J. Food Prot. *47*, 96.

GRAU, F. H.   1980.   Inhibition of the anaerobic growth of *Brochothrix thermosphacta* by lactic acid. Appl. Environ. Microbiol. *40*, 433.

HAUSCHILD, A. H. W.   1982.   Assessment of botulism hazards from cured meat products. Food Technol. *36*(12), 95.

HAUSCHILD, A. H. W. and HILSHEIMER, R.   1983.   Prevalence of *Clostridium botulinum* in commercial liver sausage. J. Food Prot. *46*, 242.

HAUSCHILD, A. H. W., HILSHEIMER, R., JARVIS, G. and RAYMOND, D. P.   1982.   Contribution of nitrite to the control of *Clostridium botulinum* in liver sausage. J. Food Prot. *45*, 500.

HIBBERT, R. G.   1983.   Potassium sorbate and propylparaben on semi-dry sausage. Policy memo 056. Food Safety and Inspection Service, U.S. Department of Agriculture.

HOUSTON, D. L.   1979.   Nitrates and nitrites. Fed. Reg. *44*, 48959.

ICMSF.   1974.   Microorganisms in Foods. 2. Sampling for Microbiological Analysis: Principles and Specific Applications. International Commission on Microbiological Specifications for Foods. University of Toronto Press, Toronto, Ontario.

ICMSF.   1980.   Microbial Ecology of Foods. Vol. II. Food Commodities. International Commission on Microbiological Specifications for Foods. Academic Press, NY.

IWATA, H., TOMISHIMA, M. and SAKAMOTO, H.   1965.   Microbiological studies on the greening of cured meat products. I. Taxonomic characteristics of lactic acid bacteria which cause the greening. Bull. Japan. Soc. Sci. Fish. *31*, 527.

JOHNSTON, R. W.   1983.   *Salmonella* in meat and poultry products. Dairy Food Sanit. *3*, 415.

JOHNSTON, R. W. and KRUMM, G. W.   1980.   The microbiological safety of canned, cured, perishable meat products. Proc. 26th Europ. Mtg. Meat Res. Workers, Colorado Springs, CO, p. 295.

KEMP, J. D., LANGLOIS, B. E. and FOX, J. D.   1981.   Effects of vacuum packaging and potassium sorbate on yield, yeast and mold growth, and quality of dry-cured hams. J. Food Sci. *46*, 1015.

KEMP, J. D., LANGLOIS, B. E. and FOX, J. D.   1983.   Effect of potassium sorbate and vacuum packaging on the quality and microflora of dry-cured intact and boneless hams. J. Food Sci. *48*, 1709.

KEMPTON, A. G. and BOBIER, S. R.   1970.   Bacterial growth in refrigerated, vacuum-packed luncheon meats. Canad. J. Microbiol. *16*, 287.

KOIDIS, P. and DOYLE, M. P.   1983.   Survival of *Campylobacter jejuni* in fresh and heated red meat. J. Food Prot. *46*, 771.

KOTULA, A. W., CHESNUT, C. M., EMSWILER, B. S. and YOUNG, E. P. 1977. Destruction of bacteria in beef patties by cooking. J. Anim. Sci. *45*, 54.
LEE, B. H., SIMARD, R. E., LALEYE, C. L. and HOLLEY, R. A. 1984. Shelf-life of meat loaves packaged in vacuum or nitrogen gas. I. Effect of storage temperature, light and time on the microflora change. J. Food Prot. *47*, 128.
LEISTNER, L., RÖDEL, W. and KRISPIEN, K. 1981. Microbiology of meat and meat products in high- and intermediate-moisture ranges. In Water Activity: Influences on Food Quality. p. 855. L. B. Rockland and G. F. Stewart (Editors). Academic Press, NY.
LILLARD, D. A. and AYRES, J. C. 1969. Flavor compounds in country cured hams. Food Technol. *23*(2), 117.
LÜCKE, F.-K, HECKELMANN, H. and LEISTNER, L. 1982. Botulismus nach verzehr von rohschinken. Experimentelle untersuchungen. Fleischwirtschaft *62*, 203.
MICROBIOLOGY LABORATORY GUIDEBOOK. 1975. Food Safety and Inspection Service, U.S. Department of Agriculture, Washington, DC.
MIDURA, T. F., NYGAARD, G. S., WOOD, R. M. and BODILY, H. J. 1972. *Clostridium botulinum* type F: Isolation from venison jerky. Appl. Microbiol. *24*, 165.
MILBOURNE, K. 1983. Thermal tolerance of *Lactobacillus viridescens* in ham. Meat Sci. *9*, 113.
MOL, J. H. H., HIETBRINK, J. E. A., MOLLEN, H. W. M. and VAN TINTEREN, J. 1971. Observations on the microflora of vacuum packed sliced cooked meat products. J. Appl. Bacteriol. *34*, 377.
NATIONAL RESEARCH COUNCIL. 1981. The health effects of nitrate, nitrite, and N-nitroso compounds. Part 1 of 2-part study by the committee on nitrite and alternative curing agents in food. Assembly of Life Sciences, National Research Council, National Academy Press, Washington, DC.
NATIONAL RESEARCH COUNCIL. 1982. Alternatives to the current use of nitrites in foods. Part 2 of 2-part study by the committee on nitrite and alternative curing agents in food. Assembly of Life Sciences, National Research Council, National Academy Press, Washington, DC.
NIELSEN, H.-J. S. 1983. Influence of temperature and gas permeability of packaging film on development and composition of microbial flora in vacuum-packed bologna-type sausage. J. Food Prot. *46*, 693.
NIELSEN, H.-J. S. and ZEUTHEN, P. 1983. Influence of phosphate and glucose addition on some important bacteria in vacuum packed bolonga-type sausage. J. Food Prot. *46*, 1078.
NIVEN, C. F. 1952. Significance of the lactic acid bacteria in the meat industry. Proc. 4th Res. AMIF Conf., p. 31. American Meat Institute, Chicago, IL.
NIVEN, C. F., BUETTNER, L. G. and EVANS, J. B. 1954. Thermal tolerance studies on the heterofermentative lactobacilli that cause greening of cured meat products. Appl. Microbiol. *2*, 26.
OBLINGER, J. L. and KENNEDY, J. E. 1980. Microbiological evaluation of selected delicatessen meats from retail supermarkets. J. Food Prot. *43*, 530.
RANDOLPH, W. F. 1979. Thermally processed low-acid foods packaged in hermetically sealed containers. Fed. Reg. *44*, 16209.
SHAPARIS, A. B. and CHRISTIANSEN, L. N. 1976. Unpublished data. Swift & Company, Oak Brook, IL.
SCHNEIDER, W., HILDEBRANDT, G., and SINELL, H.-J. 1983. D(-)-lactatekonzentration als parameter fur die bewertung des frischezustandes vorverpacter hitzbehandelter fleischer zeugnisse. Fleischwirtschaft *63*, 1198.
SHAPTON, D. A., LOVELOCK, D. W. and LAURITA-LANGO, R. 1971. The evaluation of sterilization and pasteurization processes from temperature measurements in degrees celsius (°C). J. Appl. Bacteriol. *34*, 491.
SILVERMAN, G. J., MUNSEY, D. T., LEE, E. and EBERT, E. 1983. Interrela-

tionship between water activity, temperature and 5.5 percent oxygen on growth and enterotoxin A secretion by *Staphylococcus aureus* in precooked bacon. J. Food Sci. *48,* 1783.

SMITH, A. M., EVANS, D. A. and BUCK, E. M. 1981. Growth and survival of *Clostridium perfringens* in rare beef prepared in a water bath. J. Food Prot. *44,* 9.

SOFOS, J. N. 1983. Antimicrobial effects of sodium and other ions in foods: A review. J. Food Safety *6,* 45.

STANLEY, G., SHAW, K. J. and EGAN, A. F. 1981. Volatile compounds associated with spoilage of vacuum-packaged sliced luncheon meat by *Brochothrix thermosphacta.* Appl. Environ. Microbiol. *41,* 816.

STERN, N. J. and KOTULA, A. W. 1982. Survival of *Campylobacter jejuni* inoculated into ground beef. Appl. Environ. Microbiol. *44,* 1150.

STILES, M. E. and NG, L.-K. 1979A. Fate of pathogens inoculated into vacuum-packaged sliced hams to simulate contamination during packaging. J. Food Prot. *42,* 464.

STILES, M. E. and NG, L.-K. 1979B. Fate of enteropathogens inoculated onto chopped ham. J. Food Prot. *42,* 624.

STILES, M. E., Ng, L.-K., and PARADIS, D. C. 1979. Survival of enteropathogenic bacteria on artificially contaminated bologna. Canad. Inst. Food Sci. Technol. J. *12,* 128.

SUNDBERG, A. D. and CARLIN, A. F. 1978. Relation of final internal temperature to *Clostridium perfringens* destruction in beef loaves cooked in a crockery pot or conventional oven. J. Food Sci. *43,* 285.

SURKIEWICZ, B. F., JOHNSTON, R. W. and CAROSELLA, J. M. 1976. Bacteriological survey of frankfurters produced at establishments under federal inspection. J. Milk Food Technol. *39,* 7.

SURKIEWICZ, B. F., JOHNSTON, R. W. and CAMPBELL, D. F. 1977. Bacteriological survey of chopped liver produced at establishments under federal inspection. J. Food Prot. *40,* 468.

TÄNDLER, K. and RÖDEL, W. 1983A. Manufacture and stability of thin-calibre longlife sausages. I. Manufacture. Fleischwirtschaft *63,* 202.

TÄNDLER, K. and RÖDEL, W. 1983B. Manufacture and stability of thin-calibre longlife sausages. II. Stability. Fleischwirtschaft *63,* 1170.

THOMPSON, D. R., WILLARDSEN, R. R., BUSTA, F. F. and ALLEN, C. E. 1979A. *Clostridium perfringens* population dynamics during constant and rising temperatures in beef. J. Food Sci. *44,* 646.

THOMPSON, W. S., BUSTA, F. F., THOMPSON, D. R. and ALLEN, C. E. 1979B. Inactivation of salmonellae in autoclaved ground beef exposed to constantly rising temperature. J. Food Prot. *42,* 410.

TIWARI, N. P. and KADIS, V. W. 1981. Microbiological quality of some delicatessen meat products. J. Food Prot. *44,* 821.

TODD, E. and PIVNICK, H. 1973. Public health problems associated with barbecued food. A review. J. Milk Food Technol. *36,* 1.

TODD, E., ERDMAN, I. and PIVNICK, H. 1974. Recommended procedures for preparation and vending of barbecued meats cooked in rotisseries. J. Milk Food Technol. *37,* 157.

TOMPKIN, R. B. 1983A. Nitrite. *In* Antimicrobials in Foods. p. 205. A. L. Branen and P. M. Davidson (Editors). Marcel Dekker, Inc., New York, NY.

TOMPKIN, R. B. 1983B. Indicator organisms in meat and poultry products. Food Technol. *37*(6), 107.

USDA. 1973. Meat and Poultry Inspection Manual, Part 27.9. U.S. Department of Agriculture, Washington, DC.

USDA. 1983. Meat and Poultry Inspection Regulations, Part 318.17 U.S. Department of Agriculture, Washington, DC.

VAHABZADEH, F., COLLINGE, S. K., CORNFORTH, D. P., MAHONEY, A. W., and POST, F. J. 1983. Evaluation of iron binding compounds as inhibitors of gas and toxin production by *Clostridium botulinum* in ground pork. J. Food Sci. *48*, 1445.

VRCHLABSKY, J. and LEISTNER, L.   1971.   Hitzeresistenz von laktobazillen bei unterschiedlichen a_w-werten. Fleischwirtschaft *54*, 1368.

WILKINSON, R. J., MALLMANN, W. L., DAWSON, L. W., IRMITER, T. F. and DAVIDSON, J. A.   1965.   Effective heat processing for the destruction of pathogenic bacteria in turkey rolls. Poul. Sci. *44*, 131.

WILLARDSEN, R. R., BUSTA, F. F., ALLEN, C. E. and SMITH, L. B.   1978.   Growth and survival of *Clostridium perfringens* during constantly rising temperatures. J. Food Sci. *43*, 470.

WOODS, L. F. J. and WOOD, J. M.   1982.   A note on the effect of nitrite inhibition on the metabolism of *Clostridium botulinum*. J. Appl. Bacteriol. *52*, 109.

ZEUTHEN, P.   1980.   Some observations on the bacterial growth in sliced, vacuum-packed ham in relation to pH of the product. Proc. 26th Europ. Mtg. Meat Res. Workers, Colorado Springs, CO, p. 265.

4

Fermented Meat and Poultry Products

J. N. Bacus[1]

INTRODUCTION

Fermented meat products are those that are deliberately incubated, or "aged," during their processing cycle to allow for sufficient microbial activity to alter the product characteristics. Although microorganisms generally are considered the adversary in the processing of meat, fermented products rely upon controlled microbial activity of specific types of bacteria, molds, and sometimes even yeasts. Traditionally, good manufacturing practices and proper environmental conditions were relied upon to ensure the desired type of microbial development and the extent of the microbial activity. Some manufacturers still depend upon the naturally occurring microflora to effect the desired results. However, most fermented meat processors, particularly in the United States, now employ specific starter cultures to assure the numerical dominance of the desired microorganisms at the start of the processing cycle. Controlled formulation and processing

[1]MicroSure, Inc., 1925 Lone Star Drive, Dallas, TX 75212.

Advances in Meat Research, Volume 2
Copyright 1986 by AVI Publishing Co.
All rights of reproduction in any form reserved
ISBN 0-87055-498-0

parameters still regulate the type and extent of microbial activity, but the presence of the desired microorganisms is no longer left to chance.

Fermented meat technology encompasses a thorough knowledge of meat processing with a basic understanding of microbiology and microbial metabolism. Although reference literature is not extensive, several practical reviews are available on fermented meat processing which cover either both aspects of the process, or focus on processing concerns (Bacus 1984; Terrell et al. 1978). This discussion will concentrate on the microbiological developments and technology in fermented meat manufacturing.

HISTORICAL PERSPECTIVE

Salting and drying are the oldest forms of meat preservation. Early civilizations quickly realized that raw meats must be quickly processed in order to preserve them for consumption at a later date. Initially, whole cuts, or large pieces of meat, were salted heavily on the exposed surfaces, wrapped, and set aside in a cool place, or hung to air dry. The high concentration of surface salt gradually dehydrated the meat tissue while retarding most microbial deterioration. Although today, "dry cured" hams, bacon, loins, etc, are still manufactured basically in the same way, early meat handlers learned that the preservation process could be accomplished much faster when the meat was cut into smaller chunks, mixed with the salt and spices, and then "stuffed" into flexible containers that served to hold the meat tightly and provide convenient units in which to store the product. These containers were initially the intestines of the animals that provided the meat, and were the origin of all modern-day sausage casings and the familiar shapes we associate with unique varieties of processed meats. These sausages became an effective means to preserve fresh meat and are some of the oldest forms of processed foods. Sausage from the Latin word salsus, meaning salt, was consumed by the ancient Babylonians, Romans, and Greeks, during their military campaigns and is credited as one of the factors in the success of Caesar's legions (Pederson 1979).

The careful salting and drying of meat and sausages became very common in southern Europe along the shores of the Mediterranean where most of the popular nomenclature for dry sausage originated (salami, Genoa, Toscano, Coppa, Pepperoni, Milano). Roman butchers cut pork and beef into small pieces, added salt and spices, packed the mixture into skins, or washed intestines, and hung them in special rooms to dry. They quickly learned that the proper hygiene in the cutting and formulating of the meat, coupled with control of temperature and humidity in the dry rooms, resulted in more safe and consistent products. The Roman butchers had guilds for their protection, and most formulating and processing secrets were passed from one generation to another, with an intentional lack of written documentation. Preparation and spicing of sausage became a culinary art in the Mediterranean countries and later in upper Europe. Many small, and some relatively large, processing operations soon appeared in various cities.

Although unaware of the process, early sausage makers knew that once the animal was slaughtered, it was a race between the external preservation techniques and the decomposition of the raw meats to decide the ultimate fate of the tissue. We now realize that once the inherent defense mechanisms of the live animal are destroyed, the meat tissue is subjected to rapid microbial decay. The slaughtering process affords extensive contamination of the sterile tissue with primarily gram-negative microorganisms (*Escherichia coli, Salmonella, Pseudomonas, Achromobacter*) associated with either the intestinal tract, or the environment. As a result, "fresh meat spoilage" is usually associated with aerobic, gram-negative, proteolytic bacteria which literally decompose the protein with the production of offensive odors and flavors (Niven 1961).

Salting, drying, and curing of fresh meat has proved an effective means to control the fresh meat microflora and thus preserve the tissue for later consumption. This is possible since the microbiology of salted meats is entirely different from that of fresh meat. The curing salts (sodium chloride, sodium nitrate, and sodium nitrite) and the subsequent handling methods create a different microenvironment in the meat mixture which favors the growth of specific types of gram-positive microorganisms while inhibiting the proliferation of the fresh meat microflora. This "microbial inversion," occurring during the salting and curing process, provided the accidental origin of all fermented meat products.

Once the raw meat was salted and spiced, the mixture was stuffed tightly into casings or skins which excluded air and held the sausage during aging. It also provided a convenient medium to hang the mixture for smoking and drying. Consequently, a microenvironment was selected for those microorganisms that were not only salt tolerant, but which also could grow in the absence of air. These gram-positive, fermentative types of microorganisms included the lactic acid bacteria, staphylococci, micrococci, and yeasts. As the product dried, a fermentation ensued whereby residual meat sugar, or added carbohydrates, were fermented to a variety of end products including various organic acids, carbon dioxide, alcohols, etc., that contributed to a variety of flavors and textural properties. The primary fermentation product, lactic acid, served to lower meat pH and contributed to the stabilityof these sausages against food-borne pathogens and other less desirable spoilage microorganisms. Although actually a spoilage condition, the "souring" of the product could be tolerated to a much greater extent than the fresh meat type of proteolytic spoilage, and this served to preserve the meat. If properly controlled, the resulting flavor also could make the product more acceptable to the palate, through a "tangy" sensation in combination with the salt, spices, smoke, and other imparted formulating and processing characteristics. Due to fermentation, lactic acid has a tendency to enhance the "salty" and "smoky" flavors.

MICROBIOLOGICAL CONSIDERATIONS

The microbiological contributions to dried sausage did not gain significant attention until the 1940s and 1950s. The application of early microbiological research to meat processing was for control purposes: to improve hygiene, prevent disease, and prolong shelf life. In the 1920s a few scientists suggested inoculation of sausages with nitrate-reducing microorganisms and with yeasts since the fermentation was thought to be due to yeast growth (Drake 1928; Kurk 1921). In the 1930s the contribution of bacteria to sausage processing was considered as similar to the changes brought about in the cheese industry, in which technological advances were proceeding at a much faster rate. The suggested use of pure, standardized lactic cultures as used in the cheese industry occurred in the early 1940s, but this classical work received little attention and was never commercially realized (Jensen and Paddock 1940). It has been hypothesized that either the wrong microorganisms were employed for the meat formulation and/or the pure cultures were not applied practically to the existing meat processing environment.

The commercial application of pure cultures to sausage processing did not occur until after many studies in the mid-1950s (Niven 1951; Deibel and Niven 1957; Niven et al. 1958; Niinivaara 1955). Even then, commercial usage of pure cultures did not become widespread until the late 1970s. Although similar in principle to fermented dairy products, fermented meat technology has progressed at a much slower pace. A partial explanation resides in the fact that research in meat technology has been left far behind its dairy counterpart. Meat as a research material is more difficult to standardize and control, due to its nonuniformity and non-fluid nature (Niinivaara et al. 1964). Studies with pure cultures are often complicated since the meat cannot be pasteurized, as is the case with many dairy products, to preclude the involvement of the naturally occurring, highly variable raw meat microflora. The effects of random contaminants cannot be minimized or eliminated. Raw meats, prior to experimentation, can contain millions of microorganisms that influence subsequent experiments and performance by pure cultures. In addition, early application work with pure, laboratory-grown cultures attempted to modify traditional processes to suit the pure microbial strains. The significance of the meat processing technology and prior experience was often minimized in favor of optimizing the microbiological aspects. In effect, the two technologies were not successfully merged to yield the traditional products' characteristics that were desired. Many times, the microbiological input was oversimplified with either the wrong culture(s) to produce the desired effect(s), and/or the lack of understanding as to the effects of formulation and processing parameters on the culture(s) performance. Most sausage makers also felt that the manufacturing of dried meats was more of an art than science, and they were reluctant to reveal traditional, successful practices that were inherited from each generation. As an example, some sausage makers, in an attempt to improve consistency, learned that a small portion of each batch might be retained and held over to "start," or inoculate subsequent batches. This "back-slopping technique" proved quite effective and is still practiced today, although most knowledgeable processors have refined the practice to minimize "disasters" that can occur if undesirable microorganisms achieve superiority. The "back-slop" material also consists of a wide variety of lactic acid microorganisms that continually compete for dominance and affect consistency. When used as an inoculant, "back-slop" can result in more of a "wild" flavor and texture in the final product, due to the influence of various metabolic end products from the many microorganisms involved. Initial attempts with single-strain starter cultures could not duplicate the effects of the "wild mix." Depending upon the method of preparation and propogation of the "back slop," yeasts and pathogenic microorganisms often can achieve levels that affect product characteristics and safety. This method, if properly controlled, can be used effectively; however, as our knowledge of the microenvironment has increased, we now can inoculate with the same "mix" of pure cultures to achieve the desired "wild" flavors and aromas. This precludes the development of the unwanted microbes, which are an ever-present risk with the "back-slopping" technique.

A combination of factors, particularly in the United States, led to increased understanding of fermented meat technology and usage of microbial cultures in the 1970s. Several food poisoning outbreaks attributed to dry sausage and involving coagulase-positive staphylococci occurred due to a general lack of understanding and control of the fermentation phase of the process (U.S.D.A. 1977). These incidents focused attention by meat scientists, microbiologists, and regulatory agencies on better ways to control the process. In addition, the significance of microbiology was being realized as more scientists and meat technologists gained exposure to both scientific disciplines. Several additional companies also entered the market to manufacture and sell meat starter cultures, creating competition and stimulating the research effort. Prior to 1970s, essentially only one United States company marketed cultures to the meat industry. Significant economic and energy considerations also increased the pressure to expedite the manufacturing of dry and semidry sausages to minimize initial production costs and subsequent holding times for the "aging" process. Pure cultures provided faster "aging" cycles and an additional control mechanism to minimize the number of substandard batches, achieving greater consistency from batch to batch (Fig. 4.1).

CLASSIFICATIONS OF FERMENTED MEATS

Today, the majority of fermented meat products manufactured in the United States are classified as dry and semidry sausages (Table 4.1—

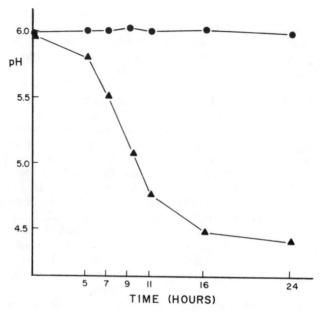

FIG. 4.1.   The effect of presence (▲) or absence (●) of lactic acid starter culture on meat fermentation (i.e., pH) at 110°F (38°C).

U.S.D.A. 1973). Although the USDA has never formally defined the categories for dry and semidry sausages, as has been done with other sausage products, they are regulated by their final moisture to protein ratio, indicating the degree of drying (Table 4.2). However, major United States manufacturers of these products have proposed good manufacturing practices for dry and semidry sausages (AMI 1982). They have defined dry sausages as "chopped or ground meat products that, as a result of bacterial action, reach a pH of 5.3 or less and are then dried to remove 25–50% of the moisture to have a final moisture to protein ratio no greater than 2.3 to 1.0." Semidry, fermented sausages are defined as "chopped or ground meat products that, as a result of bacterial action, reach a pH of 5.3 or less and undergo up to 15% removal of moisture during the fermentation and heating process. In general, the semidry sausages are not subsequently dried in a dry room, but they are packaged soon after the fermentation/heating process is completed. They are generally smoked during the fermentation cycle and have moisture to protein ratios no greater than 3.7 to 1.0." The proposed Guidelines on Good Manufacturing Practices states, in addition, that the pH reduction can be attributed to the action of lactic acid-forming bacteria, which may be added to the meat by either a commercially prepared starter culture or a "back inoculum" from a previously fermented "mother batch." Although fermentation also can be initiated by the lactic

TABLE 4.1. Sausage Classification (United States)

Classification	Characteristics	Examples
Fresh sausage	Fresh meat, (chiefly pork); uncured, comminuted, seasoned, and usually stuffed into casings; must be cooked fully before serving	Fresh pork sausage; bratwurst; bockwurst
Dry and semidry sausages	Cured meats; air dried, may be smoked before drying; served cold	Genoa salami; pepperoni
Cooked sausages	Cured or uncured meats; comminuted, seasoned, stuffed into casings, cooked and sometimes smoked; usually served cold	Frankfurters; liver sausage; braunschweiger; bologna
Cooked meat specialties	Specially prepared meat products; cured or uncured meats, cooked but rarely smoked, often made in loaves, but generally sold in sliced, packaged form; usually served cold	Loaves; head cheese; scrapple
Fresh, smoked sausages	Fresh meats, cured or uncured, stuffed, smoked, but not cooked; must be fully cooked before serving	Smoked, countrystyle pork sausage; mettwurst; kielbasa

acid bacteria occurring naturally in the meat, the Good Manufacturing Practices encourages manufacturers to use more and better control procedures so as to minimize risks.

In 1983, total dried and semidried sausages manufactured under federal inspection in the United States was 332,899,000 pounds, or 6.7% of the

TABLE 4.2. Moisture-Protein Ratios for Dry and Semidry Meat Products[a]

Product	Moisture:protein ratio (maximum)
Pepperoni	1.6:1
Genoa salami	2.3:1
Italian salami	1.9:1
Summer sausage	3.1:1[a]
Jerky	0.75:1
Hard salami	1.9:1
Thuringer	2.3:1
Dried beef	2.04:1
Air-dried sausages	2.1:1

[a] Labeling restrictions apply only if product is to be sold nonrefrigerated. Product must also have a pH ≤ 5.0.

total sausage production (4,981,273,000 lb—AMI 1984). Although relatively small in volume, this group of products is tied closely with the tradition and evolution of meat processing, but often has been the least understood.

In Europe, there are many ways to classify the numerous types of sausages. Germany, as much as any other country, is associated with sausage manufacture, and the German classification is based on the temperature treatment of either the final product or the raw materials (Tables 4.3 and 4.4). Fermented sausages, generally are non-heat-treated, although some varieties of mortadella and cooked salami (i.e., heat-treated final product) are fermented.

In a 1980 International Codex Committe (FAO/WHO Food Standards Programme) meeting on processed meat and poultry products, the proposal from the Italian delegation defined dry and semidry sausages as "product consisting of minced meat of porcine and bovine species, salted, with added spices and natural flavors, enclosed in a natural or artificial casing, possibly smoked, which has undergone a process of fermentation and gradual slow drying." Final product characteristics included a product "more or less finely minced, colour bright red characteristic of meat, slice particularly compact, and the presence of a characteristic layer of mould for some types of salami." Essential ingredients included meat "muscle" of porcine and/or bovine, porcine fat, salt, spices, and flavors. Starter cultures were described as optional "processing aids." Analytical values and types for salami were recommended at total protein (min 20%), muscle protein (min 17%), collagen protein (max 12%), water/protein ratio (max 1.5 for sliced, 1.7 for sliced-thickness not exceeding 50 mm), fat/protein ratio (max 2.2), and salt/water ratio (min 0.10). Finished products covered by the code "may be stored at ambient temperature up to the point of consumption owing to their low content of free water (a_w) and to their being products of a natural process of fermentation which contributes to the formation of their organoleptic characteristics" (FAO/WHO 1980).

TABLE 4.3. Classification (German) of Sausage/Comminuted Meat Products According to Heat Treatment by the Producer[a]

| Group | Heat treatment | | Examples |
	Ingredients	Final product	
A Raw sausage (Rohwurst)	—	—	Bratwurst, salami; mettwurst, zervelat
B1 Cooked sausages (Bruhwurst)	—	+	Frankfurter, bockwurst, bierwurst
B2 Cooked sausages (Knockwurst)	+	+	Liver sausages, blood sausage
B3 Jellied products (Sulze)	+	+	Kopfsulze, hausmachersulze
C Minced meat products (Hackfleisch)	±	±	Meat balls, hamburger

[a] Schut 1978.

TABLE 4.4. Nonheat-Treated Sausages[a]

Group	Product	Example[b]
A1 Raw sausage Rohwurst A1$_1$ Nonfermented	Fresh sausage Pork and beef	Bratwurst Thuringer (fein) (−) Nurnberger (grob)
A1$_2$ Fermented	—	Frischwurst Mettwurst Braunschweiger (+) Thuringer (+) Zervelat (+) Theewurst (+) Regensburger Knack (+) Frankfurter (+)
A11 Fermented	Dry sausage Salami types	Dauerwurst Salami Italian (+)(−) Hungarian (+)(−) Zerevelat (+) Plockwurst (+)

[a] Schut 1978.
[b] +, Smoked, −, not smoked.

With regard to fermented sausages, the European Economic Community directive 77/99/EEC considers these meat products to be "completely treated," and therefore stable at room temperature, if the water activity is less than or equal to 0.91, or the pH is less than 4.5, or the water activity is less than or equal to 0.95 and the pH is less than or equal to 5.2 (Vansteenkiste and Van Hoof 1980).

Although dried sausages are the largest group of fermented meats, other products such as cured meats (i.e. hams, bacon, beef cuts) are being examined for the use of microbial activity to accelerate "aging," provide safety, and increase shelf life. Most of this developmental work and actual production of these types of products is being done in Europe, but microbial cultures are USDA-approved additives for bacon (to reduce residual nitrite), and the USDA is considering the approval of cultures for hams in response to several industry petitions.

EFFECTS OF FERMENTATION

A microbial fermentation, or any form of acidification, has never been required by federal regulations or documented as essential in traditional manufacturing procedures. Although early sausage makers did not understand fermentation, pH, and microorganisms, they did realize that something happened during this stage of the process that affected better drying and resulted in better color, firmness, and flavor. Although pH meters were nonexistent, the sausage maker could tell when this phase was completed by feeling the firmer texture, observing the redder color, and tasting the "tang" of the raw mixture. Lack of control at this early phase could result in product failures due to undesirable odors and flavors, as well as the product "collapsing" or drying very slowly in the later drying phase.

Today, we realize that the acid development via fermentation greatly assists the processor in subsequent moisture removal, provides the desirable safety margin, and yields many of the quality attributes normally associated with these types of products (Fig. 4.2). Some dried meats are not fermented but these items, specifically beef jerky and some other meat snacks, have high surface to volume ratio or are of such small diameter that uniform drying is not much of a problem.

The myofibrillar or contractile proteins are responsible for the binding of water in meat. Water–protein interactions and protein–protein interac-

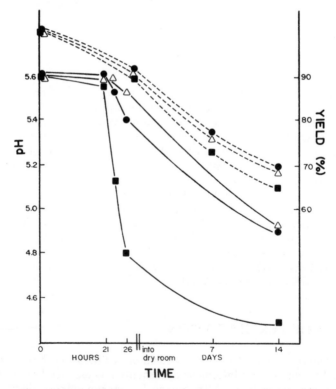

FIG. 4.2.   The effect of various starter cultures on dry sausage pH (———) and process yield (- - -) (pepperoni, 45-mm casing). ● Starter culture 1, △ starter culture 2, ■ starter culture 3.

tions determine the size of the spaces in which the water molecules are harbored in the protein network. The amount of water immobilized depends on the space available between the three-dimensional network of the filaments. In fresh meat, the minimum water-retaining capacity is observed around pH 5.0–5.1, which corresponds approximately to the isoelectric point of the myofibrillar proteins in the normal ionic environment of meat.

At the isoelectric point, the myofibrillar proteins have a maximum of charged groups on their surface and, thus, have a maximum hydrophility. This isoelectric condition exists when the number of positive charges is equal to the number of negative charges. When the pH is above the isoelectric point, some of the positive charges are removed, and there exists a surplus of negative charges. This condition results in a repulsion of the filaments, leaving more space for the water molecules. In fresh meat, the same result is observed at a lower pH than the isoelectric point.

The addition of salt to meat affects the total and relative number of charged groups on the filaments. Sodium chloride addition increases the water-retaining capacity (i.e., binding) and the swelling of meat on the alkaline side of the isoelectric point (Swift and Ellis 1956). The chloride ion is bound strongly by the positive charged groups and they are practically eliminated. The sodium ion is bound only weakly by the negative charges, and the net effect is a displacement of the isoelectric point toward a lower pH (Niinivaara and Pohja 1954) and an increased space between the filaments at or above the pH 5 level.

When meat tissue (generally containing salt) is fermented, the resulting lower pH allows water molecules to subsequently be released more readily and uniformly since the ultimate pH is closer to the isoelectric point. Inadequate fermentation can result in insufficient drying, "case hardening" of the surface, soft product, a surface "ring" and product "collapse." The lower pH also "denatures" the meat protein whereby the native protein structure or conformation (required for biological function) is altered with the unfolding of the polypeptide chain(s).

As the denaturation process continues, the extensive unfolding exposes side chains which attract one another with the consequent formation of aggregates of increasing size. Ultimately, these aggregates reach a size that they can no longer remain in solution and thus precipitate. This total process is referred to as coagulation, and it is a manifestation of the extensive denaturation initiated by the lower pH (i.e., lactic acid). The denaturation and coagulation of meat proteins also contribute to the moisture loss, and all three factors contribute to the product "firmness" that is characteristic of most fermented sausages.

MANUFACTURING ASPECTS

Fermented sausages are manufactured by formulating the meat, spice, starter culture, and cure components at cold temperatures (20° to 30°F,

−6.7 to −1.1°C), stuffing into the proper casings, incubating the meat at higher temperatures (70° to 110°F, 21° to 43°C) to effect fermentation, and subsequently drying the products at temperatures of 50° to 70°F (10° to 21°C). Some sausages are also either partially cooked, or fully cooked, following the incubation stage. Generally, semidry sausages (i.e., summer sausage) are packed soon after heat processing while dry sausages (i.e., salamis) are placed in specific drying rooms to achieve greater moisture loss (Bacus 1984).

The fermentation segment of the process is termed "greening" or "maturing" with the processing room being called the "green room," "drip room," or "aging room." The range of room sophistication, and thus environmental control, varies from processor to processor, and many consist of merely a closed room with a fan/steam pipe to a standard smokehouse or to a precisely designed environmental chamber that closely regulates temperature, humidity, and air flow. The first widespread awareness of the microbiological input to the process came in the late 1950s with the description and commercial availability of sausage starter cultures. In 1960, the USDA approved lactic acid starter cultures for use in dry sausage, pork roll, Thuringer, Lebanon bologna, cervelat, and salami as flavoring agents, protectors, and developers. Almost simultaneously, two different microorganisms were described in the United States and Europe, respectively, for use as starter cultures which initiated the development of fermented meat technology along two different paths.

Up to this time, potassium nitrate (KNO_3) had been used to effect the "curing reaction" that contributed to the color, flavor, and keeping qualities of fermented products. Historically, impure salt used in meat processing often contained saltpeter which provided a source of nitrate. The nitrate subsequently was converted microbiologically in the meat mixture to nitrite which reacts chemically with myoglobin in the meat to result in the range of "cured meat colors." It had been documented that microorganisms were required, not only to ferment the product, but also to convert the nitrate to nitrite to initiate the curing reaction. Researchers in the United States felt that once nitrite was identified as the essential curing agent, it could be added directly to the meat instead of nitrate, and the primary microbiological input would be the rapid conversion of added sugar to lactic acid. Consequently, they proposed a strain of *Pediococcus cerevisiae,* a lactic acid bacterium, for use as a meat starter in combination with a nitrite cure, or a mixed cure of nitrate and nitrite (Deibel and Niven 1957).

Strain FPI was selected from 32 strains of lactobacilli and nine strains of pediococci isolated from fermented sausage. Apparently, this strain possessed the most desirable physiological characteristics and also was capable of surviving lyophilization and rehydration. At the time, the lyophilization technique was judged the best method to afford distribution of a viable culture as reliably and inexpensively as possible. This procedure necessitated the use of a strain that was best able to survive the treatment (Table 4.5).

European researchers felt that the microbiological conversion of nitrate to nitrite was preferred, and that the responsible cultures (micrococci) also contributed to the flavor of the dried products. Rapid acid development was less emphasized, and they felt that the natural lactic microflora of the meat, in combination with the micrococci, could effect the necessary degree of fermentation. In general, European-style sausages are fermented at a lower (less than 75°F, 23.9°C) temperatures with a slower fermentation rate and higher ultimate pH (5.2–5.6) (Table 4.6). American processors prefer more rapid fermentations at higher temperatures, yielding a higher acidity (i.e., tangy) and lower final pH (4.6–5.1) (Fig. 4.3). Consequently, a strain of *Micrococcus aurantiacus* was recommended as a starter culture in Europe (Niinivaara 1955). This strain was selected from more than 700 natural isolates, based on its ability (1) to reduce nitrate; (2) to form acid from glucose in aerobic conditions; (3) to grow in media

TABLE 4.5. Physiological Characteristics of *Pediococcus cerevisiae* Strain FP1[a,b]

Characteristic	
Motility	$-^c$
Catalase	
APT broth	−
0.05% Glucose	−
CO_2 from glucose	−
Nitrate reduction	−
Litmus milk	No change
Final pH, glucose broth	3.7
Agar shake	Facultative
Acetylmethylcarbinol production	−
Hydrolysis	
Sodium hippurate	−
Esculin	$+^c$
Arginine	+
Gelatin	−
Starch	−
Growth	
10°C	+
30°C	+
45°C	+
50°C	+
5% Na°Cl, 30°C	+
10% Na°Cl, 30°C	+

[a] From Deibel *et al.*, 1961.
[b] Xylose, arabinose, mannose, fructose, galactose, sucrose, trehalose, glucose, salicin, cellobiose, and α-methyl-*d*-glucoside were fermented. Glycerol was fermented only under aerobic conditions. Lactose, maltose, raffinose, inulin, mannitol, melibiose, rhamnose, sorbose, melezitose, dulcitol, dextrin, sorbitol, and α-methyl-*d*-mannoside were not fermented.
[c] −, negative; +, positive.

TABLE 4.6. Alternative Conditions for Preparing Dry Sausage[a]

Time frame	Temperature (°F)	Relative humidity (%)
European style		
1st day	72–75 (22.2–23.9°C)	94–96
2nd day	68–72 (20.0–22.2°C)	90–92
3rd day	65–68 (18.3–20.0°C)	85–88
Drying room	53–59 (11.7–15.0°C)	75–80
American style		
24 to 48 hr to pH 4.9–5.0	80–100 (27.7–37.7°C)	90
Drying room	50–52 (10.0–11.1°C)	68–72

[a] From Bacus (1984).

containing sodium chloride; and (4) for the intensity of nitrate reduction
(Niinivaara *et al.* 1964).

Today, the primary genera of bacteria which are used as meat starter
cultures are *Pediococcus, Lactobacillus, Micrococcus,* and *Staphylococcus,*
in pure form, or in a mixture of two or three. These cultures are available
either fresh, frozen, freeze-dried, or in a low-temperature stabilized liquid
form. Although this chapter will discuss the predominant starter culture

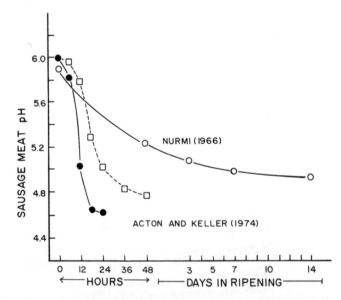

FIG. 4.3. Rate of pH reduction during fermented sausage manufacture with different forms of starter culture and varying temperatures; (●) frozen concentrate
starter culture at 38°C (100°F); (□) lyophilized culture at 38°C; (○) lyophilized
culture at 20°C (68°F) for first 3 days, then 15°C (59°F).
Adapted from Acton (1977).

TABLE 4.7. Microbial Species Described as Meat Starter Cultures[a]

Bacteria	Bacteria
Lactobacillus plantarum	*S. simulans*
L. acidophilus	*S. saprophyticus*
L. casei	*Staphylococcus* sp.
L. fermenti	*Escherichia* sp.
L. brevis	*Aerobacter* sp.
L. buchneri	*Alcaligenes* sp.
L. delbrueckii	*Achromobacter* sp.
L. curvatus	*Flavobacterium* sp.
Leuconostoc mesenteroides	*Pseudomonas* sp.
Lactobacillus sp.	*Vibrio costicolus*
Pediococcus cerevisiae	*V. halo (de) nitrificans*
P. acidilactici	*Corynebacterium* sp.
P. pentosaceus	Yeasts
Pediococcus sp.	*Debaryomyces kloeckeri*
Streptococcus lactis	*D. hansenii*
Str. diacetyllactis	*D. canterellii*
Str. acidilactici	*D. pfafii*
Micrococcus aurantiacus M53	*Debaryomyces* sp.
M. candidus	Molds
M. varians	*Penicillium expansum*
M. epidermis	*P. miczynskii*
M. conglomeratus	*P. simplicissimum*
M. aquatilis	*P. nalgiovensis*
M. kristinae	*P. candidum*
M. lactis	*P. camemberti*
M. caseolyticus	*P. comune*
Micrococcus sp.	*P. roqueforti*
Staphylococcus carnosus	*Penicillum* sp.
S. caseolyticus	*Scopulariopsis brevicaulis*
S. xylosus	*Scop. alboflavescens*

[a] Adapted from Coretti (1977) and Haymon (1984).

species that are available commercially, a wide variety of microbial species have been described, and many are used on a more limited, or custom, basis (Table 4.7).

STARTER CULTURES

Pediococci

The initial *Pediococcus* starter culture was recommended mainly for semidry sausages since it had a somewhat high optimum growth temperature and it was found in processed Thuringer sausage. In 1965, the freeze-dried culture was reevaluated with the subsequent introduction in 1968 of a frozen concentrate (Everson *et al.* 1970). The lyophilized form had proved insufficient since the required rehydration period was not very practical and yielded inconsistent results. The frozen concentrate was also made possible by corresponding advances in the technology of storing, handling, and shipping frozen materials and it eliminated the variable rehydration step. Subsequent refinements in classification techniques also indicated that the actual starter culture strain, originally designed as *P. cerevisiae,* was more correctly classified as *P. acidilactici* (Buchanan and Gibbons 1974).

Today, strains of *P. acidilactici* and *P. pentosaceus* are commercially available as meat starters (Bacus 1983; Raccach 1981). These two classifications have been used interchangably in promotional literature and in general references to meat starter cultures. The United States Department of Agriculture also recognizes *P. cerevisiae* in regulations permitting starter cultures in meat processing.

The primary function of *Pediococcus* starter is to ferment carbohydrates to lactic acid, thereby lowering meat pH (Fig. 4.4). Most strains produce 90+% lactic acid from the fermentation of glucose. They are generally preferred when using higher fermentation temperatures (in excess of 90°F, 32°C), although *P. pentosaceus* was introduced for use with relatively lower fermentation temperatures since it has a lower optimum growth temperature (35°C, 95°F). Early researchers concluded that the

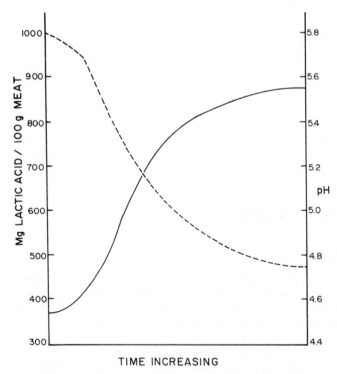

FIG. 4.4.   Comparison of pH reduction (- - -) and lactic acid development (———) in fermented sausage with *Pediococcus* starter culture at 100°F (43°C).

predominant organoleptic characteristics in semidry type products aside from the "tangy" flavor arose from the individual spicing, salt, sugar, and meat components, as well as contributions from varied processing schedules as practiced by the individual plants. Flavor contributions due to secondary microbial actions (aside from straight lactic acid production) appeared to be insignificant. Most semidry products are fermented/smoked at higher temperatures where the *Pediococcus* strains are favored.

Over the past 10 years, the major emphasis in fermented meat technology in the United States has been in understanding the role of lactic acid-producing microorganisms and the factors affecting their activity and selecting meat starters which achieve rapid and consistent lactic acid development. Other flavor and color contributions due to microbes have been minimized to yield safe, accelerated fermentations. Today, rapid acid development (i.e., 6–8 hours vs. 3–4 days traditionally) is easily obtained via most commercially available meat cultures and even shorter fermentations are being explored.

Lactobacilli

Before the introduction and subsequent use of the pediococci strains as meat starter cultures, most natural isolates from fermented meats consisted of various species and strains of lactobacilli (Deibel *et al.* 1961). Lactobacilli are still the predominant microflora in products that are "naturally fermented" from chance inoculation.

An early U.S. patent pioneering the use of a bacterial starter culture in sausage products described the effectiveness of *Lactobacillus plantarum, L. brevis,* and *L. fermente* (Jensen and Paddock 1940). These investigators used several *Lactobacillus* species to effect the meat fermentation, but they depended upon chance inoculation for nitrate reduction. With the introduction of frozen culture concentrates for sausage in 1968, interest in the *Lactobacillus* strain was renewed. In addition, the lactobacilli generally have lower growth temperatures which made them more suitable for dry sausage production. In 1974, a patent was issued that described the use of *Lactobacillus plantarum,* either alone or in combination with other lactic acid-producing microorganisms (i.e., *P. acidilactici*) for preparing dry and semidry sausages (Everson *et al.* 1974). The concept of a "mixed" starter culture was also introduced to afford the sausage manufacturer a broad range of fermentation temperatures.

Natural isolates of lactobacilli have been continually recovered as the predominant microflora from fermented meat and sausage products. Most researchers have emphasized the occurrence of *L. plantarum* as the predominant species, but *L. casei* and its subspecies, *L. casei* v. *alactosus* and *L. casei* var. *rhamnosus* are also present, although in smaller amounts (Yankov and Brankova 1978). Many natural isolates are species variants that do not conform precisely to any species, but they are highly adapted to the specific environment. Most products where "natural" or "wild" fermentations are allowed to develop are comprised of a mixed lactobacilli microflora. This accounts for the variations in flavor and other characteristics from batch to batch, depending upon which strains predominate. Often, a characteristic "wild" flavor develops due to the variety of end products that can result from mixed species fermentations.

The flavor considerations regarding semidry sausages are not totally applicable to other types of fermented sausage. The primary lactic acid fermentation is necessary but often secondary fermentations and chemical reactions play a significant role in the final flavor of the products. Lower temperature fermentations for extended times allow some metabolism by the naturally occurring microflora and enzymatic reactions in the meat have more time to be effected. Although most *Lactobacillus* meat starter cultures primarily produce lactic acid from dextrose, the slower fermentation rate provides an opportunity for other secondary reactions and does not yield the sharp "tangy" taste characteristic of semidry sausages. The wide variety of lactobacilli strains (i.e., meat starters and naturally occurring strains) probably contributes to the uniqueness of many dry sausage products.

Although most commercial *Lactobacillus* cultures are homofermentative, yielding primarily lactic acid from the fermentation of dextrose and sucrose, heterofermentative lactobacilli can often occur as natural contaminants and contribute to the sausage flavor through the production of volatile acids, alcohols, and carbon dioxide. The role of two heterofermentative lactics, *L. brevis* and *L. buchneri,* has been documented and the incorporation of heterofermentative lactics in sausage making has been suggested (Urbaniak and Pezacki 1975). *Leuconostoc mesenteroides* is a common isolate, and its heterofermentative production of ethanol and carbon dioxide, along with lactic acid, can create unique flavors and aromas due to an "effervescence effect." It has been used as a starter culture in combination with homofermentative lactics, but the extent of its activity must be controlled since excessive gas production can create problems with casing breakage and "pinholes" within the product. Control mechanisms can consist of temperature, pH, and the relative amounts of the other starters.

Micrococci-Type Starters

Micrococci-type bacteria have been used extensively for many years in European sausages and other fermented meats where typically, lower "aging" temperatures and longer processes are employed. These starters and naturally occurring microorganisms consist of specific *Micrococcus* strains and harmless, coagulase-negative staphylococci. Although most strains are only weakly fermentative, they take an active role in meat curing and flavor development (Fig. 4.5).

Meat starters are selected based on their ability to reduce nitrate and

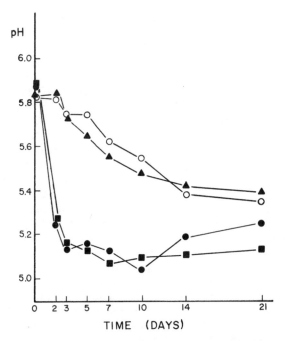

FIG. 4.5.   The effect of starter-culture-type on dry sausage pH during "aging" at 70°F (21°C). ○ Control, ▲ *Micrococcus,* ● *Lactobacillus,* ■ *Lactobacillus* plus *Micrococcus.*

nitrite, their salt tolerance, and their ability to produce acid from glucose in aerobic conditions. They are utilized as starters (generally in combination with either pediococci or lactobacilli) for their ability to accelerate the curing reaction via nitrate/nitrite reduction and the resulting intense, stable red coloration observed in the final products. Depending upon the formulation and process, perceptible flavor differences can also be achieved.

Most of the gram-positive, catalase-positive cocci strains found in dry sausage have, until recently, been regarded as "micrococci." This is also true of the natural isolates that have been selected for use as starter cultures. However, current classifications schemes have identified most of the strains as actually being coagulase-negative staphylococci. Eighty-two strains isolated from 88 commercial samples demonstrated 61% as staphylococci and 39% as micrococci. The staphylococci strains were classified as 20% *S. xylosus,* 25% *S. simulans,* and 16% *S. saprophyticus,* while the micrococci consisted of 36% *M. varians* and 3% *M. kristinae* (Fisher and Schleifer 1980). Other studies isolated micrococci and staphylococci from freshly prepared and "stored" or "aged" sausages. In freshly prepared sausages, 77% were classified as micrococci, 5% coagulase-negative staphylococci, and 18% coagulase-positive staphylococci. In "stored" sausages, the corresponding figures were 43, 41, and 17%, indicating the equal distribution of micrococci and coagulase-negative staphylococci. Of 93 strains of staphylococci isolated, 19.4% were *S. capitis,* 9.7% *S. epidermis,* 32.3% *S. xylosus* type II, 25.8% *S. saprophyticus,* 3.2% *S. haemolyticus,* and 9.7% *S. atypicus* (Simonetti and Cantoni 1983).

Subsequent isolations of 14 strains of staphylococci from dry sausage and one commercial starter culture have identified a new species as *Staphylococcus carnosus* based primarily on its DNA–DNA hybridization relationships, its biochemical reactions, and its cell wall composition (Schleifer and Fisher 1982). All strains grew facultatively anaerobically and produced, under anaerobic growth conditions, equal amounts of D- and L-lactate from glucose. All strains grew at 15° and 45°C, at salt levels up to 15%, reduced nitrate, and produced acetoin. All failed to produce coagulase and to exhibit hemolytic activity. Each isolate produced acid aerobically from glucose, fructose, mannose, mannitol, and glycerol but failed to produce acid from xylose, sucrose, maltose, xylitol, rhamnose, turanose, raffinose, fucose, and melibiose. *Staphylococcus carnosus* was selected from several coagulase-negative staphylococci strains for its superior ability to undergo polyethylene glycol-induced protoplast-transformation with plasmid DNA. Since *S. carnosus* is apathogenic and an important microorganism in food technology, it could be a suitable gram-positive strain for molecular cloning. It is being examined as a host strain for recombinant DNA and for studying the genetic organization of certain staphylococci. Several plasmids isolated from different species were readily transformed with an efficiency ranging between 4×10^6 to 2×10^3 transformations per milligram plasmid DNA (Gotz *et al.* 1983). Culture research via genetic engineering techniques or natural selection offers the potential to selectively eliminate those undesirable fermentation end products while retaining the desirable flavor compounds.

Many European processors and some United States manufacturers, particularly of Lebanon bologna, still rely on micrococci/staphylococci to effect nitrate reduction since they still employ straight nitrate cures. In the conventional, time-honored process for dry and semidry sausages, the meat mixture (meat, salt, nitrate) was placed in pans about 20 cm in depth and cured for 2–7 days at refrigeration temperatures to allow, supposedly, for the growth of nitrate-reducing micrococci with the subsequent formation of nitrite to initiate the curing reaction. However, researchers later failed to detect any microbial activity in reference to nitrate reduction, or any increase in viable bacterial counts during this holding period (Deibel *et al.* 1961). Subsequently, it was determined that lactic acid produced by the lactic-type bacteria during fermentation served as an effective hydrogen donor for nitrate respiration by the micrococci (Wessley 1960).

Currently, a variety of both *Micrococcus* spp. *(M. varians and M. kristinae)* and coagulase-negative *Staphylococcus* spp. *(S. carnosus, S. saprophyticus,* and *S. simulans)* are used as meat starters. The exact nomenclature varies extensively depending upon the classification scheme

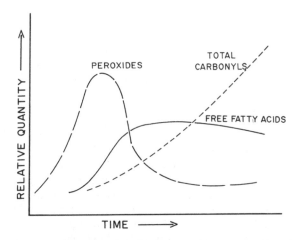

FIG. 4.6.   Generalized sequence of change in lipid fraction of pork salami during a
traditional ripening process.
From Acton (1977).

and the timing of the respective descriptors. In any event, these micrococci-type cultures are added primarily for their nitrate/nitrite reducing capabilities and for their respective contributions to flavor and product stability. Most species demonstrate lipolytic activity under aerobic
(Micrococcus) and both aerobic and anaerobic conditions *(Staphylococcus)*
(Simonetti and Cantoni 1983) (Fig. 4.6). Different strains are preferred
based on their specific lipolytic activity, and the extent of volatile fatty
acid formation (Cattaneo *et al.* 1983; Simonetti *et al.* 1983). A survey of 230
strains of *Micrococcaceae* (73 collection strains and 157 food isolates) for
butter and lard lipase activity revealed 47% of the staphylococcal food
isolates had butter lipase and 54% had lard lipase. Of dry sausage isolates,
34% had butter lipase while 32% had a lard lipase. Of four micrococci food
isolates, only one demonstrated butter lipase and none exhibited lard
lipase (Delarras 1982). Both micrococci and staphylococci demonstrate catalase activity which can be an effective antioxidant in noncooked processed meats, retarding oxidative rancidity from peroxide formation.

Molds and Yeasts

Molds and yeasts always have been associated with fermented, or
"aged" meats. Generally, their existence reflects a problem to be controlled or prevented. However, certain varieties of sausage characteristically exhibit mold growth on the product surface, and many manufacturers feel the mold is essential to achieve the unique attributes of their

product. The "white" or "gray" surface also serves a cosmetic function to which the consumer has become accustomed.

In processing establishments where the desirable mold growth is prolific, commercial starter cultures often are not required since the mold growth is readily transferred from batch to batch. These European-style sausages are fermented 3 to 4 days at 60°–75°F (15°–24°C) with 80–90% relative humidity, and subsequently dried at 60°–70°F (15°–21°C) with 75–80% relative humidity. Generally, drying conditions with less than 75% relative humidity do not afford desirable mold growth. These types of sausages traditionally are produced in countries such as Hungary, Italy, Spain, Greece, Yugoslavia, Rumania, and Czechoslavakia and, to a more limited extent, in certain localities in the United States, primarily in the San Francisco-Oakland Bay area. Most research into the types and the control of mold growth has been directed at examining potential mycotoxin production. Although potential toxin-producing strains of *Aspergillus* sp. have been isolated, aflatoxins have not been encountered during normal manufacturing conditions. Various strains of *Penicillium candidum, P. roqueforti, P. nalgiovensis,* and *Scopularia* sp. have all been associated with fermented sausage with the *Penicillium* sp. being the most desirable. *Penicillium candidum, P. nalgiovensis,* and *P. roqueforti* are approved as starter cultures in West Germany.

In addition to their cosmetic function, surface mold growth can have several important functions. The extensive mycelial coat on the product surface can reduce moisture loss, and may compensate for changes in the relative humidity of the environment, achieving a more uniform drying rate. The enzymatic activities on the surface fats and proteins can influence the flavor and aroma that are distinctive of the particular product. Large drying rooms can have a pronounced "ammonia aroma" resulting from proteolytic action. The catalase activity at the product surface can also provide a natural antioxidant, reducing oxygen penetration through the mycelial mat. Unlike most dry sausages in the United States, Italian salami does not contain chemical antioxidants, and yet, rancidity is rarely encountered. Most molds also possess nitrate reductase activity, enhancing surface color. The environmental conditions dictate the type and extent of mold growth, with the final surface color being very dependent on the stage in the respective mold life cycle. If the product is not dried correctly, the desirable white mycelia of *Penicillium* sp. can evolve into a blue-green or green coloration as the mold sporulates. Generally, this occurs with conditions of excessive humidity. Undesirable *Scopularia* sp. (i.e., brown coloration) often can occur on products where the *Penicillium* sp. initially fails to grow, particularly in spots of lower water activity. Often, the same sausage may contain mixed strains of surface molds. Although not employed widely, mold starters would be desirable to ensure a high level of the desirable strain at the start of the process. Generally, this precludes the development of undesirable mold strains and other microorganisms. The preparation of the starter culture and the inoculation procedures (i.e., surface only) are more difficult with molds, and these factors coupled with a general lack of demand have precluded the necessary research in this area.

Some European workers also have documented the utilization of certain yeasts, particularly of the *Debaryomyces* family in the manufacture of dry sausages (Coretti 1977). Yeasts are commonly associated with fermented sausage and are usually more prevalent on the surface than the interior of the product. Many "naturally fermented" products, employing "back-slopping" techniques, owe their "wild" flavors to yeast growth that is common in refrigerated, recycled, uncooked meat. Yeast growth and the production of the typical "fruity," "alcoholic" aroma is often considered a spoilage problem in most fermented sausages, but if controlled, can achieve the unique flavor and aroma attributes associated with some varieties of sausage. The yeast can also accelerate cure-color development and provide the typical, white powdery surface appearance characteristic of some European sausages, particularly from Hungary, Switzerland, and Italy. Commercial starter cultures containing yeast are available in Europe, usually consisting of various strains of *Debaryomyces hansenii* or *D. kloeckeri*, either alone or in combination with micrococci, lactobacilli, and/or pediococci. With increased curing time, i.e., lowering of pH and water activity, and lack of oxygen in the sausage's interior, the yeast count will slowly decrease, being identifiable in the raw sausage perimeter zones only (Frey 1983). Most yeast activity, yielding the characteristic flavor and aroma, occurs in the initial days of aging. Since yeast growth is accompanied with carbon dioxide production, which can yield swollen product and/or packages, only surface growth in nonsealed packages is usually desirable.

OTHER CULTURED MEATS

Although most fermented meat products are within the broad categories of dry and semidry sausages, the use of fermented meat technology and controlled microbial activity has been applied to other meat items. Specific microbial cultures are utilized to either: (1) improve the quality attributes through accelerated "aging," (2) prolong shelf life through antimicrobial properties via acid development and/or nonfermentative inhibitory effects, and/or (3) provide an increased margin of safety through activation (i.e., safety valve) in the event of product temperature abuse.

The term "cured meats" generally refers to whole-muscle meats (i.e., ham, bellies, shoulders, loins, rounds) that are either dry-cured or injected with a curing brine, followed by a various combinations of drying, smoking, and heating. Many of the more traditional products are not fully cooked during the processing cycle, but rely on the salt and the curing components, in combination with dehydration (i.e., reduced water activity), to effect an ultimately safe and stable product. Many of these products preceded the development of dried sausages and, during the required "aging" process, developed unique flavors and aromas that have become firmly associated with the product names such as Country Ham, Westphalian Ham, Proscuitto, and Dry Coppa. Obviously, enzymatic and microbial activities have contributed to these unique organoleptic properties.

With the increased technological development in meat curing formulations, equipment, and processes, many of the more traditional quality attributes associated with "aging" have been lost. In addition, the consumer emphasis on reduced salt intake and the widespread use of refrigeration has resulted ultimately in lower salt percentages, since high brine levels are no longer required for product stability. Rapid, high-temperature processes using straight nitrite cures also have decreased the intensity of the red meat-cured colors often associated with "aged" products. In attempts to regain the traditional characteristics, some European processers are utilizing microbial cultures to enhance color development and achieve "aged" flavors and aromas without sacrificing the convenience and economy of accelerated processes. Generally, *Micrococcus* and *Staphylococcus* cultures are utilized for their nitrate/nitrite conversion capabilities and their lipolytic activites, while their relatively high salt tolerance allows survival and activity in the curing brines.

Natural isolates are selected based on a criteria of good growth, formation of aroma, nitrate reduction, catalase activity, and minimal acid development (0.15–0.20 pH units) under controlled conditions. The various strains improve aroma and consistency of cured meat and generally improve color. Nitrate reduction was not related to color formation in the brine, but it was directly related to color formation in the meat (Petaejae *et al.* 1972).

Accelerated, cured meat processes have been described using starter cultures. Amino acids are liberated by the starters which react with acids formed by carbohydrate decomposition to form aroma compounds. Rapid culture growth and multiplication also inhibit undesirable microbial growth. The accelerated, cultured processes generally reduce "pickling" time and are completed safely at higher ripening and smoking temperatures (Schiffner and Oppel 1973).

Some lactic acid bacteria are also used alone, or in combination with the *Micrococcus* strains, where mild acid development is desired to enhance the color and flavor profile. Lactic acid also enhances the "salty" flavor, thereby increasing the perception of salt (i.e., traditional flavor), while the product actually contains a lower salt content. However, the extent of fermentation must be controlled to avoid an excessively "tangy" flavor which is not desirable in most of these types of products. This is usually accomplished by limiting the added carbohydrate content (i.e., less than 0.3%) or a subsequent heat treatment. Besides the flavor contribution, a limited initial fermentation can readily inhibit potential spoilage microorganisms. Greater product stability can be achieved at a higher moisture content when the pH is lower.

In the United States, the use of lactic cultures has been investigated in the production of country-style, dry-cured hams (Bartholomew and Blumer 1977). Concentrated cultures of *Pediococcus* were injected into the hams to achieve sufficient distribution. Subjective evaluations indicated that the control and the inoculated hams were similar in flavor and other quality characteristics, although the "aged" flavor increased as acidity increased with the cultured hams. Generally, white film formation which is positively correlated with increased crumbliness, softness, and tenderness, increased in inoculated hams with increased "aging" times. Ham film formation results from free amino acid precipitation (mainly tyrosine) on the ham surface and probably increases with increasing lactic acid production.

Acid development via fermentation is the primary known mechanism by which most meat starter cultures inhibit undesirable microorganisms. However, the production of other inhibitory substances and inhibition through competition for essential nutrients by meat starter cultures, and other similar food-related starters, has been repeatedly documented. These compounds include hydrogen peroxides, antibiotics, bacteriocins, etc., and the relative effects depend on the respective microorganisms involved and the environmental conditions. Selected cultures have been applied successfully to boiled ham, ground beef, bacon, beef cuts, frankfurters, dry-cured hams, mechanically deboned poultry, smoked turkey, and shrimp (Pina 1977; Reddy et al. 1970; Tanaka et al. 1980; Tezan and Yuecel 1975; Petaja 1977; Bartholomew and Blumer 1977; Raccach and Baker 1978; Moon et al. 1980). Hydrogen peroxide appears to be the major inhibitor produced by the lactobacilli cultures that have been studied (Gilliland 1980). Most research indicates that large numbers of lactobacilli are required to effect sufficient inhibition. The preservative effect of microbial additives in typically, nonfermented products is continually being investigated, but it is not in widespread commercial use, presumably due to a lack of complete understanding of the mechanism(s) and the ultimate control that prevents undesirable side effects. The technology acquired by greater understanding of the fermented meat microenvironment may eventually lead to controlled, natural microbial inhibition in nonfermented meats where acid development is not desired.

A novel application of fermented meat technology has been applied commercially to bacon processing, and it may ultimately serve as a precedent for other food products. Lactic acid cultures *(Lactobacillus* and *Pediococcus)* are added to the raw pork belly, along with the other curing ingredients, and because of the nature of the typical bacon process, survive and remain essentially inactive if the product is held under acceptable storage conditions. However, in the event of product temperature abuse, the culture "activates" and quickly ferments added sugar to lactic acid, thereby lowering product pH and rendering the product safe from food pathogens (i.e., *C. botulinum*). Due to the inherent distribution problems with a specialized and transient society, we pasteurize, or sterilize, many food products to extend shelf life. This can create some problems since the natural microflora of the products are destroyed, providing an opportunity for typically, noncompetitive food pathogens to proliferate if they survive the pasteurization process (i.e., spores), or if they are introduced post-processing. *Clostridium botulinum,* a typical spore-forming micro-organism, is not competitive in a normal microenvironment, but can grow and produce toxin when the competing organisms have been eliminated through cooking.

In 1979, the USDA approved the use of meat starter cultures for bacon processing to dissipate residual nitrite and, thus, to lower or eliminate nitrosamine formation during frying (Houston 1979). Bacon fermentation via a lactic starter and a fermentable substrate had proved an effective means to reduce residual nitrite while increasing the safety of the product (Bacus 1979; Tanaka *et al.* 1980). The presence of the culture acts as a "safety valve" to rapidly lower product pH in the event of temperature abuse. The resulting product actually becomes safer with prolonged abuse, unlike many preservative systems which are eventually overcome with time. This natural control mechanism against *C. botulinum* and other food pathogens had been applied in traditionally, fermented meats and was substantiated through more than a year of commercial bacon production (Brown 1980). Initially, lactic cultures were applied to bacon processing to reduce the pH of the product during smoking and subsequent storage, achieving product stability while lowering residual nitrite. Both factors reduce subsequent nitrosamine formation at the time of frying. It had been shown that residual nitrite can react with secondary amines in certain meat products, particularly bacon, to form nitrosamines which are proved carcinogens (Sen *et al.* 1974). Reducing the nitrite content will minimize subsequent nitrosamine formation.

Although readily feasible, the use of lactic cultures in bacon manufacturing has not been widely applied, and the nitrosamine problem has persisted. Various manufacturers have deemed the "culture process" to be too expensive. There were also fears that uncontrolled temperatures would lead to "sour bacon." Recommended solutions to the nitrosamine problem have included lowering the mandatory nitrite concentration initially added (120 ppm), although the potential threat of *C. botulinum* growth is a major concern at the lower nitrite levels.

Recently the Food Research Institute (FRI) at the University of Wisconsin, under sponsorship of the USDA, completed a study on the effects of a starter culture/fermentable substrate in conjunction with lower, ingoing nitrite concentrations on subsequent nitrosamine formation and the susceptibility of bacon to *C. botulinum* growth (Traisman 1984). The bacon was produced commercially in three plants. In each plant, a control (120 ppm nitrite, no added sugar) and two test products (80 and 40 ppm nitrite,

0.7% sugar, starter culture) were manufactured and then forwarded to FRI for inoculation with 1000 *C. botulinum* spores per gram, vacuum packaged, and incubated at 10°F (27°C). Periodically, the samples were assayed for botulinal toxin and nitrosamine formation during frying. Only four of 300 test samples taken from the three plants evidenced toxin formation through 56 days of temperature abuse. The control products from two plants demonstrated 100% toxicity, while 38% from the remaining plant became toxic. Nitrosopyrrolidine levels analyzed on 30 samples from each plant ranged from 5.2 to 38 ppb in the control bacon and less than 0.5 to 8.5 ppb, and less than 0.5 to 2.2 ppb in the 80 and 40 ppm nitrite products, respectively. Trained sensory panels rated the control and the 80 ppm test bacon as equally preferred, although not identical, while the 40 ppm test bacon scored somewhat lower, although differences were generally not statistically significant.

These results confirmed earlier findings on the effectiveness of starter cultures as a preservative mechanism to reduce the risk of *C. botulinum* in bacon processed with lower ingoing nitrite levels. It offers the meat industry an acceptable means to reduce nitrite levels (i.e., nitrosamines) and it may stimulate the USDA to provide the industry an option in bacon processing.

Initially, it was thought that lactobacilli strains namely *Lactobacillus plantarum,* was the optimum strain for use in bacon processing. However, a thorough screening process by the FRI revealed that *Pediococcus acidilactici* (strain PO2) was more heat resistant, and it was thus recommended for subsequent work in bacon processing. *Lactobacillus plantarum* strains still appear to be desirable starters, although their use is somewhat limited to more conventional bacon processes, not in excess of 12 to 14 hr or product temperatures in excess of 130°F (54.4°C). Although many heat-resistant strains of bacteria are available, few of the microorganisms tested are capable of suffecent metabolic activity in a typical bacon system containing salt, nitrite, and high fat.

This approach to food preservation via a natural "safety valve," will probably gain greater significance in the future as we demand "fresher" products with minimal processing (i.e., less canning, cooking) and more "natural" foods with fewer chemical preservatives.

FERMENTED POULTRY PRODUCTS

The application of meat fermentation techniques to poultry products only has occurred in recent years, and fermented poultry products are still not widely available. Although some of the technical aspects have been investigated, most research has focused on the control of pathogens in poultry sausages rather than product development to establish optimal formulations and processes.

Commercial realization of fermented poultry items has proceeded slowly due to several factors. The commercial success of processed poultry products (franks, bologna, salami, etc.) only has occurred in the last 10 years. Prior to this development, poultry went directly from the producer to the consumer in the whole, unprocessed form. The market for dry and semidry sausages (i.e., fermented items) also is relatively small compared to frankfurters and bologna. Hence, these markets are not as attractive to poultry processors. Traditionally, poultry is also associated with *Salmonella* and other food pathogens, and a requirement prior to consumption is fully cooking by either the processor or consumer. Unlike many fermented pork and beef products which are not fully cooked, research into alternate ways of poultry preservation (i.e., fermentation, salting, drying) has been lacking. Due to the association with *Salmonella*, USDA regulations mandate the thorough cooking of processed poultry products.

The familiar nomenclature associated with "aged," fermented red meats accounts for much of their success, and poultry does not have such product tradition and consumer acceptance in this market. The controversy in applying traditional names associated with red meat products (i.e., ham, salami, pepperoni) to similar products containing poultry, prevents potential, fermented poultry processors from capitalizing on traditional markets. This reluctance on the part of potential processors may dissipate with the success of nonfermented, processed poultry products. Processed poultry is a rapidly growing area accounting for 17.3 and 24.3% of the luncheon meat and frankfurter market, respectively, in the Western region (Theno 1984). Nationally, the percentage of poultry frankfurters has grown from less than 7% in 1977 to 15% in 1980. The success of poultry franks has expanded to other market areas of processed red meats (bologna, salami, ham, and pastrami) and will certainly result in fermented, dry and semidry sausages containing poultry.

Technically, poultry tissue is much "softer" and more sensitive to "abuse" than pork and beef. As a result, formulations and processes incorporating poultry meat must consider these characteristics and must be tightly controlled. These considerations are magnified in fermented products where acid development destabilizes the protein-water binding. The nature of poultry fat (i.e., more fluid at room temperature) makes it undesirable in coarse ground-type products unless it is emulsified with a portion of the lean tissue. However, emulsification of fat is not desirable in dry sausage since the fat "coats" the lean tissue (i.e., containing the moisture) which retards subsequent drying. This is not as much of a problem in semidry products where poultry meat containing higher fat levels would appear more feasible.

Generally, fermented sausages containing poultry utilize lean turkey or chicken meat in combination with beef or pork fat to achieve the desirable textural characteristics. Formulations comprised entirely of poultry either utilize only lean dark meat (i.e., turkey thighs) or the dark meat is combined with skins to produce the "white flecks" characteristic of salamis.

Fat content usually is restricted to a maximum of 15%, which is low compared to corresponding red meat formulations (23–32%). Formulations containing poultry also have a high initial pH value which should be considered when designing formulations (i.e., dextrose) and processes to achieve specified final pH values. Due to the higher moisture content of poultry, fermentation can proceed at a rapid pace and must be controlled via dextrose level and/or heat treatment. Characteristically, nonfermented poultry sausages often contain phosphates which must be either reduced, eliminated, or at least considered, in designing fermented products since the "buffering action" will retard the normal reduction in pH. The lactic acid development will still proceed, but the correlation of pH to actual acidity will be altered in phosphate-containing products. An additional factor to be considered in fermented poultry products is the proper drying parameters for a high moisture product. Poultry sausages, due to their lower fat content, contain high moisture levels and thus, tend to release moisture too rapidly, resulting in the product "collapsing." The use of beef/pork fat can minimize the problem of nonuniform drying (i.e., surface vs. internal). Products solely comprised of lean poultry meat must be processed to afford a uniform moisture loss and avoid the "dry texture" that often can result from excessive heating/drying. Most research has indicated larger meat particles are more desirable in fermented poultry sausages and recommend maximum heating of 115°F (46°C) if the sausage is to be fully dried (Baran and Stevenson 1975; Baran et al. 1973). However, other studies attained a 160°F (71°C) internal temperature with no apparent textural problems (Dawson 1970; Keller and Acton 1974). The different results probably are attributed to the type of tissue, the degree of emulsification, and/or the other processing parameters.

No apparent problems are experienced in the actual fermentation of poultry sausages, or combination products of red meats and poultry. The fermentation of sausages containing either chicken or turkey meat with 0, 25, and 50% ground beef demonstrated significant pH reduction, with the chicken sausages showing a lower final pH (5.1 to 5.2) than the corresponding turkey products (5.5) (Dawson 1970). This initial research utilized a lyophilized P. cerevisiae (acidilactici) starter culture which subsequently was shown to be much slower in acid development than its corresponding frozen concentrate (Keller and Acton 1974). Other studies on fermenting/drying turkey thigh meat in combination with beef kidney fat at two fat levels showed a higher amount of lactic acid (wet sample basis) in the 15% fat sausages compared to the 30% fat product. However, the lactic acid content after 0 and 12 days (pH 4.6 ± 0.9 for both) drying, when adjusted to a fat-free basis, was very similar at approximately 1.6 and 3.2%, respectively (Acton and Dick 1975). The percentage of lean tissue is a factor in determining total acidity in final sausages, and these levels were much higher than reported in all-turkey sausages (0.9%) processed similarly (Keller and Acton 1974).

Compositional changes in the above dried turkey/beef fat sausage demonstrated a significant correlation between moisture loss and the increase in protein and fat percentages. Shear values (0.22 kg/g-cm²) on sliced samples from dried product (following a 12-day drying cycle of the 15% formulated fat sausages) were similar to those observed in corresponding studies with all-turkey product utilizing poultry skin fat at about 8%. However, the lean portion of the product had "a crumbly, powdery characteristic of the muscle fibers." Apparently, the shear force values resulted from the "harder" beef fat, since the poultry muscle fibers appeared fragile and easily disrupted (Acton and Dick 1975).

Early research on fermented poultry sausage examined the general microflora and the destruction of pathogens during processing. Despite considerable destruction of salmonellae during the manufacture of turkey sausage, complete elimination was not achieved in some specific processes (Baran and Stevenson 1975). The extent of destruction of *Clostridium perfringens* and *Salmonella* sp. in a low heat process (115°F, 46°C) for fermented turkey sausage varied with the strain and amount of inoculated pathogen (Baran *et al.* 1973). Due to the higher incidence of pathogens, particularly salmonellae, in raw poultry, alternative time/temperature/pH processes will have to be established firmly to ensure pathogen destruction in any fermented products that are not fully cooked. This has been done with beef summer sausage inoculated with *Salmonella* sp. (Masters *et al.* 1981).

CHEMICAL ACIDULATION

Microbial fermentation using either specific starter cultures, or "wild fermentation," is considered biological acidulation. In fermented products where the primary function of controlled microbiological activity is to produce acid, attempts have been made to mimic the fermentation by various means of chemical acidulation, thereby avoiding any problems associated with biological additives. Attempts to add lactic acid directly to the meat have resulted in failure since the acidification of a salted meat mixture must employ a uniform, "slow-release" mechanism over an extended period of time. Direct acid addition, to achieve similar acidity levels as that of fermentation, results in the immediate "shorting" of the mixture, or a denaturing of the protein with a resulting loss of "bind." The mixture becomes "crumbly" and will not adhere to form any shape. Fermented meats first must achieve protein extraction via the addition of salt at higher pH values to form a "matrix structure" prior to the acid development, which destabilizes the protein with the accompanying moisture loss.

Chemical acidulants that have achieved limited success in certain "fermented" products generally rely on some type of "slow-release" mechanism that results in acid formation with increased temperature and/or hydration. Glucono-δ-lactone (GDL) is a common meat acidulant that was originally USDA approved for use as a "cure accelerator" to enhance cured color development. This chemical compound has a ring structure which slowly hydrolyzes on hydration yielding gluconic acid. The acidulation step is relatively absolute, ensuring the production of acid in a manner that closely parallels biological fermentation. The associated pH decrease is quite rapid and the meat mixture containing GDL must be stuffed and processed immediately to avoid premature acidulation that prevents subsequent forming of the mixture into the proper shape. GDL has achieved more success in some European formulas where minimal acidulation (0.2–0.5 pH units) is desired. In the United States, GDL is approved for use in sausage at 8 oz per 100 lb of meat, with the exception of Genoa salami where it is approved at 1 lb per hundred weight. However, at higher levels, GDL causes loss of bind in the meat blend and produces a softer, more crumbly texture. Some researchers also have suggested that GDL is conducive to rancidity development as the product "ages" (Terrell *et al.* 1977; Deibel 1974). In addition, GDL imparts a typical acrid flavor in the final product which is detectable in all types of sausages, regardless of meat combination or seasonings used (Schneider 1980). In effect, the active acidulant is gluconic acid, rather than lactic acid, which is the primary acidulant associated with traditionally fermented meats.

Attempts to further control chemical acidulation have resulted in "encapsulated" acidulants. Established chemical acidulants (GDL, citric acid, lactic acid) are encapsulated with hydrogenated palm oil which "release," or melt, at designated temperatures (usually in excess of 125°F) thereby activating the acid development. Encapsulated GDL and citric acid have been used with some success in meat items since they partially avoid premature acidulation and supposedly, "release" as the product is cooked. However, incomplete encapsulation, residual surface acidulant, and capsule breakage can still create problems, and the latter is enhanced with the normal grinding/chopping of the meat blend. Variations in the rate and the extent of temperature treatment, as can be encountered in nonuniform smokehouse processes, can also result in a range of ultimate product pHs. In some products, the "capsule" can also affect texture, flavor, and visual characteristics of the finished sausage.

Encapsulated lactic acid, utilizing a palm oil carrier that reportedly melts at 140°F (60°C) appeared to offer a close similarity to microbial acidulation, but "fermented" product comparisons using the chemical acidulant vs a range of starter cultures repeatedly favored the biological acidulation process. Although possessing a typical lactic acid flavor, the product was not "well liked by the panelists" and was easily distinguished from the starter culture sausages. Apparently, the sausage lacked the other (unexplained) products of the microbial fermentation which seem to contribute significantly to the flavor of fermented products. Performance problems were also encountered with the capsule due to incomplete melting and visual awareness (Kielniarz 1982).

Encapsulated citric acid (70% active component) has been employed successfully in a cooked, semidry sausage product to attain a pH 5.0 with reduced processing time (as compared to a corresponding starter culture process). Postprocessing inoculation with *Staphylococcus aureus* and *Salmonella* sp. demonstrated that both microorganisms failed to grow in nonrefrigerated, vacuum-packaged products manufactured by either fermentation (*Pediococcus* starter) or chemical acidulation. Apparently, encapsulated citric acid was preferred over GDL since the less active component was required to attain a lower pH. The author noted that "semidry sausages, due to their robust, tangy flavors and absence of low temperature fermented flavor notes, typical of such products as Genoa Salami, are ideal products for chemical acidulation" (Jedlicka 1984). An additional requirement for chemical acidulation, with existing encapsulated acidulants, is that the product must be fully cooked to effect complete acid development.

Recently, the USDA approved the direct addition of acidifiers in processed meat and poultry products. Acetic acid, citric acid, lactic acid, phosphoric acid, and tartaric acid can be utilized to adjust and stabilize acidity in various products at levels "sufficient for purpose." Specific meat and poultry products and exact use levels of the acidifiers must be approved via the label approval process of the Food Safety and Inspection Service (Houston 1984).

The use of chemical acidulants in "fermented" meat and poultry products, either alone or in combination with microbial cultures, will probably expand as acidulant "forms" are developed that mimic the action of microorganisms. However, the combined flavor, inhibitory, and acidulation effects of microbes will be difficult to duplicate in purely chemical form. The flavor and inhibitory attributes of specific microbial starters may be further refined and then utilized with chemical acidulants that precisely dictate the amount of acid(s) development.

CONTROL OF PATHOGENS

Most published research on fermented meats, particularly in the United States, has examined the potential growth and/or destruction of pathogens in various processes. Several excellent reviews are available on the subject (Smith and Palumbo 1983; Bacus and Brown 1981; Smith and Palumbo 1981). This chapter will summarize only the most common pathogens encountered and the practical means to control their proliferation and decrease their survival.

Traditionally, dry sausages are not subjected to any significant degree of heat treatment during their processing cycle. Although some "modern" processes employ higher temperature "finish" schedules to either halt the microbial fermentation, destroy the starter microorganisms, avoid the trichinae restrictions, accelerate drying, increase firmness, "fix" color, and/or activate chemical acidulants, the majority of true dry sausages do not reach temperatures in excess of that necessary to achieve the desirable microbial fermentation—typically, 60–115°F (16–46°C). Often, higher temperatures result in the loss of the traditional flavor, color, and texture attributes normally associated with these products. As a result, most dry sausages are basically raw meats that have been salted/cured and deliberately "aged," or incubated, to achieve microbial activity prior to drying. In Europe, most dry sausages are classified as rohwurst, or raw sausage.

These considerations, coupled with the fact that dry sausage is usually eaten by the consumer without further cooking make strict control of the product essential. Without cooking as an expedient vehicle to eliminate most food pathogens, the manufacturers of dry sausage must rely upon more historical means such as salting, curing, fermentation, and drying to control and eliminate undesirable microorganisms. Although good sanitation, employee hygiene, and good manufacturing practices must be maintained to minimize initial contamination, the ultimate control of product safety must be inherent in the formulation and process.

Almost any pathogen associated with the animal or human contact is a possibility in noncooked sausage. Fortunately, most pathogens do not compete well with the naturally occurring, nonpathogenic microorganisms that predominate in a properly cured sausage. Most gram-negative microbial pathogens (*Pseudomonas, E. coli,* and *Salmonella*) generally are inhibited by the addition of salt (generally in excess of 2%) and nitrite. The "microbial inversion" that occurs during the curing process results in a predominately, gram-positive microflora consisting of lactic acid bacteria, yeasts, micrococci, and staphylococci, etc.

The most common pathogen associated with fermented meats, particularly dry sausage, is *Staphylococcus aureus* (U.S.D.A. 1977) which also correlates to the prevalence of staphylococci in raw meats and sausage. Reports in the United States indicate that greater than 50% of the samples contain staphylococci, with some meats, such as pork cheeks and beef hearts, containing very high levels (Johnston 1980). Staphylococcal food poisoning is caused by the ingestion of a heat-stable enterotoxin produced as a by-product during the growth of certain strains of *Staphylococcus aureus*. Most food poisonings have involved Type A enteroxin. This is also true in cases in which fermented sausages have been implicated (Barber and Deibel 1972). Although other meat and food products have been implicated in this type of food poisoning, some of the conditions involved in the manufacture of fermented sausage allow for the successful occurrence, competition, and growth of *S. aureus* strains. These formulation and processing parameters include the use of a high percentage of pork raw materials, a high salt content, reduced water activity, lack of natural smoke application to the surface, and higher incubation temperatures. In general, staphylococci proliferate and produce enteroxin during the initial stages of the sausage fermentation and in the outer ⅛ inch of the product. Final product pH, heat treatment, water activity, and/or refrigeration will not preclude staphylococcal food poisoning if the toxin has already been produced in the initial fermentation stage. Proper control mechanisms in the successful production of fermented sausage must be applied during the initial formulation and processing stages (U.S.D.A. 1977).

Inhibition of staphylococcal growth is enhanced as the ratio of bacteria found in meats to staphylococci increases and the temperature of storage decreases (Peterson *et al.* 1962). Suppression of staphylococcal growth generally suppresses enterotoxin production (Niskanen and Nurmi 1976), although the reverse is not true (Haines and Harmon 1973). The beneficial effect of microbial starter cultures in inhibiting staphylococcal growth and enterotoxin production in fermented sausages has been readily demonstrated (Fig. 4.7). The large numbers of lactic acid bacteria provide a consistent controlled fermentation, accelerate the rate of acid development, and thus indirectly retard the growth of staphylococci (Nurmi 1966; Genigeorgis *et al.* 1971; Daly *et al.* 1973). In addition, certain microbial cultures also exhibit antagonistic effects on staphylococcal growth and/or enterotoxin formation through the production of inhibitory substances (e.g., hydrogen peroxide, antibiotics) and/or a competition for essential nutrients (Haines and Harmon 1973).

Industry GMPs for fermented sausages recommend that the fermentation (i.e., pH reduction) be accomplished by the addition of lactic acid-forming bacteria to the formulation and that a pH of 5.3, or less, be achieved within a prescribed time interval (Table 4.8). The recommendations are based on the assumption that the environment for *Staphylococcus aureus* is effectively controlled at pH 5.3 or less, and during initial processing, it is necessary to restrict the time the meat is held in excess of

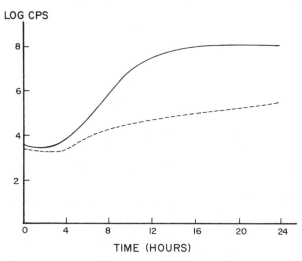

FIG. 4.7.   The effect of presence (- - -) or absence (———) *Pediococcus* starter culture on growth of coagulase-positive staphylococci (CPS) in summer sausage at 100°F (38°C).

TABLE 4.8. Recommended Time–Temperature Control for Dry Sausage
Using Constant-Temperature Processes

Maximum degree/hr[a] to reach pH 5.3	Temperatures (°F)	Allowed time by guideline[b] (hr)
1200	75 (23.9°C)	80
1200	80 (26.7°C)	60
1200	85 (29.4°C)	48
1000	90 (32.2°C)	33
1000	95 (35.0°C)	28
1000	100 (37.8°C)	25
900	105 (40.4°C)	20
900	110 (43.0°C)	18

[a] Degrees are measured as excess over 60°F (15.6°C). Degree per hour is the product of time in hours at a particular temperature and the "degrees."
[b] In variable temperature processes, each step-up in the progression is analyzed for the number of degree per hour it contributes, with the highest temperature used in the fermentation process determining the degree per hour limitation.

60°F (15.6°C). Additional recommendations encourage manufacturers to measure temperatures at the surface of the product where staphylococcal growth is most abundant and note that natural smoke will reduce the likelihood of the growth of coagulase-positive staphylococci (Fig. 4.8). Time-temperature controls are outlined for both constant temperature and variable temperature processes, and microbiological monitoring of both formulated materials and final products is encouraged (AMI 1982).

Salmonella sp. and Trichinae spiralis are also pathogens associated with fermented meats since many dried products are not fully cooked. Controlling these pathogens means decreasing their survival rate since neither proliferates in a typical, semidry and dry sausage microenvironment. Trichinae cysts are sometimes encountered in pork muscle, although the incidence in the United States is very low at <0.5% (Genigeorgis 1976). The USDA specifies treatment of pork and products containing pork to destroy potentially present trichinae cysts in products that are not "customarily well cooked in the home or elsewhere" prior to consumption (i.e., fresh pork, bacon). Other processed products, including "summer or dried sausage" must be effectively heated, refrigerated, or cured to destroy any trichinae. Nonheated (i.e., less than 137°F, 58.3°C) products must either use certified pork, via specific freezing times/temperatures, or be cured by one of several procedures specifying salt content, grind size, and time and temperature parameters (U.S.D.A. 1973). A current USDA proposal revises the trichinae control requirements to permit additional treatment methods by providing alternate combinations of time, temperature, and salt content (Houston 1983). Although a potential hazard in noncooked, fermented sausage, the low incidence of trichinae and the prescribed curing procedures generally preclude any survival. In addition, a "dilution effect" in most sausages, comprised of several meat

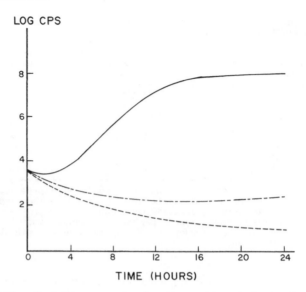

FIG. 4.8.   The effect of presence (–·–) or absence (——) of natural smoke along with a *Pediococcus* starter culture (- - -) on coagulase-positive staphylococcal growth (CPS) at 100°F (38°C).

sources, further reduces the potential existence of trichinae. Any fermented "whole cuts" (i.e., ham), representing the muscle from one animal, present more of a risk.

Salmonella also represents a potential problem since it does exist in the raw meat supply, more commonly being associated with pork and, particularly, poultry. One survey of fresh pork sausage indicated 28% of the samples contained low numbers (Genigeorgis 1976). However, salmonellae have only been implicated in several food poisoning cases attributed to dry sausage. Since 1966, the USDA has routinely analyzed dry sausage samples for *Salmonella,* but they have never isolated *Salmonella* from "finished, commercial dry sausage" although "salmonellae can be isolated from in-process samples."

Fermented meat research has demonstrated that salmonellae may be able to survive some dry sausage processes (Baran and Stevenson 1975). The ability to survive is apparently related to the amount of contamination and whether or not starter cultures are used. A common source of *Salmonella* sp. can be natural casings, if inadequately cleaned prior to use. Fortunately, *Salmonella* usually are found in low numbers and many studies have documented more effective destruction if starter cultures are used as opposed to "natural" or "wild fermentations," presumably due to controlled lactic acid development. Experimental evidence has indicated that lactic acid is an effective sanitizing agent against *Salmonella* sp. (Kampelmacher 1984). In addition, most research has inoculated salmonellae in much higher numbers than that normally encountered. In a landmark Canadian case where *Salmonella* was identified as the causative agent in food poisoning from noncooked dry sausage, the process did not employ a starter culture and the product had a pH of 6.1. *Salmonella* was also isolated from other dry sausage products manufactured by the firm with a corresponding pH range of 6.28 to 5.06. The contamination was traced to the raw pork used in the product (Saunders 1983).

Other pathogens that conceivably could occur in dry sausage are the clostridia *(C. perfringens, C. botulinum)*, although typical formulations and processes generally preclude their survival. Aflatoxins, via surface mold growth, which is characteristic of many dried salamis, have been investigated as a potential problem in commercial samples and laboratory-produced sausages. Aflatoxins have not been isolated from commercial samples, although *Aspergillus* strains capable of aflatoxin production have been isolated (Bullerman *et al.* 1969). Generally, commercial processing conditions are not conducive to aflatoxin production, and the predominant mold strains are nontoxin-producing penicillia. Laboratory sausage research has shown that the factors influencing aflatoxin production are process temperature, product moisture content, humidity, and smoking. Generally, temperatures in excess of 30°C (86°F) and high humidities (87%) favor aflatoxin production (Alvarez-Barrera *et al.* 1982). Infrequently, these conditions can be encountered in salami processing during the initial fermentation phase, although this is prior to any significant mold growth. Subsequent drying conditions do not favor aflatoxin production (55°–65°F, 60–75% RH). Any smoking of the products also will reduce mold growth, and thus potential aflatoxin production.

Many microbial cultures currently used in the production of fermented sausages also have exhibited inhibitory action against other undesirable species, including bacilli, gram-negative enterics, and yeasts (Nurmi 1966; Hurst 1973; Brankova 1976). Trials in fermented sausage demonstrate that added starter cultures effectively control enterococci and enterobacteria (Liebetrau and Grossman 1976).

Histamine has been associated with several outbreaks of food poisoning in the United States and in numerous episodes abroad (Taylor *et al.* 1978). Histamine is formed in foods by the bacterial decarboxylation of histidine and is a normal constituent of fermented foods, such as cheese, wine, and sauerkraut (Taylor *et al.* 1978), and other food products exposed to microbial degradation. Histamine concentrations in fermented meats can be variable and dependent on the length of the aging process (Cantoni *et al.* 1974; Rice *et al.* 1975; Taylor *et al.* 1978). Higher histamine levels have been found in dry sausages where a natural fermentation process is employed for an extended aging period. The addition of commercial lactic cultures appears to effectively prevent histamine accumulation through control of natural fermentation. Apparently, microbial contaminants in the naturally fermented products account for the higher levels of histamine detected (Taylor *et al.* 1978). Similar results have demonstrated that use of a starter culture greatly decreases the possibility of development of microflora that possess both tyrosine decarboxylase activity and the proteolytic activity required to produce potentially hazardous tyramine concentrations (Eitenmiller *et al.* 1978). Several reports have confirmed the lack of histamine and tyramine production by commercially available *Lactobacillus* and *Pediococcus* meat starter cultures (Rice and Koehler 1976).

SUMMARY

This chapter briefly outlines the historical development of fermented meats from a microbiological standpoint. Current classification schemes for fermented meat products are presented as well as the function of fermentation and other microbial activities in the manufacturing of various products. Specific emphasis is placed on the types of microorganisms utilized in fermented meats. The application of fermented meat technology and specific microorganisms as food additives is discussed with reference to nonfermented meat and poultry products. The status and potential of chemical acidulation is also presented. The purpose of the chapter is to provide a current description and reference list on the microbiological considerations in the processing of fermented meat and poultry products. References emphasizing production of fermented meat products are provided.

REFERENCES

ACTON, J. C.   1977.   The chemistry of dry sausages: and physical properties of the meat. Proc. Recip. Meat Conf. *30*, 49.
ACTON, J. C. and DICK, R. L.   1975.   Improved characteristics for dry, fermented turkey sausage. Food Product Develop. *9 (8)*, 91.
ALVAREZ-BARRERA, V., PEARSON, A. M., PRICE, J. F., GRAY, J. I. and AUST, S. D.   1982.   Some factors influencing aflatoxin production in fermented sausages. J. Food Sci. *47*, 1773.
AMI.   1982.   Good Manufacturing Practices, Fermented Dry and Semi-dry Sausage. Am. Meat Inst., Washington, D.C.
AMI.   1984.   Meat Facts. Am. Meat Inst., Washington, D.C.
BACUS, J. N.   1979.   Reduces nitrosamines. Food Eng. *51(5)*, 24.
BACUS, J. N.   1983.   Custom Cultures™ Technical Binder. ABC Research, Gainesville, FL.
BACUS, J. N.   1984.   Utilization of Microorganisms in Meat Processing. A handbook for Meat Plant Operators. John Wiley & Sons, Inc. NY.
BACUS, J. N. and BROWN, W. L.   1981.   Use of microbial cultures: Meat products. Food Technol. *35 (1)*, 74.
BARAN, W. L. and STEVENSON, K. E.   1975.   Survival of selected pathogens during processing of a fermented turkey sausage. J. Food Sci. *40*, 618.
BARAN, W. L., DAWSON, L. E. and STEVENSON, K. E.   1973.   Production of a dry fermented turkey sausage. Poult. Sci. *52*, 2358.
BARBER, L. E. and DEIBEL, R. H.   1972.   The effect of pH and oxygen tension on

staphylococcal growth and enteroxin production in fermented sausage. Appl. Microbiol. *24*, 891.
BARTHOLOMEW, D. R. and BLUMER, T. N.   1977.   The use of a commercial *Pediococcus cerevisiae* starter culture in the production of country-style hams. J. Food Sci. *42 (2)*, 494.
BRANKOVA, R.   1976.   Antagonism of starter cultures toward some microbial species. Proc. Europ. Mtg. Meat Res. Workers, Sofia, Bulgaria, No. 22, *G7*, 1.
BROWN, W. L.   1980.   Starter cultures—New vs old techniques. Meat Ind. Res. Conf., p. 51. Am. Meat Inst., Washington, D.C.
BUCHANAN, R. E. and GIBBONS, N. E.   1974.   Bergey's Manual of Determinative Bacteriology. The Williams and Wilkins Co., Baltimore, MD.
BULLERMAN, L. B., HARTMAN, P. A. and AYRES, J. C.   1969.   Aflatoxin production in meats. Appl. Microbiol. *18 (5)*, 718.
CANTONI, A., BLANCHI, M. A. and BERETTA, G.   1974.   Amino acids, histamine and tyramine variation during ripening of dry sausage (Salami). Ind. Aliment. *13*, 75.
CATTANEO, P., SIMONETTI, P., BERETTA, G. and BALZARETTI, C.   1983.   Micrococcaceae and ripening of dry sausage. Technol. Aliment. *6(9)*, 18.
CORETTI, K.   1977.   Starter cultures in the meat industry. Fleischwirtschaft *3*, 386.
DALY, C., CHANCE, N., SANDINE, W. E. and ELLIKER, P. R.   1973.   Control of *Staphylococcus aureus* in sausage by starter culture and chemical acidulation. J. Food Sci. *38*, 426.
DAWSON, L. E.   1970.   Utilization and acceptability of poultry in processed meat products. Proc. 14th World's Poultry Sci. Congr. Madrid, Spain, p. 749.
DEIBEL, R. H.   1974.   Technology of fermented semi-dried and dried sausages. Proc. Meat Ind. Res. Conf., p. 57. Am. Meat Inst., Chicago, Ill.
DEIBEL, R. H. and NIVEN, C. F.   1957.   *Pediococcus cerevisiae* : A starter culture for summer sausage. Bacteriol. Proc., p. 14.
DEIBEL, R. H., NIVEN, C. F. and WILSON, G. D.   1961.   Microbiology of meat curing. III. Some microbiological and related technological aspects in the manufacture of fermented sausages. Appl. Microbiol. *9*, 156.
DELARRAS, C.   1982.   Lipolytic activity of *Micrococcaceae*. Rev. Franc. Corps Gras *29 (4)*, 165.
DRAKE, E. T.   1928.   Process of curing meats. U.S. Patent 1,685,630.
EITENMILLER, R. R., KOEHLER, P. E. and REAGAN, J. O.   1978.   Tyramine in fermented sausages: Factors affecting formation of tyramine and tyrosine decarboxylase. J. Food Sci. *43*, 699.
EVERSON, C. W., DANNER, W. E. and HAMMES, P. A.   1970.   Bacterial starter cultures in sausage products. J. Agr. Food Chem. *18*, 570.
EVERSON, C. W., DANNER, W. E. and HAMMES, P. A.   1974.   Process for curing dry and semi-dry sausages. U.S. Patent 3,814,817.
FAO/WHO Food Standards Programme.   1980.   Draft code of hygienic practice for dry and semi-dry sausage. Prepared by Italy. Codex Committee on Processed Meat and Poultry Products. Eleventh Session, Copenhagen, Sept. 22–26.
FISHER, U. and SCHLEIFER, K. H.   1980.   Presence of staphylococci and micrococci in dry sausage. Fleischwirtschaft *60*, 1046.
FREY, W.   1983.   Starter cultures for raw sausage production. Fleischerei, February, p. 67.
GENIGEORGIS, C. A.   1976.   Quality control for fermented meats. J. Am. Vet. Med. Assoc. *169*, 1220.
GENIGEORGIS, C., FODA, M. S., MANTIS, A., and SADLER, W. W.   1971.   Effect of sodium chloride and pH on enterotoxin C production. Appl. Microbiol. *21*, 862.
GILLILAND, S. E.   1980.   The use of lactobacilli to preserve fresh meat. Proc. Recip. Meat Conf. *33*, 54.
GOTZ, F., KREUTZ, B., and SCHLEIFER, K.   1983.   Protoplast transformation of *Staphylococcus carnosus* by plasmid DNA. Mol. Gen. Genet. *189*, 340.

HAINES, W. C. and HARMON, L. G.   1973.   Effect of lactic acid bacteria on growth of *Staphylococcus aureus* and production of enterotoxin. Appl. Microbiol. *25,* 436.

HAYMON, L. W.   1985.   New developments in starter cultures. Proc. Meat Ind. Res. Conf. Am. Meat Inst., New Orleans, LA. In press.

HOUSTON, D.   1979.   Acid-producing microorganisms in meat products for nitrite dissipation. Fed. Reg. *44 (31),* 9372.

HOUSTON, D.   1983.   Trichina control requirements. Fed. Reg. *48 (48),* 10065–68.

HOUSTON, D.   1984.   Acetic acid, citric acid, lactic acid, phosphoric acid, and tartaric acid as acidifiers in meat and poultry products. Fed. Reg. *49 (178),* 35746.

HURST, A.   1973.   Microbial antagonisms in food. Canad. Inst. Food Sci. Technol. J. *6,* 80.

JEDLICKA, G.   1985.   Chemical acidulation. Proc. Meat Ind. Res. Conf. Am. Meat Inst. New Orleans, LA. In press.

JENSEN, L. B. and PADDOCK, L. S.   1940.   Sausage treatment. U.S. Patent 2,225,783.

JOHNSTON, R. W.   1980.   Coagulase positive staphylococci update. Presented at the ABC Res. 6th Ann. Tech. Sem., Gainesville, Florida, Feb. 17–19.

KAMPELMACHER, E. H.   1984.   International Symposium on *Salmonella.* Food Chem. News, Aug. 6, p. 17.

KELLER, J. E. and ACTON, J. C.   1974.   Properties of a fermented semi-dry turkey sausage during production with lyophilized and frozen concentrates of *Pediococcus cerevisiae.* J. Food Sci. *39,* 836.

KIELNIARZ, K. S.   1982.   Comparison of fermentation temperatures on organoleptic and microbiological properties of summer sausage. Master of Science Thesis, Iowa St. University, Ames, Iowa.

KURK, F. W.   1921.   Art of curing meat. U.S. Patent 1,380,068.

LIEBETRAU, B. and GROSSMAN, G.   1976.   The role of starter culture used for raw sausage ripening in the context of food hygiene. Hyg. Res. Beyirkes Suhl/Sitz Gotha. German Democratic Rep. *20 (5),* 489.

MASTERS, B. A., OBLINGER, J. L., GOODFELLOW, S. J., BACUS, J. N., BROWN, W. L.   1981.   Fate of *Salmonella newport* and *Salmonella typhimurium* inoculated into summer sausage. J. Food Prot. *44,* 527.

MOON, N. J., BEUCHAT, L. R. and HAYS, E. R.   1980.   Evaluation of lactic acid bacteria for extending the shelf-life of shrimp. Proc. 40th Ann. Mtg., Inst. Food Technol., New Orleans, LA.

NIINIVAARA, F. P.   1955.   The influence of pure bacterial cultures on aging and changes of the red color of dry sausage. Saomen Maataloustietellisen Seuran Julkaisuja No. 84, Acta Agralis Fennica, Helsinki.

NIINIVAARA, F. P. and POHJA, M. S.   1954.   Zur theorie der wasserbindung des Fleisches. Fleischwirtschaft *6,* 192.

NIINIVAARA, F. B., POHJA, M. S. and KOMULAINEN, S. E.   1964.   Some aspects about using bacterial pure cultures in the manufacture of fermented sausages. Food Technol., February, p. 25.

NISKANEN, A. and NURMI, E.   1976.   Effect of starter culture on staphylococcal enterotoxin and thermonuclease production in dry sausage. Appl. Microbiol. *34 (1),* 11.

NIVEN, C. F.   1951.   Sausage discolorations of bacterial origin. Am. Meat Inst. Found. Bull., p. 13.

NIVEN, C. F.   1961.   Microbiology of meats. Cir. No. 68, Am Meat Inst. Found, Washington, D.C.

NIVEN, C. F., DEIBEL, R. H. and WILSON, G. D.   1958   The AMIF sausage starter culture. Circ. No. 41, Am. Meat Inst. Found. Chicago, IL.

NURMI, E.   1966.   Effect of bacterial inoculations on characteristics and microbial flora of dry sausage. Acta Agr. Fenn. *108,* 1.

PEDERSON, C. S.   1979.   Microbiology of Food Fermentations. 2nd Edition. AVI Publishing Co., Westport, CT.

PETAEJAE, E., LAINE, J. J. and NIINIVAARA, F. P.   1972.   Starter cultures for meat curing. Fleischwirtschaft 52, 310.

PETAJA.   1977.   Starter cultures in frankfurter-type sausage. Fleischwirtschaft 57, 109.

PETERSON, A. C., BLACK, J. J., and GUNDERSON, M. F.   1962.   Staphylococci in competition. II. Effect of total numbers and proportion of staphylococci in mixed cultures on growth in artifical medium. Appl. Microbiol. 10, 23.

PINA, V. J. G.   1977.   Bacterial antagonism—The use in the preservation of boiled meat products. Fleischerei 28 (10), 43.

RACCACH, M.   1981.   Method and bacterial compositions for fermenting meats. U.S. Patent 4,303,679.

RACCACH, M. and BAKER, R. C.   1978.   Lactic acid bacteria as an antispoilage and safety factor in cooked, mechanically deboned poultry meat. J. Food Prot. 41, 703.

REDDY, S. G., HENDRICKSON, R. L. and OLSEN, H. C.   1970.   The influence of lactic cultures on ground beef quality. J. Food Sci. 35, 787.

RICE, S. L. and KOEHLER, P. E.   1976.   Tyrosine and histidine decarboxylase activities of Pediococcus cerevisiae and Lactobacillus species and the production of tyramine in fermented sausages. J. Milk Food Technol. 39, 166.

RICE, S., EITENMILLER, R. R. and KOEHLER, P. E.   1975.   Histamine and tyramine content of meat products. J. Milk Food Technol. 38, 256.

SAUNDERS, J.   1983.   Legal Judgment: Bona Foods Ltd. vs Turcotte and Turmel, Inc. Supreme Court of Ontario, Sept. 14.

SCHLEIFER, K. H. and FISHER, U.   1982.   Description of a new species of the genus Staphylococcus: Staphylococcus carnosus. Intl.. J. System. Bacteriol. 32 (2), 153.

SCHIFFNER, E. and OPPEL, K.   1973.   Utilization of bacterial cultures in manufacture of cured meat products. Fleischwirtscheft 27 (11), 207.

SCHNEIDER, H.   1980.   Dry and semi-dry sausage technology primer. Meat Industry, October p. 62.

SCHUT, J.   1978.   The European sausage industry. Proc. Recip. Meat Conf. 31, 5.

SEN, N., IYENGAR, J., DONALDSON, B. and PANALAKS, T.   1974.   Effect of sodium nitrite concentration on the formation of nitrosopyrrolidine and dimethylnitrosamine in fried bacon. J. Agr. Food Chem. 22, 540.

SIMONETTI, P. and CANTONI, C.   1983.   Coagulase negative staphylococci for dry sausage ripening. Ind. Aliment. 22 (204), 262.

SIMONETTI, P., CANTONI, C., FIGERIO, R. and PROVERA, D.   1983.   Starter cultures and ripening of dry sausages. Ind. Aliment. 22 (208), 614.

SMITH, J. L. and PALUMBO, S. A.   1981.   Microorganisms as food additives. J. Food Prot. 44, 936.

SMITH, J. L. and PALUMBO, S. A.   1983.   Use of starter cultures in meats. J. Food Prot. 46 (11), 997.

SWIFT, C. E. and ELLIS, R.   1956.   The action of phosphates in sausage products. I. Factors affecting the water retention of phosphate-treated ground meat. Food Technol. 10, 546.

TANAKA, N., TRAISMAN, E., LEE, M. H., CASSENS, R. G. and FOSTER, E. M.   1980.   Inhibition of botulinum toxin formation in bacon by acid development. J. Food Prot. 43, 450.

TAYLOR, S. L., LEATHERWOOD, M., and LIEBER, E. R.   1978.   A survey of histamine levels in sausage. J. Food Prot. 41, 634.

TERRELL, R. N., SMITH, G. C. and CARPENTER, Z. L.   1978.   Practical manufacturing technology of dry and semi-dry sausage. Proc. 20th Ann. Meat Sci. Inst., Athens, Ga.

TERRELL, R. N., SMITH, G. C. and CARPENTER, Z. L.   1977.   Practical manufacturing technology for dry and semi-dry sausage. Proc. Recip. Meat Conf. 30, 39.

TEZAN, I. and YUECEL, A.   1975.   Effect of Lactobacillus starter culture in vacuum packaged meat on Salmonella and Pseudomonas organisms. Vet. Hekimter Dernegi Dergisi 45 (4), 7.

THENO, D.   1985.   The U.S. poultry industry, past / present/future. Proc. Meat Ind. Res. Conf. Am. Meat Inst., New Orleans, LA. In press.

TRAISMAN, E.   1984.   Lactic acid cultures for meat preservation. Proc. 10th Ann. Tech. Seminar, ABC Res. Corp., Gainesville, FL, Feb. 27–29.

URBANIAK, L. and PEZACKI, W.   1975.   Die Milschsaure bildende Rohwurst-mikroflora und ihre technologisch bedingte Veranderung. Fleischwissenschaft 55, 229.

U.S.D.A.   1973.   Meat and Poultry Inspection Regulations. Washington, D.C.

U.S.D.A.   1977.   The staphylococcal problem in fermented sausage. Task Force Report. F.S.Q.S., Washington, D.C.

VANSTEENKISTE, J. P. and VAN HOOF, J.   1980.   Checking of fermented sausages for complete treatment according to EEC-directive 77/99/EEC. Proc. Eur. Mtg. Meat Res. Workers No. 26, *I*, 154.

WESSLEY, D.   1960.   The role of microorganisms in the manufacture of summer sausage. Thesis. U. of Wisconsin

YANKOV, Y. and BRANKOVA, R.   1978.   Studies on the lactobacilli species in raw-dried sausages. Proc. Europ. Meat Res. Workers, *G10*, 3.

5

Sporeforming Bacteria

F. F. Busta[1] and Peggy M. Foegeding[2]

INTRODUCTION

Contamination of meat, poultry, and their products with sporeforming bacteria may result in product spoilage or public health problems. Understanding and control of problems resulting from sporeforming bacteria require a knowledge of the physiological and biochemical properties involved in formation of the dormant resistant bacterial spore and emergence of the metabolically active vegetative cell. The ability of *Bacillus* and *Clostridium* species to cause spoilage and public health problems in food is frequently a result of the ability to form bacterial spores which have high resistance to processing and control procedures; however, the metabolic activities of vegetative cells of these genera typically are directly responsible for the detrimental effects of these organisms. *Clostridium perfringens* food-borne illness is one unique exception. Enterotoxin synthesis by *C. perfringens* is related intimately to sporulation (Frieben and Duncan 1973). This chapter will briefly review the structure, formation, inhibition, and inactivation of bacterial spores and the emergence of vegetative cells from the spore prior to reviewing the involvement of specific species of recent significance in meat and meat products or about which recent advances in knowledge have been achieved.

[1]Department of Food Science and Nutrition, University of Minnesota, 1334 Eckles Avenue, St. Paul, MN 55108. *Present address:* Food Science and Human Nutrition Department, 359 Food Service Building, University of Florida, Gainesville, FL 32611.
[2]Department of Food Science, 339 Schaub Hall, Box 7624, North Carolina State University, Raleigh, NC 27695-7624.

Advances in Meat Research, Volume 2

THE BACTERIAL SPORE

Morphology and Composition

Many gram-positive bacilli, some gram-negative organisms, and some cocci form endospores. Spores of the gram-positive bacilli, *Clostridium* and *Bacillus,* are the most common and most important in meat and other food products. Spores of all bacterial species have the same basic structure (Fig. 5.1) which consists of a central core (protoplast) surrounded, in turn, by a plasma membrane, germ cell wall, cortex, coat(s), and exosporium (in some species). The core, plasma membrane, and germ cell wall essentially represent a modified vegetative cell which is protected by the cortex, coat(s), and exosporium. The molecular contents of the core are similar to the contents of vegetative cells with a few key exceptions. Spores contain a complement of enzymes, ribosomes, DNA, and lipids not significantly different from vegetative cells of the same species. Setlow (1974,1975B) recently discovered a group of basic, low molecular weight, proteins in *Bacillus megaterium* spores but not in vegetative cells of this species. These proteins appear to have a role in stabilization of the spore DNA and serve as a reserve material for germination. Another unique feature of the core is the presence of dipicolinate anions, at least some of which are chelated 1:1 with Ca^{2+}. Spores appear to be in a relatively dry state although they are water permeable (Watt 1981). The cortex consists primarily of peptidoglycan only slightly modified from the peptidoglycan present in vegetative cell walls and is relatively uniform among spores of various species. Degradative enzymes termed spore lytic enzymes are associated with the peptidoglycan, cortex, and germ cell wall (Gombas and

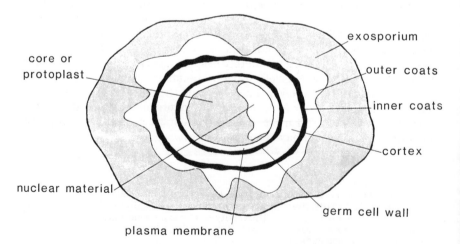

FIG. 5.1.   Diagrammatic illustration of the bacterial spore.

Labbe 1981; Boschwitz *et al.* 1983). These enzymes apparently play a role in breaking spore dormancy. Although spore coats vary among species, all are composed primarily of tenacious, keratin-like protein, present in layers around the spore cortex. Spores of many species have an exosporium composed of phospholipoprotein, protein, and glucose as the outermost layer. Spore composition and morphology have been reviewed by many authors, including Murrell (1969), Sadoff (1969), Ellar (1978), Keynan (1978), Warth (1978), and others.

The Spore Cycle

Sporulation. Events associated with sporulation and their control have been reviewed extensively (Halvorson *et al.* 1966; Bernlohr and Leitzman 1969; Doi 1969; Vinter 1969; Freese 1981; Setlow 1981). The sporulation process begins when rapid growth ceases due to nutritional deprivation which causes the cells to divide asymmetrically. In nature, cells multiply until the concentration of one or more nutrients is reduced sufficiently that the cell recognizes the deficiency as a signal for sporulation. Asymmetric septation usually depends upon a nutritional signal while subsequent developments are genetically controlled (Freese 1981). The conditions required for sporulation are exacting and different from the conditions required for growth. Some important factors affecting sporulation are the nutrient and mineral compositions, pH, temperature, and aeration of the medium (Vinter 1969). During sporulation, characteristics unique to spores such as heat and chemical resistance develop and dipicolinic acid (DPA) and calcium accumulate. The structural changes of *B. cereus* during sporulation have been described in detail by Ellar and Lundgren (1966).

The sporulation conditions affect the structure, resistance, and properties of spores (Sugiyama, 1951; Waites *et al.* 1979,1980; Labbe and Rufner 1980; Bayliss *et al.* 1981). If raffinose replaced starch in sporulation media, *Clostridium perfringens* spores produced more enterotoxin (Labbe and Rey 1979), had thicker cortexes, and altered spore coat structures (Labbe and Rufner 1980). Spores of *C. bifermentans* produced on Trypticase medium contained more DPA, were more H_2O_2 and heat resistant, and outgrew more rapidly than spores produced on Reinforced Clostridial medium (Waites *et al.* 1980). Church and Halvorson (1959) were able to increase the DPA content of spores of *B. cereus* var. *terminalis* by raising the level of yeast extract or by deleting DL-phenylalanine from the sporulation medium. Spores with higher DPA contents were more resistant to heat. Halvorson and Swanson (1969) isolated a *B. cereus* T DPA-less mutant. The mutant spores were slightly more heat resistant than vegetative cells and much less resistant than wild-type spores. Sugiyama (1951) found that *C. botulinum* spores formed at 37°C were of higher heat resistance than those produced at 41°, 29°, or 24°C. He also observed that lower Fe^{2+} concentrations in the sporulation medium decreased the heat resistance of the spores and that fatty acids in the sporulation medium decreased the heat resistance of the spores and that fatty acids in the sporulating medium affected the heat resistance. Generally, the longer the fatty acid chain, the greater the resistance. Extraction of fatty acids from the sporulation medium lowered the heat tolerance. Waites *et al.* (1979) observed smaller protoplasts, larger cortexes, and greater heat resistance of *C. bifermentans* spores produced in Trypticase medium with glucose or Reinforced Clostridial medium. A similar relationship of resistance and protoplast or cortex size was observed with *B. subtilis* (Bayliss *et al.* 1981).

The variation in chemical composition between batches of a complex medium can affect the resulting spores. *Bacillus subtilis* spores produced on Antibiotic Assay Medium Number 1 from different suppliers had different resistances to heat and glutaraldehyde and different germination rates (Hodges *et al.* 1980). *Bacillus subtilis* spores produced on a chemically defined medium showed a greater degree of reproducibility in resistance and germination.

The variability in spore properties observed as a consequence of modifications of sporulation medium has practical significance. Studies of inoculated systems are conducted using spores produced in laboratory media. The medium used may vary among studies, making comparisons difficult. More importantly, the spores of concern in meat or other food products are produced in nature, an environment not easily or perfectly mimicked in the laboratory. Consequently, the spores of real concern in foods may differ in resistance, structure, dormancy, and in other ways from laboratory-produced spores used for many experiments.

Activation. According to the definitions of Keynan and Evenchik (1969) activation of spores terminates the state of dormancy (physiological state of reluctance to germinate) but not the state of cryptobiosis (physiological state of arrested metabolism). Activated spores are refractile, nonstainable, and resistant to heat, radiation, and chemicals, but they can germinate more rapidly in suitable germination initiators (germinants) and require lower concentrations of germinants than nonactivated spores.

Heat activation is used most widely. Other agents used to activate spores include reducing agents, low pH, calcium dipicolinate, ionizing radiation, and other chemicals, such as urea and D-cycloserine (Keynan and Evenchik 1969). Activation remains an elusive phenomenon which may be affected by the composition of the sporulation and plating media (Roberts and Ingram 1967; Montville 1981), time and temperature of the heat treatment, storage time, interstrain variation (Levinson and Freeherry 1978), and length and temperature of plate incubation (Busta and Ordal 1964A). For example, some but not all strains of *C. botulinum* required heat activation for maximal enumeration on Reinforced Clostridial agar but not on Botulinum Assay medium (Montville 1981), indicating Botulinum Assay medium obviates the need for heat activation. Heat activation and activation by reducing agents were reversible during storage at low temperatures (Keynan *et al.* 1964). Spores which had reverted to dormancy germinated normally after they received a second heat activation treatment. However, Busta and Ordal (1964B) observed that *B. subtilis* spores heat activated at 75°C did not lose the ability to form colonies during 215 days at 5°C.

Germination.   Germination, measured by onset of heat or chemical lability, stainability, phase darkening, manometry, and absorbance decrease, is the irreversible transition from a heat-resistant spore to a heat-labile entity, which is not yet a vegetative cell. There is a vast amount of literature concerning germination of spores of *Bacillus* species, whereas spores of *Clostridium* species have been neglected by comparison. Spore germination involves rapid depolymerization of spore structure and storage components and excretion of about 30% of the spore weight, including the dipicolinic acid, most of the calcium and manganese, and about 50% of the peptidoglycan (Gould 1970). Physical changes that follow include loss of resistance to heat, chemical agents, desiccation, pressure, radiation, and extremes of pH. Dormancy is lost, metabolism commences, and enzymes not detected in the dormant spores become active (Gould 1970). During germination and outgrowth, protein and RNA storage forms are degraded, synthesis of ATP and ribosomal and soluble RNA begins, while synthesis of messenger RNA, protein, and DNA lags behind (Setlow 1975A; Setlow and Primus 1975). The sequences of events during germination of *B. megaterium* (Levinson and Hyatt 1966) and PA3679 (Uehara and Frank 1967) have been reported. Because the changes involved in the transition from a spore to a germinated spore to a vegetative cell (outgrowth) occur in sequence, exactly when germination begins and ends is ill defined and controversial.

Germination may be initiated or promoted by nonnutrient (metal ions, calcium dipicolinate, bicarbonate) or nutrient stimulants or germinants, by enzymatic germinants (lysozyme, spore-lytic enzyme, subtilisin, *B. cereus* T initiator protein), or by physical means (abrasion, deformation, hydrostatic pressure) (Gould 1970; Gould and Sale 1970; Mackey and Morris 1972; Smoot and Pierson 1981).

Reviews on the various germination initiators have been provided by Gould (1969, 1970) and Gould and Dring (1972). Metabolizable or nutrient initiators or germinants include particular amino acids, purine ribosides or deoxyribosides, bases, and sugars. L-Alanine is the most widely studied germinant, and alone or in the presence of suitable ions or sugars it will initiate germination of many species of *Bacillus* and *Clostridium* spores (Gould 1970). The exact mechanism(s) by which germination is initiated is unknown.

Outgrowth.   After germination, spores undergo outgrowth, which involves swelling, rupture of the spore, and emergence and elongation leading to formation of the first vegetative cell (Strange and Hunter 1969).

As with other spore and cell processes, outgrowth is affected by environmental factors such as temperature, amounts and kinds of nutrients, water activity, Eh, and pH. Strange and Hunter (1969) have reviewed the ordered sequence of events occurring during outgrowth.

It is tempting to exploit the unique properties of the cell at certain stages of the spore cycle to control spore problems in the food industry. For example, if bacterial spore germination could be blocked, the dormant spores would present little spoilage or public health problem. Conversely, if spores could be induced to germinate, much less severe inactivation treatments could be used to destroy the spores and the deleterious effects of the treatments on the food would be reduced. As a safety factor, controlling spore problems by inducing or blocking progression of spores through the spore cycle at more than one stage would be useful. In any event, further research is needed to understand the processes involved in the transitions from a vegetative cell to a dormant spore and back to a metabolically active vegetative cell. In addition, a more complete understanding of the effect of inactivation and inhibitory treatments on the vegetative cell and spore processes is needed. This information is especially scarce for anaerobic sporeforming organisms.

Inhibition, Inactivation, and Injury

Bacterial spores are dormant, nonvegetative entities which have high resistance to treatments used to inactivate or control microorganisms. Typically, bacterial spores are many times more resistant than are vegetative bacterial cells of the same species to inactivation by heat, sanitizers, drying or freezing. In addition, because of their unique structure and biochemical processes, many food preservatives react with bacterial spores in a manner which is different from the reaction with vegetative cells. The following are some examples from current literature on inhibition, inactivation, and injury of sporeforming bacteria relevant to meat and meat processing. The examples are neither all-inclusive of control procedures nor is any single example comprehensively treated. Reviews are published which comprehensively and adequately survey the literature addressing each of these topics and readers should consult such reviews for more detailed treatments.

Nitrite. Nitrite is used in cured meat products because of its antibotulinal properties and for its positive effect on cured meat color and flavor. Tompkin et al. (1978) have extensively studied the antibotulinal effect of nitrite and suggested that nitrite may react with ferredoxin (an iron-sulfur compound) or an enzyme for which iron is essential. The iron-containing compound may be necessary for energy production in the vegetative cells of and outgrowing spores of C. botulinum. Woods et al. (1981) and Woods and Wood (1982) showed that nitrite inhibits the phosphoroclastic system in *C. sporogenes* and *C. botulinum*. This energy-generating reaction probably is ferredoxin which is catalyzed in both species. Recently, Reddy *et al.* (1983) demonstrated the presence of iron-sulfur centers in *C. botulinum* vegetative cells using electron spin resonance spectra. Addition of nitrite formed iron-nitric oxide complexes, destroying the iron-sulfur clusters. Undoubtedly, destruction of the iron-sulfur center is at least partially responsible for the effective antibotulinal activity of nitrite since these centers are involved in energy production.

Chlorine.   Chlorine, a routinely used sanitizer in the meat industry, is highly effective against bacterial spores when used properly. A recent report by Foegeding and Busta (1982A) reinforced the requirement for proper use concentrations. Using a model system, they found that if *C. botulinum* spore concentrations were high (ca. 10^7 spores per milliliter) and hypochlorite concentrations were low (12 or 28 g/ml), sublethal injury rather than inactivation of *C. botulinum* 62A and 12885A spores resulted. Previously, sublethal injury of vegetative bacteria by chlorine compounds was reported by Scheusner *et al.* (1971). The sublethal spore damage was manifested by the inability to recover hypochlorite-damaged spores using a modified peptone colloid broth, 5-tube, most probable number procedure. Damaged spores could be recovered by a colony count procedure using modified peptone yeast extract agar-Lee tubes. Spores not treated with hypochlorite were enumerated essentially equally by both procedures. Hypochlorite-treated spores were sensitive to recovery media components. Sodium bicarbonate was beneficial and sodium chloride was detrimental to enumeration of hypochlorite-treated spores (Foegeding and Busta 1983B). These data illustrate the significance of assuring proper use concentrations of hypochlorite sanitizers and selection of media which will enumerate all viable spores in a hypochlorite-treated population when monitoring sanitizer effectiveness.

Heat.   Although there are many factors which contribute to the high heat resistance of bacterial spores, the basic mechanism of heat resistance has not been fully explained. Various theories have been proposed, none of which satisfactorily explain the physicochemical basis for stabilization of essential macromolecules and structures, the means by which stabilization is achieved, or the means by which destabilization is achieved. Historically, investigations into mechanisms of heat resistance involved spore fractionation and analysis of components. Thus, the unique properties imparted by the spore structure and packaging of components were lost. Collaborators in the Commonwealth Scientific and Industrial Research Organisation (CSIRO) Division of Food Research in Australia, the Food Research Institute in England, and others have begun to investigate the heat resistance of spores using nondestructive biophysical techniques and are expected to make great strides in this area. The emerging information indicates that the core contains densely packed macromolecules interacting with dipicolinic acid, calcium dipicolinate, and ions through electrostatic, hydrogen, and noncovalent bonding. The core has little intermolecular space, reduced molecular mobility, and a low water content. The combination of these factors apparently stabilizes the essential macromolecules and imparts the spore resistance to heat. The core and cortex appears to function in achieving and maintaining the critical "packaging" and low water content of the core (Murrell 1981). Many unanswered questions remain and interpretation of the existing data is controversial.

Phosphate. Use of polyphosphates in processed meats has indicated antimicrobial activity, specifically antibotulinal activity, by sodium acid pyrophosphate (SAPP) in combination with nitrite and sorbate (Wagner and Busta 1982; Nelson et al. 1983). Qualitative antagonistic effects also have been observed against C. botulinum spores by Seward et al. (1982). Recently, the influence of NaCl on these antibotulinal activities have also been observed (Wagner and Busta 1984). The effects appear to be focused on the outgrowth portion of the conversion of spores to cells but much research remains to be done before the mechanism is well understood.

Acid. Bacterial spore resistance to acid is complex and may involve the hydrogen ion concentration or the undissociated acid or both. The activation, germination, or outgrowth of the spore may be affected or the growth of the vegetative cells may be the limiting event (Blocher and Busta 1983). The minimum pH for activity of various sporeformers has been evaluated, and much effort has been directed at C. botulinum. Except in acidified processed meats, pH usually is not the controlling factor.

Much effort has been directed at sorbic acid as a possible alternative for nitrite to control clostridia in cured meats (Sofos et al. 1979A,B; Busta 1982; Sofos and Busta 1981, 1983). Besides extensive evaluation of meat processing and storage conditions, this research assisted in the identification of mechanisms of acid control of spores. Sofos et al. (1979A,B) showed that sorbic acid inhibited the germination process in C. botulinum spores in meat emulsions. Smoot and Pierson (1981) indicated that sorbic acid was a competetive inhibitor for L-alanine germination. Subsequent work on sorbic acid and other acid environments by Blocher and Busta (1982, 1984) has shown that low pH inhibits the binding of L-alanine to the receptor site on the spore and sorbic acid inhibits the connecting reactions between the binding of the germinant and the initiation of degradative reactions during spore germination. More research effort is needed to fully understand the complete mechanism of acid resistance and control of spores in meat.

BACILLUS SPECIES

Bacillus cereus

The sporeformer *Bacillus cereus* is of moderate concern in meats as a potential agent food-borne illness. It is now recognized that *Bacillus cereus* can cause illnesses with two distinct syndromes. The first well-documented report of the diarrheal type was associated with the consumption of vanilla sauce in 1950, although similar symptoms associated with bacilli in foods had been reported as early as 1906. Diarrhea appears about 12 hr after ingestion of the food. More recently a higher incidence of the other syndrome which involves vomiting has been recorded. Vomiting starts in 1–5 hr after ingestion of the toxic food. Food-borne illnesses with either syndrome caused by *B. cereus* have been reported in the U.K., United States, Canada, Japan, the Netherlands, and elsewhere. Gilbert (1979) has comprehensively reviewed these types of gasteroenteritis and recently Johnson (1984) has published an update on *B. cereus* food-borne illness.

Bacillus cereus food-borne illness has been linked to meat products on many occasions, although meats are not the vehicles of transmission in the majority of reported cases. Beef was implicated in a 1980 outbreak in New York involving 118 cases of the illness (CDC 1983A) but none of the eight confirmed outbreaks in the United States in 1981 identified meat as the vehicle (CDC 1983B). Beef, beef curry, gravy, lamb, and poultry have been implicated in outbreaks in the U.K. and Canada.

The presence of *B. cereus* spores or cells in food products not implicated in food-borne illness outbreaks also has been summarized by Johnson (1984). Meat products, often associated with rice or other carbohydrate foods, have demonstrated significant levels of *B. cereus* showing 21–100% of the samples containing viable organisms. Many dried grains and spices frequently combined with or added to meats also demonstrated high incidence of contamination by *B. cereus*. Consequently, the presence of these spores and the potential for the growth of the organism must be a recognized fact because it is so widely distributed in nature.

Methods to enumerate, identify, and characterize *B. cereus* are well documented (Goepfert 1976; Gilbert *et al.* 1981; Kramer *et al.* 1982) and have been reviewed recently by Foegeding (1985). The routine approach is to enumerate by colony count on solid media such as mannitol-egg yolk-polymyxin agar (MYP), Kim and Goepfert agar (KG), and polymyxin-pyruvate-egg yolk-mannitol-bromthymol blue agar (PEMBA). Harmon *et al.* (1984) indicated equivalent recoveries of *B. cereus* by these three media but endorsed MYP based on ease of differentiation and confirmation. The influence of medium on recovery of heat-damaged spores also influences apparent numbers of colony-forming units (Johnson and Busta 1984).

Control of *B. cereus* hazards in meat products involves inactivation of the spores or cells and the minimizing of germination and growth of any survivors or contaminants. The influence of temperature on *B. cereus* survival, spore germination, and cell growth (Johnson *et al.* 1982, 1983) indicates that spores from strains associated with diarrheal outbreaks have few dramatically different characteristics from those associated with the emetic syndrome. Germination was observed between 5° and 50°C and growth responses were recorded between 15° and 50°C. The significant role of animal protein sources of germinant or growth substrates also was reported by Morita and Woodburn (1977). *Bacillus cereus* inoculated into vacuum-packaged ham was able to reach a population in excess of 10^8 per gram in 24 hr at 30°C (Stiles and Ng 1979). A pH level at 4.35 limited growth in meat (Raevuori and Genigeorgis 1975). Reduced a_w to below 0.95 also limits growth. Prevention of *B. cereus* food-borne illness from meat products is based on the assumption that the cells or spores are present in the product and that inactivation treatments must be used to eliminate the microorganism or conditions such as temperature must be maintained where the *B. cereus* spores cannot germinate or grow.

Other Bacilli

Reports of spoilage or food-borne illness from other species of the genus *Bacillus* are not readily evident in the literature. The very heat-resistant thermophilic flat sour sporeformers are generally associated with carbohydrate foods such as sugar or starch (Ito 1981). Bell (1983) has shown experimentally that a pasteurization value of $P_{70°C}=135$ min or more for processed luncheon meat in chubs eliminated all but the spoilage bacilli. The absence of any mention of *Bacillus* sp. in a recent review on spoilage and storage life of fresh meat would indicate that any problems that might exist are minimal or unrecognized. In general, adequate temperature control of canned thermally processed, pasteurized, or raw meat products will control spoilage bacilli.

CLOSTRIDIUM SPECIES

Clostridium perfringens

The anaerobic sporeformer *Clostridium perfringens* is of major concern as a potential food-borne hazard in cooked meat products. This food-borne illness is characterized by severe diarrhea and cramps that develop 8–24 hr after ingestion of the organism. Ingestion of about 10^8 viable organisms is required for symptoms to develop. Typically vegetative cells multiply to high numbers in the meat and after ingestion sporulate in the small intestine. An enterotoxin that is serologically homologous to spore coat protein (Frieben and Duncan 1973) is released upon lysis of the sporangium. This relationship is well documented (Craven 1980; Labbe 1980; Craven *et al.* 1981; Loffler and Labbe 1983). Although enterotoxin can be detected in meat products (Naik and Duncan 1977A) preformed enterotoxin is considered rare. Of the five generally recognized types of *C. perfringens*, only type A and occasionally C are associated with food-borne illness. *Clostridium perfringens* food-borne illness has been reported in the U.K., United States, Japan, Germany, New Zealand, India, and elsewhere. Walker (1975) and Hobbs (1979) have comprehensively reviewed this gasteroenteritis, and McDonel (1980) has reviewed the mechanisms of action of the enterotoxin.

Clostridium perfringens food-borne illness is frequently associated with meat products (Shandera *et al.* 1983). In the period from 1976 to 1980, beef products were implicated as vehicles for 33% of the *C. perfringens* outbreaks. Turkey, ham, and chicken were also implicated. In 1981, 11% of the outbreaks (28), 13% of the cases (1162), and 6% of the deaths (2) in confirmed food-borne disease outbreaks were attributed to *C. perfringens* (CDC, 1983B). The largest outbreak involved 185 cases and turkey was implicated. Beef, pork, chicken, sausage, and other meats were implicated in other outbreaks.

The incidence of the spores or cells in raw meats is well documented. Bauer *et al.* (1981) reported that 39% of commercial pork sausage samples contained *C. perfringens.* Smart *et al.* (1979) isolated *C. perfringens* from 29%, 66%, and 85% of beef, pork, and lamb carcasses, respectively.

Selected lots of beef rounds in the United States also demonstrated the presence of *C. perfringens,* especially after low temperature and long time (LTLT) roasting and abusive cooling (Smith *et al.* 1980). Since these are sporeforming bacteria, their resistance in the spore state will permit them to survive many processes, such as carcass scalding, cured meat smoking, and oven roasting. The strains that produce less heat-resistant spores outnumbered those that produce more heat-resistant spores; however, both types may cause food-borne illness (Duncan and Harmon 1976).

Growth in meat products, and especially beef, is rapid over a considerable range of temperatures. Hobbs (1979) indicated no growth at <15° or >55°C. Willardsen *et al.* (1978) showed significant growth from 26° to 51°C in cooked ground beef with a maximum rate of growth between 41° and 45°C. Doubling times of 7–8 min were observed at optimal temperatures. Constantly changing temperatures that simulated beef cooking could be evaluated for their influence on growth of *C. perfringens* in beef, and a mathematical model to predict growth and inactivation for hazard assessment has been developed (Thompson and Busta 1981).

Methods to enumerate, identify, and characterize *C. perfringens* in food products are well established (Duncan and Harmon 1976). Recently, Labbe (1983) and Foegeding (1986) discussed enumeration media and confirmation tests. At present, tryptose-sulfite-cycloserine agar (TSC) with or without added egg yolk incubated anaerobically at 37°C for 24 hr, or 48 hr for injured spores, is the medium of choice to enumerate colony-forming units that produce H_2S and form black colonies. Other media may be preferable for heated spores (Labbe and Norris 1982). Frequently, refrigeration or freezing inactivates *C. perfringens*. Consequently, alpha toxin (lecithinase or phospholipase C) produced by *C. perfringens* has been proposed as an indirect after the fact measure (Harmon and Kautter 1976). Foegeding and Busta (1980) showed that, during growth and thermal inactivation, concentrations of viable *C. perfringens* and alpha toxin were directly related. Analysis of the enterotoxin is difficult. Several methods including counterimmunoelectrophoresis (Naik and Duncan 1977B; Craven *et al.* 1981) and radioimmunoassay (Stelma *et al.* 1983) have been studied with limited success. Stelma *et al.* (1985) developed an enzyme-linked immunosorbent assay (ELISA) for detection of *C. perfringens* enterotoxin directly from the surface of agar medium. This procedure may prove useful for rapid detection of toxigenic strains.

Clostridium perfringens is ubiquitous in nature and is relatively resistant to stress in the spore state. Consequently, control and prevention of the food-borne illness usually depends upon proper handling of food. This involves adequate cooking and rapid cooling if not consumed immediately. Hazard analysis procedures have been developed for control in roast beef preparation (Bryan and McKinley 1979). Educational materials are developed regularly for food handling personnel stressing temperature control—serving food hot or immediately after cooking, holding at >60°C, reheating to at least 60°C, or cooling to <10°C as rapidly as possible (Wagner and Busta 1982). Some processes such as LTLT cooking of beef have a potential to support growth of *C. perfringens* (Willardsen *et al.* 1978); thus appropriate evaluations of these hazards are essential. Thermal inactivation data obtained under simulated cooking conditions (Roy *et al.* 1981) indicated that heat resistance of the cells was dictated by the highest growth temperature they had experienced during the cooking process. These findings coupled with systematic evaluation of the LTLT cooking (Thompson and Busta 1981) should permit adequate evaluation and control of *C. perfringens*.

Chemical control of *C. perfringens* frequently is not considered. It was not treated as a concern in a recent evaluation of alternatives to nitrite (NAS 1982) since it has been only infrequently associated with food-borne illness from cured meat. The response of *C. perfringens* to nitrite is variable. In some cases it is inhibited by nitrite but high concentrations germinate the spores (Ando 1980). The inhibitory levels are above commonly employed concentrations. Reduction of a_w to <0.93, pH to <4.9, or elevation of Eh >+320 mV will also inhibit *C. perfringens* (Murrell 1979).

Clostridium botulinum

Botulism, the rare food-borne intoxication, derives its name originally from its association with sausage (*botulus* in Latin) but in recent years has been associated with meats far less than with other commodities. Nevertheless, the control of *C. botulinum* spores remains extremely visible in the entire field of meat microbiology.

The illness is caused by ingestion of the heat-labile neurotoxin that has been elaborated by vegetative cells of *C. botulinum* (Smith 1977).

Although small amounts of toxin have been observed to be associated with *C. botulinum* spores, the hazard generally develops after viable spores proceed through germination and outgrowth and cell populations proliferate in the meat product. The classic symptoms, which usually begin between 12 and 48 hr after ingestion of the toxin, include blurred vision, diplopia, photophobia, dysphagia, generalized weakness, nausea or vomiting, disphonia and dizziness (CDC 1979). Untreated, the mortality rate can be considerable, e.g., between 1899 and 1949 the mortality rate was greater than 60%. However, the mortality rate has declined significantly with early recognition, antitoxin, and respiratory assistance. In 1981, only one death was observed in the 22 cases reported to CDC (1983B). The requirements for an outbreak include an opportunity for growth and toxin formation by *C. botulinum* and ingestion of the toxic food before proper heating which would inactivate the toxin. An outbreak is usually the result of improper processing, inadequate handling, or consumer abuse. Sakaguchi (1979) has presented a comprehensive treatment on the subject of botulism.

Tompkin (1980) in his outstanding historical review of botulism from meat and poultry products evaluated outbreaks in the United States and Canada, and contrasted the key factors of meat products from these countries with those associated with products from France, Germany, Poland, Denmark, U.K. and ten other countries. He concluded that there is a very real potential for botulism in meat products, and pork historically has been the most frequently implicated. The types of products and processes related to the resistance of *C. botulinum* spores may play a significant role. Products associated with outbreaks such as underprocessed canned meatballs, liver paste, beef stew, abused pot pies, home processed chili, venison jerky, hamburger, sausage, tamales, and stew demonstrate that the spore form of *C. botulinum* constitutes the major hazard.

There are seven serotypes of *C. botulinum* identified as A through G. These are determined by antitoxin protection of mice. Type A, some B, and some F strains are heat resistant and proteolytic; type E, G, some B, and some F are psychrotrophic. To date, types C and D have not been associated with human illnesses but rather affect fowl and cattle (Lynt *et al.* 1982). As Tompkin (1980) has shown, types A and B, and on two occasions F, have been implicated in meat outbreaks. The incidence of outbreaks in Europe is much greater and type B is usually involved. Type A has been observed most frequently in the United States and Canada.

The concentration of *C. botulinum* spores in Canadian products, such as liver sausage or bacon, have been estimated to be from 0.15 to 0.064 spores per kilogram, respectively (Hauschild and Hilsheimer 1980, 1983). These workers noted that this was low compared to surveys in the U.K. (Roberts and Smart 1977) that showed 1–2 spores per kilogram of bacon or to earlier surveys of various semipreserved or raw meats that indicated 0.1 to 1 *C. botulinum* spore per kilogram. The similarity of the observations supports the premise that the frequency of contamination is low, even though the organism is present in soil. The possibility of high populations in rare samples has not been investigated. Hauschild (1982) has used these data to assess statistically botulinal hazards in cured meats and has concluded that the probability of potentially toxic bacon is the lowest probability of the cured meats and that the degree of safety among cured products varies dramatically by several orders of magnitude. This reflects processing, handling, and other factors beyond the level of *C. botulinum* spores.

The requirements for *C. botulinum* growth and toxin production have been reviewed most recently by Sperber (1982). It was noted that toxins generally are produced under the same circumstances that permit growth and that frequently *C. botulinum* growth is measured by determining the presence of toxin. Responses to temperature, Eh, pH, a_w and other environmental conditions exhibited by *C. botulinum* types A, B, and E were cataloged. Generally the conditions that result in control of the organism are of the greatest interest.

Detection of toxin usually is done with classical methodology using intraperitoneal injection of mice (CDC 1979) and observing the specific symptoms of botulism, except in antitoxin-protected mice, or if the sample was boiled. Trypsinization frequently is used to activate the protoxin, especially with nonproteolytic strains or in restrictive environments (Montville 1983). A variety of other methods based on immunological principles have been proposed but none has replaced the sensitive and specific mouse test. Recently, Ferreira *et al.* (1981) described an immunodiffusion technique for type A and Lewis *et al.* (1981) have developed an ELISA method for type G.

Methods for the detection and enumeration of *C. botulinum* spores and cells are numerous and varied and have been reviewed recently by Foegeding (1986). Enrichment procedures utilizing a variety of media are used for detection of low numbers (Kautter and Lynt 1976; ICMSF 1978). Several solid media including blood agar and liver veal-egg yolk agar are suggested for colony counts in the texts on methodology. Recently, Hauschild and Hillsheimer (1977) offered Wynnes agar plus egg yolk as an enumeration medium for *C. botulinum* in meats. Lilly *et al.* (1984) incorporated antibody into *C. botulinum* growth medium, allowing toxigenic isolates to be identified directly by the antigen–antibody precipitation zone surrounding the colonies. Inactivation of vegetative cells can be by heat treatment or with alcohol for heat-sensitive spores. Incubation can be in special systems such as roll or Lee tubes or can be in anaerobic jars or chambers. A major consideration is the environmental stress to which the spores have been exposed that may injure the spores and influence their apparent viability (Foegeding and Busta 1981).

The control of *C. botulinum* spores and cells in meat products is absolutely essential, and nitrite, frequently coupled with heat, has played one of the major roles. Christiansen (1980) has reviewed the numerous factors that influence the inhibition of *C. botulinum* by nitrite, noting that germination of spores is unaffected by nitrite and that many of the environmental factors (pH, temperature, salt, etc.) influence the ultimate inhibition. Although thermal treatments are used to inactivate *C. botulinum* spores and nitrite may influence the effectiveness of the thermal treatment or the recovery of the spores, it does not influence nitrite inhibition. The site of inhibition is in the outgrowth of the spores and may be due to specific iron-binding compounds that could be formed in the meat (Reddy *et al.* 1983; Vahabzadeh *et al.* 1983).

Thermal processes yielding an F_0 value in excess of 2.78 min should control *C. botulinum* spores in canned meats. The addition of nitrite considerably reduces the thermal process for cured meats. This same differential and interaction exists for other environmental factors and nitrite in cured meats. These interactions were extensively reviewed by the Committee on Nitrite and Alternative Curing Agents in Food (NAS 1982) and their effects on *C. botulinum* spores were evaluated.

A comprehensive study of the interactions between sodium chloride, sodium nitrite, sodium nitrate, sodium isoascorbate, polyphosphate, heat treatment, pH level, and storage temperature was summarized by Roberts *et al.* (1981) and a model to predict the probability of toxin production was offered. Interactions among the many controlling factors must be considered in each experimental design and practical application.

Irradiation as a means of control of *C. botulinum* spores has been the focus of extensive study for many years. Recently the substitution of low levels of irradiation of bacon for part or all of the nitrite appears to have promise (Anellis *et al.* 1979; Rowley *et al.* 1983). The freshness of poultry carcasses can be prolonged by irradiation without any apparent increase in the likelihood of a *C. botulinum* type E hazard (Firstenberg-Eden *et al.* 1983). Irradiation preservation of other meat and poultry products is feasible. Kreiger *et al.* (1983) have published an ionizing radiation D value determination method. They published estimates for *C. botulinum* spores in chicken, pork, and ham and a useful compilation of D values obtained from the literature for radiation inactivation of *Clostridium* spores in meat and other products.

Control by reduced temperature is effective against some strains, but cannot be considered a universal solution. Although type A is controlled by 10°C, type E and some type B can grow down to 3.3°C. However, a reduced a_w to 0.97 will control the type E, whereas, 0.94 is necessary to control type A (Sperber 1982). The control by a_w is effective on the cell growth because spores germinate at lower a_w than those inhibitory to growth. The greater inhibitory activity of NaCl over glycerol shows a similar relationship for cells and spores (Baird-Parker and Freame 1967). Furthermore, type E has no significant heat resistance in the spore form.

The addition of acid or reduction of pH is a well-recognized control method for *C. botulinum* and until recently the pH value of 4.6 was considered the maximal inhibitory level (Blocher and Busta 1983). Apparently, binding of the germinant to the initiation site does not occur at low pH; consequently, germination does not take place and the spores are inhibited (Blocher and Busta 1984). Furthermore, many strains cannot grow at these low pH levels. An extensive collection of data had indicated that only with metabiosis could *C. botulinum* grow below pH 4.6. However, recent work by Smelt *et al.* (1982) indicates that acidification of high concentrations of protein may produce environments that permit growth of *C. botulinum* down to pH 4.3 on acidifying with HCl. Although not tested with meat proteins, these observations are extremely significant when considering acidified sauces on meat products.

Controlled atmosphere packaging of foods is gaining increased attention as a food preservation method. *Clostridium botulinum* types A, B, and E can produce toxin in nitrogen-packed hamburger or sausage sandwiches (Kautter *et al.* 1981). Carbon dioxide-containing atmospheres permitted more rapid and extensive germination of *C. botulinum* types A and B spores in laboratory medium than nitrogen or nitrogen plus hydrogen atmosphere without added carbon dioxide (Foegeding and Busta 1983C). Obviously, the selective or stimulatory effect of modified atmosphere storage or new packing techniques (Ito and Bee 1980) of meat and poultry products must be and is being evaluated to assure protection from *C. botulinum* and other anaerobic and microaerophillic microorganisms of spoilage or public health concern.

Changes in production and marketing of meat products have generated concerns about potential botulinal hazards. Cerveny (1980) addressed these concerns in relation to cured meats. Others have also voiced concerns over potential hazards (Holley 1981). The greatest concern was generated by the possibility of drastically reducing or removing nitrite from cured meats. The Committee on Nitrite and Alternative Curing Agents in Food of the National Research Council produced a major document on alternatives to the current use of nitrite in foods (Widdus and Busta 1982). Sofos and Busta (1980) and Pierson and Smoot (1982) also have reviewed the possible alternatives to nitrite, especially as they related to control of botulism.

Several alternatives surfaced as having strong potential. Irradiation was a candidate. Sorbate in combination with reduced nitrite also was a possibility because it acted in concert with nitrite. Sorbate was discussed earlier. Sodium hypophosphite or fumarate esters had antibotulinal activity but had not been tested extensively for consumer use. Acidulation by lactic acid-producing bacteria also was an alternative to control *C. botulinum*.

Although not directly mentioned by the Committee, recent observations on action of various antimicrobials on bacterial spores maybe extremely useful in the near future. A review on this subject by Cook and Pierson (1983) was published recently.

One of the extremely significant results of the Committee's evaluation of nitrite alternatives was the development of long-term strategies (NAS 1982). To prevent problems from *C. botulinum* and other sporeformers, it would be useful to develop an agent that inhibits or inactivates the undesired organisms but has little toxicity toward humans. A target in the microorganism that is unique or very different from humans (e.g., an enzyme or structure) could be identified and specific agents could be devised to attack the target without affecting the human.

Suitable targets for control of *C. botulinum* toxin production might be found in the processes involved in the spore-to-cell transition, since this must take place for toxin production to ultimately occur. This transition, from activation and germination through outgrowth to cellular multiplication, almost certainly involves certain metabolic processes or enzymes that have no equivalents in humans. These unique processes would be ideal targets against which to design specific inhibitors that might serve as alternatives to conventional nitrite use in foods.

These strategies are valid and useful not only for alternatives for nitrite or *C. botulinum* but for control of any sporeformer.

Other Clostridia

The presence of spores or cells of other clostridia in raw or processed meats would be anticipated considering the many opportunities for contamination by soil and water. Ingram and Dainty (1971) indicated that in addition to *C. perfringens*, other clostridia including *Clostridium oedematiens*, *Clostridium bifermentans*, *Clostridium histolyticum*, and *Clostridium sporogenes* appear in raw meat spoilage under warm conditions. Their metabolic activities produce end products that make spoilage obvious. With the exception of *Clostridium putrefaciens*, most putrefactive clostridia do not normally develop in cured meats. Presumably this is associated with the presence of nitrite but the mechanism is far from clear. Rosset (1982) adds little to this assessment and does not indicate any special involvement of clostridia in vacuum-packaged meats. Noting that clostridia may be inoculated into meat products with additives such as spices, Ingram and Simonsen (1980) also treat clostridial spores other than the pathogens as routine spoilage hazards with moderate potential as problems. The impact of psychrotrophic or thermophilic species or strains of clostridia under raw handling or processing situations such as controlled-atmosphere storage remains to be determined.

SUMMARY

The ability of *Bacillus* and *Clostridium* species to cause spoilage and public health problems in meat and other food products frequently is a result of their ability to form resistant spores which survive processing and control procedures. Generally it is the metabolic capabilities of these microorganisms which ultimately are responsible for the adverse effect in food. Features unique to the bacterial spore have been summarized briefly as background for evaluation of current data on preservatives and other control procedures which have roles in meat preservation or meat plant sanitation and have antimicrobial properties against sporeforming bacteria.

The occurrence, detection, and control of the pathogens *B. cereus, C. perfringens,* and *C. botulinum* in meat products have been reviewed in light of the recent advances in our knowledge of the association and/or control of these sporeforming bacteria relative to meat products. Other *Bacillus* species are thought to be of minimal or unrecognized significance in meat. Other species of the genus *Clostridium* are considered only moderate potential spoilage hazards which are detected easily due to their odorous metabolic end products. To the best of our knowledge, this latter group of microorganisms has not been the subject of recent advances in meat microbiology. Undoubtedly, improved understanding of bacterial spore physiology and biochemistry will contribute substantially to our knowledge and ability to control sporeforming bacteria in meat and other food products. Research efforts are needed in this area.

REFERENCES

ANDO, Y. 1980. Mechanism of nitrite-induced germination of *Clostridium perfringens* spores. J. Appl. Bacteriol. *49,* 527.

ANELLIS, A., ROWLEY, D. B. and ROSS, E. W., JR. 1979. Microbiological safety of radappertized beef. J. Food Prot. *42,* 927.

BAIRD-PARKER, A. C. and FREAME, B. 1967. Combined effect of water activity, pH and temperature on the growth of *Clostridium botulinum* from spore and cell inocula. J. Appl. Bacteriol. *30,* 420.

BAUER, F. T., CARPENTER, J. A., and REAGAN, J. O. 1981. Prevalence of *Clostridium perfringens* in pork during processing. J. Food Prot. *44,* 279.

BAYLISS, C. E., WAITES, W. M. and KING, N. R. 1981. Resistance and structure of spores of *Bacillus subtilis.* J. Appl. Bacteriol. *50,* 379.

BELL, R. G. 1983. The effect of variation of thermal processing on the microbial spoilage of chub-packed luncheon meat. J. Appl. Bacteriol. *54,* 249.

BERNLOHR, R. W. and LEITZMAN, C. 1969. Control of sporulation. *In* The Bacterial Spore. Chapter 6, p. 183. G. W. Gould and A. Hurst (Editors). Academic Press, London.

BLOCHER, J. C. and BUSTA, F. F. 1982. Constitutents of media for recovery of sporeformers from foods. Arch. Lebensmittelhyg. *33,* 138.

BLOCHER, J. C. and BUSTA, F. F. 1983. Bacterial spore resistance to acid. Food Technol. *37(11),* 87.

BLOCHER, J. C. and BUSTA, F. F. 1984. Mechanisms of acid inhibition of bacterial spores. Abstr. Ann. Mtg. Am. Soc. Microbiol., p. 136.

BOSCHWITZ, H., MILNER, Y., KEYNAN, A., HALVORSON, H. O. and TROLL, W. 1983. Effect of inhibitors of trypsin-like proteolytic enzymes on *Bacillus cereus* T spore germination. J. Bacteriol. *153,* 700.

BRYAN, F. L. and MCKINLEY, T. W.   1979.   Hazard analysis and control of roast beef preparation in foodservice establishments. J. Food Prot. *42*, 4.
BUSTA, F. F.   1982.   Combined effects of sorbate and other inhibitory factors in cured meat products. Food Technol. Austral. *34*, 529.
BUSTA, F. F. and ORDAL, Z. J.   1964A.   Heat-activation kinetics of endospores of *Bacillus subtilis*. J. Food Sci. *29*, 345.
BUSTA, F. F. and ORDAL, Z. J.   1964B.   Lack of influence of suspending media on heat activation of *Bacillus subtilis* spores and absence of deactivation. Appl. Microbiol. *12*, 111.
CENTER FOR DISEASE CONTROL.   1979.   Botulism in the United States, 1899–1977. Handbook for Epidemiologists, Clinicians, and Laboratory Workers. USDHHS, PHS, CDC. Atlanta, GA.
CENTERS FOR DISEASE CONTROL.   1983A.   Foodborne Disease Outbreaks, Annual Summary 1980, Issued February 1983. HHS Publication No. (CDC) 83-8185. USDHHS, PHS, CDC. Atlanta, GA.
CENTERS FOR DISEASE CONTROL.   1983B.   Foodborne Disease Outbreaks, Annual Summary 1981, Issued June 1983. HHS Publication No. (CDC) 83-8186. USDHHS, PHS, CDC. Atlanta, GA.
CERVENY. J. G.   1980.   Effects of changes in the production and marketing of cured meats on the risk of botulism. Food Technol. *34(5)*, 240.
CHRISTIANSEN, L. N.   1980.   Factors influencing botulinal inhibition by nitrite. Food Technol. *34(5)*, 237.
CHURCH, B. D. and HALVORSON, H.   1959.   Dependence of heat resistance of bacterial endospores on their dipicolinic acid content. Nature (London) *183*, 124.
COOK, F. K. and PIERSON, M. D.   1983.   Inhibition of bacterial spores by antimicrobials. Food Technol. *37(11)*, 115.
CRAVEN, S. E.   1980.   Growth and sporulation of *Clostridium perfringens* in foods. Food Technol. *34(4)*, 80.
CRAVEN, S. E., BLANKENSHIP, L. C. and McDONEL, J. L.   1981.   Relationship of sporulation, enterotoxin formation, and spoilage during growth of *Clostridium perfringens* Type A in cooked chicken. Appl. Environ. Microbiol. *41*, 1184.
DOI, R. H.   1969.   Changes in nucleic acids during sporulation. *In* The Bacterial Spore. Chapter 4, p. 125. G. W. Gould and A. Hurst (Editors). Academic Press, London.
DUNCAN, C. L. and HARMON, S. M.   1976.   *Clostridium perfringens. In* Compendium of Methods for the Microbiological Examination of Foods. Chapter 35, p. 437. M. L. Speck (Editor). American Public Health Association, Washington, D.C.
ELLAR, D. J.   1978.   Spore specific structures and their function. Symp. Soc. Gen. Microbiol. *28*, 295.
ELLAR, D. J. and LUNDGREN, D. G.   1966.   Fine structure of sporulation of *Bacillus cereus* grown in a chemically defined medium. J. Bacteriol. *92*, 1748.
FERREIRA, J. L., HAMBY, M. K., ZAPATKA, F. A. and HEBERT, W. O.   1981.   Immunodiffusion method for detection of type A *Clostridium botulinum*. Appl. Environ. Microbiol. *42*, 1057.
FIRSTENBERG-EDEN, R., ROWLEY, D. B., and SHATTUCK, G. E.   1983.   Competitive growth of chicken skin microflora and *Clostridium botulinum* Type E after an irradiation dose of 0.3 Mrad. J. Food Prot. *46*, 12.
FOEGEDING, P. M.   1986.   Detection and quantitation of sporeforming pathogens and their toxins. *In* Proceedings of the 1985 IFT-IUFOST Basic Symposium, Food Microorganisms and Their Toxins—Developing Methodology. M. D. Pierson and N. J. Stern (Editors). Marcel Dekker Inc., NY.
FOEGEDING, P. M. and BUSTA, F. F.   1980.   *Clostridium perfringens* cells and phospholipase C activity at constant and linearly rising temperatures. J. Food Sci. *45*, 918.
FOEGEDING, P. M. and BUSTA, F. F.   1981.   Bacterial spore injury–an update. J. Food Prot. *44*, 776.
FOEGEDING, P. M. and BUSTA, F. F.   1983A.   Hypochlorite injury of *Clostridium botulinum* spores alters germination response. Appl. Environ. Microbiol. *45*, 1360.

FOEGEDING, P. M. and BUSTA, F. F.   1983B.   Proposed mechanism for sensitization by hypochlorite treatment of *Clostridium botulinum* spores. Appl. Environ. Microbiol. *45*, 1374.
FOEGEDING, P. M. and BUSTA, F. F.   1983C.   Effect of carbon dioxide, nitrogen and hydrogen gases on germination of *Clostridium botulinum* spores. J. Food Prot. *46*, 987.
FREESE, E.   1981.   Initiation of bacterial sporulation. *In* Sporulation and Germination. p. 1. H. S. Levinson, A. L. Sonenshein, and D. J. Tipper (Editors). American Society for Microbiology, Washington, D.C.
FRIEBEN, W. R. and DUNCAN, C. L.   1973.   Homology between enterotoxin protein and spore structural protein in *Clostridium perfringens*. Eur. J. Biochem. *39*, 393.
GILBERT, R. J.   1979.   *Bacillus cereus* gasteroenteritis. *In* Food-Borne Infections and Intoxications. 2nd edition. Chapter 10, p. 495. H. Riemann and F. L. Bryan (Editors). Academic Press, NY.
GILBERT, R. J.. TURNBULL, P. C. B., PARRY, J. M. and KRAMER, J. M.   1981.   *Bacillus cereus* and other *Bacillus* species: Their part in food poisoning and other clinical infections. *In* The Aerobic Endospore-forming Bacteria: Classification and Identification. p. 297. R. C. W. Berkeley and M. Goodfellow (Editors). Academic Press, London.
GILL, C. O.   1983.   Meat spoilage and evaluation of the potential storage life of fresh meat. J. Food Prot. *46*, 444.
GOEPFERT, J. M.   1976.   *Bacillus cereus. In* Compendium of Methods for the Microbiological Examination of Foods. p. 417. M. L. Speck (Editor). American Public Health Association, Washington, D.C.
GOMBAS, D. E. and LABBE, R. G.   1981.   Extraction of spore-lytic enzyme from *Clostridium perfringens* spores. J. Gen. Microbiol. *126*, 37.
GOULD, G. W.   1969.   Germination. *In* The Bacterial Spore. Chapter 11, p. 397. G. W. Gould and A. Hurst (Editors). Academic Press, London.
GOULD, G. W.   1970.   Germination and the problem of dormancy. J. Appl. Bacteriol. *33*, 34.
GOULD, G. W. and DRING, G. J.   1972.   Biochemical mechanisms of spore germination. *In* Spores V. p. 401. H. O. Halvorson, R. Hansen, and L. L. Campbell (Editors). American Society for Microbiology, Washington, D.C.
GOULD, G. W. and SALE, J. H.   1970.   Initiation of germination of bacterial spores by hydrostatic pressure. J. Gen. Microbiol. *60*, 347.
HALVORSON, H. O. and SWANSON, A.   1969.   Role of dipicolinic acid in the physiology of bacterial spores. *In* Spores IV. p. 121. L. L. Campbell (Editor). American Society for Microbiology, Bethesda, MD.
HALVORSON, H. O., VARY, J. C. and STEINBERG, W.   1966.   Developmental changes during the formation and breaking of the dormant state in bacteria. Ann. Rev. Microbiol. *20*, 169.
HARMON. S. M. and KAUTTER, D. A.   1976.   Estimating population levels of *Clostridium perfringens* in foods based on alpha toxin. J. Milk Food Technol. *39*, 107.
HARMON, S. M., KAUTTER, D. A. and McCLURE, F. D.   1984.   Comparison of selective plating media for enumeration of *Bacillus cereus* in foods. J. Food Prot. *47*, 65.
HAUSCHILD, A. H. W.   1982.   Assessment of botulism hazards from cured meat products. Food Technol. *36(12)*, 95.
HAUSCHILD, A. H. W. and HILSHEIMER, R.   1977.   Enumeration of *Clostridium botulinum* spores in meats by a pour-plate procedure. Canad. J. Microbiol. *23*, 829.
HAUSCHILD, A. H. W. and HILSHEIMER, R.   1980.   Incidence of *Clostridium botulinum* in commercial bacon. J. Food Prot. *43*, 564.
HAUSCHILD, A. H. W. and HILSHEIMER, R.   1983.   Prevalence of *Clostridium botulinum* in commercial liver sausage. J. Food Prot. *46*, 242.
HOBBS, B. C.   1979.   *Clostridium perfringens* gasteroenteritis. *In* Food-Borne Infections and Intoxications. 2nd edition. Chapter 3, p. 131. H. Riemann and F. L. Bryan (Editors). Academic Press, NY.

HODGES, N. A., MELLING, J. and PARKER, S. J. 1980. Comparison of chemically defined and complex media for the production of *Bacillus subtilis* spores having reproducible resistance and germination characteristics. J. Pharm. Pharmacol. *32*, 126.
HOLLEY, R. A. 1981. Review of the potential hazard from botulism in cured meats. Canad. Inst. Food Sci. Technol. J. *14*, 183.
INGRAM, M. and DAINTY, R. H. 1971. Changes caused by microbes in spoilage of meats. J. Appl. Bacteriol. *34*, 21.
INGRAM, M. and SIMONSEN, B. 1980. Meats and meat products. *In* Microbial Ecology of Foods. Vol. 2. Food Commodities. Chapter 15. ICMSF. Academic Press, NY.
INTERNATIONAL COMMISSION ON MICROBIOLOGICAL SPECIFICATIONS FOR FOODS. 1978. Microorganisms in Foods. I. Their Significance and Methods of Enumeration. 2nd edition. p. 257. University of Toronto Press, Toronto, Canada.
ITO, K. 1981. Thermophilic organisms in food spoilage: Flat-sour aerobes. J. Food Prot. *44*, 157.
ITO, K. A. and BEE, G. R. 1980. Microbiological hazards associated with new packaging techniques. Food Technol. *34(10)*, 78.
JOHNSON, K. M. 1984. *Bacillus cereus* foodborne illness—An update. J. Food Prot. *47*, 145.
JOHNSON, K. M. and BUSTA, F. F. 1984. Detection and enumeration of injured bacterial spores in processed foods. *In* The Revival of Injured Microbes. p. 241. A. D. Russell and M. H. E. Andrews (Editors). Academic Press, London.
JOHNSON, K. M., NELSON, C. L. and BUSTA, F. F. 1982. Germination and heat resistance of *Bacillus cereus* spores from strains associated with diarrheal and emetic food-borne illnesses. J.Food Sci. *47*, 1268.
JOHNSON, K. M., NELSON, C. L. and BUSTA, F. F. 1983. Influence of temperature on germination and growth of spores of emetic and diarrheal strains of *Bacillus cereus* in a broth medium and in rice. J. Food Sci. *48*, 286.
KAUTTER, D. A. and LYNT, R. K. 1976. *Clostridium botulinum. In* Compendium of Methods for the Microbiological Examination of Foods. Chapter 34, p. 424. M. L. Speck (Editor). American Public Health Association, Washington, D.C.
KAUTTER, D. A., LYNT, R. K., LILLY, T., JR. and SOLOMON, H. M. 1981. Evaluation of the botulism hazard from nitrogen-packed sandwiches. J. Food Prot. *44*, 59.
KEYNAN, A. 1978. Spore structure and its relations to resistance, dormancy, and germination. *In* Spores VII. p. 43. G. Chambliss and J. C. Vary (Editors). American Society for Microbiology, Washington, D.C.
KEYNAN, A. and EVENCHIK, Z. 1969. Activation. *In* The Bacterial Spore. Chapter 10, p. 359. G. W. Gould and A. Hurst (Editors). Academic Press, London.
KEYNAN, A., EVENCHIK, Z., HALVORSON, H. O. and HASTINGS, J. W. 1964. Activation of bacterial endospores. J. Bacteriol. *88*, 313.
KRAMER, J. M., TURNBULL, P. C. B., MUNSHI, G. and GILBERT, R. J. 1982. Identification and characterization of *Bacillus cereus* and other *Bacillus* species associated with foods and food poisoning. *In* Isolation and Identification Methods for Food Poisoning Organisms. p. 261. J. E. L. Corry, D. Roberts, and F. A. Skinner (Editors). Academic Press, London.
KREIGER, R. A., SNYDER, O. P. and PFLUG, I. J. 1983. *Clostridium botulinum* ionizing radiation D-value determination using a micro food sample system. J. Food Sci. *48*, 141.
LABBE, R. G. 1980. Relationship between sporulation and enterotoxin production in *Clostridium perfringens* Type A. Food Technol. *34(4)*, 88.
LABBE, R. G. 1983. Enumeration and confirmation of *Clostridium perfringens*. J. Food Prot. *46*, 68.
LABBE, R. G. and NORRIS, K. E. 1982. Evaluation of planting media for recovery of heated *Clostridium perfringens* spores. J. Food Prot. *45*, 686.
LABBE, R. G. and REY, D. K. 1979. Raffinose increases sporulation and enterotoxin production by *Clostridium perfringens* type A. Appl. Environ. Microbiol. *37*, 1196.

LABBE, R. G. and RUFNER, R. 1980. Ultrastructure of sporulating cells of *Clostridium perfringens* type A grown in the presence of raffinose. Canad. J. Microbiol. *26*, 1153.

LEVINSON, H. S. and FEEHERRY, F. E. 1978. Kinetics of heat activation of spores of *Clostridium perfringens*. In Spores VII. p. 34. G. Chambliss and J. C. Vary (Editors). American Society for Microbiology, Washington, D.C.

LEVINSON, H. S. and HYATT, M. T. 1966. Sequence of events during *Bacillus megaterium* spore germination. J. Bacteriol. *91*, 1811.

LEWIS, G. E., JR., KULINSKI, S. S., REICHARD, D. W. and METZGER, J. F. 1981. Detection of *Clostridium botulinum* type G toxin by enzyme-linked immunosorbent assay. Appl. Environ. Microbiol. *42*, 1018.

LILLY, T., JR., KAUTTER, D. A., LYNT, R. K. and SOLOMON, H. M. 1984. Immunodiffusion detection of *Clostridium botulinum* colonies. J. Food Prot. *47*, 868.

LOFFLER, A. and LABBE, R. G. 1983. Intracellular proteases during sporulation and enterotoxin formation by *Clostridium perfringens* type A. Current Microbiol. *8*, 187.

LYNT, R. K., KAUTTER, D. A. and SOLOMON, H. M. 1982. Differences and similarities among proteolytic and nonproteolytic strains of *Clostridium botulinum* types A, B, E and F: A review. J. Food Prot. *45*, 466.

MACKEY, B. M. and MORRIS, J. G. 1972. Calcium dipicolinate - provoked germination and outgrowth of spores of *Clostridium pasteurianum*. J. Gen. Microbiol. *73*, 315.

MCDONEL, J. J. 1980. Mechanism of action of *Clostridium perfringens* enterotoxin. Food Technol. *34(4)*, 91.

MONTVILLE, T. J. 1981. Effect of plating medium on heat activation requirement of *Clostridium botulinum* spores. Appl. Environ. Microbiol. *42*, 734.

MONTVILLE, T. J. 1983. Dependence on *Clostridium botulinum* gas and protease production on culture conditions. Appl. Environ. Microbiol. *45*, 571.

MORITA, T. N. and WOODBURN, M. J. 1977.Stimulation of *Bacillus cereus* growth by protein in cooked rice combinations. J. Food Sci. *42*, 1232.

MURRELL, W. G. 1969. Chemical composition of spores and spore structures. In The Bacterial Spore. Chapter 7, p. 215. G. W. Gould and A. Hurst (Editors). Academic Press, London.

MURRELL, W. G. 1979. *Clostridium perfringens*. In Food-Borne Microorganisms of Public Health Significance. 3rd edition. Vol. I, Chapter 12, p. 12.1. K. A. Buckle, G. R. Davey, M. J. Eyles, G. H. Fleet, and W. G. Murrell (Editors). The University of New South Wales, Kensington, NSW, Australia.

MURRELL, W. G. 1981. Biophysical studies on the molecular mechanisms of spore heat resistance and dormancy. In Sporulation and Germination. p. 64. H. S. Levinson, A. L. Sonenshein, D. J. Tipper (Editors). American Society for Microbiology, Washington, D.C.

NAIK, H. S. and DUNCAN, C. L. 1977A. Enterotoxin formation in foods by *Clostridium perfringens* type A. J. Food Safety *1*, 7.

NAIK, H. S. and DUNCAN, C. L. 1977B. Rapid detection and quantification of *Clostridium perfringens* enterotoxin by counterimmunoelectrophoresis. Appl. Environ. Microbiol. *34*, 125.

NAS. 1982. Alternatives to the Current Use of Nitrite in Foods. Natl. Acad. of Sciences, Natl. Acad. Press, Washington, D.C.

NELSON, K. A., BUSTA, F. F., SOFOS, J. N. and WAGNER, M. K. 1983. Effect of polyphosphates in combination with nitrite-sorbate or sorbate on *Clostridium botulinum* growth and toxin production in chicken frankfurter emulsions. J. Food Prot. *46*, 846.

PIERSON, M. D. and SMOOT, L. A. 1982. Nitrite, nitrite alternatives, and the control of *Clostridium botulinum* in cured meats. CRC Crit. Rev. Food Sci. Nutr. *17*, 141.

RAEVUORI, M. and GENIGEORGIS, C. 1975. Effect of pH and sodium chloride on growth of *Bacillus cereus* in laboratory media and certain foods. Appl. Microbiol. *29*, 68.
REDDY, D., LANCASTER, J. R., JR. and CORNFORTH, D. P. 1983. Nitrite inhibition of *Clostridium botulinum:* Electron spin resonance detection of iron–nitric oxide complexes. Science *221*, 769.
ROBERTS, T. A., GIBSON, A. M., and ROBINSON, A. 1981. Prediction of toxin production by *Clostridium botulinum* in pasteurized pork slurry. J. Food Technol. *16*, 337.
ROBERTS, T. A. and INGRAM, M. 1967. The effect of sporulation medium on heat activation of spores of *Clostridium botulinum* type B. *In* Botulism 1966. p. 169. M. Ingram and T. A. Roberts (Editors). Chapman and Hall, Ltd., London.
ROBERTS, T. A. and SMART, J. L. 1977. The occurrence of clostridia, particularly *Clostridium botulinum,* in bacon and pork. *In* Spore Research 1976 II. p. 911. A. N. Barker, J. Wolf, D. J. Ellar, G. J. Dring, and G. W. Gould (Editors). Academic Press, NY.
ROSSET, R. 1982. Chilling, freezing and thawing. *In* Meat Microbiology. p. 265. M. H. Brown (Editor). Applied Science Publishers, NY.
ROWLEY, D. B., FIRSTENBERG-EDEN, R., POWERS, E. M., SHATTUCK, G. E., WASSERMAN, A. E. and WIERBICKI, E. 1983. Effect of irradiation on the inhibition of *Clostridium botulinum* toxin production and the microbial flora in bacon. J. Food Sci. *48*, 1016.
ROY, R. J., BUSTA, F. F., and THOMPSON, D. R. 1981. Thermal inactivation of *Clostridium perfringens* after growth at several constant and linearly rising temperatures. J. Food Sci. *46*, 1586.
RUSSELL, A. D. 1982. The Destruction of Bacterial Spores. 333 pp. Academic Press, London.
SADOFF, H. L. 1969 Spore Enzymes. *In* The Bacterial Spore. Chapter 8, p. 275. G. W. Gould and A. Hurst (Editors). Academic Press, London.
SAKAGUCHI, G. 1979. Botulism. *In* Food-Borne Infections and Intoxications. 2nd edition, p. 389. H. Riemann and F. L. Bryan (Editors). Academic Press, NY.
SCHEUSNER, D. L., BUSTA, F. F. and SPECK, M. L. 1971. Injury of bacteria by sanitizers. Appl. Microbiol. *21*, 41.
SETLOW, P. 1974. Polyamine levels during growth, sporulation and spore germination of *Bacillus megaterium.* J. Bacteriol. *117*, 1171.
SETLOW, P. 1975A. Energy and small-molecule metabolism during germination of *Bacillus* spores. *In* Spores VI. p. 443. P. Gerhardt, R. N. Costilow, and H. L. Sadoff (Editors). American Society for Microbiology, Washington, D.C.
SETLOW, P. 1975B. Identification and localization of the major proteins degraded during germination of *Bacillus megaterium* spores. J. Biol. Chem. *250*, 8159.
SETLOW, P. 1981. Biochemistry of bacterial forespore development and spore germination. *In* Sporulation and Germination. p. 13. H. S. Levinson, A. L. Sonenshein, and D. J. Tipper (Editors). American Society for Microbiology, Washington, D.C.
SETLOW, P. and PRIMUS, G. 1975. Protein degradation and amino acid metabolism during germination of *Bacillus megaterium* spores. *In* Spores VI. p. 451. P. Gerhardt, R. N. Costilow, and H. L. Sadoff (Editors). American Society for Microbiology, Washington, D.C.
SEWARD, R. A., DEIBEL, R. H. and LINDSAY, R. C. 1982. Effects of potassium sorbate and other antibotulinal agents on germination and outgrowth of *Clostridium botulinum* type E spores in microcultures. Appl. Environ. Microbiol. *44*, 1212.
SHANDERA, W. X., TACKET, C. O. and BLAKE, P. A. 1983. Food poisoning due to *Clostridium perfringens* in the United States. J. Infect. Dis. *147*, 167.
SMART, J. L., ROBERTS, T. A., STRINGER, M. F. and SHAH, N. 1979. The incidence and serotypes of *Clostridium perfringens* on beef, pork, and lamb carcasses. J. Appl. Bacteriol. *46*, 377.
SMELT, J. P. P. M., RAATJES, G. J. M., CROWTHER, J. S. and VERRIPS, C.

T. 1982. Growth and toxin formation by *Clostridium botulinum* at low pH values. J. Appl. Bacteriol. *52*, 75.

SMITH, L. DS. 1977. Botulism. The Organism, Its Toxins, the Disease. Charles C. Thomas, Springfield, IL.

SMITH, L. B., BUSTA, F. F. and ALLEN, C. E. 1980. Effect of rising temperatures on growth and survival of *Clostridium perfringens* indigenous to raw beef. J. Food Prot. *43*, 520.

SMOOT, L. A. and PIERSON, M. D. 1979. Effect of oxidation-reduction potential on the outgrowth and chemical inhibition of *Clostridium botulinum* 10755A spores. J. Food Sci. *44*, 700.

SMOOT, L. A. and PIERSON, M. D. 1981. Mechanism of sorbate inhibition of *Bacillus cereus* T and *Clostridium botulinum* 62A spore germination. Appl. Environ. Microbiol. *42*, 477.

SOFOS, J. N. and BUSTA, F. F. 1980. Alternatives to the use of nitrite as an antibotulinal agent. Food Technol. *34(5)*, 244.

SOFOS, J. N. and BUSTA, F. F. 1981. Antimicrobial activity of sorbate. J. Food Prot. *44*, 614.

SOFOS, J. N. and BUSTA, F. F. 1983. Sorbates. *In* Antimicrobials in Foods. p. 141. A. L. Branen and P. M. Davidson (Editors). Marcel Dekker, Inc., NY.

SOFOS, J. N., BUSTA, F. F. and ALLEN, C. E. 1979A. Botulism control by nitrite and sorbate in cured meats: A review. J. Food Prot. *42*, 739.

SOFOS, J. N., BUSTA, F. F. and ALLEN, C. E. 1979B. Sodium nitrite and sorbic acid effects on *Clostridium botulinum* spore germination and total microbial growth in chicken frankfurter emulsions during temperature abuse. Appl. Environ. Microbiol. *37*, 1103.

SPERBER, W. H. 1982. Requirements of *Clostridium botulinum* for growth and toxin production. Food Technol. *36(12)*, 89.

STELMA, G. N., JR., JOHNSON, C. H. and SHAH, D. B. 1985. Detection of enterotoxin in colonies of *Clostridium perfringens* by a solid phase enzyme-linked immunosorbent assay. J. Food Prot. *48*, 227.

STELMA, G. N., JR., WIMSATT, J. C., KAUFFMAN, P. E. and SHAH, D. B. 1983. Radioimmunoassay for *Clostridium perfringens* enterotoxin and its use in screening isolates implicated in food-poisoning outbreaks. J. Food Prot. *46*, 1069.

STILES, M. E. and NG, L.-K. 1979. Fate of pathogens inoculated into vacuum-packaged sliced hams to simulate contamination during packaging. J. Food Prot. *42*, 464.

STRANGE, R. E. and HUNTER, J. R. 1969. Outgrowth and synthesis of macromolecules. *In* The Bacterial Spore. p. 445. G. W. Gould and A. Hurst (Editors). Academic Press, London.

SUGIYAMA, H. 1951. Studies on factors affecting heat resistance of spores of *Clostridium botulinum*. J. Bacteriol. *62*, 81.

THOMPSON, D. R. and BUSTA, F. F. 1981. Modeling microbial populations during meat cooking and cooling. Trans. American Society of Agricultural Engineers *24*, 1644.

THOMPSON, D. R., WILLARDSEN, R. R., BUSTA, F. F. and ALLEN, C. E. 1979. *Clostridium perfringens* population dynamics during constant and rising temperatures in beef. J. Food Sci. *44*, 646.

TOMPKIN, R. B. 1980. Botulism from meat and poultry products - A historical perspective. Food Technol. *34(5)*, 229.

TOMPKIN, R. B., CHRISTIANSEN, L. N. and SHAPARIS, A. B. 1978. Causes of variation in botulinal inhibition in perishable canned cured meat. Appl. Environ. Microbiol. *35*, 886.

UEHARA, M. and FRANK, H. A. 1967. Sequence of events during germination of putrefactive anaerobe 3679 spores. J. Bacteriol. *94*, 506.

VAHABZADEH, F., COLLINGE, S. K., CORNFORTH, D. P., MAHONEY, A. W. and

POST, F. J.   1983.   Evaluation of iron binding compounds as inhibitors of gas and toxin production by *Clostridium botulinum* in ground pork. J. Food Sci. *48*, 1445.

VINTER, V.   1969.   Physiology and biochemistry of sporulation. *In* The Bacterial Spore. Chapter 3, p. 73. G. W. Gould and A. Hurst (Editors). Academic Press, London.

WAGNER, M. K. and BUSTA, F. F.   1982.   *Clostridium perfringens* foodborne illness. *In* Microbiological Safety of Foods in Feeding Systems. p. 32. ABMPS Report No. 125. National Academy Press, Washington, D.C.

WAGNER, M. K. and BUSTA, F. F.   1983.   Effect of sodium acid pyrophosphate in combination with sodium nitrite or sodium nitrite/potassium sorbate on *Clostridium botulinum* growth and toxin production in beef/pork frankfurter emulsions. J. Food Sci. *48*, 990.

WAGNER, M. K. and BUSTA, F. F.   1984.   Effect of sodium acid pyrophosphate, sodium chloride, and/or potassium sorbate on *Clostridium botulinum* spore germination and outgrowth. Abstr. Ann. Mtg. Am. Soc. Microbiol., p. 202.

WAITES, W. M., BAYLISS, C. E. and KING, N. R.   1980.   The effect of sporulation medium on spores of *Clostridium bifermentans*. J. Gen. Microbiol. *116*, 271.

WAITES, W. M., STANSFIELD, R. and BAYLISS, C. E.   1979.   The effect of sporulation medium on the structure and heat resistance of spores of *Clostridium bifermentans*. FEMS Microbiol. Lett. *5*, 365.

WALKER, H. W.   1975.   Food-borne illness from *Clostridium perfringens*. CRC Crit. Rev. Food Sci. Nutr. *7*, 71.

WARTH, A. D.   1978.   Molecular structure of the bacterial spore. Advan. Microbial Physiol. *17*, 1.

WATT, I.C.   1981.   Water vapor adsorption by *Bacillus stearothermophilus* endospores. *In* Sporulation and Germination. p. 253. H. S. Levinson, A. L. Sonenshein, and D. J. Tipper (Editors). American Society for Microbiology, Washington, D.C.

WIDDUS, R. and BUSTA, F. F.   1982.   Antibotulinal alternatives to the current use of nitrite in foods. Food Technol. *36(12)*, 105.

WILLARDSEN, R. R., BUSTA, F. F., ALLEN, C. E. and SMITH, L. B.   1978.   Growth and survival of *Clostridium perfringens* during constantly rising temperatures. J. Food Sci. *43*, 470.

WOODS, L. F. J. and WOOD, J. M.   1982.   A note on the effect of nitrite inhibition on the metabolism of *Clostridium botulinum*. J. Appl. Bacteriol. *52*, 109.

WOODS, L. F. J., WOOD, J. M. and GIBBS, P. A.   1981.   The involvement of nitric oxide in the inhibition of the phosphoroclastic system in *Clostridium sporogenes* by sodium nitrite. J. Gen. Microbiol. *125*, 399.

Psychrotrophic Organisms

A. A. Kraft[1]

TYPES OF ORGANISMS

Psychotrophic organisms grow at low temperatures, such as 0°C, although their optimum growth temperatures may be 10°–30°C higher (Eddy 1960). Minimum growth temperatures are important in preservation of meats and poultry, but it should be emphasized that low temperature-tolerant organisms prefer higher growth temperatures. Nevertheless, microbial activity from psychrotrophs may occur at refrigeration temperatures, with ultimate spoilage, or in unusual cases, with the possibility of food-borne disease.

Although gram-negative rods may commonly cause spoilage at low temperatures, only a few different genera are significant. *Pseudomonas* species are among the most common spoilage types (Splittstoesser 1976). Formerly *Achromobacter* (now no longer recognized in Bergey's "Manual of Determinative Bacteriology," 8th edition), *Flavobacterium,* and *Alcaligenes* have been commonly involved as causative agents of meat spoilage. *Pseudomonas* generally predominates under aerobic conditions. Olson and Nottingham (1980) listed 27 genera of bacteria that include psychrotrophs, such as *Acinetobacter* and *Moraxella* (which may be consid-

[1]Department of Food Technology, Iowa State University, Ames, IA 50011.

Advances in Meat Research, Volume 2
Copyright 1986 by AVI Publishing Co.
All rights of reproduction in any form reserved
ISBN 0-87055-498-0

ered as a group comprising part of the aerobic spoilage organisms), *Aeromonas,* and others of varying significance, in addition to the genera specified above. *Alteromonas putrefaciens,* formerly *Pseudomonas putrefaciens,* although not strictly aerobic, and differing in its DNA base composition, is also a spoilage type of psychrotroph. *Corynebacterium, Microbacterium, Brochothrix thermosphacta, Arthrobacter,* and members of the Enterobacteriaceae, *Lactobacillus,* gram-positive spore formers, and others are psychrotrophs that are recognized as meat microorganisms. Their importance depends to a large extent on environmental conditions, such as those imposed by packaging materials and methods, pH, salt concentration (which also involves water activity), oxygen tension, and inhibition by competing organisms.

A numerical taxonomy study of 110 pseudomonads isolated from meat was performed by Shaw and Latty (1981) in "an attempt to determine the relationship with species listed in Bergey's Manual (8th edition) and to establish how many different types of pseudomonads are present on meat." They compared their isolates with many reference strains which included not only *Pseudomonas* species, but also *Aeromonas, Serratia, Hafnia,* and *Enterobacter.* One of the principal observations made was that the pseudomonads found on meat differed from those described in Bergey's Manual. Most of the isolates did not produce fluorescent pigment, a finding similar to that of previous investigators, and they also consisted of a low incidence of strains producing extracellular enzymes. While the information obtained was stated to be of value in identifying meat spoilage bacteria, it was not surprising that the organisms did not resemble those described in Bergey's Manual.

The work of Lahellec and Colin (1981) is important in that they emphasized that environmental conditions imposed by processing and storage are liable to influence the properties of the psychrotrophic flora of poultry, particularly for *Pseudomonas* strains. Changes in characteristics in relation to problems of classification will be discussed in more detail later.

As indicated by Olson and Nottingham (1980), psychrotrophs include almost all kinds of microorganisms, i.e., gram-positive and gram negative bacteria, aerobes and anaerobes, spore formers and nonspore formers, and motile and nonmotile organisms. In addition to bacteria, psychrotrophic yeasts and molds also are found on foods. Yeasts include members of the genera *Candida, Torulopsis, Cryptococcus,* and *Rhodotorula;* mold species include members of the genera *Penicillium, Aspergillus, Cladosporium,* and *Trichothecium.* The reader is referred to Chapter 2 of this book for details on the physiology of psychrotrophic bacteria; the prevalence of these organisms on meats and poultry will be described later.

According to Walker (1977), yeasts do not normally play a major role in spoilage of meats held at low temperatures because of competition from more rapidly growing psychrotrophic bacteria. Yeasts have more commonly been associated with foods containing high salt or high sugar concentrations, although *Candida* has been associated in several instances with refrigerated foods including beef.

Low temperatures normally do not favor growth or toxin production by pathogens, but exceptions do exist. *Staphylococcus aureus* has been reported to grow at 6.7°C with toxin production at 18°C. The lowest temperature for growth of salmonellae is stated to be 6.7°C. For *Clostridium botulinum* types A and B, 10°C allows growth with toxin formation, while type C has a 15°C minimum growth temperature; type E has been reported to grow at 3.3°C with toxin being produced slowly (Michener and Elliott 1964). *Clostridium botulinum* may not ordinarily be expected to grow in frozen poultry or meat products after defrosting because of competition from saprophytic organisms. However, as indicated above, *C. botulinum* type E can grow at low temperatures and produce toxin in vacuum-packaged smoked fish where growth of spoilage organisms is normally inhibited. Vacuum-packaged red meats are not liable to harbor *C. botulinum* type E, so this hazard is minimized at low temperatures. Psychrotrophic *Yersinia enterocolitica*-like organisms can grow on refrigerated meats and may present a hazard (Hanna *et al.* 1977).

Despite the evidence that most pathogens will not grow on foods stored below 5°C, work has continued in attempts to isolate psychrotrophic salmonellae from meats. Catsaras (1981) concluded that a strain of *Salmonella typhimurium* can grow well in minced beef at 6° and 10°C. and was "relatively psychrotrophic." Mossel *et al.* (1981) investigated salmonellae isolated from humans, raw meat, and poultry products, including 20 serotypes commonly implicated in human salmonelloses in the Netherlands. These workers showed that 65 strains grew at 7°C, 44 strains did not grow, and only one *Salmonella* strain grew at 4°C within 4 weeks. In addition, 81 strains were tested at 3°C, and none demonstrated growth within 70 days. Mossel *et al.* (1981) concluded that salmonellae "will not grow at 3°C, only very exceptional strains will grow very slowly at 4°C, and many strains will grow slowly at 7°C," but the last finding is still of little significance in view of rapid outgrowth by psychrotrophic spoilage organisms.

While bacteria usually outgrow molds and other fungi on meats, consuming oxygen necessary for fungal growth, certain molds may be considered as possible pathogens if they produce mycotoxins. Mycotoxins and their relation to human health are described in Chapter 10, and will not be dealt with in detail here. Suffice it to state that mycotoxins are compounds produced by molds that may be toxic or have an adverse biological effect on animals, including man (Bullerman 1979). The aflatoxins are of particular interest as fungal products of *Aspergillus flavus* and *A. parasiticus* because there are regulatory tolerances on the amounts permitted in foods or feeds. With regard to occurrence as products of psychrotrophic molds, mycotoxins have been detected from culture extracts of molds collected from household refrigerators (Torrey and Marth 1977). Some foods sampled have included meat products. *Penicillium* species can grow and produce mycotoxins at low temperatures. However, the significance of these findings regarding production of mycotoxins is not established.

DISTRIBUTION OF PSYCHROTROPHS

Much of the world's surface, both land and sea, exists at temperatures conducive to growth of low-temperature bacteria. It is no wonder, then, that the psychrotrophic organisms are so prevalent. Stokes and Redmond (1966) noted the preponderance of psychrophiles (which was a common term at the time) in streams, rivers, and lakes and the high numbers in soil and foods. Large numbers of psychrophiles were found in dairy products, but more important to the present review, in frozen foods, meats, and poultry. Psychrophiles were recovered at a range of 17% in frozen fish products to 93% in pork chops, with the remaining organisms being characterized as mesophiles (and rarely as thermophiles) in foods. Psychrophiles or psychrotrophs predominate in foods stored at low temperatures and these organisms, because of their dominance, will influence the characteristics and acceptability of foods.

Since fresh meats and poultry present ideal media for microbial growth, it is also not surprising that psychrotrophic organisms soon become established on meats when the products are held at low temperatures. Psychrotrophic bacteria will soon become favored when meat is kept at refrigeration temperatures (about 0° to 10°C), and will grow to large numbers within 1 to 2 weeks. The typical types of organisms have already been described. It should also be emphasized that the spread of these organisms and their subsequent growth is primarily a surface phenomenon, and deep muscle penetration and growth is not as important. In the case of ground meats and/or emulsion-type products, the greatest amount of contamination may occur from processing operations. With such products, internal bacterial growth assumes a greater role in keeping quality and wholesomeness. A study reported by Parker and Levin (1983) indicated that 64 of 65 isolates, which produced H_2S from seven samples of ground beef, were *Alteromonas putrefaciens*. These workers concluded that *Pseudomonas putrefaciens* was either absent or present in such low numbers that it could not be detected. Further, they concluded that previous work by other investigators, who isolated similar organisms from poultry, also indicated that the isolates were *Alteromonas* and not *Pseudomonas*.

In a survey done by Kuehn and Gunderson (1963) on several types of frozen chicken pot pies and pastries, the psychrophilic fungal flora was represented mainly by *Penicillium* and *Chrysosporium*. The role of molds in frozen foods has yet to be fully investigated and their significance as potential pathogens remains to be elucidated.

EFFECT OF PROCESSING, PACKAGING, AND STORAGE CONDITIONS ON TYPE OF FLORA

As temperature is lowered, growth of microorganisms is decreased until it finally stops. Psychrotrophs vary in their ability to grow at different low temperatures, and their growth may be halted at temperatures above or below the freezing point of the meat substrate.

Reduction of temperature causes an increase in the lag period and generation time; the minimum growth temperature may be regarded as that point when those two criteria become infinite (Ingram and Mackey 1976). Also, as temperatures are lowered, a selective action is exerted on a mixed flora of mesophiles and psychrotrophs on meats. This selective effect of temperature subsequently influences the types of organisms remaining as contaminants or survivors during later low-temperature holding (Olson and Nottingham 1980). Empey and Scott (1939) observed that beef from cool climates had a shorter storage life than beef in warmer areas when the meat was later chilled. The "cool" beef already had a large number of psychrotrophic bacteria from the environment as initial contaminants—it has a "built in" spoilage flora. Similar results were noted by Rey et al. (1970) in comparisons of keeping time of retail cuts from carcasses aged at high temperatures for a short time (16°–22°C for 1 to 2 days followed by 2°C for 3 or 2 days, respectively) and cuts from carcasses held continuously at low temperature (2°C) for 11 days. With long low-temperature aging, spoilage was more rapid for the retail cuts than with aging at high temperatures for a short time. A psychrotrophic spoilage flora had become established during continuous low-temperature holding of the carcasses, so that the retail cuts subsequently prepared had a high initial level of these organisms. From these observations, short time high-temperature aging may be more advantageous in limiting growth of typical spoilage types than the conventional continuous low-temperature aging practice.

In general, it is believed that gram-negative bacteria are more affected by low temperature than gram-positive bacteria. Organisms of the former type, such as *Escherichia coli,* species of *Pseudomonas,* salmonellae, and *Enterobacter* are among those susceptible to cold. Gram-positive bacteria that have been observed to suffer cold injury include *Bacillus subtilis, Clostridium perfringens,* and *Staphylococcus aureus.* The latter two organisms have been of concern as pathogens in meats but should not be a problem if low temperatures are maintained.

As indicated by Rey (1975), minimum growth temperatures for control of microorganisms in foods have been listed as about −10°C for bacteria, −12°C for yeasts, and −18°C for other fungi, although there are some exceptions. The review by Michener and Elliott (1964) details minimum growth temperatures and environmental factors affecting these temperatures for many organisms in different foods.

Vacuum packaging, other modified atmosphere packaging, and packaging materials are all related to each other with regard to spoilage. Many studies have been concerned with the effects of vacuum and gas packaging on microbial growth and inhibition of spoilage. Other work has related packaging methods to growth or toxin production by pathogens, such as *Clostridium botulinum* and other anaerobes. Obviously, the permeability of packaging materials plays an important role in considering methods designed to change the atmosphere of the package from that of conventional packaging in air.

Generally, growth of strict aerobes is suppressed by vacuum packaging, so that the typical surface spoilage bacteria are replaced by faculative anaerobes (Holland 1980). Vacuum-packaged meats will allow growth of lactic acid producers, mainly lactobacilli, some members of the Enterobacteriaceae, and *Brochothrix* (formerly *Microbacterium*). Fresh meat packaged in air has more rapid growth of aerobic spoilage organisms than occurs when the meat is vacuum packaged, but the reverse situation favors growth of anaerobic organisms (Baran *et al.* 1970). Vacuum-packaged meats are not especially prone to growth of potential pathogens, such as *Clostridium botulinum,* as long as the meats are kept refrigerated. A study of retail store products has shown that vacuum-packaged luncheon meats did not harbor potential pathogens (Steele and Stiles 1981). Although *Staphylococcus aureus* survives on vacuum-packaged meats, it does not readily produce enterotoxin, as noted in a review by Sinell (1980). Beyer and Sinell (1981) did not find evidence of a health hazard from Enterobacteriaceae in refrigerated vacuum-packaged beef trimmings, although these organisms grew to levels of about 10^5 per gram after 2 to 3 weeks.

In addition to vacuum packaging, the gaseous environment of meat packages may be altered by modified atmosphere packaging by addition of gases, or by packaging materials themselves because of their difference in gas permeability. Gases commonly added include carbon dioxide, nitrogen, and oxygen. Modified atmospheres extend the keeping time of meats by changing the dominant flora from the typical gram-negative spoilage types to that similar to the flora of vacuum-packaged meats—lactic acid producers, Enterobacteriaceae, which are relatively unimportant spoilage types, and *Brochothrix thermosphacta*. An excellent review of the latter organism has been provided by Gardner (1981), who described its ecological association with meats packaged under modified atmospheres and films providing low permeability to oxygen. Egan and Grau (1981) elucidated the role of *B. thermosphacta* in spoilage of vacuum-packaged meats, and emphasized that its spoilage capability varied with oxygen permeability of the packaging materials and the pH of the meat, with growth being favored by more permeable films and pH values higher than 5.4–5.7.

Packaging materials having low gas permeability may also provide modified atmospheres since oxygen is consumed and carbon dioxide is produced by surface organisms on meat. Under these conditions the pH also drops, thus inhibiting growth of typical spoilage organisms and inducing the eventual growth of lactic acid producers. The keeping time of fresh meat is increased by use of high-barrier packaging materials (Kraft and Ayres 1952). Further discussion of modified atmospheres and their effects on microbial flora of meats is found in Chapter 2.

Freezing and frozen storage alters the flora of meats and poultry. Spores are most resistant to these conditions. Cocci are also more resistant than rod forms, and gram-positive bacteria are normally expected to be more resistant than gram-negative ones. The phase of growth may also effect survival of bacteria; those in the stationary phase are more resistant than those in the logarithmic growth phase. These considerations have been reviewed by Speck and Ray (1977), and indicate how the initial flora may be drastically changed by freezing. A full explanation of effects of cold temperature on various microorganisms has also been offered by Ingram and Mackey (1976).

Strains of gram-positive bacteria such as *Bacillus, Clostridium, Lactobacillus, Staphylococcus, Micrococcus,* and *Streptococcus* (Olson and Nottingham 1980) are most resistant. However, not all gram-positive bacteria resist freezing and frozen storage. While spores of *C. perfringens* survive freezing, vegetative cells are very sensitive to these conditions (Trakulchang and Kraft 1977). Although gram-negative bacteria initially present on meats and poultry are generally sensitive to freezing and frozen storage, they may still survive frozen holding, particularly with the protection possibly offered by meats and poultry from dissolved solutes that lower the freezing point. Many instances of survival of salmonellae, for example, have been reported in studies of frozen meat and poultry products. Kraft *et al.* (1963) recovered salmonellae from frozen turkeys after storage at $-29°C$ for as long as 30 days. Salmonellae have been reported to persist in frozen poultry products by other workers as well (Gunderson and Rose 1948; Schneider and Gunderson 1949).

Effects of water activity on the ability of different organisms to survive or grow at low temperatures have been documented by several workers (Ingram and Mackey 1976). The use of salt in cured meat products has had wide implications for the slow-growing low-temperature type E of *C. botulinum*. The addition of salt causes an increase in the minimum growth temperature for this organism. This is also true for psychrotrophic salmonellae (Matches and Liston 1972A).

OTHER CONSIDERATIONS

One of the most important factors affecting the type of flora developing on meat and poultry is the pH. General reports have indicated that lowering the pH creates a requirement for higher growth temperature for *C.*

perfringens, C. botulinum, and salmonellae. Increasing the acidity also narrows the range of water activity at which growth of *Pseudomonas* may occur (Ingram and Mackey 1976). In work done by Rey *et al.* (1976) with pale, dark, or normal pork, proteolytic and lipolytic abilities of spoilage bacteria were reduced on pale pork, which had a low pH, as compared with normal or dark pork which had higher pH values. The most rapid rate of growth of these bacteria also occurred on the dark pork (pH about 6.1 to 6.2) as compared with normal (pH 5.9) pork or pale, soft, exudative (PSE) pork (pH about 5.8).

Ingram and Mackey (1976) reviewed many of the conditions that influence the minimum growth temperature of organisms, in addition to those already described. By inference, any processing, packaging or storage conditions affecting these factors, particularly oxygen, pH, and water activity requirements, will affect the type of flora and its metabolic activity. Additional information concerning growth of psychrotrophs as influenced by environmental factors is given in Chapter 2. Ingram and Simonsen (1980) summarized the incidence of different microbial flora on meats based upon the environment in which meat is held. Refrigerated fresh meats packed conventionally in air harbor primarily *Pseudomonas, Acinetobacter,* and *Moraxella.* If the meat is vacuum packaged, however, the dominant flora becomes lactobacilli, *Brochothrix thermosphacta,* and Enterobacteriaceae.

SIGNIFICANCE IN MEATS AND POULTRY

The most obvious effect of psychrotrophs on meat and poultry is spoilage of the products. These organisms become more significant as temperatures of storage are lowered. In developed countries, where refrigeration is a common means of preservation of meat and poultry items from producer to consumer, psychrotrophic spoilage is one of the main concerns. Reference should be made to the preceding statements regarding dominant psychrotrophic flora in relation to the packaging environment. Spoilage by *Pseudomonas* is more obvious than spoilage by lactobacilli. These considerations will be described in more detail in the next section.

BIOCHEMICAL ACTIVITY ASSOCIATED WITH SPOILAGE

The various defects produced by psychrotrophs growing on meat and poultry products have been described by Ayres (1963): "unclean," "aromatic," "fermented," "fruity," "stale," "sweet," "rancid," "bitter," "sour," and "musty" odors; colors were described as "red," "pink," "yellow," "gray," "blue," "black," and "fluorescent," and the very descriptive "dirty dishrag" odor for spoiled poultry. Off-odors are characteristic when bacterial populations reach about 10^7 cells per cm^2; continued growth leads to slime formation under typical aerobic conditions, and surface counts may reach 10^8 bacteria per cm^2. Along with the increase in bacterial populations, the products of bacterial growth become manifested.

Biochemical activity of psychrotrophic organisms producing spoilage during low-temperature storage of meat and poultry products has received considerable attention and is continually being elucidated. Much of the spoilage activity is confined to the surface of the products, since penetration into the deeper flesh by bacteria is not common during spoilage. A rather detailed discussion of the spoilage activity of different groups of the dominant flora is given in Chapter 2.

Temperature effects are very important in determining evidences of spoilage, such as lipolysis and proteolysis. Temperatures of 5°, 15°, and 20°C produced greater lipolytic and proteolytic activity than temperatures of 30°C or higher, with inhibition of activity in the range 31° to 37°C (Alford 1960; Alford and Pierce 1963). Alford et al. (1971) and Jezeski and Olson (1962) indicated that lipase and proteinase production was favored by low temperatures. All evidence indicates that enzymatic activity of psychrotrophs increases when the bacteria are grown at low temperatures as compared with higher temperatures. Lowering of the temperature from 30° to 0°C caused an increase in production of an extracellular protease by *Pseudomonas* which was isolated from a frozen chicken pie by Peterson and Gunderson (1960). However, the colony size of psychrophilic *Pseudomonas* increased when the growth temperature was increased from 0° to 30°C (Johnson et al. 1970).

When refrigerated storage was studied as to the effects of cycling of temperature, *Pseudomonas fluorescens* showed greater growth at temperatures cycling a few degrees below than at temperatures cycling above the optimum range (29°–30°C) (Howell et al. 1971).

The activity of spoilage organisms on meat was reviewed by Shelef (1981), who stated that it is generally believed that the microbial flora use the simple compounds before complex materials are degraded during the spoilage process. Free amino acids and nucleotides are utilized before proteolysis occurs from bacterial action; water-soluble proteins are attacked by proteolytic enzymes. However, if simple carbohydrates are available, such as the minimal amounts of glucose in beef, they will be attacked first, causing a slight decrease in pH. As indicated by Shelef (1981) in her review, *Pseudomonas* species will degrade glucose, but this early activity has little effect on the manifestations of meat spoilage because carbohydrate levels in meats are very low. The pH increases with the onset of spoilage and with formation of off-odor and slime as bacterial numbers reach populations in the millions per gram (or per cm^2). If the pH remains low (below 6.0) slime formation is inhibited. Lactic acid-producing bacteria can inhibit gram-negative spoilage organisms. Dubois et al. (1979) reported that bacteria isolated from ground beef were inhibited by lactic acid bacteria. Shelef (1981) suggested that carbohydrates could be utilized to produce sufficient inhibition of spoilage organisms so that shelf lifewould be prolonged.

In addition to protein, other nutrients may continue to be utilized in aerobic spoilage of meats and poultry until the supply of oxygen is exhausted. In anaerobic spoilage, nutrients are used until they are depleted when the cell population becomes high (about 10^8 per cm^2); growth then ceases (Newton and Gill 1978). The growth of spoilage organisms on the fat surfaces of meat was reviewed by Nottingham et al. (1981) who observed that bacterial spoilage of adipose tissue and muscle tissue are similar. Spoilage was well advanced before proteins and lipids of fatty tissue were degraded by bacterial enzymes. From these findings, Nottingham et al. (1981) stated that potential lipolytic activity of microorganisms was not related to their ability to spoil fatty tissue of fresh meat.

The sequence of biochemical changes in aerobically and anaerobically packaged meat has been reviewed by Ingram and Simonsen (1980).On vacuum-packaged retail cuts, the sarcoplasmic and myofibrillar proteins and other components become degraded to form H_2S, ethanol, acetoin, short-chain fatty acids, ethyl esters, and various amines.

Speck and Ray (1977) stated that low water activity and limiting low temperatures are important reasons for low bacterial populations in frozen foods. These principles, therefore, apply to frozen meat and poultry products. However, it was also observed that those characteristics of freezing that preserve the structure of frozen foods may also preserve microorganisms, although leaving them in different states of viability or injury. When freezing and thawing causes cell death or injury in varying degrees for bacteria, it also may result in increased availability of tissue fluids from the damaged substrate, thus providing a supply of available nutrients (Elliott and Michener 1965). Ray and Speck (1973) listed conditions affecting susceptibility of bacterial cells to freezing and thawing. These included strain differences, age, species, growth conditions, substrate, and actual freezing and thawing conditions. Also, destruction of microorganisms continues after initial freezing and during frozen storage; bacterial spores are most resistant. Surviving bacteria may respond differently with regard to their growth and biochemical activity after thawing. Proteolytic enzyme activity was observed by Peterson and Gunderson (1960) to be greater in defrosted foods than might be expected from the bacterial population present.

Rey and Kraft (1971) attempted to explain the relationship between organisms surviving freezing and thawing and the occurrence of spoilage in chicken by showing an increase in the proportion of biochemically active proteolytic, lipolytic, and fluorescent bacteria after freezing and thawing. Although total aerobic bacterial counts did not differ appreciably between frozen-defrosted chicken and unfrozen refrigerated chicken after both types of poultry were stored at 5°C for 5 days, the proportion of spoilage organisms was greater for the frozen poultry. Protein and fat deterioration as determined by chemical analyses followed trends similar to those of the biochemical activity of the bacteria involved in spoilage.

Even at temperatures lower than the minimum for growth, micro-organisms can contribute to spoilage of frozen foods by elaboration of extracellular proteases and lipases (Peterson 1961). Extracellular enzymes released prior to freezing remained active at temperatures as low as −18°C which was shown by the work done by Rey *et al.* (1969) with *Pseudomas* isolated from frozen poultry.

DETECTION AND ENUMERATION OF PSYCHROTROPHS

Methods for enumeration of psychrotrophic bacteria in foods are described by Gilliland *et al.* (1976). As already mentioned, it is important to know how many of these organisms are present, because their numbers are directly related to spoilage or spoilage potential of refrigerated meats. This relationship becomes more significant in considering temperature abuse of frozen foods, or premature defrosting of frozen meats and poultry items.

Generally, psychrotrophs are enumerated by plating with nonselective media, such as plate count agar (PCA) or trypticase soy agar (TSA), and incubating at a refrigeration temperature such as 7°C for 10 days. Variations of time and temperature have been used (the author uses 5°–7°C for 10–14 days). The spread plate method may be preferable to the pour plate, as there is less danger of destruction of heat-sensitive psychrotrophic bacteria. Another plating medium, which can be incubated at a temperature of 32°C for 48 hours, is Crystal Violet Tetrazolium Agar (CVTA). This medium has the advantage of inhibiting gram-positive bacteria and allowing for a more rapid determination of results than with the usual methods. However, when gram-positive organisms are of concern, such as lactics and staphylococci in cured meats, CVTA is not applicable.

Gram-negative psychrotrophs also use oxygen as a terminal hydrogen acceptor during growth, and their cytochrome oxidase system may be used as a detection method. Surface plating facilitates the use of a dye, such as a 1% solution of dimethyl-*p*-phenylenediamine hydrochloride, which will turn the oxidase-positive colonies a purple-red or maroon color.

Certain media have been developed for *Pseudomonas*. Several of these contain cetrimide (cetyltrimethylammonium bromide) and have been described by Mossel and Indacochea (1971), Solberg *et al.* (1972), and Hart *et al.* (1976). Grant and Holt (1977) described a medium for selecting *Pseudomonas* from several different substrates, including foods. Their medium functioned by inhibiting gram-positive bacteria, fungi, enteric organisms, and *Acinetobacter, Aeromonas,* and aerobic gram-negative rods, other than *Pseudomonas*.

For staphylococci subjected to low-temperature treatment in foods, addition of catalase may aid in recovery because hydrogen peroxide accumulates in cold-injured cells (Martin *et al.* 1976).

Greer (1981) described media and incubation methods to establish a more rapid method for detection of psychrotrophs in retail beef. Of the various methods compared, with incubation temperatures of 7°, 25°, and 32°C applied with different media, the aerobic plate count with PCA, following incubation at 25°C for 24 hr was stated to provide an accurate estimate of psychrotrophic populations on beef steaks. When this incubation method was used, initial bacterial loads were directly related to retail storage life at about 7°C in a display case. Greer (1981) further stated that all bacteria isolated from PCA incubated at 25°C were psychrotrophic.

When food blenders are used in the laboratory to homogenize meat samples, care must be taken not to overheat the samples which could cause death or injury of psychrotrophs at the location of the blender blades. The blender should be turned off for 1- to 2-min intervals to allow cooling before additional blending.

A "Keeping Quality Test" may be used to measure the probable shelf life or proportion of psychrotrophic spoilage organisms in the total flora of meats. The sample is plated initially, and again after a low-temperature incubation for 5–7 days. The difference in the count is then used as the estimate of keeping quality.

Many reports have been published on injury, repair, and methods for recovery of low-temperature injured bacteria of various genera and species, including those classified as psychrotrophs. Excellent reviews have been presented by Ray and Speck (1973), Speck and Ray (1977), Van Schothorst (1976), Ingram and Mackey (1976), and Busta (1976). Low temperatures may produce injured or stressed organisms such as those already described in meats and poultry, and detection or enumeration requires special procedures. As indicated by Speck and Ray (1977), injured cells may suffer "structural" or "metabolic" injury; the latter is a more extensive form of damage. Viability of injured cells can be determined after repair on a nonselective medium, and then testing on selective media. In the case of metabolic injury, there is a requirement for nutritional supplements before growth occurs. Ray and Speck (1973) listed trypticase, yeast extract, tryptone, peptone, casamino acids, cysteine, aspartic acid, glutamic acid, and biologically active peptides from trypticase as aiding in repair of metabolic injury in various bacteria. From the point of view of protection of public health in consumption of frozen meat and poultry products, recognition of freeze-injury is important because injured pathogens can be as harmful as noninjured cells. The same is true for spoilage by injured spoilage organisms (Speck and Ray 1977).

The effects of freezing in changing the microbial flora were demonstrated by Rey (1975) to cause problems in identification and classification of organisms surviving on frozen poultry meat. In her work, freezing caused significant reductions in counts of total aerobic bacteria and fluorescent *Pseudomonas*. Prolonged frozen storage for 8 weeks continued to reduce aerobic populations, but not the fluorescent *Pseudomonas*. On the other hand, the incidence of coagulase-positive staphylococci was relatively unaffected on frozen chicken as a result of the actual freezing operations (conventional air blast or liquid nitrogen) but were appreciably reduced by frozen storage. The results suggested differences in susceptibility of different types of organisms not only to the actual freezing procedures, but also to frozen storage. Also, the flora present immediately after freezing was more heterogeneous than after 8 weeks of frozen storage. Frozen storage reversed the original effects of the freezing process (Rey 1975), in that the flora isolated after the frozen storage period was almost as homogeneous in biochemical characteristics as that isolated before freezing. Psychrotrophs were less susceptible to frozen storage than to the cold shock associated with the initial freezing operation. Another possible complication in identification of injured cells is a change in the gram staining reaction, since more variability is introduced.

CONTROL OF PSYCHROTROPHS IN MEATS AND POULTRY

Many physical and chemical treatments have been suggested or are in use to control psychrotrophs and other organisms on meats and poultry. The main objective of these treatments, however, is to reduce the hazard from pathogens rather than to reduce spoilage from psychrotrophic spoilage organisms. Some of these methods have been described in earlier sections of this chapter and in Chapters 2–4. Control of psychrotrophs on or in meat and poultry products has already been described to some extent in relation to temperature of storage, freezing and thawing, packaging with vacuum or modified atmospheres, pH, and control of water activity. All these factors are involved in control of psychrotrophs and are concerned with the biochemical activity of psychrotrophs on meat substrates. With the trend toward decreased use of chemicals in food processing, it seems likely that more advantage will be taken of modified atmosphere packaging, which makes use of naturally occurring environmental gases in controlling growth of psychrotrophs on packaged meats. Pseudomonads, which commonly cause spoilage of poultry, are replaced by lactobacilli and Enterobacteriaceae when oxygen is reduced in the package environment. The practicality of treatment of large cuts of meat or carcasses with glucose as a means of retarding growth of pseudomonads is described in Chapter 2, and has been advocated as a means of control of spoilage (Shelef 1981).

Many of the possible means of control of psychrotrophs have been reviewed by Splittstoesser (1976). Moderate acidity, which lowers pH, is a commonly cited method for controlling low-temperature organisms on meats. The use of dips or sprays with acids to lower surface pH has been related to reduction in the numbers of psychrotrophic spoilage bacteria (see Chapter 2). The selective effect of pH was demonstrated by Barnes and Impey (1968) for chicken leg muscle (pH 6.4–6.7) and chicken breast muscle (pH 5.7–5.9). Both muscles allowed growth of *Pseudomonas*, but *Acinetobacter* was inhibited on breast muscle.

Since psychrotrophs generally have low resistance to chlorine sanitizers, hypochlorites have been extensively used for control of these organisms, particularly in meat-processing operations. More recently, work has been done to reduce loads of organisms by washing or spraying beef carcasses or cuts with hypochlorite solutions (Kotula *et al.* 1974; Emswiler *et al.* 1976; Marshall *et al.* 1977; Titus *et al.* 1978). Although some variation in results occurred when hypochlorite sprays were compared with water sprays, generally, the hypochlorite was more effective in reducing bacterial counts. Several variables need to be taken into account with hypochlorite sprays; pressure, flow rate, concentration, time, and method of sanitization are all important.

With poultry, spray washing and use of hypochlorite is practiced during processing operations and effectively removes or decreases bacterial populations on the surface of carcasses. Much of the control relates to cleaning of equipment as well as to prevention of build-up of psychrotrophs on equipment surfaces by decreasing psychrotrophic populations in the water supply. Use of chlorine in poultry-processing operations may provide variable results in reducing psychrotrophs on carcasses and may be limited in value if much organic material is present before its application. The review of Thomson *et al.* (1974) provides extensive information on this subject.

Psychrotrophic gram-negative rods are relatively insensitive to quaternary ammonium compounds as compared with hypochlorites.

More recently, Greer and Jeremiah (1980, 1981) have suggested that surface temperatures of retail meat cuts could be lowered by adjustment of blowers, or meat could be transferred into coolers when not on display in the retail case to reduce surface temperature. These practices had the effect of improving shelf life. The latter method, which involves extra labor and storage, may not be as practical as the alternative of lowering blower temperatures. This work also demonstrated the need for monitoring the position of meat in the display case, since surface temperatures vary with location.

Radiation offers a promising means of controlling psychrotrophs on meats and poultry, since many studies have shown that psychrotrophs generally have low resistance to radiation. The possibility exists that low-dose ionizing radiation (approximately 100 krads) may be effective in reducing surface contamination by psychrotrophs and may be an alternative to other methods.

CONCLUSIONS

From the foregoing discussion, it may be concluded that effects of low temperature on psychrotrophic organisms varies considerably with the ability of individual strains, not only species, to survive cold shock and subsequent cold storage. Populations of various types of psychrotrophs may change, causing differences in the predominant flora over time of storage. Freeze-injury and death rate also vary for bacterial populations on meats and poultry. Organisms having the greatest biochemical spoilage activity may be among the survivors and can resume their growth and activity when products are thawed. This may lead to spoilage similar to that for unfrozen meat and poultry products, or to potential hazard from surviving pathogens. Emphasis should be placed on recovery of injured cells before selective enumeration is performed, so that an adequate picture of microbial types and numbers may be obtained.

Control of psychrotrophs may lie, to a large extent, in packaging systems designed to prevent or retard growth of aerobic organisms, but care must be taken to provide adequate and continuous refrigeration so that anaerobic growth is deterred. Other control measures in common use need further investigation for application to modern meat- and poultry-processing operations.

REFERENCES

ALFORD, J. A. 1960. Effect of incubation temperature on biochemical tests in the genera *Pseudomonas* and *Achromobacter*. J. Bacteriol. *79*, 591.

ALFORD, J. A. and PIERCE, D. A. 1963. Production of lipase by *Pseudomonas fragi* in a synthetic medium. J. Bacteriol. *86*, 24.

ALFORD, J. A., SMITH, J. L. and LILLY, H. D. 1971. Relationship of microbial activity to changes in lipids of foods. J. Appl. Bacteriol. *34*, 133.

AYRES, J. C. 1963. Low temperature organisms as indexes of quality of fresh meat. Microbiological Quality of Foods. p. 132. Academic Press, NY.

BARAN, W. L., KRAFT, A. A. and WALKER, H. W. 1970. Effects of carbon dioxide and vacuum packaging on color and bacterial count of meat. J. Milk Food Technol. *33*, 77.

BARNES, E. M. and IMPEY, C. S. 1968. Psychrophilic spoilage bacteria of poultry. J. Appl. Bacteriol. *21*, 313.

BEYER, K. and SINELL, H.-J. 1981. Psychrotrophic microorganisms in vacuum packaged beef trimmings. Proc. XIth Intern. Symp. Food Microbiol., Chapter 17.

BULLERMAN, L. 1979. Significance of mycotoxins to food safety and human health. J. Food Prot. *42*, 65.

BUSTA, F. F. 1976. Practical implications of injured microorganisms in food. J. Milk Food Technol. *39*, 138.

CATSARAS, M. 1981. Growth of *Salmonella* in minced meat at low temperature. Proc. XIth Intern. Symp. Food Microbiol. Chapter 26.

DUBOIS, G., BEAUMIER, H. and CHARBONNEAU, R. 1979. Inhibition of bacteria isolated from ground meat by Streptococcaceae and Lactobacillaceae. J. Food Sci. *44*, 1649.

EDDY, B. P.   1960.   The use and meaning of the term "psychrophilic." J. Appl. Bacteriol. 23, 189.

EGAN, A. F. and GRAU, F. H.   1981.   Environmental conditions and the role of Brochothrix thermosphacta in the spoilage of fresh and processed meat. Proc. XIth Intern. Symp. Food Microbiol. Chapter 19.

ELLIOTT, R. P. and MICHENER, H. D.   1965.   Factors affecting the growth of psychrophilic microorganisms in foods. A review. Tech. Bull. 1320. U.S. Dept. of Agriculture, Washington, DC.

EMPEY, W. A. and SCOTT, W. J.   1939.   Investigations on chilled beef. Part I. Microbial Contamination acquired in the meat works. Bull. Counc. Sci. Ind. Rest. Aust. No. 126.

EMSWILER, B. S., KOTULA, A. W. and ROUGH, D. K.   1976.   Bactericidal effectiveness of three chlorine sources used in beef carcass washing. J. Animal Sci. 42, 1445.

GARDNER, G. A.   1981.   Brochothrix thermosphacta (Microbacterium thermosphactum) in the spoilage of meats: a review. Proc. XIth Intern. Symp. Food Microbiol. Chapter 14.

GILLILAND, S. E., MICHENER, H. D. and KRAFT, A. A.   1976.   Psychrotrophic microorganisms. In Compendium of Methods for the Microbiological Examination of Foods. Chapter 8, p. 173. M. L. Speck (Editor). American Public Health Assoc., Washington, DC.

GRANT, M. A. and HOLT, J. G.   1977.   Medium for the selective isolation of members of the genus Pseudomonas from natural habitats. Appl. Environ. Microbiol. 33, 1222.

GREER, G. G.   1981.   Rapid detection of psychrotrophic bacteria in relation to retail beef quality. J. Food Sci. 46, 1669.

GREER, G. G. and JEREMIAH, L. E.   1980.   Influence of retail display temperature on psychrotrophic bacterial growth and beef case-life. J. Food Prot. 43, 542.

GREER, G. G. and JEREMIAH, L. E.   1981.   Proper control of retail case temperature improves beef shelf life. J. Food Prot. 44, 297.

GUNDERSON, M. F. and ROSE, K. D.   1948.   Survival of bacteria in a pre-cooked fresh frozen food. Food Res. 13, 254.

HANNA, M. O., STEWART, J. C., ZINK, D. L., CARPENTER, Z. L. and VANDERZANT, C.   1977.   Development of Yersinia enterocolitica on raw and cooked beef and pork at different temperatures. J. Food Sci. 42, 1180.

HART, A., MOORE, K. E. and TALL, D.   1976.   A comparison of the British Pharmacopoeia (1973) and United State Pharmacopeia (1975) methods for detecting pseudomonads. J. Appl. Bacteriol. 41, 235.

HOLLAND, G. C.   1980.   Modified atmospheres for fresh meat distribution. Proc. Meat Ind. Res. Conf., pp. 21–39. Am. Meat Sci. Assoc., Am. Meat Inst. Foundation, Chicago, IL.

HOWELL, A. D., SAFFLE, R. L. and POWERS, J. J.   1971.   Temperature cycling effects on bacterial growth. 1. Pseudomonas fluorescens. J. Food Sci. 36, 778.

INGRAM, M. and MACKEY, B. M.   1976.   Inactivation by cold. In Inhibition and Inactivation of Vegetative Microbes. p. 111. F. A. Skinner and W. B. Hugo (Editors). Soc. Appl. Bacteriol. Symp. Ser. No. 5. Academic Press, NY.

INGRAM, M. and SIMONSEN, B.   1980.   Meat and meat products In Microbial Ecology of Foods. Vol. 2. Chapter 15. Intern. Commission Microbiolog. Specifications for Foods, Academic Press, NY.

JEZESKI, J. J. and OLSEN, R. H.   1962.   The activity of enzymes at low temperatures. Proc. Low Temp. Microbiol. Symp. 1961, pp. 139–155. Campbell Soup Co., Camden, NJ.

JOHNSON, M. G., PALUMBO, S. A., RIECK, V. T. and WITTER, L. D.   1970.   Influence of temperature on steady state growth of colonies of Pseudomonas fluorescens. J. Bacteriol. 103, 267.

KOTULA, A. W., LUSBY, W. R., CROUSE, J. D. and DEVRIES, B.   1974.   Beef carcass washing to reduce bacterial contamination. J. Anim. Sci. 39, 674.

KRAFT, A. A. and AYRES, J. C. 1952. Post-mortem changes in stored meats. IV. Effect of packaging materials on keeping quality of self-service meats. Food Technol. *6*, 8.
KRAFT, A. A., AYRES, J. C., WEISS, K. F., MARION, W. W., BALLOUN, S. L. and FORSYTHE, R. H. 1963. Effect of method of freezing on survival of microorganisms on turkey. Poul. Sci. *42*, 128.
KUEHN, H. H. and GUNDERSON, M. F. 1963. Psychrophilic and mesophilic fungi in frozen food products. Appl. Microbiol. *11*, 352.
LAHELLEC, C. and COLIN, P. 1981. Psychrotrophic microorganisms in spoilage and pathogenicity. Proc. XIth Intern. Symp. Food Microbiol. Chapter 25.
MARSHALL, R. T., ANDERSON, M. E., NAUMANN, H. D. and STRINGER, W. C. 1977. Experiments in sanitizing beef with sodium hypochlorite. J. Food Prot. *40*, 246.
MARTIN, S. E., FLOWERS, R. S. and ORDAL, Z. J. 1976. Catalase: Its effect on microbial enumeration. Appl. Environ. Microbiol. *32*, 731.
MATCHES, J. R. and LISTON, J. 1972A. Effects of incubation temperature on the salt tolerance of *Salmonella*. J. Milk Food Technol. *35*, 39.
MATCHES, J. R. and LISTON, J. 1972B. Effect of pH on low temperature growth of *Salmonella*. J. Milk Food Technol. *35*, 49.
MICHENER, H. D. and ELLIOTT, R. P. 1964. Minimum growth temperatures for food poisoning, fecal-indicator, and psychrophilic microorganisms. Advan. Food Res. *13*, 349.
MOSSEL, D. A. A. and INDACOCHEA, L. 1971. A new cetrimide medium for the detection of *Pseudomonas aeruginosa*. J. Med. Microbiol. *4*, 380.
MOSSEL, D. A. A., JANSMA, M. and DEWAART, J. 1981. Growth potential of 114 strains of epidemiologically most common salmonellae and arizonae between 3 and 17 C. Proc. XIth Intern. Symp. Food Microbiol. Chapter 3.
NEWTON, K. G. and GILL, C. O. 1978. The development of the anaerobic spoilage flora of meat stored at chill temperatures. J. Appl. Bacteriol. *44*, 91.
NOTTINGHAM, P. M., GILL, C. O. and NEWTON, K. G. 1981. Spoilage at fat surfaces of meat. Proc. XIth Intern. Symp. Food Microbiol. Chapter 16.
OLSON, J. C., JR. and NOTTINGHAM, P. M. 1980. Temperature. Microbial Ecology of Foods. Vol. I. Chapter 1, p. 332. Intern. Commission on Microbial Specifications for Foods. Academic Press, NY.
PARKER, L. L. and LEVIN, R. E. 1983. Relative incidence of *Alteromonas putrefaciens* and *Pseudomonas putrefaciens* in ground beef. Appl. Environ. Microbiol. *45*, 796.
PETERSON, A. C. 1961. An ecological study of frozen foods. Proc. Low Temperature Microbiology Symp., p. 157. Campbell Soup Co., Camden, NJ.
PETERSON, A. C. and GUNDERSON, M. F. 1960. Some characteristics of proteolytic enzymes from *Pseudomonas fluorescens*. Appl Microbiol. *8*, 98.
RAY, B. and SPECK, M. L. 1973. Freeze-injury in bacteria. CRC Crit. Rev. Clin. Lab. Sci. *4*, 161.
REY, C. R. 1975. Numerical taxonomy and changes in the bacterial flora on frozen chicken. Ph.D. dissertation, Iowa State University, Ames, IA.
REY, C. R. and KRAFT, A. A. 1971. Effect of freezing and packaging methods on survival and biochemical activity of spoilage organisms on chicken. J. Food Sci. *36*, 454.
REY, C. R., KRAFT, A. A., SEALS, R. G. and BIRD, E. W. 1969. Influence of temperature on some biochemical characteristics of *Pseudomonas* associated with spoilage of chicken. J. Food Sci. *34*, 279.
REY, C. R., KRAFT, A. A., WALKER, H. W. and PARRISH, F. C., JR. 1970. Microbial changes in meat during aging at elevated temperature and later refrigerated storage. Food Technol. *24*, 67.
REY, C. R., KRAFT, A. A., TOPEL, D. G., PARRISH, F. C., JR. and HOTCHKISS, D. K. 1976. Microbiology of pale, dark and normal pork. J. Food Sci. *41*, 111.

SCHNEIDER, M. D. and GUNDERSON, M. F.   1949.   Investigators shed more light on *Salmonella* problems. U. S. Egg Poult. Mag. *55,* 10.

SHAW, B. G. and LATTY, J. B.   1981.   The taxonomy of *Pseudomonadaceae* responsible for low-temperature aerobic spoilage of meats. Proc. XIth Intern. Symp. Food Microbiol. Chapter 24.

SHELEF, L. A.   1981.   Spoilage microflora and pH in fresh beef stored in an aerobic environment at 5 C. Proc. XIth Intern. Symp. Food Microbiol. Chapter 15.

SINELL, H. J.   1980.   Microbiol Ecology of Foods. Vol. I. Chapter 11, p. 332. Intern. Commission on Microbial Specifications for Foods. Academic Press, NY.

SOLBERG, M., O'LEARY, V. S. and REHA, W. E., JR.   1972.   A new medium for the isolation and enumeration of pseudomonads. Appl. Microbiol. *24,* 544.

SPECK, M. L. and RAY, B.   1977.   Effects of freezing and storage on microorganisms in frozen foods: a review. J. Food Prot. *40,* 333.

SPLITTSTOESSER, D. F.   1976.   Gram negative nonspore-forming rods. *In* Food Microbiology: Public Health and Spoilage Aspects. p. 337. M. P. de Figueiredo, and D. F. Splittstoesser (Editors). AVI Publishing Co., Inc. Westport, CT.

STEELE, J. E. and STILES, M. E.   1981.   Microbial quality of vacuum packaged sliced ham. J. Food Prot. *44,* 435.

STOKES, J. L. and REDMOND, M. L.   1966.   Quantitative ecology of psychrophilic organisms. Appl. Microbiol. *14,* 74.

THOMSON, J. E., WHITEHEAD, W. K. and MERCURI, A. J.   1974.   Chilling poultry meat–A literature review. Poult. Sci. *53,* 1268.

TITUS, T. C., ACTON, J. C., McCASKILL, L. and JOHNSON, M. G.   1978.   Microbial persistence of inoculated beef plates sprayed with hypochlorite solutions. J. Food Prot. *41,* 606.

TORREY, G. S. and MARTH, E. H.   1977.   Isolation and toxicity of molds from foods stored in homes. J. Food Prot. *40,* 187.

TRAKULCHANG, S. P. and KRAFT, A. A.   1977.   Survival of *Clostridium perfringens* in refrigerated and frozen meat and poultry items. J. Food Sci. *42,* 518.

VAN SCHOTHORST, M.   1976.   Resuscitation of injured bacteria in foods. *In* Inhibition and Inactivation of Vegetative Microbes. p. 317. F. A. Skinner and W. B. Hugo (Editors). Soc. Appl. Bacteriol. Symp. Ser. No. 5. Academic Press, NY.

WALKER, H. W.   1977.   Spoilage of food by yeasts. Food Technol. *31(2),* 57.

Salmonella

John H. Silliker[1]
and
Damien A. Gabis[2]

INTRODUCTION

From Chapter 1 on the microbial ecology of meats it is clear that salmonellae are present so commonly on raw meat and poultry that they may be considered to be a part of the normal microflora. The incidence and numbers of salmonellae in meat and poultry varies with the species of animal from which it is derived, the geographical location, preslaughter holding conditions, processing conditions and other factors. Currently technology does not exist to assure the production of carcass meat and poultry that is free from salmonellae. Further processing of carcasses into primal, subprimal, and retail cuts does not involve treatments that are destructive to salmonellae.

The problem of controlling Salmonella contamination of raw meat and poultry has been recognized on both the national and international levels. The federal (U.S.) court held that salmonellae are an inherent defect in red meats and poultry (APHA vs Butz 1974). The working group of the Codex Committee on Food Hygiene (FAO/WHO 1979) concluded that no benefits to public health or quality would arise from microbiological criteria for Salmonella on red meats and poultry because the incidence of Salmonella is so high that application of a criterion would be impracticable.

Salmonellae are pathogenic to man and animals. There is a direct link between the occurrence of salmonellae in living animals, on the meat

[1]Silliker Laboratories of California, Inc., 1139 E. Dominguez, Suite I, Carson, CA 90746.
[2]Silliker Laboratories, Inc., 1304 Halsted Street, Chicago Heights, IL 60411.

Advances in Meat Research, Volume 2
Copyright 1986 by AVI Publishing Co.
All rights of reproduction in any form reserved
ISBN 0-87055-498-0

derived from them, and human salmonellosis. On a world-wide basis, epidemiological records for food-borne disease prove that meat and poultry are the vehicles responsible for most outbreaks (Hobbs 1974). It is clear that the bulk of human salmonellosis relates directly to man's association with animals, both wild and domestic.

The animal-to-man link is only one factor in the epidemiology of human salmonellosis. Contaminated red meat and poultry provide a nidus for salmonellae which man nurtures through mishandling. Furthermore, inedible parts of the animal are processed to yield important components of livestock feeds. As a result of poor manufacturing practices (postprocessing contamination) these rendered animal by-products become recontaminated with salmonellae which, in turn, are carried into the feeds. The consumption of these feeds by livestock followed by animal-to-animal transmission completes the *Salmonella* cycle. This is not to suggest, however, that contaminated feeds are the only source of salmonellae in livestock. Epidemiological evidence indicates that there is a direct link between the presence of salmonellae in meat and poultry and human salmonellosis. Man induces salmonellosis through improper food handling practices and perpetuates salmonellosis through recontamination of rendered animal by-products, which are incorporated into livestock feeds.

SALMONELLA, THE ORGANISM

Definitions, Characteristics, and Classification

Edwards and Ewing (1972) have set forth the biochemical and physiological characteristics of the genus *Salmonella*: "The genus *Salmonella* is composed of motile bacteria that conform to the definitions of the family *Enterobacteriaceae* and the tribe *Salmonelleae*. Urease is not produced, sodium malonate is not used, gelatin is not liquefied and growth does not occur in medium containing potassium cyanide. Lysine, arginine and ornithine are decarboxylated. Acid is produced in Jordan's tartrate medium. Dulcitol is fermented and inositol is utilized by numerous strains. Sucrose, salicin, raffinose, and lactose are not fermented."

In practice, isolates not conforming to one of more than these characteristics are encountered. For example, S. *gallinarum* and S. *pullorum* are always nonmotile and nonmotile variants of motile serotypes are also found. Similarly, lactose- and sucrose-fermenting salmonellae are not as uncommon as is generally thought.

Serological analysis of salmonellae is most useful for identification of isolates and this is based on the Kauffman-White scheme (Kauffman 1966) which depends upon the detection and identification of the O (somatic) and H (flagellar) antigens. In this regard, the presence of H antigens is most specific to the genus, the O antigens being more frequently shared by other genera. Speciation based upon antigenic analysis has been of great value in epidemiological investigations and is the foundation of the *Salmonella* surveillance program administered by the Centers for Disease Control and similar programs in other countries.

Ecological Divisions of the *Salmonellae*

Salmonellae can be grouped according to host preference. First, there are those species which are more or less strictly adapted to man, including *S. typhi, S. paratyphi,* types A, B, and C, and *S. sendai.* With the exception of type B *S. paratyphi* these serotypes have no known secondary host. It is less strictly adapted to man in that infections of swine, dogs, and fowl have been reported. The other four serotypes have rarely been observed in nonhuman animals.

The characteristics of the strictly human-adapted serotypes are: (1) small dosage required to produce disease, (2) prolonged incubation time (10–20 or more days), (3) enteric fever produced via bloodstream invasion, and (4) tendency to produce permanent carriers and to become endemic.

Infections due to the human-adapted serotypes are usually the result of consumption of contaminated food or water. Person-to-person contact is not as frequently the mode of transmission.

Second, there are those serotypes that are adapted to animals, including *S. pullorum,* which occurs in poultry, *S. abortus equi,* in horses, *S. abortus-ovis,* in sheep, and *S. choleraesuis* and *S. typhisuis,* which occur in pigs. Although these serotypes are animal host-adapted, human illness from them has occurred, sometimes with serious consequences.

The third group of salmonellae infects both man and animals, there being no strong host preference. The characteristics of the disease produced by these unadapted serotypes are: (1) they usually cause gastroenteritis instead of enteric fever; (2) infection is localized in the intestine and the bloodstream is not usually invaded; (3) there is a short incubation period, rarely longer than 48 hr; and (4) the disease is of short duration and less serious than that which occurs with the serotypes that cause enteric fever. However, serious consequences can occur as a result of infection of the very young, the aged, and the infirm.

Human Disease

The vast majority of cases of human salmonellosis associated with the consumption of meat and poultry are caused by salmonellae in the third group, i.e., non-host-adapted. However, in a susceptible individual virtually any serotype may produce the more serious enteric fever syndrome. In the food poisoning syndrome, the incubation period may range from 8 to 72 hr but most frequently is 24–48 hr. Headache, abdominal cramps, vomiting, diarrhea, and general malaise are the principal symptoms. It is common to see a rise in temperature to about 38°–39°C. The acute stage of the disease lasts 2–5 days. During this time salmonellae can be isolated from the feces, but diagnosis of salmonellosis should be based both upon clinical symptoms and the isolation of *Salmonella* from the feces. With suspected food-associated salmonellosis, every attempt should be made to isolate salmonellae from the suspected foods. In most cases the organisms isolated from the patient and the suspected food will be of the same serotype. Unfortunately, analysis of suspect foods is only rarely accomplished in food-borne outbreaks. In large outbreaks, epidemiologists often use bacteriophage typing and antibiotic sensitivity patterns, in addition to serotyping of *Salmonella* isolates, to obtain a more specific or conclusive association of a food with a given outbreak. The mechanism of *Salmonella* infection in man and animals has been reviewed by Bryan *et al.* (1979).

The Infective Dose

A distinction should be made between the infective dose and the dose needed to produce symptoms. Some people may ingest salmonellae, become infected, and excrete the organism but never show symptoms. In this discussion, however, the infective dose is the number of salmonellae needed to produce symptoms.

Traditionally it has been thought that relatively large numbers of salmonellae are required to produce illness. McCullough and Eisele (1951A,B,C) reported that the dosage required to produce salmonellosis in volunteers ranged from 120,000 to 16 billion. These studies had defects in experimental design, among which were the exclusive use of healthy adult volunteers and the utilization of relatively few serotypes. Healthy adult prisoners very likely belong to a group which includes individuals most resistant to *Salmonella* infection. Furthermore, there are many hundreds of *Salmonella* serotypes and, retrospectively, it seems imprudent to draw conclusions on infective dose from challenge tests using a handful of serotypes tested against an inherently resistant population. Until recently, the data of these workers has been widely quoted and relied upon as a basis for asserting that the infective dose required to cause salmonellosis is high.

Evidence obtained subsequent to the work of McCullough and Eisele (1951A,B,C) indicates, in fact, that salmonellosis may be caused by consumption of foods containing relatively low numbers of salmonellae. Table 7.1 (Silliker 1980) summarizes estimates of the infective doses from a number of outbreaks. These data support the conclusion that relatively small numbers of salmonellae may initiate infection in a susceptible host. Bryan *et al.* (1979) cautioned that the relatively small numbers detected in foods reported in these outbreaks must be interpreted with caution because the data were obtained using Most Probable Number procedures which may give highly variable results. They caution further that some salmonellae may have died because the samples were analyzed a considerable time after the suspect foods were ingested. In all probability the

TABLE 7.1. Evidence for Low Infectious Dosage by Salmonellae[a]

Year	Product	Infecting dose	Reference
1967	Carmine dye	15,000	Lang et al. (1967)
1970	Ice cream	1,000	Armstrong et al. (1970)
1974	Chocolate candy	100	D'Aoust et al. (1975)
1975	Pancreatin (23)	200	Lipson (1976); Rowe and Hall (1975)
1975	Raw hamburger	60–2300/per 100 g	Fontaine et al. (1978)
1977	Salmonella agona	Low	Anon. (1977)

[a] From Silliker (1980).

minimum infectious dose required to produce salmonellosis is often low and the nature of the food vehicle and health status of the host, to a large degree, influence susceptibility to food-borne salmonellosis.

GROWTH, SURVIVAL, AND DESTRUCTION OF SALMONELLA

Growth

Temperature. The optimum temperature for growth of salmonellae is 35°–37°C. Environmental factors including the substrate, pH, water activity, and competing microflora affect both extremes.

Table 7.2 (Mackey et al. 1980) summarizes the minimum temperatures for growth of salmonellae in a variety of foods. The minimum growth temperature recorded was 6.7°C in chicken à la King (Angelotti et al. 1961), but growth of S. heidelberg on agar at 5.2°C has been reported (Matches and Liston 1972). The influence of chill temperatures on growth rates of Salmonella is summarized in Table 7.3 (Mackey et al. 1980). Although growth may occur at temperatures slightly above what would be considered "refrigeration," the rate is exceedingly slow. For example, Mackey et al. (1980) calculated that it would require approximately 2.5 hr at 15°C, 5 hr at 12.5°C, and 7.5 hr at 10°C for salmonellae to double in number on the surface of inoculated beef. Further, these calculations did not take into account the influence of the lag time.

Acidity (pH). Salmonella growth has been reported in broth at pH values as low as 4.05 (Chung and Goepfert 1970), but the optimum pH is generally accepted to fall between 6.5 and 7.5.

Meat products may be acidified through fermentation by lactic acid bacteria or by direct chemical acidulation with glucono-lactone or other food acids.

TABLE 7.2. Minimum Temperatures for Growth of *Salmonella* in Foods[a]

Food	Growth (°C)	No growth (°C)	Reference
Beef and pork	—	4.4–10	Gomutputra and Fabian (1953)
Chicken à la King	6.7	5.6	Angelotti *et al.* (1961)
Ham salad	—	10	Angelotti *et al.* (1961)
Cream custard	—	10	Angelotti *et al.* (1961)
Crab meat	—	5	Berry (1942)
Crab meat (sterile)	8	5	Matches and Liston (1968)
Sole	8	6	Matches and Liston (1968)
Egg	10	2	Ayres and Taylor (1956)
Egg	10	5	Stokes *et al.* (1956)
Liquid egg	11.1	7.2	Gibbons *et al.* (1944)
Ground pork	10	4	Alford and Palumbo (1969)
Ground pork	—	7	Sulzbacher (1952)
Ground beef	12.5	7	Goepfert and Kim (1975)
Ground beef	—	5	Tiwari and Maxcy (1972)
Luncheon meat	—	5	Goepfert and Chung (1970B)
Bacon	16	5	Farrell and Upton (1978)
Ground beef (vacuum packed)	12	5	Davidson and Witty (1977)
Sterile beef	8	7	Shaw and Nicol (1969)

[a] From Mackey *et al.* (1980).

The ultimate pH of fermented meats and poultry varies. Deibel *et al.* (1961) analyzed summer sausage from 9 different establishments in the United States and reported pHs varying from 4.6 to 5.3. Eight samples of dry salami, each from different establishments, showed values from 5.1 to 5.4. Three samples of Lebanon bologna showed values of 4.6–4.7. Smith and Palumbo (1973) analyzed six samples of Lebanon bologna, each from a different producer, and reported pH values ranging from 4.6 to 4.9. The greater acidity of Lebanon bologna can probably be attributed to the smoking of this product for 4 days at 35°C (Palumbo *et al.* 1973). Hungarian salami, a dry sausage subjected to a slow ripening process, is reported to show pH levels of 5.9–6.2 but sometimes rising to 6.5 (Takács *et al.* 1963). Recently the American Meat Institute (1982) published voluntary guidelines for the manufacture of semidry and dry sausage. A maximum pH of 5.3 is prescribed for both types of product.

Goepfert and Chung (1970A) investigated the fate of *Salmonella* during sausage fermentation. *Salmonella typhimurium* multiplied in a sausage emulsion during a 14 hr period at 30°C in the absence of starter culture. When a starter culture of *Pediococcus* was employed, the *Salmonella* population declined during fermentation, the magnitude of the decline ranging between 0.75 and 2.5 $\log_{10}$ units in replicate experiments. In further studies, the omission of nitrite did not change this pattern. When glucose was omitted from the emulsion, there was only a small reduction in the number of viable salmonellae during the fermentation period. With the omission of sodium chloride, salmonellae proliferated during the first 12 hr of fermentation and thereafter died as the pH dropped to 4.3 in 24 hr.

TABLE 7.3. Growth Rates of *Salmonella* at Chill Temperatures[a]

Temperature (°C)	Organism	Substrate	Generation time (hr)	References
8	*S. heidelberg*	Broth + 1% NaCl	19[b]	Matches and Liston (1972)
	S. heidelberg	English sole	28[b]	Matches and Liston (1968)
	S. heidelberg	Sterile crab	31[b]	Matches and Liston (1968)
10	*S. oranienburg*	Sterile beef	35	Shaw and Nicol (1969)
	S. oranienburg (3 strains)	Ground pork	9.4	Shaw and Nicol (1969)
	S. derby	Ground pork	12[b]	Alford and Palumbo (1969)
	S. enteritidis	Ground pork	19[b]	Alford and Palumbo (1969)
	S. thompson	Ground pork	22[b]	Alford and Palumbo (1969)
	Mixture of strains	Beef surface	17[b]	Alford and Palumbo (1969)
12	*S. heidelberg*	Broth	8–26	Mackey et al. (1980)
	S. typhimurium	Broth	12[b]	Matches and Liston (1972)
	S. derby	Broth	12[b]	
12.5	Mixture of strains	Beef surface	12[b]	
15	Mixture of strains	Beef surface	5.2–10.2	Mackey et al. (1980)
	S. oranienburg		2.9–3.5	Mackey et al. (1980)
			4.6	Shaw and Nicol (1969)

[a] From Mackey et al. (1980).
[b] Mean generation times were calculated from published growth curves and are, therefore, approximate.

The authors conceded that the combination of acidity and sodium chloride is the principal reason for the demise of salmonellae during fermentation. The survival of S. dublin and S. typhimurium during the production of Lebanon bolgna was studied by Smith et al. (1975). Populátions of S. dublin were reduced 3 to 4 $\log_{10}$ cycles during a 4-day fermentation at 35°C; whereas S. typhimurium numbers were usually reduced to undetectable levels. Baran and Stevenson (1975) studied the destruction of salmonellae during the processing of dry fermented turkey sausage and found that S. pullorum was reduced by 4.5 to 5.3 $\log_{10}$ cycles and S. senftenberg by only 1.5 to 2.0 $\log_{10}$ cycles. The final pH of the dried sausage was 5.3. The turkey sausage fermentation time of 12 hr was shorter than that employed by Chung and Goepfert (1970A), and by Smith et al. (1975), and this probably accounts for the greater survival of salmonellae in turkey sausage.

Water Activity.   The minimum a_w for growth of three Salmonella species in laboratory media was found by Christian and Scott (1953) to be 0.941. Minimum a_ws for growth were slightly lower in three foods, e.g., S. oranienburg grew in rehydrated soup at an a_w of 0.93 (Christian and Scott 1953). An a_w of 0.94 is equivalent to approximately 9.0% sodium chloride. A study of 15 Salmonella strains revealed that maximal growth rates are obtained at 0.995 a_w (Christian and Scott 1953). Growth rates decreased steeply and the length of lag times increased markedly as a_w values were lowered below the optimum.

The water activity of red meat and poultry is near the optimum for growth of salmonellae. Salt in cured meats reduces the a_w which results in an increased lag time and reduced growth rate. However, incubation temperature, competing microflora, and pH combine with a_w to influence the growth of salmonellae. Cooked cured meats, such as domestic sausages, are generally vacuum packaged and merchandized under refrigeration. Under these conditions lactic acid bacteria are the predominant flora, tending to suppress the growth of salmonellae. Chung and Goepfert (1970A) found that salmonellae rapidly died in the presence of a lactic acid bacteria starter culture during the 24 hr fermentation of a sausage emulsion at 30°C. If salt were omitted from the sausage emulsion, S. typhimurium multiplied during a 12-hr incubation at 30°–37°C, illustrating the influence of a_w. Similar findings with respect to the influence of lactic acid starter cultures on the fate of salmonellae in sausage emulsions were reported by Smith et al. (1975). Although growth may be inhibited by interactions between brine, pH, and competing microflora, salmonellae may survive for some time. For example, salmonellae survived for 2 months at room temperature in naturally contaminated salami with a brine content of 23% (Marazza and Crespi 1973). Takaćs and Simonffy (1970) reported that dried sausages contained viable salmonellae up to the time of consumption if the initial concentration was greater than 20,000 per gram.

Salmonellosis from unheated dried sausage has reportedly occurred in Canada (D'Aoust and Evans 1978). However, taking into account the limitations of surveillance data, it does not appear that either semidry or dry sausage constitutes a widespread *Salmonella* hazard. Quantitatively, the potential for cross-contamination from raw meat and poultry in the butcher shop during slicing of these products may pose the greatest risk, although epidemiological evidence for this is lacking.

Curing Salts. The influence of sodium chloride has been discussed above. Legal limits of nitrite and nitrate have minimal effect on *Salmonella* (Koelensmid and van Rhee 1964; Alford and Palumbo 1969; Goepfert and Chung 1970B; Davidson and Webb 1973; Smith *et al.* 1975).

Gaseous Atmosphere. Over one-half the fresh meat in North American is vacuum packaged in gas-impermeable films (Marriott *et al.* 1977) and substantial quantities of carcass and boned fresh meat are shipped in modified atmospheres containing elevated levels of CO_2 with various concentrations of nitrogen and oxygen (Wolfe 1980). Vacuum packaging and modified atmospheres inhibit gram-negative psychrotrophic bacteria which normally spoil fresh meat packaged under aerobic conditions. Indeed, vacuum packaging alone generates a modified atmosphere because the metabolism of meat enzymes results in accumulation of CO_2 within the package. Levels of 10–20% are reached within 4 hr after packaging and achieve a maximum of around 30% CO_2 (Ledward *et al.* 1971; Taylor 1971). There is no epidemiological evidence that storage of meats and poultry in modified atmospheres increases the *Salmonella* hazard presented by these products. To the contrary, at 10°C virtually complete inhibition of salmonellae was observed in ground meat packaged in a 60% CO_2 atmosphere, but with samples stored in air a steady increase in numbers occurred (Silliker and Wolfe 1980). At 20°C, comparable growth occurred on samples stored in air and the CO_2 atmosphere. Similarly, Luiten *et al.* (1982) found that *S. typhimurium* in beef steaks increased significantly during storage in an oxygen-permeable film at 10°C, but remained low and fairly constant in steaks packaged under vacuum or in oxygen barrier bags containing a mixture of 60% CO_2 and 40% O_2. These findings suggest that modified atmospheres may afford some protection against the growth of salmonellae in red meats stored in modified atmospheres. However, with severe temperature abuse (20°C) the CO_2 effect is minimal.

Destruction by Heat. Salmonellae are heat sensitive and ordinary pasteurizing or cooking conditions are generally sufficient to kill salmonellae in high moisture foods. As with other microorganisms, the heat resistance of salmonellae is markedly increased as a_w decreases. Extensive data on the heat resistance of *Salmonella* has been tabulated by Genigeorgis and Riemann (1979). Goodfellow and Brown (1978) determined D values of salmonellae in ground beef at temperatures generally considered to be in the subpasteurization range. D values at 51.6°, 57.2°, and 62.7°C were 51–62, 3.8–4.2, and 0.6–0.7 min respectively. They also found that the same time/temperature process which resulted in a 7 $\log_{10}$ reduction of salmonellae in the interior of a beef roast did not completely destroy the inoculum on the surface of the meat. Drying at the meat's surface resulted in increased heat resistance, which illustrates the interaction between a_w and thermal tolerance.

Certain processed meats receive no heat treatment at the manufacturing level. These include raw ground beef, raw salted and cured meats, such as fresh pork sausage, Polish, and Italian sausage, and uncooked ham and corned beef. Also in this category are salt pork, dry cured bacon, and country-cured ham — all products which are shelf stable due to low a_w. In addition, heat processing is not obligatory with semidry sausage not containing pork or with pork containing dry sausage produced under conditions assuring destruction of trichinae. Furthermore, pork-containing semidry sausage need not be heat treated if it is formulated with "certified" pork trimmings, i.e., pork that has been frozen for a sufficient length of time to assure freedom from trichinae.

Although perishable raw salted and salted cured meats, including salt pork and country-cured ham receive no heat process at the manufacturing level, they have not been indicted as important sources of human salmonellosis. They are subject to the same handling errors as are other raw meats and likely are responsible for some outbreaks, but thorough cooking of these products by the consumer is more likely to occur than with unprocessed red meats and poultry. Further, the presence of salt probably renders these items less a hazard than raw meat and poultry.

In the United States the minimum internal heat treatment given to raw pork to destroy trichinae is 137°F (58.3°C). This is within the lower temperature range lethal to salmonellae. With semidry sausages, for example, the primary intent of the heat process is the destruction of trichinae and not salmonellae. In this type of product, destruction of salmonellae depends not only on the heat treatment but also on the interactions between a_w, pH, and competing microflora during fermentation. A substantial volume of ready-to-eat cooked pork sausage products, such as Polish and Italian sausage, are commercially packaged and distributed frozen or under refrigeration. The heat treatment of these items must be sufficient to destroy trichinae but, in practice, the process significantly exceeds the "trichinae cook" of 137°F (58.3°C), thus assuring destruction of salmonellae. Postheat-processing contamination of these products is possible but there is no epidemiological evidence that they have constituted a significant salmonellosis hazard. Normally they are cooked by the consumer before consumption.

Cooked uncured meat and poultry are used in consumer-sized frozen entrees, such as "TV dinners," pot pies, and sliced cooked meat in gravy. Cooked uncured meats are also produced in bulk for distribution to food service establishments. Such items include cooked ground beef with chili, thinly sliced cooked beef, and chicken for use in ethnic dishes. Postcooking contamination with salmonellae is possible, but epidemiological evidence indicates that these products are not frequently involved as vehicles in salmonellosis outbreaks. Such items are generally cooked before serving which destroys *Salmonella*.

Commercially prepared cooked "roast beef" is distributed to foodservice establishments. These products are not necessarily prepared from primal cuts, but more often are fabricated from meat trimmings in such a manner that when sliced they have the appearance of cooked roast beef. Generally, the heat treatment used in the production of these products is sufficient to destroy most vegetative microorganisms. A notable exception is precooked roast beef.

In recent years precooked rare "roast beef" has been a significant cause of human salmonellosis in the United States (Centers for Disease Control 1981A,B). As a result of these and other outbreaks the USDA issued a regulation requiring all cooked beef and beef roasts be processed to a minimum internal temperature of 145°F (62.7°C) (Angelotti 1977). This heat-processing schedule did not permit production of rare roast beef, so representatives of the meat industry requested the USDA to develop and promulgate a regulation permitting the use of equivalent processes with lower temperatures and longer times. Subsequently, Goodfellow and Brown (1978) developed a table of equivalent heat processes which were based on the thermal destruction of salmonellae in a ground beef system using different temperatures ranging from 51.6° to 62.7°C. These equivalent processes were chosen to ensure the destruction of 10 million *Salmonella* inoculated into the center of beef roasts and to permit production of roasts with the characteristic red color of rare roast beef. The validity of these processing values was established by inoculating roast beef with salmonellae and processing them under commercial conditions. The USDA issued regulations permitting processing of roast beef within the parameters established by Goodfellow and Brown (1978). Nevertheless, outbreaks implicating precooked roast beef have occurred (Centers for Disease Control 1981A,B).

There is little doubt that a minimum internal temperature of 145°F (Angelotti 1977) or the heat-processing schedules established by Goodfellow and Brown (1978) provide for destruction of salmonellae in these products. The recent outbreaks of salmonellosis from precooked roast beef occurred mainly as a result of postcooking cross-contamination (Johnston 1983). Failure to separate raw and cooked products is the most frequent cause of cross-contamination. Often the heat-processed product is rebagged which may result in cross-contamination. Failure to adhere to the required heat processes has been responsible for some of the outbreaks.

Poultry products, primarily turkey rolls, are similar to the precooked roast beef. Salmonellosis outbreaks were traced to these products when they were first introduced in the 1960s. Inadequate heat treatment and/or postprocessing contamination were responsible. Currently, the USDA requires that poultry rolls be heated to a minimum internal temperature of 160°F (71°C) to eliminate salmonellae. In recent years poultry rolls have not been implicated in salmonellosis outbreaks (Johnston 1983).

Cooked uncured poultry products, such as boneless breasts, are sold in retail stores and to the food service industry. These must be cooked to an internal temperature of 160°F (Bailey 1974). They have not constituted a significant *Salmonella* problem (Johnston 1983).

Cooked cured meats include domestic sausage (frankfurters, bologna, etc.) and luncheon meats, e.g., pepper and pimento loaf, ham, bacon, and corned beef. The common property shared by these products are that they are cured, i.e., treated with nitrite and salt, and are subjected to heat treatment. Some are ready to eat (bologna, luncheon meats, and fully cooked hams); others are cooked before eating to improve texture and flavor (smoked ham and frankfurters); still others must be cooked before eating to ensure safety (e.g., bacon which does not recieve a heat process sufficient to destroy trichinae and usually not *Salmonella*).

The heat process applied to cooked cured meats depends upon the product. Bacon is heated to a final internal temperature between 120°–130°F (49°–54.5°C), heat being applied for the sole purpose of "fixing" the cured color. Bacon is generally thoroughly cooked by the consumer and constitutes no *Salmonella* hazard. Smoked hams must achieve a temperature of 137°F (58.3°C) for the destruction of trichinae. In all probability this is sufficient, given the time/temperature relationships applied, to eliminate salmonellae. However, smoked hams are not ready to eat and require further cooking by the consumer. Fully cooked hams must achieve a minimum internal temperature of 158°F (70°C) which provides a wide margin of safety with respect to salmonellae. By regulation, domestic sausage and luncheon meats containing pork must achieve a minimum internal temperature of 137°F (58.3°C) in order to achieve freedom from trichinae, but from a practical point of view luncheon meats and domestic sausage are processed to much higher temperatures in order to ensure satisfactory shelf life. The reader is referred to Bailey (1974) for prescribed minimum heat processes for these and related products.

Smoked and cured poultry products, such as poultry frankfurters, are required to be heated to a minimum internal temperature of 155°F (approx. 68.3°C), a process assuring freedom from salmonellae. Although the heat processes applied to cured meats and poultry will eliminate salmonellae, these products may be contaminated after heat treatment. Furthermore, salmonellae are capable of growth in these cured meats if favorable temperatures exist (Goepfert and Chung 1970B; Davidson and Webb 1973). Despite this there is no epidemiological evidence to indicate that cooked cured meat and poultry products are an important source of human salmonellosis.

The technology involved in the production of dried meats has been reviewed (International Commission on Microbiological Specifications for Foods, 1980). Cooked meat may be dried in hot air tunnels at temperatures sufficiently high to preclude growth of relevant microorganisms (above 50°C). The low temperatures used for freeze-drying cooked or uncooked meats also precludes microbial growth. Cooked products destined for drying are sufficiently heated to destroy salmonellae, whereas the freeze-drying of uncooked products is not expected to eliminate such contamination. In either case, postprocessing contamination of the dried product with salmonellae is possible. The hazard is increased if the contaminated dried meat is rehydrated and exposed to temperatures permitting *Salmonella* growth. Dried meats, however, have not been an important source of human salmonellosis.

THE RELATIONSHIP BETWEEN MEAT AND POULTRY AND HUMAN SALMONELLOSIS

On a world-wide basis, epidemiological records for food-borne disease prove that meat and poultry are the vehicles responsible for most outbreaks of salmonellosis (Hobbs 1974). The importance of salmonellosis in the countries of the world varies but, there is no doubt that it is one of the principal food-borne diseases. Todd (1978) studied these outbreaks in six countries and found that microbiological agents were by far the most important cause of food-borne illness. *Salmonella* caused 29.2% of the outbreaks in Canada, 33.5% in the United States, 86.6% in England/ Wales, 12.8% in Japan, and 27.3% in Australia. Figure 7.1 (Gangarosa 1978) summarizes data on the mode of transmission in 500 human cases of salmonellosis reported to the Centers for Disease Control between 1966 and 1975. Of these outbreaks, 40% were attributed to meat and poultry. If one considers only those outbreaks where a cause was determined, then meat and poultry were responsible for 56% of the outbreaks included in Gangarosa's study.

Food-borne illness, regardless of the etiological agent, is primarily a consumer-induced disease caused by improper food handling. Table 7.4 (Bryan 1980) illustrates this with respect to meat and poultry outbreaks. Of these outbreaks, 96% were attributable to mishandling in food service establishments and in homes. In only 4% of the outbreaks where the place of mishandling was known were improper food-processing techniques involved. There is no doubt that these data are skewed because outbreaks occurring due to mishandling in food service establishments are far more likely to come to the attention of public health authorities than are isolated episodes occurring in homes. If all outbreaks were identified, the proportion attributable to mishandling of foods in homes would be far greater than that attributable to mishandling in food service establishments. Furthermore, illness attributable to improper processing of meat and poultry is far more likely to come to the attention of public health authorities than outbreaks caused by improper handling in either food

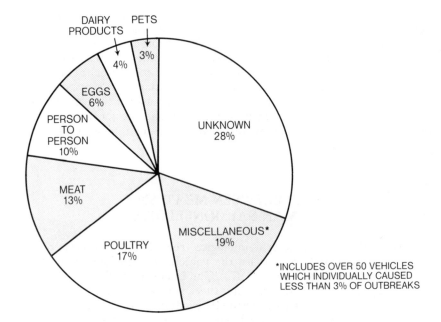

FIG. 7.1.   Mode of transmission in 500 human salmonellosis outbreaks, 1966–1975.
From Gangarosa (1978).

service establishments or homes, since, at least in the United States, meat and poultry processing is subject to federal and/or state regulations.

Salmonellae are inherently present on red meat and poultry, and so the introduction of these organisms into the food-processing plant, the food service establishment, or the home is inevitable. Prevention of red meat- and poultry-associated salmonellosis requires cooking under conditions adequate to destroy salmonellae. It requires, further, that cross-contamination between raw meat and poultry and other foods not occur. It

TABLE 7.4.   Food Handling and Salmonellae-Associated Outbreaks in the United States, 1973–1977[a]

Place	Number	Percentage	Percentage of known place
Food service establishments	322	50	65
Homes	155	24	31
Food-processing plants	20	3	4
Unspecified/unknown	150	23	—
Total	647	100	100

[a] From Bryan (1980).

also requires holding of both raw and cooked foods at temperatures low enough to prevent *Salmonella* growth.When consumers fail to apply these control measures salmonellosis results.

In a study of 49 meat and poultry-associated outbreaks of salmonellosis, Bryan (1980) found that inadequate cooking was involved in 25 incidents (51%). Turkey or roast beef was involved in 19 of the 25 outbreaks where inadequate cooking was a contributing factor.

Of these 19 outbreaks, 8 were traced to precooked roast beef prepared in meat-processing plants. The pattern with turkey was quite different,with only one outbreak being traced to improper food processing. The bulk of turkey outbreaks occurred with meals served to large numbers of people at resorts, hotels, and church or school suppers. Only a single outbreak in this group involved chicken. The incidence of salmonellae is high in both turkeys and chickens, but many more outbreaks are attributed to turkey because turkeys are larger and more often stuffed, and, hence, are more likely to be undercooked. Furthermore, turkey is often served to large groups of people, thus compounding the problems of inadequate cooking and subsequent mishandling.

Of the 49 outbreaks, 17 involved cross-contamination. In most cases the cooked product was recontaminated by equipment that had been in contact with the raw product. However, infected food handlers were involved in two outbreaks. In three of the outbreaks, illness was traced to the consumption of raw meat.

In only 6 of the 49 outbreaks was the source not traced to inadequate cooking, cross-contamination, or the consumption of raw meat. It is axiomatic that one of these three factors was *actually* involved in every one of these six outbreaks. Virtually, without exception, the genesis of salmonellosis outbreaks is related to inadequate cooking or cross-contamination.

In spite of the evidence indicating that low numbers of salmonellae may initiate infection, the fact is that in most outbreaks the offending food contains large numbers of organisms. Not only are the foods contaminated (as a result of undercooking or cross-contamination), but they also are mishandled so as to permit multiplication of the contaminating organisms. Growth of the salmonellae in the food stems from inadequate cooling of cooked products requiring refrigeration or from insufficiently high temperatures during holding for serving.

Poor refrigeration practices can account for growth of salmonellae in recontaminated cooked foods. Such temperature abuse most frequently occurs when a food is held in bulk in containers too large for the capacity of the refrigeration equipment. When this type of temperature abuse occurs the food may be in the incubation zone for *Salmonella* growth many hours before it reaches inhibitory temperatures. The rate at which food cools is related to the differential in temperature between it and the surrounding cooling medium, the type and volume of the food, and the size and shape of the container in which it is placed. Often, objections are raised to placing hot foods into the refrigerator without previously cooling to room temperature. It is fallacious to believe that prompt cooling will "sour" the food or "seal in the heat" due to the congealing of outer layers. It has been shown that the time foods remain within the temperature growth range is lessened by refrigeration before its temperature reaches 46.1°C (115°F) (Black and Lewis 1948). One study on the correlation among food volume, container size, and cooling rates found that a difference of 6 hr was necessary to lower the temperature of a 100-serving portion of chicken salad in a deep container, as compared with the same volume distributed in four shallow bowls, each containing 25-serving portions (Lewis et al. 1953).

Sliced meat can be cooled rapidly by putting the slices in shallow pans which are in contact with a bed of ice. Stocks, sauces, and gravies can be cooled rapidly by putting their containers into larger ice-filled containers or in a cold water bath. Stirring foods also aids cooling (Bryan and McKinley 1974). Cutting large roasts or cuts of cooked meats into small portions greatly reduces cooling time (Bryan and Kilpatrick 1971). Large cuts of cooked meat or poultry that cannot be cut into smaller pieces should be wrapped in foil or plastic, or stored separately in pans in refrigerators. Other foods should be divided into portions and stored in pans that are not more than 10.2 cm (4 in.) deep, and preferably only partially filled (Bryan 1978).

Food service regulations in the United States require the internal temperature of potentially hazardous foods requiring hot storage be held at 60°C (140°F) or above except during necessary periods of preparation. At this temperature, not only will *Salmonella* be inhibited, but destruction will occur with time.

In addition to those already discussed, other indirect factors contributing to outbreaks involve the preparation of foods one or more days prior to serving, as well as the use of leftover foods. In Bryan's (1980) study of meat- and poultry-associated outbreaks, one or the other of these factors were involved in 15 of 49 episodes (30.6%). The foods involved were contaminated by salmonellae due to inadequate cooking or cross-contamination, or by infected food handlers. If such foods are not held under conditions precluding *Salmonella* growth, then the dosage is significantly increased as compared with foods that are cooked and served on the same day. The use of leftover foods compounds the problem, because further handling is usually involved. Leftover food and food prepared for service at a later time should be thoroughly reheated to reach a temperature of 71.1° to 73.8°C (160°–165°F). This is frequently not done, for instance,when leftover meat or poultry is used in salads. The problem of poultry- and meat-associated salmonellosis is ironic since the epidemiology of the disease is completely understood and the measures necessary for prevention are well established. Red meat and poultry are the most important sources of human salmonellosis because these foods are inherently contaminated with salmonellae. Although technology for the reduction in the incidence of salmonellae exists (irradiation, *Salmonella*-free feeds, and the Nurmi culture—see Chapter 1), these measures are not generally applied. As a consequence, contamination of raw meat and poultry with salmonellae is expected. The requirements for destruction (principally heat treatment) of salmonellae in raw products are well established as are the requirements for prevention of cross-contamination between raw meat and poultry and other foods. Despite this knowledge, the incidence of food-borne salmonellosis is increasing and red meat and poultry remain the most important vehicles. Surely, the bulk of the salmonellosis problem relates to the consumer's failure to exercise proper control measures.

SUMMARY

If a decrease in meat- and poultry-associated salmonellosis is to be seen, improved food handling practices will be required. In the United States various laws requiring proper food handling practices exist, but enforcement is ineffective. In the home a decreased incidence of salmonellosis will result only when the homemaker is educated to apply proper food-handling practices. Government at various levels, educational institutions, and industry have made sporadic and abortive attempts to educate the public. These attempts have taken the form of discussions with consumer groups, television and radio broadcasts, newspaper articles, and pamphlets. A Gallup poll, commissioned by the federal government in 1973 (Anonymous 1974), revealed the following in a survey of American women: 74% did not know what *Salmonella* is, 66% did not know how to minimize the spread of salmonellae, and 39% thought that raw meat and poultry are inspected for the presence of *Salmonella* by federal and state inspectors. The increasing incidence of salmonellosis and this Gallup poll indicate that educational efforts made so far have been unsuccessful.

Nevertheless, consumer education and increased regulatory control of food service establishments through inspection and strict enforcement of proper food-handling practices probably have the greatest chances for success in controlling food-borne salmonellosis. Intensive regulatory control is exercised over food-processing plants but, generally, regulatory control over food service establishments is haphazard and ineffective. Food-borne illnesses result largely from negligence of consumers, not food processors. Food service establishments are ultimate consumers and as such have an abysmal record with respect to prevention of food-borne disease, including salmonellosis. Greater emphasis on the inspection of food service establishments with demand for adherence to proper food-handling practices would attack the problem at one of its two most critical points.

Regulatory control over food handling in the home is not possible, but education of the homemaker is. The mass communications and media approach to education has not been successful. Virtually no concerted effort has been directed toward teaching the principles of sanitary food handling to the group which will be responsible for prevention of food-borne disease in future years—school children. The greatest hope for reducing the incidence of home-associated food-borne illness, including salmonellosis, lies in educating tomorrow's consumer by incorporating the concepts of proper food handling practices in appropriate courses throughout the curricula in elementary and secondary schools.

In the absence of regulatory control over food service establishments and lack of effective education for food preparers in the home, it is doubtful that the incidence of human salmonellosis caused by meat and poultry will decrease.

REFERENCES

ALFORD, J. A. and PALUMBO, S. A.   1969.   Interaction of salt, pH, and temperature on the growth and survival of salmonellae in ground pork. Appl. Microbiol. *17*, 528.

AMERICAN MEAT INSTITUTE.   1982.   Good manufacturing practices. I. Voluntary guidelines for the production of dry fermented sausage. II. Voluntary guidelines for the production of semi-dry fermented sausage. American Meat Institute, Washington, D.C.

AMERICAN PUBLIC HEALTH ASSOCIATION vs. BUTZ.   1974.   American Public Health Association *et al.*, Appellants vs. Earl Butz, Secretary of Agriculture *et al.* Washington D.C. Civil Court. Suit to enjoin the Secretary of Agriculture against alleged violations of the Wholesome Meat Act. pp. 331–338. 551F. 2d 331 (D.C. Civ. 1974).

ANGELOTTI, R., FOTER, M. J., and LEWIS, K. H.   1961.   Time-temperature effects on salmonellae and staphylococci in foods. I. Behavior in refrigerated foods. Am. J. Publ. Health *51*, 76.

ANGELOTTI, R.   1977.   Cooking requirements for cooked roast beef. Fed. Reg. *42(17)*, 44217.

ANONYMOUS.   1974.   Report to the Congress. *Salmonella* in raw meat and poultry: An assessment of the problem [B-164031 (2), July 22, 1974]. U.S. General Accounting Office, Washington, D.C.

ARMSTRONG, R. W., FODOR, T., CURLIN, G. T., COHEN, A. B., MORIS, G. K., MARTIN, W. T. and FELDMAN, J.   1970.   Epidemic of *Salmonella* gastroenteritis due to contaminated imitation ice cream. Am. J. Epidemiol. *91*, 300.

AYRES, J. C. and TAYLOR, B.   1956.   Effect of temperature on microbial proliferation in shell eggs. Appl. Microbiol. *4*, 355.

BAILEY, J. W.   1974.   Encyclopedia of Labeling Meat and Poultry Products. Meat Plant Mag. (publisher), St. Louis, MO.

BARAN, W. L. and STEVENSON, K. E.   1975.   Survival of selected pathogens during processing of a fermented turkey sausage. J. Food Sci. *40*, 618.

BERRY, C.   1942.   The multiplication of bacteria in sterile crab meat. J. Bacteriol. *44*, 145.

BLACK, L. C. and LEWIS, M. N.   1948.   Effects on bacterial growth of various methods of cooling cooked foods. J. Am. Diet. Assoc. *24*, 394.

BRYAN, F. L.   1978.   Control of *Salmonella* in food service establishments. Paper presented at National Salmonellosis Seminar Jan. 10–11, 1978, Washington, D.C.

BRYAN, F. L.   1980.   Foodborne diseases in the United States associated with meat and poultry. J. Food Prot. *43*, 140.

BRYAN, F. L. and KILPATRICK, E. G.   1971.   *Clostridium perfringens* related to roast beef cooking, storage, and contamination in a fast food restaurant. Am. J. Pub. Health *61*, 1869.

BRYAN, F. L. and McKINLEY, T. N.   1974.   Prevention of foodborne illness by time-temperature control of thawing, cooking, chilling and reheating turkeys in school lunch kitchens. J. Milk Food Technol. *37*, 420.

BRYAN, F. L., FANELLI, M. J. and RIEMANN, H.   1979.   *Salmonella* infections. *In:* Food Borne Infections and Intoxications. pp. 73–130. H. Riemann and F. L. Bryan (Editors). Academic Press, NY.

BRYAN, F. L.   1980.   Foodborne diseases in the United States Jan. 10–11, 1978, Washington, D.C.

CENTERS FOR DISEASE CONTROL.   1977.   Drug-resistant *Salmonella agona*— New York. Morbidity, Mortality Weekly Rep. *26*, 129.

CENTERS FOR DISEASE CONTROL.   1981A.   Multistate outbreak of salmonellosis caused by precooked roast beef. Morbidity Mortality Weekly Rep. *30*, 391.

CENTERS FOR DISEASE CONTROL.   1981B.   Multiple outbreaks of salmonellosis associated with precooked roast beef—Pennsylvania, New York, Vermont. Morbidity Mortality Weekly Rep. *30*, 569.

CHRISTIAN, J. H. B. and SCOTT, W. J.   1953.   Water relations of salmonellae at 30°C. Austral. J. Biol. Sci. *6*, 565.

CHUNG, K. C. and GOEPFERT, J. M.   1970.   Growth of *Salmonella* at low pH. J. Food Sci. *35*, 326.

D'AOUST, J. Y. and EVANS, A.   1978.   Suspect case of human salmonellosis from a dry cured meat product—Ontario. Canad. Dis. Weekly Rep. *4(7)*, 27.

D'AOUST, J. Y., ARIS, D. J., THISDELE, P., DURANTE, A., BRISSON, N., DRAGON, N. D., LACHAPELLE, G., JOHNSTON, M. and LAIDLEY, R. P.   1975. *Salmonella eastbourne* outbreak associated with chocolate. Canad. Inst. Food Sci. Technol. J. *8*, 181.

DAVIDSON, C. M. and WEBB, G.   1973.   The behavior of salmonellae in vacuum-packaged cooked cured meat products. Canad. Inst. Food Sci. Technol. J. *6*, 41.

DAVIDSON, C. M. and WITTY, J. K.   1977.   Fate of salmonellae in vacuum-packaged ground meat during storage and subsequent cooking. Canad. Inst. Food Sci. Technol. J. *10*, 223.

DEIBEL, R. H., NIVEN, C. F., JR. and WILSON, G. D.   1961.   Microbiology of meat curing. III. Some microbiological and related technological aspects in the manufacture of fermented sausages. Appl. Microbiol. *9*, 156.

EDWARDS, P. R. and EWING, W. H.   1972.   Identification of *Enterobacteriaceae*. 3rd edition. Burgess Publishing Co., Minneapolis, MN.

FAO/WHO (Food and Agriculture Organization/World Health Organization).   1979.   Report of a FAO/WHO working group on microbiological criteria for foods. Geneva: FAO/WHO.

FARRELL, G. M. and UPTON, M. E.   1978.   The effect of low temperature on the growth and survival of *Staphylococcus aureus* and *Salmonella typhimurium* when inoculated on to bacon. J. Food Technol. *13*, 15.

FONTAINE, R. E., ARNON, S., MARTIN, W. T., VERNON, T. M., GANGAROSA, E. J., FARMER, J. J., MORAN, A. B., SILLIKER, J. H., and DECKER, D. L.   1978.   Raw hamburger: An interstate common source of human salmonellosis. Am. J. Epidemiol. *107*, 36.

GANGAROSA, E. J.   1978.   History and surveillance programs for salmonellosis. Proc. Natl. Salmonellosis Sem., Washington, D.C.

GENIGEORGIS, C. and RIEMANN, H.   1979.   Food processing and hygiene, *In* Food-Borne Infections and Intoxications. pp. 621–623. H. Riemann and F. L. Bryan (Editors). Academic Press, NY.

GIBBONS, N. E., MOORE, R. L., and FULTON, C. O.   1944.   Dried whole egg powder. XV. The growth of *Salmonella* and other organisms in liquid and reconstituted egg. Canad. J. Res. *F22*, 169.

GOEPFERT, J. M. and CHUNG, K. C.   1970B.   Behavior of *Salmonella* in sliced luncheon meat. Appl. Microbiol. *19*, 190.

GOEPFERT, J. M. and CHUNG, K. C.   1970A.   Behavior of *Salmonella* during the manufacture and storage of a fermented sausage product. J. Milk Food Technol. *33*, 185.

GOEPFERT, J. M. and KIM, H. U. 1975. Behavior of selected food-borne pathogens in raw ground beef. J. Milk Food Technol. *38*, 449.

GOMUTPUTRA, C. and FABIAN, F. W. 1953. Acids and chloramphenicol as sanitizing agents for meat contaminated with food poisoning organisms. J. Milk Food Technol. *16*, 220.

GOODFELLOW, S. J. and BROWN, W. L. 1978. Fate of *Salmonella* inoculated into beef for cooking. J. Food Prot. *41*, 598.

GRAU, F. H. 1983. Growth of *Escherichia coli* and *Salmonella typhimurium* on beef tissue at 25C. J. Food Sci. *48*, 1700.

HOBBS, B. C. 1974. Food Poisoning and Food Hygiene. Edward Arnold Ltd., London.

INTERNATIONAL COMMISSION ON MICROBIOLOGICAL SPECIFICATIONS FOR FOODS. 1980. Meats and Meat Products. Microbial Ecology of Foods. Vol. 2, Food Commodities, pp. 378–382. Academic Press, NY.

JOHNSTON, R. W. 1983. Personal communication.

KAUFFMAN, F. 1966. The Bacteriology of Enterobacteriaceae. Einar Munksgard, Copenhagen, Denmark. (Williams & Wilkins, Baltimore, MD).

KOELENSMID, W. A. A. B. and VAN RHEE, R. 1964. *Salmonella* in meat products. Ann. Inst. Pasteur de Lille *15*, 85.

LANG, D. J., KUNZ, L. J., MARTIN, A. R., SCHROEDER, S. A., and THOMSON, L. A. 1967. Carmine as a source of nosocomial salmonellosis. New Engl. J. Med. *276*, 829.

LAWRIE, R. A. 1966. Meat Science, p. 76. Pergamon Press, Oxford, England.

LEDWARD, D. A., NICOL, D. J., and SHAW, M. K. 1971. Microbiological and color changes during aging of beef. Food Technol. Austral. *23*, 30.

LEWIS, M. N., WEISER, H. H. and WINTER, A. R. 1953. Bacterial growth in chicken salad. J. Am. Diet. Assoc. *29*, 104.

LIPSON, A. 1976. Infecting dose of *Salmonella*. Lancet *1*, 969.

LUITEN, L. S., MARCHELLO, J. A., and DRYDEN, F. D. 1982. Growth of *Salmonella typhimurium* and mesophilic organisms on beef steaks as influenced by type of packaging. J. Food Prot. *45*, 263.

McCULLOUGH, N. B. and EISELE, C. W. 1951A. Experimental human salmonellosis: I. Pathogenicity of strains of *Salmonella meleagridis* and *Salmonella anatum* obtained from spray-dried whole egg. J. Infect. Dis. *88*, 278.

McCULLOUGH, N. B. and EISELE, C. W. 1951B. Experimental human salmonellosis: IV. Pathogenicity of strains of *Salmonella meleagridis* and *Salmonella anatum* obtained from spray-dried whole egg. J. Infect. Dis. *89*, 259.

McCULLOUGH, N. B. and EISELE, C. W. 1951C. Experimental human salmonellosis: III Pathogenicity of strains of *Salmonella newport. Salmonella derby* and *Salmonella bareilly* obtained from spray-dried whole egg. J. Infect. Dis. *89*, 209.

MACKEY, B. M., ROBERTS, T. A., MANSFIELD, J., and FARKAS, G. 1980. Growth of *Salmonella* on chilled meat. J. Hyg. Cambridge *85*, 115.

MARAZZA, V. and CRESPI, A. 1973. Osservazioni sulla sopravoivenza di *Salmonella cholerasuis* in insaccati naturalmente inquinati. Atti Soc. Ital. Sci. Vet. *17*, 537.

MARRIOTT, N. G., SMITH, G. C., HOKE, K. E., CARPENTER, Z. L. and WEST, R. L. 1977. Long-distance transoceanic shipments of fresh beef. J. Food Sci. *42*, 316.

MATCHES, J. R. and LISTON, J. 1968. Growth of salmonellae on irradiated and non-irradiated seafoods. J. Food Sci. *33*, 406.

MATCHES, J. R. and LISTON, J. 1972. Effect of pH on low temperature growth of *Salmonella*. J. Milk Food Technol. *35*, 49.

PALUMBO, S. A., SMITH, J. L. and ACKERMAN, S. A. 1973. Lebanon bologna: I. Manufacture and processing. J. Milk Food Technol. *36*, 497.

ROWE, B. and HALL, M. L. M. 1975. *Salmonella* contamination of therapeutic pancreatic preparation. Brit. Med. J. *4*, 51.

SHAW, M. K. and NICOL, D. J.   1969.   Effect of the gaseous environment on the growth on meat of some food poisoning and food spoilage organisms. Proc. 15th Europ. Mtg. Meat Res. Workers, p. 226.

SILLIKER, J. H.   1980.   Status of *Salmonella*—ten years later. J. Food Prot. *43*, 307.

SILLIKER, J. H. and WOLFE, S. K.   1980.   Microbiological safety considerations in controlled atmosphere storage of meats. J. Food Technol. *34*, 59.

SMITH, J. L. and PALUMBO, S. A.   1973.   Microbiology of Lebanon bologna. Appl. Microbiol. *26*, 489.

SMITH, J. L., PALUMBO, S. A., KISSINGER, J. C., and HUHTANEN, C. N.   1975.   Survival of *Salmonella dublin* and *Salmonella typhimurium* in Lebanon bologna. J. Milk Food Technol. *38*, 150.

STOKES, J. L., OSBORNE, W. W. and BAYNE, H. G.   1956.   Penetration and growth of *Salmonella* in shell eggs. Food Res. *21*, 510.

SULZBACHER, W. L.   1952.   Effect of freezing and thawing on the growth rate of bacteria in ground meat. Food Technol. *6*, 341.

TAKÁCS, J. and SIMONFFY, Z.   1970.   Das Salmonellen—Problem bei Dauerwursten. Fleischwirtschaft *50*, 1200.

TAKÁCS, J., JIRKOVSKY, M. and HEGYI, Z.   1963.   Studies on the microbiological and biochemical changes involved in the ripening process of Hungarian salami. Acta Vet. Hung. *13*, 119.

TAYLOR, A. A.   1971.   The gaseous environment of packaged fresh meat. Proc. 17th Europ. Meat Res. Workers, p. 662.

TIWARI, N. P. and MAXCY, R. B.   1972.   Comparative growth of salmonellae, coliforms and other members of the microflora of raw and radurized ground beef. J. Milk Food Technol. *35*, 445.

TODD, E. C.   1978.   Foodborne disease in six countries—A comparison. J. Food Prot. *41*, 559.

WOLFE, S. K.   1980.   Use of CO and CO_2 enriched atmospheres for meat, fish and produce. Food Technol. *34(3)*, 55.

Staphylococci

James B. Evans[1]

GENERAL TAXONOMIC FEATURES AND HABITAT

Staphylococci are gram-positive, facultatively anaerobic cocci with a tendency to grow in clusters. They are widely distributed in nature and may be frequently found as part of the microbial flora of meat and poultry products. The taxonomic boundaries of the genus were the subject of much debate and conflicting opinions until the mid-1960s (Evans 1965) when an international committee agreed that the genus should be limited to species that produced the enzyme catalase and fermented glucose under anaerobic conditions and described standardized procedures for conducting these tests (Subcommittee 1965). At about that same time methods became available for determining the "DNA base ratio" [the mol % of guanine (G) + cytosine (C) in the nuclear DNA] of bacteria. It was quickly discovered that staphylococci had a base ratio of 30 to 39% G + C, whereas, the micrococci had a base ratio of 63 to 73% G + C. This essentially settled the debate about separating these two genera (Kloos 1980).

It soon was discovered that the correlation between the phenotypic test for anaerobic glucose fermentation and the base ratio criterion was not perfect. In those instances where these two criteria do not agree, the DNA composition obviously would have greater taxonomic validity. Unfortunately, DNA analysis is not a simple procedure that can be used in routine screening of cultures in diagnostic or control laboratories. For virtually all

[1]Department of Microbiology, North Carolina State University, Raleigh, NC 27695.

Advances in Meat Research, Volume 2
Copyright 1986 by AVI Publishing Co.
All rights of reproduction in any form reserved
ISBN 0-87055-498-0

staphylococcus cultures that are of significance in food and public health laboratories, the glucose fermentation test will be positive (Evans and Kloos 1972).

The classification of staphylococci into species also was in a highly unsatisfactory and confused state until the landmark publications of Kloos and Schleifer (Kloos and Schleifer 1975; Schleifer and Kloos 1975). These workers used an extensive array of morphological, physiological, biochemical, and antibiotic sensitivity tests to study the staphylococci from human skin. Studies of the chemical structure of cell walls was particularly useful. They described nine species other than *Staphylococcus aureus*. Subsequent studies of the staphylococci from many other host species of animals and birds have added several additional species. Their taxonomic scheme has been widely accepted and has proved to be a very useful framework for clinical and epidemiological studies. A total of 23 species have been described thus far (Schleifer *et al.* 1984) and at least one miniaturized, rapid identification kit based on this identification scheme currently is commercially available (Kloos and Wolfshohl 1982; Doern *et al.* 1983).

At present it appears that only one species, *S. aureus,* is of significant practical importance on meat and poultry. Not only can this bacterium cause a variety of infections of meat animals and birds, as well as in humans, but it also is the causative agent of a major form of food poisoning if it grows to a sufficient population level in the food before it is consumed. Although *S. aureus* is one of the most phenotypically homogeneous species of bacteria known, no single diagnostic test is infallible. For many years a positive coagulase test was generally accepted as synonymous with this species, and it still remains as probably the best practical criterion for identifying *S. aureus.* However, mutants lacking this characteristic may be isolated from coagulase-positive cultures (Engels and Kamps 1982) or may be isolated from clinical sources and from other habitats. In addition, two other species in the modern classification scheme may give positive coagulase tests.

Perhaps even more important to the microbiology of meat and poultry is the discovery that subtle differences exist between *S. aureus* from humans and those from different animal species, including cows and hogs, and from poultry. Poultry strains that are otherwise typical *S. aureus* but give slow and weak, or even negative, coagulase tests have been isolated (Evans *et al.* 1983).

Other diagnostic tests that have been touted as being definitive for identifying *S. aureus* are the production of a heat-stable deoxyribonuclease and the fermentation of mannitol under anaerobic conditions. However, critical evaluation of these tests proves them to be subject to the same problems of specificity noted for the coagulase test. Of course DNA hybridization studies will provide absolute identification, but this procedure is beyond the scope of routine diagnostic application and remains the ultimate test of the research laboratory. Subdivision of *S. aureus* for epidemiological purposes may be accomplished in some circumstances by bacteriophage typing or by serological studies.

A number of selective and differential media have been developed for the isolation or enumeration of staphylococci or of *S. aureus*. Among the more common selective agents used in these media are high salt concentration, potassium tellurite, glycine, and egg yolk. Most of these media provide fairly good qualitative results but fall short of quantitative success. The best of these media currently available seems to be that developed by Baird-Parker (Stiles and Ng 1981; Van Doorne *et al.* 1982).

PHYSIOLOGICAL CHARACTERISTICS RELEVANT TO MEAT AND POULTRY

Oxygen Requirements

Staphylococcus aureus and most other staphylococci are typical facultatively anaerobic bacteria. They grow very vigorously under anaerobic conditions and even better under aerobic conditions. Occasionally one may isolate respiratory-deficient mutants, particularly from hosts that have received extensive antibiotic treatment. These organisms produce very small colonies on agar and can grow with about equal vigor anaerobically or aerobically. They are significantly more resistant to some antibiotics, particularly the aminoglycosides (Harrell and Evans 1977). As a result of their facultative nature, *S. aureus* can grow on or in meat and poultry products even when in an air-impermeable package, if the temperature and other environmental parameters are suitable.

Growth Temperature

Staphylococcus aureus strains generally have a minimum growth temperature a few degrees below 10°C and a maximum growth temperature only a few degrees above 45°C (Troller 1976). Those growth parameters are affected to a small extent by other environmental factors such as the salt level of the growth medium. Because of their minimum growth temperature, they do not grow under normal refrigeration conditions that are essential to slow the growth of psychrophilic bacteria on meat and poultry. The minimum temperature for toxin production seems to be several degrees above the minimum temperature for growth (Pereira *et al.* 1982).

Heat Tolerance

Staphylococci are nonspore-forming bacteria that do not produce any heat-resistant bodies. They are readily killed by the heat processing or cooking temperatures to which meat and poultry products normally are subjected before being consumed. The specific resistance varies somewhat among strains and, particularly, may depend to some extent on the physical and chemical environment of the bacteria during heating. Factors such as fat, salt, acidity, and moisture levels have an effect. A recent study by Verrips and van Rhee (1983) reported that their test strain of *S. aureus* had a *D* value of 66 sec at 55°C in water and 246 sec in egg yolk. In salted egg yolk it had a *D* value of 180 sec at 66°C. Occasional reports attribute extreme heat resistance to staphylococci under certain conditions, but carefully controlled experiments have failed to verify most such claims. It does, however, produce enterotoxins that will withstand boiling temperatures for as much as 30 min (Tatini 1976).

Salt Tolerance

Staphylococcus aureus and most other staphylococci will grow in media with up to 12% salt, and some growth occurs in media with 15% or more salt. Since most other bacteria other than halophilic species are much less tolerant of salinity, most selective media for staphylococci incorporate 7.5% salt. Salted meat products may act as a selective medium for staphylococci so other means such as refrigeration or acidification should be used to control staphylococcal growth and the possibility of food poisoning. It should be borne in mind that the effective salt concentration at the surface of a product will be affected greatly by factors such as drying or moisture condensation on the surface. The rate of toxin production is reduced substantially by salt levels from 1 to 10% and is prevented at 12% (Pereira *et al.* 1982).

Acid Tolerance

Staphylococcus aureus is capable of growing over a relatively wide pH range. Most strains can grow under alkaline conditions as high as pH 9.6, and under acid conditions as low as pH 5.0. A pH of 4.8 will inhibit *S. aureus* and any pH below 6.0 decreases their growth rate and greatly reduces the possibility that they may produce enterotoxin during growth (Troller 1976; Pereira *et al.* 1982).

Metabolism of Carbohydrates

Staphylococci are capable of fermenting a fairly wide range of carbohydrates. Under anaerobic conditions *S. aureus* carries out a homolactic fermentation of glucose with better than 90% of the sugar being converted to lactic acid via the conventional glycolytic pathway. Under aerobic conditions, they metabolize the glucose to CO_2 and water via the normal respiratory pathway involving the tricarboxylic acid cycle and a cytochrome-linked pathway of electron transport. Although the initial processes of phosphorylation and transmembrane uptake of other sugars may differ in some respects from these processes with glucose, the ultimate pathways of fermentation and respiration of those sugars that are utilized are essentially the same. A final pH of around 5.0 is generally reached during the anaerobic fermentation of glucose.

Metabolism of Nitrogenous Compounds

Staphylococcus aureus is capable of carrying out limited transformations of a fairly wide range of nitrogenous compounds. Polymers such as DNA are cleaved to smaller oligomers or monomers. Most strains will hydrolyze native animals proteins, but do not produce overt proteolytic spoilage of meat and poultry products under most conditions. Nitrates are reduced to nitrite, and ammonia is produced from arginine. Nevertheless there may be extensive growth of *S. aureus* on some meat products without pronounced evidence of spoilage.

IMPORTANCE IN MEAT AND POULTRY

Spoilage Problems

Since staphylococci cannot grow at ordinary refrigeration temperatures, they do not represent a spoilage problem for fresh meat and poultry. Even if these products are not adequately refrigerated, spoilage by other bacteria would take place before staphylococci became a significant factor. However, cured meat products because of their salt content are somewhat selective for staphylococci if refrigeration is inadequate. They could become a significant component of the surface slime on such products but would have relatively little effect on odor or flavor.

Food Poisoning Problems

The primary, and almost exclusive, reason for concern about staphylococci on meat and poultry products is the potential ability of many strains of *S. aureus* to produce enterotoxins that are a major cause of food poisoning. Despite some taxonomic confusion and conflicting reports in the literature, with possibly rare exceptions, the ability to produce enterotoxins appears to be confined to the one species, *S. aureus*. It is now possible to detect and identify these enterotoxins in foods by serological techniques (Freed *et al.* 1982). In order to produce sufficient toxin to cause clinically recognizable food poisoning in a human consumer, *S. aureus* must multiply in the food product to a population level in excess of 10^6 per gram before sufficient toxin is produced to cause illness in a human consumer of the food. It should be remembered that on a solid food item this bacterial population is not evenly distributed but may be highly localized. Furthermore, after the toxin has been produced the bacteria may be killed by heat or other adverse conditions that do not destroy the toxin.

Not all strains of S. aureus produce enterotoxins. However, a recent study by Olsvik et al. (1981) reported that 61% of the cultures they isolated from a variety of sources were able to produce enterotoxin. Of interest to meat microbiologists was their finding that 32 of the 46 strains of bovine origin, 9 of 11 from sheep, and 15 of 35 from humans produced enterotoxin. However, S. aureus from poultry seem much less likely to be toxin producers; Shiozawa et al. (1980) have reported that only 16 of 586 strains from poultry produced enterotoxin. On the other hand, Harvey et al. (1982) found that 95% of 139 strains of S. aureus from poultry were able to produce enterotoxin, almost exclusively of serotype D. Most strains of human origin produce types A and C enterotoxin. Fresh meats and poultry, although unlikely to be held under conditions that will permit extensive growth of S. aureus may serve as a source of these organisms for other foods where they may proliferate. Cured meats are particularly vulnerable. Ham is the most common meat item involved in staphylococcal food poisoning, which almost invariably is caused by S. aureus.

OCCURRENCE

Fresh Meats and Poultry

Staphylococcus aureus occurs with considerable frequency on the skin and nasal membranes, in the intestinal tract, and as the causative agent of a wide variety of cutaneous infections in the human population, meat animals, and poultry. Consequently, they constitute part of the bacterial flora in meat- and poultry-processing facilities and are part of the flora on the products, although normally as a minor component. For example, Stiles and Ng (1981) examined 100 retail samples of ground beef and found S. aureus counts to range from less than 100 to 4500 per gram; 16% had counts in excess of 1000 per gram. Frozen pork sausage had similar counts, but the 140 retail meat cuts examined generally had counts of less that 100 S. aureus per gram. Notermans et al. (1982) found the S. aureus population on the skin of broilers before processing to be less than 10 per gram, but after processing the counts had increased to more than 1000 per gram. The plucking and eviscerating operations were the major source of this increased population of S. aureus

Staphylococcus aureus from different animal or avian hosts have undergone some host-specific changes that help to distinguish the probable source of these organisms when they are found in meat and poultry products. These may be phenotypic changes such as the ability to coagulate bovine blood plasma or to lyse clots of human fibrin or they may be changes in bacteriophage susceptibility as well as in the serotype of enterotoxin they produce.

Cured Meats

Because of their widespread distribution, S. aureus are likely to be found on almost any item that is subject to much handling during production or packaging. However, only on products that might encounter conditions that would allow growth and multiplication of these bacteria do they constitute a threat. Cured meats clearly fall into this category. Their salt content inhibits the growth of many potentially competing microbial species, and their relatively high resistance to spoilage may lead to poorer refrigeration conditions. As a result, relatively high populations of S. aureus sometimes can be found on cured meats. Ham is the principal meat item involved in episodes of staphylococcal bacterial food poisoning.

Processed Meats

There is a variety of products that may be lumped in this category. Generally they have been exposed to considerable handling, and their production often involves grinding and mixing, the addition of spices and salts, and some level of heat processing. These conditions may result in the buildup of a considerable population of S. aureus prior to their being killed by heat processing. If the heat processing takes place in a closed container or package, subsequent recontamination is prevented. However, if enterotoxin was produced before the bacteria are killed, the toxin will not be destroyed by the heat processing. Laboratory findings must be interpreted in the light of these factors.

CONTROL

Control of S. aureus in meat and poultry products starts with procedures designed to minimize the level of contamination of the products with the organism during processing and packaging. The same procedures that are characteristic of good sanitary practice designed to minimize contamination with spoilage bacteria and other pathogenic organisms will also limit the initial level of S. aureus. This should be followed by procedures designed to prevent their multiplication. Good refrigeration will accomplish this and should be employed for any product that might support the growth of S. aureus if there is any possibility of viable cells of this organism being present. It should always be borne in mind that although heat processing or cooking will readily kill these bacteria, it will not destroy their enterotoxin that may have been produced during prior mishandling.

SUMMARY

Staphylococci are widely distributed in nature and are capable of growing on or in most meat and poultry products. They are not capable of multiplying at normal refrigeration temperatures and even when they grow in meat and poultry products only minor organoleptic changes are produced. One species, *Staphylococcus aureus,* is a major cause of food poisoning as a result of the ability of many strains of this species to produce one or more enterotoxins. Although these bacteria are killed by the usual cooking or heat-processing temperatures, the enterotoxins are much more heat resistant. Staphylococci, including *S. aureus,* are capable of growing in the presence of salt concentrations that prevent the growth of most other bacteria and therefore, grow very well on and in cured and processed meat and poultry products if refrigeration is inadequate.

REFERENCES

DOERN, G. V., EARLS, J. E., JEZNACH, P. A. and PARKER, D. S. 1983. Species identification and biotyping of staphylococci by the API STAPH-IDENT SYSTEM. J. Clin. Microbiol. *17,* 260.

ENGELS, W. and KAMPS, M. A. F. 1982. The nature of the competitive ability of spontaneous staphylocoagulase-negative mutants of *Staphylococcus aureus* with respect to growth of the parent strains in continuous culture. Antonie van Leeuwenhoek J. Microbiol. Serol. *48,* 67.

EVANS, J. B. 1965. Current views and problems relating to the taxonomy of the *Micrococcaceae.* Intern. Bull. Bacteriol. Nomen. Taxon. *15,* 111.

EVANS, J. B. and KLOOS, W. E. 1972. Use of shake cultures in a semisolid thioglycolate medium for differentiating staphylococci from micrococci. Appl. Microbiol. *23,* 326.

EVANS, J. B., ANANABA, G. A., PATE, C. A. and BERGDOLL, M. S. 1983. Enterotoxin production by atypical *Staphylococcus aureus* from poultry. J. Appl. Bacteriol. *54,* 257.

FREED, R. C., EVANSON, M. L., REISER, R. F. and BERGDOLL, M. S. 1982. Enzyme-linked immunosorbent assay for detection of staphylococcal enterotoxins in foods. Appl. Environ. Microbiol. *44,* 1349.

HARRELL, L. J. and EVANS, J. B. 1977. Effect of anaerobiosis on antimicrobial susceptibility of staphylococci. Antimicrob. Agents Chemother. *11,* 1077.

HARVEY, J., PATTERSON, J. T. and GIBBS, P. A. 1982. Enterotoxigenicity of *Staphylococcus aureus* strains isolated from poultry: Raw poultry carcases as a potential food-poisoning hazard. J. Appl. Bacteriol. *52,* 251.

KLOOS, W. E. 1980. Natural populations of the genus *Staphylococcus.* Ann. Rev. Microbiol. *34,* 559.

KLOOS, W. E. and SCHLEIFER, K. H. 1975. Isolation and characterization of staphylococci from human skin. II. Descriptions of four new species: *Staphylococcus warneri, Staphylococcus capitis, Staphylococcus hominis,* and *Staphylococcus simulans.* Intern. J. Syst. Bacteriol. *25,* 62.

KLOOS, W. E. and WOLFSHOHL, J. F. 1982. Identification of *Staphylococcus* species with the API STAPH-IDENT system. J. Clin. Microbiol. *16,* 509.

NOTERMANS, S., DUFRENNE, J. and VAN LEEUWEN, W. J. 1982. Contamination of broiler chickens during processing; incidence and origin. J. Appl. Bacteriol. *52,* 275.

OLSVIK, O., BERDAL, B. P., FOSSUM, K. and OMLAND, T. 1981. Enterotoxin production by *Staphylococcus aureus* related to the origin of the strains. Acta. Pathol. Microbiol. Scand. *B89*, 423.

PEREIRA, J. L., SALZBERG, S. P. and BERGDOLL, M. S. 1982. Effect of temperature, pH and sodium chloride concentrations on production of staphylococcal enterotoxins A and B. J. Food Prot. *45*, 1306.

SCHLEIFER, K. H., KILPPER-BALZ, R. and DEVRIESE, L. A. 1984 *Staphylococcus arlettae* sp. nov., *S. equorum* sp. nov. and *S. Kloosii* sp. nov.: Three new coagulase-negative, novobiocin-resistant species from animals. Syst. Appl. Microbiol. *5*, 501.

SCHLEIFER, K. H. and KLOOS, W. E. 1975. Isolation and characterization of staphylococci from human skin. I. Amended descriptions of *Staphylococcus epidermidis* and *Staphylococcus saprophyticus* and descriptions of three new species: *Staphylococcus cohnii*, *Staphylococcus haemolyticus*, and *Staphylococcus xylosus*. Intern. J. Syst. Bacteriol. *25*, 50.

SHIOZAWA, K., KATO, E. and SHIMIZU, A. 1980. Enterotoxigenicity of *Staphylococcus aureus* strains isolated from chickens. J. Food Prot. *43*, 683.

STILES, M. E. and NG, L. K. 1981. Use of Baird-Parker's medium to enumerate *Staphylococcus aureus* in meats. J. Food Prot. *44*, 583.

SUBCOMMITTEE ON TAXONOMY OF STAPHYLOCOCCI AND MICROCOCCI. 1965. Recommendations. Intern. Bull. Bacteriol. Nomen. Taxon. *15*, 109.

TATINI, S. R. 1976. Thermal stability of enterotoxins in food. J. Milk Food Technol. *39*, 432.

TROLLER, J. A. 1976. Staphylococcal growth and enterotoxin production-factors for control. J. Milk Food Technol. *36*, 499.

VAN DOORNE, H., PAUWELLS, H. P. and MOSSEL, D. A. A. 1982. Selective isolation and enumeration of low numbers of *Staphylococcus aureus* by a procedure that relies on elevated temperature culturing. Appl. Environ. Microbiol. *44*, 1459.

VERRIPS, T. and VANRHEE, R. 1983. Effects of egg yolk and salt on *Micrococcaceae* heat resistance. Appl. Environ. Microbiol. *45*, 1.

9

Miscellaneous Pathogenic Bacteria in Meat and Poultry Products

Frank L. Bryan[1]

[1]Department of Health and Human Services, Public Health Service, Centers for Disease Control, Atlanta, GA 30333. *Present address:* Food Safety Consultation and Training, 2022 LaVista Circle, Tucker, GA 30084.

Advances in Meat Research, Volume 2
Copyright 1986 by AVI Publishing Co.
All rights of reproduction in any form reserved
ISBN 0-87055-498-0

TABLE 9.1. Classification of Meat- and Poultry-Borne Pathogens

A.	Pathogenic bacteria transmissible to man by ingestion of raw or undercooked meat and poultry
	Arizona hinshawii
	Bacillus anthracis
	Campylobacter jejuni
	Campylobacter coli
	Escherichia coli (enterotoxigenic, enteroinvasive, and enteropathogenic strains)
	Francisella tularensis
	Salmonella ((most serovars)
	Yersinia enterocolitica
	Yersinia pseudotuberculosis
B.	Pathogenic bacteria transmissible to man by ingestion of cooked or otherwise heat-processed meat or poultry that may become contaminated after heat processing
	Any of the above
	Bacillus cereus
	Clostridium botulinum
	Clostridium perfringens
	Shigella
	Staphylococcus aureus
	Streptococcus pyogenes
C.	Pathogenic bacteria sometimes present in animals and their milk, but meat- and poultry-borne transmission unproved
	Brucella
	Coxiella burnetii
	Mycobacterium bovis
	Streptobacillus moniliformis

INTRODUCTION

Pathogenic bacteria in meat or poultry products can be transmitted to man by several means (Table 9.1). They may be transmitted during ingestion of raw meat or raw poultry but transmission can also follow the ingestion of cooked products which have been mishandled. They may also be transmitted when animal tissues are handled or when aerosols or dust from them are inhaled. Furthermore, other bacteria are found in meat or poultry, but the role of these organisms in causing diseases in man is unknown. Some overlapping exists among categories in Table 9.1 because some agents have more than one mode of transmission. Time and place factors, as well as, information not yet available will, no doubt, reclassify some of these organisms in the future.

Meat and poultry are commonly reported vehicles for the etiologic agents of food-borne diseases. In the United States, for example, they account for over 50% of the reported outbreaks for which a vehicle was ascertained (Table 9.2; Bryan 1980). Beef (particularly roast beef), ham, and turkey are the most commonly reported vehicles, and staphylococcal

According to Modes of Transmission

D. Pathogenic bacteria transmissible by contact with animal tissue or
      by inhalation of aerosols or dust
      Bacillus anthracis
      Brucella
      Campylobacter fetus subsp. *intestinalis*
      Chlamydia psittaci
      Coxiella burnetii
      Erysipelothix rhusiophathiae
      Francisella tularensis
      Listeria monocytogenes
      Leptospira
      Pseudomonas mallei
E. Pathogenic bacteria present in animals, but role in meat-borne
      transmission to man unknown
      Brucella
      Chlamydia psittaci
      Coxiella burnetii
      Erysipelothrix rhusiopathiae
      Atypical mycobacteria
      Leptospira
      Listeria monocytogenes
      Pseudomonas mallei
F. Other bacteria sometimes on meat and poultry reported in the
      literature as pathogens, but proof is lacking
      Aeromonas
      Citrobacter
      Klebsiella
      Proteus
      Providencia
      Streptococcus faecalis
      Streptococcus faecium

TABLE 9.2. Number and Percentage of Food-Borne Outbreaks Reported in the United States, 1968–1977, Involving Meat and Poultry as Vehicles[a]

Year	Number of outbreaks	Number of outbreaks in which vehicle was ascertained	Outbreaks attributed to meat, poultry, or foods containing them		Outbreaks attributed to foods in which meat or poultry may have been an ingredient	
			Number	%	Number	%
1968	290	226	170	75	11	5
1969	326	275	194	71	15	5
1970	297	206	146	71	14	7
1971	320	249	142	57	11	4
1972	301	247	125	51	18	7
1973	307	237	86	36	21	9
1974	456	312	139	45	13	4
1975	497	379	195	51	33	9
1976	438	266	120	45	33	12
1977	436	269	103	38	56	21
Total	3668	2666	1420	54	225	8

[a] U.S. Department of Health and Human Services, Centers for Disease Control, 1969–1977.

TABLE 9.3. Number of Meat and Poultry Products as Food-Borne Vehicles in Outbreaks

Disease	Beef (specified)	Beef (unspecified, possibly roast beef)	Roast beef	Ground beef	Cured beef	Foods containing beef	Pork	Cured pork (ham)	Sausage	Foods containing pork	Lamb	Other meats
Arizonosis												
Bacillus cereus gastroenteritis		1				1				1		
Botulism				1		5			1			6
Clostridium perfringens gastroenteritis	9	11	36	14	1	11	4		1		1	
Salmonellosis	4	13	22	8	2	3	13	6	4			2
Shigellosis												
Staphylococcal intoxication	9	4	7	7	4	4	23	105	7	5	1	2
Streptococcal group D gastroenteritis			3	1		1		2	1			
Hepatitis A									1			
Toxoplasmosis				1								
Trichinosis				7			39		42	6		6
Chemical poisonings	1						2			4		
Disease of unknown etiology	24	44	85	81	11	49	18	77	31	16	5	3
Total	47	73	153		18	74	99	191	87	32	7	19
		⎵ 226						409			26	
			488									
Percentage	3.4	5.2	11.0	8.8	1.3	5.3	7.1	13.7	6.3	2.3	0.5	1.4
		16.2										
			35.1					29.4			1.9	

a U.S. Department of Health and Human Services, Centers for Disease Control, 1969–1977.
b Listed in another category, but gravy was served with the food.

food poisoning, salmonellosis, and *Clostridium perfringens* enteritis are the most commonly reported diseases (Table 9.3). (These diseases are discussed elsewhere in this book.) Other less common food-borne diseases, however, are acquired as a result of eating meat and poultry or dishes made from them.

The purpose of this chapter is to describe the role that pathogenic bacteria, which have been isolated from meat and poultry and which have not

Reported in the United States, 1968–1977[a]

Meat, general				Poultry					Totals	
Unspecified meats	Luncheon meats	Liver	Gravy[b]	Turkey	Chicken	Duck	Poultry salad	Foods containing poultry	Total outbreaks in which meat or poultry were vehicles	Percentage of outbreaks in which meat or poultry were proved/ or suspicious vehicles
			1						1	25
1								1	5	39
					2			1	16	14
4	1		10 (13)	29	6			1	139	90
5	3	1	1 (3)	39	15	1	11	4	157	44
		1		1	2				4	8
5	6	2	3	23	16		16	3	252	8
1		1		1					11	65
	2								3	9
									1	100
									100	94
									10	9
16	22	3	18 (20)	91	52	3	22	22	693	31
32	34	8	32 (36)	185	91	4	51	32	1392	
⎣___ 74 ___⎦				⎣_____ 363 _____⎦						
2.3	2.4	0.6	2.3 (2.6)	13.3	6.5	0.3	3.7	2.3		
⎣__ 5.3 __⎦			4.9	⎣_____ 26.1 _____⎦						

been previously discussed in this volume, either have been or might be transmitted by meat or poultry, via ingestion, contact or inhalation routes. The pathogens are described here in alphabetical order to aid in retrieving information. This arrangement, however, should not imply relative importance; classification in Table 9.1 and epidemiologic data about the diseases provide this. The ecology of the agents, the epidemiology of the diseases they cause, and preventive and control measures are emphasized.

ARIZONA HINSHAWII

Bergey's "Manual of Determinative Bacteriology" (Le Minor and Rohde 1974) classifies *Arizona* as a *Salmonella (Salmonella arizonae)*, but others do not (Edwards and Ewing 1972). Because of the classification and ecological similarities of *Arizona* to *Salmonella*, reference is made to the discussion in Chapter 7. Poultry or eggs have been the implicated vehicles of all reported food-borne outbreaks of arizonosis (Bryan 1979).

Prevention and Control

Prevention of infections by *Arizona hinshawii* can be accomplished by thorough cooking of poultry, prevention of cross-contamination, holding of cooked poultry at a temperature above which this species grows (regulations usually require 60°C or above), rapid chilling of cooked poultry that is to be served several hours or a day or more after cooking, and thorough reheating of leftovers. Recommended cooking and reheating temperatures for poultry are 74°C or above. Prevention of cross-contamination can be accomplished by thoroughly washing hands after handling egg shells or poultry, by using one set of cloths to clean areas soiled by raw poultry, and another set to clean equipment used for cooked foods; by not using the same equipment for processing raw poultry and cooked foods; and by properly cleaning and disinfecting utensils and equipment after they contact raw poultry or eggs.

BACILLUS ANTHRACIS

Three clinical forms of anthrax—cutaneous, inhalational, and gastrointestinal—are known (Brachman 1983). Cutaneous anthrax is the most common form. It develops primarily on exposed skin, usually at the site of a scratch or abrasion after a person handles infected animals or contaminated carcasses or hides. After an incubation period of 2 days or less, a small, red (often pruritic) spot that resembles an insect bite or pimple develops. As the lesion evolves, extreme edema occurs. Necrosis begins and a characteristic asteristic black scab forms. Nearby lymph nodes become tender, and the infection spreads from the nodes to blood, with rapid development of bacteremia and toxemia.

An animal dying of anthrax excretes *B. anthracis* in its feces, urine, saliva, and any discharge of blood. As the carcass is opened, heavy contamination can spread to surroundings. Furthermore, aerosols and dust containing *B. anthracis* spores are produced during processing of contaminated animal hair, wool, hides, and similar products. When these spores are inhaled, they are deposited in the lungs, where they are taken up by alveolar phagocytes and carried to lymph glands. There, the spores germinate and vegetative cells multiply and elaborate toxins. Bacteremia and toxemia develop when *B. anthracis* and toxins reach the bloodstream. Symptoms first simulate influenza; these are followed by acute dyspnea, labored breathing, profuse sweating, cyanosis, shock, and collapse. Such infections are frequently fatal as a result of respiratory failure.

Gastrointestinal anthrax, which is the rarest form, is characterized by a high temperature, general weakness, anorexia, malaise, headache, insomnia, abdominal pain, bloody diarrhea, nausea, and vomiting of blood and bile. The clinical course can progress through toxemia, shock, and cyanosis to death. This syndrome develops 2–5 days after ingestion of contaminated meat. Also, primary anthrax of the pharynx may possibly arise from ingestion of contaminated meat.

Anthrax still occurs commonly in nonindustrialized regions of the world and sporadically in the industrialized regions as animal (particularly goat) hair, hides, skins, and bones originating from principally Africa, Asia, and the Middle East are handled (Dutz and Kohout 1971; Turner 1980). Few cases are now reported in the United States.

Reservoirs

Soil is the principal reservoir of spores of *B. anthracis* and herbivores, especially cattle, sheep, horses, and goats, are at risk of becoming infected during grazing. Spores have been isolated from bone meal fertilizer. Neutral or alkaline soils, along with rainy, warm weather, are conducive to their development.

Meat-Borne Outbreaks

Several meat-borne outbreaks of anthrax have been reviewed by Bryan (1979). These have resulted from the ingestion of raw or inadequately cooked meat from infected animals that were either found dead or slaughtered because of illness. In additional reports, seven cases of anthrax, of which all but one died, occurred after malodorous beef and duck were eaten (Nalin *et al.* 1977), and 33 cases (3 deaths) were traced to eating sausage in Spain (Christie 1980).

Prevention and Control

Several measures can be taken to prevent and control anthrax in animals and in their products. Animals in endemic areas should be vaccinated. Any animal suspected of having died of anthrax should be autopsied to confirm diagnosis, and the carcass cremated, if possible. Suspected feeds and fertilizers should be tested, and incinerated if they contain spores of *B. anthracis*. Herds from which infected animals are found should be quarantined for 2 weeks after the last case is identified, and all animals in the herd should be vaccinated during an outbreak. The public must be educated so that dead or dying animals will not be eaten. Antemortem evaluations should be made of meat-source animals, and their carcasses and organs examined during postmortem inspections, particularly in endemic regions.

Employees of plants that manufacture products made from high-risk animal by-products should be made aware of the hazards and should be immunized. Cuts and abrasions should be kept clean and covered. Workers in dusty contaminated areas should be issued respirators and urged to wear them. Raw products should also be decontaminated, and ways to prevent and control dissemination of dust and aerosols should be put into effect. A preventive program should also include regular cleaning of equipment and work areas, as well as maintaining and requiring the regular use of facilities for washing, showering, and storing clothing. Specimens of lesions suspicious of being anthrax should be cultured for *B. anthracis,* and the lesions should be observed daily for a week.

BRUCELLA SPP.

Brucellosis is manifested by fever, chills, sweating, malaise, weakness, body aches, headache, anorexia, and weight loss, usually without any localized signs. The incubation period is 1–3 weeks.

Reservoirs

The major reservoirs of brucellae are cattle, sheep, goats, swine, horses, and dogs. Reindeer, caribou, moose, bison, yaks, and camels are also sometimes infected. Fowl and other birds are seldom infected.

Brucellae have a propensity for localizing in the male genitalia, uteri of pregnant females, and in the mammary glands of lactating females. Abortions occur, and aborting females can extensively contaminate their immediate environment. Another source of contamination is urine from infected animals. Infected animals may shed brucellae in their milk for years.

Animals can become infected by drinking contaminated milk, by licking aborted fetuses, placentas, or the genitalia of infected animals. Infection can also occur through abraded skin, nasopharanyx, conjunctivae, and udder. Infections may occur intravaginally from infected animals during either coupulation or artificial insemination.

The principal modes of transmission to man are (1) direct contact with infected animals or the handling of contaminated tissues, including meat, or touching discharges, and (2) ingestion either of raw milk from infected animals (usually goats or cows) or of cheese made from such raw milk. Morales-Otero (1929, 1930) demonstrated in human volunteers that infection occurred more readily through the abraded skin than through the gastrointestinal tract. Large numbers (1 milliliter of a 24-hour broth culture in milk for 5 to 7 days) of *B. abortus* had to be ingested to elicit mild symptoms. Dust-borne or aerosol-borne transmission is also possible.

Food Sources

Numerous outbreaks and individual cases of brucellosis have been traced to the ingestion of raw milk, primarily that from goats (Bryan 1979 1983). There is also a possibility that brucellosis is acquired during ingestion of raw or insufficiently cooked meat, but the evidence is weak. A slaughterhouse worker developed brucellosis after drinking swine blood (Loffler 1931). Seventeen slaughterhouse workers developed brucellosis; nine had eaten meat heated on steam radiators, but seven denied any contact with meat (Levine 1943). In both of these incidents the possibility of infection through the skin or airborne transmission cannot be excluded. In another episode, eight of ten persons contracted brucellosis after a picnic meal at which inadequately cooked goat's meat was eaten (Molinelli *et al.* 1948).

Furthermore, food may become contaminated with brucellae through contact with excreta and organs from infected animals and by dust and fomites that have been contaminated by these articles. Such a possibility is intensified in rural regions where people live in intimate contact with animals that harbor brucellae.

Growth and Survival

Brucellae are quite resistant to environmental stresses and survive for weeks in soil, manure, and water. They survive in milk for hours and in milk products for weeks. They also survive well in meat products. For example, *Brucella suis* was recovered from hog carcasses after 21 days of refrigerated storage. *Brucella melitensis* was isolated from hams after they were cured in covered pickle brine for 21 days. *Brucella abortus* survived in sausage for 175 days. Brucellae are killed in less than 20 min at temperatures between 60° and 63°C, and in seconds at temperatures above 70°C. [See Bryan (1979) and Gillespie and Timoney (1981) for a review of their survival in these substrates.]

Contact Infections

Most cases of abattoir-associated brucellosis are acquired as a result of brucellae penetrating skin abrasions (Buchanan *et al.* 1974). The airborne route of transmission, however, may also be important (Jackson and Western 1975).

Prevention and Control

Brucellosis eradication programs are based on vaccination, testing, and slaughter. In such a program, cattle that are retained for breeding should be vaccinated between the ages of 4 to 7 months. Positive serological reactions are indicative of infection, and animals with such reactions should be removed from the herd and slaughtered. Swine and cattle should be kept apart in separate pens and fields.

Prevention of brucellosis in persons in high-risk occupational groups (farmers, meat-packing and rendering plant workers, and veterinarians) depends on the eradication of infected animals. Wearing protective gloves when handling infected animals or their tissues, using protective glasses to avoid splash droplets to the eye, and carefully dressing cuts on employees who handle meat also help.

Pasteurization or boiling of milk is essential for the prevention of brucellosis in areas where there are infected animals. Aging of cheeses for at least 90 days kills or greatly reduces the quantity of brucellae in these products. These practices can reduce the likelihood of transmission by these foods, but they will not eliminate the disease. Only the eradication of infected animals will do this.

CAMPYLOBACTER JEJUNI AND CAMPYLOBACTER COLI

Campylobacter jejuni and *Campylobacter coli* (formerly referred to as *Campylobacter fetus* subsp. *jejuni* and, before that *Vibrio fetus*) cause an enterocolitis. Numerous reports of isolations of *Campylobacter* are made at laboratories that look for it. In some laboratories, it is the most common pathogenic bacteria isolated from stool specimens from patients with acute enterocolitis.

The infection is acquired orally. Apparently the infective dose can be small; as few as 500 organisms have caused illness (Robinson 1981). After an incubation of 1 to 7 days, diarrhea (usually watery and sometimes containing cellular exudate, blood or pus) and severe abdominal pain occur. The illness may be preceded or accompanied by malaise and fever. Aches of head, back, and limbs may occur, along with sweating and rigor. The abdominal pain can be so severe that appendicitis is suspected. See Butzler and Skirrow (1979) for more details.

Reservoirs

Campylobacter enterocolitis, like salmonellosis, is a zoonosis. Campylobacters are found in a wide variety of animal hosts. They have been isolated from swine, cattle, sheep, rabbits, and goats, and from the cecal contents of chickens, ducks, turkeys, and wild birds. Detailed reviews are given by Blaser and Reller (1981), Doyle (1981), and Smibert (1978). In animals, *C. jejuni* and *C. coli* have caused abortion in cattle and sheep, hepatitis in fowl, and scours in swine and calves.

Following a milk-borne outbreak, the duration of excretion of *Campylobacter* varied. In a study by Wright (1981), more than 50% of persons studied ceased shedding within 2 weeks, over 20% ceased shedding after 4 weeks, and more than 5% ceased shedding after 6 weeks. The last known carriers stopped excreting *C. jejuni* after 9 weeks.

Food Sources

Poultry is often contaminated with campylobacters. These organisms were isolated from 94% of 50 chicken carcass rinses collected from a poultry-processing plant. Counts were as high as 1.1×10^5 per carcass (Smeltzer 1981). In a processing plant, *C. jejuni* was isolated from 36 of 50 (72%) chickens both at the start and end of processing, and it was still present in 24 (48%) after refrigerated delivery to simulated time of sale (Simmons and Gibbs 1979). In a further study, these investigators found *C. jejuni* in 28 of 35 (80%) processed chickens and in 11 of 12 (92%) processed turkeys at the simulated time of sale. *Campylobacter jejuni* was isolated from 2.1% of 140 rinses from chicken necks and whole dressed broilers that had been purchased at local outlets (Smith and Muldoon 1974). Of 100 whole market chickens purchased 1 per week over a 5-week period from each of 20 different stores in Ontario and rinsed in bags, 62% were positive for *C. jejuni* (Park *et al.* 1981). These investigators tested the same number of chickens using the same procedure in Ohio and found 54% positive for this organism. *Campylobacter jejuni* was isolated from 22% of 82 samples of frozen chickens from retail stores (Norberg 1981). It was isolated from 32% of peritoneal cavities of chilled chicken carcasses and from 36% of frozen carcasses from retail stores (Hartog and de Boer 1981). These researchers also isolated this organism from 67% of chilled chicken livers, but they recovered it from only 4% of frozen chicken livers. Thirty-six percent of the counts in the chilled livers were greater than 10^3 CFU/g. *Campylobacter jejuni* was isolated from 51 of 60 chicken livers and from 57 of 64 chicken gizzards, but they recovered it from only 1 of 86 turkey gizzards and from none of 86 turkey livers (Christopher *et al.* 1982). *Campylobacter jejuni* was found on 37% of 40 chicken carcasses and on 19% of 22 chicken livers (Oosterom and Beckers 1981). Campylobacters were isolated from 60% of chickens and from all samples of minced meat (mostly pork) tested (Kaijser and Svedhem 1981). These organisms were isolated from 18 of 40 processed broiler carcasses in Australia (Shanker *et al.* 1982). All of these isolates came from 20 samples from two processing plants, but none were isolated from two other plants. Counts ranged from 1.5×10^3 to 4.8×10^6 per carcass. The investigators reported that 82% of the isolates from chicken were the same biotype as 98% of isolates from persons with enteric infections who lived in the same locale. Luechtefeld and Wang (1981) isolated *C. jejuni* from 94% of 33 swab samples from 33 freshly dressed turkey carcasses, but from only 34% of 83 carcasses that had been placed overnight in tanks of chlorinated ice and water.

Investigators in four poultry slaughterhouses showed that cross-contamination occurs widely. For example, Hartog and de Boer (1981) showed extensive contamination of equipment, and that 73% of samples from the peritoneal cavity harbored *C. jejuni;* cooling water contained up to 3×10^3 CFU/ml and air near scalding tanks and in evisceration areas yielded 5 to 6 CFU/m^3.

Contamination with *C. jejuni* of carcasses and cuts of meat has also been observed. Calves usually have low densities (ca. 1 to 10 per cm^2 from flanks). After chilling carcasses and deboning of veal this organism was recovered even less frequently. Small numbers were recovered from equipment during processing but not after cleaning (Gill and Harris 1982A). It was isolated from 56% of 100 samples from cut surfaces of pig carcasses before chilling and from 32% after chilling. It also was isolated from 42% of 100 samples from liver surfaces (Rosef 1981). It was found on 38% of 58 pork, 24% of 59 mutton, and 2% of 58 beef carcasses (Stern 1981). Hudson and Roberts (1981) isolated it from 59 of 100 pig carcasses, but not from beef or lamb carcasses.

In a survey of abattoirs and butchers' shops, Bolton *et al.* (1982) isolated campylobacters from the carcasses of 32% of 117 samples from beef carcasses, 70% of 126 samples from sheep carcasses, and 56% of 90 samples from pig carcasses. These bacteria were isolated from 54 of 142 (38%) of swabs from knives, cleavers, and saws, from 15 of 56 (27%) of swabs from cutting blocks, and from 21 of 69 (30%) of swabs from hooks, racks, and scales. These organisms, however, were not recovered from 170 swabs taken from wholesale butchers and 100 from 20 retail butchers. Death of the organisms from slaughter to retail is probably due to their oxygen sensitivity.

Growth and Survival

Campylobacters do not multiply well in or on food products. For example, *C. jejuni* (10^5) had a lag of 2 days in cooked meat medium at 37°C and took another 2 days to reach 10^8, whereas *Clostridium perfringens*, *Salmonella typhimurium*, and *Staphylococcus aureus* reached 10^9 within 1 day in cooked meat medium. In *Brucella* broth (pH 6.9), *C. jejuni* multiplied at temperatures from 32° to 45°C (Doyle and Roman 1981). The number of organisms declined at 47°C and at 25°, 27°, and 30°C. The most rapid generation time of 1.24 to 1.34 hr occurred at temperatures from 42° to 45°C; slow growth (5.88 to 11.1 hr generation time) occurred at 32°C. In *Campylobacter* agar (pH 5.7–5.9), the maximum growth temperature was between 43° to 45°C, and the minimum growth temperature was between 34° to 36°C. *Campylobacter jejuni* increased from 10^4 to 10^9 in 6 hr in sterile meat (pH 6.4) stored at 37°C (Gill and Harris 1982B). In competition with normal flora, *C. jejuni* increased from $10^{5.5}$ to about 10^7 in about 25 hr but decreased to less than 10^3 in 50 hr as normal flora increased and exceeded 10^8.

When sterile meat slices (pH 5.8 and 6.4) were inoculated with campylobacters they declined more than 3 log within 10 days at 25°C and at -1°C at the lower pH. Only slight declines were observed when the higher pH products were stored at -18° and -1°C (Gill and Harris 1982B). Campylobacters can multiply within the pH range of 4.9 to 9.5; the most rapid growth is between pH 6 and 8. According to Gill and Harris (1982B), the growth requirements of *C. jejuni* are such that it could not grow on normal (pH 5.5–5.8) meat, but it could grow on high-pH, dark, firm, dry (DFD) meat only at temperatures around 40°C.

In reduced *Brucella* broth (adjusted to pH 4.0 or less) that was incubated at 42°C, *C. jejuni* exhibited a 5 $\log_{10}$ decrease within 4 hr, a 3 $\log_{10}$ decrease within 8 hr at pH 4.5, and slight growth at pH 5 (Doyle and Roman 1981). In the same broth incubated at 25°C, a 5 $\log_{10}$ decrease occurred at pH 3.5 or less in 4.5 hr. At pH 4 this decrease took 24 hr. It took 48 hr for this decrease at pH values of 4.5 and 5.0.

Several studies have been made on the ability of campylobacters to survive storage environments. A culture of *C. jejuni* grown in a microaerobic atmosphere at 42°C for 2 days survived on chicken and minced meat at 4°C for 1 week and while frozen at -20°C for 3 months (Svedhem *et al.* 1981). The survival of *C. jejuni/coli* in ground beef liver was not affected by storage at 4°C for 6 days, but they decreased considerably in both ground beef liver and chicken samples stored at -20°C for 12 weeks (Hanninen 1981). This organism was shown to survive when packaged in air or CO_2 for 24 days at 4°C (Blankenship and Craven 1982). Organisms declined more rapidly on raw chicken in an air atmosphere (4 $\log_{10}$ decrease) than in a CO_2 atmosphere (1 $\log_{10}$ decrease). Stern and Kotula (1982) reported that *C. jejuni* declined three orders of magnitude after 3 days of storage at -15°C in ground beef and, subsequently, their numbers remained relatively constant.

Campylobacters are not particularly resistant to high temperatures. For example, none of 13 strains tested by Svedham *et al.* (1981) survived heat treatment at 60°C for longer than 20 min, but some survived this temperature for 15 min, 57.5°C for 30 min, and 55°C for 60 min. At oven temperatures of 190° and 218°C, *C. jejuni* decreased to less than 30 cells per gram after internal temperatures reached 70°C. For 100-gram meat balls, a decrease from 10^7 CFU/g to nondetectable levels took less than 10 min after the internal temperature reached 60°C (Stern and Kotula 1982). *D* and *z* values for campylobacters in various substances are given in Table 9.4.

TABLE 9.4. *D* and *z* Values for *Campylobacter jejuni* in Various Substances

Substrate	D values (minutes)	z values (°C)	Reference
Peptone broth	D_{49} = 14.9–15.2		Blankenship and Cravens, 1982
	D_{51} = 4.9–7.02		
	D_{53} = 1.71–2.7	4.62–5.07	
	D_{55} = 0.64		
	D_{57} = 0.25	4.62	
Chicken	D_{49} = 20.5		
	D_{51} = 8.77–9.27		
	D_{53} = 4.55–4.59		
	D_{55} = 2.12–2.25	5.91–6.35	
	D_{57} = 0.79–0.98	5.91–6.35	
Sterile skim milk	D_{50} = 3.5–5.4		Doyle and Roman, 1981
	D_{55} = 0.74–1.00		
Peptone-yeast	D_{50} = 2.2		Gill and Harris, 1982B
extract broth	D_{55} = 0.7		
	D_{60} = 0.26–0.95		
	D_{65} = 0.22		
	D_{70} = 0.19		

Meat- and Poultry-Borne Outbreaks

Up to the present time, raw milk has been the most important vehicle of campylobacters that have caused human illness (Bryan 1983). Water from a community supply was implicated as a vehicle in an outbreak that afflicted more than 2000 persons (Vogt *et al.* 1982). Of more concern in this text, however, is the role of meat and poultry as vehicles. Raw beef liver was a suggested source for a single case (Soonattrakul *et al.* 1971), and ingestion of raw beef serum was responsible for another (Dolman 1957).

Poultry and meat have been implicated as a vehicle on a few occasions. An investigation of an outbreak of campylobacteriosis involving 89 Dutch military cadets implicated chicken as the vehicle. Chickens were killed, skinned, and cooked over a wood fire by each cadet. It is quite likely that *Campylobacter* either survived the cooking or that recontamination occurred during eating of the chickens with bare hands (Brouwer *et al.* 1979). Fifteen persons developed *Campylobacter* enterocolitis following a meal of Chinese fondue which included chicken liver. There was a statistically significant association between chicken livers and the disease (Mouton *et al.* 1981). Raw hamburger was considered as a probable vehicle in an outbreak involving 34 soldiers in the Netherlands (Oosterom and Beckers 1981). Twenty-one of 140 people developed diarrhea and other gastrointestinal symptoms within 6 days (all but one within 4 days) of attending a dinner dance. *Campylobacter jejuni* was isolated from three of ten persons from whom specimens were collected. Chickens that appeared pink and very undercooked were the most likely vehicles (Skirrow *et al.* 1981). The biotype (2) responsible for the outbreak was the type most likely to be associated with poultry (Skirrow and Benjamin 1981). Chicken was also suspected as the vehicle in an outbreak of campylobacterosis following a wedding breakfast. The chicken had been cooked earlier in the morning and allowed to cool before serving (Hayek and Cruickshank 1977). Three persons who ate medium rare steak from the same source developed diarrhea; two of them had repeated episodes after eating steaks from the same lot on a second occasion. *Campylobacter jejuni* was isolated from the remaining steaks (Health and Welfare Canada 1982).

By comparing epidemiologic histories of 114 patients with those of 90 control persons, Kist (1981) observed a statistically significant association ($P < 0.05$) between eating poultry and developing *Campylobacter* enterocolitis within 48 hr. No such association was made with either contact with ill persons or contact with dogs. Of the ill group, three members of a family became ill 2 days after eating a roasted goose. Two patients were believed to have contracted their infections by eating poultry on an airplane.

A prospective study of 55 patients having *C. jejuni* enterocolitis in a Swedish urban community showed that the patients had eaten chicken within a week of their illness significantly more often than had a corresponding control group. Also, seven of nine of the persons who ate the chicken had prepared the chickens themselves. There was no evidence of transmission of *Campylobacter* to food prepared by two cooks who were working (one in a hospital kitchen that served 1000 meals per day) while still being asymptomatic excreters (Norkrans and Svedhem 1982). Many of the infected persons (75%) had acquired their infections outside Sweden.

Contact Infections

Farmers, abattoir workers, or butchers have acquired septicemic infections caused by *Campylobacter fetus* subsp. *intestinalis* from contact with animals or their tissues (Retting 1979). A meat-packing plant worker developed gastroenteritis and septicema after he cut his finger on a machine (Park *et al.* 1973).

Prevention and Control

From what is known about *Campylobacter* at this time, it appears difficult to keep this organism from infecting animals. All means to keep fecal matter from carcasses should be used. Spray washing of carcasses will be helpful, but some campylobacters, nevertheless, will be spread to carcasses and primal cuts of meat in abattoirs. Campylobacters from contaminated carcasses may be spread to equipment surfaces and to hands of workers and then spread to other carcasses. Effective end-of-the-day or -shift clean-up and disinfection of surfaces can eliminate the spreading of these organisms at the start of the next operation, but as carcasses or cuts of meat pass through the operation, contaminated ones will start the cross-contamination cycle again. Cleaning is, of course, necessary to prevent other problems and should be actively applied at each establishment where meat and poultry are processed or otherwise handled.

The few reported poultry-borne campylobacterioses have been related to inadequate cooking, therefore, "thorough" cooking is as essential a control measure, as is pasteurization of milk. Campylobacters will most likely be on the surface of cuts of meat, and will be mixed throughout in ground (minced), rolled, or fabricated meat. Cooking of whole cuts should be such that surface regions reach 60°–70°C for a few minutes. These temperatures should be reached in the geometric center regions of ground, rolled, or fabricated meat. Lower temperatures, within the range of 50° to 60°C, can also be effective at killing campylobacters, but sufficient time within this temperature range must be provided. Cooked foods should be held at or above these temperatures.

Although data suggest that the quantity of campylobacters on meat and poultry and the prevalence of contaminated items will be reduced as meat passes through retail channels, cross-contamination will still occur. Cross-contamination should be avoided through such routine practices as using separate equipment to process raw and cooked meat and poultry or thoroughly cleaning equipment after processing raw meat and poultry; using separate cleaning cloths so that one set is used for equipment in areas where raw foods are handled and another set is used in areas where cooked foods are handled; and using utensils, waxed paper, and disposable gloves, so as not to touch cooked meat and poultry.

Although campylobacters do not multiply at temperatures below 30°C, cooked meat and poultry should not be kept at room temperature. Storage of cooked foods in large covered containers during periods of refrigeration might lead to multiplication because such foods remain warm at reduced redox potentials for several hours.

CHLAMYDIA PSITTACI

Psittacosis is a flu-like disease manifested by fever, severe headaches, and pneumonia and is caused by *C. psittaci*. This organism is transmitted to man by dust or aerosols that are contaminated with fecal matter or nasal excretions of infected avian species. Outbreaks of psittacosis and conjunctivitis have occurred among turkey processing plant workers (Bryan 1979).

COXIELLA BURNETII

Coxiella burnetii is enzootic in cattle, sheep, goats, dogs, rodents, and birds in many regions of the world. Large numbers are shed from infected animals in milk, urine, and feces, and in uterine discharges at parturition. Placentae may contain very high quantities. Because of the high level of environmental contamination, *C. burnetii* becomes airborne. Human beings are usually infected by *C. burnetii* in aerosols, but they may acquire this organism when bitten by insects, by handling infected animals or their internal tissues or hides, or by drinking raw milk from infected animals. Abattoir workers have acquired *C. burnetii* and consequently developed Q fever (which resembles influenza) by inhalation of aerosols created by spraying or sawing carcasses, dropping meat and organs on tables and floors, pressure release of compression lines used on offal lines, and splattering of blood or other body fluids (Bryan 1979). An outbreak involving 149 cases in slaughterhouse workers followed their inhalation of aerosols caused by sick animals (Blidaru *et al.* 1982).

ERYSIPELOTHRIX RHUSIOPATHIAE

Erysipeloid is a cutaneous lesion, caused by *E. rhusiopathiae*, that is characterized by a slowly progressive, self-limited, purplish-red, painful swollen area on the finger or arm. Often a sense of burning, throbbing, and itching accompanies the wound. The swelling may even be so severe as to limit movement of joints. The lesion and swelling occur 1–4 days after being jabbed by a bone, spine, or knife while handling pork, poultry, fish, shellfish, or bones. Erysipeloid is an occupational disease of fishermen, fish handlers, farmers, poultry-plant workers, abattoir- and meat-processing workers, butchers, and veterinarians.

Food-borne transmission is rarely reported and such reports are questionable. In one such report, a person developed malaise, generalized pruritus, and erysipeloid eruption localized in the ears and cheeks within a few hours after he ate salt pork. Anemia occurred and the patient died 2 months after onset of illness (Fiessinger and Brovet 1934).

Erysipelothrix rhusiopathiae is resistant to salting, pickling, and smoking and has survived for 1–3 months in meat that has undergone such treatment (Reed 1965). It survives for long periods in soil, water, and putrefying meat (Gillispie and Timoney 1981).

The wearing of gloves and frequent hand washing are preventive measures.

ESCHERICHIA COLI

Escherichia coli resides in the lower part of the intestinal tract of warm-blooded animals. It is the most common oxygen-tolerant bacterium in the large bowel of human beings. Most strains of *E. coli* are harmless commensals, but pathogenic strains can cause enteric illness either by elaborating a cholera-like enterotoxin or by penetrating the intestinal epithelium as *Shigella* does (Bryan 1979; Sack 1975).

Enterotoxigenic strains colonize the gut and elaborate enterotoxin, which causes secretion of salt and water into the lumen. Mild to severe diarrhea (rice-water stools) with profound dehydration and shock without fever ensue. During recovery, toxigenic strains are cleared from the small bowel, but they colonize the large intestine without causing any effect on the mucosa. Patients remain asymptomatic carriers as long as the organisms stay in the bowel. Enterotoxigenic strains produce either a heat-stable toxin that resists 100°C for 15 min or a heat-labile toxin that is antigenic and destroyed at 60°C within a period of 30 min; both types of toxins may be produced.

Enteroinvasive strains cause an illness that is manifested by fever, chills, headache, myalgia, abdominal cramps, and profuse watery diarrhea. Feces sometimes contain blood, mucus, and abnormally high numbers of epithelial cells. The term enteropathogenic also appears in the literature; it refers to strains which have caused gastroenteritis in infants.

Food Sources

Because of the omnipresence of *E. coli* in feces of animals, it commonly reaches carcasses and cuts of meat during slaughtering and processing. This organism can multiply on equipment surfaces, so its presence on meat may not indicate direct fecal pollution. There are numerous reports of *E. coli* on meat during slaughtering and processing. For example, it has been found in ground beef (Goepfert 1966; Reis *et al.* 1980; Tamminga *et al.* 1982), sausage (Reis *et al.* 1980), and on poultry (Kim and Stephens 1972; Shooter *et al.* 1974). Only a part of the *E. coli* flora on foods is pathogenic. Of 240 *E. coli* isolates from foods, only 19 (8%) were enterotoxigenic (Sack *et al.* 1977). Toxigenic isolates were found on 10% of sausage, 7.5% of hamburger, and 5% of keebe (beef and wheat) (Reis *et al.* 1980).

Meat-Borne Outbreaks

On rare occasions, meat or meat products have been implicated as vehicles of outbreaks. In their review of outbreaks of food-borne diseases in England and Wales, Vernon and Tillett (1974) reported on an outbreak caused by serotype 0127 in which veal, ham, and egg pie were implicated as the vehicles. An illness characterized by severe abdominal cramps, initially watery diarrhea followed by grossly bloody diarrhea, and little or no fever, was associated with eating at restaurants of the same fast-food chain in two widely separated states (Riley *et al.* 1983). There was a statistically significant association with the ingestion of hamburgers, dehydrated onions, and pickles. Stools of the 9 of 12 patients yielded *E. coli* 0157:H7 that was neither invasive nor toxigenic by routine tests, but it produced nonbloody diarrhea in infant rabbits. This serotype was also isolated from a sample of frozen raw beef patty from a suspect lot in one of the states. It was hypothesized that undercooked hamburger meat was responsible for the outbreak.

As with other organisms on the surface of carcasses and cuts of poultry and meat, *E. coli* can be spread to equipment surfaces and then to other foods (cross-contamination). Following the introduction of frozen broilers into 60 kitchens, swabs of cutting boards, utensils, tables, sinks, spice tins, taps, and cleaning cloths frequently yielded the test strain of *E. coli*. These organisms were found even after cleaning (de Wit *et al.* 1979).

Escherichia coli is commonly found on the hands of workers in the food industry. It was isolated from 12 of 34 food workers after they washed their hands in sterile buffered water (Horwood and Minch 1951). Hands of 13 of 100 butchers were contaminated by *E. coli* after they left a meat line in a processing plant (Pether and Gilbert 1971). It was also recovered by these investigators from 14% of finger tips of persons 15 min after 10^4 cells were applied, and from 1% of their fingers after 60 min.

Prevention and Control

Raw foods of animal origin will frequently be contaminated by *E. coli*, so thorough cooking is an important control measure. It will contaminate cooked foods when touched by food handlers or when in contact with equipment that previously was used for raw foods, or which had been wiped with cleaning cloths that had also been used in raw-food areas. Prevention of such contamination (by hand washing after defecation and after handling raw meat and raw poultry, by thoroughly washing kitchen equipment, and by using separate cleaning cloths in raw-food areas from those used in cooked-food areas of a kitchen or processing plant) are important, but difficult to achieve, preventive measures. Outbreaks can often be prevented by storing cooked foods in a manner that prevents multiplication of *E. coli*.

FRANCISELLA TULARENSIS

Francisella tularensis can be transmitted to man by several means: (1) bites of blood-sucking arthropods [ticks, deer flies, certain other biting flies, mosquitoes, and (rarely) lice, mites, and fleas] which have previously bitten infected animals; (2) direct or indirect inoculation of the skin or eye during skinning, dressing, or otherwise handling of diseased animals, particularly wild rabbits; (3) ingestion of stream or well water which has been polluted by the bodies, urine, or feces of infected animals; (4) ingestion of insuffiently cooked meat from infected animals; and (5) inhalation or ingestion of dust or aerosols from contaminated urine, soil, grain, hay, hides, fur, or wool. Very few organisms can cause infection when they enter the body by the respiratory or intradermal routes, whereas very large numbers (10^{10}) were required to cause illness by gargling and swallowing (Hornick et al. 1966).

Meat-Borne Outbreaks

Most reports of tularemia that has been acquired by ingestion are difficult to interpret because the infected persons usually also skinned or otherwise handled the meat (Bryan 1979). There are a few reports, however, among members of families, some of which did not touch the carcasses or meat. Also, some patients have had no ulcers or skin involvement.

Reported meat-borne outbreaks have incubation periods of 8 to 24 hr. The disease is manifested by nausea, vomiting, abdominal pain, diarrhea, fever (around 40°C), chills, headache, thirst, convulsions, and delirium. Ulcerative lesions of the buccal mucosa, pharynx, and intestine with subsequent lymph involvement can also occur. The disease is often fatal.

Growth and Survival

Francisella tularensis can survive in insufficiently cooked meat. Following one such outbreak, rabbit meat had been breaded and fried by the victims. Although the meat had a brown crust, the region near the bone showed red strands of muscle and red juice. An extract of the red muscle was ingested into guinea pigs and death resulted (Freese et al. 1926).

Prevention and Control

The only method in preventing intestinal tularemia is to thoroughly cook wild rabbit meat. Well-water supplies should be protected, and stream water should not be ingested. Persons who skin and dress wild rabbits and fur-bearing mammals (e.g., muskrats) should wear rubber or plastic gloves and both hands and gloves should be disinfected afterward. Hunters and others who walk in tick-infested areas should wear protective clothing, use insect repellent, and examine their bodies frequently for ticks. Sheep shearers, fur handlers, and other persons who are exposed to potentially contaminated dust or aerosols should wear face masks.

LEPTOSPIRA SEROVARS

Leptospires localize in certain tissues and organs, especially the kidneys. Leptospirosis is manifested by fever, headache, chills, malaise, vomiting, muscular aches, and conjunctivitis. The incubation period is 4–19 days.

During the acute phase of leptospirosis in lactating animals, leptospires may be spread in milk. Milk, however, has leptospirocidal properties (Kirschner *et al.* 1957). The main portal of entry of leptospires is through the skin, especially when it has been cut or abraded or has become sodden from long contact with water. The mucous membranes of the eyes, nose, and throat can also be penetrated.

Leptospires are present in the infected animal's urine, and can reach meat and the internal organs of animals during processing. Leptospires that reach the stomach would most likely be killed rapidly by stomach acids, but infection could, theoretically, penetrate the alimentary tract anterior to the stomach. Dolman (1957) referred to a case of leptospirosis that occurred in a man 8 days after he ate ham that had been stored in a cellar. The ham exhibited evidence of rat gnaws and, presumptively, was polluted with rodent urine.

Infection can occur among abattoir workers who have contact with infected animals, their urine, kidneys, or meat or organs that have been contaminated by urine. Inhalation of contaminated air can also be a means of transmission. Agricultural workers (such as rice field workers) who wade in irrigated or flooded fields which have been polluted by rodent or other animal urine have also become infected.

Prevention of this disease is difficult. The most effective method of prevention is to increase farm and household animal resistance by immunization. Improving or maintaining sanitation and controlling rodents are also helpful.

LISTERIA MONOCYTOGENES

Listeria monocytogenes is widely distributed in nature. It has been isolated from soil taken from both agricultural and nonagricultural land, from vegetation, and from feces of humans and other animals. Listeriosis is frequently recognized in sheep and cattle. Poultry is often contaminated by *L. monocytogens*. For example, Kwantes and Isaac (1971) isolated this organism from 20 of 35 (57%) market poultry and later (1974) from 17 of 51 (33%). Gitter (1976) isolated it from 10 of 68 swab samples from poultry (mostly frozen) purchased at 26 different shops and supermarkets.

Listeria monocytogenes has also been isolated from meat and meat products. Gudkova *et al.* (1958) isolated it from viscera of pigs on a farm at which several persons with mononucleosis due to *L. monocytogenes* had ingested pork from pigs of the infected herd. Between 10 and 30% of egg-processing plant and slaughterhouse workers harbored *L. monocytogenes* during surveys (Kampelmacher and van Noorle Jansen 1969). The carrier state is relatively brief, usually without diarrhea (Bojsen-Moller 1972). Poultry plant workers have developed conjunctivitis when handling birds that were infected with *L. monocytogenes* (Bowmer *et al.* 1979).

Listeria monocytogenes grows well at refrigeration temperatures of 4° to

6°C. It is relatively heat resistant. It has been isolated from pasteurized milk and from fried eggs with congealed whites and soft yolks. Furthermore, it has survived temperatures ranging from 63° to 100°C. See Bryan (1979) for review and references. Gouet *et al.* (1978) showed that *L. monocytogenes* multiplied in ground beef, particularly in the presence of pseudomonads. Lactobacilli inhibited growth of the organisms.

Because meat and poultry are frequently contaminated with *L. monocytogenes* and it multiplies at refrigerated temperatures and can survive temperatures that exceed those sometimes used in cooking, prevention is more difficult to achieve than it is for the more common food-borne pathogens.

MYCOBACTERIUM BOVIS AND OTHER MYCOBACTERIA

There is little evidence of transmission of *Mycobacterium bovis* from meat or poultry. One reason is that several million *M. bovis* cells are required to cause infection of experimental animals by the intestinal route (Francis 1973). The same is probably true for man. Such a level of contamination would probably be unlikely unless liver, lungs, mesentery, udder, intestines, or other parts that are sites of extensive lesions would be eaten (Shrader 1939; Francis 1958, 1973). Today, flesh of cattle seldom contains *M. bovis,* and carcasses are rarely retained or condemned for tuberculosis during meat inspection (Francis 1973). In Egypt, however, 11% of 4050 buffalo carcasses were found to harbor virulent tubercle bacilli (El Mossalami *et al.* 1972).

The so-called atypical mycobacteria cause tuberculosis or similar diseases, but unlike *M. tuberculosis,* there is no evidence of person-to-person spread with the atypical form. These organisms have been isolated from chickens, swine, cattle, and sheep. For example, *Mycobacterium avium* infects birds (including domestic poultry), pigs, and some other animals. *Mycobacterium xenopi* is found in coastal areas and tidal estuaries and infects sea birds. Soil and water are sources of mycobacteria for animals. Eggs, meat, and both raw and pasteurized milk and milk products have been found to be contaminated (Tison *et al.* 1966). Atypical mycobacteria can survive the time-temperature exposure of pasteurization of milk (Chapman *et al.* 1965; Scammon *et al.* 1963). In spite of the presence of atypical mycobacteria in foods, food-borne transmission is unknown (Bryan 1979).

PSEUDOMONAS (ACTINOBACILLUS) MALLEI

Pseudomonas mallei causes glanders in horse species. Serious outbreaks have occurred in members of the cat family fed contaminated horse meat in zoological parks (Hart 1916). Evidence that human beings have acquired this disease from eating meat, however, is lacking.

Man can become infected occasionally when in close association with diseased animals. The disease is characterized by pain and swelling at the point of infection, usually the hand, lip, or eye. Nearby lymph glands also swell, and ulcers often develop in the mouth or nasal passages. Skin abscesses and pustules, joint inflammations, high fever, lung involvement, and septicemia occur, and patients usually die within 4 weeks. This disease could potentially be acquired when persons touch contaminated nasal passages, lungs, or lesions, or when they inhale aerosols that are generated during processing.

Control of the disease in animals involves early diagnosis and elimination of the infected animals. This disease has been eradicated from the United States, Western Europe, and Australia, but sporadic cases are still reported in South America, Africa, and Eastern Europe.

Pseudomonas pseudomallei is closely related to *P. mallei*. It causes melioidosis, which closely resembles glanders, in man. The organism is found naturally in soil water, particularly in low-lying and rice-growing regions. This disease cannot be considered a zoonosis.

SHIGELLA DYSENTERIAE, SHIGELLA FLEXERNI, SHIGELLA BOYDII, AND SHIGELLA SONNEI

Shigellae penetrate the intestinal lumen, invade colonic epithelial cells, multiply within them, and pass into adjacent cells to cause an acute inflammatory reaction. After an incubation period of 1 to 7 days (usually less than 4 days), diarrhea, abdominal pain, fever, and often vomiting and tenesmus occur. Stools may contain blood, mucus, or pus.

Food-Borne Outbreaks

Shigellae are host-adapted to man and other primates. Convalescent carriers are important in the spread of food-borne shigellae. Cooked foods are touched while they are cut, sliced, chopped, mixed or otherwise handled. A person who is shedding shigellae may contaminate his hand while wiping or washing after defecation. If this person either fails to or inadequately washes his hands and then touches foods before these organisms die due to the acid reaction of the skin, the food is likely to be contaminated. Frequently, such contaminated foods are kept for several hours within a temperature range in which shigellae can multiply (Bryan 1978). Salads, particularly potato salads, are commonly reported vehicles. Turkey salad has been implicated in a few outbreaks (Bryan 1979).

Prevention and Control

Prevention is accomplished by requiring that persons who have diarrhea refrain from handling foods. Also, convalescents of shigellosis should not handle foods until their stools are shown to be free of shigellae. This requires three culture-negative stools, each collected at least a week apart. Teaching food workers safe food-handling techniques and to wash their hands after going to the toilet is essential for prevention. Chilling prepared foods which are not to be served immediately, and keeping such foods at either hot or cold temperatures at which shigellae cannot grow are important preventive measures, along with cooking and reheating foods to time-temperature values that will kill shigellae.

STREPTOCOCCUS FAECALIS AND STREPTOCOCCUS FAECIUM

It is questionable whether S. faecalis and S. faecium (the enterococci) cause food-borne illness. Sporadic articles in the medical and scientific literature, along with surveillance reports, have implicated these bacteria as pathogens, and meat products were sometimes implicated as vehicles. The reported illnesses have simulated either staphylococcal food poisoning or C. perfringens enteritis. Large numbers of enterococci, however, have been ingested in several foods without reports of illnesses.

Human volunteer studies have shown conflicting results (Bryan 1979). For example, Deibel and Silliker (1963) performed extensive tests with 23 strains of enterococci, nine of which had been previously implicated in food-borne disease outbreaks. These were grown in different substrates and incubated for different times; some were disrupted by sonic treatment. In no instance did any of the cultures produce illness in any of the persons who ingested them. On the other hand, Sedova (1970) reported that strains of S. faecalis subsp. liquefaciens had enteropathogenic properties. Freshly isolated strains caused illness in 71% of the volunteers, but after 6 months of transfer and storage, test strains entirely lost their enteropathogenic properties.

One habitat of enterococci is the alimentary tract of man and many other animals. Some strains, however, are found on vegetation. Enterococci are commonly isolated from foods (including meat and poultry) and from the environment of food processing and food service establishments. They can multiply in the presence of 6.5% NaCl, at pH 9.6, at 10° and 45°C, and they can survive 60°C for 30 min.

Prevention and Control

Because enterococci are common organisms in the intestinal tract of animals, including man, and are often contaminants of equipment in food processing and service establishments, it is difficult to keep them out of foods. They also survive thermal processing better than do most other vegetative cells, so heat processes should be carefully designed and practiced. Rapid chilling and holding foods at low temperatures (<5°C) or holding at temperatures of 55°C or higher are necessary to prevent their multiplication. After cooking, foods may be contaminated with enterococci from cross-contamination or worker's hands. Multiplication of the organisms during storage is also a possibility so that thorough reheating to a temperature of 74°C or above or lethal time-temperature exposures are necessary to eliminate any enterococci that reach foods.

STREPTOCOCCUS PYOGENES

Streptococcus pyogenes is the causative agent of septic sore throat, tonsillitis, scarlet fever, and a number of other pyogenic and septicemic infections. Following outbreaks of *S. pyogenes* infections, sequelae such as rheumatic fever can develop.

Reservoirs

Man is a primary reservoir of *S. pyogenes*. Many persons harbor group A streptococci in their throats for weeks after onset of infections. Active and healing skin infections are also important sources of streptococci that reach foods. This organism is also a common cause of mastitis in dairy cattle.

Meat- and Poultry-Borne Outbreaks

In the past, milk-borne epidemics were common (Bryan 1979, 1983). In the last decade or two, foods containing eggs were the most commonly reported vehicles. Occasionally, meat- or poultry-containing foods have been identified as vehicles. For example, hams were contaminated during slicing, boning, grinding, and in sandwich preparation. The sandwiches were kept at room temperature overnight and until the late afternoon when they were served. Over 100 persons who ate the sandwiches developed either scarlet fever or septic sore throat (Getting *et al.* 1943). Chicken salad was the vehicle of a pharyngitis, caused by a group G streptococci, involving 72 persons. The chicken salad had been prepared by a person who developed pharyngitis a day before. The salad was refrigerated overnight in a 40-quart pan, in which the contents would cool very slowly (Stryker *et al.* 1982). Stew and either eggs or meat sandwiches have been reported as vehicles in other outbreaks (Bryan 1979).

Contact Infections

Group A streptococcal skin infections have occurred among persons who handle meat in abattoirs and meat-processing plants. Eight outbreaks were reported in the United Kingdom (Fraser *et al.* 1977) and others have been reported in the United States by Tsai *et al.* (1979). Workers in a chicken-processing plant have become infected (Barnham *et al.* 1980). These meat- and poultry-processing plant workers are at risk because they often suffer trauma to their hands while working, and handling meat contaminated by streptococci provides opportunities for transfer.

Prevention and Control

A review of the outbreaks provides obvious, food-borne preventive measures. Persons having infected lesions or sore throats should not touch cooked foods, particularly eggs, or prepare salads. Cooked foods and prepared salads should be cooled either in shallow pans (less than 10 cm high), in refrigerators, or by some other rapid means.

YERSINIA

Diseases caused by *Yersinia enterocolitica* and *Yersinia pseudotuberculosis* have several manifestations. Acute forms are enteritis, pseudoappendicular syndrome (acute appendicitis), septicemia (typhoid-like or hepatitis-like illness), scarlatiniform fever (fever and skin eruptions), and localized infections (such as abscesses). Secondary immunological complications that have occurred are erythema nodosum (fever, eruptions, and fatigue), arthritis (pain and swelling of joints), thyroid disease (goiter and related symptoms), and glomerulonephritis (edema and hypertension). The enteritis form of yersiniosis is manifested by abdominal pain, fever, diarrhea, nausea, and vomiting; it cannot be distinguished from salmonellosis, shigellosis, and *E. coli* diarrhea without cultural or serological tests. Serotypes 03, 08, or 09 are the types most often implicated in human illness.

Animals are important reservoirs of *Yersinia*. *Yersinia pseudotuberculosis* has been found in the digestive tract or feces of a wide variety of mammals and birds. Poultry and rodents are frequently infected. Swine are major sources of *Y. enterocolitica*. These bacteria are often recovered from cecal or fecal material, mesenteric lymph nodes, throats, and tongues of pigs. Isolations have been made from cattle, sheep, chickens, and rodents (Swaminathan *et al.* 1982).

Food Sources

Because of their wide presence in animals, *Yersinia* would be expected to contaminate meat and poultry. Beef samples obtained from retail markets in West Germany yielded *Y. enterocolitica* at a 10.8% level (Leistner *et al.* 1975). Two of the isolates were of serotypes that have caused illness in human beings. This organism was isolated from 15 of 61 samples of beef in Japan (Inoue and Kurose 1975). In the United States *Y. enterocolitica*-like organisms were isolated from 10 of 98 surface-swab samples of vacuum-packaged beef and were also isolated from lambs (Hanna *et al.* 1976). These organisms were isolated from 66 of 150 samples of vacuum-packaged beef knuckles, but they were isolated from only 4 of 150 samples of hanging beef knuckles (Johnson *et al.* 1982). *Yersinia enterocolitica*-like organisms are now classified as *Yersinia enterocolitica sensu stricto, Yersinia intermedia, Yersinia frederikenii,* and *Yersinia kristensenii.*

Serotypes of *Y. enterocolitica* that have been associated with human illness have been isolated from samples of pork as well as from specimens from pigs. Leistner *et al.* (1975) isolated *Y. enterocolitica* from 10 of 29 samples of pork from retail markets in Germany. Serotype 03 was isolated from 75 of 142 pork tongues from 34 different butcher shops in 19 Belgian communities (Wauters and Janssens 1976). In Japan, however, only two isolations of 03 and one of 05 were made from 300 samples of pork (Asakawa *et al.* 1979). Serotype 03 was recovered by these investigators from only 2 of 571 fecal samples from butchers and from only 2 of 50 chopping blocks. In the same country, other environmental-related serotypes were isolated from 27 of 40 pork samples (Inoue and Nagao 1976). Although 163 samples of muscle tissue and 60 samples of raw ground pork were free of this organism. It was found in a sample of pork liver (Narucka and Westerndoorp 1977). Schiemann (1980) isolated *Y. enterocolitica* from 49% of 128 samples of raw pork (mostly from tongues and ground pork) and from 7% of 169 samples of processed pork products from retail stores in Canada. Although the majority of the isolates were untypeable, serotype 03 and 05 were the predominate typeable strains.

Poultry has also yielded environmental-related serotypes of *Y. enterocolitica.* These strains were isolated from 35 of 121 samples of chicken from retail markets in Germany (Leistner *et al.* 1975). In Japan, they were recovered from 16 of 40 samples of chicken (Inoue and Nagao 1976). In the United States, three of 75 samples of turkey meat yielded these organisms (Guthertz *et al.* 1976). In Sweden, *Y. enterocolitica* (mostly nontypeable strains) was isolated from 24.5% of 82 samples of frozen chicken from retail stores (Norberg 1981). It was isolated in much higher frequency than *Salmonella* (1.2%). In the Netherlands, it was isolated from 73 of 108 samples of poultry carcasses from processing plants and from retail outlets. Chicken salad has also been shown to be contaminated with *Y. enterocolitica* (Hurvell *et al.* 1982). Isolations of *Y. enterocolitica* have been made from milk and a number of other foods (Swaminathan *et al.* 1982; Lee *et al.* 1981; Bryan 1983).

Food-Borne Outbreaks

Although a number of common-source outbreaks have been reported, vehicles are seldom identified. Those identified include raw milk, pasteurized chocolate milk, pasteurized milk, tofu (fermented soybean curd packed in water), and water (Bryan 1983). Epidemiological associations have been made between illness and ingestion of meat, but laboratory confirmation is lacking. In Czechoslovakia, Rakovsky *et al.* (1973) observed that the seasonal incidence of *Y. enterocolitica* infections coincided with the period during which pig feasts are held. In the Netherlands, Keet (1974) attributed human yersiniosis to the custom of eating tartar (raw meat). In Japan, Zen-Yoji *et al.* (1974) considered pork as an important source of *Yersinia* that caused human infections.

Growth and Survival

In nutrient broth, *Y. enterocolitica* has been reported to grow at temperatures between 1° and 44°C by Sutherland and Varnam (1977). Nilehn (1969) reported that most strains of *Y. enterocolitica* could not grow at 43°C or above. On raw beef, it has grown at 0°C according to Hanna *et al.* (1979). These investigators observed that *Y. enterocolitica* and *Y. enterocolitica*-like organisms grew in round steaks at 1°–5°C when either wrapped in polyvinyl chloride or vacuum packaged. Larger numbers accumulated in the more oxygen-permeable film than in the vacuum packages. *Pseudomonas* spp. developed rapidly on the steaks stored in polyvinyl chloride, whereas lactic acid bacteria became dominant on the vacuum-packaged steaks. Hanna *et al.* (1979) further observed that large increases in counts of *Y. enterocolitica* occurred on either raw or cooked beef and pork when cuts were stored at 7°C for up to 10 days, and even greater increases occurred when they were held at 25°C for 24 hr.

Yersinia are about average in respect to pH and a_w. The pH range for growth of *Y. enterocolitica* is 4.4–9.0; the optimal pH range is from 7 to 8 (Hanna *et al.* 1977; Stern *et al.* 1980; Kendall and Gilbert 1980). Several strains were inhibited in brain heart infusion broth containing 5 to 7% NaCl (Stern *et al.* 1980).

Freezing can adversely affect survival of *Y. enterocolitica* in meats. Large reductions of this organism were observed when roast beef was stored at −23°C for 28 days (Hanna *et al.* 1977). In ground beef, survival of this organism declined 83% in 30 days when stored at −20°C, and many survivors were sublethally injured (El Zawahry and Rowley 1979). Upon storing ham for 7 days at −10°C, almost a 2 $\log_{10}$ decrease of *Y. enterocolitica* was observed by Asakawa *et al.* (1979). Leistner *et al.* (1975) observed only a slight decrease in numbers of this organism in chicken stored at −18°C for 90 days.

The effects of thermal treatments on *Y. enterocolitica* appear similar to these effects on other Enterobacteriaceae. $D_{62.8}$ values for *Y. enterocolitica* in sterile whole milk range from 0.7 to 17.0 sec (Francis *et al.* 1980). In roast beef, 10^6 *Y. enterocolitica* decreased to nondetectable levels when heated to temperatures of 60° to 62°C (Hanna *et al.* 1977).

Prevention and Control

Yersinia reach raw meat and poultry from intestinal and oral cavity contents, hides, feathers, and processing equipment. Therefore, raw meat must be considered to be contaminated. Cooking meat and poultry to internal temperatures of 60°C or above for a few minutes should kill these organisms unless the level of contamination is quite high. Efforts to prevent cross-contamination from raw meat and raw poultry to cooked foods are essential aspects of a control program. Recommended temperatures (<7°C) that prevent growth of other pathogenic food-borne bacteria, unfortunately, do not prevent the growth of *Y. enterocolitica*, although they do prolong lag periods.

OTHER BACTERIA

Several of the Enterobacteriaceae (such as *Klebsiella, Enterobacter*) and other gram-negative bacteria (such as *Aeromonas hydrophila, Aeromonas sobria, Plesiomonas shigelloides,* and *Pseudomonas aeruginosa*) produce enterotoxins (Bryan 1979). These organisms can contaminate meat and poultry and are potential food-borne pathogens. For example, Cooke *et al.* (1980) isolated *Klebsiella* from about 25% of cold meat in a hospital kitchen. The counts often exceeded 10^3 organisms per gram. These organisms were also commonly found in the kitchen. Numerous other bacteria are potential food-borne pathogens (Bryan 1979, 1982).

SUMMARY

This chapter reviews information about pathogens that can be transmitted by direct contact with or by ingestion of meat or poultry or by inhalation of dust or aerosols generated from these products. The information covered includes discussion, when applicable, about reservoirs, food sources, meat- and poultry-borne outbreaks, growth and survival, contact infections, and preventive and control measures.

REFERENCES

ASAKAWA, Y., AKAHANE, S., SHIZAWA, K. and HONMA, T. 1979. Investigations of source and route of *Yersinia enterocolitica* infection. Contrib. Microbial. Immunol. *5,* 115.
BARNHAM, M., KERBY, J. and SKILLRIN, J. 1980. An outbreak of streptococcal infection in a chicken factory. J. Hyg. *84,* 71.
BLANKENSHIP, L. C. and CRAVENS, S. E. 1982. *Campylobacter jejuni* survival in chicken meat as a function of temperature. Appl. Environ. Microbiol. *44,* 88.

BLASER, M. J. and RELLER, L. B.   1981.   *Campylobacter* enteritis. New Engl. J. Med. *305*, 1444.

BLIDARU, I., LAMBA, N. and PETRESUE, C.   1982.   [A Q fever episode in a municipal slaughter house.] Bacteriol. Virusol. Parazitol. Epidemiol. *27*, 179.

BOJSEN-MOLLER, J.   1972.   Human listeriosis. Diagnostic, epidemiological, and clinical studies. Acta Pathol. Microbiol. Scand. Suppl. *B229*, 1.

BOLTON, F. J., DAWKINS, H. C. and ROBERTSON, L.   1982.   *Campylobacter jejuni/coli* in abattoirs and butcher shops. J.Infect. *4*, 243.

BOWMER, E. J., CONKLIN, R. H. and STEEL, J. H.   1979.   Listeriosis. *In* CRC Handbook Series in Zoonoses. Section A. Bacterial, Rickettsial, and Mycotic Disease. J. H. Steel (Editor). CRC Press, Boca Raton, Florida.

BRACHMAN, P. S.   1983.   Anthrax. *In* Infectious Diseases.A Modern Treatise of Infectious Processes. 3rd edition. pp. 939–944. P. D. Hoeprich (Editor). Harper and Row Publ., Hagerstown, MD.

BROUWER, R., MERTENS, M. J., SIEM, T. H. and KATCHAKI, J.   1979.   An explosive outbreak of *Campylobacter* enteritis in soldiers. Antonie van Leeuwenhoek J. Microbiol. Serol. *45*, 517.

BRYAN, F. L.   1978.   Factors that contribute to outbreaks of foodborne disease. J. Food Prot. *41*, 816.

BRYAN, F. L.   1979.   Infections and intoxications caused by other bacteria. *In* Food-Borne Infections and Intoxications. 2nd edition. pp. 211–297. H. Riemann and F. L. Bryan (Editors). Academic Press, NY.

BRYAN, F. L.   1980.   Foodborne diseases in the United States associated with meat and poultry. J. Food Prot. *43*, 140.

BRYAN, F. L.   1982.   Diseases Transmitted by Foods. 2nd edition. Centers for Disease Control, Atlanta.

BRYAN, F. L.   1983.   Epidemiology of milk-borne diseases. J.Food Prot. *46*, 637.

BUCHANAN, T. M., FABER, L. C. and FELDMAN, R. A.   1974.   Brucellosis in the United States 1960–1972. An abattoir associated disease, Parts I, II, and III. Medicine (Baltimore) *53*, 403, 415, 427.

BUTZLER, J. P. and SKIRROW, M. B.   1979.   *Campylobacter* enteritis. Clin. Gastroenterol. *8*, 737.

CHAPMAN, J. S., BERNARD, J. S. and SPEIGHT, M.   1965.   Isolation of mycrobacteria from raw milk. Am. Rev. Respir. Dis. *91*, 351.

CHRISTIE, A. B.   1980.   Infectious Disease Epidemiology and Clinical Practice, 3rd edition. Churchill Livingstone, Edinburgh.

CHRISTOPHER, F. M., SMITH, G. C. and VANDERZANT, C.   1982.   Examination of poultry giblets, raw milk and meat for *Campylobacter fetus* subsp. *jejuni*. J. Food Prot. *45*, 260.

COOKE, E. M., SAZEGER, T., EDMONDSON, A. S., BRAYSON, J. C.and HALL, D.   1980.   *Klebsiella* species in hospital food in kitchens: A source of organisms in the bowel of patients. J. Hyg. *84*, 97.

DE WIT, J. C., BROEKHUIZEN, G. and KAMPELMACHER, E. H.   1979.   Cross-contamination during the preparation of frozen chickens in the kitchen. J. Hyg. *83*, 27.

DIEBEL, R. H. and SILLIKER, J. H.   1963.   Food poisoning potential of the enterococci. J. Bacteriol. *85*, 827.

DOLMAN, C. E.   1957.   The epidemiology of meat-borne diseases. *In* Meat Hygiene. WHO Monogr. Ser. No. 33, p. 11. World Health Organization, Geneva.

DOYLE, M. P.   1981.   *Campylobacter fetus* subsp. *jejuni:* An old pathogen of new concern. J. Food Prot. *44*, 450.

DOYLE, M. P. and ROMAN, D. J.   1981.   Growth and survival of *Campylobacter fetus* subsp. *jejuni* as a function of temperature and pH. J. Food Prot. *44*, 596.

DUTZ, W. and KOHOUT, E.   1971.   Anthrax. Pathol. Ann. *6*, 209.

EDWARDS, R. R. and EWING, W. H.   1972.   Identification of Enterobacteriaceae. 3rd edition. Burgess Publ. Co., Minneapolis, MN.

EL-MOSSALAMI, E., EL-AMROUSI, S. and ZEIDAN, M. 1972. Tuberculosis in buffalo carcasses. Egypt. J. Vet. Sci. *9*, 1.
EL-ZAWAHRY, Y. A. and ROWLEY, D. B. 1979. Radiation resistance and injury of *Yersinia enterocolitica*. Appl. Environ. Microbiol.*37*, 50.
FIESSINGER, W. and BROVET, G. 1934. The occurrence of *Campylobacter jejuni* in fresh food and its survival under different conditions. Presse Med. *42*, 889.
FRANCIS, D. W., SPAULDING, P. L. and LOVETT, J. 1980. Enterotoxin production and thermal resistance of *Yersinia enterocolitica* in milk. Appl. Environ. Microbiol. *40*, 174.
FRANCIS, J. 1958. Tuberculosis in Animals and Man. A Study in Comparative Pathology. Cassell, London.
FRANCIS, J. 1973. Very small public health risk from flesh of tuberculous cattle. Austral. Vet J. *49*, 496.
FRASER, C. A. M., BALL, L. C., MORRIS, C. A. and NOAH, N. D. 1977. Serological characterization of group A streptococci associated with skin sepsis in meat handlers. J. Hyg. *78*, 283.
FREESE, H. L., LAKE, G. C., and FRANCIS, E. 1926. Four cases of tularaemia (three fatal) with conjunctivitis. Publ. Health Rep. *41*, 369.
GETTING, V. A., WHEELER, S. W. and FOLEY, G. E. 1943. A food-borne *Streptococcus* outbreak. Am. J. Publ. Health *33*, 1217.
GILL, C. O. and HARRIS, L. M. 1982A. Contamination of red-meat carcasses by *Campylobacter fetus* subsp. *jejuni*. Appl. Environ. Microbiol. *43*, 977.
GILL, C. O. and HARRIS, L. M. 1982B. Survival and growth of *Campylobacter fetus* subsp. *jejuni* on meat and cooked food. Appl. Environ. Microbiol. *44*, 259.
GILLESPIE, J. H. and TIMONEY, J. F. 1981. Hagan and Bruner's Infectious Diseases of Domestic Animals. 7th edition. Comstock Publ. Associates, Ithaca and London.
GITTER, M. 1976. *Listeria monocytogenes* in "oven-ready"poultry. Vet. Rec. *99*, 336.
GOEPFERT, J. M. 1976. The aerobic plate count, coliform and *Escherichia coli* content of raw ground beef at the retail level. J. Milk Food Technol. *39*, 175.
GOUET, P. H., LABADIE, J. and SERRATORE, C. 1978. Development of *Listeria monocytogenes* in monoxenic and polyxenic beef mixtures. Zentrabl. Bakteriol. Hyg. I. Abt. Orig. *B166*, 87.
GUDKOVA, E. I., MIRONOVA, K. A., KUSMINSKII, A. S. and GEINE, G. O. 1958. A second outbreak of listeriotic angina in a single populated locality. J. Mikrobiol. Epidemiol. Immunobiol. *29*, 1373.
GUTHERTZ, L. S., FRUIN, J. T., SPICER, D. and FOWLER, J. L. 1976. Microbiology of fresh comminuted turkey meat. J. Milk Food Technol. *39*, 823.
HANNA, M. O., ZINK, D. L., CARPENTER, Z. L. and VANDERZANT, C. 1976. *Yersinia enterocolitica*-like organisms from vacuum packaged beef and lamb. J. Food Sci. *41*, 1254.
HANNA, M. O., STEWART, J. C., CARPENTER, Z. L. and VANDERZANT, C. 1977. Effect of heating, freezing, and pH on *Yersinia enterocolitica*-like organisms from meat. J. Food Prot. *40*, 689.
HANNA, M. O., STEWART, J. C., CARPENTER, Z. L., ZINK, D. L. and VANDERZANT, C. 1979. Isolation and characteristics of *Yersinia enterocolitica*-like bacteria from meats. Contrib. Microbiol. Immunol. *5*, 234.
HANNINEN, M. L. 1981. Survival of *Campylobacter jejuni/coli* in ground refrigerated and in ground frozen beef liver and in frozen broiler carcasses. Acta Vet. Scand. *22*, 566.
HART, G. H. 1916. Glanders in wild animals kept in zoological gardens. J. Am. Vet. Med. Assoc. *49*, 659.
HARTOG, B. J. and DE BOER, E. 1981. *Campylobacter jejuni* in poultry products from retail outlets and in poultry slaughter houses. *In Campylobacter*, Epidemiology, Pathogenesis and Biochemistry. p. 270. D. G. Newell (Editor). MTP Press, Lancaster, PA.

HAYEK, L. J. and CRUICKSHANK, J. G. 1977. *Campylobacter* enteritis (letter). Brit. Med. J. *2*, 1219.

HEALTH AND WELFARE CANADA. 1982. Campylobacter food poisoning from steaks—Ontario. Canad. Dis. Weekly Rep. *8(36)*, 177.

HORNICK, R. B., DAWKINS, A. T., EIGELSBACH, H. T. and TULIS, J. J. 1966. Oral tularemia vaccine in man. Antimicrob. Agents Chemother. *6*, 11.

HORWOOD, M. P. and MINCH, V. A. 1951. The members and types of bacteria found on the hands of food handlers. Food Res.*16*, 133.

HUDSON, W. R. and ROBERTS, T. A. 1981. The occurrence of Campylobacter on commercial red-meat carcasses from one abattoir. *In Campylobacter*, Epidemiology, Pathogenesis, and Biochemistry. p. 273. D. G. Newell (Editor). MTP Press, Lancaster,PA.

HURVELL, B., DANIELSSONTHAM, M. L. and OLSSON, E. 1982. Zoonotic aspects of *Yersinia enterocolitica* with special reference to its ability to propagate at low temperatures. *In* Psychotrophic Microorganisms in Spoilage and Pathogenicity. pp. 393–400. T. A. Roberts, G. Hobbs, J. H. B. Christian, and N. Skovguard (Editors). Academic Press, London.

INOUE, M. and KUROSE, M. 1975. Isolation of *Yersinia enterocolitica* from cows intestinal contents and beef meat. Japan. J. Vet. Sci. *37*, 91.

INOUE, M. and NAGAO, H. 1976. Isolation of *Yersinia enterocolitica* from bovine cecal contents, commercial meat and meatshops. J. Japan. Vet. Med. Assoc. *29*, 612.

JACKSON, R. S. and WESTERN, R. A. 1975. Modes of transmission of abattoir-associated brucellosis—Virginia. Brucellosis Surveillance Annual Summary, 1973. p. 12. Centers for Disease Control, Atlanta, GA.

JOHNSON, R. W., HARRIS, M. E., MORAN, A. C., KRUMM, G. W. and LEE, W. H. 1982. A comparative study of the microbiology of commercial vacuum-packaged and hanging beef. J. Food Prot. *45*, 223.

KAIJSER, B. and SVEDHEM, A. 1981. The occurrence of *Campylobacter jejuni* in fresh food and its survival under different conditions. *In Campylobacter*. Epidemiology, Pathogenesis and Biochemistry. p. 74. D. G. Newell (Editor). MTP Press, Lancaster, PA.

KAMPELMACHER, E. H. and VAN NOORLE JANSEN, L. M. 1969. Zentrakbl. Bakteriol. Parasitenk., Infektionskr. Hyg. Abt. 1: Orig. *A211*, 353.

KEET, E. 1974. *Yersinia enterocolitica* septicemia. Source of infection and incubation period identified. N.Y. State. J. Med. *74*, 2226.

KENDALL, M. and GILBERT, R. J. 1980. Survival and growth of *Y. enterocolitica* in broth media and in food. *In* Microbial Growth and Survival in Extremes of Environment. pp. 215–226. G. W. Gould and J. E. L. Corry (Editors). Soc. Appl. Bacterial. Tech. Ser. No. 15. Academic Press, London.

KIM, T. K. and STEPHENS, J. F. 1972. Drug resistance and transferable drug resistance of *Escherichia coli* isolated from "ready-to-cook" broilers. Poult. Sci. *51*, 1165.

KIRSCHNER, L., MAGUIRE, T. and BERTAND, W. S. 1957. Further evidence of the antileptospiral effect of milk: Electron microscopic studies. Brit. J. Exp. Pathol. *38*, 357.

KIST, M. 1981. *Campylobacter* enteritis epidemiological and clinical data from recent isolations in the region of Freiburg, West Germany. *In Campylobacter*. Epidemiology, Pathogenesis, and Biochemistry. p. 138. D. G. Newell (Editor). MTP Press. Lancaster, PA.

KWANTES, W. and ISAAC, M. 1971. Listeriosis. Brit. Med. J. *2*, 296.

KWANTES, W. and ISAAC, M. 1974. *Listeria* infection in west Glamorgan. *In* Problems of Listeriosis. Proc. 6th Intern. Symp. on Listeriosis. pp. 112–114. M. Woodbine (Editor). Leicester University Press, Survey.

LEE, W. H., VANDERZANT, C. and STERN, N. 1981. The occurrence of *Yersinia* enterocolitica in foods. *In Yersinia enterocolitica.* pp. 161–171. E. J. Bottone (Editor). CRC Press, Boca Raton, FL.

LEISTNER, L., HECHELMANN, H., KASHIWAZAKI, M. and ALBERTZ, R. 1975. Nachweis von *Yersinia enterocolitica* in Faeces und Fleisch von Schwein, Rindern, und Geflugel. Fleischwirtschaft *55*, 1599. (Ger.).

LEVINE, M. G. 1943. Brucellosis in packing-house workers. J. Ind. Hyg. Toxicol. *23*, 451.

LE MINOR, L. and ROHDE, R. 1974. Genus IV. *Samonella* Lignieres 1900, 389. *In* Bergey's Manual of Determinative Bacteriology. 8th edition. pp. 298–318. R. E. Buchanan and W. E. Gibbons (Editors). Williams and Wilkins Co., Baltimore, MD.

LOFFLER, W. 1931. Besonderheiten der Febris undulans Bang des Menschen. Schweiz. Med Wochenschr. *61*, 968. (Gr.).

LUECHTEFELD, N. W. and WANG W-L, L. 1981. *Campylobacter jejuni* in a turkey processing plant. J. Clin. Microbiol. *13*, 266.

MOLINELLI, E. A., BASSO, G. and MIYARA, S. 1948. [Human brucellosis in the Republic of Argentina.] *In* Primera Reunion Interamericana de la Brucellosis. p. 711. Ediciones del Hospital General, Mexico, D. F. (Span.)

MORALES-OTERO, P. 1929. Experimental infection of *Brucella abortus* in man; preliminary report. P. R. J. Publ. Health Trop. Med. *5*, 144.

MORALES-OTERO, P. 1930. *Brucella abortus* in Porto Rico.P. R. J. Publ. Health Trop. Med. *6*, 3.

MOUTON, R. P., VELTKAMP, J. J., LAWWERS, S. and BUTZLER, J. P. 1981. Analysis of a small outbreak of *Campylobacter* infections with morbidity. *In Campylobacter.* Epidemiology, Pathogenesis, and Biochemistry. p. 129. D. G. Newell (Editor).MTP Press, Lancaster/Boston/The Hague.

NALIN, D. R., SULTAVA, B., SAHMUJA, R., ISLAM, A. K., RAHIM, M. A., ISLAM, M., COSTA, B. S., MAWLA, N. and GREENOUGH, W. B., III. 1977. Survival of a patient with intestinal anthrax. Am. J. Med. *62*, 130.

NARUCKA, V. and WESTENDOORP, J. F. 1977. Studies for the presence of *Yersinia enterocolitica* and *Yersinia pseudotuberculosis* in clinically normal pigs. Tijdschr. Diergeneesk. *102*, 299.

NILEHN, B. 1969. Studies on *Yersinia enterocolitica* with Special Reference to Bacterial Diagnosis and Occurrence in Human Acute Enteric Disease. Munksguard, Copenhagen.

NORBERG, P. 1981. Enteropathogenic bacteria in frozen chicken. Appl. Environ. Microbiol. *42*, 32.

NORKRANS, G. and SVEDHEM, A. 1982. Epidemiological aspects of *Campylobacter jejuni* enteritis. J. Hyg. *89*, 163.

OOSTEROM, J. and BECKERS, H. J. 1981. *Campylobacter* outbreak in a military camp: Investigations, results and further epidemiological studies. *In Campylobacter.* Epidemiology, Pathogenesis, and Biochemistry. p. 107. D. G. Newell (Editor). MTP Press, Lancaster, PA.

PARK, C. E., STANKCIEWICZ, Z. K., LOVETT, J. and HUNT, J. 1981. Incidence of *Campylobacter jejuni* in fresh eviscerated whole market chickens. Canad. J. Microbiol. *27*, 841.

PARK, C. H., McDONALD, F. K., TWOHIG, A. M., and COOK, C. B. 1973. Septicemia and gastroenteritis due to *Vibrio fetus.* S. Med. J. *66*, 531.

PETHER, J. V. S. and GILBERT, R. J. 1971. The survival of salmonellosis on fingertips and transfer of the organisms to foods. J. Hyg. *69*, 673.

RAKOVSKY, J., PAUCKOVA, V. and ALDOVA, E. 1973. Human *Yersinia enterocolitica* infections in Czechoslovakia. Contrib. Microbiol. Immunol. *2*, 93.

REED, R. G. 1965. Listeria and Erysipelothrix. *In* Bacterial and Mycotic Infections of Man. pp. 752–762. R. J. Dubos and J. G. Hirsh (Editors). Lippincott, Philadelphia, PA.

REIS, M. H. L., VASCONCELOS, J. C. and TRABULSI, L. R. 1980. Prevalence of enterotoxigenic *Escherichia coli* in some processed raw food from animal origin. Appl. Environ. Microbiol. *39*, 270.

RETTING, P. S.   1979.   *Campylobacter* infections in human beings. J. Pediatr. *94*, 855.

RILEY, L. W., REMIS, R. S., HELGERSON, S. D., McGEE, H. B., WELLS, J. G., DAVIS, B. R., HEBERT, R. J., OLCOTT, E. S., JOHNSON, L. M., HARGRETT, N. T., BLAKE, P. A. and COHEN, M. L.   1983.   Hemorrhagic colitis associated with a rare *Escherichia coli* serotype. New Engl. J. Med. *308*, 681.

ROBINSON, D. A.   1981.   Infective dose of *Campylobacter jejuni* in milk. Brit. Med. J. *1*, 1584.

ROSEF, O.   1981.   [*Campylobacter fetus* subsp. *jejuni* as a surface contaminant of fresh and chilled pig carcasses]. Nord. Vet-Med. *33*, 535. (Nor.).

SACK, B.   1975.   Human diarrheal disease caused by enterotoxigenic *Escherichia coli*, Ann. Rev. Microbiol. *29*, 333.

SACK, R. B., SACK, D. A., MEHLMAN, I. J., ORSKOV, F. and ORSKOV, I.   1977. Enterotoxigenic *Escherichia coli* isolated from food. J. Infect. Dis. *135*, 313.

SCAMMON, L. A., PICKETT, M. J., FROMAN, S. and WILL, D. W.   1963.   Nonchromogenic acid-fast bacilli isolated from tuberculous swine. Am. Rev. Respir. Dis. *87*, 97.

SCHIEMANN, D. A.   1980.   Isolation of toxigenic *Yersinia enterocolitica* from retail pork products. J. Food Prot. *43*, 360.

SEDOVA, N. A.   1970.   [A study on the role of enterococci in the etiology of food poisoning]. Vopr. Pitan. *29*, 82. (Rus.).

SHANKER, S., ROSENFIELD, J. A., DAVEY, G. R. and SORRELL, T. C.   1982. *Campylobacter jejuni:* Incidence in processed broilers and biotype distribution in human and broiler isolates. Appl. Environ. Microbiol. *43*, 1219.

SHOOTER, R. A., COOKE, E. M., O'FARRELL, S., BETTELHEIM, K. A., CHANDLER, M. E. and BUSHROD, F. M.   1974.   The isolation of *Escherichia coli* from a poultry packing station and an abattoir. J. Hyg. *73*, 245.

SHRADER, J. H.   1939.   Food Control. Wiley, New York.

SIMMONS, N. A. and GIBBS, F. L.   1979.   *Campylobacter* spp. in oven-ready poultry. J. Infect. Dis. *1*, 159.

SKIRROW, M. B. and BENJAMIN, J.   1981.   The classification of "thermophilic" *Campylobacters* and their distribution in man and animals. *In Campylobacter*. Epidemiology, Pathogenesis, and Biochemistry. pp. 40–44. D. G. Newell (Editor). MTP Press, Lancaster, PA.

SKIRROW, M. B., FIDOE, R. G. and JONES, D. M.   1981.   An outbreak of presumptive food-borne *Campylobacter* enteritis. J. Infect. Dis. *3*, 234.

SMELTZER, T. I.   1981.   Isolation of *Campylobacter jejuni* from poultry carcasses. Austral. Vet. J. *57*, 511.

SMIBERT, R. M.   1978.   The genus *Campylobacter*. Ann. Rev. Microbiol. *32*, 637.

SMITH, M. V. and MULDOON, P. J.   1974.   *Campylobacter fetus* subspecies *jejuni (Vibrio fetus)* from commercially processed poultry. Appl. Microbiol. *27*, 995.

SOONATTRAKUL, W., ANDERSON, B. R. and BRYNER, J. H.   1971.   Raw liver as a possible source of *Vibrio fetus* septicemia in man. Am. J. Med. Sci. *261*, 245.

STERN, N. J.   1981.   Recovering rate of *Campylobacter fetus* ssp. *jejuni* on eviscerated pork, lamb, and beef carcasses. J. Food Sci. *46*, 1291.

STERN, N. J. and KOTULA, A. W.   1982.   Survival of *Campylobacter jejuni* inoculated into ground beef. Appl. Environ. Microbiol. *44*, 1150.

STERN, N. J., PIERSON, M. D. and KOTULA, A. W.   1980.   Effects of pH and sodium chloride on *Yersinia enterocolitica* at room and refrigerator temperatures. J. Food Sci. *45*, 64.

STRYKER, W. S., FRASER, D. W. and FACKLAM, R. R.   1982.   Foodborne outbreak of group G streptococcal pharyngitis. Am. J. Epidemiol. *116*, 533.

SUTHERLAND, J. P. and VARNAM, A. H.   1977.   Methods of isolation of potential importance of *Yersinia enterocolitica* in foods stored at low temperatures. J. Appl. Bacteriol. *43*, xiii. (Abstr.).

SVEDHEM, A., KAIJSER, B. and SJOGREN, E.   1981.   The occurrence of *Campylobacter jejuni* in fresh food and survival under different conditions. J. Hyg. *87,* 421.
SWAMINATHAN, B., HARMON, M. C. and MEHLMAN, I. J.   1982.   A review: *Yersinia enterocolitica.* J. Appl. Bacteriol. *52,* 151.
TAMMINGA, S. K., BEUMER, R. R. and KAMPELMACHER, E. H.   1982.   Microbiological studies on hamburgers. J. Hyg. *88,* 125.
TISON, F., DEVULDER, B., ROOS, P. and TACQUET, A.   1966.   Techniques et resultats de la recherche des mycobateries dan les viandes. Ann. Inst. Pasteur (Lille). *18,* 167. (Fr.).
TSAI, T. F., WATSON, W. N., HAYES, P. S., FACKLAM, R. R., and FRASER, D. W.   1979.   Mode of spread of group A streptococci in an abattoir outbreak of wound sepsis. *In* Pathogenic Streptococci. pp. 118–119. M. T. Parker (Editor). Reedbooks, Surrey.
TURNER, M.   1980.   Anthrax in humans in Zimbabwe. Central Afr. J. Med. *26,* 160.
U.S. DEPARTMENT OF HEALTH AND HUMAN SERVICES, CENTERS FOR DISEASE CONTROL.   1969–1977.   Foodborne Disease Surveillance Annual Summaries, 1968–1978. Centers for Disease Control, Atlanta, Georgia.
VERNON, E. and TILLET, H. E.   1974.   Food poisoning and *Salmonella* infections in England and Wales, 1969–1972. Publ. Health *88,* 225.
VOGT, R. L., SOURS, H. E., BARRETT, T., FELDMAN, R. A., DICKINSON, R. J. and WITHERRELL, L.   1982.   *Campylobacter* enteritis associated with contaminated water. Ann. Intern. Med. *96,* 292.
WAUTERS, G. and JANSSENS, M.   1976.   Carriage of *Yersinia enterocolitica* by slaughtering pigs. II. Search for *Yersinia enterocolitica* in pig tongues. Med. Mal. Infect. *6,* 517.
WRIGHT, E. P.   1981.   Duration of excretion period of *Campylobacter jejuni* in human subjects. *In Campylobacter.* Epidemiology, Pathogenesis, and Biochemistry. p. 110. D. G. Newell (Editor). MTP Press, Lancaster, PA.
ZEN-YOJI, M., SANCI, S., MARUYAMA, T. and YANAGOWA, Y.   1974.   Isolation of *Yersinia pseudotuberculosis* from swine, cattle and rats in an abattoir. Japan J. Microbiol. *18,* 103.

10

Fungi and Mycotoxins in Meats

James J. Pestka[1]

INTRODUCTION

Fungi characteristically are unable to grow rapidly on animal tissue. Bacteria are better adapted physiologically and are encountered, therefore, almost exclusively in the early microbial decay of animal flesh. It is for this reason that fungi are of only minor concern to most producers and processors of meats. However, when meat-preservation techniques such as drying, curing, and freezing are employed, fungi can compete effectively with bacteria and become the dominant microflora. A knowledge of the specific reasons why certain fungi colonize meat and poultry is thus essential in order to prevent economic losses during meat storage and to maximize desirable fermentations of certain cured meats. In the past three decades, some molds have been found to produce highly toxic metabolites known as mycotoxins. One of these compounds, aflatoxin B_1, is the most potent liver carcinogen known. Mycotoxins may be present in meats as tissue residues carried over from contaminated feeds or as a direct result of mold growth and toxigenesis. Significant questions therefore exist as to whether meat-borne mycotoxins pose a threat to human health. The purpose of the following chapter is twofold: (1) to provide an overview of the physiology and taxonomy of fungi associated with meat; and (2) to review recent research on mycotoxin contamination of meats.

[1]Department of Food Science & Human Nutrition, Michigan State University, E. Lansing, MI 48824.

Advances in Meat Research, Volume 2
Copyright 1986 by AVI Publishing Co.
All rights of reproduction in any form reserved
ISBN 0-87055-498-0

GROWTH OF FUNGI IN MEAT PRODUCTS

Physiological Considerations

Yeasts and filamentous fungi comprise the group of microorganisms known as the fungi, of which it has been estimated that there are between 50,000–200,000 species (Kobayashi 1980). Fungi are inherently different from bacteria on the basis of their (1) larger size, (2) modes of reproduction, (3) slower growth rate, (4) typical eukaryotic characteristics such as a well-defined nucleus, mitochondria, and endoplasmic reticulum, and (5) insensitivity to many antibiotics that are effective against the prokaryotic bacteria. Since the fungi commonly referred to as "yeasts and molds" are ubiquitous, they are introduced into animal tissue at the time of slaughter and throughout meat processing. Fungal counts in fresh beef and poultry range typically between 10^2 and 10^5 per gram (Jay 1979). However, it is only under certain environmental conditions that fungi compete successfully with bacteria in meats. Critical parameters which affect the growth of bacteria and fungi on a rich nutrient source such as meat include temperature, water activity (a_w), pH, and oxidation-reduction potential (Eh). Jay (1978), in an excellent review of the subject, has stated that although fungi tolerate wide variations in temperature, pH, and water activity, they are dominated by bacteria in meats because of their relatively slow growth rates and high Eh requirements. For a yeast or mold to spoil a meat product, ample oxygen usually must be present and some other environmental parameter changed so as to inhibit dominant bacterial groups and allow the slower-growing fungi to colonize the substrate.

Fungal Colonization of Meats

Spoilage manifestations of moldy meats include stickiness, "whiskers," "black spots," "white spot," "green patches," fat decomposition, and off-odor (Frazier and Westoff 1978). In some cases, molds are believed to give quality attributes to products such as fermented meats and aged beef. Early studies of mold colonization of meats dealt with the stability of beef transported at sea (Brooks and Hansford 1923; Wright 1923). Jay (1978) summarized reports in the literature during the past 60 years and found that only about 20 different mold genera have been isolated from meats—the aspergilli and penicillia being the ones most commonly encountered. Other molds found in meat spoilage are *Thamnidium, Mucor, Rhizopus, Cladosporium,* and *Sporotrichum.* Processes, which most commonly select for fungal growth in meats, are drying, curing and aging, and low-temperature storage.

Dried Meats.   Water activity plays a critical role in the fungal spoilage of meats. Reduction of water activity in fresh meat to 0.96 is adequate to inhibit bacteria and to select for fungal growth (Banwart 1979). While drying fresh lean meat to 20% moisture inhibits most bacteria, yeasts, and molds, a level of 15% moisture is needed to inhibit xerotolerant species of fungi (Ingram and Simonsen 1980). Humidity at which dried meat is stored is equally critical. Macara (1943) studied the growth of molds in dried meat at 20°, 28°, and 37°C at relative humidities ranging from 75 to 90% and found that meats stored at 90% relative humidity had demonstrable mold growth between 5–6 days. However, onset time for mold spoilage increased to 36–40 days when the dried meat was stored at 75% relative humidity.

Cured and Aged Meats. The ripening and storage conditions used for certain cured and aged meats potentiates the growth of several genera of fungi. In some cured products, fungal growth is considered spoilage and is prevented by light smoking and vacuum packaging. In other products, such as country-cured hams and Hungarian- and Italian-type fermented sausages, molds are desirable as part of a "natural" fermentation process (Leistner and Ayres 1968). This is primarily because the esthetic appearance of mold on these special cured meats is traditionally expected by the consumer. It has been further suggested that improved flavor of molded cured meats is related to inhibition of fat oxidation, proteolytic and lipolytic changes, or inhibition of spoilage bacteria. Molded sausages also may dry in a slow uniform manner resulting in improved quality and reduced weight loss.

In the production of country-cured hams, the hams are dry cured, with or without smoking, and aged for between 6 and 24 months (Bullerman *et al.* 1969B). Aging is usually done in an environment such as a room or attic where humidity and temperature are not regulated. The resulting ham often has massive fungal growth, usually green, covering the flesh. Country-cured hams are produced typically in the southern United States.

European-type salamis are prepared by encasing ground beef and pork mixed with spices and curing agents and subjecting these to a ripening period in which the humidity is dropped from 95 to 75%. Hungarian-type sausages are smoked lightly during ripening, whereas Italian types are not smoked. Fungal growth usually occurs during the first 5 days of ripening and is dictated by the characteristic microbial flora of the ripening chamber (Ciegler *et al.* 1972).

Sampling cured meats from 32 different United States and European producers, Leistner and Ayres (1968) isolated 307 fungal strains from country cured hams and fermented sausages. *Aspergillus* and *Penicillium* were predominate in the country-cured hams, and were found in 90 and 83% of the samples, respectively. Other genera isolated from the ham samples were *Cladosporium* (30%), *Rhizopus* (13%), *Alternaria* (13%), *Scopulariopsis* (8%), *Pacilomyces* (8%),and *Oospora* (8%). The presence of *Cladosporium* in many samples was significant because this fungus is proteolytic and capable of producing deep-seated black spots in the ham.

The authors observed that country-cured hams wrapped in paper and held at ambient humidity and temperature during the ripening process were heavily molded on the flesh portions but not on the skin or fat. Fatty portions of the wrapped hams exhibited only moderate oxidization even after 9 to 12 months. Unwrapped hams held at low relative humidity (65%) during ripening had little mold growth but their fat became strongly oxidized after several months. In the fermented sausages, the authors found *Penicillium, Scopulariopsis,* and *Aspergillus* in 89, 41, and 33%, respectively, of the samples examined. Minor flora of the fermented sausages included *Rhizopus* (11%), *Mucor* (4%), and *Mortierella* (4%). Prevalent penicillia species in the cured meats were *P. expansum, P. janthinellum,* and *P. chrysogenum.* Most of the aspergilli isolated were members of the *A. glaucus* group and included *A. ruber, A. repens, A. amstelodami,* and *A. chevalieri.* Aspergilli generally grew better in the low a_w country-cured hams than in the higher a_w fermented sausages where the penicillia were predominant.

In a related study, Sutic *et al.* (1972) isolated 562 fungi from 356 country cured hams. Of these, 403 were *Penicillium,* 121 were *Aspergillus,* and the remainder were *Cladosporium, Alternaria,* and other genera. Again, aspergilli were most often isolated from hams stored under dry conditions, whereas penicillia were associated with humid storage conditions. As was found in the previous study, members of the *A. glaucus* group predominated among the aspergilli.

The most common way of "inoculating" a fermented sausage is simply by hanging it in a room that has been used for aging and molding of sausages for many years and thus contains high concentrations of desirable mold spores. However, fungi isolated from fermented meats can be used as starter cultures for country-cured hams and European-type fermented sausages. Leistner (1984) has recently reported on the successful use of *Penicillium nalgiovense* and *P. chrysogenum* as starters for European salamis. There is need for further systematic studies of quality attributes of fermented meats inoculated with pure fungal cultures. Major considerations in selection of starter strains are their potential for pathogenicity, antibiotic production, and toxigenicity. Fungal strains found naturally in fermented meats are generally nonpathogenic, but a small number of these can produce mycotoxins. This topic will be dealt with in detail later in the chapter.

Cold and Frozen Storage of Meats.   Cold or frozen storage often tends to decrease the a_w of meats, thus simultaneously selecting for psychrotrophic and xerotolerant fungi. None of these are known to be pathogenic or mycotoxigenic. Table 2.9 (Chapter 2) summarized growth temperature and water activity minima for some major spoilage molds. One of the most economically important forms of psychotrophic mold spoilage is a dark discoloration of meat known as "black spot." Beef, mutton, pork, veal, lamb, and rabbit are prone to this spoilage. Black-spotted portions of meat must be cut away and discarded resulting in carcass weight loss. Gill *et al.* (1981) isolated 20 fungal strains that produce black spot colonies on meat and fat tissue. Strains were identified as *Cladosporium cladosporioides, Cladosporium herbarum, Penicillium hirsutum,* and *Aureobasidium pullulans* (Table 2.9) and all were found capable of growing at $-1°C$ on sterile meat slices. All but *P. hirsutum* could penetrate 4–7 mm into the tissue. Another type of meat spoilage known as "white spot" is caused by *Chryosporium pannorum (Sporotrichum carnis)* and occasionally *Acremonium* sp. *(Cephalosporium* sp.) (Lowry and Gill 1983A). Growth of black spot and white spot fungi at subzero temperatures is relatively slow and only proceeds if bacterial growth is inhibited by meat desiccation (Gill and Lowry 1982; Lowry and Gill 1983A). "Whiskers," the term given to the cottony gray-black growth found in beef stored in cold rooms, is caused by species of *Thamnidium, Mucor,* and *Rhizopus* (Frazier and Westhoff 1978). One of the whisker fungi, *Thamnidium elegans,* grows at temperatures below $-5°C$ on supercooled (unfrozen) medium (Lowry and Gill 1983A). Although it has a relatively high a_w requirement, *T. elegans* grows rapidly enough to compete successfully with psychrotrophic bacteria at or near $0°C$.

Growth of whisker fungi on meats is sometimes considered desirable. Tenderness and flavor of beef is often enhanced in various food services by storage of carcasses in coolers at $2°–4°C$ for 2 to 4 weeks. Whisker growth that occurs during these holding operations often corresponds to increases in aged flavor and tenderness. While it has been suggested that *Thamnidium* releases proteases which tenderize beef (Ingram and Dainty 1971), it is more likely that the tenderized flavor in aged beef is actually a result of endogenous enzymes in the animal tissue. Nevertheless, it is interesting to note that Williams (1957) patented a process whereby beef can be aged only 48 hr after inoculation with whisker-forming *Thamnidium.* Kotula *et al.* (1982) found that *Thamnidium elegans, Mucor mucedo,* and *Chaetostylum fresenii* proteolyzed litmus milk and gelatin at 24° and 18°C but not at 4°C and that all strains hydrolyzed tributyrin at 24°, 18°, and 4°C. The authors suggested that the lack of proteolytic activity by the whisker fungi at 4°C and the impracticality of aging beef at 18° and 24°C preclude the feasibility of using these for beef tenderization. Furthermore, lipolytic action by these strains might actually contribute to the development of rancidity. It is apparent that further studies are needed to justify the use of whisker inoculums, particularly using substrates and holding conditions which closely mimic actual food service operations.

Yeast Growth in Meats

Jay (1978) surveyed the incidence of yeasts in meat products and found that the species *Debaromyces, Candida, Torulopsis,* and *Rhodotorula* were most frequently isolated. Yeasts, typically present only in low numbers in fresh meats, can compete with bacteria if the meat surface becomes dry

(Ayres *et al.* 1980). Some yeasts are psychrotrophic and grow on meat at subzero temperatures. Jay (1979) found that in refrigerated ground beef, psychotrophic yeasts and bacteria grew very slowly. When stored at 5°C for 15 days, yeast counts increased 2 logs while the bacterial population increased 4 logs. In contrast, a yeast microflora of 10^6 per cm^2 developed in lamb loins wrapped in gas-permeable plastic film during storage at $-5°C$ for 20 weeks, competing successfully with gram-negative psychrotrophic bacteria (Lowry and Gill 1983B).

Finished products, such as frankfurters, luncheon meats, bacon, and sausages, are also susceptible to yeast spoilage. Yeasts grow in packaged frankfurters but are inhibited by CO_2 concentrations greater than 15% (Ogilvy and Ayres 1953). Meat curing brines often contain *Debaromyces* sp. which tolerate high salt concentrations and assimilate nitrite (Mrak and Bonar 1938; Wickerham 1959) and can thus contaminate meats.

POTENTIAL PRESENCE OF MYCOTOXINS IN MEATS

Fungi can cause three basic types of diseases in humans: (1) mycoses, (2) allergies, and (3) mycotoxicoses. A mycosis is defined as an invasion of living tissue by a fungus, while an allergy is a hypersensitivity to a fungal antigen. A mycotoxicosis is a toxic manifestation in an animal resulting from ingestion or exposure to a fungal metabolite. Whereas mycoses and allergies to fungi probably are not a major concern in the consumption of meats, there is a potential for mycotoxins to enter meat products either by indirect carry over from animal feed to edible tissue or by direct fungal growth on meats.

Mycotoxins are a heterogeneous group of nonpolar low molecular weight compounds produced as part of fungal "secondary" metabolism. At this time, yeasts are not known to produce mycotoxins. Toxigenic fungi are ubiquitous and can grow in various agricultural commodities in the field, or, appear postharvest during storage and processing. It should be emphasized that not all fungi are toxigenic. Furthermore, production of mycotoxins by toxigenic fungi is not simply concurrent with growth but is dependent on the temperature, relative humidity, and moisture content of the substrate. Thus, weather conditions during a particular growing season actually dictate whether mycotoxins will be present in a commodity. Some proposed functions of mycotoxins are that: (1) they are involved in differentiation or sporulation of the fungus; (2) they act as antibiotics which help the fungus compete with other microorganisms; (3) they enhance the pathogenicity of the fungus in plants; (4) they enhance the ability of fungi to colonize the gastrointestinal tract of insects; and (5) they are waste products. As yet there is a lack of substantiating evidence for any of these mechanisms.

TABLE 10.1. Natural Sources and Toxicity of the Major Mycotoxin Groups

Group	Sources	Toxic effects
Aflatoxins	Corn, peanuts, cottonseed, treenuts, sorghum	Hepatotoxic, hepatocarcinogenic, teratogenic
Ochratoxins	Barley, corn, oats, rye	Nephrotoxic, teratogenic
Zearalenones	Corn, wheat	Hyperestrogenism
Trichothecenes	Corn, wheat	Emesis, feed refusal, necrosis of GI tract, immunotoxic
Sterigmatocystin	Grains, green coffee	Hepatotoxic, hepatocarcinogenic
Penicillic acid	Corn, beans	Acute toxicity
Patulin	Apple juice	Stomach lesions
Citrinin	Barley, wheat, oats	Nephrotoxic
Cyclopiazonic acid	Corn, peanuts	Necrosis of GI tract, hepatotoxic

Many mycotoxins have been discovered because they are causative agents of toxicoses in livestock and poultry. Typically, a fungus is isolated from feed associated with an animal toxicosis of unknown etiology and the organism is then shown to produce, in culture, factors which are toxic to test laboratory animals. These factors are subsequently extracted, purified, and chemically characterized using the animal bioassay. The toxicology of many of the purified mycotoxins have thus been studied. Based on these investigations and human epidemiological evidence, potentially harmful effects of mycotoxins are sometimes extrapolated to man. Mycotoxins, which are of the greatest possible significance to meats, are the aflatoxins, ochratoxins, zearalenones, and trichothecenes. Table 10.1 summarizes natural sources and toxic manifestations of these and other mycotoxins.

Aflatoxins

Occurrence. The aflatoxins, a family of difuranocoumarins, produced by toxigenic strains of *Aspergillus flavus* and *A. parasiticus,* have received the greatest notoriety because of their ability to act as hepatotoxins and hepatocarcinogens. These toxins were first identified during the early 1960s in association with an epidemic known as "Turkey X disease" in which over 100,000 turkey poults died after ingesting toxic peanut meal (Austwick 1978). Nearly concurrent with this was the discovery that aflatoxin contamination of cottonseed meal was the cause of trout hepatoma epidemics in hatcheries in the western United States (Sinnhuber *et al.* 1965). Given the proper humidity and temperatures, *A. flavus* is capable of growing and elaborating aflatoxins on almost any organic substrate. Agricultural commodities that can be contaminated by the aflatoxins in-

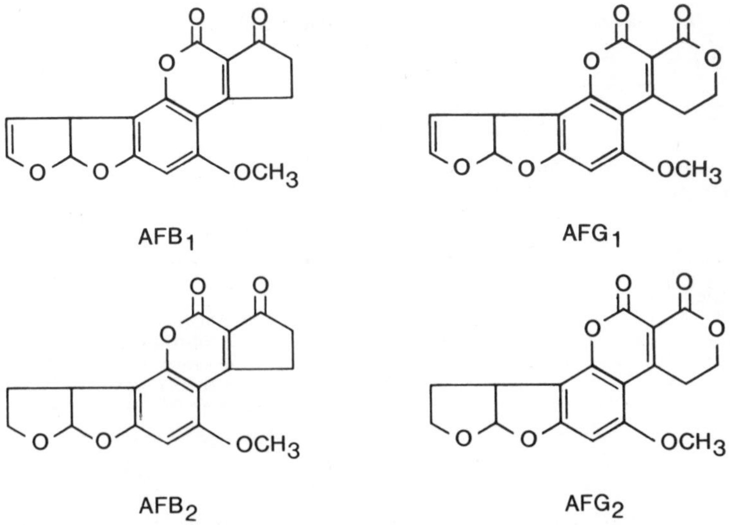

FIG. 10.1.   Structures of naturally occurring aflatoxins.

clude corn, peanuts, cottonseed, cassava, copra, and many types of tree-nuts (Davis and Deiner 1978). Figure 10.1 shows the structure of four naturally occurring aflatoxins, aflatoxin B_1 (AFB_1), aflatoxin B_2 (AFB_2), aflatoxin G_1 (AFG_1) and aflatoxin G_2 (AFG_2), of which AFB_1 is encountered most often in nature.

Toxic Effects and Metabolism.   Aflatoxins can be acutely toxic, carcinogenic, mutagenic, and teratogenic (Busby and Wogan 1979). The rank order for toxicity, carcinogenicity, and mutagenicity among the four naturally occurring aflatoxins is $AFB_1 > AFG_1 > AFB_2 > AFG_2$, indicating that the unsaturated terminal furan of AFB_1 is critical for determining the degree of biological activity of this mycotoxin family. AFB_1 is acutely hepatotoxic with LD_{50}s ranging from 0.3 to 40 mg/kg depending on the species. At high levels, toxicity occurs in 3–6 hr after ingestion and is evidenced by necrosis of the hepatocytes, derangement of the normal clotting mechanisms, and capillary fragility. This can lead to widespread hemorrhaging and eventual death (Carlton and Szczech 1978; Cysewski *et al.* 1968). In 1974, acute aflatoxin toxicity occurred in an area of India in which 106 people died from consumption of moldy, aflatoxin-contaminated corn (Van Rensburg 1977). At chronic levels, aflatoxins cause marked decreases in productivity and the immune response of domestic animals (CAST 1979). Reduced growth rate in livestock and poultry is the most common effect of aflatoxin in feed.

Species susceptible to AFB_1-induced hepatocarcinogenesis include the rat, monkey, marmoset, ferret, trout, and salmon. Rainbow trout are one the most sensitive of the species; as low as 4 ppb of AFB_1 in the diet for 12 months is adequate to cause liver tumors in test animals (Sinnhuber et al. 1968). Epidemiological studies have demonstrated that a positive correlation exists between current exposure to aflatoxins in foods and the incidence of primary human liver cancer in areas of Africa, India, Southeast Asia, and China (Shank 1978). In the United States there is no epidemiological evidence that aflatoxins cause human liver cancer (CAST 1979). Although aflatoxin intake in the Southeast is 9 times greater than in the entire United States, the actual incidence of liver cancer is lower in the Southeast than in the country as a whole.

Extensive studies on the metabolic fate of the aflatoxins and their toxic mode of action have been conducted. These compounds, like other nonpolar xenobiotics, are metabolized primarily in the liver by microsomal mixed-function oxidases and cytosolic enzymes. AFB_1 metabolism has been extensively reviewed by Busby and Wogan (1979) and Campbell and Hayes (1976). Figure 10.2 identifies and gives the structures of some of the major metabolites of AFB_1, most of which are further detoxified by conjugation with glucuronic acid or sulfate and eliminated via urine and feces. AFM_1 which results from hydroxylation of AFB_1 at the 4 position, has about 3% of the mutagenic potency of AFB_1 in the Salmonella mutagenesis assay (Wong and Hsieh 1976) and is also less toxic and carcinogenic. AFM_1 has been shown, however, to be excreted in the milk of animals which have ingested AFB_1. Stoloff (1980) in a summary of several studies estimated that cows ingesting AFB_1 in diet at a level 300 ng/g will produce milk containing 1 ng/ml AFM_1 24 hours later. Detectable AFM_1 disappears 4–5 days after withdrawal from AFB_1-contaminated feed. The FDA has set an action level of 0.5 ng/ml for AFM_1 in milk because of potential danger to growing children who ingest large quantities of milk. Aflatoxicol (AFL) results from the reversible reduction of the cyclopentenone carbonyl of AFB_1 by cytoplasmic enzymes. Formation of AFL is not considered to be a true detoxification mechanism since this metabolite has about 23% the mutagenic potency of AFB_1 (Wong and Hsieh 1976) and is nearly as carcinogenic as AFB_1 in trout and rats (Schoenhard et al. 1981; Nixon et al. 1981). Two other major AFB_1 metabolites, AFQ_1, resulting from ring hydroxylation of the carbon B to the cyclopentenenone carbonyl, and AFP_1, resulting from o-demethylation, have 1 and 0.1%, respectively, the mutagenic potency of the parent aflatoxin.

The carcinogenicity and mutagenicity of AFB_1 most likely results from the formation of a reactive epoxide at the 2,3 position of the terminal furan and its subsequent covalent binding to nucleic acid (Essigmann et al. 1982). This and other related reactions are summarized in Fig. 10.3. One of these nucleic acid adducts 2,3-dihydro-2,3-(N^5-formyl-2',5',6'-triamino-4-oxo-N^5-pyrimidyl)-3-hydroxyaflatoxin B_1 (AFB_1-FAPyr) can last for weeks after initial formation. Covalent binding of the 2,3-epoxide to nucleophilic moieties in proteins is also likely, but specific characterization of these adducts has not yet been carried out. An important means of

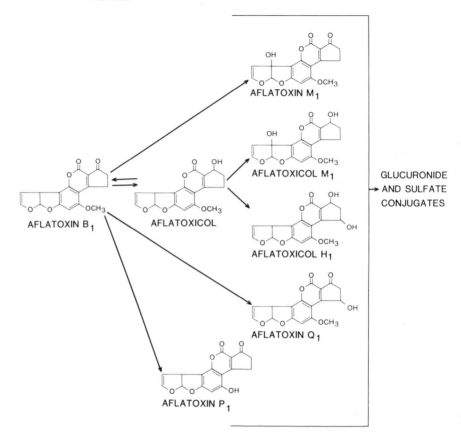

FIG. 10.2.   Polar metabolites of aflatoxin B_1.

detoxifying the active AFB_1 epoxide is via formation of a glutathione conjugate (Moss *et al.* 1983). Another major metabolite, 2,3-dihydro-2,3-dihydroxyaflatoxin B_1 (AFB_1-diol) appears after spontaneous or enzymatic reaction of the 2,3-epoxide with water (Lin *et al.* 1977; Neal and Colley, 1979) and after the degradation of AFB_1-modified DNA (Wang and Cerutti, 1980). A functional role for AFB_1-diol in aflatoxicosis has been postulated on the basis that, under neutral and alkaline conditions, the metabolite becomes a dialdehydic phenolate ion which is capable of forming Schiff base adducts with amino groups of cellular proteins (Neal *et al.* 1981).

Accumulation in Animal Tissue.   There is concern that AFB_1 and its metabolites accumulate in animal tissue and are thus carried into meat products. Early investigations of this topic are reviewed by Rodricks and

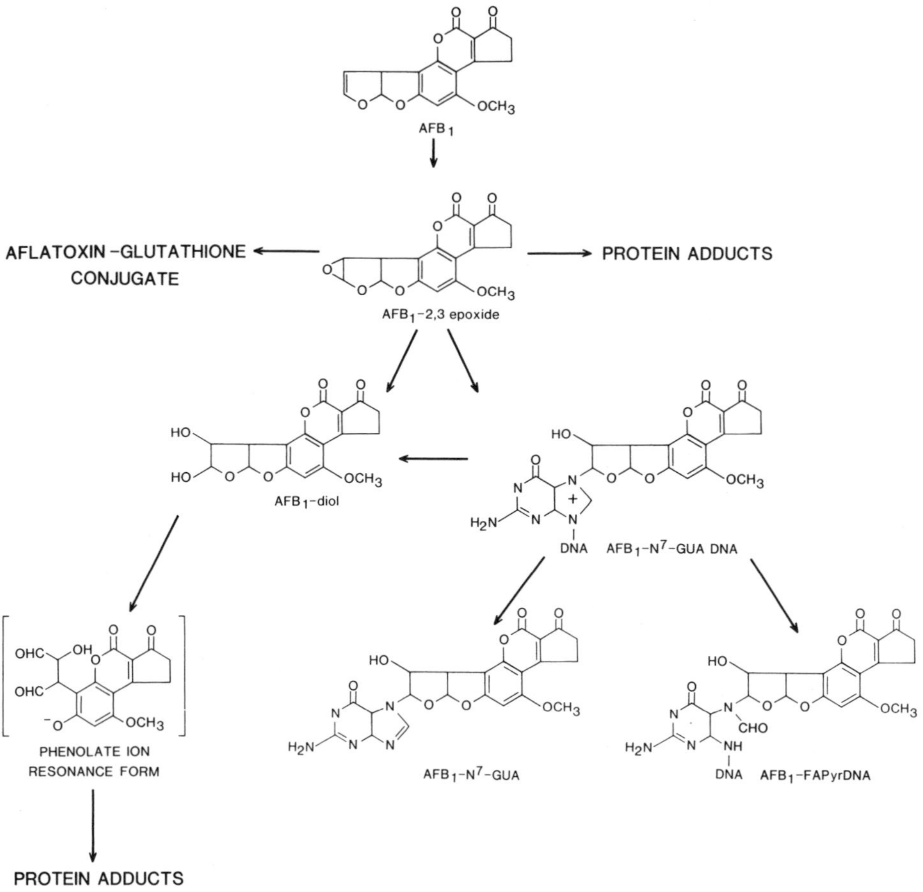

FIG. 10.3.   Fates of metabolically active 2,3-expoxide intermediate of aflatoxin B_1.

Stoloff (1977) and Stoloff (1979). Factors affecting aflatoxin residue accumulation in tissue include species of animal, level of exposure, health status of animal, and the time after cessation of aflatoxin exposure that the tissues are analyzed. Original studies of aflatoxin carry over were based on appearance of ^{14}C-labeled AFB_1 in urine, feces, and various organs. Wogan et al. (1969) found most of the ^{14}C-labeled AFB_1 that was injected (ip) into rats was eliminated within 24 hr in the urine and feces with about 8% remaining in the liver; similar results were found for the mouse and mink. Luthy et al. (1980) performed a comprehensive study in which excretion of ^{14}C-labeled AFB_1 and its metabolites was followed for 9 days in pigs. Approximately 71% of the label was released in the feces and urine, of which only 11% was extractable in methylene chloride. Tissue analyses revealed that the highest ^{14}C activities were in the liver followed by kidney and lung, most of which was neither extractable or dialyzable. General conclusions from this and earlier tracer studies are that (1) a major portion of administered AFB_1 is rapidly metabolized to water-soluble conjugates (probably glucuronide, sulfate, or glutathione metabolites), which are excreted in urine and feces; (2) most of the residues remaining in tissue and plasma are in a bound form; and (3) only small fractions of residues in feces, urine, and tissue, are actually AFB_1 or biologically active metabolites, such as aflatoxicol, AFM_1, or AFQ_1.

Identification and quantitation of specific aflatoxin residues in tissues was initially hampered by the lack of suitable sensitive detection methods. Improved cleanup procedures, two-dimensional TLC, and HPLC now allow detection of AFB_1 and related metabolites at levels below 0.1 ng/g tissue (Stubblefield and Shotwell 1981; Trucksess and Stoloff 1981; Gregory and Manley 1981). Table 10.2 summarizes recent studies of the accumulation of AFB_1 and AFM_1 in swine. While data vary slightly among investigators because of different detection methods, the general conclusions remain the same. Pigs fed diets containing between 100 to 1253 ng/g AFB_1 for various time periods have detectable amounts of AFB_1 and AFM_1 in their tissues at the immediate conclusion of the experiments. Total residues appear to be dependent on dose levels but independent of dose duration. Primary sites of accumulation are liver and kidney, with maximal reported levels approaching 1–2 ng/g of both AFB_1 and AFM_1. Accumulation in muscle is much less than in liver or kidney. These results are not surprising since the latter two organs are primary sites of xenobiotic metabolism and elimination. A single study which analyzed for AFL in swine found that the metabolite accounted for only 1% AFB_1 + AFM_1 accumulation in liver but that it was not detectable in kidney or muscle (Trucksess et al. 1982). An important conclusion from these studies was that low level aflatoxin residues can be greatly reduced by withdrawing pigs from contaminated feed and placing them on clean feed for a single day. Furthermore, residues are completely eliminated by a 4-day withdrawal period (Furtado et al. 1982). In regard to possible accumulation of water-soluble conjugates of AFB_1 in swine tissue, Gregory et al. (1983) analyzed tissues from the withdrawal study of Neff and Edds (1981) and reported that water-soluble conjugates were also completely removed after a 4-day withdrawal period.

Most carryover studies on the cow have dealt with AFM_1 residues in milk. These have been adequately reviewed by Rodricks and Stoloff (1977) and Stoloff (1980). Recent investigations on aflatoxin residues in other edible tissues of cows indicate, as with swine, that more AFB_1 and AFM_1 accumulate in kidney and liver than in muscle (Table 10.3). Both dietary and oral administration studies show, however, that the kidney accumulates the most residues and that these are primarily AFM_1 with lesser amounts of AFB_1 and AFL. The AFB_1 and AFM_1 residues remain in the liver and kidney 7 days after oral dosing but are completely eliminated from cattle tissue within 18 days after withdrawal from the contaminated

TABLE 10.2. Aflatoxin Residues Detected in Tissues from Swine Fed Dietary AFB$_1$

Dietary AFB$_1$ (ng/g)	Dose interval (days)	Withdrawal time (days)	Tissue residue (ng/g)						Reference
			Liver		Kidney		Muscle		
			(AFB$_1$)	(AFM$_1$)	(AFB$_1$)	(AFM$_1$)	(AFB$_1$)	(AFM$_1$)	
100	28	0	0.23	—[a]	—	—	0.19	—	Jacobson et al. (1978)
400	28	0	1.51	—	—	—	1.04	—	
866	21	0	0.18	0.29	ND[b]	0.85	—	—	Neff and Edds (1981)
		1	ND	0.08	ND	Tr[c]	—	—	
		2	ND	ND	ND	ND	—	—	
1253	21	0	0.40	0.68	0.16	1.12	—	—	Furtado et al. (1982)
		1	ND	0.10	ND	0.17	—	—	
		2	ND	ND	ND	0.09	—	—	
551	42	0	0.85	0.28	0.60	0.58	0.33	0.08	
		1	0.12	ND	0.13	0.07	Tr	Tr	
		2	Tr	ND	Tr	ND	ND	ND	
		4	ND	ND	ND	ND	ND	ND	
300	70	0	0.51	0.58	0.20	0.61	0.19	0.15	Miller et al. (1982)
600	70	0	1.57	1.07	0.25	0.91	0.02	ND	
400	14	0	0.35[d]	0.89	0.15	1.46	ND	ND	Trucksess et al. (1982)
		1	0.02	0.04	0.11	0.01	ND	ND	

[a] Not determined.
[b] Not detectable by method used.
[c] Trace, not quantifiable.
[d] 0.01 ppb aflatoxicol detected.

TABLE 10.3. Aflatoxin Residues Detected in Tissues from Cows Dosed with AFB$_1$

AFB$_1$ dose	Dose interval (days)	Withdrawal period (days)	Liver AFB$_1$	Liver AFM$_1$	Kidney AFB$_1$	Kidney AFM$_1$	Muscle AFB$_1$	Muscle AFM$_1$	Reference
387 ng/g diet	123	0	0.37	1.07	0.09	4.82	0.002	0.1	Richard et al. (1983)
387 ng/g diet	105	18	ND[a]	ND	ND	ND	ND	ND	(1983)
0.35 mg/kg/day	3	1	7.12	6.09	1.32	56.64	0.46	1.13	Stubblefield et al. (1983)
0.35 mg/kg/day	3	7	0.03	0.023	0.02	0.11	ND	ND	
0.5 mg/kg/day (0.5)	1	2.5	5.1[b]	4.3	3.3[c]	20	[d]	[d]	Trucksess et al. (1983 A)

Tissue Residues (ng/g)

[a] None detected.
[b] 0.85 ng/g AFL detected.
[c] 2.6 ng/g AFL detected.
[d] Not determined.

diet. It appears that the cow might require a longer withdrawal period than the pig for complete elimination of aflatoxin residues from tissues, although further studies clarifying this are needed.

Examination of aflatoxin residue data for turkey and chicken reveals that poultry also accumulate low levels of AFB_1, AFM_1, and AFL in liver and kidney and that these residues are eliminated after a 2 to 7-day withdrawal period (Table 10.4). The turkey had a higher rate of carryover of AFM_1 in liver than did the chicken. Gregory et al. (1983) determined that initially 55–90% of the total detectable aflatoxin residue in turkey tissue existed as water-soluble conjugates (probably glucuronides and sulfates) and that these residues tended to be eliminated more slowly than free AFB_1 and its nonpolar metabolites. It is interesting to note that Chen et al. (1984) found that even though the birds were fed more AFB_1 in diet than AFB_2, a greater proportion of AFM_2 carried over into broiler tissue than AFM_1. Eggs produced by hens ingesting 8000 ng/g dietary AFB_1 for 7 days also contain detectable AFB_1 and AFL (0.02 to 0.2 ng/g) but residues disappear when the hens are given a 7-day withdrawal period (Trucksess et al. 1983).

Table 10.5 summarizes the reported feed:tissue ratios of AFB_1 to AFB_1 and AFM_1 in pig, steer, turkey, and chicken. In all four species, feed:tissue ratios are much higher for kidney (79-30,769) and liver (251-19,512) than for muscle (938-200,000). Chickens apparently have the least ability to carry over AFB_1 into tissue. Cow kidney has the highest feed:tissue ratio, 79, of all the organs examined among the species. These values are generally lower than those discussed in an earlier review by Rodricks and Stoloff (1977)—a likely result of improved analytical techniques.

Cooking has little effect on aflatoxins (Furtado et al. 1981). Although prevention of any detectable aflatoxin residues in meats is most desirable, it is not economically feasible to preclude the use of feeds contaminated with low to moderate amounts of aflatoxins. Several alternatives are available. For example, withdrawal of aflatoxin-contaminated feed could be an effective means of eliminating aflatoxin residues from the tissues of food-producing animals. However, it would not be practical to routinely implement such a control program among livestock and poultry producers. Another approach for decreasing aflatoxin residues would be to detoxify contaminated feed by a chemical or physical method. Ammoniation of feed has been shown to be very effective in decreasing total aflatoxins in foods (CAST 1979). Up to this time, the United States FDA has not given approval for this process because of the lack of adequate data on the identity or toxicity of substances formed by the ammoniation of aflatoxins. Further research on this alternative and other detoxification methods is thus warranted. The only remaining approach is to attempt to balance the potential health impact of aflatoxins in tissues vs the economic benefits of using contaminated feed.

Until recently, the FDA action level for total aflatoxins in feeds and non-dairy foods was 20 ng/g, since it was believed there is minimal risk to

TABLE 10.4. Aflatoxin Residues Detected in Tissues from Poultry Fed Dietary AFB$_1$

Dietary AFB$_1$ dose (ng/g)	Dose interval (days)	Withdrawal period (days)	Tissue residues (ng/g)						Reference
			Liver		Kidney		Muscle		
			AFB$_1$	AFM$_1$	AFB$_1$	AFM$_1$	AFB$_1$	AFM$_1$	
500 (Turkey)	21	0	0.1 (0.28)[a,c]	0.44 (0.37)	—	—	0.03(ND)[b]	ND	Gregory et al. (1983)
		1	0.08 (0.23)	0.02 (0.40)	—	—	0.01	ND	
		2	0.02 (0.06)	0.06 (0.42)	—	—	ND	ND	
		3	0.01 (0.02)	0.02 (0.22)	—	—	—	—	
8000 (Chicken)	7	0	0.41[d]	ND	0.23[e]	0.03	ND[f]	ND	Trucksess et al. (1983B)
		7	0.01	ND	ND	ND	ND	ND	
2057 (Chicken)	35	0	0.17	0.06	0.05	0.10	0.09	0.02	Chen et al. (1984)
		1	0.10	0.04	ND	ND	0.04	0	
		2	ND	ND	ND	ND	ND	ND	

[a] Number in parentheses indicates water-soluble conjugates.
[b] Not detected.
[c] Traces of AFL detected.
[d] 0.18 ng/g AFL detected.
[e] 0.09 ng/g AFL detected.
[f] 0.07 ng/g AFL detected.

TABLE 10.5. Average Ratios of AFB_1 in Feed to AFB_1 and AFM_1 in Tissue

Species	Feed: tissue ratio[a,b] $(AFB_1 : AFB_1 + AFM_1)$			Reference
	Liver	Kidney	Muscle	
Pig	1,316	1,103	—[c]	Neff and Edds (1981)
Pig	489	467	1,343	Furtado et al. (1982)
Pig	251	444	938	Miller et al. (1982)
Pig	323	250	200,000	Trucksess et al. (1982)
Steer	268	79	3,974	Richard et al. (1983)
Turkey	926(769)[d]	—	16,667 (25,000)[d]	Gregory et al. (1983)
Chicken	19,512	30,769	—	Trucksess et al. (1983B)
Chicken	8,943	13,713	18,700	Chen et al. (1984)

[a] Calculated on basis of AFB_1 in feed.
[b] Analyzed within 24 hr after completion of feeding regimen.
[c] Not determined.
[d] Value in parentheses indicates value determined for water soluble AFB_1 and AFM_1 conjugates.

human health in consuming food contaminated at this level. In order to be exposed to meat containing AFB_1 or aflatoxin metabolites near this level, the feed animal would have to be exposed to dietary AFB_1 at levels significantly higher than 1 µg/g (a level at which many species exhibit toxic responses). A similar argument was the basis for raising the FDA action level of aflatoxin in cottonseed meal from 20 to 300 ng/g when it is used as a feed ingredient for beef cattle, swine, and poultry. After detailed analysis of potential safety risks versus economic benefits of using aflatoxin contaminated meal, the FDA concluded that increasing the allowable levels of aflatoxins in cottonseed meal feed ingredients did not pose a toxicological threat to humans since (1) the meal would be diluted approximately tenfold in the final feed mixture, (2) the final aflatoxin residues in edible tissue and eggs would be less than 0.03 ng/g using an average feed:tissue ratio of 1000. It was specified that this revision was *not applicable to cottonseed meal used for dairy cattle* where feed:milk ratios of AFB_1:AFM_1 have been reported to range between 46 and 646 (Stoloff 1980). Similar modifications in action levels for peanut meal and corn used in feeds might be expected in the future as the scientific data base on aflatoxin toxicity and carryover improves.

The risk from ingestion of water-soluble and covalently bound macromolecular aflatoxins forms might also be questioned. Although also present at very low levels in animal tissue, free aflatoxins may be cleaved from glucuronide, sulfates, nucleic acids, and proteins during digestion and subsequently absorbed from the intestine. Jaggi et al. (1980) tested this hypothesis by preparing in vivo water-soluble and macromolecular-bound forms of radio labeled AFB_1 and feeding these to rats. Based on radioactivity covalently bound to liver DNA (a measure of potential carcinogenicity), the macromolecule-bound AFB_1 derivatives were at least 4000 times less active than AFB_1 with respect to covalent binding to rat liver DNA, and the water-soluble conjugates were at least 100 times less potent than free AFB_1. It was concluded by the authors that the risk of cancer to humans who consume liver or meat containing such aflatoxin residues is negligible when compared to the risk from intake of aflatoxins from nuts, milk, and other sources.

Occurrence in Meats after Fungal Colonization.   Aflatoxins may appear in meat products as a direct result of the growth of toxigenic aspergilli. Bullerman et al. (1969A) found that fresh beef, bacon, and ham could support the growth of inoculated A. flavus and A. parasiticus as well as of aflatoxin production. Storage at 20°C for 14 days was optimal for toxin production with levels in beef exceeding 600 ng/g, however, meats stored at 10°C became spoiled by bacteria and yeast before significant Aspergillus growth. Thus, products less susceptible to bacterial spoilage, such as bacon and ham, could potentially support aflatoxin production when subjected to ample oxygen and temperature abuse. It is thus good practice for the consumer to discard products of this type when heavy mold contamination is apparent on them.

The fermentation conditions used for country cured hams and aged salamis hypothetically make these meat products especially susceptible to colonization by toxigenic aspergilli. Aflatoxins are elaborated when Italian-type and Hungarian-type salamis, summer sausages, and country-cured hams are inoculated with A. flavus or A. parasiticus before aging (Bullerman et al. 1969B; Alvarez-Barrera et al. 1983). Toxin production is greatest at temperatures near 30°C and relative humidities greater than 85% but can be inhibited by aging the meats at temperatures between 10° and 15°C and relative humidities below 80%. Smoking and curing ingredients also tend to inhibit aflatoxin elaboration (Bullerman et al. 1969B; Meier and Marth 1977). It is important to note that A. flavus and A. parasiticus are rarely encountered in fermented meat products. For example, of 562 fungi isolated from country-cured hams, only three were A. flavus (Sutic et al. 1972). Leistner and Ayres (1968) detected only one strain of A. flavus from the 307 mold strains isolated from country cured hams and European-type salamis. Even if spores of toxigenic aspergilli are present on a meat, they must successfully compete with other molds in order to colonize and produce aflatoxins. Up to this time, there have been no reports of aflatoxins being detected in fermented meat products taken from the market shelf. Thus, the danger of human aflatoxin exposure by this route is probably minimal.

Ochratoxins

Occurrence and Toxic Effects.   The ochratoxins are a group of seven related isocoumarin derivatives linked to phenylalanine (Figure 10.4) that

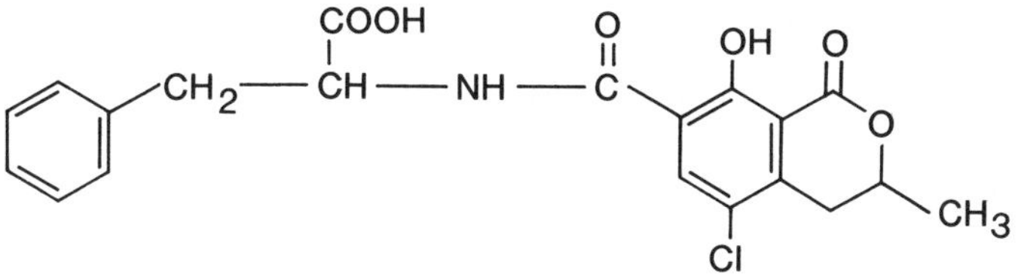

FIG. 10.4.   Structure of ochratoxin A.

are produced by species of *Aspergillus* and *Penicillium* (Busby and Wogan 1979). Ochratoxin A (OA), the most commonly encountered of the group, is highly nephrotoxic to monogastric animals and has also been shown to be immunotoxic and teratogenic. OA is frequently detected in Scandanavian and Balkan countries and occasionally in the United States in commodities such as barley, corn, wheat, oats, rye, peanuts, hay, and green coffee beans (CAST 1979). The toxin has been related to endemic kidney disease in swine and poultry in Denmark and Sweden. During the course of the swine disease, pigs fed diets containing 200 ng/g OA develop pale swollen kidneys characterized by atrophy of the proximal tubules and interstitial cortical fibrosis (Krogh 1977). These symptoms are similar to those occurring in humans during the course of endemic Balkan kidney disease of Yugoslavia, Bulgaria, and Romania. The incidence of this human disease can be correlated to OA content of foods by regions in the Balkan countries (CAST 1979).

Accumulation in Animal Tissue.   OA accumulates to significant levels in meat and poultry tissue under both experimental and natural conditions. Table 10.6 summarizes OA accumulation data for several species and indicates that the primary sites of residues were the kidney with lesser amounts in liver and muscle. Krogh *et al.* (1979) determined that there was no difference in OA residue levels in kidney, muscle, liver, and fat of swine fed 1000 nanograms per gram dietary OA for 3 months or 2 years. Feed to tissue ratios for pig and chicken kidney were less than 100 indicating extensive carryover of OA. Following oral administration, the biological half life of OA in swine tissues is 4.5 days indicating that a several week withdrawal period would be needed to eliminate OA residues after exposure to contaminated feed (Krogh *et al.* 1976). In regard to ruminants, *in vitro* and *in vivo* studies reveal that OA is rapidly detoxified by the action of proteolytic enzymes in the rumen, which cleave phenylalanine from the isocoumarin of OA (Stoloff 1979).

Field surveys of market meat and poultry demonstrate the presence of OA in tissue, primarily kidney. Josefsson (1979) reported that of 90 abnormal appearing pig kidneys from 6 Swedish slaughter houses, 22 contained

TABLE 10.6. OA Residues Detected in Tissues of Food Animals Tissue Residue

Species	Dietary OA (ng/g)	Dose interval	Withdrawal time (days)	Liver (ng/g)	Kidney (ng/g)	Muscle (ng/g)	Reference
Pig	1000	3 Month	0	11.4	26.8	9.5	Krogh et al. (1979)
Chicken	500	14 Days	0	13	124	3.3	Frye and Chu
	5000	14 Days	0	80	124	8.4	(1977)
Chicken	1000	8 Week	0	ND[a]	ND	ND	Prior et al.
	2000		0	24	41	ND	(1980)
			1	ND	16	—[b]	
			2	ND	ND	—	
Calf	430	87 Days	0	ND	Tr[c]-5	—	Patterson et al. (1981)

[a] Not detected.
[b] Not determined.
[c] Trace.

OA at levels greater than 2 ng/g with the highest detectable concentration being 88 ng/g. Other similar studies in Sweden, Denmark, and Yugoslavia have reported OA in between 25 to 40% of pig and poultry carcasses that were selected on the basis of abnormal kidneys (Stoloff 1979).

As in the case of AFB_1, cooking apparently has little effect on OA. When OA-contaminated ground muscle, fat, diced kidneys, and sliced blood pudding were fried at 150°–160°C, losses in total toxin averaged only about 20% (Josefsson and Moller 1980). In view of the potential dangers of having OA in human foods, Danish health authorities have devised a system whereby all suspect pig kidneys are analyzed for the toxin (Stoloff 1979). Should OA be detected, the whole carcass is condemned and the source of the contaminated pig feed determined and eliminated. In the United States, regulations concerning the presence of OA in meat or plant products do not exist, due to the apparent low incidence of the toxin in this country.

Occurrence in Meat after Fungal Colonization.   Both A. ochraceus and P. viridicatum, species which often produce ochratoxin A, have been isolated from country-cured hams in several studies (Leistner and Ayres 1968; Sutic et al. 1972; Strzelecki et al. 1969). Escher et al. (1973) found that both of two strains of A. ochraceus isolated from country-cured hams produced OA and ochratoxin (OB) in culture and in hams; however, none of six P. viridicatum strains yielded the OA or OB in culturing on ham. Optimum conditions for toxin production were 25°–30°C and a total moisture content of 45%. After 21 days incubation, one-third of the toxin was found in mycelia on the ham surface while the remainder penetrated the meat to a distance of 0.5 cm. Systematic market studies of ochratoxin occurrence in marketplace aged cured hams and sausage have yet to be conducted.

Zearalenones

Occurrence and Toxic Effects. The zearalenones are a group of resor-
cyclic lactones, produced by members of genus *Fusarium,* that have es-
trogenic effects on a number of animal species (CAST 1979). Zearalenone
(Fig. 10.5A), the parent compound, is often found in temperate regions in
corn, wheat, sorghum, barley, and oats. While not acutely toxic, high
levels of zearalenone interrupt normal estrus in sows and cause vulval
swelling and enlargement of the uterus. Testicular atrophy and mammary
gland hyperplasia develop in young males exposed to zearalenone. Other
species affected by zearalenone include rats, mice, lambs, monkeys, and
humans. In regard to meat quality of food producing animals, it is interesting to note that high dietary levels of zearalenone retard growth of
rats and cause a 40% decrease in α R fibers in the vastus lateralis with a

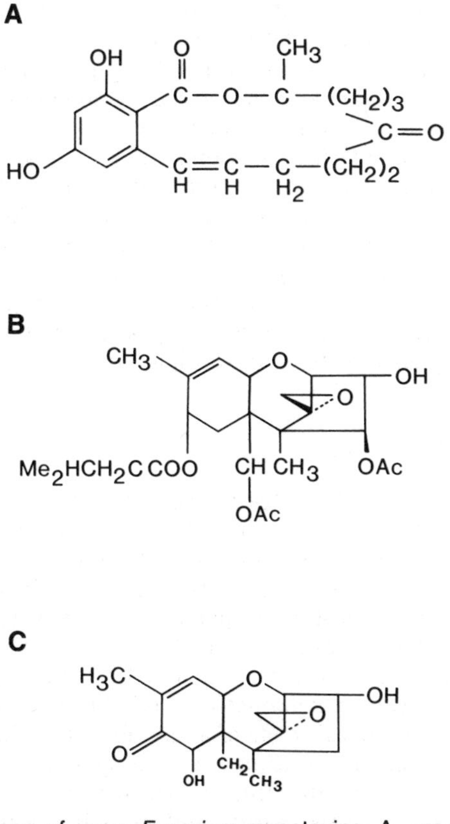

FIG. 10.5. Structures of some *Fusarium* mycotoxins: A—zearalenone; B—T-2
toxin; C—deoxynivalenol.

corresponding increase in α W fibers (Keissling 1982). In the United States, no regulations concerning the presence of zearalenone in foods or feeds currently exist. *Fusarium* toxins are not likely to be present in meats, since these molds are not typically encountered on stored or cured meats.

Accumulation in Animal Tissue.   Zearalenone is rapidly metabolized in pig, cow, rabbit, rat and man, and is eliminated in urine and feces primarily as glucuronide and sulfate conjugates (Mirocha *et al.* 1981). Oral intubation of rats with ^{3}H-labeled zearalenone does not result in appreciable radioactivity accumulation in liver, kidney, spleen, ovary, brain, or uterus (Mirocha *et al.* 1977). Dailey *et al.* (1980) found that ^{14}C-labeled zearalenone administered to laying hens at 10 mg/kg of body weight did not accumulate in edible tissues but that persistent levels of lipophilic metabolites remained in egg yolks at relatively high (2 μg/g) concentrations. Dairy cows fed diets containing 2 μg/g of unlabeled zearalenone for 7 weeks did not accumulate the mycotoxin (detection limit 4 ng/g) in tissue or milk (Shreeve *et al.* 1979). In contrast, Mirocha *et al.* (1981) found that when cows were fed diets containing 25 μg/g zearalenone for 7 days, a feed to tissue ratio (zearalenone to free zearalenone plus zearalenone conjugates) of 17 resulted in milk, indicating a very high potential for carryover. Further clarification of the potential for carryover of zearalenone in edible tissue, milk, and eggs is likely with improved analytical procedures, such as the HPLC procedure described by Turner *et al.* (1983).

In relation to carryover studies, zearalanol (Ralgro), a derivative of zearalenone, is being used as a growth promoter in livestock because of its anabolic qualities (Hurd 1977). The rationale for using this derivative is that, unlike diethylstilbestrol, residues apparently do not accumulate in tissues nor does it exert potent uterotropic effects.

Trichothecenes

Occurrence and Toxicity.   Besides zearalenone, toxins known as the trichothecenes are produced by certain fusaria. Among the over 40 known trichothecenes, a group of sesquiterpenoids containing a trichothecane nucleus (Fig. 10.5B,C), those most often identified in *Fusarium* culture filtrates are T-2 toxin, diacetoxyscirpenol, and deoxynivalenol or vomitoxin (CAST 1979). When applied to the shaved skin of guinea pigs, these compounds produce a strong dermatitic reaction indicated by severe local irritation, inflammation, desquamation, and general necrosis (Busby and Wogan 1979). The biological mode of action for trichothecenes is believed to be via the inhibition of initiation or the elongation-termination steps of protein synthesis. Actively dividing tissues such as bone marrow, lymph nodes, spleen, thymus, testes, ovary, and intestinal mucosa appear most susceptible to these toxins. Acute LD_{50}s for mice injected (iv) with T-2 toxin, diacetoxyscirpenol, and deoxynivalenol are 5.2, 23, and 70 mg/kg, respectively. The potential danger of trichothecenes to human health was first realized in the 1940s during several massive outbreaks (1942–1947) of fatal alimentary toxic aleukia in the Soviet Union where overwintered grain containing the toxins was ingested (Joffe 1978). Ironically, recent evidence implicates the Soviet Union in using trichothecenes in "yellow rain" chemical warfare in Southeast Asia and Afghanistan (Marshall 1982). The effects of ingesting sublethal doses of trichothecenes over a long period of time are still unknown.

Members of the genus *Fusarium* occur both as saprophytes in soil and decaying vegetation and as parasites in cultivated plants. Toxigenic *Fusaria* are often isolated from agricultural commodities such as corn, wheat, barley, and oats (CAST 1979). Until only recently, actual detection of the preformed toxins has been limited by the lack of suitable analytical methods. Vesonder *et al.* (1973) first isolated the trichothecene, deoxynivalenol, as an emetic principle and feed refusal factor in *Fusarium*-infected corn. The toxin has since been found to occur in the parts per million range in grains produced by the United States, Canada, Japan, China, South Africa, and Austria. Although T-2 toxin has also been isolated in a few feed-associated mycotoxicoses, deoxynivalenol appears to be the most common naturally occurring trichothecene. In many cases, zearalenone and deoxynivalenol occur simultaneously.

Accumulation in Animal Tissue.   Research on metabolism and carryover of trichothecene toxins has dealt primarily with T-2 toxin. Table 10.7 summarizes feed to tissue ratios of ^{3}H-labeled T-2 toxin to total tritium in liver, muscle, and milk of the cow, chick, and swine. The results suggest that liver was the primary site of residue accumulation. The chick carried over more T-2 toxin and T-2 metabolites into edible tissue than the pig, based on the respective feed to tissue ratios for liver, 41 vs. 91, and muscle, 77 vs. 500. The lactating cow had higher feed to tissue ratios than the other species but comparisons are not possible since the cow study employed a threefold longer withdrawal time. Yoshizawa *et al.* (1981A)

TABLE 10.7. Average Ratios of ^{3}H-Labeled T-2 Toxin in Feed to Total Tritium in Tissue

Species	Withdrawal period	Feed : tissue ratio						Reference
		Liver		Muscle		Milk		
Cow	3 Days	1667	(0.54)[a]	3333	(1.15)	2500	(0.89)	Yoshizawa *et al.* (1981)
Chick	1 Day	42	(0.56)	77	(1.06)	—[b]		Chi *et al.* (1978)
Swine	1 Day	91	(0.29)	500	(1.29)	—		Robison *et al.* (1979)

[a] Number in parentheses indicates plasma to tissue ratio of total tritium residues.
[b] Not determined.

suggested that because plasma:tissue ratios among the species are very close to 1.0 (Table 10.7), residues of T-2 metabolites in edible tissues could be estimated from the residues in plasma. Two of the major metabolites of T-2 toxin found in tissue *in vivo* are toxic and have been identified as a hydroxy derivative and a deacetylated hydroxy derivative of the toxin (Yoshizawa *et al.* 1981B). Recently, Swanson *et al.* (1982) reported carryover of diacetoxyscirpenol from feed to swine tissue. Similar studies on deoxynivalenol have not been reported.

Other Mycotoxins

Besides those mycotoxins described above, numerous others have been identified. Only limited information exists on the role of these toxins in human health or on their potential presence in meats.

Sterigmatocystin.   Sterigmatocystin (Fig. 10.6A), the parent compound of a family of toxins known as the sterigmatocystins, is produced in cultures of *Aspergillus flavus* and *A. versicolor* (Busby and Wogan 1979). Like the aflatoxins, sterigmatocystins are hepatotoxic and hepatocarcinogenic. Although isolated from severely molded wheat, barley, rice, and pecans, sterigmatocystin is rarely found naturally and thus unlikely to occur as residue in fresh meats. However, under ideal growth conditions, pure cultures of sterigmatocystin-producing fungi can elaborate toxin in aged cured meats. Halls and Ayres (1973) found that 10 of 16 isolates of *Aspergillus versicolor* from country-cured hams were capable of producing sterigmatocystin. When three of these were inoculated onto sterile ham slices, they were shown to produce the toxin at levels as high as 800 ng/g. Sterigmatocystin has not been detected in market hams or sausages, although its presence has not been systematically investigated.

Penicillic Acid.   Penicillic acid is a highly reactive unsaturated lactone (Fig. 10.6B) produced by species of *Aspergillus* and *Penicillium* in corn (Busby and Wogan 1979; Davis and Diener 1978). Penicillic acid is moderately toxic to animals and binds directly to sulfhydryl groups or to free amino groups of proteins. Orally administered ^{14}C-labeled penicillic acid is rapidly metabolized and excreted with most residual activity remaining in the blood (Park *et al.* 1977). Ciegler *et al.* (1972) determined that 10% of 346 *Penicillum* cultures isolated from mold-fermented salamis produced penicillic acid in liquid media. When 5 of these mold strains were inoculated onto sausages and ripened for 70 days, toxin was not detected. It was hypothesized that if penicillic acid was formed during the aging of meats, it would react with amino acids in the meats and be rendered nontoxic.

Patulin.   Patulin is another reactive unsaturated lactone (Fig. 10.6B) produced by aspergilli and penicillia (Davis and Diener 1978). Commonly

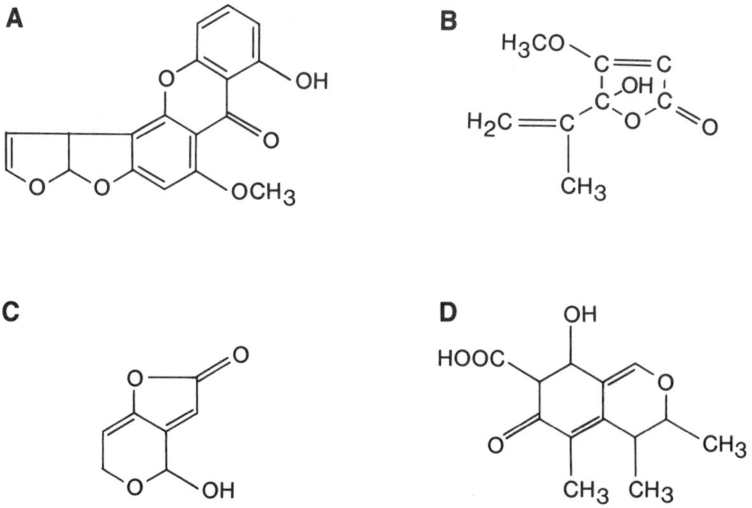

A

B

C

D

FIG. 10.6.   Structures of other naturally occurring mycotoxins: A—sterigmato-cystin; B—pencillic acid; C—patulin; D—citrinin.

isolated from apples, it is moderately toxic to animals and has been reported to cause stomach lesions. Patulin is rapidly metabolized in rats (Dailey *et al.* 1975) and since the toxin is not found in livestock feeds, is unlikely to accumulate in meat and poultry products.

Citrinin.   Citrinin is a moderately toxic compound (Fig. 10.6D) also produced by *Aspergillus* sp. and *Penicillium* sp. (Davis and Diener 1978). It has been detected in barley, wheat, and other grains. Citrinin is nephro-toxic and has been suggested, along with ochratoxin A, to be involved in swine kidney disease. However, its occurrence is relatively rare and thus probably does not constitute a residue problem in animal tissues. Under experimental conditions, however, *Penicillium viridicatum* can produce citrinin in country-cured hams (Wu *et al.* 1974).

Cyclopiazonic Acid.   Cyclopiazonic acid is another toxic metabolite of species in the *Penicillium* and *Aspergillus* groups. It is a natural contaminant of corn and peanuts and is often coproduced with aflatoxin (Gallagher *et al.* 1978). Leistner (1984) reported that cyclopiazonic acid is the major mycotoxin produced by penicillia isolated from mold-fermented salamis suggesting that these meat proucts should be surveyed for this mycotoxin. Norred *et al.* (1985) recently found that when rats were dosed with [14C] cyclopiazonic acid, skeletal muscle tissue contained 48% of the radioactive dose 6 hr after either intraperitoneal or intragastric administration. After 72 hr, between 3 and 8% of the dose still remained in the muscle. These results indicate that future perspectives should include a thorough understanding of both cyclopiazonic acid metabolism in animals and the degree of carryover of this mycotoxin into poultry and livestock tissues.

SUMMARY

Growth of spoilage fungi in meats is generally precluded by bacterial competition. Changes in environmental parameters that inhibit bacteria, however, may select for the slower-growing fungi. Successful control of undesirable fungi is especially dependent on adequate monitoring of water activity and temperature. Dried, fermented, or cold-stored meats have reduced water activities that select for xerotolerant fungi. Decreased holding temperatures often select for psychrotropic molds and yeasts. While modern techniques such as vacuum packaging and controlled atmosphere storage of meats can inhibit aerobic fungi, investigations on the potential of fermentative yeasts to grow in such environments are warranted. It should also be noted that under experimental temperature abuse, fresh and stored meats can support the growth of molds and mycotoxin production. Thus, consumers should discard heavily molded products of this type.

Fungi are believed to give quality attributes to certain aged and cured meats. These are primarily esthetic, although improved flavor, texture, and preservation characteristics have been suggested to result from growth of desirable molds. Further studies, similar to those conducted on the lactic acid bacteria and micrococci, are needed regarding the efficacy of using mold starter cultures in aged, fermented meats (Leistner 1984).

From a health standpoint, fungal species isolated from fermented meats are nonpathogenic but a few are capable of producing mycotoxins in meat under appropriate environmental conditions. While it is unlikely that these toxigenic molds would be the predominant flora of country-cured hams and sausages, a systematic market survey for mycotoxins of fermented meat products produced at various sources should be conducted. A major obstacle to this approach is the excessive time and cost required to perform a typical mycotoxin analysis. Usually, lengthy extraction and chromatographic cleanup steps are needed before actual quantitation of the mycotoxin. Identification and quantitation of the toxin then involves thin layer chromatography, high performance liquid chromatography, gas chromatography, or mass spectroscopy. Recently, analytical enzyme immunoassays have been devised for AFB_1, AFM_1, ochratoxin A, T-2 toxin, and zearalenone (Liu et $al.$ 1985; Pestka et $al.$ 1980, 1981A,B,C) that allow rapid and specific quantitation of the toxins at the picogram level without the cleanup problems encountered by other methods. While these assays have been applied primarily to plant products and milk, they might similarly be used to screen for the presence of mycotoxins in fermented meats.

It has been experimentally established that low levels of mycotoxins and their metabolites are carried over from feeds to the edible tissues of food-producing animals. Generally, the degree of mycotoxin carryover is related to total dose level rather than duration of dose. Carryover of aflatoxins has been most thoroughly studied and is subject to strict regulation at the feed level because of the ability of these toxins to act as carcinogens. Ochratoxin A residues in meat may also pose a significant health problem in certain European countries and are therefore monitored by regulatory authorities. It has been recently determined that there are sporadic incidences of *Fusarium* toxins, particularly deoxynivalenol and zearalenone, in North American wheat and corn. It is not yet known whether these compounds have an effect on human health when present in the diet. Although guidelines for zearalenone have not been established, the Canadian government has regulated against the presence of deoxynivalenol in wheat products while the United States Food and Drug Administration has set a nonenforceable "level of concern" for grains used in processing and animal feeds. Suitable information regarding feed to tissue carryover of *Fusarium* toxins and cyclopiazonic acid is lacking. Since these compounds are likely to be present in the diet of food-producing animals, further data on their potential to appear as residues needs to be developed.

A market survey of southeastern beef, hog, and chicken liver performed by the U.S. Department of Agriculture during 1977, a year of high aflatoxin contamination in corn, revealed no detectable aflatoxins at the 0.5 ng/g level (Stoloff 1979). Relatively little, however, is known of the actual levels of residues of other mycotoxins in fresh meats at the market level. Again, there is need for systematic assessment of this possibility, perhaps using enzyme immunoassay or some other screening procedure. For example, a light microscopic immunoperoxidase localization technique has been devised for the detection of AFB_1 covalently bound to liver macromolecules (Pestka *et al.* 1983). Another approach might involve the use of mycotoxin plasma level as a diagnostic "indicator" of tissue contamination, as has been proposed for T-2 toxin (Yoshizawa *et al.* 1981). Development of a comprehensive data base on mycotoxin tissue residues in market-ready meats would greatly enhance our ability to make rational judgments on the risks and benefits of using feed contaminated with mycotoxins at low to moderate levels.

ACKNOWLEDGMENTS

This work was supported by the Michigan State Agricultural Experiment Station and USDA Grant No. 83-CRSR-2-2257. I thank C. Chen, J. F. Gregory, P. D. Lowry, R. D. Stubblefield, and M. W. Trucksess for prepublications and unpublished data used in this chapter.

REFERENCES

ALBAREZ-BARRERA, V., PEARSON, A. M., PRICE, J. F., GRAY, J. I., and AUST, S. D. 1983. Some factors influencing aflatoxin production in fermented sausages. J. Food Sci. *47*, 1773.

AUSTWICK, P. K. C. 1978. Aflatoxicosis in poultry. *In* Mycotoxic Fungi, Mycotoxins, Mycotoxicoses, An Encyclopedic Handbook. Vol. 2. Chap. 3.61, p. 279. T. D. Wyllie and L. G. Morehouse (Editors). Marcel Dekker, NY.

AYRES, J. C., MUNDT, J. O., and SANDINE, W. E. 1980. Meat and meat products. *In* Microbiology of Foods. Chap. 17. G. Hefta (Editor). W. H. Freeman and Co., San Francisco, CA.

BANWART, G. 1979. Food spoilage. *In* Basic Food Microbiology. Chap. 8, p. 433. G. Banwart (Editor). AVI Publishing Co., Westport, CT.

BROOKS, F. T. and HANSFORD, C. G. 1923. Mold growth upon cold-store meat. Trans. Brit. Mycol. Soc. *8*, 113.

BULLERMAN, L. B., HARTMAN, P. A., and AYRES, J. C. 1969A. Aflatoxin production in meats. I. Stored meats. Appl. Microbiol. *18*, 714.

BULLERMAN, L. B., HARTMAN, P. A. and AYRES, P. A. 1969B. Aflatoxin production in meats II. Aged dry salamis and aged country cured hams. Appl. Microbiol. *18*, 718.

BUSBY, JR., W. F. and WOGAN, G. F. 1979. Mycotoxins and mycotoxicoses. *In* Food-Borne Infections and Intoxications. 2nd edition., Chap. 11, p. 519. H. Riemann and F. L. Bryan (Editors). Academic Press, NY.

CAMPBELL, T. C. and HAYES, J. R. 1976. The role of alfatoxin metabolism in its toxic lesion. Toxicol. Appl. Pharmacol. *76*, 199.

CARLTON, W. W. and SZCZECH, G. M. 1978. Mycotoxicoses of laboratory animals. *In* Mycotoxic Fungi, Mycotoxins, Mycotoxicoses, An Encyclopedic Handbook. (Vol. 2 Chap. 3.7, p. 333. T. D. Wyllie and L. G. Morehouse (Editors). Marcel Dekker, NY.

CAST. 1979. Aflatoxin and Other Mycotoxins: An Agricultural Perspective. Report No. 80. Council for Agricultural Science and Technology, Ames, IA.

CHEN, C., PEARSON, A. M., COLEMAN, T. H., GRAY, J. I., PESTKA, J. J. and AUST, S. D. 1984. Tissue deposition and clearance of aflatoxins from broiler chicken fed a contaminated diet. Food. Chem. Toxicol. *22*, 447.

CHI, M. S., ROBISON, T. S., MIROCHA, C. J., BEHRENS, J. C. and SHIMODA, W. 1978. Transmission of radioactivity into eggs from laying hens administered tritium labeled T-2 toxin. Poult. Sci. *57*, 1234.

CHU, F. S. and UENO, I. 1977. Production of antibody against aflatoxin B$_1$. Appl. Environ. Microbiol. *33*, 1125.

CIEGLER, A., MINTZLAFF, A-J., WEISLEDER, D. and LEISTNER, L. 1972. Potential production and detoxification of penicillic acid in mold-fermented sausage (salami). Appl. Microbiol. *24*, 114.

CYSEWSKI, S. J., PIER, S. J., ENGSTROM, G. W., RICHARD, J. L., DOUGHERTY, R. W. and THURSTON, J. R. 1968. Clinical features of acute aflatoxicosis in swine. Am. J. Vets. Res. *29*, 1577.

DAILEY, R. E., BLASCHKA, A. M. and BROUWER, E. A. 1975. Absorption, distribution, and excretion of [^{14}C] patulin by rats. J. Toxicol. Environ Health *3*, 479.

DAILEY, R. E., REESE, R. E. and BROWER, E. A. 1980. Metaboism of [^{14}C] zearalenone in laying hens. J. Agr. Food Chem. *28*, 286.

DAVIS, N. D. and DIENER, U. L. 1978. Mycotoxin. *In* Food and Beverage Mycology. Chap. 14, p. 397. L. R. Beuchat (Editor). AVI Publishing Co., Westport, CT.

ESCHER, F. E., KOEHLER, P. E. and AYRES, J. C. 1973. Production of ochratoxins A and B on country cured ham. Appl. Microbiol. *26*, 17.

ESSIGMANN, J. M., CROY, R. G., BENNETT, R. A., and WOGAN, G. N. 1982. Metabolic activation of aflatoxin B$_1$: Patterns of DNA adduct formation, removal, and excretion in relation to carcinogenesis. Drug Metab. Rev. *13*, 581.

FRAZIER, W. C. and WESTHOFF, D. C. 1978. Contamination, preservation, and spoilage of meats. *In* Food Microbiology. Chap. 13. J. E. Vastyan and J. W. Bradley (Editors). McGraw-Hill, NY.

FRYE. C. E. and CHU, F. S. 1977. Distribution of ochratoxin A in chicken tissues and eggs. J. Food Safety *1,* 147.

FURTADO, R. M., PEARSON, A. M., GRAY, J. I., HOGBERG, M. G. and MILLER, E. R. 1981. Effects of cooking and/or processing upon levels of aflatoxin in meat from pigs fed a contaminated diet. J. Food Sci. *46,* 1306.

FURTADO, R. M., PEARSON, A. M., HOGBERG, M. G., MILLER, E. R., GRAY, J. I., and AUST, S. D. 1982. Withdrawal time required for clearance of aflatoxins from pig tissues. J. Agr. Food Chem. *30,* 101.

GALLAGHER, R. T., RICHARD, J. L., STAHR, H. M. and COLE, R. J. 1978. Cyclopiazonic acid production by aflatoxigenic and non-aflatoxigenic strains of *Aspergillus flavus.* Mycopathologia *66,* 31.

GILL, C. O. and LOWRY, P. D. 1982. Growth at sub-zero temperatures of black spot fungi from meat. J. Appl. Bacteriol. *52,* 245.

GILL, C. O., LOWRY, P. D., AND DiMENNA, M. E. 1981. A note on the identities of organisms causing black spot spoilage of meat. J. Appl. Bacteriol. *51,* 183.

GREGORY, J. F. III and MANLEY, D. 1981. High performance liquid chromatographic determination of aflatoxins in animal tissues and products. J. Assoc. Off. Anal. Chem. *64,* 144.

GREGORY, J. F. III, GOLDSTEIN, S. L. and EDDS, G. T. 1983. Metabolite distribution and rate of residue clearance in turkeys fed a diet containing aflatoxin B_1. Food. Chem. Toxicol. *21,* 463.

HALLS, N. A. and AYRES, J. C. 1973. Potential production of sterigmatocystin on country cured ham. Appl. Microbiol. *26,* 636.

HURD, R. N. 1977. Structure activity relationships in zearalenones. *In* Mycotoxins in Human and Animal Health. p. 379. J. V. Rodricks, C. W. Hesseltine, and M. A. Mehlman (Editors). Pathtox Publishers, Inc., Park Forest South, IL.

INGRAM, M. and DAINTY, R. H. 1971. Changes caused by microbes in spoilage of meats. J. Appl. Bacteriol. *34,* 21.

INGRAM, M. and SIMONSEN, B. 1980. Meats and meat products. *In* Microbial Ecology of Foods, Vol. 2, Food Commodities. Chap. 15, p. 333. J. H. Stilliker, R. P. Elliot, A. C. Baird-Parker, F. L. Bryan, J. H. B. Christian, D. S. Clark, J. C. Olson, and T. A. Roberts. (Editors). Academic Press, NY.

JACOBSON, W. C., HARMEYER, W. C., JACKSON, J. E., ARMBRECHT, B. and WISEMAN, A. G. 1978. Transmission of aflatoxin B_1 into tissues of growing pigs. Bull. Environ. Contam. Toxicol. *19,* 156.

JAGGI, W., LUTZ, W. K., LUTHY, J., ZWEIFEL, U. and SCHLATTER, C. 1980. *In vivo* covalent binding of aflatoxin metabolites isolated from animal tissue to rat-liver DNA. Food. Cosmet. Toxicol. *18,* 257.

JAY, J. M. 1978. Meats, poultry, and seafoods. *In* Food and Beverage Mycology. p. 129. L. R. Beuchat, Editor. AVI Publishing Co., Westport, CT.

JAY, J. M. 1979. Occurrence and significance of specific yeasts and molds in meats, poultry, and seafoods. *In* Food Mycology Chap. 5, p. 44. M. E. Rhodes (Editor). G. K. Hall and Co., Boston, MA.

JOFFE, A. Z. 1978. *Fusarium poae* and *F. sporotrichoides* as principal causal agents of alimentary toxic aleukia. *In* Mycotoxic Fungi, Mycotoxins, Mycotoxicoses, An Encyclopedia Handbook. Vol. 3. Chap. 3.10, p. 21. T. D. Wyllie and L. G. Morehouse (Editors). Marcel Dekker, Inc., NY.

JOSEFSSON, E. 1979. Study of ochratoxin A in pig kidneys. VarFoeda *31,* 415.

JOSEFSSON, B. G. E. and MOLLER, T. E. 1980. Heat stability of ochratoxin A in pig products. J. Sci. Food Agr. *31,* 1313.

KIESSLING, K.-H. 1982. The effect of zearalenone on growth rate, organ weight, and muscle fibre composition in growing rats. Acta Pharmacol. Toxicol. *51,* 154.

KROGH, P. 1977. Ochratoxins. *In* Mycotoxins in Human and Aniaml Health. p. 489.

J. V. Rodricks, C. W. Helleltine, and M. A. Mehlman (Editors). Pathotox Publishers, Inc., Park Forest South, IL.

KROGH, P., ELLING, F., HALD, B., LARSEN, A. E., LILLEHOJ, E. B., MADSEN, A. and MORTENSEN, H. P.   1976.   Time-dependent disappearance of ochratoxin A residues in tissues of bacon pigs. Toxicology 6, 235.

KROGH, P., ELLING, F., FRIIS, C., HALD, B., LARSEN, A. E., LILLEHOJ, E. B., MADSEN, A., MORTENSEN, H. P., RASMUSSEN, F. and RAUNSHOV, U.   1979.   Porcine nephropathy induced by long-term ingestion of ochratoxin A. Vet. Pathol. 16, 466.

KOBAYASHI, G. S.   1980.   Fungi. In Microbiology. Chap. 45, p. 830. B. D. Davis, R. Dulbecco, H. N. Eisen, and H. S. Ginsberg (Editors). Harper and Row, NY.

KOTULA, A. W., CAMPANO, S. G. and KINSMAN, D. M.   1982.   Proteolytic and lipolytic activity of molds isolated from aged beef. J. Food Prot. 45, 1242.

LEISTNER, L.   1984.   Toxigenic penicillia occurring in feeds and foods: A review. Food Tech. in Australia 36, 404–406.

LEISTNER, L. and AYRES, J. C.   1968.   Molds and meats. Fleischwirtschaft 48, 62.

LIN, J., MILLER, J. A. and MILLER, E. C.   1977.   2,3-Dihydro-2-(guan-7-yl)-3-hydroxy-aflatoxin B_1, a major acid hydrolysis product of aflatoxin B_1-DNA or ribosomal RNA adducts formed in heopatic microsome-mediated ractions and rat liver in vivo. Cancer Res. 37, 4430.

LIU, M-T., RAM, B. P., HART, L. P., and PESTKA, J. J.   1985.   Indirect enzyme-linked immunosorbent assay for the mycotoxin zearalenone. Appl. Environ. Microbiol. 50, 332–336.

LOWRY, P. D. and GILL, C. O.   1983A.   Private communication. Meat Industry Research Institute of New Zealand, Hamilton, New Zealand.

LOWRY, P. D. and GILL, C. O.   1983B.   Private Communication. Meat Industry Research Institute of New Zealand, Hamilton, New Zealand.

LUTHY, J., ZWEIFEL, U. and SCHLATTER, C. H.   1980.   Metabolism and tissue distribution of (C^{14})aflatoxin B_1 in pigs. Food. Cosmet. Toxicol. 18, 253.

MACARA, T. J. R.   1943.   Dried meat, II. The growth of moulds on dried meat. J. Soc. Chem. Ind. 62, 104.

MARSHALL, E.   1982.   Yellow rain: Filling in the gaps. Science 217, 3.

MEIER, K. R. and MARTH, E. H.   1977.   Production of aflatoxin by Aspergillus parasiticus NRRL-2999 during growth in the presence of curing salts. Mycopathology 61, 77.

MILLER, D. M., WILSON, D. M., WYATT, R. D., McKINNEY, J. K., CROWELL, W. A. and STUART, B. P.   1982.   High performance liquid chromatographic determination and clearance time of aflatoxin residues in swine tissues. J. Assoc. Off. Anal. Chem. 65, 1.

MIROCHA, C. J., PATHRE, W. V. and CHRISTENSEN, C. M.   1977.   Zearalenone. In Mycotoxins in Human and Animal Health. p. 345. J. V. Rodricks, C. W. Hesseltine, and M. A. Mehlman (Editors). Pathotox Publishers, Inc., Park Forest South, IL.

MIROCHA, C. J., PATHRE, S. V. and ROBINSON, T. S.   1981.   Comparative metabolism of zearalenone and transmission into bovine milk. Food. Cosmet. Toxicol. 19, 25.

MOSS, E. J., JUDAH, D. J., PRZYBYLSKI, M. and NEAL, G.   1983.   Some mass-spectral and NMR analytical studies of a glutathione conjugate of aflatoxin B_1. Biochem. J. 210, 227.

MRAK, E. M. and BONAR, L.   1938.   A note on yeast obtained from slimy sausage. Food Res. 3, 615.

NEAL, G. E. and COLLEY, P. J.   1979.   The formation of 2,3-dihydro-2,3-dihydroxy aflatoxin B_1 in vitro by rat liver microsomes. FEBS Lett. 101, 382.

NEAL, G. E., JUDAH, D. J., STRIPE, F. and PATTERSON, D. S.   1981.   The formation of 2,3-dihydroxy-2,3-dihydro-aflatoxin B_1 by the metabolism of aflatoxin B_1 by liver microsomes isolated from certain avian and mammalian species and the possible role of this metabolite in the acute toxicity of aflatoxin B_1. Toxicol. Appl. Pharmacol. *58*, 431.

NEFF, G. L. and EDDS, G. L. 1981. Aflatoxin B_1 and M_1: Tissue residues and feed withdrawal profile in young growing pigs. Food Cosmet. Toxicol. *19*, 739.

NIXON, J. E., HENDRICKS, J. D., PAWLOSWKI, N. E., LOVELAND, P. M. and SINNHUBER, R. O. 1981. Carcinogenicity of aflatoxicol in Fischer 344 rats. J. Natl. Cancer Inst. *66*, 1159.

NORRED, W. P., MORRISSEY, R. E., RILEY, R. T., COLE, R. J. and DORNER, J. W. 1986. Distribution, excretion, and skeletal muscle effects of the mycotoxin, [^{14}C] cyclopiazonic acid in rats. Food. Chem. Toxicol. In press.

OGILVY, W. S. and AYRES, J. C. 1953. Post-mortem changes in stored meats. V. Effect of Carbon dioxide on microbial growth on stored frankfurters and characteristics of some microorganisms isolated from them. Food Res. *18*, 121.

PATTERSON, D. S., SHREEVE, B. J., ROBERTS, B. A., BERRETT, S., BRUSH, P. J., GLANCY, E. M. and KROGH, P. 1981. Effect on calves of barley naturally contaminated with ochratoxin A and groundnut meal contaminated with low concentrations of aflatoxin B_1. Res. Vet. Sci. *31*, 213.

PARK, D. L., DAILEY, R. E., FRIEDMAN, L. and HEATH, J. L. 1977. The absorption, distribution, and excretion of ^{14}C-penicillic acid by rats. Ann. Nutr. Aliment. *31*, 919.

PESTKA, J. J., GAUR, P. K. and CHU, F. S. 1980. Quantitation of aflatoxin B_1 and aflatoxin B_1 antibody by an enzyme-linked immunosorbent microassay. Appl. Environ. Microbiol. *40*, 1027.

PESTKA, J. J., STEINART, B. W. and CHU, F. S. 1981A. Enzyme-linked immunosorbent assay for the detection of ochratoxin A. Appl. Environ. Microbiol. *41*, 1472.

PESTKA, J. J., LEE, S. S., LAU, H. P. and CHU, F. S. 1981B. Enzyme-linked immunosurbent assay for T-2 toxin. J. Am. Oil Chemists Soc. *58*, 940.

PESTKA, J. J., LEE, Y. K., LAU, H. P. and CHU, F. S. 1981C. Comparison of a radioimmunoassay and an enzyme-linked immunosorbent assay for the analysis of aflatoxin M_1 in milk. J. Assoc. Anal. Chem. *64*, 294.

PESTKA, J. J., BEERY, J. T. and CHU, F. S. 1983. Indirect immunoperoxidase localization of aflatoxin B_1 in rat liver. Food Chem. Toxicol. *21*, 41.

PRIOR, M. G., O'NEIL, J. B. and SISODIA, C. S. 1980. Effects of ochratoxin A on growth response and residues in broilers. Poult. Sci. *59*, 1254.

RICHARD, J. L., PIER, A. C., STUBBLEFIELD, R. D., SHOTWELL, O. L., LYON, R. L. and CUTLIP, R. C. 1983. Effect of feeding corn naturally contaminated with aflatoxin on feed efficiency, physiological, immunological, and pathological changes and tissue residues in steers. Am. J. Vet. Res. *44*, 1294.

RODRICKS, J. V. and STOLOFF, L. 1977. Aflatoxin residues from contaminated feed in edible tissues of food-producing animals. *In* Mycotoxins in Human and Animal Health. p. 67. J. V. Rodricks, C. W. Hesseltine, and M. A. Mehlman (Editors) Pathotox Publishers Inc., Park Forest South, IL.

ROBISON, T. S., MIROCHA, C. J., KURTZ, H. J., BEHRENS, J. C., CHI, M. S., WEAVER, G. A. and NYSTROM, S. D. 1979. Transmission of T-2 toxin into bovine and porcine milk. J. Dairy Sci. *62*, 637.

SCHOENHARD, G. L., HENDRICKS, J. D., NIXON, J. E., LEE, D. J., WALES, J. H., SINNHUBER, R. O. and PAWLOWSKI, N. E. 1981. Aflatoxicol-induced hepatocellular carcinoma in rainbow trout and the synergistic effects of cyclopropenoid fatty acids. Cancer Res. *41*, 1011.

SHANK, R. C. 1978. Mycotoxicoses of man: Dietary and epidemiological conditions. *In* Mycotoxic Fungi, Mycotoxins, Mycotoxicoses, An Encyclopedic Handbook. Vol. 3. Chap. 3.9, p. 1. T. D. Wyllie and L. G. Morehouse (Editors). Marcel Dekker, Inc., NY.

SHREEVE, B. J., PATTERSON, D. S. P. and ROBERTS, B. A. 1979. The "carryover" of aflatoxin, ochratoxin, and zearalenone from naturally contaminated feed to tissues, urine and milk of diary cows. Food. Cosmet. Toxicol. *17*, 151.

SINNHUBER, R. O., WALES, J. H., ENGEBRECHT, R. H., AMEND, D. F., KRAY, W. D., AYRES, J. L. and ASHTON, W. E. 1965. Aflatoxins in cottonseed meal and hepatoma in rainbow trout. Fed. Proc. *24*, 627.

SINNHUBER, R. O., WALES, J. H., AYRES, J. L., ENGEBRECHT, R. H. and AMEND, D. L. 1968. Dietary factors and hepatoma in rainbow trout. J. Natl. Cancer Inst. *41*, 711.

STOLOFF, L. 1979. Mycotoxin residues in edible animal tissues. *In* Interactions of Mycotoxins in Animal Production. p. 157. NAS, Washington, DC.

STOLOFF, L. 1980. Aflatoxin M_1 in perspective. J. Food. Prot. *43*, 226.

STRZELECKI, E., LILLARD, H. S. and AYRES, J. C. 1969. Country cured ham as a possible source of aflatoxin. Appl. Microbiol *18*, 938.

STUBBLEFIELD, R. D. and SHOTWELL, O. L. 1981. Determination of aflatoxins in animal tissues. J. Assoc. Off. Anal. Chem. *64*, 964.

STUBBLEFIELD, R. D., PIER, A. C., RICHARD, J. S. and SHOTWELL, O. L. 1983. Fate of aflatoxins in tissues, fluids, and excrements from cows dosed orally with aflatoxin B_1. Am. J. Vet. Res. *44*, 1750.

SUTIC, M. J., AYRES, J. C., and KOEHLER, P. E. 1972. Identification and aflatoxin production of molds isolated from country cured hams. Appl. Microbiol. *23*, 656.

SWANSON, S. P., COPPOCK, R., and BUCK, W. B. 1982. Analysis of diacetoxyscirpenol in animal tissues. Paper 045, presented at the 82nd Annual Meeting of the Am. Soc. Microbiol., Atlanta, GA, June 7–12, 1982.

TRUCKSESS, M. W. and STOLOFF, L. 1981. High Performance liquid chromatographic determination of aflatoxicol in milk, blood, and liver. J. Assoc. Off. Anal. Chem. *64*, 1083.

TRUCKSESS, M. W., STOLOFF, L., BRUMELY, W. C., WILSON, D. M., HALE, O. M., SANGSTER, L. T. and MILLER, D. M. 1982. Aflatoxicol and aflatoxins B_1 and M_1 in the tissues of pigs receiving aflatoxin. J. Assoc. Off. Anal. Chem. *65*, 884.

TRUCKSESS, M. W., RICHARD, J. C., STOLOFF, L., McDONALD, S. and BRUMELY, W. C. 1983 A. Absorption and distribution patterns of aflatoxicol and aflatoxins B_1 and M_1 in blood and milk of cows following oral administration of aflatoxin B_1. Am. J. Vet. Res. *44*, 1753.

TRUCKSESS, M. W., STOLOFF, L., YOUNG, K., WYATT, R. D. and MILLER, B. L. 1983 B. Aflatoxicol and aflatoxins B_1 and M_1 in eggs and tissues of laying hens consuming aflatoxin-contaminated feed. Poult Sci. *62*, 2176.

TURNER, G. V., PHILIPS, T. D., HEIDELBOUGH, N. D. and RUSSEL, L. H. 1983. High pressure liquid chromatographic determination of zearalenone in chicken tissues. J. Assoc. Off. Anal. Chem. *66*, 102.

VAN RENSBURG, S. J. 1977. Role of epidemiology in the elucidation of mycotoxin health risks. *In* Mycotoxins in Human and Animal Health. p. 699. J. V. Rodricks, C. W. Hesseltine, and M. A. Mehlman (Editors). Pathtox Publishers Inc., Park Forest South, IL.

VESONDER, R. F., CIEGLER, A. and JENSEN, A. 1973. Isolation of the emetic principle from *Fusarium* infected corn. Appl. Microbiol. *26*, 1008.

WILLIAMS, B. E. 1957. Method for aging meat. U.S. Patent 2,816,836.

WICKERHAM, L. J. 1959. Presence of nitrite assimilating species of *Debaromyces* in lunch meats. J. Bacteriol. *74*, 832.

WANG, T. V. and CERUTTI, P. A. 1980. Spontaneous reactions of aflatoxin B_1 modified deoxyribonucleic acid *in vitro*. Biochemistry, *19*, 1692.

WOGAN, G. N. 1969. Metabolism and biochemical effects of aflatoxins. *In* Aflatoxin. Chap. 6, p. 152. L. A. Goldblatt (Editor). Academic Press, NY.

WONG, J. J. and HSIEH, D. D. 1976. Mutagenicity of aflatoxins related to their metabolism and carcinogenic potential. Proc. Natl. Acad. Sci. U.S.A. *73*, 2241.

WRIGHT, A. M. 1923. Molds on frozen meats. New Z. J. Sci. Technol. *A6*, 208.

WU, M. T., AYRES, J. C. and KOEHLER, P. E.   1974.   Production of citrinin by *Penicillium viridicatum* on country cured ham. Appl. Microbiol. *27,* 427.

YOSHIZAWA, T., MIROCHA, C. J., BEHRENS, J. C. and SWANSON, S. P.   1981A. Metabolic fate of T-2 toxin in lactating cow. Food. Cosmet. Toxicol. *19,* 31.

YOSHIZAWA, T., SAKAMOTO, T., AYANO, Y., and MIROCHA, C. J.   1981B.   3'Hydroxy T-2 and 3'hydroxy HT-2 toxins: New metabolites of T-2 toxin, a trichothecene mycotoxin in animals. Agric. Biol. Chem. *46,* 2613.

11

Parasitic Organisms

K. D. Murrell,[1] R. Fayer[1] and J. P. Dubey[1]

INTRODUCTION

Although the importance of food-borne parasites to public health has long been recognized, new information has intensified the concern of public health authorities and food scientists worldwide over this problem. This stems from both the reassessment of the frequency and distribution of certain of these parasites and recent recognition that certain species might be more pathogenic than formerly believed. For example, up to approximately 40% of the United States adult population have antibodies to *Toxoplasma gondii*. Although acquired toxoplasma infection seldom results in clinical disease, 40% of infants born to women who become infected while pregnant may develop clinical disease. It is estimated that over 3000 babies are born of mothers with primary infections, of these, each year 5–15% die, 18–23% suffer blindness or brain damage, and 58–77% of those who appear normal develop active infections later in life. The high prevalence (20–30%) of *T. gondii* in livestock and the fact that it can be transmitted in improperly cooked meat has serious implications for the meat industry. Similarly, the well-characterized transmission of trichinosis by pork has received increased attention because its prevalence in pork might be higher than earlier studies indicated (Schad and Murrell 1984) and that some cooking technologies, such as microwave cooking, might be inadequate for heat inactivation of the muscle stage. Also important to the food industry may be the discovery that *Sarcocystis* (closely related to *T. gondii*) found in beef and pork can infect humans and pro-

[1]Animal Parasitology Institute, ARS, USDA, Beltsville, MD 20705.

Advances in Meat Research, Volume 2
Copyright 1986 by AVI Publishing Co.
All rights of reproduction in any form reserved
ISBN 0-87055-498-0

duce diarrhea, nausea, and fever. The thermal death curve for *Sarcocystis* spp., important for food preparation, has yet to be determined.

Changes in the movement of human populations and in the adoption of certain cultural and agricultural practices appear to be exacerbating the "old" problems of beef and pork cysticercosis. In the United States, influxes of parasite-infected immigrants from underdeveloped countries have resulted in increases in both the prevalence of cysticercosis in meat animals and in clinical human cases. Current control procedures based on meat inspection are recognized widely as inadequate and research to find new detection methods has received increased encouragement. There is now new awareness that certain parasites of pets and livestock, such as those causing zoonotic toxacariasis and hookworm disease, might be transmitted by meat and milk; the significance of these modes of transmission for public health currently is being actively investigated.

Control procedures traditionally invoked to interrupt the transmission of such food-borne parasites as trichinae and the cysticerci have not proved to be effective enough to ensure a completely safe meat supply. Just as important, adequate control measures for food-borne toxoplasmosis, sarcocystosis, and the recently recognized important helminth parasites are either lacking or inadequate. This chapter will address these needs and highlight some of the current major research areas such as the development of more sensitive meat inspection methods, including antemortem serodiagnosis. The discussions will also highlight research needed to gain a better understanding of the biology and epidemiology of these food-borne parasites.

The examples cited above are part of the basis of the growing belief of public health authorities, food scientists, and parasitologists that the importance of food-borne parasites has hitherto been underestimated and that renewed interest in this problem will lead to a more accurate assessment of their importance to and control in the food industry. Communication between parasitologists and food scientists should be increased; the opportunity afforded by this review will be an important step in achieving this. Because food microbiologists and technologists have produced an impressive record of coping with food health problems, their involvement and expertise is needed to both assess the importance of food-borne parasites and to develop appropriate controls.

PROTOZOAN PARASITES

In the protozoan subphylum Apicomplexa, there is a large group of parasites known as the coccidia. At least nine genera are commonly occurring parasites of domestic and wild animals. *Eimeria, Isospora,* and *Cryptosporidium* usually develop in the intestinal tract. The infected animal sheds infections units called oocysts in the feces. These initiate a similar intestinal cycle in other hosts. *Cystoisospora, Besnoitia, Hammondia,*

Frenkelia, Sarcocystis, and *Toxoplasma* have added to the complexity of this basic developmental cycle by encysting in extraintestinal sites in one or more additional host species. Of all these genera, two are known to infect humans: *Toxoplasma* and *Sarcocystis*.

Toxoplasma gondii: Toxoplasmosis

Public Health Significance. Estimates range as high as half a billion people throughout the world that have had *Toxoplasma* infections based on the findings of antibody in their serum. Most of these infections are inapparent or manifest only mild clinical flu-like symptoms that disappear after a few days. Others are more severely affected with a variety of clinical symptoms depending on the organ most affected. Some die as a result of infection. Those most at risk to serious consequences from clinical toxoplasmosis include pregnant women, the elderly, and immunocompromised persons. However, anyone of either sex or of any age that has not developed immunity from prior exposure to *Toxoplasma* can develop severe clinical toxoplasmosis if they acquire large numbers of organisms in the infectious stages in a short period of time. In the United States serological surveys indicate infection rates ranging from 0 to 44% of the populations examined (Fayer 1981). Of 3274 serum specimens examined by the Communicable Disease Center in Atlanta in 1982, 25.8% of this population were positive (Walls, personal communication). Approximately 3300 neonatal infections of toxoplasmosis are diagnosed annually in the United States, resulting in an estimated annual cost of approximately 222 million U.S. dollars for hospitalization, institutionalization, and special education (Wilson and Remington 1980).

Biology and Life Cycle. *Toxoplasma gondii* can parasitize nearly all warm-blooded vertebrate species and can infect nearly all organs (Dubey 1977; Frenkel 1973). However, it develops through its entire life cycle only in the small intestine of domestic and wild cats. In this location a sequence of asexual, sexual, and oocyst stages develop (Fig. 11.1). Cats can acquire infection by eating animal tissues containing cysts containing asexual banana-shaped organisms called cystozoites or bradyzoites, by eating tissues from acutely infected animals with rapidly multiplying banana-shaped tachyzoites, or by ingesting oocysts from the feces of other cats (Fig. 11.1). Epidemiological evidence indicates that cats acquire *Toxoplasma* infections in nature by eating cysts from tissues of infected animals. After ingestion of the cysts, five asexual stages designated types A to E develop sequentially; these differ from one another in morphology and location. Following asexual development, male and female stages (gametocytes) develop, fertilization takes place, and the fertilized female gamete develops into an oocyst which becomes surrounded by a protective wall. The oocyst enters the lumen of the intestine and is shed in the feces.

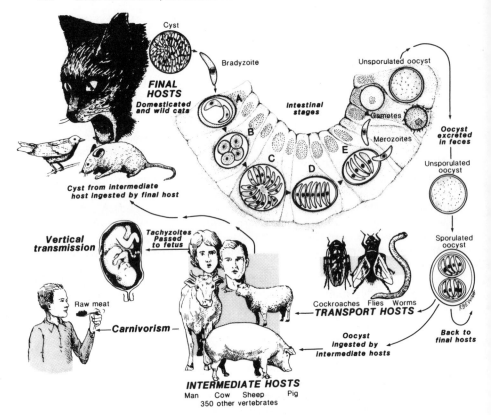

FIG. 11.1.   Outline of the life cycle of *Toxoplasma gondii* showing final and intermediate hosts and sources of infection.

It is not immediately infectious for cats or other vertebrate hosts, requiring 2–3 days in an aerobic environment for sporulation. When sporulated, the oocyst contains two sporocysts each containing four banana-shaped sporozoites; the oocyst measures approximately 10 μm in diameter.

Sporulated oocysts are infections for virtually all warm-blooded vertebrates. Ingested sporozoites are liberated from oocysts in the small intestine of the vertebrate and develop as rapidly multiplying tachyzoites throughout the body. After a few tachyzoite multiplicative cycles in various tissues, the organisms encyst predominantly in muscles, brain, and liver. The cysts are 10 to 100 μm in diameter and contain several hundred lunate-shaped bradyzoites surrounded by a resilient wall. Cysts do not harm the host and probably remain viable for the life of the host. Carnivorism of a vertebrate host with encysted *Toxoplasma* by another vertebrate results in digestion of the cyst wall, release of bradyzoites, and infection of the carnivorous vertebrate, be it man or beast.

Epidemiology and Distribution. *Toxoplasma* is found worldwide but is more prevalent in the tropical and temperate regions than in the Arctic or hot arid regions. It has also been reported to be more prevalent at low altitudes. Variations in prevalence is most probably related to cat population, climate, sanitation, and cultural habits.

Toxoplasma is transmitted to susceptible hosts via two life cycle stages; the oocyst shed in cat feces and the cyst in animal tissues. Transmission by the cyst stage may occur among carnivores or omnivores but does not account for infection of strictly herbivorous meat animals. Infection in grazing or grain-fed animals is mostly the result of oocyst contamination of pastures, barns, feed storage facilities or water sources via infected cat feces. As a result of infection by eating, for example, a mouse or bird with latent *Toxoplasma*, a single nonimmune cat might shed as many as 20 million oocysts per day in about 20 grams of feces. These oocysts might be dispersed throughout the environment mechanically by water or wind, by boots, shovels or farm implements, or biologically when slugs, cockroaches, earthworms, flies, or birds ingest oocysts at one site and deposit them at another. Oocysts have been reported to remain infectious for as long as 18 months but climatic factors such as freezing, heating, sunlight, and drying shorten their longevity. Surveys conducted on meat animals in North and South America, Europe, Africa, Asia, and Australia attest to the success of the oocyst as an infectious stage (Fayer 1981). Of 16, 293 cattle, 9,654 sheep, and 17,499 pigs examined worldwide the prevalence ranged from lows of 0, 0, and 1% to highs of 99, 96, and 98% with averages of 25, 31, and 29%, respectively. Prevalence in other meat animals such as chickens, turkeys, rabbits, horses, and goats has not been as well documented. These figures primarily reflect the presence of antibody in serum from respective meat animals. However, of those species studied there appears to be differences in response to infection, the tissues in which cysts develop, and the longevity of cysts. Therefore, direct extrapolation from the finding of serum antibody to relative risk of infection from eating beef, pork, lamb, or other meat is not possible.

Among food animals, *Toxoplasma* infection is most common in pigs and sheep. Infection rates vary with husbandry. For example, *Toxoplasma* infection is found more frequently in pigs and chickens raised in backyards than in those raised in large-scale commercial facilities. The chance of an animal acquiring *Toxoplasma* infection increases with age; therefore, fewer young animals are infected. Infection in lambs (6–8 months old- is about one-half of that in older ewes (Waldeland 1976). Little information is available concerning the prevalence of *T. gondii* cysts in edible tissues of food animals, raised for human consumption. Although viable cysts have been demonstrated in as many as 73% of pigs and 40% of sheep in some studies in Europe (Čatár *et al.* 1969; Waldeland 1976), it has been rarely found in cattle. Differences in techniques and tissues examined may have influenced these findings. Attempts at recovery of viable *T. gondii* from food animals in the United States are summarized in Table 11.1.

TABLE 11.1. Isolation of *Toxoplasma gondii* in Laboratory Animals Inoculated with Tissues from Animals Slaughtered for Meat in the United States

Host	Location	No. examined	Percentage infected	Tissues inoculated into laboratory animals	Reference
Pig	Baltimore	50	24	Diaphragm	Jacobs et al. (1960)
	California	50	32	Pork loin	Remington (1968)
	Georgia	91	3.2	Salivary glands	Dienst and Verma (1965)
	Tennessee	120	0.8	Brain	Eyles et al. (1959)
Sheep	Baltimore	86	9.3	Diaphragm	Jacobs et al. (1960)
	California	50	4	Chops	Remington (1966)
Cattle	Baltimore	60	0	Diaphragm	Jacobs et al. (1960)
	California	50	0	Diaphragm	Remington (1968)
	Baltimore	100	0	Mammary glands	Jacobs (1973)
	Ohio	350	0	Mixed tissues[a]	Dubey and Streitel (1976)
Horses	Ohio	500	1.4	Mixed tissues[a]	Al-Khalidi and Dubey (1979)
Chickens	Baltimore	108	3.6	Ovaries, brain, leg muscles	Jacobs and Melton (1966)

[a] Tissues were fed to *Toxoplasma*-free cats and the feces of cats were examined for oocysts. Other isolations were made in mice.

Studies in other countries were similar. Studies on longevity and infectivity of cysts in tissues of sheep, goats, cattle, and pigs inoculated orally with oocysts of the GT-1 strain reveal some interesting results. Using the pepsin digestion technique to demonstrate cysts, *T. gondii* cysts persisted in edible tissues until market age (Table 11.2). Cysts were found not only in skeletal muscles but also in visceral tissues. *Toxoplasma* cysts persisted less frequently in beef than in other meat animals. Preliminary results indicate that oocysts of some isolates of *T. gondii* may be more infectious to cattle (Fayer and Frenkel 1979).

Other studies must now be conducted with other common meat animal species, including horses, chickens, and turkeys, to identify and quantitate possible sources of human infections.

Humans, like other carnivores, can acquire toxoplasmosis by ingestion of oocysts from plant materials or other foods contaminated by cat feces or ingestion of uncooked animal tissues containing cysts or tachyzoites of *Toxoplasma*. As with herbivorous meat animals, the relatively high rate of infection among strict vegetarians in the United States and India reflects infection by oocysts. The presence of infected cat feces in many false attics of houses and the ability of this material to contaminate the living area below offer one explanation for a high prevalence of *Toxoplasma* antibody in Costa Ricans (Frenkel and Ruiz 1980). Similarly, cultural habits related to the preparation of food influence the transmission of *Toxoplasma* from meat to humans. A higher prevalence of *Toxoplasma* was found among Russian women in Kiev who tasted raw chopped meat during prep-

TABLE 11.2. Persistence of *Toxoplasma gondii* Cysts in Tissues of Food Animals Fed Oocysts

| Host | Days postinoculation | No. of animals positive for cysts/No. of animals examined | | | Reference |
		Liver	Brain	Thigh muscles	
Goats	335–441	6/6	5/6	6/6	Dubey (1982)
Sheep	97–173	6/8	4/8	6/8	Dubey (1984)
Cattle					
Cows	98–190	2/5	ND[a]	2/6	Dubey (1983)
Calves	256, 267	2/2	1/2	0/2	
Pigs	91–171	2/8	8/8	5/8	Dubey *et al.* (1984)
Horses and ponies	33–476	0/13	2/13	3/13	Dubey (1985)

[a] ND, No data.

aration for cooking than among those who did not taste the meat, among Hawaiians and Filipinos known to enjoy raw meat, especially pork, than among Caucasians and Japanese in Hawaii who usually cook meat, and among affluent whites in New York City who prefer raw ground meat (steak tartare) than among poor blacks. Outbreaks of toxoplasmosis related to ingestion of undercooked meat were reported in five medical students from Cornell University who hurriedly ate hamburgers at a dormitory snackbar, for 110 students at a university in Brazil who ate unidentified meat, and for four people who ate kibee nayee, a Syrian recipe made with raw beef (Magaldi *et al.* 1969; Kean *et al.* 1969). Whether beef in these epidemics was the primary source of infection or was contaminated with infected pork or mutton was not determined.

Clinical Disease. Infection in man is usually asymptomatic, but clinical illness largely results from destruction of host cells by multiplying organisms. Specific clinical symptoms reflect those tissues or organs involved.

In acute primary infections symptoms might include fever, malaise, skin rash, pneumonia, myocarditis, hepatitis, lymphadenopathy, and encephalitis. Women who acquire the infection during pregnancy might transmit it to their fetuses yet remain asymptomatic themselves. Some congenitally infected neonates might have all the symptoms previously described accompanied by encephalomyelitis and retinochoroiditis. Subacute toxoplasmosis, often observed in neonates, is prolonged and usually affects the brain and eye where immune mechanisms might be impeded. The onset of clinical neurologic and ophthalmic toxoplasmosis in congenitally infected children might be delayed until adulthood. Chronic toxoplasmosis usually lasts for months or years and might be asymptomatic unless cysts rupture. Reactivation of chronic to acute toxoplasmosis might result from the loss of immunity in aging persons or in immunosuppressed persons such as those receiving organ transplants or those being treated for neoplasms or collagen-vascular disease. Patients with acquired immunodeficiency disease syndrome (AIDS) might develop acute, fatal encephalitis due to toxoplasmosis.

Infections in animals is usually not clinical but, as in man, acute toxoplasmosis may involve a number of organs and a variety of clinical signs. Reproductive problems are one of the main clinical manifestations of toxoplasmosis in livestock, particularly in sheep, goats, and pigs. *Toxoplasma* can cause fetal death and resorption, abortion, stillbirth, weak offsprings, and is the main cause of losses in lambs in Norway, New Zealand, Australia, England, and perhaps other countries. Congenital infection occurs when sheep become infected during pregnancy and is usually a one-time event. Adult sheep do not have other clinical signs of toxoplasmosis. Congenitally infected lambs grow normally if they survive 2 weeks after birth. Goats are even more susceptible to toxoplasmosis than sheep and even adult goats can die of toxoplasmosis. Young pigs can die of toxoplasmic pneumonia, and epizootics of swine toxoplasmosis are common in Japan. Cattle rarely suffer from clinical toxoplasmosis and true toxoplasmosis has not been described in horses. Sporadic and widespread epizootics of clinical toxoplasmosis occur in rabbits, hares, minks, poultry, and marsupials (Siim *et al.* 1963; Obendorf and Munday 1983). *Toxoplasma* infection is common in dogs, cats, and other pets, but clinical disease is not common and when it does occur, young ones die of pneumonia.

Diagnosis in Humans and Animals.   *Clinical Diagnosis.*   The diagnosis of clinical infections is aided by the identification of the organism in smears or tissue sections, serologic examination, and the isolation of *T. gondii* by animal inoculation. Tachyzoites and cysts can be recognized in impression smears from biopsy fluid or tissue after staining with Giemsa or in tissue sections stained with hematoxylin and eosin. Tachyzoites are lunate-shaped in smears but appear as oval to round in cross section. Cysts are usually few. The periodic acid-Schiff (PAS) reaction can be used to identify the cysts, since the cyst wall is PAS-negative but the bradyzoites are PAS-positive. The determination of antibody to *T. gondii* is also helpful. A negative test might exclude toxoplasmosis, while a positive test generally indicates past exposure. The antibody titer does not always correlate with duration of infection (McCabe and Remington 1983). Isolation of the organism in laboratory animals can be definite but the results may not be obtained for 4 weeks.

Clinical toxoplasmosis in other animals rarely is diagnosed during the life of the host. The diagnosis of ovine abortion due to *T. gondii* is of paramount importance to the sheep industry because the ewes that have aborted are useful for future breeding. In addition to identifying the organism in placenta or fetal tissues, finding antibody to *T. gondii* in fetal fluids is diagnostic because maternal antibody in sheep does not cross the placenta. However, in humans, maternal IgG crosses the placenta while the large IgM molecule does not. Therefore, tests to diagnose toxoplasmosis in neonates are directed toward identifying IgM in the blood of infants as well as unusually high levels of maternal IgG.

Surveys for Subclinical Infections.   Serologic tests and the recovery of the organism from animal tissues or excretions are commonly used and each has advantages. Antibody specific to *T. gondii* can be determined in human and animal sera using any of the several serologic tests (Dubey 1977; McCabe and Remington 1983). The Sabin-Feldman dye test is the most sensitive and specific test for *Toxoplasma* but is not reliable for cattle and chicken sera. Although a positive *T. gondii* antibody titer indicates past exposure, it cannot predict the current parasitologic status of the organism in the host because antibodies might decline to an undetectable level with passage of time and antibodies might not be detectable in early acute infections. Thus, the host might be infected with *T. gondii* yet have no detectable antibody, and a host might have antibody but not be infected.

In numerous studies, antibodies to *T. gondii* frequently have been detected in bovine sera; whereas, only very few studies have attempted to isolate the organism from beef in the United States. Thus, more work is needed on isolation procedures before it can be assumed that eating of raw beef does not constitute any human health hazard from toxoplasmosis. The determination of meat animals infected with *T. gondii* is best achieved by isolating the organism with a pepsin-HCl digestion procedure. In this procedure, a meat sample is ground and digested in acid pepsin solution and after incubation and washing, the digest is inoculated parenterally into *Toxoplasma*-free mice. The mice are then examined for *Toxoplasma* infection (Dubey 1977). This is the best method to accurately demonstrate *Toxoplasma* cysts in meat because there might be only a few cysts per 100 grams of tissue and these are unlikely to be detected histologically.

Determination of *Toxoplasma* oocysts in feline feces is also important epidemiologically. Oocysts in cat feces are demonstrated best by fecal concentration methods using sugar or salt solution.

Treatment of Humans and Animals.   For acute toxoplasmosis either sulfadiazine, sulfamerazine, sulfamethazine or triple-sulfa plus pyrimethamine are usually the medications of choice. Folic acid might be given to counteract the effect of pyrimethamine on bone marrow. Because of teratogenic effects of pyrimethamine, pregnant women or animals should receive clindamycin (McCabe and Remington 1983). These drugs only retard the multiplication of *T. gondii* and none are known to kill cysts in tissues.

Prevention and Control.   To avoid contamination of the home environment with oocysts from cat feces the following preventive measures should be taken: feed cats dry, canned or completely cooked food; stop cats from hunting birds and rodents; empty cat litter boxes daily, before oocysts sporulate; wear gloves or wash hands after working with soil and before touching the face or eating; cover children's sandboxes when not in use; prevent aerosols in the laboratory during centrifugation or biologic samples thought to be infected with *Toxoplasma;* boil drinking water from sources frequented by cats. To avoid transmission from infected meat, cook meat to 66°C or higher and wash hands after handling raw meat. Freezing is not a reliable method of destruction of organisms in meat. On farms and in animal-rearing facilities contamination of feed and water with cat feces should be avoided by: substituting rodenticides and traps to obviate a need for cats hunting rodents; securing feed storage areas to prevent cats from entering; promptly removing cat feces from buildings, stalls or cages, and flushing, burning or burying them to eliminate oocysts; feeding cats dry, canned or cooked food and providing separate water to prevent cats from sharing facilities with other animals.

Sarcocystis spp.: Sarcocystosis

Public Health Significance. Two types of *Sarcocystis* infection are known in man. One type is the intramuscular cyst stage probably acquired via feces from a carnivore and the other type includes intestinal stages that develop after ingestion of raw infected meat. Because the actual sources of infection for the intramuscular cyst stage are unknown and because it is unlikely that human flesh is consumed often enough by carnivores to maintain a human-carnivore cycle in nature, it is hypothesized that such infections are accidental zoonoses, possibly existing in nature in a nonhuman primate-carnivore cycle. Since only about 40 such infections have been reported worldwide, most originating in tropical areas, this type of *Sarcocystis* infection does not represent a significant public health problem. Two sources for the human intestinal infection are known: ingestion of raw beef and raw pork (Fig. 11.2). However, little documentation exists regarding the public health significance of such infections. There are several possible reasons for this lack of information. The life cycles and epidemiology of *Sarcocystis* spp. have been described only recently. The sporocyst stage shed in the feces of infected humans is relatively small and often is overlooked in examination of feces. Finally, considering the excellent sanitation system utilized for disposal of human sewage in the United States, these infections are rare in humans.

Biology and Life Cycle. *Sarcocystis* species are obligate two-host parasites, usually requiring an herbivorous intermediate host and a carnivorous final host. The specificity of these parasites is usually greater for the intermediate host than for the final host. Either host might be infected simultaneously with several species of *Sarcocystis*.

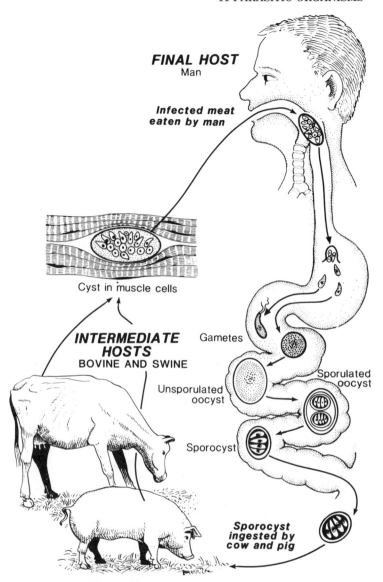

FIG. 11.2. Outline of the life cycle of *Sarcocystis hominis* and *S. suihominis* showing final and intermediate hosts and sources of infection.

For *Sarcocystis hominis,* domestic cattle are the intermediate hosts and for *Sarcocystis suihominis* domestic swine are the intermediate hosts. Humans and such nonhuman primates such as cynomolgus and rhesus monkeys and chimpanzees serve as final hosts, which become infected by eating mature cysts containing zoites (= cystozoites or bradyzoites) found in meat. Using information derived from experimental studies with other species of *Sarcocystis* the following events are thought to occur in the final host. Within the gastrointestinal tract, digestive enzymes break down the cyst wall releasing the banana-shaped zoites. The liberated zoites enter goblet cells lining the small intestine. Within a few hours the intracellular zoites differentiate into male and female gametes. Fertilization occurs, a wall forms around the zygote, and the zygote matures into an oocyst. Oocysts are found in the lamina propria of the intestine, beneath the epithelium. Here they mature (sporulate) eventually containing two sporocysts each with four sporozoites. Oocysts and sporocysts that have broken out of oocysts move to the intestinal lumen and pass in the feces of the carnivore. The prepatent period is approximately 1 week but is highly variable and might not actually begin in some individuals for 2 or 3 weeks. The patent period might last 2 or 3 months, although shedding of sporocysts becomes intermittent after about 3 weeks. Reinfection is common and there appears to be no immunity in the final host.

Cattle become infected by ingesting the oocysts or sporocyst of *S. hominis*. Similarly, pigs become infected with *S. suihominis*. When these oocysts or sporocysts are exposed to digestive enzymes and bile the walls break down releasing sporozoites which penetrate the small intestine and eventually come to rest within cells lining arteries. These sporozoites remain inactive for 1–2 weeks. The nucleus then proliferates rapidly forming a first-generation schizont (= meront). Numerous banana-shaped merozoites released from such schizonts enter the bloodstream and develop into second-generation schizonts in cells lining capillaries throughout the body. Approximately 4 weeks after infection, merozoites from second-generation schizonts enter the bloodstream where some develop into two or more progeny. Merozoites from second-generation schizonts or those that develop in the bloodstream enter muscle cells where they eventually give rise to the cyst stage. Early cysts are difficult to see. They contain only a few metrocytes, round noninfectious parasites that give rise to the banana-shaped infectious zoites found in mature cysts beginning 2–3 months after infection. Only those cysts containing zoites are infectious to the carnivore final host—man and nonhuman primates.

Epidemiology and Distribution. Although domestic animal species throughout the world have a very high prevalence of *Sarcocystis* infection, the species of *Sarcoystis* infecting each host animal species have rarely been clearly identified. Within the United States infection rates for cattle, sheep, and pigs have been reported at 75–98, 50–100 and 44–75%, respectively (Levine 1973). Both *S. hominis* and *S. suihominis* are known to occur in Europe, but no attempts have been made to identify these species in naturally infected food animals in North America. However, sporocysts of *S. hominis* were discovered in the stools of Asian immigrants in the

United States. Whether infections were acquired in the United States or were brought from Asia is unknown. Thus, identification of parasite species is important; infected cattle might harbor species from dogs, cats, or humans or any combination thereof. *Sarcocystis cruzi* with a cattle–dog (coyote, fox, wolf) cycle is transmissible only from cattle to canids to cattle, and likewise with other species. Although cattle or pigs may have multiple species infections, only *S. hominis* and *S. suihominis* are infectious to humans.

Although the longevity of infective oocysts or sporocysts of *Sarcocystis* in the environment has not been determined, oocysts of related coccidian parasites have been found infective a year or more after being shed.

Clinical Disease. The species of *Sarcocystis* known to infect specific meat animals are listed in Table 11.3 and the pathogens are identified. The severity of clinical illness in meat animals is directly related to the number of sporocysts ingested. For all pathogenic species, acute illness parallels the development of second-generation schizonts and the blood-borne second-generation merozoites. Typical clinical signs observed at this time include fever, anemia, depression of or lack of appetite, weight loss, hypersalivation or runny nose, nervousness, muscle weakness, and occasionally muscle twitching. Severely affected animals that do not die might linger for weeks or months in a generalized poor condition with loss of hair or wool, especially the loss of the switch from the tail of cattle, and generalized muscular atrophy. Some develop signs of disease in the central

TABLE 11.3. Species of *Sarcocystis* in Meat Animals

Intermediate host	*Sarcocystis* species	Final hosts	Clinical illness in intermediate host[a]
Cattle (*Bos taurus*)	cruzi	Dog, coyote, wolf, fox, raccoon (?)	+
	hirsuta	Cat	±
	hominis	Man, rhesus monkey, baboon	Un
Water buffalo (*Bubalus bubalis*)	levinei	Dog	Un
	fusiformis	Cat	Un
Sheep (*Ovis aries*)	tenella	Dog, coyote, fox	+
	gigantea	Cat	Un
	medusiformis	Cat	Un
	arieticanis	Dog	+
Goat (*Capra hircus*)	capracanis	Dog, coyote, fox	+
	hircicanis	Dog	+
Pig (*Sus scrofa*)	miescheriana	Dog, fox, wolf	+
	suihominis	Man, chimpanzee, rhesus monkey, cynomolgus monkey	+
Horse (*Equus caballus*)	fayeri	Dog	+
	equicanis	Dog	Un

[a] Un = Unknown; +, illness in the herbivore host; ±, mildly pathogenic.

nervous system including ataxia, nystagmus, opisthotonus, lateral recumbency with a walking gait, and, finally, death. During or shortly after the onset of the acute disease, milking cows reduce or cease milk production. Pregnant animals often abort. Young animals might fail to grow well even after recovery. Detailed clinical laboratory findings, gross pathology, and histopathology have been summarized by Dubey and Fayer (1983). In most cases, even though animals are infected with pathogenic species and may harbor numerous cysts, infection is probably acquired gradually at low levels and clinical signs are not evident.

Canid and felid final hosts rarely have clinical illness from infections regardless of the number of parasites ingested. Human final hosts have exhibited clinical illness. Information acquired from five studies in which 20 volunteers ate raw beef known to be infected with S. hominis indicates that 12 became infected and passed sporocysts in their feces beginning 9–39 days later. Only one volunteer became ill. Symptoms included nausea, stomachache, and diarrhea within 3–6 hr after eating the beef and lasted 24–36 hr. Segmental enteritis was found associated with the presence of Sarcocystis in six persons in Thailand where cysts in local beef and the custom of eating raw beef suggested it to be the source of infection (Bunyaratvej et al. 1982). Of six rhesus monkeys and four baboons fed S. hominis-infected beef, all became infected but none had clinical illness. Information acquired from three studies in which 15 volunteers ate raw pork known to be infected with S. suihominis indicates that 14 became infected and passed sporocysts in their feces beginning 10–17 days later. Twelve persons exhibited acute clinical symptoms, including bloat, nausea, inappetence, stomachache, vomiting, dry heaves, diarrhea, coldness and sweating, dyspnea, rapid pulse, and fever. In one of these studies, Sarcoystis-infected pork from the same pigs was cooked well done and fed to nine other volunteers. None developed clinical symptoms. Of one chimpanzee, two rhesus, and two cynomolgus monkeys fed raw infected pork, all became infected but none had clinical illness. Whether clinical signs in humans that ate raw meat were caused by Sarcocystis or by other agents in raw meat is uncertain.

Diagnosis in Humans and Animals.   In meat animals, the clinical signs of acute sarcocystosis provide a presumptive diagnosis. Some animals might also show excessive salivation or runny nose, loss of body hair, abortion, reduced milk production, or death. For a short time during peak acute illness the serum enzymes lactic dehydrogenase (LDH), creatine phosphokinase (CPK), or aspartate aminotransferase (SGOT) may be elevated. Serologic tests may be helpful in confirming the diagnosis. The indirect hemagglutination test and ELISA have been used in the laboratory but are not yet available commercially. Definitive diagnosis depends on finding parasites and lesions in sick animals. This is especially difficult because of the relatively short life span of second-generation schizonts and the fact that by the time animals become sick or die these stages have usually disappeared. Hemorrhage and nonsuppurative inflammation are often found in tissues from acutely infected animals. The finding of large numbers of immature cysts in muscle biopsies or after death is indicative of a recent clinical infection. The presence of large numbers of mature cysts without inflammation is of little value because these cysts might accumulate over a long period of time from numerous light infections.

Diagnosis of sarcocystosis in the final hosts—humans or other carnivores—is based on finding sporocysts in the feces. This is best accomplished by standard laboratory fecal flotation procedures using saturated sugar solution or zinc sulfate followed by examination with bright field microscopy.

Treatment of Humans and Animals. Anticoccidial drugs including amprolium, salinomycin, monensin, and other compounds have been found effective in prophylactically preventing development of sarcocystosis in food animals. Therapeutic treatment has not been successful once clinical signs become evident.

No effective prophylactic or therapeutic treatment is known for stages in the carnivore final host or in humans.

Prevention and Control. The key to prevention and control of sarcocystosis in meat animals is the elimination from the environment of the sporocyst stage in carnivore feces. Any control measures designed to prevent carnivores from becoming infected and to prevent fecal contamination of feed and water will break the cycle. Such measures were described for control of toxoplasmosis. In addition every effort should be made to bury, incinerate, or otherwise remove dead livestock from farms, fields, or grazing areas to prevent domesticated and feral carnivores from acquiring infections.

To prevent human intestinal infection, meat should be cooked or frozen before it is eaten. In two studies of beef from retail food stores infectious *S. cruzi* (infectious for dogs but not humans) was present in various roasts, steaks, and hamburger but not in processed meats, such as frozen hamburger patties or minute steaks, beef bologna, frankfurters or in hamburger cooked to 60°C (140°F) or higher.

HELMINTH PARASITES

Trichinella spiralis: Trichinosis

Public Health Significance. Since its discovery in 1835, the parasite *Trichinella spiralis* has had a prominent role in food hygiene (Campbell 1979). *Trichinella spiralis* is acquired from wild animals and domestic pigs by the ingestion of infected muscle; the severity of the disease is usually proportional to the number of worm larvae ingested and is characterized by fever, gastrointestinal symptoms, myositis, periorbital edema, and eosinophilia. By the beginning of the 20th century trichinosis was recognized as an important public health problem in Europe, the United States, and Central and South America. During the past 50 years or so, human trichinosis has declined in the United States and Europe. For example, estimates from diaphragm muscle samples taken from cadavers throughout the United States show that the incidence in humans had declined from 16.7% in the early 1940s (Wright et al. 1943) to 2.2% in 1970 (Zimmerman et al. 1973). Over the period 1977–1981, an average of 137 human cases were reported to the CDC annually (Schantz 1983A). Nevertheless, trichinosis remains a public health problem in the United States primarily because the disease is enzootic in swine, the major source of human trichinosis (Schantz 1983A). There are published estimates that up to 300,000 humans in the United States are exposed to *T. spiralis* each year, the vast majority of whom apparently develop only subclinical infections (Zimmerman 1975). The decline of human and swine trichinosis in Europe has been even more dramatic during this century, a reflection probably of the strict inspection of pork at slaughter for the presence of encysted larvae (Ruitenberg et al. 1983). This continuing inspection, however, represents an economic burden and is difficult to apply when there are high rates of hog slaughter (Leighty 1983). In contrast to the declining incidence of trichinosis in industrialized western countries, the number of reported cases appears to be increasing in Africa and Asia. African countries now reporting human trichinosis include Egypt, Kenya, Tanzania, and Senegal, and in Southeast Asia the number of reported cases in Laos, Thailand, China, and Japan has risen markedly in the last 20 years (Ruitenberg et al. 1983). The public health significance and challenge of trichinosis is that this disease accounts for numerous human cases of painful, serious illness, occasionally death, and yet is entirely preventable.

Biology and Life Cycle.   *Trichinella spiralis* is nearly unique among helminth parasites in that all stages of development occur within a single host (Fig. 11.3); over 100 species of mammals have been reported to be susceptible to some degree of infection (Zimmerman 1970). The infective stage is the encysted muscle larva which might remain viable in the host's musculature for many years; it might also survive for long periods in decaying and putrifying muscle (Kozar 1969), attributes which confer a high probability of successful transmission. The survivability of encapsulated larvae in carrion has been considered as analogous to the free-living stages of many other parasitic nematodes (Campbell 1983).

The adult worms are small and slender with slightly tapered anterior ends, a common feature of the superfamily Trichuroidea (Fig. 11.4A). The males measure 1.4–1.6 mm in length by 40–60 μm in diameter, and have two pseudobursal flaps at the posterior end with two pairs of papillae between the flaps; the pseudobursae aid in embracing the female during

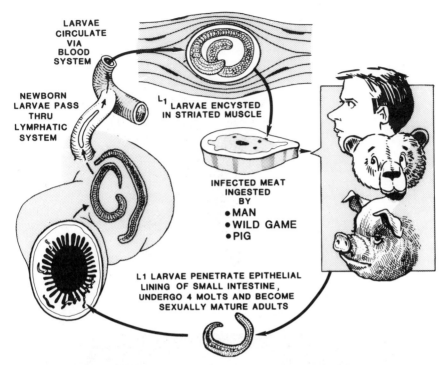

FIG. 11.3.   Outline of the life cycle of *Trichinella spiralis* showing wide host specificity range.
From Murrell (1986).

coitus. The female is a little more than twice as long as the male, 2.2–3.6 mm, and about one and a half times as broad. The vulva is situated near the middle of the esophageal region. An important feature is the presence of a column of cells called stichocytes that are associated with the capillary-like esophagus; the secretions of these cells contain potent antigens which play important roles in the host's response to the parasite (Despommier 1977), and are of great value in serodiagnosis (Gamble *et al.* 1983).

When man consumes raw or rare flesh infected with cysts of *Trichinella* (Fig. 11.4B), the cysts are digested out of the muscle in the stomach; the larvae (L₁ or first stage) are resistant to gastric juice. After passage to the small intestine, the larva burrows beneath the columnar epithelium and lies just above the lamina propria, completely enveloped by tissue (Despommier *et al.* 1978; Gardiner 1976). There the larva undergoes four molts within about 36 hr and develops into an adult worm (Ali Kahn 1966; Kozek 1971). Still within the intestinal tissue, the male and female worms mate. After fertilization the females begin to discharge live, newborn larvae as early as 4–7 days postinfection (Gardiner 1976). Production of

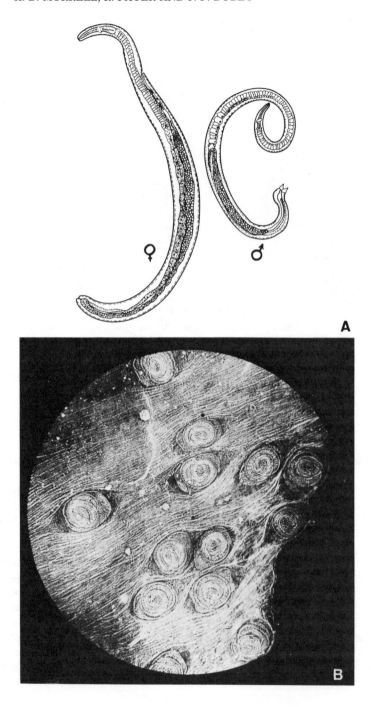

larvae may continue for quite some time, 4–16 weeks or more, depending on host species, until the worms are finally expelled from the intestine; the longevity of adult worms in the human intestine is not known with certainty (Larsh 1963). The newborn larva (about 100 μm long by 6 μm in diameter) makes its way into the lamina propria where it enters a draining lymph or blood vessel and is carried to the arterial circulation via the thoracic duct (Gardiner 1976; Harley and Galliccho 1971). The newborn larva is capable of migrating out of the blood vessel and invading nearly any tissue, but can survive only in a skeletal muscle cell. Invasion of the muscle cell induces changes which culminate in a new host unit termed the "nurse cell" (Despommier 1975). The larva begins to coil and the nurse cell completes the formation of the cyst around the larva by 17–21 days postinfection (Fig. 11.4B). By this time, the encysted larvae are gastric digestion-resistant and infective. The cyst size in man averages 400 μm by 260 μm; the encysted larvae have grown from 800 to 1000 μm in length and are now fully infective. Unusual for nematodes of this group, these larvae are sexually differentiated (Kozek 1976). In/man, calcification of the cyst may begin within 6 months to a year, a process which eventually leads to death of the encysted larva (Zimmermann 1975).

Electron microscopic studies describe more precisely the position of the adult worm within the epithelium (Wright 1978). The serial row of epithelial cells in which the worms lie exhibits a fusion of their lateral cell membranes close to the surface of the worm. Importantly, the worm apparently lies directly in the cell cytoplasm and is not surrounded by a host membrane. This worm–cell relationship is comparable to that of the muscle larva (L_1) and its differentiated muscle nurse cell. The duration of the intestinal phase is determined by the host's immune response to the adult worm; the response appears to be essentially an intestinal inflammation which drives the worm from the intestinal tissues and into the lumen where they are expelled from the host (Larsh 1963).

The distribution of encysted larvae among skeletal muscles is not random or equitable. In pork, although larvae are found in all striated muscles, the greatest densities of muscle larvae are found in the diaphragm, tongue, masseters, and neck muscles (Olsen et al. 1964; Herrera 1979; Matoff and Komandarev 1963). Zimmerman (1970) estimated that 25–30% of the total number of muscle larvae present in the carcass were contained in the hams and about 20% were present in the shoulder or Boston butts cuts. Although muscle larvae are believed to survive and mature to the infective stage only in striated muscle, Hill (1957) reported recovering infective larvae from experimentally infected pig liver, testes, brain, lung, pancreas, urinary bladder contents, and heart. However, Hill's report has been criticized by Matoff and Komandarev (1963) who

FIG. 11.4.   (A) Drawing of male and female adult T. spiralis. (B) Slide compression of pig diaphragm muscle showing encysted T. spiralis larvae. From Murrell (1986).

attempted to verify these earlier studies. They suggest that the larvae recovered from nonskeletal muscle were due to the accidental contamination of tissues by knives and other tools. The presence of larvae in heavily infected pigs might be expected in such viscera as stomach, small intestine, and urinary bladder because these organs possess striated muscle in their walls (Matoff and Komandarev 1963).

The basis for the predilection of *T. spiralis* larvae for anterior striated muscles is unclear, although some workers believe that it reflects a larval preference for those muscles which are highly active and consequently possess the richest supply of blood (Stewart and Giannini 1982). This preference might also be determined in part by the larva's positive taxis to a 120 mV action potential and/or increased negativity of the sarcolemma characteristic of more active muscles (Hughes and Harley 1977; Stewart and Giannini 1982). Considerable muscle cell alteration, including macromolecular and micromorphological alteration, occurs as a result of larval penetration and has been well reviewed by Stewart and Giannini (1982) and Despommier (1983A). Briefly, an invaded muscle cell exhibits loss of striations, disorganizations of contractile filaments, hypertrophy and displacement of nuclei, and dissolution of myofilaments. Accompanying these changes during the first few days of infection are decreases in myoglobin, ATP, phosphocreatine, and creatine, producing significant alterations in the contraction kinetics of infected skeletal muscle. Between 4 and 20 days after cell invasion, the cellular DNA and RNA increase, as does the proliferation of sarcoplasmic reticulum, polyribosomes, and protein synthesis. The alteration of host cell myofibril metabolism is probably a consequence of the larva's demands for nutrients. This nutritional requirement is reflected in the extensive hyperplasia of the T-tubular system, probably associated with increased active uptake of substances by the parasitized cell to support demands of both the perturbed cell and the growing larva. A marked increase in larval glycogen content occurs during the growth phase which is probably a requirement for further development after the larva is ingested by another host. All these changes appear to be directed toward altering the striated myofibril into a nurse cell (Purkerson and Despommier 1974) which provides the larva with suitable habitat in which to grow and develop (Stewart and Giannini 1982).

An important but neglected aspect of the biology of *T. spiralis* is the nutrition of the adult and larval stages. Available evidence strongly suggests that the adult worm obtains its required nutrients from the host's intestinal contents and/or from the intestinal epithelial cells in which it resides (Stewart 1983A). Alteration of the infected rat's oral intake of food by intravenous alimentation appears to favor worm survival (Castro *et al.* 1976). On the other hand, starvation of the mouse for 12 hr lowered the female worms' fecundity as was shown in studies by Stewart *et al.* (1980).

The nutritional requirements of the muscle larvae are perhaps of more interest since an understanding of this aspect might suggest strategies for improving treatment of the infected host. Yet this phase too has received little study. The available information recently was reviewed by Stewart (1983A). There is agreement that the encapsulated muscle larvae incorporate host dietary amino acids, glycogen, phosphorus, lipids, cholesterol, and thymidine. Certainly these activities are only part of the host–parasite interaction that produces the infective muscle larvae and permits their survival within the cyst for long periods of time. Information is especially needed on the mechanisms that select and promote the influx of needed nutrients through the cyst's double membrane; the cyst wall exhibits a highly selective character because the encysted larvae appear highly invulnerable to host immune effector mechanisms and many anthelmintics (see below). For the future, greater interest in these biological features must be encouraged.

The reproductive biology of parasites is of great interest not only for its intrinsic importance but also because it offers a potential area for developing better control methods, i.e., inhibition by chemical mediators that can confuse sexual attraction and mating (Bone 1982). In spite of the scarcity of published work on *T. spiralis'* sexual behavior, there is reasonable support for the belief that pheromone attraction among adult worms occurs (Despommier 1982). *In vitro* studies have demonstrated that female worms produce a water-soluble molecule(s) with attractive properties for male worms (Bonner and Etges 1967; Belosevic and Dick 1980). *In vivo* experiments with unisexual and bisexual infections in mice have supported these *in vitro* experiments and have further produced evidence that male worms might produce a repellent that keeps other males at some distance, tending to produce a more widely dispersed or random distribution within the intestinal habitat (Sukhedo and Croll 1981). As pointed out by Despommier (1983A), because all female worms in an infection tend to become fertilized and the normal sex ratio is two females to one male worm, each male generally must mate twice. Therefore, to accomplish this, a female attractant would have to be strong enough to override a male repellent. Confirmation of these findings is needed to encourage the isolation and characterization of these sex attractants and repellents.

The fecundity of the female worm is of interest since the number of newborn larvae produced bears a direct relationship to both the level of risk in infected meat and the degree of clinical illness suffered by the host, especially humans. Most of the information available on this aspect of the parasite's reproductive biology is derived from careful studies using rodents as hosts, and generally the estimates for these animals range from 200 to 1600 infective larvae produced by each female (Villela 1970). Similar investigations have not been made in swine, the host of primary importance for human infection, although very rough estimates were made by Zimmermann (1970A): 105 to 112 muscle larvae produced for each infective larva administered. This contrasted with a similarly derived figure of 300 muscle larvae produced for each infective larva ingested which was reported by Olsen *et al.* (1964). The actual number of newborn larvae produced by each female worm cannot be estimated because no efforts were made to determine average number of female worms maturing in paired pigs.

Of the many interesting features of the biology of *T. spiralis,* none are perhaps more critical to both the invasion of the host tissues and to the immunodiagnosis and potential immunological control of the parasite than the stichosome Fig. 11.4A) and its secretory products. The structure and role of this organ have been well reviewed (Despommier 1983A) and only certain aspects will be mentioned here. The stichosome consists of a row of secretory cells that contain granules of different sizes and morphology. These granules are secreted by the developing intestinal worm and are depleted by about the 30th hr of infection. Although the functional properties of these granules are as yet not known, they are strongly antigenic. Speculation on their function revolves mainly around the possibility that they are enzymes that act to assist in tissue invasion and worm nutrition. Histochemical tests indicate that the stichosome cells contain acid phosphatase and ATPase, but not alkaline phosphatase (Ruitenberg 1972). Recently, Rhoads (1983) isolated a metalloprotein with superoxide dismutase (SOD) activity from the secretions of muscle larvae maintained in culture. Although definitive proof that this enzyme originates in the stichosome is lacking, the fact that the culture procedure also stimulates the secretion of stichosome antigens provides strong circumstantial evidence that it is a stichocyte product. The intriguing aspect of this finding is that SOD might play a role in defending the worm against the highly destructive superoxide radical commonly produced by host inflammatory cells; the antimicrobial, antitumor, and antiparasitic activity of phagocytic leukocytes is believed to be, at least in part, due to their elaboration of superoxide anions. If the possession of SOD proves to be effective *in vivo* in modulating the activity of the host's inflammatory cells, the ability of the parasite to survive at least moderate assault by the host's immune cells (Larsh 1963) will be more comprehensible.

The stichosome secretions, as indicated previously, contain some of the most dominant of the worm's antigens. These antigens have been partially purified and immunochemically characterized (Despommier and Müller 1976; Despommier and Laccetti 1981A,B) especially those associated with the large particle component (S_3). In addition to their value as immunodiagnostic antigens (see below) they have been shown to be protective in mice (Despommier and Laccetti 1981A,B) and swine (Murrell and Despommier 1983). All these features underscore the importance of defining completely the biochemical and functional nature of the stichosome and its products, especially if better chemical and immunological control procedures are to be developed.

Epidemiology and Distribution.   The worldwide distribution of human and animal trichinosis has been the subject of several reviews (Kim 1983; Ruitenberg *et al.* 1983; Steele 1983). During this century, the incidence of trichinosis in humans and in swine has decreased significantly in Europe and North America (Steele 1983) although the infection rates in United States in cadavers and swine are still among the highest in the world (Zimmermann *et al*. 1973; Zimmermann and Zinter 1971). The rather slow decrease of the prevalence in the United States, which currently does not have a mandatory inspection requirement, might be attributed to: (1) increased number of urban common-source outbreaks responsible for large numbers of human cases per episode; (2) increased number of epidemics caused by sources other than pork; and (3) the importance of trichinosis from other countries (Ruitenberg *et al*. 1983). In some countries, such as the U.S.S.R., the large majority of human cases are now traceable to wild animal meat (Bessonov 1980). An example of the importance of sporadic, sole-source outbreaks on the overall prevalence of human trichinosis is the experience of Germany. During the period of 1860 to 1890, an average of 450 human cases per year was reported, but after the introduction of inspection of slaughtered swine, periods as long as 17 years passed without any clinical cases being reported (Kim 1983). However, large outbreaks occurred in 1950 (436 cases), 1967 (263 cases), 1977 (71 cases), and 1982 (318 cases); in the latter instance, raw pork was eaten by participants in a festival given by a brewery. The failure of the slaughter inspection to prevent all transmission of *T. spiralis* from pig to man is of concern. It is illustrative of the problem of sole reliance on inspection to realize that in 1976 only one pig out of 32,210,876 inspected in West Germany was found infected by the trichinoscopic method (Steigler 1978). Similarly, although no infected slaughter hogs have been detected in the Netherlands between 1926 and 1962, epidemiological studies have detected infected pigs at several farms (Ruitenberg *et al*. 1983).

In recent years the Scandinavian countries have experienced very low incidences of human and swine trichinosis. Denmark, for example, has not had a reported case in man or swine since 1910 (Steele 1983), although a very low prevalence appears to exist still in wild foxes in that country (Clausen 1978). The prevalence of trichinosis in man and swine have also decreased in eastern European countries, although the rates are generally somewhat higher than those in Western Europe. This is especially true in Poland, where the number of human cases averaged 582 per year from 1946 to 1965; the incidence has been declining in recent years and no major epidemics have been reported (Kozar 1970). All swine in Poland are subjected to inspection and the prevalence is reported to be less than 0.015%. Steele (1983) should be consulted for detailed information on the prevalence rates for swine and human trichinosis in Yugoslavia, Hungary, Bulgaria, Czechoslovakia, and the U.S.S.R.; these countries have also experienced marked declines in human trichinosis, especially since World War II. Similar reports on declining incidences of trichinosis have been made by Greece, Italy, and Spain, although occasional outbreaks do occur. Italy especially has experienced several epidemics in which the infected meat was determined to be fox and horse meat (Pampiglione 1971; Bellani *et al*. 1978). Occasional outbreaks of human trichinosis have occurred in the British Isles, but these are even more rare than in continental Europe (Harvey and Kershaw 1964). Ireland has experienced several episodes since 1957, most of which have been traced to pork products and there is concern that trichinosis may become epidemic (Kim 1983). Trichinosis is endemic among wild animals, especially foxes, rodents, and wild bears in Austria, Switzerland, Belgium, Portugal, and France, but reports of human cases are extremely rare; the prevalence in domestic swine is also very low or nonexistent (Kim 1983; Steele 1983). However, trichinosis is considered to be an important zoonosis in Spain, where it is frequently detected in wild and domestic animals, especially in rats, dogs, and foxes. The infection rate in pigs in 1965 for all of Spain was only 0.0007%, but the accuracy of this figure has been questioned (Kim 1983). The introduction of veterinary inspection has reduced the incidence of human trichinosis from several hundred cases per year in 1971–1975 to only 15 cases in 1978 (Martinez-Gomez 1979).

Trichinosis is now recognized as prevalent throughout much of Africa. Unconfirmed human cases were reported in Egypt in the 1970s which prompted surveys of slaughter pigs; over 4.5% of more than 40,000 samples were found to be infected (El-Nawawi 1981). In Cairo, Morsy et al. (1981) found infection in 3.5% of stray cats examined. Until its discovery in Kenya in 1961 (Forrester et al. 1961), trichinosis was not thought to exist south of the Sahara. Subsequently, human outbreaks have been reported in Senegal and Tanzania (Nelson 1982). Infections in wild animals, especially in the spotted hyena (*Crocuta corcuta*), appear to be the main maintenance host for *Trichinella* in Africa, rather than infections in swine and domestic rodents. The species isolated from Africa has been designated *T. nelsoni* because of certain distinguishing biological characteristics (Boev and Sokolova 1981), especially its low infectivity to rats and domestic pigs (Nelson 1982).

Detailed and comprehensive data on the presence and extent of trichinosis in Asia are lacking. In the Near East, trichinosis appears to have existed in Lebanon for quite some time (Steele 1983), with pork being the primary source. Sporadic reports of human infections also have been reported from Iran, India, Indonesia, and Laos, although sylvatic trichinosis is known in Iran, Afghanistan, India, and Indonesia (see reviews by Kim 1983; Steele 1983). Several outbreaks of human trichinosis have been reported from northern Thailand during the past 20 years, suggesting that trichinosis might be an emerging problem in that region. Surveys show that more than 10% of hill tribe pigs are infected and 0.1% of Nham, a local fermented pork dish, might contain *T. spiralis* larvae (Dissamaran and Aranyakanada 1974; Steele 1983).

Human trichinosis cases in China are rare although enzootic infections occur throughout the country (Gould 1970A). Recently, a documented human outbreak among Hong Kong Chinese arising from ingestion of pork was reported (Pun et al. 1983) and two other recent outbreaks among humans are known, one involving 58 cases caused by consumption of raw bear meat (WHO 1982).

The first human cases of trichinosis were reported in Japan in 1974. A group of hunters apparently contracted the disease after eating raw bear meat (Yamaguchi 1978). No human cases have been reported from the Philippines or from Korea (Kim 1983), and extensive efforts to determine the presence of *T. spiralis* in wild animals have not yet been made.

Although occasional human cases of trichinosis occur in Australia, and New Zealand, it appears to be endemic only in New Zealand, as small foci maintained in a sylvatic cycle (Cairns 1966; Mason 1978).

In the Pacific area enzootic trichinosis occurs only in the Hawaiian Islands. Wild pig meats appears to be the most common source for humans although infection is also prevalent in wild rats of the genus *Rattus* (Alicata 1970).

Trichinosis is enzootic in Latin America in both wild and domestic animals, especially in the southern regions and in Mexico (Neghme 1979). The status of human infections has been reviewed by Neghme (1979), Kim (1983), and Steele (1983), and need not be detailed here except to point out that comprehensive studies have not been carried out uniformly throughout this region and, because of this, the true prevalence of domestic and sylvatic trichinosis is not known. Frequent epidemics are reported in Chile, Uruguay, Argentina, and to a lesser extent, in Mexico.

Trichinosis in wild and domestic animals occurs in North America, especially among the former. Sporadic outbreaks may occur among humans in Canada, chiefly due to the consumption of bear meat (Cameron 1970), although other meat sources, such as pork, have been implicated (Tanner 1979; Kim 1983). Most infections in Alaska and Greenland are also traceable to inadequately cooked bear, especially polar bear, and walrus meat which have relatively high rates of infection (Rausch 1970; Thorborg *et al.* 1948; Roth 1949). The number of human cases in Canada was 31 in 1976, 23 in 1977, and 32 in 1978 (Tanner 1979).

The United States has one of the world's highest rates of *T. spiralis* infection among both humans and animals, and the disease is still considered an important public health problem (Schantz 1983A). The most recent investigation of the prevalence in humans, by examination of human cadaver diaphragm samples, indicated that 2.2% of the population of the United States was infected (Zimmermann *et al.* 1973). Over the last several decades, the mean annual number of reported clinical cases and deaths appears to have stabilized at between 100 and 150 cases, with the most frequent reports of cases originating from New England and the Middle Atlantic states (Schantz 1983A). However, Zimmermann (1975) argues that the actual annual number of human infections are mild or subclinical and are frequently overlooked or misdiagnosed. The signs and symptoms of human trichinosis simulate those of a wide variety of other diseases (see the following) and infection can easily be attributed to other infections, especially viral influenza (Murrell and Nelson 1983). Another important aspect of the reported declining mortality and infection rate among humans is probably a marked reduction in naturally occurring larval densities of *T. spiralis* in pork (Zimmermann 1975; Schantz 1983A). In the

United States, excepting Alaska, trichina-infected pork always has been a major source of human infection; in Alaska the vast majority of cases arise from the ingestion of bear and walrus meat (Schantz 1983A). Trace-back studies implicate pork products such as fresh sausage, summer sausage, and dried or smoked sausage as the source of infection in about 80% of cases (Zimmermann 1975; Schantz 1983A). Not uncommonly, ground beef is implicated, but this probably arises from adulteration with ground pork (Schantz 1983A). Accidental contamination of other species of meat with infected pork by use of either unclean butcher's knives or chopping blocks might sometimes occur (Gibson 1958), although intentional adulteration of ground beef might occur more frequently.

Typically, a large number of cases stem from a common source. For example, in 1981, 46 cases of trichinosis, including one death, were diagnosed in Providence, Rhode Island during November to December. The infections resulted from communal eating of two pigs purchased directly from a farm; the pork was prepared in ethnic dishes (Indochinese) requiring raw or partially cooked pork (CDC 1982). As pointed out by Schantz (1983A), traditionally, the largest outbreaks of human trichinosis have occurred among ethnic groups with preferences for raw or only partially cooked pork. Autopsy studies show that infection rates are much higher in persons of middle European descent (Italian, German, Polish, and/or Portuguese) (Zimmerman et al. 1973; Schantz et al. 1977). According to Schantz (1983A) approximately 70% of the human cases during the period 1975–1981 arose from the ingestion of raw meat; the remainder is believed to have eaten inadequately cooked meat.

The sources of implicated meats during the period 1975–1981 have been analyzed (Schantz 1983A). For domestic pork-associated cases, the infected meat was purchased from a local supermarket, butcher shop, or in other commercial outlets in 81% of the traceable cases. Only 5% of the pork was purchased in a restaurant; purchase of infected pork directly from a farm represented nearly 14% of the cases. Of the 132 human trichinosis cases arising from the consumption of wild animal meat (mostly Alaska), all animals were obtained by hunting and trapping.

Human infections resulting from the ingestion of infected horse meat occurred recently in the province of Reggio Emilia, Italy (Bellani et al. 1978). Epidemiologic investigations by Montovani et al. (1980) led them to postulate that ingestion of an infected rat by a horse resulted in contamination of the meat which was readily transmitted to local people who ate raw horse meat. Experimental studies confirmed that the horse is a susceptible host for T. spiralis (Pampiglione et al. 1978). Although such events appear to be rare relative to infections transmitted by pork and game animals, they serve to warn that the consumption of any mammalian meat, raw or only partially cooked, carries with it at least some risk of becoming infected because T. spiralis is known to infect more than 100 species of mammals, with 40 species in the United States alone (Zimmermann 1970B).

As pointed out earlier, the major source of *T. spiralis* for humans in the United States is the domestic pig. Periodic prevalence studies on swine have revealed a rather marked decline in infection rates among pigs during the last 85 years, although the prevalence varies considerably from one region to another (Zimmermann and Brandley 1965; Zimmermann and Zinter 1971; Murrell 1983). For example, the prevalence of *T. spiralis* in slaughter hogs nationally has decreased from 1.4% around the turn of the century to 0.63% in 1952 and 0.125% in 1970 (Zimmerman 1975). These low rates are influenced by the preponderance of midwestern hogs in the samples, which account for the majority of production in the United States. Although few in number, regional prevalence studies indicate that swine reared in the eastern United States are infected considerably more frequently than are midwestern- and western-raised hogs (Zimmermann and Zinter 1971; Murrell 1983). Zimmermann (1975) considered this difference a reflection of the greater reliance on the feeding of garbage among eastern hog producers in contrast to midwestern producers who are primarily grain feeders. Associated with the decline in the national prevalence rate for swine trichinosis is the fall in the number of larvae per gram (LPG) of pork muscle; this factor has undoubtedly had a major influence on the annual number of clinical human cases reported because the degree of illness is proportional to the numbers of larvae ingested (Murrell and Nelson 1983). In midwestern-raised hogs, 85% of muscle samples analyzed contained fewer than 10 LPG (Zimmermann and Brandley 1965). Schad and Murrell (1984) observed that 82% of samples from eastern hogs contained less than 10 LPG. However, the decline in prevalence of infection in hogs and in the larval densities should not be interpreted too optimistically in assessing the risk of human infection. Zimmermann (1975) estimates that a swine prevalence rate of 0.1% means that in the United States about 105,000 infected carcasses are processed by the packing industry which, in turn, yield approximately 40 million potential meal exposures each year.

The downward trend in the prevalence of trichinosis has been most dramatic among garbage-fed hogs, traditionally regarded as the primary source for human infections (Hall 1937). The prevalence fell from 11.0% in 1950 to 2.2% in 1959 (Schwartz 1960). In 1952, legislation was passed requiring the cooking of garbage before feeding it to swine in order to control swine vesicular exanthema. Following an increase in the prevalence of trichinosis in garbage-fed swine to about 5% in the early 1960s, it again fell to around 0.5% subsequent to the initiation in 1962 of a national hog cholera program which placed further emphasis on the cooking of garbage (Zimmermann and Brandley 1965; Jeffries *et al.* 1966; Zimmermann and Zinter 1971). Although evidence for the importance of garbage in swine trichinosis is circumstantial, it is biologically compatible with our understanding of the life cycle of *T. spiralis* (see above). Therefore, it is only reasonable to expect that adequate cooking of garbage (boiling for 30 min) will reduce *T. spiralis* transmission in swine fed garbage containing meat scraps, particularly pork, and that cooking regulations must be enforced adequately. Unfortunately, these regulations do not apply to the feeding of household scraps to pigs. This feature can be of significance since outbreaks of human trichinosis do occur among people who purchase pigs for home use directly from small or part-time operations not formally engaged in the commercial feeding of garbage (CDC 1982; Murrell 1983).

Despite its apparent importance, the practice of feeding garbage cannot be considered the only source for swine infections (Fig. 11.5). In-depth epidemiological studies on swine trichinosis, conducted on farms with on-going transmission, are surprisingly few given the importance of this aspect in the domestic cycle of trichinosis. However, there is sufficient evidence that other sources of swine infection might be important, especially for grain-fed hogs. Chief among these is transmission via infected farm rats, although considerable controversy exists regarding their actual importance. Some workers regard the rat as simply a bystander or "indicator" of the presence of trichinosis on a farm (Zenker 1871; Madsen 1974; Kozar 1969; Merkushev 1970). Cameron (1970) claimed that domestic swine actually have a great aversion to rats, and, hence, doubted that rats could play an important part in infecting pigs. However, Murrell *et al.* (1983) experimentally showed that grain-fed hogs given access to dead, infected rats consumed enough tissue within a few hours to become infected. Most field data supporting the idea that rats might be important as reservoir hosts on hog farms come from prevalence studies (Cironeanu 1974; Moynihan and Musfeldt 1949A,B; Smith 1980), a circumstantial association that awaits more direct evidence. Campbell (1983) suggests

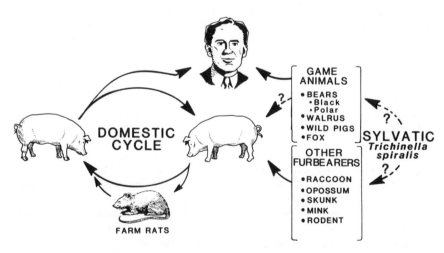

FIG. 11.5. Transmission patterns of the sylvatic and domestic cycles of *T. spiralis*. Note uncertainty in transmission of *T. spiralis* of wild animals to the domestic pig.

that introduction of trichinosis into a farm rat population could be amplified and propagated by rat cannibalism, with rats therefore representing
an offshoot of the domestic cycle ("recipients"). He also points out that the
crucial question of whether rats "donate" infection to pigs cannot be answered as yet because of insufficient evidence.

Another possible mode of infection to swine that has received little
consideration is infection by hog cannibalism. In an investigation of a
farm identified as the source of infected slaughter hogs in Iowa, Rothrock
(1965) concluded that a very likely means of transmission was the farmer's
practice of leaving a pig that had died in the lot to be eaten by other swine.
This suggestion was supported by his failure to find infected rats on the
premises. Although the owner had fed raw garbage some years before, he
had stopped that practice when cooking became mandatory. A similar
finding from investigation of an Illinois farm was offered by Levine (1978),
although infected rats were caught on the farm in question. These observations should be given more serious consideration by investigators because even in well-managed total confinement hog operations, there is
frequently a long time interval between the death of a hog and its eventual
removal from the pen (Murrell 1982). There is experimental evidence that
eating of only a small sample of muscle, especially a tail, can result in
transmission of *T. spiralis* (Zimmerman *et al.* 1962).

Another source of swine infection regarded as important is the introduction of sylvatic trichinosis *via* wild animal carcasses (Fig. 11.5). Kozar
(1969) concluded that the introduction of trichinae from wild animals
occurs far more frequently than generally assumed, a view shared by
Zimmerman (1970B). Evidence for this transmission route was also provided by trace-back studies in which two infected Iowa herds were located
where the feeding of carcasses of wild animals was practiced (Andrews *et
al.* 1969); however, other possible sources of infection were not eliminated.
Although *T. spiralis* is widely prevalent among wildlife, the evidence that
sylvatic trichinosis is an important source of infection is mainly indirect,
and, in fact, the few experimental studies that have been carried out
indicate that some wild animal isolates have low infectivity for swine
(Rausch 1983; Nelson 1982; Boev and Sokolova 1981). Zimmermann *et al.*
(1956) reported success in infecting pigs with isolates of *T. spiralis* from
Iowa fox, mink and opossum, but no data were offered to compare their
rates of infectivity with the pig strain. Clearly, more careful experimental
and epidemiological studies are needed to evaluate the importance of wild
animal *T. spiralis* in the domestic pig–man cycle.

Related to the problem of the relevance of sylvatic trichinosis is the
current uncertainty of the systematics of *Trichinella*. Rausch (1983) and
Dick (1983) have recently reviewed the basis of the confusion in the taxonomy of the genus. Isolates from Kenya and Arctic carnivores have been
given separate species names (*T. nelsoni* and *T. nativa,* respectively) by
Britov and Boev (1972) and an unusual form isolated in Russia from a
raccoon and raptorial birds which does not induce the formation of a mus-

cle capsule (*T. pseudospiralis*) was discovered by Garkavi (1972). Analysis of enzyme polymorphism among these isolates revealed some differences between them (Flockhart *et al.* 1982), which coupled with other biological and genetic features (Dick and Chadee 1981, 1983) indicates that in addition to their differences in pig infectivity these wild animal strains are distinguishable from the domestic pig–man strain. Especially important to control of trichinosis is the capability of the Arctic strain to withstand freezing sufficient to kill *T. spiralis* in pork. Although evaluation of freezing resistance of the Arctic isolate in pork has not been reported, this isolate can withstand freezing for at least 12 months in bear muscle (at −15°C) and fox muscle (at −15°C) (Dick 1983), while the pig strain is killed by freezing at −15°C for 20 days (see below). Because the freezing susceptibility of only a few pig isolates have been examined, some caution in generalizing about the effectiveness of freezing should be exercised. Although the Arctic strain, like the Kenya strain, has a very low infectivity for domestic pigs (Rausch 1983; Kovalchuk 1981; Nelson *et al.* 1966), there is concern that the present requirements for killing trichinae in meat by freezing might need to be modified should other more resistant strains become adapted to the domestic pig–man cycle. In some instances, though, these larvae have lost their high resistance to freezing after transfer to laboratory rodents, indicating resistance might be more a function of the host's muscle biochemistry than the parasite (Campbell 1983). It would be of interest to assess the influence of the Arctic carnivore host's muscle habitat upon the freezing susceptibility of the pig strain of *T. spiralis*. More study of the potential for wild animal strains of *Trichinella* (especially those in the United States) to infect pigs and the importance they play in the epidemiology of swine trichinosis may be required in order to base control on documentable facts and not assumption.

Lichtenfels *et al.* (1983) have questioned whether the biological, biochemical, and karyotype data used to justify the designation of the Kenyan isolate (*T. nelsoni*), the Arctic isolate (*T. nativa*), and the nonencapsulating isolate (*T. pseudospiralis*) are adequate and prefer to term them subspecies of *T. spiralis* until more conclusive evidence is offered, especially since they could detect no morphological differences among the isolates. Dick (1983) also prefers, from his careful genetic analysis, not to refer to the isolates as separate species since gene flow between the isolates is evident by their ability to interbreed. These subspecies might be in the process of becoming truly reproductively isolated in nature, a state that would make separate species designation more acceptable.

Despite long standing interest, understanding of the epidemiology of swine trichinosis is surprisingly inadequate. It is doubtful that an effective control program for trichinosis in the United States can be designed without first filling these gaps in our knowledge.

Clinical Disease.   Stated simply, the severest manifestations of the disease or infection in humans are due to the larval offspring of the viviparous female worms and normally not to the adult worms in the intestine. Extensive invasion of the striated muscles and the epithelial lining of the small intestine stimulates a pronounced inflammatory response to the worm and its released antigens; it is this host defensive response that produces illness and sometimes death. A considerable amount of study of the pathology and pathophysiology of *T. spiralis* infection in experimental animals has been carried out and this literature has been recently reviewed in detail by Weatherly (1983), Castro and Bullock (1983), Gould (1970B), and Stewart (1983B).

Most human cases are mild or subclinical. The severity of clinical trichinosis perhaps is greatly dependent upon the intensity of infection, as measured by the number of larvae per gram of muscle tissue ingested; infections with fewer than 1 larva per gram are asymptomatic. Those with more than 100 larvae per gram are critical (Hall and Collins 1937). However, Pawlowski (1983A) noted that other host factors, such as age, sex, race, general health status, and individual resistance factors require caution in accepting such generalizations. For example, infections of over 1000 larvae per gram were often moderate and not necessarily fatal in Kikuyu males infected with the Kenyan strain of *T. spiralis* (Forrester *et al.* 1961). Cadaver studies in the United States reveal that more than 50% of positive muscle samples had 10 larvae or less per gram of diaphragm; only 0.9% had more than 100 larvae per gram. Similar findings have been reported from other countries (Pawlowski 1983A). Therefore, the opportunities to carry out careful clinical research on symptomatic human cases are infrequent and even less commonly are such cases convenient to qualified laboratories and investigators.

The initial consequences of infection occur within the first week after ingestion of infected meat, during the intestinal phase; this period is associated with the development of larvae to the adult stage within the lamina propria of the small intestine. Gastrointestinal symptoms occur in only a small percentage of trichinosis cases and do not present a picture specific for trichinosis. Of these symptoms, loss of appetite, constipation, abdominal cramps and pain, nausea and weight loss, and diarrhea, some basis for physiological etiology has been determined experimentally only for the latter; readers are referred to Castro and Bullock (1983) for discussion of this aspect. Because these symptoms may be mild or easily confused with other etiologic agents of gastroenteritis, infection with *T. spiralis* is misdiagnosed at least occasionally, or not diagnosed (Zimmerman 1975). The worm-induced inflammation of the intestinal mucosa may persist for 1–2 months until the worms are eliminated from the gut by the expulsion response or until treatment with an anthelmintic drug.

The most pronounced symptoms of infection coincide with the penetration of newborn larvae into muscle cells, beginning about 7 to 9 days after exposure. The larvae will only complete their development in striated skeletal myofibrils (Stewart 1983B; Despommier 1983A). This cell invasion triggers a strong host inflammatory response (Weatherly 1983), especially in extraocular muscles, masseters, muscles of the larynx, tongue, diaphragm, neck, intercostal muscles, and muscles attached to tendons and joints. The muscle fibers become edematous and enlarged due to infiltration of neutrophils, eosinophils, lymphocytes, and tissue histiocytes. Inflammation reaches its peak at about 5 to 6 weeks of infection and appears to diminish when the larva is completely encapsulated (Grove *et al.* 1977; Gould 1970B). The acute muscular clinical phase is characterized by muscle and joint pain, anorexia, emaciation, pyrexia, dyspnea, periobital edema, eosinophilia, malaise, laryngitis, conjunctivitis, photophobia, respiratory manifestations, skin eruptions, and occasionally, in severe infections, myocarditis, endocarditis, encephalitis, and meningitis. As with the gastrointestinal phase, the symptoms associated with the muscle phase frequently may be confused with acute arthritis, influenza, lymphocytic choriomeningitis, bacillary dysentery, measles, mumps, scarlet fever, nephritis, and mononucleosis (Zimmermann 1975; Pawlowski 1983A). Allergic vasculitis is often present in moderate and severe trichinosis (Ozeretskovskaya 1978). Vascular leakage of fluid most easily is seen as a periorbital edema, conjunctival hemorrhage, and frequently as splinter hemorrhages of the nailbeds on the fingers and toes (Pawlowski 1983A).

The convalescent phase usually begins a few months after infection and might continue for several years, until the destruction of the muscle larvae is complete. In some patients, muscle pain, weakness, and fatigue may continue for months or years. The death of the larvae probably coincides with completion of cyst calcification, which in man may require 18 months or more (Gould 1970B; Weatherly 1983).

Myocarditis is a frequent and perhaps the most serious complication of trichinosis and may lead to acute congestive cardiac failure, usually 4–8 weeks after infection (Andy *et al.* 1977). Although the vast majority of patients who survive trichinosis recover completely, a few undoubtedly continue to suffer from cardiac manifestations. These cardiac manifestations are due to inflammation and healing by interstitial fibrosis; larvae cannot successfully encyst and survive in heart muscle (Despommier 1983A).

The pig apparently tolerates infection with *T. spiralis* very well (Zimmerman 1975), and clinical disease has not been diagnosed in the field. Experimental infections in pigs produced the characteristic eosinophilia, retarded weight gains in very heavily infected pigs, but had no effect on hemoglobin, packed cell volume, white blood cell count or leukocyte differential counts (Strafuss and Zimmermann 1967). For reasons that are not clear, muscle larvae densities (1000 larvae per gram) that would be life-threatening in humans do not appear to produce significant clinical effects in domestic swine (Beck 1970).

In addition to differences encountered between host species in development of *T. spiralis* infections, the clinical course of trichinosis might differ from subspecies to subspecies (Forrester *et al.* 1961; Ozeretskovskaya

1978). With the recent discovery of *T. pseudospiralis,* the form that does not induce muscle encapsulation in mammals and birds, interest has developed on the potential for this species to infect man. So far, no human infections with this species have been reported. However, comparative studies of *T. spiralis* and *T. pseudospiralis* in monkeys (*Macacus fasciolaris*) demonstrated that these primates were susceptible to the latter and that they developed clinical and pathological reactions similar to that induced by *T. spiralis* (Kociecka *et al.* 1981; Teppema *et al.* 1981). The finding that primates, and perhaps man, are susceptible to *T. pseudospiralis* might have important consequences from the standpoint of control since little is known of that species' thermal death point or susceptibility to curing procedures. If it should become established in the domestic trichinosis cycle, the applicability of current standards for inactivating the trichina by cooking, freezing, or salt curing is unknown.

As pointed out previously, the host's immune response is important in the development of disease, chiefly because of the inflammatory response to the parasite and its antigens. The intestine is the initial site of infection and, consequently, experiences the initial immune response. Characteristically, the adult worms persist perhaps up to 6 weeks in man (Wakelin and Denham 1983), after which the worms are expelled from the intestine (Larsh 1963). The expulsion is a consequence of an immunologically mediated inflammation; experimental data with laboratory hosts indicate that the response is dependent upon T cell or thymus-derived lymphocytes. T cells themselves are apparently not the direct cause of worm expulsion (Wakelin and Denham 1983), but might instead specifically trigger the cellular and biochemical chain of events that characterize the inflammatory changes strongly associated with worm expulsion (Larsh and Race 1975). Humans with conditions that restrict their ability to mount an immune response may fail to eliminate the adult worms, or at least suffer a protracted intestinal infection, and develop higher muscle larvae densities. Consequently, they may develop more critical forms of disease (Pawlowski 1983A).

Antibodies also might play an important role in regulating the infection, but the experimental evidence for it is less firm. As cited by Wakelin and Denham (1983) there is considerable circumstantial evidence that humoral antibody is an important effector mechanism against migrating and muscle-invading newborn larvae, perhaps in concert with inflammatory cells (MacKenzie *et al.* 1978). There is a very prominent cellular response to the muscle larvae, especially prior to the formation of the capsule. Despommier (1983B), however, believes that much of the evidence for antibody or protective response to the tissue stages is derived from nonrealistic or abnormal experimental conditions and as a consequence the results may be misleading. There is also evidence that antibodies may act upon the intestinal worms, causing worm damage and reduced fecundity. Antibodies may also play a role in intestinal expulsion by their mediation of immediate hypersensitivity (reagins) and Arthus reaction, both of which initiate inflammation (Wakelin and Denham 1983).

Diagnosis in Man and Animals. Because the symptoms of mild trichinosis are largely not pathognomonic, diagnosis is often difficult, and because it is not a common disease it is frequently not considered as a possible diagnosis. Generally, diagnosis is based on: (1) clinical history, (2) physical examination, (3) serological tests, (4) direct demonstration of the parasite in the muscles or intestine, and (5) differential diagnosis (Pawlowski 1983A).

Trichinosis should be a prime suspect when a group of people present themselves with symptoms after having shared a common meat source. If the meat implicated can be obtained, it should be examined by either direct microscopic examination of pressed muscle to look for encysted larvae or by pepsin-HCl digestion of the meat to recover larvae (Gould 1970B).

Physical examination might reveal such suggestive symptoms of trichinosis as periorbital edema and hemorrhagic lesions in the eyeballs associated with fever, myalgia, and malaise.

Serological tests are now quite sensitive and specific enough for trichinosis, especially the enzyme-linked immunosurbent assay (ELISA). A variety of other serological tests have been developed for diagnosis of human trichinosis (Ljungström 1983). Complete reliance upon serology for diagnosis of human trichinosis is not recommended, however. Patients with very low infection levels or immunocompromised conditions might generate either very delayed or low antibody titers.

Great interest exists in both Europe and the United States in the application of the ELISA for antemortem testing of slaughter swine (Leighty 1983; Ruitenberg et al. 1983). Improvements in automation of the ELISA procedure eventually might permit the use of serodiagnosis under modern, high-volume slaughterhouse conditions. Until recently, the ELISA for swine trichinosis suffered from frequent false-positive reactions, but this condition has been greatly improved by the use of partially purified *T. spiralis* antigens (Seawright et al. 1983; Gamble et al. 1983), especially if the antigen was purified by monoclonal antibody affinity chromatography (Gamble and Graham 1983). Successful introduction of the inspection procedure could result in a marked improvement in efforts to lower the trichinosis infection rates in man and swine.

An important hallmark of human and animal trichinosis is the development of eosinophilia. Eosinophilia of 500 cells per mm^3 or more is the earliest and most consistent laboratory sign of trichinosis, usually occurring by the second or third week after infection and persisting during the symptomatic period (Pawlowski 1983A).

Demonstration of worms by direct tests is the most reliable procedure for diagnosing trichinosis. This is usually accomplished by microscopic examination of muscle biopsies (Murrell and Nelson 1983). Some caution should be exercised in interpreting the finding of larvae in muscle preparations. It is possible that the recovered larvae are the result of an earlier infection and are not responsible for the present symptoms.

These techniques are also applicable to the direct diagnosis of trichinosis in swine and other animals. In Europe, the laborious and costly trichinoscopic examination of slaughter swine has been mandatory since the late 19th century. Recently, modification of the artificial gastric juice digestion procedure has been made that makes this the most sensitive of the direct procedures. Originally introduced for large-scale swine inspection in the United States by Zimmerman (1967), it has been refined and adapted to more efficient machinery for rapid digestion in Denmark (Thomsen 1977). This "Mechanically Assisted Pooled Sample Digestion" method is now the official inspection procedure in Denmark, Norway, Sweden, and Finland and there are indications that other European countries will adopt this method (Skvogard and Petersen 1983). Cost estimates for this method in Denmark are 7–10 cents per head in a plant processing 5000 hogs per day. It should be noted, however, that this method, when employing 1-gram samples in a 100-gram pool, may fail to detect up to 36% of the swine bearing one cyst or less per gram of muscle.

Treatment of Humans and Animals. The treatment of human trichinosis has been recently reviewed (Pawlowski 1983A; Murrell and Nelson 1983; Campbell and Denham 1983). The efficacy of treatment depends on the intensity and duration of infection and on the character and intensity of the host's response. Guidelines for treatment have also recently been proposed by the International Commission on Trichinellosis:

1. *Intestinal stage.* Removal of adult worms from the intestine is necessary to stop the production of newborn larvae. This can be accomplished by several anthelmintics, such as thiabendazole (50 mg/kg for 5 days), pyrantel (10 mg/kg for 4 days), and mebendazole (in adults 200 mg/day for 4 days); mebendazole should not be given in the first trimester of pregnancy.
2. *Muscle stage.* Corticosteroids are the drugs of choice in acute trichinellosis because of their antiinflammatory and antiallergic action. The usual dose is 40 to 60 milligrams of prednisolone per day, taken until the fever and allergic signs subside. In life-threatening infections, higher doses might be required. Bed rest is always necessary, and any cardiac, circulatory, neurologic, or pulmonary complications might need additional, intensive, specific treatment.
3. *Moderate or mild infection.* Because corticosteroids might suppress the intestinal inflammatory response to the adult worms, immune expulsion may not occur, thereby prolonging the period of production of newborn larvae and muscle invasion. The use of corticosteroids, therefore, should be restricted to patients with fever, allergic symp-

toms, high leukocytosis, and eosinophilia; antipyretic and analgesic
treatment alone might produce satisfactory results.

4. *Chronic infection.* Trichinosis is a self-limiting disease in both intestinal and muscular phases, and recovery usually occurs within a few
months. In sporadic cases, myalgia and weakness have been known
to persist for several years. In these cases evidence of an active process shown by muscle biopsy examination might justify the use of
larvicidal drugs such as mebedazole or thiabendazole (Pawlowski
1983A).

Only limited studies on chemotherapy for swine infections have been
carried out. Generally, the benzimidazole drugs appear as effective in
swine as in humans. Campbell and Denham (1983) have reviewed drug
studies in animals.

Prevention and Control.   Approaches toward control or prevention of
trichinosis in humans varies somewhat in different countries. Based on
reported prevalence data for both swine and humans, the most effective
control procedure is direct inspection of pork at slaughter, either by microscopic or "trichinoscopic" examination or by a pooled sample digestion
method as practiced in Europe (Ruitenberg *et al.* 1983). In the United
States, inspection of slaughter hogs was discontinued in 1906 (Campbell
1983) and since then control procedures have been based on two programs:
(1) destruction of trichinae in ready-to-eat pork products; and (2) education
of the consumer of the necessity for adequate cooking of fresh pork.

In general, this program has been very successful in that few if any
human outbreaks have been traced to products covered by regulations,
especially since the enactment of The Wholesome Meat Act of 1967 as an
amendment to the Federal Meat Inspection Act, which extended coverage
of the regulations to include all state and local meat inspection services
and processors (Zimmermann 1975).

Perhaps the chief weakness in this control program is its inability to
cover fresh pork cooked in the home or home-processed into ready-to-eat
products. These products, when improperly prepared, are the most important sources of human trichinosis in the United States (Schantz 1983A).
To help eliminate or reduce this hazard, consumer and producer education
has received considerable emphasis by the USDA, chiefly through publications such as USDA Leaflet No. 428, entitled, "Trichinosis, How It Affects
You, How It Affects Your Hogs, What You Can Do About It," and "FACTS
About Trichinosis" (Leighty 1983). The USDA recommends that consumers consider that all pork may be infected with trichinae and should be
handled by: (1) cooking to 77°C (USDA 1982); or (2) freezing, if less than 6
inches thick, to −15°C for 20 days, −23°C for 10 days, or −30°C for 6 days.
These freezing recommendations do not appear to apply to wild game meat
infected with the Arctic subspecies of *T. spiralis.*

Recently, some confusion and consternation have resulted from published findings that infected pork cooked to 77°C and above in microwave ovens sometimes still yielded infective trichinae (Zimmerman and Beach 1982; Carlin *et al.* 1982; Kotula *et al.* 1982). The experimental evidence indicates that the observed failure of microwave cooking to consistently destroy trichinae in pork stems not from some peculiar resistance of the larvae to microwaves but instead to the tendency of such cooking to produce nonuniform temperatures throughout the meat (Kotula *et al.* 1983A). The thermal death point of *T. spiralis* larvae in pork was originally determined to be 55°C by Ransom and Schwartz (1919) and a time-thermal death curve was recently derived by Kotula *et al.* (1983B). The larvae are destroyed at 55°C if held 4 min at that temperature, killed nearly instantaneously at 60°C, but could survive up to 47 min at 52°C.

Processing regulations for pork products are specified in Government publications (FSQS 1973). Pork products which are sold as ready-to-eat must be processed in a manner that does not require further cooking to destroy trichinae. In inspected establishments, pork muscle tissue is heated to at least 58°C throughout. Pork products intended for consumption without prior cooking must be made trichina-safe by freezing; temperature requirements vary depending upon the thickness of the pork product except that any product might be processed by freezing to −35°C in its center or by freeze-drying (Leighty 1983). Curing procedures for the destruction of trichinae are specified in the Federal Meat Inspection Regulations (FSQS 1973), although other procedures might be acceptable after official review (Zimmerman, 1975; Leighty 1983).

Currently, interest has been revitalized in developing an irradiation procedure for pork to kill encysted trichinae (Sivinsky 1983). Both gamma emissions and X rays have been shown to be highly effective in either sterilizing the encystal larvae so that they fail to reproduce in the next host (8,000–10,000 rads) or in preventing their establishment in the host's intestine altogether by irradiation at 15,000 rads (Schwartz 1921; Gould *et al.* 1952; Gibbs *et al.* 1964). Although biologically efficacious, the adoption of food irradiation will depend greatly on its demonstrable safety, its cost/benefit advantages for the meat industry, and on consumer acceptance of irradiated pork.

Control of human trichinosis could be achieved in the United States by some manner of direct or indirect inspection at the slaughterhouse, as has been achieved in Europe (Ruitenberg *et al.* 1983). Leighty (1983) reviewed the obstacles that must be overcome if animal inspection is to be adopted by the packing industry in the United States. Militating against direct inspection by either trichinoscopy or pooled sample digestion methods is the large number of hogs slaughtered per year (91 million in 1981), often at kill rates of 1000 hogs per hour and the increasingly large number of plants that process the hogs into pork products within a few hours after slaughter, preventing the retention of carcasses overnight while tests are performed. If 91 million hogs are slaughtered annually, each penny of the cost of inspection would increase the cost of annual inspection by $910,000, a very unattractive prospect for the packing industry. These aspects have made development of an indirect antemortem testing by means of a rapid, automated serological test, such as the ELISA, the object of considerable effort by the Food Safety and Inspection Service (FSIS) over the past 12 years (Leighty 1983) and by Government agencies in Europe (Ruitenberg *et al.* 1983). On the basis of limited laboratory field trials, the ELISA has performed well, although in very lightly infected hogs (around 1 to 10 larvae per gram of diaphragm or less) circulating antibody is frequently not detected for 6 weeks or more after infection (Gamble *et al.* 1983), leaving a window of about 4 weeks in which infected hogs could escape serological detection. However, this aspect may be improved by further refinement of the testing procedure. It is also probable that such lightly infected hogs may not cause clinical disease unless very large quantities of pork were consumed; the larval densities in the pork loin, ham, and belly muscles are generally 3 to 5 times smaller than in the diaphragm (Kotula and Murrell 1981). The prospects for an antemortem serological test for swine trichinosis are, on the whole, promising but it appears that commercial adoption of such a procedure is still some time in the future.

Although the adoption of a serodiagnostic test for inspection or the irradiation of pork to render it trichina-safe could have a significant impact on the pork industry and the incidence of human trichinosis in the United States, sufficient epidemiological evidence has accumulated (Murrell 1983) to indicate that a considerable amount of infected pork passes through slaughterhouses that are too small to expect the incorporation of sophisticated technology for inspection. For these plants, alternative procedures might have to be considered, such as direct trichinoscopy or pooled sample digestion.

Prevention and control of *T. spiralis* infections in swine rests solely on stopping ingestion by hogs of meat containing trichinae. This effort requires, however, identification of the sources of infected meat for swine, an aspect which has not been defined clearly in the United States (Murrell 1983). Although the data are largely circumstantial, they do strongly support the belief that the feeding of uncooked garbage is a major culprit. Ideally, the elimination of all garbage feeding would have a favorable impact, but this is unrealistic given the economic attractiveness of recycling through hogs the tremendous amount of food waste generated in the United States. Instead, strong enforcement of garbage cooking regulations in the 34 states that allow the practice is necessary. These regulations have recently been upgraded (Swine Health Protection Act 1983) and stipulate that all garbage must be boiled for 30 min in a licensed facility before being fed to swine. Unfortunately, these provisions do not apply to the feeding by a farmer of his own household garbage.

Although the evidence that wildlife strains of *T. spiralis* are infective for swine is scant (see above), the practice of feeding wild animal carcasses or meat scraps to pigs should be discouraged. All swine producers, hunters, and trappers should be informed of the possible dangers of this practice, in addition to being warned that wild game may harbor trichinae infective to humans unless well cooked before consumption. Such an educational effort could easily be achieved by the inclusion of a warning attached to hunting and trapping licenses as is done in Canada, and by the publishing of information in sportsmen's magazines and farm publications (Zimmermann 1975; Murrell 1983). Custom butchers should also be informed of the danger in mixing wild animal meat with pork and of the need for safe disposal of carcass remains.

Even though the evidence is so far incomplete, the role of rats in transmission of *T. spiralis* to hogs should be given serious consideration. Greater educational efforts could be made to encourage all operators of hog farms, including the small and part-time operators, to practice effective rodent control.

Hopefully, epidemiological studies eventually will identify all of those management practices that are associated with the highest risk of swine trichinosis. This would allow serious consideration for designing specific control methods that would be targeted to those producers at highest risk. Among the potential control approaches that could be employed in this manner are vaccination, prophylactic and therapeutic drug treatment, and the development of swine strains with higher resistance to infection (Murrell 1983). Again, these control methods probably would not be feasible or necessary for all swine in the United States, but only applicable to those herds showing the highest prevalences or risks of swine trichinosis.

Regardless of the nature of potential control efforts, their chances for success depend primarily upon a strong commitment on the part of industry, government agencies, and the public. Encouragingly, this dedication and commitment are being exhibited by several of these groups, especially the National Pork Producers Council in the United States which is providing leadership through its Trichina-Safe committee, and the prospects of achieving the control success achieved in other regions, especially Europe, appear more promising now than at any time in the past.

Taenia saginata: Beef Cysticercosis

Public Health Significance. *Taenia saginata* can be transmitted to humans by the ingestion of the larval or cysticercus stage which is encysted in the meat of bovines; in humans the parasite develops to the adult tapeworm stage in the intestine and produces the condition termed taeniasis. Although taeniasis has been known since ancient times, and has been much studied, there are still many gaps in our knowledge of the biology of the parasite, clinical features of the disease, and its epidemiology. This probably accounts for the persistence of the problem and the frequent failures in control efforts (Pawlowski 1983B). The problem continues also for the modern livestock producer and packer whose cattle might suffer condemnation at slaughter because of the presence of the cysticercus stage in the tissue, producing the condition known as bovine cysticercosis or beef measles. Bovine cysticercosis is prevalent not only in underdeveloped regions such as East Africa where it is widespread, but also occurs frequently in the developed countries of Europe and in the United States. The high standards of meat inspection in the United States have not yet succeeded in eliminating this infection which is most commonly seen in feedlot cattle in western and southwestern states (Hird and Pullen 1979).

Because human tapeworm infections are not reportable to health authorities in any state, accurate data concerning this disease are not available. However, during the years 1968–1981 when the National Center for Disease Control controlled the release of the cestocidal drug niclosamide, information obtained from physicians requesting the drug to treat their patients provided some insight on the number of cases of *T. saginata* diagnosed in the United States. Data from CDC indicates 443 patients were treated for *T. saginata* in 1981 (Schantz 1983B). Elsewhere, the prevalence of *T. saginata* taeniasis may reach 50% or more, especially in certain regions in Africa, in East Europe and in Caucasian and south-central Asian U.S.S.R. republics (Pawlowski 1983B). Infection rates among cattle worldwide are extremely variable, but might also be quite high. Recent estimates for slaughter cattle range from 0.0002% in the United States in 1981 (Snyder and Murrell 1983) to 9% in Belgium (Geerts et al. 1980) 20% in Kenya (Grindle 1978), and even higher in Ethiopia (Pawlowski 1983B). As will be discussed below, these estimates are almost certainly too conservative because of the inefficiency of current meat inspection procedures (Dewhirst et al. 1967). Within the United States, the incidence varies greatly; in 1981, the incidence per 1000 head was 1.79 for California, 2.27 for New Hampshire, 0.69 for Washington, 0.49 for Arizona, and 0.004 for both Iowa and Wisconsin. The economic losses due to bovine cysticercosis are difficult to estimate. In Kenya, Grindle (1978) estimates the loss per animal slaughtered at around $5.00. For all countries, the need to maintain meat surveillance represents a significant economic burden.

Biology and Life Cycle. The adult stage of *Taenia saginata* is a flat tapeworm consisting of a scolex or head with 4 suckers for attachment, a neck column, and a chain or strobila of approximately 1000–2000 proglottids or segments; the total length may vary between 4 and 12 m. The proglottids are formed at the distal end of the neck, and undergo a maturation process during their movement toward the end of the strobila. The proglottid is composed of both male and female reproductive organs and rudimentary nervous and excretory systems. Fertilization is cross-proglottids and results in the production of an egg-filled uterus in the mature gravid proglottid; the number of lateral branches of the gravid uterus ranges from 18 to 32 on each side and is of some use in species determination (Pawlowski and Schultz 1972). Gravid proglottids, about 20 mm long and 5 to 7 mm wide detach singly from the strobila and independently pass out of the intestine through the host's anus (Fig. 11.6). Generally, an infected person harbors one tapeworm, although in some regions of the world, e.g., Asia Minor, multiple infections are frequent (Pawlowski 1983B). The adult tapeworm normally localizes in the jejunum, about 50 cm below the duodenojejunal flexure, and rarely enters the gall bladder or

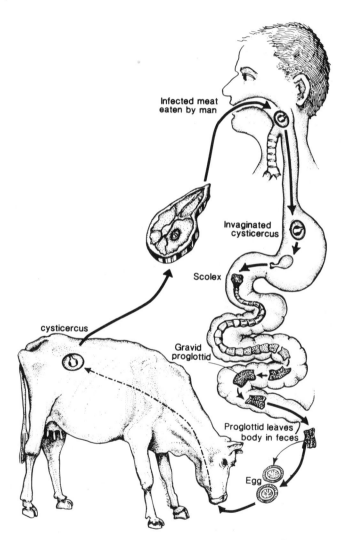

FIG. 11.6.   Life cycle and transmission pattern of the beef tapeworm, *Taenia saginata.*

nasopharynx (Pawlowski and Schultz 1972). The life span of *T. saginata* in man can be as long as 30 or 40 years.

Taenia saginata is capable of producing a very large number of eggs and an individual proglottid may contain about 80,000 eggs (Penfold *et al.* 1937A); because each strobila can shed 6 to 9 gravid proglottids per day, a single infected individual may contaminate the environment with one-half million eggs or more each day. The proglottid can migrate actively through the anus and, therefore, is not dependent upon defecation to gain access to the environment. The movement of the proglottid during extrusion from the intestine and anus expels most of the eggs from the uterus. The mature egg or embryophore contains the larval stage termed the onchosphere; immature eggs that are passed can complete development outside the host. About 50% of the embryophores escaping the proglottid are fully developed (Silverman 1954). The spheroid onchosphere is about 30 μm large and possesses 6 hooklets and a pair of penetration glands. Ingestion of the egg by cattle (Fig. 11.6) is followed by disintegration of the outer embryophore and induction by gastric juices of activation of the onchosphere. Aided by its hooks and penetration glands, the onchosphere penetrates the bovine intestinal mucosa and within a couple of hours enters the blood or lymphatic system present in the submucosa (Slais 1970).

Although the path by which the larva reaches the site for further development is not known in detail (Pawlowski 1983B), it probably is the circulatory system. The primary localization of developing cysticerci is the dilated lymphatic spaces in the skeletal muscles or the heart; localization in organs such as liver and lung results in degeneration of the larvae, as early as 20 days after ingestion (Slais 1970). Invasion of the heart muscle also is associated with a higher rate of aborted larval development although some do reach full development as cysticerci. During development, the larva develops a cavity and an immature scolex, and by 10–12 weeks after infection the cysticercus is infective for man. The infective cysticercus is composed of an invaginated scolex within a vesicle or bladder filled with fluid. The size is about 7–10 mm by 4–6 mm. The bladder wall is a multilayered complicated tissue and quite distinctive; the small bladder can be visible to the unaided eye as early as 10–14 days after infection (Voge 1963). The longevity of the cysticerci is reported to be as short as a few months and as long as 3 years (Penfold *et al.* 1937B; Van den Heever, 1967). Whether this variability reflects strain differences in host or parasite, or host immunity is not altogether clear (Soulsby 1965). Death of the cysticercus is accompanied by calcification (Neveu-Lemaire 1936). It is likely that only fresh, viable cysts containing clear fluid are infective for humans (Soulsby 1965).

Man appears to be the only definitive host for *T. saginata*. However, the cysticercus may develop successfully in domestic Bovidae and it has been suggested that certain species of Asian wild goats, African gazelle, and antelope are susceptible (Soulsby 1965). The reindeer of northern Siberia,

U.S.S.R. also has been shown to be a suitable intermediate host (Safronow 1960). Although suggestive findings are reported occasionally, there is no convincing evidence that man can serve also as an intermediate host for *T. saginata,* as is the case for *T. solium* (Pawlowski and Schultz 1972).

Epidemiology and Distribution. *Cysticercus bovis* is widespread in most cattle-rearing countries of the world. Prevalence data reported by individual countries are often misleading since the wide variability by region or province might be obscured by a single overall prevalence statistic. However, the global distribution of *T. saginata* in humans and in cattle has recently been summarized and reviewed by Pawlowski (1983B) and Van Kooy and Robijns (1968). The highly endemic areas are Central and East African countries, Caucasian and South-Central Asian U.S.S.R. republics, Near-East countries, and certain regions of Yugoslavia (Bosnia, Montenegro) (Urquhart 1961; Dada 1980; Schandevyl and Vercruysse 1982; Prokopenko 1968; Petrovic *et al.* 1982). Moderate infection rates are reported for Europe, Southeast Asia, and South America, while the United States, Canada, and Australia report low incidences of *T. saginata* (Soulsby 1965; Pawlowski 1983B; Snyder and Murrell 1983). Interestingly, the prevalence of *C. bovis* has increased in many developed countries since World War II. For example, in Germany, meat inspection data show that bovine cysticercosis increased from 0.37% in 1910 to 2% in 1960; in Halle and Frankfurt/Oder it was reported as 7% in the 1960s (Ockert 1965; Mielke 1969). Slaughterhouse data from Prague show the infection rate in cattle increased from 0.3% in 1945 to 3.1% in 1964 (Pawlowski and Schultz 1972). A sharp rise also was reported in England (Silverman 1955). In the United States, over the past 20 years 80% or more of infected cattle have originated from California, Arizona, New Mexico, and Texas, the four states bordering Mexico (Hird and Pullen 1979; Schultz 1971); the prevalence in California is about 20 times the national level (Schultz *et al.* 1970). By and large, the transmission of bovine cysticercosis in developed countries is sporadic and epizootic, while that in the less well developed countries and pastoral or nomadic communities is enzootic (Pawlowski 1983B).

The reasons for the persistence and, in some regions, increases in human and cattle infections with *T. saginata* are uncertain but it is suggested that population displacements due to wars, increased consumption of beef, especially rare beef, and stresses placed on sewage treatment plants are important factors (Greenberg and Dean 1958; Adonajlo *et al.* 1976; Hird and Pullen 1979).

Transmission of cysticerci to man is dependent upon the ingestion of raw or inadequately cooked beef. The human fondness for rare or semirare beef is especially pronounced in some regions (Pawlowski 1983B): beef tartar in the U.S.S.R., basterma in the Middle East, shish kebab in India, larb in Thailand, and raw or slightly roasted meat in Central and East Africa, especially in Ethiopia (Carmichael 1952). Hence, these regions tend to experience higher prevalences of infection. Because the adult *T. saginata* tapeworm can be very long-lived, the time span is sometimes limited only by that of the host (Pawlowski and Schultz 1972).

As pointed out above, man is a very prolific disseminator of eggs. The transmission of infective eggs may be direct or indirect. The direct mode occurs perhaps only occasionally when there is close attention of humans with their cattle. For example, human carriers might cause large outbreaks among feedlot cattle by handling and feeding cattle with contaminated hands (Urquhart 1961) or the passage of proglottids into the feed during feeding chores (Slonka *et al.* 1978), and by indiscriminate defecation in and around feed storage facilities.

Indirect transmission of infection from man to animals involves the contamination of the external environment, the accumulation and spread of infective eggs in it, and subsequent contamination of cattle feed and water (Pawlowski 1983B). Recent studies have implicated contamination of hayfields, hay, silage, and other feeds by infected farm workers (Schultz *et al.* 1969; Slonka *et al.* 1975). Hird and Pullen (1979) point out that the act of defecation might not be necessary for transmission of eggs because the proglottids of *T. saginata* are motile and might pass through the anus and expel eggs either around the perianal skin or drop unobserved to the ground, thus contaminating cattle feed. Another potentially important avenue of transmission is the contamination of field crops by irrigation water from workers defecating or washing in an irrigation ditch or canal (Guilhon 1975; Adonajlo *et al.* 1976). Defecation by infected humans on cattle pastures or the border hedge or thorn bush used as a latrine is an important factor in transmission in underdeveloped regions, especially East Africa (Soulsby 1965). Noteworthy are the findings of Ockert and Obst (1973) that examination of 10 infected persons yielded 68 onchospheres from fingernail dirt, up to 700 from water used for hand washing, and over 50,000 per liter of water used for soaking of underwear. Effluent from sewage treatment plants should be regarded as a potentially important source of eggs for environmental contamination, especially when used on agricultural lands. Taeniid eggs can survive many sewage treatment processes and pass still viable into the fluid effluent or dried sludge (Silverman and Griffiths 1955). This problem has been exacerbated by introduction in recent years of various chemicals and detergents in households and industry which inhibit the operation of the sewage treatment process. Outbreaks in the United States and Australia have been attributed to sewage effluent (Schultz *et al.* 1969; Rickard and Adolph 1977).

The survival and fate of taeniid eggs have been reviewed in detail by Gemmell and Johnstone (1977). Taeniid eggs are capable of surviving long periods in the environment and are resistant to moderate desiccation, disinfectants, and low temperatures (4°–5°C) (Froyd 1962). Some reports indicate that the eggs can remain infective for 4–6 months, depending on the moisture content of the microenvironment. For example, in liquid manure a longevity of 71 days, in river water 33 days, and on pasture 154 days was observed (Jepsen and Roth 1952).

Mechanical transmission by sea gulls, which have fed on raw sewage sludge, can contaminate pasture with eggs which pass through their digestive tracts (Silverman and Griffiths 1955). Potential mechanical transmission of eggs by sparrows, grackles, and pigeons also has been demonstrated by Dewhirst (1983). Other agents that can serve as mechanical vectors or hosts for the dissemination of taeniid eggs are earthworms (Lonc 1980) and carabid beetles (Bly et al. 1978). Recent reports from Australia suggest that the dispersal of taeniid eggs is rapid and occurs over considerable distances (up to 80 m within 10 days); this vigorous dissemination is probably aided, in addition to bird and arthropod agents, by the wind (Lawson 1980).

Prenatal infection of calves has been reported (McManus 1960; Slais and Mann 1976), but the importance of this infection route in the epidemiology of the infection is not clear (Hird and Pullen 1979).

The relative paucity of detail on the epidemiology of bovine cysticercosis is a concern to health and agricultural authorities and several aspects have been highlighted as needing more study (WHO-FAO 1976): factors that modify the infectivity and survival of eggs, the contributions of prenatal and neonatal infection to survival of cysticerci in cattle, the prevalence of antenatal infection in endemic areas, factors or agents which have an ovicidal effect during the processing of sewage, factors involved in the survival of cysticerci, and the influence of different environmental, husbandry, and social conditions.

Clinical Disease.   There are no pathognomonic symptoms of adult *T. saginata* infections in humans, making clinical diagnoses difficult. Pawlowski and Schultz (1972) analyzed the reports on over 3100 affected patients and concluded that the following were the most frequent symptoms observed: discharge of the proglottids (93.0%), abdominal pain (35.6%), nausea (34.4%), loss of weight (21.0%), change in appetite (17.0%), and headache (15.5%). About 50% of the patients exhibited a lowered volume and acidity of gastric secretion. The observed headache and occasionally observed anal irritability, urticarial skin rash, eosinophilia, and elevated levels of IgE might be due to allergic sensitization by the excretory-secretory products of the tapeworm (Nepote et al. 1974; Lapierre 1953); numerous antigens have been identified in the proglottids of *T. saginata* adults (Geerts et al. 1979). Examination of intestinal mucosa biopsy specimens often reveals slight inflammatory responses (Gasparov et al. 1962). Only rarely does the adult tapeworm cause severe gastrointestinal problems which require surgery. Among these instances are appendicitis and cholecystitis (Upton 1950; Kim et al. 1981).

Light or moderate infections are well tolerated in cattle and are not associated with any clear clinical picture. Heavy experimental infections are reported to induce fever, muscle stiffness, and degenerative myocarditis (Soulsby 1965; Pawlowski 1983B). The muscle tissue reactions to the parasite were described in detail by Machnicka et al. (1977) and are characterized by a cellular infiltrate around the cyst, primarily eosinophils and lymphoid cells. Necrosis frequently is associated with the inflammatory border. Blazek *et al.* (1982) observed that the tissue reactions in neonatal infections (calves less than 4 days old) differed in several respects from the responses around cysticerci in calves several months of age: the inflammatory foci were smaller, the cellular response was considerably less, eosinophils were lacking, and fewer lymphoid cells were seen. Of significance, the antibody response in these neonates was weak; Soulsby (1965) observed that cysts remained viable much longer in calves infected within a few days of birth than in calves infected at several months of age. Further, calves infected at a few days of birth could be reinfected with a challenge dose of eggs 10 months later, while calves first infected at 4 to 6 months of age were resistant to challenge infection suggesting to Soulsby (1965) that some degree of immunological tolerance was induced by early postnatal infection. However, epidemiological studies in East Africa have produced conflicting data and appear to show that dairy calves infected within a few weeks of life develop life-long immunity (Urquhart 1961). Interestingly, these animals often nurture the initial cysticerci for long periods, often up to 4 or 5 years of life; in contrast, others have reported that the developing immunity in cattle to infection can destroy the cysticerci within 9 months if the calves were mature at the time of initial infection (Penfold and Penfold 1937). Although the experimental data are scant, it appears that host age, infection size and, perhaps, *C. bovis* strain can influence the longevity of the cyst and host immunity (Urquhart 1961).

Diagnosis in Humans and Animals.   In the case of *T. saginata*, the segments have muscular activity and can migrate out of the anus into the underclothes. Such an event greatly facilitates diagnosis. The eggs are not shed continuously from the proglottids of *T. saginata* but rather are squeezed out as the proglottids break away from the main strobila of the tapeworm. Therefore, they are not distributed uniformly throughout the stool and stool examination is not as reliable for diagnosis as with other helminths. Thick fecal smear are accurate in 77% on single examination whereas simple sedimentation methods are less than 70% accurate. The anal swab method is very useful for *T. saginata* infections because of their motility and is effective in at least 85% of the cases.

Species identification of taeniid infections is important. This is done most commonly by pressing the proglottid between two glass slides and counting the uterine branches. In *T. saginata,* each segment contains 18 or more uterine branches, while, in contrast, *T. solium* segments usually have less than 12. Some parasitologists, at least, would dispute the reliability of basing the species' differentiation upon the number of uterine branches and insist that a more accurate identification should be based upon the structure of the rostellum or the ovaries, vaginal sphincter, and cirrus pouch of the mature segments.

Diagnosis in cattle normally is done at slaughter by direct inspection. Meat inspection personnel employ specific procedures to detect lesions of

C. bovis during postmortem inspection, procedures which involve the incision of muscle tissue and palpation of other tissues (Snyder and Murrell 1983). The external and internal masseter muscles are incised parallel to the plane of the mandible from the angle of jaw down to their attachments to the zygomatic process. The surfaces of these muscles are carefully examined for cysts of the parasite. The tongue is palpated from tip to base to detect embedded cysts in this organ. If cysts are suspected in the tongue, it is then incised. The heart is incised and the cut surfaces examined for the presence of *C. bovis* cysts. The cysts are usually found embedded in the cut surfaces, and rarely on the external or internal surfaces of the heart.

When a lesion of *C. bovis* is detected in a carcass, all carcasses represented by that lot are subjected to the following required procedures: Additional incisions are made in the external and internal masseter muscles and the heart and close observation is made of the esophagus and all cut surfaces of the carcass. If a lesion of *C. bovis* is detected, the carcass is subjected to further examination by a veterinarian to determine disposition of the carcass and viscera. The inspector thoroughly incises the lateral and medial masseter muscles, the heart, diaphragm, and pillars of the diaphragm; the tongue is carefully examined and incised if necessary. The esophagus and all exposed muscle surfaces also are carefully examined. If a cyst is discovered in any of these sites a transverse incision is made in each shoulder to expose the biceps brachii and a second incision is made in the round exposing a cross section of those muscles.

Carcasses in which lesions of *C. bovis* are detected are condemned for use as human food if the condition is considered extensive or the musculature of the carcass is discolored or edematous. Carcasses are considered extensively infected if lesions are discovered in two of the usual inspection sites (heart, diaphragm, masseter muscles, esophagus, tongue, or exposed musculation) and in two sites exposed by the incision through the shoulder and the round.

Carcasses with lesions not considered extensive are passed for human food as restricted carcasses. Such carcasses are subjected to heat or freezing requirements prescribed in the Federal meat inspection regulations. A carcass with a single lesion (dead or alive) is considered infected and is subjected to heat or freezing requirements.

The postmortem examination for cysticercosis is notoriously insensitive. Because cattle are often lightly infected, direct meat inspection misses many infections. Studies by Dewhirst *et al.* (1967) indicate that the error rate may be 25%, and in regions where cysticercosis infections are infrequent, inspectors might miss even a higher percentage. Because of this problem, efforts are being made to develop more reliable antemortem techniques for detection. Chief among these are serological methods. However, a specific, sensitive test for slaughterhouse use has not been developed. Although there have been developed tests such as complement fixation, immunofluorescence, counterimmunoelectrophoresis, indirect hemagglutination, immunodiffusion, and intradermal tests, all suffer from varying degrees of nonspecificity or lack of sensitivity (Gemmell and Johnstone 1977; Craig and Rickard 1981). The most promising method, however, is an enzyme-linked immunosorbent assay (ELISA). Until recently, it too lacked sufficient specificity to be reliable, especially in areas where the liver fluke, *Fasciola hepatica*, is endemic (Geerts *et al.* 1981). However, recent improvements in antigen purification have eliminated much of the ELISA's nonspecificity problems; importantly, the antigens can be derived from more available species of *Taenia*, such as *T. crassiceps* and *T. hydatigena* (Harrison and Sewell 1980, 1981; Geerts *et al.* 1981; Craig and Rickard 1980). Another important reason for the attractiveness of the ELISA is its adaptability to the automated equipment that would be necessary for large-scale use in modern packing houses.

The immunodiagnosis of bovine cysticercosis eventually might be useful also for the diagnosis of cattle on feedlots. Infected cattle could then be drug-treated before going to slaughter, thereby reducing the economic losses experienced by the producer. An additional benefit would be the improvement in epidemiological studies that attempt to identify the sources of transmission.

As pointed out by Pawlowski (1983B), the destruction of cysticerci in retained carcasses is an important problem which is not being addressed to the satisfaction of meat hygienists and economists. Cysticerci can be killed in meat by freezing at $-10°C$ for 10 days, the most common practice in the United States (Hird and Pullen 1979). However, 6 days at $-15°C$ is also sufficient to kill the cysticerci (Hilwig *et al.* 1978) and this shorter period might prove to be more economical. Alternatively, heating to temperatures above 56°C is allowed by USDA regulations for inactivation of cysticerci in meat. Salting is reported to be effective in rendering infected meat safe although there is some dispute about this (Jacobs 1962).

Gamma irradiation has been shown to be effective in killing *C. bovis* encysted in meat although the levels of radiation were very high (300 krads and above), levels which induced changes in the quality of the meat (Van Kooy and Robijns 1968; Pawel 1968). However, lower doses (10 krad) might inhibit the development of the cysticercus in the intestine of the definitive host (Taylor and Parfitt 1959). More research is needed to evaluate this procedure for postmortem control of cysticercosis in meat.

Treatment of Humans and Animals.   At present the drug of choice for human taeniasis is niclosamide, which has a reported efficacy of between 85 and 95% (Pawlowski 1970). There are few strict contraindications for its use except during the first trimester of pregnancy. More recently, a new drug, praziquantel, has been introduced and its potential appears to be very promising (Pawlowski 1983B). Single doses of 10 milligrams per kilogram in humans are up to 95% effective in removing tapeworms, including the scolex; failure to remove the scolex results in regeneration of the strobila. Importantly, praziquantel causes destruction and degeneration of the strobila without release of distal gravid proglottids and the side effects are minimal (Groll 1980).

Praziquantel and mebendazole both have been evaluated for treatment of cattle. Again, praziquantel appears to be the drug of choice. Subcutaneous injection or peroral administration of praziquantel at 100 mg/kg has been reported by several investigators to be 100% effective in killing all cysticerci present in cattle (Walther and Koske 1979). If praziquantel becomes economical for mass treatment of cattle, especially in enzootic areas, it could be a very effective control for prevention of transmission of infection to humans.

Prevention and Control.   One obvious method of interrupting transmission of *T. saginata* to cattle is to eliminate human infections. However, this is not an easy task anywhere, and efforts to have employees of cattle feedlot operations submit to examination and treatment by public health agencies have not enjoyed much success in the United States, probably because of certain sociological and legal problems associated with immigration status. In enzootic areas, some attempts at mass chemotherapy of humans have been attempted, with moderate success (Pawlowski 1983B). Permanent improvements in infection rates usually occur, however, when there are great improvements in sanitary and economic conditions, such as have occurred in Israel (Pawlowski and Schultz 1972). This general effect, aided by improvements in drug therapy for cysticercosis and taeniasis, improved meat inspection procedures and in public health education, appears to have the greatest potential for real control of bovine cysticercosis.

Some thought and research effort has been given to the idea of vaccination of cattle as a control (Rickard and Williams 1982). Although this approach would have little application in regions such as the United States, which experience only sporadic epizootic outbreaks, vaccination could have an important role in enzootic areas. Success has been achieved experimentally in instances in which older animals have been vaccinated orally with irradiated eggs (Urquhart 1966), and intramuscularly with onchospheres (Gallie and Sewell 1976) and excretory-secretory antigens derived by *in vitro* cultivation of onchospheres (Rickard and Adolph 1976). Calves appear more difficult to immunize, although they have been shown to be protected by maternal antibody via the colostrum when the dams were vaccinated with *in vitro* culture-derived antigens (Rickard *et al.* 1977). Moderate protection also has been obtained in mature cattle vaccinated with culture antigens or onchospheres of an ovine tapeworm, *T. hydatigena* (Wikerhauser *et al.* 1970; Rickard *et al.* 1982); the interest in this latter species lies in the greater availability of material for large-scale vaccine production. Although a candidate vaccine for commercial production has not yet emerged, the research on this is progressing, and the results offer some reasons for optimism.

Taenia solium: Pork Cysticercosis

Public Health Significance. The two parasites of major importance in taeniasis-cysticercosis are the tapeworms *Taenia solium* and *T. saginata,* both of which are obligatory parasites of the intestines of man. Both parasites and the infection caused by their larval stages (cysticercosis) are widespread; Stoll (1947) estimated that 39 million people were infected with *T. saginata* and 2.5 million with *T. solium* worldwide. However, these estimates were based on poor epidemiological information and most authorities today believe that taeniasis-cysticercosis is increasing in many countries (WHO-FAO 1976). Factors contributing to this probably relate to the worldwide increase in and intensification of livestock production and trade, large-scale intercountry migrations of people, the popularization of camping with the increase in promiscuous defecation, overtaxing of sewage treatment facilities, and increased use of sewage as fertilizer.

Although the adult stages of these tapeworms are generally innocuous in man, the larval or cysticercus stage of *T. solium (Cysticercus cellulosae)* can infect both man and pig (see pp. 349–359 for discussion of *T. saginata).* Man as an intermediate host for *T. solium* is vulnerable to very serious complications because the brain is a frequent site of localization. For this reason *T. solium* is considered a serious public health problem wherever it occurs.

Biology and Life Cycle. Details on the life cycle and biology of *T. solium* recently were reviewed by Pawlowski (1983B), Hird and Pullen (1979), and Verster (1969). The adult form of *T. solium* resembles closely that of *T. saginata* (see earlier). The length is a little shorter, usually less than 3 m, and is composed of fewer than 1000 proglottids. The mature proglottid, although similar to that of *T. saginata,* contains only about one-half the number of lateral uterine branches (7–13). The eggs are difficult to differentiate between the two species (Pawlowski 1983B). There are usually fewer than 50,000 eggs in a single *T. solium* proglottid and only about five segments are released daily, containing about 250,000 eggs (versus 750 million for *T. saginata*) (Webbe 1967). An important distinction is the lack of motility of *T. solium* proglottids which results in their being shed as connected segments; this presents a greater likelihood of massive infection in a single intermediate host such as a scavenging pig that consumes human feces (Hird and Pullen 1979).

Internal autoinfection leading to the development of human cysticercosis has been a long-held belief and is cited repeatedly by authors (Fig. 11.7). Pawlowski (1983B) and Webbe (1967) question whether this is a frequent occurrence, however. Experimentally, a short period of peptic digestion can prepare the onchosphere for tissue invasion and migration, but there is as yet little unequivocal data that eggs or gravid proglottids enter the stomach by vomiting or reverse peristalsis, a required step for

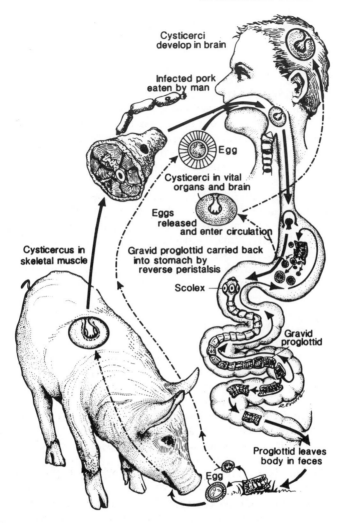

Cysticerci
develop in brain

Infected pork
eaten by man

Egg

Cysticerci in vital
organs and brain

Eggs
released
and enter circulation

Cysticercus in
skeletal muscle

Gravid proglottid carried back
into stomach by
reverse peristalsis

Scolex

Gravid
proglottid

Proglottid leaves
body in feces

Egg

FIG. 11.7.   Life cycle and transmission patterns of the pork tapeworm, *Taenia solium*.

true autoinfection to occur. Alternatively, man can become infected, like pigs, with the cysticercus stage by accidental ingestion of eggs (Fig. 11.7).

The distribution of the cysticercus stage within the body of the intermediate host (pig, man) has been studied by several authors (Yoshino 1933; Hsieh 1960; Acha and Aquilar 1964; Delfand and Jeffrey 1973). In pigs, the cysticerci are fairly evenly distributed throughout the liver, brain, skeletal muscle, and myocardium. A similar distribution appears to occur in humans, although there is frequent localization in the central nervous system. The cysticercus of *T. solium* is bigger than that of *T. saginata* (5–20 mm in diameter). After 2 to 3 months development, the cysticercus appears as a glistening pearly white cyst, with the scolex or head deeply invaginated into the fluid-filled bladder; the scolex bears four suckers and an apical crown of hooklets. When humans ingest infected pork, the larvae are digested out of the meat or tissue, the scoleces evaginate from the bladder, attach to the wall of the proximal portion of the ileum, and develop into a complete worm or strobila in about 3 months. The tapeworm begins to excrete proglottids after about 2 months and can live for many years.

The host specificity of *T. solium* is less restricted than that of *T. sanginata*. Although man is the natural definitive host, infections also can be established in subhuman primates and golden hamsters. In addition to the pig and, less frequently, man, a variety of other wild mammals have been reported as intermediate hosts, although the confirmation of some of these records is suspect (Pawlowski 1983B). There is evidence that there may be subspecies of *T. solium* with distinct host preferences (Heinz and Aron 1966).

Epidemiology and Distribution. In contrast to the distribution of *T. saginata*, *T. solium* infection is most prevalent in poor communities, and only rarely in highly developed countries. The world regions endemic for *T. solium* are Central and South America, Central and South Africa, Southeast Asia, and South and East Europe (FAO/WHO/OIE 1974). Pawlowski (1983B) has summarized the surveys for swine cysticercosis in these regions and the estimate is that about 3% of pigs in Central and South America are infected; Mexico has a rate of about 1%. In Southeast Asia, India, Thailand, Taiwan, and Korea appear to have the highest prevalences; one study in South Korea found 7.4% of the pigs infected on Cheju Do Island (Han 1969). Infection rates in the U.S.S.R. and East Europe have declined during the last 20 years to less than 1 in 10,000. It should be noted that the reported prevalences for both humans and swine are no doubt conservative because of the inherent difficulty of making specific diagnoses in humans and of detecting light infections in pigs using routine meat inspection procedures (Herbert and Oberg 1974). In the United States, only 6 of about 88 million hogs slaughtered in federally inspected plants were detected during 1981 (FSIS 1981). Human cysticercosis infections, however, have been on the rise in the United States in recent years (Schantz 1983B), probably attributable to the presence of a large immigrant population coming from Latin America, particularly Mexico.

The persistence of *T. solium*-cysticercosis in man and pigs is essentially due to social and economic factors, especially poor hygienic practices. Although internal autoinfection in people is probably infrequent, external autoinfection with eggs transmitted from anus to mouth or through dirty hands or contaminated food is more likely (Webbe 1967). Because of the generalized nature of larval infection in pigs, the ingestion of proglottids by scavenging pigs is probably the most common route of transmission to swine, although in comparison to bovine cysticercosis, epidemiologic data on infection of swine are poor. Information on the survival and spread of *T. solium* eggs in the external environment is also very limited. As pointed out by Pawlowski (1983B), the limiting factors for transmission are the smaller number of human carriers, coming primarily from rural communities, more restricted range of both human and pig hosts, and more frequent private uninspected slaughter of pigs and local consumption of most pork. Also important to the epidemiology of pork cysticercosis is the avoidance of eating raw pork compared to beef, especially among people having religious prohibitions of pork consumption (Moslems, Orthodox Jews). The well-established public health educational efforts to reduce transmission of trichinosis have undoubtedly also had some impact on reducing transmission of pork cysticercosis.

Another sources, as indicated for bovine cysticercosis, is the use of inadequately treated human excrement as fertilizer, either as sludge or liquefied for irrigation (Herbert and Oberg 1974).

Clinical Disease. Clinical disease associated with the adult form of *T. solium* is mild in man and similar to that of *T. saginata* (see earlier). Far more serious may be infection with the larval cysticercus form, especially, if the central nervous system is involved. Cerebral cysticercosis is usually classified according to its location: (1) ventricular-cisternal, (2) meningeal, (3) parenchymal, and (4) mixed. These localizations are often accompanied by a myriad of signs and symptoms, including seizures, hydrocephalus, headaches, dizziness, arterial thrombosis, loss of vision, and nausea (Grisolia and Wiederholt 1982). Cerebral cysticercosis is, on a worldwide basis, one of the most common parasitic diseases of the central nervous system.

Cysticerci which develop in the muscle tissues cause little or no pain unless they encroach on nerve endings, although when they die and calcify (1–20 years, according to Dixon and Hargreaves 1944) they can cause considerable inconvenience. Ocular cysticercosis, however, is a more frequent cause of clinical disease; the most common locations are vitreous humor and subretinal. The inflammatory response to the parasite may lead to retinal detachment or atrophy, iridocyclitis, and chorioiditis. Although myocardial cysticercosis frequently occurs in massive infections, clinical signs rarely result (Pawlowski 1983B).

The host pig response to the cysticercus is mild. Pathological manifestations are said to be associated with the death of the larvae and the release of antigens, although this can vary with the tissue type in which the cyst occurs (Herbert and Oberg 1974). Careful study of the cysticercus encysted in pig muscle by Willms and Merchant (1980) revealed that the cyst is surrounded by a prominent inflammatory response, similar to that described in the parenchyma of the central nervous system of the pig (Hernandez-Jauregui *et al.* 1973). The reaction corresponded to a chronic granuloma with many eosinophils. Little damage to the parasite membrane surface (tegument) was observed, prompting them to conclude that the host's inflammatory response can cause parasite damage only after a very long time.

Diagnosis in Humans and Animals.   Specific diagnosis of human intestinal infection with *T. solium* is solely dependent upon finding the scolex or proglottids in the stool since detecting the free eggs in a fecal examination or on an anal swab will not permit specific differentiation from *T. saginata;* however, the reliability of the number of lateral uterine branches as a taxonomic character has been questioned (Verster 1969). Routinely, a scolex can be found after drug treatment and with careful scrutiny an experienced observer can make a specific diagnosis. However, in regions in which *T. solium* is nearly absent and *T. saginata* common, and in cases where the number of uterine branches clearly exceed 20 on one side of a proglottid, diagnosis of the former is usually not troublesome (Pawlowski 1983B).

Diagnosis of human cysticercosis may require biopsy of nodules appearing as slight elevations of the skin. Ocular cysticercosis can be detected by opthalmoscopy. Computer tomography is now generally used to visualize the location and size of most cysticerci in the central nervous system.

Immunodiagnosis of human cysticercosis also is complicated by a variable or weak immune response to the cysticerci, especially to those localized in the central nervous system (Flisser *et al.* 1980). The immunological impairment or immunomodulation of the immune response in humans has been suggested (Flisser 1980). Recently, a solid-phase radioimmunoassay using protein A and tested on both sera and CSF of patients was reported to provide good agreement with diagnosis made by other means (Heiner *et al.* 1982). A major problem with many serologic tests employing crude extracts of adult or larval *T. solium* is a high degree of nonspecificity (Schantz *et al.* 1980; Diwan *et al.* 1982). Currently, efforts are being made to improve the specificity of these tests by antigen purification procedures (Flisser *et al.* 1980), and it is possible that a suitable serologic test can be developed.

Currently, serologic detection of infection in pigs is even more unreliable, since they exhibit unacceptable levels of sensitivity and specificity (Pawlowski 1983B). It can be expected that this situation will also be alleviated by improvements in the immunodiagnosis of human cysticercosis.

At present, direct meat inspection by organoleptic means is the only acceptable diagnostic procedure for pork cysticercosis. Fortunately, postmortem detection of cysticercosis in swine is easier than in cattle because lightly infected carcasses are more infrequent, making detection easier (Hird and Pullen 1979).

Treatment of Humans and Animals. The drug of choice for the adult tapeworm is niclosamide (Yomesan) (Pawlowski and Schultz 1972). More recently, praziquantel in single doses of 10 mg/kg has been highly effective (Rim *et al.* 1979). In addition, praziquantel is reported to be effective in humans against taeniidae cysticerci. It is important that humans found to be infected be treated immediately and kept isolated until free of the intestinal infection because of the danger of spreading the infection.

Several drugs have now been found to be effective against the cysticerci in pigs: praziquantel (Liu 1981), flubendazole (Tellez-Giron *et al.* 1981), and fenbendazole (Cho *et al.* 1982). In countries such as Mexico where in some regions the prevalence in pigs may exceed 4 or 5%, representing a considerable economic loss because of carcass rejections, the application of mass chemotherapy on swine operations might be justifiable.

Prevention and Control. The most promising approach toward interrupting transmission from man to animals in those areas in which improvements in sanitation and living standards cannot be expected to occur quickly is to detect and treat all infected humans. Although the limitations associated with mass diagnoses are not inconsiderable, this approach has had some success in East Europe and the U.S.S.R. (Pawlowski and Schultz 1972). Also of potentially great value in endemic regions would be the institution and enforcement of veterinary meat inspection. Infected carcasses should be condemned or boiled until the whole carcass turns grey. Freezing at −10°C for at least 14 days is generally accepted for rendering pork incapable of transmitting cysticerci, although, recently, Robinson and Chambers (1976) reported that under blast-freezing conditions complete devitalization of pork cysticerci could be achieved at −15°C for 75 min. Some research has been carried out on inactivating cysticerci in pork by gamma irradiation, but the data are too incomplete to permit any recommendations (Pawel 1968; Verster *et al.* 1976). The consensus among most authorities is that real control of *T. solium,* while being aided by meat inspection, etc., will not be adequately achieved without fundamental changes in the economic, social, and sanitary conditions in endemic areas.

SUMMARY

The problems of food-borne parasite are receiving greater concern as public health authorities and food scientists become more informed of recent revelations about their occurrence and implications in human disease. The association between some of these parasites and clinical illness has only recently been established. Other, more well-known parasites, continue to frustrate efforts to eradicate them from the food supply. It is the intent of this chapter to present the salient aspects of these parasites related to their distribution, transmission, biology, pathogenesis, and treatment. Special emphasis is placed on needs for further research and on critical evaluation of current control efforts.

REFERENCES

ACHA, P. N. and AGUILAR, F. J.   1964.   Studies on cysticercosis in Central America and Panama. Am. J. Trop. Med. Hyg. *13*, 48.

ADONAJLO, A., KOZAKIEWICZ, B., PAWLOWSKI, Z. S. and ROKOSSOWSKI, H.   1976.   Transmission fo *Taenia saginata* in rural areas. Wiad. Parazytol. *22*, 499.

ALI KAHN, A.   1966.   The post-embryonic development of *Trichinella spiralis* with special reference to ecdysis. J. Parasitol. *52*, 248.

AL-KHALIDI, N. and DUBEY, J. P.   1979.   Prevalence of *Toxoplasma gondii* infection in horses. J. Parasitol. *65*, 331.

ALICATA, J.   1970.   Trichinosis in the Pacific Islands and adjacent areas. *In* Trichinosis in Man and Animals. p. 465. S. E. Gould (Editor). Charles C. Thomas, Springfield, IL.

ANDREWS, J. S., ZINTER, D. E., and SCHULZ, N. E.   1969.   Evaluation of the trichinosis pilot project. Proc. 73rd Ann. Mtg. U.S. Anim. Health. Assoc., p. 332.

ANDY, J. J., O'CONNELL, J. P., DADDARIO, R. C. and ROBERTS, W. C.   1977.   Trichinosis causing extensive ventricular mural endocarditis with superimposed thrombosis. Am. J. Med. *63*, 824.

BECK, J. W.   1970.   Trichinosis in domesticated and experimental animals. *In* Trichinosis in Man and Animals. Chap. III, p. 61. S. E. Gould (Editor). Charles C. Thomas, Springfield, IL.

BELLANI, L., MANTOVANI, A., PAMPIGLIONE, S. and FILIPPINI, I.   1978.   Observations on an outbreak of human trichinellosis in northern Italy. *In* Trichinellosis. p. 534. C. W. Kim and Z. S. Pawlowski (Editors). University Press of New England, Hanover, NH.

BELOSEVIC, M. and DICK, T. A.   1980.   Chemical attraction in the genus *Trichinella*. J. Parasitol. *66*, 88.

BESSONOV, A. S.   1980.   Changes in the epizootic and epidemic situation of trichinellosis in the USSR. *In* Trichinellosis. p. 365. C. W. Kim, E. J. Ruitenberg, and J. S. Teppema (Editors). Reedbooks, Chertsey, England.

BLAZEK, K., SCHRAMLOVA, J. and KURSA, J.   1982.   Pathology of neonatal infection of calves with *Cysticercus bovis*. Folia Parasitol. (Praha) *29*, 147.

BLY, S., STERBA, J. and DYKOVA, I.   1978.   Results of an artificial feeding of eggs of *Taenia saginata* Goetz, 1782 to various beetle species. Folia Parasitol. (Praha) *25*, 257.

BOEV, S. N. and SOKOLOVA, L. A.   1981.   Primary diagnostics of sibling-species of Trichinellae. Wiad. Parazytol. *27*, 483.

BONE, L. W.   1982.   Chemotaxis of parasitic nematodes. *In* Cues That Influence Behavior of Internal Parasites. p. 52. W. S. Bailey (Editor). Agricultural Research Service, U.S. Department of Agriculture, New Orleans, LA.

BONNER, T. P. and ETGES, F. J.   1967.   Chemically mediated attraction in *Trichinella spiralis*. Exp. Parasitol. *21*, 53.

BRITOV, V. A. and BOEV, S. N.   1972.   Taksonomicheskii rang trichinell razlichnykh shtammov i kharakter ikh tsirkuliatsii. Vest Akad. Nauk Kaz SSR *28*, 27 (in Russian).

BUNYARATVEJ, S., BUNYAWONGWIROJ, P., and NITIYANANT, P.   1982.   Human intestinal sarcosporidiosis. Report of 6 cases. Am. J. Trop. Med. Hyg. *31*, 36.

CAIRNS, G. C.   1966.   The occurrence of *Trichinella spiralis* in New Zealand pigs, rats and cats. New Z. Vet. J. *14*, 84.

CAMERON, T. W. M.   1970.   Trichinosis in Canada. *In* Trichinosis in Man and Animals. p. 374. S. E. Gould (Editor). Charles C. Thomas, Springfield, IL.

CAMPBELL, W. C.   1979.   History of trichinosis: Paget, Owen and the discovery of *Trichinella spiralis*. Bull. Hist. Med. *53,* 520.

CAMPBELL, W. C.   1983.   Epidemiology I: Modes of transmission. *In Trichinella* and Trichinosis. Chap. 13, p. 425. W. C. Campbell (Editor). Plenum Press, NY.

CAMPBELL, W. C. and DENHAM, D. A.   1983.   Chemotherapy. *In Trichinella* and Trichinosis. Chap. 10, p. 335. W. C. Campbell (Editor). Plenum Press, NY.

CARLIN, F., ZIMMERMAN, W. and SUNDBERG, A.   1982.   Destruction of trichina larvae in beef-pork loaves cooked in microwave ovens. J. Food Sci. *47,* 1096.

CARMICHAEL, J.   1952.   Animal-man relationships in tropical diseases in Africa. Trans. Roy. Soc. Trop. Med. Hyg. *46,* 385.

CASTRO, G. A. and BULLOCK, G. R.   1983.   Pathophysiology of the gastrointestinal phase. *In Trichinella* and Trichinosis. Chap. 6 p. 209. W. C. Campbell (Editor). Plenum Press, NY.

CASTRO, G. R., JOHNSON, L. R., COPELAND, E. M. and DUDRICK, S. J.   1976.   Course of infection with enteric parasites in host shifted from enteral to parenteral nutrition. J. Parasitol. *62,* 353.

ČATÁR, G., BERGENDI, L. and HOLKOVÁ, R.   1964.   Isolation of *Toxoplasma gondii* from swine and cattle. J. Parasitol. *55,* 952.

CENTERS FOR DISEASE CONTROL.   1982.   Common-source outbreaks of trichinosis–New York City, Rhode Island, Morbidity Mortality Weekly Rep. *31,* 61.

CHO, K. M., ARAKI, T., TAKAICHI, S., SEGAWA, T., SHIINA, T. and YAMADA, S.   1982.   Fenbendazole in *Cysticercus cellulosae*. Proc. Intern. Pig Vet. Soc. Congr., Mexico, p. 179.

CIRONEANU, I.   1974.   Trichinellosis in domestic and wild animals in Rumania. *In* Trichinellosis. p. 549. C. Kim (Editor). Intext Educational Publishers, NY.

CLAUSEN, B.   1978.   Ecological factors in spreading *Trichinella spiralis* in Denmark. *In* Trichinellosis. p. 541. C. W. Kim, and Z. S. Pawlowski (Editors). University Press of New England, Hanover, NH.

CRAIG, P. S. and RICKARD, M. D.   1980.   Evaluation of "crude" antigen prepared from *Taenia saginata* for the serological diagnosis of *T. saginata* cysticercosis in cattle using the enzyme-linked immunosorbent assay (ELISA). Z. Parasitenk. *61,* 287.

CRAIG, P. S. and RICKARD, M. D.   1981.   Studies on the specific immunodiagnosis of larval cestode infections of cattle and sheep using antigens purified by affinity chromatography in an enzyme-linked immunosorbent assay (ELISA). Intern. J. Parasitol. *11,* 441.

DADA, B. J. O.   1980.   Taeniasis, cysticercosis and echinococcosis/hydatidosis in Nigeria: III. Prevalence of bovine and porcine cysticercosis, and hydatid cyst infection based on joint examination of slaughtered food animals. J. Helminthol. *54,* 293.

DESPOMMIER, D. D.   1975.   Adaptive changes in muscle fibers infected with *Trichinella spiralis*. Am. J. Pathol. *78,* 477.

DESPOMMIER, D. D.   1977.   Immunity to *Trichinella spiralis*. Am. J. Trop. Med. Hyg. *26,* 68.

DESPOMMIER, D. D.   1982.   Behavioral cues in migration and location of parasitic nematodes, with special emphasis on *Trichinalle spiralis*. *In* Cues That Influence Behavior of Internal Parasites. p. 110. W. S. Barley (Editor). Agricultural Research Service, U.S. Department of Agriculture, New Orleans, LA.

DESPOMMIER, D. D.   1983A.   Biology. *In Trichinella* and Trichinosis. Chap. 3, p. 75. W. C. Campbell (Editor). Plenum Press, NY.

DESPOMMIER, D. D.   1983B.   Private communication. School of Public Health, Columbia University, NY.

DESPOMMIER, D. D. and LACCETTI, A.   1981A.   *Trichinella spiralis:* Partial characterization of antigens isolated by immunoaffinity chromatography from the large-particle fraction of the muscle larvae. J. Parasitol. *67*, 332.

DESPOMMIER, D. D. and LACCETTI, A.   1981B.   *Trichinella spiralis:* Proteins and antigens isolated from a large-particle fraction derived from the muscle larva. Exp. Parasitol. *51*, 279.

DESPOMMIER, D. D. and MÜLLER, M.   1976.   The stichosome and its secretion granules in the mature muscle larva of *Trichinella spiralis.* J. Parasitol. *62*, 775.

DESPOMMIER, D. D., SUKHEDO, M., and MEEROVITCH, E.   1978.   *Trichinella spiralis:* Site selection by the larva during the enteral phase of infection in mice. Exp. Parasitol. *44*, 209.

DEWHIRST, L.   1983.   Personal communication. Agricultural Experiment Station, University of Arizona, Tucson, AZ.

DEWHIRST, L. W., CRAMER, J. D. and SHELDON, J. J.   1967.   An analysis of current inspection procedures for detecting bovine cysticercosis. J. Am. Vet. Med. Assoc. *150*, 412.

DICK. T. A.   1983.   Species and infraspecific variation. *In Trichinella* and Trichinosis. Chap. 2, p. 31. W. C. Campbell (Editor). Plenum Press, NY.

DICK, T. A. and CHADEE, K.   1981.   Biological characterization of some North American isolates of *Trichinella spiralis. In* Trichinellosis. p. 23. C. W. Kim, E. J. Ruitenberg, and T. S. Teppema (Editors) Reedbooks, Surrey, England.

DICK, T. A. and CHADEE, K.   1983.   Interbreeding and gene flow in the genus *Trichinella.* J. Parasitol. *69*, 176.

DIENST, R. B. and VERMA, M. P.   1965.   Isolation of Toxoplasma from salivary glands and saliva of pigs with asymptomatic infections. Am. J. Trop. Med. Hyg. *14*, 558.

DISSAMARAN, R. and ARANYAKANADA, P.   1974.   Surveillance of trichinosis in Thailand. J. Thai. Vet. Med. Assoc. *26*, 29.

DIWAN, A. R., COKER-VANN, M., BROWN, P., SUBIANTO, D. B., YOLKER, R., DESOWITZ, R., ESCOBAR, A., GIBBS, C. and GAJDUSEK, D. C.   1982.   Enzyme-linked immunosorbent assay (ELISA) for the detection of antibody to cysticerci of *Taenia solium.* Am. J. Trop. Med. Hyg. *31*, 364.

DIXON, H. B. F. and HARGREAVES, W. H.   1944.   Cysticercosis (*Taenia solium*). Quart. J. Med. *13*, 107.

DUBEY, J. P.   1977.   *Toxoplasma, Hammondia, Besnoitia, Sarcocystis,* and other tissue cyst-forming coccidia of man and animals. *In* Parasitic Protozoa. Vol. 3. p. 101. J. P. Kreier (Editor). Academic Press, NY.

DUBEY, J. P.   1982.   Repeat transplacental transfer of *Toxoplasma gondii* in dairy goats. J. Amer. Vet. Med. Assoc. *180*, 1220.

DUBEY, J. P.   1983.   Distribution of *Toxoplasma* cysts and tachyzoites in cattle inoculated with *Toxoplasma gondii* oocysts. Vet. Parasitol. *13*, 199.

DUBEY, J. P.   1984.   Experimental toxoplasmosis in sheep fed *Toxoplasma gondii* oocysts. Intern. Goat Sheep Res. *2*, 93.

DUBEY, J. P.   1985.   Persistence of encysted *Toxoplasma gondii* in tissues of equids fed oocysts. Am. J. Vet. Res. *46*, 1753.

DUBEY, J. P. and FAYER, R.   1983.   Sarcocystosis. Brit. Vet. J. *139*, 371.

DUBEY, J. P. and STREITEL, R. H.   1976.   Prevalence of *Toxoplasma* infection in cattle slaughtered at an Ohio abbatoir. J. Am. Vet. Med. Assoc. *169*, 1197.

DUBEY, J. P., MURRELL, K. D., and FAYER, R.   1984.   Persistence of encysted *Toxoplasma gondii* in tissues of pigs fed oocysts. *45*, 1941. USDA–ARS, Beltsville Agricultural Research Center, Beltsville, MD.

EL-NAWAWI, F. A.   1981.   Swine trichinellosis in Egypt. Arch. Lebensmittelhyg. *32*, 156.

EYLES, D. E., GIBSON, C. L., COLEMAN, N., SMITH, C. S., JUMPER, J. R., and JONES, F. E.   1959.   The prevalence of toxoplasmosis in wild and domestic animals of the Memphis region. Am. J. Trop. Med. *8*, 505.

FAO/WHO/OIE.   1974.   Animal Health Yearbook for 1973. Food and Agriculture Organization, Rome, Italy.

FAYER, R.   1981.   Toxoplasmosis update and public health implications. Canad. Vet. J. *22*, 344.

FAYER, R. and FRENKEL, J. K.   1979.   Comparative study for calves of oocysts of feline coccidia: *Besnoitia, Hammondia, Cystoisospora, Sarcocystis*, and *Toxoplasma* J. Parasitol. *65*, 756.

FLISSER, A.   1980.   The immunology of human cysticercosis. *In* Molecules, Cells and Parasites in Immunology. p. 125. C. Larradle, K. Willms, L. Ortiz-Ortiz, and M. Sela (Editors). Academic Press, NY.

FLISSER, A., WOODHOUSE, E. and LARRALDE, C.   1980.   Human cysticercosis: antigens, antibodies, and non-responders. Clin. Exp. Immunol. *39*, 27.

FLOCKHART, H. A., HARRISON, S. E., DOBINSON, A. R. and JAMES, E. R.   1982. Enzyme polymorphism in *Trichinella*. Trans. Roy. Soc. Trop. Med. Hyg. *76*, 541.

FORRESTER, A. T. T., NELSON, G. S. and SANDER, G.   1961.   The first record of an outbreak of trichinosis in Africa, South of the Sahara. Trans. Roy. Soc. Trop. Med. Hyg. *55*, 503.

FRENKEL, J. K.   1973.   Toxoplasmosis. Parasite life cycle, pathology and immunology. *In* The Coccidia. p. 343. D. M. Hammond (Editor). University Park Press, Baltimore, MD.

FRENKEL, J. K. and RUIZ, A.   1980.   Human toxoplasmosis and cat contact in Costa Rica. Am. J. Trop. Med. Hyg. *29*, 1167.

FROYD, G.   1962.   Longevity of *Taenia saginata* eggs. J. Parasitol. *48*, 279.

FSIS.   1981.   Statistical Summary: Federal Meat and Poultry Inspection for Fiscal Year 1981. USDA, Washington, DC.

FSQS.   1973.   Meat and Poultry Inspection Regulations. p. 125. Food Safety and Quality Service, USDA, Washington, DC.

GALLIE, G. and SEWELL, M.   1976.   Experimental immunization of six-month-old calves against infection with the cysticercus stage of *Taenia saginata*. Trop. Anim. Health Prod. *8*, 233.

GAMBLE H. R. and GRAHAM, C. E.   1983.   Immunodiagnostic antigens for swine trichinosis isolated using monoclonal antibodies. Am. J. Vet. Res. *45*, 67.

GAMBLE, H. R., ANDERSON, W. R., GRAHAM, C. E. and MURRELL, K. D.   1983. Serodiagnosis of swine trichinosis using an excretory-secretory antigen. Vet. Parasitol. *13*, 349.

GARDINER, C. H.   1976.   Habitat and reproductive behavior of *Trichinella spiralis*. J. Parasitol. *62*, 865.

GARKAVI, B. L.   1972.   *Trichinella* ot enota poloskuna in Mat-ly dokl. Vsesouizn. Konf. po probleme trikheinellez cheloveka i zhivotnykh., Vil'nius, AN Litov. SSR. p. 53.

GASPAROV, A., SMIRCIC, P. and FILIPOVIC, B.   1962.   Morphological changes in the mucosa of the small intestine in taeniasis. Med. Pregl. *15*, 451.

GEERTS, S., KUMAR, V. and AERTS, N.   1979.   Antigenic components of *Taenia saginata* and their relevance to the diagnosis of bovine cysticercosis by immunoelectrophoresis. J. Helminthol. *53*, 293.

GEERTS, S., KUMAR, V., CEULEMANS, F., AND MORTELMANS, J.   1981. Serodiagnosis of *Taenia saginata* cysticercosis in experimentally and naturally infected cattle by enzyme linked immunosurbent assay. Res. Vet. Sci. *30*, 288.

GEERTS, S., KUMAR, V., and VAN DEN ABBECLE, O.   1980.   *Taenia saginata* cysticercosis in Belgium. VI. Tijdschr. Diergeneesk. *49*, 365.

GELFAND, M. and JEFFREY, C.   1973.   Cerebral cysticercosis in Rhodesia. J. Trop. Med. Hyg. *76*, 4.

GEMMELL, M. A. and JOHNSTONE, P. D.   1977.   Experimental epidemiology of hydatidosis and cysticercosis. Advan. Parastiol. *15*, 311.

GIBBS, H. C., MacQUEEN, K. F., and PULLIN, J. W.   1964.   Further studies of the effects of gamma radiation on pork infected with *Trichinella spiralis*. Canad. J. Publ. Health *55*, 191.

GIBSON, T. E.   1958.   The transmission of trichinosis by butchers' knives. Ann. Trop. Med. Parasitol. *52,* 48.
GOULD, S. E.   1970A.   History. *In* Trichinosis in Man and Animals. p. 3. S. E. Gould (Editor). Charles C. Thomas, Springfield, IL.
GOULD, S. E.   1970B.   Anatomic pathology, Ch. 9. *In* Trichinosis in Man and Animals. p. 147. S. E. Gould (Editor). Charles C. Thomas, Springfield, IL.
GOULD, S. E., VAN DYKE, J. G. and GOMBERG, H. J.   1952.   Effect of X-rays on Trichina larva. Proc. 49th Ann. Mtg. Am. Assoc. Pathol. Bacteriol. p. 323.
GREENBERG, A. E. and DEAN, B. H.   1958.   The beef tapeworm, measly beef and sewage—A review. Sewage Ind. Wastes *30,* 262.
GRINDLE, R. J.   1978.   Economic losses resulting from bovine cysticercosis with special reference to Botswana and Kenya. Trop. Anim. Health Prod. *10,* 127.
GRISOLIA, J. S. and WIEDERHOLT, W. C.   1982.   CNS cysticercosis. Arch. Neurol. *39,* 540.
GROLL, E.   1980.   Praziquantel for cestode infections in man. Acta Trop. *37,* 293.
GROVE, D. I., HAMBURGER, J. and WARREN, K. S.   1977.   Kinetics of immunological responses, resistance to reinfection, and pathological reactions to infections with *Trichinella spiralis.* J. Infect. Dis. *136,* 562.
GUILHON, J.   1975.   Le rôle de la pollution hydrique dans l'étiologie et l'épidemiologie de la cysticercose bovine et du téniasis humain. Rec. Med. Vet. *151,* 39.
HALL, M. C.   1937.   Studies on Trichinosis. IV. The role of the garbage-fed hog in the production of human trichinosis. Publ. Health Rep. *52,* 873.
HALL, M. C. and COLLINS, B. J.   1937.   Studies on trichinosis. II. Some correlations and implications in connection with incidence of trichinae found in 300 diaphragms. Publ. Health Rep. *52,* 512.
HAN, H. R.   1969.   A survey on *Cysticercosis cellulosae* infection in swine of Cheju-Do. Korean J. Publ. Health *6,* 23.
HARLEY, J. P. and GALLICCHO, V.   1971.   *Trichinella spiralis:* Migration of larvae in the rat. Exp. Parasitol. *30,* 11.
HARRISON, L. J. S. and SEWELL, M. M. H.   1980.   The antigenic activity of chromatographic fractions of saline extract of *Taenia saginata* (Goezt, 1782) proglottids. Vet. Immunol. Immunopathol. *1,* 361.
HARRISON, L. J. S. and SEWELL, M. M. H.   1981.   A comparison of the enzyme linked immunosorbent assay and the indirect hemagglutination technique applied to sera from cattle experimentally injected with *Taenia saginata* (Goezt, 1782). Vet. Immunol. Immunopathol. *2,* 67.
HARVEY, P. W. and KERSHAW, W. E.   1964.   Low incidence of latent trichinosis near Blackpool compared with incidence elsewhere in England and Wales. Brit. Med. J. *2,* 1632.
HEINER, D. C., MILLER, B., GOLDBERG, M. A., and MEYERS, A.   1982.   A new diagnostic test for cerebral cysticercosis. Pediat. Res. *16 (4 part 2),* 223A.
HEINZ, H. J. and ARON, L.   1966.   Studies on *Cysticercus cellulosae.* S. Afr. J. Med. Sci. *31,* 61.
HERBERT, I. V. and OBERG, C.   1974.   Cysticercosis in pigs due to infection with *Taenia solium* Linnaeus, 1758. *In* Parasitic Zoonoses. p. 199. E. J. L. Soulsby, (Editor), Academic Press, NY.
HERNANDEZ-JAUREGUI, P. A., MARGUEZ-MONTER, H. and SASTRE-ORTIZ, S.   1973.   Cysticercosis of the central nervous system in hogs. Am. J. Vet. Res. *34,* 451.
HERRERA, J. L.   1979.   Estudio sobre preferente localizacion de larvas de *Trichinella spiralis* (Owen 1835) en los musculos del cerdo *(Sus scrofa domestica).* Rev. Iber. Parasitol. *39,* 233.
HILL, C. H.   1957.   Distribution of larvae of *T. spiralis* in the organs of experimentally infected swine. J. Parasitol. *43,* 574.
HILWIG, R. W., CRAMER, J. D. and FORSYTH, K. S.   1978.   Freezing times and temperatures required to kill cysticerci of *Taenia saginata* in beef. Vet. Parasitol. *4,* 215.

HIRD, D. W. and PULLEN. M. M.   1979.   Tapeworms, meat and man: A brief review and update of cysticercosis caused by *Taenia saginata* and *Taenia solium*. J. Food. Prot. *42*, 58.

HSIEH, H. C.   1960.   Experimental transmission of *Cysticercus cellulose* in Taiwan monkey (*Macacus cyclopis*) (Swinhoe, 1862). Formosan Sci. *14*, 66.

HUGHES, W. L. and HARLEY, J. P.   1977.   *Trichinella spiralis:* Taxes of the first-stage migratory larvae. Exp. Parasitol. *42*, 363.

JACOBS, L.   1962.   Parasites in food. *In* Chemical and Biological Hazards in Food. Chap. 14, p. 248. J. C. Ayres, A. A. Kraft, H. E. Snyder, and H. W. Walker (Editors). Iowa State University Press, Ames, IA.

JACOBS, L.   1973.   New knowledge of toxoplasmosis. Advan. Parasitol. *11*, 631.

JACOBS, L. and MELTON, M. L.   1966.   Toxoplasmosis in chickens. J. Parasitol. *52*, 1158.

JACOBS, L., REMINGTON, J. S. and MELTON, M. L.   1960.   A survey of meat samples from swine, cattle and sheep for the presence of encysted *Toxoplasma*. J. Parasitol. *46*, 23.

JEFFRIES, J. C., BEAL, V., JR., MARTISHAW, T. R. and ZIMMERMAN, W. J.   1966. Proc. 70th Ann. Mtg. U.S. Lvstk. Sanit. Assoc., p. 349.

JEPSEN, A. and ROTH, H.   1952.   Epizootiology of *Cysticercus bovis*—resistance of the eggs of *Taenia saginata*. Proc. 14th Intern. Vet. Congr. London *2*, 43.

KEAN, B. H., KIMBALL, A. C., and CHRISTENSON, W. N.   1969.   An epidemic of acute toxoplasmosis. J. Am. Med. Assoc. *108*, 1002.

KIM, C. W.   1983.   Geographic distribution and prevalence. *In* Trichinella and Trichinosis. Chap. 14, p. 445. W. C. Campbell (Editor). Plenum Press, NY.

KIM, Y. H., CHI, J. G. and CHO, S-Y.   1981.   A case of *Taenia saginata* infection involving gallbladder and common bile duct. Korean J. Parasitol. *19*, 167.

KOCIECKA, W., VAN KNAPEN, F., RUITENBERG, E. J., GELEIJNSE, M. E. M. and TERLINGEN, J. B. A.   1981.   *Trichinella pseudospiralis* and *T. spiralis* infection in monkeys. II. Clinical aspects. *In* Trichinellosis. p. 205. C. W. Kim, E. J. Ruitenberg, and J. S. Teppma (Editors). Reedbooks, Ltd., Surrey, England.

KOTULA, A. W. and MURRELL, K. D.   1981.   Unpublished data. USDA-ARS, Beltsville Agricultural Research Center, Beltsville, MD.

KOTULA, A. W., MURRELL, K. D., ACOSTA-STEIN, L., LAMB, L. and DOUGLAS, L.   1983A.   Destruction of *Trichinella spiralis* during cooking. J. Food Sci. *48*, 765.

KOTULA, A. W., MURRELL, K. D., ACOSTA-STEIN, L., LAMB, L. and DOUGLAS, L.   1983B.   *Trichinella spiralis:* Effect of high temperature on infectivity in pork. Exp. Parasitol. *55*, 15.

KOTULA, A. W., MURRELL, K. D., ACOSTA-STEIN, L. and TENNENT, I.   1982. Influence of rapid cooking methods on the survival of *Trichinella spiralis* in pork chops from experimentally infected pigs. J. Food. Sci. *47*, 1006.

KOVALCHUK, E. S.   1981.   Ecological questions of speciation in *Trichinella*. Ekologiya *5*, 67.

KOZAR, Z.   1969.   Incidence of Trichinellosis in Poland and Its Control. PWRIL, Warszawa.

KOZAR, Z.   1970.   Trichinosis in Europe. *In* Trichinosis in Man and Animals. p. 423. S. E. Gould (Editor). Charles C. Thomas, Springfield, IL.

KOZEK, W. J.   1971.   The molting pattern of *Trichinella spiralis*. I. A light microscope study. J. Parasitol. *57*, 1015.

KOZEK, W. J.   1976.   *Trichinella spiralis:* Size of F_1 generations produced in mice by transplanted females or from infections with known numbers of male and female larvae. Rev. Biol. Trop. *24*, 175.

LAPIERRE, J.   1953.   Un cas d'eosinophilie exceptionnellement éleucé au cours d'un taeniasis à *Taenia saginata*. Ann. Parasitol. Hum. Comp. *28*, 126.

LARSH, J. E., JR.   1963.   Experimental Trichiniasis. Advan. Parasitol. *1*, 213.

LARSH, J. E. and RACE, G. J.   1975.   Allergic inflammation as a hypothesis for the expulsion of worms from tissues. A review. Exp. Parasitol. *37*, 251.

LAWSON, R. 1980. The dispersal of taeniid eggs. New Z. J. Zool. 7, 606.

LEIGHTY, J. C. 1983. Regulatory action to control *Trichinella spiralis*. Food Technol. 37, 95.

LEVINE, N. D. 1973. Protozoan Parasites of Domestic Animals and of Man. Burgess Publ. Co., Minneapolis, MN.

LEVINE, N. D. 1978. Unpublished data. University of Illinois, Urbana.

LICHTENFELS, J. R., MURRELL, K. D. and PILITT, P. A. 1983. Comparison of three subspecies of *Trichinella spiralis* with scanning electron microscopy. J. Parasitol. 69, 1131.

LIU, X. G. 1981. Treatment of *Cysticercosis cellulosae* with praziquantel. Lianoning Anim. Husb. Vet. Med. No. 4, p. 32.

LJUNGSTRÖM, I. 1983. Immunodiagnosis in man. *In* Trichinella and Trichinosis. Chap. 12, p. 403. W. C. Campbell (Editor). Plenum Press, NY.

LONC, E. 1980. The possible role of the soil fauna in the epizootiology of cysticercosis in cattle. I. Earthworms—the biotic factor in a transmission of *Taenia saginata* eggs. Angew. Parasitol. 21, 133.

MACHNICKA, B., SLAIS, J., ZDARSKA, Z., SCHRAMLOVA, J., HULINSKA, D. and STERBA, J. 1977. Experimental studies on bovine cysticercosis. Acta Parasitol. Polon. 25, 55.

McCABE, R. E. and REMINGTON, J. S. 1983. The diagnosis and treatment of toxoplasmosis. Eur. J. Clin. Microbiol. 2, 95.

MacKENZIE, C. D., PRESTON, P. M., and OGILVIE, B. M. 1978. Immunological properties of the surface of nematodes. Nature (London) 276, 826.

McMANUS, D. 1960. Prenatal infection of calves with *Cysticercus bovis*. Vet. Res. 72, 847.

MADSEN, H. 1974. The principles of the epidemiology of trichinelliasis with a new view on the life cycle. *In* Trichinellosis p. 615. C. W. Kim (Editor). Intext Educational Publishers, NY.

MAGALDI, C., ELKIS, H., PATTOLI, D., and COSCINA, A. L. 1969. Epidemic of toxoplasmosis at a university in Sao-Jose-dos-Campos, S. P. Brazil. Rev. Latino Amer Microbiol. Parasitol. 11, 5.

MARTINZ-GOMEZ, F. 1979. Short report concerning trichinellosis in Spain (1977 and 1978). Wiad. Parazytol. 25, 592.

MASON, P. C. 1978. *Trichinella spiralis* in New Zealand. New Z. Vet. J. 26, 215.

MATOFF, K. and KOMANDAREV, S. 1963. On the problem of occurrence of infective muscle trichinae in organs devoid of striated muscles. Z Parasitenk. 23, 197.

MERKUSHEV, A. V. 1970. Trichinosis in the Union of Soviet Socialist Republics. *In* Trichinosis in Man and Animals. p. 449. S. E. Gould (Editor). Charles C. Thomas, Springfield, lL.

MIELKE, D. 1969. Ein Beitrag zum Taeniose—Zystizerkose—Problem. Deut. Gesundheitsws. 24, 470.

MONTOVANI, A., FILIPPINI, I. AND BERGOMI, S. 1980. Indagini su un'epidemia di trichinellosi umana verificatasi in Italia. Parassitologia 22, 131.

MORSY, T. A., SADEK, M. S. M. and HAMID, M. Y. A. 1981. Intestinal parasites of stray cats in Cairo, Egypt. J. Egypt. Soc. Parasitol. 11, 331.

MOYNIHAN, I. W. and MUSFELDT, I. W. 1949A. A study of the incidence of trichinosis in swine in British Columbia. Canad. J. Comp. Med. 13, 224.

MOYNIHAN, I. W. and MUSFELDT, I. W. 1949B. A study of the incidence of trichinosis in rats in British Columbia. Canad. J. Comp. Med. 13, 152.

MURRELL, K. D. 1982. Unpublished data. USDA-ARS, Beltsville Agricultural Research Center, Beltsville, MD.

MURRELL, K. D. 1983. Preslaughter control of swine trichinosis. Food Technol. 37, 87.

MURRELL, K. D. 1986. Trichinosis. *In* Clinical Medicine. Spittell, J. A., Jr. (Editor). Harper & Row, Philadelphia, PA.

MURRELL, K. D. and DESPOMMIER, D. D. 1984. Immunization of swine against *Trichinella spiralis*. Vet. Parasitol. 15, 263.

MURRELL, K. D. and NELSON, G. S.   1983.   Trichinosis. *In* Hunter's Tropical Medicine. 6th Edition. G. T. Strickland (Editor). W. B. Saunders Co., Philadelphia, PA.

MURRELL, K. D., GAMBLE, H. R. and SCHAD, G. A.   1984.   Experimental transmission of *Trichinella spiralis* to swine by infected rats. Proc. Helminthol. Soc. Wash. *51*, 66.

NEGHME, A.   1979.   Trichinellosis in Latin America: Report for 1976–1978. Wiad. Parazytol. *25*, 586.

NELSON, G. S.   1982.   Carrion-feeding cannibalistic carnivores and human disease in Africa with special reference to trichinosis and hydatid disease in Kenya Symp. Zool. Soc. Lond. No. 50, p. 181.

NELSON, G. S., BLACKIE, E. J. and MUKUNDI, J.   1966.   Comparative studies on geographical strains of *Trichinella spiralis*. Trans. Roy. Soc. Trop. Med. Hyg. *60*, 471.

NEPOTE, K. H., PAWLOWSKI, Z. S. and SOULSBY, E. J. L.   1974.   Immunoglobulin levels in patients infected with *Taenia saginata*. *In* Parasitic Zoonosis, Clinical and Experimental Studies. p. 241. E. J. L. Soulsby (Editor). Academic Press, NY.

NEVEU-LEMAIRE, M.   1936.   Taeniasis. Traité d'Helminthologie Medicale et Veterinaire. Vigot Frères, Paris.

OBENDORF, D. L. and MUNDAY, B. L.   1983.   Toxoplasmosis in wild Tasmanian wallabies. Austral. Vet. J. *60*, 62.

OCKERT, G.   1965.   Uber die Verbreitung einiger Darmparasiten unter die Bevolkerung des Bezirkes Halle. Z. Artzl. Fortbild. *59*, 850.

OCKERT, G. and OBST, J.   1973.   Dissemination of encapsulated onchospheres by tapeworm carriers. Monat. Veterinaermed. *28*, 97.

OLSEN, B. S., VILLELLA, J. B. and GOULD, S. E.   1964.   Distribution of *Trichinella spiralis* in muscles of experimentally infected swine. J. Parasitol. *50*, 489.

OZERETSKOVSKAYA, N. N.   1978.   Pathogenesis, Pathomorphology and clinics of trichinellosis: Treatment of trichinellosis. *In* Trichinelly i Trichinelliez. p. 165. S. N. Boev, V. I. Bondareva, and I. B. Sokolova (Editors). Akademija Nauk Kazahskoj SSR. (Russ).

PAMPIGLIONE, S.   1971.   Observations and research on an epidemic in the province of Trento. Parassitologia *13*, 241.

PAMPIGLIONE, S., BALDELLI, R., CORSINI, C., MARI, S. and MANTOVANI, A.   1978.   Infezione sperimentale del cavalla con larvae di trichina. Parassitologia *20*, 183.

PAWEL, O.   1968.   Devitalization of cysticerci by gamma irradiation. *In* Elimination of Harmful Organisms from Food and Feed by Irradiation. p. 91. Panel Proceedings Series. International Atomic Energy Agency. Vienna.

PAWLOWSKI, Z. S.   1970.   Inorganic tin compounds as the alternative drug in human taeniarhynchosis. J. Parasitol. *56*, 261.

PAWLOWSKI. Z. S.   1983A.   Clinical aspects in man. *In* Trichinella and Trichinosis. Chap. 11, p. 367. W. C. Campbell (Editor). Plenum Press, NY.

PAWLOWSKI, Z. S.   1983B.   Taeniasis and cysticercosis. *In* Parasitic Zoonosis. Vol. I, CRC Handbook Series in Zoonosis. p. 313. J. H. Steele CRC Press, Inc., Roca Raton, FL.

PAWLOWSKI, Z. S. and SCHULTZ, M. G.   1972.   Taeniasis and cysticercosis *Taenia saginata*. Vol. 10. Advan. Parasitol. *10*, 269.

PENFOLD, W. J. and PENFOLD, H. B.   1937.   *Cysticercosis bovis* and its prevention. J. Helminthol. *15*, 37.

PENFOLD, W. J., PENFOLD, H. B. and PHILLIPS, M.   1937A.   The criteria of life and viability of mature *Taenia saginata* ova. Med. J. Austral. *24*, 2.

PENFOLD, W. J., PENFOLD, H. B., and PHILLIPS, M.   1937B.   *Taenia Saginata:* Its growth and propagation. J. Helminthol. *15*, 41.

PETROVIC, Z., RADOVIC, M. and LAUSEVIC, B.   1982.   Significance and problems of taeniasis in some parts of Yugoslavia. Acta Vet. *32*, 31.

PROKOPENKO, L. I.   1968.   Approaches and methods of taeniarhynchosis eradication in the U.S.S.R. Proc. 8th Intern. Congr. Trop. Med. Malaria, Teheran, p. 233.

PUN, K. K., WONG, W. T. and WONG, P. H. C.   1983.   The first documented outbreak of trichinellosis in Hong Kong Chinese. Am. J. Trop. Med. Hyg. *32*, 772.
PURKERSON, J. and DESPOMMIER, D.   1974.   *In* Trichinellosis. p. 7. C. Kim (Editor). Intext Educational Pub., NY.
RANSOM, B. H. and SCHWARTZ, B.   1919.   Effects of heat on trichinae. J. Agr. Res. *17*, 201.
RAUSCH, R. L.   1970.   Trichinosis in the Arctic. *In* Trichinosis in Man and Animals. p. 348. S. E. Gould (Editor). Charles C. Thomas, Springfield, IL.
RAUSCH, R. L.   1983.   Contemporary concepts of the taxonomy of nematodes in the genus *Trichinella* Raillet, 895. *In* CRC Handbook Series in Zoonosis. Vol. II. Section C, p. 325. J. H. Steele (Editor). CRC Press, Inc., Boca Raton, FL.
REMINGTON, J. S.   1968.   Toxoplasmosis and congenital infection. Birth Defects *4*, 49.
RHOADS, M. L.   1983.   *Trichinella spiralis:* Identification and purification of superoxide dismutase. Exp. Parasitol. *56*, 41.
RICKARD, M. D. and ADOLPH, A. J.   1976.   Vaccination of calves against *Taenia saginata* infection using a "parasite-free" vaccine. Vet. Parasitol. *1*, 389.
RICKARD, M. D. and ADOLPH, A.   1977.   The prevalence of cysticerci of *Taenia saginata* in cattle reared on sewage-irrigated pasture. Med. J. Austral. *1*, 525.
RICKARD, M. D. and WILLIAMS, J. F.   1982.   Hydatidosis/Cysticercosis: Immune mechanisms and immunization against infection. *In* Advances in Parasitology. p. 229. J. R. Baker and R. Muller (Editors). Academic Press, NY.
RICKARD, M. D., ADOLPH, A. and ARUNDEL, S.   1977.   Vaccination of calves against *Taenia saginata* using antigens collected during *in vitro* cultivation of larvae: Passive protection via colostrum from vaccinated cows and vaccination of calves protected by maternal antibody. Res. Vet. Sci. *23*, 365.
RICKARD, M. D., BRUMLEY, J. L. and ANDERSON, G. A.   1982.   Field trial to evaluate the use of antigens from *Taenia hydatigena* onchospheres to prevent infection with *Taenia saginata* in cattle grazing on sewage-irrigated pasture. Res. Vet. Sci. *32*, 189.
RIM, H. J., PARK, S. B., LEE, J. S. and JOO, K. S.   1979.   Therapeutic effects of praziquantel (Embay 8440) against *Taenia solium* infection. Korean J. Parasitol. *17*, 67.
ROBINSON, J. T. R. and CHAMBERS, P. G.   1976.   Observations on cysticercosis in Rhodesia. II. The survival time for *Cysticercus cellulosae* cysts at low temperatures. Rhodesian Vet. J. *7*, 32.
ROTH, H.   1949.   Trichinosis in Arctic animals. Nature (London) *163*, 805.
ROTHROCK, T. P.   1965.   Trichinosis in an Iowa swine herd. J. Am. Vet. Med. Assoc. *146*, 366.
RUITENBERG, E. J.   1972.   Acid phosphatases in the intestinal cells of two nematode larvae: *Anasakis* sp. and *Trichinella spiralis*. *In* Comparative Biochemistry of Parasites. p. 283. H. Van den Bossche (Editor). Academic Press, NY.
RUITENBERG, E. J., VAN KNAPEN, F. and ELGERSMA, A.   1983.   Incidence and control of *Trichinella spiralis* throughout the world. Food Technol. *37*, 98.
SAFRONOW, M. G.   1960.   O gelminto faunie denej w Tomponskom i olenjekskom rajonach jakutskoj ASSR (in Russian). Tr. Irkutsk Nauch.-Issled Inst. Sel. Khoz. Wa. 3.
SCHAD, G. A. and MURRELL, K. D.   1984.   Unpublished data. University of Pennsylvania, Philadelphia.
SCHANDEVYL. P. and VERCRUYSSE, J.   1982.   Cysticercosis in cattle in Senegal. Vet. Parasitol. *11*, 267.
SCHANTZ, P. M.   1983A.   Trichinosis in the United States—1947–1981. Food Technol. *37*, 83.
SCHANTZ, P. M.   1983B.   Personal Communication. Centers for Disease Control, DHHS, Atlanta, GA.
SCHANTZ, P. M., JURANEK, D. D. and SCHULTZ, M. G.   1977.   Trichinosis in the

United States. 1975. Increase in cases attributed to numerous common source outbreaks. J. Infect. Dis. *136*, 712.

SCHANTZ, P. M., SHANKS, D. and WILSON, M. 1980. Serologic cross-reactions with sera from patients with echinococcosis and cysticercosis. Am. J. Trop. Med. Hyg. *29*, 609.

SCHULTZ, M. G. 1971. Parasitic diseases along the Mexican-USA frontier. Helminthol. Abstr. *41*, 309.

SCHULTZ, M. G., HALTERMAN, L., RICH, A. and MARTIN, G. 1969. An epizootic of bovine cysticercosis. J. Am. Vet. Med. Assoc. *155*, 1708.

SCHULTZ, M. G., HERMOS, J. A. and STEELE, J. H. 1970. Epidemiology of beef tapeworm infection in the United States. Publ. Health. Rep. *85*, 169.

SCHWARTZ, B. 1921. Effects of X-rays on trichinae. J. Agr. Res. *20*, 845.

SCHWARTZ, B. 1960. Trichinosis in the United States. Proc. 1st Intern. Conf. Trichinellosis, Warsaw, Poland.

SEAWRIGHT, G. L., DESPOMMIER, D. D., ZIMMERMANN, W. J. and ISENSTEIN, R. 1983. Enzyme immunoassay for swine trichinellosis using antigens purified by immunoaffinity chromatography. Am. J. Trop. Med. Hyg. *32*, 1275.

SIIM, J. C., BIERING-SØRENSEN, A. and MØLLER, T. 1963. Toxoplasmosis in domestic animals. Advan. Vet. Sci. *8*, 335.

SILVERMAN, P. H. 1954. Studies on the biology of some tapeworms of the genus *Taenia*. The morphology and development of the taeniid hexacarth embryo and its enclosing membranes, with some notes on the state of development and propagation of gravid segments. Ann. Trop. Med. Parasitol. *48*, 356.

SILVERMAN, P. H. 1955. Bovine cysticercosis in Great Britain from July 1950 to December 1953 with some notes on meat inspection and the incidence of *Taenia saginata* in man. Ann. Trop. Med. Parasitol. *49*, 429.

SILVERMAN, P. and GRIFFITHS, R. 1955. A review of methods of sewage disposal in Great Britain, with special reference to the epizootiology of *Cysticercus bovis*. Ann. Trop. Med. Parasitol. *49*, 436.

SIVINSKY, J. 1983. Irradiated pork. Nat. Hog Farmer, August 15, 1983. p. 16.

SKVOGAARD, N. and PETERSEN, K. 1983. Personal communication. Danske Slagterier, Copenhagen, Denmark.

SLAIS, J. 1970. The Morphology and Pathogenicity of the Bladder Worms: *Cysticercosis cellulosae* and *Cysticercus bovis*. Academia, Prague.

SLAIS, J. and MANN, I. 1976. Morphological determination of the age of *Cysticercus bovis* in very young calves with cysticercosis. Folia Parasitol. (Praha) *23*, 321.

SLONKA, G., MOULTHROP, J., DEWHIRST, L., HOTCHKISS, P., VALLAZA, B. and SCHULTZ, M. 1975. An epizootic of bovine cysticercosis. J. Am. Vet. Med. Assoc. *166*, 678.

SLONKA, G. F., MATLUCH, W., MORPHET, E., MILLER, C. W. and BAYER, E. V. 1978. An outbreak of bovine cysticercosis in California. Am. J. Trop. Med. Hyg. *27*, 101.

SMITH, H. J. 1980. Trichinosis—A zoonotic time bomb. Canad. Agr. *25*, 22.

SNYDER, G. R. and MURRELL, K. D. 1983. Bovine cysticercosis. *In* Practices in Veterinary Public Health and Preventive Medicine. G. Woods (Editor). Iowa State Press, Ames. In press.

SOULSBY, E. J. L. 1965. Cestodes of cattle. *In* Textbook of Veterinary Clinical Parasitology. Vol. I. Chap. 30. Helminths. F. A. Davis, Philadelphia, PA.

STEELE, J. H. 1983. Trichinosis. *In* CRC Handbook Series in Zoonosis. Vol. II. Section C, p. 293. J. H. Steele (Editor). CRC Press, Inc., Boca Raton, FL.

STEIGLER, H. 1978. Die Ergebnisse der amtlichen Schlattier—und Fleischuntersuchung 1976. Fleischwirtschaft *58*, 77.

STEWART, G. L. 1983A. Biochemistry. *In Trichinella* and Trichinosis. Chap. 4, p. 153. W. C. Campbell (Editor). Plenum Press, NY.

STEWART, G. L. 1983B. Pathophysiology of the muscle phase, *In Trichinella* and Trichinosis. Chap. 7, p. 241. W. C. Campbell (Editor). Plenum Press, NY.

376   K. D. MURRELL, R. FAYER AND J. P. DUBEY

STEWART, G. L. and GIANNINI, S. H. 1982. *Sarcocystis, Trypanosoma, Toxoplasma, Brugia, Ancylostoma* and *Trichinella* spp.: A review of the intracellular parasites of striated muscle. Exp. Parasitol. *53*, 406.

STEWART, G. L., KRAMAN, G. W., REDDINGTON, J. J. and HAMILTON, A. M. 1980. Studies on *in vitro* larva position by adult *Trichinella spiralis*. J. Parasitol. *66*, 94.

STOLL, N. R. 1947. This wormy world. J. Parasitol. *33*, 1.

STRAFUSS, A. C. and ZIMMERMANN, W. J. 1967. Hematologic changes and clinical signs of trichinosis in pigs. Am. J. Vet. Res. *28*, 833.

SUKHDEO, M. V. K. and CROLL, N. A. 1981. The location of parasites within their hosts: Factors affecting longitudinal distribution of *Trichinella spiralis* in the small intestine. Intern. J. Parasitol. *11*, 163.

TANNER, C. E. 1979. Report on trichinellosis in Canada. Wiad. Parazytol. *25*, 585.

TAYLOR, E. C. and PARFITT, J. W. 1959. Destruction by irradiation of parasites transmitted through butcher's meat. Intern. J. Appl. Rad. Isotop. *6*, 194.

TELLEZ-GIRON, E., RAMOS, M. C. and MONTANTE, M. 1981. Effect of flubendazole on *Cysticercosis cellulosae* in pigs. Am. J. Trop. Med. Hyg. *30*, 135.

TEPPEMA, J. S., BLOMJOUS, F. J. E. M., ELGERSMA, A. and RUITENBERG, E. J. 1981. *Trichinella pseudospiralis* and *T. spiralis* in monkeys. III. Pathological aspects. *In* Trichinellosis. p. 209. C. W. Kim, E. J. Ruitenberg, and J. S. Teppema (Editors). Reedbooks, Ltd. Surrey, England.

THOMSEN, D. U. 1977. The approved version of the stomacher method for *Trichinella* control. Danish Vet. J. 60, 337.

THORBORG, N. B., TULINIUS, S. and ROTH, H. 1948. Trichinosis in Greenland. Acta Pathol. Microbiol. Scand. *25*, 788.

UPTON, A. C. 1950. Taeniid proglottids in the appendix. Possible association with appendicitis. Report of cases. Am. J. Clin. Pathol. *20*, 1117.

URQUHART, G. 1961. Epizootiological and experimental studies on bovine cysticercosis in East Africa. J. Parasitol. *47*, 857.

URQUHART, G. 1966. Bovine cysticercosis. Proc. 1st Intern. Congr. Parasitol. Vol. II. pp. 829, 839.

USDA. 1982. Press release. 417–82, April 12, 1982.

VAN DEN HEEVER, L. W. 1967. On the longevity of *Cysticercus bovis* in various organs in a bovine. J. Parasitol. *53*, 6.

VAN KOOY, J. G. and ROBIJNS, K. G. 1968. Gamma irradiation elimination of *Cysticercus bovis* in meat. *In* Elimination of Harmful Organisms from Food and Feed by Irradiation. p. 81. Int. Atomic Energy Agency, Vienna.

VERSTER, A. 1969. A taxonomic revision of the genus *Taenia* Linnaeus, 1758. Onderstepoort J. Vet. Res. *36*, 3.

VERSTER, A., DUPLESSIS, A. J. and VAN DEN HEEVER, L. 1976. The effect of gamma radiation on the cysticerci of *Taenia solium*. Onderstepoort J. Vet. Res. *43*, 23.

VILLELLA, J. B. 1970. Life cycle and morphology. *In* Trichinosis in Man and Animals. Chap. II, p. 19. S. E. Gould (Editor). Charles C. Thomas, Springfield, IL.

VOGE, M. 1963. Observations on the structure of cysticerci of *Taenia solium* and *Taenia saginata* (Cestoda: Taeniidae). J. Parasitol. *49*, 85.

WAKELIN, D. and DENHAM, D. A. 1983. The immune response. *In* Trichinella and Trichinosis. Chap. 8, p. 265. W. C. Campbell (Editor). Plenum Press, New York, NY.

WALDELAND, H. 1976. Toxoplasmosis in sheep. The prevalence of Toxoplasma antibodies in lambs and mature sheep from different parts of Norway. Acta Vet. Scand. *17*, 432.

WALTHER, M. and KOSKE, J. K. 1979. The efficacy of praziquantel against *Taenia saginata* cysticercosis in naturally infected calves. Z. Tropenmed. Parasitol. *30*, 401.

WEATHERLY, N. F. 1983. An anatomical pathology, *In Trichinella* and Trichinosis. Chap. 5 Campbell, W. C. (Editor). Plenum Press, NY.

WEBBE, G. 1967. The hatching and activation of taeniid ova in relation to the development of cysticercosis in man. Z. Tropenmed. Parasitol. *18,* 354.

WHO-FAO. 1976. Research needs in taeniasis-cysticercosis (memorandum). Bull. W.H.O. *53,* 67.

WIKERHAUSER, T., ZUKOVIC, M. and DZAKULA, N. 1970. Vaccination against bovine cysticercosis. J. Parasitol. *56,* 369.

WILLMS, K. and MERCHANT, M. T. 1980. The inflammatory reaction surrounding *Taenia solium* larvae in pig muscle: Ultrastructural and light microscopic observations. Parasit. Immunol. *2,* 261.

WILSON, C. B. and REMINGTON, J. S. 1980. What can be done to prevent congenital toxoplasmosis. Am. J. Obstet. Gynecol. *138,* 357.

WORLD HEALTH ORGANIZATION. 1982. Abstracts of recent Chinese publications on helminthiasis. WHO/HELM/82.5, p. 4.

WHO-FAO, 1976. Research needs in taeniasis-cysticercosis (memorandum). Bull. W.H.O. *53,* 67.

WRIGHT, K. A. 1978. *Trichinella spiralis*—an intracellular parasite in the intestinal phase. Proc. 4th Intern. Congr. Parasitol, Warszawa. August 19–26, 1978. Short Communications. Sect. C, p. 150.

WRIGHT, W. H., KERR, D. B. and JACOBS, L. 1943. Studies on Trichinosis. XV. Summary of the Findings of *Trichinella spiralis* in a Random Sampling of Other Sampling of the Population of the United States. Publ. Health Rep. *58,* 1293.

YAMAGUCHI, T. 1978. Report on Trichinellosis in Japan. Wiad. Parazytol. *24,* 114.

YOSHINO, K. 1933. Studies on the post-embryonal development of *Taenia solium.* Parts I, II, III. Taiwan Igak Kai Zasshi *32,* 1392.

ZENKER, F. A. 1871. Zur lehre von der trichinenkrankheit. Deut. Arch. Klin. Med. *8,* 387.

ZIMMERMAN, W. J. 1967. A pooled sample method for post-slaughter detection of trichiniasis in swine. Proc. 71st Ann. Mtg. U.S. Lvsk. Santit. Assoc., p. 358.

ZIMMERMAN, W. J. 1970A. Reproductive potential and muscle distribution of *Trichinella spiralis* in swine. J. Am. Vet. Assoc. *156,* 770.

ZIMMERMAN, W. J. 1970B. The epizootiology of trichiniasis in wildlife. J. Wildl. Dis. *6,* 329.

ZIMMERMAN, W. J. 1975. Trichinosis. *In* Meat Hygiene. 4th edition. p. 187. J. A. Libby (Editor). Lea and Febiger, Philadelphia, PA.

ZIMMERMAN, W. J. and BEACH, P. J. 1982. Efficacy of microwave cooking for devitalizing trichinae in pork roasts and chops. J. Food. Prot. *45:* 405.

ZIMMERMAN, W. J. and BRANDLEY, P. J. 1965. The current status of trichiniasis in U.S. swine. Publ. Health. Rep. *80,* 1061.

ZIMMERMAN, W. J. and ZINTER, D. E. 1971. The prevalence of trichinosis in swine in the United States, 1966–70. Health Serv. Mental Health Admin. Health Rep *86,* 937.

ZIMMERMAN, W. J., SCHWARTE, L. H., and BIESTER, H. E. 1956. Incidence of trichiniasis in swine, pork products and wildlife in Iowa. Am. J. Publ. Health *46,* 313.

ZIMMERMAN, W. J., HUBBARD, E. D., SCHWARTE, L. H. and BIESTER, H. E. 1962. Trichiniasis in Iowa swine with further studies on modes of transmission. Cornell Vet. *52,* 156.

ZIMMERMAN, W. J., STEELE, J. H., and KAGAN, I. G. 1973. Trichiniasis in the U.S. population, 1966–1970: Prevalence, epidemiologic factors. Health Serv. Rep. *88,* 606.

12

Viruses in Meat and Poultry Products

Dean O. Cliver[1]

The past 20 years have brought a general awareness that a significant portion of the diseases transmitted through foods are caused by viruses (Cliver 1983). There has been a long-standing tendency of clinicians to ascribe intractable illnesses, including simple gastroenteritis, to viruses even when the diagnosis was totally intuitive. Now, at last, enough is known about viruses and their transmission through foods to confirm some of these diagnoses, and perhaps to refute others.

PROPERTIES OF FOOD-BORNE VIRUSES

Because viruses occupy a peculiar niche at the border between living and nonliving things, it is important to describe some properties that are unique to viruses before discussing the practical aspects of the subject. One might speak of a "life cycle," even though viruses lack many of the properties of living things, and assign it two stages: the particulate and the replicative.

[1]Food Research Institute, World Health Organization Collaborating Centre of Food Virology, and Department of Bacteriology, University of Wisconsin—Madison, Madison, WI 53706.

Advances in Meat Research, Volume 2
Copyright 1986 by AVI Publishing Co.
ISBN 0-87055-498-0

The Particulate Phase of the Viral Cycle

Viruses are transmitted as small, simple, inert particles. The size, shape, and composition of the viral particle are the bases on which viruses are classified. "Small," in this case, denotes diameters of 25 to 100 nm for food-borne viruses, with most of the important ones being near the lower end of the range. "Simple" conveys the fact that most have only two chemical components: nucleic acid (either RNA or DNA, ordinarily double-stranded only in particles more than ca. 50 nm in diameter, usually in a random coil) and a coat of protein (usually in single layer, but sometimes double). A few viruses have an outermost envelope of lipid-containing material which results in their being very labile; however, few of these are food-borne. The nucleic acid contains the information needed to direct a host cell to produce more virus. The coat protein shields the nucleic acid from the rigors of the environment, serves as the basis for selective attachment of the virus to specific receptors of potential host cells, and is the antigen to which the host's body reacts in producing immunity against the viral infection. The particle is "inert" in the sense that it cannot carry out any life process, including motion, reproduction, reaction to environmental stimuli, or adaption to the conditions around it; therefore, it cannot replicate outside of a susceptible living cell.

The Replicative Phase of the Viral Cycle

The inertness of the viral particle is deceptive: viruses are capable of causing infections, or they would not be discussed here. The infectious potential of viruses is specific at two levels, the species (e.g., viruses that infect humans seldom infect swine, and vice versa) and tissue or organ (e.g., viruses that infect the lungs seldom infect the intestines, and vice versa).

In general, a virus particle first contacts the plasma membrane of a human or animal host cell and only attaches if a suitable receptor is present. The host cell then is induced to engulf the viral particle, which sheds its coat protein and loses its particulate shape. The nucleic acid that is liberated from the particle functions to direct the host cell to produce components of virus, which then assemble within the cell to become progeny viral particles. In the process, the cell may abdicate whatever special functions it is supposed to perform in the body, or may even die as a result of the infection. In either case, the progeny viral particles escape the host cell and proceed to infect other cells on which there are receptors; some may escape the host's body and perhaps reach other hosts. If enough cells become infected and abdicate their bodily functions, the abnormality that results may be recognized as disease. Virus diseases are sometimes severe, but few of them are fatal: antibodies are produced by the host's body against the antigens of the viral coat, and these and some nonspecific substances usually suffice to eliminate the viral infection. Whether the infection is transient or fatal, the virus produced in one infected host must be released and reach another susceptible host, or the virus would cease to exist as an infectious entity. Many viruses pass directly from one infected host to another, by what is called "contact" transmission. However, a significant number of them are also transmissible through "vehicles" (food and water).

VIRUS TRANSMISSION THROUGH FOODS

The transmission of viruses through foods is not a common event. Even though such transmission is recorded with significant frequency, it is clear that viruses infectious for humans do not depend on this mode for their persistence as species.

General Principles of Virus Transmission

The route by which a virus leaves an infected host's body depends first upon the site of the infection. Viruses that infect the respiratory tract are likely to be exhaled, or sneezed or coughed out, with aerosols. Viruses that infect the intestinal tract are shed with feces. Viruses that infect the skin may be shed with exudates from the lesions. Viruses that infect the kidneys or lactating mammary glands are shed with urine and milk, respectively. Any of these may be transmitted by "contact," which is, unfortunately, a very ill-defined term. The essence of contact transmission may be that virus was transferred from an infected individual to a susceptible individual by touching, but this only gets the virus from the outside of one person to the outside of another. If someone who has a cold sneezes, and someone else inhales the virus-containing aerosol, this would usually be considered contact transmission, even though the two persons never touched each other. By contrast, virus shed in feces might be transferred from the hands of one person to another, but would cause infection only if the newly soiled hand entered the susceptible person's mouth. This, too, would be contact transmission. It seems safe to say that the majority of virus infections, almost regardless of the type of virus involved, are transmitted by contact.

Indirect transmission of a virus may involve a vector (a living animal that carries the virus from place to place, with or without being infected itself), a fomes (an inanimate object on which virus is deposited), or a vehicle (food or water). When virus-contaminated food or water is ingested, infection usually begins in the lining of the small intestine (often the ileum) and may later spread to other organs in which the symptoms of illness are produced. Ingestion of tissue from an infected animal might also be expected to transmit virus directly to a human consumer; however, very few viruses of animal disease are infectious for humans. Finally, there are instances in which tissues of animals raised as human food may serve as the source of viruses that cause disease in other animals.

Modes of Viral Contamination of Foods

The presence of virus in meat as a result of infection of the source animal is a relatively minor concern to human health, but is often classified as "primary contamination" because it takes place before the event of slaughter, meaning that virus is already present when the raw material becomes food (Cliver 1983). Any subsequent contamination is called "secondary contamination"; the virus is introduced during processing, storage, distribution, or final preparation. Secondary contamination should be the easier to prevent but is far the more frequent and significant to human health in that few viruses infectious for humans infect food-source animal species.

The viruses of human origin that are transmitted through meats and other foods are ordinarily shed via the human intestines, in feces. Fecal contamination of food may take place through unsanitary handling of the food by an infected individual or by exposure of the food to water that is contaminated with feces. Vectors, such as flies and other insects, as well as fomites have been suspected of carrying viruses to meats and other foods, but it is very difficult to make a case for this on the basis of the epidemiological record. The epidemiological record, as it happens, is composed almost entirely of outbreaks of hepatitis A transmitted via food, so we shall spend some time in discussion of this disease.

Reported Transmission of Viruses through Meat and Poultry Products

Unfortunately, it appears that only a small proportion of the food-borne viral disease that occurs is recorded in such a way as to be accessible for summaries such as the following.

Hepatitis A (HA). This disease is caused by a small, round virus that has recently been classified in the enterovirus group (particles about 28 nm in diameter, containing single-stranded RNA). It is transmitted by the fecal-oral route, principally by person-to-person contact, and has an incubation period ranging from 15 to 50 days, with a median of about 28 days. Although many infected persons experience no symptoms whatever, jaundice and severe debility possibly lasting 6 weeks are frequently seen. Shedding of the virus occurs during the last 10–14 days before, and declines shortly after, the onset of symptoms (Center for Disease Control 1980). Given the long incubation period of the disease, the common shedding of the virus before onset of illness, and the significant incidence of inapparent infections, it is remarkable that so many outbreaks of food-borne hepatitis have been investigated and recorded. Even so, it is certain that only a small proportion of the outbreaks that occur are being recorded.

HA leads, by a considerable margin, all other viral diseases recorded as being transmitted through foods. The available record does not reflect the true incidence of food-borne HA, or the relative incidence of HA among food-borne viral diseases. The record derives largely from outbreaks investigated by the U.S. Centers for Disease Control (CDC). Many outbreaks of HA that occurred elsewhere in the world either were not recorded, or else the records were not accessible for compiling this summary.

Records from the CDC for the 5-year period 1975–1979 have been compiled recently (Cliver 1983). They show a total of 160,203 cases of HA reported in the United States for the period, of which 64 (0.04%) were attributed to reported water-associated outbreaks and 656 (0.41%) were attributed to recorded food-associated outbreaks. Although only a small proportion of HA cases in the United States are associated with vehicular transmission, significant numbers of illnesses occur in this way, and the impact on some segments of the food industry is quite important.

The WHO Manual on Food Virology lists 117 recorded outbreaks of HA in which the vehicle was drinking water, and 153 in which the vehicles were various foods (Cliver 1983). Forty-six of the 153 food-associated outbreaks showed shellfish (bivalve mollusks) as the vehicle, whereas only 13 outbreaks involved meat, food containing meats, and sandwiches that may have contained meats. No poultry meats were implicated in these outbreaks. The eight outbreaks in which meat or meat-containing vehicles were clearly implicated are summarized in Table 12.1. Sandwiches that may have contained meat are listed among the vehicles in five other outbreaks comprising a total of 294 cases (Denes et al. 1977; McCollum 1961; Meyers et al. 1975). All of these outbreaks, except the one in Amsterdam, either took place in the United States or involved members or associates of the United States military abroad, showing again the difficulty of obtaining such information for outbreaks occurring outside the United States. Food handlers were the sources implicated, with the sole exception of the incident in which a sewer backed up into a New Jersey delicatessen. In this instance, food was contaminated by the sewage, but later also by two food handlers who had become infected as a result of the sewer backup (Center for Disease Control 1965). Direct human contamination of food is typical of HA outbreaks involving any food vehicle other than shellfish. Polluted water is a less frequent source of contamination and insect vectors have yet to be implicated in an outbreak.

Other Human Enteric Viruses. Market surveys to detect viruses in meats have yielded disparate results. A survey by the U.S. Food and Drug Administration yielded human enteroviruses from market samples of ground beef; 3 of 12 samples collected in Cincinnati, Ohio, yielded viruses, including polioviruses 1, 2, and 3 and echovirus 6 (Sullivan et al. 1970).

TABLE 12.1. Outbreaks of Hepatitis A Transmitted via Meats or Sandwiches Containing Meats

Year	Vehicle(s)	Cases	Location	Source of virus	Reference
1962–1963	Roast pork, salad, sandwiches	44	Cafeteria of school for U.S. Air Force dependents, Bushey Hall, England	Food handler (manager)	Center for Disease Control, 1963
1965	Cold cuts	67	Delicatessen in New Jersey	Sewer backup, two infected food handlers	Center for Disease Control, 1965
1965	Cold cuts, salads, etc.	66	Delicatessen in New York	Food handler (owner)	Center for Disease Control, 1966
1969	"Sloppy Joe" sandwiches	9	Delicatessen in New Jersey	Food handler (manager)	Center for Disease Control, 1969
1973	Garnished hamburger sandwiches, spaghetti	31	Restaurant in Arizona	Food handler	Leger *et al.* 1975
1974	Ham	15	Wedding reception in Michigan	Unknown	Center for Disease Control, 1976
1977	"Submarine" sandwiches	18	Benefit for a baseball team, Pennsylvania	Food handler (amateur)	Center for Disease Control, 1977
1977	Spiced, raw ground beef	21	Butcher shop, Amsterdam, The Netherlands	Food handler (butcher)	Noordam and Coutinho, 1977

Eight of eight samples in a survey of ground beef in the area of Montreal, Canada contained plaque-forming agents that were assumed to be viruses but were not identified (Idziak and Srivastava 1975). Larkin (1982) reports previously unpublished instances of isolation by the U.S. Food and Drug Administration of poliovirus 1 from market samples of chicken parts, pork and beef loaf, and bologna. In contrast to these findings, a survey of ground beef and luncheon meat, among other market foods, in Madison, Wisconsin yielded no viruses (Kostenbader and Cliver 1977). Negative virological test results were also reported in a survey of ground meat (a mixture of beef and pork) from markets in seven communities in the Netherlands (Northolt and Kapsenberg 1976). It seems most likely that such contamination of ground beef as occurs would result from mishandling by infected persons, by analogy to the outbreak of HA associated with spiced, raw ground beef that is listed in Table 12.1. However, it should be noted that the product that caused the HA outbreak, which was called "tartar" and was sold for consumption raw, probably received more intimate hand contact in the process of mixing in the seasonings than would be normal for ground meat in general. Bovine and swine carcasses surveyed at slaughter have yielded animal viruses on occasion, but apparently not human viruses (Kostenbader and Cliver 1977; Northolt and Kapsenberg 1976).

In addition to the enteroviruses and the HA virus, which also appears to be an enterovirus, there are small, round viruses ("Norwalk-like agents"), which cause gastroenteritis. A great proportion of recorded food- and water-borne disease each year is listed as gastroenteritis of unknown etiology or as acute infectious nonbacterial gastroenteritis. In recent years, it has been shown that some of these illnesses are caused by small, round viruses that produce gastroenteritis with an incubation period of approximately 24–48 hr. In addition to diarrhea, the illness is expected to include vomiting in at least 50% of the cases and to have a duration of 12–60 hr. Among 430 outbreaks of food-borne acute gastroenteritis of previously unknown etiology reviewed recently, only 18 (4%) showed this pattern of illness, compared to 22 (23%) among 96 outbreaks where water was involved in transmission (Kaplan et al. 1982). Blood serum from persons involved in some of these outbreaks was available for testing and showed a significant rise in level of antibody against the Norwalk virus (one of the small, round viruses shown to cause this kind of gastroenteritis) in one food-associated and four water-associated outbreaks. It appears that this kind of viral gastroenteritis is less frequently transmitted through foods than through water, but additional study is certainly warranted. There has been at least one outbreak of viral gastroenteritis, affecting approximately 30 persons, in which the diagnosis was confirmed by the demonstration of the virus in the stools of a patient. The vehicle was ham sandwiches served to a private party at a restaurant; the source of the contamination evidently was not identified (Appleton 1980). It may be that methods will eventually be devised for detecting these gastroenteritis viruses in foods and water, but the evidence now accumulating is based solely on improved diagnostic tests applied to those who have become ill. Even though evidence thus far suggests that viral gastroenteritis is transmitted less frequently via foods than via water, most of the rest of the picture that is emerging resembles that seen in the transmission of HA. Therefore, it seems likely that the small, round gastroenteritis viruses represent a significantly greater threat to human health, as they may be transmitted through foods, than the enteroviruses that have been the object of most food virology research. This presents a dilemma, since the enteroviruses can be detected as they occur in foods, and the gastroenteritis viruses cannot (see later). It may well be that the enteroviruses serve best as indicators of fecal contamination or to suggest the presence of other viruses that are a greater threat to human health, at least when the source of contamination is polluted water, rather than an infected food handler (see later; Cliver 1983).

In addition to the agents that have been discussed in this section, a number of other viruses have been identified with some frequency in human diarrheal stools. It is entirely possible that these agents cause gastroenteritis in humans, but they will not be discussed here because they have not yet been associated with transmission via vehicles.

Agents of Animal Disease.   Several viruses and at least one *Chlamydia* (a bacterium that is an obligate intracellular parasite and thus is often discussed along with viruses because of similarities in modes of transmission and in research methods) that are agents of disease in food-source domestic animals are at least occasionally transmitted in ways that might be described as "food-associated." This topic is described in detail elsewhere (Cliver 1979; 1983) and will be addressed only briefly here.

Zoonoses are animal diseases that are transmissible to humans, although they are not ordinarily transmissible from person to person. *Chlamydia psittaci,* the agent of ornithosis (a disease of several species of poultry), occasionally causes airborne outbreaks of illness among poultry slaughter plant workers but has been reported to have infected a consumer only once, when a woman who had bought some ducks eviscerated them at home (Andrews *et al.* 1981). Infection is apparently contracted by inhalation, and not by ingestion with food. Creutzfeld-Jakob disease, a progressive degeneration of the human brain that has been proposed to be caused by an agent that may resemble a virus, may be contracted by eating brains of sheep that have a similar affliction, but the evidence to date is circumstantial (Alter *et al.* 1975, 1977). The viruses that cause rabies, Rift Valley fever, and swine vesicular disease (an illness that resembles foot-and-mouth disease clinically but is caused by a virus related serologically to coxsackievirus B5 of humans) are all known to be transmissible to humans but have not been known to cause infections via foods. None of these zoonotic agents is definitely known to be transmissible from animal to animal via food, although all (with the possible exception of the hypothetical virus of Creutzfeld-Jakob disease) must occur in foods on occasion.

Viruses of animal disease that have a significant potential to be transmitted via food or food by-products and scraps include those that cause foot-and-mouth disease, hog cholera, rinderpest, African swine fever, and Newcastle disease of poultry. The first of these are by far the most noteworthy. The viruses of foot-and-mouth disease (there are several serological types) belong to the picornavirus group of small, round viruses containing single-stranded RNA but differ from the enteroviruses that have been discussed above in that they are rapidly inactivated at pH 3, whereas the enteroviruses are fairly stable at this pH. The acid lability of the foot-and-mouth disease viruses is such that the acid generated in muscle during the process of rigor mortis is apparently sufficient to eliminate the virus from the muscle tissue of the hoofed animals that may be infected by it at the time of slaughter. However, viruses sequestered in lymph nodes, bone marrow, and large blood clots are not accessible to this acid and are quite persistent, even through many heating processes. The potential of these viruses to withstand all but the most rigorous heat treatments in the nonmuscular tissues named has led in the past to the worldwide transmission of foot-and-mouth disease and, at present, to some very costly embargoes of animal foods (Blackwell 1980). The agents of the other animal diseases listed can all be transmitted on a worldwide basis via animal tissues, causing outbreaks, but all are significantly larger and more complex than the foot-and-mouth disease viruses, and none has shown the persistence and ability to withstand heating that the latter have.

Perspectives

The evidence that has been reviewed shows that animal and poultry meats have a significant potential for transmitting viral diseases of animals, especially foot-and-mouth disease, but are not frequently vehicles for viruses infectious for humans. Essentially all outbreaks of viral disease that have been known to occur in humans as a result of ingestion of meats have been caused by viruses that emanated from the human intestinal tract. These may reach meats directly from the infected person, or by way of contaminated water. There is no indication that meats are more likely than other foods to become contaminated with human intestinal viruses, and if the meat is cooked after contamination (as some other foods are not), there is little risk to human health. It is possible that contaminated meats may protect viruses against thermal inactivation more than other foods do; this will be discussed in a later section.

Although meats as such may not play a large role in virus transmission, there is certainly evidence that the foot-and-mouth disease viruses are transported on a worldwide basis by milk and milk products (Blackwell 1980). There is evidently some risk of transmitting Newcastle disease of poultry through eggs and egg products. Meat scraps, which are valuable protein supplements for animal feed, have transmitted several viral diseases of animals if fed uncooked. Finally, it might be mentioned that heart valves from swine are now an article of international commerce; they are used as prostheses in open heart surgery in the United States but are usually imported, often from countries where foot-and-mouth disease occurs. The foot-and-mouth disease viruses and other viruses of animal disease that might be present in these heart valves have been shown to be inactivated by a glutaraldehyde treatment that was devised for the purpose (Cunliffe *et al.* 1979).

In general, then, meats may occasionally transmit viruses from animal to animal and, in the event of contamination with human enteric viruses, may serve as vehicles in the transmission of viruses among humans. However, the viruses that infect animals seldom represent a threat to human health as they occur in meats ingested as food.

INACTIVATION OF VIRUSES IN FOODS

Contamination of meats, or any other food, with viruses should be avoided when possible. This means that no infected animal should voluntarily be used as food and that opportunities for contamination with human viruses should be minimized by proper hygienic practices and by excluding infected persons, at least if they are overtly ill, from handling foods. However, it should be noted that once an animal has been slaughtered, there is no further opportunity for virus replication. That is, the quantity of virus present at the time of slaughter, or on the occasion of secondary contamination, is the greatest quantity of virus that will ever be present in the food. Thereafter, the virus may retain its infectivity (persist) or lose it (be inactivated), but it will not increase in quantity. Under certain circumstances, there is a strong possibility that the virus will have been inactivated before any opportunity for transmission arises.

Spontaneous Inactivation

Viruses are inert and cannot multiply in foods. Individual particles of virus will lose infectivity randomly, at a rate that is a function of the kind of virus, the nature of the food, and the temperature. It was stated above the foot-and-mouth disease virus would be inactivated by the acid that develops in muscle, and that enteroviruses are more stable in acid conditions. Virus inactivation is likely to be generally imperceptible at temperatures below freezing in meats. At temperatures above freezing, inactivation might occur as a result of the temperature and due to the enzymatic action of the proteolytic bacteria that develop in the meat. However, when ground beef was inoculated with coxsackievirus A9, a virus that had been shown to be exceptionally susceptible to protease, the virus persisted at levels near those inoculated until the meat had been stored for at least 8 days at 4° or 23°C and was no longer fit to eat (Herrmann and Cliver 1973). This suggests that meat is a fairly bland environment from the standpoint of viral persistence and that the "shelf life" of a contaminating virus is likely to exceed that of the meat at room temperature or below.

Thermal Inactivation

Virus inactivation will be more rapid at higher temperatures. Heating coxsackievirus A9 for 6 hr at 49°C in Thuringer sausage produced a 99% loss of infectivity (Herrmann and Cliver 1973). Cooking temperatures are even more destructive (Filppi and Banwart 1974; Sullivan et al. 1975). Even in accidental (as opposed to experimental) contamination, heat transfer to the interior of ground beef is critical because the virus is likely to be present throughout the substance of the food. On the other hand, solid cuts of meat are likely to contain viruses of human origin only at their surfaces, inasmuch as the virus has not infected the food-source animal but has been added during subsequent handling (secondary con- tamination). Foot-and-mouth disease viruses, by contrast, will be present throughout the carcass of an infected animal and are likely to persist in lymph nodes and major blood clots of deboned meat, and perhaps even in marrow if deboning has been mechanically performed. Therefore, heat penetration is critical to the inactivation of foot-and-mouth disease viruses in all meats, whether ground or not. When lymph nodes from infected cattle were mixed with beef in the preparation of ground beef products, complete inactivation (no further infectivity detectable by injection of meat extracts into the tongues of susceptible cattle) required heating bulk ground beef to an internal temperature of 98.8°C and meatballs to 93.3°C (Blackwell et al. 1982). Internal indicator discs were devised that changed color irreversibly when the desired temperature had been attained.

Other Modes of Inactivation

Heat is, by far, the most generally useful means of inactivating viruses in meats. It is noteworthy, in the prevention of secondary contamination, that disinfectants which are strong oxidizing agents (e.g., chlorine), may eliminate viruses from contaminated water or food-contact surfaces; other classes of disinfectants, however, tend to be ineffective. Fermentation of experimentally contaminated Thuringer sausage batter for 24 hr to 30°C produced an 84% reduction in the level of coxsackievirus A9 (Herrmann and Cliver 1973). Freeze-drying of virus-contaminated meat can be ex- pected to cause substantial inactivation of virus (Heidelbaugh and Giron 1969). Subsequent storage of freeze-dried products is likely to cause accel- erated virus inactivation, not because of the low moisture level directly, but because the low-moisture foods are likely to be stored at higher temperatures (Cliver et al. 1970). Ionizing irradiation of meats will almost certainly produce a dose-dependent inactivation of any virus that might be present; approximately 90% inactivation of experimentally inoculated coxsackievirus B2 was obtained with doses of cobalt-60 γ-rays near 0.75 Mrad (Sullivan et al. 1973).

Food Factors in Inactivation

As has been mentioned, meats seem to constitute a fairly bland environment from the standpoint of virus persistence. Protein and fat seem to offer some protection to virus during heating. All meats tend to be high in protein; virus inactivation was significantly less rapid during cooking in high-fat ground beef than in lower-fat preparations experimentally inoculated with enteroviruses (Filppi and Banwart 1974; Sullivan et al. 1975). Food components apparently serve as "radical scavengers" and mitigate the effects of ionizing radiation to some extent. Other than the adverse effect of acid on the viruses of foot-and-mouth disease, no component of meat is known to be significantly antiviral.

DETECTION OF VIRUSES IN MEAT AND POULTRY PRODUCTS

Consumer illnesses are one way of demonstrating that food contains a virus. When an outbreak occurs, it is still desirable to test the suspect food in the hope of detecting virus by laboratory techniques. Alternately, it may be possible on some occasions to determine that food contains virus and prevent it from being eaten, thus avoiding the consumer illnesses that would otherwise result. Regardless of the reason for testing food for viral contamination, the cost is likely to be substantial. However, the expense of the laboratory work may prove small when contrasted to the costs incurred in the aftermath of consumer illness.

Infectivity Methods

The reason for concern over the presence of viruses in food is their potential for producing infection. Therefore, it is appropriate that all of the methods presently in use for detecting food-borne viruses are based on the infectivity of the contaminating virus (Cliver et al. 1983A, B). That is, the virus is considered to have been detected when it produces a perceptible infection in a laboratory host, such as a cell culture. Laboratory animals or embryonated eggs might also be used on occasion, but cell cultures are by far the most frequently selected host system for this purpose.

Cell cultures are produced either from tissues obtained from an animal at death (while the individual cells are still alive) or from lines of cells that have been maintained *in vitro* over many generations. The choice of cells for the purpose depends, first, on viruses that one wishes to detect: viruses that are infectious for humans or are of human origin are detected in cells derived from humans or other primates, whereas one would use swine cell cultures to detect porcine viruses, etc. The selection and use of cell cultures for detection of food-borne viruses is discussed in detail elsewhere (Cliver *et al.* 1983A, B). Suffice it to say here that the care and maintenance of cell cultures are demanding tasks and should be undertaken only by someone who can give them close attention for some period. It is also possible to purchase some types of cell cultures ready for use in virus detection (Kostenbader and Cliver 1979), although this does not obviate learning how to maintain them and interpret whatever effects a virus may produce.

It is usual to test a sample in more than one type of cell culture, even if one is seeking only viruses infectious for humans, to afford a broader spectrum of viral susceptibility than any one cell culture type can afford. This may be done by splitting the sample extract and inoculating two types of cultures in parallel, or by harvesting the inoculum from one type of cell culture and inoculating it into another, in series (Kostenbader and Cliver 1977). No matter what cell cultures are used, there is still no method available that will detect the HA virus or the Norwalk-like agents, so there are serious limits on what can be accomplished by infectivity testing.

In any case, a sample must be processed before it can be inoculated into cell cultures. For solid foods, such as meats, this entails making a fluid suspension of the sample, dissociating the virus from the food solids, and removing the food solids from the suspension. To be able to test this fluid extract in a reasonable number of cell cultures, it may also be desirable to remove excess fluid from the suspension before inoculating the food extract into the cultures. For reasons that have been discussed, the focus in devising detection methods has been on ground beef, in contrast to meats from other species or to beef that has not been comminuted. An array of test procedures has been reviewed elsewhere (Cliver *et al.* 1983A, B). Without going into great detail, it is possible to divide the process into a sequence of steps and consider the various ways in which these steps may be performed. First, suspension of the sample in fluid may be done by mixing, grinding, or homogenization. Alkaline fluids are usually used to suspend the sample, so as to ensure that the final pH of the suspension will be at least 7. The least rigorous method is probably sufficient to recover virus introduced by secondary contamination, whereas very rigorous suspension methods, augmented by the action of trichlorotrifluoroethane to break down host cells and liberate virus, may be needed for primary contaminants. Separation of the food solids from the suspension may be accomplished either by centrifugation or by filtration and may be assisted by a polycation coagulant that causes flocculation of the food solids. Finally, the extract may be inoculated in large volumes (at least 1 ml/cm^2 of cell culture monolayer) into cell cultures or be concentrated beforehand by ultrafiltration, ultracentrifugation, or other means. Inasmuch as the cost of the cell cultures used in testing is a substantial element in the cost of the entire test, the decision to inoculate large volumes of sample extract or to concentrate is of great importance. Finally, one may maintain the inoculated cells with fluid medium and look for virus effects by means of a microscope or with medium solidified with agar to look for local areas of degeneration of the cell sheet (plaques; this cannot be done when the large-volume inoculation procedure has been used). Elapsed time is likely to range from 2 days to 2 weeks. Whether the putative virus effect is seen microscopically or as a plaque, confirmation of the viral cause is required (Cliver *et al.* 1983A, B). Detection procedures based on infectivity can be exquisitely sensitive, for a single enterovirus particle, which may theoretically suffice to initiate cytopathic effects or a plaque, weighs just over 10^{-17}g. The limitations of the methods published to date are that (1) they have usually been developed with ground beef, to the exclusion of other meats; (2) the extraction and concentration procedures have been developed mainly with enteroviruses and may not be successful in recovering larger, more complex viruses; and (3) there is no indication whatever that they can detect the HA and Norwalk-like viruses, which are the agents most likely to infect humans via foods.

Serological Methods

Conventional viruses have an outer coat of protein or lipid-containing envelope with external glycoproteins. These surface proteins are antigenic: they will induce production of antibody in a host and will react specifically with the antibody that they have evoked. Therefore, it should be possible to detect viruses such as the agent of HA and the Norwalk-like viruses on the basis of antigen–antibody (serological) reactions. If detection, rather than identification, is the goal, one would seek a method that would give a very clear signal even when minimal quantities of virus were present. In fact, there are no serological tests that will produce a clear signal with quantities of virus as small as a single particle, but methods such as the radioimmunoassay and enzyme immunoassay procedures do amplify the signal produced by the reaction with a relatively small quantity of antigen so as to yield a positive test result. Many possibilities exist, but there is as yet no serological procedure that has been fully developed for the detection of any virus in any food. Given the need for such methods, it is likely that this will take place, subject to the following constraints: (1) the quantity of antigen detectable by a serological method at its best will probably never equal the small quantity of infectious virus that can be detected when a suitable host system is available; (2) if the requisite quantity of antigen is present in a large sample of food, it will be necessary to extract and concentrate the virus with great efficiency to permit serological detection; and (3) the detection of any "new" virus by serological means will require the production of antiserum capable of reacting specifically with that virus. Much more work along this line remains to be done before, for example, the HA virus that may be present in a food sample can be detected by serological means.

Indicator Systems.   Given the manifest difficulties of detecting food-borne viruses either on the basis of their infectivity or their ability to react with homologous antibody, one might well wish for an "indicator," the presence of which would suggest strongly that viral contamination had occurred, and perhaps that infectious virus was present in the sample being tested. Unfortunately, no bacterium or other agent has been identified, the presence of which would strongly suggest the presence of virus (Berg 1978). The presence of human enterovirus in a food suggests that the HA virus or Norwalk-like agents may also be present, both because it suggests that fecal contamination has occurred and because the inactivation characteristics of the enteroviruses *may* resemble those of the HA and Norwalk viruses more closely than do those of any bacterial indicator. This is far from an ideal situation, in that the detection of the enteroviruses is difficult and costly, and they are likely to occur as cocontaminants only when the contamination derives from many people (e.g., by way of sewage). The more frequent case, in which a single food handler is the source of virus, is unlikely to introduce more than one type of virus to the food at a time, in that viruses interfere with each other in a single host so that multiple infections are exceptional. Therefore, if one found an enterovirus in a food as a result of mishandling by an infected person, the HA or Norwalk agents probably would *not* also be present. At present, there is no solution to this unsatisfactory situation.

PREVENTION

It can be seen that viruses sometimes occur in meats and may cause human illnesses. It seems appropriate, therefore, to consider what can be done to prevent virus transmission by these vehicles.

Prevention of Infections

All viruses are produced in the course of infections. There are many reasons for trying to avoid infections of food-source animals. Aggressive sanitation programs, to avoid both on-farm and between-farm transmission of viruses, are needed. To the degree that antibiotics in animal rations have at times been used as an alternative to sanitation, it should be remembered that antibiotics are ineffective against viruses. Vaccinations should be used when possible. Sanitation on the way to slaughter is also important, for many types of viruses can be transmitted among animals as they arrive at the facility, unless slaughtering is done within a few hours of arrival (Kostenbader and Cliver 1977).

Prevention of infections in persons who handle foods is largely a function of community and personal hygiene. Proper waste disposal facilities and adequate housing are important in preventing virus transmission in the community.

Prevention of Contamination

Since viral infections do occur and many of them are not detected in time to prevent contamination of food, in-plant sanitation is critical. Water conservation is being required in many plants and is leading to some changes in established cleaning procedures; plants that are in this situation are advised to obtain the services of a knowledgeable microbiologist to determine that they are minimizing opportunities for cross-contamination of product. Beyond this, personnel must be given facilities that are conducive to personal hygiene and proper food handling practice on the job. Unfortunately, there are as yet no definitive practices for the removal of viruses from fecally contaminated hands; this is a subject in need of study. Meanwhile, the diligent use of soap and water by personnel after defecation is certainly an appropriate approach to hand cleaning. Any change in operations that reduces intimate hand contact with the product will also reduce chances of contamination with viruses.

Decontamination

From one point of view, food that has been contaminated with fecal virus or other infectious agents can never be made "wholesome" again. However, it seems likely that viral contamination of meats occurs much more often than does transmission of the virus to consumers via meats as vehicles. This means that in many instances virus that has been introduced into the food has been inactivated before the food is eaten. Thorough cooking, as is usually done in the United States with pork and poultry, can be a useful safeguard; however, one must keep in mind that there have been outbreaks of viral disease in which cooked meats have been recontaminated before being served. This is a problem of the food service, rather than food-processing, industry, but it still represents a hazard to consumer health. At the very least, persons who are ill in any way (particularly with gastroenteritis) should be prevented from handling food in both plants or restaurants. Viral infections in food handlers are sometimes inapparent or are manifested only after the individual has been shedding virus for some time. Only proper personal hygiene and close supervision of food handling practices can prevent contamination of food in these instances.

SUMMARY

Meats do not serve frequently as vehicles in the transmission of viruses to humans. Most of the viruses of animal disease that may occur in meats and related products are principally a threat to animal, rather than human, health; however, the incidence of agents such as the foot-and-mouth disease viruses in meats has important economic consequences. Viruses causing human disease that are transmitted via meats emanate principally from human intestines and contaminate the food as a result of direct mishandling or by way of polluted water. Some of the human viruses that contaminate meats can be detected by laboratory tests, but at present this is not true of the agents of HA and of Norwalk-like gastroenteritis. Thorough cooking can inactivate viruses in meats, but cooking is not practiced with all meats, and contamination after cooking has also been known to occur. Conventional good food handling practice seems likely to minimize the opportunities for viral contamination of meats.

ACKNOWLEDGMENT

From the College of Agricultural and Life Sciences, University of Wisconsin—Madison.

REFERENCES

ALTER, M., FRANK, Y., DOYNE, H. and WEBSTER, D. D.   1975.   Creutzfeldt-Jakob disease after eating ovine brains? New Engl. J. Med. *292*, 297.

ALTER, M., HOENIG, E. and PRATZON, G.   1977.   Creutzfeldt-Jakob disease: possible association with eating brains. New Engl. J. Med. *296*, 820.

ANDREWS, B. E., MAJOR, R. and PALMER, S. R.   1981.   Ornithosis in poultry workers. Lancet *1*, 632.

APPLETON, H.   1980.   Small round viruses in outbreaks of food poisoning. *In* Viral Enteritis in Humans and Animals. p. 237. F. Bricout and R. Scherrer (Editors). Editions INSERM, Paris.

BERG, G.   1978.   Indicators of Viruses in Water and Food. Ann Arbor Science, Ann Arbor, MI.

BLACKWELL, J. H.   1980.   Internationalism and survival of foot-and-mouth disease virus in cattle and food products. J. Dairy Sci. *63*, 1019.

BLACKWELL, J. H., RICKANSRUD, D., McKERCHER, P. D. and McVICAR, J. W.   1982.   Effect of thermal processing on the survival of foot-and-mouth disease virus in ground meat. J. Food Sci. *47*, 388.

CENTER FOR DISEASE CONTROL, U. S. DEPARTMENT OF HEALTH, EDUCATION, AND WELFARE.   1963.   Hepatitis Surveillance, Report #15.

CENTER FOR DISEASE CONTROL, U. S. DEPARTMENT OF HEALTH, EDUCATION, AND WELFARE.   1965.   Hepatitis Surveillance, Report #24.

CENTER FOR DISEASE CONTROL, U. S. DEPARTMENT OF HEALTH, EDUCATION, AND WELFARE.   1966.   Morbidity and Mortality Weekly Report *15*, 9.

CENTER FOR DISEASE CONTROL, U. S. DEPARTMENT OF HEALTH, EDUCATION, AND WELFARE.   1969.   Morbidity and Mortality Weekly Report *18*, 70.

CENTER FOR DISEASE CONTROL, U. S. DEPARTMENT OF HEALTH, EDUCATION, AND WELFARE.   1976.   Foodborne and Waterborne Disease Outbreaks, Annual Summary 1974.

CENTER FOR DISEASE CONTROL, U. S. DEPARTMENT OF HEALTH, EDUCATION, AND WELFARE.   1977.   Morbidity Mortality Weekly Rep. *26*, 247.

CENTER FOR DISEASE CONTROL, U. S. DEPARTMENT OF HEALTH AND HUMAN SERVICES.   1980.   Hepatitis Surveillance, Report #45.

CLIVER, D. O.   1979.   Viral infections. In "Food-borne Infections and Intoxications," 2nd edition. Chap. 6, p. 299. H. Riemann and F. L. Bryan (Editors). Academic Press, NY.

CLIVER, D. O.   1983.   World Health Organization Manual on Food Virology. World Health Organization, Geneva, Switzerland.

CLIVER, D. O., KOSTENBADER, K. D., Jr. and VALLENAS, M. R.   1970.   Stability of viruses in low moisture foods. J. Milk Food Technol. 33, 484.

CLIVER, D. O., ELLENDER, R. D. and SOBSEY, M. D.   1983A.   Methods for detecting viruses in foods: Background and general principles. J. Food Prot. 46, 248.

CLIVER, D. O., ELLENDER, R. D. and SOBSEY, M. D.   1983B.   Methods to detect viruses in foods: Testing and interpretation of results. J. Food Prot. 46, 345.

CUNLIFFE, H. R., BLACKWELL, J. H. and WALKER, J. S.   1979.   Glutaraldehyde inactivation of exotic animal viruses in swine heart tissue. Appl. Environ. Microbiol. 37, 1044.

DENES, A. E., SMITH, J. L., HINDMAN, S. H., FLEISSNER, M. L., JUDELSOHN, R., ENGLENDER, S. J., TILSON, H. and MAYNARD, J. E.   1977.   Foodborne hepatitis A infection: A report of two urban restaurant-associated outbreaks. Am. J. Epidemiol. 105, 156.

FILPPI, J. A. and BANWART, G. J.   1974.   Effect of the fat content of ground beef on the heat inactivation of poliovirus. J. Food Sci. 39, 865.

HEIDELBAUGH, N. D. and GIRON, D. J.   1969.   Effect of processing on recovery of poliovirus from inoculated foods. J. Food Sci. 34, 239.

HERRMANN, J. E. and CLIVER, D. O.   1973.   Enterovirus persistence in sausage and ground beef. J. Milk Food Technol. 36, 426.

IDZIAK, E. S. and SRIVASTAVA, A. N.   1975.   The isolation of virus from comminuted meat. Canad. Inst. Food Sci. Technol. J. 8, 219.

KAPLAN, J. E., FELDMAN, R., CAMPBELL, D. S., LOOKABAUGH, C. and GARY, G. W.   1982.   The frequency of a Norwalk-like pattern of illness in outbreaks of acute gastroenteritis. Am. J. Publ. Health 72, 1329.

KOSTENBADER, K. D., Jr. and CLIVER, D. O.   1977.   Quest for viruses associated with our food supply. J. Food Sci. 42, 1253.

KOSTENBADER, K. D., Jr. and CLIVER, D. O.   1979.   Purchased cell cultures for detecting foodborne viruses. J. Food Prot. 42, 888.

LARKIN, E. P.   1982.   Detection of viruses in foods. In Methods in Environmental Virology, Chap. 10, p. 221. C. P. Gerba and S. M. Goyal (Editors). Marcel Dekker, NY.

LEGER, R., BOYER, K., PATTISON, C. and MAYNARD, J.   1975.   Hepatitis A: Report of a common-source outbreak with recovery of a possible etiologic agent. I. Epidemiologic studies. J. Infect. Dis. 131, 163.

McCOLLUM, R. W.   1961.   An outbreak of viral hepatitis in the Mediterranean fleet. Mil. Med. 126, 902.

MEYERS, J. D., ROMM, F. J., TIHEN, W. S. and BRYAN, J. A.   1975.   Food-borne hepatitis A in a general hospital. J. Am. Med. Assoc. 231, 1049.

NOORDAM, A. L. and COUTINHO, R. A.   1977.   Unpublished data. City of Amsterdam Health Dept., The Netherlands.

NORTHOLT, M. D. and KAPSENBERG, J. G.   1976.   Onderzoek naar enterovirussen in vlees en gehakt. Rapport nr., 57/76 Zoön. Rijks Instituut voor de Volksgezondheid, Bilthoven, Netherlands.

SULLIVAN, R., FASSOLITIS, A. C. and READ, R. B., Jr.   1970.   Method for isolating viruses from ground beef. J. Food Sci. 35, 624.

SULLIVAN, R., SCARPINO, P. V., FASSOLITIS, A. C., LARKIN, E. P. and PEELER, J. T.   1973.   Gamma radiation inactivation of coxsackievirus B-2. Appl. Microbiol. 26, 14.

SULLIVAN, R., MARNELL, R. M., LARKIN, E. P. and READ, R. B., Jr.   1975.   Inactivation of poliovirus 1 and coxsackievirus B-2 in broiled hamburgers. J. Milk Food Technol. 38, 473.

13

Perspective on Potentially Fruitful Research Areas

C. F. Niven, Jr.[1]

INTRODUCTION

Meat and poultry microbiology is concerned primarily with the inhibition or prevention of growth, or the destruction of spoilage or pathogenic microorganisms that may contaminate the product. In light of today's largely streamlined technology it is only the exceptional case that microorganisms play any functional role in the processing of any meat or poultry food. It has not always been so.

Even well into the present century the practice of aging beef and other red meats was rather commonplace, the purpose being to tenderize the meat and to develop characteristic flavors. No doubt, this practice was encouraged through lack of refrigeration capacity, and many consumers came to expect the strong characteristic flavor resulting from surface growth of what is now considered generally to be spoilage microorganisms. "Whisker" development on the carcass surface resulting from mold growth was considered to be a desirable feature. Poultry was considered to be ready to eat by some consumers figuratively when "it fell off the hook." The dramatic increase in refrigeration capacity has accompanied a gradual waning of the popularity of aged meat by the connoisseur.

The technology of meat curing has undergone an even more dramatic evolutionary change. Extending into the early part of this century swine were slaughtered largely in the fall of the year so advantage could be

[1]2100 Belford Drive, Walnut Creek, CA 94598.

Advances in Meat Research, Volume 2
Copyright 1986 by AVI Publishing Co.
All rights of reproduction in any form reserved
ISBN 0-87055-498-0

taken of cooler weather. Hams were dry cured by rubbing the surface with a mixture of salt, sugar, and nitrate and then stacked for a period of several weeks. The muscle tissues became cured through gradual diffusion of the curing mixture into the interior. Nitrite, essential for the curing action, resulted from nitrate reduction largely through bacterial action (micrococci) on the surface and then by diffusion into the interior. Putrefactive spoilage ("bone sours") resulting from the growth of *Clostridium putrefaciens* in the bone joint fluid was not uncommon. Spoilage of this nature resulted from bacterial growth prior to diffusion of the curing salts into the sensitive areas.

Aging of dry-cured hams required several months and often was accompanied by surface growth of molds and bacteria. It is believed that surface growth contributed at least in part to the characteristic flavor of these hams. This type of ham is produced today as country-cured hams but they are considered only to be a specialty item. Interior spoilage has been greatly reduced through adequate refrigeration during the curing process. Nitrite generally is added directly to the curing mix and the cure may be enhanced through direct injection of a curing brine into the vicinity of the bone joints.

With the advent of readily available mechanical refrigeration, brine curing of hams largely replaced the dry cure procedure. Vascular pumping has virtually eliminated interior spoilage and the possibility of any role that bacteria might play has gradually faded. Nevertheless, a widespread belief persisted in the industry that bacteria, somehow, played an important function in the development of the ham flavor. This belief was strengthened by the ham curing procedures that were practiced in England and Europe where curing brines were reused many times with the deliberate attempt to encourage bacterial growth in the cover brine. The bacteria ultimately attained huge populations in these brines, and, no doubt contributed to the ultimate ham flavor.

Reuse of curing brines never received widespread acceptance in the United States, but because of the difficulty in cleaning the wooden tierces between use a modest level of bacteria developed in the brine and on the meat surfaces, particularly if the hams were cured more than 10 days. The microorganisms are predominately psychrotrophic, salt-tolerant lactic acid bacteria (Deibel and Niven 1958, 1959). Yeasts and nitrate-reducing micrococci were found near the surface of the brine. Deliberate inoculation of the pickle used to pump the hams—either pure or mixed cultures— failed to yield an improved ham flavor (Deibel and Niven 1957).

Considering the current streamlined curing techniques in America, including intramuscular injecting of the boned ham, the use of curing adjuncts and enhancers, and the virtual elimination of any holding period prior to thermal processing, there is little chance that bacteria play any role in the curing procedure. They are, however, essential in the production of the large class of deliberately fermented meat and poultry foods as discussed in Chapter 4.

FRESH MEATS AND POULTRY

Nature of Spoilage Microorganisms

As discussed in Chapter 2, by far the most important group of bacteria that limit the shelf life of refrigerated meats and poultry are members of the genus *Pseudomonas*. These surface contaminants are psychrotrophic strict aerobes that require a high water activity (a_w) for growth.

In their elegant study on the taxonomy of the various species of the genus *Pseudomonas*, it is unfortunate that Stanier *et al.* (1966) did not include in their collection various *Pseudomonas* strains from the surface flora of fresh meats, poultry, and fish. There is a need for extensive taxonomic studies on this important group of spoilage organisms so that they can be better related to other established members of the genus (Buchanan and Gibbons 1974). A valuable contribution in this respect already has been made by Shaw and Latty (1982).

Similarly, further work is needed on the taxonomy of the genera *Moraxella* and *Acinetobacter*, also encountered as spoilage organisms on fresh meats, poultry, and fish. Like *Pseudomonas*, they are aerobic psychrotrophic surface contaminants that have characteristics similar to each other. Earlier literature on the microbiology of meat placed these bacteria in the genera *Achromobacter* and *Flavobacterium*. Thornley (1967) has contributed to our knowledge on the taxonomy of these bacteria.

When permitted to grow extensively on the surface of meats and poultry these spoilage bacteria, particularly the pseudomonads, discolor the meat, yield a slimy surface, and synthesize malodorous compounds. There is a need to know considerably more about the substrates in meat juices that are attacked by these microorganisms, as well as the nature of the offensive metabolites, and the biochemical pathways for their formation. Such studies might yield valuable information on the taxonomy of these organisms and may give better insight into their control. Pittard *et al.* (1982) reported that the metabolites are largely sulfides, esters, and acids that are derived from amino acid metabolism.

Spoilage Control

Under the usual marketing conditions chilled fresh meats and poultry innately have a relatively short refrigerated life prior to onset of spoilage. To effectively extend shelf life requires either minimizing the initial contaminating levels, removal of the surface contaminants on the meat surfaces, retarding or preventing growth of the contaminants, or a combination of these factors. Chapter 1 discusses the sources of the surface contaminants and steps that may be taken to minimize the initial levels. Because of the nature of the animal and the slaughter and dressing techniques that are employed, poultry appears to be the most difficult product to handle in a satisfactory manner. Much additional research of a technological nature is needed to improve upon poultry slaughtering methodology to minimize contamination from equipment, as well as cross-contamination from one carcass to another and also to prevent carcass contamination with fecal contents. The effectiveness of the scalding and defeathering operations for reducing surviving bacterial population levels but without undue damage to the skin needs careful review. To improve upon present methods without impairing efficiency may require radical departure from current practices.

Swine slaughter presents similar problems because of the retention of the skin on the carcass. Cattle and sheep slaughter appears to offer the greatest possibility for improvement because the highly contaminated hide is removed. Attention to elementary principles of good hygiene practices should prove to be effective, keeping in mind that puncture or incision through an unclean hide with unclean instruments, as well as contamination from the anus and oral cavity, are the common portals of entry of contaminants onto the surface of an otherwise sterile carcass.

Another approach to extending refrigerated shelf life is to remove the contaminants that are introduced onto the surface during slaughter. Stringer (1982) reviewed efforts that have been employed in this respect. High-pressure water sprays (hot or cold), or hypochlorite or acetic acid sprays have been attempted with varying degrees of success. Very high-pressure water sprays appear to be most effective. A 3% acetic acid spray also is effective in that a residual effect is retained for retarding growth of surviving contaminants. For example, the *Acinetobacter/Moraxella* group fails to grow at low pH values.

To intelligently approach efforts to physically remove microorganisms from surfaces requires knowledge of the manner in which bacteria attach themselves and become colonized onto solid surfaces. Surface active agents may prove to be beneficial for their removal.

In addition to efforts to physically remove contaminants from meat surfaces, one should be mindful of the potential benefits of high-energy radiation (beta, gamma, X ray) for killing the contaminating bacteria without harming appearance or palatability characteristics of the meat. Meat spoilage psychrotrophs, particularly the pseudomonads, are among the most radiation sensitive of all bacteria.

A third method for the control of spoilage in fresh meats and poultry is to retard or prevent growth of the surface contaminants. Refrigeration is effective but has its limits due to the psychrotrophic nature of many of the surface contaminants. Freezing would be the ideal method but, unfortunately, consumer resistance continues to be encountered. Packaging in oxygen-impermeable films has proved to be very effective in prolonging the refrigerated life of fresh meats and has gained widespread acceptance in the institutional trade. It appears to be receiving increasing, although modest, acceptance in the retail trade.

Dehydration, modified atmospheres, fermentation, salting, or curing are other measures that can be employed to retard spoilage, but most of these measures significantly change the appearance or palatability characteristics of fresh meat or poultry. The use of organic acids and citrate buffer on fresh meats is discussed in Chapter 2.

Not to be overlooked is the use of combinations of preservative methods, each of which may be marginally effective, but when combined, prove to be synergistic. This well-established principle in food preservation has been reviewed by Ingram and Mackey (1976), Ingram and Simonsen (1980), and Leistner (1978). The potential of various synergistic preservation combinations has not been exhausted and should be exploited further.

CURED MEATS

When meat is cured, a selective microbiological medium is produced. As a result of the addition of salt and nitrite, plus a fermentable sugar, the important fresh meat spoilage bacteria, the *Pseudomonas-Moraxella-Acinetobactor* group is no longer able to grow. Instead, various lactic acid bacteria *(Lactobacillus, Leuconostoc, Streptococcus, Pediococcus), Micrococcus, Brochothrix,* as well as various yeasts, become important potential spoilage microorganisms. The fresh meat spoilage flora are essentially gram negative, whereas cured meat spoilage flora are largely gram positive.

Most of the cured meat microflora, particularly the lactic acid bacteria, are rather poorly defined taxonomically and are in need of a good deal of systematic study. Some are difficult to culture in artificial media because of their fastidious nutritional requirements, and as a result, were largely ignored or went unrecognized in earlier studies (Niven 1952). Adequate media, e.g., APT agar and broth now commercially available, have made it possible to easily culture them. Because of the very nature of the environment imposed upon them, most species that are associated with cured meats are rather salt tolerant, and capable of growing at low temperatures.

One important species that is well defined is *Lactobacillus viridescens* (Niven and Evans 1957), a heterofermentative, heat-and salt-tolerant species that is capable of growing at low temperatures. It is the most common species responsible for greenish discolorations of cured meats. The discoloration results from the oxidation of the cured meat pigment by hydrogen peroxide that accumulates as the organism is permitted to grow in the presence of oxygen. The substrate(s) existing in the meat juices that is oxidized by the organism to yield hydrogen peroxide is not known. Its identity, as well as the biochemical pathway for its oxidation, might ultimately prove helpful in the control of this important spoilage problem.

Meat curing and processing are undergoing continual changes and improvements, most of which are aimed toward streamlining the procedures or the adoption of cost-cutting measures. Examples are the use of curing adjuncts and enhancers, extenders, acidulants, tumbling or massaging, reforming, and use of lower salt and nitrite levels in response to consumer pressures. The microbiologist should be mindful that meat curing establishes a rather delicate ecologic balance with respect to the surviving flora and the ability of subsequent contaminants to grow in or on the product. It, therefore, behooves the microbiologist to critically examine the consequences of any changes that are introduced in curing or processing, no matter how subtle the change might appear. Attention should be paid to any changes in the spoilage picture that might occur. More especially, the effect of the change must be assessed with respect to its influence upon growth of potential pathogens.

CANNED MEATS

Chapter 3 reviews the various types of canned meats currently produced. They range from meats intended to be kept under refrigeration (e.g., canned ham) and which receive only heat pasturization, to those meats that receive a full process ($F_0 \geq 2.78$) to assure safety from a botulism hazard.

Of greatest interest are the luncheon meats and canned hams weighing three pounds or less that are considered to be shelf stable, yet receive a relatively mild heat treatment, generally in the range of $F_0 = 0.1-0.7$. These canned meats have enjoyed a most remarkable safety record in respect to freedom from botulism outbreaks.

Numerous studies have been conducted in an attempt to explain the safety of these products. Much of the earlier literature is confusing. However, excellent reviews have been published by Tompkin (1983) and by Hauschild (1982). There is general agreement that stability and safety of these canned cured meats results from a combination of the heat treatment, the inhibitory properties of added salt and nitrite in the curing mix, and a consistently low initial spore population. These factors appear to be in delicate balance and a significant change in any one of them may drastically alter stability and safety. The heat treatment, even though relatively mild, is sufficient to injure any *Clostridium botulinum* spores that may be present. Even though the spores may germinate in the canned products, outgrowth is prevented by the presence of nitrite and salt. Studies indicate that a reduction in amount of heat applied requires higher concentrations of the curing salts to maintain stability. An increase in spore levels through inoculation requires either higher thermal processing values or higher levels of curing salts to restore stability.

There is need for considerably more information interrelating quantitatively these factors with respect to stability and safety of shelf-stable canned cured meats. The multifactorial nature of such investigations greatly complicates the experimental approach. An excellent contribution has already been made by Roberts *et al.* (1981A, B, C).

Any attempt to reduce the level of salt and nitrite in these canned products to gain a possible marketing advantage should be approached with extreme caution. A canned, uncured product such as beef stew that is only lightly salted to taste (no nitrite) requires a full thermal process ($F_0 \geq 2.78$) to assure safety. It then stands to reason that as salt and/or nitrite levels are reduced in shelf-stable canned cured meats a point will be reached where a hazard of unacceptable proportions will be encountered. These parameters need to be much better defined prior to any deliberate manipulation of the curing mix for these shelf-stable canned meats.

The exact mechanism of the bacteriostatic effect of nitrite is unknown. It is a powerful oxidizing agent and probably attacks a number of chemicals both inside and outside the cell. Its bacteriostatic effect is greatly increased by lowering the pH, but it becomes progressively more unstable in an acid environment. Bacteriostasis seems to be associated with the calculated concentration of the hypothetical undissociated nitrous acid (Castellani and Niven 1955). Tompkin *et al.* (1978) and Christiansen (1980) speculated that nitrite reacts with the iron in ferredoxin that is involved in electron transport among the clostridia. Resistance to nitrite varies from species to species and with the medium in which it is tested. Considerably more research is needed to elucidate the exact mechanism of action of this most important chemical used in meat curing.

FOOD-BORNE INFECTIONS AND INTOXICATIONS

In addition to measures to control contamination and growth of potential spoilage microorganisms in or on meat and poultry foods it is important to avoid all possible contamination with human pathogens. Unfortunately, many of the pathogenic microorganisms are not host specific and, therefore, are capable of infecting both humans and domestic animals. Therefore, meat and poultry frequently harbor microorganisms considered to be dangerous to the human. Some cause active infections while others are responsible for intoxications as a result of synthesis of toxins when permitted to grow in or on meat and poultry foods.

Salmonella

As reviewed in Chapter 7 the great majority of *Salmonella* serotypes are not host specific and therefore are capable of cross-infecting humans and meat animals and poultry. The existence of a cycle of infection from animal by-products, to feed, to the farm animal, to meat, poultry, milk or eggs, and back to the by-products, is well documented through numerous epidemiological studies. Such cycles serve as reservoirs for human infections.

Because of the ubiquity of salmonellae in nearly all warm- and many cold-blooded animals there appears to be general acceptance of their presence in the environment and in unprocessed meat and poultry foods. On the other hand, costs in terms of both human and animal health as a result of *Salmonella* gastroenteritis outbreaks would seem to warrant continuous efforts to minimize the frequency of their occurrence. Monetary incentives to the feed manufacturer, the livestock and poultry producers, the abattoir, and the food service establishment should provide encouragement to minimize frequency of food contamination.

Technological innovations continue to appear that hold promise in reducing the incidence of *Salmonella* infection. The microbiologist should play a key role in evaluating the effectiveness of innovations as they arise. Without the aid of some radical discovery eradication appears to be impossible; but reduction in frequency appears feasible.

The following are some steps that should aid in any integrated approach aimed toward reducing the frequency of *Salmonella* contamination of foods and salmonellosis outbreaks among humans and domestic livestock:

1. Reduce the incidence of *Salmonella* contamination in rendered animal by-products. Contamination of these feed ingredients is known to be one of the steps in the continuation of the *Salmonella* infection cycle. The rendering procedure voids the product of any *Salmonella* contamination, and their presence in the rendered product clearly indicates recontamination as a result of poor manufacturing practice. This source of contamination should be corrected.

2. Follow good hygienic measures in the preparation of feed mixes for poultry and livestock. Use only constituents that are known to have low incidence of *Salmonella* contamination.

3. Exploit to the fullest the principle of competitive exclusion wherein, for example, the gastrointestinal tract of the newly hatched chick is colonized with flora from the feces of healthy adult poultry (Barnes *et al.* 1980). Efforts to identify the responsible flora should be actively pursued.

4. Follow good husbandry practices in the growing of poultry and livestock. It is known that otherwise healthy animals kept under good hygienic conditions, and well fed, are relatively resistant to salmonellosis.

5. Avoid stress conditions, thirst, and hunger among the animals and poultry being shipped to slaughter. Adopt practicable measures to shorten the time period between leaving the farm and slaughter. Only a few hours are required for the interim between the harvesting and canning of tomatoes. The same practice should be followed in the slaughter of poultry and livestock. Marketing channels for cattle and swine generally are not conducive to effective control of *Salmonella* infections.

6. Develop and adopt new and improved slaughter procedures that will aid in preventing cross-contamination among carcasses.

7. Encourage or enforce good hygienic practices in food processing and preparation, particularly among the food service establishments. Conduct a continuing education program, beginning in the public schools, concerning good hygienic practices to follow in food preparation and handling in the home.

To test the adequacy and effectiveness of any control measure the microbiologist must have at his disposal accurate and rapid tests for determining the presence or absence of salmonellae. Historically, testing for salmonellae has been tedious and cumbersome, especially when the demands of the control official require a sensitivity for detecting less than one viable cell per gram of sample. Fortunately, improved and more rapid tests are becoming available, such as the enzyme immunoassay method or the DNA–DNA hybridization technique (Fitts et al. 1983). It should be kept in mind that, to be effective, no test needs to be 100% accurate, nor can one test a problem out of existence. The ultimate aim should be to reduce the incidence of Salmonella contamination to a low enough level that routine testing would no longer be required.

Campylobacter

Campylobacter fetus subsp. jejuni has been recognized as an animal pathogen for a number of years. Only after 1970 was it realized that this subspecies was an important taxon in causing disease, not only in domestic animals, but also gastroenteritis in humans. This subspecies, now generally designated as C. jejuni, is considered to be a more common etiologic agent for gastroenteritis than Salmonella. Since C. jejuni is considered to be basically an animal pathogen, campylobacteriosis is designated as a zoonosis. Like Salmonella, even low population levels of the microorganism can cause infection in the human.

Like Salmonella, this species is widespread in nature. It occurs in the intestinal tract of a wide variety of animals, both domestic and wild. It is a common contaminant on fresh meats and, especially, poultry. It is believed that meat and poultry are the original sources of the microorganism in human disease outbreaks, although in numerous instances evidence is circumstantial rather than direct. Raw milk and untreated water also have been implicated in a few outbreaks.

Campylobacter jejuni is an unusual microorganism in that it requires a low oxygen and high carbon dioxide tension for growth. Temperature limits for growth reside between 32° and 45°C. Perhaps because of its high optimum growth temperature it is more commonly found in the poultry intestine. Doyle (1981) reviewed this species and its significance in human health.

The epidemiology, symptoms, and nature of human campylobacteriosis are very similar to salmonellosis. Therefore, any measures taken to reduce the incidence of either one should help to control the other.

Staphylococcus aureus

Staphylococcus continues to be a common type of food poisoning associated with the consumption of cured meats. Historically, ham has been the most common meat food involved, most likely because of the tendency for abuse of this product by the food service establishment or consumer after it has been cooked and prepared for eating. Incidence appears to be waning, perhaps, because of the gradual loss in popularity of the large bone-in ham. Cured meats permit rapid growth of the salt-tolerant *Staphylococcus aureus* while inhibiting growth of many other species.

Enterotoxin production in sufficient quantity to yield symptoms requires the attainment of population levels in excess of a million per gram of food. To reach these levels requires the holding of contaminated prepared food for at least several hours at a warm growing temperature prior to consumption. Thus, there is no excuse for an outbreak of staphylococcus food poisoning except for ignorance or laxity by the food preparer or consumer. Although much additional research is needed on this species and its toxins it is likely that such research will fail to reduce the incidence of staphylococcal intoxication to a significant degree. There are some foods, however, that are occasionally associated with staphylococcus food poisoning through no fault of the consumer. Cheddar cheese, for example, can contain toxic concentrations of enterotoxin if *Staphylococcus aureus* is permitted to grow in the milk during cheese manufacturing. Barber and Deibel (1972) reported the occurrence of staphylococcus food poisoning from fermented sausages as the result of contamination and growth of enterotoxigenic strains in the sausage during the ripening process. For further information on staphylococcus food poisoning the reader is referred to Chapter 8.

Other Pathogens

Other chapters in this book, particularly Chapters 5 and 9, present details on other pathogens of interest to the food microbiologist. The investigator should be aware of each of these species, their physiological characteristics that permit their growth in meat and poultry foods, factors that affect their viability, and methods for their detection and identification. Any technical or technological developments for their control must be evaluated through appropriate testing procedures.

Prevention of botulism through control procedures is unique because of the stringencies placed upon avoiding this hazard. In this instance the food being processed is not tested directly for the organism or its spores. Rather, strict control is placed upon the formulation and thermal process for shelf-stable low-acid foods to assure adherence to a well-established safe process. No microbiological testing procedure could ever approach the stringency required to avoid this potential hazard.

FERMENTED MEAT FOODS

Throughout history numerous varieties of sausages of varied ethnic origin have evolved in which bacterial fermentation is allowed to produce a characteristic tangy flavor and to help preserve the product (Chapter 4). Traditionally these sausages were cured with a mixture of salt, nitrate, and sugar, plus a mixture of spices. Chance contamination was relied upon for nitrate reduction needed for the curing action (generally micrococci), and for lactic fermentation (various lactic acid bacteria). Some received a terminal heat treatment, others received a "cold smoke," while others were dried at cool temperatures to yield a shelf-stable product. Failures were not uncommon as a result of malfermentations.

Today, most fermented sausages are cured by the direct addition of nitrite as one of the curing constituents, thus eliminating the necessity for bacterial reduction of nitrate. In addition, starter cultures are added to assure a lactic fermentation. The first commercially available starter culture was a freeze-dried *Pediococcus* sp. originally isolated from a fermented sausage variety (Deibel *et al.* 1961). The manufacture of fermented sausages has much in common with cheese fermentation.

A successful sausage starter must be capable of growing vigorously in sausage emulsions under anaerobic conditions, must carry out a homofermentative lactic fermentation to avoid gassiness, must not produce undesirable odors or flavors or be actively proteolytic, should have a reasonably wide temperature range for growth, must be inactivated through a moderate terminal heat process, must not discolor the cured meat pigment, and must be harmless to human health. Adherence to all of these characteristics virtually limits the choice to the homofermentative lactic acid bacteria *(Lactobacillus, Pediococcus,* and *Streptococcus).*

Starter cultures can be selected to fit a particular set of environmental conditions needed to produce the desired sausage. Traditionally, this has been accomplished through culture isolations from natural sources wherein desired fermentations have occurred as a result of chance contamination. This technique has achieved widespread success in cheese, pickles, bread, sausage, as well as numerous other food fermentations.

Today the microbiologist has other methods for strain selection at his disposal. For example, artificial mutagenesis can be employed using various techniques to effect the mutation, followed by selection of those mutants having the desired characteristics. This technique has been successful in strain selection used in a number of industrial fermentations.

A more precise technique is the deliberate manipulation of the organism's genetic structure through use of recombinant DNA technology. Theoretically, through use of this technique, the desired characteristics could be "built-in" to a starter culture—most likely through use of inducible plasmid-encoded enzyme systems.

Genetic exchange between bacteria can be effected through transformation in which purified DNA is taken up directly by a recipient culture, by transduction through use of a temperature transducing phage, or by conjugal transfer of plasmid DNA from a donor to a recipient.

Molecular biology and genetic engineering have not received widespread attention in the food industry, possibly because of the required sophistication, and cost. Possibilities, however, are unlimited in attaining those objectives that otherwise could not be attained. Although their origin is lost in antiquity, the development of additional varieties of tasty, fermented sausages through use of unique starter cultures and substrates offers enticing possibilities.

CONCLUSIONS

From both a nutritional and an economic standpoint, meat and poultry constitute a major part of the human diet. It, therefore, behooves those who are associated with this important industry to devote increasing effort and attention to economic production, quality improvement, spoilage prevention, assurance of safety, new product development, and by-product utilization. The microbiologist should play a significant role in each of these areas.

The microbiologist should maintain vigilance in attempting to identify the responsible etiologic agent in an alleged meat- or poultry-borne illness. The unusual causative pathogen may be easily overlooked. Chapter 9 discusses a number of species that have been implicated in food-borne disease outbreaks. Not to be overlooked are chemicals and viruses (Chapter 12) as possible responsible agents. On the other hand, care should be taken not to be misled by an existing harmless species that may constitute a high proportion of the flora in the food examined. In too many instances enterococci have been implicated as being responsible for a food poisoning outbreak only on the basis that this ubiquitous and versatile group of microorganisms comprised the dominant flora in the sample examined.

Tissue culture of both plant and animal cells has become a common laboratory practice. In light of advances that have been made in both cellular and molecular cloning techniques it is possible that we are but a step away from economical culture of tissues for edible purposes. Such a procedure would eliminate the necessity to dispose of inedible by-products, such as hides, hair, horns, and hooves. It should be possible to control flavor, texture, and composition through the use of tissue cultures to achieve highly desirable foods from the standpoint of nutrient content.

Meat and poultry microbiology has not kept pace with dairy microbiology. Historically, dairy microbiology has dominated the entire field of food microbiology. The microorganisms associated with, and so well defined in the dairy industry, largely represent those that inhabit a rather restricted ecologic niche in nature. Many might very well be mutants derived from parent strains that have acquired the ability to ferment lactose, a sugar that is restricted in its occurrence in nature. Acquisition of this character would give the microorganism a distinct competitive advantage in dairy foods. A similar selective environment generally does not exist for those microorganisms that inhabit fresh meats and poultry, for example, and therefore a much wider spectrum of species would be expected to develop in these products.

When considerably more information becomes available on the general aspects of meat and poultry microbial ecology we shall be much more confident in dealing with problems concerned with preservation, spoilage prevention, and safety. Technical and technological developments in the past several decades permit much greater flexibility in the marketing of these important foods. Further developments should provide much greater rewards.

Unfortunately, in recent years there appears to have been a significant reduction in research and development effort by the meat- and poultry-processing industry. This deficiency leaves the industry in a rather tedious and vulnerable position, particularly with respect to their ability to cope effectively with unforeseen developments. This situation imposes increasing demands upon colleges and universities who have appropriate departments and staff to aid in filling the void. Unfortunately, most of these institutions are experiencing increasing constraints because of severe budget limitations. The need is great to find a solution to this problem, so that adequate funding can be devoted especially to needed areas of fundamental research.

REFERENCES

BARBER, L. E. and DEIBEL, R. H. 1972. Effect of pH and oxygen tension on staphylococcal growth and enterotoxin formation in fermented sausage. Appl. Microbiol. 24, 891.

BARNES, E. M., IMPEY, C. S. and COOPER, D. M. 1980. Competitive exclusion of salmonellas from the new hatched chick. Vet. Rec. 106, 61.

BUCHANAN, R. E. and GIBBONS, N. E. 1974. Bergey's Manual of Determinative Bacteriology. 8th edition. The Williams & Wilkins Company, Baltimore, MD.

CASTELLANI, A. G. and NIVEN, C. F., JR. 1955. Factors affecting the bacteriostatic action of sodium nitrite. Appl. Microbiol. 3, 154.

CHRISTIANSEN, L. N. 1980. Factors influencing botulinal inhibition by nitrite. Food Technol. 34, 237.

DEIBEL, R. H. and NIVEN, C. F., Jr. 1957. Studies on the microflora of commercial ham curing brines and their significance in curing. Proc. 2nd Intern. Symp. Food Micorbiol., Cambridge, England, p. 149.

DEIBEL, R. H. and NIVEN, C. F., Jr. 1958. Microbiology of meat curing. I. The occurrence and significance of a motile microorganism of the genus Lactobacillus in ham curing brines. Appl. Microbiol. 6, 323.

DEIBEL, R. H. and NIVEN, C. F., Jr. 1959. Microbiology of meat curing. II. Characteristics of a Lacotobacillus occurring in ham curing brines which synthesizes a polysaccharide from sucrose. Appl. Microbiol. 7, 138.

DEIBEL, R. H., NIVEN, C. F., Jr. and WILSON, G. D. 1961. Microbiology of meat curing IV. A lyophilized *Pediococcus cerevisiae* starter culture for fermented sausage. Appl. Microbiol. *9,* 239.

DOYLE, M. P.   1981.   *Campylobacter fetus* subsp. *jejuni:* An old pathogen of new concern. J. Food Prot. *44,* 480.

FITTS, R., DIAMOND, M., HAMILTON, C. and NERI, M.   1983.   DNA–DNA hybridization assay for detection of *Salmonella* spp. in foods. Appl. Environ. Microbiol. *46,* 1146.

HAUSCHILD, A. H. W.   1982.   Assessment of botulism hazards from cured meat products. Food Technol. *36,* 95.

INGRAM, M. and MACKEY, B. M.   1976   *In* Inhibition and Inactivation of Vegetative Microbes, p. 111. F. A. Skinner and W. B. Hugo (Editors). Academic Press, NY.

INGRAM, M. and SIMONSEN, B.   1980.   *In* Microbial Ecology of Foods, Intern. Commission Microbiol. Specifications for Foods, p. 333. Academic Press, NY.

LEISTNER, L.   1978.   *In* Food Quality and Nutrition, p. 553. W. K. Downey, (Editor). Applied Science Publishers, London.

NIVEN, C. F., JR.   1952.   Significance of the lactic and bacteria in the meat industry. Proc. 4th Res. Conf., p. 31. American Meat Institute, Chicago, IL.

NIVEN, C. F., JR. and EVANS, J. B.   1957.   *Lactobacillus viridescens* Nov. spec., a heterofermentative species that produces a green discoloration of cured meat pigments. J. Bacteriol. *73,* 758.

PITTARD, B. T., FREEMAN, L. R., LATER, D. W. and LEE, M. L.   1982.   Identification of volatile organic compounds produced by fluorescent pseudonomads on chicken breast muscle. Appl. Environ. Microbiol. *43,* 1504.

ROBERTS, T. A., GIBSON, A. M. and ROBINSON, A.   1981A.   Factors controlling the growth of *Clostridium botulinum* Types A and B in pasteurized, cured meats. I. Growth in pork slurries prepared from "low" pH meat (pH range 5.6–6.3). J. Food Technol. *16,* 239.

ROBERTS, T. A., GIBSON, A. M. and ROBINSON, A.   1981B.   Factors controlling growth of *Clostridium botulinum* Types A and B in pasteurized, cured meats. II. Growth in pork slurries prepared from "high" pH meat (range 6.3–6.8). J. Food Technol. *16,* 267.

ROBERTS, T. A., GIBSON, A. M. and ROBINSON, A.   1981C.   Prediction of toxin production by *Clostridium botulinum* in pasteurized pork slurry. J. Food Technol. *16,* 337.

SHAW, B. G. and LATTY, J. B.   1982.   A numerical taxonomic study of *Pseudonomas* strains from spoiled meat. J. Appl. Bacteriol. *52,* 219.

STANIER, R. Y., PALLERONI, N. J. and DOUDOROFF, M.   1966.   The aerobic pseudomonads: A taxonomic study. J. Gen. Microbiol. *43,* 159.

STRINGER, W. C.   1982.   Removing microbes from meat surfaces. *Proc. Meat Ind. Res. Conf.* p. 81. Amer. Meat Sci. Assoc. Chicago, IL.

THORNLEY, M. J.   1967.   A taxonomic study of *Acinetobacter* and related genera. J. Gen. Microbiol. *49,* 211.

TOMPKIN, R. B.   1983.   Nitrite. *In* Anti-Microbials in Foods. p. 205. A. L. Branen and P. M. Davidson (Editors). Marcel Dekker, NY.

TOMPKIN, R. B., CHRISTIANSEN, L. N. and SHAPARIS, A. B.   1978.   Enhancing nitrite inhibition of *Clostridium botulinum* with isoascorbate in perishable canned cured meat. Appl. Environ. Microbiol. *35,* 59.

Index

Oxidase, 201
Oxidation, 5. *See also* Redox potential
Oxidation-reduction potential, 278. *See also* Redox potential
Oxogluconic acids, 63
Oxygen, 2, 5, 53–56, 75, 77, 80, 196, 201, 203, 217, 401, 405
 concentrations, 4–5, 78–79
 consumption, 78
 free gasses, 80
 permeability, 6, 79, 109, 216, 268, 400
 requirements. *See* Requirements, oxygen
 residual, 78
 scavaging system, 79
 transmission rate, 102

P

Pacilomyces, 279
Package
 air impermeable, 233
 atmosphere, 78
 gas permeable, 77, 108, 196, 282
 modified atmosphere, 75
 moisture impermeable, 109
 oxygen free, 80
 oxygen permeable, 268
 oxygen impermeable, 109, 400
 plastic bag, 77
 vacuum, 65, 77–80, 193
Packaging, 1, 62, 81, 102, 106
 aerobic, 200
 anaerobic, 200
 bulk, 62–63
 conditions, 75
 controlled atmosphere, 180
 film, 6, 79
 gas flush, 80
 materials, 108–109, 192, 196, 197, 217, 268, 282, 400
 modified atmosphere, 196, 203, 217
 oxygen free, 80
 vacuum, 6, 55, 63–65, 67, 72, 75, 77–80, 91, 99–101, 108, 113, 196, 203, 217, 268, 279, 302
 vacuum, bacon, 101
 vacuum, beef, 79
 vacuum, DFD meat, 64

vacuum, lamb, 65, 67
vacuum, refrigerated cooked poultry, 100
Parasites, 2, 311–366, 386
 helminth, 312, 325–365
 life cycles, 313–314, 320–321, 326, 332, 350–353, 360–362
 protozoan, 312–325
Parma. *See* Ham
Pasteurization, 217, 250, 402
Pasture, 28
Paté, 100
Pathogenic bacteria. *See* Bacteria, pathogenic; Pathogens
Pathogenicity, 280, 282
Pathogens, 63, 68, 105, 181, 193, 311–366. *See also* Microorganisms, pathogenic; Bacteria, pathogenic
 cold tolerant, 64
 enteric, 68, 94
 potential, 56
Patulin, 283, 300–301
Pediococcus, 107, 136–139, 141, 145, 147, 154, 156, 214, 401, 407
 P. acidilactici, 137–139, 149, 151
 P. cerevisiae, 4, 134, 137–138, 151
 strain FPI, 134–135
 P. pentosaceus, 107, 137–138
Pelleted meal. *See* Meal, pelleted
Penicillic acid, 283, 300–301
Penicillium, 4, 137, 144, 159, 192, 194, 278–281, 294, 300–301
 P. camemberti, 137
 P. candidum, 137, 144
 P. comune, 137
 P. corylophilum, 74
 P. chrysogenum, 280
 P. expansum, 137, 280
 P. hirsutum, 74
 P. janthinellum, 280
 P. miczynskii, 137
 P. nalgiovensis, 137, 144, 280
 P. roqueforti, 137, 144
 P. simplicissimum, 137
 P. viridicatum, 269, 301
Pens, holding, 19, 28–29
 sale, 28
Pepperoni, 93, 124, 129, 132
Peptidoglycan, 166, 169
Perianal region, 33

Encyclopedia of
World Sport

FROM ANCIENT TIMES TO THE PRESENT

David Levinson and Karen Christensen, editors

New York   Oxford
Oxford University Press
1999

Oxford University Press

Oxford   New York
Athens Auckland Bangkok Bogotá Buenos Aires Calcutta
Cape Town Chennai Dar es Salaam Delhi Florence Hong Kong Istanbul
Karachi Kuala Lumpur Madrid Melbourne Mexico City Mumbai
Nairobi Paris São Paulo Singapore Taipei Tokyo Toronto Warsaw

and associated companies in

Berlin   Ibadan

First published in 1996 by ABC–CLIO, Inc.
130 Cremona Drive, P.O. Box 1911
Santa Barbara, California 93116-1911

First issued as a one-volume editon in paperback and cloth by Oxford University Press
198 Madison Avenue, New York, New York 10016

Oxford is a registered trademark of Oxford University Press

Library of Congress Cataloging-in-Publication Data
Encyclopedia of world sport / general editors, David Levinson, Karen
   Christensen.
        p.   cm.
     Condensation of 3 vol. work published in 1996.
     Includes bibliographical references (p.   ) and index.
     ISBN 0-19-513195-9 (cloth) / ISBN 0-19-512778-1 (pbk.)
        1. Sports--Encyclopedias.   I. Levinson, David, 1947-   .
   II. Christensen, Karen.
   GV567.E55   1998
   796'.03--dc2198-27052

Berkshire Reference Works Staff
Bonnie Dyer-Bennet
Qiang Li
John Townes
Alan Trevithick
Susan Walton
Patricia Welsh

10 9 8 7 6 5 4 3 2 1

Printed in the United States of America
on acid-free paper

Editorial Board

General Editors

Contents

The Contributors, *ix*

Preface, *xv*

Encyclopedia of World Sport

Contributors

Andrea Abbas
Keele University, UK
Masculinity

Harvey Abrams
State College, Pennsylvania
Art
Literature

E. John B. Allen
Plymouth State College, New
    Hampshire
Skiing, Alpine
Skiing, Nordic

Gary Anderson
International Shooting Union
Shooting, Pistol
Shooting, Rifle

G. Whitney Azoy
Lawrenceville School, New Jersey
Buzkashi

William J. Baker
University of Maine at Orono
Basketball
Traditional Sports, Africa
Religion

John Bale
Keele University, UK
Environment
*Track and Field, Running and
    Hurdling*

Ralph B. Ballou, Jr.
Middle Tennessee State University
Horse Racing, Steeplechase

Robert Knight Barney
Centre for Olympic Studies,
    University of Western Ontario,
    Canada
Olympic Games, Modern

Dawn Bean
United States Synchronized
    Swimming
Swimming, Synchronized

A. Gilbert Belles
Western Illinois University
Handball, Court
Handball, Team

Kendall Blanchard
University of Tennessee at Martin
*Traditional Sports, North and South
    America*

Tim Boggan
USA Table Tennis
Tennis, Table

Anne Bolin
Elon College, North Carolina
Bodybuilding

Gherardo Bonini
European Community Historical
    Archives, Florence, Italy
Motocross
Motorcycle Racing

Douglas Booth
University of Otago, New Zealand
Surfing

Linda A. Bowlby
World Sidesaddle Federation
Horseback Riding, Sidesaddle

Maynard Brichford
University Archives, Urbana,
    Illinois
African Games
Politics

Anthony Bush
Waltham Cross, UK
Polo, Bicycle

Michael B. Camillo
World Pulling International
Truck and Tractor Pulling

Kevin Gray Carr
Amherst College, Massachusetts
Judo
Jujutsu

Richard Cashman
University of New South Wales,
    Australia
Cricket

Joan M. Chandler
University of Texas at Dallas
Media

Timothy J. L. Chandler
Kent State University, Ohio
Camogie
Hurling
Rugby Fives

Jeffery A. Charlston
George Washington University,
    Washington, D.C.
Skating, In-Line

Garry Chick
University of Illinois at Urbana-
    Champaign
Aggression
Billiards
Formula 1 Auto Racing
Mesoamerican Ball Game

Karen Christensen
Berkshire Reference Works, Great
    Barrington, Massachusetts
Imaginative Literature (sidebar)
Softball (sidebar)
Cricket (sidebar)

Annie Clement
Florida State University at
    Tallahassee
Law, Sports

Tony Collins
Sheffield Hallam University, UK
Rugby League

Mary Conti
American Horse Shows Association
Horseback Riding, Eventing
Horseback Riding, Hunters and
    Jumpers
Horseback Riding, Vaulting
Horseback Riding, Western

Pamela Cooper
Allentown, Pennsylvania
Marathon and Distance Running

Frank Cosentino
York University, Toronto, Canada
Football, Canadian

Sally Crawford
Deerfield, Illinois
Aerobics
Conditioning
Exercise

Scott A. G. M. Crawford
Eastern Illinois University
Barrel Jumping
Coursing
Croquet
Darts
Diving
Golf
Highland Games
Horseback Riding, Gymkhana
Indy Auto Racing
Korfball
Movies
Netball
Pedestrianism
Polo, Water
Race Walking
Shinty
Skating, Ice Speed
Sled Dog Racing
Swimming, Distance
Tug of War

Simon J. Crawford
Illinois Wesleyan University
Parachuting

Michael Cronin
DeMontfort University, Leicester,
    UK
Bobsledding

Lewis C. Cuyler
Berkshire Sculling Association,
    Pittsfield, Massachusetts
Rowing

Michael G. Davis
Truman State University, Missouri
Tai Chi

Wolfgang Decker
Deutsche Sporthochschule Köln,
    Cologne, Germany
Chariot Racing

Lisa Delpy
George Washington University,
    Washington, D.C.
Management and Marketing

Michael A. DeMarco
Journal of Asian Martial Arts
Wushu

Richard Dingman
International Jugglers Association
Juggling

Jon Griffin Donlon
Baton Rouge, Louisiana
Cockfighting
Hunting

Peter Donnelly
McMaster University, Ontario,
    Canada
Mountain Climbing
Rock Climbing

Andrew Doyle
Auburn University at Montgomery,
    Alabama
Intercollegiate Athletics

Margaret Carlisle Duncan
University of Wisconsin at
    Milwaukee
Tae Kwon Do

Eric Dunning
Centre for Research into Sport and
    Society, Leicester, UK
Spectators
Violence

Tom Dunning
University of Tasmania, Australia
Animal Baiting

Brooke Dyer-Bennet
Monterey, Massachusetts
Drag Racing

Bonnie Dyer-Bennet
Berkshire Reference Works (staff)
Biathlon
Trampolining

Mark Dyreson
Weber State University, Utah
Armed Forces Games
Technology
War and Sports

Henning Eichberg
Gerlev Idrætschøjskole, Slagelse,
    Denmark
Volkssport

Raymond Farrell
British Association for Sport &
    Law, Manchester Metropolitan
    University, UK
Legal Issues in Sport

Albert J. Figone
Humboldt State University,
    California
Gambling

Dennis J. Foster
Masters of Foxhounds Association
    of America
Fox Hunting (sidebar)

Joel S. Franks
San Jose State University, California
Ethnicity

Richard Friary
Skate Sailing Association
Sailing, Ice Skate
Sailing, Icewing and Roller Skate

Marco Galdi
ANSA News Agency, Rome, Italy
Umpires and Umpiring

David W. Galenson
University of Chicago, Illinois
Tennis

Heiner Gillmeister
University of Bonn, Germany
Tennis, Real

Matti Goksøyr
Norges Idrettshøgskole, Oslo,
    Norway
Ski Jumping

Allen Guttmann
Amherst College, Massachusetts
Diffusion
Modernization
Ritual
Sumo

Astrid Hagenguth
New York, New York
Skating, Figure

Steve Hick
Falls Church, Virginia
Cudgeling

Hajime Hirai
Shiga University, Shiga, Japan
Baseball, Japanese

Richard Holt
Katholieke Universiteit, Leuven,
    Belgium
Patriotism
Cycling (sidebar)

Ronald L. Holt
Weber State University, Utah
Martial Arts

Maxwell Howell
University of Queensland,
    Indooroopilly, Australia
Football, Australian

Reet Howell (deceased) affiliated
    with Queensland University of
    Technology, Australia
Traditional Sports, Oceania

Joan Hult
University of Maryland at College
    Park
Speedball
Women's Sports, North America

Duncan Humphreys
University of Otago, New Zealand
Skateboarding
Snowboarding

Steven J. Jackson
University of Otago, New Zealand
Lacrosse

Wesley V. Jamison
Worcester Polytechnic Institute,
    Massachusetts
Animal Rights

Ian F. Jobling
University of Queensland at
    Brisbane, Australia
Swimming, Speed

Don Johnson
East Tennessee State University
Literature

Gary Kemp
University of Waikato, New Zealand
Olympic Games, Modern (sidebar)

Jane Kidd
British Equestrian Centre, UK
Horseback Riding, Dressage

Donald G. Kyle
University of Texas at Arlington
Olympic Games, Ancient
Pentathlon, Ancient

Horacio A. Laffaye
Yale University School of Medicine,
    Connecticut
Polo

Mary Lou LeCompte
University of Texas at Austin
Rodeo

Michael Letters
University of Queensland at
    Brisbane, Australia
Football, Gaelic

David Levinson
Berkshire Reference Works, Great
  Barrington, Massachusetts
Extreme Sports
Stickball

Katherine Lincoln
Bernardsville, New Jersey
Carriage Driving

Sigmund Loland
Norges Idrettshøgskole, Oslo,
  Norway
Skiing, Freestyle

John Lowerson
University of Sussex, Brighton, UK
Bowls and Bowling
Foxhunting
Hockey, Field

John W. Loy
University of Otago, New Zealand
Aggression
Definitions
Sociology

Stu Luce
National Air Racing Group
Air Racing

Ruth P. Ludwig
Balloon Federation of America
Ballooning

John McClelland
University of Toronto, Canada
Acrobatics

C. D. (Kit) McConnell
Auckland, New Zealand
Leadership

Robin McConnell
Massey University (Albany), New
  Zealand
Coaches and Coaching
Leadership

Richard V. McGehee
Southeastern Louisiana University,
  Hammond
Baseball, Latin American
Gymnastics
Pan American Games

Heather McMorrow
Tacoma, WA (formerly of United
  States Luge Association)
Luge

M. J. McNamee
Cheltenham and Gloucester College
  of Higher Education, UK
Values

Teresa Baksh McNeil
Cuyamaca College, El Cajon,
  California
Jai Alai
Pelota

Anita H. Magafas
Western Illinois University
Horseback Riding, Endurance

Maurice Mars
University of Natal Medical School,
  South Africa
Drugs and Drug Testing

Tony Mason
University of Warwick, UK
Soccer

Walter D. Miller
Monument, Colorado
Soaring

Andrew W. Miracle
Cleveland State University, Ohio
Aggression

Timothy Mitchell
Texas A & M University
Bullfighting

Linda Mojer
American Amateur Racquetball
  Association
Racquetball

William J. Morgan
University of Tennessee, Knoxville
Philosophy

Morris Mott
Brandon University, Canada
Curling
Hockey, Ice

Susan Nattrass
Vashon, WA
Shooting, Clay Target

John Nauright
University of Queensland at
  Brisbane, Australia
Football, Gaelic

Dennis Pagen
United States Hang Gliding
  Association
Hang Gliding

Victoria Paraschak
University of Windsor, Ontario,
  Canada
*Native American Sporting
  Competitions*

Roberta J. Park
University of California at Berkeley
Physical Education

A. R. Parr
Broad Haven, Pembrokeshire,
  Wales
Sand Yachting

Katharine A. Pawelko
Western Illinois University
Tobogganing

Benny Josef Peiser
Liverpool John Moores University,
UK
Karate

Gertrud Pfister
Institut für Sportwissenschaft,
Berlin, Germany
Women's Sports, Europe

Richard Pillsbury
Georgia State University, Atlanta
Stock Car Racing

Philip A. Pines
Trotting Horse Museum, Goshen,
New York
Horse Racing, Harness and Trot

Bill Plummer III
American Softball Association
Softball

Michael B. Poliakoff
Pennsylvania Department of
Education, Harrisburg
Wrestling, Freestyle
Wrestling, Greco-Roman

S. W. Pope
Human Kinetics Press, Champaign,
Illinois
Basketball

Rudi Prusok
American Single Shot Rifle
Association
Shooting, Single-Shot

Rivka Rabinowitz
Pierre Gildesgame Maccabi Sports
Museum, Israel
Maccabiah Games

Benjamin G. Rader
University of Nebraska, Lincoln
Baseball, North American

Gerald Redmond
University of Alberta, Edmonton,
Canada
Commonwealth Games

Shirley H. M. Reekie
San Jose State University, San Jose,
California
Sailboarding
Sailing
Yachting

Roland Renson
Katholieke Universiteit, Leuven,
Belgium
Archery
Traditional Sports, Europe

Mary E. Ridgway
University of Texas at Arlington
Disabled Sport

James Riordan
University of Surrey, UK
Worker Sport

Joachim K. Rühl
Deutsche Sporthochschule Köln,
Cologne, Germany
Jousting

Allan J. Ryan
American College of Sports
Medicine
Medicine

Yasuhiro Sakaue
Fukushima University, Japan
Kendo

Thomas F. Scanlon
University of California at
Riverside
Mythology

Andy Seeley
US Amateur Confederation of
Roller Skating
Skating, Roller

Roland Seiler
Sport Science Institute, Switzerland
Orienteering

K.G. Sheard
Centre for Research into Sport and
Society, Leicester, UK
Rugby Union

Ron Shepherd
East Melbourne, Victoria, Australia
Cycling

Stan Shipley
University of London, UK
Boxing

Fumiaki Shishida
Waseda University, Japan
Aikido

Martti Silvennoinen
University of Jyväskylä, Finland
Baseball, Finnish

Ronald A. Smith
Pennsylvania State University
Football, American

Chet Snouffer
U.S. Boomerang Association
Boomerang Throwing

Kathleen M. Spence
U.S. Badminton Association
Badminton

B. James Starr
Howard University, Washington,
D.C.
Duathlon
Triathlon

Sharon Kay Stoll
University of Idaho, Moscow
Ethics

Nancy L. Struna
University of Maryland, College
    Park
Leisure

Kim Taylor
University of Guelph, Ontario,
    Canada
Iaido

David Terry
Ruislip, Middlesex, UK
Cross-Country Running
Track and Field, Jumps and Throws

George Theriault
New London, New Hampshire
Sailing, Parawing

Jeffrey R. Tishman
Associated Press Archives
Fencing
Pentathlon, Modern

John Townes
Berkshire Reference Works (staff)
Arm Wrestling
Canoeing and Kayaking
Falconry
Flying Disc
Footbag
Gay Games
Ice Boating
Karting
Kite Flying

Motor Boating
Rafting
Senior Games
Shuffleboard
Skiing, Water
Tennis, Paddle
Tennis, Platform
Truck Racing
Vintage Auto Racing

Alan Trevithick
Berkshire Reference Works (staff)
Asian Games
Bandy
Horseshoes
Paddleball
Pigeon Racing
Snowshoe Racing
Takraw
Traditional Sports, Asia
Trapball
Volleyball

Horst Ueberhorst
Wachtberg-Niederbachern,
    Germany
Gymnastics—Turnen (sidebar)

Wray Vamplew
De Montfort International Centre
    for Sports History and Culture,
    UK
Horse Racing, Thoroughbred

Robin S. Vealey
Miami University, Ohio
Psychology

Mark V. Wiley
Charles E. Tuttle Publishing
    Company, Tokyo, Japan
Martial Arts, Philippines

Ian D. W. Wright
Squash Rackets Association, UK
Squash Rackets

Daniel G. Yoder
Western Illinois University
Commercialization
Fishing

Darlene Young
Western Illinois University
Powerlifting
Weightlifting

Philip B. Zarilli
University of Wisconsin, Madison
Martial Arts, South Asia

Frank Zarnowski
Mount St. Mary's College,
    Emmitsburg, Maryland
Track and Field, Decathlon

Dean A. Zoerink
Western Illinois University
Rounders

Preface

Sports tell us about who we are, and who we want to be. Sports are about myth—about legendary physical prowess, determination, stamina, and teamwork. Whether and how the mythic importance of sport can survive labor disputes and commercialization is one of the great questions for sports enthusiasts today. But we have no doubt that sports can and will survive as an important, even essential, part of many people's lives. Sports bring peoples and nations together. They create a shared language, shared passions; they highlight our aspirations and values, our ways of interacting with one another, and our appreciation of competition, achievement, and adventure.

We talk about "sport" and we talk about "sports." By "sport" we mean the social processes and institutions that make up what we think of as the sporting world. This world is a complex mix of people, activities, events, rituals, and material objects, as well as the beliefs and values associated with the practice of sports. By "sports" we mean actual games and practices, such as football, gymnastics, and stock car racing.

The *Encyclopedia of World Sport* is the definitive reference on the history, practice, and culture of sport. What we have put together is a collection of authoritative articles on every Olympic sport and on dozens of other sports as well, together with articles examining the history and evolution of sport as a social phenomenon and social institution. We discuss the events and influences shaping the contemporary sporting world in articles on aggression and violence in sports and on sports ethics, psychology, media, law, and medicine. We describe, too, the development of women's sports, and the business and politics of sports today.

Sports are not only about winning or losing on the field. They are about months and years of training, expense, and sacrifice for the chance, often remote, of a few hours—or a few seconds—of glory. They are about fame and fortune: sports are big business around the globe, stakes are high, and competition is fiercer than ever before.

But the issues range far beyond training and money. Sport is a vital aspect of the human experience, an endeavor that, perhaps more than anything else, connects people worldwide. Basketball and soccer (football) are more universally known, and loved, than any religion or food or political system.

The *Encyclopedia of World Sport* is a book for the sports fanatic, of course, the person who arranges his or her calendar by the dates of the World Series, and for the millions of people who read the sports pages every day, can't miss Wimbledon or the Olympics, and tune in to sports talk shows. Fans who want to know what the games are, how they're played, who won and why, will find fascinating and surprising information here.

But the book is also intended for the many people who can't figure out why sports are such a big deal. It's about how sports and the rest of life fit together, and how sports reflect our ideas about patriotism, achievement, community, competition, fairness, and equality. Our coverage of sport as one of society's most vital institutions is the single most important feature of the *Encyclopedia of World Sport*. The best, and worst, of a society can be seen on the sports field. Because people pay so much attention to sports, fields and tracks have become the places where important contemporary issues—such as cheating, drug use, violence, celebrity, sexual harassment, and the use of technology—are played out, and sometimes worked out.

There have been cultures in which sport was not valued, but they are few. In most places and times—from ancient Greece to Nazi Germany—sport has expressed people's beliefs and served many purposes: ritualistic and religious expression, military valor, nationalism, community building, character formation, and, of course, money making. Sport affects many aspects of our lives, from how we resolve conflicts to how we think about the human body and about our identities as male or female.

There are three ways of thinking about the connection between sport and society. First, the way sports are organized and played can be seen as a reflection of other institutions in a particular society. From this perspective, the composition of an American football team reflects the management structure of

U.S. corporations, with a single leader, the quarterback (CEO), finesse players called running backs and receivers (corporate division heads), offense (marketing), and defense (legal department).

Second, sport may be viewed as a symbolic expression of core values, a reflection of how a society sees achievement, individuality, fairness, cooperation, and teamwork. Because sports take place in public, they can play an important role in communicating these core values to all members of a society, and especially to its children.

These first two interpretations suggest that sport is basically conservative: a set of activities that reinforces the existing social order. A third interpretation takes the opposite view and sees sport as an agent of social change. In this view, Title IX, the U.S. law that opened college sports to women, also promoted greater participation by women in other aspects of society. Similarly, the success of African athletes in the Olympics has called attention to African achievement and potential in other areas of human endeavor.

When we began work on the *Encyclopedia*, we took account of the fact that sport has become global, creating global connections and building a global community around issues such as women's participation in sports, preserving traditional games, and improving access to sports for all members of society. Sport is ancient, but most sports we know today are less than 150 years old, and they have spread around the world as a result of colonialism, commerce, and educational exchange. Clearly, Americanization is having a dramatic effect on the practice of sport around the world, just as the British Empire had in the last century. But it is equally clear that the reverse is also occurring, and sports that few Americans have heard of—takraw, for example, an important Southeast Asian footbag sport—are spreading to other parts of the world.

When we began this work, we didn't know how truly global our efforts would become. One example— how we searched for an author for an entry on polo— illustrates something of how we compiled this volume. A British contributor suggested an Italian colleague then based in Norway, who responded by email, suggesting the person who agreed to write the entry: an Argentinean surgeon and polo player working at a Connecticut hospital only 150 miles from our offices in western Massachusetts. In the end, the entries were written by 150 contributors from 15 countries and every continent.

The most popular game on the global village green is undoubtedly association football—futbol, bollfoer, calcio, fussball, labdarugó, podosfairiki, voetbal, and known to us in the United States as soccer—but the range of global sports is enormous and has never before been covered in a single work, in any language. We chose to be inclusive when we planned the *Encyclopedia of World Sport*. We included all activities that could be characterized as sports by the following definition: (1) competition between two or more individuals or teams; (2) rules of play that allow a winner to be determined; (3) a primary goal of victory; (4) victory determined by the relative physical ability of the competitors, although strategy and chance may also play a role. We have tried to cover all activities— both sports currently contested and many that are now obsolete—that fit this definition.

We have also included articles on sports in which the outcome is determined mainly by the physical ability of animals that are trained or controlled by humans (as well as an article on animal rights). Some of these are equestrian sports, and also bullfighting, cockfighting, dog racing, pigeon racing, animal baiting, and chariot racing. We also cover competitive activities that rely on mechanical technology and nonhuman energy: auto racing in several forms, as well as speed boat racing, air racing, and other sports. Some experts do not consider these activities to be sports because of their reliance on nonhuman energy and the absence of direct human competition. However, their competitors, sponsors, and spectators certainly do, and all these activities also depend on human skill, knowledge, and physical ability.

We have by design placed less emphasis on sporting statistics—scores, averages, and records. To provide statistical details on every sport, we would have had to reduce the coverage we have given the history of sports, the culture of sports, sports in society, and the global nature of sport. This does not mean we have ignored sport statistics and individual athletes; many articles provide information on world records and discuss individuals who have played a pivotal role in the development of a sport because of their pioneering efforts or record-breaking performances.

We have also included articles on the traditional sports of all regions of the world, as well as extensive coverage of modern sports important in Asia, Oceania, Africa, and the Americas. Many articles cover a great variety of types of sport under a general heading. To add texture and context to the volume, and to show the human side of sports through the ages, we have added short extracts of primary text—ranging from the first jousting list and a foxhunting song to a poster for Soviet Workers Sport.

We could not have compiled a work of such scope without the Internet, which enabled us to put together an international team of contributors who shared our excitement about covering an incredible array of more than 300 sports played from ancient times to the present. In working on encyclopedia projects we have found that the subject of a work determines the process of compiling it. Our team of sports experts quickly agreed on rules, looked to the goal, recruited the best team-mates, and raced to the finish line.

Sports participants and journalists sometimes feel that scholars emphasize the negative aspects of modern sports—injuries or drug use, for example—at the expense of any focus on character building, fair play, and the joy of competition. But our scholarly editors and contributors (historians, sociologists, anthropologists, geographers, psychologists, and doctors) are enthusiasts as well as scholars. One is an Olympic gold medalist, others are coaches at the college or community level, and many help to run clubs and local sports organizations. We also recruited writers from national and international sports or-ganizations, and, finally, had some entries written by staff writers.

Appropriately, this work has been a team effort from the beginning. Our staff at Berkshire Reference Works, the editorial board, and all our contributors have our thanks for prompt and careful work, and for their wonderful sporting spirit. Allen Guttmann, an early member of the editorial board and key person in developing this work, also translated several articles. We are also grateful for the assistance and enthusiasm shown by the North American Society for the History of Sport and by scholars Michael Salter, Phillips Stevens, Michael Smith, and Gigliola Gori, and would also like to thank Heather Cameron, Todd Hallman, Susan McRory, Jeff Serena, Kristi Ward, Tony Sloggett, and Rolf Janke at ABC-CLIO and Linda Robbins and Ellen Chodosh at Oxford University Press in New York.

Susan Walton deserves much praise for the extraordinary editorial job she undertook: condensing the three-volume library edition of this work into a lively and coherent single volume. Susan brought her varied knowledge, and enthusiasm for unusual books, to the sometimes overwhelming task of creating a new volume on world sport.

We hope that this book will bring the broader issues—and the fascinating and complex history—of sport around the world to a wide international audience. This is the first time that work of such global scope has been compiled and as such, undoubtedly has omissions we will want to correct in future editions. We look forward to hearing from readers, who can write to us at the address below or via our web site:

David Levinson & Karen Christensen
Berkshire Reference Works
P O Box 177
Great Barrington, Massachusetts 01230 U.S.A.
http://www.berkshire-reference.com

Acrobatics

Acrobatics is the practice of performing physically unusual feats with one's body. Principally the art of jumping, tumbling, and balancing, it often involves apparatus such as poles, one-wheel cycles, and flying trapezes. The somersault is the fundamental tumbling act of acrobatics. Acrobatics, with a long recorded history and many noted practitioners, has hovered on the fringes of dance and the theater and provided an aesthetic alternative to sport.

History

The history of acrobatics is the history of its constant marginalization—but also its constant presence. From the early Egyptians to the European Middle Ages, acrobatic feats (particularly somersaults) were an integral, if unofficial, element of funeral rites. Acrobatic stunts have always seemed morally as well as physically dangerous. The ambiguous status of acrobatics may derive from its forgotten symbolism. Whether walking a tightrope or performing a somersault, the acrobat is exposing himself to the possibility of serious injury and thus defying death. The acrobat who survives the danger to which he has willfully exposed himself embodies our belief that immortality is possible.

By definition, an acrobat is one who "walks [Greek *bateo*] on the extremity [Greek *akra*]," to mean on tiptoe, but that might also denote walking on one's hands (ancient Greek statuettes depict acrobats doing so). Either way, an acrobat walks in an unnatural and inherently unbalanced manner. Subsequently, the term "acrobat" came to designate a gymnast who walked on ropes or otherwise performed while hanging from them.

"Acrobatics entered the modern languages only in the limited sense of rope-walking. The subsequent popularity of the word and its extension to the range of physical activities traces largely to advances in the techniques and technology of rope gymnastics. The invention of the flying trapeze (1859) and the exploits of Blondin and Farini, who in 1859 and 1860 walked on tightropes across the Niagara gorge, took acrobatics literally to new heights. The development of the great traveling circuses and the rise of the music hall gave acrobatics both a venue and a new respectability. Acrobatic feats were performed purely for spectacular and monetary purposes, offering the vicarious thrill of watching performers gratuitously risk their lives.

Acrobats and dancers performed on the same stage, and some acrobats rivaled dancers in celebrity, but acrobatics and dance were clearly distinct specialties. Acrobatics was also part of the *commedia dell'arte,* the traditional Italian theater that required actors to perform stunts viewed as more appropriate to the circus. But by the end of the 17th century the *commedia dell'arte* had been largely relegated to the fairground.

In early modern times acrobatics was the prerogative of the Italians, who tended to valorize acrobatics by a combination of agility and equilibrium—the display of mind over matter. Later it came to be an Eastern European specialty characterized by exhibitions of great strength. The appearance in the West of the Peking (Beijing) Circus in the 1970s profoundly altered Western perceptions of acrobatics; the Chinese stress lightness more than strength. Chinese acrobats introduce humor into their acts, suggesting that acrobatics has become so institutionalized in Asiatic culture that there is nothing to fear.

Finally, the Cirque du Soleil (founded in the 1980s)

added to acrobatics a new notion of a narrative based on elements drawn from the *commedia dell'arte*. The Cirque's shows are not simply a string of acts ordered on principles of spectacle. Each act is part of a story; the flow is mimetic as well as rhetorical and aesthetic. The acrobatic spectacle involves the working out of human problems and relations as well as the increasing emotional thrill of witnessing the marvelous and the death-defying.

Rules and Play

Hovering as it does on the edge of sport, acrobatics has traditions more than rules, and the winners are those who best perform the most complex feats and survive intact. The successful performance of acrobatic feats requires considerable physical exertion, the painstaking acquisition of unusual athletic skills, and a high degree of muscular and psychological control. Acrobats are less motivated by the creed of faster, higher, stronger and by the quest for records than by the goal of performing more inventively than others. Since the ultimate purpose of acquiring acrobatic skills is not to compete but to acquire even more spectacular skills, acrobatics remains outside the realm of sport. The basic criteria by which we appreciate acrobatics—control, gracefulness, innovation—are not susceptible to objective measurement.

Defying death was for a mortal an appropriately symbolic part of ancient funeral ceremony, but doing so for reasons of pure spectacle is an act of hubris. Acrobatics has thus traditionally been both applauded and derided. Complete respectability has always eluded acrobatics. Perhaps for that reason, the practitioners have almost always been outsiders—or portrayed themselves as such—to Western European culture.

Acrobatics cannot be conventionally competitive. Yet some Olympic sports are judged more on aesthetic than on quantified bases—gymnastics and figure-skating—and so a form of acrobatics might someday achieve Olympic status. Whether this happens or not, acrobatics is certain to retain its appeal as an activity both exciting and appealing to watch.

—JOHN MCCLELLAND

Bibliography: Borassatti, Giustiniano. (1753) *Il ginnasta in pratica, ed in teorica.* Venice: Gio Battista Rossi. Burgess, Hovey. (1976) *Circus Techniques: Juggling, Equilibristics.* New York: Drama Book Specialists. Sparshott, Francis. (1988) *Off the Ground. First Steps to a Philosophical Consideration of the Dance.* Princeton, NJ: Princeton University Press.

Aerobics

Aerobics is a system of exercises designed to promote the supply and use of oxygen in the body. These exercises include biking, running, dancing, rowing, skating, and walking (the term "aerobic" means "with oxygen," or "living and working with oxygen"). The system originated and remains primarily a fitness activity, but has also developed into an intense competitive sport: "the toughest two minutes in sport." Aerobic exercise increases cardiorespiratory fitness, the heart's ability to pump blood and deliver oxygen throughout the body. The result is increased endurance, energy, weight control, and ability to manage stress, and decreased blood pressure, heart disease, and cholesterol levels.

History

The word "aerobics" is relatively new to sport and exercise. In 1968, Dr. Kenneth Cooper, a U.S. Air Force physician, published a book, *Aerobics,* based on his research on coronary artery disease. Cooper developed his aerobics exercise program as preventive medicine, to improve health and fitness. Aerobics developed a prescription for exercise. The book identified the quantity, kind, and frequency of desirable exercise. Cooper's books have been translated into many languages, reflecting his belief that aerobics, exercise, and preventive medicine are universal. The Congress of International Military Sports adopted Cooper's aerobics program for the countries of Sweden, Austria, Finland, Korea, and Brazil as well as the United States. The aerobics program spread to civilian populations worldwide. In Brazil, runners ask "Have you done your Cooper today?" when they want to know if you've run or jogged.

The same year that Cooper published *Aerobics,* Judy Sheppard Missett began an aerobic exercise program called "Jazzercise," a highly choreographed group of exercises set to music. The program incorporated muscle group work with new dance trends. In 1969, Jackie Sorenson started "Aerobic Dance," also a choreographed set of dance patterns set to music intended to increase cardiovascular fitness. By the early 1970s, aerobics, aerobic dance, and dance exercise were used interchangeably to describe the combination of exercise and dance movements set to music. Most early participants were women.

In the late 1970s, the name "aerobic dancing" was shortened to "aerobics" to attract more men. Coeducational classes were offered, and the aerobics boom followed, soon becoming international. Aerobics classes were held in churches, community centers, schools, and health clubs. Jane Fonda and Richard Simmons contributed to the tremendous growth of aerobics. U.S. instructors began to train new instructors in other countries. In the United States in 1978 an estimated 6 million people participated in aerobics, rising to 19 million by 1982, and 22 million in 1987. Forty-five percent of the aerobics participants were women aged 30–50 who used aerobics as their sole form of exercise. Ten percent of the participants were instructors. Today more than 25 million people participate in the aerobics industry and virtually every community offers aerobics classes. Televised aerobic dance classes are frequent, and aerobics videos are readily available. The social support and reinforcement of the group exercise situation also help account for its popularity.

Training and educational organizations emerged to guide this fast-growing industry, develop safe and effective programs, and promote aerobics internationally. In the United States, the International Dance Exercise Association (IDEA) and the Aerobic and Fitness Association of America (AFAA) developed into two of the largest in the world. In 1990 IDEA had over 23,000 instructor members in over 70 countries.

Rules and Play
Cooper's original exercise plan has diversified in both content and style while retaining its original purpose. As a fitness activity, a well-designed aerobic dance class consists of five segments: the warm-up or pre-stretch (10 minutes), the aerobic segment (20–45 minutes), cool down (5–10 minutes), strength work (10–20 minutes), and the final stretch (5–10 minutes). The rhythmic movements also help to develop balance and coordination. Aerobic activity began as "high impact," with both feet off the floor at any given time, characterized by running or jogging in place, jumping jacks, and small jumps or hops. This placed tremendous stress on the joints, and many participants developed impact-related injuries. Thus, "low impact" aerobics was developed: one foot is always on the floor; the routines are characterized by marching in place and traveling from one side of the room to the other. Next came variable impact aerobics, which combines the intensity of high impact moves with the safety of the low impact variety. Other types of aerobics include water aerobics, sculpting, strength, abdominal, sports conditioning, and circuit or interval classes. Step aerobics, developed by Gin Miller, took the aerobics industry by storm. This style involves stepping up and down from a platform 15 to 30 centimeters (6 to 12 inches) high while performing different step combinations.

Competition
Aerobics became a competitive sport in 1983, when Karen and Howard Schwartz created the National Aerobic Championship (NAC). Today its format and rules are the international standard for aerobic competition. In 1989, Howard Schwartz founded the International Competitive Aerobics Federation (ICAF), which became the governing body of the sport and continues to develop new guidelines. The new sport's growth has been impressive. The first World Aerobic Championship was held in 1990, with 16 countries represented. Thirty-five countries were represented in 1994. The World Aerobic Championships have been broadcast to over 150 nations each year since 1995.

Championship aerobics has been called the "toughest two minutes in sports." It is a rigorous display of both compulsory and freestyle moves choreographed according to specific rules into a two-minute routine set to music. The performance showcases tremendous strength, flexibility, and endurance as well as creativity and dance. The eight categories of competition are: Novice Men's Individual, Novice Women's Individual, Masters Division M (over 35) men's individual, Masters Division M women's individual, Advanced Men's Individual, Advanced Women's Individual, Advanced Mixed Pair (male/female combination), and Advanced Teams (of three; any gender combination).

The novelty of aerobics has passed, and, arguably, its popularity has peaked. Nevertheless, as an activity that many people find a practical way to achieve fitness, aerobics seems likely to retain its niche in the world of sports.

—SALLY CRAWFORD

Bibliography: Cooper, Kenneth. (1977) *The Aerobics Way.* New York: M. Evans and Co. Mazzeo, K. S., and L. M. Mangili. (1993) *Fitness through Aerobics and Step Training.* Englewood, CO: Morton Publishing.

African Games
The African Games began 1965 as a force for African solidarity and a means of uniting the continent against South Africa's apartheid system. By 1995, determined African leadership with International Olympic Committee (IOC) support had held six African Games, and South Africa had become a participant. The games had tested the Olympic ideal of athletic competition as a means of securing peaceful international understanding while increasing cultural and national identity on a continent whose populous and relatively young nations had many contrasting cultural and political traditions.

History

Attempts were made to hold All-Africa games in Algiers in 1925 and Alexandria in 1929, but these failed due to colonial politics, language differences, poor communications systems, and economic difficulties, then the Depression and World War II stymied further attempts. Athletes of African descent performed well in the Olympics, although few Africans participated on their national teams. In 1928, a Moroccan won the marathon while competing for France and Americans of African descent were successful in track events.

The end of colonial rule in the decades after World War II brought the creation of 32 new African nations, 17 in 1960 alone. Many of the new national governments included a culture, youth, and sports ministry, and various sports competitions were held within the continent. In 1959, French-speaking athletes competed in games at Bangui (what is now the Central African Republic). In the independence year of 1960, East and West African games were held. The same year, former French colonies held the Games of Friendship in Tananarive (now the capital, Antananarivo), Madagascar. In 1961, athletes from France and 22 African countries participated in the second games at Abidjan, Côte d'Ivoire. The third Games of Friendship were held in April 1963, in Dakar, Senegal. French athletes joined those from 19 francophone and 5 anglophone countries in competing in track and field, boxing, soccer, cycling, swimming, basketball, volleyball, handball, and judo. Women competed in track and field and basketball. Athletes from Mediterranean Africa, such as Egypt, Tunisia, Algeria, and Morocco, participated in the Mediterranean Games and athletes in anglophone Africa took part in the Commonwealth Games. By 1968, 45 African countries were involved in international sports. The nations most active in Olympic sporting events were Egypt, Tunisia, Morocco, Ethiopia, Ghana, Sudan, Kenya, and Uganda.

The first African Games opened July 1965 at Brazzaville. More than 1,000 individuals from 30 nations competed in track and field, swimming, basketball (male and female), soccer (association football), handball, volleyball, boxing, cycling, judo, and tennis. Soccer attracted the largest crowds. Despite lingering rivalries between former French and British colonies and instances of pushing, holding, and striking, the soccer federation reacted favorably to the games' management and the progress they represented.

In December 1966, 32 nations in the three-year-old Organization for African Unity (OAU) formed the Supreme Council for Sports in Africa. Composed of sports ministers, national sports committee heads, National Olympic Committee presidents, IOC members, and sports federation presidents, the Supreme Council's general purpose was to coordinate and promote sports, but the "primary motivating force" was "an attack on South Africa's apartheid sport." The Supreme Council led in staging the African Games and opposing South African participation in international sports. Its policy of racial apartheid led to South Africa's disbarment from the 1964 and 1968 Olympics and expulsion from the Olympic movement in 1970.

Postponed by a 1969 coup in Mali, the second African Games opened in Lagos, Nigeria, in January 1973, with delegations from 41 countries and 50,000 spectators. In July 1978, the third African Games opened with nearly 3,000 athletes from 45 nations assembled before 70,000 spectators in Algiers. Media coverage was extensive. The Algerian team of 265 athletes dominated. Henry Rono of Kenya won gold medals in the 10,000 meters and the 3,000 meter steeplechase. The report to the IOC commended the games for "transcending the current political divisions."

The fourth African Games were held in Nairobi, Kenya, in August 1987. Approximately 4,000 competitors from 38 nations participated. After nine years during which the games had been postponed twice, the tenacity of the Supreme Council for Sports in Africa and the Organizing Committee helped stage the Nairobi games, which were funded by a variety of sources, including the People's Republic of China.

Egyptian President Hosni Mubarak opened the fifth African Games in Cairo in September 1991. Forty-two nations participated in 16 sports. Meeting before the games, the General Assembly of African National Olympic Committees admitted South Africa and Namibia to membership. The IOC provided substantial financial support. It reported that "the situation is a lot better" than in previous games. Egypt, Nigeria, and Kenya dominated the games, and newcomer Namibia won several medals.

The sixth African Games were held in Harare, Zimbabwe, in September 1995, when a South African team participated for the first time. A cash crisis caused by drought, World Bank restrictions, and a lack of sponsors limited participation and hampered the preparation of venues.

Nevertheless, as conditions permit, African Games are likely to continue. African athletes have proved themselves competitive internationally, a situation that intracontinental competitions can only improve.

—MAYNARD BRICHFORD

Bibliography: Allison, Lincoln, ed. (1986) *The Politics of Sport.* Manchester: Manchester University Press. Baker, William F., and James A. Mangan. (1987) *Sport in Africa.* New York: Africana Publishing Company. Avery Brundage Collection. Box 196, University of Illinois Archives. Lapchick, Richard E. (1975) *The Politics of Race and International Sport, The Case of South Africa.* Westport, CT: Greenwood Press. *Olympic Review* (September 1977; August–September 1978; April–June 1987; October 1987; September–November 1991; August–September 1995). Ukah, Matthias O. (1990) "Socio-cultural Forces in Growth of All African Games." *Journal of the International Council for Health, Physical Education and Recreation* 26, 2: 16–20. Wagner, Eric A., ed. (1989) *Sport in Asia and Africa.* New York: Greenwood Press.

Aggression

The relationship between sport and aggression has been studied extensively for decades, yet investigators still have only an incomplete understanding of the link between the two. That there is a link seems certain, and researchers in various disciplines continue trying to refine their understanding of it in ways that will illuminate both sport and society.

In the first half of the 20th century, many psychologists assumed that participation in sports might allow individuals to vent their aggressive tendencies. Generally, these assumptions arose from the view that aggression is an internal drive based on frustration and/or instinct. However, more recent research shows the opposite—participation in sports is likely to increase an individual's aggression.

Sport psychologists distinguish between *hostile* and *instrumental* aggression. The primary purpose of hostile aggression is to inflict physical or psychological injury on another; the main aim of instrumental aggression is to attain an approved goal, such as winning a game. These two forms of aggression can be distinguished clearly in most sport situations, although not necessarily in extreme contact sports such as boxing and ice hockey. Recent research suggests that instrumental aggression in sport may spill over into hostile aggression outside of sport, for example, male athletes involved in sexual assault against women.

History

Historically, some argued that sport developed as a constraint on aggression, or at least as a means to channel aggression into culturally acceptable forms. Others have contended that sports do not necessarily increase aggression, but rather reflect and enhance the dominant values and attitudes of the broader culture.

Yet another school of thought has proposed that sport creates a separate moral sphere, distinct from the real world, in which the goal of winning is more important than the rules of the game. Others consider that when athletes are overly aggressive; they are overconforming to what they see as acceptable within the sport. Display of machismo, playing with pain, or intentionally injuring an opponent may be "grounded in athletes' uncritical acceptance of and commitment to what they have been told by important people in their lives ever since they began participating in competitive programs. Where winning is valued above all else, athletes may use aggression to show their total commitment to sport or to winning in sport.

Aggression and the Individual

Individuals who participate in sports seem to exhibit higher levels of aggression than those who do not. However, this may be because sports attract people who are naturally more aggressive than nonathletes.

Some sports are more likely to be associated with violence and inappropriate aggression. When provoked, for example, participants in contact sports reveal much higher levels of aggression than those in noncontact sports. Research also shows that aggression may give players an edge when used early in a contest, or they may show aggression if they fail in the sport. Other factors also influence aggression during sports events. For example, the presence of officials in organized sports increases the number of fouls since the athletes assume it is the referees' job to control inappropriate aggression.

Studies of martial arts suggest that sport participation does not necessarily promote aggression. For example, one study showed that among 13-to-17-year-old delinquents, the group that was taught the philosophical elements of Tae Kwon Do—respect for others, maintaining a sense of responsibility, for example—along with the physical component lowered their aggression levels, compared to those who were not taught the philosophy or engaged in activities other than Tae Kwon Do.

Aggression and the Group

Some scholars have argued that games are models of culturally relevant activities and provide the greatest opportunity to practice and to learn these activities. American football is an unmistakable model of warfare, for example, with its "men in the trenches" (offensive and defensive linemen), "field generals" (quarterbacks), efforts by teams to move the ball into "enemy territory" and, ultimately, scoring by "invading" the opponent's end zone. Cross-cultural studies too show a positive association between the existence of combative sports and the prevalence of warfare in particular cultures. Not all sports fit this model, though. Baseball, in contrast, cannot be so directly linked with any single culturally relevant activity, although running, clubbing, and missile throwing were all important activities in human evolutionary history.

Aggression is appropriate, even essential for success in war, but what happens to individuals with heightened levels of aggression in peacetime or when there is no active war in which to channel their aggression? Recently, this question—still controversial—has been raised about violence toward women. Several studies indicate that athletes are disproportionately represented among rapists and others who abuse women physically. Other investigators suggest that sports contribute to male dominance by linking maleness with acceptable aggression while belittling women and their activities. Some researchers believe that athletes are unfairly stereotyped because they are more visible and are typically held to higher standards.

Aggression and Fan Violence

Violence by sport spectators or fans has become an issue of considerable concern. Soccer (association football) hooliganism in Great Britain has received much attention as have violent confrontations between European soccer fans. What is it about sports that excites spectators to violent aggression? One theory is that it directly results from observing athletes' aggression; another links it to fans' desire to establish their own social identity; a third proposes that spectator violence is a kind of ritual.

Drugs, especially alcohol, are another common element in spectator aggression. During the 1995 U.S. National Football League season, a national audience was treated to a game-long spectacle of fans throwing snowballs and ice at players, coaches, and officials on the field, as well as at each other, during a game between the New York Giants and the San Diego Chargers. Alcoholic beverages were subsequently banned from Giants Stadium for the next home game to be played there. Drugs have also been implicated in aggressiveness by players. In particular, steroids, usually taken surreptitiously by athletes, appear to heighten aggressiveness.

Aggression, Sport, and Mass Media

Instant replays have brought an interesting but chilling phenomenon in modern sport spectatorship. Scoring plays or other exciting or exceptional plays are commonly replayed. But also commonly replayed are tactics that involve exceptional aggressiveness, such as a "good hit" or a particularly devastating down-field block in American football. This replaying occurs even when the violent moves have little apparent effect on the outcome of the game or the particular play. Aggressive acts that lead to actual violence—fights among players—are frequently replayed or rebroadcast on sports shows. Spectators seem to enjoy exhibitions of aggression and even violence, while players in many sports believe that aggressive play is instrumental in winning.

Precisely how sports and aggression are linked is unclear, but that they are linked seems certain. Sports may be one way to teach young people how and when to use violent forms of aggressive behavior. Young athletes observe the behavior of role models and learn from interactions with coaches, parents, and others. This may well have long-lasting consequences for individuals and for society.

Can there be sport without increased aggression? Studies suggest that sport could be reformed so that it would not necessarily lead to increases in aggression. Spectators and players both would experience sport in a different way. Nevertheless, it seems likely that sport could be enjoyed without the promotion of inappropriate aggression.

—ANDREW W. MIRACLE, GARRY CHICK, AND JOHN W. LOY

See also Violence.

Bibliography: Buss, A. H. (1961) *The Psychology of Aggression.* New York: Wiley. McPherson, Barry D., James E. Curtis, and John W. Loy. (1989) *The Social Significance of Sport.* Champaign, IL: Human Kinetics. Messner, Michael A., and Donald F. Sabo. (1994) *Sex, Violence and Power in Sports: Rethinking Masculinity.* Freedom, CA: Crossing Press. Russell, G. W. (1993) *The Social Psychology of Sport.* New York: Springer-Verlag.

Aikido

Aikido is a Japanese martial art that includes techniques for bare-handed wrestling, using weapons, and dealing with the armed enemy and also has a spiritual component. Aikido is known for its joint-twisting and pinning techniques (*kansetsu-waza*) and its thrusting and stunning blows (*atemi-waza*). The advanced student is a master of techniques to break the opponent's balance or ward off a thrust or grasp. Aikido techniques can kill or injure, but fundamentally their purpose is to seize and control the opponent. All of the principles of swordsmanship (eye contact, proper distance, timing, and cutting methods) are incorporated into aikido movements. Various schools of aikido exist, and the methods of training and spiritual teachings vary from school to school. Aikido is a competitive sport, but controversy remains on the question of whether this conflicts with its origins as a solitary practice.

History

Aiki, the core concept of aikido, can be traced to martial arts literature of the Edo era. In *Toka Mondo* (Candlelight Discussion), the master of Kito-ryu Jujutsu wrote in 1764 that aiki means that two fighters come to a standstill in a martial arts bout when they have focused their attention on each other's breathing. Many other authors in the 1800s gave similar definitions. In 1982, the volume *Budo-hiketsu Aiki no Jutsu* (Secret Keys to Martial Arts Techniques) gave a new definition of the term: aiki is the ultimate goal in the study of martial arts and may be accomplished by "taking a step ahead of the enemy." The prerequisites for such a preemptive move are to read the enemy's mind and use a battle cry. Unfortunately, no details on specific exercises have been recorded.

Aikido was promoted throughout Japan by Morihei Ueshiba (1883–1969), a student of multiple martial arts. He derived the major techniques of aikido from the Daito-ryu Jujutsu style, which he learned from Sokaku Takeda (1860–1943) in Shirataki, Hokkaido, between 1915 and 1919. Aikido became an official term when it was approved at a conference of the Dai-Nippon Butoku-Kai, the association of all martial arts in Japan. Ueshiba and his gifted disciples are responsible for the current position of aikido as a popular Japanese martial art. Ueshiba and his followers decided that aikido is a way to become one with the universe or harmonize with the movement and rhythm of nature.

Rules and Play

Aikido's unique practice system is one of the features that has drawn many followers. The training is made up mainly of the practice of kata. A kata is a formalized series of movements that imitate sword and spear cuts and thrusts. Practiced in a formal manner that resembles a dance routine, kata contain 20 to 30 stopping, pivoting, cutting, and thrusting movements. Participants repeat these movements many times to refine technique and coordination.

Two issues complicate the practice of aikido. Diver-

sification is one. Traditionally, the Japanese people are inclined to favor a school of great prestige and authority. But recently, as part of a general shift toward accepting different values shared by people in other parts of the world, young people are joining aikido schools because they are operated by a truly gifted teacher with a likable personality rather than large and traditionally credited schools.

The second issue is the rigid policy of prohibiting competition enforced by some aikido schools. Now that more students are showing an interest in competitive aikido, it will be increasingly difficult for the traditional schools to justify this prohibition. Competitive aikido does have a "negative" side in that contestants have a tendency to place priority on winning. But trainees also have a wonderful opportunity to develop unflinching courage, a tense and serious attitude, and practical self-defense skills.

Aikido Today

Aikido, originally meant to be "a martial art of harmony and unification," is currently suffering a chaotic division while simultaneously growing in popularity. The absence of an objective method to measure students' skills and strength resulted in the phenomenal growth of different styles and schools, each of which has different philosophies and training methods. Miscommunication and mistrust abound among members of different organizations.

Aiki-kai

Aiki-kai, the association founded by Morihei Ueshiba, has been promoted internationally since World War II, and is said to be the school of aikido with the greatest number of followers. Ueshiba's son, Kisshomaru (1921–) inherited his father's foundation and demanded that his students practice aikido only for self-discipline and truth-seeking. This pacifist policy is now widely accepted, but some of Morihei Ueshiba's most distinguished disciples disagreed with Kisshomaru and left his school to establish their own. They include:

JAA (Japan Aikido Association)

Kenji Tomiki (1900–1979) founded the JAA in 1974. and created a randori (training match) system of aikido. His new proposal caused a sharp conflict of opinions on what aikido should be.

Yoshin-kan

Gozo Shioda (1915–1994), founded his own school in Tokyo with the backup of businesses, emphasizing mastery of basic techniques. He made a great contribution to the promotion of aikido after World War II.

Ki no Kenkyu-kai (Ki Society)

Koichi Tohei (1920–) founded the Ki Society and left Aiki Kai in 1974. He describes aikido as a way to assimilate man into the "Ki" of the universe.

Yoseikan Minoru Mochizuki (1907–) built Yoseikan in Shizuoka, where he developed a unique system for all-around martial arts training with integrated judo and karate techniques.

The increasing international popularity of aikido is attributable to Aiki-kai and other aikido schools' activities outside Japan. Aikido was introduced to the United States by Kenji Tomiki in 1952 when he traveled through 15 states with a team of judo instructors. According to the aikido magazine *Aiki Journal,* aikido has the greatest numbers of followers in France, the United States, Japan, Germany, and England, respectively. Beyond a general interest, westerners are drawn to aikido because kata practice is well suited for the elderly or female trainees who learn aikido for physical fitness or self-defense. Also, westerners view this type of aikido as a way of Zen meditation or a means to gain insight into Eastern mysticism and philosophies.

The traditional ban on aikido competition stymies making aikido an Olympic event, although an increasing number of groups are working to organize international tournaments. At the same time, both the spiritual and physical components of aikido appeal to westerners. The sport divided within itself is likely to continue bridging the gap between East and West.

—FUMIAKI SHISHIDA

Bibliography: Pranin, Stanley. (1991) *The Aiki News Encyclopedia of Aikido.* Tokyo: Aiki News. Westbrook, Adele, and Oscar Ratti. (1979) *Aikido and the Dynamic Sphere.* Rutland, VT, and Tokyo: Charles E. Tuttle.

Air Racing

Air racing began as a sport about 6 years after Orville and Wilbur Wright's 12-second flight at Kitty Hawk, North Carolina, in December 1903. Since that 1909 event, air racing has developed into a competitive sport with four basic classes according to type of aircraft.

History

The first air race was sponsored by James Gordon Bennett, publisher of the *New York Herald,* who lived in Paris. Bennett offered a cash prize and a trophy for "the best speed record by an airplane over a closed course" at an air meet to be held annually. The first such prize would be awarded at the International Air Meet scheduled for Rheims, France, in August 1909. Daily contests for speed, altitude, and time and distance. Twenty-eight pilots and thirty-eight airplanes entered this historic event. Hubert Letham of France won the altitude contest by climbing to the amazing altitude of 153 meters (503 feet). Henry Farman won the time and distance prize of $10,000; he stayed aloft for just under 3 hours, 5 minutes, and flew 180 kilometers (112 miles). Glenn Curtiss, the American "dark horse," won the main event. The first air meet in the United States was held the following year.

Air racing expanded next into races involving aircraft capable of taking off and landing in open water. To stimulate interest in designing and developing seaplanes, Jacques Schneider, an affluent French aviation enthusiast, offered a trophy for an annual race. The first of the Schneider Cup races took place April 1913 in Monaco. England dominated the Schneider series, winning five of the eleven competitions and taking permanent possession of the trophy by winning three consecutive races in 1927, 1929, and 1931. By 1931 the winning speed had increased to 547 kph (340 mph).

After World War I air racing in the United States expanded greatly because of the hundreds of ex-military pilots and several thousand military surplus aircraft (including an estimated 6,000 Curtiss Jennys). Many of these pilots turned to "barnstorming" to make a very marginal living. Some of the air shows featuring the barnstorming acts also included one or more speed competitions. Barnstorming was halted in 1926, when the U.S. Congress passed various laws regulating aviation.

Speed became a primary goal in aviation. In 1920 a trophy to promote higher speeds was offered by newspaper publisher Ralph Pulitzer. The United States Army and Navy were intensely interested in developing faster, more powerful aircraft, and allocated funds to improve the performance of planes they entered in the Pulitzer race. The first of this series was held in 1920. When the series was discontinued after the 1925 race, the winning speed had increased by almost 100 mph.

Air racing grew in popularity with the inception of the National Air Race series, organized under the sanction of the National Aeronautics Administration and first held in September 1926 in Philadelphia. However, military expenditures for development of racing aircraft soon dried up and for the next thirteen years the National Air Races would feature civilian designed and tested aircraft. The series is well remembered for two trophies awarded during the meet: the Thompson and the Bendix.

The Thompson Trophy events held between 1930 and 1939 were closed course speed races featuring unlimited aircraft (no restrictions on horsepower or airframe modifications). Pilots whose names are recognized today flew in the Thompson races: Charles "Speed" Holman, James Doolittle, James Wedell, and Roscoe Turner, who kept the trophy after winning three consecutive times. When the series resumed after World War II some of the pilots who had flown the races before the war returned to try again.

The Bendix Transcontinental Speed Classic was inaugurated in 1931. Pilots were timed against the clock in the first dash from Los Angeles to Cleveland. Jimmy Doolittle won the 1931 race in a Laird Super-Solution with an average speed of 375 kph (223 mph).

The National Air Races resumed in Cleveland in 1946. Bendix offered two cross-country trophies: one for piston engines and one for jet aircraft. The four-day event also featured a women's race and several consolation races for the slower ex-wartime planes.

World War II fighter and jet planes continued to dominate the National Air Races until 1949 when a P-51 flown during the Thompson race lost control and crashed into a home near the airport, killing the pilot, a woman in the house, and her 13-month-old baby. The public outcry that followed concerning civilian safety during air races has haunted air race promoters ever since.

Later in the 1940s, a group of pilot/designers who felt the warbirds were too expensive and wanted a more competitive class began designing small race planes, which first appeared at the 1947 National Air Races. Weighing about 227 kilograms (500 pounds) and with 80-horsepower engines, these tiny planes could fly a smaller radius course, bringing them closer to the stands where the spectators could see them.

The next important development came with the first Reno National Championship Air Race in 1964. Three classes of airplanes raced: Formula I's, Sport Biplanes, and the vintage World War II aircraft now designated "Unlimiteds." In 1995 the Reno National Championship Air Race celebrated their 32d consecutive event, making this the longest running series in air racing. The AT-6 class was added in 1969.

Air races are still held all around the United States and in Europe. Most of these events have featured one or two racing classes, usually limited by the size of the field or the prize money available. In Europe, since

1970 much interest has been in the Formula I class. Annual races are held in both France and England under the direction of the International Formula I Air Race Association.

Rules and Play

Air racing is divided into four classes.

Unlimited

Unlimited air racing aircraft are the fastest racing machines in regular competition in the world. Their roots stem directly from the Thompson Trophy of the postwar era, which were ex-military fighter aircraft. After 1949, Unlimited air racing almost totally disappeared, but was revived with the advent of the Reno National Championship Air Races in 1964 and has since grown steadily in popularity. The aircraft themselves may still be ex–World War II fighter aircraft, but there the kinship ends; most have been highly modified and achieve performance far beyond that of stock military fighters.

Average winning speeds in Unlimited competition are well in excess of 650 kph (400 mph). The current record in the class for average race speed is now in the neighborhood of 775 kph (480 mph).

The Unlimited class of air racing has only two major restrictions: The aircraft must be propeller driven and must have a piston-type engine. Extensive modifications may be made to engines and to airframes, and most Unlimited aircraft of today have clipped wings, modified fuselages, cut-down canopies, and highly exotic racing engines, as well as many other smaller refinements engineered into these racers for one purpose: speed! Unlimited Aircraft race on a closed-pylon course and use an "air start," with the aircraft in formation extending back from the pace aircraft.

T-6

This "round-engined" plane, one of the world's leading training aircraft, has been around for many years and became a racer in 1968. To make the new T-6 class competitive, it was decided to race them in a stock configuration, which makes the events extremely close and exciting. Stock means that the parts, engine configuration, etc., must have been standard on some type of T-6/SNJ/Harvard aircraft as assembled by North American or Canadian manufacturers. A T-6 was considered a 290 kph (180 mph) aircraft, and these speeds were typical in the early years of the class. Now, however, an aircraft that is not at least in the 320 kph (200 mph) category is not competitive.

Formula I

International Formula I racing aircraft first raced at the 1947 Cleveland National Air Races. The idea in creating this class of racing was to provide aircraft that could be designed and built for a relatively low cost, would be safe to fly, and would provide close competition. The Formula I's continue to meet all of these standards and more. In the 1960s a rule change permitted engines of 200 cubic inches; at the same time, the class name was changed to International Formula I.

Formula I craft are normally built and often designed by those who race them. Many others are versions of popular types in which the builder has incorporated some original ideas. A Formula I aircraft is usually constructed of steel tube and fabric with wood wings, and all are powered by four-cylinder, 200 cubic inch engines that deliver 100 horsepower.

Biplanes

Single-place sport and aerobatic biplanes first flew as a racing class aircraft in that first Reno race in 1964. The early participants and many that compete today were built from plans. The majority of these aircraft are raced by the pilots who built them. Construction materials and methods are much the same as those used in the Formula I class. By class rules, the average sport biplane is 4.6 to 5.2 meters (15 to 17 feet) long and has a wingspan of 5.2 to 5.8 meters. They are normally powered by a Lycoming 0–290 engine of 125 horsepower and are restricted to an engine that displaces no more than 290 cubic inches.

With continued improvements in both materials and design, air racing seems likely to grow in popularity. As long as there are at least two airplanes still flying, there will be an air race somewhere.

—STU LUCE

Alpine Skiing
See Skiing, Alpine

Animal Baiting

Animal baiting is a form of animal fighting in which men undertake the harassment, torment, or provocation of one animal by another for the purposes of entertainment, which usually includes wagering. For the past several centuries, men (and most participants are men) have set dogs on other animals such as bulls, bears, badgers, and rats. The defenders of this sport emphasized its value in producing a desirable masculinity based on the values of courage and bravery. Critics opposed the inhumane treatment of animals.

With a few notable exceptions, such as bull fighting, all forms of animal baiting have been prohibited and are practiced only clandestinely.

History

Cockfighting, which dates back 2,500 years, is the oldest recorded type of animal fighting. Virtually a worldwide practice, cockfighting is an indigenous sport almost everywhere. Apart from cockfighting, dog fighting has been and remains perhaps the most widespread type of animal baiting. Various societies practice other types of animal fighting, frequently involving animals indigenous to the region: elephant fighting in India, tarantula fights in South Africa, and fish fights in China. Matches between different animals such as between boars and tigers have occurred in India and between bulls and bears in Spain. Some fights pit human beings against other animals, the most famous being the Spanish bullfight.

The best documented occurrences of animal baiting are from Great Britain during the 17th century, when it became an important public recreation. Since the late 18th century, middle-class moralists have condemned this sport as an undesirable public recreation of the poor. This eventually led to its illegality in the mid-19th century. In the 20th century, it became a rare, clandestine sport rather than a popular, public sport. The principal animals used in the sport were bulls, bears, badgers, and rats. Bull baiting, the most popular type of animal baiting, was held on special occasions, often at fairs, wakes, and even at elections. It always occurred in the open, usually a publican's yard, an open field, or a marketplace.

Rules and Play

The various forms of animal baiting have their own rules and conventions, although with the same underlying idea: endurance wins. In bull baiting, men attached the bull to a strong stake and unleashed dogs on it. The dogs seized the bull about the head. The one who retained its hold the longest won a prize for his master. Frequently the bulls tossed the dogs high into the air. Owners attempted to catch them before they fell to the ground and were injured.

Bear baiting was similar, though held indoors. Men tethered the bear to a wall with strong collar and chain. One man further controlled the bear with a rope fastened to the collar. This allowed the man to help a dog that the bear had grabbed and "hugged" with a sharp pull of the rope that would bring the bear to its knees, causing it to release the dog. A well-trained dog could

BAITING THE OPOSSUM.

An Account of a Well Matched Fight between a Young Terrier Bitch, Belonging to Mr. Ferguson, and an Opossum, Brought from New South Wales by Mr. Jenkins.

News has been received from London, of this extraordinary match, which excited exceeding interest amongst the sporting fraternity in the Old Dart.

Local boys need no introduction to the fighting attributed of the Vulpine Opossum, our bushy-tail, whose remarkably strong claws have left many a mark on incautious Europeans, both man and dog.

Mr. Ferguson's young terrier bitch was about sixteen months old, liver and white, weight about 25 1/2 lbs. Mr. Jenkin's opossum from New South Wales was supposed to be about three years old and weighed 27 lbs.

The bitch and opossum fought on the 6th January, 1829, and the day being very rough, the fight was obliged to take place in a barn instead of Hempton Green, Norfolk, as had been contemplated, to the vexation of numbers, who could not get admission at any price; so much stir did the affair make in the neighborhood.

A great deal of betting took place previous to the match, at guineas to pounds, Possey the favourite. Some of our Norfolk knowing and learned country swells, who were acquainted with the nature of the beast, (after seeing the excellent trim he was got into by his trainer Jemmy Neal) even went as high as three to two, and it was said that even two to one was offered on the New South Wales favourite.

ROUND 1ST. Possey looked very fit, shook his bushy tail, and darted at the bitch as quick as lightening, caught her by the shoulder, and tore a piece out of it; he then drew back, made another spring at the fore leg, but missed it. Meantime, the bitch was not idle—she made several attempts at a hold, but the gentleman's furry coat deceived the poor bitch, who brought away a mouthful of his outer garment every time she sprung at him; at length, she caught him where the Irishmen put their lundy, and punished him severely, while he returned by making use of his claws, with which he scratched dreadfully. At length he got away, and was taken to his house; and after two minutes rest, began.

ROUND 2ND. Both darted at one another, their heads met, and both were knocked over. Returning, Possey seized the bitch by the throat, and almost knocked all the wind out of the bitch (four to one on Possey freely offered—no takers). The bitch fought shy till she got a little wind, then made for him, seized his proboscis, and pulled him about in good style, in spite of his claws which made dreadful havoc with the bitch; Possey got away and was taken to his house. This lasted nine minutes and a half.

ROUND 3RD. The bitch made first play, and began by taking Mr. Possey by the nose, where she held him, and pulled him about for two minutes and a half he keeping his claws in exercise all the while when she lost her hold, and sprang at his neck (which in the previous round she had cleared of the fur) which she lacerated in a shocking manner, when he got away and was led to his house. Possey became rather weak from the loss of blood, but was restored by something being applied to his nostrils.

ROUND 4TH, AND LAST. The bitch again made for the foreigner's neck, where she left the marks of her toothy work; she then seized him by the shoulder, got an excellent hold, and for the first time Possey uttered a dismal yell, and, on getting away, made for his house, from whence he could no more be brought to the scratch. The bitch was consequently declared the winner.

The fight lasted thirty-seven minutes.

—Pierce Egan. (1832) Book of Sports.
Reprinted in Ingleton 1952, 119.

grab the bear by the nose or lower jaw and pull its head between its legs, causing a complete somersault that left the bear helpless at the end of a chain.

Bull running was a variant activity. It was usually held on a holiday. It began with the baiting of the bulls, usually with liquid irritants or a red effigy. This was followed by a free-for-all through the streets of the town. It was similar to contemporary bull running in France and Spain, the most famous being at Pamplona.

Badger baiting was another form of the sport. Again the animal was tied to a stake and a dog was loosed on it, worrying it while the badger fought back with its jaws and claws. A variation of this sport was badger drawing, in which a badger was placed in a box. The dog's master held the dog by the scruff of its neck and by the tail, letting the dog into the box and then drawing it out by the tail. Wagering was based on how many times the dog could successfully draw the badger from the box.

Rat baiting or rat killing was also popular. Men placed dogs, usually terriers, in a small, wire-enclosed pit with a large number of rats. The dogs killed the rats by shaking them before the rats could bite. The dog that killed the most rats in the shortest time won; five seconds per rat was good work. A rare variation of this form of the sport was a competition among men and dogs involving who could kill the most rats, men using their teeth to tear off the head of the rat.

A final "sport" was throwing rocks at cocks, which was often held on Shrove Tuesday. A promoter charged twopence for three throws. The customer attempted to knock the bird down long enough to reach it and grab it before it regained its feet. If successful, he kept the prize.

These sports had gender, class, and racial components, and attacks and defenses of them involved these issues. Some individuals denounced the popular recreations of the poor, but not the blood sports of gentlemen, such as fox hunting, shooting, and fishing. Many males advocated animal-fighting sports. Their arguments were race- and gender-based, emphasizing the values of bravery, valor, and courage of the English "race." The defenders endowed the dogs that participated in the various baitings with these values, which the Anglo-Saxon youth of Great Britain needed to defend Empire.

Opposition to animal baiting began in the late 18th century, with opponents holding their opinions for different reasons and from different political points of view. The middle class led the movement against these popular sports. Rational and radical individuals opposed the indifference to suffering and pain of a pre-humanitarian age, while conservative moralists valued social control and feared these sports because they attracted large crowds in a revolutionary age. The opposition culminated in the introduction of the Bull-Baiting Bill of 1800 in the British Parliament. Further success came in 1835 with the passage of the Act Against Cruelty of Animals. The sports, however, were not to be legislated out of existence, and both the practices and opposition to them continued.

Given recent concerns with animal rights, as well as overall changes in cultural values, it seems unlikely that animal baiting will again emerge as a public sport. The lure of such blood sports remains strong in some individuals, however, making it unlikely that animal baiting will ever disappear entirely.

—TOM DUNNING

See also Animal Rights; Cockfighting.

Bibliography: Dundes, Alan. (1994) *The Cockfight: A Casebook.* Madison: University of Wisconsin Press. Fitz-Barnard, L. (1983 reprint) *Fighting Sports.* Surrey, UK: Saiga Publications. Ingleton, Geoffrey Chapman, ed. (1952) *True Patriots All or News from Early Australia as in a Collection of Broadsides.* Sydney: Angus and Robertson. Malcolmson, Robert W. (1973) *Popular Recreations in English Society, 1700–1850.* Cambridge: Cambridge University Press. Walvin, James. (1978) *Leisure and Society, 1830–1950.* London: Longman.

Animal Rights

The animal rights movement is a product of the late 20th century, when many accepted relationships between humans and the environment have come under scrutiny. Contemporary animal rights advocates see their cause in very broad terms: a general attempt to protect animals from human exploitation, defined as the use of animals (or their parts) in scientific research, consumer products, and sport. Those involved in the movement range from people with philosophical objections to those who actively protest to those who engage in sometimes violent action against facilities that use animals. The movement has already affected sports such as horse racing, rodeo, and fox hunting.

History

Historians and social scientists trace the contemporary animal rights movement to the 19th-century antivivisection movement, which opposed the use of animals for scientific research. Originally a Puritan reaction to both the Industrial Revolution and Victorian materialism, the antivivisection movement responded to perceptions of the increasing human exploitation of, and intrusion into, the natural world.

The Victorian antivivisection movement used sensationalized publicity, popularized exposes of animal mistreatment, and apocalyptic literature to mobilize public sentiment against animal experimentation, animal baiting, and the use of animals in sport. The movement depended heavily on aristocratic noblesse oblige for support and played heavily upon public sensibilities concerning morality and brutality.

The movement had little impact upon the use of animals and eventually disintegrated. However, the symbolic reaction against the use of animals did not disappear, but left the reformist animal welfare movement as its legacy. The cause was perpetuated by less radical groups that sought reform of societal attitudes toward animals. Through the turn of the century these groups continued working to abate animal suffering. Antivivisection sentiments reemerged briefly in the 1950s in response to various scientific phenomena, but animal welfare groups still predominated. Beginning in the 1960s, the cause of animal protection was transformed from reformist calls for animal protection into the radical calls for societal redemption.

The contemporary animal rights movement has evolved to question virtually all forms of animal use and control. Using publicity, exposes, and apocalyptic literature, the movement has framed the issues surrounding the status of animals in moralistic terms. However, unlike its progenitor, the radical animal rights movement extends rights-based claims for moral consideration and legal protection to animals.

Philosophies

The movement's claim to moral equivalency between human and nonhuman animals originates in two opposing philosophical schools. Utilitarianism cites the creed, "The greatest good, for the greatest number, for the longest time," as its justification. Animal liberationists argue that since animals and people both feel pain and pleasure, that the utilitarian creed should be expanded to include nonhuman animals.

The moral rights argument emphasizes similarities in the physiology, and therefore the inherent value, between higher mammals. Proponents argue that since nonhuman animals have consciousness, expectations, and desires, they likewise have personal autonomy and moral rights.

The Animal Rights Movement

The animal rights movement consists of various organizations, which can be subdivided into roughly three categories with different beliefs and goals. Some see animals as objects of compassion, deserving protection, but acknowledge some boundaries between species. Their goals include avoiding animal cruelty, limiting animal populations, and adopting animals. Others believe that animals deserve moral and legal consideration, with a balance between human and nonhuman interests, and that there is some hierarchy of animals. Their explicit goals include the elimination of all unnecessary suffering by reducing and replacing existing uses of animals. A third group argues that animals have absolute moral and legal rights to personal autonomy and self-determination, with equal rights across species, especially among higher vertebrates. They seek total and immediate abolition of all animal exploitation and use moralistic rhetoric and public condemnation in conjunction with civil disobedience and direct actions to protest the use of animals.

Several reasons explain this increase in awareness of animal rights and the expansion of what those rights are. Since the 1970s, researchers who have studied primates and marine mammals have concluded that these animals have thinking ability, complex social groups, and even forms of language. These conclusions have accentuated human empathy with animals. At the same time, evolutionary theory has indicated that humans and animals are biologically related, and indeed that humans share a distant though long-ago ancestry with other primates; in effect, scientists have argued that animals are much more similar to humans than previously thought. If indeed animals can think and feel and are intelligent, if they are physically similar to people, if they are evolutionary brothers and sisters of humans, and if animals act almost "human," then why should they not be treated as the moral equivalent of people?

Implications for Sports

The implications of this philosophy for sports cannot be overstated. Indeed, the impact of the animal rights movement upon sport is ubiquitous in nature and global in geography.

In England, blood sports such as foxhunting have come under attack by the Hunt Saboteurs, an animal rights group whose protests and confrontational disruptions of fox hunts have been highly publicized. The Saboteurs oppose hunters who exploit the animals for mere pleasure. In response, some hunts now chase human marathon runners rather than foxes, ending when the hounds catch the runners, and a good time is had by all. In continental Europe, the movement is found in all sporting contexts. In Spain, animal rights activists protest bullfighting, albeit unsuccessfully. In Germany, catch-and-release fishermen have been attacked by animal rights activists, and the promenades of Vienna find activists accosting the Viennese for wearing fur. In Australia, the animal rights movement opposes kangaroo hunts, while in Africa animal rights groups protest big game trophy safaris and claim to have been responsible for the shift toward noninjurious "photo-safaris." In the Arctic, animal rights groups protest subsistence trapping as well as trophy hunting, and they have significantly affected both the fur industry and sportsmen. In the United States, rodeos have been forced to justify their existence in the face of animal rights publicity. They have been picketed, and they now include contingency plans for disruptions caused by animal rights activists in their overall event planning. From greyhound racing to pig wrestling, from pigeon shoots to rattlesnake roundups, animal rights activists have periodically appeared at events to protest and disrupt, thus gaining publicity for their cause. Whether it be deer hunting to control overpopulation or provide pleasure, whether it be falconry or competitive sheep herding, animal rights activists believe that the animals involved have the right to be left alone, regardless of human justifications.

A striking example of the potential success of the animal rights movement came in California in 1990. California voters passed an initiative on the state ballot that banned mountain lion hunting despite the opposition of hunting, gun, and agricultural groups. This is significant to sportsmen for a variety of reasons. First, the California Department of Fish and Game (CDF&G)

Animal Rights
and Billfishing

"If animals have inalienable rights, as some animal rights activists argue, how can hunters and fishermen justify killing them?"

A case in point involves the tag-and-release program adopted by the Billfish Foundation in response to diminished fish numbers and the negative public perception of trophy fishing. Supporters contend that this program allows the thrills associated with the sport without damaging existing fish populations, all the while providing scientific research intended to perpetuate the species. In this program, sport anglers cooperate with researchers who tag the billfish, then release them to collect data.

Animal rights activists contend that billfishing is cruel and unacceptable. The tag-and-release program fails to account for the rights of the individual fish. Activists also assert that tag-and-release fails as a conservation tool because the struggle involved in landing some big game fish results in death or exhaustion to the fish; big-game fishing is the cause of, not the solution to, diminished game fish numbers. They likewise insist that very little "science" has actually emerged from the program. But more important, animal rights activists criticize the morality of subjecting fishes to repeated pain and exhaustion, hooking them, playing them, damaging them to the point of death, then releasing them, all for the pleasure of humans. The activists scoff at the idea of killing animals to save them. They ask, "How can people justify killing, torture, and maiming, all in the name of pleasure?"

Indeed, they attack all forms of fishing as repugnant. Nonetheless, they argue that subjecting an innocent animal to repeated torture through catch-and-release is worse than killing the animal outright. Hence they oppose the Billfish Foundation, and all such organizations, who in their ethical calculus fail to account for the rights of the fish they catch.

—*Wesley V. Jamison*

had determined that mountain lions were sufficiently numerous to allow a lotteried hunt. Although the lion had been both hunted and protected numerous times in state history, biologists for the CDF&G believed that population growth justified a hunt as a management tool. Animal rights activists, however, disputed the scientific justification, arguing instead that hunting the lions was immoral and evil. Second, the animal rights groups who passed the initiative contained a significant minority who wanted to ban hunting outright. The leadership of the animal rights groups agreed that an outright ban on hunting was premature and would have failed. Instead they identified legislative strategy with a high likelihood of passing, banning the hunting of individual, charismatic larger animals. A 1996 California initiative to rescind the legislation protecting the cats, and thus subjecting them to hunting, was re-

soundingly defeated. Activists intend to extrapolate the success in California to other areas of sports. As a result, other states such as Oregon and Colorado have passed bans on specific types of hunting as well as hunting of certain species.

Some observers argue that animal rights activists, although highly visible at sporting events, have had little success in ending them. Nonetheless, the very presence of the activists indicates that the movement is growing, and the dismissals of the movement's impending demise have been greatly exaggerated.

—WESLEY V. JAMISON

Bibliography: Dizard, Jan. (1994) *Going Wild: Hunting, Animal Rights, and the Contested Meaning of Nature.* Amherst: University of Massachusetts Press. Jasper, James, and Dorothy Nelkin. (1992) *The Animal Rights Crusade: The Growth of a Moral Protest.* New York: Free Press. Regan, Tom. (1985) *The Case for Animal Rights.* Berkeley: University of California Press. Sperling, Susan. (1988) *Animal Liberators: Research and Morality.* Berkeley: University of California Press.

Archery

Archery involves the loosing of an arrow from a string fastened tightly to each end of a curved bow, with the goal of hitting a target. Both recreational and competitive target shooting are popular in many countries, and bows and arrows are also used in hunting.

History

What is sport today was first done for hunting, defense, and, apparently, ritual. Bows and arrows appear as hunting equipment in prehistoric cave paintings in Spain and France, and stone arrowheads have been found in many excavations as archaeological evidence of early human hunters. Evidence of archery can be found almost everywhere, indicating that it did not spread from one place to others but originated independently in various places. Bows and arrows were also used as lethal weapons in warfare. The training of these military skills led to competitions, which can be considered as prototypes of organized sport.

Archery was often linked with magic and full of symbolism. Among the ancient Hittites, for example, it was part of a magic rite to cure impotence or homosexuality. A magical formula then confirmed that he was cured and that all female elements had been expunged. It is often difficult to differentiate where, when, and how archery was practiced "for its own sake." The links with hunting, warfare, and ritual are never far away, but they have throughout history often been invoked as a rationalization for practicing shooting for pleasure.

Tutankhamen's tomb, discovered in Egypt in 1922 by Howard Carter (1873–1939), revealed, among other artifacts for hunting, bows, arrows, quivers, arm guards, and a bow case belonging to the king's hunting chariot. Drawings show that the king hunted with bow and arrow from a sitting or standing position, and also from a moving chariot. He displayed these hunting skills not out of economic necessity, but for pure enjoyment. These royal hunting scenes also symbolized the king's military preparedness and his physical fitness.

The motif of the king hunting with bow and arrow in a two-wheeled chariot is also frequently found in Ancient Mesopotamia, where King Asshurnasirpal was depicted in 9th- and 7th-century B.C.E. reliefs, performing his hunting skills before spectators.

Archery contests are described in Homer's epic poems, the *Iliad* and the *Odyssey*. A series of sporting contests were organized in honor of the Greek hero Patroclus, who had been killed by Hector during the siege of Troy. As part of these funeral games, Achilles had a ship's mast set up in the sandy soil, with a pigeon tied to it by one leg, for the archery contest. Teucrus, who won first shot, hit the ribbon and the pigeon flew off. The second archer, Meriones, snatched the bow from Teucrus and aimed at the bird as it circled in the clouds. His arrow struck the bird in the chest, went right through its body, and came down to bury its tip in the ground at the archer's feet. This scene is an early predecessor of popinjay shooting, which appeared on the program of the modern Olympic Games in 1900 and 1920.

Roman soldiers trained in archery but excelled more in handling the sword. Until the 5th century C.E. Roman legionaries shot their bows by drawing the string to the chest, instead of the longer draw to the face, which gives the arrow far more accuracy. Saint Sebastian, a Roman officer of the Imperial Guard, was martyred by being pierced with arrows because of his Christian faith around C.E. 300. He became the patron saint of many medieval archery guilds.

Archery seems to have been among the first sports for which records were set. A Turkish inscription from the 13th century praises Sultan Mahmud Khan for a shot of 1,215 arrow lengths. A 17th-century miniature also portrays archers on Istanbul's Place of Arrows, where shots of astounding length were recorded.

Just as Attila and his Huns had terrorized the eastern borders of Europe with his horsemen-archers in the 5th century, Genghis Khan rode westward with his Mongolian cavalry in the 13th century. The Mongols used powerful composite bows, and their archery tradition survives in present-day Mongolia, where champion archers enjoy much prestige. The so-called Mongolian draw or thumb lock for drawing the bowstring refers to this cultural heritage.

Kyudo, the traditional Japanese art of archery, is a branch of Zen Buddhism, in which the bow and arrow are used as a means to achieve a spiritual goal via physical and mental discipline. The famous samurai warriors were not only expert swordsmen but also skillful archers. They practiced shooting from a galloping horse, which is still known today as *yabusame.* A gallery in one of the ancient religious temples in Kyoto served as a shooting range in the so-called Oyakazu contest, which took place between 1606 and 1842 and consisted of shooting a maximum number of arrows in a period of 24 hours through an aperture of 4.5 meters (14 feet, 9 inches) without touching the walls of the gallery. Interest in this contest dropped off after 1686, when an archer scored 8,132 successes with 13,053 arrows; it seemed virtually impossible to break this record.

The Toxophilite Society of London, formed in 1781 for the practice of archery as a sport, sparked the great revival of archery at the end of the 18th century and influenced later societies. At that time the game varied from one society to another, but rules for scoring, the number of arrows to be shot, and the distances for shooting slowly evolved in an attempt to standardize the sport of competitive archery. Archery, until then linked with the lower classes, was now rapidly adopted by the wealthy "leisure class." The archery field thus became an arena of fashion, coquetry, and elegance.

In England, the first Grand National Meeting was held at York in 1844. It was agreed to shoot a "York Round," which consisted of shooting 72 arrows at 100 yards (91 meters), 48 at 80 yards (73 meters), and 24 at 60 yards (55 meters). The championship of Great Britain is still based on these rules, decided upon by the Archers of the United Kingdom. Women competed for the first time in the second Grand National Archery Meeting of 1845, although some had already been members of various societies previously. Queen Victoria herself, before her accession to the throne, had been both a patron of the Queen's Royal St. Leonard's Archers and had actively shot with them.

The English archery tradition spread to the United States, where the first archery club was founded in 1828 on the banks of the Schuylkill River, under the name the United Bowmen of Philadelphia.

A Royal Archer

During the period of the Commonwealth, Oliver Cromwell's iron fist reigned over England and King Charles II had to seek refuge on the Continent. From 1651 to 1656 he first stayed in France and later in Germany. In 1656 Charles moved his residence to Bruges in Flanders.

Generally speaking his sojourn in Bruges was marked by its peacefulness. There was something in Charles' character through which he soon won all the hearts . . . not only those of lovesick ladies. The rough Irishman Lord Taaffe, once declared of him: "May I never drink wine, if I had not rather live in six sous a day with him than have all the pleasures of the world without him." But of course, where Charles came, pleasures and amusements were never far away.

From the very year of their arrival, Charles and his brother Henry, Duke of Gloucester, were registered as members of the old Saint George Crossbow Guild of Bruges. Later Charles also became an active member of the Saint Sebastian (archery) guild and the Saint Barbara (culverin) guild. Here follows the English translation of the original report, laid down in the Saint George Guild Book:

Charles II, King of Great Britain, enforced to leave his throne because of riots, has established his residence within the walls of Bruges.

On the 11th June 1656, the Gild has been shooting the bird of honour in the presence of His Majesty and His Highness the Duke of Gloucester, his brother, with many other noblemen both from England and from this Country, as well as the members of the illustrious Guild.

The King shot as first and he hit the popinjay; his brother continued shooting until the popinjay was finally shot down by mister Pieter Pruyssenaere, wine merchant, residing in the Old Castle . . .

Only two weeks after their entrance in the Saint George Crossbow Guild the Stuarts were already present at the shooting grounds of another guild: the Saint Sebastian Archers. Honouring the English longbow traditions, the king and his brother made archery their favorite sport and daily they were seen practising in the gild's lanes. As the king and his brother were not familiar with Flemish long-distance shooting, the Saint Sebastian Archers even arranged for two special butts at shorter distance to meet this problem.

—*Roland Renson, "Play in Exile"*

In the United States, the Civil War (1861–1865) helped renew interest in archery. After the war, former Confederate soldiers were no longer permitted to use firearms. Two war veterans, the brothers William (1846–1918) and Maurice (1844–1901) Thompson spent the period from 1866 to 1868 in the wilderness of Georgia's swamps and Florida's Everglades, living mostly on the game they killed with bow and arrow. Maurice Thompson's book *The Witchery of Archery,* published in 1878, captured their love of the sport. The book was widely read and interest in archery spread throughout the country. American archery tackle had rapidly improved and was now at least of equal quality to the English. Archery declined, however, almost as rapidly as it had expanded. Americans sought their thrills in rival fashionable outdoor games such as tennis, rowing, baseball, and golf.

Archery was also exported to the British colonies. In Australia, for instance, it was one of the rare socially acceptable competitive sports for women, and was organized in mixed clubs.

Rules and Play

In 1931 the Fédération Internationale de Tir à l'Arc (FITA) was founded at Lwow, Poland, with representatives from Belgium, France, Poland, and Sweden. This started a new era in international archery. FITA rules and regulations were internationally adopted. The United Kingdom joined one year later. Archery was voted back into the Olympic Games at the meeting in Mexico City in 1968.

In the single FITA round, competitors shoot six sets of six arrows from distances of 90, 70, 50, and 30 meters (98, 77, 55, and 33 yards). Women's rounds have distances of 70, 60, 50, and 30 meters (77, 66, 55, and 33 yards). In Olympic competitions a double round is shot, which comprises 72 arrows at the same distances.

Archery lends itself to a variety of organized forms. Shooting from a wheelchair, for example, has become a standard sport among many paraplegic athletes. An alternative to formal target archery is field shooting, based on conditions as they might be encountered in hunting. This more "natural" type of archery has also become standardized and is practiced either as the Field Round or as the Hunters Round. They include:

- Flight shooting, or shooting for maximum distance. Distances of over 1,100 meters (1,200 yards) have been recorded.
- Clout shooting, or shooting arrows with a high trajectory to fall into a target zone, marked by circles on the ground.
- International crossbow shooting, which is regulated by the Union Internationale de Tir à l'Arbalète (UIA), founded in 1956 in Switzerland, the land of the legendary Wilhelm Tell. Several variants exist both in traditional crossbow types (for instance, the bullet crossbow, still practiced in Belgium) and in the targets.
- Popinjay shooting, practiced both at a tall mast, from which feathered "birds" have to be shot down, but and also horizontally in lanes.

Archery across Cultures

In Africa archery is still used for hunting among isolated groups such as the San and Khoi-speaking peoples in the Kalahari and foragers in the rainforests of Central Africa, who employ rather small bows and poisoned arrowheads.

North American Indians have always been associated with the bow and arrow. Bow types and arrow forms varied widely among the different tribes. The Inuits of North Alaska moved archery indoors in winter and used miniature bows and arrows for shooting at small wooden bird targets hung from the roof of the communal center. After the Spanish introduced horses in the 16th century, the Indian archers quickly adapted themselves to shooting from horseback. Contests included shooting for accuracy at an arrow standing upright in the ground; arrows arranged upright in a ring; an arrow locked in a tree; a suspended woven grass bundle or a roll of green cornhusks.

Archery is also widespread in indigenous South America. Shooting contests are usually organized as contests of dexterity in which the archers aim at a stationary or a mobile target. Shooting for the longest distance is also common. A thrilling variant (for instance, among the Yanomamö of the Brazil-Venezuela border) consists of shooting blunt arrows at opponents who try to parry their blows.

The British Legacy

The traditional English longbow occupies a special position in archery's evolution. The secret of the longbow lay in the natural properties of yew (*Taxus baccata*), which was cut in such a way that a layer of sapwood was left along the flattened back of the bow. The heartwood of yew withstands compression, while the sapwood is elastic; both return to their original straightness after the bow is loosed. This combination had already been applied in prehistoric times, as shown by Neolithic bows discovered in a peat bog in Somerset, England. The Saxons used bows for hunting purposes only, not for warfare, as they considered only man-to-man combat with hand-held weapons appropriate. This would change, however, after the Norman invasion of England in 1066, in which William the Conqueror used massed archery.

A more proficient longbow, probably developed by the Welsh, would make England a first-class military power. Folktales celebrated the lore of bow and arrow and featured such legendary bowmen as Robin Hood.

Of special importance for the spread of the English longbow was the victory in 1346 at Crécy, where the English archers completely routed the Genoese cross-bowmen of the French army. Edward III's victorious army, largely outnumbered by the enemy, consisted of some 13,000 men, half of whom were archers. The yeoman archer became feared and respected and was therefore imitated on the continent, where the swift longbow was adopted side by side with the much more precise but slow-to-load crossbow.

The first law concerning archery was passed in the 12th century; it absolved an archer from charges of murder or manslaughter if he accidentally killed a man while practicing. From the 13th to the 16th century all servants, laborers, yeomen, and other menfolk were enjoined to have their own bows and to practice at the butts on Sundays and holy days. Target archery thus gradually lost its exclusive military character and also became a social pastime. During the reign of Henry VIII (1491–1547) several acts were promulgated to encourage archery. One ordered all physically fit men under the age of 60, except for clergymen and judges, to practice shooting the longbow.

Militarily speaking, however, firearms made the bow obsolete. Despite all the official encouragement and the publication of a specialized treatise on archery, called *Toxophilus, the Schole of Shootinge* in 1545, the bow's decline had begun.

Continental Archery

The Frankish knights who joined the First Crusade (1096–1099) became acquainted with a new weapon, the crossbow, a bow made by fastening a bow at right angles to a stock or tiller. This instrument proved so deadly that it was forbidden to Christians by the second Lateran Council of 1139—another antiwar decree that has never been observed!

By the end of the 13th century special elite troops had been set up within the urban militias; these were the guilds of the crossbow-men. These guilds obtained their charters and received privileges during the 14th century. In the course of the 15th century the military role of the crossbow and longbow guilds was seriously affected by the invention of firearms. More and more, the archery guild's main pursuit was representing the prestige and status of the leading citizens, thus losing their role in military training but maintaining their traditional social status and political power.

Popinjay shooting still is a popular sporting activity in the northern (Flemish) part of France, in Belgium (mostly in Flanders but also in Wallonia) and in the Catholic southern provinces of the Netherlands. A few cities in Italy still keep their medieval crossbow tradition alive. During the magnificent yearly Palio della Balestra in Gubbio or San Marino, two rival societies of crossbow-men compete each other in full medieval attire, accompanied by their flag wavers and drum corps. Numerous *Schützen* (rifle clubs) societies in Austria, Germany, and Switzerland found their origins in archery guilds.

Archery's Precarious Olympic History

Originally archery was included in the Olympics only at the request of the national archery association of the host country. International rules did not exist; the rules of the host country were used. Archery first appeared during the 1900 Games held in Paris and consisted of horizontal target shooting (*tir au berceau*) both with the crossbow and with the handbow and vertical popinjay shooting (*tir à la perche*) with the handbow.

Archery reappeared during the 1904 Olympic Games, when women first participated. All competitors, male and female, were Americans. During the so-called Anthropological Days, American archers competed against a number of "savages" from different parts of the globe. Where the white Americans put practically all their arrows at the four-foot-square target board at 40 yards, the "savages" hardly hit the target at all. This carnivalistic event with racist undertones upset Olympic head Pierre de Coubertin, who called it a vulgar experiment not to be repeated.

For the 1908 Olympic Games, held in London, clear, concise rules of competition were drawn up. The competing teams consisted of women and men from Britain, men from France, and a lone male competitor from the United States.

Olympic archery next appeared in 1920 in Antwerp, Belgium. Archery was Belgium's national sport par excellence, but it was rather idiosyncratic. Only archers from Belgium, France, and the Netherlands showed up, and there were no women's events.

The codification of international rules in 1931 initiated a new era in international competition and in 1972 archery reappeared at the Munich Olympics. It has remained an Olympic sport since then and has expanded in terms of number of nations competing and number of competitors.

Archery is an activity and a sport dating back thousands of years and has been practiced in many cultures. Despite almost entirely disappearing as a military, hunting, and ritual activity, archery still remains a recreational and competitive sport. And, while it is perhaps too highly specialized to exert mass appeal, loyal archers will continue to loose their arrows, worldwide.

—ROLAND RENSON

Bibliography: Acker, William R. B. (1965) *Japanese Archery.* Rutland, VT: Tuttle. Guttmann, Allen. (1978) *From Ritual to Record.* New York: Columbia University Press. Loades, Mike. (1995) *Archery: Its History and Forms.* Knebworth, UK: Running Wolf Productions (video). Paterson, W. F. (1984) *Encyclopaedia of Archery.* New York: St. Martin's Press. Renson, Roland. (1976) "The Flemish Archery Gilds: From Defense Mechanisms to Sports Institutions." In *The History, the Evolution and Diffusion of Sports and Games in Different Cultures,* edited by P. P. De Nayer, M. Ostyn, and R. Renson. Brussels: BLOSO, pp. 135–159. Schröter, Harald. (1983) *Roger Ascham, Toxophilus: The Schole of Shootinge. London 1545.* St. Augustin: Richarz.

Arm Wrestling

Arm wrestling is a contest of strength and will power. The two contestants sit or stand facing each other across a table or other flat surface. Each places one elbow on the table, holding an arm upright at a V-shaped angle, and griping the opponent's hand with knuckles facing out. When the match begins, each person presses in an arc toward the table, attempting to force the opponent's forearm, wrist, and hand onto the surface beneath. The arm wrestler who succeeds is the victor. In the mid-1990s, an estimated 100,000 men and women competed seriously in organized arm wrestling.

Wrist wrestling is a specific form of arm wrestling, which uses a particular technique in which the opponents grip each other's unused arm across the table. In contrast, arm wrestlers grip a peg or other object with the free hand or keep it loose.

History

It is generally believed that ancient peoples practiced arm wrestling as a specialized form of wrestling. The arm wrestling common today is usually traced to the indigenous people of North America, where European settlers later adopted it. One traditional name for the sport, Indian wrestling, refers to these origins.

In addition to spontaneous individual matches, arm-wrestling tournaments have long been conducted at fairs, taverns, and other social settings. Organized arm wrestling gained momentum in the 1960s with a movement to coordinate and publicize it as a serious competitive sport. This modern arm-wrestling movement was originally most active in California, Connecticut, Virginia, and Pennsylvania. It subsequently spread to other regions of North America and other nations. In India, where it is called punjah, it is among the most popular of sports, and national championships there attract thousands of spectators. Arm wrestling has also become increasingly recognized in Russia and other states of the former Soviet Union, and in Brazil and England. In 1988, organized arm wrestling gained major corporate backing when Heublein, a liquor company, began to sponsor a large annual circuit of tournaments called the Yukon Jack World Arm-Wrestling Championships.

Rules and Play

Each arm wrestling match is called a pull. Contestants press their arms and hands in a downward arc toward the table. In right-hand matches, they press counterclockwise and in left-hand matches clockwise. Each opponent presses in the same direction, but because they are facing each other their arms and hands strain in opposite directions. A match ends in a pin, when one opponent forces and keeps the other's forearm, wrist, and hand down. Matches are not timed, so their length depends on the time it takes for a pin to occur. A pull may last less than a minute or may be several minutes long. Flashing is a term used to describe a contest in which one opponent pins the other especially quickly.

Organized, sanctioned events have specific rules and guidelines for conducting and judging matches. Tournaments are generally organized by weight classes and gender. Typical basic weight classes include divisions for less than 75 kilograms (165 pounds), between 75 and 90 kilograms (166 and 198 pounds), and over 90 kilograms (199 pounds). Official matches often take place on special tables equipped with elbow pads, a pinning mat, and gripping pegs.

Arm wrestlers use specific strategies in the way they hold themselves and use their muscles and energy. In standard arm wrestling, contestants have more mobility, and they emphasize techniques that use their shoulders, arms, and hands. Basic movements (which have many variations) include the shoulder-roll, in which the wrestler exerts pressure from the shoulder and triceps; the hook and drag, which emphasizes the use of wrist and triceps to press the opponent's arm down; and the top roll, which focuses on bending the opponent's wrist.

While arm wrestlers are often large and obviously muscular, many successful competitors are small and wiry or of average size. Although strong, well-developed upper arms and shoulders give a wrestler an obvious advantage, well-developed tendons and ligaments in the forearm and hand are particularly important. In addition to physical strength, psychological attributes and technical strategies are vital to suc-

cess. A contestant must have the will power to maintain determination and sometimes endure intense physical pain during the strenuous match. They develop techniques to focus their mental energy and to gain a psychological advantage over their opponents.

Contemporary arm wrestling reflects its varied history. Some aspects of the sport are very colorful, and emphasize belligerence and machismo. Others treat it as serious athletic activity that focuses on technique and discipline. The sport's top athletes are similarly diverse. Some contestants are flamboyant, with extravagant tattoos and costumes. They have outrageous nicknames and growl, pound the table, or engage in other antics before a match, reflecting both a sense of showmanship and intent to intimidate opponents. Other arm wrestlers are more subdued and approach the sport with quiet discipline and concentration.

The sport's largest sanctioning body is the nonprofit World Armsport Federation (WAF), based in Scranton, Pennsylvania. The WAF coordinates regional and national affiliated organizations in over 50 countries, including the American Arm-Wrestling Association (AAA) in the United States. Smaller independent arm-wrestling associations also sponsor tournaments. Some private entrepreneurs organize tournaments as profitable business ventures.

The number of organized tournaments with cash prizes has increased since the 1980s, but arm wrestling remains primarily an amateur sport, and most arm wrestlers wrestle for fun. Many tournaments do not have cash prizes, and even for the top wrestlers, prize money usually only covers travel costs and other expenses.

Although likely to remain a popular amateur pastime, arm wrestling is at the same time edging toward a more professional image. The major goals of many contemporary proponents of arm wrestling are to change the sport's rough-and-tumble image and increase appreciation of it as a serious athletic competition.

—JOHN TOWNES

Bibliography: Berkow, Ira. (1995) "Wrist Wars on the Waterfront." *New York Times* (26 August). Jordan, Pat. (1987) "In Florida: 'Lock Up!' And the Pulse Pounds." *Time* (2 November). Junod, Tom. (1993) "Arms and the Man." *Sports Illustrated* (14 June).

Armed Forces Games

Armed forces games are the sports competitions engaged in among branches of the military with the goals of entertainment, training, and morale-building. The games themselves include such staples as track and field competitions, boxing and wrestling, various forms of football, and baseball.

History

Members of armies have long practiced various sports to hone their warrior skills or break the monotony of camp life. By the mid-19th century most military leaders in industrializing nation-states thought modern soldiers needed athletic competitions to practice their military craftsmanship, to teach the essentials of "teamwork, and to inculcate nationalism. Modern armies began to sponsor sporting competitions during the Industrial Revolution. In the midst of one of the first "modern" wars in world history, the U.S. Civil War (1861–1865), troops played sports for diversion from combat, and the intermingling of soldiers from various regions played an important role in making baseball the United States' "national pastime."

Following the Civil War, sports retained an important connection with the U.S. military. Advocates promoted them both as morale-builders and means of enhancing military preparedness. National Guard units helped to spread modern sports throughout the United States, and armories served as centers of the new sporting life. In the active services, sports had become a central feature of military life. A baseball craze swept the U.S. Navy during the 1890s. By the end of that decade every ship in the North Atlantic Squadron had a baseball team. Armed forces teams also competed in boxing, fencing, football, track and field, rowing, and other sports. In 1897 the armed services created a Military Athletic League.

Other industrialized nations also employed sporting competitions to inspire martial nationalism in their armed forces. The major imperial powers of the late 19th century—Great Britain, France, and Germany—used sports to train their armies and navies. Japanese sailors learned baseball from U.S. naval crews. The colonial powers, including the United States, also used sports in efforts to impose Western styles of civilization on the peoples of Asia, Africa, and the Pacific.

The outbreak of World War I entrenched sporting competitions in the military practices of the major powers. The armed forces athletic competitions during World War I wove sports even more firmly into the fabric of American life. Indeed, in the wake of the war, the United States attempted to re-create through sport some semblance of a community of nations by reinvigorating the tottering Olympic movement with an armed forces competition, believing that an athletic festival could help restore war-ravaged Western civilization.

The Inter-Allied Games of 1919 initiated by Elwood S. Brown, a leader of the YMCA movement and the director of athletics for the American Expeditionary Force (AEF) were modeled on the Olympic Games.

The games brought nearly 1,500 athletes from Australia, Belgium, Brazil, Canada, China, Cuba, Czechoslovakia, France, Great Britain, Greece, Guatemala, Haiti, Italy, Japan, Liberia, Montenegro, Nicaragua, New Zealand, Panama, Poland, Portugal, Romania, Serbia, South Africa, and the United States to Paris to compete. No athletes from the defeated Central Powers—Germany, Austria-Hungary, and the Ottoman Empire—were invited. The success of these games kindled a resurgence of the modern Olympic movement in the wake of the "Great War." The "Military Olympics," however, was never repeated by the Allied armies.

In the years since, national armed forces competitions have continued to be an important institution in many countries. In the United States the military service academies compete in intercollegiate sports, and the Army-Navy football game has historically occupied an important place in the national fascination with college football. Well-organized sports programs play a prominent role in the U.S. military. Many other nations also use sports as training devices and morale builders for armed services.

Sports with important warfare components, such as shooting contests, the modern pentathlon, and the biathlon have remained a part of the Olympic program and been dominated by military competitors. Since World War II armed services in many nations have adopted sporting competitions and served as training grounds for world-class athletes.

The end of the century has brought change to the military, with the end of the Cold War and the rise of international peacekeeping efforts. The role of the military and of soldiers is no longer as clear-cut as it once was. This suggests that armed forces games will retain their importance in maintaining cohesion, identity, and morale, but matter less as a means of sharpening combat skills.

—MARK DYRESON

Bibliography: Baker, William. (1982) *Sports in the Western World.* Totowa, NJ: Rowman and Littlefield. Guttmann, Allen. (1994) *Games and Empires: Modern Sports and Cultural Imperialism.* New York: Columbia University Press. Mrozek, Donald. (1983) *Sport, an American Mentality, 1880–1910.* Knoxville: University of Tennessee Press. Pope, Steven. (1995) "An Army of Athletes: Playing Fields, Battlefields, and the American Military Sporting Experience, 1890–1920." *Journal of Military History* 59 (July):

435–456. Wythe, Major G., Captain Joseph Mills Hanson, and Captain C. V. Burger, eds. (1919) *The Inter-Allied Games of 1919.* New York: Games Committee.

Art

Human beings have always seem interested in depicting sport events and sport heroes and heroines in art and they have done so over the course of history in many media. These include traditional canvas paintings in oil, graphic arts such as lithographs, posters, serigraphs, the medallic arts such as coins and medals; ceramic arts; sculptures in stone or metal; architecture and design of sports stadiums and facilities; film and photography; and on postage stamps. We have been enriched as human beings with the art that has been left to us from different civilizations and cultures over the centuries, which ranges from images on utilitarian objects such as vases to priceless treasures, such as the statue of the Discus Thrower (Discobolus) by the ancient Greek artist Myron (5th century B.C.E.). The original bronze statue no longer exists; we have only the replicas made by Roman artists in marble.

Sport Art in the Classical World

The ancient civilizations of Egypt, Sumer, Greece, and Rome left numerous examples of sport art. Ancient paintings on the walls of tombs in Sumer and Egypt show in great detail the various types of sports and games of their cultures, including over 400 wrestling scenes at the tombs of Beni Hasan. Greek ceramic vases with elaborate paintings of wrestling, boxing, running, jumping, and other sports fill whole rooms in dozens of museums from Athens to New York. Reliefs carved in stone show elaborate scenes of wrestlers, ball players, runners, and judges engaged in athletic performances, while statuary sculpted in marble honors ancient Olympic athletes from over 2,000 years ago.

The Greeks also created pottery of incredible beauty that was painted with the everyday scenes. Among the many subjects are hundreds of ceramic scenes of sports illustrated in fine art books worldwide. The Greeks were unique among civilizations ancient and modern. They glorified the beautiful body and depicted their many gods as humans. Their statues and paintings of the gods reflected the image of the perfect body: lean, muscular, athletic, and naked. In the gymnasium, students and athletes trained naked, and outside, the statues honored the best of them, also naked. The beautiful bodies were the idols of the society, because the quest for Greek education was perfection.

The Romans primarily copied Greek bronze statues in bronze or marble. These statues also fill museums around the world and show us chariot racers, boxers, wrestlers, pankratiasts (who practiced a combination of boxing and wrestling), runners, and athletes cleaning up after the competition. The Romans, however, were more inhibited and when making replicas of Greek artworks, they covered all genitals with fig leaves (one way to tell an original Greek piece from a Roman copy).

But their differences went far beyond aesthetics, and this is reflected in surviving artworks. The Romans found the Greek sports meaningless and preferred the Etruscan sport of gladiatorial fighting. Whereas the Greeks educated their youths to seek perfection, the Romans educated theirs for warfare. Artworks that survived show the bloody combats of armed men in mortal combat, men fighting against wild animals, and great naval combats in flooded arenas.

The Romans also created artwork with their buildings, such as the Colosseum, which served as sports venues. Officially known as the Flavian Amphitheater, it was constructed in the 1st century C.E. and was the scene of gladiatorial combats, animal hunts, and naval battles. Nearby was the Circus Maximus, an enormous site where great, bloody, and violent chariot races took place.

During the "Dark Ages," sport changed as the nature of life changed, and a new activity appeared called the *tournament,* in which two riders on horseback would race toward each other with long poles and try to knock each other off their horses. Tournament produced art in the form of magnificent suits of armor. Emerging from France in the 11th century, it spread throughout Europe. The magnificent suits of armor now in museums today testify to the skilled work of the craftsmen who made them and the equipment used in the contests. Many illustrations of *tournements* exist in 15th-century manuscripts.

Sport Art in the Modern World

The industrial revolution brought further changes in the art of sport. The price of books dropped with the industrialization of printing processes, and by the 19th century, almost anyone could buy a book or penny magazine. Illustrations of famous riders and their horses proliferated in England. As boxing grew in popularity, it too became a frequent subject of illustration. By the late 19th century books were appearing on sport subjects, almost always with illustrations. By the 20th century photography had become advanced enough that sports were being photographed and illustrated in daily newspapers.

Photography led to moving pictures, and sport on film is another art form. The most famous filmmaker in this genre is Leni Riefenstahl, who created the film *Olympia* at the 1936 Berlin Olympic Games. Her use of slow motion, close-ups, and editing created an unforgettable image of athletes in dramatic action. Since then, numerous films have been made with sport as a subject. Among the most famous films dealing with sports are *Chariots of Fire, Rocky* and its sequels, and *Requiem for a Heavyweight.*

Printing has greatly expanded the availability of art in general by allowing numerous copies to be made at a low cost, but few can afford the originals. However, coins and medals depicting sports themes and motifs are one type of art that is collectable and affordable. Since 1952 the Olympic Games have been commemorated on coins and today many dozens of such coins are produced by numerous nations. The medals presented to athletes at the Games are great pieces of art, designed by medallic artists and rendered into metal on huge presses that stamp blank pieces of bronze, silver, or gold-plated bronze into works of art.

Posters are common in sports art. Readily available, thousands of sport scenes are depicted on posters, including baseball, football, basketball, ice hockey, tennis, and track and field stars. During the Olympic Games posters are produced by the millions. The 1912 Olympics in Stockholm had one single poster design; the 1980 Moscow Olympics had almost 1,000.

The art of sport is voluminous and as varied as the nations on this earth. It is there for us to view, study, admire, and wonder that sport is so important that man immortalizes himself through permanent images.

—HARVEY ABRAMS

See also Literature; Movies.

Bibliography: Bandy, Susan J., ed. (1988) *Coroebus Triumphs: The Alliance of Sport and the Arts.* San Diego, CA: San Diego State University Press. Kozar, Andrew J. (1992) *The Sport Sculpture of R. Tait McKenzie.* Champaign, IL: Human Kinetics. Rhodes, Reilly, ed. (1990) *Sport in Art from American Museums.* New York: Universe Publishing. Yalouris, Nicolaos, ed. (1979) *The Eternal Olympics: The Art and History of Sport.* New Rochelle, NY: Caratzas Bros.

Asian Games

The Asian Games were first held under the auspices of the International Amateur Athletic Federation and are now regulated by the Olympic Council of Asia. The first Asian games were held in 1951. Athletes came from Afghanistan, Burma (Myanmar), Ceylon (Sri Lanka), India, Indonesia, Iran, Japan, Nepal, the Philippines,

Siam (Thailand), and Singapore. Six events were featured: track and field, basketball, cycling, football, swimming, and weight lifting. The fact that the games included no traditional Asian sports indicates how "western" international sport culture had become by the postwar period.

The Asian Games have always been highly politicized, although perhaps no more than other international sports events. Israel attended the first games, but Syria did not. Iran attended but Iraq did not. Pakistan, only recently separated from India, refused to attend the first games. Communist China and Vietnam were also absent because India refused to recognize either government.

Athletes from 18 countries attended the second Asian Games, which were hosted in 1954 in Manila, the Philippine capital.

Perhaps fittingly, Japan's Emperor Hirohito opened the third Asian Games in 1958, which were staged in Tokyo. His speech to athletes assembled from 20 countries was very short—three sentences—but no doubt meant much to a Japan so recently defeated by western forces. Japan was again triumphant on the field. There was some irony in the choice of Jakarta, Indonesia, as the site of the fourth Asian Games in 1962, since it was Japan that had created, during its occupation of the erstwhile Dutch East Indies, the basis for an organized Indonesian sports program.

Sukarno's conduct during the fourth Asian Games irritated the members of the International Olympic Committee (IOC), who felt that their authority was being challenged. Sukarno was unmoved and, in fact, immediately began to experiment with a new international structure for sports in the "nonwestern" world, calling it "The Games of the Newly Emerging Forces" (GANEFO).

Insofar as GANEFO came into creation in clear opposition to the western powers, both the Soviet Union and communist China supplied money and sent athletes to the few GANEFO events that were staged. Indonesia also received enough support from emerging nations in Asia and Africa that the IOC felt obliged to back off from its threats of expulsion: most GANEFO states had athletes at the Tokyo Olympic Games in 1964. In fact, although GANEFO did not survive long after Sukarno's ouster in 1965, the affair showed the West that Asian nations could indeed organize alternate games.

During the fifth Asian Games in Bangkok, Thailand in 1966, the government issued a special set of postage stamps featuring "modern" sports, that is to say, the western sports that were, and still are, featured at these

Southeast Asian Games

The Southeast Asian Games are biennial games, modeled on the Asian Games and the Olympics, for the nations of the region—Burma, Cambodia, Laos, Malaysia, Thailand, Vietnam, Brunei, Indonesia, the Philippines, and Singapore. The games were established in 1959. The first games were held in 1959 in Bangkok, and the Thais took most of the gold and silver medals in the 12 featured sports, all of which were "Western" Olympic-style events.

As is the case with all international athletic bodies, the Southeast Asian Games have often been affected by sociopolitical factors. For instance, in 1965, Singapore became the seventh member of the federation—in the same year it became an independent republic. Pressed by political and economic concerns, some countries found it difficult to attend all of the games, so that, at the eighth games, held in Bangkok, only Thailand, Burma, Malaysia, and Singapore took part.

Thailand has tended to garner most of the medals throughout the games' history, but Indonesia has recently been close behind. At the eighteenth games (1995), with 10 countries participating, Thailand earned most of the gold, followed by Indonesia and the Philippines.

—Alan Trevithick

events. At the next games in 1970, also in Bangkok, closing ceremonies featured a spectacular fireworks display and an entirely Asian assembly of contestants singing "Auld Lang Syne." These games, as before, were dominated by Japanese athletes.

The seventh Asian Games, held in Tehran, Iran, in 1974, were chiefly notable for the participation of mainland Chinese athletes for the first time.

Israel, though, was barred from the next games, in Bangkok in 1978, six years after the infamous terrorist attack on Israeli athletes at the Olympics in Munich. One Thai organizer rationalized the expulsion with the comment, "Like a neighbor whose house is on fire, you want to move away from them." This was surely one of the low points in sports "internationalism."

In 1982, for the ninth games, the event moved back to its birthplace, New Delhi, where the government of Indira Gandhi is said to have spent nearly $1 billion for the construction of new facilities.

The next games were staged in Seoul, South Korea, whose government believed Korea's international prestige would rise as a result. Athletically, this effort paid off, in that South Korean athletes came in a close second to China in the achievement of medals.

However, there were domestic political problems during the Seoul games, and these sometimes threatened to crowd news of Korean sports victories off the front page. Most people noticed a heavy police presence, and five universities, hotbeds of opposition to the Korean government, were shut down during the course of the games. While Korean students battled their government, Japanese Prime Minister Yasuhiro Nakasone took the occasion to apologize to the Korean people for the oppressive period of Japanese colonialism. The Chinese again outdid their Japanese rivals.

In 1990, mainland China hosted the games. Beijing, determined to make the most of what was to be China's biggest-ever international gathering, directed massive resources to the games. A few traditional Asian games were featured in exhibition, notably kabbadi, the Indian game of team pursuit and capture, but most events were modern and western. The 1994 games were hosted by Hiroshima, Japan, and signaled a new era in the life of that once-devastated city. The Hiroshima Games also featured a first: an ex-Soviet Asian Republic, Kazakhstan, attended. Its athletes won two gold medals in wrestling and demonstrated anew that Asia is not a changeless geographical entity.

—ALAN TREVITHICK

Bibliography: Kanin, D. (1982) *A Political History of the Olympic Games.* Boulder, CO: Westview Press. Knuttgen, Howard G., Ma Qiwei, and Wu Zhonguan, eds. (1990) *Sport in China.* Champaign, IL: Human Kinetics Books. Wagner, Eric A. (1989) *Sport in Asia and Africa: A Comparative Handbook.* New York: Greenwood Press.

Auto Racing

See Drag Racing; Formula 1 Auto Racing; Indy Auto Racing; Karting; Stock Car Racing; Truck Racing; Vintage Auto Racing

Badminton

Badminton, called the world's fastest racket sport, is played with rackets and shuttlecocks on a court divided by a net. Initially a form of recreation, it is now an Olympic sport with a professional tour. It is a major sport in most countries of northern Europe and southeast Asia, and virtually the national sport in Indonesia and several other countries. Denmark, Sweden, England, Holland, and Germany lead the European nations in their interest. The International Badminton Federation lists approximately 1.4 million as registered with national badminton associations around the world, although the actual number of people who play badminton is estimated at 10 times that figure.

History

Evidence of games similar to badminton appears as early as the 1st century B.C.E. in China, where Ti Jian Zi, or shuttlecock kicking, became popular. The game of Ti Jian Zi involved hitting a shuttlecock with one's feet or hands, or occasionally with a bat. The game also was popular in Japan, India, and Siam, and spread to Sumeria and Greece.

In 14th-century England, the game of battledore shuttlecock, involving a racket or paddle and a shuttlecock, was widely played. Using no nets or boundaries, this was primarily a means of testing players' skill in keeping the shuttlecock in play as long as possible. By the late 16th century it had become a popular children's game, the object still being to hit the shuttlecock to each other, or to oneself, as long as possible.

During the 17th century, the game's social status rose as it became a pastime for British royalty and the leisured classes. Early English settlers in America also enjoyed the game at this time. In the 1800s, the seventh Duke of Beaufort and his family were avid players at his Gloucester estate, called Badminton House. At this estate, a "new game" of badminton battledore, involving a net and boundaries, evolved; thus, the name "badminton." By 1867, a formal game of badminton was being played in India by English officers and their families, who developed the first rules. During the following three decades, badminton evolved into a competitive indoor sport, and clubs were formed throughout the British Isles. Beginning in the 1920s, badminton spread to northern Europe and North America and from India throughout the rest of Asia.

By 1979 the game had become truly professional; in 1985 it became an Olympic sport (with a 1992 debut in Barcelona), and was included in the Pan American Games in 1995. The International Badminton Federation, formed in 1934, governs all international badminton competition and has more than 125 member nations. A year-round international grand prix circuit worth $2 million a year in prize money currently attracts the top players to touring careers.

Rules and Play

Badminton differs from other racket sports in its use of a shuttlecock that must not touch the ground. These factors make badminton a fast game requiring quick reflexes and strong conditioning; top athletes have recorded smashes of over 320 kilometers (200 miles) per hour.

All officially sanctioned competition around the world is played indoors (recreational badminton is played outside as well). The badminton court measures

The 1930s Badminton Rage

In the 1930s that badminton became the fastest-growing sport in the United States. Americans' worked fewer hours and had more leisure and many used this time to play badminton. Educational institutions, the Young Men's Christian Association, and hundreds of newly formed clubs offered badminton instruction. A New York beauty salon even installed a court on its rooftop to allow customers to get their exercise while their hair set.

Interest in badminton in the 1930s was also generated by professional players, well-known athletes who enjoyed the sport, and Hollywood movie stars who played the game for fun and fitness. Badminton professionals like George "Jess" Willard, Bill Hurley, Jack Purcell, Ken Davidson, and Hugh Forgie performed exhibitions in movie houses and staged badminton comedy shows and "badminton on ice" performances. Athletes from other sports who played badminton included tennis stars Sidney Wood and Hazel Wightman, Chicago Cubs slugger Larry French, Seattle Rainiers baseball player Freddie Hutchison, University of Southern California football coach Howard Jones, and Stanford football star Ernie Nevers. Hollywood stars who played badminton during the rage of the 1930s included Douglas Fairbanks, Joan Crawford, James Cagney, Claudette Colbert, Bette Davis, Boris Karloff, Dick Powell, and Ginger Rogers.

–Kathleen M. Spence

17 feet by 44 feet (5.2 meters by 13.4 meters) for singles play and 20 feet (6.1 meters) by 44 feet for doubles play. Competitive badminton is played in five events: men's singles, women's singles, men's doubles, women's doubles, and mixed doubles. A badminton game consists of 15 points, except for women's singles in which a game is 11 points. The best of three games constitutes a match. Points can be scored only by the serving side.

A typical rally in badminton singles consists of a serve and repeated high deep shots hit to the baseline (clears), interspersed with dropshots. If and when a short clear or other type of "set-up" is forced, a smash wins the point. More often than not, an error (where the shuttlecock is hit out-of-bounds or into the net) brings an end to a rally rather than a positive winning play. A patient player who commits few or no errors often wins by simply waiting for the opponent to err. In doubles, there are fewer clears and more low serves, drives, and net play. Again, the smash often ends the point.

The traditional feathered shuttlecock is used in all major badminton competitions. The badminton net stands 5 feet (1.524 meters) high at the center of the court and 5 feet, 1 inch (1.550 meters) at each end post. Badminton rackets, made of wood until the 1950s, today are made of various blends of carbon, boron, aluminum, and steel, are very light, and can be strung very tightly with natural gut or synthetic string.

Major Events and Players

Major international badminton competitions include the Olympic Games, the Thomas Cup and the Uber Cup, the World Badminton Championships, and the Sudirman Cup. The World Badminton Championships were initiated in 1977 to provide individual championships that would complement other competitions. The World Championships are currently held every odd-numbered year. The Sudirman Cup is the World Mixed Team Championship, instituted in 1989. The record-holder for most individual world badminton titles and World Championships titles [1977–present]) is the legendary U.S. player Judy Devlin Hashman, with 17. By nation, players from Denmark have won more individual world titles (77) than any other country. Indonesia holds the most men's team world titles (9), and China and Japan are tied for the most women's team world titles (5). Currently, Indonesian players dominate international competition. China is also near the top in international badminton competition. Chinese players captured four medals at the 1996 Olympics; South Korea and Malaysia took four and two, respectively.

Badminton's diversity—as an uncomplicated and lively backyard game to a multimillion-dollar professional sport—suggests that it is likely to remain popular at several levels. Although growing more visible, it has yet to achieve the status or cachet of tennis, and whether it will ever do so remains an open question.

—KATHLEEN M. SPENCE

Bibliography: Bloss, Margaret Varner, and R. Stanton Hales. (1994) *Badminton.* Dubuque, IA: Brown & Benchmark. Davis, Pat. (1983) *Guinness Book of Badminton.* London: Guinness Superlatives Ltd. United States Badminton Association. (1995) *Badminton '95* (USBA Official Media Guide). Colorado Springs, CO: United States Badminton Association.

Ballooning

Ballooning is both a recreational and a competitive sport in which the balloonist, in a craft lifted by either hot air or gas, relies on the wind and controls height and direction by monitoring and responding to weather conditions. The pilot must understand the complex micrometeorological conditions that govern wind. A balloon in flight floats literally lighter than air; however, a typical four-place system can weigh as much as 363 kilograms (800 pounds). While some balloonists compete in championship events, fly paying passengers, or fly balloons as advertising billboards, most enter the sport for the sheer beauty of flight.

History

Ballooning marked the beginning of manned flight. Credit for inventing and developing lighter-than-air craft generally goes to the Montgolfier brothers. Sons of a paper manufacturer near Annonay, France, Joseph (1740–1810) and Jacques Etienne (1745–1799) began building model balloons out of paper laminated with tafetta. Believing that the lifting power came from smoke, they powered their balloons with smoke from burning wet straw under the paper envelope. On 19 September 1783, the Montgolfiers launched a balloon carrying a sheep, a cock, and a duck.

That same year, J. A. C. Charles (1746–1823), working with Ainé and Cadet Robert, built an envelope out of silk coated with varnish. They filled it with hydrogen, made by pouring sulfuric acid over iron filings.

In November 1783, the first manned balloon, built by the Montgolfiers, was launched from the Bois de Boulogne. Pilâtre de Rozier (1756–1785) and copilot Marquis d'Arlandes (1742–1809) became the first live humans in recorded history to fly, and spent most of their time aloft putting out small fires in the balloon caused by the burning straw. Their aircraft would later become known as a hot air balloon. Later that year, Charles and Ainé Robert launched in a hydrogen-filled balloon from the Tuilleries Gardens, and gas ballooning grew in popularity in Europe and the United States.

It wasn't until 1960 that hot air ballooning again made its presence felt. That year, Paul Edward Yost (1919–), an aeronautical engineer under contract to the U.S. Navy, launched a tiny aerostat lifted by a small propane burner from Bruning, Nebraska. Yost began building hot air balloons for sport flying. His contribution resulted in the explosive growth ballooning has since enjoyed.

Rules and Play

The sport of ballooning is influenced less by rules than by a goal: to ascend and descend safely when and where the pilot chooses. Rules of safety and laws of aerodynamics govern ballooning; competitive ballooning rules are set by the ballooning divisions of the Fédération Aéronautique Internationale (FAI).

Hot air balloons, cheaper and less complex to rig, are the most popular form of balloon flight. They contain three components. The envelope is the fabric "balloon" part of the system, holds the hot air used for lift, and is constructed of panels of nylon or polyester, usually sealed with urethane or silicone. The basket hangs from the envelope by aircraft cables. Most baskets are woven from wicker or rattan. The burner and fuel system are the "engine" of the hot air balloon. The burner is attached to a frame over the pilot's head, and is connected by fuel hoses to the tanks stored in each corner of the basket. Hot air balloons lift when propane burners heat the air inside the envelope, making it less dense; gas balloons rise when the pilot jettisons weights. Pilots of hot air balloons descend by cooling the gas; gas balloon pilots vent gas to reduce altitude.

Recently, some manufacturers have been experimenting with a hybrid balloon called a Rozier. This is a gas-balloon sphere surrounded on the bottom half by a hot air balloon cone; a tiny propane burner heats the air inside this cone, which then warms the helium, expanding it and increasing lift. Rozier balloons have proven useful for long-distance flights.

Balloon pilots are trained much like pilots of any other aircraft, with ground and flight training covering equipment operation; weather; aviation regulations of the pilot's country; emergencies; and launch, flight, and landing procedures. A balloon joins the air mass within which it flies and goes wherever that air mass goes and so are called "aerostats"; they are static within the air. The pilot can vary the direction of flight somewhat by adjusting the altitude of the aircraft—air currents at various levels can differ by as much as 90 degrees of the compass. Flying with the wind, the aerostat can rarely fly back to its launch site, so a chase crew follows the flight on the ground.

Ideal weather for ballooning consists of high pressure, light surface winds, and moderate winds at higher elevations. Too much wind means the pilot will probably elect not to fly. Balloons normally fly within three hours of sunrise or sunset, when the air near the ground is most stable and the winds most predictable. As the sun heats the earth's surface, thermals and higher winds often develop, which are not conducive to ballooning. The balloonist must also learn to take advantage of various aspects of the terrain that may affect the flight. Winds flow differently in the wide, flat expanses of the plains than they do in wooded, mountainous areas. Yet both can be good areas for ballooning.

Each country with an active ballooning community has its own balloon federation. The two most active are the British Balloon and Airship Club (BBAC) and the Balloon Federation of America (BFA). The BFA is the largest group of balloonists in the world. Balloonists compete in local, regional, national, and world championship flying events, or to set world records. The FAI organizes balloon records into category (gas, hot air, or Rozier) and size of balloon. Within these are records for altitude, distance, and duration.

Ballooning is a sport limited by technology. Apparently fearless balloonists continue to try to conquer new routes and longer distances. Rozier balloons may permit balloonists to attain long-sought goals, which will be quickly replaced by new aspirations. Like their crafts, balloonists' imaginations soar.

—Ruth P. Ludwig

Bibliography: Crouch, Tom. (1983). *The Eagle Aloft.* Washington, DC: Smithsonian Institution Press. Ludwig, Ruth. (1995). *Balloon Digest.* Indianola, IA: Balloon Federation of America. Wirth, Dick. (1982) *Ballooning, the Complete Guide to Riding the Winds.* New York: Random House.

Bandy

Bandy, sometimes known as "winter football," combines elements of soccer (association football) and ice hockey. Rules and tactics are similar to those of soccer, but the game is played on ice, and the skating players use wooden sticks, as in ice hockey, to strike and control a small ball. Organized and competitive bandy originated in England in the late 19th century; the modern game is more popular in Scandinavia, Russia, and the Baltics. World championship bandy competition is administered by the International Bandy Federation, which was established in 1955. Bandy was played as a demonstration sport at the 1952 Oslo Olympics, but it has not achieved the same level of popularity as its closest rival, ice hockey.

History

Early references to "bandy" may designate a variety of games, some of which bear little resemblance to the modern sport. This is because the English word "bandy" originally meant simply to toss a ball back and forth and referred to no particular game. A game resembling modern bandy was played in England as early as the 12th century. Also, a French bandy-like game was being played on the other side of the channel. Whether these games were called bandy is uncertain: a later source, from the 15th century, refers to "bandy-ball," but has the players using straight sticks. Games resembling modern bandy have also been known as bandy-ball or bandy-cad—and sometimes as cambuca, hurley, or shinty. Playing on natural ice or frozen fields, teamed contestants fought to control either a flat puck-like object or a ball. This may explain why the game never developed much in England: the unreliability of natural icing during English winters precluded a predictable competitive calendar.

A version of the game, known as "shinny," was popular in America, from New England to Virginia, during the latter half of the 18th century and was known for violence and general lack of discipline. Shinny was particularly popular on early college campuses until it was banned at Princeton in 1787 because of the mayhem that generally accompanied it and it was heavily regulated at other schools.

A National Bandy Association was formed in England in 1891, and the first international match was played the same year between the English Bury Fen team and a Dutch team from Haarlem. Bandy was started in Sweden in 1894. Swedish bandy grew quickly, with almost 200 local bandy associations by 1926 and 445 by 1990. Organized bandy came to Russia in 1898, where it quickly became popular. Bandy was organized in Norway by 1903 and in Finland by 1908. The sport was played for a time in Denmark, Switzerland, and Austria, but it did not thrive and has now been all but abandoned.

The Swedes and the Russians are credited with developing bandy as a sophisticated and competitive sport. In Russia, bandy has never achieved the popularity of soccer (association football), but matches drew crowds of thousands during World War II, and the sport still retains loyal fans.

Rules and Play

In modern bandy, each team has 11 players, including the goalkeeper. All players wear ice skates, and all but the goalkeeper hold crooked sticks. The cork or plastic ball is usually red and always brightly colored.

The game is played in two 45-minute periods and teams trade after the first period. Tie scores are acceptable, except when championships are at stake, in which case two 15-minute periods are added, followed by "sudden death" if the game is still tied.

Dangerous play, defined as hitting or body-blocking with the stick, is forbidden. The stick may not be raised above shoulder height, be used to strike another player's stick, or to interfere with any player who does not control the ball. Such rules are apparently well observed; incidence of injury is about half that encountered in ice hockey.

As a hybrid of two extremely popular sports, soccer and hockey, bandy seems unlikely to become more widespread. Its survival for at least 800 years, though, suggests equally that it will retain a modest following indefinitely.

—Alan Trevithick

Bibliography: Aspin, Jehoshaphat. (1925) *A Picture of the Manners, Customs, Sports and Pastimes of the Inhabitants of England.* London: J. Harris. Edelman, Robert. (1993) *Serious Fun: A History of Spectator Sports in the USSR.* New York and Oxford: Oxford University Press. Gomme, Alice Bertha. (1898) *The Traditional Games of England, Scotland, and Ireland.* London: David Nutt. Harste, Ann K. (1990) "Soccer on Ice." *The Physician and Sports Medicine* 18 (November): 32. Strutt, Joseph. (1876) *The Sports and Pastimes of the People of England.* London: Chatto and Windus.

Barrel Jumping

Barrel jumping, although presumably considered recreation by those who practice it, is a competitive sport in which ice skaters attempt to propel themselves over as many barrel-like objects in a row as possible. Style is immaterial as only distance matters in scoring. Barrel jumping is not an Olympic sport, but does have a world championship competition.

History

Types of skate jumping have been attempted throughout the history of skating. Some evidence suggests that long-distance skating competitions in 19th-century Holland incorporated natural obstacles such as fences, gates, and walls. The founding father of the modern sport of barrel jumping is Irving Jaffee, a former Olympic speedskating champion. Barrel jumping has been criticized for its daredevil element. Yet one must be in superior condition, with incredible control and daring, to successfully compete in the risky sport.

Rules and Play

The basic premise of barrel jumping is that skaters work up a head of steam by skating around a rink and then attempt to leap over a series of 16-inch (41-centimeter) diameter barrels that look like solid steel drums but are made out of fiberboard or cardboard. In barrel-jumping competitions, the barrels provide a soft, cushioned landing compared to the severe impact of clearing the barrels and landing on the ice. Competitive barrel jumping begins with 12 barrels. Three attempts are allowed at each distance. There are no scoring marks for style. The winner is the contestant who goes the farthest distance. The world record is held by a Canadian, Yvon Jolin, who has jumped 18 barrels, 8.9 meters (29 feet, 5 inches).

Safety is paramount, so suspension-type helmets, hip and spine protectors are mandatory. The majority of accidents result in sprains, torn muscles, and bruising. The most severe injuries are to the knee.

With an average weight of 75 kilograms (165 pounds), the body build and type for barrel jumping resembles that of a track-and-field long jumper. For the last decade Canadians have dominated the sport, and they consistently win the Culligan World Cup, an international team award added at the 1978 world championships. The Canadians have emphasized age-range competitions to extend both the participatory base and longevity of barrel jumpers. They have instituted Pee Wee, Bantam, Midget, Juvenile, and Senior competitions as well as female divisions and have record lists of winning performances on natural as well as artificial surfaces. In 1971 the Canadian barrel jumping clubs regrouped to form the Fédération de Saut de Barils du Quebec Inc. In Canada, at least, barrel jumping's future is secure.

—SCOTT A. G. M. CRAWFORD

Bibliography: Sheffield, R., and R. Woodward. (1980) *The Ice Skating Book.* New York: Universe Books. Widmark, R. (1996) Materials and items received and transcript of personal telephone interview (23 January).

Baseball, Finnish

Pesäpallo (Finnish baseball) is a good example of how aspects of a foreign game can be assimilated into a popular pastime of another culture. With origins in an informal game played by villagers and country people in a rather free-for-all fashion, Finnish baseball has evolved into a more competitive and formal sport with organized clubs, standardized rules, uniforms, and modern equipment.

The development of Finnish baseball has clear connections to the industrialization of its native country in the 20th century. The rules and organization of the game have evolved with the population migration into towns and cities and the increasing commercialism of contemporary life.

History

The modern game of Finnish baseball is based on the traditional game of "king's ball," in which a ball of birch bark (later a fist-sized leather ball) was pitched straight up in the air and hit by a player wielding a board or long racket. A similar game was played in German-speaking areas as *Schlagball*, in Nordic countries as *långboll*, and in Russia as *lapta*. All were peasant, or "folk" games, played outdoors, and in principle anyone could participate.

A good deal of improvisation and something of a carnival atmosphere characterized this early game. There was no clear method for keeping score, players taunted each other freely and vigorously, and games regularly ended in open quarrel and stone throwing.

Modern Finnish baseball was the brainchild of Lauri "Tahko" Pihkala (1888–1981), a journalist, philosopher, sport historian, and critic of modern competitive sport. Pihkala's primary interests lay in national defense and in the educational possibilities of sports.

In 1914, Pihkala initiated modifications to king's ball to create what he envisioned as a more functional, disciplined, and competitive game. He viewed the original game as a confused "crowd game" that did not offer players sufficient scope for exercising responsibility and initiative.

As early as 1907, Pihkala had watched baseball games in the United States and sought to incorporate aspects of American baseball into his developing concept of Finnish baseball. Pihkala saw American baseball as a hitting and running game in which the rules produced more frequent exchanges of teams "at bat," speeding up the game. He viewed the American game as a form of "trench warfare" and proposed developing Finnish baseball into a "mobile war" between bases, in conformity with the basic Finnish military doctrine of forest warfare, which was to "fire and move" (i.e., shooting or throwing a hand grenade, and then plunging ahead) (Klemola 1963, 51–52, 237).

Rules and Play

The contemporary game is guided by a set of conventional rules and tactics developed over the years since Pihkala's campaign to "modernize" the sport. It is played on a field measuring 40 by 94 meters (131 by 308 feet) (somewhat smaller for women's teams) with standard-sized bats and balls.

Like American baseball, the Finnish game has nine innings, and each team fields nine players. Eight members of the fielding team are positioned around the field, and the *lukkari* (pitcher) attempts to prevent the batter from getting a hit. Unlike the horizontal pitches in American baseball, Finnish pitches are vertical (straight up), which gives the pitcher greater tactical opportunities to mislead the batter and precludes power pitching. The ball must be pitched so that it falls on home plate if it is not struck.

A batter has three chances (strikes) to get on the field. Once he has gotten on base, succeeding players attempt to get on base themselves and advance the preceding players in the field. As in American baseball, a player is out if the ball reaches the base before he does. A run is scored when a player makes the circuit of three bases and reaches home plate. The batting team has at least nine attempts, plus one after each run, to get onto the field. When the batting team has burned three times, by failing to reach the base before the ball, the teams change places.

One major difference between American and Finnish baseball is that the Finnish ball field has a rear boundary over which the batter may not hit the ball. Hitting the ball beyond the boundary is known as an "illegal strike." As a result of this limitation, players are less likely to advance more than one base at a time.

Finnish baseball has become a game for all sections of the population and, since the 1920s, has been incorporated into the physical education program in the public schools. Team games are concentrated mainly in population centers, but there are also good teams in sparsely populated areas, where the game is even more popular than soccer (association football).

—MARTTI SILVENNOINEN

Bibliography: Karkkainen, P. (1992) "Pesäpallo—Finnish baseball: history and presentation of the national game." Presented at the first International Society of History in Sports and Physical Education seminar, "Sport and Cultural Minorities," 8–13 June, Turku, Finland. Klemola, H. (1963) *Tahkon latu. Lauri Pihkala eilen ja tänään* [Tahko's trail: Lauri Pihkala in the past and present]. 75-vuotispäivän juhlakirja. Helsinki: Otava. Laitinen, E. (1983) *Pesäpallo: Kansallispeli 60 vuotta* [Pesäpallo: a national game in 60 years]. Saarijärvi, Saarijärven: Offset Ky. Pihkala, L. (1932) *Pesäpallo itsekurin ja päällikk mielen kouluna* [Pesäpallo as a school self-discipline and commander-spirit]. Pesäpalloilijan vuosikirja.

Baseball, Japanese

Baseball has been played in Japan for more than a century, and many Japanese regard the sport as a part of their culture. Over 4,000 Japanese high school teams compete for the national championship each year. Only about 50 teams can advance to the two major national championship tournaments, held in spring and summer at Koshien Stadium, the Mecca of high school baseball. The stadium, with a capacity of over 50,000, is packed with students, parents, and alumni who come from all over the country by chartered bus.

Professional baseball is popular in Japan, too. The annual total attendance for the two professional leagues is estimated at over 20 million. During the season, games are telecast live almost every night. Tabloid newspapers featuring scores and players' gossip sell millions of copies every day. Baseball players are national and local heroes for many Japanese. A 1996 survey showed being a baseball player the most popular career choice for elementary school boys.

Since its introduction into Japan in the second half of the 19th century, the sport developed a unique character to fit the Japanese social and cultural climate. Indeed, Japanese baseball is a completely different type of sport from the game North Americans are familiar with, although the rules and regulations are almost identical.

History

Baseball was brought to the Japanese in the early 1870s by Americans teaching English and Western culture at colleges in Tokyo. The game instantly became a popular extracurricular activity among college students and clubs were formed by students at prestigious colleges.

By the early 20th century, intercollegiate games had become a major spectator phenomena, with colleges recruiting high school stars, and the Keio-Waseda three-game series became one of the country's biggest baseball events. The rivalry was so heated that, lest their supporters fight each other and possibly cause riots, Keio and Waseda authorities decided to cancel the series in 1906. It was not resumed until 1925.

The first 30 years of the century were the golden age of amateur baseball. The Tokyo Six Universities League, whose members are Keio, Waseda, Meiji, Hosei, Rikyo, and Tokyo Universities, was organized in 1925. Thousands of spectators packed the stadium and millions of people all over Japan listened to the games on radio. Major college clubs toured the continental United States and brought the latest knowledge and equipment back to Japan. College and semiprofessional teams from the United States visited Japan. Major League All-Stars and All-American teams, including such legendary players as Babe Ruth, Jimmy Foxx, and Lou Gehrig, played exhibition games in Japan.

Semiprofessional teams were founded and sponsored by private corporations, as well as by public-sector organizations such as the Japan National Railways. Their national championship tournament started in 1927.

Social and Cultural Climate

Some effort has been made to explain why baseball became so popular in such a relatively short period in a country with no tradition of Western sports. Controlled by the feudal Tokugawa dynasty, Japan had closed its doors to the West until the 1850s. As information on advanced technologies, Western science, and culture flowed in after the Meiji Restoration of 1868, a sense of crisis deepened among the nation's leaders and spread to ordinary people. Adopting the goal of catching up with and getting ahead of the West, Japanese eagerly and industriously adopted Western civilization—including Western sports. Besides baseball, rowing, rugby football, soccer (association football), and tennis were introduced into Japan.

Although the Japanese were good pupils, their understanding of Western culture tended to be superficial. It was impossible, or at least difficult, for them to fully appreciate the internal meaning of the culture. Baseball was no exception, and the Japanese adapted the psychology of baseball to their own cultural norms: "The Japanese found the one-on-one battle between pitcher and batter similar in psychology to sumo and the martial arts. It involved split-second timing and a special harmony of mental and physical strength" (Whiting 1989, 28).

Ichiko College played a significant role in the early age of Japanese baseball. Most of the graduates of the school enrolled in the prestigious Imperial University of Tokyo and were expected to become national leaders, and their values, such as samurai spirit and Zen meditation, were strongly reflected in the game. The organization and structure of Ichiko's baseball club were remarkably different from those of Western sports clubs. It was called Bu, which is closer to a military squad than a club. Bu was based on a rigid vertical hierarchy among students, and its members were required to be thoroughly loyal to the Bu. This version of baseball was spread widely, as Ichiko's graduates became instructors and coaches at other colleges and high schools.

Baseball's popularity was further increased by business interests and technological advancements. Major newspapers were competing for sponsorship of tournaments to increase their circulation when radio stations started live broadcasting in 1927. Meanwhile, private railroad companies built stadiums along their train lines.

The Baseball Control Act, designed to promote the healthy development of baseball after problems occurred, led to the establishment of Japan's first professional team. Since the act prohibited amateurs from playing with professionals, the *Yomiuri Shinbun,* a major national newspaper, which was planning to invite the Major League All-Stars in 1934, had to organize the All-Japan team, whose players were naturally regarded as professionals. The first professional team, established in 1934, was named the Tokyo Giants the next year. Even though the Japan Professional Baseball Association was formed in 1936 by seven clubs, professional baseball gained support slowly in its early days. World War II interrupted baseball's development. Nationalists and militarists insisted that baseball should be banned because it came from the enemy, the United States.

Baseball and the Media

The Japanese returned to baseball quite quickly after World War II. The professional baseball league and the Tokyo Six Universities League resumed their activities in 1946. The National High School Baseball Summer Tournament was revived in the same year. In the 1950s professional baseball firmly established its status as the most popular spectator sport in Japan.

One of the unique characteristics of Japanese professional baseball is that every club, with the exception of Hiroshima Carp, has been financed by large corporations for promotional purposes. In the early age of professional baseball, most clubs were owned either by railroad companies or by multimedia conglomerates. For instance, the Yomiuri Giants, formerly the Tokyo Giants, are a subsidiary of the Yomiuri Shinbun Group, whose members include a major nationwide newspaper and a major television network. Other clubs, such as the Hanshin Tigers and Kintetsu Buffaloes, are owned by private railroad companies.

The 1960s and 1970s constituted the era of the Yomiuri Giants. With superstars like Sadaharu Oh (1940–) and Shigeo Nagashima (1936–), they won nine Japan Championships in a row from 1965 to 1973. The club drew the largest crowds in both leagues, and its annual home game attendance consistently exceeded 3 million. The Giants remain the most popular team, but no longer dominate baseball.

The Globalization of Japanese Baseball

Japanese baseball is now entering a new era of globalization. In the past, despite international exchanges in baseball, they were essentially one-way relations. Japanese baseball imported most of its knowledge and technology from the United States in the early days. International games, frequently held in the early 20th century, dwindled after World War II. In professional baseball, exchange activities with U.S. major leagues were limited to importing players and hosting exhibition games. Japanese baseball was virtually isolated for quite a long period.

All this has changed since the mid-1980s. At the amateur level, international exchanges have been as active as ever, particularly since baseball was admitted to the Olympic Games in 1984. All-Japan national teams have participated in many international tournaments. At the professional level, satellite television channels,

which started service in the mid-1980s, have been televising major league games from the United States, and cable television stations have a channel exclusively for U.S. sports. These changes in the mass media have made many Japanese feel closer than ever to major league baseball in the United States. This tendency was further intensified when Hideo Nomo (1968–), ace pitcher of the Kintetsu Buffaloes, began playing with the Los Angeles Dodgers in 1995.

Baseball in Japan has a long history at both the amateur and professional levels. The social and cultural conditions surrounding Japanese baseball have helped to make it quite a different game from its counterpart in the United States. But as the globalization of the sport continues, baseball in Japan is likely to be reconstructed again in a worldwide framework.

—HAJIME HIRAI

Bibliography: Cromartie, Warren. (1991) *Slugging It Out in Japan: An American Major Leaguer in the Tokyo Outfield.* New York: Kodansha International. Oh, Sadaharu. (1984) *Sadaharu Oh: A Zen Way of Baseball.* New York: Times Books. Whiting, Robert. (1989) *You Gotta Have Wa.* New York: Macmillan.

Baseball, Latin American

North Americans tend to think of baseball as "theirs," but it is as much a "national sport" in several Latin American countries as it is in the United States. Baseball is more popular than soccer in Cuba, Nicaragua, the Dominican Republic, Puerto Rico, and Panama and is important in Venezuela and Mexico. Good baseball is played also in Colombia, El Salvador, Honduras, and Netherlands Antilles. Cuba's first professional league was founded in 1878, only two years later than the U.S. National League, and the game had been introduced in many areas of Latin America and the Caribbean before the start of the 20th century.

Cubans learned baseball while attending school in the United States and brought the game back to Cuba as early as the 1860s. They in turn took the game to Puerto Rico, the Dominican Republic, the Yucatán Peninsula of Mexico, and Venezuela. Baseball interest in Mexico was also strongly affected by that nation's close relations with the United States. Baseball was being played in Panama (still part of Colombia at the time) by people from Britain and the United States as early as 1882.

Cuba

In 1866 Nemesio Guillot, a young Cuban attending school in the United States, brought baseball equipment and enthusiasm for the game with him when he returned to his country. Shortly thereafter another Cuban, Esteban Bellán, played baseball while attending Fordham University and then joined the Troy Haymakers, a charter member of the National Association, in 1871, the first year of professional league play in the United States. The Havana Baseball Club was founded in 1872 as Cuba's first professional team, and the Matanzas Club was established in 1873.

Soon baseball popularity spread throughout the island, and Sunday afternoon games were being played in nearly every town. Cuban immigrants organized baseball teams in the United States, and U.S. major league teams began to visit the island, the Philadelphia Athletics playing a series of exhibition games against Cuban professionals in 1886.

Baseball was viewed as a form of expression of Cuban national spirit, as opposition to Spanish colonialism grew through the later years of the 19th century, and colonial authorities viewed participation in the game with suspicion, banning the sport for a year in 1873 and again 1895 when the war for independence began.

The popularity of the game and the competitive successes of Cubans and Cuban national teams grew throughout the 20th century, one of the many high points being construction of Havana's Cerro Stadium in 1946. While opportunities in Cuban sport before 1959 were largely limited to a small and relatively wealthy elite, baseball (along with boxing) was available to all and even allowed players to earn a living through participation in the professional game. Professional play was dominated by two teams, Havana and Almendres. During this period many Cuban players participated in summer baseball in the United States, and Cuban professionals were prominent on team rosters of Latin American countries. Black Cubans played in the U.S. Negro Leagues before major league baseball was integrated.

Cuba has dominated international amateur baseball competition. Through 1995, Cuba has won 9 of the 12 Pan American Games titles (including the first, in 1951, and the last 7), 12 of the 17 Central American and Caribbean Games titles, and 21 of the 24 World Amateur Championships they have participated in through 1994.

Puerto Rico

Puerto Rico's first baseball game was played in 1896; a Spanish Army officer brought the sport from Cuba. United States soldiers stationed in Puerto Rico after the Spanish-American War (1898) helped popularize baseball. Government, company, and school teams were organized throughout the island, and players inducted into the military during World War I played the game in army camps. Professional play in the Puerto Rican Winter League began in 1938–1939.

In international amateur baseball Puerto Rico won the World Championship in 1951 and the Central American and Caribbean Games title in 1959. Puerto Rico has also won medals in the Pan American Games and the Olympic Games, including a bronze in the 1988 Olympics.

Dominican Republic

Baseball was introduced in the Dominican Republic by Cubans who left their country after civil war began there in 1868. The game became popular all over the country, but first developed mainly in the area of sugar refineries in the southeastern part of the island, where there was no work during the sugarcane growing season and baseball filled the days of the "dead time." Important contributions to Dominican baseball were made by immigrants from the British Virgin Islands and other British colonies of the Caribbean.

In the early 20th century, many amateur baseball teams existed, particularly around the cities of Santo Domingo, Santiago, and San Pedro de Macorís, and in 1907 the first professional team, Licey, was formed in Santo Domingo. The presence of U.S. troops in the country from 1916 to 1924 favored the spread of baseball interest, as did the imposing influence of the country's most prominent fan, President Rafael Trujillo, during his 31 years of absolute political power. In the 1930s Negro League barnstormers toured the island each winter.

In 1937 Trujillo's agents bought the best talent that could be found in the U.S. Negro Leagues to assure a championship for the dictator's Ciudad Trujillo (as Santo Domingo was then called) Dragons, but this extravagance ended professional baseball in the Dominican Republic for thirteen years, until the lowering of the race barrier in the U.S. major leagues gave Dominican ballplayers a new opportunity to earn a living at their game and opened the Dominican Republic to another invasion, this time from American professional baseball interests.

From the mid-1950s onward connections increased between U.S. and Dominican baseball. Dominican professional league play was conducted in summer from 1951 through 1954, but with more and more of the top Dominicans playing summers in the United States, the country adopted a winter schedule (in 1955), so that both their players and Americans could play the two seasons and thus augment their incomes. However, after free agency in the U.S. majors allowed salaries to rise to astronomical figures, the stars of both nationalities had second thoughts about risking injury by playing relatively low-paying winter ball, even if their U.S. teams would permit it.

With the loss in 1959 of Cuba as a source of players, U.S. professional teams stepped up scouting operations in the Dominican Republic and, beginning in 1977, established year-round rookie training camps, such as the Dodgers' academy, Campo Las Palmas.

Through 1972, Dominican Republic amateur teams had hosted the World Amateur Championship once and won the tournament in 1948. The national team also won the Pan American Games in 1955 and the Central American and Caribbean Games in 1962 and 1982.

Mexico

Games had been held by American sailors in Guaymas and American railroad construction workers in Nuevo Laredo in 1877, and several Mexican baseball clubs became active in the 1880s and 1890s, especially in Mexico City, Veracruz, and in northern Mexico where they played Texas teams. Also in the 1890s Cuban immigrants introduced baseball in Yucatán, where it expanded rapidly and took on a life almost independent from developments of the sport elsewhere in Mexico. By 1904 there were leagues for amateurs and also for semiprofessionals. By 1926 there were more than 150 amateur baseball teams in the capital and an extensive schedule of games was played on Sundays. In the 1920s there were also several professional teams playing in the capital and elsewhere, and in 1925 the Mexican Professional League (summer) was organized. The Franco-Inglés field in Mexico City was the scene of most baseball action, and Ernesto Carmona was recognized as the foremost exponent of the sport. The Mexican Pacific Coast League (professional winter play) was organized in 1945, and teams of northwestern Mexico have won the Caribbean World Series twice since Mexico's first participation in the championship in 1971.

Panama

In 1882, 22 years before the isthmus's independence from Colombia, Americans and British played baseball in Panama, as did young Colombians attending school in the United States when they returned for their school vacations. In the 1890s the game was still mainly played by foreigners in Panama City, and when a club was established in Colón, on the Caribbean side of the isthmus, in 1892, players traveled by train to play inter-city matches. Around 1913 baseball activity became clearly divided between Panamanian teams and those consisting mainly of foreigners in the Canal Zone. A few U.S. professional players were included in Canal Zone teams. The racial segregation that existed in the Canal Zone led to the formation of Colored Leagues, whose players were largely Antillean men imported to construct the canal. From 1926 to 1935, the National League became firmly established; it would become the Professional League. Amateur and Juvenile Leagues were also founded. By this time the social background of baseball players had changed considerably from the elites of the first clubs to largely a middle- and working-class composition.

The years 1935–1943 were dominated by semiprofessional play, with black players making up 70 to 75 percent of the rosters (and 95 percent on the teams that won the national championships most years). Although professional players had been increasingly employed on Panamanian and Canal Zone teams since 1932, the move toward professionalism was completed with establishment of the nation's Professional League in 1946.

In 1952 the Isthmian League of the Canal Zone disappeared and interest in Panamanian professional play decreased until 1962, when a short-lived experiment attempted to revitalize the Professional League by combining it with Nicaragua's. Under worsening economic conditions, the Professional League continued until its demise in 1972. The quality of amateur baseball also fell off during this period, as did the numbers of Panamanian players employed by minor and major league teams in the United States.

Venezuela

Baseball was introduced in Venezuela in 1895 by the Cuban Emilio Cramer. However, the game developed more slowly there than in some other Caribbean nations. The New York Yankees' appearance in Venezuela in 1947 sparked local interest in professional baseball, and the Venezuelan Winter League has maintained its strong position in the country. Venezuela has hosted the Caribbean (and Inter-American) Series nine times and won the championship seven times.

Nicaragua

The introduction of baseball in Bluefields, on the northern coast of Nicaragua, in 1889 is attributed to an

American resident of the area, who wanted to lure the locals away from cricket. The first organized league competition in Nicaragua was held in Managua in 1911–1912, with five local teams participating. Bóer, founded as a neighborhood club in Managua in 1905, won, beginning a long if erratic tradition that still survives.

Military intervention in Nicaragua by the United States occurred occasionally in the late 19th and early 20th centuries, and from 1912 to 1933 Marines were almost continuously present. Marines stationed in Managua fielded baseball teams and supplied officials for Nicaraguan baseball competitions.

In 1915 the first enclosed field went into operation and the first nationwide league play was held, featuring teams from Managua, Granada, Masaya, Chinandega, and León. Sunday baseball games were important social occasions and were often attended by the nation's president and high government and church officials. Betting by fans and by the competing teams added interest to the games.

In the 1930s professional baseball was established in Nicaragua. Like his Dominican counterpart, Trujillo, Nicaragua's strongman, Anastasio Somoza, had his baseball team, Cinco Estrellas. The Nicaraguan professional Winter League functioned from 1956 to 1966, and Cinco Estrellas won the Inter-American Series title in 1964. The Sandinista years brought more emphasis on increasing mass participation in sport, but now professional caliber baseball is again a national passion.

Nicaragua has participated in the World Amateur Championships since 1939 and hosted the tournament several times, first in 1948, upon completion of the National Stadium, and most recently in 1994. The national team won the Central American Games baseball competition in 1977, 1986, and 1994, but has finished no higher than second place in the more competitive amateur tournaments, including the Central American and Caribbean Games, the Pan American Games, and the World Amateur Championships.

International Amateur and Professional Competition

Latin American amateur baseball is important at all levels from juvenile to adult recreational and elite play. The highest level of international competition is the World Amateur Championships, but fiercely contested baseball also occurs in the Pan American Games and other regional games.

Baseball has been an Olympic demonstration sport seven times: 1912, 1936, 1952 (Finnish baseball), 1956, 1964, 1984, and 1988. It became a medal sport in 1992.

At the 1984 Games, Nicaragua and the Dominican Republic (the latter a last-minute replacement for Cuba, which boycotted the Games) finished low in the eight-team tournament. Puerto Rico won the silver medal in 1988, again in the absence of a boycotting Cuba, and Cuba won the gold medal in 1992 and in 1996.

An international tournament, the Caribbean World Series, is used to determine the Latin American professional baseball regional champion each year. Dominated by Cuba before that country dropped professional sports in 1961, this tournament (including four years in the early 1960s when the competition was known as the Inter-American Series) has since been won most by teams from Puerto Rico (8) and Dominican Republic (8).

—RICHARD V. McGEHEE

Bibliography: Bjarkman, Peter C. (1994) *Baseball with a Latin Beat: A History of the Latin American Game.* Jefferson, NC: McFarland. Klein, Alan M. (1991) *Sugarball: The American Game, the Dominican Dream.* New Haven, CT: Yale University Press. Pettavino, Paula J., and Geralyn Pye. (1994) *Sport in Cuba: The Diamond in the Rough.* Pittsburgh: University of Pittsburgh Press. Ruck, Rob. (1991) *The Tropic of Baseball: Baseball in the Dominican Republic.* Westport, CT: Meckler.

Baseball, North American

Baseball has long occupied a large place among North American sports. As early as the 1850s, sporting sheets began to argue that "base ball" was uniquely "America's game," and by the end of the 19th century it was the most popular team sport in North America. Although millions of young men (and a few women) played amateur or semiprofessional baseball, the professional game soon became ascendant. In 1903 the National and American leagues signed an agreement establishing the present structure of the professional game. Beginning in 1905, each season (except 1994 due to a players' strike) ended with a "World Series" between the championship teams of the two leagues.

Baseball's significance extends far beyond the playing field. Apart from sheer entertainment, references to baseball and the employment of baseball motifs abound in literature, music, painting, drama, politics, and religion, indeed in nearly every facet of American life. The game has given towns and cities, as well as occupational, ethnic, and racial groups, deeper emotional existences. Baseball's heroes have reflected some of America's most fundamental values. Finally, with its capacity for quantification and its slow, deliberate pace, both of which allow fans to collect and digest memories of the game's past, baseball has possessed a special power to connect past and present.

History

Modern baseball evolved from informal bat and ball games, the roots of which can be traced to 17th- and 18th-century England. In the early 19th century, boys played one or another of these games—called variously "old cat," "one-old-cat," "barn ball," "town," "rounders," "base," and even "base ball"—on empty lots, village greens, and cow pastures. During the 1840s and 1850s two styles of play, the Massachusetts (favored in New England and southern Ontario) and the New York games, competed for popularity.

A major turning point in baseball's evolution came in the 1850s, when New Yorkers, in particular clerks and artisans living in impersonal boardinghouses and experiencing profound changes in their lives and work, organized dozens of formal "base ball" clubs. Led by the Knickerbockers (formed in 1845), representatives of these clubs wrote and revised the rules of play, appointed game officials, scheduled matches, and in 1858 created the first national association.

Deriving its name from the four bases that form a diamond (the infield) around the pitcher's box (later called the mound), teams in the New York game consisted of nine players who used a leather-covered ball and wooden bats. Teams remained at bat until three outs were made; then the team that had been in the field took a turn at bat. An inning consisted of one turn at bat for each team and nine innings constituted a game. Each time a batter or "striker" touched all of the bases without being put out a run scored. The team with the most runs after the completion of nine innings won.

New York's central place in commerce and communications helped its form of baseball spread rapidly. Tours by the famed Excelsiors of Brooklyn to upstate New York and to Philadelphia and Baltimore in 1860 attracted attention across the continent to New York's game. In 1863, New York area teams first contended for a self-proclaimed national championship, and, during the same year, the Young Canadians of Woodstock awarded themselves a silver ball for the first Canadian championship. The U.S. Civil War (1861–1865) brought together massive numbers of young men, which encouraged the sport's growth; after the war veterans of both the Union and Confederate armies returned home enthusiasts of the game.

The early players comprised what contemporaries called a "fraternity," a term that implied that the ball-players were members of a single brotherhood regardless of differences in club membership, ethnicity, social class, or religion. The fraternity set itself apart from the urban masses by establishing a special body of customs and rituals and by donning colorful uniforms similar to the volunteer fire departments and militia units of the day. Off the diamond, the early players frequently gathered to eat, drink, wager, talk, and even dance.

League Formation

The early clubs initially neither charged gate fees nor paid their players, but commercialism quickly entered the sport. In 1858 fans paid 50 cents each to watch a three-game championship series between all-star teams from New York and Brooklyn, and in 1862 an ambitious Brooklynite, William H. Cammeyer, built an enclosed field and charged fans a fee to watch games there. The "enclosure movement," as the drive to build fences around fields and charge an admission fee was called, introduced a new era of baseball history that heralded the beginning of professional baseball. To take advantage of gate fees, teams began to play more games, to embark upon long summer tours, to recruit athletes on the basis of playing skills rather than sociability, and even to pay outstanding players.

Professional baseball benefited from urban rivalries. The success in 1869 of Cincinnati's Red Stockings in winning 54 games without a single defeat provoked envy in other cities. In both Canada and the United States, small businessmen, politicians, and civic boosters united to form joint-stock company baseball clubs. The clubs usually expired after a year or two, but out of the ruins of the old, new clubs frequently arose to replace them. From 1871 through the 1875 season, several of these professional clubs competed for a championship pennant sponsored by a loose confederation known as the National Association of Professional Base Ball Players.

Professional baseball entered another era in 1876 when William A. Hulbert (1832–1882), president of a Chicago club, and Albert Spaulding (1850–1915), player, manager, and soon-to-be sporting goods magnate, set about organizing a replacement for the National Association. Determined that the league would become the premier circuit of professional clubs representing only the larger cities, the National League prohibited clubs in cities with a population of less than 75,000 from joining, required any club wishing to join the circuit to have the approval of the existing clubs, and provided each team with a territorial monopoly. By banning

The Doubleday-Cooperstown Myth

In the early twentieth century, sporting goods magnate Albert Spalding decided to challenge octogenarian sportswriter Henry Chadwick's long-held claim that baseball had evolved from the English boys' game of rounders. To resolve the dispute, Spalding appointed a special committee of seven men (including two U.S. senators) "of high repute and undoubted knowledge of Base Ball."

Rather than research the question the committee placed its faith in the recollections of old-timers. One of the elderly respondents, Abner Graves (after some prodding and perhaps direction from Spalding), reconstructed from his memory the day in 1839 when Abner Doubleday is said to have invented baseball in Cooperstown, New York. Without bothering to take additional testimony from Graves or corroborate his account from other sources, the committee concluded in 1907 that Graves's story was the "best evidence obtainable to date" of the game's origins. Doubleday, a Civil War hero who had written a two-volume memoir without once mentioning baseball, let alone seizing the opportunity to stake his claim as its creator, had died in 1893. Although Henry Chadwick described the committee's work as a "piece of special pleading which lets my dear old friend Albert escape a bad defeat," its conclusions were quickly accepted by nearly everyone as established truth.

During the 1930s, a group of businessmen in Cooperstown decided to offset some of the ravages of the Great Depression by promoting their village as the site for a national baseball hall of fame and museum. The plan won the endorsement of organized baseball, and in 1936 sportswriters chose as charter members to the Hall of Fame Ty Cobb, Babe Ruth, Honus Wagner, Christy Mathewson, and Walter Johnson. In 1939 the major leagues commemorated the "centennial" of baseball's creation with ceremonies at Cooperstown and the U.S. Post Office issued a commemorative stamp. The Baseball Hall of Fame and Museum has subsequently become something of a national shrine and is visited by thousands of fans annually.

Ironically, at the very time that the museum in Cooperstown came into being, an industrious librarian in New York City began a reexamination of baseball's origins. In 1939, Robert Henderson discovered a little book of children's games authored by Robin Carver. The tiny tome, published in 1829, a full decade before Doubleday's alleged invention of baseball, included the rules for a game called "Base, or Goal Ball." Modern researchers (including those employed by the Hall of Fame) have added support to Henderson's evolutionary theory of baseball's early history. Nonetheless, the Doubleday-Cooperstown myth continues to enjoy wide acceptance in American popular culture.

—*Benjamin G. Rader*

In the 1880s professional baseball shared in the nation's booming prosperity. No fewer than 18 leagues (including leagues with Canadian teams) appeared, although several expired after only a season or so. In 1882, the American Association, dubbed the "Beer Ball League" because brewery owners sat on the boards of directors of six of its clubs and it permitted beer to be sold at games, challenged the National League's hegemony over big league baseball. Beginning in 1884 and ending in 1890, the National League champions met those of the American Association in a post-season "World Championship" series.

Professional baseball reflected the changing ethnic composition of both Canada and the United States. Perhaps upon discovery that recent immigrants had limited entrepreneurial opportunities in more respectable and less risky enterprises, a disproportionate number of Germans, German Jews, and later the Irish could be found among club owners. Likewise, an unusually large number of German and Irish names appeared on late 19th-century player rosters, suggesting that these ethnic groups may have found in professional baseball a means of upward social mobility. During the first half of the 20th century increasing numbers of old-stock players from the countryside and new ethnics from southern and eastern Europe, as well as a few Native Americans, entered the big league ranks.

Opportunities for African Americans in professional baseball were another matter. Although blacks played amateur baseball from at least the 1860s on, as early as 1867 the National Association of Base Ball Players specifically excluded black clubs from membership, and the National League informally enforced a "color ban" against blacks from its founding in 1876. Yet a few blacks did play on racially integrated professional teams in other leagues; in 1884 Moses Fleetwood Walker and his brother Weldy played with Toledo in the American Association. In the late 1880s and in the 1890s, the era when racial segregation became the rule for much of the United States, white leagues ended racially integrated baseball.

In the 1880s conflicts between the National League franchise owners and the professional players escalated. They clashed in the first place over player drinking. The players resented restrictions on their personal behavior and the player reservation system that had been put into place in 1879. The reserve clause in contracts prevented players from offering their services to the highest bidders. The players also believed that they were not getting a fair share of baseball's additional earnings. Player grievances climaxed in the formation

Sunday games, prohibiting the sale of liquor at ball parks, and charging a 50-cent admission fee, the league also sought without complete success to obtain the patronage of the middle class.

of a separate Players League in 1890. With three big leagues competing for the loyalties of fans and the superior leadership offered by Albert Spaulding, the National League crushed the upstart league after only one season. In 1891, the American Association also collapsed, leaving only a 12-team National League as a major league circuit.

The National League drifted aimlessly through the 1890s, confronted with the absence of the popular World Championship Series, the lack of superior teams in the largest cities, and an economic depression. In earlier times, the league had deliberately cultivated an image of Victorian propriety, but in the 1890s it acquired a notorious reputation for brawling, both on the field and in the stands. In 1900, Byron Bancroft (Ban) Johnson (1863–1931), a former sportswriter and president of the Western League, mounted a challenge to the National League. Johnson renamed his loop the American League and began to raid National League teams for players.

In 1903, the leagues signed a pact agreeing to recognize each other's reserved players and established a three-man commission to oversee all of professional baseball. The agreement protected the reserved rights of minor league teams to their players, but provided that at the conclusion of each season the majors could "draft" players from the franchises of the minors at set prices. Although the National Agreement of 1903 did not provide for a championship series, in 1905 the leagues agreed upon a mandatory postseason World Series.

The Golden Age
The first half of the 20th century may have been baseball's Golden Age. The game gained in acceptability among all social groups; in 1910 William Howard Taft established the tradition of the president of the United States opening each season by throwing out the first ball. "Take Me Out to the Ball Game," written by vaudevillian Jack Norworth in 1908, soon became the game's unofficial anthem. Between 1909 and 1923, the major league teams went on a stadium-building binge; great civic monuments of steel and concrete replaced shaky, wooden structures. Minor league baseball grew from 13 circuits in 1903 to 51 leagues in 1950.

Baseball exploded in popularity at all levels. Twilight leagues and Sunday School leagues sprang up across the continent. Boys grew up reading baseball fiction, learning the rudiments of the game, and dreaming of one day becoming diamond heroes themselves. Newspapers carried detailed accounts of games, as well as stories about the game during the off season (Hot Stove League). Beginning in the 1920s, radio began to broadcast play-by-play descriptions of games.

In the meantime the game experienced fundamental changes on the playing field. Long ago, pitchers had stopped gently tossing the ball to the hitters with a straight arm and underhanded; a gradual relaxation of the rules permitted overhanded pitching in 1884, and in 1887 the hitters lost the privilege of asking for a pitch above or below the waist. In 1893 the league adopted the modern pitching distance of 60 feet, 6 inches (18.44 meters). Offensive and defensive tactics slowly grew more sophisticated.

Beginning in the 1860s, infielders inched away from their respective bases and managers began to place their quickest man at shortstop. In the next decade, a few catchers donned masks and fielders put on gloves. At first, the skin-tight gloves (with the ends cut off to improve throwing) were used exclusively to protect the hands from the sting of the ball. In the 1890s with the extension of the pitching distance, teams turned more to bunting and the ingenious hit-and-run play.

The first two decades of the 20th century came to be known as the "deadball era," or the "era of the pitcher." The adoption of rules providing for counting the first two foul balls as strikes (National League in 1901 and American League in 1903), increasing the width of home plate from a 12-inch (30 centimeters) square to a five-sided figure 17 inches (43 centimeters) across in 1900, and allowing the application of spit to the ball by pitchers, along with the appearance of big, strong-armed pitchers and the conservative tactics of managers resulted in an age of extraordinarily low offensive output. Except for John "Honus" Wagner (1874–1955) and Ty Cobb (1886–1961), the major stars of the day were such pitchers as Cy Young (1867–1955), Christy Mathewson (1880–1925), and Walter Johnson (1887–1946). Long-time field managers John J. McGraw (1873–1934) of the New York Giants and Connie Mack (1862–1956) of the Philadelphia Athletics also occupied much of baseball's public limelight.

For unknown reasons, the 1920s witnessed a sudden reversal in offensive production. Traditionally, the surge in hitting has been attributed to the introduction of a more resilient ball, using more balls per game, outlawing the spitball in 1920, and the growing popularity of "free swinging" by the hitters. Recent research emphasizes the importance of George Herman "Babe" Ruth (1895–1948). Led by the free-swinging Ruth, batting averages, scoring, and home runs soared. While repeatedly leading the league in home runs, Ruth himself became the game's preeminent hero. With Ruth's rise from lowly origins, his enthusiasm for the game, and his towering home runs, no other player in baseball history so won the awe and adoration of baseball fans.

During the Golden Age, great dynasties, most in the larger cities, ruled major league play. From 1900 to 1969, when the leagues were divided into divisions, New York City franchises won 41 pennants. Beginning with Ruth's arrival in New York, the Yankees became synonymous with success; they won 29 flags in 39 years. In general, franchises located in larger cities drew more fans and commanded larger revenues; they were thus better able to purchase superior players from other big league clubs or minor league franchises. Only the St. Louis Cardinals, led by their astute general manager Wesley "Branch" Rickey (1881–1965), who created a system of developing new talent through the ownership of minor league teams (the farm system), seriously contended with the Yankee dynasty.

Ruth's Homeric feats during the 1920s helped to counter the negative effects of the Black Sox Scandal of 1919. Although a court acquitted eight Chicago White Sox players for fixing the 1919 World Series, Judge Kenesaw Mountain Landis (1866–1944), the newly appointed commissioner of baseball, banished them from organized baseball for life. The scandal also sparked the 1921 reorganization of baseball. The new National Agreement gave sweeping powers to a single commissioner to suspend, fine, or banish any parties in baseball who had engaged in activities "detrimental to the best interests of the national game." Although Landis (who served until 1944) rarely used his vast powers to discipline the team owners, he employed them widely against the players. In 1922, the U.S. Supreme Court further strengthened major league baseball by exempting it from federal antitrust laws in *Federal Base Ball Club of Baltimore, Inc. v. National League of Professional B.B. Clubs and American League of Professional B.B. Clubs*, 259 U.S. 200.

The Great Depression and World War II dealt powerful blows to professional baseball. During the economic crisis of the 1930s, the establishment of an annual All-Star game between the best players in the two leagues (beginning in 1933), the introduction of night baseball with electric lighting at Cincinnati in 1935, and the founding of the Hall of Fame in Cooperstown, New York, in 1936, all failed to draw crowds to games. The big leagues even considered closing down during U.S. participation in World War II (1941–1945), but President Franklin D. Roosevelt, believing big league play would be good for morale, urged that baseball

continue. With many of the best players drafted into the armed forces, the quality of play suffered.

Fearful that major league baseball might be discontinued during World War II and aware of the popularity of women's softball, Philip K. Wrigley (1894–1977), chewing gum magnate and owner of the Chicago Cubs, organized the All-American Girls Baseball League in 1943. While women had played versions of baseball and softball on college campuses and occasionally on barnstorming teams since the last quarter of the 19th century, ball-playing by women experienced a sharp growth in popularity during the 1930s and 1940s. Stressing a combination of feminine beauty and masculine playing skills, the league initially prospered in mid-sized, midwestern cities. Reflecting the postwar trend toward at-home diversions and the return to a more restrictive conception of femininity, the league folded in 1954.

Race Relations

The war years also represented a turning point in baseball's race relations. Excluded from white leagues since the 1880s and 1890s, African Americans carved out a separate baseball sphere. In the late 1880s the black barnstorming Cuban Giants (formed in 1885) booked some 150 games a season, but barnstorming reached its heyday in the first half of the 20th century. Barnstorming black teams played other itinerant black teams, town teams scattered across North America and the Caribbean basin, and occasionally, during the off season, "all-star" big league white teams. While skill levels were high among the barnstormers, showmanship, which often entailed the employment of black stereotypes, was a fundamental part of the barnstorming game. The founding of the Negro National League in 1920 ushered in another era of professional black baseball, and teams frequently combined barnstorming with league play. League baseball reached the height of its popularity in the early 1940s. For more than two decades, Leroy "Satchel" Paige (1906–1982), a pitcher, was the star attraction of black baseball.

Despite substantial opposition from fellow club owners, in 1945 Branch Rickey, the general manager of the Brooklyn Dodgers, signed Jackie Robinson (1919–1972), a multisport African American star at the University of California at Los Angeles and a player in the Negro National League, to a contract to play with the Dodgers' Montreal farm club in 1946. The next year, amidst great fanfare, Robinson joined the parent team. Given baseball's distinction as the "national pastime" of the United States, the game's racial integration had vast symbolic importance. If the racial wall of the national game could be breached, it seemed manifest to many that other barriers to blacks should be removed as well.

Yet the entry of Robinson into the big leagues failed to herald the end of racial bigotry in baseball. Racial integration proceeded slowly; it was 12 years before the last big league club, the Boston Red Sox, finally employed a black player. Integration was uneven. In 1959 the National League had twice as many blacks as the American League. Finally, studies consistently found that blacks had to outperform whites to make team rosters and that blacks were commonly the victims of "stacking," that is, more frequent relegation to "noncentral" playing positions such as the outfield or first base.

The Troubled Years

In the second half of the 20th century, baseball entered more troubled times. After an initial resurgence of attendance in the late 1940s, crowds declined during the 1950s. The growth of sprawling independent suburbs and the appearance of television encouraged a larger trend away from inner-city and public forms of leisure to private, at-home diversions. Unlimited telecasts of big league games damaged minor league attendance and support for semiprofessional baseball. In the 1950s thousands of semipro teams folded and minor league baseball became a shell of its former self. The major leagues fared only somewhat better. Average game attendance remained below the 1948–1952 seasons until 1978, and even after that lagged behind the population growth of the metropolitan areas served by big league clubs. Baseball's television ratings were also weak, falling to about half that of regular season professional football games. Ironically, the rapid growth of Little League baseball (founded in 1939 and composed of preadolescent boys) after World War II may have seriously damaged attendance at all other forms of baseball.

Big league baseball responded to the postwar woes in several ways. Reflecting changing population centers and the advantages of air travel, several franchises, led by the Boston Braves moving to Milwaukee in 1953, relocated, and the number of franchises expanded from two eight-team loops in 1960 (the same as it had been since 1903) to 28 teams in two leagues of six divisions by 1994. Big league baseball became a truly international sport when it planted franchises in Montreal (1969) and Toronto (1977); both Montreal and Toronto had fielded teams for 55 and 78 years, respectively, in the powerful International League. Frequently abetted by subsidies from local governments, baseball also en-

tered a new stadium building era. Efforts to capitalize on media, especially television, were only partly successful. Large disparities in media revenues between small and large city franchises endangered the game's financial stability.

The empowerment of the players added to the woes of the owners. With the appointment in 1966 of Marvin J. Miller as executive director of the Major League Baseball Players Association (which had been formed in 1956), the players won a series of victories over the owners. The right to salary arbitration (1972) and free agency (1976) triggered a cycle of escalating salaries; average annual salaries soared from $29,000 in 1970 to more than $1 million in 1992. Efforts by the owners to stem the effects of arbitration and free agency resulted in a seven-week strike in 1981 and a strike at the end of the 1994 season, closing down the World Series and delaying the start of the 1995 season.

The Divisional Era

Baseball in the divisional era (1969–present) witnessed the demise of team dynasties. During the 1980s, only 3 of 26 clubs failed to capture at least one divisional flag, and teams in smaller cities won just as many, indeed overall more, flags than the cities in the largest metropolitan areas. The major leagues implemented an amateur draft in 1965, which allowed franchises to draft (in reverse order of their standings in the previous season) the rights to unsigned amateur players, thus reducing the longstanding recruiting advantages of richer franchises. Also, women and men with vast financial resources became big league owners; they were less concerned than their more impoverished predecessors about earning profits from baseball. Finally, free agency—the right gained by veterans in 1976 to sign with any franchise—may have encouraged rather than discouraged competitive balance.

A new style of play also characterized the divisional era. The hitting revolution of the 1920s had encouraged an emphasis on the home run; in the 1940s and 1950s, the stolen base nearly disappeared as the game featured slugging at the expense of finesse, but in the divisional era dazzling speed and specialized pitching joined sheer brawn. Aided by the expansion of new talent by including players of African and Hispanic descent, the stolen base returned to baseball. All earlier stolen base records fell. As managers turned increasingly to relief pitchers, the number of complete games hurled by one pitcher dropped from about seven in ten at the beginning of the century to about one in ten in the divisional era.

Baseball Perseveres

Although baseball in the second half of the 20th century no longer occupied the dominant position among North American sports that it had once enjoyed, it persevered remarkably. The game seemed to fulfill needs to establish connections with the past. During the 1980s and 1990s, major and minor league attendance increased and an auxiliary culture of baseball memorabilia flourished. Baseball books, especially those of a historical nature, far outsold those on any other sport, and, in 1994, Ken Burns turned to baseball as the subject of the most monumental historical television documentary ever made.

—BENJAMIN G. RADER

See also Rounders.

Bibliography: Goldstein, Warren. (1989) *Playing for Keeps: A History of Early Baseball.* Ithaca, NY: Cornell University Press. James, Bill. (1988) *The Bill James Historical Baseball Abstract.* New York: Villard Books. Rader, Benjamin G. (1992) *Baseball: A History of America's Game.* Urbana: University of Illinois Press. Thorn, John, and Peter Plamer, eds. (1993) *Total Baseball.* New York: Outlet Books. Voigt, David Quentin. (1983) *American Baseball,* 3 vols. University Park: Pennsylvania State University Press.

Basketball

Basketball is a recreational and competitive sports with widespread appeal across age, gender, class, regional, and national lines, which reflects the game's broadly based origins and early development. The game is played by two teams of five players, who attempt to score points by throwing a ball through an elevated hoop attached to a pole.

Basketball was made in the United States, but by a Canadian. Devised by and for young white Protestant male competitors, it was quickly adopted by Catholics, Jews, African Americans, and females. Originally designed for exercise and the inculcation of moral values, it soon became a commercial pastime celebrated the world over.

Whatever the global appeal of soccer (association football), basketball is the game most played and most watched by people around the world. Hoops rattle throughout Asia, as well as Africa and South America. Professional leagues thrive in Europe, and even in distant Australia. In the United States, basketball attracts more participants and spectators than do football and baseball combined. In all, basketball is played by an estimated 200 million people on all continents. No other sport has enjoyed such recent increases in popularity, both in terms of those who play and the number of spectators.

Some of basketball's appeal can be explained by its unique status as a team game that is relatively simple, inexpensive, and easy to produce. People happily play one-on-one. In its organized form, the game requires only five players at a time, half as many as a baseball or football team. Compared to most team sports, basketball needs little space and minimal equipment to play, and it leaves participants with few bruises and broken limbs. It can be played, and enjoyed, by female youths on a playground court or by an over-the-hill gang of businessmen on lunch break as well as by seasoned collegians and professionals.

The International Federation of Amateur Basketball has governed international play since the 1930s; the Olympics are the principal forum for competition. The United States, Soviet Union, and Yugoslavia have dominated international hoops since the 1950s. In recent years, televised competition has enhanced both the scope of basketball's global appeal and the quality of play.

History

Basketball was literally created overnight, the result of an assignment posed by a physical education teacher in December 1891 at a Young Men's Christian Association (YMCA) training college in Springfield, Massachusetts. A Canadian student, James Naismith (1861–1939), rose to the challenge of constructing an active indoor winter game that would prove attractive to young men. He typed up a rudimentary set of rules, had a janitor nail up peach baskets along the railing at each end of the Springfield gym, and invited his colleagues to toss a soccer ball into one of the two baskets.

The first game consisted of two 15-minute halves, with 5 minutes' rest between. Naismith's physical education class numbered 18, so 9 men played on each team. Players had to pass the ball; no dribbling was allowed at first. That inaugural game was hardly a spectacle that anyone would recognize today.

Within its first decade basketball changed dramatically. Dribbling quickly became an acceptable means of moving the ball around the court. Standard team size was readjusted to seven, and finally set at five. The value of a field goal, originally set at three points, was changed to two points; foul shots, too, counted three at first, but were soon changed to one. Equipment also changed. By 1895 the old soccer ball was replaced by a slightly larger leather-covered basketball; peach baskets gave way to mesh-wire baskets with strings and pulleys that released the ball, and finally to a bottomless cord net fixed to an iron rim. Metal screens also made an early appearance behind baskets, in order to keep balcony spectators from guiding or deflecting shots. As more solid substance provided greater consistency for angled shots, wooden backboards became standard by the turn of the century.

In 1895, Naismith left Springfield for medical school and a YMCA job in Denver, largely leaving the supervision of basketball to his old Springfield colleague, Luther Gulick (1861–1918). Within the following year, Gulick and the YMCA passed the mantle of guardianship over to the Amateur Athletic Union (AAU). Committed to amateur ("gentlemanly") sport, the AAU required players and teams to pay a fee and "register" their intention to comply with the amateur code and to compete only against other registered teams.

This policy played havoc with the many teams sponsored by local YMCAs, athletic clubs, settlement houses, churches, schools, and colleges who not only competed with each other but also indiscriminately played against whatever local or touring professional teams they could schedule. Professional squads made their presence felt early in the history of basketball. In November 1896, a team in Trenton, New Jersey, rented the Masonic Temple, charged 25 cents for admission, and shared the profits after paying expenses. They also introduced a distinctive piece of equipment. A 12-foot-high mesh-wire fence, presumably designed to keep the ball in play, separated players from spectators. For more than two decades, professionals played within a cage of mesh-wire or net, causing basketball to be called the "cage" game.

Never did the AAU register a majority of the basketball teams in the United States. In 1905 seven coaches of powerful college teams drew up their own set of rules. Three years later the newly formed National Collegiate Athletic Association (NCAA) assumed responsibility for the rules governing college basketball. Finally, in 1915 the NCAA, AAU, and YMCA joined forces in establishing a single rules committee to oversee any further changes in basketball throughout North America.

While refining its form and governance, Naismith's new game expanded rapidly. Nearby colleges and athletic clubs embraced it as a competitive antidote to onerous gym exercises during New England's frigid winters. One of the first converts to the game was Senda Berenson (1861–1954), a gymnastics instructor at Smith College. Early in 1892 she introduced the game to her female students, but divided the court into three equal sections and kept players confined to a single section in order to avoid exhaustion. Within the following year this distinctive form of "women's basket ball" was being played not only at neighboring Mt. Holyoke College but also at distant Sophie Newcomb College in New Orleans, Louisiana, and at the University of California in Berkeley.

For a time, though, basketball remained primarily a YMCA commodity. Its place of origin—an aggressive new training college for YMCA leaders—ensured immediate widespread exposure. Copies of Springfield's campus weekly, the *Triangle*, were mailed out regularly to every YMCA in North America. In the January 1892 issue of the *Triangle*, Naismith described his new game and heartily recommended it to YMCA leaders everywhere. Those leaders, in turn, wrote to the editor of the *Triangle* with news about the popularity of basketball as it was introduced to more than 200 YMCA gyms in the United States and Canada.

Many of those YMCA chapters and gyms were set on college campuses, especially in the Midwest and Pacific coast regions. Moreover, Springfield graduates—Naismith's old classmates and fellow athletes—found teaching and coaching jobs in college programs, where they eagerly introduced basketball.

High schools especially responded to that gospel, for the game proved useful for physical education classes and interscholastic competition. The women's game was played with great passion, particularly in Iowa, Oklahoma, Missouri, and Texas high schools. By 1900 high school championship tournaments were held in conjunction with commercial exhibitions in Boston, Buffalo, and Chicago. In 1903 Gulick created a Public School Athletic League for New York City and supervised the construction of basketball courts in both elementary and high schools throughout the city. Within a decade, more than a dozen of the major cities in the United States sponsored similar city-wide leagues for public school athletes.

Basketball also thrived in rural and small-town schools. Hoops not only fed rural school and town pride; it also provided entertainment sorely lacking in remote places. After 1909, when the agricultural colleges of Iowa and Montana produced the first high school state basketball tournaments, land-grant institutions from Maine State College to Washington State College fulfilled their public service purposes by providing space and publicity for annual high school championship playoffs. In the 1920s national tournaments for public and parochial (Catholic) high schools began; by 1925 more than 30 state championship teams were competing at the National Interscholastic Tournament at the University of Chicago.

Early professional leagues also held tournaments to close out their seasons, but barnstorming proved to be the more lucrative route. Around the turn of the century, the Buffalo "Germans" and the New York "Wanderers" emerged as the premier professional teams that traveled afar competing with the best local talent available in armories, dance halls, and high school gyms. Their successors included the Troy Trojans and "Globe Trotters" from upstate New York, but the most successful of all the early touring teams was the Original Celtics. Founded in Manhattan in 1914, the Original Celtics capitalized on the use of the automobile as a popular means of transportation. At their barnstorming pinnacle in the 1920s, they often appeared in southern and western towns previously unreached by the railway.

The loosely structured, theatrical character of professional basketball made the game uniquely attractive to ambitious first-generation Americans. Heroes of the cage game had names like Dehnert, Holman, Lapchick, Friedman, Borgmann, Husta, and Chismadia. All were of East European or Irish heritage; most were Catholic or Jewish. African Americans, too, laid early claims on professional basketball as a means of fun and success. Founded in 1922, the all-black Harlem Renaissance Five quickly became the strongest opposition to the dominance of the Original Celtics.

Most spectator sports took a beating during the economic troubles that began in 1929, but the Depression worked to the advantage of high school and college basketball in the United States. As unemployment mounted, families found themselves unable to spend freely on commercialized amusements, causing social life in the local college and school to take on more importance. Basketball became a weekly social events. At the end of the decade of the 1930s, no less than 95 percent of all U.S. high schools sponsored varsity basketball teams.

A newly formed program, the Catholic Youth Organization (CYO), also made much of basketball's sociable and socially healthy potential. Begun in 1930 as an antidote to juvenile delinquency in Chicago, the CYO was the Catholic equivalent to the Protestant YMCA and the Jewish Young Men's Hebrew Association (YMHA). The CYO initially received most publicity for its sponsorship of interracial boxing tournaments, but basketball was always high on its agenda. Chicago's CYO and B'nai B'rith champions met annually on the basketball court.

Basketball also went visibly international in the 1930s. At the hands of YMCA enthusiasts, the game had been introduced all over the world shortly after its cre- ation. By 1930, fifty nations had adopted the sport. Despite the economic hardships, representatives from Asia and Africa as well as Europe convened in 1932 to form the International Federation of Amateur Basketball (FIBA). Chinese and Japanese students who had learned the game from YMCA missionaries before World War I introduced basketball at the University of Berlin in the mid-1930s. Nazi propagandists overlooked the game's YMCA origins and gave it their stamp of approval on the grounds that basketball required not only speed and stamina but also an aggressive spirit that allegedly characterized the true German. At the Berlin Games of 1936, basketball became an official Olympic sport. Unfortunately, most of those games were played outdoors in a downpour of rain, with a U.S. squad beating a Canadian team, 19–8.

By the mid-1930s, American basketball was thriving at the college level, particularly in New York City where promoter Ned Irish (1905–1982) arranged doubleheaders at Madison Square Garden featuring the best western teams against eastern powers St. John's University, New York University, and Long Island University.

Building on the foundation of these intersectional doubleheaders, the National Invitational Tournament (NIT) was created in 1938 as the first intercollegiate championship playoff. Some 16,000 spectators turned out to see Temple University win the first NIT. Impressed with that successful event, college coaches in 1939 created the NCAA tournament. Their first playoffs, at Northwestern University, suffered from inadequate publicity. The NCAA tournament remained second fiddle until 1951, when scandals discredited the NIT.

Despite the game's growth during the 1930s, it was perceived by the American public as a second-rate sport. Not only did it lack the cachet of a major professional organization until the late 1940s, it had modest national media coverage save the minuscule game summaries of YMCA, professional barnstorming teams, or amateur contests in local daily newspapers. The most significant watershed in basketball's rise to international stature came during World War II. U.S. servicemen introduced the game to people the world over, and government-sponsored cultural exchange tours fueled a steady flow of U.S. teams and coaches to all parts of the globe.

The Post–World War II Era

The American collegiate game enjoyed the national and international limelight until the early 1950s.

Coached by the winningest coach in basketball history—Adolph Rupp (1901–1977)—Kentucky was the biggest winner of the period. Apart from a few tournament appearances by southern schools, basketball languished in football's shadows in part because the region's most talented black players were excluded from the leading teams and national tournaments. Formidable black college teams (for example, 1950s power Tennessee A&I coached by African American John McLendon, a Naismith student from Kansas) were forced to compete exclusively against each other in relative obscurity. Gamblers wagered millions of dollars weekly on the major games, triggering a national controversy in 1950–1951 when several New York City teams were implicated in a point-shaving scandal.

By the time of this well-publicized scandal, the previously unpopular professional game was in the midst of a fundamental transformation. The pros were renowned for their physical, pushing, grabbing, and defensively oriented style played by a tough, beer-drinking, ethnically diverse group of industrial workers, many of whom had served stints in the military. Respectability came in 1946 when 11 businessmen—skilled in hockey and entertainment promotion—organized the Basketball Association of America (BAA) and brought a cleaner brand of basketball to a mainstream, middle-class audience. The newly formed BAA competed with a less profit-oriented and more knowledgeable, civic-minded National Basketball League (formed in 1937)—located in smaller midwestern, industrial cities. The two struggling leagues merged and formed the National Basketball Association (NBA) in 1949. The number of NBA franchises shrank to eight teams in 1954 as the well-financed, large-city franchises forced the smaller ones to relocate or fold. By the end of its first decade, the young NBA unquestionably showcased the best basketball in the world.

The African American Influence
The transformation of the professional game into its elegant, fast-paced, high-scoring contemporary mode derived from an increasingly innovative style of play centered around big men and an emergent generation of innovative African American players. The conservative horizontal offenses of the 1940s became more daring and vertical in the 1950s when quick forwards like "Jumping" Joe Fulks (1921–1976) and Kenny Sailors (1922–) popularized the jumpshot, and coaches developed tall players and built teams around them. As late as 1947, only 25 players on the 12 NBL teams were 6 feet, 6 inches (1.98 meters) tall or taller, reflecting the

popular wisdom that large players were too clumsy and ill suited to the game's demands. Those stereotypes were forever shattered by George Mikan (1924–) (6 feet, 10 inches [2.08 meters]), Bob Kurland (1924–) (7 feet [2.13 meters]) and Ed Macauley (1928–) (6 feet, 8 inches [2.03 meters]), whose dominance near the basket prompted the young NBA to widen the free throw lane and penalize goal tending. The most revolutionary rule change in the professional game, however, was the introduction of the 24-second clock in 1954, which prevented deliberate offensive stalling and thereby increased scoring by 30 percent over the following five years.

The influence of a black basketball aesthetic was just as revolutionary. Derived from the faster, louder, stop-and-go play of the cement, urban (particularly Harlem) courts, young black players learned that the game was not just about weaves and standard patterns, but also about explosive speed, deception, and slam dunks. Like improvisational jazz music of the 1950s, the emergent black style of play defied the established standards of traditional "white" performance. The Harlem Globetrotters was the most innovative team of the era, whose stars Reece "Goose" Tatum (1921–1967) and Marques Haynes (1926–) integrated improvisational bits from professional comedians and circus clowns into their performance. Organized in 1927 by a Jewish immigrant, Chicagoan Abe Saperstein, the barnstorming 'Trotters took their exciting court antics to the farthest reaches of the globe.

Despite the stellar quality of black basketball, the American professional ranks remained racially segregated until the early 1950s. Earl Lloyd (1928–), Chuck Cooper (1926–), and Nat "Sweetwater" Clifton (1922–) were the first African Americans to play in the NBA in 1950, but the league remained 80 percent white as late as 1960. Though the way was opened up by the Harlem Renaissance, Globetrotters, and several collegiate teams, it was in the NCAA's Division I that the African American style burst through the locked doors of integrated national competition. Black collegians Bill Russell (1934–), Wilt Chamberlain (1936–), Elgin Baylor (1934–), Oscar Robertson (1938–), and Connie Hawkins (1942–) elevated the game to new levels in the 1950s and 1960s.

At the height of the civil rights movement in the United States, two white coaches devised systems that made black style integral to their teams' personas and became the two longest running dynasties in basketball history. Arnold "Red" Auerbach (1917–), a feisty street-smart strategist born in Brooklyn to Russian Jewish immigrants, became coach of the Boston Celtics in 1950 and assembled a superb, balanced team around center Bill Russell. They won 11 NBA championships between 1959 and 1969. John Wooden (1910–), a devout Muscular Christian from small-town Indiana, built powerhouse teams at the University of California at Los Angeles (UCLA) around stellar centers such as Lew Alcindor (1947–) (later Kareem Abdul-Jabbar) and won nine national titles between 1964 and 1975.

Women's Basketball

Between the late 1940s and early 1960s, U.S. women's basketball became a true varsity sport. Teams had six players, and the court was divided so that the three forwards did the scoring and the three guards covered the backcourt. In 1971 the U.S. Congress passed Title IX legislation, which prohibited sex discrimination at federally funded academic institutions. Thereafter, teams were reduced to five and women were freed from the limits imposed by the halfcourt game. Increased funds to women's athletics attracted first-rate coaches such as former collegian and Olympic star Pat Head Summitt (1952–) of Tennessee, who recruited players from a growing pool of quality high school talent. When the NCAA took control of women's basketball in the late 1970s the large universities with strong programs (such as UCLA, Tennessee, Virginia, Texas, and USC) eclipsed traditional small college powerhouses and shifted the production of women's basketball from New England and the Midwest to southern and western states. The NCAA's prestigious Final Four tournament conferred the truly national scope of women's basketball in 1982 and through increased network television coverage, expanded attendance 90 percent during the decade by the early 1990s.

The Olympics embraced women's basketball in the 1976 Montreal Games. The Soviets won the gold medal in the 1976 and 1980 Games against an impressive field that included strong Chinese and Korean teams. In the aftermath of the 1976 Games, collegiate All-American stars Ann Meyers (1955–) of UCLA and Nancy Lieberman (1958–) of Old Dominion dominated U.S. women's basketball. Both played in the 1976 Olympics, but their influence came later when they became the first women to be drafted by men's professional teams, and then led the short-lived Women's Professional League in 1979–1980. Four years later the United States, led by African American stars Cheryl Miller and Lynette Woodard (the first female member of the Harlem Globetrotters), defeated the Soviets 83–60 in the 1984 Games. In 1988 they repeated by defeating Yugoslavia for another gold medal, which firmly estab-

lished them as the world power of women's basketball. In recent years, the women's traditional "finesse" game has increasingly come to resemble the speedier, powerful, vertical male version.

The Modern Era

The era of stalwart professional dynasties ended with the creation of a rival professional league—the American Basketball Association (ABA)—in 1967, which shifted the NBA's balance of power. By 1976, when the NBA absorbed four ABA teams, professional salaries averaged $110,000—more than twice what baseball and football players made. Moreover, the NBA Players' Association won a collective-bargaining agreement, severance pay, first-class airfare, disability, medical insurance, and pensions. Despite the improvement in players' salaries and overall play, however, the NBA limped along in television ratings and profitability throughout the 1970s. For the first time since the advent of the 24-second clock, the NBA enhanced the drama by adopting the three-point shot (from 23 feet, 9 inches [7.23 meters]).

The American professional game continues to provide the model for global competition. A U.S. "Dream Team" took advantage of revised FIBA eligibility rules that permitted professional athletes' participation in the Olympics, to trounce all their opponents at the 1992 Barcelona Games by unprecedented margins. The Dream Team's success propelled the game into the most geographically diffused and commercially lucrative phase of any sport in history. Even in places without a strong basketball tradition, like Britain, attendance for England's National Basketball League has soared from an early 1970s' average of 7,500 to 330,000 in 1985. The game's popularity since the 1970s continues untrammeled in Latin America, and now China claims more players than the entire population of Europe. Efforts are currently under way to establish a professional league in Asia, with likely locations for teams in Tokyo, South Korea, Taiwan, and the Philippines.

Basketball has enjoyed even greater success on the European continent where NBA stars are celebrated in Italian, Spanish, and French newspapers and glossy magazines. Since 1987, basketball has been Italy's second most popular sport. More than half the members of the national Spanish junior team are currently playing college ball in the United States. Moreover, of the 21 foreign players on NBA rosters in 1995, 14 had attended U.S. universities.

The renaissance of big-time college basketball came in the 1979 NCAA title game when two of the three dominant players of the 1980s—Earvin "Magic" Johnson (1959–) and Larry Bird (1956–)—were pitted against each other for the first time. The 6 foot, 9 inch "Magic" destroyed the stereotypical notions of how size dictated positions and, along with Bird, elevated creative passing and teamwork. Magic's dexterity and court vision brought the brilliance of the black aesthetic to new heights. The Magic-Bird rivalry catapulted the month-long NCAA tournament atop the pinnacle of international sport just beneath the Olympics and World Cup competitions. Gross receipts for the NCAA tournament have increased from eight million dollars in 1979 to over 184 million dollars in 1995. The rivalry also sparked unprecedented interest in both the game and the basketball player as a marketable celebrity. Buoyed by the advertising agency's success in marketing athletic shoes and sportswear (e.g., Nike, Reebok, and Converse) with superstar endorsers, basketball stars, especially Michael Jordan (1963–), have become some of the world's highest paid athletes and most recognizable personalities.

The game's hold on the American imagination is reflected in the emergence of a cadre of successful basketball films. Unlike baseball, football, and boxing, basketball was largely ignored by filmmakers until the late 1970s, but recently has become part of a pervasive sports, media, and entertainment enterprise. Since the 1970s filmmakers have moved away from silly, frivolous scripts to ones that dramatize the contradictory nature of basketball in contemporary society. The commercial success of *White Men Can't Jump* (1991) and the artistic recognition conferred upon the documentary *Hoop Dreams* (1995) illuminate the importance of urban playgrounds as breeding grounds of big-time talent, the centrality of the black aesthetic, and the game's promise of social mobility for millions of young people throughout the world.

—WILLIAM J. BAKER AND S. W. POPE

Bibliography: George, Nelson. (1992) *Elevating the Game: Black Men and Basketball.* New York: HarperCollins. Hult, Joan S., and Marianna Trekel, eds. (1991) *A Century of Women's Basketball: From Frailty to Final Four.* Reston, VA: National Association for Girls and Women in Sport. Neft, David S., and Richard M. Cohen. (1991) *The Sports Encyclopedia: Pro Basketball.* New York: Grosset & Dunlap.

Biathlon

Biathlon is a challenging combination of cross-country skiing and target shooting. The competitor skis a desig-

nated loop with a specially adapted .22 rifle harnessed on his or her back, pausing to shoot at a specified number of ranges along the route. Biathlon requires athletes to master the physical and mental demands of two somewhat conflicting disciplines—the strength and stamina to ski a long course and the self-control to concentrate upon arriving at the shooting range. Biathlon has been an Olympic event for men since 1960. Today there are Olympic events for both men and women, as individuals and relay teams, and national and international competitions for junior athletes as well.

History

The ancient origin of biathlon is revealed in rock carvings found in Norway that date from about 2000 B.C.E., which show two hunters on skis stalking animals. Modern biathlon has military origins in Scandinavia, where the terrain and climate required troops to be trained and equipped for combat in winter conditions. The earliest recorded biathlon event occurred in 1767 between "ski-runner companies" who guarded the border between Norway and Sweden. In the late 1930s, the Finnish Army, outnumbered 10 to 1 but outfitted with skis, routed the Russians from their border.

The first international biathlon competition was held as a demonstration event at the 1924 Winter Olympics in Chamonix, France, and repeated at the Winter Olympics of 1928, 1936, and 1948. After 1948, biathlon was dropped from the Olympic program in response to the antimilitary sentiment that followed World War II.

In 1948, the Union Internationale de Pentathlon Moderne et Biathlon (UIPMB) was founded to promote both sports as Olympic events. The UIPMB instituted annual World Championships for biathlon in 1957 and it was first included as an individual event for male athletes at the Winter Olympics in Squaw Valley, California, in 1960. In 1966 the biathlon relay was introduced at the World Biathlon Championships and added to the Olympic program in 1968. The first Women's World Championships were held in Chamonix, France, in 1984, and women's biathlon events were included at the 1992 Winter Olympics in Albertville, France.

Rules and Play

There are three race events in biathlon—individual, sprint, and relay—each with different distances, rules, and penalties. Competitors ski a set number of loops of the course depending on the event, taking four stops for shooting.

The equipment used in biathlon competition has changed over the years. From 1958 to 1965, competitors used NATO caliber rifles, first 3.08 and then large bore .223. In 1978 the .22 caliber was adopted as the official rifle.

Skiing technique shifted from the classic, diagonal cross-country stride, but in 1985 the "skating" technique was introduced. This revolutionized the physical techniques of the sport and required new equipment: longer ski poles and shorter, stiffer skis. Skating has also reduced race times. World Cup winners have "cleaned" every set of targets and finished a 20-kilometer race in under one hour.

—BONNIE DYER-BENNET

Bibliography: *United States Biathlon Association Bulletin.* (1994) 14, 2.

Biathlon (Cycling and Running)

See Duathlon

Billiards

Billiards is a group of games played with balls on a rectangular table. In carom billiards, players score points by knocking a ball into another using a long, tapered cue stick. In the other general form, players score when they drive balls into any of six pockets in a table by first hitting them with the cue ball, which the player strikes with the cue. Games played on pocket billiards tables include English billiards, snooker, and pocket billiards, also known as pool. Each game, especially pool and carom billiards, varies by country or region. Local differences in rules and game etiquette are common. Billiards are played for recreation and in competition.

History

Billiards probably developed from one of the late-14th- or early-15th-century outdoor lawn games in which players hit balls at targets with sticks. It was first played on the ground, often on measured plots that were dug out to provide boundaries. The earliest mention of pool as an indoor table game is in a 1470 inventory list of the accounts of King Louis XI of France (reigned 1461–1483). The word billiards probably descends from Latin terms for ball and from the Old French word *bille* (a piece of wood), which refers to the stick. The term "cue" is derived from the French *queue,* meaning "tail," and probably refers to the practice of striking a ball with the small, or tail, end of the billiard mace.

France's Louis XIII (reigned 1610–1643) and Louis XIV (reigned 1643–1710) were avid pool players. The latter is generally credited with spreading the game

through Europe. Mary Stuart, queen of Scotland, was an early patron of billiards. In 1586, while imprisoned in the castle at Fotheringay, her playing table was taken away, apparently as part of her punishment. A few months later she was beheaded and, according to some sources, her body was wrapped in the cloth stripped from the table.

Billiards arrived in the Americas some time before 1709. The game flourished in 18th-century America, and most towns had public billiards tables. By the mid-1830s, billiards tables were to be found as far west as Bent's Fort outpost on the Santa Fe Trail in Colorado.

Rules and Play

Modern billiards are played on three basic table types: the pocketless carom table, the English table, and the pocket billiards, or pool, table. The first billiards tables were constructed of wood and subject to warping. Substituting slate, easy to smooth and nonwarping, proved the single most important improvement in tables. Uniformly resilient rails around the table became possible with Goodyear's 1839 development of vulcanizing. Skilled play also requires a good cloth covering, but by the middle of the 19th century improved textile technology had made good cloth (often felted) universally available.

Billiard balls were initially turned from wood, in the late 19th century from celluloid and later from cast phenolic resin. Modern balls range in diameter from $2^1/_{16}$ to $2^{27}/_{64}$ inches (roughly 5 centimeters), depending on the game. Larger balls are used in carom games while snooker and English billiards require small balls.

The cue probably appeared between 1679 and 1734 and had replaced other sticks by the second half of the 18th century. Throughout the 18th century, players adapted various practices and techniques to improve their control; these included angled and oblong tips, the roughening of tips, chalking cues, leather-tipped cues, and the horizontal spin, still used today. This is commonly called "English" in the United States, although the English refer to it as "side." Modern cues are tapered, wooden rods about 1.4 meters (57 inches) long and weighing between 397 and 624 grams (14 and 22 ounces). Aluminum and fiberglass are also used.

Four types of billiards are played today: carom, or French billiards; English billiards; snooker; and pocket billiards, or pool.

Carom Billiards

Carom, or French billiards, is played on a table with no pockets and with three balls: one red, one white, and

The Drama of Billiards

The first dramatic mention of the game appears in Shakespeare's play *Antony and Cleopatra,* written around 1609. In Act II, scene v, Cleopatra suggests to her handmaiden Charmian, "Let's to billiards." Although history indicates that the game did not exist in ancient Egypt, Shakespeare's mention suggests that he regarded billiards as a suitable diversion for royalty in his own time (Hendricks 1974). With respect to comedy, pocket billiards often provided slapstick material for early Hollywood short films starring the likes of Laurel and Hardy, the Three Stooges, and W. C. Fields. In addition to being one of the world's great jugglers, Fields was an expert pool player.

The dark side of the game was suggested in Meredith Wilson's Broadway musical *The Music Man* when con artist Professor Harold Hill, played by Robert Preston, declared, "There's trouble in River City," in reference to a pool parlor. Billiards play has also been featured in several films, including *From Here to Eternity, Irma la Douce,* and *Sleuth,* as well as numerous television shows (Mizerak 1990). Pool and pool players have been the focus of at least two significant films. The first of these, the 1961 film *The Hustler,* starred Paul Newman and Jackie Gleason as the legendary player Minnesota Fats. The movie is based on a novel by Walter Tevis and depicts the seamy life of a pool hustler, "Fast Eddie" Felson (Newman). Newman reprised this role in the 1986 film *The Color of Money,* for which he received an Oscar. In that film, Newman's character mentors a young pool hustler played by Tom Cruise. When *The Hustler* appeared, pocket billiards in the United States was suffering from a steep post–World War II decline in popularity. The film is credited with reviving interest in the game during the 1960s and 1970s (Mizerak 1990; Shamos 1995). By the mid-1980s, interest in pool had again waned. This time, *The Color of Money* and its two handsome stars stimulated a resurgence of the game, resulting in the opening of "upscale" pool rooms across the country that bear little resemblance to the dark and dissolute pool parlors of the 1920s and 1930s (Shamos 1995).

—*Garry Chick*

one distinguished by two or three red or black spots. A point, or carom, is scored when a player's cue ball is propelled into the two object balls, the red ball, and the opponent's cue ball in succession. The player continues his or her turn (known as an "inning") until he or she fails to score. Scoring and rules of carom billiards differ regionally. The winner is the first player to reach a predetermined number of points, usually 50.

English Billiards

English billiards combines attributes of the carom game and the pocket game. It is played with three balls: a red, a white, and a spot white. Players score by knocking balls into pockets.

Snooker

Snooker may be played on any pocket billiards table and uses 22 balls, including the white cue ball, 15 red balls, and 6 numbered, colored balls, each worth a specific number of points. Players begin by striking a red ball with the cue ball; if successful, they attempt to pocket any of the nonred balls. The player with the highest total score after all of the balls have been pocketed is the winner.

Snooker is extremely popular in Great Britain and former British colonies. Large billiard rooms in the United States sometimes have snooker tables, but its popularity is minimal compared to pocket billiards.

Pocket Billiards

Pocket billiards, commonly known as pool, is played with a cue ball and up to 15 object balls. Each ball is numbered and has a distinctive color. Numbers 1 though 8 are solid-colored and numbers 9 through 15 are white with a wide stripe of a distinctive color. Pocket billiards games probably come in more variety than any of the other general game types described above (the Billiards Congress of America rules and records book lists 26, but local variations in these make the actual number much larger). Rules and popularity of the games depend on where they're played. Currently, the three most popular pocket billiards games, which are played in officially sanctioned tournaments, are straight pool, also known as 14.1 continuous; eight ball; and nine ball.

Straight Pool

In straight pool, the 15 numbered balls are grouped with a triangular plastic or wood rack, the apex of the triangular group toward the head of the table. Each is worth one point when pocketed. A match consists of a number of "blocks" agreed upon by the players. Each block consists of an agreed-upon number of points—usually 150 in tournament play. Players must "call," or designate, each shot before shooting. As long as the called ball goes into the correct pocket, all other balls pocketed (in any pocket) as a result of the shot are worth one point.

Straight pool was the game of choice for tournament play in the United States for most of the 20th century. Many of the legends of pocket billiards derive from "runs"—the number of balls pocketed consecutively without losing turn. Willie Mosconi (1913–1993) holds the officially recognized run record of 526 balls, made at a 1954 exhibition.

Nine Ball

In recent years, nine ball has supplanted straight pool as the primary tournament game. Nine ball is played with the balls numbered 1 through 9, which are racked in a diamond shape with the 1 ball at the head of the diamond and located on the foot spot. The 9 ball must be in the center of the rack and the remaining balls may be located randomly. Nine ball is termed a "rotation" game in that the balls must be shot in consecutive numerical order. However, they need not be pocketed in numerical order. The game is won by the player who legally pockets the 9 ball. The number of balls pocketed is not important.

Tournament play has embraced nine ball due to its fast pace, unpredictability, spectacular shot making, and clever safety play. Since shots need not be called, some element of luck is involved—especially on the break. Because of this, weaker players can often defeat stronger ones. Tournaments require players to win the majority of a designated number of games, typically best of nine.

Nine ball also has the reputation of being a gambling game, and for that reason has been banned in some billiards parlors and taverns from time to time.

Eight Ball

The most popular form of pocket billiards is eight ball. The object of eight ball is not to score points, as in straight pool, but to pocket a set of the object balls, either those numbered 1 through 7 (termed "solids" or "low") or those numbered 9 through 15 (termed "stripes" or "high"), followed by the 8 ball. When a player has pocketed all of his or her balls, he or she may then attempt to pocket the 8 ball and thereby win the game. House rules are probably more common in eight ball than in any of the other billiards games.

Billiards in one form or another is played in nearly every country around the world. World championship tournaments are held for both amateurs and professionals in three-cushion billiards, snooker, and various pocket billiards games. In addition, women are making inroads into a game long dominated by men. National- and international-level championships have been held for women since the mid-1970s. In recent years, billiards had enjoyed a surge of popularity.

—GARRY CHICK

Bibliography: Billiard Congress of America. (1995) *Billiards: The Official Rules & Records Book.* Iowa City, IA: Billiard Congress of America. Hendricks, William. (1974) *William Hendricks' History of Billiards.* Roxana, IL: William Hendricks. Mizerak, Steve, with Michael E. Panozzo. (1990) *Steve Mizerak's Complete Book of Pool.* Chicago: Contemporary Books.

Biodynamics
See Physical Education

Boating
See Ice Boating; Motor Boating; Sailing; Yachting

Bobsledding

Speed, ice, and danger are the key qualities of bobsledding, perhaps one of the most exciting sports for participants and spectators both. Bobsledding involves a two- or four-person team riding a specially designed sled down an steep, icy course. The "bob" that reaches the end in the shortest time wins. Bobsledding has been an Olympic sport since 1924 and is growing in popularity, although limited by the number of runs and the high cost of participation.

History

As an organized and identifiable sport, bobsledding goes back more than 100 years. The sled and the luge were common in the mountainous regions of Europe and North America throughout the 19th century. Developing from local transport forms, both had increasingly been used for recreation by visitors to mountain areas as they sought new thrills and new ways of traveling down mountainsides at great speed. This group of people consisted primarily of those wealthy enough to spend part of the winter in places such as St. Moritz. At the forefront of this search for new thrills were the British, and in 1875 a group of tourists were responsible for the invention of the Skeleton. The Skeleton took the basic form of a sled with the addition of a sliding seat that would enable the rider to travel down a slope while lying on his or her stomach. The Skeleton could be controlled by shifting the rider's weight on the seat. The Skeleton took the old sled and luge to new speeds while opening minds to the possibility of new and future forms of downhill travel that would be used primarily for sport.

The first identifiable bobsled was designed in 1886 by Wilson Smith, an Englishman. This idea was advanced by Christian Mathias, a St. Moritz, Switzerland, blacksmith. It consisted of a plank crossed by six or so pieces of wood, then laid over two sledges. The front sled was mounted on a pivot and steered by two strings. At the back, a primitive harrow acted as a brake.

Those brave enough to board these early contraptions had to restrict their runs to the high frozen banks of roads in the Alpine regions. As the bobsled became a more frequent sight, and specific roads were used on a more regular basis, organized clubs developed, the first founded in 1896 by Lord Francis Helmsley of Britain at St. Moritz, the spiritual home of the bobsled.

Roads were not ideal bobsled runs, and the clubs began to consider building dedicated runs. The first was built by the St. Moritz club in 1903. This first run was 1,600 meters (1,750 yards) long and linked le Parc Badrutt with Celerina. The first national championships were held in Germany at Oberhof in 1907, with the winning team receiving a trophy donated by Crown Prince William of Prussia. Subsequently, bobsled clubs emerged in Germany, Romania, and France, as well as Switzerland.

Increasing spread of bobsled as a sport led to calls for standardization. During the early 1920s there were international moves to organize a winter sports week recognized by the International Olympic Committee as the Winter Olympics. These first Winter Olympics were held at Chamonix in France in 1924 and played host to the first four-man bobsled event. The International Olympic Committee was the catalyst for the formation of the IBTF, which in turn introduced standardized rules and regulations for bobsledding in 1924. The two-man bobsled competition was introduced in 1932, and with the four-man bobsled forms the basis of all bobsled competitions. Until the Second World War the nations joining the IBTF were either those with traveling wealthy elites or those with snow.

Over the years the rules changed to include new technological developments and to encourage greater safety. These included the adoption of amateur status in 1927, the banning of women from competing in 1933, the introduction of maximum weight limits for bobsled teams in 1939, 1952, 1966, and 1978, and the introduction of a uniform and standard bobsled for all competitors in 1984.

Rules and Play

Each bobsled team makes four runs down the course, a chute of packed ice that twists and turns down an incline. The team with the lowest aggregate time is the winner. All internationally recognized runs are between 1,200 and 1,600 meters (1,313 and 1,750 yards) and the run to the finish line down a gradient of between 8 and 15 percent. The first section of the run lasts for 50 meters and allows team members to push the bob from the start to build up momentum before

Cool Runnings

*C*ool Runnings is a 1993 film that charts the experience of a group of track-and-field athletes who failed to qualify for the Jamaican team going to the Seoul Summer Olympics. In a desperate search for Olympic glory, they discover a former U.S. bobsledder and coach living on the island who had once dreamt of taking Jamaican sprinters and transforming them into a bobsled team. Although he is a disillusioned drunk, the coach, played by the late John Candy, is convinced of the Jamaicans' desire for Olympic glory and sets about training them. Although lacking funding, official support, training facilities, and a bobsled, and with only three months to go before the start of the Games, the Jamaicans make it to Calgary. The film depicts their attempts to raise money, their first experience of winter weather, and their dogged attempts to learn how to bobsled. Despite the odds being stacked against them and opposition from the bobsledding fraternity, the Jamaicans qualify for the Olympic finals. By embracing their Jamaican identity and by sledding brilliantly in the second round, the team wins over their fellow bobsledders and the Jamaican Olympic officials and capture the world's imagination. The final run meets with disaster and the Jamaican sled crashes. From adversity, however, springs success. All the conflicts in the film are resolved and the Jamaicans are heralded as the true sporting winners.

The film did much to promote bobsledding. Although based on real events, the film is largely fictional. The romance, however, was real. The Jamaicans who went to Calgary had never seen snow before; their first-ever run on ice was only days before their final qualifying run, and they really did raise their funding from such strange sources as T-shirt sales and the release of a reggae record. Some of the profits from the film were put back into the sport and the interest encouraged the Red Stripe beer company to sponsor the team. At the 1994 Winter Olympics in Albertville the Jamaicans finished fourteenth and ahead of traditional bobsled nations such as the United States, France, and Italy.

—*Mike Cronin*

jumping in. Once in the bob, the frontman will take control and will attempt to keep the bob on the straightest course. The other members sit as low as possible to offer the least wind resistance, thereby increasing the speed of the bob.

Since the 1950s the weight limits for both competitions have been standardized to eliminate any advantage for heavier teams. The four-man bob must not weigh in excess of 630 kilograms (1,389 pounds), and the two-man bob no more than 375 kilograms (827 pounds). The bob itself is a sectionalized steel structure that is positioned on four blades. The front of the bob is covered with a streamlined plastic cowling, and the whole machine is steered by cables attached to the blades. Since the introduction of the bobsled to the Olympics, teams from Germany have won the most medals (25), followed by Switzerland (21) and the United States (14).

Bobsledding as a competitive sport has been dominated by the Winter Olympics. Although the IBTF has held World Bobsled Championships every year since 1930, these do not reach the same global audience as the Olympics. This has stunted the growth of bobsledding compared to other winter sports, such as skiing or ice skating, which receive regular media coverage through their national and international championships.

The more fundamental problems that have held back any wider growth of bobsledding are the limited availability of runs and the expense. By 1988 the IBTF recognized 19 official runs, only 3 of which, Calgary (Canada), Lake Placid, New York (United States), and Sapporo (Japan) were outside the European Alpine area. At present even a second-hand bobsled will cost up to $15,000. Bobsledding is not a sport that the viewer or spectator can then go out and try.

The nations that have joined the IBTF and who have competed in the Winter Olympics over the last 50 years are, in the main, those nations with access to snow who have come late to the event, or those with a political agenda. Nations such as Andorra, Bulgaria, Sweden, Chinese Taipei, Venezuela, and the former Yugoslavia have joined the ranks of bobsled nations as a result of their wider cultural and sporting links with Alpine sports events. The participation of the former German Democratic Republic since 1973, the former Soviet Union since 1980, and China since 1984 has its roots in the sporting agenda of the communist nations. A new spread of bobsled has taken place in the last 10 years to nations with no background in winter sports. This has included the involvement of Australia, Mexico, and Jamaica in recent Winter Games. These nations have relied on private funding, foreign coaches, and huge amounts of travel, as there are no domestic training facilities. By and large, bobsledding is still dominated by the original areas where the sport was taken up and the same class of athlete. At present over 30 different nations are affiliated with the International Bobsleigh and Tobogganing Federation (IBTF).

The spectacle of two or four men traveling down a 1,600-meter (1,744-yard) course at speeds approaching 130 kilometers (78 miles) per hour, thereby suffering a centrifugal force of up to 4g's as they approach a bend, makes bobsledding in particular one of the most fascinating winter sports for participant and spectator alike. While other sports may be in decline, bobsledding is growing and increasing in popularity, especially, and in many ways surprisingly, in countries where snow is seldom, if ever, seen.

—MICHAEL CRONIN

Bibliography: "Bobsleigh and Olympism." (1984) *Olympic Review* 206 (December): 1003–1030. Kotter, K. (1984) "Le bobsleigh et la federation internationale de bobsleigh et de tobogganing." *Message-Olympique* (June): 59–66. Mallon, B. (1992) "On Two Blades and a Few Prayers." *Olympian* 18, 6: 54–55. O'Brien, A., and M. O'Bryan. (1976) *Bobsled and Luge.* Canada: Colban.

Bocce
See Bowls and Bowling

Bodybuilding

Bodybuilding is defined as working out with weights to reshape the physique by adding muscle mass and increasing separation and definition of the various muscle groups. The practice is distinct from other types of resistance training (e.g., bodyshaping, bodysculpting, and fitness training) in that it is the visible result of training—large, well-defined muscles—that is judged rather than any ability developed in the course of building those muscles. Appearance counts; the athletic component—lifting weights—is not presented but re-presented through a series of poses. Opinion is divided on the question of whether bodybuilding is a bona fide sport. Many men practice bodybuilding, but only a small proportion of bodybuilders compete. In contrast, most women who lift weights exclusively to build larger muscles are either active competitors or aspire to compete. Bodybuilding competitions are well established internationally, but the sport has yet to achieve Olympic status.

History

Modern bodybuilding descended from the mid-19th-century health reform movements, including the muscular Christianity movement, that emphasized exercise and heralded a cult of manliness that, by the end of the century, was embraced through exercise, athletics, and weight training. Eugene Sandow is credited with generating intense interest in bodybuilding in Europe and the United States. First appearing in 1893 at the Chicago World's Fair, this strongman and physique showman represented a new ideal of muscular manhood. Strength and stoicism replaced passivity and turning the other cheek in a cultural form that linked athleticism and religion.

At the same time, as the population became more sedentary, concern for public health increased. Muscular masculinity replaced the prevalent masculine models of the thin, wan intellectual and the corpulent businessman of the 1800s. For women, the Gibson Girl dominated the scene from the late 1800s to World War I. "The Gibson Girl was a healthy, strong, athletic, albeit corsetted ideal" (Bolin 1992a, 85).

An industry quickly developed to support physical culture: the invention of resistance training machines, the use of various types of weights, and the widespread availability of training/exercise programs. The world's first major bodybuilding contest was held in Britain in 1901, followed in 1903 by the first such competition in the United States, sponsored by Bernard MacFadden. Physique competition was the focus of the show, with the athletic feats and strength displays relegated to a supporting position—an unprecedented approach at a time when bodybuilding was more often an exhibition tacked on after weightlifting contests. Twenty years later, MacFadden's 1921 physique contest spawned one of the best-known U.S. bodybuilders, Angelo Siciliano, who later changed his name to Charles Atlas and claimed the title of the Most Perfectly Developed Man in America. Atlas perpetuated the ideal of a muscular masculinity through his mail-order courses on physical development. He embodied the industrial self-made man, who, through hard work (i.e., Atlas's program of exercise), could overcome hardship (i.e., being weak).

In the 1930s, physique contests began to gain in popularity. The Amateur Athletic Union (AAU) inaugurated its first Mr. America Contest in 1939. Other national contests followed, facilitating the promotion of local and regional bodybuilding contests as qualifying events, thereby boosting the sport economically and socially.

Joe Weider and his brother Ben are regarded as a driving force in the modern history of bodybuilding and Joe remains a major promoter of bodybuilding as a sport and way of life in the 1990s. Their goal was to make bodybuilding into a genuine sport. In 1946, the Weiders founded the International Federation of Bodybuilding (IFBB), which today has 134 member countries.

The era of bodybuilding spanning the 1940s and 1950s continued to incorporate the health concerns of the physical culture movement and to provide opportunities for physique competitors through contests such as Mr. America and Mr. Universe. Steve Reeves became a public figure in bodybuilding via his subsequent career in Hollywood's Hercules movies.

In the 1960s, bodybuilding included multiple amateur and professional contests at the national and international levels in the United States and Europe. European bodybuilding was dominated by the Mr. Universe competition. In 1965, the Mr. Olympia bodybuilding championship was created by the IFBB. By the 1990s it would become the highest award possible in international bodybuilding competition.

The 1960s can be regarded as the beginning of the Arnold Schwarzenegger era in the United States. The 1970s were punctuated by the publication of Charles Gaines and George Butler's book *Pumping Iron* (1974), followed by the movie of the same name, which helped popularize and increase national recognition for the sport. Bodybuilding became more competitive, and the standards of perfection demanded greater expertise in the knowledge of dieting, nutrition, and training.

By the 1980s, bodybuilding had been reborn. Professional bodybuilders and the gyms where they train have been transformed into elite clubs with resistance machines, aerobic classes, stair climbers, stationary bikes, tanning beds, computerized diets, and personal trainers. Professionals could earn money through personal training, endorsements of fitness commodities, guest performances, and seminars. Health clubs expanded and became co-ed during this time. The popularization of bodybuilding ultimately converged health spas with the development of elite gyms and led to the decline, but not disappearance, of barbell clubs and hardcore gyms. The elite gyms are often expansive facilities catering to the public at large as well as providing a setting for the professional.

Rules and Play

Rigorous training, a strategy for continual muscle development including size, shape, proportion and body symmetry, disciplined dieting and nutrition, posing practice, and the preparation of a choreographed posing routine are integral components of bodybuilding competition. Competitive bodybuilding is organized formally at both the amateur and professional levels through a number of associations, each with a bureaucracy, by-laws, agendas, membership fees, contests, promotions, and personnel consisting of judges, promoters, competitors, and fans.

Competitive bodybuilders train toward their competitions throughout the year, varying it as their contest approaches. During the off-season, they work to acquire as much muscle as possible. Pre-contest training frequently involves lighter weights and more repetitions, and super sets (two exercises performed back-to-back without rest in between). Simultaneously, bodybuilders increase aerobic activity to acquire the necessary leanness.

Bodybuilding is one of only a few sports where a rigorous diet is such a central feature in training. Participants have estimated that diet is 90 to 98 percent of pre-contest preparation. Since success for the competitor demands a lean body coupled with significant muscle mass in a symmetrical form, fat is the enemy of the competitive physique. For bodybuilders diet entails modifying the relative proportion of carbohydrates, protein, and fats in the calories consumed. The diet typically consists of five to seven small meals a day, with no more than 10 to 20 percent fat. The ultimate goal is to reduce body fat to a very low percentage, preferably 7 percent or lower for men and 10 to 12 percent or lower for women.

For the day of the competition, bodybuilders strive to have a physique that has "peaked"—one that has achieved its potential in terms of maximum leanness, muscularity, vascularity, striations, and skin thinness and tautness. Fluids under the skin can obscure the muscles and can be avoided through the manipulation of diet. A peak may be missed, sometimes by a few hours or several weeks, because the diet strategy did not work or it was not followed closely enough.

Local, state, and national competitions usually consist of two segments: the morning, or pre-judging, portion when most of the judging decisions are made and the evening contest, in which the finalists and winners are announced and awarded.

The day of the competition includes a backstage "pumping up" through exercise and lifting light weights, wherein blood is brought to the surface resulting in vascularity and muscle fullness. The competitor's body is stained with a temporary tanning agent, and posing oil is applied to give shine and enhance the visibility of the muscle. Sometimes an oil that causes the skin to feel hot and appear vascular may also be used.

Judging occurs as the competitors display their physiques through mandatory poses and the presentation of a short choreographed routine set to music. The standard of excellence for bodybuilders is the "X." The lower portion of the "X" signifies the ideal of large flaring thighs, with a thin waist and wide shoulders and back (*latissimus dorsi*). Contestants are evaluated for symmetry or proportions, muscular development, vascularity, skin tightness and tone, leanness, muscle fullness, muscle shape, and the overall configuration of their physiques. In the evening, the competitors, depending on their placing, will have an opportunity to present their choreographed routine. After presentations of the routines, each class of competitors will engage in a posedown. Hard rock-and-roll music is usually played and the audience cheers on their favorite contenders, who engage in a drama of comparison. Men and women in their classes move around the stage and may stand next to an archcompetitor in a symbolic duel of muscles and body parts.

In nonprofessional competitions weight classes dominate and height classes are used by some organizations. Other additional classes include novice classes, teen classes, and masters classes that may be further subdivided by age. Professional competitions include no class divisions.

The Culture of Bodybuilding

Historically, bodybuilding for men has been associated with the working classes and blue-collar professions where physical efficacy is a component. Bodybuilding was born in hardcore gyms (the term *hardcore* is usually used in reference to gyms where weightlifting is marked by intensity, commitment, and seriousness), and, at the amateur level, hardcore gyms are still the site of choice for competition training. Their atmosphere cannot be replicated in the social milieu of the modern health club. A hardcore gym offers various advantages for potential competitors: the presence of mentors—former competitors and active competitors—to help the novice bodybuilder learn all aspects of the sport as well as a pool of other serious lifters from which to find a training partner. There is camaraderie in such gyms, but also unspoken but powerful rules of respect and the sanctity of training. There is a no-nonsense atmosphere, embellished with pictures of professional bodybuilders and local competitors. A particular kind of clothing has come to be associated with hardcore bodybuilding: tank tops, tee shirts, sweatshirts, sweatpants, and "baggies" designed for the workouts. Contemporary bodybuilders, unlike their predecessors, come from all professions, following an influx of white-collar men that began in the 1980s.

These elite centers have lost some of the sense of camaraderie and family forged by the subculture of bodybuilding in its earlier days. By the end of the 1980s the single-owner, hardcore gyms were on the verge of extinction. Competitive women's bodybuilding has a different cultural role. The female bodybuilder is in a position to contribute to the social redefinition of womanhood and femininity, which involves challenging the notion that the muscularity that embodies power and privilege is the "natural" purview of men.

Centered as it is on the body, bodybuilding still occupies a somewhat marginal position in an age that favors the mental over the physical.

Women and Bodybuilding

Women's bodybuilding has a briefer history than men's, and is distinct from it. Health reform in the mid-19th century at the time of early feminism led to the innovative idea that exercise was healthful for women and that women's muscles could be beautiful, contradicting the prevailing view of middle-class femininity as frail and ethereal, which continued through the turn of the century. Early on, Sandow and MacFadden both promoted the benefits of exercise and muscle development for women.

MacFadden may be counted as one of the first to promote the ancestor of modern women's bodybuilding contests. From 1903 to 1905, he staged a series of local and regional physique competitions culminating in a grand competition with a prize for the "best and most perfectly formed woman." Paradoxically, MacFadden's very success placed the development of women's physical culture back in the closet for some time. In 1905, he hosted the Madison Square Garden Mammoth Physical Culture Exhibition, which included the finale of MacFadden's women's competition. Shortly before the competition, Anthony Comstock of the Society for the Suppression of Vice, had MacFadden's offices raided for the spreading of pornography. The offensive items were posters of the finalists of the women's physique competition, who were dressed in white formfitting, leotard-like exercise wear, along with a photo of one of the men's winners in a leopard-skin loincloth and other items (Todd 1991, 3–8). MacFadden was arrested and found guilty of dissemination of pornography, although the trial's publicity served to promote his physique extravaganza even more. MacFadden, however, ceased all publication and promotion of women's physiques. Women's physique exhibitions continued to be relegated to sideshow strength performances through the early decades of the 1900s of women like Sandwina, who displayed her strong and beautiful figure at the Barnum and Bailey Circus in 1910.

Weight training for female athletes was introduced in the 1950s, and women's competitive bodybuilding emerged as a sport about 20 years later. Competitions began in 1975 just before the first competitive powerlifting contests for women in 1977. The social movements for gender equality in the 1960s were a major influence in bringing women into the sports arena. Women's bodybuilding found a home in the hardcore gyms where men trained, and it moved, along with male bodybuilding, from these gyms into scientific and contemporary pavilions of nutrition and training, which opened their doors to the public and became part of the modern fitness industry of the 1980s. The first Miss (now Ms.) Olympia was held in 1980, establishing the zenith of women's international titles.

Bodybuilding Today

The question of whether bodybuilding is a sport continues to be debated among sports researchers and within organizations. The detractors of the bodybuilding-as-sport position claim physical exertion does not actually occur in the competition itself, which is limited to posing displays of muscularity. Supporters contend that posing and presenting choreographed routines is indeed a physically demanding and grueling activity.

Joe Weider is the driving force behind the National Physique Committee, which organizes amateur and professional bodybuilding on the local, state, regional, and national levels. For some years, the only other organization for competitive bodybuilders was the Amateur Athletic Union. In the late 1980s, "natural" contests and bodybuilding organizations (those that drug test, using polygraph and/or urine testing methods) began emerging. This has occurred in part as a result of a generalized increase in public awareness of anabolic steroid use among athletes. Natural organizations include the World Natural Bodybuilding Federation (WNBF), which sponsors professional bodybuilding and the National Gym Association (NGA), a WNBF-affiliated amateur organization. The recent growth of "natural" (drug-free) bodybuilding organizations and their increasing popularity is a positive sign for the sport.

The use of anabolic steroids among competitive bodybuilders remains a concern. As a result, widespread drug testing became routine in many professional sports, including some bodybuilding organizations and within the Olympics. Steroid use also inflamed the existing debate over what constitutes femininity, as some female bodybuilders were using the drugs to increase their muscle mass too.

Bodybuilders, meanwhile, continue their quest for Olympic status for what they view as a true sport.

—ANNE BOLIN

Bibliography: Bolin, Anne. (1992a) "Vandalized Vanity: Feminine Physiques Betrayed and Portrayed." In *Tatoo, Torture, Adornment and Disfigurement: The Denaturalization of the Body in Culture and Text,* edited by F. Mascia-Lees. Albany: State University of New York Press, 79–90. Chapman, David L. (1994) *Sandow the Magnificent: Eugene Sandow and the Beginnings of Bodybuilding.* Urbana: University of Illinois Press. Klein, Alan. (1993) *Little Big Men: Gender Construction and Bodybuilding Subculture.*

Albany: State University of New York Press. McLish, Rachel. (1984) *Flex Appeal.* New York: Warner Books. Schwarzenegger, Arnold. (1985) *Encyclopedia of Modern Bodybuilding.* New York: Simon and Schuster. Weider, Betty, and Joe Weider. (1981) *The Weider Book of Bodybuilding for Women.* Chicago: Contemporary Books.

Boomerang Throwing

While the boomerang has existed for nearly 15,000 years in Australia, boomerang throwing as an organized sport began in the 1970s in Australia and the United States. Now the sport is practiced worldwide, both for recreation and in competition, with International Team Cup Challenges and World Team and Individual championships held every two years. Distance remains a factor in scoring a throw; others include time aloft, elapsed time between throw and return, and others.

History

While traditionally thought of as an Australian artifact, boomerangs and their cousins, nonreturning throw sticks, have been discovered throughout the world. The oldest wooden boomerangs are from Wyrie Swamp in South Australia and appear to be 8,000 to 10,000 years old. Depictions of boomerangs also appear in Arnhem Land rock paintings believed to be more than 15,000 years old. The nonreturning, low-flying throw stick was used for hunting ground game.

Recent research has stunned the boomerang world with discoveries that the oldest boomerang might not be Australian. A boomerang made from a mammoth's tusk was discovered in southern Poland in 1987 and has been dated at 23,000 years old. Egyptian throw sticks and returning boomerangs were discovered in King Tutankhamen's tomb (1350 B.C.E.) in 1927 by Howard Carter.

Rules and Play

The rulebooks of the U.S. Boomerang Association and the Boomerang Association of Australia are the two standards after which most countries pattern their contests.

Boomerang competition includes eight standard events: Accuracy, Trick Catch, Australian Round, Fast Catch, Maximum Time Aloft, Endurance, Doubling, and Juggling. With the exception of Maximum Time Aloft, every boomerang must fly a minimum of 20 meters out to register a score.

Accuracy is similar in concept to darts, except the competitor throws from the bull's-eye on the ground. A

Seventeen-Minute Boomerang Flight Sets World Mark

On 8 August 1993, a sunny Sunday afternoon at Mingo Park in Delaware, Ohio, John Gorski launched his boomerang. Seventeen minutes and six seconds later, he caught it within 40 meters of the launch point. The boomerang was made by Jonas Romblad (1970–), age 23, of Stockholm, Sweden, who was in attendance when the flight occurred. Romblad, a student of aeronautical engineering at the Royal Institute of Technology in Stockholm, designed the boomerang from a composite made of high-tech materials, including Kevlar and carbon fiber. While the specialized boomerang was designed to climb and hover in the air for the Maximum Time Aloft event, normal flight times would be 30 to 40 seconds without some form of thermal assist. The World Record in competition is 2 minutes, 59 seconds by Dennis Joyce (1956–) of Newport News, Virginia. The previously recognized feat was a 14-minute throw in Sydney, Australia, which disappeared out over Sydney Harbor.

Gorski threw the boomerang on the soccer fields at Mingo Park at 3:10:08 P.M. EDT. The boomerang settled into a thermal and rose dramatically, soaring to over 200 meters in the air before beginning a gradual descent back down onto the field. All told, the boomerang drifted 150 meters to the north, hovering over the Olentangy River for several minutes before reversing course and drifting back almost due south for another 225 meters. It then turned and, descending, headed north once again, and was caught less then 40 meters from the launch point at 3:27:14 P.M.

"I couldn't believe I got it back," an elated Gorski recounted later. "I thought, 'I'm never going to see this boomerang again,' but then it stopped drifting and just hung there." However, no one dreamed that the boomerang, which seemed destined for the town of Marion, 20 miles north, would actually reverse course and be caught in the park. Tournament director Chet Snouffer summed it up as, "An unbelievable, once-in-a-lifetime experience! He caught the perfect wave and surfed it right into the record books!"

—Chet Snouffer

---

perfect score is 50. The boomerang cannot be touched after its release until it comes to a complete stop.

Trick Catching catches are made with one hand, behind the back, under the leg, and with the feet.

Australian Round tests distance, accuracy, and catching ability.

Fast catch involves making five throws and catches as quickly as possible with the same boomerang.

Maximum Time Aloft times the longest of five throws to stay in the air.

Endurance tests fast-catching ability over a five-minute period.

The final two events are further challenges requiring specialized boomerangs. Doubling involves throwing two boomerangs at the same time, catching both upon return. Juggling takes two identical boomerangs. They are kept alternating in the air for as many throws as possible without a drop. Long-distance throwing is a separate event, held when the space is available.

Surprisingly, it is not Australia but the United States that has dominated international competition since its outset. In November 1981, a U.S. team of 10 boomerang throwers went to Australia to challenge the Australians at their native sport. It was the first such international competition in history. Unexpectedly, the Americans came away victors by sweeping the three-test series. The Australians came to the United States in 1984 and evened the score, winning the Lands' End Boomerang Cup.

International Team Championships began in 1987, with five U.S. teams and two European teams competing in the United States.

Competitions are held worldwide, with local, regional, national, and international events filling the calendar. Nearly three dozen tournaments are now held annually in the United States, and the sport continues its international growth. National boomerang clubs are springing up from New Zealand to the Netherlands, Japan to Brazil, and throughout Europe, Russia, and Asia. While the United States Boomerang Association lists over 500 members, it is estimated that there are now hundreds of thousands of recreational boomerang throwers in the country, based upon sales estimates by the many cottage industry manufacturers of boomerangs and witnessed by the recent involvement of national team sponsors and boomerang distributors.

Boomerang Throwing Worldwide

Different cultures value different aspects of the boomerang. Australians show a distinct conservative bent toward preserving the purity of the shape, materials, and competitive events of boomerang throwing. In France, where extreme sports are in vogue, throwers value world record performances and hold tournaments designed specifically for world record attempts. Radical shapes and bright colors hallmark the French creations. The French teams are renowned for their aggressive, flamboyant style in competition. On the other hand, German craftsmen typically value the boomerang's craftsmanship at least as much as its performance. German and Swedish engineers go to great lengths to craft intricate strip-laminated and inlaid boomerangs as well as boomerangs made from high-tech materials like carbon fiber, fiberglass, and Kevlar. While craftsmanship and design are important to the Americans, they seem more pragmatic in their approach to the sport. Performance is the bottom line, and winning the tournament can be more important than setting a record or having the best-looking boomerang. Radical designs, use of a variety of materials, and the addition of weights and flaps with duct tape and holes drilled for wind resistance characterize the U.S. scene. Although open space—the sole requirement for boomerang throwing—is in short supply, Japan is importing and selling hundreds of thousands of boomerangs every year. The indoor boomerang made of foam plastic accounts for the bulk of sales.

The boomerang has stood the test of time. Its popularity continues to grow exponentially in these increasingly complex times, perhaps due to its inherent simplicity. Thrown here, it lands here. The boomerang represents the cycle of life and reminds us of one great universal truth—what you throw out does indeed come back to you.

—CHET SNOUFFER

Bibliography: Darnell, Eric, and Ruhe, Benjamin. (1985). *Boomerang: How to Throw, Catch, and Make It.* New York: Workman Press. Smith, Herb A. (1975) *Boomerangs: Making and Throwing Them.* Littlehampton, UK: Gemstar. Snouffer, Chet. (1994) *The Leading Edge.* Newsletter of the Free Throwers Boomerang Society, 1980–1994. Delaware, OH: Leading Edge Boomerangs.

Bowls and Bowling

The terms "bowling" and "bowls" refer to a series of loosely related sports that have been adapted and refined to such an extent that many of their common origins are no longer obvious. The games' most common element is the use of a heavy ball that is tossed or rolled underarm to reach its target. That is the "bowl" itself—it is the action that is "bowling." Success is measured either by the bowl's proximity to a target or by knocking standing targets over. These sports come from all over the world and have been shaped by much transplanting and adaptation. In some areas, several types of bowling now exist side by side, with seasonal overlaps. Bowling is practiced both competitively and for recreation.

History

As with other ball games, the origins of bowling have been traced to ancient Egypt, where tombs of circa 500 B.C.E. contained simple bowling implements. There are scattered classical references, but the game's key developments go back to late-medieval Europe as part of rural folk festivals.

Generally, it was the later impact of industrialization

The Most Famous Game of Bowls

The most famous game of bowls in history, if it ever actually took place, was played by Sir Francis Drake and other captains of the English fleet as they waited for the appearance of the Spanish Armada, the large fleet assembled to invade England, on 19 July 1588. The story claims that Drake and the captains were playing after dinner on the green of the Pelican Inn, at Plymouth Hoe in southwest England, when news was brought that the enemy navy had been sighted. Drake is said to have replied, "We have time enough to finish the game and beat the Spaniards, too," which he duly did. Historians have argued about the actual event ever since, because the story did not appear in print for another 40 years or so. Some have claimed that Drake would have been far too anxious to fight to have wasted time playing a game. Others have surmised that since the tide was running against the English fleet that afternoon, it would have been better to occupy the time in play until it turned. Drake's comment was also seen as a means of reassuring the men and boosting morale. Whatever the truth, the story has become a mainstay of English naval heroism and was a favorite among artists trying to portray the roots of Victorian imperialism. It is also supposed to represent the calm, phlegmatic approach to life and its priorities that bowls is claimed to engender—the natural sense of English superiority that has proved so arrogant in its treatment of foreigners ever since.

—John Lowerson

and urban life that prompted the emergence of many modern bowling games. Traditional folk activities were then refined, changed, and codified as they were selected to meet the leisure needs of the new bourgeoisie.

The process of bowling's modernization has been largely dominated by Europe and North America, although many less well-recorded ethnic versions probably survive outside those areas. They occur in three main broad categories: thrown bowls with Latin-European origins; rolled bowls from the British tradition; and skittle/pin games adapted by North Americans from older European models. Each variety also uses a different playing surface—in thrown balls, sand or gravel; in British bowls, grass or artificial copies; in pin games, wooden lanes.

Rules and Play

The Latin-European Tradition: Bocce and Pétanque/Boule

Italy and France have produced two main games, codified relatively recently, with broad similarities. They are predominantly open-air activities, played on long, rectangular pitches originally improvised from rough village spaces during hot, dry summers. These have surfaces of raked sand or gravel on which the tossed balls fall and stick, rather than roll. Both games are still often played informally in the village and cafe tradition by men of all ages, but they have now acquired national and international competitive networks and, in many cases, dedicated indoor facilities that allow for year-round play in urban areas and participation by women and children.

Bocce (literally "bowls") is the Italian variant of bowling. Almost inevitably it is claimed to go at least as far back as classical Rome, with Emperor Augustus and others cited as keen players. By the Middle Ages bowling had become rather more popular and intensely localized, with many regional variations in style and rules. Since about 1900 it has paralleled the industrialization of Italy with organization and partial standardization, which has transformed the humble game into sport.

Bocce uses an "alley" or "rink" approximately 18.3 meters long by 2.4 meters wide (60 feet by 8 feet). Increasingly, common indoor facilities provide several of these side by side, as do dedicated areas found in many public parks. The small target ball, the pallino, is then tossed from one end and must land at least $1^{1}/_{4}$ meters (5 feet) beyond the peg. Each player then aims to throw his bowl, which is heavier than the pallino, as close as possible to the target.

Italy stages regional competitions, reinforcing the country's strong regional rivalries. International play is largely limited to Italy and France, which occasionally compete at adult and juvenile levels in grandly titled tournaments. With its peasant origins, it remains male-dominated, although a small number of women play. Despite its growing complexity, its appeal lies in its being a "sport simpatico e popolare," in the words of a recent enthusiast—something essentially part of an Italian summer.

The quintessentially French pétanque, or boule, has many similarities to bocce. It grew out of regional peasant cultures and was adapted for the needs of a cafe society. The game has been codified and organized, although it is probably more widely followed for recreational rather than competitive purposes. It has attracted a significantly wider international following than bocce has achieved.

Pétanque's origins lie in southern France, where it emerged as "jeu provençal"; it has much in common with that game, which still survives as a minority interest. However, boule players throw from a stationary position without the short run-up common to jeu and bocce. The word pétanque is an amalgam of two

French words meaning "feet tied together"—a fanciful description of the standing throw.

A small wooden target, the cochonnet, is thrown about 6 to 10 meters (20 to 33 feet), after which players throw their balls so they come to rest as close to the target as possible. Skill in bypassing an opponent is highly regarded.

Outdoors, like bocce, pétanque's season lasts from April to October, but the game has found a growing winter popularity in France where it is often played in covered equestrian centers whose rough riding surfaces offer ideal playing fields. Although its popularity depends very heavily on a warm and relaxed French cafe and village image, pétanque has grown considerably both as an urban and an exported activity in recent decades. It remains male-dominated in France, but women and children play in some of the countries in which it has been enthusiastically adopted. The French created a Fédération Française de Pétanque et Jeu Provençal in 1945 and an international federation later. The sport eventually spread to other parts of mainland Europe, including Belgium, Switzerland, and Spain, and to North Africa, the United States, and China. World championships have been organized since 1959, with France dominating them. The British started a national Open Championship in 1986.

Bowls: The British Contribution
Rolling wooden bowls toward a jack has been practiced in Britain since the early Middle Ages. Southampton claims to have the oldest continually played-over greens, dating from the 1290s. It was the lowland Scots who kept up and refined the tradition of bowls, playing on flat, seaside turf adjoining their golf links. A Scot, W. W. Mitchell of Glasgow, first codified the rules in 1849. Thereafter, the game was reintroduced to England and began a spate of growth that took it overseas as well.

In England, bowls was soon divided into two main types. Both variants use specially prepared grass greens, although one is now much influenced by artificial and indoor facilities. The culturally dominant form, and the most adaptable to overseas and indoor play, has been the Lawn, or Flat, Green code. The other variant, Crown Green, uses a deliberately contoured area that is difficult to replicate with indoor artificial surfaces.

Lawn bowls has emphasized its amateur purity, although many of its star players in recent decades have had commercial links with the production and retailing of bowls services and products. The game is played on a flat square of between 31 and 41 meters (33 and 44 yards) that is usually divided into rinks up to $5^1/_2$ me-

ters (18–19 feet) wide, so that several matches can go on simultaneously. The Crown Green may be either square or rectangular, but must be a minimum of 25 meters (30 yards) wide. It usually rises to a central crown up to 35 centimeters (14 inches) high and the surface may be irregular. The Lawn jack (target) is white and some 6.4 centimeters ($2^{17}/_{32}$) inches in diameter; the Crown jack is marginally smaller. Both variations use bowls that were originally turned from heavy woods, but rubber and then synthetic composites became much more common in the 20th century. Players normally have a set of four bowls each and scoring depends on proximity to the jack. As the game has become more formalized, strict dress codes have appeared. What was once a sign of class distinction still serves to differentiate between the casual bowler playing on a municipally owned green and membership in a private club.

As bowls' popularity grew, so did the complexity of its organization. A web of regulatory bodies emerged, reflecting both rival games and tensions within them. Essentially, for the two codes of play, there are three governing organizations: two for the Lawn game and one for Crown.

Crown bowls has developed similarly, but in ways that reflect its strong regional roots in the north of England and the major role played in its development by professionals and semiprofessionals.

The maleness of both varieties of bowls was taken for granted in the early years of its popularity, and the role of women was restricted to making refreshments at tournaments. By the end of World War I, however, female interest in the game had grown, at least among the middle classes, and a parallel women's game emerged. This has been largely restricted to the Lawn code, although a small number of women play Crown bowls. In turn, this led to two national organizations matching the men's. The English Women's Bowling Association was founded in 1931, to be followed by the English Women's Bowling Federation. Both organize national tournaments. Women's play still tends to be largely segregated, but this is exacerbated in the eyes of many by dress codes that seem archaic at the end of the 20th century—particularly regarding the shape of the hats the women invariably wear. It has, however, appealed much more readily to all ages than the men's games did originally and has a strong juvenile element as well as a number of mother-daughter tournament teams. Both men's and women's associations now have links with a body that unites the representative groups from the four nations of the British Isles (England,

Scotland, Wales, and Ireland) in the British Isles Bowls Council, formed in 1962.

Lawn Green in particular served another purpose. It became another of the bonding agencies that spread throughout the British Empire and the Commonwealth. Expatriates took it with them to Australia, New Zealand, Canada, Africa, and onward. All the governing bodies are linked by the International Bowling Board, formed in 1905, which oversees the game throughout the world.

Bowls' greatest limitation has been its role as a seasonal game. Although that may have fit the requirements of preindustrial society, its seasonal nature has been at odds with growing urban demands for year-round participation. The answers have been the significant growth of indoor play, benefiting from artificial light and protection from the weather, and sharing facilities with other games. It remained a distinctly eccentric pursuit until the 1960s when a boom started that has continued since, but the phenomenon was largely confined to the south of England until the later 1980s. Television has played a major role in increasing bowls' popularity by enhancing the sense of competition. This has accompanied a steady rise in the number of local leisure center buildings with multiuse halls. The development of portable artificial surfaces using plastic-based "grasses" has made it possible to produce indoor rinks with varying characteristics suitable to the level of play. It has proved easier for Lawn than Crown play to be replicated indoors.

Ten-Pin Bowling and the Americanization of Skittles
Skittles shares similar claims of antiquity as other forms of bowls, but is said to have emerged fully in the late Middle Ages when German parishioners were persuaded to roll stones against wooden clubs set up to represent the forces of evil. Martin Luther is said to have played and to have fixed the number of skittles at nine. Variants were played in England, one version of which used a wooden disk, the "cheese," instead of stones or balls. As it developed, European skittles became closely identified with recreational drinking, and was often played in alleys erected alongside inns. It accompanied European settlers to the New World, with Dutch, German, and British migrants playing their own regional versions. Outdoor games in places such as New York City's Battery Park were increasingly superseded by indoor play, but there was also a great deal of gambling, which led many state authorities to ban the pin games. There is a compelling but unproved legend that the change from nine to ten pins was a cunning

way around that prohibition. Whatever the case, the new game achieved growing popularity throughout the United States.

Bowling became a popular activity in many new suburban neighborhoods but often was a sport mainly for working-class men. Much of that changed in the 1950s, when the game was mechanized with automated clearing and restacking of the fallen pins. The spread of the automobile and high levels of plant investment in suburban alleys along with refreshment facilities made it attractive to teenagers of both sexes, women, and families. By then, bowling had become just as important for pleasure as for organized competition. It also became a symbol of exportable American culture to other parts of the world, especially where U.S. forces had bases during the cold war decades. The game was exported to Britain by the 1960s, and a British Ten-Pin Bowling Association was formed in 1961. It has enjoyed a steady resurgence there since the 1980s, and there are now some 40,000 players. Some European cities have also acquired bowling alleys, but perhaps the greatest growth spurt has been in Japan, where a 504-lane Tokyo site was long claimed to be the world's largest.

Individuals or small teams (the most popular for competitive play is five) play on two of the single lanes into which the building is divided. These have a highly polished wooden floor that requires special shoes and offers least resistance to the moving bowls. Each lane is 18.3 meters (60 feet) long by 1.1 meter (3 feet, 6 inches) wide. At the other end stand the ten bottle-shaped pins, 38.1 centimeters (15 inches) tall and weighing between 1.53 and 1.65 kilograms (3 pounds, 6 ounces and 3 pounds, 10 ounces). They are usually made of maple and are placed on marks in a three-foot triangle with its apex toward the player. The bowls (balls) vary in size, according to the skills and strength of the player.

Many players compete only with friends, but most rinks have locally sponsored leagues representing various community and commercial associations. Bowling rules were standardized by the American Bowling Congress (ABC) formed in 1895. A Women's International Bowling Congress (WIBC) appeared in 1916. Both were linked until 1939 with the International Bowling Association (IBA) but are now governed by the Fédération Internationale des Quilleurs (FIQ), founded in 1951. The games' variations have been genuinely international—many winners in the various team events have come from outside the United States. The WIBC has also organized annual championships since it was founded, and these have attracted around 80,000 entrants in recent decades. In 1961 the WIBC inaugurated the

Queen's Tournament and offered prize money. In addition, a male professional circuit emerged with some 2,000 players, forming a Professional Bowler's Association in 1958. A Professional Women's Bowling Association appeared in 1959. Frequently televised, professional matches indicate the commercial importance of a game that is said to attract some 7 million bowlers in organized U.S. leagues alone. These leagues have been linked since 1943 by the National Bowling Council, which represents commercial interests as well as players. This, in turn, has fostered various juvenile organizations, such as the Young American Bowling Alliance, formed in 1982, which encourages competitive collegiate bowling. Beyond these associations, at least 80 million Americans are said to play at least once a year.

Ten-pin has come to dominate the North American bowling scene, but there are other developments of the older immigrant import that frequently share the standard facilities. Candlepin, popular in the eastern United States, uses cylindrical pins that taper at both ends. A frame consists of three balls. Another variant, duckpins, was developed by two professional baseball players, Wilbert Robinson and John J. McGraw, at a bowling alley they owned jointly. Duckpins also has a three-ball frame. In the United States—especially in its stronghold, New England—duckpins is organized by the National Duck Pin Bowling Congress, founded in 1927.

The most important of the alternatives to ten-pin appeared just across the U.S. border in Canada before World War I, when Thomas J. Ryan, a Toronto businessperson, developed a less-demanding and faster version of the game. His version, called Canadian Fivepin, uses five smaller pins in a standard alley. The game caught on rapidly in Canada among leagues and both sexes. Rules were formalized after the foundation of a Canadian Bowling Congress in 1926 that today presides over 20,000 leagues with more than 600,000 players.

More recently, many bowling games have received heavy media attention. Television's sharp focus on the games' intimacy and restricted playing space has given them a new role in the world of sports and more fans than their previously localized nature had attracted. This has also done a great deal to increase participation in games whose equipment and space requirements are relatively simple.

—JOHN LOWERSON

Bibliography: Freeman, Garth. (1987) *Petanque: The French Game of Bowls.* Leatherhead, UK: Carreau Press. Harrison, Henry. (1988) *Play the Game: Ten Pin Bowling.* London: Ward Lock. Lowerson, John. (1993) *Sport and the English Middle Classes, 1870–1914.* Manchester: Manchester University Press. Martin, Joan L., Ruth E. Tandy, and Charlene Agne-Traub. (1994) *Bowling.* Madison, WI: William C. Brown and Benchmark. Phillips, Keith, ed. (1990) *The New BBC of Bowls.* London: BBC.

Boxing

Boxing, amateur and professional, is a stylized form of gloved fistfighting that is governed by international rules. The primary division in the sport is between amateur and professional. What distinguishes both prizefighting and modern boxing from unarmed fighting intended to maim is a code of rules under which no blows may be inflicted below the waistline and none after the opponent has gone down.

History

"Boxing" is an Old English term that 600 years ago meant fighting with the fists. Until the end of the 19th century the real sport was prizefighting, using bare knuckles, for money. Precepts from the sport have affected cultural practice in a way few sports have: fights between enemies, fights between boys, have tended to follow prizefighting rules. (The terms "boxing" and "prizefighting" are now used synonymously.)

The first written rules of prizefighting were published by Jack Broughton (1704–1789) in London in 1743. Broughton taught gentlemen to box using the "mufflers" (gloves) he is said to have invented, although earlier boxing academies existed in nearby streets. Most people would have learned the rules of boxing from participation in the sport itself. The weekly newspaper *Bell's Life in London and Sporting Chronicle* dominated and directed the sport from 1822 until the 1870s. Starting in 1841 the editors also published a boxing yearbook called *Fistiana*, which soon modified Broughton's Rules.

Weight and bulk counted most when fighters were in close, so the notion of science, which became part of the sport in the late 18th century, was mainly concerned with punching or stopping a punch. Movement of the feet, advance and retreat, linked skill to manliness, and international matches soon followed.

Thomas Molineaux, a black man from Virginia, fought the best men in Britain between 1810 and 1815, and his two losing battles with Tom Cribb (1781–1848) for the English championship attracted unprecedented public attention. Molineaux died in poverty in 1818.

Paris also adopted boxing. The country already enjoyed *savate*, which had national and regional cham-

"The Fight".

Reader, have you ever seen a fight? If not, you have a pleasure to come, at least if it is a fight like that between the Gas-man and Bill Neate. The crowd was very great when we arrived on the spot. The odds were still on Gas, but only about five to four. [Mr.] Gully had been down to try Neate, and had backed him considerably, which was a damper to the sanguine confidence of the adverse party. About two hundred thousand pounds were pending. The Gas says he has lost 3000£ which were promised him by different gentlemen if he had won. He had presumed too much on himself, which has made others presume on him.

I felt the sun's rays clinging to my back, and saw the white wintry clouds sink below the verge of the horizon. "So," I thought, "my fairest hopes have faded from my sight!—so will the Gas-man's glory, or that of his adversary, vanish in an hour." The time drew near, I had got a good stand; a bustle, a buzz, ran through the crowd, and from the opposite side entered Neate, between his second and bottle-holder. He rolled along, swathed in his loose great-coat, his knock-knees bending under his huge bulk; and with a modest, cheerful air, threw his hat into the ring. He then just looked around, and began quietly to undress; when from the other side there was a similar rush and an opening made, and the Gas-man [Tom Hickman] came forward with a conscious air of anticipated triumph, too much like the cock-of-the-walk. He strutted about more than became a hero, sucked oranges with a supercilious air, and threw away the skin with a toss of his head, and went up and looked at Neate, which was an act of supererogation. The only sensible thing he did was, as he strode away from the modern Ajax, to fling out his arms, as if he wanted to try whether they would do their work that day. By this time they had stripped, and presented a strong contrast in appearance. If Neate was like Ajax, "with Atlantean shoulders, fit to bear" the pugilistic reputation of all Bristol, Hickman, might be compared to Diomed, light, vigorous, elastic, and his back glistened in the sun, as he moved about, like a panther's hide. All was ready. They tossed up for the sun, and the Gas-man won. They were led up to the *scratch*—shook hands, and went at it.

In the first round every one thought it was all over. After making play a short time, the Gas-man flew at his adversary like a tiger, struck five blows in as many seconds, three first, and then following him as he staggered back, two more, right and left, and down he fell, a mighty ruin. Neate seemed like a lifeless lump of flesh and bone, round which the Gas-man's blows played with the rapidity of electricity or lightening, and you may imagined he would only be lifted up to be knocked down again. It was as if Hickman held a sword or a fire in that right hand of his, and directed it against an unarmed body. They met again, and Neate seemed, not cowed, but particularly cautious. I saw his teeth clenched together and his brows knit close against the sun. He held out both his arms at full length straight before him, like two sledge-hammers, and raised his left an inch or two higher. The Gas-man could not get over this guard—they struck mutually and fell, but without advantage on either side. It was the same in the next round; but the balance of power was thus restored—the fate of the battle was suspended. No one could tell how it

would end. This was the only moment in which opinion was divided; for, in the next, the Gas-man aiming a mortal blow at his adversary's neck, with his right hand, and failing from the length he had to reach, the other returned it with his left at full swing, planted a tremendous blow on his cheek-bone and eyebrow, and made a red ruin of that side of his face. The Gas-man went down, and there was another shout—a roar of triumph as the waves of fortune rolled tumultuously from side to side. This was a settler. Hickman got up, and "grinned horrible a ghastly smile," yet he was evidently dashed in his opinion of himself; it was the first time he had ever been so punished; all one side of his face was perfect scarlet, and his right eye was closed in dingy blackness, as he advanced to the fight, less confident but still determined. After one or two rounds, not receiving another such remembrancer, he rallied and went at it with his former impetuosity. But in vain. His strength had been weakened,—his blows could not tell at such a distance,—and he obliged to fling himself at his adversary, and could not strike from his feet; and almost as regularly as he flew at him with his right hand, Neate warded the blow, or drew back out of its reach, and felled him with the return of his left.

To see two men smashed to the ground, smeared with gore, stunned, senseless, the breath beaten out of their bodies; and then, before you recover from the shock, to see them rise up with new strength and courage, stand ready to inflict or receive mortal offense, and rush upon each other "like two clouds over the Caspian":—this is the high and heroic state of man! About the twelfth round it seemed as if it must have been over. Neate just then made a tremendous lunge, and hit Hickman full in the face. He hung suspended for a second or two, and then fell back, throwing his hands in the air, and with his face lifted up to the sky. All traces of life, of natural expression, were gone from him. His face was like a human skull, a death's head, spouting blood. The eyes were filled with blood, the nose streamed with blood. the mouth gaped blood. He was like a preternatural, spectral appearance, or like one of the figures in Dante's *Inferno*. Yet he fought on after this for several rounds, still striking the first desperate blow, and Neate standing on the defensive, and using the same cautious guard to the last, as if he had still all his work to do; and it was not until the Gas-man was so stunned in the seventeenth or eighteenth round that his sense forsook him and he could not come to time, that the battle was declared over. When the Gas-man cane to himself the first words he uttered were, "Where am I? What is the matter?" "Nothing is the matter, Tom,—you have lost the battle, but you are the bravest man alive." Neate instantly went up and shook him cordially by the hand, and seeing some old acquaintance, began to flourish with his fists, "Ah, you always said I couldn't fight— What do you think now?" But all in good humor, and without any appearance of arrogance; only it was evident that Bill Neate was pleased that he had won the fight. The carrier-pigeons now mounted into the air, and one of them flew with the news of her husband's victory to the bosom of Mrs. Neate. Alas for Mrs. Hickman!

—Condensed from William Hazlitt, "The Fight," in *The Round Table: A Collection of Essays on Literature, Men, and Manners* (1817). Edinburgh: Archibald Constable and Co.

pionships and allowed blows with the feet (see Cudgeling), but boxing swept France in a few years immediately before World War I. British boxers started crossing the English Channel, and a cluster of African American fighters, including the world heavyweight champion, Jack Johnson (1878–1946), stayed to ply their trade. The first major French fighter was Georges Carpentier (1894–1975), who won all the way up to heavyweight, but lost at that level to Jack Dempsey (1895–1983) in 1921.

Boxing, as opposed to prizefighting, used rules written by a Cambridge University athlete, John Graham Chambers (1843–1883) and published by Sir John Sholto Douglas (1844–1900), a contemporary scholar who was the eighth Marquis of Queensberry. These brief rules, which appeared in 1867 and came to be known as the Queensberry Rules, distinguished between boxing competitions and contests. According to these rules, competitions were for amateurs as well as professionals. These bouts were limited to three rounds in about ten minutes and were usually decided on points. Contests, in contrast, were tests of endurance that continued until one man could no longer fight; they were confined strictly to professionals. Only in the latter code was it specified that new gloves of fair size and best quality be used, so Queensberry Rules assumed the superiority of contests over competitions. Amateurs sparred, professionals fought, and both boxed sportingly according to Queensberry. Common to both codes were timed rounds and one-minute rests between rounds; gloves were to be used, and wrestling was not allowed. The 10-second count ending a contest was not referred to under competitions, and attempting to knock the opponent out while sparring was frowned upon in amateur competitions.

Promoting prizefighting was never a safe business proposition. The ropes and stakes and the rest of the paraphernalia had to be transported to an unadvertised, and often remote, place to avoid interference from hooligans or police. A prizefight was a breach of the peace. The fewer people who knew where and when the match was on, the better able were the organizers to give the slip to magistrates and to collect the spectators' money. By contrast, boxing under Queensberry Rules, usually an indoor sport, was controllable. The public house, music hall, or people's palace had a door at which everyone was obliged to pay to gain admission, and the enormous industrial boom that started in the 1880s allowed male workers to join the queue for leisure time and sport especially.

Between the two world wars, the sport of boxing expanded in two ways. First, professional boxing made unheard-of profits, and second, both amateur and professional boxing became popular in Europe and the United States. Meanwhile, the ubiquitous color bar in professional rings began to be relaxed. When Joe Louis (1914–1981), an African American, won the world heavyweight title in Chicago in 1937 the sport's desegregation process had just started. Black men were not permitted to win British professional championships until 1948. (The amateur ranks had dropped their social class barrier back in 1880 and never seem to have bothered with a racial one.)

Rules and Play

Boxing matches take place in a roped-off, elevated area (the ring) surrounded by spectators. Contestants wear protective gear, including helmets and gloves. The traditional boxing stance consists of the fighter turning his or her left side toward the opponent with both fists raised, the left fist advanced and the right covering the chin. To move around the ring, the boxer steps forward with the left foot. The right foot follows without overtaking the left, thus preserving the original, highly stable stance. To move back, the boxer simply reverses this order. The body should be bent slightly forward from the hips. Boxers around the world use the same rules, positions, and movements, except for a minority of left-handers called "southpaws," who box right side first.

Contestants are classed by weight, from flyweight to heavyweight.

Amateur and professional boxing remain distinct. Amateur boxing organizations will not tolerate boxers competing for money, but modern professional boxers were invariably introduced to the sport as amateurs. The professional level of the sport has always attracted greater public interest.

Professional Boxing

Britain and the United States traded domination in the early days of organized professional boxing. In the 1880s bare-knuckles prizefighting had refused to give way to boxing with gloves, but the contest between the new and old styles was decided in 1891, when English-born Bob Fitzsimmons (1862–1917) knocked out Kildare-born "Nonpareil" Jack Dempsey (1862–1895) under Queensberry Rules in New Orleans for the world middleweight championship.

Immigrants from countries with a boxing culture brought the sport to the United States. England, Ireland, Australia, New Zealand, and South Africa all contributed their customs, as did Central European Jewish immigrants, from the earliest days until after World War II. One of the most famous boxers from this background was Benjamin Leiner, who as Benny Leonard fought over 200 contests and reigned as world lightweight champion from 1917 to 1925. Italian immigrants contributed the legendary Rocky Marciano (1923–1969), the heavyweight who never lost a professional fight. African Americans have done equally well in the professional fighting arena, dominating the weights since Louis's 1937 victory.

Poverty was (and still is) the common denominator that impelled many athletes into professional boxing. Boxing generally thrives where the living is not easy. From the mid-20th century, boxers from less-developed countries began to replace white men. From Mexico to South Korea, poorer countries have produced more and more boxers, especially at the lighter weights.

Later, cinema and radio further increased the popularity of boxing even more without commanding great sums of money from advertising. With the advent of television, particularly during the reign of heavyweight Muhammad Ali (born Cassius Clay in 1942, he rejected this name on his conversion to Islam in the early 1960s), the rewards for successful professional boxers (except fly and bantamweight) have skyrocketed. Ironically, the quality of much televised boxing, in which the focus on knockouts has driven the artistry out of the sport, has declined.

Amateur Boxing

The first championships for amateurs were contested at three weights (light—under 140 pounds [52 kilograms, or 10 stone in the older British system of weight]; middle—under 158 pounds [59 kilograms]; and heavy) in 1867 at Lillie Bridge, a London stadium. The Queensberry Rules were written for this occasion, but boxing was only part of a two-day open-air program of general athletics, bicycling, and wrestling for gentlemen from newly formed London sports clubs and the universities of Oxford and Cambridge. The organizing committee excluded "riffraff," so laborers, artisans, and tradesmen were not able to compete. Subsequently, six of the boxers and the editor of a weekly newspaper, the *Referee*, met to form the Amateur Boxing Association (ABA), which allowed blue-collar workers to enter its annual championships each spring. The ABA competitions, held first in 1881 with an extra weight division (the "feather" class at 126 pounds [47 kilograms, or 9 stone]), proved such an attraction for spectators that the Lillie Bridge event was soon discontinued. The real amateur sport developed, not among

the comfortably off, but in boys' clubs in the uglier parts of cities, near factories, docks, and railway arches.

In the United States the social integration of wealthy clubs with the hoi polloi came much later. The Golden Gloves tournament was started by the *Chicago Tribune* in 1926 and became annual a few years later. However, the spread of the sport to the rest of the world was erratic. The Olympic Games program first included boxing at St. Louis in 1904, when U.S. boxers won all seven titles (the British made a clean sweep at the London Games four years later). Boxing was dropped for the 1912 Games, but returned in 1920 and has been retained ever since.

International Amateur Boxing

The organization of international amateur boxing began in 1920 with the formation in Paris of the Fédération Internationale de Boxe Amateur. Only five countries were represented, and the elected president was an Essex man, John Herbert Douglas (185?–1930). World War II ended the introductory phase of international amateur boxing. When the sport resumed after the war, countries were split into two hostile camps: capitalist and communist. The communists eschewed professional sport as degrading and subsidized their amateurs with state funds. Amateur boxing in capitalist countries largely lacked government support, but compensated with television fees and sponsorship from industry and business. In both systems excellence at sport was considered vital for national prestige. In market economies, professional boxing siphoned off gifted amateurs.

Africa, Asia, and the Middle East became involved in boxing through the amateur version. The International Amateur Boxing Association was formed in London in 1946. Tournaments organized by the Arab Boxing Union involve associations from Iraq to Algeria; and the Oceanic Federation, which includes Australia, has successfully staged its championships in the tiny mid-Pacific island of Tahiti.

The World Amateur Boxing Championships were first held in Havana, Cuba, in 1974. They bridged the four-year gap between Olympics and tapped the huge television fees available for supposedly amateur athletics. Boxers get medals, pride, and satisfaction, but no cash unless they turn professional. Scoring changed for international tournaments after chauvinistic judging and crowd misbehavior brought disgrace to the sport at the 1988 Olympics in Seoul, South Korea. Five ringside judges, equipped with computers, had to register points as they saw them scored, but only those points signified by a majority within a second of each other were counted toward the final result. The new system, hated initially, has rapidly gained devotees since it was tried at the Barcelona Olympics in 1992, and the increased impartiality, with its low, measured scores is adjudged a triumph in the management of amateur boxing.

Boxing and the Body

The physical dangers of boxing have long been known. At the National Sporting Club in London, the self-styled home of modern boxing, four boxers died within 41 months at the turn of the century. Amateur fights have produced far fewer fatalities, presumably because their bouts are shorter. Boxing's governing bodies and medical associations inevitably disagree about whether punches to the head cause cumulative brain damage. This debate has become more urgent as the focus of the sport leans more toward raw power. Even so, the headguards in amateur fights, obligatory since the late 1980s, are generally unpopular with both boxers and spectators. Argument rages about the guards' value in reducing concussions, but they have lessened the number of cut eyes and detached retinas.

Despite these dangers, boxing is unsurpassed at developing and maintaining physical fitness. In recent years some women have appreciated this and taken to the sport. In addition, boxing can test character, determination, and valor. Boxing feints, the movement of the feet, the skill in a rally, are all elements that can be appreciated by the aesthete, inside or outside the ring. Indeed, ABA rules published in 1880 state that style should be a factor in judges' decisions. Many boxing fans believe that the sport should heed the spirit of these rules and remember that the goal is not to maim, but to hit, stop blows, and avoid being hit. For boxing to prosper, the slide from artistry toward power must be reversed in the ring and appreciated by those outside.

—STAN SHIPLEY

Bibliography: Fleischer, Nat, and Sam Andre. (1980) *A Pictorial History of Boxing.* London: Hamlyn. Gorn, Elliott J. (1986) *The Manly Art: Bare-Knuckle Prize Fighting in America.* Ithaca, NY: Cornell University Press. Hartley, R. A. (1988) *History & Bibliography of Boxing Books.* Alton, Hampshire, UK: Nimrod Press. Shipley, Stan. (1993) *Bombardier Billy Wells: The Life and Times of a Boxing Hero.* Tyne and Wear, UK: Bewick.

Bullfighting

Bullfighting is practiced primarily in Spain and to a lesser extent in Mexico, Central America, South America, southern France, and Portugal. Its existence depends on (1) a large and constant supply of "noble" or "brave" bulls (i.e., bulls specially bred to charge aggressively in a straight line); (2) a large and constant supply of young poor men; (3) large numbers of hero-worshipping people addicted to thrilling displays of raw physical courage; (4) a smaller number of aficionados obsessed with technical and historical details; and (5) generations of taurine writers and intellectuals who consider bullfighting a fine art rather than a sport. In any given year, approximately 10,000 bullfights are held worldwide, usually in the context of a local religious fiesta that may also include running bulls or brave cows through the town streets, as in the famous festival of Pamplona.

Although bullfighting possesses many ritualistic aspects, it is misleading to call it a ritual. In a true ritual, such as the Catholic Mass, the officiate and communicants are engaged in deliberately symbolic activity; their every word and action has an agreed-on spiritual referent; everything is rigidly predetermined, nothing is left to chance. None of these qualities can be found in a bullfight. There is no deliberately symbolic activity, only simple signals such as handkerchief waving and clarion calls. The bullfighter's actions do not "stand for" anything beyond themselves, and the spectators are always entitled to disagree about them. A great deal is left to chance as it is impossible to predict the behavior of bulls, crowds, or matadors beforehand. There is always a fair chance that the performance will turn sour and anticlimactic, or tragic and ugly.

The rules of a typical bullfight call for a four- or five-year-old bull to be "picced" in his withers with a long lance, further weakened by *banderillas* and risky or flashy cape passes, then killed with a sword thrust by a man wearing decorative rather than protective clothing. Since picadors' (mounted riders who pierce the bull with lances during the first stage of the fight) horses now wear thick padding, the element of cruelty to animals is incidental rather than central to the actual mechanics of the bullfight, more apparent than real. Bullfighting has been a de facto ecological preserve for the Iberian *toro bravo*, a species as rare and unique as the American buffalo, cherished and pampered by ranchers. For another, the archaic concept of manhood that animates the spectacle requires a worthy opponent at all times (women toreros exist but they are still regarded as anomalies, as are midget and comic bullfighters). That is why Hispanic publics always shout out their disapproval if they perceive that a bull is being mishandled and mistreated. Nevertheless, the psychology of both bullfight performers and spectators is thoroughly sadomasochistic, as could hardly be otherwise in a show that features public killing and needless risk of human life. For the thoughtful student of world sports, bullfighting raises questions of a moral or ethical nature much more serious than the ones raised by overwrought animal-rights activists.

History

A predatory species of mammal known as *Homo sapiens* and a herbivorous mammal species known as *bos taurus* had gone forth and multiplied with particular success in the Iberian peninsula. Mythology tells us that when Hercules had to steal bulls, he went to what is now the province of Cádiz in southern Spain. Apart from being used as food, the bull was in all likelihood a totemic figure and/or sacrificial victim for the races that populated Iberia during the Bronze Age. Local cults were later blended with beliefs and practices common to the entire Mediterranean area—chief among them the cult of Tauromorphic Bacchus, or Dionysus, firmly entrenched in the Hispania of Roman days. But the Visigoths who occupied Hispania when Rome fell had no interest in animal-baiting, and the grand amphitheaters were abandoned and never used again.

In the hinterlands, however, the bull continued to play the role of magical agent of sexual fertility, especially in wedding customs that called for the bride and groom to stick darts into a bull tied to a rope. The object was not to fight the beast—certainly not to kill him—but to evoke his fecundating power by "arousing" him, then ritually staining their garments with his blood. This nuptial custom evolved into the rural *capea*, or bull-baiting fiesta, which in turn led to grandiose urban spectacles organized to celebrate military victories or royal weddings. The common people were permitted to crowd into gaily decorated plazas (one in Madrid had room for 60,000 spectators) and watch their lords, mounted on gallant steeds, lancing bulls.

Until the 18th century, vast herds of aggressive Iberian bulls roamed freely and bred themselves with no interference from the human species. When knightly bullfighting was in flower, the elite sent their peons into the wilds to round up as many bulls as they could. But not every wild bull had the right amount of *bravura* (focused aggressiveness) to make the aristocrat look good with his lance; thus, large numbers of bulls were supplied in the hope that enough of them would act out their roles convincingly.

As bullfighting on foot became more popular in the 1700s, the demand for bulls increased accordingly, specifically for bulls that could be counted on to charge, not flee. So the landed blue bloods did the same thing with the bulls that they had done with themselves in earlier epochs: They developed techniques for testing *bravura*, then perpetuated the blood of the bravest through consanguineous mating. Whether or not we think that aristocrats were a superior species, it is unquestionable that the animals they bred were and are amazingly consistent in their power, size, and aggressiveness. Hundreds of brave cattle ranches are now in existence to supply the roughly 25,000 bulls killed every year by Spanish matadors. The many brands of brave bulls that constitute the indispensable raw material for today's *corridas* (program of bullfights for one day, usually six) descend from only five different *castas* or bloodlines, all developed in the 18th century. The prestige of a particular brand of bulls was traditionally based on the number of horses, toreros, or innocent bystanders they had killed or maimed. On several occasions, bulls being shipped to a bullfight by train escaped from their railroad crates to wreak havoc. Cossío's taurine encyclopedia lists hundreds of notorious bulls.

Rules and Play

In a rural fiesta, no one is in a hurry to see the bull dead; when the time comes to kill him, any method will do, from a shotgun to a mass assault with knives. In the urban *corrida*, however, it is crucial to show efficiency and know-how; the bull is to be dispatched cleanly (at least in theory) and in three timed *suertes*, or acts—picador, *banderillas*, and matador. Daily experience in the slaughterhouse gave certain ambitious plebeians the necessary knowledge and skill, and the boldest discovered they could earn more money by doing their jobs in public in the manner of a duel: man against monster. The guild system then dominant in the workaday world served as the model for turning bullfighting into a true profession with rules, regulations, hierarchism, apprenticeship, and seniority.

The first professional bullfighters were men completely immersed in the ethos of the 18th-century urban slum. They detested the effeminate aristocratic fashions imported from France and proudly affirmed "pure" native concepts of male honor, along with bold and insolent styles of dressing, walking, talking, and killing. Among the rank and file of the down and outs, the readiness to kill or die with a maximum of nonchalance was the only route to prestige. Bullfighting on foot appealed chiefly to violent men who had nothing to lose and something to prove. Ironically, the sport has always enjoyed enthusiastic support among the same poor masses who would never have chosen bullfighting as a way to escape poverty; masses who, in other words, were either resigned to their lowly fate or hopeful that through hard work and daily sacrifice they could somehow find a better life, but who were willing, all the same, to deify those few who were neither resigned nor inclined to hard work. Bullfighters were rebels in a rigidly stratified society, violators of the general law of submission to circumstances. But the violation of one value system implies adherence to another.

The code matadors lived by was called *vergüenza torera* or *pundonor.* Both terms possess a certain connotation of "touchiness" that descends quite directly from the oldest, most benighted tradition of Spanish honor obsessions. Simply put, *vergüenza torera* is a bullfighter's willingness to place his reputation ahead of his own life. This is not a mythical or romantic notion but a genuine code of conduct. Flashy flirtation with death has both financial and psychological rewards: By all accounts, the heady delusion of omnipotence and heroism that matadors experience is quite addictive. A retired bullfighter is like a reformed alcoholic, always on the verge of a relapse into his favorite vice. Sometimes death is the only sure cure. Those bullfighters who best embody the imprudent honor code receive positive reinforcement from the crowds—rewarded, as it were, for their appetite for punishment. Toreros who stray from the code are negatively reinforced in the form of jeers, taunts, thrown objects, and malicious reviews. Readers of *Death in the Afternoon* may recall Ernest Hemingway's witty, catty, and often vicious disparagement of the bullfighters of his day.

Throughout the 19th century, the popular concept of bullfighting was that of a martial art. Matadors were considered to be warriors; their "suits of light" were a kind of super-uniform, and their performances were so many episodes of a grandiose national saga. Unlike other European nations during this period, Spain saw its colonial possessions shrinking instead of expanding. For many Spaniards, the *corrida* may have been a gratifying fantasy of national potency to make up for the less-than-glorious reality.

The military origins of bullfight music have been firmly established by scholars. Every change of *suerte,* or scene, in a bullfight was, and is, signaled by a bugle call; the melodies are much the same as those used in infantry and cavalry barracks. The *pasodoble,* the stirring music played even today by bullring bands, descends directly from the military march. Over 500 of them were composed, and the band was always on hand to set the right tone of militancy. Following the loss of Spain's colonies to the United States in 1898, numerous bullfights were organized in which people wore the national colors and bullfighters made inflammatory speeches. During the Spanish Civil War (1936–1939), both sides sponsored *corridas;* bullfighters would parade with clenched fists or fascist salutes, whichever was appropriate. And in the darkest days of their country's isolation under Franco, Spaniards flocked to bullrings to reaffirm their identity with something they knew was their own and which they took to represent their finest qualities. However barbarous its origins, however sordid some of its practices, the *fiesta de toros* had truly become Spain's *Fiesta Nacional.*

For every successful matador paraded around the bullring on the shoulders of ecstatic fans, there is an invisible army of forgotten young men who tried and failed. Like certain marine species that give birth to thousands of young in the hopes that a few will reach maturity, the overwhelming majority of would-be matadors have been eliminated by environmental factors, each harsher than the last. The bull's horns are the most basic, physical agent of this process of natural selection. For many Spanish youth, the beginning was the end. From 1747 to 1995, at least 170 young aspirants were killed by goring, along with 142 *banderilleros,* 70 picadors, 59 full matadors, and 4 comic bullfighters. These statistics do not include toreros killed during ranch tests or private parties, nor do they include *capeas* (amateur bullfights), which have arguably been festal Spain's major device for maiming young bodies and crushing hopes. Doctors specializing in *taurotraumatología,* or horn-wound surgery, are accustomed to working on the pierced thighs, ruptured rectums, and eviscerated scrota of bullfighters. When an apprentice torero recovers from his first goring and reappears in the ring, his manager anxiously watches for any sign that his valor or his determination have been compromised. The all-powerful element of luck will still preside over his career. To be successful, a man must meet a noble and cooperative bull at the right moment; he must also have *padrinos,* or godfathers, a good manager, opportunities, a crowd-pleasing personality, grace, flair, and a whole series of other qualities that are difficult to isolate but nevertheless mean the difference between glory and mediocrity.

In view of this brutal selection process, it might well be asked why any young man in his right mind would want to be a bullfighter. Poverty is the answer most often given to this question. Many portions of the Spanish populace have been condemned to misery, illiteracy, and lack of opportunity. Harsh as they have been, however, these social conditions are not sufficient in themselves to explain matador motivation. They obviously do not tell us why bullfighters who were already immensely wealthy—such as Espartero or Belmonte or Paquirri—remained in the plazas, or why so many men who had actually found good jobs wanted only to fight bulls. Additional motivational factors include self-destructive tendencies and unusually powerful oedipal conflicts. With an activity that has been one of the only means of advancement in a rigidly stratified society, whose wellspring is passion and whose lifeblood is the ritual combat between two animal species, where a lucky and skillful few succeed where so many hundreds fail, where so many frustrated men hound their sons into bullrings to avenge their own defeats, where critics dip their pens in poison and crowds go from adulation to mockery in a second, we cannot help but find sado-masochistic behavior patterns. In general, matadors are men obsessed with insurmountable violent masculine role models and rivals; their ambition is directly correlated with the obstacles placed in their path. Violence becomes identified with fullness of being; winning or losing, brutalizing or arranging to be brutalized, the bullfighter keeps his buried fantasies of omnipotence alive. Hemingway idolized masochistic matadors with adolescent enthusiasm, but in many ways they are like compulsive gamblers who throw caution to the winds and unconsciously play to lose all. Unlike gamblers, bullfighters go for broke in front of huge crowds of people egging them on; so in the last analysis, the taurine honor code is a matter of mass cultural psychology. Countless bullfighters have confessed to fearing the crowd's reactions more than the bulls themselves. Mass desire is as potentially sadomasochistic as individual desire: It will polarize around any expert manipulator of violence, seemingly autosufficient and untouchable in his charisma. The dramatic death of a matador in the line of duty (caused most often by his socially sanctioned suicidal honor), and his subsequent deification in popular lore, simply carry the whole idolatrous process to its logical conclusion.

From a historical point of view, bullfighting has been nothing less than a microcosm of Spain, a nation built not on individuals but on quasi-familial factions, where a "strong man" ultimately derived his strength from the debility of his supporters and the weak got nowhere without patriarchs, caudillos, godfathers, political bosses, and other men who bestowed rewards and punishments in accordance with their mood swings. Until recently, the Spanish political system served to keep most Spaniards out of politics altogether, instilling in them a fatalistic attitude vis-à-vis the whims of authority. The office of presidente of a bullfight still represents this legacy of arbitrary despotism. Fraud and influence peddling were once endemic on the "planet of the bulls." Horns were shaved, half-ton sandbags were dropped on bulls' shoulders, critics were bribed. (One of the cruel ironies of bullfighting is that the most honest and reputable critics are also the ones most determined to preserve the authentic risk of human life upon which the whole enterprise is founded.) Beyond tricks and venality, we can see that bullfighting's personalistic patronage system mirrors that of the larger society. The provincial fiesta de toros was a cautionary tale about what could happen to people without connections or friends; small-town mayors anxious to please their supporters had no qualms about acquiring the largest, most fearsome bulls for penniless apprentice toreros to struggle with and occasionally succumb to. Sooner or later a would-be bullfighter must find protectors/exploiters, the more the better, or he will get nowhere. El Cordobés wandered for years without such connections, and when he finally found them they were desperate gambling types much like himself who were willing to take a chance on a brash newcomer. The other side of this coin of unfair exclusion is unfair inclusion, young men from the right families, prodigies favored from the beginning by cattle breeders, impresarios, and critics. Traditionally, the whole point of a matador's career was to go from being a dependent, a client, a receiver of favors in a more or less corrupt system of personalistic patronage, to being a dispenser of favors and patronage—the boss of his cuadrilla, or team, a landowner, a big man in his community, a pillar of the status quo, idolized by impoverished and oppressed people. A whole web of complicities make bullfighting possible—including local religious belief systems. The fiesta de toros is always held in honor of a patron saint, a kind of supernatural protector in touch with an arbitrary central authority that can be cajoled into doing favors for his "clients."

Like old-fashioned Spanish political oratory, bullfighting can be seen as a series of dramatic public gestures. Every bullfighter is a potential demagogue, a man who stirs up the emotions of a crowd to become a leader and to achieve his own ends. A bullfighter gains power and wealth only when he learns how to sway the masses, to mesmerize them, to harness their passion for his private profit. The matador rides to the top of society on the backs of mass enthusiasm. But no bullfighter could sway the masses if they were not disposed to be swayed. As soon as we become spectators of the spectators, we find their mobile and emotional disposition to be intimately related to popular concepts of power, authority, justice, and masculinity. Without heed to experts or critics, bullfight spectators evaluate artistic merit or bravery on their own and express their views instantly and unselfconsciously. The downside of this refreshing spontaneity, however, is that popular value judgments tend to be arbitrary, impulsive, and irreflexive. The impulsive evaluations of bullfight crowds rattle and unnerve bullfighters, sometimes leading them to commit acts that result in serious injury or death. At the Almería Fair in 1981, for example, the normally cautious Curro Romero was gored in an attempt to appease a hastily judgmental crowd. Afterwards the public was very sorry, of course, as sorry as it had been in 1920 after hounding Joselito into fatal temerity at Talavera and in 1947 when it drove Manolete to impale himself on the horns of Islero. *Blood and Sand,* the famous bullfighting novel by Blasco Ibáñez, ends with this description of the public: "The beast roared: the real one, the only one."

At the very least, the public judges the taurine performance in an arbitrary, capricious, and personalistic manner. Since the decisions of the bullring *presidente* form part of the entire affair, they too fall under the scrutiny—and often the vociferous condemnation—of the spectators. Like old Spain itself, the bullfight is a *mise en scène* of an authoritarian power in an uneasy relationship with a blasphemous and rebellious underclass. For many Spanish writers, the crowd's impulsive style of reacting to duly constituted authority was the worst evil of bullfighting, one that reconfirmed Spaniards in their submission to the despotic whims of the powerful. As the very embodiment of arbitrary might, the *presidente* possesses total immunity and his decisions cannot be appealed. The public's only recourse is to whistle, hoot, or insult. Thus, in much the same manner as the old African monarchies described by anthropologists, the *corrida de toros* permits a ritualistic contestation of power that is momentarily gratifying but essentially without consequence. In his own way, of course, the matador polarizes the crowd's criteria of dominance and submission: Whatever power he has must be seen in terms of popular concepts of power (who deserves to have it and who doesn't) worked out long ago during Spain's traumatic history of civil conflicts. According to one Spanish sociologist, "The bullfight spectator believes in certain qualities inherent in a man that constitute manliness, and precisely because he believes in them he goes to see bull-

fights." It would be correct to picture the bullfight as a dramatization of machismo, as long as we remember that machismo is primarily a psychological mechanism of compensation that provides a fantasy image of superiority in the absence of real sociopolitical power. Perhaps a bullfighter's manly hyperbole serves to mediate between personal and national inferiority complexes. In any event, the evidence would seem to be on the side of those who argue that bullfighting is the legacy of obscurantism, that it is emblematic of the manipulability of the people, their gullibility, their irrational hero-worship, their civic immaturity. It would surely be an exaggeration to see bullfighting as the "cause" of Spain's former political backwardness, but it was certainly no cure.

The bullfight is a spectacle of killing and gratuitous risk of life. It is extremely difficult for human beings to gaze upon such transgression without being aroused in some way. Even reactions of horror and nausea confirm that violent spectacle is inherently erotic. Properly defined, disgust is nothing but negative arousal, caused by the fear of degradation that accompanies the desire to give way to the instincts and violate all taboos. In reality, most people do not transgress one taboo after another and set off on the primrose path to ruin. Culture (whether in the form of Spanish bullfighting or American "slasher" movies) is there to provide official fantasy gratification as a safe substitute for the real thing. Order must be preserved even as desire requires some sort of release. The majority of Spaniards and many foreigners enjoy the titillating taurine spectacle without guilt or moral qualms of any kind. The group norms that hold sway at a bullfight enable each spectator to feel his or her physiological arousal as entirely appropriate. Intense stimulation actually increases commitment to the group's rationalization of it. This is the sociopsychological mechanism that has permitted Spaniards to experience titillation at bullfights and associate it, at a conscious level, with patriotism, manly ideals, integrity, honor, art, and so on. What happens to this happy group consensus when a goring occurs and the transgressive nature of bullfighting is fully manifested? Community norms are already in place that will provide cognitions appropriate to the intense arousal spectators experience. These stand-by norms quickly forge a new group consensus whose conscious elements are pity, grief, forbearance, resignation, and ultimately, reaffirmation of all the heroic qualities that led the matador to risk his life in the first place. The normative emotionality that takes shape around the fallen bullfighter goes far beyond the bullring in its sociocultural implications and lasts for many years after the tragedy. There is still plenty of cultural debris left over from the emotional explosions that accompanied the deaths of star matadors.

—TIMOTHY MITCHELL

Bibliography: Hemingway, Ernest. (1932) *Death in the After-noon.* New York: Charles Scribner's Sons. Mitchell, Timo-thy. (1991) *Blood Sport. A Social History of Spanish Bull-fighting.* Philadelphia and London: University of Pennsylvania Press. Tynan, Kenneth. (1955) *Bull Fever.* New York: Harper & Bros.

Buzkashi

Buzkashi (goat dragging) is a spectacular, volatile, and often violent equestrian game played primarily by Turkic peoples in northern Afghanistan. Central Asian in origin, buzkashi also occurs, for the most part as a self-conscious folkloristic survival, in the Muslim re-publics of the former Soviet Union north of the Oxus River and in China's Xinjiang Province. During the 1980s and early 1990s, buzkashi was played among Afghan refugees near Chitral and Peshawar in Pakistan where, however, it bears no cultural relationship to Pakistani polo. In both its principal forms—i.e., the traditional-grassroots game (*tudabarai*) and modern-governmental sport (*qarajai*)—the central action is much the same: riders on powerful horses congregate above the carcass of a goat or calf, lean from their sad-dles, struggle with each other to grab the carcass off the ground, and then try to keep sole control of it while rid-ing away at full speed. While regarded primarily as playful fun, both forms of buzkashi also exist as an im-plicitly political events in which patron/sponsors seek to demonstrate and thus enhance their capacity for controlling events.

History

The origins of buzkashi are impossible to trace pre-cisely, but it doubtless sprang from nomadic forebears of the same Turkic peoples (Uzbek, Turkomen, Kazakh, Kirghiz) who remain its core players. Equestrian no-mads, these groups spread westward from China and Mongolia between the 10th and 15th centuries. The game quite likely developed, in much the same way as American rodeo, as a recreational variant of everyday herding or raiding activity. No evidence supports the lurid notion, advanced to horrify tourists during the 1960s and 1970s, that the game was originally played with live human prisoners.

In recent generations other ethnic groups in north-

ern Afghanistan have started to play buzkashi: Tajiks, Hazaras, and even Pushtun migrants from south of the Hindu Kush whose new prominence in the north was supported by central government policy. Another key development dates from 1955 when the central govern-ment, based in Kabul, hosted its first tournament on the birthday anniversary of King Mohammed Zahir. From the mid-1950s to the early 1980s, successive na-tional regimes hosted similar buzkashi competitions in Kabul. With the collapse of the authority of the central government during the Afghan-Soviet War (1979–1989), the tournament fell apart. In the 1990s, as political chaos continues, buzkashi has largely re-verted to its original status as a locally based pastime north of the Hindu Kush.

Rules and Play

Whatever its form and occasion, buzkashi depends on sponsorship of both the champion horses and riders and of the ceremonial event in which buzkashi is played. In the traditional, rural context of northern Afghanistan, both types of sponsorship are exercised by *khans,* men of social, economic, and political impor-tance who constitute the informal and ever-shifting power elite of local life. The *khans* breed, raise, and own the special horses whose bloodlines are proudly chron-icled and whose success in buzkashi contributes to owner status. *Khans* likewise employ specialist riders (*chapandazan*) for their prize horses. Most important of all is their sponsorship of the celebratory events called *toois* at which buzkashi is traditionally played. These are scheduled for winter, both because it is the agricultural slack season and because horses and rid-ers can play then without overheating.

Khans stage *toois* to celebrate ritual events such as a son's circumcision or marriage. While the ritual itself is generally a private, family affair, it provides the occa-sion for much wider gatherings whose centerpiece is a day or several days of buzkashi. It also represents a sta-tus-oriented initiative in which the social, economic, and political resources of the sponsor (*tooi-wala*) are publicly tested. If those resources prove sufficient and the *tooi* is a success, its sponsor's "name will rise." If not, the *tooi-walla*'s reputation can be ruined. Prepara-tions include the amassing of funds for food and prize money and the recruitment of nearby hosts for the hundreds of invited guests who, the sponsor hopes, will accept invitations to attend. Equally hopeful but like-wise problematic is the expectation that the guests will present the sponsor with cash gifts to help defray the costs of the *tooi.*

After a ceremonial first day's lunch, everyone mounts and rides to the buzkashi field: sponsor, closest associates, invited *khans,* their sizable entourages (including prize horses, *chapandazan,* and assorted associates who have come in the name of "friendship" but can be quickly mobilized in case of serious conflict), and the local populace. The field itself typically consists of a barren plain, unbounded and undemarcated, on the village periphery. A goat or calf carcass lies in the middle. (While the term buzkashi specifically refers to "goat," calf carcasses are often used because, it is said, they last longer.) Without ceremony but in accordance with Muslim law (*hallal*), the animal has been bled to death, decapitated, and dehooved to protect contestants' hands. An eviscerated carcass makes for faster play, but purists tend to favor a heavier, ungutted animal so that only real power, rather than mere quickness, will prevail.

Most traditional buzkashis begin without fanfare and gather intensity as more and more participants arrive. Any number may take part, and some games involve hundreds of riders at once. A morning or afternoon session consists of several dozen play cycles, each of which starts with the riders forming an equestrian scrum over the dead calf. With their horses lurching, rearing, and trying to hold position, riders lean down from the saddle and grab at the carcass. More horses and riders batter their way toward the center of an ever-growing, ever more fiercely contested mass of wild movement. Lunging half-blind in the melee, one rider manages to grab hold of the carcass briefly, but, as a saying goes, "Every calf has four legs," and other riders quickly wrench it away. The calf is trampled, dragged, tugged, lifted, and lost again as one competitor after another seeks to gain sole control. There are no teams although friendly riders (or the riders of friendly *khans*) may sometimes assist each other. Everyone has the right to try, but play is monopolized in practice by the *chapandazan* in their distinctive fur-trimmed headgear. Meanwhile the "town crier" (*jorchi*) shouts the amount of prize money offered. The longer a given play cycle is contested, the greater that amount grows and the fiercer the competition.

Finally one horse and rider emerge from the mass (*tudabarai*), take the calf free and clear, and drop it in uncontested triumph. Play stops for a brief moment while the town crier launches into a stylized praise chant for the rider, the horse, and most of all the horse owner:

Oh, the horse of Hajji Ali,
On him rode Ahmad Gul.
He leapt like a deer.

He glared like a leopard.
How he took it away.
How he showed what he is.
How the name of Hajji Ali rose.
How we all hear his name.
How his pride is complete.

Prizes for the victorious rider once took the form of carpets, rifles, and even horses. Now almost all are cash, with amounts depending on *tooi* sponsor liberality and sometimes exceeding $100. The horse owner's sole reward is prestige or "name," that amorphous but most important currency of traditional Afghan life.

Barely has the chant finished before the next play cycle starts. Cycle follows cycle with no sense of cumulative score. The last cycle each day, typically played with a carcass in shreds, has special value, and the winning rider proudly departs with the tattered calf dangling across his saddle. The visiting *khans* and their entourages then retire for dinner and sleep at one or another of the nearby host houses where every event of the past day is reviewed in conversation: whose horse did well, whether the prize money was sufficient, and—most of all—what happened in case of serious dispute. Disputes and the issue of who can control them represent the darker, less readily admitted core of interest in buzkashi.

Three factors contribute to dispute in traditional buzkashi. First, the play activity itself is already full of physically brutal contact. Second, the question of being sufficiently "free and clear" for a score is notoriously subjective and difficult to adjudicate. And third, the horse-owner *khans,* whose horses and riders compete, are very often rivals of each other in the real-life game of local politics. Indeed it is during buzkashi that such rivalries and alliances, otherwise hidden by the diplomatic niceties of day-to-day existence, are revealed in all their disruptive potential.

It takes little to trigger a dispute. Had a victory claimant really gotten the carcass "free and clear" before dropping it? Was one rider guilty of grabbing another's bridle or whipping him in the face? Did the *chapandaz* of Mujib Khan have a rope secreted in his sleeve in order to enhance his grasp of the carcass? Suddenly the violent pushing and shoving, hitherto "for fun," now becomes "for real." Each *khan's* entourage coalesces around him. The current play cycle is abandoned and the air is full of angry shouts as everyone tries to gain control of an increasingly uncontrollable situation.

While outright fighting is rare, an aggrieved group may leave the buzkashi and go home rather than suffer perceived injustice. Such defection tarnishes the reputation of a *tooi* and thus of its *tooi-wala*. More typically the shouting and jostling gradually subside as one or another of the *khans* makes himself heard and emerges in the role of peacemaker. Much prestige thereby attaches to him. He has, after all, demonstrated an ability to control volatile events, to impress his will on a dynamic that had shifted from playful to political. Now his "name will rise" in the countless tellings and retellings of this buzkashi. Such reputational gain can then be of considerable importance as potential followers calculate the benefits of attaching themselves to a patron or of taking sides in a real-world dispute over land, water, livestock, or women.

Beginning in the mid-1950s, Afghanistan's central government likewise began to enlist buzkashi in its efforts at political impression management. The Afghan National Olympic Committee was charged with staging a "national tournament" in Kabul each year on the birthday of King Mohammed Zahir. Provincial contingents were organized in the north (as yet unlinked by all-weather roads to the rest of the country), and the game itself was transformed into a more or less codified sport (*qarajai*) with uniformed teams, authorized referees, a demarcated field of play (the *qarajai*), a cumulative scoring system, and severe penalties (including arrest) for any form of dispute during play. Only the players (typically 10 or 12 per team) and the referees (usually military officers) were allowed on the field. Horse-owner *khans,* their *tooi*-sponsorship role now co-opted by the government, had to sit on the sidelines. And instead of having the vague "free-and-clear" objective of *tudabarai,* players now had to carry the calf around a flag and drop it in clearly marked circle (the *daiwra*). The king assumed the role of national *tooi-wala,* hosting the tournament banquet and presented the championship medals. The tournament allowed Kabul residents to rub elbows with rustic horsemen from the distant north. And the northerners returned home each year with fresh tales of a broader Afghanistan and potent impressions of the central government's capacity for control.

By the time of the king's fall from power in 1973, the Kabul buzkashi tournament had become a fixture in the national calendar. Subsequent nonroyalist regimes retained the October timing but shifted the occasion

first (under President Mohammed Daoud, 1973–1977) to United Nations Day and then (under communist rule) to the anniversary of the 1917 Bolshevik Revolution. Always presented in the name of sheer play and fun, Kabul buzkashi tournaments continued to serve as a symbol both of Afghan national unity and of governmental capacity for dispute-free control. The nationwide collapse of Afghan government control in the early 1980s was reflected in the year-by-year disintegration of Kabul buzkashi. In Daoud's era, the tournament had lasted 12 days and featured ten provincial teams in a precisely orchestrated round-robin. From 1980 onward, fewer teams came each year. By 1983 the Soviet puppet government had abandoned all pretense of staging buzkashi.

During the Afghan-Soviet War (1979–1989), buzkashi was played in Pakistan's North West Frontier province by refugees based in Peshawar and Chitral. Many of the same *khans* and riders who had dominated the game in prewar Afghanistan now formed the core of competitions played on Fridays in the winter months. Now, however, the principal *tooi-wala* role shifted to several men whose newly developed renown rested on their leadership of local refugee relief efforts. As usual, all was done in the name of fun, but soon the new breed of sponsor-entrepreneurs were competing to attract resource-rich spectators from the fast-growing expatriate community: diplomats, United Nations personnel, and directors of nongovernmental aid organizations. Thus ingratiated with their "guests," these *tooi-walas* in exile promoted themselves as conduits for international aid to the refugee community.

By the mid-1990s, the central government in post-Soviet Afghanistan was still too weak to resume the national tournament and the main locus of buzkashi had reverted to the northern provinces. Some traditional *khans* still sponsored *toois,* but local warlords and militia commanders were replacing them in the primary sponsorship role.

—G. WHITNEY AZOY

Bibliography: Azoy, G. Whitney. (1982) *Buzkashi: Game and Power in Afghanistan.* Philadelphia: University of Pennsylvania Press. Michaud, Roland, and Sabrina Michaud. (1988) *Horsemen of Afghanistan.* London: Thames and Hudson.

Camogie

Camogie is a modified form of hurling with 12 players per team and is Ireland's national field sport for women. The game resembles hurling (an exclusively male sport), although physical contact is more restricted. Players score points by successfully hurling a ball between crossbars on goal posts.

History

Camogie was first played in 1904, when Irish women had limited opportunities to participate in sport. Female members of the Gaelic League, the national language movement, decided to found a game that was both distinctly Gaelic and strictly female. In developing camogie in and around Dublin, they modified the Irish national field game of hurling but maintained use of the stick, which symbolized Irish nationalism and Gaelic culture. The Camogie Association of Ireland, founded in 1904, still governs the sport.

The game did not spread much beyond Dublin until the development of competition in the universities, with women from Dublin, Belfast, Cork, and Galway competing in the annual intervarsity competition, the Ashbourne Cup, first held in 1915. However, while subscribing to the ideals of the Gaelic Athletic Association (GAA), the Camogie Association remained distinct, giving Irish women a voice in the fostering of nationalism, feminism, and Gaelic sport.

In the 1930s, the Camogie Association tried to increase its sphere of influence beyond the major Irish cities. It reorganized on a national basis and founded an All-Ireland championship for county teams, mirroring the organization of hurling. The game has contin-ued to spread. Now its areas of strength, like its rules and style of play, parallel even more closely those of its brother game, hurling.

Rules and Play

The camogie field is a maximum of 110 meters (120 yards) long and 68 meters (75 yards) wide. The stick (*camog*) is shorter and lighter than hurling's "hurley" (*caman*) and the ball is also lighter than the "slitter" (*sliothar*). The rules of camogie closely resemble those of hurling, although the "H"-shaped goal posts of hurling have been modified by the addition of a second crossbar. One point is scored when the ball passes between the crossbars, and three points are scored when the ball is driven below the lower crossbar and into the goal.

Camogie has shown few signs of catching on outside of Ireland, and its proponents seem not to aspire to international status. However, within Ireland, the sport continues to be enjoyed in its own right and to express both nationalist and feminist sentiments.

—TIMOTHY J. L. CHANDLER

See also Hurling.
Bibliography: Carroll, Noel. (1979) *Sport in Ireland.* Dublin: Department of Foreign Affairs.

Canoeing and Kayaking

Canoeing is the use of a popular and versatile category of small, lightweight, narrow craft with a shallow bottom. Initially used for transportation, canoeing is now a popular recreational and competitive sport with Olympic status. Contemporary canoes come in two basic styles, known as Canadian canoes and kayaks. Canadian canoes usually have an open deck; kayaks are enclosed with a small passenger cockpit. They are usually powered and steered by paddles held by the canoeist.

Canadian-canoe paddles have a blade (the wide section placed in the water) at one end. Kayak paddles have blades at both ends. The term canoeing refers specifically to the use of Canadian-style canoes, while the use of kayaks is called kayaking. Both are frequently referred to as canoes because of their common characteristics. Competitive canoe races, for example, often include divisions for kayaks.

History

Canoes were important in many cultures largely because of their versatility. Their design allows them to move very efficiently in both shallow and deep water, permitting travel on open seas or through rivers and lakes. Canoes were used to carry warriors into battle, or for fishing and hunting. A direct ancestor of the modern Canadian canoe was the bark canoe developed by Native Americans. These lightweight canoes could be carried (portaged) over the land, and they could be easily repaired.

The pointed kayak was developed by the Aleuts and Inuit of the far northern Arctic regions of America and Greenland. Kayaks were made by wrapping animal skins over a frame of wood or bone. These kayaks were very fast and maneuverable. Their covered, watertight decks protected the kayaker in turbulent, cold waters. If a kayak capsized, the passenger could right the boat by shifting his weight and maneuvering the paddle while he was underwater, a move now called an Eskimo roll.

Other methods of transportation gradually took over in the mid-19th century, and canoes were used more for recreation and competitive sport. In North America, people on wilderness vacations rode in canoes operated by expert guides. Recreational canoes also were used at resorts. Early interest in canoe sports was particularly strong in Europe. John McGregor, a lawyer, was an important early booster of the canoe in England and Europe, and his writings about the Rob Roy canoe—actually a kayak—promoted interest in that vessel.

In the late 19th and early 20th centuries, recreational canoeing continued to gain worldwide popularity. Specialized canoes and kayaks were developed, along with new competitive racing sports. Numerous organizations were formed to promote sport canoeing, including the American Canoe Association in 1880. In 1924, an international canoeing organization, the Internationella Representantskapet for Kanotidrott (IRK) was formed in Europe. Canoe racing was officially included in the Olympics for the first time in the 1936 Games in Berlin. After World War II, the IRK was succeeded by the International Canoe Federation.

In the middle and latter 20th century, canoeing benefited from the increasing emphasis on physical fitness and the popularity of outdoor activities. New local and national canoeing associations were formed, including the United States Canoe Association and the American White-Water Affiliation.

Rules and Play

Paddling is the basic skill of canoeing. Each individual movement of the paddle through the water is called a stroke. There are many styles and combinations of strokes. People develop personal paddling styles, and canoe enthusiasts often debate the merits of specific strokes.

Canadian-canoe and kayak paddling are both based on similar basic strokes and principles, but there are also differences. Because canoe paddles have only one blade, it is awkward to shift from one side to the other, so canoeists usually paddle primarily on one side of the boat (some do alternate sides in races and other circumstances). In open Canadian canoes, kneeling is the most efficient position for paddling in many situations. Canoeists also paddle from an upright sitting position, especially in calm waters. In kayaks, the paddler is usually seated in the cockpit, or on top of the hull, with legs extended in front. Kayakers can also more easily shift their strokes from one side to the other because they hold their paddles in the center with the two blades extending over the hull.

There are three basic categories of stroke for both canoes and kayaks. Power strokes propel the canoe forward, stop it, or push it backward. Turning strokes exert force on one side to either change the canoe's direction or to correct its course. The stabilizing, or bracing, stroke, is used to keep the craft level and upright.

A single stroke may combine the actions of a power, turning, or stabilizing stroke. The J-stroke, for example, is a basic movement that simultaneously propels the canoe and keeps it on a straight course by combining a forward stroke with a turning movement. The strokes also depend on the number of paddlers. A solo paddler must concentrate both on steering and powering the boat. When two or more people are paddling, these responsibilities are shared.

Paddles have differing sizes, shapes, and weights

that also determine which strokes are used. One paddle might be lightweight or have a narrow blade to make it easier to use, while another may be larger and heavier to provide more power. The blades and handles are often angled or shaped to make specific types of paddling more efficient.

White-water sports are a special category of boating. White-water paddling and rafting require specialized skills and fast reflexes, because the vessels move very quickly in turbulent water, among rocks, and other obstacles. In contrast to calm-water canoeing, where paddling is necessary to move the vessel forward, fast-moving currents naturally propel white-water craft. So the ability to slow down, stop, and turn quickly become the priorities. In addition to riding the crest of the fast-moving currents to go forward, white-water paddlers also steer into quieter eddies to slow down, to rest, and to aim their boats for the next stage of the run. In rapids, the white-water canoeist must also paddle across or against the currents when necessary.

Canoeists and rafters usually plan their runs in advance using maps and guidebooks published by boating organizations and publications. They rate individual rivers by categories of difficulty, so people can choose sites within their level of ability. While individual ratings methods may vary, rivers are generally designated as Class I—the calmest—to Class VI—the most difficult.

White-water paddlers and rafters also "read the river": study the water on the site before making an actual run, to judge water levels and other changeable conditions. These advance precautions are also advised for those who are using canoes and kayaks on water that appears calm, to avoid being caught in unexpected stretches of rapids or other hazards.

Safety is an important consideration in all forms of canoeing and kayaking. The canoe should be equipped with life jackets for passengers, and with other flotation devices and features to make it easier to turn the boat upright if it capsizes or is swamped. Warm clothing is also advised under cold conditions. In white-water boating and other risky situations, boaters wear helmets and other protective equipment.

Competitive Canoeing

Prominent canoeing sports include wild-water racing, slalom white-water events, and sprint or marathon racing on flat water. Many events include divisions for both canoes and kayaks, with canoes designated as C (or OC for open canoes) and kayaks as K. Classifications are also based on the number of people the boat can hold. A two-person Canadian canoe is classified as a C2; a one-person kayak is a K1. In addition to the Olympics, formal events with strict criterion sanctioned by a canoeing organization are held in many localities and on a national and international level. The specific race categories and rules may vary, depending on the guidelines of the sponsoring organization. Informal races are also popular.

Slalom canoe races are held either on rapidly running rivers or on artificial courses with simulated rapids, rocks, and other obstacles.

Wild-water races also take place on running rivers. However, the object in wild-water racing is to complete the course as quickly as possible, with no defined course of gates (except to mark dangerous sections).

Other types of canoe racing take place on calmer, open lakes, rivers or artificial pools. These include long-distance marathon races or short sprints. Here, endurance and the ability to paddle fast are the required skills. Sprint courses are often 500 meters (547 yards), 1,000 meters (1,094 yards), or as long as 10,000 meters (10,940 yards) or more. Marathon courses may be much longer.

Canoe polo is a fast-paced water sport in which teams of players in small one-person kayaks attempt to score points by maneuvering and passing a ball into the opponent's goal.

Other canoe and kayaking sports include mass-races, which are informal events with a large number of canoeists racing on open water. Competitions are also held in poling, sailing, and other specialized canoe sports. At times canoeing is incorporated with other activities into multisport endurance events. A triathlon that with activities like cycling or running, for example, may include a section where the participants paddle a canoe.

As means of transport, canoes have been replaced except in remote areas under extreme conditions. Their popularity for recreation and competition, however, appears unchallenged.

—JOHN TOWNES

Bibliography: Harrison, David. (1993) *Sea Kayaking Basics.* New York: Hearst Marine Books. Ray, Slim. (1992) *The Canoe Handbook.* Harrisburg, PA: Stackpole Books.

Carom Billiards
See Billiards

Carriage Driving

Carriage driving is an amateur equestrian sport in which drivers, horses, and vehicles are judged for appearance and performance in multiple events. The sport has no professional component and lacks Olympic status, although local, national, and international competitions are held regularly.

History

Coach driving began as a purely commercial practice, with professional coachmen paid to transport passengers and evolved into a sport of the affluent, the only people who could afford the vehicles, horses, and personnel needed. The creation of breeds suitable for carriage sports was likewise slower than those for flat racing and polo. Cross-breeding eventually produced carriage horses with the power of cold bloods and the speed and competitiveness of hot bloods.

The precursors of modern carriage-driving competitions, driving clubs were first instituted in England. Since 1958 there has been a British Driving Society, and the Coaching Club has been in existence for over 125 years. The Ascot race meeting traditionally has an enclosure for coaching club members.

Two critical elements fused at the beginning of the 19th century to lay the foundation of coaching as a sport in Europe and the United States. First, construction of roads became scientific and uniform, providing a safe and stable surface for carriages. Second, suspension systems for carriages came into vogue, and carriage design and workmanship lessened the tenor of carriage travel. Organized carriage driving competitions have existed in central Europe and Germany for a hundred years.

Four-in-hand driving as a hobby contracted sharply after World War I. Organized contests for carriage drivers did not develop until after World War II, and multinational European contests were initiated in the 1950s. Driving contests of the time generally included two phases: dressage and marathon. As a formally recognized international sport with uniform rules, however, combined driving has only recently passed the quarter-century mark.

Rules and Play

In 1969, the Fédération Equestre Internationale (FEI) drafted a set of standardized rules for carriage driving competitions, based on ridden three-day tests. The first test, dressage, includes two parts: presentation and the driven dressage test. Presentation requires that horses, equipment, driver, and grooms be cleanly turned out and correctly outfitted. The rules for this competition are based primarily on 19th-century driving standards. Opinion remains divided over whether such a "beauty" contest ought to be included in a combined driving event. Proponents suggest that it adds to the appeal of the sport and underscores the need for attention to detail the sport requires. Critics decry presentation as outdated and elitist. Scoring is based on how close a driver and team come to achieving perfection.

The second phase is known as the marathon, although the distance covered is usually about 17 miles (27 kilometers). This phase tests the fitness and stamina of the team and the driver's ability to maneuver the team through obstacles and complete the distances within a prescribed pace.

The greatest spectator appeal is during the final phase of the marathon. Drivers, belted onto their carriage seats, must drive with enough speed not to incur penalty points, as their grooms—acting as navigators—shout reminders from their posts on the backs of the marathon vehicles. They prompt drivers when needed to keep them on course through the confusing maze of gates, and they often throw their weight to one side or the other around a turn to shift the cart on the track, freeing a wheel or avoiding its entrapment on a gatepost or tree. As in dressage, penalties are scored and the low score wins.

A veterinary check before the final competition, the obstacles competition (colloquially known as the cones competition), verifies the horses' fitness to compete in the concluding contest, which tests the driver's ability to negotiate a technical course, as well as the horse's state after a grueling cross-country test the previous day.

In Europe, driving is a sport enjoyed by all ages, whereas in the United States it is primarily an adult sport. Most of the top drivers traditionally have been men, although the ranks of experienced women drivers have grown.

Throughout the world, carriage driving is an amateur sport. Prize money is minimal, and there are virtually no sponsorships of drivers or horses. Despite its amateur status, however, competitions, especially in Europe, draw sizable numbers of spectators.

Eastern European countries, traditionally preeminent in driving competitions, have had difficulty maintaining their state-owned stud farms and training centers as their economies change. However, despite the loss of state funding, carriage driving remains a popular sport throughout Europe and is gaining popularity in North America and elsewhere around the world. During the 1995 World Pairs Driving Championship in Poznan, Poland, a record number of countries competed.

Like many equestrian sports, carriage driving requires an investment of time, money, and training that restricts its serious practice to the affluent, particularly given its amateur status and lack of prize money. Its popular appeal seems likely to remain limited but secure.

—KATHERINE LINCOLN

Bibliography: The Duke of Edinburgh. (1982) *Competition Carriage Horse Driving.* Macclesfield, UK: Horse Drawn Carriages Limited. Pape, Max. (1982) *The Art of Driving.* New York: J. A. Allen.

Chariot Racing

Chariot races survive today only in the form of harness racing, a sport far less thrilling and less dangerous than the chariot races of classical times. The origins of chariot racing are not fully known, but it was a major public sport and spectacle in ancient Greece and Rome. It declined with the decline of Rome and, with the chariot, has disappeared as a cultural activity.

History

Chariot racing could not have emerged before the domestication of horses and the invention of the two-wheeled light chariot, preconditions fulfilled at the beginning of the second millennium B.C.E., but it is not known for sure where the first races took place. Archeological evidence suggests that eastern Anatolia played a leading role in the first phase of horse-taming and chariot-making; other possible sites include Mesopotamia, among the Hittites, or in ancient Egypt. By the middle of the second millennium B.C.E., it was known not only in Egypt and the ancient Near East but also in India and among the Mycenean Greeks. (Somewhat later, chariots appeared in China as well.) Chariots were culturally important as status symbols, which gave the chariot race a certain aristocratic flair. The oldest depictions of chariot races come from late Mycenean Greece in the 13th century B.C.E. In Greece, the sport experienced its first great flowering.

The first unambiguous evidence is the first depiction of a chariot race on a late Mycenean amphora from the city Tiryns in southern Greece. On this 13th-century B.C.E. vase, as in later sources, chariot racing appears in conjunction with a funeral ritual. The most vividly detailed account appears in Book XXIII of Homer's *Iliad* where he describes the chariot race as the most splendid sporting event in the funeral games held in honor of Achilles' friend Patroclus, slain by the Trojan hero Hector. Homer's account of the race is more than twice as long as his report on the other seven athletic events, a statement about the importance of chariot racing.

Grave Inscription for Crescens.

Crescens, charioteer for the "Blues," of moorish birth, 22 years old.

With the four-horse chariot he won his first victory when L. Vipstanius and Messalla were the consuls [ca. C.E. 115–116] on the day of the races in honor of the birthday of the divine Nerva in the twenty-fourth race with the following horses: Circius, Acceptor, Delicatus, Cotynus. From the consulship of Messalla to the races for the birthday of the divine Claudius in the consulship of Glabrio [ca. C.E. 124–125] he started 686 times and won 47 times. In single races, he was victorious 19 times, in double races 23 times, in triple races 5 times. Once he overtook the entire field from behind. 8 times he won with a lead. 38 times he won by means of a final spurt. He won 130 second places and 111 third places. In prize money, he took in 1,558,346 sesterces.

After the Homeric age, chariot racing remained a popular sport for centuries. No important athletic meet was complete without a chariot race, and the chariot race was often the high point of an athletic festival. Until the very end of the race's Greek history it remained an aristocratic—at times even a royal—property, unsurprising given the expense of a stable of horses and the costs of sending a four-horse chariot to Olympia.

Chariot races figure frequently in the visual arts of Etruscan civilization, where they clearly had a significant place, especially in the first half of the 5th century B.C.E. In eleven different tombs, chariot races can be seen in frescoes of the highest quality and are a motif in ceramics and in stone and bronze reliefs. The depictions of chariot races—and other sports—in tomb frescoes strongly suggest that they were a part of funeral games in honor of the deceased. Etruscan evidence shows characteristics of the sport unknown in Greek iconography—such as the use of a crash helmet and the custom of knotting the reins tightly at the charioteer's back.

Chariot races reached their height of popularity in Roman times, in Rome's huge *Circus Maximus*. The satirical poet Juvenal's famous reference to *panem et circenses* ("bread and circuses") expressed his dismay at a public depoliticized and deprived of its rights by the ancient equivalent of food stamps and football games. Victorious charioteers enjoyed great fame and received immense sums in prize money. The Romans left monumental material evidence of their passion for chariot racing. From the *Imperium Romanum* 74 large-format structures have survived, some of them in excellent condition. Outside of Rome, the chief geographical centers of chariot racing were southern Spain, North Africa, and the Near East (Syria, Palestine, Egypt). The northernmost "circus" was constructed in what is now the German city of Trier (*Augusta Treverorum*).

The last chariot races held in the city of Rome took place in 549 C.E. under Totila, king of the conquering Ostrogoths. When the seat of empire was shifted to Byzantium (renamed Constantinople), chariot races continued until the Crusaders seized the city in 1204.

After the fall of Rome, the passion for chariot races survived in the Hippodrome at Constantinople, the capital of the Byzantine Empire, where they became a part of official state ceremony. Although the seizure of the city by Crusaders, in 1204, briefly interrupted the races, they resumed after the intruders were expelled and continued until the conquest of Constantinople by the Ottoman Turks in 1453.

The rule that declared the owner of the chariot to be the victor, rather than the charioteer, allowed women who were otherwise excluded from the Olympic Games to become Olympic victors. The first was the Spartan princess Cynisca, whose victor's inscription proudly testifies to her lineage. Among the later victors was Queen Berenice, the wife of Ptolemy III of Egypt.

Rules and Play

Conventions of chariot racing varied by region. Rome provides one example: The chariots started when the games' sponsor dropped a white cloth. At the same time, a mechanical device opened the gates of the starting boxes (*carceres*), which were staggered across the width of the stadium in order to give every chariot an equal opportunity to reach the breakpoint.

The usual distance for a race was seven rounds, approximately 4 kilometers (2.5 miles). Since roughly 15 minutes were required to complete a race, it may have been possible hold up to 24 races in a day. Between races it was customary to keep the spectators entertained with running, jumping, and throwing events or other "pause fillers." The standings of the factions were indicated by means of a movable "scoreboard" consisting of seven artificial dolphins or seven oversized eggs.

Most charioteers (*agitatores* or *aurigae*) came from the lower classes. Success, which sometimes meant frequent changes in team membership, brought not only great fame but also a substantial income. Roman chariot races are best understood, from a sports-historical perspective, if one compares them with modern soccer (association football) games; they even kept detailed statistics.

Professional charioteers lived dangerous lives. A spill could all too easily take a driver's life. In an attempt to safeguard the charioteer from an accidental death, protective gear was developed; there were leather pads for the thighs and chest, and a leather crash helmet too. The charioteer carried a sharp knife with which, in the event of a crash, he could free himself from entangling reins.

Chariot racing enjoyed a brief revival in the 14th and 15th centuries when Renaissance scholars rediscovered Greek and Roman sports and were inspired to imitate the ancients. In Florence and elsewhere, they staged chariot races. They were not very successful and never reached the appeal of classical times centuries earlier.

—WOLFGANG DECKER

Bibliography: Cameron, Alan. (1976) *Circus Factions: Blues and Greens at Rome and Byzantium.* Oxford: Clarendon Press. Decker, Wolfgang. (1992) *Sports and Games of Ancient Egypt,* trans. by Allen Guttmann. New Haven, CT: Yale University Press. Humphrey, John H. (1986) *Roman Circuses: Arenas for Chariot Racing.* London: B. T. Batsford.

Climbing
See Mountain Climbing; Rock Climbing

Coaches and Coaching

Coaching has emerged as a critical profession in 20th-century sports. A coach plays a key role in an athlete's success, influencing both the athlete's performance and sense of personal fulfillment and, in the case of team sports, team culture and cohesion. A coach's primary responsibility remains the athlete, and the 1979 Bill of Rights for Young Athletes of the American Coaching Effectiveness Program endorses the philosophical ethos of the American Alliance for Health, Physical Education, Recreation and Dance (AAHPERD) Bill of Rights for Young Athletes, drawn up in 1979. Coaches place athletes first and winning second. People in sports generally seems to agree with the ethical guidelines of the Australian Coaching Council (ACC):

Respect the talent of all athletes and seek to develop their potential

Treat each athlete as a unique individual

Learn as much as you can about your sport and the disciplines which contribute to athlete excellence

Make sure that the period of time with you is a positive experience and self-enhancing for the athlete

Never deceive or mislead the athlete

Be fair and considerate

Be dignified and controlled and teach athletes to be likewise

Actively discourage the use of ergogenic or behavior-modifying drugs

History

Variants of coaching existed in early times. Ancient Greece and Rome had informal training for such activities as running, archery, and gladiatorial skills. The term *coach,* however, did not enter our vernacular until the latter 19th century, when "trainers" worked with teams or individual athletes through private clubs, or "masters" undertook coaching and instructional activities at private schools or colleges. *Professional* coaching positions did not become common until the mid-1900s.

Several factors are associated with the rise in coaching roles, both amateur and professional: the status of sport, the rise of international and national competition, the development of specialized knowledge and equipment, the organization of formal coaching schemes, the inclusion of physical education programs in educational institutions, and the ever-growing popularity of professional sport.

Coach Education and the Practice of Coaching

Formal coach education programs and accreditation have evolved since World War II. Canada and Australia both have internationally recognized coaching courses that develop common philosophies or areas of content across hemispherical boundaries. Instruction covers communication, teaching skills, athletic technique, biomechanics, sport psychology, leadership and management, nutrition, training, and group dynamics.

Expert advisers may be used to optimize the coaching role. The 1990s display the trend toward increasing collaboration between coaches and sport psychologists, recognizing that the mental aspect is as critical as the physical. The sport psychologist emphasizes goal setting, relaxation skills, visualization, motivation, and coping and concentration skills. This union is still developing toward a full and complementary partnership on all levels, including the international level.

Professional associations for coaches, both sport-specific and generic, abound, and programs, conferences, and journals are readily accessible to coaches for advice and information on new philosophies and technologies. Coaches have been the subject of assessment scales, such as the CBAS SCP, to provide insights from observers and athletes on coach personalities and practices.

Women as Coaches

An unexpected and unwelcome effect of Title IX, the 1972 U.S. law that opened intercollegiate sports to women, was a dramatic decrease in the number of women in management positions in sports. This has been especially controversial in the most visible of management positions, the on-field coach. It is argued that coaches of women's teams should always be women, because women's sports should be controlled by women, because women are more sensitive to the needs of women athletes, and because having men as coaches creates new problems such as sexual harassment and physical abuse. They also point out that there are virtually no women coaches of men's teams. Others argue, however, that coaches should be selected based on their knowledge and experience, and if this principle is followed in sports such as basketball and soccer at least some coaches will be men. In December 1998 the issue again became the subject of public debate when critics complained that 5 of the 12 coaches in the Women's Basketball Association were men.

Coaches have many responsibilities, to themselves, their athletes, and the public. They must respond favorably to the numerous pressures resulting from public expectation, parental concern, athlete diversity, ethical issues, constant technological and physiological advances, and staffing issues, while maintaining personal satisfaction, self-esteem, and positive relationships in both the personal and professional spheres in order to function successfully. Since a coach is held liable by others for team/athlete performance results, outstanding coaches usually receive considerable public recognition and media attention for their coaching triumphs. They often become part of a virtual sport folklore that includes well-known figures such as Vince Lombardi (1913–1970) in American football, Fred Allen (1920–) in rugby, John Wooden (1910–) in basketball, and Joyce Brown in netball.

A fundamental element of athlete success lies in an athlete's complete acceptance of the coach's philosophies and actions. Young athletes' positive sport experiences are influenced by their coaches. Although the athletes may become more self-determining and self-directed in their learning and development, they still value the athlete-coach relationship to the highest levels.

Women and members of certain ethnic groups have been markedly underrepresented in coaching, reflecting the dominance of white men in sport. For example, the Black Coaches Association (BCA) in the United States has suggested that African Americans hold a disproportionately small number of coaching positions in the 1990s. For women seeking to coach, the situation is further compounded by the female's dependency on male coaches. In addition, the processes of coach selection may utilize informal networks that are currently oriented toward males or white males. Given the cultural diversity of athletic groups, gender and ethnic sensitivity would most likely enhance coach-athlete relationships and team dynamics, in addition to fostering player self-esteem. Following general societal trends, coaching seems likely to become more diverse; for example, the National Basketball Association is actively working to increase the number of its African-American coaches.

—ROBIN MCCONNELL

Bibliography: McKee, S. (1994) *Coach.* Mechanicsburg, PA: Stackpole Books. Martens, R. (1991). *Successful Coaching.* Champaign, IL: Leisure Press. Walton, G. M. (1992) *Beyond Winning: The Timeless Wisdom of Great Philosopher Coaches.* Champaign, IL: Leisure Press.

Coaching (Four-in-Hand)
See Carriage Driving

Cockfighting

Cockfighting, the contesting of specially bred male chickens, is a blood sport, that subset of sports heavily reliant on the likelihood of injury, bloodletting, or death. In cockfighting, throughout its many variations, the bird acts as a surrogate for the owner or handler. While wagers may ride on the performance of a particular rooster, the communal display of virile zeal is more important.

From this perspective, the human participant in a cockfight, in spite of the obvious violence, views him- or herself (more frequently him) as taking part in a sport, not engaging in animal cruelty. In his well-known study of Balinese cockfighting, Clifford Geertz explores the notion that cockfighting reflects the basest component of humanity. Yet he shows too that cockfighting is multifaceted, with elements that extend beyond the gory spectacle.

History

The chicken's history is considerably more glorious than its present. Thought to be prophetic, the chicken bird was pampered, cultivated, and desired both for its special relationship with the sun and as a provider of magic-laden plumes. Partly for this reason, the keeping of chickens, though not necessarily for food, spread from Southeast Asia through much of Africa, up through Iran, and through many Pacific islands. Long-

ago Aryan invaders of India learned to enjoy cockfights and held the birds in great esteem. By 1000 B.C.E. they forbade any peoples under their control to eat chicken.

Evidence shows that the birds were raised, presumably for sport and ritual, by the Celts, Gauls, and ancient Britons. Chickens were reportedly introduced into Greece about 524–460 B.C.E. with the associated sport spreading throughout Asia Minor and Sicily. From Rome, the pastime moved northward and became popular throughout Italy, Germany, Spain and its eventual colonies, and through England, Wales, and Scotland. In some areas, especially among maritime nations quick to see the advantages, fowl were reared for food. Chickens could well endure the life at sea and provided fresh meat and eggs, but were also used to forecast the future and for entertainment.

Cockfighting is so old and widely distributed that examples of its imprint on language, design, and decoration are easy to find. In today's English language, examples include the words "cock's egg," a malformed egg, and "cockney," a "malformed" variation of the English accent. Because of roosters' image of pugnacity and courage, an insouciant fellow may be called a "coxcomb" and an overconfident person "cocky" or "cocksure." A disappointed person may be described as "crestfallen."

The magic quality of the cock greeting the dawn is evidenced by the rooster-shaped windvanes and weathervanes that grace so many barns and homes. Since antiquity, images and language using the cock motif have been commonplace when trying to convey ideas related to courage, durability, magic, robustness, patriotism, and aggressiveness. The cock is virtually the national symbol of France, and is frequently used on clothing and other advertising.

Rules and Play

Cockfighting is very widespread and exists in several forms. Depending on geography, cocks fight "bare-heeled," with attached blades, or with "spurs," "harpoons," or "gaffs." Tools attached to the fowl for the fight may be made from ivory, tortoise shell, bone, specially prepared chicken spurs (superimposed over the bird's normal one), plastic, brass, and even alloy cut from jet turbine engine blades. And there are "boxing" events in which the fowl's real spur is covered by padded "gloves" to keep from severely injuring his opponent.

Cockfighting is still an important pastime available across America, Europe, and elsewhere. Magazines cater to enthusiasts, and several craftspeople, like specialist jewelers, fabricate the blades, gaffs, and harpoons used

Bath Prophecy.

On the 30th of March 1809, the destruction of the city of Bath was to have been effected by a convulsion of the earth, which should cause "Beacon-hill to meet Beechen Cliff." This inauspicious junction was said to have been foretold by an old woman, who had derived her information from an angel. This reported prophecy rendered many of the inhabitants truly unhappy, and instigated crowds of visitors to quit the city. The portentous hour, 12 o'clock, passed, and the believers were ashamed of their former fears. The alarm is said to have originated with two noted cock-feeders, who lived near the aforementioned hills; they had been at a public house, and, after much boasting on both sides, made a match to fight their favorite cocks on Good Friday, which fell on this day; but fearing the magistrates might interfere, if it became public, they named the cocks after their respective walks, and in the agreement it was specified that "Mount Beacon would meet Beechen Cliff, precisely at twelve o'clock on Good Friday." The match was mentioned with cautions of secrecy to their sporting friends, who repeated it in the same terms, and with equal caution, until it came to the ears of some credulous beings, who took the words in their plain sense; and, as stories seldom lose by being repeated, each added what fear or fancy framed, until the report became a marvelous prophecy, which in its intended sense was fulfilled; for the cocks of Mount Beacon and Beechen Cliff met and fought, and left their hills behind them on their ancient sites, to the comfort and joy of multitudes, who had been infected by the epidemical prediction.

—*From Willaim Hone, ed.*, The Year Book of Daily Recreation and Information, *1832.*

in the bouts. Though certainly part of a fringe entertainment in most of the West, cockfighting provides a sound enough infrastructure to support a number of businesses. In some areas of the world the sport is fully engaged in the economy, much as baseball is in the United States.

Descriptions of cockfights around the world suggest much general similarity in rules and play.

Although there are local, regional, and national differences, cockfights around the world have a number of common features. Common structural features include the differential valuation of different categories of fights, a regional basis for betting, betting being an integral part of virtually every fight, protocol enforced regarding the wagering and the performance of the cock handlers, and, usually, an attempt to match fowl in some reasonable way (usually by size).

In addition, cockfights usually progress through a predictable series of steps: (1) bout preliminaries including picking cocks, prepping them, and showing them to the crowd and competition; (2) the business of betting; (3) placing the cocks in the ring and the almost invariable fighting that follows; (4) resolution of bets; and (5) initiation of the next bout. The fight itself continues until one of the cocks is killed or is so injured that it cannot continue. It seems that the goal is not for one cock to kill the other, but for the birds to display "heart" and gameness.

A Louisiana Cockfight

The southern Louisiana cockfights observed by the author took place in a very new cockpit that had been near a small, rural complex containing a horse track, bars, and small restaurants. The contemporary-style metal quick-fab building featured basic bleachers and a simple bar. The pit building fronted a large parking area and boasted an attractive, well-lit sign with its name and the word "cockpit" prominently displayed. Nothing about the situation seemed furtive, although other pits are frequently in out-of-the-way locations.

The pit was assembled from metal reinforcing-bar and hardware cloth. The ring or pit was raised slightly above the surrounding earth. Concrete covered most of the area, but not the pit or a small rectangular area into which dead chickens were tossed and in which the heel attachments were put on. There were both a main pit and a "drag" pit available where long or unusual fights could be finished.

The birds, which are lavished with attention and generally fed special meals as part of the preparation, were kept in custom-built individual carriers. Matches were made among the breeders and owners. The game cocks were informally presented to the crowd.

Wagering, clearly important to the event, generally occurs at this point. Bets may be trivial—buying the next round of drinks—but overall the event was a form of "serious play." The fights between evenly matched birds are straightforward, but are also part of a variety of competition patterns. Each region offers particular styles of organizing the matches, including informal pairs, derbies, melees, and other increasingly complex forms.

Before each fight, the contestants were examined by an "official" who looked under the wings and into the eyes, shook the game cock, and thrust a lemon down over each spur to verify that the weapon was well attached and sturdy. Last, the official wet a cotton ball and wiped down the metal weapons. He squeezed the remaining water into the cock's mouth and discarded the ball. The cocks were then paired by weight and weapon. Their attachments are designed to be uniform for a fair event, not to be more brutal, as is sometimes claimed. The weapons may be edged so they can both slash and pierce. In Louisiana these competitors are called "slashers." Gaff cockers claim the slashers are less sophisticated and more brutal.

Once in the pit area, the fighting cocks quickly assume their combat positions, with feathers out and chest forward. Beady eyes glinting, the competitors clash after a few cackled threats. Their strikes are extraordinarily fast. The target is clearly the opponent's head, which involves leaping up, twisting around, and stabbing backward with the metal spurs or other heel appliance. Often the exchange continues until one bird is dead. At that point the winner may also be in poor condition, possibly having been gouged in the eyes or repeatedly stabbed in the head, body, and wings. Sometimes if a bird is "chicken" the match is ceded and the appropriate neck wrung. Most fights are fast, but long bouts are not unusual. These involve lengthy periods of one of the birds chasing his opponent around and around the ring—a standoff resolved either by one bird's sudden action or by an owner stopping the match. As their courage ebbs and flows, the birds fluff up for the attack or smooth down to try to escape.

Participants in cockfighting events often openly show adoration for their birds, fondling, petting, and cooing soothingly to them. Because the game fowl's *raison d'être* is to seek dominance among his kind, cockfighters see their role as a positive one of support, not a negative one of predatory delight in the fights. Cockfighters believe their birds are happiest when allowed to exhibit prowess in the fight, contesting the ground with a fairly matched opponent.

Depending on your point of view, the cocker is not a rebel but a traditionalist. The modern cocker, considered a pariah in many circles, is subjected to increasing pressure to conform to the different, though not necessarily more salubrious, values and behaviors of his or her antagonists. When opponents of cockfighting call participants barbarians, villains, scofflaws, and so on, they valorize the pursuit in some people's minds. The journals serving the fraternity are saturated with descriptions of participants as "good men," "the best sort of man," "a man's man," and so on. It is easy to get the implication about nonparticipants.

—JON GRIFFIN DONLON

Bibliography: Donlon, J. (1990) "Fighting Cocks, Feathered Warriors, and Little Heroes." *Play & Culture* 3: 273–285. Dundes, Alan. (1994) *The Cockfight: A Casebook.* Madison: University of Wisconsin Press. Geertz, Clifford. (1972) "Deep Play: Notes on the Balinese Cockfight." *Daedalus, The Journal of the American Academy* 101 (Winter): 1–37. Smith, Page, and Charles Daniel. (1975) *The Chicken Book.* Boston: Little, Brown.

Commercialization

The commercialization of sports is that aspect of the sports enterprise that involves the sale, display, or use of sport or some aspect of sport so as to produce income. Some experts prefer the term "commodification of sport" as a label for the same process.

Interest in the commercialization of sport has existed for several decades, but only in recent years has the phenomenon has been taken seriously on a larger scale. The first attention came from a small group of critical, mostly leftist writers, who have now been joined by people from all political and social perspectives.

History

The commercialization of sport is not a cultural universal, but a product of unique technical, social, and economic circumstances. Sports in the colonial United States were usually unstructured, spontaneous activities that the participants initiated, coordinated, and managed. Only in the latter part of the 19th century did organized sport cross the ocean from Great Britain and arrive in America. At that time, urbanization forced a large number of people to live in new settings and to abandon traditional leisure activities, which included drinking, carousing, and gambling. The dominant class sought to replace them with activities such as baseball, horseracing, and boxing.

Setting the stage for future commercialization, industry moved to meet the burgeoning desire for organized sports. The most prominent producer of sports equipment was Albert Spaulding. In 1876, he opened the A. G. Spaulding and Brothers Company. Spaulding's ability to influence the organizers of the various professional sports leagues allowed him to sell his goods and to capture a virtual monopoly on sporting goods by the latter part of the 19th century. But others quickly followed, and by the beginning of the 20th century, began producing their own lines of sports equipment.

During the first two decades of the 20th century, the growth in sales of sporting goods and services glittered brighter than ever. Commercial spectator sports attrracted the interest of much of the population. Commercialized sports was one of several male bastions. However, the by the 1920s, women began to take an interest in both watching sports and participating in sports. Although the commercialization of sports slowed during the Great Depression and World War II, by the early 1950s it had solidly established itself as feature of modern Western culture.

Professional Sports

Professional sports, a big business that has grown rapidly over the last three decades, may be the epitome of commercialization, its influence pervasive throughout. Athletes, support personnel (managers, coaches, officials, media persons, lawyers, and agents), and sports team owners benefit handsomely from the willingness of sports fans to pay to watch their favorite sports and to purchase the commodities endorsed by sports personalities. Hundreds of professional athletes earn well over $1 million a year. Before 1977, $1 million contracts did not exist. By 1994 there were well over 200 professional athletes who earned salaries in excess of $1 million. In 1990, reported average 1989 salaries for athletes in four different professional sports stood at $577,200 in the National Basketball Association, $490,000 in the national baseball leagues, $212,000 in the National Football League, and $156,000 in the National Hockey League. *Forbes*'s 1994 list of the top-earning athletes included basketball stars Michael Jordan at $30 million and Shaquille O'Neal at $17 million, golfers Jack Nicklaus at $15 million and Arnold Palmer at $14 million, and boxers Micheal Moore and Evander Holyfield at $12 million each. In most cases, athletes' endorsements make up over 90 percent of their earnings.

Owners of professional sports franchises are some of the wealthiest people in the world. They continue to make large profits from their sports teams. In the United States there are about 110 professional sports franchises, including football, basketball, baseball, and hockey. The combined revenues of these four sports leagues equaled $5.1 billion in 1993. In addition to the money from gate receipts and television revenues, owners realize profits through the buying and selling of franchises. Sports franchises are very profitable short- and long-term investments. For example, the Dallas Cowboys football team was purchased for $600,000 in 1960. In 1989 the team sold for $140 million.

The profits for the players, owners, and other associates of professional sports come from various sources. One source, the fares paid at the gates for the opportunity to see one's favorite professional players or teams, continues to increase. By 1998, with good seats, $3 hot dogs, and $15 parking fees, it costs over $200 for a family of four to go to National League Football and National Basketball Association games.

Olympic Games

The ideal of the modern Olympic Games stands in stark opposition to the commercialism of sports. However, many commentators have argued that this idealism has been compromised to the point that the Olympics is currently the epitome of commercialism. In the early part of the 20th century 98 percent of the Games' amateur competitors made no money from their participation. In contrast, today's Olympic athletes are far from amateurs. The International Olympic Committee recognized the inevitable creep of commercialism and professionalism, and instead of requiring participants to be amateurs they merely ask that participants have an "amateur spirit."

The Games have also come under criticism because of the movement toward corporate sponsorship. While most Olympic administrators recognize the need for support from the private sector, there is concern about how much help and control should be exchanged. Private enterprises that range from soft drink producers to automobile companies compete to be an official sponsor of the games. For example Coca-Cola paid $22 million for the guarantee that no competitive soft drinks be allowed to display the Olympic symbol for the Seoul Games.

Intercollegiate Sports

Sports at the university and college level, many argue, are big-time entertainment businesses, not collections of students striving merely to achieve physical, mental, and moral health. Over the past 140 years, student control has been replaced, and the commercial aspect of the activities has grown immensely. Many universities have athletic budgets in excess of $12 million, football bowl games generate $30 million for the teams, teams for the men's intercollegiate basketball championships earn $1.37 million, and the National Collegiate Athletic Association has annual profits of approximately $9 million.

Mass Media

The mass media have been linked to the commercialization of sports. They exist in a symbiotic relationship with sports, each benefiting greatly from the other. Sports employs all forms of the mass media. Books and magazines that specialize in particular sports are published regularly. Newspapers often devote up to one-third of their nonadvertising space to sports coverage. Radio stations all over the country have changed their menu to include 24-hour coverage of sports.

However, television has affected sports most profoundly. Television and sports are involved in a relationship in which the economic stakes are very high.

Television contracts for the coverage of professional, Olympic, and college events reach billions of dollars. The return on the investment by the major television networks is just as impressive.

Television has altered individual sports in the effort to accommodate larger viewing audiences. In some sports, additional time-outs have been implemented to allow for more commercials. In tennis, the rules regarding play-offs have been changed to allow matches to fit into prescribed schedules. The scheduling of events in the Olympic Games has been modified not to provide athletes with the optimum conditions for peak athletic performances, but to allow large audiences in the United States to view events at more convenient times.

Gambling

A rise in gambling on sporting events has been an indirect consequence of these phenomena. Great Britain and Las Vegas permit some legal gambling. However, it is likely that more money is bet on sports illegally. According to McPherson, Americans lose an estimated $200 million on sports bets annually. The link between sports and gambling is complex. For example, the profits from legalized gambling are often used to build sports facilities and to operate many youth sports programs.

Social Consequences

How does this commercialization affect the individual and society? Proponents of modern sport argue that capitalist systems have made more sports available to more people. They contend, too, that the owners, producers, and distributors of sports are simply responding to the demands of sports consumers.

Critics of commercialization reject this view and argue that in reality only a small segment of society—the wealthy—have access to many sports. In addition, some critics also argue that commercialization via television especially has turned sport yet another form of passive entertainment. In addition, it is argued that commercialized sports, when used to display social status, effectively divides society. Finally, critics complain that commercialized sport is another way of defining life in terms of the purchase price rather than an inner sense of meaning and achievement. Despite these criticisms, there is little doubt that sports continues to become more and more commercial and the process is spreading to the non-Western world.

—DANIEL G. YODER

See also Gambling; Management and Marketing.

Bibliography: Benjamin, D. (1992) "Pro vs. Amateur." *Time* (July 27): 64–65. Kasky, J. (1994) "America's Best Sports Buys." *Money* (October): 158–170. Kelly, J. R., and G. Godbey. (1992) *The Sociology of Leisure.* State College, PA: Venture. Lane, R. (1994). "The Forbes All-Stars." *Forbes* (December): 266–278. McPherson, B. D., J. E. Curtis, and J. W. Loy. (1989) *The Social Significance of Sport: An Introduction to the Sociology of Sport.* Champaign, IL: Human Kinetics. Rader, B. G. (1990) *American Sports: From the Age of Folk Games to the Age of Televised Sports.* 2d ed. Englewood Cliffs, NJ: Prentice-Hall. Sage, G. H. (1990) *Power and Ideology in American Sport: A Critical Perspective.* Champaign, IL: Human Kinetics.

Commonwealth Games

The Commonwealth Games were inaugurated as the British Empire Games in Hamilton, Ontario (Canada), in 1930, with 400 competitors representing 11 countries. Since then they have been celebrated on 14 other occasions and grown considerably in status. The festival has undergone name changes that reflect the growing political maturity of member countries, and the changing relationship of Great Britain to its former empire. From 1930 to 1950, the games were known as the British Empire Games; from 1954 to 1962 as the British Empire and Commonwealth Games; from 1966 to 1974 as the British Commonwealth Games; and since 1978 as the Commonwealth Games.

History

In 1891, the Englishman John Astley Cooper (1858–1930) proposed an "Anglo-Saxon Olympiad" and/or "Pan-Britannic Gathering" to celebrate industry, culture, and athletic achievements among the English-speaking nations of the world (including the United States). Then in 1911, as part of the "Festival of Empire" coronation celebrations for George V (1865–1936), an "Inter-Empire Sports Meeting" was held in London. Teams representing Australia, Canada, New Zealand, South Africa, and the United Kingdom competed, with the Canadian team emerging victorious. The First British Empire Games were held at Hamilton in 1930.

By 1930, some disenchantment surfaced at the perceived lack of sportsmanship demonstrated at the Olympic Games and resentment at the domination of U.S. athletes. The empire, too, was less of a force in international affairs. The prospect of some more "private" competition was therefore appealing, and perhaps a way of partly restoring some prestige.

Sixteen countries were represented at London in

1934. The games at Sydney in 1938 provided a happy event that contrasted sharply with the "Nazi Olympics" in Berlin only 18 months earlier. Because of World War II a dozen years would pass before athletes of the empire could meet again in friendly competition, in neighboring New Zealand.

The games at Vancouver in 1954 produced the Bannister-Landy "mile of the century," one of most dramatic moments in sports history, and heralded the larger and more sophisticated spectacles of the modern era, now aided by air travel and television. Cardiff, in 1958, attracted the largest assembly to date: 35 nations sent more than 1,100 athletes, ten world records were broken, and the games' record book was almost rewritten. But there were protest demonstrations because South Africa's team was believed to be selected "on the basis of color rather than ability"; and these were the last games in which South Africa competed until 1994.

No fewer than 15 world records were set in swimming alone at the 1966 games in Kingston, as this quadrennial festival continued to provide Olympic-caliber competition for Commonwealth athletes. More world records were set at Edinburgh four years later, when the queen attended the games for the first time. In Christchurch, New Zealand, in 1974, perhaps the greatest excitement came when Filbert Bayi of Tanzania defeated New Zealander John Walker in the 1,500 meters (1,640 yards) in the new world record time of 3 minutes, 22.2 seconds. The games at Edmonton, Alberta (Canada) in 1978 were threatened with a boycott by African nations over the simmering issue of sporting contacts with South Africa, particularly the rugby rivalry between New Zealand and South Africa. The Commonwealth nations were committed to the Gleneagles Agreement of 1977, which prohibited sporting contacts with the Republic of South Africa. Although Nigeria still did not participate at Edmonton, diplomacy won the day and allowed other African nations to compete in what has been described as one of the finest Commonwealth celebrations.

Recent Games

Through no fault of the Scottish hosts, the 1986 games in Edinburgh were the unhappiest of all, plagued by a boycott of virtually all African and Caribbean nations, as well as the most populous in the Commonwealth, India, over the issue of the British government's refusal to implement sanctions against South Africa. Although the 1990 games in Auckland, New Zealand, finished with a large deficit also, the celebration itself was a great success. This process of renewal continued at the 1994 games in Victoria, aided by the return of South Africa to the competition, the republic having rejoined the Commonwealth less than three months before the games. Sixty-three of the 67 Commonwealth nations participated in the Victoria games. The 1998 games are scheduled to be held in Kuala Lumpur, Malaysia.

—GERALD REDMOND

Bibliography: Dheensaw, Cleve. (1994) *The Commonwealth Games.* Victoria, British Columbia: Orca Book Publishers. Mathews, Peter, ed. (1986) *The Official Commonwealth Games Book.* Preston, UK: Opax Publishing and the Commonwealth Games Consortium.

Conditioning

Conditioning is a systematic process of repetitive, progressive exercise or work, involving the learning process and acclimatization to the workload. In general, it refers to the physical or mental preparation for a sport or competitive event. The goal is usually increased performance, performance being any mental or physical effort subjected to psychological or physiological measurement or assessment. Some components of conditioning are muscular strength and endurance, flexibility, cardiorespiratory fitness, and body composition. Another important aspect of physical conditioning for sport is injury prevention.

History

At one time, conditioning was a part of everyday life as physical labor meant physical conditioning. The other major form of physical conditioning was preparation for battle or war. Strength conditioning seemed to be the major component of physical training as warriors prepared for battle. Ancient myth and folklore include accounts of strong men such as Samson, Hercules, and the Greek warrior Milo, who was said to have carried a calf up to a hayloft each night and then retrieved it each morning. As the calf gained weight Milo gained strength, until he was carrying a full-grown cow up and down a ladder daily.

The early Greeks have had a profound and lasting effect on conditioning for sport and competitive events. The Greek Spartans were motivated and conditioned by a strong spirit of militarism. Physical conditioning was preparation for life as a soldier. Young men spent the greatest part of their youths in training for the army. The Romans also believed in physical training to prepare young men for the rigors of battle. Military exercises and games took precedence over any

Muscles and Femininity.

And, ladies, when some jealous and false prophet arises to decry your noble efforts by drawing a forbidding picture of your great-great-grandchildren as huge, muscular amazons divested of sweet womanly charms by too steady encroachment on the field where men alone are fitted to excel, believe him not! By some happy provision of kind Nature, no matter if the woman's biceps grow as firm as steel, the member remains as softly rounded, as tenderly curved, as though no greater strain than the weight of jeweled ornaments had been laid upon them. This is a comforting assurance, and one that may induce many hitherto prudent ladies to lay aside old fashioned prejudice and join the growing host of womankind in the bowling alley.

—Margaret Bisland, "Bowling for Women,"
Outing 16 (April 1890): 33–36.

other form of exercise. The Greek Athenians, however, believed in conditioning for sport and for the welfare of the whole body.

With the appearance of professional athletes in Greek society, the *gymnastes* came into existence. These men helped to condition and prepare athletes for their sport. They used their knowledge of anatomy, physiology, and nutrition to keep the athletes in good competitive shape. Later, the medical *gymnastai* became important to the development of conditioning. Their concern was conditioning the athlete and maintaining him at a high peak of physical efficiency. The greatest of all Greek trainers was Herodicus of Megara. a doctor as well as an athletic trainer and mentor to Hippocrates.

Physical conditioning was revived during medieval times, and included in practice of chivalry. The idea of chivalric conditioning was to train the young men to be strong in mind, body, and spirit.

With the rise of modern nationalism came the need for more organized and directed physical conditioning. Individual nations needed to have strong and healthy soldiers to defend their national borders. Communist countries were particularly strong in their pursuit of strength and conditioning. The former East Germany required fitness training for everyone. Mao Zedong (1893–1976) of China said that "the youth of China are encouraged to get fit, keep fit, and spur on the revolution."

Russia has been a key influence in the development and promotion of conditioning for the strength of the nation and preparation for sport. After the Russian Revolution of 1917 the Communist party recognized physical exercise as a means of improving the strength of the country and its people. From this idea of increasing military strength came the birth of Soviet athletics in 1918. By 1921, more than 150 sports clubs had been formed and 6,000 physical education instructors had been trained. During World War II, the Soviet Union credited the physical fitness of its soldiers and the general public with helping its people withstand months of hunger and fatigue. In addition, the Soviets have conducted much scientific research on the training of athletes.

England, France, and the United States have also influenced the development of conditioning in sport. During the last decades of the 19th century and the early decades of the 20th century the physiological study of human performance began. The United States has been at the forefront of much of modern performance research. Biological sciences like anatomy, physiology, biomechanics, kinesiology, and nutrition, as well has chemistry, have provided vast quantities of knowledge that broadened the scope of conditioning and sport. Technology and technological devices have now become the ultimate tools in the measurement of performance.

Components of Conditioning

Physical conditioning for sports participation prepares athletes for high-level performance and protects against injury. Improper conditioning is a major cause of injuries. Muscular imbalance, improper timing, inadequate muscle or tendon strength, inadequate cardiovascular function, problems related to flexibility, and problems related to body composition are some of the causes of sports injuries and poor performance.

Proper conditioning includes four components. The first is cardiorespiratory conditioning. Through aerobic conditioning the cardiorespiratory system (heart, lungs, and circulation) functions more efficiently. With proper cardiovascular training the heart becomes a bigger, stronger, more efficient pump capable of doing more work with less effort. The lungs also benefit by becoming more efficient at passing air through the lungs, thus increasing vital capacity. Circulation improves by increasing blood flow, meaning that more oxygen and fuel are delivered to the muscles.

The second component is muscular strength and endurance. Increases in muscular strength are associated with increases in muscle mass and productivity. Increases in muscular endurance are associated with improved blood flow to the working muscles. Resistance training, which increases the tension on the muscle, promotes both strength and endurance.

Flexibility, the third component, helps to increase the range of motion around a joint by lengthening the muscles, tendons, and ligaments connected to the bone, thus allowing for increased freedom of movement.

Body composition, or the percentage of body fat, is the fourth component. It is important for athletes to maintain a lean body mass for optimal performance as well as to avoid injuries.

Six principles of conditioning are important to optimal performance.

1. *Specificity* is training the specific component primarily used in competition. If an athlete needs a particularly large amount of muscular strength, then heavy weight training is essential to proper preparation for the event.
2. *Intensity* is the percentage of one's maximum capacity being used while training.
3. *Duration* is the amount of time the exercise or conditioning bout continues.
4. *Frequency* is the number of times per week an athlete trains.
5. *Progression* is the gradual increase in intensity and duration of conditioning. As the body adapts to training modes the exercise load can be increased.
6. The *overload* principle is related to progression. Overload means that to improve any aspect of physical conditioning the athlete must continually increase the demands placed on the appropriate body systems.

Physical conditioning has evolved from conditioning for military strength to a highly technological aspect of performance in sport. As this ever-changing field continues to grow, new and exciting concepts will be investigated to continually test the peaks of human performance.

—SALLY CRAWFORD

See also Aerobics; Exercise; Medicine.
Bibliography: American College of Sports Medicine. (1992) *ACSM Fitness Book.* Champaign, IL: Leisure Press. Arnheim, Daniel D. (1989) *Modern Principles of Athletic Training.* St. Louis, MO: Times Mirror/Mosby College Publishing. Sharkey, B. J. (1984) *Physiology of Fitness.* Champaign, IL: Human Kinetics Publishers.

Coursing

Coursing—the development, breeding, and preparation of racing dogs, as well as the competition itself—is one of the world's oldest sports. The greyhound eventually came to the fore as the swiftest animal that could be domesticated and trained to run at breathtaking speeds over a variety of distances.

History

Dog racing has evolved over millennia; the trained dog held an important place in ancient Egypt and Assyria and in the Mayan civilization. Unlike many breeds that have been transformed over the centuries—for example, such bull-baiting types as the boxer, bulldog, and mastiff—the greyhound has remained virtually unchanged.

Lord Orford is credited with founding the first coursing club in Swaffham in 1776. Other clubs were formed in Britain, and in 1836 an unofficial national championship came into being, called the Waterloo Cup after Liverpool's Waterloo Hotel. Hotel proprietors and publicans frequently found themselves promoting greyhound race meetings, since the taproom and the racetrack seemed to complement each other. Conducted in a climate of unlimited gambling, these meetings brought together crowds of spectators eager to speculate and make merry.

In 1858 a National Coursing Club was set up to monitor the sport in England. Even more than horse racing, coursing lent itself to chicanery and deception. Most often there was the subterfuge of substituting one greyhound for another, so careful scrutiny was critical if the sport's reputation was to be maintained. Coursing qualified as a popular blood sport in Victorian England (along with boxing and foxhunting), and some groups came to oppose it because the dogs usually killed the live hare released to encourage them to run.

The invention of the mechanical hare and, later, an electrified hare on a circular track saved the sport. The first attempt at creating a mechanical hare took place at Welsh Harp, Hendon, in 1876. The "hare" was mounted on a rail and moved by means of a rope and pulley system. The major drawbacks of the system, and the reason this innovative gadget was unsuccessful, was that it was set up on a straight track of 400 yards. This meant that the quickest greyhound would win again and again, thus all but eliminating the important gambling elements of luck, tactics, lane draw, and guile. The shape of the track was changed to a circle or oval. Meanwhile, in certain regions of Britain greyhound racing became hugely popular and attracted wildly enthusiastic crowds made up mostly of working-class men eager to drink ale and wager on a succession of closely contested races.

Although the mechanical hare's prototypes were

"Heeded lyke a snake".

In a short history of greyhound racing, *Roots of the Greyhound,* published by the Greyhound Hall of Fame and Museum in Abilene, Kansas, appears one of the earliest descriptions of a perfectly contoured greyhound. The words still apply to a champion Hall of Famer today. The poetic description was written by Dame Juliana Berners in the *Boke of St. Albans* (1486):

A greyhound should be heeded lyke a snake,
And neckyd lyke a drake,
Backed lyke a bream,
Footed lyke a catte,
Taylled lyke a ratte.
—*Scott A. G. M. Crawford*

tested in England, it was an American, Owen Patrick Smith, who shaped greyhound racing as it exists today. In 1912 in South Dakota, Smith successfully tested a mechanical hare (otherwise known as a mechanical lure), and two years later used it on a greyhound racing track that he established in Tucson, Arizona. The first recorded race with the electric hare took place in 1920 at Emeryville, California. Smith went on to organize the International Greyhound Racing Association.

An American, Charles Munn, who introduced the now-electrified form of greyhound racing to its native England in 1925. Despite early indifference, Munn eventually found a partner for his venture, Gen. A. C. Critchley, and set up an experimental track in 1926 at Belle Vue, Manchester. They could not have selected a better site, since the area was primarily populated by working-class people who were excited by the sport and who wagered passionately on the outcome.

Tracks sprang up in most of the major cities of Great Britain in the late 1920s, offering cheap gambling and a night out for ordinary working people who found it difficult to go to horse-racing. Sixty-two companies with a total capital of 7 million pounds were registered for greyhound racing in 1927 alone. Britain was "going to the dogs" and by 1932 the annual attendance at licensed tracks in London had risen to 6.5 million. Several of the leading tracks drew 200 to 300 bookmakers. In the pre–World War II era, greyhound racing became Scotland's second-most-popular spectator sport after soccer (association football).

Sports historian Richard Holt describes the "rich tradition of potions and tricks" that was part and parcel of the greyhound racing culture. The common practices of concealing a dog's true form and cloaking the champion performer created an atmosphere in which deception and guile posed no moral or ethical

dilemma, but rather were integral elements in an unpredictable, unfolding drama.

In 1925, the advent of night racing played a key role in popularizing greyhound racing as a spectator sport in the United States. During its early years the sport was plagued by criminal elements who took advantage of the quick profits that could be make by "doctoring" a dog or bribing an untrustworthy dog handler. Eventually, dog owners and racetrack promoters saw to it that the sport was regulated and closely supervised. This helped establish credibility and integrity in the sport. In 1932, with the legalization of greyhound racing gambling at on- and off-course locations in Florida (parimutuel betting), the sport's future was assured. Two years later, greyhound racing and parimutuel betting were enjoying success at U.S. tracks as far north as Massachusetts.

Rules and Play

Greyhound racing continues to be an exhibition of pure speed. Races tend to be no more than 550 meters (601 yards), but 950-meter (1,039-yard) marathons do occur. At these distances the greyhound maintains an average speed of 60 kilometers (37 miles) per hour—faster than harness horseracing (48 kilometers [30 miles] per hour), but slightly slower than flat horseracing over similar distances (62 kilometers [39 miles] per hour).

Betting is an important element of the sport for many fans. People attending greyhound races receive charts that list the physical characteristics and performance records of the dogs in each race.

Nighttime greyhound racing has a singular ambiance and setting. The configuration of the track; the darkened backdrop and brightly illuminated track; the lean, lithe dogs with their handlers; and the intense involvement of wagering spectators all come together to create a kind of working man's theater. Nevertheless, greyhound racing continues to find it difficult to compete with the mystique of horseracing and the tradition of the Kentucky Derby.

Greyhound racing is established in 18 U.S. states. Florida has 15 of the 51 tracks, closely followed by southern New England, which has 6 tracks in 5 states. Within the United States the sport is controlled by the American Greyhound Track Operators Association, with headquarters in Miami, Florida. Among spectator sports in the United States, greyhound racing ranks sixth. In 1988, the revenue from the 51 U.S. dog tracks generated $225 million in tax dollars. In Great Britain, the sport continues to be associated with working-class communities. A 1995 *Economist* obituary on union leader Sam McCluskie opened with the comment, "There are leaders of British trade unions whom one could still imagine owning a racing greyhound."

—SCOTT A. G. M. CRAWFORD

Bibliography: Holt, R. (1989) *Sport and the British: A Modern History.* Oxford: Oxford University Press. Raitz, K. B., ed. (1995) *The Theater of Sport.* Baltimore: Johns Hopkins University Press.

Cricket

Cricket, a bat and ball game played by two teams, has long been regarded as the archetypal English game, and its complex and even archaic rules baffle those who have not grown up in cricket-playing countries. The leisurely pace of cricket has inspired much reflection and literature. Others make lofty claims for the game as a moral and healthy pastime; one Australian clergyman even claimed that had Adolf Hitler played cricket World War II would not have occurred.

History

Cricket's origins are obscure; it is still not clear whether the word cricket refers to the target that is defended (the three stumps that make up the wicket) or the implement used to defend this target, the bat. The derivation of the word cricket is also uncertain. Some scholars argue that the word is related to the Flemish or Low German *krick-stoel,* a low stool similar to the earliest types of wicket. Others contend that cricket derives from the Old English *cryce* or Middle Flemish *crick,* literally a staff for leaning on. Uncertainty about cricket's prehistory has encouraged fanciful attempts to establish its ancient antecedents. Some writers have attempted to link cricket with bat-and-ball folk games such as stool-ball, trap-ball, tip-cat, cat-and-dog, and club-ball, suggesting that they were the acorn from which the mighty oak cricket sprang. Others have posited a connection between cricket and folk games such as *creag,* a game played by the Prince of Wales in 1299–1300. No evidence supports any of these claims.

The first authentic reference to cricket dates to 1598, and it seems clear that cricket was played in the south of England in the 16th century. Increased references to the game in the 17th century suggest that the game was becoming more popular in both city and country. The involvement of wealthy landowners who patronized the game from the late 17th century helped transform an informal intervillage pastime to a more organized sport. Aristocrats with time and money to

---

Cricket (as explained to a foreign visitor).

You have two sides one out in the field and one in.

Each man that's in the side that's in goes out and when he's out he comes in and the next man goes in until he's out.

When they are all out the side that's out comes in and the side that's been in goes out and tries to get those coming in out.

Sometimes you get men still in and not out.

When both sides have been in and out including the 'not outs'

That's the end of the game.

Howzat!

—*Marylebone Cricket Club*

---

lavish on leisure played an important role in establishing and codifying the rules of the game; one reason consistent rules were desirable was the substantial bets (up to £10,000) placed on matches. From 1711 articles of agreement were often drawn up for individual matches. These articles set out the core rules of the game and were later incorporated into the versions of the "laws" drafted in 1744, 1771, 1774, and 1788. By the end of the 1700s rules covered the form of the bat, ball, stumps, and bails; the size of the wicket; methods of batting and bowling; and methods of dismissal. The essential rules of the game were completed by the next century with the evolution from underarm to roundarm bowling in 1835 and the legalization of overarm (over the shoulder) bowling in 1864.

Cricket was transformed in the 18th century largely because it fired the imagination of a number of aristocrats. Cricket appealed to English aristocrats because it was a complex and leisurely game amenable to subtle distinctions of class. The aristocrat could lead the side and bat, leaving the more physically taxing fast bowling to the estate laborer. Another aspect of the game's appeal may have been that it conjured a romantic vision of bucolic bliss and class cooperation on rustic swards on sunlit afternoons while England was rapidly becoming urban and industrial.

Village cricket clubs also flourished; 1,000 were reported in England and Wales in this century. Competition grew more demanding in the 1740s, and matches were played between teams representing counties. Teams designated as "All England" also took the field.

From the 1730s to the 1770s, cricket found a London home at the Artillery Ground, Finsbury, the grounds of the Honourable Artillery Company, which was partly enclosed, enabling gate entry charges. Lord's cricket ground was established at the same time. The 1740s brought intervillage cricket games for women, particularly in the counties of Surrey and Sussex. The rise of more organized cricket for women paralleled that of the men's game. Some of the games were robust and boisterous and involved gambling. Arguably, women cricketers achieved greater acceptance in the 18th century than later. Their matches were advertised in the press, gate-entry was charged, and large crowds watched. However, after the novelty wore off they were treated with indifference.

The second great transformation in cricket—the spread of the game throughout England and abroad and its growth into a highly profitable mass spectator sport—was not so much the achievement of the gentlemen of the MCC at Lord's as of the working-class professionals whose role has not been properly acknowledged until recently. The professionals, or teams made up predominantly of professionals, took the game overseas to Canada and the United States in 1859, to Australia in 1862, and to Australia and New Zealand in 1864. Their tours overseas proved immensely profitable and did much to stimulate interest in overseas cricket. The success of the Australians, who in 1878 performed very creditably against the best English sides, helped install cricket as an international game, and indigenous traditions soon developed. International matches, which were played regularly from 1877, came to be known as tests.

Class distinctions were incorporated into all facets of the game: the amateur was segregated from the professional in terms of accommodation and dining, and he even entered the field from a different gate. The amateur had his name and initials recorded in the schoolbook, the professional was identified by surname only. It was also thought proper that England should be captained by an amateur; not until 1953, when the Yorkshireman Len Hutton became captain, was England captained by a professional.

The era before World War I has been called the Golden Age of cricket, when the game itself was a form of imperial cement that bound the British Empire together. An Indian prince, K. S. Ranjitsinhji, who was selected to play for England in the 1890s, became a potent symbol of empire. "Ranji" declared that cricket was "one of the greatest contributions which the British people have made to the cause of humanity." Similarly lofty claims were made for cricket as character building. One Australian official was convinced that cricket encouraged "cleanliness of mind and thought."

The major changes in the game in the 19th and 20th centuries relate to improvements in facilities, technology, and equipment and changes in the form of competition and styles of play: the introduction of three- and four-day competition, the beginning of five-day test (international) matches, and limited overs contests.

Twentieth Century

The 20th century has seen significant growth in international cricket competition and an ever-expanding program of international tours and contests. Many new competitors have been accorded test status, including South Africa (1889), West Indies (1928), New Zealand (1930), India (1932), Pakistan (1952), Sri Lanka (1981), and Zimbabwe (1992). Many other nations have acquired associate status, including Bangladesh, the Netherlands, Canada, Kenya, and the United Arab Emirates. The expansion of international competition led to the creation of a world cricket authority, the Imperial Cricket Conference (later the International Cricket Conference) in 1909.

International cricket for women dates from the 1930s, when England toured Australia in 1934–1935 and played three tests. Since then a number of other women's teams have played test cricket, including New Zealand, India, and teams from the West Indies, until it was established on a surer basis in the 1970s. The staging of a World Cup for women's cricket—two years before the men—was an inspired idea that helped to revive interest in the game. Since cricket is still regarded as a man's game, there remains an onus on women who play cricket to prove their femininity.

The 20th century has been notable for major controversies that rocked the cricket world and altered the character of the game. The first was the infamous Bodyline series of 1932–1933. There was much debate about the tactics employed by the English captain, Douglas Jardine, to curb the Australian run-machine, Sir Donald Bradman. Jardine instructed his chief bowler to bowl *at* the batsmen in an intimidating fashion and in a manner many considered unfair and not in the spirit of the game. The series strained relations between Australia and England until a cricket solution, a change in the rules, was devised.

The introduction of a new form of cricket, limited overs, in English domestic cricket in 1963 had wide ramifications. The experiment resulted from dwindling interest in three-day domestic cricket. A limited overs match could be completed in a day and a result was always achieved, eliminating the draw. The abbreviated format, which encouraged innovative play, proved an instant success. Although it took some time for officials to fully comprehend the potential of the abbreviated game, limited overs internationals were played from 1971, and the 1975 World Cup in England—exclusively composed of limited overs matches—proved a huge success.

Advances in television also greatly extended the popularity of cricket in the 1970s. The game translated well on television, for from the mid-1970s slow-motion replays helped unravel some of the intricacies of the game. This television-related boom in cricket made the game attractive to Australian media tycoon Kerry Packer, who virtually hijacked world cricket after he was denied exclusive Australian television rights. In a daring raid, Packer signed up the majority of the world's best cricketers—offering players far more generous payment—and established a rival cricket circuit. For two seasons Establishment cricket and World Series were locked in deadly combat, and a number of court cases ensued before a truce was worked out in May 1979. Packer's great innovation in this period of crisis was to popularize limited overs cricket and night play, which proved commercially attractive.

Rules and Play

Cricket is played by two sides with 11 players each, who take turns batting the ball bowled to them by the bowler. Play occurs at both ends of rectangular-shaped areas, with wickets consisting of three stumps at each end of a 22-yard (20-meter) grass pitch in the center of an oval or field. An over (now six balls) is bowled from one end to one batsman, followed by an over at the other end, by another bowler, to the second batsman. A batsman can hit the ball (on the full or the bounce) to any part of the field and a run or runs are scored when both batsmen safely reach the other end. If the ball reaches the boundary, four runs are scored; if the ball crosses the boundary without bouncing, six runs. A unique feature of cricket is that batsmen do not have to run when they hit the ball: they can continue to bat for hours and, in international cricket, for days on end.

Underarm bowling was the norm initially, but the laws were altered in the 1800s to allow round arm and eventually overarm bowling. The laws of cricket dictate that the ball should be bowled (with a straight arm) and not thrown. New traditions developed as the game became more popular in the 19th century: the English three-day county game was instituted in 1864, and international contests known as Test matches began in 1877, which came to be played over five days. An ab-

breviated form of cricket, limited overs, was introduced in 1963 and soon became popular.

Cricket boasts a rich language of fielding positions such as "fine leg," "gully," "silly mid on," as well as terms for specialist balls that include "bosie," "googly," "wrong-un," "Chinaman," and "zuter." Phrases such as "sticky wicket" and "it's not cricket" have assumed many broader meanings outside cricket. It is now more popular in many Commonwealth countries than it is in Britain.

Spread of the Game

The British took cricket with them to all parts of their empire, though they made very limited attempts to encourage the indigenes of Asia and Africa to play the game. For almost a century in India (from the time of the first cricket club at Calcutta in 1792) cricket was a game for European soldiers, merchants, educators, and missionaries, and the local population were not encouraged to play. Indian teams were not formed until the mid-19th century and it was not until the late 1800s that they played against European teams. In the 20th century, however, cricket became the most popular sport on the subcontinent, in India, Pakistan, and Sri Lanka. The support of cricket by comprador communities, such as the Parsis of Bombay, and by many Indian princes endowed the game with glamour and status. Cricket on the subcontinent was able to reinvent itself to fit in with local culture and society.

In the West Indies, too, cricket was initially a white man's game. C. L. R. James, in the cricket classic *Beyond a Boundary,* shows how West Indian cricket, although part of colonial oppression, was domesticated and transformed into a vehicle for the liberation struggle. Creolized West Indian cricket developed its own rich traditions—including cricket as carnival—and produced outstanding teams that dominated world cricket from the mid-1970s to the 1990s.

British settlers established cricket clubs early in European settlement in Australia and New Zealand. For Europeans living in remote parts of the empire playing cricket was a way to maintain their culture in remote and exotic locations. Cricket comes close to being the national game of Australia, and it is also popular in New Zealand and South Africa, where it ranks second to rugby. Each of these countries reinvented cricket to suit its particular climate, culture, and society. The hard and firm wickets of Australia encouraged fast and leg spin bowling and more certain shot making.

Although cricket was exported at an earlier period than soccer, it spread far less, remaining confined to the former British Empire. Various explanations for this have been put forth. It is likely that cricket's failure to spread, for example, from local elites of Philadelphia and other social bastions to the broader population in North America was because these elites preferred to maintain cricket as an exclusive game. Cricket also failed to find a niche in Ireland, though rugby was played there, possibly because cricket was the archetypal English game.

Cricket as a sport has been a great survivor in that it has been able to reinvent itself many times over. It has evolved from the era of gentlemen who loved to gamble, to the time of the professional, to the amateur era, to the more commercial and professional era following World Series Cricket. In the 1980s and 1990s the balance of cricket has shifted away from England. The game itself will remain as it began: quintessentially English.

—RICHARD CASHMAN

Bibliography: Altham, H. S., and E. W. Swanton. (1962) *A History of Cricket.* 2 vols. 5th ed. London: Allen and Unwin. Cashman, Richard, et al., eds. (1996) *The Oxford Companion to Australian Cricket.* Melbourne: Oxford University Press. Frith, David. (1987) *Pageant of Cricket.* Melbourne: Macmillan. Moorhouse, Geoffrey. (1983) *Lord's.* London: Hodder and Stoughton. James, C. L. R. (1963) *Beyond the Boundary.* London: Hutchinson. McPhee, Hilary, and Brian Stoddart. (1995) *Liberation Cricket: West Indies Cricket Culture.* Manchester: Manchester University Press. Rundell, Michael. (1985) *The Dictionary of Cricket.* London: Allen and Unwin.

Croquet

Croquet is a sport that pits individuals against each other. Each player tries to hit wooden balls through wire arches, to hit a post in the ground, and to hit his opponent's ball. Surpassed by tennis in Great Britain in the 19th century, it is today more of a recreational activity than competitive sport, although intense competition has not disappeared entirely, neither on back lawns nor on the smooth lawns of croquet clubs.

History

Croquet probably evolved from a game called *palle mall* in which players hit a ball (*palla*) with a mallet (*maglio*) through a series of iron rings. The modern form of croquet originated in France in the early years of the 19th century and was immediately recognizable by its unique mallet. This mallet, in its French peasant form, had a broomstick as a handle. The word "croquet" derives from the French word *croc,* meaning something shaped like a hook or a crook.

The sport of croquet was transplanted from France to Ireland, where there are records of its being played regularly after 1852. Once introduced to England, it flourished. Walter James Whitmore promoted and publicized the sport in England. The game's stellar figure both as player and tactician, Whitmore became the unofficial world champion with his 1867 victory in the Moreton-on-Marsh, England, Croquet Open Championship. In 1868, the All England Croquet Club was formed.

Croquet might have come to rival cricket as a major outdoor English sport had another new sport not arrived that quickly became a public passion. Tennis was so popular that players took up all available grass space. By 1875, the All England Croquet Club had to add the words "and Lawn Tennis Club" to its title. Five years later the demise of croquet was apparent out when the croquet club changed its name to the All England Lawn Tennis Club.

Croquet's international expansion was led by the American National Croquet League, founded in 1880, and the first Australian croquet club, founded at Kyneton, Victoria, in 1866. The Australian Croquet Council was founded in 1950. (Australia now leads the world with over 6,000 registered players.) In 1896 the Croquet Association was founded.

In the 19th century croquet provided an important vehicle for women to move beyond the traditional boundaries of home, church, and school and to seek a role in some quasi-athletic pursuit. Sociologist Jennifer Hargreaves, however, says that although croquet was "a highly sociable and fashionable pastime," women's entrance into athletics saw them stereotyped as the weaker sex capable of "doing" only gentle and respectable games. In other words, it was only acceptable for women to perform "the smallest and meanest of movements." Even with croquet, it was felt that it might be more appropriate for women to play croquet's indoor variations—Parlor Croquet, Table Croquet, and Carpet Croquet—instead of the outdoor variety.

During the 1860s, 1870s, and 1880s conservative groups in Britain and the United States feared the downfall of women who let themselves be carried away by the excesses of such sports as bicycling and croquet. An article in the *American Christian Review* in 1878 described the consequences of such involvement:

1. A social party.
2. Social and play party.
3. Croquet party.
4. Picnic and croquet party.

An Anglo-American Match.

It was not far to Longmeadow, but the tent was pitched and the wickets down by the time they arrived. A pleasant green field, with three wide-spreading oaks in the middle and a smooth strip of turf for croquet.

"Welcome to Camp Laurence!" said the young host, as they landed with exclamations of delight.

"Brooke is commander in chief, I am commissary general, the other fellows are staff officers, and you, ladies, are company. The tent is for your especial benefit and that oak is your drawing room, this is the messroom and third is the camp kitchen. Now, let's have a game before it gets hot, and then we'll see about dinner."

Frank, Beth, Amy, and Grace sat down to watch the game played by the other eight. Mr. Brooke chose Meg, Kate, and Fred; Laurie took Sallie, Jo, and Ned. The English played well, but the Americans played better, and contested every inch of the ground as strongly as if the spirit of '76 inspired them. Jo and Fred had several skirmishes and once narrowly escaped high words. Jo was through the last wicket and had missed the stroke, which failure ruffled her a good deal. Fred was close behind her and his turn came before hers, he gave a stroke, his ball hit the wicket, and stopped an inch on the wrong side. No one was very near, and running up to examine, he gave it a sly nudge with his toe, which put it just an inch on the right side.

"I'm through! Now, Miss Jo, I'll settle you, and get in first," cried the young gentleman, swinging his mallet for another blow.

"You pushed it; I saw you; it's my turn now," said Jo sharply.

"Upon my word, I didn't move it; it rolled a bit, perhaps, but that is allowed; so stand off, please, and let me have a go at the stake."

"We don't cheat in America, but you can, if you choose," said Jo angrily.

"Yankees are a deal the most tricky, everybody knows. There you go!" returned Fred, croqueting her ball far away.

Jo opened her lips to say something rude, but checked herself in time, colored up to her forehead and stood a minute, hammering down a wicket with all her might, while Fred hit the stake and declared himself out with much exultation. She went off to get her ball, and was a long time finding it among the bushes, but she came back, looking cool and quiet, and waited her turn patiently. It took several strokes to regain the place she had lost, and when she got there, the other side had nearly won, for Kate's ball was the last but one and lay near the stake.

"By George, it's all up with us! Good-by Kate, Miss Jo owes me one, so you are finished," cried Fred excitedly, as they all drew near the finish.

"Yankees have a trick of being generous to their enemies," said Jo, with a look that made the lad redden, "especially when they beat them," she added, as, leaving Kate's ball untouched, she won the game by a clever stroke.

—*Louisa May Alcott*, Little Women *(1869)*

---

5. Picnic, croquet, and dance.
6. Absence from church.
7. Imprudent or immoral conduct.
8. Exclusion from the church
9. A runaway match.
10. Poverty and discontent.
11. Shame and disgrace.
12. Ruin.

Despite such gloomy pronouncements, croquet flourished as a women's sport. In America, long before women took part in competitive tennis or basketball tournaments, their first venture into competition sport was with croquet in the 1860s.

Rules and Play

Croquet is unusual in that it is not a team sport. Almost without exception, croquet consists of one individual challenging another. Although many of the descriptions make it seem as complex and cerebral as chess, the essence of the game is its simplicity. The object of the sport is to score points by striking the ball through each of the hoops in the proper order and hitting the stake. Each player, in turn, tries to make a point or to *roquet*. This means to hit an opponent's ball with one's own. If a competitor scores a point he or she is entitled to another stroke. If not, the next player takes a turn.

In virtually every individual sport, the structure of the competition allows a degree of involvement by even an outplayed player. Not so in croquet. During a Washington, D.C., challenge tournament in the late 1980s a competition took place in which a competitor started and continued playing at such a level of excellence that he completed the whole course without yielding his turn. It was a dazzling, bravura performance in which his competitor's only physical action was to doff his hat and shake the winner's hand.

The MacRobertson International Shield is croquet's top honor. The Croquet Association, with its headquarters at the Hurlingham Club, organizes all of the major championship events. In the United States croquet has been organized since 1976 by the United States Croquet Association. Croquet has caught on in the British Commonwealth and is played today in Australia, New Zealand, and South Africa.

Croquet was and is an elitist activity. In the early

days of the sport, croquet hoops on a lawn showed the house owner to be on the cutting edge of fashion. Today, club memberships still tend to be expensive and exclusive.

—SCOTT A. G. M. CRAWFORD

Bibliography: Baltzell, E. D. (1995) *Sporting Gentlemen.* New York: Free Press. Hargreaves, J. (1993) "The Victorian Cult of the Family and the Early Years of Female Sport." In *The Sport Process,* edited by E. G. Dunning, J. A. Maguire, and R. E. Pearton. Champaign, IL: Human Kinetics. Lidz, F. (1995) "Mallets Aforethought." *Sports Illustrated* 83, 10 (14 September).

Cross-Country Running

Cross-country running is described from the earliest times of foot messengers to boys' games of hunt the hare or fox. Cross-country running needs little explanation; participants run long distances off rough ground roads or tracks. It is a competitive sports for men and women and at one time enjoyed Olympic status, but many people run cross-country simply because they enjoy it and for the exercise.

History

In Kazakhstan, Uzbekistan, and Tajikistan, day-long races across country were held. In Europe, at least as early as the middle of the 14th century, the sport of cross-country running emanated from hunting. A poem written sometime around 1560 records "when we play hunt the fox, I out run all the boyes in the schoole."

Important to the sport in northern England and southern Scotland was the adaptation of the 18th-century sport of steeplechasing (a race to a church steeple on horseback). The 1830s saw many foot steeplechases, particularly in the lowlands of Scotland. Ireland had races at Cavan and Tipperary in the early 1840s. The courses included fences, hurdles, ditches, brooks, and even the swimming of rivers. The distance commonly run was three-quarters to 1.5 miles.

By the beginning of the 1800s, the sport was a pastime at many English schools. By the 1840s, the sport reached Oxford University where two clubs, the Kangaroo Club and the Charitable Grinders, organized steeplechase runs.

The paper-chase stems from at least 1856 when it is mentioned in the journal *Household Words.* Paperchasing consisted of laying a trail of paper by two runners called the hares, one of whom would lay false trails. They were followed after an interval of 10 minutes by runners called hounds. The paper-chase survived only until about 1930.

Cross-country running quickly spread to several other countries. In the United States, hare and hound clubs appeared in the Boston, New York, and Philadelphia areas in the late 1870s. Australia had several clubs in Melbourne and Sydney in the late 1880s. but cross country in New Zealand did not develop until after 1917. In South Africa, there were paper-chases in Durban as early as 1883 over a course of earth banks and hurdles.

Northwest Europe also took up cross-country running. Championship races commenced in France in 1889, and between 1896 and 1925 there were even professional cross-country championships in France. Neighboring Belgium ran its field race in 1896; Denmark held a 15-kilometer (9.4-mile) race in 1901 (the distance was reduced to 8 kilometers in 1918). Sweden began its championships in 1907 with 8-kilometer races. Finland entered the scene in 1913 and Paavo Nurmi, one of the greatest runners of all time, clocked up seven victories. In the same year, Germany ran the *Waldlauf* (forest run) over 7,500 meters (4.7 miles), increasing the distance to 10,000 meters (6.2 miles) by 1920. The Dutch championships began in 1919 with 5-kilometer (3.1-mile) races, but within five years the distance became 10 kilometers.

Cross-country running was introduced in the Olympics at the Stockholm Games in 1912. The 1920 race was held at Antwerp over a one-lap course that started and finished in the stadium. The race at Paris in 1924 was a disaster. It was run over 10,650 meters (6.6 miles) from and to the stadium on a very hot day (36 degrees Celsius [97 degrees Fahrenheit]). Forty runners started, but only teams from Finland, the United States, and France finished, in that order. Only 15 runners finished the race; the remainder were taken to the hospital. After this disaster, cross country was dropped from the Olympics; it has since been considered but not readopted.

The International CC race between 1929 and 1972 saw various other countries competing on an irregular basis. Spain, Italy, Switzerland, and Luxembourg competed in Paris in 1929. The 1950s and 1960s saw interest from the North African countries of Tunisia, Morocco, and Algeria. The 1960s were also notable for other English-speaking countries such as South Africa, New Zealand, Canada, and the United States taking part.

The Balkan states introduced the Balkan championships in 1957. The following year the International Amateur Athletic Federation agreed with the International Cross Country Union (CCU) that the latter's championships be an IAAF-permitted competition.

Teams now compete from all continents. In 1990 the IAAF introduced the IAAF Cross-Country Challenge, 11 races in which runners could take part and score points, if 8 or more nations took part, with prizes for the first 12 for both men and women.

Women's Cross Country

Women's cross country can be traced back to the late 1870s, when middle-class women in the London and Dublin areas ran hare and hound races. France was the first to organize a national championship, which began in 1919. In England cross-country running began in 1923, with national championships following in 1930, while Belgian women were competing in the 1920s. The first women's international was at Brussels when France beat Belgium in 1930. At Douai, Belgium, in 1931 there was a three-cornered match between France, Belgium, and England, won by the latter. A return match was held in England the following year and another in 1938.

The English Cross Country Union (ECCU) instituted a women's 4-kilometer (2.5-mile) international championship in 1967 at Barry, South Wales, in conjunction with the men's event. Up to 1975 the United States and England vied for team honors; the Soviet Union then became dominant. The following year the course was lengthened to approximately 5 kilometers (cross-country courses are not measured as accurately as formal running tracks). Norwegian Grete Waitz won five titles in six years between 1978 and 1983; Lynn Jennings of the United States captured three victories in the period 1990 to 1992, when 6 kilometers (3.75 miles) was the usual distance.

In 1990 the first under-20 junior competition was held, and since that time either the Ethiopians or Kenyans have usually taken the team prize. Continued interest among younger competitors suggests that cross-country has a secure, if modest, future.

—DAVID TERRY

Bibliography: Bloom, M. (1977) *Cross Country Running*. Mountain View, CA: World Publications. Fraser, I. (1968) *The Annals of Thames Hare and Hounds*. London: Thames & Hudson.

Cross-Country Skiing
See Skiing, Nordic

Cudgeling
Cudgeling, or European stick fighting, is an umbrella term that covers various similar practices around the world.

Fencing with sticks for sport is probably as old as warfare. The Egyptians have the oldest known record of a fencing match in the form of a temple relief from 1200 B.C.E. It depicts two fencers with blunted sticks and masks, one of whom says: "On guard, and admire, what my valiant hands shall do!"—an old but always popular way of boasting.

History

Asia
The Indian art of *silambam* emphasizes the use of a 1.2-meter (4-foot) staff. After seven years' training, practitioners advance to other weapons and may use their bare hands. *Gatka* is a stick- and knife-based martial art from India and Pakistan. Gatka is the traditional fighting art of the Sikhs, a religious group in the Punjab, neither Muslim nor Hindu. It is practiced today by members of the 3H Foundation, the followers of Yogi Bhajan, a Sikh leader and teacher. Sikhs have traditionally filled rolls of military and police in India. British influence is seen in the use of a singlestick (a meter-long piece of bamboo with a leather handle) in place of the sword for the lower levels of training. The techniques are practiced to drumbeats and performed with a high stepping movement that is taught with a chanted mantra. Horseback techniques are still taught.

Kalaripayattu, based in the southern Indian state of Kerala, is a composite martial art. After two phases of weaponless training, the third phase of Kalaripayattu training is training in the use of various weapons, which begins with the short staff and quarterstaff and progresses to weapons such as the spear and shield, sword and shield, daggers, knives, battle axes, and so on.

In the Philippines, when Fernando Magellan was killed by the sharpened stick of a local chief during a failed landing attempt on his round-the-world voyage in 1521, the Spaniards had made their first bloody experience with "arnis." Arnis, kali, and escrima are the national weapon arts of the Philippines. All three have in common the use of the stick in combat, either as itself or as a replacement for or representative of the sword or knife. They have had full contact events with stick that is much like old cudgeling or backswording in 18th-century Europe. After conquering the island group, the Spanish tried to root out this art. It was passed on for centuries only in secrecy or family circles. But with Philippine independence after World War II arnis appeared in public again, now as a stick fencing sport with 0.76-meter (30-inch) long rattan sticks.

Europe

The cudgel or singlestick was the practice weapon for military sword, broadsword, or saber. The earliest known manual of European fencing delineates techniques that are illustrated in other medieval documents depicting the training of knights or squires and entertainments conducted with stick or sword indiscriminately.

In England, from the Middle Ages, the common man had to train at cudgel and buckler. Singlestick and cudgel play was a bulwark of rugged English manliness in the 19th century, according to *Tom Brown's School Days,* in which a backswording event that involves two men trying to draw blood from each others' scalps with cudgels is recounted with relish. As recently as 1886, the British army used singlestick drill to train recruits for combat.

The quarterstaff, a stick 1.8 meters by 3 centimeters (6 feet by $1^1/_4$ inches), was also a medieval weapon that survived to modern times. Developed from a common peasant weapon, it was mentioned in the training manuals of many countries. It formed the basis of training with two-handed weapons. The pugil stick fights that the U.S. Marines were force to drop from training in 1985 for reasons of safety appear to be from the same set of techniques.

Stick fighting remained popular until Italian masters formalized saber fencing into a nonfatal sporting/training form with metal weapons in the late 19th century. Few of these "extinct" fencing styles remain from a long tradition of European fencing. Those that survive in the main are subsumed with the styles studied in association with savate, a French form of unarmed combat.

Modern Sport and Combat

The survival of European stick fighting is associated with savate—French footfighting. Savate may have originated in pancration, a sport in the original Olympics that combined wrestling, boxing, and other techniques. Roman legions carried it and cestus, an armored glove for punching, along with them. Many local styles existed; and some, like Cornish wrestling and *lutte breton,* survive.

The link between the French *stic* and foot fighting systems began in the early 1700s with chausaun (from the name of the deck shoe worn by sailors), a combat system that includes the use of the belaying pin (a shipboard tool shaped something like a bowling pin and used to manage the rigging), along with kicks and hand strikes practiced by sailors on ships. In other

Village Sports.

[To Mr. Hone.] You may know, perhaps, that the inhabitants of many of the villages in the western counties, not having a fair or other merry-making to collect a fun-seeking money-spending crowd, and being willing to have one day of mirth in the year, have some time in the summer what are called *feasts;* when they are generally visited by their friends, whom they treat with the old English fare of beef and plumb pudding, followed by the sports of single-stick playing, cudgelling, or wrestling: and sometimes by those delectable inventions of merry Comus, and mirthful spectacles of the village green, jumping in the sack, grinning through the horse-collar, or the running of blushing damsels for that indispensable article of female dress—the plain English name of which rhymes with a *frock.*

Single-stick playing is so called to distinguish it from cudgelling, in which two sticks are used: the single-stick player having the left hand tied down, and using only one stick both to defend himself and strike his antagonist. The object of each gamester in this play, as in cudgelling, is to guard himself, and to fetch blood from the other's head; whether by taking a little skin from his pericranium, drawing a stream from his nose, or knocking out a few of those early inventions for grinding—the teeth. They are both *sanguine* in their hope of victory, and, as many other ambitious fighters have done, they both aim at the *crown.*

In cudgelling, as the name implies, the weapon is a stout cudgel; and the player defends himself with another having a large hemisphere of wicker-work upon it. This is called the *pot,* either from its likeness in shape to that kitchen article, or else in commemoration of some ancient warfare, when the "rude forefathers of the hamlet," being suddenly surrounded with their foes, sallied forth against them, armed with the *pot* and *ladle.*

Single-stick playing, and cudgelling, would be more useful to a man as an art of self-defense, if he were sure that his enemy would always use the same mode of fighting: but the worst of it is, if a Somersetshire single-stick player quarrel with a Devonshire wrestler, the latter, not thinking himself bound to crack the stickler's head by the rules of the game, will probably run in and throw him off his legs, giving such a violent shock to his system that the only use he will be able to make of his stick will be that of hobbling home with it.

—*W. Barnes, letter to the editor, Mr Hone,*
of The Year Book of Daily Recreation
and Information, *1832*

parts of France foot fighting systems were called savate, for shoe.

Savate itself was established in the 1800s. It started as a unification of many of the different foot fighting styles across the various provinces of France, along with various hand defense techniques. Canne is the use of one or more short sticks, each held in one hand. Many of these stick fighting arts did not survive the transition to the saber foil and the end of carrying canes in public and the sword in war.

La canne de combat is still practiced by about 10,000 people in France as well as a few hundred in Belgium, the Netherlands, Spain, Italy, and the United States. The Association Française de Boxe Française, Savate et Disciplines Assimilés has a committee dealing with the sport. World championships are held yearly and attract players from all over Europe. La canne de combat is basically fencing using a small (tapered) stick handled with one hand.

Baton is taught as an exercise and timing drill. This uses an opposing hand grip about a foot wide. The stance and grip is very similar to the greatsword stances illustrated in German woodcuts and to the halberd guard position of Swiss woodcuts. It is slower than la canne but the strikes are very powerful.

The current French association has attempted to suppress or limit the influence of the combative lines to make savate popular as a sport and reduce the danger of training. This involved limiting both kicks and strikes, separating la canne, and dropping the study of lutte parisienne, baton, fouette, knife, and panache. These changes came at the cost of much of the old tradition, although a few enthusiasts still teach the combative form. In the 1980s several of these formed a group dedicated to preserving combative style of savate, which they called Savate Danse Du Rue. In Marseilles a school of chaussoun preserves the art as a cultural activity and a rough sport called chaussoun Marseilles rather than as a functional fighting system. The Academy of French Martial Arts in Dallas continues the French fighting tradition in the United States. That cudgeling will pass into history, however, seems a distinct possibility.

—STEVE HICK

See also Fencing; Martial Arts, Philippines.
Bibliography: Delahaye, M. (1986) *Savate, Chaussoun, et Boxe-Française*. Paris: Editions Française Reder. Khalsa, Nanak Dev Singh. (1991) *Gatka: As Taught by Nanak Dev Singh Khalsa, bk. 1. Dance of the Sword : Beginner Levels I, II & III*. 2d ed. Amsterdam: GT International. Reed, P., and R. Muggerridge. (1984) *Savate, the Martial Art of France*. Phoenix, AZ: Paladin Press.

Curling

Curling is a sport in which participants slide "rocks" or "stones" along a sheet of ice toward a "house." The competition is between two four-player teams or "rinks."

The objective is to score more points than the other team. Points are awarded at the completion of each end to the team with rocks closest to the "tee."

The attractions of curling resemble those of golf. At the highest competitive levels of play, the sport represents a fascinating test of skill and strategy, and it particularly highlights players' capacity to perform well under pressure. The game can also be enjoyed by recreational players because almost anyone can make a shot occasionally, and serious injuries are rare.

History
For nearly two hundred years, students of the history of curling have argued over whether the sport was "invented" in Scotland or in continental Europe. It now seems clear that curling as we know it developed primarily in Scotland. From early in the 16th century until early in the 1800s, the Scots played according to local rules that dictated varying numbers of players and shots and rinks of assorted dimensions as well as stones of diverse shapes and sizes. Then, in the early 1800s, when improved means of transportation made it possible for curlers to compete against distant opponents, uniformity of rules became desirable. This uniformity was accomplished in large part through the formation in 1838 of the Grand Caledonian Curling Club (it became the Royal Caledonian Curling Club in 1843, after it received royal patronage).

While Scots were developing the modern game of curling, they were also exporting it. Thus, over the course of about 150 years, from the 1760s to the 1910s, curling appeared in England, Sweden, New Zealand, Switzerland, Norway, Austria, Italy, France, and the United States. It was played for a time in Ireland, Russia, and even China. Most important, curling began in Canada. By early in the 20th century, the sport was more popular and more skillfully played in Canada than it ever had been anywhere.

The hotbed of curling in Canada was the prairie region of the southern and central parts of the current provinces of Manitoba, Saskatchewan, and Alberta. The prairies were settled between the 1870s and the 1920s. Among the immigrants to the region were significant numbers of Scottish people who came either from Scotland itself or from eastern Canada. Also, commercial agriculture drove prairie agriculture; in summer many people were extremely busy, but in winter they had plenty of leisure time. Finally, excellent natural ice could be maintained inside covered rinks for three or four months a year, much longer than in other parts of the world where curling had a following.

Hacks, Shoes, and the Delivery of the Rock

Early Scottish curling took place on frozen rivers, streams, and lakes. The curlers had to carry with them a portable foot grip, usually called a "crampit." The crampit encouraged a delivery from a sideways position.

In Canada, in the last half of the 19th century, curling moved indoors. Permanent holes or "hacks" were cut in the ice, and as time went on leather or rubber was inserted in the holes. The hack allowed a curler to keep the shoulders square to the target and therefore to be a more efficient athlete. In particular, the hack allowed a curler to be much more accurate with "take-out" shots.

The "slide" developed as a follow-through from the face-the-target delivery. Early in the 20th century the slide evolved, especially in the prairies of Canada, where curlers played a knock-out style that often required heavy weight. The momentum from delivering a fast rock carried the curler a few feet forward out of the hack. Since the 1960s special curling shoes have been manufactured. They have featured brick, stainless steel, or some other sliding material.

Nowadays a top male or female curler in the act of throwing a rock is a beautiful athletic sight. He or she is using footwear that allows for the kind of smooth, balanced delivery that curlers a century ago could not even have imagined.

—Morris Mott

Prairie Canadians curled both more and better than did other peoples. From the 1880s to the 1950s, they introduced and promoted most of the techniques and strategies that gradually made curling a more impressive and demanding athletic contest. They developed the sliding delivery, which resulted from—and at the same time encouraged—a style of play based on "hits" rather than "draws." Although every curler was an amateur, the top players on the prairies became as serious about their sport as any professional athlete.

In the latter part of the 19th century and the first part of the 20th, then, Canadians took the Scottish game of curling to new heights of popularity and skill. However, curling was not yet popular internationally. It did not become so until after World War I and especially after World War II.

Between the 1920s and the 1990s, the sport became truly international, due largely to the availability of "artificial ice." In the prosperous 1940s, 1950s and 1960s artificial ice rinks were built in many cities in Canada, England, Scotland, and the United States and also in warm countries where the natural ice game had not been well established. Curlers now had consistent ice, and they had it, theoretically at least, 12 months of the year.

In Canada, the prairies remained the most impor-tant curling region, but clubs sprung up in every province and territory. Women started to participate in significant numbers early in the 20th century, and by the 1980s there were nearly as many females as males on the ice. By the 1990s there were over a million curlers in Canada, far more than anywhere else.

Meanwhile, in the United States, curling achieved a reasonable degree of popularity by the turn of the 20th century, but lost appeal until after World War II. Then, with the gradual adoption of artificial ice rinks, curling developed a large following. By the 1990s the United States Curling Association oversaw men's and women's curling in 27 states in the union, with some 15,000 registered curlers.

In Scandinavia, curling became an important sport in Norway and Sweden and recently it has gained a foothold in Denmark, Finland, and Iceland. By the 1980s, Norway had over 1,000 curlers.

In continental western and southern Europe, curling first gained prominence at the turn of the 20th century as an outdoor sport played at Alpine resorts. The hotels catered to Scottish and English tourists who wanted to play the sport. During the interwar period the continental Europeans started to curl in significant numbers. By the 1990s in Europe, curling had its largest following in Alpine countries: Switzerland, France, and Germany. Each had a few thousand curlers. Smaller numbers of aficionados resided in Austria, Italy, the Netherlands, Belgium, Liechtenstein, Luxembourg, Andorra, Bulgaria, Hungary, the Czech Republic, Romania, and Russia.

In Britain, curling gained adherents. In Scotland, the home of the sport, curling was given a boost early in the 20th century by the construction of indoor rinks. After World War II, ice hockey declined in popularity and curling benefited from the greater availability of ice. It was further stimulated after the 1950s by the Scots' desire to match the skill of Canadians in international matches. By the 1980s Scotland had some 30,000 curlers.

Curling was introduced in a number of other countries after the 1960s, including such unlikely ones (given their climates) as Mexico, South Africa, and Côte d'Ivoire. The next spurt in popularity seems likely to occur in the Pacific Rim. In the 1980s and 1990s curling associations were formed in Japan, Australia, New Zealand, and Korea to serve a steadily growing number of participants.

Since the 1960s the highlights of the curling year have been the world championship events. These championship events are administered by the World Curling Federation, made up of 31 curling associations. This federation was founded in 1966 (as the International Curling Association) in part to oversee the unofficial world men's championship event that the Scotch Whisky Association had arranged annually since 1959. It was also founded in order to apply for status for curling as an official sport at the Winter Olympic Games, a goal achieved with the curling competitions for men and women at the 1998 Winter Olympics in Japan.

Rules and Play

The dimensions of the sheet of ice or "rink" on which a game occurs may vary slightly. In Canada the sheet is generally 44.5 meters (146 feet) long and 4.3 meters (14 feet, 2 inches) wide; for international competitions the sheet is the same length but 4.75 meters (15 feet, 7 inches) wide. Some of the most important rules of curling may be identified by referring to the lines drawn on the ice.

"Hacks" are placed at each hack line; rocks are thrown from a hack. The back line marks the farthest point a rock may travel down the sheet and still remain in play. "Sweepers" may assist a rock from tee line to tee line. When delivering a rock, a player must release the stone before it reaches the near hog line from the hack; at the other end, the rock must stop beyond the hog line (but before the back line) in order to remain in play. The area between the hog line and the tee line, not including the house, has become in very recent years a "free guard zone." With its first two shots, a team may establish "guards" in this zone. The opposing team may not remove these guards with its first shot in some jurisdictions or with either of its first two shots in other jurisdictions.

The future of curling seems very promising. It is now an Olympic sport, which means much international exposure. It is now almost always played on artificial ice and the climate no longer determines who can participate. It can be enjoyed by young as well as old, by men as well as women and, as thousands of Scots, Canadians, and others can attest, by serious athletes as well as those who just want an opportunity to visit and laugh with their friends.

—MORRIS MOTT

Bibliography: Lukowich, Ed, Eigil Ramsfjell, and Bud Sumerville. (1990) *The Joy of Curling: A Celebration.* Toronto: McGraw-Hill Ryerson. Mott, Morris, and John Allardyce. (1989) *Curling Capital: Winnipeg and the Roarin' Game, 1876 to 1988.* Winnipeg: University of Manitoba Press. Welsh, Robin. (1969) *A Beginner's Guide to Curling.* London: Pelham Books.———. (1985) *International Guide to Curling.* London: Pelham Books.

Cycling

Cycling is the fastest form of human-powered motion. A cyclist travels short distances twice as fast as by running and long distances more than three times as fast. The most efficient vehicles ever invented, bicycles are used for transportation, recreation, and sport, but worldwide, their main use is for everyday travel. However, in affluent regions, especially North America, Europe, and Australasia, bicycles are used extensively for recreation. The speed of cycling also invites competition.

History

The bicycle evolved from a two-wheeled vehicle without pedals known as a hobby horse, propelled by the rider's feet. This was modified around 1820 into a machine with foot treadles and a driving shaft. Around 1865, Pierre Lallamont, a Frenchman, introduced the velocipede, with a large front wheel and a smaller rear wheel, both made of wood and metal. The early bicycles were so uncomfortable that they were known as "boneshakers." They had to be pedaled furiously to achieve a speed as fast as running. Mass production began in the 1860s.

The world's first recorded bicycle race was held in 1868 over a distance of 1,200 meters on a track at Saint-Cloud, a Paris suburb. In the same year, track races for women were held in France. The first recorded cycling road race was between Paris and Rouen, a distance of 123 kilometers (76 miles), in 1869. Both men and women competed in this race. About the same time, races were held in other countries, including Australia, England, and the United States.

The 1870s brought much lighter vehicles with larger front wheels to increase their speed. The classic "high bicycle" was the fastest thing on the road and could outdistance a galloping horse. High bicycles were used for traveling long distances and for competitive sport. As early as 1873, riders on high bicycles completed a 1,300-kilometer (808 miles) ride across Britain in 14 days.

By 1890 the dangerous high bicycle was being supplanted by "safety" bicycles with smaller, equal-sized wheels. These new bicycles also had pneumatic tires and a chain drive, making them considerably faster. While a champion rider could reach 40 kilometers per hour (25 miles per hour) in a sprint on a high bicycle, a safety bicycle rider could achieve 50 kilometers per hour (31 miles per hour).

Cycle sport first became organized in the 1870s in

England, which at that time was the leading country in the production of bicycles. Class differences were reflected in the establishment of separate amateur and professional cycling events. Amateurs were "gentlemen" who competed for enjoyment and accepted no financially valuable prizes. Professional riders were paid and entertained the working classes. Cycle sport was essentially a male pastime in England, and most people opposed strenuous cycling by women. Nevertheless, there were some female competitors in France and the United States. The international control body, the Union Cycliste Internationale (UCI), was established in 1896.

In the 1890s, cycling on specially constructed tracks with steeply banked sides became enormously popular throughout Europe, North America, and Australia. Almost every city had a cycle track, whether surfaced with dirt, wood, asphalt, or concrete. Sprint and handicap races were held over a variety of distances. Track bicycles had a fixed drive and no brakes or gears—a tradition that continues today. At the same time, cycle racing on roads thrived throughout the world. Professional road racing flourished in France and Belgium with the establishment of such place-to-place races as the Paris-Brest-Paris, Paris-Brussels, Paris-Roubaix, and in 1903 the most famous of all, the Tour de France. The early races were grueling events over bad roads with single "stages" (non-stop distances) up to 500 kilometers (311 miles) in length.

Of the many road races in the United States, the most popular was the annual Pullman Race in Chicago, Illinois. In Australia, the first Warrnambool-Melbourne cycle race was held in 1895. However, in England there was concern about the dangers of cycle racing on public roads, which led to the ban of "massed-start" racing. The only form of road racing permitted was time trialing. The enormous interest in the speed of cycling led to contests between cyclists and horses and cyclists and trains. Records were often set by cyclists behind other cyclists who took turns to make the pace. In special track races in the 1890s cyclists were paced by several teams of four, five, or even six riders on tandem bicycles. After 1898, pacing was done by motorbikes.

At the start of this century, the prospect of using bicycles for maneuvers and dispatch in warfare led to the formation of cyclist divisions in armies around the world. Some French soldiers enjoyed riding through fields and forests, leading to the first cyclocross contests. Cyclocross was taken up by European road racers as a way of maintaining fitness during winter, when roads were often icy and dangerous.

Race Across America

The Race Across America (RAAM) is a grueling annual bicycle marathon from California to the East Coast. The race was founded in 1982 to bring greater recognition to ultramarathon cycling, a sport that pushes human limits. During the race, the participants cycle almost continuously, taking only very short rest breaks. In addition to extreme physical challenges, participants must contend with monotony, frustration, and other psychological barriers. In some instances, riders experience hallucinations during the race.

John Marino, the event's founder, broke the transcontinental bicycling record in 1978 by riding from Santa Monica, California, to New York City in 13 days, 1 hour, and 20 minutes. He later decided to organize a transcontinental race and recruited three other top ultramarathon cyclists to help: John Howard, who had won six national cycling championships; Lon Haldeman, who in 1981 broke Marino's transcontinental record; and Michael Shermer, who in 1981 established a north-south cycling record. Shermer, Haldeman, and Marino formed a business, Ultra-Marathon Cycling Inc., to organize an annual event with the new name "Race Across America."

The routes and specific distances of the RAAM change yearly, but they always average around 4,800 kilometers (3,000 miles) and have so far always started in California. Routes have ended in Atlantic City, New Jersey; Savannah, Georgia; and other East Coast cities. The average speed of the participants is an important measurement because of the variations in routes. The typical field for the actual RAAM ranges from 20 to 40 racers, not all of whom finish. The inaugural year for the women's division,1984, was marked by a dramatic finish-line sprint between Shelby Hayden-Clifton and Pat Hines, who tied at 12 days, 20 hours, and 57 minutes. In 1989 the race was opened to teams, with four-person relay and tandem divisions added. This aspect was expanded in 1992 with a new race called Team RAAM. Four-person team races tend to be faster and have more competitive sprints because each racer cycles for shorter distances and can rest while his or her teammates take over the lead.

—John Townes

Rules and Play

At competitive speeds most of a cyclist's power is used to push aside the air through which he or she passes. This greatly influences the various ways cycle racing is conducted. For example, racing cyclists crouch to reduce their air resistance. This can be lessened by a further 20–30 percent when a cyclist "drafts" behind another, so riding in groups plays a major part in the tactics of cycling. At higher altitudes the atmosphere is less dense and air resistance is lower than at sea level. Consequently, some cycling records have been set at high-altitude venues despite it being more difficult for riders to breathe.

Competitive cycling began as and remains a sport with many variations.

Time Trialing
Unpaced time trialing, called *contre la montre* (against the clock) in France, has also been called "the race of truth." Individual trials over standard distances and times were the main form of road racing in England for the first half of this century.

Track Cycling
Track cycling has gradually declined during this century, but is still held in Europe and other countries, culminating in the annual world championships. Track cycling is the major element of the Olympic cycling program. Track races include the following events:

- The 1,000-meter sprint. Two cyclists usually start slowly seeking a tactical advantage. Riders may even stop still, balancing on their pedals for several minutes. The final 200 meters is ridden flat out.
- Pursuit races. Two cyclists or teams of cyclists start off on opposite sides of the track. If one cyclist or team of cyclists catches the other, the race is over. Otherwise, the winner is the first to cross the finish line.
- *Keirin.* A special form of track racing that originated in Japan in 1948. Nine riders start from separate stalls and follow a motorbike, which gradually increases the pace before pulling out with about a lap and a half to go, leaving the riders to contest the final sprint. *Keirin* is dangerous but extremely popular in Japan and has now been included in the world championships.

Road Racing
Road racing is held worldwide, but the most popular series of races form the professional European road-racing circuit. This consists of classic, one-day place-to-place races and stage races, including the three-week Giro d'Italia (Tour of Italy), Vuelta de España (Tour of Spain), and the most famous of all, the Tour de France.

Olympic Games
Track and road cycling have been included in all Olympic Games of the modern era, starting in Athens in 1896. The top Olympic cycling nations have been France, Germany, Italy, and Great Britain. Olympic cycling events consist of track and road events for men and women, and include both individual and team events. The types of Olympic cycling event have varied over the years. Tandem races were part of the program from 1906 to 1972. Women's events were included for the first time in 1984. Mountain bike races were introduced in 1996 and triathlons will be introduced at the Sydney Olympics in 2000.

BMX
BMX (bicycle motocross) is a competition over a short dirt track (typically 300 meters [328 yards]) with humps and banked corners. BMX competitors ride small, single-geared bicycles with 50-centimeter (20-inch) wheels, and wear helmets and other protective clothing. BMX is a family sport. Competitors range in age from 4 to over 45, with separate races for males and females. However, it is most popular with boys of ages 11–12. BMX originated in Santa Monica, California, in 1969 and quickly spread to other countries. National championships are held in more than 30 countries, and world championships occur each year under the control of the UCI. Another form of riding, "freestyle," consists of acrobatic stunts done on a BMX bicycle. "Observed trials" is a contest in which riders traverse extremely difficult terrain on a special low-geared BMX bicycle. By balancing on the pedals and hopping their bicycles, riders can jump over logs and rocks or even climb waterfalls. The objective is to complete the course without putting a foot to the ground ("dabbing").

Mountain Bike Racing
Mountain bike racing also began in California in the 1970s. Tough, versatile bicycles were developed for racing down fire trails, and then wide-range gears were added for riding up them. Races were held throughout the United States and the first national championships were organized in 1983. Many male and female riders with backgrounds in cyclocross and road racing have taken up mountain biking. Although it involves rugged terrain similar to that popular with cyclocross riders, techniques differ.

The sport of mountain biking was enthusiastically adopted in Europe and Australia, and the first world championships were held in 1987. Commercial sponsorship has led to pressure for shorter courses with several laps so spectators and television cameras can watch the racers more easily. World championships now consist of cross-country races of about two hours' duration, and downhill races in which competitors wear full-face helmets and body armor. Separate men's and women's events are held. Mountain biking has been incorporated under the UCI and was included in

Cycling—Tour de France

The Tour de France cycle race is the largest annual sporting event in the world. Stretching to approximately 4,000 kilometers (2,500 miles)—the precise itinerary and distance vary from year to year—but always including a voyage round France taking in the Pyrenees and the Alps, it lasts for three weeks in July. The success of Irish and Colombian riders and of American Greg Lemond (c.1960–)as well as several Australians and East Europeans has recently given the Tour a remarkable global appeal, enhanced by live television film taken mostly by camerapersons perched on the back of motorcycles close to the riders. The best riders must be able to sprint, race against the clock, and climb, day after day, week after week. The greatest of them have become probably the most widely known sporting heroes in 20th-century continental Europe.

The development of the modern bicycle in the 1890s led to classic races, such as the Paris-Bordeaux and the Paris-Roubaix. These were promoted by the new sporting press, especially the daily sports and cycling paper, *Le Vélo*, which alienated one of its main backers, the conservative Baron de Dion. He founded a rival paper, *L'Auto*, whose first editor, Henri Desgranges, backed an idea to organize a race around France. The magnitude and daring of the project captured public attention.

The first Tour was only two-thirds the length of later races and was run day and night in six stages. Desgranges decided to abandon the night stages and lengthen the race itself to go round the whole country, taking in Alpine passes and what were little more than rough tracks in the high Pyrenees.

It was more than a race; it was an epic, a kind of heroic story through which France would come to know itself. The "giants of the road," as they were known, passed through historic sites and scenes of great deeds in the French past. As many as a third of the country would actually see the race go by, organizing local festivities to coincide with it. Perhaps more than any other great sporting event, the Tour is rooted in the landscape and culture of its host country. As a showcase for France it is superb, and tourist towns now pay vast sums to feature in the race.

The Tour is run in teams. The teams were originally sponsored by bicycle manufacturers but are becoming increasingly beverage- and fashion-based. Despite complex deals within and between teams, the Tour is primarily about individual achievement. The main riding group *(le peleton)* is preceded by a massive advertising caravan. The winner, supported by his "servants" (the *domestiques* or supporting riders), is the best overall performer with the lowest aggregate time. There is a prize for the best climber (the "King of the Mountains") and a coveted points prize for the best sprinter as well as a host of other minor awards.

The great riders have become household names, men possessed of seemingly miraculous powers of endurance. (The Tour is limited to men, although a women's Tour de France was launched in 1984.) The epithets attached to their names, as French literary critic Roland Barthes remarked in a famous essay, "Le Tour de France comme épopée" in *Mythologies* (1957), seemed to derive "from an earlier age when the nation reverberated to the image of a handful of ethnic heroes: Brankart le Franc, Bobet le Francien, Robic le Celte" and so on.

The race is run over a period of just over three weeks with 21 stages (in 1996); a stage is a single day with designated starting and finishing point (usually a town or mountain resort called an "étape," which pays handsomely for the privilege). Hence the tour is both a single cumulative race and a series of one-day races.

Heroic feats are part of the popular mythology of the Tour. As riders pass over the great mountain passes—the Tourmalet, the Galibier, the Alpe d'Huez—the deeds of past champions are recalled. Men like the tall, graceful Italian, Fausto Coppi, the "champion of champions," setting out alone across the Alps in 1952 to win a magnificent stage or Bartali, "Gino the Pious," praised by the pope, who first won in 1938 and then again after a gap of 10 years, a feat never repeated since.

Belgians have played a great part in the Tour, especially those from Flanders, who dominated around World War I. The greatest of all was a rider who devoured four successive titles from 1969 to 1972 and another in 1974: Eddy Merkcx (1945–), the "Cannibal," who also won an unprecedented number of other classics.

Two French riders who have won the Tour five times. Jacques Anquetil (1934–1987), the winner in 1957 and again in four successive years from 1961, was a specialist in racing against the clock. His rivalry with the unfortunate Raymond Poulidor (1936–), seemingly destined to be second, caught the attention of even the austere General Charles de Gaulle. Next came "the Badger," Bernard Hinault (1954–), a Breton, like Poulidor from a peasant family, who took charge of the Tour in the 1980s. After a bad fall close to the end of the fourteenth stage of the Tour in 1985, he remounted, blood streaming from a broken nose, to ride across the line on the way to his fifth title.

Hinault's record sixth title was denied him in 1986 by the first American to win the race, Greg Lemond, who repeated his success in 1989. Lemond's success delighted the sponsors of the race. For the Tour has its eye firmly on the global marketplace and is becoming less French in the process despite the guiding hand of Jacques Goddet, who has ruled the race for so long, since the Desgranges era. Recent winners have been Irish and Spanish, most notably the remarkable Spaniard Miguel Indurain (1964–), whose amazing lung capacity and quiet authority made the Tour his from 1991 to 1995.

—*Richard Holt*

the 1996 Atlanta Olympics. Given the sport's near-universal appeal, cycling's future innovations seem likely to receive enthusiastic receptions as well.

—RON SHEPHERD

See also Duathlon; Triathlon.

Bibliography: Cripps, Cecil. (1990) *Racing the Wind!* Melbourne: Vetsport Promotions. Liggett, Phil. (1992) *The Complete Book of Performance Cycling.* London: Collins Willow. Watson, Roderick, and Martin Gray. (1978) *The Penguin Book of the Bicycle.* Harmondsworth, UK: Penguin Books.

Darts

Darts is a recreational activity and sport that evolved in the 20th century from military training and a historical legacy of soldiering, combat, and armed engagement. Darts are now played virtually all over the world with the most competitive play often taking places in taverns and pubs, where in some nations, such as England, regular dart leagues meet several evenings per week.

History

Darts or "dartes" were in use as early as the Middle Ages. Archers used heavily weighted hand arrows in close combat and threw them at archery targets for recreation. Anne Boleyn gave a set of darts to her husband Henry VIII and, in the 16th century, a popular children's game was "blow-point," in which a type of arrow was forced through a pipe and directed at a numbered target. The Pilgrims shipped darts on board the *Mayflower*.

Darts as a sport is primarily a modern, 20th-century activity. The sport took off as a result of one of the most celebrated cases in "sports law." In 1908 at Leeds Magistrates' Court, England, the judicial system focused on the nature and function of darts. Was it a game of chance or skill? If the former it would be prohibited from the domain of licensed premises. However, if it could be proved that the key ingredient was skill then it would be legally admitted into pubs. In a dramatic moment, "Foot" Anakin, the publican who had allowed games of darts inside his pub, turned in a bravura performance. He put three darts in the single 20 and followed this up by throwing three double 20s. The case against Anakin was dismissed and darts in British pubs became not only legal but also *the* premier pub sport.

The National Darts Association of Great Britain (NDA) was founded in 1953. The country's first major competition was inaugurated in 1938–1939 and players sought the Lord Lonsdale Trophy. Since 1962 the NDA has supervised this trophy competition as well as three pairs championships (men's, women's, and mixed) and two individual championships (one open, the other for women). The World Darts Federation World Cup was inaugurated in 1977. A year later that same body instituted the Europe Cup. Both championships are held biennially.

Darts is regularly played by 6 million people in Great Britain, making it the country's leading participation sporting pastime. There are pub and club competitions, and tournaments at league, super league, and professional levels.

The traditional setting of darts—a closed space in which alcohol flows freely and smoking is not discouraged—has created several misconceptions about the sport and its participants. Darts players are serious and intense, though the returns for success are slight compared to other sports. Rhythm and confidence are said to be the keys to success.

Rules and Play

Dart boards are made of bristle, cork, or elm wood. The standard match board is numbered 1 to 20 in the following clockwise sequence: 1, 18, 4, 13, 6, 10, 15, 2, 17, 3, 19, 7, 16, 8, 11, 14, 9, 12, 5, and 20. The board is split into 20 triangular sections, which meet two center rings. The outer ring scores 25, and the inner ring (the bull's-eye) scores 50. The dart board design suggests that the ends of tree trunks were the probable model for dart boards.

The outer ring is divided into sections called "doubles." A dart landing in one of these sections scores exactly double the value of the respective triangular section. This is also the traditional finish to a game of darts. Each player must conclude on an exact double of the number required to win the game. The only exception is if 50 is needed, when a "bull's-eye" counts as double 25.

The inner ring is known as the "treble." All darts landing here score three times the value of the respective triangular section. All the other areas of the triangular sections of the dart board, between the double segment and the treble segment, and between the treble segment and the outer ring score the relevant number.

A standard dart board has a diameter of 45.7 centimeters (18 inches). Each player is allocated three darts. The average length of a dart is 15.3 centimeters (6 inches) long. While the point is made of steel, the barrel or midsection of the dart is plastic, wood, or brass. The tail portion is of feathers, paper, or plastic. Dart players search fastidiously for the perfect amalgamation of weight and balance in a dart.

In competitions the board is hung so that the center is 1.72 meters (5 feet, 8 inches) above the floor. The darts are flighted in, and fired from, a distance of 2.43 meters (8 feet), 2.59 meters (8 feet, 6 inches), or 2.74 meters (9 feet).

Games begin with a high number and go to zero with competitions opening (and closing) with a double. Standard starting totals are 1001, 501, and 301.

Variations on the standard game include "Darts Baseball," "Fives," "Halve It," "Closing," "Scram," and "Shanghai." A traditional pub favorite and one that lends itself to an informal recreational activity rather than a "serious" sport is "Around the Clock," which can be played with an unlimited number of players. Players take turns, after scoring a double, trying to place a dart in each sector beginning at 20 and working their way down to 1.

World Darts

Although primarily a British sport, darts enjoys some cosmopolitan exposure, especially in Commonwealth countries. The Australian Darts Council was founded in 1927. The Darts Federation of Australia was created in 1976 to facilitate Australia's entry to the World Darts Federation, which had been set up in 1975. Australia hosted the World Cup in 1985 and has won the Pacific Cup four times.

Over 100,000 "darters" practice in the United States, Puerto Rico, and Guam. The American Darts Organiza-

tion hosted the 1979 World Cup (the first major championship held outside of the United Kingdom) and controls a circuit of professional tournaments worth over $1 million a year in purse money.

Darts organizations continue to lobby for acceptance of darts as an Olympic sport—so far without success. Perhaps there is still a question whether darts is truly a sport or merely a pastime.

—SCOTT A. G. M. CRAWFORD

Bibliography: Barnes, S. (1994) "Mortgage Money Rides on Point of a Dart." *Times* (London), 3 January. Vamplew, W., K. Moore, J. O'Hara, R. Cashman, and I. Jobling. (1992) *Oxford Companion to Australian Sport.* Melbourne: Oxford University Press.

Decathlon
See Track and Field, Decathlon

Diffusion

Why do the young men of Munich, Rio de Janeiro, and Nairobi play soccer (association football) while their counterparts in Madras prefer cricket? Why do the Japanese and the Cubans, two cultures otherwise very different, share a love of baseball? How can we explain national differences in preferences for sports? The key is the relative political, economic, military, and cultural power of the nations involved. A nation that exercises political or economic or military power usually, but not always, exercises cultural power as well.

Thus, cricket and soccer are among the most widely diffused team games because both took shape when their country of origin, Great Britain, was unquestionably the world's most powerful nation. Enthusiasm for the Tour de France and similar races in Belgium, Spain, and Italy shows the French sphere of cultural influence. In the late 19th century, when the United States began to challenge Great Britain's global hegemony, baseball became popular in Japan and in the Caribbean. After World War II, from which the United States emerged dominant globally, Europeans suddenly discovered the joys of basketball and volleyball.

Cricket was the first modern ball game. Its rules were codified in 1744 and the Marylebone Cricket Club was founded in 1787. Between these dates, the British decisively defeated the French in a series of imperial conflicts fought principally in Asia and North America. By the time Nelson's victory at Trafalgar in 1805 and Wellington's at Waterloo in 1815 confirmed British hegemony, men (and occasionally women) of British birth or ancestry were playing cricket in Philadelphia and New

York as well as in Toronto, Kingston, Adelaide, and Cape Town. As part of the British effort to pacify and to administer the Indian subcontinent, the British taught cricket to the sons of Indian princes (who were horrified to learn that cricket balls were made of leather, a "jutha" or "unclean," material).

Cricket remains popular throughout the Commonwealth, but it has never been widely played elsewhere except among men and women of British origin. Soccer, not cricket, was destined to become the world's most popular sport. When the Football Association was formed in 1863, soccer got its name (derived from "association football"). Great Britain was near the zenith of its imperial power.

That year an Irish pupil from Killarney introduced soccer to his Belgian classmates at the Maison de Melle, a school for the nobility and the upper middle class. A German student brought the game to Germany in 1874. A Dutch boy who had studied at an English boarding school founded the Haarlemsche Football Club in 1879. Although Englishmen living in France had been playing soccer as early as 1864, Parisian schoolboys did not begin to imitate them for twenty years. By 1896, soccer had reached Hungary, introduced by a schoolboy whose parents had emigrated to England, when he returned to Budapest on a holiday visit.

In Italy, schoolboys played less of a role than they did in France, Germany, Hungary, and the Low Countries. British sailors introduced soccer in the 1880s when they docked and went ashore in Genoa, Leghorn, Naples, and other peninsular ports, but it was Britons "in trade" in Turin and Milan, the industrial and financial centers of northern Italy, who first organized viable teams. Initially, the teams were composed entirely of Britons. Then, in 1887, Edoardo Bosio, a businessman from Turin, visited England and discovered the game, which he promptly introduced to the employees of his firm. By 1898, there was a Federazione Italiana del Football.

British merchants, bankers, railroad manufacturers, and educators diffused soccer throughout Latin America, an area dominated by British capital and entrepreneurial expertise well into the 20th century.

In Mexico, British mine owners and other businessmen established a cricket club in 1827. But by 1890, when U.S. investors in the Mexican economy surpassed the British, baseball had appeared. British influence waned; U.S. influence waxed; baseball became Mexico's most popular sport. The game had already spread to Cuba by 1864, again introduced by a student. Cuban patriots who fled after the failure of their first war for independence (1868–1878) sought solace in baseball during their exile in Santo Domingo and sowed the seeds for today's crop of Dominican major leaguers.

The 1870s were also the years when Japan, closed for centuries to Western influence, opened its ports and began to modernize. After the Meiji Restoration (1868) that returned political power from the Tokugawa family to the emperor, U.S. educators were invited to reform the Japanese educational system. Horace Wilson, teaching at what is now Tokyo University, introduced baseball in 1873. The game spread relatively slowly, but three prestigious universities—Meiji, Keio, and Waseda—formed an intercollegiate league in 1914. In 1936, two years after a tour by a U.S. team that included George Herman "Babe" Ruth, a professional league was launched.

Basketball, invented in 1891 by James Naismith at Springfield's YMCA Training School, reached the Far East a mere four years later when Willard Lyon established the first Chinese YMCA at Tientsin. Lyon's colleagues carried the game to the Philippines and to Japan. Their efforts to propagate basketball bore early fruit. At the first Far Eastern Championship Games, held in Manila in 1913, basketball was part of the program.

Other YMCA workers attempted to interest Europeans in the newly invented game, but they made little headway until World War I, when the United States became a military ally of Britain, France, and Italy. At the Inter-Allied Games held to celebrate victory, a basketball tournament was part of the program (U.S. servicemen defeated a team of French soldiers, who had just learned the game, 93–8).

Between 1918 and 1939, the most important development in the global diffusion of modern sports was the progress of the Olympic Games. When Pierre de Coubertin, a French aristocrat, revived the ancient games at Athens in 1896, all but 2 of the approximately 300 athletes were Europeans or North Americans. Among the Olympians, there was 1 Chilean and 1 Australian. The 3 Africans who sailed to London for the 1908 games were white, as were 19 of the 21 Africans who competed in Stockholm in 1912. The other 2 were an Egyptian fencer and an Algerian marathon runner. The Los Angeles Games of 1932 were another breakthrough in terms of diffusion. An Argentine, Juan Zabala, won the marathon—Latin America's second gold—and Japanese swimmers astonished the world by winning 11 of a possible 16 medals in their events. Only after World War II did Kenyans and other representatives of sub-Saharan Africa begin to play a prominent role at the Olympics. The International Olympic Committee itself began, in 1894, with 12 European members, an American, an Argentinian, and a New Zealander. Asian members were added in 1908 (Turkey) and 1909 (Japan). The first Africans, both of European descent, were elected in 1910 and 1913. It was not until 1981 that the first women were elected to the International Olympic Committee.

One surprising postwar development has been the penetration of typically American games into areas once dominated by sports of British, French, or German origin. In Spain, Italy, Belgium, and Turkey, basketball is the second or third most popular sport (after soccer). The 32 teams of Italy's professional league draw two million fans a year to their games. The French still prefer soccer, rugby, and cycling, but have become increasingly fascinated by surfboards, in-line skates, hang-gliders, and other artifacts of *les sports californiens*. In Australia, Japanese sponsors have joined the Cincinnati Reds, the California Angels, and six other U.S. clubs in establishing an eight-team professional baseball league (1989).

The most intriguing sign of a further shift in this global balance is the popularity in Great Britain of American football (a game derived, ironically, from British rugby). Two years after the birth of the London Ravens in 1983, a 38-team British American Football League was formed. Anheuser-Busch, which has underwritten Channel 4's production costs for telecasts of National Football League games, organized a semiprofessional Budweiser League that grew to nearly 200 teams by 1988. The NFL moved next to Europea, where Trans World Sport has arranged for television coverage of nascent football leagues in France, Germany, Italy, Spain, and elsewhere. In 1991, the NFL launched a World League of American Football that included teams representing London, Barcelona, Frankfurt, and several U.S. cities. The venture faltered and was suspended but has now been revived as a purely European league.

Will the London Monarchs ever be the equal of the San Francisco Forty-Niners? Perhaps not, but other teams have turned the tables and "beaten them at their own game." When Australian cricketers vanquished the English at the London's Oval in 1882, they simultaneously affirmed their membership in the British Empire and their own national identity. When a team of schoolboys from Tokyo challenged and defeated the overconfident U.S. baseball players at the Yokohama Athletic Club in 1896, the joyful news was telegraphed the length and breadth of Japan.

The global diffusion of modern sports, however, has not been universally acclaimed. In parts of the Islamic world, fundamentalists have attempted to stop the spread of women's sports and other manifestations of Western influence. European defenders of traditional sports have formed organizations, like the Vlaamse Volkssport Centrale (1980), to preserve and revive folk games. Radical scholars writing from a Marxist perspective had condemned the displacement of older forms of games as "cultural imperialism" or as "cultural genocide."

The radical critique of sport diffusion tends to overlook the fact that there is probably no such thing as an "authentic" traditional culture. All but the most isolated cultures borrow and adapt from one another. The more powerful nations have a favorable balance of sports trade, but they too import sports. The popularity of Asian martial arts among the middle classes of Europe and the United States is a case in point. It is also true that those who have adopted a foreign sport have usually adapted it (which is exactly what Americans did when transforming rounders into baseball and rugby into gridiron football). Even when adopters are not adapters, they come to feel that the sport they have borrowed is their very own, an authentic expression of who they are. People follow the fortunes of their team at the World Cup because they believe that soccer is *their* game and the players are representatives of them as a nation. It is doubtful, when Brazilians celebrated their World Cup triumph in 1994, that many of them worried about Charles Miller's role, a hundred years earlier, in bringing the game to São Paulo from England. Soccer is, in the words of Pele, "the greatest joy of the people." And something similar can be said about modern sports wherever they are played.

—ALLEN GUTTMANN

Bibliography: Arbena, Joseph L., ed. (1988) *Sport and Society in Latin America: Diffusion, Dependency, and Mass Culture*. Westport, CT: Greenwood Press. Baker, William J., and J. A. Mangan, eds. (1987) *Sport in Africa*. New York: Africana. Bale, John, and Joseph Maguire, eds. (1993) *The Global Sports Arena*. London: Frank Cass. Guttmann, Allen. (1994) *Games and Empires: Modern Sports and Cultural Imperialism*. New York: Columbia University Press. Mangan, J. A., ed. (1992) *The Cultural Bond: Sport, Empire and Society*. London: Frank Cass.

Disabled Sports

The evolution of sports for people with disabilities began after World War II, which brought significant increases in service-connected injuries such as paraplegia, quadriplegia, and amputation. Therapists and physicians in many countries use vigorous physical and recreational activities as integral parts of rehabilitation. Sport integrates the individual into society and helps to enhance self-esteem. Today, sport for the disabled is a means for athletes with disabilities to attain a high level of physical fitness and compete with fellow athletes from all over the world. The sports also help counter the still-common view that athletes with disabilities are not "real" athletes. Sport shifts the focus from the athlete's disability to his or her ability.

The Paralympics are for athletes with physical and sensorial disabilities (in contrast to the Special Olympics, which serve mentally retarded youth and adults). Physical disabilities include spinal cord injuries, amputations, blindness, cerebral palsy, and other conditions, such as arthritis, osteogenesis imperfecta, and dwarfism. Many countries have national research and training centers to provide the optimal environment, facilities, and equipment for athletes with disabilities to training for their specific sports.

History

The oldest international organization on sport for persons with disabilities is the Comité International des Sports des Sourds (Committee International on Silent Sports [CISS]). It was founded in 1924 in conjunction with the first international competition for athletes with disabilities, the World Games for the Deaf in Paris. In conjunction with this event, CISS has conducted Summer World Games every four years since 1924 and Winter World Games since 1949.

In 1944 the National Spinal Injuries Centre of the Stoke Mandeville Hospital in Aylesbury, England, was founded. Wheelchair sports were included as part of the rehabilitation process of war veterans. Ludwig Guttmann introduced England's first organized wheelchair sports program on the front lawn of the Stoke Mandeville Hospital in 1948. Those activities are known as the Stoke Mandeville Games. Guttmann expanded these games to include bowling, table tennis, and field events in which wheelchair athletes competed. After 1960, weightlifting, fencing, and swimming were added.

In 1958, following the first National Wheelchair Games held in the United States, the National Wheelchair Association (now called Wheelchair Sports, USA) was organized to establish rules and regulations governing all wheelchair sports except basketball, which was governed by the National Wheelchair Basketball Association, founded in 1949. During this same period Guttmann founded the International Stoke Mandeville Games Federation (ISMGF), which governed the international games.

In 1960 the First International Games for Disabled of an Olympic nature were held in Rome for spinally paralyzed athletes under the auspices of the International Stoke Mandeville Games Federation. This marked the beginning of the Olympics for the Disabled, which were held every fourth year in the same country (if possible) as the Olympic Games from 1960 through 1980. After 1980, the International Olympic Committee (IOC) requested that disabled athletes no longer use the term Olympics, and the games continued under the name Paralympics.

In 1968, Eunice Kennedy Shriver founded Special Olympics to help erase misconceptions about people with mental retardation. Special Olympics was established to provide year-round sports training and athletic competition in a variety of Olympic-type sports for children and adults with mental retardation. It is founded on the belief that people with mental retardation can, with proper instruction and encouragement, learn, enjoy, and benefit from participation in individual and team sports, adapted as necessary to meet their needs. Sports training and competition is offered in 23 Olympic-type sports (summer sports, winter sports, and demonstration sports) open to anyone ages eight and up.

The number of sports for the disabled increased slowly. While basketball, swimming, and archery have been practiced by athletes with disabilities for a number of years, only recently have such sports as tennis, wheelchair rugby (murder ball), volleyball, and winter skiing become popular. These changes occurred following pressure from athletes, coaches, and scientists.

In 1984, for the first time in Olympic history, at the Los Angeles Olympics, two wheelchair races were included as demonstration events. The aim of such demonstration events is to integrate sports for athletes with disabilities into the international sports movement, while preserving the identity of sports for disabled athletes. Sixteen wheelchair athletes representing eight countries competed. The women's wheelchair 800-meter (875-yard) race was won by Sharon Rahn Hedrick of the United States with a time of 2:15.50. The men's wheelchair 1500-meter (1604-yard) race was won by Paul Van Winkle of Belgium with a time of 3:58.50, as over 90,000 cheering fans yelled their appreciation.

In 1988 the Paralympics were held in Seoul, Korea, following the Olympics. Over 4,000 athletes from 60 countries participated in the Seoul Paralympics. Three hundred and seventy world records were set, in addition to over 600 Paralympic records. For the first time in the history of disabled sports, athletes with disabilities were selected for participation in IOC drug testing. Athletes were screened under the same procedures in place for able-bodied competitors.

Special sports included Goalball (for blind and visually impaired athletes), which uses a 5-pound (2.3-kilogram) ball with bells in it hurled by three members of each team into the opponent's goal. Guide runners assisted blind and visually impaired runners in competing in track events. Tandem biking allowed blind and visually impaired athletes to team with sighted riders to compete in cycling. Other sports included judo, swimming, table tennis, wheelchair tennis, weight lifting, wheelchair basketball, sitting and standing volleyball for athletes with amputations, boccia, fencing, and equestrian events.

The 1992 Paralympic logo, "Sports Without Limits," was designed to express the effort to create full social integration of people with disabilities through participation in sporting events. An estimated 60,000 spectators and millions of television viewers witnessed the opening ceremony, when Spanish Paralympic archer Antonio Rebollo shot a flaming arrow across the length of the stadium and lit the Olympic flame. Sixty-two countries were represented by approximately 3,000 athletes competing in 16 sports over a 14-day period. Such numbers represent the progress of athletes with disabilities worldwide. The United States won a total of 176 medals (76 gold), with Germany second (171 total; 61 gold), followed by Great Britain.

Over 7,000 athletes representing 140 countries converged on New Haven, Connecticut, to participate in the 1995 Special Olympics World Games. The Olympic torch was delivered from Athens, Greece, to the opening ceremonies at the Yale Bowl. U.S. President Bill Clinton took part in the ceremony and television networks covered the games. For the first time the World Games included a marathon.

These games showcased the abundance of sports and recreation opportunities now available for individuals with mental retardation. One of the most notable is Special Olympics Unified Sports, a program that combines, on the same team, athletes with and without mental retardation. The aim of Special Olympics Unified Sports is to provide Special Olympics athletes the opportunity for meaningful training and competition with nondisabled teammates. Unified Sports has been especially successful in schools, where they help bridge the gap between students without disabilities and their special education peers.

Outlook

The 1996 Atlanta Paralympics, held immediately after the 1996 Summer Olympics, may have been to the disabled sports movement what Los Angeles 1984 was to the Olympic movement in the United States—bringing media attention, awareness, and sponsorship to the Games and providing a funding base for disabled sports. The Atlanta Paralympics brought together nearly 4,000 elite athletes with physical or visual impairments, representing over 100 nations. Athletes competed in 19 sports, 14 of which were Olympic sports.

In 1984 Claudine Sherrill wrote, "The ultimate athlete can be anyone, disabled or able-bodied, who demonstrates the capacity to dream, the unwavering intent to be the best, and the willingness to pay the price of long, hard and strenuous training."

—MARY E. RIDGWAY

Bibliography: Adams, R. C., and J. A. McCubbine. (1991) *Games, Sports, and Exercises for the Physically Disabled.* 4th ed. Philadelphia: Lea and Febiger. Allen, A. (1981) *Sports for the Handicapped.* New York: Walker and Company. Sherrill, C. (1986) *Adapted Physical Educational and Recreation.* 3d ed. Dubuque, IA: Wm. C. Brown Publishers.

Diving

A dive is a head-first entry into the water, straightforward or intricate depending on how the diver performs the dive and what he or she does between leaving the platform and hitting the water. Diving has flourished throughout the 20th century and is now a component of swimming competitions held at all levels of competition. At the international level, from the 1970s on the most successful divers (men and women) have been from the United States, Italy, Germany, the then Soviet Union, and China. English swimming authority Pat Besford articulates an apt and evocative definition of diving: "This complicated sport demands acrobatic ability, the grace of a ballet dancer, iron nerve, and a liking for heights."

History

One of the earliest historical records of diving is from 480 B.C.E. Called "Tomba del Tuffatore" (the "tomb of the diver"), it is a huge burial chamber to the south of Naples, Italy, that houses, high up on a roof slab, a painting of a male athlete diving from a small elevated platform. The first book on diving apparently was published in Germany in 1843. In the 18th and 19th centuries, diving was popularized by the Germans and the Swedes, who, took various pieces of apparatus to the beach and used these to perform gymnastic stunts prior to entering the water.

Competitive diving began in Great Britain in 1883 with the Amateur Swimming Association setting up the first plunging competition. The plunge was a head-first crouching dive, rather like the modern racing dive off starting blocks. The Swedish divers Johannson, Hagberg, and Mauritzi came to London during the late 19th century and entertained crowds with exhibitions of what was called "fancy diving" from a 10-meter platform erected at Highgate Ponds. These exhibitions inspired the 1901 formation of the world's first official diving organization, called the Amateur Diving Association.

Springboard diving was on the program for the first time at the 1904 St. Louis Olympics and platform diving was introduced at the 1906 Athens Olympics. Women first took part at the 1912 Stockholm Olympics. Diving is a popular activity at the club, school, and university level but generally draws international attention only every four years at the Olympics when diving events are widely televised.

Rules and Play

Today the Fédération Internationale de Natation Amateur—the world governing body for aquatics—lists nearly 90 different types of dives that may be performed at various levels of difficulty. Some of the basic dive types are forward dives with the body facing the water and the dive made forward; backward dives with the back to the water and rotating away from the board or platform; reverse dives with the diver facing forward, but the rotation of the body back toward the board; inward dives with the back to the water and rotating inward toward the board or platform; twisting dives made from either starting position with the body twisting in the air; armstand dives made from the platform only—the diver begins the movement sequence from a motionless handstand on the platform's edge.

Diving body positions include tuck, pike, straight, and free. Tuck means that the body is bent at the knees and at the hips, with the knees held together and drawn to the chest; pike means that the body is bent at the waist with the legs straight; straight means that the body is not bent; and free refers to a combination of two or more of these positions.

Degree of difficulty is key to scoring. The standard Olympic Diving Table rates the toughness of dives from a low of 1.2 to a high of 3.5. The reverse three-and-one-half somersault is rated a 3.5 degree of difficulty, the highest for any springboard dive. The degree of difficulty factor means that a flawless uncomplicated dive may score as well as the most advanced of dives performed poorly. A panel of seven judges awards points according to the following highly subjective formula:

- Failed dive—0 points;
- Unsatisfactory dive—.5–2 points
- Deficient dive—2.5–4.5 points
- Satisfactory dive—5–6 points
- Good dive—6.5–8 points
- Very good dive—8.5–10 points

After displaying the score numbers, judges discard the high and low scores. The remaining scores are then multiplied by a factor of three-fifths and by the dive's degree of difficulty. Diving competitions, as with gymnastics and figure skating events, have a history plagued by acrimonious exchanges over accusations of unfair scoring. At the 1956 Olympics in Melbourne the head coach of the U.S. men's diving team, Karl Michael, accused the Russian and Hungarian judges of colluding. This controversy led to new rules that dictated that (1) scoring would be done electronically (judges would no longer hold up cards), (2) no national coaches would serve as judges, and (3) if judges were deemed incompetent they could be removed from the panel.

Diving is a bruising activity. Platform divers are more missile than body as they hurtle through the air to hit the water at speeds of as much as 80 kilometers per hour.

Men's springboard diving (the 3-meter board) has been marked by the enduring presence and depth of U.S. diving, due largely to well-supported programs at local and college levels. At both the 1932 and 1964 Olympics the three medal winners were from the United States. The United States has also had great success in platform diving (from a 10-meter-high fixed platform). The 1970s, 1980s, and 1990s have shown the strength of women's diving in the Germanys, the Soviet republics, Cuba, and China.

The world record high dive of 53.9 meters (176 feet, 10 inches) was performed by Oliver Favre of Switzerland in France in 1987. The women's record is 36.8 meters (120 feet, 9 inches), by American Lucy Waidle in Hong Kong in 1985. However, in terms of awesome human feats, no competitive dives into diving pools can compare to the soaring dives of the Pentecost Islanders of the South Pacific. The Islanders engage in land diving, a sport similar to bungee jumping, from heights of from 25 to 80 feet, with long fiber ropes tied to their ankles to stop their dive before they hit the ground.

—SCOTT A. G. M. CRAWFORD

Bibliography: Barber, G., ed. (1984) *Olympic Gold 84.* Kensington, New South Wales: Bay Books. Eaves, G. (1969) *Diving: The Mechanics of Springboard and Firmboard*

Techniques. New York: A. S. Barnes and Company. Smith, D., with J. H. Bender. (1973) *Inside Diving.* Chicago: Henry Regnery Company.

Drag Racing

Two cars, start and finish lines, and someone to yell "Go!" basically defines drag racing as a casual form of recreation. Professional drag racing involves sophisticated cars, highly trained drivers, special courses, and much money. At all levels, the goal of the sport is to cross the finish line first.

History

Drag racing apparently got started in the 1930s in southern California, before cars had become a national obsession but after they had become commonplace. Young men began beefing up old junkers and testing them. Two guys, their cars side by side, waiting for the light to change at an intersection, revved their engines, challenging each other to a duel: who could get away quickest? Unable to catch up to the cars they pursued, the police could not stop the game. The threat of restrictive legislation led to a search for suitable, and safe, venues for races. This led to races on the bed of Muroc Dry Lake, and then to official timing in 1937 by the Southern California Timing Association (SCTA), which imposed strict penalties on members found guilty of drag racing on streets.

In 1950 the SCTA ran a hot rod-versus-motorcycle race at a former naval air field near Santa Ana, California. The success of this event led to more local airstrips becoming available as drag strips. In 1951 *Hot Rod* magazine proposed a much needed National Hot Rod Association (NHRA), whose regulations would ensure nationwide conformity of requirements. Thus the NHRA was born and oversaw the booming development of the sport through the 1950s. Over 25 years, drag racing became a regionally popular spectator sport, a lucrative sport for the winners, and a highly organized motor sport with very strict safety regulations devised in conjunction with the Specialty Equipment Manufacturers Association (SEMA). International recognition was granted to the sport in 1965 when it was finally accepted by the Fédération Internationale de l'Automobile. Drag racing also exists in more restricted forms in Australia, Canada, England, Germany, Italy, Japan, New Zealand, and Sweden, but it has never achieved the professionalism nor the popularity that it has in the United States.

Rules and Play

Everything from street cars to motorcycles to highly engineered race cars are used for drag racing. The most

The Pits

Before and between races the pit crew working might be found scouring junk yards for school bus engine blocks, or preparing the dragster trailer for the next racing event by stocking it with everything from compressed air to head gaskets. At a race the pit crew is responsible for making the car run perfectly; for towing the car to the starting line and starting it, because these cars have been stripped to the bare bones for weight and have no starters; for pushing the car back to the starting line, because, again to save weight, most of the cars have no reverse gear; for towing the car from the finish end of the track back to the pits; and for doing anything to the car that needs doing between runs. Since the driver knows how the car is running, how the clutch feels, and so on, the driver and pit crew work together to improve on the car's performance. When there is no problem to attend to, the pit crew does routine maintenance; changing the oil and filter, refueling, putting in new spark plugs, adjusting the tire pressure, and always refolding and repacking the parachute. Sometimes a blower (equivalent of a carburetor), an engine block, or heads must be changed. As the racing event progresses, contestants are eliminated, quickening the time between elimination rounds. If a major engine job needs to be done under this kind of time pressure, the pit crews work feverishly against the clock in order to get their car back on the starting line in time for the next run. An interesting aspect of drag racing is that a good deal of camaraderie exists between the racers, and an eliminated driver and crew can often be found helping another crew get their car back on the starting line, ready to race.

—Brooke Dyer-Bennet

highly engineered cars produce up to 1,500 horsepower. In U.S. drag racing, engine capacity is limited to 800 cubic inches. The different competition classes are divided by the type of fuel used—"gas" (ordinary pump gas)—and "fuel" (methanol or nitro-methane [top fuel]) or by the type of car driven, unmodified or modified.

What has evolved into the pure dragster (also called a "rail" or a "slingshot"), is a long chassis built of metal tubing, with two small bicycle-like tires in front and two massive, treadless tires in the rear, all of which support a 1,000–1,300 pound motor, mounted today behind the driver and between the rear wheels. A "funny car" (or "flopper") is basically a "rail" with a fiberglass body—made to resemble a flashy passenger car—that lowers over the cockpit, driver, and engine. The faster cars have at least one attached parachute that the drivers open at the end of each run to assist the brakes in stopping the vehicles. Cars must meet exacting technical standards for their competition class and go through a technical inspection prior to each race. Drivers are licensed by the NHRA and must wear SEMA-approved safety equipment, including fireproof suits, gloves, boots, and helmets with face shields.

The race track consists of a two-lane paved strip one-quarter mile (402 meters [440 yards]) in length (plus a "shut-down" area of at least 200 meters [220 yards]), and at least 15 meters (50 feet) in width.

At the start of a race, two competitors line up side by side on the starting line. A "Christmas Tree" (a pole with a vertical series of lights) stands 20 feet down the course from the drivers, dividing the lanes. The top light is red, the next five are yellow, the sixth green, and the seventh red. The drivers start their engines, spin their rear tires until they are hot and tacky, and maneuver their cars so that the front wheels break an infrared light beam—part of a timing device that is connected to another set of lights at the finish—ensuring that neither driver has a distance or time advantage. When the green bulb lights up, the cars leave from a standing start attempting to beat each other, or sometimes the clock, to the finish line. Starting before the green light is on illuminates the bottom red light and disqualifies the driver, as does straying outside one's marked lane. Racers compete in a series of elimination rounds against other cars in their class, ultimately resulting in one winner.

Although the goal of the race is to cross the finish line first, records are kept of the peak speeds reached in an area beginning 66 feet (20 meters) before the finish line and ending 66 feet after it. It is possible to lose a race but capture an event's speed record.

Professional drag racers are people who support themselves by drag racing, by often receiving expense money and appearance money as well as by sometimes winning the prize money. Professional classes of drag racing have become so expensive to compete in, due to the costs of high-tech equipment and spare parts necessary to remain competitive, that from year to year elite levels have dozens, not thousands, of competitors. These cars usually have either one major sponsor—such as "The Hawaiian," Don "The Snake" Prudhomme's car, sponsored for years by the U.S. Army—or multiple sponsors whose decals or logos ornament the cars.

One reason for the sport's popularity is that spectators tend to identify with the participants and can also race themselves, if licensed to, even in the family car. Thus, the highest percentage of racers competes in the "sportsman" classes, made up of people who earn their living doing something else, but who compete, sometimes against the professionals, for the prize money.

An increasing number of drivers are women, including superstar Shirley "Cha Cha" Muldowny (1940–),

who set the women's world record for the lowest elapsed time—4.974 seconds—at the NHRA Keystone Nationals at Reading, Pennsylvania, in 1989.

For the spectator, drag racing events are exciting even in the pits—which are accessible to the public. Watching a drag race includes experiencing the thunderous sound waves of powerful engines, observing quick, colorful elimination rounds, and inhaling the aromas of hot rubber and fuel. Drag racing is a sprint rather than a marathon and appeals to people who are thrilled by a combination of mechanical ability, lightning reflexes, power, and courage; as drivers or spectators, both are plentiful.

—BROOKE DYER-BENNET

Bibliography: *National Dragster.* (1960–) Glendora, CA: National Hot Rod Association.

Dressage
See Horseback Riding, Dressage

Drugs and Drug Testing

Drug use, commonly referred to as "doping," is defined by the International Olympic Committee (IOC) as "the administration of or use by a competitive athlete of any substance foreign to the body or any physiological substance taken in abnormal quantity or taken by an abnormal route of entry into the body with the sole intention of increasing in an artificial and unfair manner his/her performance in competition." The word *dope* is either derived from the French *du* (to dip or layer) or, more likely, from the Dutch *dop,* a spirit made from grape skins. The phrase *Dutch courage* refers to the taking of an alcoholic beverage or drug (or a *dop*) before undertaking a difficult or unpleasant task.

History

Doping probably has a history as long as that of organized contest, with competitors in the ancient Olympics fortifying themselves with strychnine-laced alcohol or mushroom potions, possibly hallucinogenic, to mask fatigue and pain. Nineteenth-century endurance athletes were known to take heroin, cocaine, caffeine, strychnine, and alcohol in their attempts to improve performance. The third Olympic Games held in St. Louis in 1904 produced an early doping scare when a U.S. entrant in the marathon took ill after consuming a mixture of strychnine and egg white. As new drugs and natural hormones have become available, they have rapidly been assimilated into the sporting sphere.

Hero for a Day—Ben Johnson and the Steroid Scandal of the 1988 Seoul Olympics

On Saturday, 24 September 1988, Canadian sprinter Ben Johnson set a world record in the 100-meter event at the 1988 Seoul Olympic Games before an on-site crowd of 70,000 and with an estimated 2 billion others watching via television. His time of 9.79 seconds was 0.04 seconds faster than his previous world record of 9.83 seconds set in Rome in 1987. By nightfall on Monday, 26 September 1988, Ben Johnson had been disqualified because of his use of anabolic steroids, specifically stanozolol, in what was to become the most controversial event of the Games—indeed, some say, in the history of the Olympics.

The international impact of Johnson's disqualification was evident in newspaper headlines around the world. "Fastest Junkie on Earth" (*London Daily Star*), "Drugs turn Johnson's medal into a piece of fool's gold" (*Baltimore Sun*), "CHEAT!" (London *Daily Mirror*), and "The fastest man in the world—a doping sinner" (Germany's *Abendzeitung*). The impact of the Johnson affair was particularly dramatic in Canada. This may have been due not only to the nation's historical lack of success at the Olympics but, perhaps more importantly, the event had tarnished Canada's reputation as an honest, moral, fair-playing nation. Arguably, Ben Johnson had become the watershed of modern steroid use. Almost every subsequent scandal uses Johnson as the marker by which to measure its nature and significance.

An intriguing question emerges concerning why Ben Johnson became the focal point even though he was only one of at least ten athletes disqualified for drug use at Seoul and the total number of disqualifications there were less than the 1984 Los Angeles Games. In addition to Canada's national embarrassment, it may have been the fact that the IOC had publicly stated its intention to crack down on cheating; it may have been the fact that the 100-meter final is traditionally one of the most prestigious events in the Olympics; it may have been the fact that Ben Johnson had broken a world record, beating his much more recognized U.S. rival, Carl Lewis; and perhaps it was due to the fact that the world had been deceived—a global audience had witnessed human history in the making only to have their collective memory betrayed.

From the very beginning Johnson maintained his innocence and there were various conspiratorial theories put forth by coaches and administrators. However, in the end Johnson told his story, admitting his long history of steroid use and that an injury prior to the Seoul Olympics had put additional pressure on him to speed up the rehabilitation process. The Dubin Inquiry established by the Canadian government revealed that the problem was endemic in elite sport. Sadly, after Johnson's two-year ban by the International Amateur Athletic Federation had expired, he returned to competitive track and field only to test positive a second time.

—Steven J. Jackson

Attitudes toward doping have changed over the years. At the 1956 World Games in Moscow, it became apparent that the Soviet athletes' performances had been improved by the use of the male anabolic steroid hormone testosterone. The initial response was not outrage but an attempt by a U.S. physician to produce a safer anabolic steroid so that U.S. athletes could compete at an equal level—equity through abuse. The final product was methandrostenolone, or Dianabol, and the birth of a new culture of drug abuse in gymnasiums.

Antidoping investigation, with its associated punitive measures, was first introduced into the Olympic movement at the Mexico City Olympic Games in 1968. The tests used, however, were relatively primitive, with little legal certainty that the results obtained were valid. In 1983, gas chromatography and mass spectrometry brought major advances in the confirmation of doping. Further refinements in 1995 have increased the sensitivity of these tests and will result in a greater yield of positive results.

Doping Defined

Doping measures are either work enhancing (ergogenic) or growth stimulating (anabolic). Short-term effects are generated by taking drugs such as stimulants or by undergoing blood transfusions just prior to the sporting event. In certain events such as shooting or archery, (beta) blockers are taken to slow down the heart rate and reduce hand tremors. Diuretics may be used to lose weight and so enable competitors to participate in lower weight categories in sports such as wrestling, or they may be used to help mask the use of drugs. Effects of drugs may be sustained over the longer term, by administering the drugs during training on a regular basis. These are usually hormones such as anabolic steroids and growth hormones (or their derivatives or analogues) or hormones that induce natural anabolic steroid production. The effect of such anabolic drugs combined with rigorous strength training programs is to cause an increase in lean muscle mass, and apparently greater physical strength. Similarly, the hormone erythropoeitin may be used during the buildup to the competition phase of training to increase the number of circulating red blood cells, which improves endurance.

Detection is based on the presence in the athlete's urine of substances that are not normally produced by the body. Athletes are deemed to have supplemented their body's normal hormone production or to have induced excessive hormone production if the concentration in the urine exceeds the normal range of the healthy population at large, or if the ratio of one naturally occurring hormone to another is outside the normal, or nonpathological, range.

Blood sample analysis is required to detect hormones or blood transfusion. The provision of a blood sample involves a physically and emotionally invasive procedure, requiring the consent of the individual to what would otherwise be deemed unlawful assault. Recent changes in drug testing rules now make provision for blood sampling.

The underlying reason for doping in competitive sport can usually be traced to monetary and personal gain. Prestige is another reason and encompasses national and personal esteem and that of the coach and institution. Some athletes dope to keep up with competitors who are *already* doing better through doping.

The list of banned substances varies from sport to sport, but those prohibited generally include anabolic agents, amphetamines, corticosteroids, peptide hormones and their analogues, stimulants, narcotic analgesics, and (beta) blockers. Blood transfusion and the use of certain drugs to mask the presence of illegal substances in the urine are also banned.

The Drug Debate

Central to the debate on the use of drugs in sport is whether they should indeed be banned in all forms. Some people argue individuals have the right to choose what they wish to eat, drink, inhale, inject, or catheterize themselves with and that whether or not there are adverse consequences to their actions, either immediate or delayed, the individual is free to choose.

The counterargument is based largely on the notion of fair play and the medical dictum of *primum non nocere*—in the first instance, do no harm. The concept of fair play is inherent in most sports where rules have evolved to ensure both equality and safe participation. The victor should ideally be the best athlete, whose success has been achieved through inherited natural endowment and hard training. The concept of fairness held by most opponents to drug enhancement is evident in the International Olympic Committee (IOC) definition, "increasing in an *artificial* and *unfair* manner his/her performance in competition" [emphasis added].

The second principle is that a physician should do no harm to the patient. The prescription and administration of hormonal supplementation, stimulants, narcotic analgesics, diuretics, (beta) blockers, and blood transfusions is, by statute in most countries, the func-

tion of physicians. Most drugs involve some risk, and medical justification is lacking to transfuse blood to a perfectly healthy individual.

The international administrating bodies of most sports contend that doping is wrong and should cease. The relative conviction of the various sporting codes in support of this stance can be assessed by the difference in the severity of the punishment meted out to offenders.

Drug Testing

Drug testing has developed into a large industry, which requires not only testing of competitors at athletic competitions but also worldwide random, out-of-season testing. Any attempt to impede the detection (by taking other drugs that alter the rate of excretion of the banned substances from the body or by introducing uncontaminated urine into the bladder by catheterization) is also considered an offense.

In-competition testing procedure involves the identification of the athletes to be tested, the collection of a specimen from the athlete, the safe transmission of the sample to an accredited laboratory, the subsequent analysis of the sample, and finally notification of the governing authority and the athlete of the results. The protocol for each of these steps has developed with experience both in the field and in the courts of law, and each is governed by a set of procedures designed to minimize reprieve based on a legal loophole.

The process for random unannounced out-of-season testing is similar. While there is general acceptance of the rules of the international governing bodies, the risk exists that national sporting authorities may tip off an athlete under their jurisdiction of an impending out-of-season test. This may be done either to avoid the associated bad publicity or to ensure, through avoidance of the test, the continued success of the athlete and the nation. Several major sports have sought to minimize this problem by handing over the task of out-of-season testing to independent drug testing companies with established networks of sampling officers around the world.

The impact of doping on sport is profound, and those involved in the medical care of athletes cannot be ambivalent on the issue. Dr. R. Voy, former chief medical officer of the United States Olympic Committee, has stated, "Instead of being a competition and celebration of the body human, the Olympics have in some ways become a mere proving ground for scientists, chemists, and unethical physicians. In my opinion, despite renewed concern about drug use in sports, the Olympic ideal will never fully recover from the impact of this problem until it is absolutely, verifiably eliminated"

—Maurice Mars

Bibliography: Strauss, R. (1987) *Drugs and Performance in Sports.* Philadelphia: W. B. Saunders. Voy, R. (1991) *Drugs, Sport, and Politics.* Champaign, IL: Leisure Press. Wadler, G. I., and B. Hainline. (1989) *Drugs and the Athlete.* Philadelphia: F. A. Davis.

Duathlon

The term *duathlon* (originally biathlon) describes a multisport endurance race that combines competition in two distinct disciplines. Typical duathlons require participants to bike and run in some combination for specified distances. The objective is for the athletes to complete the components as rapidly as possible. The fastest contestant wins. Top performers earn awards by either winning the races outright or by doing well within their specified five-year age (and gender) group.

History

The earliest forms of multisport races were dual-discipline events that often involved swimming and running. The form persisted for some time and there have been duathlons that involve all combinations of swimming, biking, and running. Additionally, other sport "disciplines" such as in-line skating have appeared in the mix.

Early impetus seems to have come from distance runners who would dive in for a swim following a long run. According to Tinley, David Pain organized the earliest quasi-formalized multisport event in 1972. He threw himself a birthday party that had attendees race a 10-kilometer (6.2-mile) run followed by a 0.8-kilometer (one-half-mile) swim. Two years later Don Shannahan and Jack Johnstone, friends of Pain, organized the first triathlon that involved the two disciplines from the biathlon plus biking.

In the late 1970s and early 1980s, triathlon received a good deal of publicity. Adherents flocked to the sport. The Triathlon Federation of the United States, which came to be known as Tri-Fed U.S.A., emerged as the national governing board (NGB) for multisport endurance events (triathlon and duathlon) in 1982. (In 1996 the name was changed to U.S.A. Triathlon to bring it into conformity with other U.S. regulatory bodies for Olympic sports. Seven years later the International Triathlon Union (ITU) appeared as a confederation of NGBs. They sought to gain Olympic status for triathlon and to enhance professional competition. This marked an implicit lessening of the status of duathlon—now a poor relation in the multisport world.

Still, the world has embraced the sport for various reasons, although areas lack competitive swimmers. Several countries have climates that make for a short outdoor season, and others have too high a level of water pollution to permit safe competitive swimming.

Rules and Play

Although technically the term *duathlon* covers any combination of two endurance disciplines, typical events come in one of two primary forms. Most duathlons are run-bike-run affairs. Of the remainder, many consist of a run of specified length followed immediately by biking another distance. People involved in the sport regard the prevalent form as both more triathlonlike and more difficult because it is usually harder to run immediately after biking.

The Powerman Duathlon series boasts among the richest of multisport purses in the world. The original Powerman race was held in Zofingen, Switzerland, in 1989.

The commercial value of duathlon and triathlon in the United States is visible in the statistics: Between the early 1970s and the early 1990s, the number of runners and bikers increased substantially. By 1991 nearly 1.5 million people were erstwhile participants in one of triathlon's disciplines.

The point of duathlon and triathlon is to develop a *general* athletic excellence. Athletes at the pinnacle of their sport have traversed in both directions between multisports events and their individual discipline. Thus, an impressive list of stars in individual sports has tried multisport events with varying success. Few stars from single disciplines have dominated multisport events. Instead, they've learned the dictum of ITU President Les McDonald that competing in multisport events means more than just performing well at the individual sports.

—B. James Starr

Bibliography: Souza, Ken, with Bob Babbitt. (1989) *Biathlon: Training and Racing Techniques.* Chicago: Contemporary Books. Tinley, Scott, with Mike Plant. (1986) *Winning Triathlon.* Chicago: Contemporary Books.

Environment

The relationships between sport and environment are varied and complex. The environment undoubtedly influences sports and organizers of sports events have made many attempts to neutralize the environment's impact—heat, cold, rain, slope—by changing the environment and by creating artificial environments in which to play sports. Increasingly, however, it is recognized that sports also affect the environment, and that artificial environments can have a negative effect on nature.

Effect of the Natural Environment

Sports can be categorized by environmental factors. Specialized environment sports *require* certain environmental conditions to take place at all; sailing requires wind and water, skiing needs snow and slope. More commonly, though, we think of how the environment affects particular events and how the physical environment affects outcome and performance. Sports that are sensitive to conditions are best suited to "environment-less" days. Ideally the ground should be flat and dry; the weather warm, dry, and bright but overcast; little or no wind; and with excellent visibility.

Environmental Advantage Sports

In some sports, changeable conditions may affect competitors in different ways. In golf, for example, players starting on a clear morning have an advantage over those struggling over a wind-swept course later in the day. Any sport taking place in an arena too small to allow all participants to take part at the same time is open to the possibility of a change in the weather affecting the participants unequally. Indeed, the microclimate differs from place to place *within* most stadiums at any single time. The effect of an apparently constant environmental condition during the course of an event can be highly misleading. Take, for example, a 100-meter sprint. It has been shown that even within a 100-meter stretch, the wind swirls in several directions, affecting to various degrees athletes in different lanes. In a soccer game, a strong wind may exist in the first half, hence affecting one of the teams either positively or negatively, but die away in the second half and affect neither side.

The unpredictability of the environment may bring unexpected results. In baseball the ball may strike a pebble and glance off in an unexpected direction. The type of soil within baseball fields and cricket pitches varies from place to place. This may constitute a home field advantage, the opposing team being less familiar with the texture of the field. Likewise, differences in altitude may affect performance.

Playing Surface

Traditionally, most playing surfaces have been made of natural or seminatural materials such as grass, clay, water, or snow. Changes during the course of an event, or differences from place to place, in such surfaces can affect the outcome of a sports event. Snow-covered fields lead to soccer (association football) postponement; rain-outs are common in cricket and baseball; unseasonably mild weather has often led to the cancellation of ski events.

Player Comfort

Environmental factors also contribute to player comfort during an event and discomfort may hurt performance.

Sunshine

Indigenous peoples from places as disparate as Mexico and Australia enlisted sporting activities or at least games in their ritualistic attempts to appease the elements or to call for their gods to grant them bountiful harvests. The athletes of ancient Greece are said to have trained in the full heat of the day to strengthen their bodies yet they also covered themselves in exotic oils to offset the harmful effects of the same rays. There is even a theory that some of the events of the ancient games were held in the light of the full moon; now would not that debunk many a myth relating to origins of modern sport? It is said that nations and cultures are products of their climate and geography. Sports are similarly products of their environments; winter sports and aquatics most obviously spring to mind. The greatest exportation of sport as a cultural form came with the cultural imperialism that followed the rise of the British Empire. This saw the proselytization of what were essentially cold climate sports to hot climates. When considered logically, cricket is hardly a suitable game to be played under the ravages of the Australian or the South African sun, let alone the oppressive heat and humidity of the Indian subcontinent. Similarly, rugby played on the concrete-like grounds of outback Queensland or the Veldt is not a pleasant experience. However, such sports were avidly adopted by the young colonies of the empire and soon they challenged the motherland for supremacy in the games that formed her very cultural core. Australians proved to be more than a match at cricket whilst the New Zealand All Blacks of the Edwardian era were virtually unbeatable. And, in the greatest game of all, warfare, these colonial upstarts also proved themselves superior to the pale, wan, and apparently unathletic British conscripts. Clearly, it was the far healthier environment, the sun, clean air, and the vigorous outdoor lives these young colonials experienced that had produced this eugenic miracle, or so the story went. Undoubtedly, their lifestyles were in the main more physical and their diets and living environments more wholesome, yet it was also the very finest and the fittest from these young nations that volunteered to fight.

As tennis, golf, swimming, and athletics began to establish themselves as world sports, the countries that were best endowed in terms of the climate initially gained the ascendancy. Australians and Americans dominated the rankings, as their players could always be assured of at least a good (sunny) summer and in such places as California, Queensland, and Hawaii the sun apparently always shone. Talent abounded and opportunity and access existed for all aspiring hopefuls in these sunshine states. The need for scientific coaching and training was minimal, as just doing it was enough. This soon changed as sport became more and more commercialized and as it was enlisted in the race for ideological supremacy. It was no longer sufficient just to be able to swim or play in the sun. Much sport came to require a systematized regime of professionals, ranging from physiologists to business managers. The sun alone was no longer enough.

—Peter A. Horton

For example, at the 1968 Olympic Games in Mexico City the high altitude and lower oxygen concentration caused physical distress to many long-distance runners. Times in events over 1,500 meters were slower than expected. In the case of the sprints and jumps, however, performances were thought to be greatly enhanced.

Temperature matters to player comfort because sports differ in their activity levels. For example, in swimming, evaporation heat loss is curtailed and most body cooling takes place via convection and conduction. High temperatures can be extremely hazardous in long-distance cycling and running events. During the 1908 Olympic marathon in London and the 1954 Empire Games marathon in Vancouver, several runners collapsed from excessively high temperatures. Low temperatures can be hazardous in sports where the hands are important, such as rugby, football, or field hockey. Also, speed and power events tend to be performed poorly in cold conditions. One of the problems is isolating the effect of the weather or other environmental factors from other factors that may influence outcomes. Take, for example, the effect of an assisting wind in the case of sprinters. Not all sprinters achieve their best times in wind-assisted races. Hence, wind is not the only factor influencing performance, and it is dangerous to assume cause and effect in such situations.

Spectator Comfort

Many of these effects also apply to spectators. Spectators must tolerate the same conditions as the players, but are much less active. If spectators anticipate discomfort, they may not attend and thus affect the sport's finances. Environmental factors may also affect economics in that marketing often takes potential attendance into account in planning the amount of food, programs, and other concessions to be available for sale at a particular event.

Neutralizing the Environment

The interference of the physical environment, its unpredictability, and the risk to comfort, performance, and economics have led the sports business to try to neutralize this interference in two basic ways: the decision not to recognize environment-assisted performances, and the attempt to replace natural environments with artificial ones. In the first case, in track and field, performances in certain events are not recognized for record purposes in winds over a certain strength.

In the second case, sport history is filled with attempts to create artificial environments. Early baseball, cricket, and soccer (association football) took place in natural environments; the desire for better performance and less unpredictable environments led to cutting grass and rolling grass playing surfaces. Later, grass was replaced by plastic so that games could be played in adverse weather conditions. The situation in track and field has been similar—from grass to cinder to synthetic tracks. Artificial snow sculpted to form runs is commonly found on ski slopes where natural snowfall cannot be guaranteed.

Moving sports indoors controls many environmental effects. Indoor sports arenas are now large enough for football, soccer, track and field, swimming, skating, and, in modified form, golf, sailing, wind surfing, climbing, show jumping, and rodeo. Indoor environments for sports range from the high school gymnasium to the fully domed super stadium. In Toronto the distinction between an indoor and outdoor sports facility is blurred by the presence of the SkyDome with its retractable roof.

In recent years, scientists have recognized the possibility that global warming will affect sports. Such an occurrence threatens to limit the geographic area over which certain sports can take place. Skiing is the best-researched example. Global warming may raise winter temperatures, leading to a reduction in snowfall and hence a shortening of the skiing seasons.

The Effect of Sports on the Natural Environment

Some observers believe that sport is intrinsically anti-nature; others argue that sports have positive effects on the environment. A golf course in the Arizona desert brings a splash of greenery to an otherwise arid area. In Britain, the construction of golf courses has been said to increase the number of botanical and zoologic species in the course area. On the other hand, the very same sport and many others have been shown to pollute the environment.

Such pollution has been well researched in the case of golf. Japan, for example, is experiencing the most rapid rate of increase in golf courses. In 1956 there were 72 golf courses, by 2000, an estimated 3,000. Given the limited open space, forests, usually near the foot of mountains, have been felled to satisfy the demand. Herbicide, germicide, pesticide, coloring agents, organic chlorine, and other chemical fertilizers that are carcinogenic or may cause health problems are some of the many substances used to maintain the courses. Widespread damage to bird, insect, animal, and human life has been reported. Pesticide abuse is now seen as a problem requiring serious regulation. Golf is one sport that has witnessed the emergence of anti-golf ecological movements. The Global Anti-Golf Movement is a network of ecological organizations that is fighting against golf as a sport that destroys the natural environment.

Detailed studies also exist of the effect of ski facilities in mountain areas. During ski piste construction the natural terrain is modified to such an extent that soil erosion occurs, which in turn inhibits the regeneration of vegetation. The artificial modification of mountain slopes for improved skiing covers substantial areas of many alpine zones.

The development of urban stadium complexes has spillover effects in the form of increased traffic generation and its resultant pollution. Traffic congestion around older, inner-city stadiums is often perceived by local residents as a greater nuisance than crowds, noise, or fan hooliganism. Stadium and arena-based sports involve the removal of the entire natural ecosystem and the creation of an artificial environment. Motor sports create lead and noise pollution. Even wind surfing can produce some damage to water courses; nesting birds can be driven away from sites where the sport takes place. Orienteering lies at the other end of the spectrum and its effects are (almost) undetectable.

Sport is not independent of broader global concerns. In its bid for the 2000 Olympic Games, Sydney enlisted the help of Greenpeace Australia in formulating environmental guidelines for what were billed as the first "Green Games," aimed at promoting global sustainability. Included in the plans was an Olympic village, to be named Newington, which would become the world's largest solar-powered suburb when the Games are over, complete with energy-efficient orientation and landscaping. Critics contend, however, that the air travel and product marketing associated with the Games would far outweigh any environmental gains from such projects.

As environmental concern grows in the decades ahead, its impact on sport, and the effects of sport itself, will need to be carefully monitored. Moves to ban environmentally unfriendly sports may grow in significance; at the same time, sport may, through its "need" to eliminate many environmental effects, unwittingly contribute to the very degradation that threatens it.

—JOHN BALE

Bibliography: Bale, John. (1994) *Landscapes of Modern Sport.* Leicester, UK: Leicester University Press. Galtung, Johan. (1984) "Sport and International Understanding: Sport as a Carrier of Deep Culture and Structure." In *Sport and International Understanding,* edited by M. Illmarinen. Berlin: Springer-Verlag, 12–19. Moon, Y., and D. Shin. (1990) "Health Risks to Golfers from Pesticide Use on Golf Courses in Korea." In *Science and Golf,* edited by A. Cochran. London: Spon, 358–363.

Ethics

Ethics, one of the four branches of philosophy, is the study of right and wrong, good and bad. Specifically, ethics is moral philosophy or philosophically thinking about the moral questions, problems, and judgments that occur in our everyday lives. In the philosophy of sport, current writings focus on the why and how of sport ethics; they use applied ethics to focus on current social issues. These writers give presumably common-sense solutions to current problems. Current thinking about ethics in sports concerns both ethics and the social community, and formal written codes for professional athletes.

Ethics and the Social Community

Most writing today on sport ethics issues is directed toward the perceived immoral or unethical nature of the sport community, focusing on the immoral or unethical conduct of players, coaches, fans, administrators, or parents. Some of the current social issues in sport today are:

1. The nature of competition. Is it good or bad? Should we compete, and if so, how?
2. The importance of rules. What is the role of rules within the contest? Why do rules fail? What social problems occur because of unethical conduct in relation to the rules?
3. Sportsmanship and fair play. What are the social problems of poor sportsmanship? What has sport become? Does anyone play fairly?
4. Commercialization. Does commercialization negatively affect the ethical character of the player, the fan, the administrator? Should we commercialize or not? How does commercialization affect the nature of the game and the integrity of the organization?
5. Performance enhancement and drug abuse. What are the ethical concerns of performance-enhancing drug use? Should rules outlaw drug usage? What do drugs do to the validity of the performance?
6. Gender equity. Should opportunities for men and women be equal or equitable? What effect does the status quo have on the participating female?
7. Racism. What are the ethical concerns and ramifications of racism in the sporting experience? How does racism affect athletes? What should the experience be for the minority athlete? What eth-

ical and legal issues are preeminent in discussing racism in sport?
8. Youth sport. Should children be in competitive experiences? What role should youth sport play in the lives of children? What do children learn from youth sport? What medical problems occur because of overuse and too much competition in children?
9. Intercollegiate sport. Should intercollegiate sport exist? What are the ethical problems with intercollegiate sport? What solutions are available?

Professional Ethics

In sport, as elsewhere, professional ethics is the stated or implied professional conduct that each organization deems important. The acceptable professional conduct can be general or specific. Most governing bodies of sport organizations have stated codes of ethical conduct or codes of sportsmanlike behavior. For example, the National Federation of High School Activities Association as well as most of its state governing bodies have stated codes of fair play conduct. The National Youth Sport Coaches Association, under the umbrella of the National Alliance for Youth Sport, has explicit statements of acceptable ethical behavior.

Attention to ethics in sport tends to increase when unethical behavior is uncovered. Although the image of the perennial good sport is (at least) exaggerated, it nevertheless seems fair to say that more unethical behavior is appearing in sports. Studying the ethical questions involved may at least heighten awareness of the situation and perhaps reduce the problem.

—SHARON KAY STOLL

Bibliography: Andre, J., and D. N. James. (1991) *Rethinking College Athletics.* Philadelphia: Temple University Press. Bissinger, H. G. (1990) *Friday Night Lights: A Town, a Team, a Dream.* Reading, MA: Addison-Wesley. Fraleigh, W. (1984) *Right Actions in Sport: Ethics for Contestants.* Champaign, IL: Human Kinetics. Jeziorski, R. J. (1994) *The Importance of School Sports in American Education and Socialization.* New York: University Press of America. Kohn, A. (1986) *No Contest: The Case against Competition.* Boston: Houghton Mifflin. Miracle, A. W., and C. R. Rees. (1994) *Lessons of the Locker Room: The Myth of School Sports.* Amherst, NY: Prometheus Books. Simon, R. (1991) *Fair Play: Sports, Values, and Society.* Boulder, CO: Westview Press. Sperber, M. (1991) *College Sports, Inc.: The Athletic Department vs. the University.* New York: Henry Holt. Stoll, S. K. (1993) *Who Says It's Cheating?* Dubuque, IA: Kendall Hunt.

Ethnicity

Through sport, people have crossed racial and ethnic borders and shown time and again that bigotry can lose. However, borders, particularly racial borders, endure and racism's border guards seem ever vigilant. Those of us who look at the Michael Jordans and Peles and optimistically argue that things have gotten better in recent years and will get even better in the future haven't been paying that much attention to human history. Far too many of us have not noticed or chosen not to notice what literary critic Elaine Kim has referred to "racism's traveling eye," which shadows our movements across the borderlands.

Sport has long been identified as an assimilating tool in multiethnic and multiracial societies such as the United States. From one perspective, sport can be viewed as a tool of the dominant culture to encourage or compel assimilation. A century ago government-run boarding schools for American Indians promoted athletic programs in order to make students over into "the white man's image." Similar kinds of programs were developed to "Americanize" white, Latin, and Asian immigrants. From another perspective, sport appears as an opportunity for individuals to make themselves over. By taking up a sport supported by the dominant culture, an ethnic minority group member is extended the freedom to fit in.

Among those who criticize sports as a means of assimilation model are a number of thoughtful intellectuals who have articulated intriguing views on ethnicity, race, and culture. They reject assimilation as a useful analytical tool while redefining multiculturalism in such a way that it allows us to better see cultural convergence and separation among distinct social groups as well as the dynamic relationship between power and culture. Gloria Anzaldua, for example, writes that in North America different racial and ethnic groups have constructed a "borderland." For Anzaldua, a borderland is terrain on which "two or more cultures edge each other, where people of different races occupy the same territory."

To situate sporting institutions and practices as constituting a borderland through which people of various racial and ethnic groups travel makes us consider seriously the contradictory character of sport's relationship to society and power. On the one hand, sport has offered individuals from marginalized and exploited groups opportunities to develop and reinforce meaningful ethnic communities, to forge a bridge across cultural boundaries, to acquire a sense of liberation and even mastery. This is not to mention that commercialized sport has expanded the income and social status of a handful of athletes from historically oppressed and exploited racial and ethnic groups. On the other hand, sport has encouraged and buttressed racial and ethnic boundaries while supporting interrelated gender, class, and other socially constructed hierarchies.

Border Crossings

Sport can help develop an ethnic identity among people. For example, the largely agricultural people migrating to the United States from Japan during the late 1800s and early 1900s were like others possessing agrarian backgrounds in that they defined themselves politically in localistic terms. They identified themselves by way of their connections with family, kin, village, and region, and their identity with a place called Japan was not so close. In the United States, Japanese immigrants tried as well as they could to transplant their localistic social networks, while many seemingly displayed relatively little interest in seeming either Japanese or American.

However, in 1905 an early sign of a Japanese American ethnic identity in the United States surfaced when Tokyo's Waseda University baseball team toured cities like Los Angeles, San Francisco, and Seattle. The Japanese immigrants in these cities reportedly attended Waseda's games with various college, high school, and other amateur teams in significant numbers and rooted for the Japanese team enthusiastically. In the process, they seemingly crossed boundaries between family and locality to link with other Japanese emigrants. In other words, they signaled the emergence of Japanese American communities in West Coast cities.

Communities, for many us, seem to cross regional and national borders. If political scientist Benedict Anderson is correct, then nations are "imagined communities" and nationalism is the effort to build and maintain a sense of community among people who have little chance of seeing each other face to face. Sport has played an often underestimated role in engendering "imagined communities" among colonized people of color. Historian and political activist C. L. R. James has chronicled the relationship between colonialism, race, and sport in his classic *Beyond a Boundary;* it is a book about cricket, but as James reminds us: "What do they know of cricket who only cricket know?"

His *Beyond a Boundary* forcefully breaks down the stereotype of cricket as strictly an elitist, white Englishman's sport. Indeed, the English colonizers brought their love of cricket to the West Indies. They sought to use cricket as a way to Anglicize as much as they thought possible the less plebeian black West Indians. However, even if cricket was intended as a helpmate for British hegemony, black West Indians found in cricket multiple possibilities, some of which could well have troubled the colonizers.

James and many of his fellow black cricketers honored the ethos of fair play underlying cricket even if the source of this ethos was created by the English colonizers. However, by playing well against whites and doing so within the framework developed by English Victorians, black West Indian cricketers nurtured a sense of pride in themselves and in their own way helped construct a bridge among people of color throughout the British Empire.

From the playground and sandlot to the professional arena, sport can aid the formation of racial and ethnic identities and communities across other social distinctions. The famous stars and teams often reflected and reinforced racial and ethnic pride, but so might the local athlete and the neighborhood team. Ethnic community leaders, moreover, often considered sport important in resolving social problems and conflicts disrupting their communities.

For Japanese Americans, this belief that sport could serve as a social bond was carried over into World War II; a time when the U.S. government interned over 100,000 West Coast Japanese Americans in concentration camps. Sports such as baseball, softball, and basketball helped maintain a sense of community among Japanese Americans during an immensely stressful period in their lives.

Sport could also bring solace and joy to people such as the Filipino migrant workers, overworked and underpaid while laboring in Alaska during the early 1930s. In multiethnic, multiracial modern England, sociologist John Hargreaves has written, "Ethnic sport is growing in importance as ethnic minorities attempt to assert their independence and to establish their own cultural identities in a largely hostile society." Hargreaves informs us that during the 1980s, West Indians in Manchester organized "a thriving centre catering for a wide range of social, cultural, and recreational interests, among which sports are prominent." Manchester residents of African ancestry established their own football league, while blacks in London operated the Muhammad Ali Sports Development Association "to develop the talents and aspirations and confidence of young blacks."

While they could have done more, community

sporting practices have often been relatively accessible to female participation. Women of Asian ancestry have had to struggle against the stereotype of them as physically, intellectually, and emotionally passive. However, in numerous Chinese American and Japanese American communities women eagerly played basketball and softball, as well as other sports.

Historically and today, the international movement of people of African, Asian, Latin American, Middle Eastern, Pacific Islander, and European ancestry has often meant the transplantation of sporting traditions along with the transplantation of communal ties. In 19th-century United States, European immigrants and their children played "old world" sports, as well as baseball, basketball, and American football. Irish games were played in cities such as Worcester, Massachusetts, where a large Irish working-class population resided. The Scottish Caledonia games attracted enthusiastic participation. German immigrants and their children organized and joined turnverein societies in American communities from St. Louis to El Paso to San Francisco. Asian immigrants to the United States also transplanted sporting traditions. For example, sumo wrestling tournaments were held by Japanese plantation workers in Hawaii before the turn of the century.

"Star" athletes seemingly reinforced community ties among members of racial and ethnic groups. Jackie Robinson's impact on African Americans is difficult to gauge. However, historian Jules Tygiel argues that the racial integration of mid-20th-century Euroamerican-organized professional baseball by Robinson encouraged the subsequent development of the American civil rights movement.

Robinson and black heavyweight champion Joe Louis became visible symbols of many African American aspirations during the first half of the 20th century. In her *Making a New Deal,* historian Liz Cohen claims that Joe Louis's popularity bridged the racial and cultural distinctions within Chicago's working class in the 1930s. In rooting for the great heavyweight, a Polish and African American worker could create a common ground between them that might otherwise have been lacking—a common ground from which a relatively effective labor movement was launched in the 1930s.

In the United States, renowned athletes like boxer John L. Sullivan, baseball players Joe DiMaggio and Hank Greenberg, and football player Jim Thorpe became ethnic symbols for Irish Americans, Italian Americans, Jewish Americans, and Native Americans, respectively. Similarly, the leading West Indian cricket players connected in a meaningful way to the experiences of black Caribbeans. Likewise, professional baseball players associated with the U.S. Negro leagues and Caribbean leagues were often considered community heroes. This was so not just because they were highly accomplished ballplayers, but because they remained tied personally to the communities they were perceived as representing.

Of course, nowadays we are used to the notion that the "superstars" of sport transcend social boundaries. We are also becoming used to the notion that many of our sport idols might possess a different racial and ethnic identity than our own, while they get paid an enormous amount of money for playing games and advertising athletic shoes or breakfast cereals. Few can argue that sport has allowed some black athletes such as basketball star Michael Jordan and soccer star Pele to seemingly traverse racial barriers and become enormously admired and enormously wealthy. In the past and in the present, other athletes associated with marginalized and exploited racial and ethnic groups have crossed cultural boundaries to become universally respected and frequently well paid.

However rich and famous many of these athletes became, it is important to remember that some of the more moving stories in sport history revolve around the efforts of highly gifted amateur and professional athletes to endure and even contest racial and ethnic discrimination. The German Jewish athletes who were denied places on Hitler's Olympic team come to mind. Of course, Jackie Robinson's experience is well known. Less known is the courage of another baseball standout, Henry Aaron, who faced down unspeakable racism as he chased and moved ahead of Babe Ruth's home-run record.

That all sorts of people also cheered Aaron on is a reminder that star athletes can provide something of a common ground for people of different racial and ethnic groups. But even for lesser-known athletes, sport can cross otherwise powerful racial and ethnic barriers. Athletic teams organized in the Hawaiian Islands have historically been more multiethnic and multiracial than in other regions in the American empire. One can look at the all too unique rosters of Hawaiian football, basketball, and baseball teams in the 1920s, 1930s, and 1940s and note the existence of Asian, Hawaiian Islander, Hispanic, and Anglo last names. Hawaii, indeed, was arguably well ahead of the U.S. mainland in using sport to enhance democratic and egalitarian experiences and nurturing highly skilled athletes of Hawaiian Islander and Asian ancestry.

Sport, therefore, has allowed significant numbers of people of diverse racial and ethnic groups to move beyond ethnocentric assumptions developed about them. In many cases, it has even helped connect them as an "imagined community," prepared to battle racism, nativism, and colonialism. It has given opportunities for some of them to make money and achieve honors. It has given everyone wonderful stories of courageous struggles against bigotry and discrimination. However, if through sport people can achieve movement across socially constructed boundaries, then it is important to note that there have been people who seem freer to travel about than others. In other words, sport has its border guards, discouraging movement for some while allowing movement for others. It has made some borders more porous, while strengthening other racial and ethnic boundaries.

Sport and the Border Guard

If we just go back 400 or 500 years, we can see how sport can reinforce cultural barriers between people. By the 1700s, the Europeans characterized many of America's indigenous people as lazy. These Europeans defined hunting and fishing as sport and performing agricultural labor as work. Since many Native American groups depended at least in part upon hunting and fishing, they did quite a lot of it, much to the dismay of Europeans and then Euroamericans. The perception that Native Americans spent so much of their time engaging in "sport" and not in useful labor strengthened Europeans and Euroamericans in their beliefs that Native Americans were culturally and, perhaps, innately inferior.

A somewhat similar kind of cultural barrier was erected in California during the mid-19th century. Before the United States obtained California as a consequence of the Mexican War, horse racing and other displays of equestrian skills ranked among the Californians' favorite pastimes. These equestrian events possessed a utilitarian value since so much of the region's economy was based upon cattle ranching and the horse-riding skills of the people who worked on these ranches. Nevertheless, those from the United States who came to California during and after the Gold Rush generally frowned upon these Mexican pastimes. This was especially true among those Americans known as Sabbatarians. These pious Protestants professed a belief in hard work from Monday through Saturday but allowed that Sunday was, according to their interpretation of God's will, a day of rest; a day of rest from work but also from play.

Sunday, however, was a favored day for Mexican

Catholics to engage in horse racing, as well as put on bullfights and other activities that repulsed good Protestant Americans. In the early 1850s, the Anglo-controlled town government of San Jose banned horse racing. At about the same time, the California state legislature distressed the state's Mexican population by passing a Sunday law that declared as illegal on Sunday many of Mexican Californians' favorite sporting activities.

In California and throughout the 19th-century United States, the sporting practices of immigrants and children of immigrants often provoked nativistic responses. Immigrants were often seen as too inclined to patronize such "disreputable" activities as prize fights and too little inclined toward hard work and sobriety. Of course, class issues intertwined with the development of industrial capitalism weighed heavily here; especially when it came to Sunday sporting and recreational practices. Its industrial capitalists often viewed Sunday laws favorably, because they would encourage a rested and sober workforce ready for 50 to 60 hours of labor from Monday through Saturday.

Into the 20th century, people identified with other racial and ethnic groups have been stereotyped as more interested in play than in work. Often such stereotyping becomes clearly racist, because it connects a person's interest with some kind of innate predisposition. In the United Kingdom, Jennifer Hargreaves writes: "Whereas the successes of white women in sports are assumed to be the result of dedicated training and self-sacrifice (or drug-taking, particularly in the case of Eastern Europeans), the visibility of elite black sportswomen is assumed to be because they are genetically predisposed to be superior athletes."

Of course, the view that people of African ancestry harbored innate talents for at least certain sports, especially sports requiring considerable running and jumping, has scarcely been unique to the United Kingdom. The issue of whether blacks are naturally gifted athletically has long provoked controversy and has long helped construct a racial ideology in the United States, the UK, and elsewhere. Ironically, among the early supporters of athletic competition in Europe and North America there was little doubt that whites were more naturally gifted athletes than nonwhites. Indeed, for many, athletic competition buttressed Social Darwinism; races did exist and some races were more fit than others. Athletic competition, according to these racial ideologues, demanded brains, discipline, and "pluck," as well as coordination and strength. Nonwhites might claim the latter two characteristics, but when it came to intelligence, discipline, and courage, they were lacking.

Therefore, sport helped draw the color line in the United States and it helped justify European imperialism. To the extent that people of color might display some ability to compete athletically, they were simply showing that they were "white inside." The dominant racial ideology was scarcely disturbed at all. At the same time, some Europeans and Euroamericans who regarded people of color as not so closely bound by their natures also considered sport as a civilizing tool. If East or West Indians learned cricket, then those "natives" would take one step closer to Western Civilization, while, hopefully, gaining new respect for their colonizers.

Within the United States, sport took on a highly visible role in supporting a racial hierarchy. Major league baseball and other professional baseball organizations affiliated with it barred African Americans from team rosters in the 1880s and backed "Jim Crow" segregation until after World War II. While prominent as jockeys for many years, African Americans found that by the 20th century commercial horse racing had drawn the color line as well. Occasionally during the late 19th century and early 20th century, blacks such as Paul Robeson might play for college football teams and some African American boxers were prominent.

Black heavyweight champions such as Jack Johnson and Muhammad Ali expressed an unapologetic awareness that they challenged white supremacy. Johnson, in particular, aroused white resentment and quests for "white hopes" to unseat him from his heavyweight throne during the 1900s and 1910s.

Non–African American athletes of color have also faced discriminatory treatment in the world of sport. A few athletes of indigenous, Asian, and Latin American ancestry have reached the higher echelons of competitive sports. However, for decades a racial ideology has proclaimed all people of color as lacking the characteristics of true sporting champions. At the dawn of the 20th century, U.S. sportswriters expressed astonishment that prizefighters of Mexican ancestry and Asian ancestry could manage adeptly in the boxing ring. Such athletes were perceived as generally lacking the white man's fortitude. When it seemed clear that some Asian boxers, in particular those hailing from the Philippines, were challenging white supremacy time and again in the boxing ring, the state of California tried to ban Filipino boxers in 1930.

Recreational sport has offered too many instances of racial and ethnic hierarchies as well. Swimming pools and other recreational facilities were declared off limits to Americans of color for decades. Private golf clubs and athletic clubs not only have restricted membership to white Americans, but they have banned Jews and others normally identified as white.

Even if unintentional, such discrimination persists, as Jennifer Hargreaves asserts is the case in the United Kingdom. Race, gender, and class factors combine, Hargreaves maintains, to limit the participation of British women of Asian ancestry in recreational sports. Asian women are stereotyped as not interested in participating in sports. Thus, their need for physical health and fun is ignored by recreational policy-makers. At the same time, many recreational activities remain too costly to be accessible to working-class Asian women.

In recent decades, the relationship between racial ideology and sport has been altered. The success of athletes of color in many competitive sports has, of course, weakened the argument that people of European ancestry are athletically superior. Instead, too many of those involved in sports in one form or another now argue that people of African ancestry possess some natural abilities that make them particularly adept in sports that require a great deal of running and jumping, such as basketball. On the other hand, it has also been claimed that people of African ancestry have a natural tendency to fail at competitive water sports.

The fact that numerous athletes of color have achieved fame and fortune should not divert us from looking at the downside of all this. As sociologist Harry Edwards points out, the stereotype of blacks as naturally inclined toward athletics more than likely dissuaded African Americans from seeking careers more realistic than those of professional athletes and more beneficial, in the long run, to themselves, their families, and communities. Even those very few athletes of color who do become well known remain subject to discrimination. Disproportionately their employers and coaches are white. If team players, they disproportionately play positions that supposedly require more athleticism and less intelligence. And very often they will hear how naturally gifted they are from pundits and fans and how intelligent and hardworking their white teammates are.

Admittedly, the last decade or so has seen less in the way of overt racial and ethnic hostility in the sporting world. Yet such hostility or indifference to such hostility persists. "Football hooliganism" emerging in the United Kingdom during the 1970s has expressed a white racial chauvinism frightening in its openness. But even more frightening is the silence expressed by many clubs and players in response to crowd abuse of players of color.

Racial and ethnic conventions seem rooted in the historical development of sport; especially commercialized sport. Indeed, commercialized sports have long marketed race and ethnicity as a sound business practice. For years, professional baseball's New York Giants sought a Jewish player who would attract Jewish fans to New York's Polo Grounds. Moreover, racial integration of post–World War II professional baseball would not have been undertaken if baseball entrepreneurs such as Branch Rickey were not convinced that terminating "Jim Crow" baseball made good business sense. In San Francisco, a prize-fight promoter in the 1930s was so anxious to attract Jewish customers that he used the services of a non-Jewish boxer because he possessed a Jewish-sounding last name. Meanwhile, in Los Angeles, prize-fight promoters employed boxers of Mexican and Filipino ancestry to lure fans of Mexican and Filipino ancestry.

The close ties between commercialized sport and manufacturers of athletic shoes combined with the knowledge that such highly expensive shoes have found a market among African American ghetto youth has been and remains troubling. Consequently, there are two sure places to see an African American male on television; during a telecast of a sporting event or in an advertisement showing him jumping, running, or being physically intimidating.

—JOEL S. FRANKS

Bibliography: Edwards, Harry. (1973) *The Sociology of Sport.* Homewood, IL: Dorsey Press. Eisen, George, and David K. Wiggins, eds. (1994) *Ethnicity and Sport in North American History and Culture.* Westport, CT: Greenwood Press. Hargreaves, Jennifer. (1994) *Sporting Females: Critical Issues in the History and Sociology of Women's Sports.* London and New York: Routledge. Hargreaves, John. (1986) *Sport, Power and Culture: A Social and Historical Analysis of Popular Sports in Britain.* New York: St. Martin's Press. James, C. L. R. (1983) *Beyond a Boundary.* New York: Pantheon Books. Lapchick, Richard. (1986) *Fractured Focus: Sport as a Reflection of Society.* Lexington, MA: D. C. Heath and Co. Riess, Steven A. (1989) *City Games: The Evolution of American Urban Society and the Rise of Sports.* Urbana and Chicago: University of Illinois Press.

Exercise

Exercise is a component of physical activity or physical fitness and is a structured activity specifically planned to develop and maintain physical fitness. Physical fitness has been defined by the U.S. President's Council on Physical Fitness and Sports as "the ability to carry out daily tasks efficiently with enough energy left over to enjoy leisure time pursuits and to meet unforeseen emergencies." The position of the American Alliance for Health, Physical Education, Recreation, and Dance (AAHPERD) is that "physical fitness is a multifaceted continuum extending from birth to death. Affected by physical activity, it ranges from optimal abilities in all aspects of life through high and low levels of different physical fitness, to severely limiting disease and dysfunction."

Since early in human development, people have realized the benefits of being physically fit. Only recently have contemporary societies actively engaged in exercise to obtain varying levels of physical fitness.

History

From the beginning of humankind's existence on earth, movement of the human body has been an integral and necessary part of human life. Exercise as physical labor was an essential and mandatory part of life. In the early hunting and gathering days there was no use for exercise as we define and use it now. People moved all day in order to survive.

Their exercise, however, was not for labor alone. They engaged in activities of a warlike nature, and in times of peace they practiced these skills as recreational pastimes. Dance was an important aspect of early physical activity. It was interwoven into many areas of the lives of the early hunters and gatherers. The earliest evidence of organized exercise, running, occurred in 3800 B.C.E. at Memphis in Egypt. However, ritual races around the walls of Memphis may have actually predated 4100 B.C.E. Drawings dating from 3300 B.C.E. show a form of high jumping, with children jumping over the linked arms of other children.

The ancient Greeks are credited with instituting and promoting the idea of exercise and athletics. The Greeks placed more emphasis on exercise than any previous society. The Athenians exercised and played for the sheer enjoyment of it. They admired a beautiful body and actively strove to attain it. They believed in both a healthy body and a healthy mind and felt that these two concepts worked together to create the whole person. The Spartans, by contrast, were motivated by militarism. Physical exercise was undertaken to develop strong bodies to withstand the rigors of war.

The Greeks held the first Olympic Games in 776 B.C.E. The Games convened every four years until they were discontinued in C.E. 394. The modern Olympic Games reconvened in 1896, in Athens, Greece, a fitting tribute to the ancient Greeks who had placed such emphasis on these games in their culture. The Romans never embraced the games as the Greeks did. The Romans, like the Spartans, were a military nation, so military exercises took precedence over games. However, the Romans were known to bring Greek athletes to their cities to watch the gladiatorial games and professional exhibitions, as they did appreciate the physical pursuits of these athletes.

On the other side of the world there were also some strong early influences of Eastern exercise and physical activity in the form of the martial arts. Historians believe that the martial arts began in India with the practice of Veda. Later Taoism and Zen were documented in Asian cultures. The martial arts practice a highly disciplined type of exercise that combines the workings of the mind and the body.

With the decline of the Roman Empire, the Christian concept of life began its dominance, which continued for many centuries. Most recreational or physical activities had to be approved by the church and mandated a strong religious theme. Germany is credited with developing in the early 19th century a system of physical exercises that became a model for many other European nations in modern times. Denmark, Sweden, and Finland followed the German lead of implementing gymnastic-type programs to increase the fitness levels and health of their citizens. England also adopted and developed a strong sport and exercise culture. The athletic and sport traditions of England were transplanted to America by the early colonists; from both North America and Britain these traditions spread throughout the world.

The industrial period began during the mid-18th century and lasted to the end of World War II in 1945. This period was marked by the development of the steam engine and electrical power. The population showed a shift from rural life to urban life, from farms to cities. This was the beginning of a less physically challenging way of life. A small but vocal group of educators and reformers in both England and the United States in the mid-1800s advocated exercise for both men and women for increased health.

Health Benefits

Following World War II, increases in illness and disease attributed to lack of activity grew at alarming rates. Exercise became medicine; however, the concept was not really a new one. It was Hippocrates, the 5th-century B.C.E. Greek physician, who said: "All parts of the body which have a function, if used in moderation and exercised in labours in which each is accustomed, become thereby healthy, well-developed and age more slowly;

but if unused and left idle they become liable to disease, defective in growth, and age quickly."

In the early 1950s, British physician Jeremy N. Morris developed what has become known as the "exercise hypothesis." He found that workers who were more active were at less risk for coronary artery disease. This idea helped to jump start the exercise revolution of the 1970s.

In the 1970s, exercise was seen as a way to combat the rising incidence of cardiovascular disease and to counteract the effects of stress, excess weight, smoking, drugs, and alcohol. Running, aerobic dance, high-impact aerobics, and the "no pain, no gain" mentality flourished. The 1980s marked the beginning of the wellness revolution. This revolution looked at many aspects of lifestyle, including diet, stress reduction, and elimination of tobacco, drugs, and alcohol as a means to a healthier life, rather than focusing exclusively on exercise. During the 1990s, there has been an even gentler and more diverse approach to exercise. The "no pain, no gain" mentality is gone, and walking has taken the place of running and high-impact aerobics as the exercise of choice.

Exercise has many benefits, supported by an erwhelming amount of research. Weight management, increased longevity, and improved quality of life are all widely recognized effects of regular exercise.

Other benefits of exercise include reductions in coronary heart disease, cholesterol levels, and atherosclerosis. With regular exercise, blood pressure is lowered and the effects of pulmonary disease are decreased or diminished. Osteoarthritis, osteoporosis, back pain, and recovery from surgery have all been found to benefit from a regular exercise program, and such a program can reduce the chances of getting cancer. There are also psychological benefits to exercise. Research shows that people who are physically fit are also more likely to be psychologically fit. The symptoms of stress, depression, and anxiety are all reduced by a regular exercise program, while self-esteem is raised.

Components of Exercise

There are many different types of exercise. Exercise could mean running a marathon to one person and walking the dog or taking the stairs instead of an elevator to another person. The key is physical movement. There are four major components to physical fitness that should be addressed when exercising. Cardiorespiratory fitness is the heart's ability to pump blood and deliver oxygen throughout the body. Walking, running,

cycling, aerobic dance, and swimming are examples of exercises that increase cardiorespiratory fitness. Muscular fitness is the second component of physical fitness and is usually obtained by some sort of weightlifting exercise program. There are two components to muscular fitness: muscular strength—how much weight one can lift—and muscular endurance—how many times one can lift a weight. Flexibility or range of motion is the third component of physical fitness. Flexibility is important for the performance in sport activities as well as for functioning in daily life. Stretching exercises will help improve the flexibility of the body's muscles and joints. The last component of fitness concerns body composition, the portion of body weight that is made up of fat. The level of body fat can affect the risk of developing health problems, including heart disease, high blood pressure, and diabetes. Some of the same exercises recommended for cardiorespiratory fitness and muscular fitness are also recommended for controlling body composition.

Along with the four components of exercise are the principles of exercise training. The first, specificity, is the idea that the adaptation of the body or change in physical fitness is specific to the type of training undertaken. To increase cardiovascular fitness, one must specifically train the cardiovascular system. The second principle is overload: to improve any aspect of physical fitness one must continually increase the demands placed on the appropriate body systems. Progression, or increasing the level of the activity, is important to increased fitness levels. Everyone has different capabilities of progression, so this progression should be slow to avoid injury or fatigue.

There has been much research on the frequency, duration, and intensity of exercise, three additional components of exercise training. To develop and maintain fitness, exercise must be performed regularly. A frequency of about three to five times a week is thought to be sufficient. The intensity of exercise has been the subject of much debate and research. In the past, it was thought that in order to reap the health benefits of exercise one needed to exercise at 80 percent of maximum heart rate. However, in more recent years, researchers have found fitness benefits at only 50 percent of maximum heart rate. Exercise heart rate has been found to be a reliable way to gauge exercise intensity. Duration of exercise is related to the intensity of the exercise. If the exercise is of a high intensity then the duration does not need to be as long; if the exercise is of low intensity then the duration must be longer to derive similar effects. All of these components and principles of exercise need to be considered when considering an exercise program.

The exercise boom is alive and well. According to American Sports Data (ASD), the number of people who participated 100 times or more in at least one fitness activity in the previous 12 months numbered 42.2 million. The U.S. running population was 30.4 million and the number of people using home exercise machines has increased tremendously. Since 1991, in-line skating has increased 51 percent and mountain biking 16 percent. Exercise and wellness constitute a long-term trend that is here to stay.

—SALLY CRAWFORD

See also Aerobics; Conditioning; Medicine.

Bibliography: American College of Sports Medicine. (1992) *ACSM Fitness Book.* Champaign, IL: Leisure Press. Gavin, James. (1992) *The Exercise Habit.* Champaign, IL: Leisure Press. Hoeger, W., and S. Hoeger. (1992) *Lifetime Physical Fitness and Wellness.* Englewood, CO: Morton Publishing. Sharkey, B. J. (1990) *Physiology of Fitness.* Champaign, IL: Human Kinetics.

Extreme Sports

Extreme sports is the generic label used for sports that in some way go beyond—in endurance, testing the limits, or danger—traditional sports. The label was promoted in the 1990s by athletes, promoters, the sports equipment industry, and advertisers to bring mainstream attention to these sports and, at the same time, to differentiate them from related sports. While most sports now classified as extreme have all existed for some time and most have governing bodies and regional and world competitions, extreme sports as a category of sports achieved their highest level of public exposure in 1995 with the First Extreme Games held in June in Newport, Rhode Island. These games were given 45 hours of week-long coverage on the ESPN (Entertainment and Sports Programming Network) cable network and have been popular ever since. The games included street luge, eco-challenge, skysurfing, sport climbing, barefoot water ski jumping, in-line skating, BMX dirt biking, mountain biking, and bungy jumping. To some extent, all of these sports are extensions of already existing sports or recreational activities:

street luge—skateboarding, roller skating, luge, tobogganing
eco-challenge—orienteering, canoeing, rafting,
   kayaking, swimming
skysurfing—sky diving, surfing
sport climbing—rock climbing
barefoot water ski jumping—water ski jumping,
   trick water skiing
in-line skating—roller skating, skateboarding
BMX dirt biking—bicycle racing, motorcross
mountain biking—bicycle racing, cross-country
   racing
bungy jumping—diving

What differentiates these sports from the related ones varies with each activity and might involve changes in the rules, the combining of different events, use of different equipment and venues, and a greater degree of risk to the athletes. Additionally, some extreme sports have been called "outlaw" sports because they have been banned in some jurisdictions as too dangerous. In street luge, for example, the participants lie flat on their backs on wheeled luges or "rails" and race downhill on roads. When these roads are used also by pedestrians, bikers, and vehicles, the sport is dangerous for both the competitors and others. Perhaps the common feature of extreme sports and what makes them extreme are requirements of the activities that make the sport especially dangerous and/or that test the limits of human physical ability or endurance.

Extreme sports are international with the Extreme or X Games attracting competitors from dozens of nations. Different sports have developed in different nations—skysurfing in France, barefoot ski jumping in Australia, and some sports such as street luge, sport climbing, eco-challenge, and mountain biking draw participants from a variety of nations. For the most part, however, competitors are from Western nations, with most coming from the United States, Australia, Canada, Germany, New Zealand, France, and England. Some sports, such as sport climbing and eco-challenge, draw competitors who are in their thirties and forties, but most competitors in the other sports are usually in their twenties or even teens. Most extreme sports draw only male competitors, with only eco-challenge and sport climbing having significant numbers of women competitors. Sport climbing is the only extreme sport with separate divisions for men and women. All extreme sports, except for eco-challenge and skysurfing, are individual sports.

—DAVID LEVINSON

Falconry

Falconry is a form of hunting in which birds of prey are trained to find and kill game for their human owners. It is an ancient sport that was once extremely popular, and although it is far less prevalent today, it still has numerous enthusiasts in many parts of the world. An important element of falconry is the training of the birds—a slow, complex process that requires patience, skill, and careful attention to detail. For many falconers this aspect of the sport, together with the appreciation of watching the magnificent birds in flight and the opportunity to preserve and display the birds for others, is just as important as the actual hunt.

Falcons are members of the Falconidae family, a category of hawks. They are powerful, fast birds of prey that swoop down and catch their quarry in their claws and talons. Eagles and other birds of prey are also used in the sport on a more limited basis; however, technically, falconry refers specifically to the use of falcons. When other species of hawks are used, the sport is called hawking. Nevertheless, people often refer to the general use of any of these birds as falconry.

History

Falconry is believed to have started in Asia and the Middle East, possibly as early as 2000 B.C.E. Falconry spread to Europe in the centuries following the death of Christ. It became especially popular in the British Isles during the Middle Ages. The wealthy often had prized collections of birds, and they employed staffs of skilled trainers to manage them. In Europe, falconry was among the sports governed by feudal laws in the Middle Ages that restricted hunting and the ownership and use of sporting animals based on social class. These became known as the Forest Laws. These laws were relaxed in the following centuries, but vestiges remained into the 19th century. While all people could participate in falconry, specific types of hawks and falcons were designated for each class. Only members of the royalty could own gyrfalcons, the largest falcons.

Interest in falconry diminished around the 17th century, as the emphasis in hunting shifted more to the use of guns and to other hunting animals such as dogs. The sport, however, has been carried on by individual falconers and by regional and national organizations, such as the North American Falconers Association.

In the mid-20th century, development significantly reduced the amount of open and accessible countryside necessary for falconry and many species of birds were in danger of extinction from chemical pesticides and other environmental threats. Their use became carefully regulated, and breeding programs were initiated to rebuild the population. In the 1990s, these programs have shown signs of success, and once-rare species are becoming reestablished.

Rules and Play

There are approximately 40 individual species of falcons, ranging in length from about 15 centimeters (6 inches) up to 60 centimeters (2 feet) or more. Several different falcons can be trained for the sport of falconry. The gyrfalcon is among the largest species of falcon used. The peregrine, another large falcon, is considered one of the world's fastest animals, with a flying speed as fast as 320 kilometers per hour (200 miles per hour). Merlins are smaller peregrines that are typically used in falconry. Kestrels are small, long-winged falcons that live primarily in woods and grassy areas. They are among the most common species of falcon and are considered easy to train.

During a hunt, the falcon is brought to a site attached by leather leg straps to a special perch or to the hand of the falconer, which is protected by a large leather glove. The bird is released to fly after its quarry, which may be other airborne birds or ground-dwelling animals. Many kinds of game animals are hunted in the sport of falconry, including rabbits, ducks, pheasants, grouse, and squirrels. After the kill, the bird is trained either to fly back to the master's glove, return to the perch, or stay with the dead prey until it is retrieved by its master. Small bells or radio transmitters are attached to the bird so it can be easily located in the field by sound or radio signal.

The sport's heritage is a basic element of its appeal for many falconers. Etiquette, methods of training, and care date back to the earliest days of the sport. These grew out of the very specific demands that are required to care for the birds, as well as a respect for the traditions and values embodied by the sport. Falconry's extensive vocabulary of specific terms for equipment, training, hunting procedures, and other facets of the sport date back to its early years.

Falcons and other predatory birds are difficult to breed in captivity. Traditionally, very young birds, or eyasses, are taken from their nests (eyries) in the wild soon after their birth, before they can fly or leave the nest on their own. They are also captured in their very early stages of flight or when they are migrating during their first year. Capture of wild bird species is now regulated. Many localities require falconers to obtain special permits prior to capturing the young birds. Falconry is also subject to laws covering the game that is hunted by the trained birds. Many areas have specific hunting seasons for falconers, similar to those for other types of hunters. Hawks of all types have an instinctive fear and mistrust of humans, so their training is undertaken very carefully. The exact procedures vary for different species, to reflect differences in their habits and temperaments.

The first basic step in training is adapting the wild bird to captivity and the presence of people. This process, called manning, takes place indoors in special houses called mews. The trainer gradually makes the bird accept him by visiting it regularly and feeding it by hand. Once a degree of trust has been established, the bird is trained to perch on the falconer's gloved hand. During training and at other times, the bird's legs are attached to leather straps, called jessups, to restrain it from flying away. In its early captivity, or later when a bird in training is being moved from its usual perch to another location for training or hunting, the head is often covered with a hood to keep it calm. In the past, the eyes of young birds were temporarily sewn shut.

Eventually the bird is taken outside to become readjusted to the open air, a process known as weathering. During this phase, the birds are attached to outdoor perches for regular periods during the day. Then they are allowed to fly while attached to leather straps. The birds are trained to hunt with the use of meat attached to lures and string, which are swung out for the bird to catch. Gradually they are trained to fly loose and hunt without flying away permanently from their demarcated territory, or from the master's control when taken to another location for a hunt.

Unfettered birds sometimes do fly off, no matter how well they have been trained. Falconers accept this as inevitable. A small but dedicated cadre of enthusiasts will continue practicing falconry, losses notwithstanding.

—JOHN TOWNES

See also Hunting.
Bibliography: Ford, Emma. (1992, 1995) *Falconry: Art and Practice.* London: Cassell.

Fencing

Fencing is the art and sport of swordsmanship using blunted weapons. For more than 100 years and until quite recently, it was the only combative sport open to both men and women, although men and women compete apart from each other. It is the only combative sport with neither weight classes nor height restrictions. It is an activity that one can begin during childhood and continue for the rest of one's life. It requires few players—two is sufficient—and needs no specially built venue or expensive equipment.

History

Fencing is an activity of the most pronounced antiquity. Perhaps the earliest reference to a fencing match appears in a relief carving in the temple at Madinet-Habu near Luxor in upper Egypt built by Ramses III about 1190 B.C.E. The fencers depicted there are using weapons with well-covered points and masks similar to those currently in use.

Every other ancient civilization—Chinese, Japanese, Persian, Babylonian, Greek, and Roman—practiced swordsmanship as a sport as well as training for combat. Curiously, European swordsmanship—the most immediate antecedent of modern fencing—did not develop until after the advent of gunpowder and firearms in the 14th century. Until that time, men wielded ever-heavier swords to cleave through ever-more-ponderous armor. And strength was more critical than skill. However, ballistic weapons rendered armor obsolete, making speed, mobility, and skill more important. This led to the development of lighter swords used with faster, more subtle handwork for better use in close quarters and the art of fencing arose.

German fencing masters were the first to organize themselves into guilds, such as the famous Marxbruder of Frankfort, in 1480. Other such associations flourished throughout Europe. The masters of these schools of fencing advocated techniques and styles of play that included wrestling and boxing tricks, in addition to swordsmanship. In Great Britain, such a fraternity was the Corporation of the Masters of Defence, founded under letters patent issued by King Henry VIII sometime before 1540. Until Henry's act swordsmen were regarded with disfavor and suspicion in Britain. The London city fathers regarded fencing schools as dens of iniquity that encouraged dueling, brawling, and all manner of ruffianism.

The Italian masters were the earliest to advocate the use of the point in preference to the cutting edge for subtlety and effectiveness, which led to the development of the rapier. From then on, swordsmanship grew detached from tricks of wrestling and boxing.

From the 16th to the 18th centuries, prize fights consisted of displays and tests of swordsmanship. These were frequented by all ranks and segments of the population and patronized by members of the royal family. Champions met challengers in bouts at a variety of weapons, such as singlesticks, quarterstaffs, and backswords, and the blood flowed freely. At the end of the 18th century, James Figg (ca. 1695–1734), the champion of the Corporation of Fencing Masters (as well as the first British boxing champion), introduced pugilism into these prize fights. Since fisticuffs was easier to learn than swordplay, and less likely to be fatal, these encounters soon eclipsed fencing in popularity. Fencing found itself relegated to provincial contests and fairs, where the old ways were held fast.

Learning to use a sword was difficult. The wounds resulting from it often became infected and loss of vision was a risk. But three innovations made fencing more appealing to prospective students concerned with their safety. The first of these came in the 17th century, when a light practice weapon was developed. It was called a foil because its point had been flattened—or "foiled"—and then padded to reduce the chance of injury. The second was the development of rules of engagement known as "conventions"—in which the valid target was limited to the breast and the fencer who initiated the attack had precedence unless completely parried by the defender. Fencing with foils thus became a "conversation" of blades. The third innovation—the invention of the quadrille wire-mesh fencing mask by the French master La Boïessière père and the English master Joseph Boulogne, Chevalier de St. George (ca. 1739–1799), at the close of the 18th century—was the final step necessary to make fencing a completely safe activity. (They actually reinvented the mask, which had been lost to history since the time of the ancient Egyptians.)

Once the mask was in widespread use, more complex "phrases" (exchanges of blows) could become possible and foil fencing as it is now known developed. The rules and conventions already mentioned prevented the play from degenerating into a brawl. These conventions are the basis of modern foil and sabre fencing.

While foil fencing was developing, dueling continued concurrently, and a more realistic fencing experience was considered desirable. The *épée de combat* was transformed from a combat weapon of affairs of honor to a weapon of sport. Its target was expanded from that of foil to simulate a real duel and conventions were discarded. Verisimilitude was enhanced when épée competitions were conducted outdoors, on terrain of grass or gravel; with street shoes and regular trousers de rigeur; finally, bouts were fenced to the best touch (that is, for one hit).

Rules and Play

A modern fencer uses one of three types of weapons—the foil, the épée, or the sabre. Competitions for men or women are conducted at all three weapons; although until quite recently, women competed exclusively at foil. Fencing meets may be conducted as individual or team events. Even in team events only two fencers compete against each other at any one time. Teams are usually made up of three or four on a side, with each competitor meeting each competitor on the opposing squad.

In the earlier years of the 20th century, fencers were frequently three-weapon men and practiced all three arms. As time passed, the size of the starting fields and the duration of competitions, as well as their concomitant expenses, kept increasing. The desire for success led increasingly to specialization in one weapon, at most two.

The modern foil has a slender, flexible blade, quadrilateral in cross-section, and a small, circular guard centrally mounted. The blade is a maximum of

90 centimeters long. Foil fencers try to score, using the point of their weapon only, by hitting their opponent on the torso.

The modern épée has a wide blade, more rigid than that of a foil, Y-shaped in cross-section, and a large circular guard that may be centrally or eccentrically mounted. The blade is a maximum of 90 centimeters (35 inches) long. Epée fencing observes no conventions, and touches are made with the point only anywhere on an opponent.

The modern sabre has a flexible blade, usually T-, Y-, or I-shaped in cross-section, and a large guard that curves around the knuckles and may be centrally or eccentrically mounted. The blade is a maximum of 88 centimeters (34 inches) long. In sabre fencing, touches made with either the point or one of the two cutting edges count if they land above the opponent's hips (a tribute to saber's cavalry origins).

With all three weapons, bouts in a round-robin pool are of 4 minutes' duration. Direct-elimination contests are encounters of 10 or 15 minute's duration, depending on the maximum number of touches.

To avoid injuries, fencers wear a heavy wire-mesh mask with a thick canvas bib to protect the head and neck. They also wear thick canvas or nylon jackets and knickers and a padded glove on the hand holding the weapon. When competing, fencers also wear equipment that permits electric scoring apparatus to function.

Until the advent of electric scoring devices, fencing matches were adjudicated by a jury composed of a "president" and four "assistants." Since the invention of the mask, no innovation in fencing has had so great an impact on the sport as the advent of electrified scoring. It has completely eliminated the need for assistants, leaving only the president to officiate. Epée was electrified in time for the 1935 world championships at Lausanne, Switzerland; foil was electrified for the 1955 world championships in Rome, Italy; and sabre was electrified for the 1989 world championships in Denver, Colorado. Electrification of the sport has increased the startup and maintenance costs considerably and has had a debilitating effect on the technique of competitors since its introduction. Also, in spite of the objectivity of the equipment, biased officials remain entrenched and are among the biggest hazards of the sport.

Much of the history of modern fencing is connected with the Olympic Games. Fencing was one of the eight sports on the program of the 1896 Olympic Games. It shares with only three other sports (athletics, swimming, and gymnastics) the distinction of being on the program of every Olympic Games observance.

The record for the most championships won by any fencer is seven. Aladar Gerevich (1910–) of Hungary won in sabre individual and team between 1932 and 1960. He is also the only athlete in any sport to win an Olympic championship in six different Olympic observances. The record for the most medals of any types is 13 held by Edoardo Mangiarotti (1920–) of Italy in foil and épée, individual and team, between 1936 and 1960; he won five gold, five silver, and three bronze.

At the end of the 19th century, the international competitions at foil and épée were dominated by the French and the Italians and those at sabre by Hungary. Then, about 1960, Russia became the dominant nation in all three weapons, with occasional successes by Poland and Romania. After 1972, there was another reordering, which included a resurgence of fencing in Italy and later in France, as well as a new flourishing in Cuba and China.

A renaissance of interest in fencing occurred simultaneously in the United States and Great Britain during the last decade of the 19th century, nearly concurrent with the revived interest in the Olympic Games and the expansion of collegiate sports. The Amateur Fencers League of America (AFLA) was founded in 1891. In Great Britain, the Amateur Fencing Association (AFA) of Great Britain was founded in 1902.

The U.S. Fencing Association (USFA), as the AFLA has called itself since 1981, administers the sport in the United States, conducting its national championships and other important events. It is the American member of the International Fencing Federation (FIE), which was founded in 1913 because of disputes over the rules governing foil at the 1908 Olympics and the rules governing épée at the 1912 Olympics. The FIE establishes the official rules of the sport and conducts the world fencing championships, the junior world championships (for competitors under 20 years of age), and the cadet world championships (for competitors under 17 years of age), as well as the fencing events of the Olympic Games.

The U.S. Fencing Coaches Association (USFCA), founded in 1941, administers the teaching of fencing in the United States and is the American member of the International Academy of Arms (AAI), the international governing body of fencing masters.

Collegiate fencing in the United States is administered by the National Collegiate Athletic Association (NCAA), which conducted its first fencing championship in 1941; the Intercollegiate Fencing Association (IFA), which was founded in 1894 by Columbia, Harvard, and Yale; and the National Intercollegiate Women's Fencing Association (NIWFA), which was founded in 1929 by Bryn Mawr, Cornell, New York University, and the University of Pennsylvania. Collegiate fencing flourished for decades in the United States, but over the past twenty years, owing to the pernicious policies of the NCAA and USFA, sponsorship of collegiate fencing teams has declined precipitously.

Interscholastic fencing still exists in some parts of the United States, such as New York City and New Jersey, but it owes its recent decline to the shoddy operation of collegiate fencing. The sport has shown no recent signs of a resurgence.

—JEFFREY R. TISHMAN

Bibliography: Castle, Egerton. (1969) *Schools and Masters of Fence: From the Middle Ages to the Eighteenth Century.* York, PA: George Shumway. De Beaumont, Charles L. (1970) *Fencing: Ancient Art and Modern Sport.* South Brunswick, NJ: A. S. Barnes.

Films
See Movies

Fishing
Fresh- and saltwater fishing both began as means of obtaining food. Both have evolved into competitive and recreational sports practiced in all but the most impoverished countries. The catch less frequently consumed; depleted stocks and animal-rights concerns have made catch-and-release fishing more common. Although some have questioned their status as a true sport, it is generally agreed that both fresh- and saltwater fishing meet the definition. Both fresh- and saltwater fishing are often considered elite sports.

Freshwater Fishing
Fishing for food is the mother of sport fishing. The earliest writing about sport fishing comes from 8th century Japan. Even in that very early culture, the sport was apparently quite socially prestigious. This thread of class distinction was to follow the sport until the modern day.

One of the earliest English writings on freshwater fishing came from Dame Juliana Barnes, who wrote *Treatyse of Fyshinge wyth an Angle* in 1496. She indicated that fishing in English-speaking cultures was also a sport of aristocrats, a tradition that continued for several centuries. British ironmonger Izaak Walton read Dame Juliana's book and went on to author the most influential book on the subject ever written. Not only did his book, *The Compleat Angler,* now in its 121st edition, address fishing technique, but also the

---

Bass Fishing

The bass family is a small group of freshwater sunfishes known as Centrarchidae that includes, among other species, the largemouth bass, the smallmouth bass, and the spotted bass. These fish are common to North America, although in recent years they have been successfully transplanted to several other countries (Bennett 1970). American anglers had pursued bass for at least a century before the construction of large dams in the 1940s. However, with the emergence of large impoundments of fresh water in the southern part of the country, fishing for bass became accessible and increasingly popular.

Bass are a predatory species and can be taken with a variety of techniques and equipment. This includes the use of natural baits, lures, and artificial flies. The largemouth bass is the most common of the basses. The world-record largemouth, a 22.25 pound lunker, was taken in 1932 in Georgia. Most bass weigh between 1 and 3 pounds, although several fish over 18 pounds are caught each year (Harbour 1979).

Waterman (1982) noted that bass fishing boomed into the consciousness of the American angler in the 1960s. Part of this was undoubtedly the result of bass fishing tournaments and the Bass Anglers Sportsman's Society (B.A.S.S.). B.A.S.S. signed up its first member in 1968, about six months after the first bass tournament, which took place in 1967 when an enterprising young insurance salesman envisioned that money could be made from tightly structured fishing contests. Within a decade, B.A.S.S. had 250,000 members. The concept started out slowly but today bass tournaments are held on virtually every large lake and river in the United States. The Bass Anglers Sportsman's Society today has over 500,000 members in 52 countries, sponsors a weekly fishing series on television, and publishes four different periodicals on the sport of tournament bass fishing (Burek 1992).

A small but visible group of professional bass fishermen composed almost entirely of white, middle-aged males competes in elite bass tournaments. Just like professionals in other sports, these men have loyal fans who follow their activities. They are sponsored by the manufacturers of fishing equipment. In return, they are walking billboards for a dazzling array of boats, recreational vehicles, tackle, fishing clothing, and electronic fishing equipment (Taylor 1988).

—*Daniel G. Yoder*

---

philosophy of the sport. Many English people, even today, consider all fish except trout and salmon "coarse fish." Freshwater sport fishing remains extremely popular in the British Isles and most parts of Europe.

Freshwater sport fishing traveled across the Atlantic Ocean with the colonists. At this point, documentation on fishing practices becomes sparse. We do know that the Puritans looked down on fishing as a waste of precious time. Nevertheless, Americans began fishing in earnest in the early 1800s. They favored not the high-class trout and salmon of the English but the

Angling Song.

I would seek a blest retreat
To my mind.
Oh: remove me from the great,
And a rural pleasant seat
Let me find.

In a vale pray let it be
That I love:
Where the blackbird on the tree,
piping forth its melody,
Fills the grove.
Let a limpid stream I pray
Murmur near,
That at eve sweet Echo may
Sound of village bells convey
To mine ear.
There I'd watch the speckled trout,
Every shy,
In the water play about,
Or perhaps leap fairly out
At a fly.
Let a steeple stand in view,
That should be:
And the poor man's cottage too,
'Twill remind me what to do
In charity.
As my poultry, let the poor,
Without dread,
From the village cot or moor,
Crowd around my wicker door,
To be fed.
Thus my time I'd pass away
With delight:
Blithe as lambkins at their play,
Social, innocent and gay,
Morn and night.
Think not this is a fancied view—
You'll be wrong:
From a well-known spot I drew,
And of me you've nothing new,
But a song.

—The Angler's Progress, 1820,
Newcastle, England, by Mr. Charnley

the American sporting scene. About 40 million freshwater anglers fish in the United States.

Rules and Play

Worldwide, freshwater fishing equipment and techniques are fairly standard. The fishes pursued run the gamut from big to small, reclusive to bold, flashy to down-home. Each species requires different techniques or equipment. One of the most visible and popular fish groups, the salmon group, includes different varieties of trout, whitefish, and salmon, which are scattered over the cold waters of much of the world and are prized both as sport fish and for their taste. Trout and salmon anglers tend to be a particular breed. Perhaps more than any other angler they are defined by technique and a special ethos, and they are likely the most exclusive of all anglers. While fish in this family may be caught by various methods, fly fishing for trout is the most well known.

Members of the pike family—a large, predatory group of fishes—are very popular game fish. They too range over a large part of the world. Generally, these fish are caught with either small, live bait fish or with artificial baits that resemble this type of forage. Pike are noted for their fighting ability, but not usually considered great table fare. Also popular is the catfish family.

In North America the bass family rivals trout in popularity. This class includes a variety of sunfish and bass. Bass fishing originated in the southern United States. Since the early 1800s it has been exported to many other countries with varying degrees of success. Whereas trout fishers are interested in technique, style, and simplicity, bass fishers surround themselves with the latest fishing technology and seem less concerned with method.

Fly Fishing

Fly fishing, whether for trout or for bass, is the most formal—and many feel the most prestigious—type of fishing. Flies are artificial fish attractants that often resemble the insects on which fish feed. Anglers cast a relatively heavy line with a fly attached to its end with a relatively light fishing rod. Although the art of fly fishing may intimidate many novice anglers, the basic skills of presenting the fly to the fish are not difficult, although advanced skills and techniques come only after years of study and practice. In fly fishing, it is the weight of the line that provides the momentum to carry the fly to the fish. Over the past 60 years, important changes have taken place in fly rods, reels, and most importantly fly-fishing lines.

rough-and-tumble bass, walleye, and muskellunge found in the new frontier. From the mid-1850s, the growth of freshwater fishing in America is closely linked to the development of fishing equipment. Perhaps the most significant development for freshwater fishing in the United States was the invention of the Kentucky reel. This reel, combined with another U.S. fishing contribution, the split bamboo rod, allowed anglers to cast a bait considerably farther. By the late 1800s freshwater fishing was a permanent fixture on

Fishing with Lures

Fishing with lures is similar to fly fishing except that the lure is usually much larger and heavier. The lure is cast out and then retrieved in such a way as to make a fish strike or bite the hook. Lures come in an incredible variety of styles, materials, colors, and shapes. Most lures are made from wood, plastic, and metal and contain from one to five hooks. Some lures appeal more to specific types of fish; others are appealing to a great variety of fish species.

Fishing with Natural Bait

Fishing with natural bait is at the other end of the spectrum. This is likely the oldest and most common method of fishing; ancient anglers were forced to use the baits they found. The equipment, although diverse, is considerably less varied than the baits used. Natural bait anglers use minnows of different species, a variety of worms, crayfish, shrimp, insects, salamanders, frogs, caterpillars, and mollusks. The secret of using natural baits is to match the bait with the preference of the fish at the particular time and location. Each bait requires a particular method of attachment to the hook. Most countries and all states in the United States have restrictions regarding the types of natural baits allowed and the methods for using them.

Freshwater Fishing Equipment

There are five basic types of rod and reel combinations. Spinning rods and reels are designed to cast a weighted artificial bait a considerable distance. The reel used in this combination is "open faced": the angler can see the line as it comes off an exposed spool. Spin casting combinations are similar except that the reel is "closed faced." This reduces the chances of tangled line but also the distance of the cast. Fly-casting combinations consist of a relatively long rod and a very simple reel. In fly fishing the reel merely acts as a place on which to store line. Bait-casting outfits are the most accurate. The rod is stiff and the reel can be manipulated to allow for accurate casts. Trolling rods and reels are much heavier than their bait-casting cousins. They are used out of moving boats and are cast only very short distances.

Challenges

The central controversy in freshwater fishing is the idea of self-imposed handicaps. The sporting quality of the activity is based on the principle of a "fighting chance." However, the new technology that has provided sophisticated means of catching fish has also reduced the opportunity for an equal contest between fish and fisher. Highly technical sonar equipment can detect not only the presence of fish but their size and type. Electronic temperature gauges also help the angler pinpoint the prey. Anglers must be aware of changes in the relationship between freshwater fish and man. Obviously, fish have not made the advances that man has made. Many argue that the game of catching fish is now grossly unfair.

Saltwater Fishing

Most saltwater fishing takes place in the world's estuaries, the diverse and very fertile areas where freshwater rivers and streams enter the ocean. While these brackish waters have very low salinity, they are considered saltwater, and thus the fishing there is considered saltwater as well. Saltwater fishing differs from freshwater fishing in two principal ways: Tidal ebb and flow and daily changes in sunlight, temperature, and other weather control the fish, and the fish species are far more diverse than their freshwater counterparts.

Tarpon and the bonefish spurred the growth of inshore fishing. Striped bass inexplicably disappeared from the U.S. Atlantic coast from 1900 to 1930. By this time, the nucleus of saltwater fishing had shifted to Florida. Tarpon had long been considered uncatchable with light fishing gear, but enthusiasts persisted, and eventually techniques and equipment were developed for catching large specimens of the powerful fish. Soon, another fish of the Florida Flats, the bonefish, was sharing center stage with the tarpon.

The Pacific tuna served as the impetus for saltwater fishing farther off shore. At the turn of the last century, a few California anglers brought in large Pacific tuna weighing over 45 kilograms (100 pounds). The Catalina Tuna Club was a prestigious fishing club that catered to the rich and occasionally eccentric, including American author Zane Grey (1872–1939), a great promoter of deep-water fishing. By the 1940s, saltwater fishing was firmly established, although its growth was slowed temporarily by World War II.

Rules and Play

Saltwater fishing may best be divided into in-shore fishing and off-shore fishing. One of the most popular types of in-shore fishing is surf fishing. The angler wades as far out into the water as possible, keeping in mind the incoming waves that may be four feet high and very powerful. On other occasions the fisher stands on a rock jetty that protrudes out into the water, and casts as far as possible, a practice some purists do not consider true surf fishing. Nevertheless, by the

Fishing Spiritualized.

Every Fisher-man hath his proper baytes, agreeable to the nature of those fishes that hee trowleth or angleth for. For at a bare hooke no Fish will bite. The case-worme, the dewe-worme, the gentile, the flye, the small Roache, and suche-like, are for their turnes according to the nature of the waters, and the times, and the kindes of fishes. Whoso fisheth not with a right bayte, shall neuer do good. Wee that are spirituall fishermen, haue our seurall baites suitable to the stomackes we angle for. If we obserue not the natures of our auditors, and fit ourselves to them, we shall not do wisely. Let such as will not bee led by love bee drawne by feare. But with some the spirit of meeknes will doe most, and loue rather than a rodde doth more good and we shall do indiscreetly, to deale roughly with such. For as the water of a spacious and deepe lake, being still and quiet by nature, by ruffling windes is moued and disquieted; so a people tractable by nature, by the rough behauiour of the Minister may be as much turmoyled and altered from his nature.

The fisherman baiteth not his hook that the fish might only take it, but be taken of it. The red-worme, the case-worme, maggot-flies, small flie, small roche, or such like, are glorious in outward appearance to the fish. So the riches, prioritie, authoritie, of the world, are but pleasant bayts laid out for our destruction. The fisherman's bayte is a deadly deceite: so are all the pleasures of the world. As all the waters of the riuers runne into the salt sea, so all worldly delights, in the saltish sea of sorrows finish their course. Wherefore mistrust worldly benefits as baites, and feed not upon them in hungry wise.

—A Booke of Angling or Fishing. Wherein is shewed, by conference with Scriptures, the agreement between the Fisherman, Fishes, Fishing of both natures, Temporall and Spirituall. *By Samuel Gardiner,* Doctor of Divinitie. *Matthew iv. 19.* "I will make you fishers of men." *London: Printed for Thomas Purfoot, 1606*

---

mid-1970s there were approximately 1 million surf anglers, making it probably the most rapidly growing type saltwater fishing. Surf fishing is most popular on the Atlantic and Pacific coasts of the United States. Surf fishing appeals to anglers with an individualistic bent; surf anglers are on their own, with no mate or guide to help them find and catch fish.

The equipment for surf fishing is critical. The spinning reel is most commonly used for fishing the surf. This reel allows the angler to continually cast long distances and to retrieve artificial lures or baits at a high rate of speed. Surf casting rods must be strong and flexible enough to cast large bait, but sensitive enough to detect small taps by cautious fish; most are fairly long and have a long rod butt, which provides the necessary two-handed leverage.

Most surf fishers prefer artificial lures, which allow surf fishers to be proactive rather than reactive. One of the oldest lures is the metal squid, variously sized and shaped, which look like the fish's natural food. Plugs are also used extensively by surf fishers, but they are less popular. They are usually made from wood and plastic and tend to be lighter than squids. Occasionally surf anglers do use natural bait, either cast and retrieved like an artificial lure or held motionless on the bottom using a large lead weight or "sinker."

Fishing from rocky shores and piers, also very popular, closely resembles surf fishing. Man-made jetties are especially productive areas for saltwater fishing, because smaller bait fish tend to congregate around areas with underwater structures such as piers and jetties, larger game fish move in to feed. Fishing around jetties is done both with artificial baits and with natural baits, which are retrieved and still fished.

These saltwater fishing techniques involve special hazards. For the beach surf fishers, ocean tides and waves can be deadly. Anglers have been washed off their feet with unexpected waves, and some have been stranded on points when tides have risen. Jetties have the reputation of being the most dangerous of all fishing areas. The jetties' rocks are usually covered with moss. The combination of poor footing and rushing waters from waves and swells can lead to disaster. Night fishing, popular in these areas, adds yet another level of risk. Specialized equipment and techniques for surf and rock fishers, such as cleated footwear and flotation devices, reduce some of the danger.

Trolling for fish, either on the surface or at considerable depth, is the most effective method of catching world-record saltwater species. By pulling a lure or a natural bait from a slow moving boat, one is able to cover a great amount of water. Anglers do not have to concern themselves with the fatigue they might experience in surf fishing. They can have their equipment in the water at all times. Much trolling is provided by charter boats because the cost of equipment is too great for many anglers, but many smaller vessels also troll for in-shore and off-shore species. Trolling reels are not designed for casting. They are often heavy, dependable, and built for extended use. The rods are usually somewhat shorter and heavier than those used for surf fishing. Outriggers are long poles that extend 3 to 6 meters (10–18 feet) from the sides of boats. These allow the lures and baits to be trolled away from the boat's wakes at different depths and with different actions. With outriggers several anglers, as many as eight, are able to simultaneously fish from a single boat. On the heavier lines, anglers can fish for marlins and sailfish, and on the lighter or "flat" lines anglers can fish for species such as wahoo, albacore, and dolphin.

Party boat fishing, which started in the last half of the 19th century, is designed for the saltwater angler who wants to fish but lacks the necessary skill and/or equipment for solo participation. Party boats were especially popular on the West Coast and, initially, in the East. Recently, they have become popular in Florida. The early boats were not specifically designed to allow a large number of people to fish simultaneously; they were merely large boats that were modified to more or less serve the purpose. As the sport became more popular and profitable, boats were designed with large decks that allowed up to 100 anglers to get bait from a central location and conveniently fish over the sides of the boat. Party boat fishing consists of fishing straight down off the sides of the boat. The boat stations itself over the fishing area (sometimes a shipwreck or a reef) and anglers simply release line on the reel until the bait is at the proper depth. A variety of species can be taken, including grouper, snappers, shark, flounder, salmon, and others.

Party boats are often equipped with the latest in sonar equipment to detect underwater structures, such as wrecked ships, that attract game fish. Some of this equipment is sensitive enough to detect the fish themselves.

Charter boats are similar to party boats, but generally carry only small groups. This fishing is usually more exciting, with greater chances of catching trophy fish of various species, but also considerably more expensive than party boat fishing. These boats are also used to fish big game fish of the open sea, a pursuit once confined to the rich.

The fastest-growing and most prestigious form of saltwater fishing is fly-fishing, with in-shore fly-fishing the most popular. Freshwater fly fishers are able to convert without too much difficulty, and other saltwater anglers are realizing the thrill of the challenge of taking large, strong fish with relatively light tackle. Saltwater fly-fishing includes in-shore fishing and off-shore fishing. More species and a greater number of fishing areas are available to the in-shore angler. It is also less expensive than its off-shore counterpart. Hot spots for fly-fishing for saltwater species, both in-shore and off-shore, include the waters of Florida, Australia, the Caribbean, and the Gulf of Mexico.

Popular species pursued by fly fishers include bonefish, tarpon, snook, sea trout, barracuda, channel bass, cravelle, and mackerel. Open sea, big game fish include various tuna species, including the bluefin tuna. Most anglers consider the swordfish the greatest big game fish of all. They are found on the deep water edges of off-shore banks throughout the warm waters of the world. The most common way of catching swordfish is to skip an artificial or a natural bait past them while trolling. First, however, it is necessary to locate them. Tall platforms mounted on fishing boats allow anglers to see swordfish from long distances because "swords" often bask very near the water's surface. Marlin and sailfish, both notable fighters, are also popular big game fish.

Sharks are the final category of big game fish. Anglers are slow to recognize them as worthy game until they experience the strength and endurance of them on a line. Although there are many species of sharks in the world's ocean waters, only mako, white, tiger, porbeagle, and thresher sharks are recognized as game fish by the International Game Fishing Association (IGFA). The white shark is the largest game fish in the world. Special care must be taken when fishing for sharks; even those species that are not man-eaters are equipped with several rows of teeth and powerful tails that can injure or kill careless anglers. In addition, sharks have razor-sharp skin consisting of thousands of denticles that make the skin feel like sandpaper.

Competitive Fishing
Fresh- and saltwater fishing competitions use similar formats. These competitions include record-keeping and organized fishing tournaments. The IGFA, organized in 1940, is now responsible for both saltwater and freshwater records. Although tournaments are organized to fish for a variety of saltwater species, probably the most popular and visible tournaments are for billfish such as marlins and sailfish. Winners are judged

on the number of fish caught within a specified time and the weight of the fish.

Limits to Fishing

Both fresh- and saltwater fishing face the issue of limits. For freshwater fishing, wide-scale pollution of fresh water has become a major threat to the sport. Many lakes and streams in several countries no longer contain fish because of an increase of insecticide residues, industrial wastes, and acid rain. Peaking in the late 1970s, with alarming deaths of freshwater fish in many countries, the trend seems to have been reversed. Serious threats to the resources, however, still remain. For saltwater fishing, in-shore and off-shore species are in fact dangerously low. Restrictions on the length of seasons, types of equipment, and fishing techniques have been imposed in an effort to reverse the trends. In addition, at least for many of the big game fish, the catch-and-release concept has firmly established itself. Amazing results have been realized for some species of saltwater game fish, but for others the outlook is less than bright.

Given the varieties of fishing and the many reasons for which people fish, the sport seems likely to stay as heterogeneous as it is today. The one constant may be the age-old, universal belief among those who fish: the biggest fish is always the one that gets away.

—DANIEL G. YODER

See also Animal Rights.

Bibliography: Boyle, R. (1995) "Management School." *Outdoor Life* 195 (April): 53–60. Cagner, E. (1976) *The Lore of Sportfishing*. New York: Crown. McNally, Tom. (1993) *The Complete Book of Fly Fishing*. 2d ed. Camden, ME: Ragged Mountain Press. McPherson, B. D., J. E. Curtis, and J. W. Loy. (1989) *The Social Significance of Sport: An Introduction to the Sociology of Sport*. Champaign, IL: Human Kinetics. Netherby, Steve. (1974) *The Experts' Book of Fresh Water Fishing*. New York: Simon and Schuster. Scharff, R. (1966) *Standard Handbook of Salt-Water Fishing*. New York: Thomas Y. Crowell. Sternberg, Dick. (1982) *The Art of Fresh Water Fishing*. Minnetonka, MN: Cy DeCosse Inc. Tryckare, Tre, Ewart Cagner, and Bernt Dybern. (1976) *The Lore of Sportfishing*. New York: Crown. Waterman, C. F. (1981) *A History of Angling*. Tulsa, OK: Winchester Press. ———. (1982) "The Bonefish Flats." In *Waters Swift and Small*, edited by C. Woods and D. Seybold. Tulsa, OK: Winchester Press.

Flying Disc

Flying discs are lightweight objects shaped like saucers that players throw and catch. "Flying disc" is a generic term, and discs are often referred to as a "Frisbee," which actually is the trademarked name of the most famous brand of them. Since the 1950s flying discs have become extremely popular recreational products. According to its manufacturer, Mattel Corp., over 100 million Frisbees have been made since the product was introduced in 1957, and they annually outsell baseballs, basketballs, and footballs. Flying disc has also been a competitive sport since 1958.

History

The contemporary lightweight flying disc is believed to have originated in a game college students invented by tossing metal pie plates or cookie-tin tops among themselves for amusement. This fad was generally thought to have started in the 1930s and 1940s, but some accounts trace it back as far as the 19th century. It is not known where this game started either. It has been attributed to several schools. The plastic flying disc as a recreational product was developed in the late 1940s and the 1950s. The idea apparently occurred to more than one person simultaneously, and several versions were sold in that era.

The genesis of the specific product known as the Frisbee—the version that made flying discs popular— is clearer. Fred Morrison, a building inspector and pilot in California, in 1948 developed a small flying disc made of plastic. He first named his invention the "Flyin' Saucer" and later the "Pluto Platter." In 1956, Morrison sold the rights to the product to Wham-O, a San Gabriel, California, company. Wham-O changed the name of the Pluto Platter to Frisbee in 1958. Backed by Wham-O's marketing skill, the Frisbee soon achieved great popularity.

The origin of the name "Frisbee" is also open to question. The most frequent explanation is that it refers to the Frisbie Baking Co., whose containers were originally thrown by students. However, one of the cofounders of Wham-O once said he took the name for the product from an old comic strip.

The flying disc has become a prominent feature of popular culture. Initially, the design and performance of these plastic discs (which have also been called "flying saucers") reflected the nation's fascination with space flight and science fiction. In the 1960s and 1970s, the gentle flight characteristics of the discs became associated with the relaxed attitudes of the counterculture. Casual players simply enjoy the act of tossing and catching the disc as a relaxing way to spend time. The flying disc also reflects the increased emphasis on sports and exercise that emerged after 1970. Flying

Ultimate

The sport of Ultimate is a fast-paced game played according to a simple set of rules, with no referee. Played with a Frisbee, the game combines elements of soccer, football, and basketball. Every player is a quarterback and every player is a receiver.

Ultimate was first played by a group of high school students in 1968 in the parking lot of the Columbia High School in Maplewood, New Jersey. Within a few years the sport had spread to colleges throughout the United States; the first intercollegiate Ultimate game took place on 6 November 1972 in New Brunswick, New Jersey, between players from Rutgers and Princeton.

A regulation game of Ultimate is played by two teams of seven players on a field measuring 70 yards by 40 yards (64 meters by 36 meters) with 25-yard (23-meter) deep endzones. At the start of each point, the teams line up in front of their respective end zones; a point is scored when the offensive team completes a pass within the defensive team's end zone. The disc (Frisbee) may be advanced in any direction by completing a pass to a teammate. Possession changes sides when a pass is not completed; the defense immediately takes possession and becomes the offense. According to participants, Ultimate depends on a spirit of sportsmanship and fair play. Players are responsible for their own foul and line calls and resolve their own disputes. Competitive play is encouraged but never at the expense of respect between players, adherence to the rules, or the basic joy of play. Under the rules of the game, behavior such as taunting opponents, dangerous aggression, intentional fouls, or a "win-at-all-costs" attitude is contrary to the spirit of the game and must be discouraged by all players.

—John Townes

discs are also used in a wide range of challenging competitive sports and in exercise programs in schools.

Rules and Play

Flying discs are designed to move forward through the air with a spinning motion. The specific characteristics of this movement depend on a combination of factors, including the force of the throw, the speed of the spin, and the angle of flight. A disc can be thrown so that it slowly floats to its destination or it can be made to fly in a fast, direct path. The skill of throwing a disc is based on the ability of a player to control these variables. These include the way the disk is held in the fingers and the angle and speed of the arm and wrist movements as it is thrown.

Flying discs are also widely used in competitive games and sports and for physical conditioning. In "Guts," individual players or teams, generally with five players on each side, face each other, and toss the disc back and forth. Their goal is to throw it as hard and fast as possible to prevent opponents from catching it. (The origin of Guts is not known, but it is believed to be a safer version of a game that college students once played with a circular saw blade!) Ultimate is a field sport played with a flying disc. Freestyle flying-disc events are displays of especially dramatic and creative movements. Canine Frisbee, in which dogs catch and retrieve discs, is also popular.

Numerous variations of bowling and other traditional games have also been tailored for the flying disc. Disc Golf is a variation of its namesake, played with specially designed discs rather than golf balls and with poles as the targets instead of holes. There are at least 500 Disc Golf courses in the United States, often in public parks. Serious flying-disc players also attempt to break records, such as those listed in the *Guinness Book of Records*.

A newer flying disc, known as the Aerobie, became popular in the 1990s. The Aerobie is hollow at the center, and is designed to fly especially far, commonly 200 yards or more. The Aerobie was recorded in one edition of the *Guinness Book of Records* as the object thrown farthest in the world, a record set with a 383.13-meter (419-yard) toss by Scott Zimmerman of San Francisco.

Disk Throwing Competitions

In 1958, the first International Frisbee Tournament was held in Escanaba, Michigan. Wham-O executive Ed Headrick founded the International Frisbee Association to promote disc sports in 1967.

In 1985, the first World Flying Disc Conference was held in Helsinborg, Sweden, with 19 nations represented, which led to the formation of the World Flying Disc Federation. This organization was accepted as a member of the General Association of International Sports Federations in 1987.

New designs and materials may bring flying discs further into the high-tech age. The spirit, however, generally remains much as it was when students threw pie plates.

—John Townes

Footbag

Footbag is a popular contemporary sport based on kicking a stuffed, pliable ball that is usually about two inches in diameter. Players keep the footbag moving in the air using only their feet, legs, or thighs. "Footbag" is a generic name for the sport; it is also known as Hacky Sack, which is the trademarked name of one of the most popular brands of footbag. From the most casual of origins, footbag is now established as both a recreational and competitive sport.

History

Footbag is similar to older kick-based sports. One of its oldest ancestors is believed to be a game that originated in China around 2600 B.C.E. in which an object filled with hair was kicked for sport and military conditioning. Another forerunner, Asian shuttlecock, dates back approximately 2,000 years, using a feathered disc that was kicked and passed by players.

The contemporary sport of footbag was developed in the western United States in the early 1970s by John Stalberger and Mike Marshall, two friends who enjoyed kicking around a small stuffed sock for enjoyment and physical conditioning. They called this pastime "hacking the sack," and they began to develop and promote their hobby as a sport. After Marshall died in 1975, Stalberger continued to promote the footbag. He invented a footbag game called Net. Experimenting with footbags of different sizes and materials resulted in the Hacky Sack, which he patented in 1979. In 1983, he sold the rights for the Hacky Sack to Wham-O. Supported by the promotional resources of Wham-O, the footbag gained many enthusiasts and became a fad in the early 1980s. From there it has evolved into an established form of recreation and exercise, and many other makers of footbags and accessories have emerged.

In 1983 the World Footbag Association (WFA), based in Steamboat Springs, Colorado, was formed as an official promotional and players' organization. By late 1995, the WFA's membership had surpassed 34,000 and was increasing at a rate of 600 new members per month. To promote the footbag as a form of physical education, the WFA sponsors many demonstrations and classes in schools.

The first National Footbag Championship tournament was held in Oregon City, Oregon, in 1980. It has since become an annual event and was renamed the World Footbag Championships in 1986. Approximately 150 players from various nations were registered to play in the 1995 World Footbag Championships held in San Francisco.

Rules and Play

Many different games have been developed for the footbag. These include completely new games as well as older sports that have been adapted to use the footbag instead of balls. Proponents contend that footbag is a valuable form of exercise that develops endurance, coordination, balance, and mental concentration in unique ways because of its emphasis on seldom used muscles and movements.

Most footbag games do not allow any movements in which the player uses their hands, arms, or upper torso to control the bag. With some exceptions, only the feet and lower body are supposed to touch the footbag while it is in play. One of the principles of the sport is the use of kicks on alternate sides of the lower body to keep the footbag in motion.

The sport's most basic format is known as Footbag Consecutive, which is played either informally or in competition. Consecutive play can be an individual activity or played by pairs or teams who pass the footbag among themselves. In basic Consecutive, players keep the footbag in the air for as long as possible and perform as many kicks as they can before they either miss the footbag, lose control of it, or become too tired to continue. By 1997 Ted Martin had set a new record with 63,326 kicks over a period of 8 hours, 50 minutes, 22 seconds. In 1980, Jack Schoolcraft and Will Wingert established a Men's Doubles record of 2,069 kicks in 25 minutes. In 1995, Tricia George and Gary Lautt made 123,456 kicks over 19 hours, 19 minutes, 20 seconds.

Footbag Freestyle emphasizes the individual display of especially creative and dramatic kicks and routines, which are scored by a panel of judges. The rules of Freestyle are more lenient regarding the use of the upper body to allow players greater freedom and variety in their actions. Players choreograph their routines to music and incorporate many elements to add to the impact of their displays.

Footbag Net is played by pairs of individuals, doubles, or larger teams. Its rules, strategy, and scoring combine elements of volleyball and tennis. Players stand on either side of the net and kick the footbag back and forth, attempting to score points by making spikes and other shots their opponents cannot return. Two kicks can be made per side in singles play, while three kicks are allowed in doubles (but a doubles player cannot make two consecutive kicks). A game is played to 11 or 15 points, and a match is won by the victor in two out of three games. Players are ranked in regional and national tournaments to qualify for the World Championships. The best Net players are able to make spectacular shots, kicking their feet high in the air as they hit the fast-moving footbag.

In Footbag Golf, players move the footbag around a specially designed course with the goal of kicking it into a series of holes. The basic format and scoring are similar to the traditional game of golf.

Like other sports that combine elements of more

popular pastimes, footbag may never gain a mass following. Its distinctive qualities, though, will likely retain it a loyal following.

—JOHN TOWNES

See also Takraw.
Bibliography: *Footbag World Magazine* (Golden, CO).

Football, American

American football is a ball game played by teams of 11 members each. Based on the English game of rugby, it involves kicking, passing, and carrying an oblong ball with pointed ends originally made out of pigskin. Tackling is a prominent aspect of the game, and players wear helmets and heavy padding. The aim is to get the ball passed the goalposts; various points are assigned depending on how this is done. It has remained a game played almost exclusively by boys and men, though a few women have challenged this tradition. Touch football is a recreational version of the game that involves no tackling.

History

American football developed from the 1870s to the early 1900s. In the 1860s and early 1870s, many American collegians were playing forms of soccer, while Harvard students, refusing to play soccer, had created a game more akin to English rugby than soccer. The game first became popular in the elite colleges of the East. Led by Yale's Walter Camp (1859–1925), rugby football rules were changed to reflect America's desire for a more scientific, rational game.

Most colleges were playing a variation of association football, but the soccer-like game was short-lived despite the rules being codified on several campuses. Harvard was the only major school not playing a form of soccer. The Harvard men called their pastime the Boston game, in which a player could catch or pick up the ball and then kick it or even run with it. The opportunity to run with the ball was a key development of a nonsoccer game in America.

Other colleges continued to play a variation of association football, and competitions became more common. In 1873, a convention was organized to formalize rules for this game. Harvard absented itself, protesting the soccer game as inferior to its own—an action that drastically changed the history of American football. While Yale, Princeton, Columbia, and Rutgers agreed to common rules, Harvard kept its own. Soon Yale asked Harvard to play a football game, but Harvard would only agree if rugby rules were the basis. Yale, to save face, agreed to "concessionary" rules, but they were really those of rugby. Some Princeton men traveled to New England to see the contest. Wanting to play the more prestigious Yale and Harvard in the future, Princeton had to change to the rugby game.

Once Princeton accepted rugby, a convention was called in 1876, in which the future "Big Three" and Columbia adopted standard rugby rules and formed an Intercollegiate Football Association (IFA). The IFA decided to initiate a Thanksgiving Day championship contest between the two leading teams of the previous year. Yale and Princeton were chosen for the first of the traditional Thanksgiving Day games, and the two schools continued to dominate the game for the next two decades. The Thanksgiving Day tradition spread across America as "a holiday granted by the State and the nation to see a game of football" (*New York Herald*, 1 December 1893, 3).

The rest of the colleges and schools accepted the rules formalized by the eastern elites. Walter Camp, the "father" of American football, remained involved in football and rule changes for the next half-century. Camp, more than any other individual, created the American version of football. In 1880, he suggested possibly the most radical rule in football history, one giving continuous possession of the ball to one team after a player was tackled. Camp proposed a "scrimmage" in which the team in original possession would snap (center) the ball back to a quarterback who would hand it to another back in a logical play. Camp, by the early 1880s, suggested incorporating the notion of "downs," in which one team was given three attempts (downs) to make 5 yards (4.5 meters) or lose possession of the ball. The 5-yard chalk lines created a "gridiron" effect and a new name for the game. The consequence of the short distance to be gained in three attempts created the need for exacting plays, the development of signals for calling the plays, and the introduction of players running interference for the ball carrier, another modification of rugby. Mass plays led to the charge of brutality in the late 1800s. The sport had defenders in high places, though, including President Theodore Roosevelt.

Rules and Play

A description of the rules of American football calls into question the original plan for a "rational" game. Football is played by two teams of 11 players on a field 100 yards long. Each team tries to gain possession of the ball and get it across the opponents' goal line, thus scoring a touchdown and earning 6 points. If a team with the ball does not advance 10 yards in 4 tries—Camp's "downs"—it yields the ball to the other team; it may also pick up a dropped ball or intercept a passed ball and gain possession that way. Strategies and tactics used to win have become highly sophisticated with much position specialization, off-season training, game and play analysis by the coaching staffs, and for a few years at the professional level even the use of instant replay to check the accuracy of official's on-filed decisions.

College and Professional Football

The professional game has been traced to the payment of Walter "Pudge" Heffelfinger (1867–1954), the acknowledged greatest college player of the 19th century. The Allegheny Athletic Association near Pittsburgh paid two players—Heffelfinger and Donnelly—to beat the rival Pittsburgh Athletic Club. Heffelfinger received the enormous sum of $500, plus travel expenses, and Donnelly received $250 plus expenses.

Other "amateur" teams began paying their players in western Pennsylvania, upper New York, and especially Ohio. Most of the better players were collegians, who at times played on Saturdays for college teams and competed under assumed names for pro teams on Sundays. Some of the players were professional baseball players as well as collegians.

Ohio led the way in the professional game. Collegians such as Knute Rockne (1888–1931) of Notre Dame and the great African American stars, Paul Robeson (1898–1976) of Rutgers and Fritz Pollard (1894–1986) of Brown, played in Ohio. While the crowds at professional games did not compare to the best of the colleges, interest in football was increasing when World War I temporarily halted the game.

Two of the most important pro franchises were a result of industry-sponsored teams—the Green Bay Packers and the Chicago Bears. In Wisconsin in 1919, Curly Lambeau (1898–1965), a Notre Dame dropout, received $500 from the Indian Packing Company of Green Bay to organize a team, the Green Bay Packers. The following year George Halas (1895–1983), a former University of Illinois player, organized a team with money from the Staley Starch Company of Decatur, Illinois. He soon joined a group in 1920 that was the forerunner of the National Football League (NFL). Green Bay and Chicago, along with the New York Giants and the Washington Redskins, dominated the NFL until the end of World War II.

The relationship between the professional and intercollegiate game has been long and close in many ways. The star players of the professional teams were mostly

---

Football Shapes Up

The year 1905–1906 was probably the most critical to the development of American football. In that year, intercollegiate football, the leader in the evolution of the American game, went through a crisis of ethics and brutality. During the middle of the season, President Theodore Roosevelt, feeling the pressure of the "muckrakers" attacking football, called a White House conference of football authorities from the Big Three, Harvard, Yale, and Princeton. Led by Walter Camp, the Big Three agreed in the future to "carry out the letter and in spirit the rules of the game of football, relating to roughness, holding and foul play." It was not enough. A number of institutions banned football at the end of the season including Columbia, Northwestern, California, and Stanford. Harvard, the leading educational institution in America, banned it for several months. Following the death of a Union College halfback in its final game with New York University, 13 institutions met to choose between banning or reforming football. Out of this meeting a second reform meeting was called at the end of December 1905, at which 68 institutions from across the nation took part. This meeting of faculty and college administrators was the beginning of the National Collegiate Athletic Association, the eventual governing body of intercollegiate athletics in many American colleges. Rule changes resulted to counter brutal play, including lengthening the yardage needed to retain the ball to 10 yards, prohibiting runners from hurdling the line, placing a neutral zone between the two teams, and introducing the forward pass. While the forward pass was unsuccessfully fought by Walter Camp, it was greatly limited by restrictions placed on its use. The pass at first was used sparingly, and generally only as a desperation device. However, restrictive rules were eventually eased, and with the appearance of the forward pass, the modern twentieth-century game was created.

—Ronald A. Smith

---

collegians from the time of Heffelfinger in the 1890s. Many college coaches had played professional football. The midwestern Big 10 Conference and the Ivy League in the East were so concerned about pro football in the mid-1920s that they prohibited (at the cost of employment) employees of their athletic departments from taking part in professional football games as players or officials. The case of Harold "Red" Grange (1903–1991), a star halfback from the University of Illinois, led to an outcry by colleges against the pros for signing a player before he graduated from college, and prompted an NFL agreement with the colleges not to sign any football player before his eligibility was completed or his class had graduated. The so-called "Red Grange Rule" lasted for more than a half century, when the agreement could no longer stand up under federal antitrust law.

It was clearly more important for the pros to feed off the colleges than for the colleges to benefit from the pros. Pro football gained stature because it increasingly used the colleges as "farm teams" of the professional clubs. In an attempt to ensure an equitable distribution of college players within the professional ranks, the annual draft of college players was devised in 1936.

College coaches and other college athletic officials feared the growth of professional football. At about the same time the NFL came into existence, college coaches formed the Football Coaches Association (FCA). One of the association's first actions in 1921 was to unanimously resolve that "professional football was detrimental to the best interests of American football and American youth and that football coaches [should] lend their influence to discourage the professional game." The fear of pro football hurting the college game continued through the century. It was seen early in creation of the "Red Grange Rule," and it continued with such 1960s actions as forbidding the mention of pro football in college football telecasts and the successful lobbying to pass federal legislation to prohibit pro football from televising games on Saturdays, when college football is traditionally played. The fear of the pros was a major stimulus in the 1960s decision to allow unlimited substitutions (two platoon football) to increase fan interest, which was being lost to the more exciting pro game.

College football far outstripped professional football until the 1960s. The college game took advantage of claiming to be amateur, with athletes playing for the honor of their alma mater. Even though the college game had been developed on a commercial model with huge stadiums, highly paid coaches, and subsidized athletes (either overtly or covertly), the athletes were still viewed as amateurs. The positive virtue of "amateurism" added to the luster of football traditions of "homecoming," pep rallies, "tailgating," cheerleaders, and marching bands. Season-ending bowl games added to the interest.

Both college and professional teams lacked a large number of African American players during the first half of the 20th century. There were blacks in the NFL until the "color line" was drawn in 1933. Football remained segregated until the end of World War II, when the Los Angeles Rams of the National Football League and the Cleveland Browns of the All-American Football Conference added black players shortly before Jackie Robinson (1917–1972) desegregated professional baseball.

Television and Football

The introduction of television dramatically affected college and pro football following World War II. Games were first telecast in 1939, and by about 1950, the growth of television made commercial telecasts of sport contests profitable. Colleges were concerned that telecasts would have a negative impact on attendance at stadiums, and in 1951 members of the National Collegiate Athletic Association decided to control the number of telecasts of their football games. From 1951 to 1984, the NCAA plan provided for national and regional telecasts each Saturday during the season. This monopoly existed first to limit games on TV and preserve gate receipts. Later, when the NCAA contract with television networks was worth over $65 million per year, television revenues going to big-time colleges became more important than preserving stadium attendance. A power struggle erupted between the smaller NCAA institutions and those that had regular game telecasts. The smaller institutions, demanding a greater percentage of television funds, helped spur the creation of the College Football Association (CFA). The CFA was created in 1976 to promote big-time football. Within five years, the CFA helped sponsor a legal suit against the NCAA by the Universities of Oklahoma and Georgia to break up the NCAA football TV monopoly. A 1984 U.S. Supreme Court decision went against the NCAA, and colleges were thereafter free to create their own television plans. The result was an oversupply of games and lower fees being paid to most institutions.

The professional National Football League had different results from television. The league's popularity rose greatly after its championship game in 1958, when the Baltimore Colts defeated the New York Giants in a dramatic overtime contest seen by millions on television. In that decade, the NFL solution to protect stadium attendance was to prevent televising within a radius of 75 miles without permission of the home team. Second, the NFL decided to pool television money, dividing the TV revenues equally among all the teams. This brilliant decision allowed smaller market teams, such as the Green Bay Packers and the Pittsburgh Steelers, to remain financially competitive.

Competition from a new league also had an impact on professional football. Lamar Hunt (1932–), disgruntled at being unable to purchase an NFL franchise, formed the American Football League (AFL) in 1960, which soon received a multimillion-dollar television contract from the National Broadcasting Corporation (NBC). The AFL received recognition, and in 1966 the NFL, which fought the AFL, accepted a merger of the two leagues. The merger, under the NFL name, became official as a 26-team league in 1970. A playoff between the NFL and AFL beginning in 1967 added excitement and created greater wealth. The championship was called the Super Bowl, and Green Bay won the first two contests. The Super Bowl, a kind of American holiday, has had some of the highest ratings in television history, easily surpassing baseball's World Series in popularity. The NFL introduced Monday Night Football to supplement the traditional Sunday games beginning in 1970. For two decades, Monday Night Football surpassed all regular televised sporting events in popularity.

Professional football's increase in wealth from television has spurred both new labor disputes and competing leagues. Players formed the National Football League Players Association in 1956, but the union was not recognized by NFL owners until 1968. A desire for a larger share of the profits eventually led to several players' strikes between 1968 and the mid-1980s. New football leagues, also looking at the growing wealth in the professional game, were formed. Of these the only survivor has been the NFL-established World League of American Football (WLAF) with teams in Europe and North America. The WLAF acts like a farm system for the NFL and expanded the college football feeder system.

Harvard's innocent rebellion against soccer has had consequences no one could have foreseen. American football has spread to other countries and shows no sign of slowing down.

—RONALD A. SMITH

Bibliography: Neft, David S., Richard M. Cohen, and Rick Korch. (1992) *The Sports Encyclopedia: Pro Football.* New York: St. Martin's Press. Porter, David L., ed. (1987) *Biographical Dictionary of American Sports: Football.* Westport, CT: Greenwood Press. Smith, Robert. (1988) *Sports and Freedom: The Rise of Big-Time College Athletics.* New York: Oxford University Press. Weyand, A. M. (1926) *Football, Its History and Development.* New York: D. Appleton.

Football (Association Football)
See Soccer

Football, Australian

Australian Rules Football is a unique Australian sport that evolved in Melbourne in the 19th century. It is played on an oval field by teams of 18 players who attempt to get the ball across their opponents' goal line. Players may not run with the ball; they advance it by dribbling, kicking, and punching it.

History

Earlier forms of football had previously been played in the Port Phillip District of New South Wales (later Victoria), but these would have been soccer, rugby, or

Gaelic football. In 1844 a hurling match was held at Batman's Hill between representatives of Clare and Tipperary, and on Christmas Day 1845 the *Port Phillip Herald* advertised various old country sports, including a "grand match of the old English game of football," which could have been the folk variant of the game.

The genesis of the new game can be attributed to one individual, Thomas Wentworth Wills (1835–1880). On July 10, 1858, he wrote to *Bell's Life,* a newspaper, suggesting that as the cricket season was over a football club should be formed, with a committee of three or more to draw up rules. It is obvious he mainly wanted to keep cricketers fit, though he felt that trampling on the cricket fields in the off-season would be good for them. He followed this letter up with an approach to the Melbourne Cricket Club Committee and after consideration they asked him to create such a game. The novel *Tom Brown's Schooldays,* which was published in 1857 and was being read in Melbourne at this precise time, espoused the creed of "muscular Christianity." The time was opportune for the delineation of a football code in Melbourne.

An impromptu game was subsequently played between members of the Melbourne Cricket Club and "others who happened to be present in August of 1858," next "about fifty gentlemen" played the game, and then 26 players from Melbourne played against a like number from South Yarra. Football interest grew rapidly, and formal rules were developed in May 1859 by seven men from the Melbourne Cricket Club.

Handling was allowed, but a player could run no farther than was necessary to kick the ball. Eventually, the rules stipulated that an individual could run, but the ball had to be bounced every 5 or 6 yards (4.5 or 5.5 meters). If there was a "mark," that is, if the ball was caught cleanly, the player with the ball would have an unobstructed kick. This rule perseveres in the modern sport of rugby as well as Australian Rules. A unique innovation was to allow for a no-offsides rule, which clearly distinguished the game from rugby. By 1874 points were gained by kicking through the posts rather than carrying the ball between them.

Rules and Play

The game is played on an oval field by two teams of 18 players. There are four goalposts at each end of the field. If the ball is kicked through the center posts, the team is awarded 6 points; if the kick goes between the outside posts, the team is awarded 1 point. There is no offside, and no goalie, and it is essentially a kicking and catching game, with points scored only by kicking. The ball is

Letter from Thomas Wentworth Wills.

Sir,—Now that cricket has been put aside for some months to come, and cricketers have assumed somewhat of the chrysalis nature (for a time only 'tis true), but at length will again burst forth in all their varied hues, rather than allow this state of torpor to creep over them, and stifle their now supple limbs, why can they not, I say, form a foot-ball club, and form a committee of three or more to draw up a code of laws? If a club of this sort were got up it would be of vast benefit to any cricket-ground to be trampled upon, and would make the turf quite firm and durable; besides which, it would keep those who are inclined to be stout from having their joints encased in useless superabundant flesh. If it is not possible to form a foot-ball club, why should not these young men who have adopted this new-born country for their mother land, why I say, do they not form themselves into a rifle club, so as at any rate they may some day be called upon to aid their adopted land against a tyrant's band, that may some day "pop" upon us when we least expect a foe at our very doors. Surely our young cricketers are not afraid of the crack of the rifle, when they face so courageously the leather sphere, and it would disgrace no one to learn in time how to defend his country and his hearth. A firm heart, a steady hand, a quick eye, are all that are requisite, and with practice, all these may be attained. Trusting that some one will take up the matter, and form either of the above clubs, or at any rate, some athletic games.

I remain, yours truly, T. W. Wills.
—*Bell's Life*, 10 July 1858.

kicked or hand-passed between teammates and features high leaps, or "marks" for the ball. Although the sport is now national in scope, its greatest following is in the state of Victoria.

Though there have been attempts to spread the adoption of the game to other countries, even Ireland because of its predilection for hurling and Gaelic football, it has not made significant inroads elsewhere. The heroes of the sport, because of its regional nature, have not been truly national heroes, particularly in comparison with those of the summer sport of cricket.

Commercialism is increasingly eroding the fundamental reasons for the emergence of this unique game, and it is in danger of losing its traditional roots. It is becoming more and more a spectacle engineered by public relations and mass consumption experts who mainly wish to market a game for a consumer-oriented society. This rampant commercialization is in danger of creating larger-than-life figures who become more distant from (and unlike) the ordinary fan, who is the basis for the game's popularity. Local clubs are gradu-

ally losing meaning as spectators are asked to change their affiliations from their local community team to a city or even a state conglomeration.

—MAXWELL HOWELL

See also Cricket; Rugby League; Rugby Union.

Bibliography: Atkinson, Graeme. (1982) *Everything You Ever Wanted to Know about Australian Rules Football But Couldn't Be Bothered Asking.* Melbourne: Five Mile Press. Stewart, Bob. (1983) *The Australian Football Business.* Kenthurst: Kangaroo Press. Vamplew, Wray, Katharine Moore, John O'Hara, Richard Cashman, and Ian Jobling. (1992) *The Oxford Companion to Australian Sport.* Melbourne: Oxford University Press.

Football, Canadian

Canadian football has followed a circuitous path to arrive at its present state as a game very similar to American football. The two are distinguished by the size of the field, the number of tries, or downs, a team gets (three in Canada), and the slightly larger team of 12 players.

History

Early on, rugby became the game of choice among the new settlers. Thirty-seven "Laws of Football played at Rugby School" were declared and codified on 28 August 1845. By the 1860s, it was being played in Canada, particularly Montreal. By 1874, McGill had its own hybrid version of the rules codified for its own use. That same year, a Montreal team challenged Harvard to a game, and the two teams discovered that they were using different rules to play what they considered the same game. Harvard ended up adopting rugby as a game. American and Canadian versions of football continued to influence each other as the years went by.

Canadian football was much like the country that created it in that it was bound to British tradition and yet increasingly subject to influences from the United States. By 1882, the traditional English scrummage, the unpredictable way of putting the ball into play, was removed. Unlike the Americans, who had replaced it with the snapback system of putting the ball into play, the Canadians "heeled" it, that is, the center put the ball into play by tapping it with his heel to the quarterback. On either side of the center was a "scrim support" to protect the center and delay any rush from the opposition. The rule change also meant that possession took precedence over spontaneity.

By 1892, a reorganized Canadian Rugby Union was formed. The new organization governed the sport and was responsible for a national championship contest. The field was set at a length of 110 yards (100 meters) with a 25-yard (22.9-meter) goal area and a width of 65 yards (59.5 meters). There were 15 players on a side, and a game consisted of two 45-minute halves. The only two values remaining in Canadian football today are the safety touch and the rouge or single point given when a kick is not returned from the end zone. The field dimensions are the same with one exception. Since 1986 the Canadian Football League changed its end zone to 20 yards (18 meters).

Today, teams must gain 10 yards in three downs or lose possession.

By 1909, the game was neither rugby in the traditional sense nor football in the modern. There were 14 players; the ball was still being heeled out, and there was no interference and no forward passing. It was a sport developing its own approach, somewhat removed from its British roots, but always with them in mind, and consistently emulating the American refinements. By 1921, more changes had been made. Teams were reduced to 12 to a side as they are today, and the ball could be snapped back, although the quarterback had to stay 5 yards behind the snapper. That year was also the first that the Dominion Championship, or the Grey Cup Game as it was increasingly called, became an East-West affair.

The forward pass was approved for all leagues in 1931. Recruitment of American players and coaches began in earnest after Warren Stevens of Syracuse University led the Montreal Amateur Athletic Association's "Winged Wheelers" to an undefeated season and the Grey Cup in 1931. In a bid to halt the flow of American talent and develop the Canadian talent pool, the Canadian Rugby Football Union imposed a residence rule requirement for 1936. Players had to live in the community they represented for one year prior to the season.

After the end of World War II, amateur status was often overlooked. In 1946, the Canadian Rugby Football Union allowed teams to carry five American "imports," and the residence rule of 1936 was abolished. Not all teams rushed to embrace the new reality.

The popularity of the game increased as did the dependence on American talent. The term "rugby" disappeared as a descriptor, replaced by "football" since it was more easily understood by American prospects. In 1956, the touchdown was increased in value from five to six points, and the following year the American names for the positions of center, guard, tackle and end replaced the Canadian snap, inside wing, middle wing, and outside wing. The twelfth position was retained, but its name was changed from flying wing to wing-back, and later to slot back, flanker, or wide out.

Meanwhile, the two dominant leagues in the coun-

try from the West and the East formed the Canadian Football Council in 1956, which was renamed the Canadian Football League (CFL) in 1958. It was organized into Eastern (Hamilton, Toronto, Ottawa, and Montreal) and Western (Winnipeg, Saskatchewan, Edmonton, Calgary, and British Columbia) Conferences in 1960.

Since 1965, the CFL has described its players as "imports" (those who played football outside Canada prior to their seventeenth birthday) and "nonimports" (those who had not played football outside Canada prior to their 17th birthday). For all intents and purposes, imports were Americans and nonimports Canadians.

In the 1960s and 1970s, CFL football grew in popularity until a series of influences minimized its acceptance. A contentious "Designated Import Rule" passed in 1970 allowed two American quarterbacks to substitute freely and virtually guaranteed that a Canadian would not play at that position. Some referred to the Canadians' status as "nonimportant." In the 1980s, a lucrative television contract was canceled, leaving teams in the CFL to scramble to make up the shortfall in revenue. The Montreal Alouettes folded in 1987 immediately prior to the season. The league found itself competing with major league baseball and other entertainment options for the public's favor and money. By 1993, the league expanded into the United States when it added the Sacramento Gold Miners. The following year, teams from Las Vegas, Shreveport, and Baltimore joined, and in 1995, Memphis, Tennessee, and Birmingham, Alabama, became members of the CFL.

Rules and Play

The CFL game today differs from the American chiefly in its size of field, no fair catch, unlimited motion by the backs, three downs to make 10 yards, 20 seconds to put the ball into play, and a single point awarded for a punt or missed field goal when the returning player is tackled in or the ball is kicked out of the goal area. In 1995, the CFL moved to two divisions that would play for the Grey Cup. In the North were Toronto, Hamilton, Ottawa, Winnipeg, Saskatchewan, Edmonton, Calgary, and British Columbia. In the South were Baltimore, Shreveport, Memphis, Birmingham, and San Antonio. Rosters per game were set at 37: The North could carry 14 imports, 3 quarterbacks and 20 nonimports; the South was allowed to carry whomever it wished. A $2.5 million (Canadian) salary cap was in place.

Baltimore, now known as the Stallions, won the Grey Cup in 1995. It was the first American team to do so. The return of the NFL to the Maryland city resulted in the shifting of the CFL franchise to Montreal, to be known as the Alouettes, for the 1996 season. The four other American teams withdrew from the league. In the Western Division were British Columbia, Calgary, Edmonton, Saskatchewan, and Winnipeg. In the Eastern Division were Montreal, Ottawa, Toronto, and Hamilton. In 1996, the CFL again became an all-Canadian city format.

—FRANK COSENTINO

Bibliography: Cosentino, Frank. (1995) *The Passing Game: A History of the CFL.* Winnipeg: Bain & Cox.

Football, Gaelic

Gaelic football includes elements of rugby and soccer (association football), as well as its own distinctive characteristics. Each team has 15 players; points are scored when players propel the ball past their opponents' goal line. Closely tied to Irish nationalism and national culture, Gaelic football is a central cultural activity in Ireland and an important sporting activity among emigrant Irish communities in Britain, North America, and Australasia. Within Ireland, spectating is also an important component of Gaelic football. The All-Ireland finals regularly attract capacity crowds of nearly 80,000 at Croke Park in Dublin, Ireland's largest sporting stadium. Although it is played in several other countries, Gaelic football is a significant part of popular culture only in Ireland.

History

Gaelic football has its origins and primary roots in various forms of football played in Ireland since at least the 7th century. The game assumed a distinctly Gaelic identity in the 1800s, when the Gaelic Athletic Association (GAA) was formed to organize Irish sports, codify their rules, and resist British sports such as soccer and rugby. The Irish Football Association formed in 1880 and the Combined Irish Rugby Union formed in 1881. As a result, English codes of football began to dominate in Ireland as other forms of English culture also expanded. The GAA was closely tied to the nationalist movement in Ireland, particularly the Irish Republican Brotherhood (IRB), and received support from many leading Irish nationalists. The first Gaelic football championship was held in 1887 between Young from Louth and Commercials from Limerick, who were victorious. From 1889, teams representing counties competed for the football championship.

The GAA is the largest sporting organization in Ireland today. It has over 2,800 affiliated clubs that have as members 182,000 football players and 97,000 hurlers. The membership of the GAA, at home and abroad, is

Bloody Sunday

Gaelic football moved to the center of Irish nationalist consciousness during the events surrounding an exhibition match, perhaps arranged in conjunction with Irish republican activities, although the evidence is not clear. The match was held at Croke Park on Sunday, 21 November 1920. The match was played between Dublin and Tipperary and proceeds were designated to buy arms for the Irish Volunteers, who were fighting against British rule. On the same day, a group led by Michael Collins shot dead 12 British officers and wounded several others in Dublin because British soldiers had infiltrated Irish nationalist organizations. A quarter-hour into the football match, British troops (Black and Tans) and Dublin police entered the stadium and began firing at the field and on the crowd of 10,000 spectators. Numbers killed have varied between 12 and 14, but one of the dead was Michael Hogan, a back from Tipperary, who later had a stand at Croke Park named after him. "Bloody Sunday" was thus indelibly etched on the memory of Irish nationalists and Gaelic footballers.

—*John Nauright and Michael Letters*

over 800,000. Gaelic football is Ireland's most popular participation sport with approximately 250,000 men and women playing, or about 20 percent of the adult population.

Rules and Play

Gaelic football is played on a field that is 140–160 yards (129–147 meters) long and 84–100 yards (77.5–92 meters) wide. At each end of the field there is a goal that looks like a combination of a soccer goal and rugby union or American football goalposts. Three points are scored for a goal when a player kicks the ball into the lower goal, as in soccer, and one point is scored when the ball is kicked between the posts above the crossbar. Scoring is rendered in the form of team A 2–7 and team B 1–9, which means that team A won the game 13–12 after adding three points for each goal recorded in the first column plus one point for each in the second. Teams consist of 15 players, including one goalkeeper. Players can carry the ball but must bounce the ball off the turf or their feet after every four steps. Passing occurs through long and short kicks or by slapping or punching the ball with the hand to a nearby teammate; throwing is not allowed. Players may not pick up the ball from the ground unless they first get their toe under the ball. The ball may also be played on the ground or in the air as in soccer. Games consist of two 35-minute halves.

The All-Ireland championships are conducted in the summer, while the National League is played during the winter. Gaelic football competitions also occur in Australia, New Zealand, Canada, the United States, England, and Scotland.

Football and Politics

Gaelic football and other GAA sports were some of the first modern sports to be openly political in context. In 1887 the GAA prohibited participation by anyone who had played, watched, or supported "foreign" (meaning British) games, by any member of the British occupying forces, particularly the Royal Irish Constabulary and the Dublin Police, or by anyone who was suspected of working or spying for the British. With the formation of the Irish Free State in 1922, Gaelic football and other Irish games came to symbolize the expression of Irish culture, losing some of the overtly political associations. In Northern Ireland, however, Irish sports remained tied to the nationalist struggle of Irish Catholics who sought a united and independent Ireland.

Gaelic football competitions are important to members of emigrant Irish communities as they serve to maintain cultural ties to Ireland. While many Irish and Irish-descended people move into local sports such as American football or Australian football, the existence of Irish sporting competitions continues a link to Irish sporting culture and life. As with other elements of Irish culture, Gaelic football has spread to other communities within North America and Australasia as a subcultural activity. The similarities between Gaelic and Australian football, for example, allow talented players to participate in both games quite easily. The game and its identity, however, remain firmly Gaelic.

—JOHN NAURIGHT AND MICHAEL LETTERS

Bibliography: Sugden, John, and Alan Bairner. (1993) "National Identity, Community Relations, and the Sporting Life in Northern Ireland." In *The Changing Politics of Sport,* edited by Lincoln Allison. Manchester: Manchester University Press.

Formula 1 Auto Racing

Formula 1 (F1) cars are single-seat vehicles built according to specifications developed by the Fédération Internationale de l'Automobile (FIA) and used only to race. Most F1 races are now held on specially constructed racecourses, although some, such as the Grand Prix of Monaco, are still contested on city streets or country roads that have been closed and prepared for the race but are otherwise used for normal traffic. Racing-only courses for F1 events are closed, but they are designed to simulate features that are encountered in ordinary everyday driving, including acceleration, straight-line speed, cornering, braking, and endurance. Drivers comprise the elite corps of auto racers and reach F1 only after demonstrating exceptional skills in lower levels of racing, such as Formula 3 or sports cars. Though now much safer than in its earlier years, F1 is still probably the most dangerous of all internationally contested sports.

History

The first international race, from Paris to Bordeaux and back, took place in 1895 and was won by a French Panhard that averaged 24 kilometers per mile (15 miles per hour). The first Grand Prix race was held at Le Mans, France, in June 1906 and required 12 laps of a 100-kilometer (62.14-mile) circuit, six to be completed on each of two consecutive days. Grand Prix–style road racing enjoyed a brief flowering in the United States, beginning with the American Grand Prize race held at Savannah, Georgia, in 1908. Grand Prize racing continued through 1916, but was superseded in popularity by the Indianapolis 500, first held in 1911.

World War I put a halt to auto racing in Europe, but in 1921 Grand Prix races were held in both France and Italy. The early 1920s saw numerous technical developments in race cars, including supercharging, exotic fuels, brakes on all four wheels, and aerodynamic body styles. In 1926, the first world championship was instituted, though it was for manufacturers, rather than drivers.

Grand Prix racing always had nationalistic overtones, and this trend reached its zenith in the 1930s. While the French and Italian teams continued with minor modifications to their existing cars, the Germans, under Hitler's intense nationalism, designed entirely new cars. These vehicles had powerful engines, but their superiority was due more to revolutionary chassis and running gear designs that gave them better road-holding and handling than the competition. By 1937, German domination was such that, of the 12 Grands Prix in which their cars raced, 7 were won by Mercedes while Auto Union took the other 5.

In the early post–World War II era, Grand Prix racing was revived using cars that had survived the war. A new set of technical specifications, or formulas, for international Grand Prix auto racing was institutionalized in 1948 with Formulas 1 and 2. A World Driver's Championship was created in 1950 and a manufacturer's championship in 1958.

Formula 1 Cars

The first Grand Prix cars were derived largely from passenger cars. A second phase of Grand Prix cars, from the 1920s through the 1950s, typically were streamlined, front-engine, rear-drive roadsters, though the Auto Unions of the 1930s were mid-engine models. Finally, since 1960 all F1 cars have been mid-engined with the engine behind the driver's cockpit and in front of the rear wheels. In the 1970s, F1 car bodies were wedge-shaped with inverted airfoils both front and rear to create aerodynamic downforce that permitted cars to corner at far greater speeds than previously possible. Wind tunnel and track testing, in addition to rule changes, have led to some modification in car shapes since the 1970s.

In the early years of Grand Prix racing, specifications for cars commonly changed yearly. Currently, formulas established by the FIA run for several years at a time. The primary stipulations limit engine displacement and minimum car weight, although virtually all aspects of car design are regulated to some extent.

For 1966 through 1988, unsupercharged engines were limited to 3.0 liters while supercharged engines could be no more than 1.5 liters. This was an extremely popular formula, and numerous technological advances in racing car design occurred while it was in effect. These included the use of exotic materials in the construction of cars, such as Kevlar and carbon fiber, and the incorporation of design principles derived from the aircraft industry.

Renault changed F1 racing in 1977 with the introduction of a new 1.5-liter turbocharged engine. Though these engines could produce far more horsepower than normally aspirated 3.0-liter engines, abrupt changes in the power curves of early turbocharged engines made cars using them difficult to drive. These problems were eventually overcome, and the world champion drivers from 1983 through 1988 all drove cars with 1.5-liter turbocharged engines.

FIA regulations for F1 for 1996 stipulate that engines must be 4-stroke, reciprocating, unsupercharged, with no more than 12 cylinders, and have a maximum displacement of no more than 3.0 liters.

Cars are designated by the names of the manufacturers of their chassis and engines. In a few cases, including BRM, Honda, Ferrari, Mercedes, Maserati, Alfa Romeo, Porsche, Vanwall, and Matra, companies made both chassis and engine, but today most F1 cars are hybrids with a chassis constructed by one manufacturer fitted with an engine produced by another. Most successful engines have been built by major auto manufacturers, including Honda, Ford, BMW, and Renault, although, among smaller companies, Ferrari has been singularly successful. In recent years, the most success-

ful chassis have been built by specialized race car manufacturers, including Williams, McLaren, and Benetton.

Formula 1 Drivers

Formula 1 is the pinnacle of auto racing. Few drivers ever manage to compete at that level; of those who do, few succeed. From 1950 through 1993, 543 different drivers competed in F1 and 124 captured World Championship points. However, only 70 won races and, of those, 17 only won once. In 1995, 34 different drivers contested F1 races but only 18 scored championship points.

Formula 1 racing is a very dangerous sport, and drivers, track personnel, race team crew members, and spectators have been killed or injured during events. Since 1950, 24 drivers have lost their lives from injuries received during races, practice, or qualifying rounds. Others have been killed while testing F1 cars or racing other types of cars. Fortunately, advances in the design and construction of tracks, cars, and driver equipment (fireproof suits, helmets, etc.) have made modern F1 racing much safer. No drivers died in sanctioned F1 events after 1982 until the tragic losses of rookie driver Roland Ratzenberger in qualifying and three-time world champion Ayrton Senna during the race at the 1994 San Marino Grand Prix. The recent safety record is all the more remarkable because retirements (cars withdrawing) during races due to collisions between cars and crashes resulting from cars leaving the track have become more common in recent years while retirements due to mechanical failures have decreased.

Successful F1 drivers must combine excellent athletic skills, such as strength, stamina, and quick reactions, with keen vision (though some wear glasses) and the ability to concentrate. Because of the enormous acceleration, braking, and cornering forces generated by F1 cars, drivers are put under tremendous physical stress. Drivers also must withstand the effects of vibration, heat, and physical wear-and-tear on hands, feet, and other parts of the body through contact with car controls or bodywork in the cockpit.

Formula 1 Races

FIA regulations require at least 8 and no more than 16 F1 Grands Prix per year, each contested by no more than 26 cars. Starting grid alignment is determined by qualifying, with the fastest driver in the pole position. When the cars are properly aligned on the grid after a formation lap around the track, a red light is displayed by the starter. Anytime between 4 and 7 seconds after the red light is illuminated, the starter switches on a green light to start the race. Under current regulations, race distance is the fewest number of complete laps that exceed a total distance of 305 kilometers (189.5 miles). Races are limited to two hours. If the race is slowed due to weather or another reason, the driver in the lead is shown the checkered flag at the end of the lap during which the two-hour limit is reached.

Due to restricted fuel capacity, F1 cars must make at least one, and more often two, pit stops during races to refuel and take on new tires. Quick pit stops figure prominently in winning or losing races, and teams practice pit stops intensely. Tires can usually be changed in 5 to 10 seconds so the duration of pit stops depends more on the amount of fuel replenished. Good pit stops usually take less than 15 seconds.

During races, electronic telemetry constantly provides information about the engine and chassis to pit crews. In the cars, liquid crystal display instruments inform the driver of engine speed, fuel remaining, water temperature, lap times, and other variables.

Miniaturized TV cameras mounted on the cars transmit the experience of F1 speed to viewers around the world. It is estimated that some 30 billion viewers followed the 1993 season on TV, making F1 among the world's most popular spectator sports.

—GARRY CHICK

Bibliography: Chimits, Xavier, and François Granet. (1994) *The Williams Renault Formula 1 Motor Racing Book.* New York: Dorling Kindersley. Griffiths, Trevor R. (1993) *Grand Prix.* London: Bloomsburg Publishing. Hodges, David, Doug Nye, and Nigel Roebuck. (1981) *Grand Prix.* New York: St. Martin's Press. Nye, Doug. (1992) *The Autocourse History of the Grand Prix Car 1966–91.* Richmond, UK: Hazleton Publishing.

Foxhunting

Foxhunting is a traditional English sport in which mounted riders chase their quarry, usually a fox, until it either escapes or is killed. It remains a sport of the leisured, monied classes, and is heavily criticized by animal-rights proponents.

History

The prehistoric pursuit of wild animals with hounds, initially for food and then for thrills, had many regional variations, and by the Middle Ages the prized English quarry had become deer, hunted in strictly defined and enclosed parks where farming was largely banned. Subsequent changes in agriculture opened up a wider countryside for hunting when whole swaths of grass, divided by hedges and small woods or "coverts" and

---

The Idealized Huntsman: John Peel (1776–1854).

John Peel was a "yeoman" (small farmer) in Caldbeck, Cumberland, on the edge of the English Lake District. Although far from wealthy, he was so addicted to foxhunting that he kept two horses and his own pack of hounds for 55 years. His knowledge of the landscape and the sport was legendary. A jovial character, he was seen as the epitome of the English sporting character of honest values. For many people he has long been more famous than many sporting aristocrats and is far better known than Hugo Meynell. The reason for this lies in a song that was composed around 1820 by his friend, John Woodock Graves, who also set it to an old folk tune, "Bonnie Annie"; it names his horse and some of the hounds. The song has passed into English culture as an expression of rural virtue, nationalism, and manly spirit. It has been adapted as a regimental march and been taught to generations of English schoolchildren. Here are three of the verses and the chorus, sung between them:

> D'ye ken John Peel with his coat so gay?
> D'ye ken John Peel at the break of day,
> D'ye ken John Peel when he's far, far away,
> With his hounds and his horn in the morning?
>
> Yes, I ken John Peel, with Ruby too,
> Ranter and Ringwood, Bellman and True,
> From a find to a check, from a check to a view,
> From a view to a death in the morning.
>
> D'ye ken John Peel with his coat so gay?
> He lived in Troutbeck·once on a day,
> Now he has gone far, far away,
> We shall ne'er hear his voice in the morning.
>
> *Chorus*
> 'Twas the sound of his horn brought me from my bed,
> And the cry of his hounds which he oft-times led,
> For Peel's "View hallo" would awaken the dead,
> Or the fox from his lair in the morning.
>
> —*John Lowerson*

---

suitable for fast riding and jumping, were created, providing new habitats for foxes and their natural prey. This was reinforced when aristocrats and the landed gentry changed from chasing stags to hunting foxes and made what had once been regarded as vermin a socially acceptable quarry. By the mid-18th century the sport was widely established but comparatively disorganized and informal. To this circumstance, Hugo Meynell (1735–?), a wealthy country gentleman, brought a sporting revolution. He took over a pack of hounds in Leicestershire, in the English Midlands, in

1753 and introduced scientific breeding and a new fast mode of riding. His hunt, the Quorn, became the model for a boom in foxhunting that has barely slowed since.

Foxhunting is an adaptation of the prehistoric and medieval chase that justifies its existence as an exterminator of vermin. English in its origins, it has an international following that finds "Britishness" attractive. Since its "scientific" reorganization in the 18th century the sport has grown because it provided a means by which affluent city-dwellers could adopt the lifestyle of the landed elite and boost their own social prestige. Modern economics have changed its financing and strengthened it in the process, and changes in the transportation systems, once feared, have actually boosted participation. With artistic and literary underpinnings, it represents the essence of rural life for far more people than those who actually hunt. Its security is, however, threatened by changes in attitudes toward animal rights and toward social hierarchies, and the hunting field is now often literally a battleground between the sport's supporters and saboteurs. Yet its cultural impact remains far wider than many people realize.

Rules and Play

Modern foxhunting is a sport of custom, ritual, and etiquette rather than rules and bureaucracy. Essentially noncompetitive, it defines itself in terms of older usage wherein "sport" is a contest with nature. Although there are formal associations of Masters of Fox Hounds and Hunt Secretaries, national organization is minimal. Each hunt has its own agreed "country," and these vary in size according to the subtle complexities of the local terrain. Men and women hunt in roughly equal numbers, a Victorian innovation, and about a third of Masters are female.

On the two or three days a week when most hunts take place, a "field" of mounted riders follows their pack of carefully bred and trained hounds (always numbered in twos or "couples") to a different meeting place, where the hunt begins. If a fox is located, it is chased until it either escapes or is killed. Although the justification for foxhunting is the killing of vermin, its appeal for most participants lies in the thrill and risks of fast cross-country riding, the attraction of the winter landscape, and in the social relationships the sport engenders. Large numbers of people follow most hunts by foot, bicycle, or motor vehicle.

Full participation in hunting is comparatively expensive; participants must maintain and transport individual horses and purchase the correct accessories. Most established hunts have a uniform in which the

Foxhunting in North America

Foxhunting has existed in North America since colonial days although it was not highly organized until much later. Night hunters, farmers, and landed gentry were the early foxhunters. Much of what little is recorded on early foxhunting comes from letters written by Lord Fairfax and from the diaries of George Washington. Washington, the first president of the United States, was an ardent foxhunter who owned his own pack of hounds. Washington's diaries are laced with frequent references to foxhunts near the nation's capitol. On one occasion Congress was in session as hounds ran near the capitol; the congressmen ran outside to watch the hounds, and some jumped on horses and joined the chase. The earliest established North American foxhound club was the Montreal Hunt in Canada (1826). In the United States, the Piedmont Foxhounds were established in Virginia in 1840, and the Rose Tree Foxhunting Club in 1859.

Through the years, American (Canada and the United States) foxhunting has evolved with its own distinct flavor, noticeably different from the British. The most obvious is that in the Americas the emphasis is the chase rather than the kill with a desire that the fox get away so it can be chased another day. A successful hunt ends when the fox is accounted for by entering its hold in the ground, called an earth. Once there, the hounds are rewarded with praise from their huntsman and that is the end of the chase. The generic term *foxhunting* applied to red fox, gray fox, coyote chasing, and bobcat chasing. What animal is hunted depends on the geographic location of the hunt. Today in America the coyote has become a significant quarry as well as the fox. Foxhunting exists in 34 states and 5 Canadian provinces.

*—Dennis J. Foster, Masters of Foxhounds
Association of America*

buttons are the key distinctive feature. Established full members and hunt servants usually wear scarlet coats (often known as "pink" after a London tailor), others black. The actual apparatus of the hunt, particularly the pack of hounds, is maintained largely by members' subscriptions, topped up by "cap" fees charged to visitors and hunt followers. This has become almost universal since the late-Victorian agricultural depressions made it almost impossible for individual landlords to follow the customary practice of keeping hounds at their own expense. It has long been argued that this cooperative financing made the sport more "democratic."

Foxhunting and Social Status

Social ambition has always fueled the sport's growth. When new roads were built across 18th-century England, they allowed an increasing number of prosperous Londoners to visit the "Shires," the Midland counties where the sport was strongest. The construction of the railways a century later was initially seen as a threat, dividing up the hunting countryside. Instead, they offered a major boost, speeding up the transport of horses and allowing city-dwellers to commute for a day's sport. This pattern of social stratification survives despite agricultural vicissitudes and a continued shift in the economic power of the traditional landed leadership.

Foxhunting also fostered two satellite sports. Most hunts arranged "point-to-point" races at the end of the season, run across the countryside. These continue, now formalized into the steeplechase, or National Hunt fence-jumping winter calendar of horse-racing, using normal racetracks. The Grand National is the peak of these. The other sport, show jumping, ritualizes the testing of a natural course in the context of an arena while its riders wear hunting clothing.

Against social acceptability, however, other problems have emerged. One has been a significant shift in farming activity due to membership in the European Union. Considerable areas of grass and woodland, with their attendant hedgerows, have been replaced by vast plowed areas that offer poor wildlife habitat and inhibit fast riding; they also do not hold a fox's scent as well as grass.

The fundamental shift in attitudes to animals and social deference has also affected the sport. An undercurrent of protest that has existed throughout the 20th century became stronger since the early 1980s with the emergence of groups committed either to the legal banning of the sport or to disruption of events and intimidation of participants. The League Against Cruel Sports stands first among these and still limits its activities to orderly protest and parliamentary lobbying. Around it, however, have emerged bodies committed to the active sabotage of hunts and, if necessary, to arson, personal violence, and bomb threats.

Opposed to these groups is an umbrella defense organization, the British Field Sports Society. The battle is now fought in the media, in politics, and in the hunting field; some farmers and local authorities have now banned the hunts from their land. Recent legislation has attempted to curb sabotage, but the battles rage and many hunts now use police protection or employ private security firms, which raise costs considerably. The protesters argue that foxhunting is a vicious and inefficient form of vermin control that has more to do with social prestige than rural necessity. Hunt supporters claim they are victims of an urban-rural rivalry at the heart of British society and that banning foxhunting, with its wide social dependencies, would both reduce the spectacle of country life and do serious damage to local economies.

Although the sport is very much associated with carefully constructed images of "Englishness," it is not restricted to that country. Scotland and Wales each have a few hunts, limited by local mountainous terrain. Ireland has nearly 30. The sport is less costly there than in England and this has attracted both English and transatlantic participants. In Australia, as elsewhere, Anglophiles have adapted the sport to local conditions, sometimes breeding from imported foxes to provide a quarry. Portugal, Spain, and Italy have hunts run on very English lines. But by far the most important growth has been in North America, where the legacy of colonialism merged with the leisure wishes of a 19th-century plutocracy to encourage this "gentry" activity. The United States has had some 130 hunts; while most are associated with the East Coast former colonies, the midwest and desert states have also seen small numbers of hunts emerge. Their quarry is usually the native gray fox, and much of the sport's justification comes less from the need to control vermin than the marking of social exclusiveness that membership provides.

Foxhunting has had an even greater impact than this distribution would suggest by providing an iconography for the English countryside and literature. Landed aristocrats sought to have themselves and their horses and hounds immortalized by specially commissioned painters. These and their many imitators had a much wider importance than their immediate patronage suggests; cheap prints brought an idealized rural world centered on the hunts to a huge public.

Perhaps the sport's most surprising impact has been in providing colloquial phrases now common in British and American life without their users' realizing their origins. When a scholar is described as "prominent in his field," he little realizes that it once referred to a fast-riding risk taker, and when we are told to "Have a nice day," few know that it is a modification of hunting's traditional greeting, "Have a good day," with its promise of a fast ride and a good kill.

—JOHN LOWERSON

See also Animal Rights.

Bibliography: Blackwood, Caroline. (1987) *In the Pink*. London: Bloomsbury. Jackson, Alastair. (1989) *The Great Hunts: Foxhunting Centres of the World*. Newton Abbot, UK: David and Charles. Lowerson, John. (1993) *Sport and the English Middle Classes, 1870–1914*. Manchester: Manchester University Press.

Frisbee
See Flying Disc

Gambling

Gambling is a multibillion-dollar industry, some legal, some illegal. A gamble in sports, as elsewhere, is essentially the bettor's informed guess of the winner of a contest and his or her willingness to give up a sum of money if wrong. If right, however, a gamble will leave the bettor richer by that sum of money multiplied by the odds—a ratio whose two parts represent chances of winning and chances of losing. Even the luckiest gambler loses far more than he wins, but this has apparently curtailed the growth of sports' gambling little if at all.

In some countries where sports are highly commercialized, estimates place the profits generated by both legal and illegal gambling as larger than the combined profits of several of the largest manufacturers. In many societies, the difference between buying a football card from a local bookie and buying stocks lies in cultural definitions of worthiness; one is disreputable and illegal, the other is an investment and praiseworthy. Both are gambles, and at some point for many people gambling becomes indistinguishable from the normal involvement with element of chance that is part of living.

Gambling has brought a marked increase in interest in sport, especially by men. Although often far from the event, the viewer now assumes partial responsibility for the contest outcome, as if his personal participation is as essential as that of the actual participants in terms of outcome.

History

Gambling on sports events has a long history and is common in many cultures, two innovations have shaped modern sports betting and bookmaking in the United States. The first and more obtrusive was television. From the early 1950s, live telecasts of sports steadily gained popularity and generated huge profits for owners. Professional sport franchise owners, especially in football and baseball, and players with new collective bargaining agreements and favorable court decisions were able to accumulate huge amounts of wealth. Sports betting was the unrecorded part of the flood of money that television generated.

The second invention involved not technology but an idea—the bookmaker's point spread. For 200 years sponsors of sports betting (that is, bookmakers) had wrestled with the problem of setting the stakes in an event in which one party (that is, a horse, fighter, or team) appeared clearly superior. In mid-19th-century England, different weights or handicaps were assigned to faster horses in a race; but rarely did the weights equalize or bring the field together. A really fast horse running against a slower one could most often pick up the extra 9 kilograms (20 pounds) of handicapped weight, take the track, and win easily. To entice more bettors, bookmakers began to offer different odds so that an unlikely horse assigned long odds would reward his backers with a rare but handsome return. The bookmaker's goal was to attract different amounts of betting at different odds so that no matter which horse won, the payout would be the same, guaranteeing the bookie a profit.

In a prize fight or a contest between two teams, one fighter or team was likely to be favored, sometimes heavily. If a bettor wished to wager on a heavily favored fighter or team, $6 might have to be wagered to win $1, while if the bettor chose the underdog, $5 would be returned for a $1 bet. The bookmaker was adjusting the odds to the strength of the bettors' opinions—in this case producing about five times as much betting on the favorite as on the underdog to protect his commission no matter who won. The bookmaking trade used the odds to split the payoffs profitably, until the early 1920s or 1930s when the point spread was introduced. Before World War II, giving or taking points was rare. After the war it became standard practice, especially in football and basketball.

With the point spread no odds are offered. Even money is bet by everyone and the bettor stakes $11 to win $10—the difference is the bookie's commission. No odds are posted with the point spread; the favored team must win by a set number of points. The underdog bettor's team may lose the contest but its backer wins the bet if the margin of defeat is less than the number of points offered.

Since the inception of the point spread a substantial number of collegiate basketball players in the United States have been involved in "fixing" scandals. These scandals have involved either a favored team playing to stay under the point spread (that is, "shaving points") or one of the teams outright losing or "dumping" the game. "Shaving" is more common since the game still can be won and players are less likely to draw attention to their manipulation. For the most part, professional and college football have evaded these scandals.

The Attraction of Betting

In sports gambling, bettors derive their primary satisfaction from the feeling of "knowing" something, of outsmarting the cosmos by choosing correctly. When a bettor wins, he ascribes it to superior power of analysis. When a bettor loses, it's bad luck. Bettors love to bet, but also enjoy the game. Because the sports bettor believes the game can be figured out, sports betting is the ideal outlet for satisfying gambling desire.

"Real" sports bettors represent a minority, but still an appreciable fraction, of the sports audience, and a disproportionate number of those who constitute the passionate following. More numerous are those who desire a little stimulant to their involvement. If one makes a small side bet with a friend, the game becomes more interesting. The first type is the "habitual bettor," the second the "casual bettor." Between them, they form the backbone of the adult sports betting audience.

Thoroughbred and harness horse racing are devices for legal betting, and the $2 bettor is no more interested in the horse as an animal than in a playing card as an artistic illustration. The democracy of horse racing, which attracts more customers each year than any other sport in the United States, is totally based on the equal opportunity to cash a bet. Without the opportunity to bet, openly, under supervision that guarantees the winners will be paid off and ensures a fair contest, horse racing and other events such as dog racing and jai alai would not draw crowds. And, such sports have been losing interest in recent years as government-sponsored lotteries and other forms of betting have become commonplace in the United States. A few historic events, such as the Kentucky Derby, transcend betting interest and become entertaining, competitive sports events steeped in tradition for millions who do not bet. But these events are exceptions.

In other sports, betting is less fundamental but not necessarily less present. Horse racing, dog racing, and jai alai are legalized and licensed for betting by some states, and they do not exist where they are not. Other sports such as professional baseball and basketball are automatically legal and need no licensing (except for business purposes), while betting on them is illegal (except in Nevada, and professional football in Oregon). Boxing requires licensing for a different reason—in theory to protect the health and safety of the contestants—but does not involve legalized betting. Betting in illegal sports such as cockfighting is common.

The reasons for this distinction between licensed and unlicensed professional sports become apparent when the requirements for attracting bettors are presented. First, the event wagered on must be sufficiently complex to provide suspense and mental stimulation, but simple enough to be easily followed.

Second, there must be the conviction that the contest is truly unpredictable—that is, the outcome is not prearranged.

Third, the contest being bet on must occur frequently with its result easily accessible to all interested parties.

Further, the bettor needs continuity. The comparable event must recur, time after time, to allow one to get even after losing.

Finally, there must be someone to bet with. A large body of other bettors, with similar interests, must exist to create a "market"—in the sense of the floor of a stock market—where pools of winnings can be formed by collecting from losers. Gambling is not practicable without someone to function as a broker, whether it's an illegal bookmaker, a legal one, the operator of a pool, or the state.

U.S. Betting Corruption

The problem of "manipulation" or fixing of sporting events has plagued sports betting since its beginnings. Manipulation in state-run betting is certainly possible, but less likely since the state's elaborate security machinery is designed to prevent such occurrences. However, anyone who bets has, or quickly acquires, sensitivity to the possibility of "fixing" results and realizes that humans can manipulate without detection, if so inclined.

Boxers can easily manipulate an event. Two people are in the ring, and if one does not hit quite as hard as he could, or falls down when hit, it is relatively difficult to prove they did so deliberately. Yet boxing remains one of the biggest betting sports, because it meets the four necessary conditions so well. More importantly, there is a public feeling that most major fights are honest, because the stakes are high (not only in terms of the winning purse, but also status for future earnings) and because each boxer faces the real physical danger of injury in the ring and, if suspected of manipulating the outcome, physical attack from "losers of big money."

"Point betting" has also led to serious problems with "fixing" in sports gambling, primarily in collegiate basketball. With "point betting" or the bookmakers' point spread, the suspense in an event can become even greater, and more prolonged, in a one-sided game. Suppose Michigan is a 15-point favorite over Indiana, a fact that has already established the belief that Michigan is most likely to win and is considered the superior team. Sure enough, Michigan dominates the football game and is leading 21–0 in the fourth quarter, content to end the game that way, not going out of its way to embarrass the loser unnecessarily. But right down to the last play, an Indiana touchdown and an extra point can decide the bet, one way or the other. A 21–7 Michigan victory, every bit as good in the league standings as a 21–0 victory, would be a 15-point bettor's defeat (or an underdog's bettor's triumph). The element of hazard and suspense has been prolonged and intensified. Point-spread betting is even better for basketball than for football, since so many points are scored quickly, and late-game margins can fluctuate so rapidly.

But every benefit contains its drawbacks—crookedness, to be blunt, is much easier. To play badly enough to lose deliberately to an inferior team requires both a callous moral sense and substantial risk of arousing suspicion. Both are blunted if a favorite can guarantee that a bet on the underdog will pay off, without giving up his own victory. All a team has to do is win by a margin smaller than the point spread—which was set illegally in the first place.

Such a rationale has been behind the fixing scandals that have plagued college basketball since the early 1930s. Involved teams that were favored attempted to play well enough to win "under the points" without actually losing. If the game got out of hand and the favored team lost, that was a shame—but the bet's success was not altered.

Recently, there have been numerous debates regarding the legalization of sports betting. All of the established sports have pronounced their opposition to legalized betting, based on the fear that athletes might perceive that society through governmental action is putting a stamp of approval on sports betting. With this view, athletes might still bet on themselves to win and play as hard as possible. However, sooner or later, there is a loss and to get even the only result that athletes can guarantee is to lose the next time out. While the above concern appears realistic, sports promoters probably have a stronger interest in ensuring that sport remains for fans (especially children) an event based on the illusion that winning is "all that counts." Under legalized betting, this would subtly change to "winning the bet," and the media will invariably reflect this view, as they now do in horse racing coverage. Children will just as inevitably quickly learn to become bettors rather than sports fans. Whether this is harmful or desirable from the standpoint of society, morality, mental health, economics, and ideation may be endlessly debated with no resolution.

Scandals outside the United States

Over the past decade soccer (association football) has become big business in France. Many clubs have annual budgets of over 200 million francs ($37 million). However, rumors have abounded of bribes, tax evasion, fraud, and doping. In 1993, France's Olympique de Marseilles soccer team were national heroes. Not only had Marseilles won the French league championships for the fifth consecutive year, but it had also become the first French club to win the European Cup ("Corrupt" 1993). Shortly after the team completed its season, one of Marseilles's players, Jean-Jacques Eydelie, was arrested and charged with attempting to bribe members of a rival team. Although Marseilles and eight other French league clubs had already been investigated on various charges (including "fixing" of games), this was the first time hard evidence had surfaced in connection with French soccer.

Outside Europe, soccer's immense popularity has also been accompanied at times by scandal. In Malaysia, government sources have reported that 85 percent of Malaysia's Premier League matches were fixed in 1994. Police investigations portray an even more dismal picture as they estimated that 95 percent of Malaysian match outcomes were rigged, with betting on certain games running as high as $2 to $4 million. Malaysian soccer fans, however, have not lost faith in their players even as they continue to be charged with fixing games and continue to jam stadiums to cheer their heroes.

The lure of beating the odds has made gambling the enormous enterprise it is today and, legally or illegally, the practice is certain to continue. The question of whether gambling should be more widely legalized remains a major issue.

—ALBERT J. FIGONE

Bibliography: Koppett, Leonard. (1981) *Sports Illusion, Sports Reality: A Reporter's View of Sports, Journalism and Society.* Boston: Houghton Mifflin. McPherson, B. D., J. E. Curtis, and J. W. Loy. (1989) *The Social Significance of Sport: An Introduction to the Sociology of Sport.* Champaign, IL: Human Kinetics. Rosen, Charles. (1978) *Scandals of 51: How the Gamblers Almost Killed College Basketball.* New York: Holt, Rinehart & Winston. Sasuly, Richard. (1982) *Bookies and Bettors: Two Hundred Years of Gambling.* New York: Holt, Rinehart, and Winston.

Gay Games

The Gay Games are a group of international athletic contests for homosexual men and women. Held once every four years in a designated city, they feature a week of competitions in swimming, track and field, tennis, and many other sports. The name derives from the word "gay," which is a term that refers to homosexuals. The word also refers to the community and culture of homosexuals.

History

The Gay Games originated in 1982, founded by Dr. Tom Waddell, a gay physician who competed in the decathlon in the Olympic Games. While the event is primarily oriented to the gay community, Waddell also wanted the Gay Games to help reduce stereotypes of homosexuals and to foster a larger sense of unity among all people.

The basic format of the Gay Games is similar to that of the Olympics, and the event became the Gay Games only because the U.S. Olympic Committee filed suit to prevent use of the name Gay Olympics. Each quadrennial event often also has a separate name based on a theme. The first two Gay Games were in San Francisco; Gay Games III took place in Vancouver, British Colum-

bia, in 1990. Gay Games IV were held in New York City in June 1994, and Gay Games V took place in Amsterdam, Holland, in August 1998.

The first Gay Games in 1982 had a field of approximately 1,300 athletes competing in 16 events. By 1994, Gay Games IV featured approximately 11,000 athletes from 44 countries, with events representing over 30 sports held at 42 different locations in the New York area. In subsequent years, the games have expanded in scope and spending. The first Gay Games had an operating budget of approximately $100,000. The 1994 Gay Games budget was over $6 million, and the event was estimated to have brought $100 million in added tourism and other revenue into the New York City economy.

The multifaceted event reflects the diversity that exists within the international gay community. In many respects, its events, athletes, and spectators are indistinguishable from those in other athletic tournaments. The Gay Games have been largely accepted by people who are not gay, and many cities compete to be selected as the site. In other ways, however, the Gay Games have reflected issues, lifestyles, and social and cultural interests that are more specific to the gay community.

Events

Sports represented in the Gay Games have included track and field events and endurance marathons, ice hockey, swimming, tennis, wrestling, figure skating, volleyball, flag football, in-line skating, rock climbing, martial arts, bodybuilding, softball, competitive aerobics, golf, billiards, bowling, croquet, squash, cycling, and many others. The Gay Games also feature events that are not based on athletic ability to augment the other contests. The scheduled roster for the 1998 games included bridge, chess, ballroom dancing, and other recreational activities. In addition to mainstream sports and recreational activities, the less conventional aspects of gay culture are also represented in the games. One of the more unusual Gay Games events has been the Pink Flamingo, a swimming relay in which participants are dressed in drag and other flamboyant costumes and hand off a plastic flamingo during the relay switch-offs. In 1994, the first international same-sex ice-dancing skating competition was held at the Gay Games.

Reflecting its basic purpose as an international celebration, the Gay Games also feature activities other than athletics, including an extensive arts and cultural festival. Events sponsored by other organizations or individuals take place in the cities where the games are held.

Athletes of all ability levels may participate in the Gay Games. There are no eligibility requirements based on current or past performance in a sport. Participants are encouraged to focus on camaraderie and accomplishing "personal bests" rather than victory. The field for competitions has included participants of many different skill levels.

However, some debates have arisen over how to balance the competitive and noncompetitive aspects of the Gay Games. As in other tournaments, winners receive awards based on how they place in the events. Some people believe that too much emphasis on serious competition detracts from the open philosophy the games are based on. Others, however, contend that the most accomplished athletes at the games should be awarded.

The Gay Games have also reflected larger issues, such as the differences and conflicts that sometimes exist among different segments of gay people and between the gay community and heterosexual society. In 1994, for example, critics of homosexuality tried to stop the New York City administration from supporting the presence of the Gay Games there. While most participants in the games are open about their sexual orientation, some athletes have competed anonymously to avoid facing discrimination in their personal lives by revealing their sexual orientation. On occasion, open displays of the more unconventional aspects of gay life have also caused discomfort and criticism.

The Gay Games have also been affected by the disease AIDS (acquired immune deficiency syndrome), which has been a major crisis in the gay community in the 1980s and 1990s. Gay Games founder Tom Waddell died at age 49 of AIDS in 1987. Participants and spectators in the games have included people infected with the HIV virus (which causes AIDS). In 1994, the administration of President Bill Clinton temporarily relaxed government immigration restrictions by granting a ten-day waiver to allow HIV-infected athletes from other nations to enter the United States to participate in the Gay Games. In addition to other personal reasons for participating in the Gay Games, HIV-infected athletes have often taken part in them to inspire and to demonstrate that people with the virus can continue to live vigorous lives.

As a source of solidarity for the gay community, as well as a forum for athletic competition, the Gay Games seem well established; also well established is the likelihood that they will continue to generate some controversy.

—JOHN TOWNES

Bibliography: Clines, Francis X. (1994) "Let the Games and the Lobbying Begin." *New York Times,* 17 June. Schaap, Dick. (1987) "The Death of an Athlete." *Sports Illustrated,* 27 July.

Gliding
See Soaring

Golf

Golf is a ball-and-stick game in which participants try to hit the ball into holes placed at fixed distances around a grass course. They must contend with natural and artificial obstacles such as sand traps and trees. Scoring is based on the number of strokes needed to complete the round; low scores win. Golf is unique among ball games in matching a single human being's skill against the forces of nature; it is the only ball game that one can legitimately play against oneself. Golf is generally stereotyped as the national game of Scotland, and St. Andrews, Fife, is recognized as its birthplace. The game also claims a rich multicultural heritage that leads back to the Scottish game of shinty, Cornish and Irish hurling, and even to ancient Egyptian fertility rituals. There are also those who argue for a Dutch origin in the game of *Kolf* or *Kolven.*

History

The Royal and Ancient Golf Club was founded in 1754, and the first universal rules were drawn up at the Royal and Ancient Golf Club at St. Andrews in 1822. The world's first golf tournament took place in 1860 on the Prestwick course in western Scotland, but the game itself was played well before the 18th century—as early as 1457, King James II prohibited the game because it was interfering with archery practice.

A list of 13 rules, the *Articles and Code of Playing Golf, St. Andrews, 1754,* is the oldest surviving official document on the sport. The St. Andrews Golf Club assumed the title "Royal and Ancient" as a result of the patronage of King William IV in 1834.

Golf profited indirectly from the Catholic-tinged Protestant culture of Scotland. James VI of Scotland, for example, encouraged the adoption of a continental sort of Sabbath observance: after church, people were to be allowed to engage in appropriate recreational activities such as golf.

During the 1700s the game spread to England, and Scottish emigrants played a vital role in spreading it around the world. New Zealand's association was founded by a golf lover and Scotsman, C. R. Howden, who carried his love of the game there. Despite the lack of suitable land, the golfers set up a nine-hole course in the town green belt at Mornington and fenced it off from wandering stock. Without the grazing animals, however, the grass grew so long that play eventually became impossible.

In 1919 the Royal and Ancient Club, St. Andrews, became the international organization for golf. Since the 1960s and especially since the mid-1980s golf has experienced an extraordinary increase in corporate sponsorship and television money. Ever more celebrity players—men and women—emerge from countries all over the world.

Golf around the World

Golf is now a major international sport and as nations enter the modern world economy, golf courses are soon to follow. In some sense, golf can be said to be the sport of international business, although its appeal is much broader. Following its establishment in Scotland, golf spread to other English-speaking nations. The first mention of golf in Canada was a Christmas 1824 announcement of a golf outing at Priest's Farm, Montreal. The Scottish connection and influence was considerable: the founding president of Canada's (and North America's) first golf club—the Montreal Golf Club (1873)—was Scottish émigré Alexander Dennistoun.

The development of golf in Australia was also markedly influenced by Scotland. In the 20th century Australia has contributed much to international golf including innovative designs for golf clubs and several leading players. Great Britain has seen extraordinary development of golf during the 20th century. Conservative estimates suggest that more than 2 million men, women, and children regularly play golf. Modern developments—oversized driving clubs shaped out of space-age materials, vast television, cable and satellite coverage of golfing events, Ryder Cup teams crossing the Atlantic on the Concorde—have not interfered with the strength and stability that the game seems to draw from its autocratic heritage there.

United States

Scotland remains the traditional home of golf, but the United States has become the dominant golf nation in the 20th century. The sport grew from 1,000 clubs in 1900 to 6,000 by 1930. The Professional Golfers' Association (PGA) was founded in 1916 and in that year the first PGA championship took place on the Bronxville, New York, course. The versatile athlete Babe Didrikson Zaharias (1914–1956) transformed the women's game into a major sport.

In a nation that stresses individual achievement, it is not surprising that the development of golf is often marked by the careers of several leading golfers. The United States' two premier golfers in the 1920s were Walter Hagen (1892–1969) and Bobby Jones (1902–1971). Hagen, who won four British Opens, is recognized as much more than a great golfer, for he virtually single-handedly changed the exclusionary nature of golf clubhouses. Hagen was a flamboyantly dressed showman and an innovator in shot making and sports psychology. His favorite one-liner was, "Who's going to be second?"

Bobby Jones, meanwhile, played such a complete game that in tournament after tournament he dominated his opponents by a wide margin. In 1930 Jones won the "Grand Slam" of his time—the British Open, U.S. Open, U.S. Amateur, and British Amateur. Jones continued to exert a tremendous influence over golf even after his retirement from tournament play. He built the Augusta (Georgia) National Course and supervised the first Masters Tournament in 1934.

In the 1930s and 1940s the leading U.S. golfer was Byron Nelson (1912–). In 1945 he won 18 tournaments. The standard of golf is so high in the 1990s that no current golfer could hope to challenge Nelson's record total. Following Nelson came Ben Hogan and Sam Snead (1912–). The major development of golf in the post–World War II United States can be summarized in two names, Arnold Palmer (1929–) and Jack Nicklaus (1940–). Palmer internationalized the game by going to Great Britain and succeeding in the British Open. His cheerful persona and genial disposition, as well as his golfing skills, endeared him to millions. Jack Nicklaus further popularized the game because he had won in his twenties—and continued to enjoy success after the age of 50 on the senior tour. In the mid-1980s, the number of excellent professional golfers increased and no one golfer dominated as in the past. In fact, some have suggested that golf lost followers for several years because of the similarity of the players, which made some events boring to the viewer. In the 1990s, European and Asian golfers have made a tremendous showing on the both the men's and women's professional tours, increasing the appeal of the game. The rise of the European game has been demonstrated by the European team's victories in the 1995 and 1997 Ryder Cup events over the American team.

While golf is now a global sport, the contrasting protocols of British and U.S. golf are intriguing. Transatlantic radio commentator Alistair Cooke (1985) noticed at least one cultural quirk:

So the British, of all ages, still walk to the course. On trips to Florida or the American Desert, they still marvel, or shudder, at the fleets of electric carts going off in the morning like the first assault wave of the Battle of El Alamein. It is unlikely, for sometime, that a Briton will come across in his native land such a scorecard as Henry Longhurst rescued from a California club and cherished till the day he died. The last on its list of local rules printed the firm warning: "A player on foot has no standing on the course."

Caddies

Linguistically, the word caddie had a French root (*cadet*), and then in Scotland, the word came to be spelled "caddie." Originally caddies cleaned and carried clubs, marked the holes, and indicated the exact location of the cup and green (the sticks that were used eventually became a permanent addition to the game and were known as "flagsticks"). In the pre-tee-peg era, the caddies sprinkled a small mound of sand on the driving area so that the golfer could more easily strike and drive the ball. Caddies are vitally important in professional golf and advise the golfer on club selection, course conditions, and provide encouragement. Caddies receive a share of the golfer's winnings in the tournament.

Professional Golf

The development of professional golf is graphically illustrated by the growth of the PGA tour. In 1950 it was hosted by 12 cities, largely in California, Arizona, and Texas. Twenty years later the tour embraced 30 cities, and by 1997 there were some 50 tournaments across the nation on the men's PGA tour and 38 tournaments on the LPGA women's tour. The two tours are coordinated so that the events complement rather than compete with each other. In addition, there are 35 events on the men's European PGA Tour and 37 events on the men's Senior PGA Tour. There is also a Japan Tour, although it is not as highly rated as the major tours.

For professional golfers, the most important victories are achieved at the four major tournaments. For men these are the Masters, the British Open, the U.S. Open, and the PGA Championship. For women they are the Dinah Shore, U.S. Women's Open, LPGA Championship, and du Maurier Classic. These tournaments are so important that a professional golfer is not truly successful until he or she wins at least one. Excellent golfers who fail to do so are often described as "the best golfer never to win a major." A case in point is American golfer Mark O'Meara, who finally won his first and then his second major in 1998, following a highly successful career.

The growth of amateur golf in the United States has also been phenomenal as well. It has been estimated that 21.7 million Americans play at least one round of golf and spent $20 billion on golf and golf-related services per year (Stoddart 1994). American colleges and universities are now a major venue for amateur golf and many professionals come from the college ranks.

In the United States, spectator facilities have become important in the Tournament Players clubs built by the PGA since 1980. These massive architectural creations, with grass amphitheaters and colossal spectator mounds, capitalize on a sport that is "part golf course, part theater." The exemplar is the Augusta National Golf Club, site of the Masters, which has taken on a legendary, heroic, and mystical aura.

Golf in Society

Some sports experts believe that golf is the most popular sport of the 1990s, with more people playing golf, more people watching golf, and more golf courses built than ever before. While golf may not be the most popular sport of the decade, it is certainly true that it is very popular and has grown in popularity. There seems to be a number of reasons for this. First, golf is a relatively expensive sport, with the cost of equipment, club memberships, and greens fees and the boom economies in Europe and Asia in the 1990s have given people more money to spend on activities such as golf. Second, a round of golf can take a long time to play relative to many others recreational sports and thus has benefited from the increase in leisure time available to some people. Third, in the United States and Europe there has been an increase in both permanent and seasonal living in warmer locales, where golf can be played year-round. Fourth, golf is a life sport that is not as strenuous as some other sports such as singles tennis and therefore people play for longer periods of time. Fifth, golf is a sport that is highly sociable in that there is much opportunity for golfers to talk as the game progresses. And, sixth, golf, as the sport of business, has benefited from the increase in business activity over the decade.

Despite—or perhaps because of—its popularity, golf has been subject to a number of criticisms. Perhaps the oldest criticism is that golf is elitist and discriminatory, with Jews, blacks, and the nonwealthy often excluded from play by private clubs with restrictive membership policies and the high cost of playing the game. Annual dues range from several hundred dollars to six-figure totals for the most expensive metropolitan areas. Golf in the United States has been accused of discriminating against minority groups. In a 1995 *Sports Illustrated* profile, golf celebrity Tom Watson noted that he gave up his membership in the Kansas City Country Club in 1990 "over its blackballing of a prospective Jewish member."

Golf has been accused of showing a grave insensitivity to race relations. For example, during the worst years of South Africa's apartheid system one of the country's so-called homelands (satellite states set up to avoid granting political rights to blacks in South Africa itself), Bophuthatswana, organized an annual rich golf tournament at the Sun City resort. Despite the international sports boycott of South Africa and warnings from the U.S. State Department, Jack Nicklaus, Lee Trevino, and other big-name players continued to attend the tournament. Similarly, there have been very few successful African American professional golfers and critics argue that the success of Tiger Woods (an American of African American and Asian ancestry) in 1997 and 1998 does not erase a history of limited African American participation. The PGA has taken steps to address this situation in recent years.

Another criticism is the suggestion by some that golf is not a sport, but a mere game, because it does not require extraordinary strength, speed, or agility. Golf is obviously a sport and does require various physical skills including strength, hand-eye coordination, agility, and the ability to judge distances. Perhaps what makes golf unique as a sport is the need to use these different skills in sequence as one drives, plays fairway irons, and then putts from hole to hole over the course. Driving requires strength, iron shots require precision, and putting requires a delicate touch.

Golf has also been singled out as a sport that is damaging to the environment, both because the environment is altered to create golf courses and because chemical herbicides and pesticides are used to maintain the courses. Golf has addressed this criticism by moving to build some courses on land—such as waste dumps—that is not suitable for human habitation and also by letting sections of courses that are usually out of play return to their natural states of growth.

Interestingly, golf is free of the major criticisms leveled at other sports including player and owner greed, player violence, spectator violence, cheating, gambling excesses, and illegal drug use. Quite to the contrary, professional golfers are held up as role models who work hard, play fair, compete with themselves, help their fellow players, are polite to fans, and are humble in both victory and defeat.

Golf in Popular Culture

Golf lends itself to wonderful storytelling. Great comics frequently spike their repertoire with "tall tales" and amusing anecdotes about golf. P. G. Wodehouse, the artful creator of Jeeves and Wooster, delighted in parodying upper-crust English eccentricity. He adored golf and repeatedly used it as an artistic backdrop for gossip, romantic intrigue, and melodrama. In *Chester Forgets Himself* Wodehouse describes one luckless golfer: "He never spared himself in his efforts to do it [the ball] a violent injury. Frequently he had cut a blue dot almost in half with his niblick."

Alec Morrison, in an anthology of golf writing, gives a taste of golf literature, from the erotic (James Bond's golf match with Goldfinger), to the existential (John Updike's Rabbit Angstrom savoring the cerebral ecstasy of a glorious five-iron shot), to the farcical (Dan Jenkins and *The Dogged Victims of Inexorable Fate*).

H. M. Zucker and L. J. Babich profile 48 golf films in their *Sports Films*. The 1980 movie *Caddyshack* with Chevy Chase, Bill Murray, and Rodney Dangerfield offers hilarious clowning. *Follow the Sun* (1951) is a nicely told story of Ben Hogan's life, with Glen Ford in the starring role. Real-life golfers Sam Snead, James Demaret, and Cary Middlecoff have cameo roles. In the 1952 classic *Pat and Mike,* Pat Pemberton (played by Katherine Hepburn) becomes a professional touring athlete (golf and tennis), Mike Conovan (played by Spencer Tracy) is her manager, and Babe Zaharias displays her considerable athletic gifts as a golf champion.

—SCOTT A. G. M. CRAWFORD

Bibliography: Cayleff, S. E. (1995) *Babe, The Life and Legend of Babe Didrikson Zaharias.* Urbana: University of Illinois Press. Crosset, T. W. (1995) *Outsiders in the Clubhouse— The World of Women's Professional Golf.* Albany: State University of New York Press. Morrison, A. (1995) *The Impossible Art of Golf: An Anthology of Golf Writing.* New York: Oxford University Press. *One Hundred Years of Golf.* (1971) Dunedin: Otago Golf Club. Wind, H. W. (1975) *The Story of American Golf.* New York: Alfred A. Knopf.

Greyhound Racing
See Coursing

Gymkhana
See Horseback Riding, Gymkhana

Gymnastics

Gymnastics is an international sport, recreational and competitive both. At its most basic level, gymnastics is designed to increase strength and flexibility through the practice of a broad range of specified exercises and movements done both on floor mats and various apparatus. As a competitive sport today, *artistic gymnastics* includes six events for men (floor exercise, high bar, parallel bars, pommel horse, rings, and vault) and four for women (floor exercise, uneven bars, balance beam, and vault). *Modern rhythmic gymnastics* is a women's sport in which light hand apparatus is used to accompany dance movements.

Gymnastics is one of the most popular Olympic events. Once nearly exclusively a European sport, gymnastics has become universally practiced, although its development is still minor in Africa and much of Latin America and Asia. International competition in artistic gymnastics since 1952 has been dominated by men and women of the former Soviet Union, Japanese men, and Romanian women, with additional top performances from Germany, Czechoslovakia, and other European countries and more recently from China and the United States.

History

Some form of gymnastics has existed since the earliest known sport activity. Tumbling and balancing activities were performed in China and Egypt before 2000 B.C.E. In the second millennium B.C.E. Minoan athletes on Crete not only tumbled and balanced, but grasped the horns of a charging bull and vaulted with a front handspring to a landing on the animal's back. As part of their practice of skills needed in war, the ancient Romans used wooden horses to practice mounting and dismounting. This apparatus evolved into the gymnastics vaulting and pommel horses, early models of which were built to look like horses with saddles or at least had one end curved upward like a horse's neck. The three sections of the gymnastics horse still retain the names *neck, saddle,* and *croup.*

It was not until the late 18th and early 19th centuries that a modern form of gymnastics began to take shape. Around that time many pieces of gymnastics apparatus were invented, mostly by Germans. Danish, Swiss, and Italian educators also promoted gymnastics activity. In the early 19th century, important contributions to gymnastics originated in Sweden, and gymnastics activity began in the United States.

In the United States, German and Swiss immigrants established Turnverein clubs (American Turners) and Czechoslovakians established Sokol clubs (American Sokols). The American Turners promoted the introduction of physical education classes in American schools, and most early school physical education activity involved gymnastics. In the late 1800s many schools favored Swedish gymnastics, a highly structured system of exercises that used specialized apparatus and was advocated as having healthful benefits for both men and women. The Young Men's Christian Association (YMCA) has also been an important force in promoting gymnastics. The Amateur Athletic Union (AAU) held its first national gymnastics championships in 1888 and controlled the sport for the next half century until conflicts with the National Collegiate Athletic Association (NCAA) and other considerations eventually led to formation of the U.S. Gymnastics Federation in 1962.

College gymnastics competition grew after that time, and the NCAA held its first national gymnastics championships in 1938. However, NCAA competition was for men only until 1980. A national gymnastics championship for women was first held in 1969, sponsored by the American Association for Health, Physical Education and Recreation's Division for Girls and Women's Sport, and the Association for Intercollegiate Athletics for Women sponsored championships for women from 1971 until 1982, when the NCAA gained control of this function.

Gymnastics Festivals

A remarkable European tradition is that of gymnastic festivals involving huge numbers of athletes of all ages, the emphasis being on participation rather than competition. In the Gymnaestradas, Turnfests (Turnverein associations), and Slets (Sokols), thousands of performers participate in mass demonstrations, team and individual competitions, and workshops involving rhythmic and artistic gymnastics, acrobatics, folk dancing, and related activities. In the 1965 Gymnaestrada in Vienna, more than 10,000 athletes from over 30 countries (perhaps 80 percent women) participated. In 1975 in Berlin, even with a boycott by Eastern Bloc countries, over 12,000 athletes (including a 2-year-old and a group from Sweden averaging 50 years old) from 36 countries presented 312 Gymnaestrada performances for the enjoyment of 250,000 spectators. Turnfests and Slets are also held in the United States. In the fourteenth American Sokol Slet, held in 1977, more than 3,000 athletes from 70 American and Canadian Sokol units took part and over 1,000 competed. Reports of this event noted that the last Sokol Slet in Czechoslovakia had 275,000 athletes and 350,000 spectators.

Events No Longer Competed

International gymnastics competitions of the past included many activities no longer performed. The first modern Olympic Games in Greece in 1896 featured rope climbing, flying rings, and special team and combined events, and later Olympics included Indian club swinging (1904 and 1932), rope climb (1904, 1924, and 1932), Swedish System gymnastics (1920), flying rings (1920), side horse vault for men (1924), and tumbling (1932). Early World Gymnastics Championships included pole vault, broad jump, shot put, rope climb, and 100-meter sprint. An exclusively gymnastics program did not appear in the World Gymnastics Championships until 1954.

In the United States until the 1960s, men's AAU, club, school, and college gymnastics meets included flying rings (swinging rings), rope climb, tumbling, and trampoline, in addition to the international events. Women's competition included tumbling and trampoline and earlier, even flying rings and parallel bars. Because of the poor showing of the United States in international gymnastics competition, especially relative to its cold war adversary, the Soviet Union, these special events were dropped in order to encourage American gymnasts to concentrate on the international events. They had disappeared from most U.S. gymnastics meets by the mid-1970s.

In the flying rings event the gymnast was swung by a teammate to initiate his routine, and then had to maintain a large swing throughout his sequence of skills. Moves such as dislocates, inlocates, and uprises were used at the ends of each swing in order to build and maintain height. Handstands and iron crosses were held through entire swings. The event was exciting and dangerous because of the great heights involved. At Santa Monica, California, quadruple flyaways have been performed on flying rings set up on the beach.

Rope climb was an exciting event in which the gymnast, using hands only, was timed from a seated position on the floor to the top of a 6.1-meter (20-foot) rope (greater heights were used in some competitions). The world record time for this event is a nearly unbelievable 2.8 seconds.

Tumbling was conducted along a strip of mats, commonly 18 meters (60 feet) long, and four passes were required, with a time limit for the entire performance of forward and backward tumbling. Trampoline competition involved the judging of skills performed during a set number of contacts with the trampoline bed (usually eight or ten). Commonly two or three such sequences were performed by each contestant, with a time limit for the entire presentation. The skills consisted of somersaults, with or without twists, and with landings allowed on the feet, stomach, and back.

Sports closely related to gymnastics in which local and international competitions continue to be held include trampoline and sport acrobatics, the latter consisting of tumbling and group balancing with teams of two, three, and four athletes. The U.S. Sports Acrobatics Federation was formed in 1975, and annual national championships began the next year. Biennial world championships have been held since 1974.

—*Richard V. McGehee*

In most countries competitive gymnastics is organized and administered under the control of a national federation. World Gymnastics Championships and World Cups offer opportunities for international competition at the highest level, as do the European and U.S. Championships and multisport festivals such as the Olympic, World University, Goodwill, Commonwealth, Pan American, and Central American and Caribbean Games.

Rules and Play

The rise of international gymnastics competition after World War II generated a great need for rules standards and improved judging. The first *Code of Points* was formulated by the International Gymnastics Federation in 1949 in order to have guidelines for use at the 1950 World Gymnastics Championships. Subsequent editions of the code added more specific rules and defined difficulty levels of skills.

The word *gymnastics* once connoted almost any form of exercise, including calisthenics and the use of light and heavy apparatus. Today the terms *developmental* or *educational gymnastics* still refer to a broad spectrum of basic movement and manipulative activities for children and young people. Educational gymnastics activities promote the development of strength, flexibility, balance, coordination, and agility, as well as courage and self-reliance.

Competitive gymnastics includes two distinct sports: (1) artistic gymnastics, consisting of six men's and four women's events, and (2) modern rhythmic gymnastics, an activity for women that makes use of light hand apparatus such as hoops, balls, ropes, clubs, and ribbons.

Artistic Gymnastics (Olympic Gymnastics)

In artistic gymnastics competition, individual skills are combined into routines that are evaluated by a panel of judges (five, at the higher levels). Gymnastics judging has evolved from strictly defined traditional ideas of good form to greater emphasis on higher difficulty, with less concern about details of form. The marks of four acting judges are reported to the head judge, who discards the high and low marks and averages the two middle marks to determine the gymnast's score. The head judge also evaluates the exercise, but that score is used only if it differs significantly from the average of the two middle scores or unless the two middle scores differ from each other by more than a set amount.

Competitions may include compulsory and/or optional routines. Compulsories are prescribed routines that all gymnasts at a particular level must perform. Judging then becomes a task of evaluating each gymnast's execution and form in the prescribed exercise (since difficulty and composition are the same for all competitors).

Optional routines are composed individually by each gymnast, which complicates judging. Women are scored on difficulty, combination (or composition), and execution to arrive at a score of up to 9.4; an additional 0.6 points may be awarded if they include especially difficult skills. Men are judged on difficulty, presentation, and special requirements for 9 points, with up to 1 point awarded for additional highly difficult skills. Ten is the maximum score. Deductions or ranges of deductions are prescribed for each type of error. For optional vaulting, each vault has a predetermined point value based on its difficulty, similar to compulsories.

Standard positions for somersaults and twists include: (1) pike (straight legs with body bent at hips); tuck (bent legs with body bent at hips); and (3) straight or layout (body straight). Rotations become more difficult as the distance from the rotational axis to each part of the body increases. Thus, twists are easiest in layout position and somersaults are easiest in a tuck, and judging of difficulty takes this into consideration (e.g., a layout double back somersault is worth more than one done piked, which in turn is worth more than one in tuck position).

International championships have three forms of competition: (1) team competition (compulsory and optional exercises; 6-member teams with low score omitted), (2) individual all-around finals (optionals by 36 best gymnasts from the team competition), and (3) individual event finals (optionals by 6 best gymnasts on each apparatus in the team competition).

Gymnastics judging evaluates routines as objectively as possible, but some subjectivity is inevitable. Each judge views a performance from a somewhat different position, and personal criteria come into play when ranges of deductions are allowed for specific classes of faults. Judges' scores have also reflected their political allegiances, and in international competitions, judges have been removed for giving biased scores.

Men's Events

Men's artistic gymnastics consists of horizontal bar (high bar), parallel bars, floor exercise, rings, pommel horse, and vault. An additional category, all-around, is treated as an event, and awards are given to the top finishers in all-around.

Horizontal Bar (High Bar). The horizontal bar is a flexible steel bar, about 2.8 centimeters (1–1/8 inches) in diameter and 2.4 meters (7 feet, 10 inches) long, mounted approximately 2.6 meters (8 feet, 6 inches) above floor level. Skills on the horizontal bar consist of swinging and vaulting types of movements. Swinging movements are done either with the trunk and legs close to the bar (in-bar moves) or with the body fully extended from the hands (giant swings). In competitive routines there should be no stops, body parts other than the hands or soles of the feet are rarely in more than momentary contact with the bar, releases of one and both hands from the bar are common, and dismounts often consist of multiple somersaults (triples have been done), sometimes with one or more twists. In high-level routines of recent years, one-arm giant swings and release moves from one-arm giants have become common.

Parallel Bars. The parallel bars are flexible wooden rails 3.5 meters (11 feet, 6 inches) long. For competition the height is set at about 1.7 meters (5 feet, 8 inches) above the floor. Movements consist of swings, vaults, balance positions (held for 2 seconds), and slow movements emphasizing strength (e.g., presses to handstands). The bars are released and regrasped with one hand at a time or with both hands simultaneously (and with the gymnast above or below the bars). Most skills involve movement of the body in the plane of the central long dimension of the bars. However, the bars may be worked with the body moving perpendicularly to the bars or circling a position on the bars, and with both hands placed on the same bar. In competitive routines only the hands and, occasionally, the upper arms are ever in contact with the bars.

Pommel Horse (Side Horse). The pommel horse is a leather- or fabric-covered cylinder 35.5 centimeters (14 inches) in diameter and 162.5 centimeters (64 inches) long. The pommels are set about 40 to 45 centimeters (16 to 18 inches) apart and the height of the horse for competition is 1.25 meters (4 feet, 2 inches) to the top of the pommels. All movements on the horse are swinging movements (no stops are permitted and neither are slow movements employing obvious strength). Only the hands should touch the horse.

Vault (Long Horse). The vaulting horse is the same apparatus as the pommel horse, with the pommels removed. For competition the height to the top of the horse is 1.35 meters (4 feet, 5 inches). The horse is vaulted along its length, with an approach run of up to 25 meters (27 yards).

Rings (Still Rings). The rings are wooden and are spaced 50 centimeters (20 inches) apart and suspended from a height of about 5.6 meters (18 feet, 6 inches). Ring activities include swinging movements, held positions, and slow movements emphasizing strength. Advanced competitive optional routines require two handstands, one reached with strength (press) and one with swing. One additional static strength element is required; it and the two handstands must be held two seconds.

Floor Exercise (Free Calisthenics). This event utilizes a square floor area, 12 meters (40 feet) on each side, and is performed on a mat 3.2 centimeters (1¼ inches) thick. Tumbling skills are combined with balance and positions and movements emphasizing flexibility and strength. In competition all parts of the floor area and all directions should be used, and a time limit of 50 to 70 seconds is placed on the exercise.

Women's Events

Women's artistic gymnastics consists of uneven bars, balance beam, floor exercise, and vault. All-around scores are totaled from the four women's events.

Uneven Bars (Uneven Parallel Bars). The uneven bars were originally an adaptation of the men's parallel bars, and thus the bars were identical to the men's bars but with one bar set higher than the other. Uneven bar work evolved toward greater swinging motions, which required modification of the apparatus to withstand the large forces produced. In the late 1960s guyed bars with the rails extending only over the distance between the uprights began to be used.

The bars are worked in the direction perpendicular to their length, with many of the skills being very similar to those used in men's horizontal bar work.

Balance Beam. The balance beam was originally wooden, 5 meters (16 feet, 4 inches) long and 10 centimeters (4 inches) wide. For competition the beam height is set at 1.2 meters (47 inches). In the 1970s beams began to be thinly padded and covered with a material giving the feel of suede leather. Competitive routines consist of tumbling, balance, and gymnastic movements.

Floor Exercise. The same floor area and the same mat are used as in the men's event. Movements are continuous and involve tumbling, gymnastic, and dance movements, as well as momentary balance positions.

Vault (Side Horse Vault). The vaulting horse for women is the same apparatus as that used in men's vaulting. However, the vaults are performed across the short dimension of the horse, and its height for competition is set at 1.2 meters (47 inches).

Turnen—"Patriotic Gymnastics"

Along with Swedish gymnastics and English sports, a form of physical exercise called *Turnen* form the basis of modern European physical culture. Friedrich Ludwig Jahn (1778–1852), a German teacher, proclaimed in 1811 that the purpose of his "art of gymnastics" (*Turnkunst*) was to restore balance to the educational process by adding physical activity as a necessary counterweight to the excessive cerebration of 19th-century schools. *Turnen* was intended by him as a way for refined young men to become truly manly. But Jahn's primary goals were patriotic. He envisioned *Turnen* as a way to train able-bodied defenders of the *Vaterland*. The system he referred to as "patriotic gymnastics" was an expression of political nationalism.

Jahn's immediate objective was to end the Napoleonic occupation of Germany; the anti-French element of his nationalistic program was eventually widened to include the rejection of everything non-German (which explains his choice of the invented term *Turnen* rather than the Greek term *gymnastics*). Jahn's ideas also contained racist and anti-Semitic elements. For him, the value of *Volkstum* (peoplehood) took priority over all other religious, cultural, social, and political ideals.

In the course of time, Jahn became increasingly narrow-minded and obsessive. His speeches and writings were often full of empty pathos. They were marred by grossness, crudity, and intolerance. "It goes without saying," he wrote, "that every real man endeavors to give his children-to-be a mother from his own people. . . . Anyone who has children by a non-German wife has spurned fatherland and fatherhood."

Ironically, this fanatical patriot was distrusted, disliked, and persecuted by his own government. Once the French had indeed been driven out of Germany and Napoleon decisively defeated at the Battle of Waterloo (1815), Jahn's abrasive rhetoric was less welcome than it had been. His uncompromising approach to every question led to a number of bitter disputes over the "correct" forms of *Turnen,* most notably in the town of Breslau. The Prussian Ministry of Education decided, on June 12, 1818, to assert its authority over the Hasenheide gymnastics grounds. When Jahn defiantly announced his intention to proceed as before, he was arrested and imprisoned. *Turnen* was banned.

The ban was eventually lifted, in 1842, when King Friedrich Wilhelm IV issued a decree officially recognizing physical exercise as a necessary and indispensable part of boys' education, stipulating that *Turnen* be introduced into the curriculum. At the same time, *Turnvereine* (gymnastics clubs) became legal once again. As centers of progressive thought and action, *Turnvereine* began to spring up all over Prussia and elsewhere in Germany. In many places, these clubs took on the character of political organizations, where physical exercises were accompanied by lively discussions of political, social, intellectual, and ethical questions.

—*Horst Ueberhorst*

Modern Rhythmic Gymnastics (Modern Gymnastics)

The women's sport of rhythmic gymnastics appeared in its current form in the 1984 Olympic Games. Four of the five possible activities (ball, hoop, clubs, ribbon, rope) are contested to determine an all-around winner. Six-member team exercises are performed in the Modern Gymnastics World Championships but not, after 1956, in Olympic competition. Competitors must move vigorously within a square floor area measuring 12 meters (40 feet) on each side, performing dance skills and exhibiting grace, balance, and flexibility, while manipulating and maintaining control of their apparatus. They must use all of the area, involve the entire body and handle the apparatus with both left and right hands, and move in harmony with the motion of the hand apparatus and corresponding to the rhythm and mood of the music. Time limits are used for both team and individual exercises and there are special requirements for skill difficulties.

Gymnasts and Their Training

The ideal body type for gymnastics is short and light. Gymnastics skills require great strength and flexibility, as well as balance and explosive power. Ages and sizes of competitive gymnasts have been decreasing progressively as their selection and training has become more demanding. The two top female gymnasts in the 1992 Olympics were 15 years old, 137 centimeters (4 feet, 6 inches) tall, and one weighed 31.7 kilograms (70 pounds) and the other 31.3 kilograms (69 pounds).

To produce the strength, flexibility, and power essential for competitive gymnastics requires long hours of strenuous practice, and training procedures are designed to develop not only these physical qualities but also the great courage required to perform intrinsically dangerous movements.

In socialist societies such as the former Soviet Union, other Eastern European countries, China, and Cuba, young children selected on the basis of body type and other physical attributes may be given opportunities to develop into competitive gymnasts through participation in state-supported training facilities and special schools. In countries such as the United States, the development of young gymnasts has been carried out in schools and organizations such as Turners, Sokols, and YMCAs. However, the intensity and level of work required to produce elite gymnasts today is available only in private training facilities, usually paid for by parents. Recognizing the financial cost of these private facilities, USA Gymnastics initiated a program of stipends paid to a small number of the most talented young gymnasts to offset their training costs. Male gymnasts tend to maintain and even improve performances beyond the peak age for female gymnasts, and their training may continue during col-

lege years with the support of athletic scholarships. Collegiate gymnastics is also available for females, but today college-age women are generally considered too old to be involved in the highest level of the sport. One of the most important contributions to the development of gymnastics in the United States was the establishment of the USGF Junior Olympics program, which provides compulsory exercises and guidelines for several levels of age-group competition for both girls and boys.

Gymnastics in the Olympics

After World War II, and especially since the early 1960s, gymnastics has grown phenomenally in the United States. Much of this growth has been due to the greatly increased coverage of gymnastics on television, and especially to the Olympic performances of Olga Korbut in 1972 and Nadia Comaneci in 1976.

International gymnastics competition before World War II was dominated by Western European countries. Except for the anomalous 1904 Games in St. Louis, Americans did not participate in Olympic gymnastics until 1920. With the entrance of the Soviet Union into Olympic competition in 1952 and the rise of Japan as a gymnastics power, the picture changed radically. Over this period, men's team medals were won by the Soviet Union (10), Japan (9), East Germany (5), China (2), Finland (2), and one each by the United States, Germany, Hungary, Italy, and Switzerland. Fewer countries participated in women's gymnastics during this period and the Soviet Union was even more dominant, winning the team gold medal in all ten Olympic Games in which they participated (Romania won in 1984). Most individual medals were won by the Soviet Union (39.4 percent) and Japan (30.5 percent), with others going to China (6.1 percent), East Germany (4.5 percent), the United States (3.7 percent), and 13 other countries (all European except for three medals to the two Koreas, for a total of 15.8 percent). In the 1996 Olympics Russia won the overall team gold and 5 individual medals; Belarus took 4.

In the 1984 Olympic Games 19 countries were represented (2 entries are allowed per country), and Canada, Romania, and West Germany won the gold, silver, and bronze all-around medals. In both 1988 and 1992, 23 countries were represented, and the Soviet Union (called the Unified Team in 1992) won both the gold and bronze. In 1996 Spain won the team gold, Bulgaria the silver, and Russia the bronze. Modern Gymnastics World Championships have been held since 1963.

The continued spectacular performances of young

gymnasts in the Olympics and other international events have undoubtedly contributed to gymnastics' growing popularity. In women's gymnastics, a sport in which athletes may be has-beens at the age of 17, the key question is age: how young is too young?

—RICHARD V. McGEHEE

See also Acrobatics.

Bibliography: Goodbody, John. (1983) *The Illustrated History of Gymnastics.* New York: Beaufort. Murray, Mimi. (1979) *Women's Gymnastics: Coach, Participant, Spectator.* Boston: Allyn and Bacon. Ryan, Joan. (1995) *Little Girls in Pretty Boxes: The Making and Breaking of Elite Gymnasts and Figure Skaters.* New York: Doubleday. Turoff, Fred. (1991) *Artistic Gymnastics: A Comprehensive Guide to Performing and Teaching Skills for Beginners and Advanced Beginners.* Dubuque, IA: Wm. C. Brown.

Handball, Court

Court handball is played worldwide for recreation and exercise. Players use gloved hands to hit and return a ball against the wall of a marked court. It is often called Irish handball, or one-wall, three-wall, or four-wall handball, combines elements of fives, squash, pelota, racquetball, and jai alai, but does not resemble team or Olympic handball.

History

Evidence of court handball's origins is indirect but substantial. In 2000 B.C.E. Egyptian priests of Osiris were depicted on tombs striking a ball with their hands. Similar evidence appears in pre-Columbian sites in the Americas dated 1500 B.C.E. Sculptures, bas-reliefs, and decorated pottery show people hitting balls with their palms. Artifacts depicting games with a ball rebounding from a wall are found only in the land of the Chichimeca people of the Mexican plateau.

In Scotland, 1427, King James I blocked a cellar window that interfered with his handball (unfortunately also blocking his escape route when assassins struck). In the 17th-century church authorities disliked wall handball, fearing that stained glass windows would be damaged. A 1782 watercolor by John Nixon in Monaghan Museum shows two men playing handball against the wall of the Castle Blaney ruins. Catholic teaching orders took the game to South Africa, Australia, and the Americas.

Modern court handball began in Ireland with the 1884 founding of the Gaelic Athletic Association. Around the same time, an Irish immigrant built a handball court in New York City, then spread the game to other cities. The U.S. Amateur Athletic Union (AAU) adopted the sport and conducted the first tournament in 1897. The AAU held the first four-wall championship in 1919 and the first one-wall championship in 1924. The Young Men's Christian Association (YMCA) built courts and conducted its own national tournaments from 1925 through 1958.

In 1951, the Amateur Handball Union was founded and subsequently became the United States Handball Association (USHA). The YMCA, USHA, and AAU developed and adopted new standard rules for four-wall handball in 1958. In 1961, the USHA split from the AAU to allow professionals from other sports to compete as amateurs in handball.

Rules and Play

Court handball can be played by two, three, or four players on a court with one, three, or four walls. The game requires speed, strength, skill, strategy, quick reactions, and agility. Only the serving side can score. The front wall, side walls, back wall, and ceiling may be used for shots that ricochet and rebound with great velocity. The first side to reach 21 points (or gain a 2-point margin after 21) wins.

Play begins with a service from the marked zone. The service shot must hit the front wall and rebound to the floor beyond the service zone before hitting a side wall, back wall, or ceiling. Opponents must return shots to the front wall before the ball hits the floor a second time. The ball may ricochet off side walls or the ceiling on its way to the front wall.

Abraham Lincoln: Handball Player

On the day the Republican Party nominated him to run for president, Abraham Lincoln was in Springfield, Illinois, playing handball. In a vacant lot on North Sixth Street, near his law office, Lincoln joined a regular contingent of locals who enjoyed playing the game.

The court was a glorified alleyway between two buildings that served as front and back walls. One wall was the office of the *Illinois State Journal*. The players fashioned side walls with boards. There were seats for players waiting or spectators watching.

William Donnelly assumed duties as caretaker of the court. He recorded that "Mr. Lincoln was not a good player. He learned the game when he was too old, but he liked to play and did tolerably well."

In another contemporary account, *Intimate Memories of Lincoln*, Rufus Rockwell Wilson remembered: "A further personal knowledge of Mr. Lincoln which impressed me was his love of handball. Immediately south of the Journal office, I saw Mr. Lincoln play handball a number of times. . . . His suppleness, leaps, and strides to strike the ball were comical in the extreme."

Historians cannot find evidence of Lincoln playing handball after moving to Washington. But it was a part of his life in Springfield.

—*A. Gilbert Belles*

Court handball is played in national and international tournaments, but it is not an Olympic event. Its simplicity and diversity should guarantee continued popularity.

—A. GILBERT BELLES

See also Jai Alai; Paddleball; Pelota; Racquetball; Rugby Fives; Squash Rackets.
Bibliography: McElligott, Tom J. (1984) *The Story of Handball: The Game, the Players, the History.* Dublin: Wolfhound Press.

Handball, Team

Team handball is a fast-paced, physically demanding game that combines elements of soccer and basketball. The game is also called Continental handball, European handball, or Olympic handball. An 11-player recreational version is still played outdoors in Europe; competitive handball is an indoor game.

History

Team handball extends back 3,000 years to ancient Greece. In the *Odyssey,* Homer described a game invented by Anagalla, a princess of Sparta: "O'er the green mead the sporting virgins play, their shining veils unbound along the skies, tossed and retossed, the ball incessant flies." Alexander the Great (356–323 B.C.E.) played handball on what the Greeks called a *sphairisterion,* or ball court.

The origin of modern team handball remains murky. Some sources place it in Germany in the mid-1800s, developed as a game for training gymnasts, then modified and moved outside onto a large field. Others claim that modern team handball evolved soon after the start of the 20th century in Scandinavia. Swedish sources refer to seven-player handball in 1907. Danish advocates credit Fredrik Knudsen with codifying the seven-player game in 1911.

By 1928, the game was established, and the International Amateur Handball Federation (IAHF) was founded. As host of the 1936 Olympics, Germany added men's team handball to the Berlin Games., using the outdoor, European version with 11-player teams. The game was introduced into Canada in the 1940s by prisoners of war. French immigrants teaching in the Canadian secondary schools, especially in Quebec, taught and coached the game. Eastern Europeans supported the game in large numbers, surpassing the Scandinavians in participation. In 1946, the International Handball Federation replaced the old IAHF, but the game was not included in the 1948 Olympic Games.

The indoor version of team handball was introduced to the United States about 1959 by European immigrants living in metropolitan New York and New Jersey, and the United States Team Handball Federation was established. High schools and colleges began playing team handball. The sport gained popularity when Germany announced that it would add men's team handball (the indoor variation with seven players) to the 1972 Olympic Games in Munich. Women's team handball was included in the 1976 Games in Montreal.

Rules and Play

Indoor team handball is played on courts 40 by 20 meters (131 by 65 feet). A team has six court players and a goalie. The objective is to throw a hard leather ball (18 centimeters [7 inches] in diameter, 60 centimeters [24 inches] in circumference) into the opponent's goal net (2 meters [6.5 feet] high by 3 meters [9.8 feet] wide) while simultaneously defending one's own goal.

Players may throw the ball with their hands, propel it with any part of the body above the knee (no kicking), or advance it by dribbling an unlimited distance. However, they must pass or shoot within three seconds of stopping. The ball may not be carried more than three steps. The game is played in two continuous 30-minute halves with no time-outs and a 10-minute half-time.

Team handball, established and popular, has a solid future.

—A. GILBERT BELLES

Bibliography: Blazic, Branko, and Zorko Soric. (1975) *Team Handball.* Winnipeg: Winnipeg Free Press.

Hang Gliding

Hang gliding fulfills a dream mankind has harbored since the beginning of recorded thought: flying freely like a bird. Wearing large "wings," hang gliders launch themselves from high places and soar as long as they can.

History

With their wings of feathers and wax that melted when they flew too near sun, the Greek heroes Icarus and Daedalus are the best-known, though possibly apocryphal, early aviators. Later stories of Chinese soldiers ascending on large kites are probably based on fact. Leonardo da Vinci, Sir Isaac Newton, and Samuel Johnson all explored the possibilities of manned flight. But it was a German engineer, Otto Lilienthal (1848–1896) who developed the first practical flying wing, actual hang gliders controlled by shifting his weight, and launched them on foot from a small hill he built near Berlin. The Wright brothers' success was partially based on Lilienthal's research, and their practice with gliding craft directly led to their development of powered flight.

Hang gliding revived in the late 1940s when a National Aeronautics and Space Administration (NASA) scientist, Dr. Francis Rogallo, and his wife, Gertrude, developed a controllable kitelike wing, later known as the Rogallo wing. Australian water-skiers used the wing to become airborne. They inspired a young American designer, Richard Miller, to build a larger wing. He successfully launched himself unaided (a foot-launch) from a southern California slope in 1965. The activity was termed *hang gliding.*

The sport spread around California in the late 1960s and took off in the early 1970s. Currently hang gliding is practiced worldwide; local and national organizations are governed by the Commission Internationale de Vol Libre (CIVL), or free flight association.

Rules and Play

Hang gliders now use a highly sophisticated light wing, which they call a glider, to run off a mountain or be towed aloft. It usually consists of a framework of aircraft aluminum and stainless steel cable covered by a sail made of Dacron. Curved aluminum rods called

battens are inserted in the sail to hold the airfoil shape. These gliders are flexible and known as flex-wings. Other types of hang gliders are made from more rigid materials such as fiberglass. These designs, known as rigid-wings, perform better than flex-wings but are typically heavier, more complex, and costlier. Flex-wings and rigid-wings compete in separate classes.

The well-equipped pilot needs a harness, a hammocklike enclosure to attach the pilot to the glider. The harness is made of strong webbing and allows the pilot to rest comfortably for hours while shifting his or her weight for control. Pilots wear helmets and carry parachutes for safe descents. All competition pilots and most recreational pilots use altimeters to indicate altitude and variometers, a sensitive vertical-speed indicator invaluable for finding lift and avoiding sink.

A hang glider relies on natural currents and updrafts. When wind strikes hills, ridges, and mountains, it is deflected upward, creating lift. Also, warm bubbles or columns of air known as thermals arise from the ground and often climb to great heights. Pilots find these sources of lift and pass back and forth or circle to stay within their confines. Since conditions vary daily, they need a great store of experience, insight, and intuition.

In early competition, pilots sought only to stay aloft as long as possible, perform maneuvers, and land with precision. Contests incorporated these skills with duration, spot-landing tasks, and pylon courses. Later, when glider performance and pilot skill improved, soaring and cross-country tasks were added. By the late 1980s, this format had been refined to include rounding distant turn points and racing to a goal, often as distant as 100 miles.

A national meet typically lasts a week, with one six-hour task flown daily in individual competition only. International meets involve both individual and team standings. A country's team usually consists of five to eight pilots; the top three pilots of each day are counted in team scoring. For almost 15 years, British were almost unbeatable. However, the U.S. team won the world title in 1993 on their home turf, California, and the French, Australians, Swiss, and Germans now match the British in organization and training. Participants in international meets come from North and South America, Europe, Asia, Australia, and South Africa. Few African or Middle Eastern nations compete in major meets. This may change; truly some of the world's best flying takes place over drier areas, where thermals climb to 6,000 meters (20,000 feet) and more. Surely their lure, too, will prove irresistible.

—DENNIS PAGEN

Bibliography: Pagen, Dennis. (1995) *Hang Gliding Training Manual.* Mingoville, PA: Sport Aviation Publications. Wills, Maralys. (1992) *Higher Than Eagles.* Marietta, GA: Longstreet Press.

Harness and Trot Racing
See Horse Racing, Harness

Highland Games
Scottish Highland Games are a unique mix of cultural identity (kilt, bagpipes, and caber), traditional track and field activities (running, jumping, and throwing), and aesthetic movement as visual tapestry (sword dancing). Speed and strength are paramount assets to highlanders, who revere Conall, a man with almost mystical powers who travels to the highlands and learns from a wise man guru all he must know of life and diligently practices lifting the "stone of manhood."

History
The Celtic prince Malcolm Canmore is credited with holding the first Scottish Highland Gathering on the Braes of Mar in 1044, highlighted by a Sword Dance and a hill race. Beyond recreation and socializing, the activities focused on military skill and displaying the capabilities of clan members as warriors, first, and athletes. The first reliably documented gathering was held in 1314 to commemorate the Scots' victory over the English at the Battle of Bannockburnat.

Many of the events in these first Highland Games can be traced to the Irish Tailtin (or Tailteann) Games, which originated in 1829 B.C.E. and survived until the 12th century C.E.

The Highland Games changed irrevocably following the crushing of the Jacobite movement in 1746; the Act of Proscription denied Highlanders traditional dress and the carrying of arms. This Disarming Act choked Highland culture and imprisoned a once-free feudalistic society. The Highland Gatherings created in the early 1800s no longer featured clan competition and grassroots athleticism but spectacles and pageants and community galas. The landed aristocracy took over what were once the people's games.

An 1848 visit by Queen Victoria and Prince Albert to the Braemar Gathering made Highland Gatherings fashionable, and landowners all over the Highlands began to emulate the gathering at Braemar in their territories. The next quarter century saw Highland Gatherings at their most numerous.

Scottish migration in the last half of the 19th century took the Highland Games all over the British Em-

pire. These transplanted activities, however, never captured the flavor of the genuine Highland Gathering.

In the 20th century, the royal family's attendance again has transformed a rural outdoor community picnic into a massive international get-together.

Rules and Play
Some events associated with Highland Games activities are essentially traditional amateur track and field athletics. Several throwing activities, including three types of "throwing the weight," are singular to Highland Games. In the hammer throwing event the weight is either 16 or 22 pounds (7.3 or 10 kilograms), with a solid wooden shaft. The 28-pound (12.7-kilogram) weight is thrown for distance, while the 56-pound (25.5-kilogram) weight is thrown for both distance and height.

The most well known (and least understood) Highland Games activity is tossing the caber. It was originally known as "ye casting of the bar." The goal is not distance but style: a perfect toss goes end-over-end and finishes in a twelve o'clock or straight position. Cabers vary in size and weight. Braemar has three varieties: 17 feet, 3 inches and 91 pounds (5.3 meters and 41.3 kilograms); 17 feet and 114 pounds (5.2 meters and 51.7 kilograms); and 19 feet, 3 inches and 120 pounds (5.9 meters and 54.4 kilograms).

Several judges lift the caber lift to a vertical position and hold it until the athlete comes forward and grasps it. With a firm grip, he stands slowly, jogs and then breaks into a steady run to build up the momentum of the caber. Often his run is not straight; his running movement, an up and down motion, is transmitted to the caber and causes it to sway and perhaps move away from his shoulders. To compensate, the athlete alters his path to keep the caber's center of gravity directly above his shoulder. As the throwing line is approached, the athlete stops and flexes the legs. This has a braking effect on the lower part of the caber, which, still within his grasp, is an extension of his arms. The part of the caber not within his grasp immediately rotates forward at great speed like the spoke of a wheel, with the wheel-hub being the athlete's hands.

Timing and coordination now become vital. He must pull vigorously on the end of the caber as it leaves his shoulder. This vicious pulling upward, followed by a last powerful push of the thin end of the caber, immediately sets up an equal and opposite reaction in the other end of the caber, which is forced downward. If the caber tosser has given the caber sufficient angular momentum it will land on the heavier end, and continue to describe a perfect, absolutely straight semicircle. Caber tossing and other Scottish sports are likely to continue among Scots and unlikely to become popular elsewhere.

—SCOTT A. G. M. CRAWFORD

Bibliography: Fittis, R. S. (1891) *Sports and Pastimes of Scotland.* Paisley, UK: Alexander Gardner. *Illustrated London News.* (1848) (September 23): 182–184. Jarvie, G. (1991) *Highland Games: The Making of the Myth.* Edinburgh: Edinburgh University Press.

Hockey, Field

Field hockey is so called to distinguish it from ice hockey. It began, apparently, like other stick-and-ball games but developed into a minority pursuit of adolescents in the English ruling classes. In later Victorian England it was adapted as an exclusive sport for the new middle classes.

History

Field hockey has deep roots. In ancient Egypt, tomb images from four millennia ago show men playing games with hooked sticks. More reliable material appears in medieval Europe, where men playing with hooked sticks appear in stained-glass windows in Canterbury and Gloucester cathedrals.

The name "field hockey" may stem from the French *hocquet*, a shepherd's crook, or "hookey," named after the bent stick. By the 18th century it was recorded as a seasonal game played by English schoolboys and young men with very localized rules and considerable violence.

Suitably modified, hockey proved ideal for the needs of the widening Victorian male elite. It offered a cold-season complement to cricket, whose grounds it often used, with a similar team ethic, fast action skills, and most essential, a refuge for amateurism in increasingly professional mass sports. It has acted as an agent of gender separation; only the rules have converged.

Hockey associations emerged beginning in the late 1800s: the National Hockey Union in the Bristol area from 1887 to 1895 and the Hockey Association, formed in the London area in 1886, which became the English national body. Other constituent nations of Great Britain formed their own associations. At present, 2,000 clubs (plus 500 schools) are affiliated with the Hockey Association.

The late 19th-century British codification and organization soon spread throughout the British Empire and beyond. In most white "dominions" (Canada was too cold), hockey soon became acceptable for expatriate officers and businessmen. In Australia, New Zealand, and southern Africa, clubs grew around British bases. On the Indian subcontinent, field hockey became more popular than elsewhere in the empire. When India and Pakistan separated after independence in 1947, each had a strong base for continued growth.

In Europe, Belgium, Germany, France, Spain, and the Netherlands soon fostered clubs, and a mixture of emulation and national rivalries before World War I advanced this "friendly" and "peaceful" sport's development. Argentina, Brazil, and Venezuela all joined in, each with a few clubs. A spread into central and eastern Europe was given an extra push after World War II when the sport became one of many symbolizing Soviet "progress," with state subsidies and facilities.

Rules and Play

The game has been standardized, for both sexes, with 18 rules. It is played on a pitch 91.5 meters (100 yards) by 54.9 meters (60 yards), with similar divisions to soccer. Both sides field 11 players, wielding wood and composite sticks curved at the striking end; these are based on an "Indian" design of 1936 that shortened the customary stick to increase power. The ball, adapted from cricket, is usually white plastic. All players wear shinguards, the goalkeepers heavy padding and helmets. A game consists of two halves of 30 to 35 minutes, with a 10-minute break when players change ends.

A popular sport for women in secondary schools and colleges, the game is played competitively by 75 countries. A men's team from England played the first "international" against Ireland in 1895, then went on to play mainland European countries, as did English women's sides. Serious international play between men's teams started with the 1908 Olympics in London, which England won. Hockey appeared again at the Olympics in 1928, with competitions generally dominated by India.

Women's Field Hockey

Female hockey emerged mostly from the drive to provide healthy mothers for Britain's elite during late-Victorian eugenic uncertainties. The All England's Women's Hockey Association was established in 1895 and readily adopted the male rules of play. An attempt to join with the male Hockey Association was firmly repelled. Women developed regional and international matches and played seriously. By 1939 England had 2,100 women's clubs, with a smattering throughout the empire.

Constance Applebee introduced the game in the

United States, and remained the most influential figure in the sport for decades. In 1922 she helped found the U.S. Field Hockey Association, which became the governing body for the 14,000 U.S. women who now play. It was 1980 before women were allowed to play at the Olympics.

Most of the 4.5 million people who play worldwide are probably committed to relatively nonserious, friendly recreational play, which they can continue as long as they remain fit. At competitive levels, questions of sponsorship, star players, and their ethics have emerged, products of the high costs involved in training and international play. But the game remains proudly "amateur," less purist than it was but closer to its origins than many other games.

—JOHN LOWERSON

Bibliography: Axton, W. F., and Wendy Lee Martin. (1993) *Field Hockey.* Indianapolis: Masters. Miroy, Neville. (1986) *The History of Hockey.* Laleham on Thames, UK: Lifeline.

Hockey, Ice

Ice hockey, an action-packed test of skill, courage, speed, endurance, and teamwork, has been called "the fastest game on earth." Played on an ice rink by teams of six players, hockey is one of the most popular sports in the world. It is played in over 40 nations, and in the 1990s women's ice hockey has emerged as a popular international sport.

History

Ice hockey's nearest ancestor is probably medieval and early modern forms of "shinny," "hurley," "bandy," or "hockey," popular games sometimes played on ice. Some paintings suggest that by the 17th century some players of shinny-on-ice wore skates. By the middle of the 19th century forms of bandy or hurley or hockey (from the French "*hoquet,*" the shepherd's crook) were frequently played on ice in the northeastern United States and what is now Canada.

Indoor ice hockey began in 1862, when young men in Montreal created rules for indoor hockey or shinny to be played on a new indoor skating facility called the Victoria Rink. The early rules combined codes from lacrosse, polo, shinny, and rugby. The first game played before spectators occurred in 1875.

Over the next few years the modern game of hockey evolved quickly. The rubber ball was replaced by a block of wood and then a hard rubber puck. The number of players on a team dropped from nine to seven.

"Face-offs" were introduced to begin play or to renew play after a stoppage. Offside became a reasonably well-defined concept: for the time being, no forward passing was allowed. Tripping, holding, and other fouls were identified.

Hockey played by Montreal rules soon spread across Canada. By early in the 1890s eastern Canada had dozens of teams, and a few had been formed in the west. (In some parts of the Maritimes the Montreal game replaced a different type of hockey played according to "Halifax" rules.)

From 1888 to 1893 Lord Preston of Stanley was Governor General of Canada (1841–1908). An enthusiastic supporter of ice hockey, he donated a cup to be presented to "the leading hockey club in Canada" as determined in matches arranged by trustees. Almost immediately, winning the Stanley Cup became the objective of serious hockey clubs across Canada.

Openly professional teams and leagues emerged early in the 20th century, first in Pennsylvania and northern Michigan in the United States, then in Canada. Between 1908 and 1912 pro leagues emerged all across Canada. By 1914 Canada's two strongest pro leagues were the National Hockey Association, with a total of six teams in the cities of Quebec, Montreal, Ottawa, and Toronto, and the Pacific Coast Hockey League, with franchises in Victoria, Vancouver, and New Westminster.

Between the 1880s and World War I hockey gained a foothold in other countries including England, Scotland, Switzerland, Austria, Finland, France, the Netherlands, Hungary, Germany, Bohemia, Belgium, Australia, Russia, and Sweden. In 1908 an International Ice Hockey Federation (IIHF) was formed by representatives from France, England, Switzerland, and Belgium. Germany joined in 1909. In 1910 the IIHF arranged for the first European hockey championship—not a "world" championship because a world hockey championship without a Canadian team would have been absurd.

In the 1920s hockey spread to Italy, Spain, Poland, and elsewhere. More important, Canada and the United States joined the IIHF after sending teams to compete against Europeans at the first Winter Olympic Games held in 1920 in Antwerp, Belgium.

In Canada, the professional major leagues were the main attraction; by 1924 they had been reconfigured or established as the National Hockey League (NHL), the Pacific Coast League; and the Western Hockey League. Some important rule adjustments were made: goalies were allowed to leave their feet to make saves;

"The Series of the Century"

Nearly every Canadian over the age of 30 knows where he or she was on 28 September 1972, at the moment Paul Henderson (1943–) scored the winning goal with thirty-four seconds to play in the final game of the 1972 "Series of the Century." This goal allowed Canadians to claim that they played hockey better than anyone. Barely.

Since the 1950s Canadians had watched with some concern as Soviet teams piled up victories in international tournaments. But they had assumed that the best Canadian professionals would whip the Eastern Europeans easily. In 1972 the pros had their chance.

The first four games were played in Canada, and they proved humiliating for the NHL and to some extent for all Canadians. The NHL all-stars won one game and tied another, but their opponents beat them convincingly in the other two. Furthermore, the Soviets exposed weaknesses in the NHL style of play; the main weakness being unimaginative offensive play.

When the series moved to Moscow for the final four games, however, the Canadians revealed more of their strengths. They could make brilliant individual rushes. They were superior on face-offs. Above all, they *wanted* the puck, especially along the boards and in front of each net. They lost the fifth game, but overcame incompetent officiating to win the last three matches.

It is rather ironic that the final victory resulted from overconfidence on the part of the Soviets. They led 5–3 after the second period. Early in the third period they played as if the game were under control, and just before Henderson scored his winning goal two Soviet players had relaxed in their own end and allowed the puck to squirt away from them.

The Canadian victory was a remarkable display of tenacity and focus. But when the Canadian pros returned from Moscow they were aware that their game had been tried and found wanting in many respects. They would have to improve to meet the future challenges that were certain to come.

—Matt Mott

forward passes were allowed in the neutral zone; penalty shots were awarded if a player with a clear path to the net was fouled from behind; and six-man hockey replaced seven-man hockey. Competition for the Stanley Cup remained keen, as did competition for the best players. The Western League could not match NHL salaries and in 1926 sold the rights to its players to the NHL, which became Canada's only major professional league. In pro hockey, the National Hockey League was the major league whose teams used amateur or minor league teams (notably the American League) as farm clubs.

In the 1930s hockey established a small following in countries such as Japan, South Africa, Latvia, and New Zealand, and became very popular in the United Kingdom.

From 1942 to 1967 the NHL had six teams: the Montreal Canadiens, Toronto Maple Leafs, Boston Bruins, New York Rangers, Detroit Red Wings, and Chicago Black Hawks.

In the six-team era the pace of play was faster and the shooting harder than either had been in earlier decades. In 1943 the NHL (followed by other leagues) introduced the center red line. A team could now pass the puck from one zone into another—from its own zone into the neutral zone as far as the red line. This "stretched" the defensive team and created more open ice. The shooting became harder because of the development of the "slap shot" (where the player does not sweep the puck forward but instead slaps or whacks the puck after raising his stick) in the 1950s and the adoption of the curved blade in the 1960s. In the 1960s the harder shots motivated almost all goalies to follow Jacques Plante (1929–1986), the superb Montreal netminder, who in 1959 donned a face mask.

From the 1940s through the 1960s, children's hockey became a major trend in Canadian amateur hockey. Kids' hockey in Canada, much like Little League baseball in the United States, became "professionalized," or at least pretty serious business.

Internationally, the main story was the Soviet Union's rise. Although played, the sport developed no significant following until after World War II. The Soviet government promoted hockey because it was an Olympic sport (the more popular sport of bandy was not), and valuable international prestige could be gained from Olympic victories. From the mid-1950s to the late 1960s, the highlight of world championship or Olympic tournaments was almost always the match between Canada and the Soviet Union. One team or the other won 13 of the 16 championships from 1954 through 1969; Swedish teams won twice, and the American team once.

Rules and Play

The objective of ice hockey is to score more goals than the opposing side by propelling a "puck" (a hard, black, rubber disk, 3 inches [7.6 centimeters] in diameter and $5^1/_2$ to 6 ounces [154 to 168 grams] in weight) into a "goal" (a cage-like structure, 6 feet [1.8 meters] wide by 4 feet [1.2 meters] high, placed on a goal line—there is a goal at each end of the playing surface about 10 feet [3 meters] out from each end board). A game is 60 minutes long, broken into three 20-minute periods. Teams have 15 to 20 players, of whom 6 play at a time.

A penalized team may be required to play with 5 or even 4 players for a specified period.

Hockey players move on skates and use sticks (made of wood or, recently, aluminum) with a blade on the end to handle, pass, or shoot the puck. Top players can skate 25 to 30 miles (40 to 48 kilometers) per hour, and they regularly shoot the puck more than 100 miles (160 kilometers) per hour.

The game's speed is probably its major source appeal for spectators. Another is the (sometimes barely) controlled violence. Players collide at high speeds; they frequently whack or shove each other with sticks. Fighting is common. In amateur leagues, fighters are usually banished from the game, but in professional leagues they are simply penalized and ruled off the ice for a few minutes, usually two or five.

Looking beyond speed and violence, anyone who watches an elite-level game for a few minutes will not fail to appreciate the coordination and skill of the best players. Their skating features not only balance and agility; they turn sharply, stop and start quickly, switch in a split-second from backwards to forwards or forwards to backwards. They control the puck with dekes, feints, and changes of pace.

Growth of Ice Hockey

In 1967 the NHL expanded from 6 to 12 teams; the owners realized that to obtain a lucrative contract with U.S. television network contracts, the league needed a presence in more than four U.S. cities. The World Hockey Association, formed in 1972, disbanded in 1979 and four of its teams were absorbed into the NHL. At the end of the 1970s the NHL had grown to 21 teams.

Two trends accompanied his expansion: signing European stars, especially from Finland and Sweden, and escalation of players' salaries, due in part to competition between leagues for players and in part to the effective leadership of the National Hockey League Players' Association. The one club that was consistently excellent was the Montreal Canadiens, who took six Stanley Cups from 1968 through 1979.

Internationally, the IIHF maintained its annual world championship tournaments—more than one since 1961 representatives of different countries were placed into "pools" by their level of play. The Soviet Union, Czechoslovakia, and Sweden dominated play, especially before the Canadians reentered the competitions in 1977. The real excitement in international hockey came when the Soviet national team played professionals from North America, as it did in 1972 against a team of NHL all-stars and in 1974 against

World Hockey Association all-stars. Since 1979 the NHL, again the one major professional league., has expanded to 26 teams.

In the 1980s teams in the league began to sign players from Eastern European countries, Sweden, and Finland, a trend that accelerated with the collapse of the Soviet Union. More Americans were appearing on NHL rosters, so that by the mid-1990s just over 60 percent of all NHL players were native Canadians, compared to 95 percent in the mid-1960s.

The year 1979 ushered in an era characterized by two remarkable teams and one remarkable player. The New York Islanders won four straight Stanley Cups from 1980 through 1983, and the Edmonton Oilers, who gained Stanley Cup victories in five of the seven seasons from 1984 through 1990. From 1979 through 1988 the Oilers were led by Wayne Gretzky (1961–), who later played with the Los Angeles Kings, the St. Louis Blues, and the New York Rangers. Gretzky is the NHL's all-time leading scorer and certainly the greatest player of his time, perhaps of all time.

Children's hockey became more serious in Canada and elsewhere, and international competitions now occur for young boys barely into high school. Hockey also became popular among women. Early in the 1990s, three women played in goal for minor pro teams. The first officially sanctioned IIHF women's world championship tournament was held in Ottawa in 1990. Women's hockey was a popular Olympic sport in 1998 with the United States defeating Canada for the gold medal.

—MORRIS MOTT

See also Bandy.
Bibliography: Diamond, Dan, and Joseph Romain. (1988) *Hockey Hall of Fame: The Official History of the Game and Its Greatest Stars.* Toronto: Doubleday Canada. Diamond, Dan, ed. (1992) *The Official National Hockey League Stanley Cup Centennial Book.* Toronto: McClelland & Stewart. Dryden, Ken, and Roy MacGregor. (1989) *Home Game: Hockey and Life in Canada.* Toronto: McClelland and Stewart. Hollander, Zander, ed. (1993) *The Complete Encyclopedia of Hockey.* 4th ed. Detroit: Visible Ink Press. McFarlane, Brian. (1994) *Proud Past: Bright Future: One Hundred Years of Canadian Women's Hockey.* Toronto: Stoddart Publishing. Young, Scott. (1990) *The Boys of Saturday Night: Inside Hockey Night in Canada.* Toronto: McClelland and Stewart.

Horse Racing, Harness (Trotting)

In the United States, harness racing began early in the 1800s as a pastime on country roads, village main streets, and prominent city avenues. Later in the 19th

Breeding

Mares are chosen for breeding on the basis of their conformation, past performance, and pedigree. But even when a mare scores high in all these categories, the foals she produces may not be the answer to a horseman's dream. Breeding farms are only as successful as their band of broodmares, so when they acquire a mare, they give serious attention to her maternal family. Good-sized mares with good conformation are sought. And if they happen to be known for their gait, speed, and gameness, the chances are better that the breeder may come up with a winner.

The same guidelines can be applied in the selections of stallions, namely, the best of bloodlines that trace back through a dominant male line to the founder of a prominent family. A horse's record of speed, manner, soundness, and conformation is also studied.

Careful thought and planning go into the selection of the proper stallion for a mare from a strong maternal family. If a mare has particular shortcomings—if she is bad gaited on the turns or has an obvious conformation fault—then she should not be bred to a horse with the same problems. Theoretical bloodline approaches to breeding include two basic types: outcross and close-breeding. Outcrossing, a successful as well as practical form of breeding, is the mating of a sire and dam whose bloodlines have little in common. Those who follow this system are quick to point out that outcross breeding produces "hybrid vigor" in the foal. However, a true hybrid is not possible from only American stock, because nearly all American harness horses trace back to one ancestor, Hambletonian. To produce a true hybrid, an American Standardbred would have to be crossed with the pure blood of a foreign trotter.

Close-breeding involves common ancestors and breaks down into three categories: linebreeding, inbreeding, and incest. Linebreeding, which combines common ancestors from the fourth or third and fourth generations, can be effective. However, to be correct according to the early definition of linebreeding, it should connect the horses through the male line of the sire and sire of the dam. But these breeding patterns are theoretical. The proof is in the trying. It is recommended that only superior horses be used for inbreeding because inbreds from the same stock will produce an inferior strain over a prolonged period.

On a Standardbred farm, the owner or manager is on 24-hour duty. The breeding season for horses starts about February 15. Although this is not the time of year breeding would occur naturally, racehorse breeders must take into account the fact that the universal birthdate for all horses is January 1. This practice simplifies keeping records of horses' ages. Since the average gestation period is eleven months, the foal is dropped soon after the new year. This gives the newborn a chance to grow up before the yearling sales later that same year. Generally, breeding goes on through June, although some farms extend the season into July in order to get as many mares as possible in foal. There has been some discussion about changing the universal birthday to some date in mid-year, which would give the farms an opportunity to breed the horses in the warmer months, as nature prefers, and would fit the mare's normal reproductive cycle.

—Philip A. Pines

century Americans began to think of it as a sport, known as "trotting." Trotting was considered the great national pastime, and the names of both horses and horsemen become household words. The term "harness racing" came at the end of the century, when turf writers sometimes used it.

History

John H. Wallace is credited with establishing the breed of the trotting horse known as the Standardbred. His *Trotting Supplement* to the *American Stud Book* in 1867 was the first step in that direction. Horses of all breeds were admitted, but Wallace soon cut off all doubtful pedigree lines. The founding father of today's Standardbreds is Messenger, who arrived in the United States five years after the Revolution and sired at least 600 foals. The trotters he produced became known for their trotting action, speed, and gameness that placed them in a class by themselves.

Originally, trotters and pacers were ridden to saddle. But their gaits lent themselves to being hitched to wagons and racing carts known as sulkies, light two-wheeled carriages constructed for a single person.

For most of the 19th century, sulkies were made with high wheels. In 1892, the new bike-wheel sulkies quickly replaced the high wheelers; they were faster, negotiated the runs better, and placed the driver behind the horse, reducing wind resistance.

The 1939 establishment of the U.S. Trotting Association 1939 unified harness racing, but the real revolution occurred in 1940, when artificially lighted night races were introduced at Roosevelt Raceway in Westbury, New York. The raceway lost a considerable amount of money in its first two years, but as attendance and pari-mutuel handle (the total amount of money wagered) increased, new tracks opened and old tracks reopened. The Western Harness Racing Association was organized in 1946 and developed harness racing on the West Coast.

Rules and Play

Today's standard sulky is based on a single-shaft design created by aeronautical engineer Joe King. It featured an arched shaft over the horse's back connected to the back pad of the harness. A small crossbar on the shaft provided foot support.

A harness horse either trots or paces. If he trots, his legs move in diagonal pairs—front right and rear left together, front left and rear right together. A pacer does the opposite: the right front and right rear legs move at the same time, followed by the front and rear legs on the left side of his body. These gaits, the trot and the pace, are inherited by most Standardbreds. Training produces the ability to maintain them at high speed over long distances. Rarely are both gaits found in the same field of horses, and generally—especially where money is involved—trotters compete against trotters and pacers do battle with their own kind.

A pacer is readily identified by his side-swaying motion. Where the trotter's body is usually balanced in the center, the pacer is constantly shifting his weight from side to side, which creates the rocking motion that inspired their nickname, "side-wheelers." Most pacers racing today wear hopples (or hobbles)—leather or plastic straps that are designed to go around a horse's legs on each side of its body and keep the horse on gait.

Drivers need strength and the ability to make split-second decisions; they must control their tempers, fears, and nervousness since horses sense a driver's indecisiveness and respond accordingly. Driver and a harness horse must race as a unit, understanding each other, responding through the senses, by touch and by word.

Harness racing used to be known as an old man's sport. Today the average driver is around 40. As long as a driver stays in good physical condition he can compete actively for many years longer than athletes in other sports.

—PHILIP A. PINES

Bibliography: Pines, Philip A. (1980) *The Complete Book of Harness Racing*. New York: Arco Publishing.

Horse Racing, Steeplechase

Steeplechase is a horse race over an obstacle course of jumps, water hazards, and other features intended to replicate natural conditions. In its modern form, steeplechase owes its existence to impromptu point-to-point races following a fox hunt. Later these races were formalized and run under the auspices of a hunt. These events were a means of keeping the horses ready for the next fox hunting season. Men and women compete on equal terms as owners, trainers, and riders, as do amateur and professional riders.

Hat Pins and Hunches.

Ye lads who love a steeplechase and danger freely court, sirs,
Hark forward all to Liverpool to join the gallant sport, sirs,
The English and the Irish nags are ready for the fray, sirs,
And which may lose and which may win, 'tis very hard to say, sirs.

—*Old song*

History

Tradition has it that in 18th-century Ireland, following a hunt, the riders raced each other toward a distant steeple. Another version has it that, after a fruitless hunt, a rider suggested a race toward a church spire. At the conclusion of the race, the promoter was said to have remarked "what great sport it was without those ...hounds."

Later, steeplechase came to occupy the time between hunting seasons. Gradually, these races, usually under the auspices of a hunt, became independent sporting events in the forms of timber racing, hurdle racing, and point-to-point races. With increasing popularity and more spectators, they moved to permanent facilities. The most famous British course is Aintree, the home of the Grand National Steeplechase, which began in about 1839 and was so named in 1847. Aintree is designed to mimic the obstacles encountered during the hunt, while allowing viewers to watch the whole race. The governing body for steeplechase events in England is the National Hunt Committee.

In the United States, steeplechase came into its own after the Civil War, although "jump" racing had existed since the 1830s. The Maryland Hunt Cup race was established in 1894 and established tracks and hunt clubs held steeplechase events. To codify the inconsistent rules, the National Steeplechase Association (NSA) was founded in 1895 and still governs the sport. Aintree's reputation as a challenging course prompted a group of American sportsmen to build a replica (or as close as possible) of Aintree at Gallatin, Tennessee, in the late 1920s.

Rules and Play

The steeplechase course is between four and five miles long. Obstacles—around 30—have been standardized as "national fences," which are in place at most tracks. In the United States, steeplechase events are classified as timber and hurdle races, with approximately eight major races sanctioned by the National Steeplechase

Association. Purses in these races have reached $100,000.

In the early steeplechase events, women rode in races planned especially for them, but soon entered major races and competed successfully against men.

Steeplechase is popular in Australia and New Zealand, England, Ireland, Wales, Scotland, France, and the United States. The running of the Sport of Kings Challenge further evidences its international character; the event has been held at several different sites, including Morven Park (Virginia), Callaway Gardens (Georgia), Cheltenham (England), and Leopardstown (Ireland). This is a million-dollar series. Sponsored by the International Steeplechase Group (ISG), the Challenge's primary goal is to advance the sport of steeplechase around the world.

—RALPH B. BALLOU, JR.

Bibliography: Rossell, John E., Jr. (1974) *The Maryland Hunt Cup, Past and Present.* Baltimore: Sporting Press. Woolfe, Raymond G., Jr. (1983) *Steeplechasing.* New York: Viking Press.

Horse Racing, Thoroughbred

Although often called the sport of kings, Thoroughbred horse racing was not the prerogative of the elite: it was the sport of all, a common interest of peer and peasant, of lord and laborer. Horse racing emerged when horses were the basic means of transport. Like today's automobiles, they were also status symbols, their quality an overt display of their owners' wealth. Ownership inevitably engendered rivalry, which led to the organization of races, initially matches between two horses but later formalized races with several entrants.

History

Many race meetings in Great Britain into the early 19th century were not just for Thoroughbred racehorses. All but the major meetings might include events for half-bred horses, hunters, and occasionally even ponies. This mix was permitted partly to ensure an adequate supply of horses. Non-Thoroughbreds were also allowed to compete because most race meetings were primarily social events, the high point of the social calendar for the local populace. If possible they wanted to race, not merely watch. Hence farmers raced, and frequently rode, their half-breeds, while the gentry entered their Thoroughbred hunters and racing stock.

Match races at the elite level, with only two horses competing, continued well into the 19th century. However, most Thoroughbred racing was against all comers, for which owners paid only a sweepstakes entry. Three major forms emerged: handicaps, in which (theoretically) all horses had an equal chance because they carried weights allotted according to their perceived ability; weight-for-age events where the older animals carried higher weights to compensate for their greater maturity; and racing where all horses carried the same weight in which the best horse should emerge victorious, gaining not just kudos and prize money but also the seal of approval for breeding.

The prime examples of the latter type of race are the so-called Classics for second-season (i.e., three-year-old) horses that were established in the late 18th and early 19th centuries in England. These comprise the St. Leger (1778), run over 1 mile, 6 furlongs, and 132 yards at Doncaster; the Derby (1780), over 1 mile and for fillies only; the Oaks (1779), over 1.5 miles at Epsom; and the 2000 Guineas (1809) and 1000 Guineas (1814), over 1 mile at Newmarket, the latter restricted to fillies. Only outstanding horses ever capture the "Triple Crown" of St. Leger, Derby, and 2000 Guineas. The U.S. equivalent is to secure the Kentucky Derby (1875) at Churchill Downs, the Preakness Stakes (1873) at Pimlico, and the Belmont Stakes (1867) at Belmont, run respectively over 1.25, $1^3/_{16}$ miles, and 1.5 miles.

Until the late 1800s, onlookers paid nothing unless they wished to view from the stand (if there was one). Clearly money could be made from a race crowd, yet entry remained free. To profit reasonably, enclosed meetings would have to be held more frequently than existing social gatherings. But lacking certainty that enough spectators would come, enclosure awaited rising real incomes, sufficient leisure time, and improved transportation.

These conditions fulfilled, entrepreneurs developed enclosed racecourses and charged entry. This occurred first in Australia, although credit often goes to the British course at Sandown Park, established in 1875. Gate money courses signaled the widespread commercialization of racing in which courses competed both for spectators and horses and, in turn, increased prize money impinged on those directly involved in satisfying the demands of the owners—the jockeys, trainers, and breeders.

Even before the enclosed course, racing had begun to change as long-distance heats were generally abandoned, races for heavyweight jockeys were increasingly difficult to find, more two-year-olds were being raced, and sweepstakes (in which many owners each paid a stake into the prize fund to enter their horses) were replacing matches for plates and other nonmonetary

Horseback Riding: Breeding

Equines play a role in almost every culture, and the myriad horse breeds of the world are valued companions for sport, ceremony, transportation, farming, and innumerable other activities. Over the centuries, each breed has been developed, with humankind's intervention, to enhance its unique traits that often determine the capacity for which the horse is best suited.

Today, in competition, individual horses are exhibited to judges in horse show breeding classes—also referred to as halter, in-hand, model, or bella forma classes—to compete to best represent the breed standard. Judges evaluate each horse's conformation, substance, and quality, penalizing heavily those animals with transmittable unsoundness, such as crooked legs or poor temperament. Often the horses are walked and trotted so that judges can rate their movements and performing potential. Classes are divided by age and sex of the horse, but breeds are grouped together so that their qualifications are measured against common standards.

Breed registries throughout the world record the names of horses best representing the essential qualities of their breed, and accept or reject horses for registry based on pedigree and appearance. Horses are often selected for specific equestrian disciplines because their breed standards are well suited to the nature of the sport.

The Arabian is one of the oldest and purest breeds in the world and has been used as founding stock for many of the modern breeds. A versatile, refined, and intelligent breed, the Arabian finds success in English and Western Pleasure classes, and is also popular in endurance riding because of its shorter spine and extra rib that give it excellent heart and lung capacity. The Arabian stands 14.1 to 15.1 hands (a hand measuring 10 centimeters [4 inches]), in predominant colors of bay, brown, chestnut, gray, and black.

Thoroughbreds were originally bred for racing, but have proven to be excellent jumping, dressage, and eventing horses as well. With a tall, athletic build, spirited temperament, and noble bearing, the Thoroughbred is one of the most popular modern breeds. Thoroughbreds range from 15 to 17 hands on average and appear in a variety of colors, with bays being predominant.

The American Quarter Horse, with a muscular, compact body and quick reflexes, has long been a favorite of Western riders. Quarter Horses are intelligent and strong and with proper training show natural talent for herding and ranch work. Quarter Horses stand approximately 15 hands and tend to appear in varying solid colors or as roans.

Morgan horses, a uniquely American breed founded in the 19th century by Justin Morgan, are known for their gentle temperament, physical power, and versatility. Morgans are also characterized by a short body, solid legs, and energetic gaits, making them popular mounts in all areas of the competition world, from driving and three-day eventing to dressage and hunting. Morgans are usually bay, brown, chestnut, liver chestnut, or black and range from 14 to 15.2 hands on average.

Color breeds are distinguished by their color or markings, and although they are frequently associated with Western riding, are used in many equestrian disciplines. Some popular color breeds include the Palomino, with its golden coat and cream-colored mane and tail; the Appaloosa, noted for its spot patterns; and the Pinto, with large patches of color—either brown and white ("skewbald"), or black and white ("piebald")—on its body. Paint horses are Thoroughbreds or quarter horses with Pinto-like coloring, while albino horses have completely white hair founded in pink skin.

The American Saddlebred is a tall, athletic, flashy, and elegant horse with a long neck and a lean, muscular body. A native American breed, it is renowned for its animated, high-stepping gaits and special ability to produce the smooth rack and slow gait. American Saddlebreds, which average 15 to 16 hands and appear predominantly as chestnuts, bays, and blacks, are popular mounts both under saddle and in-harness.

National Show Horses are a mix of Arabian and American Saddlebred breeding and display the outstanding qualities of both breeds. They are shown both in-harness and under saddle, where they display brilliant, animated gaits and carry their heads high. These refined animals appear in chestnut, bay, and gray, and stand between 15 and 16 hands.

The Tennessee Walking Horse is heavier in build than the Saddlebred, but is otherwise similar in size and appearance. The most unusual feature of the Tennessee Walking Horse is its unique running walk, in which the front feet are lifted high and straight while the back feet take long strides, providing a smooth ride.

Standardbreds have bloodlines leading back to the Thoroughbred, Morgan, and Hackney. They are characterized by strong legs, stamina, and a mild temperament and work mostly in-harness racing and driving classes. Slightly smaller than Thoroughbreds, Standardbreds may be brown, bay, chestnut, black, or gray.

The Trakehner, Hanoverian, and Holsteiner are large, solid European breeds with agreeable dispositions. They make excellent sport horses, having proven abilities in dressage, jumping, carriage work, and driving. Standing at 15.3 to 17 hands on average, these breeds are often bay, chestnut, or black in color.

The Selle Français, or French Saddle Horse, is a versatile mount originating from the northern part of France. Athletic and even-tempered with a build similar to the Thoroughbred, these horses excel in dressage, eventing, jumping, racing, and as general-purpose riding mounts. Averaging 15.3 to 16.2 hands, they commonly appear as bays and chestnuts.

The Andalusian, or Spanish purebred, influenced many American breeds when it was brought to the new continent by the conquistadors. A strong, brave, and athletic horse, it is used with success today in dressage and bullfighting. The Andalusian is typically gray and stands 16 hands high on average.

Lipizzaner horses, originally bred in Austria, are intelligent, athletic, and willing to learn. Trained and exhibited by the Spanish Riding School of Vienna, the horses have become world-famous for their extremely advanced dressage capabilities. Performing dramatic balletlike movements set to classical music, the highly trained horses are billed as the "Dancing Stallions" for their displays. Lipizzaners are usually gray or white and stand slightly smaller than their close relative, the Andalusian.

The Paso Fino and its close relative, the Peruvian Paso, are small, compact horses originating from Latin America. The Peruvian Paso is distinguished from the Paso Fino by a motion called *termino*—a lateral swinging of its legs from the shoulder. Both the Paso Fino and the Peruvian Paso have arching necks, gentle temperaments, and distinct four-beat gaits. They stand at approximately 14 hands and come in gray, bay, and chestnut.

Draft, or "cold-blooded" horses, are big, heavy, and strong. Draft horses can be as tall as 18 hands and weigh more than 1 ton. With their massive size, easygoing dispositions, and capability to pull several tons, draft horses work primarily in-harness. The Clydesdale, Percheron, Belgian, and Shire are the major draft horse breeds.

Pony breeds generally do not exceed 14.2 hands; they come in a variety of colors and markings. Because of their size, ponies such as the Shetland, Exmoor, Dartmoor, Welsh Mountain, Connemara, Chincoteague, and Pony of the Americas make popular mounts for children. These ponies come from environments and backgrounds that make them hardy, strong, and sure-footed. The Hackney Pony is an exception, being shown almost exclusively in-harness and displaying high-stepping action and show ring presence similar to the American Saddlebred. The five-gaited Icelandic Horse, standing under 14.2 hands, is strong enough to carry a grown rider and is used mostly for transportation. Falabellas, or miniature horses, at a maximum of 8.2 hands, are too small to be ridden, but make unique pets.

—Mary Conti

awards. All these can be explained by a growing commercial attitude on the part of owners. Sweepstakes races meant that owners risked less for the chance of winning more. Racing younger horses meant that investment in expensive bloodstock could yield a return earlier than before. Once younger horses ran, shorter races and lighter jockeys inevitably followed: owners did not have to be in racing for the money to appreciate the foolhardiness of risking the breakdown of valuable horseflesh.

U.S. horse racing lagged behind Britain, partly because it lacked an overarching administrative and legislative body comparable to the Jockey Club, founded in 1750 and virtually in charge of British racing by the mid-19th century. However, turf abuses via race-fixing and the use of drugs in the 1890s brought the imposition of repressive state legislation that forced U.S. racing to clean itself up and restructure administratively. The American Jockey Club was established in 1894, but its power has been weakened by the independent state racing commissions. Its prime function has been to maintain the *American Stud Book,* the official record of Thoroughbred breeding in the United States and Canada.

One distinctive American innovation was the monkey-on-a-stick style of riding in which the saddle was pushed forward and the stirrups and reins shortened so that the jockey rode with knees bent, crouching along the horse's neck. When U.S. riders invaded the British turf in the last decade of the 19th century, their success quickly led to an abandonment of the English style, modeled on the erect seat of the hunting field. Another American trademark has been the dirt tracks, often much smaller than in Britain, thus offering spectators a better view.

By the 1860s, horse racing had become a highly visible sport in Australia, although authorities had been reluctant to sanction a vehicle for gambling and public amusement in a penal settlement. The first recorded meeting for Thoroughbreds was in Sydney's Hyde Park in 1810; in the mid-1820s permanent race clubs had emerged to administer the sport; and by midcentury the turf had cemented its position as an integral part of colonial community activity.

Since then, Australian racing has generally followed international trends. In one respect, however, Australian racing remains unique. Its most important race, the Melbourne Cup, always scheduled for the first Tuesday in November, is a handicap in which the best horse does not necessarily win. This reflects an Australian culture where "tall poppies" are cut down and "battlers" given a "fair go"—the uncertainty engendered by the handicapping also appeals to the Australian gambler.

Elsewhere in Asia most international attention focuses on Japan, where the past two decades have witnessed vast investment in bloodstock and in racing itself. The Japan Cup, a weight-for-age event, was inaugurated in 1981 as the richest race in the world. Run at Tokyo's Fuchu racecourse on the last Sunday in October, it attracts high-quality horses from all over the racing world.

With the exception of France, European racing remained relatively unintegrated until well into the era of economic unity. In Paris, however, the Prix de l'Arc de Triomphe had been started in 1920 with the intention of attracting the best horses in Europe. As a weight-for-age event, it is an end-of-season test between age groups as well as countries.

Jockeys, Trainers, and Owners

Other things being equal, and often when they are not, the skill of the jockey determines the result of a race. Fred Archer (1857–1886) was a master of his profession. At age 17, he won the first of 13 consecutive English jockey championships in a career that boasted

Observations on Horse Racing.

The commonest jockey-boy in this company of man-nikins can usually earn more than the average scholar or professional man, and the whole set receive a good deal more of adulation than has been bestowed on any soldier, sailor, explorer, or scientific man of our generation.
—J. Runciman, "The Ethics of the Turf,"
Contemporary Review, April 1889

Betting is the manure to which the enormous crop of horse racing and racehorse breeding in this and other countries is to a large extent due.
—R. Black, *The Jockey Club and Its Founders,* 1891

All men are born free and equal; and each man is enti-tled to life, liberty and the pursuit of horse racing.
—Banjo Patterson, "Australian Declaration of Independence," in his *Racehorses and Racing,* 1914

2,748 winners, including 21 classics. His skill brought him wealth and fame. But in 1886, at the height of his profession, he needed to lose 11 pounds to ride St. Mirin in the Cambridgeshire, the only major British race he had never won. The effort of losing weight left him so weak that he succumbed to typhus and on the anniversary of his wife's death shot himself while in a delirious state.

Archer's quick rise and dismal end highlight several aspects of a jockey's life. In a field dominated by males, young men can burst almost overnight from poverty and obscurity into riches and popularity, but they face constant job insecurity in a labor market where riders far outnumber available mounts—a more acute prob-lem with the advent of women jockeys. Nutritional knowledge has eased but not surmounted the problem caused by racing's insistence on riding weights well be-low those required by most sportsmen.

At the inaugural running of the Kentucky Derby in 1875, 14 of the 15 riders were African Americans. That year also witnessed the turf debut of Kentucky-born jockey Isaac Murphy, designated the "Black Archer" by British racing writers for his upright riding position and coolness in an exciting finish. He was the first jockey to win three Kentucky Derbies and had a career winning record of 44 percent. Another African Ameri-can to make racing history was 17-year-old Cheryl White, who in 1971 became the first black woman to win a Thoroughbred race when she rode Jetolara to vic-tory at Waterford Park, West Virginia.

At the beginning of the 19th century, most trainers were essentially training grooms, low-paid servants with few social graces, looking after perhaps 15 to 20 of the master's horses. Racing's commercialization changed this as public trainers came to the fore; well-educated individuals caring for perhaps 100 animals from a variety of owners and charged with getting a horse fit by way of diet and exercise.

Few owners can consider racing as a money-mak-ing concern; in aggregate, the costs of horse ownership have always exceeded available prize money. Most own-ers lose money and most are prepared to do so, viewing racing as consumption—conspicuous in some cases—rather than investment. Some view it as a hobby they must pay for; others use ownership to ob-tain social cachet. In recent years, with expenses rising, multiple ownership has emerged to allow the industry to maintain the number of horses in training. Even more of an impact has been made by international owners, particularly Middle Eastern billionaires, who have globalized their racing activities almost without regard to costs. Indeed, not content with dominating the owners' and breeders' tables, the Maktoum family, made rich by Dubai's oil, have created a state-of-the-art racecourse at Nad Al Shiba, which hosts the Dubai World Cup, the richest horse race in the world.

The greatest financial contribution to racing in the 20th century has come from the totalizator (or "tote"). Under this system, the aggregate pool of bets on all horses is divided amongst those who bet on the win-ning horse, less deductions to cover operating cost and to make contributions to the racing industry. In all countries a percentage of the turnover has been spent to improve the quality of racing and spectator facilities.

Breeding

All Thoroughbred racehorses worldwide are descended in a direct male line from three stallions imported into England, the Byerley Turk (born ca. 1680), the Darley Arabian (born 1700), and the Godolphin Barb (born 1724), though ironically there is no record of any of the trio ever having raced. The Turk was captured at Buda in 1688 and ridden as a charger by Captain Byerley be-fore being put to stud in England; Thomas Darley pur-chased his Arabian in Aleppo in 1704 and dispatched it to his Yorkshire estate; and the Barb, really a Yemeni stallion, was imported to stand at stud for the earl of Godolphin. The value of this eastern blood lay in the toughness and stamina of the desert horses, which combined in selective breeding with the best of British stock produced the modern Thoroughbred.

Secretariat (1970–1989) will always feature in any history of American horse racing: he was the first two-year-old to be unanimously voted Horse of the Year and won the Triple Crown in 1973 (running away with the Belmont Stakes by an awe-inspiring 31 lengths). Few Americans at the time remained unaware of the feats of "Big Red," as he affectionately became known.

To produce outstanding animals like Secretariat has always been the ambition of breeders, but they attempted to do so unscientifically. The first attempt to fill this lacuna came with Bruce Lowe's "figure system" in the 1890s, which ranked the families of the 50 brood mares in the original *Stud Book* of 1791–1814 according to the number of classic winners they had produced. Although marred as a guide to breeding success by concentrating on absolute rather than proportionate performance, it drew attention to the important role of the female line in bloodstock development, a contribution previously largely neglected. In more recent times, more scientifically based genetic research has assisted breeders, but there is no magic formula. A judicious union of selected strains of blood is likely to secure more good horses than random coupling, but great horses have inflicted some wretched offspring on the racing world.

Gambling

Organized racing began as matches for wagers between owners of quality horses; several centuries later it provides a daily opportunity for betting. For most people interested in racing, the Thoroughbred racehorse was, and still is, little more than a mechanism for gambling. In most countries betting has provided a lifeline for racing in that a portion of the totalizator takings has been injected into the sport. Nowhere more so than in Japan, where subsidized admission reduces the cost of entry to less than 75 cents, subsidized prize money means that up to 14 races will be on the program, and augmented club profits ensure excellent viewing and betting facilities. Up to 200,000 spectators are attracted to the major events.

Most countries in which horse racing occurred adopted the totalizator when its technology became sufficiently effective in the late 19th century. In Britain, however, the tote was not legalized until 1929 and until it was, an on-course monopoly was held by that figure almost unique to British racing, the bookmaker. Such individuals had first appeared in the late 18th century, offering to take bets against any horse: if sufficient bets were forthcoming and the odds manipulated correctly, bookmakers stood to win no matter which horse was first. Some were extraordinarily successful: the unfortunately named Fred Swindell began

his early-19th-century working life as an engine-cleaner, but left £146,000 ($584,000).

Gambling aided racing, but it also encouraged deception. Notable ringers include the 1984 Fine Cotton substitution in Australia in which, backed in a $2 million plunge, the much better performing but disguised Bold Personality won a novice handicap. The authorities took severe action including warnings-off and license suspension, but as long as betting continues, especially on handicaps, which offer an incentive not to perform to one's best, racing will always be susceptible to corruption. Indeed, the turf is perhaps the classic case of insider trading.

—WRAY VAMPLEW

Bibliography: Bedford, Julian. (1989) *The World Atlas of Horse Racing.* London: Hamlyn. Pollard, Jack. (1988). *Australian Horse Racing.* Sydney: Angus & Robertson. Turner, Michael, and Gerry Cranham. (1992). *Great Jockeys of the Flat.* Middlesex, UK: Guinness. Vamplew, Wray. (1976) *The Turf: A Social and Economic History of Horse Racing.* London: Allen Lane. ———. (1989) "Horse Racing." In *Sport in Britain: A Social History,* edited by Tony Mason. Cambridge: Cambridge University Press. Zuccoli, Carlo. (1992) *The Fields of Triumph: Guide to the World of Racing.* Milan: Monographic.

Horseback Riding, Dressage

Dressage is the oldest and most artistic of the equestrian sports. The aim is to train the horse to achieve the powerful natural movements it can make when free when the horse is carrying the weight of the rider and at the command of the rider.

History

The Greeks were probably the first to practice dressage; on the Parthenon frieze there are horses in such advanced movements as the *levade* and *piaffe.*

Modern dressage began during the Renaissance and the first great master was the Neapolitan nobleman Federico Grisone, who founded a riding academy in Naples in 1532. In 1550 he published *Gli ordini di cavalcare,* which earned him an international following, furthered by Britain's one and only great master, William Cavendish, Duke of Newcastle, who wrote *Methode et invention nouvelle de dresser les chevaux* (A General System of Horsemanship) in 1658.

The country that became the most enthusiastic about dressage was France after two Frenchmen studied at the Neapolitan school and returned to their country to teach, write, and turn dressage into a highly fashionable activity. Louis XIV made Versailles a center for dressage and the most famous dressage master of all time, François Robichon, Sieur de la Guerinière, was at work during his reign. The principles he established are those used today and are the ones that paved the way for more artistic freedom of action.

In the 20th century, Germany replaced France as the leading dressage nation. Two 19th-century German dressage masters, Louis Seeger and Gustav Steinbrecht, influenced this change.

All of these masters were *manege* riders developing the art of controlling and showing off their horses' abilities in small arenas. In the 20th century, however, dressage became competitive. The spur was its inclusion in the 1912 Olympic Games at Stockholm, where it was at first more a test of obedience than of gymnastic ability —its goal today. The competitors were cavalry officers, who dominated the sport for the first half century. In 1921 the Fédération Equestre Internationale (FEI) was formed to act as the governing body of equestrian sports.

Rules and Play

The FEI stipulates that the object of dressage is the harmonious development of the physique and ability of the horse. This makes the horse calm, supple, loose, and flexible, but also confident, attentive, and keen, thus achieving perfect understanding with his rider. These qualities are judged by the freedom and regularity of the paces; the harmony, lightness, and ease of the movements.

Skill in dressage lies in the ability to persuade the horse to perform the required movements gymnastically and with power but without resistance. This absence of resistance (known as submission) is an important aspect of dressage. Building the power is useless if done at the cost of the horse's cooperation. Swishing tails, stiffness in the back, or not accepting the bit (avoiding the rein aids by either sticking the head in the air or bending the neck so the head comes close to the chest) show a lack of harmony and are severely penalized.

Training precedes competition. It begins with the variations within the paces themselves. The young horse learns a working trot, canter, and medium walk, but with training will learn to vary the length of his strides and body outline. Collecting must be a gradual process for it entails great suppleness and development of the muscles; only after two or three years of training can a true collected walk, trot, and canter be performed.

Collecting the paces is alternated with extending them. The horse is progressively elasticized and power in the hindquarters developed so that he can take longer and longer steps, but without quickening, for that vital ingredient in dressage—rhythm—must be maintained.

The horse must be taught to go backward and to stand still with the legs forming four sides of a rectangle (known as a square halt). He has to move around his hind legs within the radius of a circle just his own length. This is known as a pirouette, and although relatively easy at the walk, needs great collection in the canter (it is not performed at the trot).

The dressage horse also has to go sideways. The prettiest of the lateral movements is the half pass during which the horse moves across an arena almost parallel to the long side, bent in the direction he is going and with both the front and hind legs crossing.

Lateral work, extensions and collections, and flying changes turn the dressage horse into a better and better gymnast until eventually (in usually three to four years) the talented, well-trained horse learns the most advanced movements in competitive dressage—the *piaffe* and *passage*—both very collected variations of the trot.

Much of dressage is noncompetitive, lending itself to demonstrations and displays. Noncompetitive dressage is the ancient form of dressage and is the one practiced by such famous exponents as the Spanish Riding School in Vienna and the Cadre Noir in Saumur, France.

Dressage involves two types of competitive tests. In the straight test, horse and rider perform set movements. In the Freestyle (also known as Kur), riders choreograph their own programs and set them to music. First tried internationally in 1979, the Freestyle set to music has enjoyed increasing popularity and helped to turn dressage into a more widely known sport. In countries such as the United Kingdom and the United States, it has become the fastest-growing equestrian sport.

In a dressage competition the rider and horse perform a series of movements in an arena measuring 20 by 60 meters (22 by 66 yards) for international events and 20 by 40 meters (22 by 44 yards) for some national events. Marks from 0 (movement not executed) to 10 (excellent) are given by a judge or judges for each movement. These movements are assessed in a series of set tests. The competitor with the highest total points wins.

Freestyles are judged for technical and artistic quality. Artistic marks are given for rhythm, energy, and elasticity; harmony between horse and rider; choreography, well-calculated risks, and choice of music and its interpretation. Specialized, expensive, and time consuming, dressage training is not for all equestrians. Its beauty will keep it alive.

—JANE KIDD

Bibliography: Klimke, Reiner. *Basic Training of the Young Horse.* (1985) London: J. A. Allen & Co. Podhajsky, Alois. *The Complete Training of Horse and Rider.* (1973) London: Wilshire Book Co. Watjen, Richard. *Dressage Riding.* (1958) London: J. A. Allen & Co.

Horseback Riding, Endurance

Endurance riding is defined as "an athletic event with the same horse and rider covering a measured course within a specified maximum time." Great effort and courage are required from the horse and rider, who travel together for great distances over varying terrain, altitude, and weather conditions.

History

Distance riding began during westward expansion in the United States. Organized endurance rides began in the mid-1800s, but not for sport. Pony Express riders delivering mail, the settlers seeking the promise of land and a new life, and the U.S. Army Cavalry needing to maintain order in the vast land expanse of the West— all practiced endurance riding, although not always with today's concern for safety.

The first known modern and organized competitive ride held in the United States was sponsored by the Morgan Horse Club of Vermont in 1913. In the 1920s, the U.S. Army Cavalry introduced the United States Mounted Service Cup competition. Endurance riding, as an organized sport, is thought to have had its official beginning in 1955 at the Tevis Cup, the Western States Trail Ride, a 100-mile grueling ride from Nevada to California that follows the Gold Rush trails.

In 1987 the American Endurance Ride Conference (AERC) sanctioned 646 rides with 2,300 AERC registered riders participating for a combined 700,000 miles (1.1 million kilometers) covered. In the late 1980s, approximately 250 competitive rides were held in the United States annually, with a combined membership of nearly 4,000 people.

Rules and Play

Endurance rides fall into three categories: (1) 25 miles, a "straight out horse race" and takes approximately 1.5 hours; (2) 50 miles, with two check stops of 1 hour each and two spot checks, lasting about 4.5 hours; and (3) 100 miles, which contains three 1-hour checks and several spot checks and takes about 11 hours. All three rides occur in a 24-hour period, and the horses are under strict veterinary control. The first horse to finish in acceptable condition—that is, the horse is able to continue—wins. An additional award

It Ain't Over Til I'm Over.

Time and again, I have endured articles about the drama and the pressure of running up front. "Who can name anything as stressful as leading the North American Championships and fighting off the second place horse?" they ask. To which I reply, "I can!" How's about cut-off times at vet checks, getting caught in the dark on a 50, fear of being lapped by the 100s, or knowing throughout my last loop that everyone else is waiting impatiently for me to cross the finish line, so they can start the awards meeting?

What do these perpetual front runners know about the problems we turtles face? What do they know about happily finishing a ride only to have the timer wake up and comment, "Oh, you're not lost?" or "Trotting across the finish line, so they can start the awards meeting?" Don't get me wrong. I still get my kicks, even though I am a member of the "rear guard." It's everyone else who seems to have a problem with it!

The "To Finish Is To Win" motto is especially useless on the finish line timer. This timer is bribed by people who have fast horses for sale to say especially cruel things like, "We were worried about you," or "I figured you were the Number 23 we were waiting on." It's O.K., I'm used to this routine. After making his obligatory derogatory comment, he'll yawn, fold up his chair, pull up the sign, and walk back to camp with me. . . .

Since I see no signs of a turnaround in my career of distance riding, I've decided to accept my slow poke status and count my blessings. There are, after all some good things about being a turtle, such as:

1. I get more hours in the saddle for the money. I bet I hurt for days longer than the winner, and after all, why else would we choose this sport if our goal is not inflicting the maximum amount of pain on our bodies.

2. If I start at the front of the pack, I'll see everyone by the end of the race. It's a great way to meet friends.

3. Everyone is happy to see me when I get to ride (with the possible exception of the finish timer). They're happy to see someone they can beat.

4. It doesn't slow my horse down when I get off to jog . . . I'm as fast as he is!

5. If I ever get tired of endurance, I can always show my horse in western pleasure classes.

6. Races to the finish are more creative. For instance, in a typical battle for who's last, my friend Ruth and I brought our horses to a halt just short of the finish line. We then dropped the reins to see which horse would voluntarily cross the line first. When neither horse budged, we counted to three and then sneezed. When my horse crossed first, I apologized, because after all it really was her turn to be "not last." Her reply summed up our problem perfectly . . . she sighed, "That's O.K. Beauford is just a victim of inertia."

—Angie McGhee

is presented to the one horse who does not necessarily have the best finishing time but is judged to be in the "best condition."

The sport's popularity owes much to the allure of being outdoors on horseback, away from the noise and stress of the world, and to a feeling of connection with those who lived under rougher but simpler conditions. Too, endurance riding is a challenge, yielding the satisfaction of completing the distance involved. The long hours together in unfamiliar places bond horse and rider, and a contest primarily against natural forces creates esprit de corps among the riders. Anyone can participate. The horse is the equalizer, freeing each party from role expectations and age differences. It is a generalist sport with few professional participants; personal training and athletic stamina count most. No specific type of horse is required for endurance competition, although several breeds do very well.

Although a relatively new sport, endurance riding has changed since competition began in the United States. The first rides involved volunteers, with few qualifying standards or care for the safety of the horse or rider. Many horses died in competitions for big money purses in the mid-1800s. Today, most are sponsored by regional or national organizations with requirements that protect horse and rider and cover equipment. Coming in "best condition" instead of in "first place" originated in the 1920s with the United States Cavalry 300-mile ride, known as the U.S. Mounted Service Cup. Horses are now checked by veterinarians.

Veterinarians are also gathering information on how the ride affects the horses' health. Horse owners use this information to improve health and conditioning practices; veterinarians use the data to guide them in keeping the horses fit and healthy.

Many European countries boast their own championship rides. In 1979 the European Long Distance Rides Conference (ELDRIC) was formed. The competitions are based on a point system and are open to riders from all participating nations. Member countries include Austria, Belgium, France, Germany, Great Britain, Holland, Italy, Portugal, Sweden, Switzerland, and Norway. The United States and Australia are considered associate members.

Great Britain also offers long-distance rides, some of which ELDRIC has sanctioned, and one of which, the Goodwood 100, is run under FEI rules. There are also two organizing bodies: the Endurance Horse and Pony Society of Great Britain and the British Horse Society's Long Distance Riding Group. Two other countries, South Africa and West Germany, are actively involved

in distance and endurance riding, and they sponsor events on an annual basis.

Several countries have gone beyond the basic endurance ride to introduce novel challenging events. Examples include the pioneer rides, which are multiday rides covering historic routes; ride and tie events, which combine jogging and riding with plenty of exercise for horse and rider; competitive driving, a horse and carriage competition; and special international events such as the Elite 100 Mile competition, a ride intended to separate "the best from the rest." The Race of Champions, started in 1984, stirred up controversy because it was the first ride to require stiff entry qualifications: the horse had to have previously finished in the top 10 over 500 miles (800 kilometers) or more of competition, and had to have completed at least two one-day 100-mile rides. It also required all entrants to carry a minimum weight (rider plus tack) of 155 pounds (58 kilograms).

In its short history, endurance and distance riding has grown into a recognized, international equine sport. Development and professionalization of the sport are the natural result of increased interest and participation. At the heart of horseback riding events is the bond between the horse and rider, and the pure recreation pleasure participants derive from this interaction. The challenge now is to retain the fun associated with endurance riding.

—ANITA H. MAGAFAS

Bibliography: Paulo, Karen. (1990) *America's Long Distance Challenge.* North Pomfret, VT: Trafalgar Square.

Horseback Riding, Eventing

Three-day eventing, also called combined training, tests the horse and rider in three areas: dressage, speed and endurance, and stadium jumping. One of the three Olympic equestrian disciplines, it is popular throughout the world, with concentrated interest in Europe, North America, Australia, and New Zealand.

History

The tradition of three-day eventing began as a test of the cavalry mount, which needed to gallop long distances, negotiate the natural obstacles found on cross-country trips, and perform demanding parade movements, and the cavalry rider, who required strong riding abilities, control, and sharp reflexes.

Until 1948, the U.S. Army trained and fielded U.S. teams for international and Olympic competition. However, after World War II the cavalry was disbanded. The American Horse Shows Association (AHSA), the national equestrian federation, with the United States Equestrian Team (USET), formed in 1949, assumed the cavalry's responsibilities in this area, including team selection and training for dressage, show jumping, and three-day eventing. A dedicated organization, the United States Combined Training Association (USCTA) was founded in 1959, for the Pan American Games in Chicago. The AHSA today provides rules and regulations for all recognized events, with the USCTA maintaining a grading system to certify the progress of more than 10,000 competitors nationwide.

Three-day eventing history in European countries, Australia, and New Zealand follows a similar historical timeline. All countries participating in combined training events maintain individual national federations to govern the sport and comply with Fédération Equestre Internationale (FEI) rules for international competition.

International contenders compete at high-profile competitions, such as the Olympic Games, World Equestrian Games, and events like Burghley, Blenheim, and Badminton in the United Kingdom and Essex, Fair Hill, and Radnor in the United States, in addition to smaller-scale competitions in individual countries.

Rules and Play

Three-day events and horse trials are generally held during temperate months. Eventing attracts a spectrum of competitors of different ages and backgrounds and, through its progressive "tiered" system, allows riders and horses with varying degrees of experience to participate. Many different breeds of horses participate in three-day eventing, but Thoroughbreds and Thoroughbred-crosses are the most popular.

In three-day eventing competitions, horse and rider teams are evaluated by a panel of judges, called a ground jury, on dressage, cross-country/endurance, and stadium jumping. From easiest to most difficult, horse trials are offered at five levels: novice, training, preliminary, intermediate, and advanced.

In both horse trials and three-day events, the first day tests competitors in dressage. The horse must appear supple, obedient, and attentive and show regular paces and light, easy movements. Horses are not expected to be as collected as pure dressage mounts, although higher-level events demand more from competitors.

On the second day, riders and horses compete in the endurance phase. At horse trials, this consists only of the timed cross-country course in which competitors leap from a starting gate to gallop over challenging natural terrain, negotiating imposing obstacles such as corner fences, ditches, zigzags, water jumps, banks, and oxers all situated on varied ground.

At a three-day event, unlike a horse trial, competitors contend with three additional elements in the endurance phase: two sections of roads and tracks and a steeplechase.

The third day of a horse trial or three-day event is the stadium jumping phase. Held in an arena, this phase allows competitors to prove that their mounts can maintain suppleness, obedience, and jumping ability after the rigors of the endurance phase.

When all phases are completed, penalty points are added to produce the final score for each horse and rider combination. The competitor with the lowest number of overall penalties wins.

Three-day eventing, or combined training, is an immensely popular sport within the equestrian world. The competitor base has grown significantly, with the strongest growth taking place at the novice and training levels. World-class events draw more spectators and major sponsorships every year.

—MARY CONTI

Bibliography: Rodenas, Paula. (1991). *Random House Book of Horses and Horsemanship.* New York: Random House. Wofford, James C. (1995) *Training the Three-Day Event Horse and Rider.* New York: Howell Book House.

Horseback Riding, Gymkhana

Gymkhana describes a series of contests with ponies rather than horses. Such competitions introduce young people to equitation (steeplechasing, dressage, three-day eventing, and showjumping). The term gymkhana comes from the Hindi gend-khana, meaning "racket court."

History

Gymkhanas have become synonymous with pony clubs. The first pony club was established in 1928 in England, but the concept of a youth-oriented "learn to ride" movement quickly gathered momentum in the United States. Today, the pony club movement is worldwide with 22 national societies. Pony clubs, which accept members to the age of 21, have three primary goals: (1) to encourage young people to ride, (2) to provide them with an all-around education about horsemanship, and (3) to inculcate values regarding sportsmanship and correct behavior.

Rules and Play

Riders in a traditional gymkhana complete a straight, meandering, or circular obstacle course. Organization and rules are kept simple and basic. The first rider to complete the course wins the contest. Other gymkhana events include those for best-groomed horse, most smartly dressed rider, handkerchief catching, and wrestling on horseback. Such activities focus on making riders comfortable around horses.

The great charm of gymkhana is that, despite its intensely competitive nature, the framework of the competition and the contests themselves generate high levels of enjoyment. Gymkhana may be a unique synthesis of comedy and cut-throat competition. Here is an athletic arena in which thousands of highly motivated young children, riding spirited ponies, throw themselves into frantic games such as the sack race and the potato race. In the tacking competition, riders must lead their horses to the other end of the ring and tack up, saddle, and mount their horse. The winner is the first rider back to the starting point. In musical chairs, the familiar stop-and-get-a-seat elimination game has to be performed by riders dismounting at speed, and quickly leading their horse to an unoccupied seat.

Another popular aspect of gymkhanas is costume classes and musical rides. The former is simply a clothes extravaganza such as one would observe at a fancy dress ball. In musical rides, riding sequences are choreographed and set to a piece of music. Teams of riders and horses carry out certain movement sequences, for example, a figure-eight or a serpentine, and display the ability to make smooth transitions in gait as they go from walk to trot to canter.

Some have criticized gymkhana for the alleged rough treatment of ponies and a lack of serious horsemanship. Nevertheless, many riders who eventually succeed at national, world, and Olympic levels started as youthful novices in pony clubs.

—Scott A. G. M. Crawford

Bibliography: Evans, N. (1995) *The Horse Whisperer*. New York: Delacorte Press. Gordon-Watson, M. (1987) *The Handbook of Riding*. New York: Alfred A. Knopf.

Horseback Riding, Hunters and Jumpers

Hunter and jumper competitions mimic the conditions that foxhunters might encounter, but under controlled conditions. The course uses obstacles that mimic natural barriers, walls, and obstacles. It is a popular sport in North and South America and Europe with men and women competing equally.

History

Modern hunter and jumper equestrian activities are based on the foxhunting tradition. Until Henry I ascended the throne in Britain in the 12th century, only those of royal blood could participate. King Henry granted a charter allowing more widespread participation among the classes.

Gradually, hunting enthusiasts in Britain and America began to seek ways to display the talents of horse and rider in a more controlled environment. As the popularity of hunter seat riding spread, larger outlets dedicated solely to equestrian exhibition emerged. Competitions moved out of the fields and into the show ring, allowing timed jumper divisions and classes stressing equitation to increase in number.

Early shows were judged subjectively; competitors were evaluated by to individualized, variable criteria. In the United States, showing became organized and regulated in 1917 with the establishment of the American Horse Shows Association (AHSA), the national equestrian federation of the United States and the national governing body of equestrian sports.

Rules and Play

The AHSA annually awards medals for three styles of equitation—Hunter Seat, Saddle Seat, and Stock Seat—and oversees more than 2,500 shows as well as American participation in national championships and the Olympics. The British counterpart is the British Equestrian Federation.

In formal show activities, dress is part of the tradition. The hunter rider wears beige, gray, or rust breeches; high boots; a tailored jacket in black, navy, or dark green; a collared shirt for women, shirt and tie for men; and a black velvet safety helmet with a harness. While show jumper riders wear the same attire for most jumper events, riders don white breeches with a black, green, or bright red jacket, high boots, a collared shirt, and helmet for the important Grand Prix event. Hunter and jumper mounts are outfitted with a saddle that is contoured to allow both horse and rider to jump comfortably (called a "close contact" saddle), a bridle with an appropriate bit, and optional pieces of equipment such as leg wraps or bell boots to protect the legs and hooves.

Hunter Seat Equitation

Hunter seat, or English-style riding, is used for all jumping and stresses balance, flexibility, and security both on the flat and over fences. The hunter seat rider must exhibit an erect upper body, lowered heels, raised eyes, and gentle hands held low over the horse's withers or neck.

Hunter seat equitation on the flat is based upon the mastery of correct position at three different gaits, each of which has its own requirements and adjustments.

At the walk, the rider should display classic form while eliciting a forward, energetic walk from the horse.

To move up into a trot, a two-beat gait in which the horse raises its foreleg and opposite-side hind leg concurrently as diagonal pairs, the rider applies pressure equally with both legs to the horse's sides.

A rider asks a horse to canter through a combination of rein and leg pressure.

A secure, balanced riding seat at the three gaits establishes the necessary position for jumping.

The positions assumed while jumping are the half seat and the two-point position. The half seat is used when approaching a jump, and entails lightening out of the saddle and leaning slightly forward to encourage the horse to move upward over the fence. The rider's position while the horse is airborne is called the two-point position, referring to the two points of the body that have contact with the horse in jumping—the thigh and lower leg.

In competition, hunter seat equitation classes are conducted both on the flat and over fences and are divided according to the age of the rider. Riders are judged on their success in creating controlled, elegant ride using the hunt seat.

Hunter Division

Hunt seat riders can participate in hunter division classes. The routines in hunter classes are the same as in hunter equitation, except that the horse is evaluated on its jumping style and overall ability to work as a fox hunter. Classes are broken down by age of the rider and the horse's showing experience, and mounts must be alert, obedient, mannerly, and responsive to the rider, with smooth gaits and talent for jumping.

Jumpers

One of the three Olympic equestrian disciplines, show jumping is a sport of power, speed, grace, and courage. In jumper classes, the horse and rider are judged solely on their ability to complete a course of jumps within a set time limit and without knocking down any obstacles. All riders finishing without time or jumping penalties are invited back for the jump-off—a round in which several jumps are removed or adjusted to make a challenging, condensed course where time and speed

factor into the outcome. The winner of the jump-off, and thus the class, is the rider who finishes the shortened course with the fewest penalties in the fastest time.

International competitions may have more demanding formats, such as additional rounds or speed classes. Most international team competitions, however, including major championships and the Olympics, follow the format of the Prix des Nations, or Nations' Cup: four riders per team jump two rounds, and, if with the lowest score discarded there is an equality of faults, a timed jump-off takes place with the speediest horse and rider combination per nation sent out to claim the title.

Hunter riders, who must perfect mounted balance and control, often go on to become top competitors in the jumper divisions, where they can earn prize money. Although horses in the jumper division do not need to be well-mannered or stylish, favored hunter breeds such as the Thoroughbred, part-Thoroughbred, and Warmblood also make popular jumpers due to their athleticism, intelligence, and spirit. Jumper riders and horses usually begin in Preliminary level classes, then move up to Intermediate and Open/Grand Prix events as they gain experience, success, and prize earnings. Grand Prix competition continues to increase in popularity as a spectator sport, attracting sponsors and participants from around the world.

—MARY CONTI

Bibliography: Decker, Kate Delano-Condax. (1995) *Riding: A Guide for New Riders.* New York: Lyons & Burford. Morris, George. (1990) *Hunter Seat Equitation.* New York: Doubleday.

Horseback Riding, Sidesaddle

Today's sidesaddle rider participates in a variety of equine activities. What began as a graceful and secure way for ladies to ride now provides an alternative way for women to enjoy horseback riding.

History

Although it was a form of riding centuries earlier, by the 12th century, sideways riding was popular in Italy, Spain, and southern France. Within the next two centuries the style progressed northward, where it flourished among the nobility, both male and female, in England and France.

The earliest known "sidesaddles" were little more than pillows attached to a man's saddle to permit the lady to ride pillion style behind the man. While the pillion was popular with the masses, noblewomen were

Riding Astride for Girls (1923).

The fact that the side saddle offers a stronger seat is to my mind its greatest asset. The build of many girls and women handicap them in gaining a secure seat astride. A fat person is particularly at a disadvantage in regard to grip on a cross saddle and when her horse gives an awkward move, her legs are apt to fly out, and her hands to catch hold of her horse's mouth for support. In a side saddle however, such a rider often acquires a firm seat, for there is something definite for her to hold on to, and the leaping head (lower pommel) comes down over her left leg, keeping it in its proper place.

As a rule it takes a much shorter time to gain a side saddle seat because the best and strongest seat astride consists mainly in balance which takes far longer to develop than grip. Although for the first lesson or two both riders may make the same progress, at the end of a month the side saddle rider will be the furtherest advanced. For this reason I believe it is often sensible for those who have never ridden as children, and who do not desire a long apprenticeship, to adopt the latter style. Particularly is this applicable to those who do not intend to ride regularly but only as an occasional means of exercise. The side saddle affords them sufficient security for them to enjoy the sport, while astride they might become totally discouraged.

Among the real horsewomen there are only an exceptional few, say, over thirty years old, who still stand by the cross saddle. Also, while even an indifferent side saddle rider usually stays on when a horse bucks or kicks, it takes a much greater proficiency to do this astride. The same applies when a horse refuses to jump. If the side saddle rider sits square in her saddle there is small chance of her going off, as the pommels prevent her legs from slipping.

Of course there is no comparison in the appearance of the two styles. The girls in the side saddle always looks better. If she is slender and has a good figure she never shows to better advantage than in a well cut habit. If inclined to be fat, her size will be exaggerated astride, while she can look very well in a side saddle provided that she takes pains with her appearance.

When riding saddle horses in the Show Ring, the side saddle rider not only has the advantage of her own appearance but that of her horse as well. In the first place, the judge can see the whole side of her mount with the exception of the small flap of the saddle. If the steed has a long back, the side saddle covers it up, while if his back is one of his good points, it is set off to the best advantage. Moreover, if the saddle is adjusted properly and set well back it will also show off a horse's front.

—Ivy Maddison, *Riding Astride for Girls.*
New York: Henry Holt (1923)

mounted on their own steeds. The saddle that arose for their use started with a small platform or foot-rest called a planchette. Most all of these early sidesaddles had horns; some had horns on the front and the back of the saddle that were useful for handholds.

Catherine de Medici, the daughter-in-law of Francis I of France (1515–1547), has been given the most credit for improving the sidesaddle. Queen Elizabeth I of England was credited with helping the sidesaddle rise in popularity. Between Elizabeth's 1558 ascent to the throne and the early 20th century, no proper Englishwoman would ride in any other style.

The style of the sidesaddle changed very little for nearly 300 years, other than changes to make the saddle fit the horse and rider more comfortably.

The invention of the leaping horn about 1830 far overshadowed previous modifications. By midcentury the leaping horn could be found all over Europe. Importing the idea to the United States seemed to take longer, and the leaping horn was not common until after the Civil War. Even then it was thought of as an expensive luxury needed only by those who went hunting or planned to jump their mounts. During the last half of the century the pommel on the off side of the saddle began to disappear and was gone by the turn of the century.

Sidesaddle riding reached its peak just before World War I and fell out of favor between the two world wars. Several factors contributed, but the emancipation of women, the dire financial straits of the 1930s, and the decline in the number of families who could afford servants to help with the buckles and straps on a lady's saddle all played a part.

Rules and Play

The U.S. bicentennial celebration of 1976 triggered a rush for historical items—including sidesaddles. A similar resurgence of interest occurred in Europe during the 1970s, spurring manufacturers to create innovative, updated designs to fit the new market. All have larger trees and offer longer seat sizes, to accommodate today's larger horses and riders.

Over 2,000 sidesaddle riders practice in the United States and at least that many throughout the rest of the world. Riders who are physically challenged make up 10 percent of these riders. The sidesaddle offers some significant advantages to those who have injuries and physical limitations.

The unique structure of the saddle provides a secure seat that requires little strength or agility. The basic riding position is similar to the astride seat except for the position of the right leg. The right thigh is pressed against the upright pommel to maintain a secure grip. The rider's weight is centered over the horse's back by placing her weight on her thigh rather than her seatbones. For the rider to be secure, the saddle must fit properly.

The modern sidesaddle rider competes in special sidesaddle classes or in open classes against astride riders. Most events are judged on the performance of the horse rather than the saddle used or the style of riding. While a majority of the sidesaddle riders show in pleasure classes, today's riders have expanded their talents to include jumping, contest classes, trail classes, and even team penning. In the costume class, the beautiful period outfits worn in previous centuries make a statement of grace and beauty. Additional events in which aside riders participate include parades, drill teams, and historical reenactments.

More riders are taking up the sport. Some women have discovered that riding aside allows them the freedom to express themselves through their riding; they consider riding aside a feminine art form that should be preserved and cultivated. The timid rider may find she becomes bolder when in a sidesaddle. No longer concerned with etiquette and modesty, the modern rider is adapting the sidesaddle to modern needs. Sidesaddles offer distinct advantages to riders who, for one reason or another, cannot ride astride in comfort. Older riders may find that riding aside allows them to enjoy their horses many decades past the time they would abandon astride saddles. Perhaps, with the aging of the baby boom, sidesaddle will become the style of choice for even more riders.

—LINDA A. BOWLBY

Bibliography: Bowlby, Linda A. (May 1986) "Showing Side Saddle." *Appaloosa World* 6, 11: 46–47+. Macdonald, Janet. (1993) *Teaching Side-saddle.* London: J. A. Allen & Co. Owen, Rosamund. (1984) *Art of Side-Saddle Riding.* London: Trematon Press.

Horseback Riding, Vaulting

Vaulting is the art of gymnastics on a moving horse and dates to ancient times. Modern vaulting developed in Germany in the 1930s and involves compulsory and freestyle events in a number of formats.

History

Early riders needing to mount fast used techniques that are the nexus of modern-day vaulting movements. Ancient drawings from Scandinavia, Africa, and Greece show figures jumping onto horses from the ground or using lances similar to today's vaulting poles. Later depictions from classical Greece and Rome portray equestrian acrobat exhibitions and races in which the jockeys stand upright on horseback while onlookers cheer.

Roman cavalrymen used vaulting to retrieve objects from the ground while riding and to mount quickly in danger. Native Americans practiced moves such as hanging on the side of the horse to escape enemy fire battles. Vaulting performance gained popularity as entertainment in the 18th century when Jacob Bates, a French riding master, began to entertain crowds at fairs with horsemanship exhibitions. He, in turn, inspired Philip Astley, an ex-cavalry sergeant who developed the modern-day circus, to feature equestrian vaulting demonstrations—often called "trick riding"—in his events.

Modern vaulting began in 1930s Germany, where it was used to improve riders' technique. As word of vaulting's benefit spread, the sport gathered international interest. In the late 1960s, the American Vaulting Association (AVA) was founded, and vaulting became a competitive sport in the United States. By 1985 the American Horse Shows Association (AHSA), the U.S. national equestrian organization, had assumed regulation of the sport and the Fédération Equestre Internationale (FEI) had officially recognized vaulting as an international discipline. The world championships have taken place every two years since 1986.

Rules and Play

Modern competitions are judged by the smooth and correct execution of compulsory exercises and freestyle programs by the vaulter's sympathy and harmony with the horse during the event. The four event categories are: team, individual women's, individual men's, and pairs, or pas de deux.

Equines used must be at least six years old and sound. Any breed is acceptable, but successful mounts are those that allow for free gymnastic motion as well as mounting and dismounting at different gaits. Horses with a heavy, draft horse–like build are excellent choices. In vaulting events, the horse is outfitted with a surcingle, a wide strap with two handles called grips, in place of a saddle, with thick pads for protection and to prevent the vaulters from sliding. A longeur stands at the center of the circle and controls the horse's path and gaits using a whip and the longe line attached to the horse's snaffle bit.

Like competitive gymnasts, vaulters tend to be in their teens and early twenties due to the sport's physical flexibility demands. They need no formal training in equitation. Also like gymnasts, they wear colorful leotards and nonskid slippers.

Vaulting competitions are either team or individual events, with compulsory and freestyle, or Kur, classes, both performed at a canter to the left. The six required compulsories stress balance, rhythm, and stability.

- *Basic Riding Seat:* The vaulter sits on the surcingle with his or her legs wrapped around the horse and arms outstretched to the sides.
- *Flag:* The vaulter kneels on the surcingle, then extends the right leg behind and the left arm in front of his or her body, absorbing the motion of the horse so as to maintain limb stillness.
- *Mill:* The vaulter sits forward in the surcingle, then lifts the right leg over the front of the horse to assume sidesaddle position. After holding the sidesaddle position, the vaulter then lifts the left leg over the back of the horse to face backwards. The motion is repeated until the vaulter reassumes the forward position.
- *Scissors:* The vaulter performs the swinging movement like gymnasts on the stationary horse.
- *Stand:* The vaulter assume a completely upright position, standing forward on the horse's back and absorbing motion with the knees.
- *Flank:* The vaulter performs a handstand, then folds the body in half, with both legs together. The legs are swung to the left or right of the horse to assume a side seat position. The vaulter then must swing the legs in an arc over the horse and land firmly on the opposite side ground.

The team Kur competition is a five-minute freestyle routine set to instrumental music. All eight team members compete, but no more than three vaulters may be on the horse at one time. Pas de Deux is a pairs event with two separate freestyle sections, Kur I and Kur II.

Agility is the primary focus in vaulting. In the compulsories, the exhibitors are scored only on performance, which incorporates mechanics, form, security, balance, and consideration of the horse. For the Kur, judges evaluate degree of difficulty: height achieved above the horse, complexity of movements, changes in direction, and demands of suppleness and strength. The composition score considers use of space, variety, artistic merit, pace, and creativity. Time allotments and falls are noted, and a general impression score based upon presentation of the horse and the salute, exit, and

---

Some Horses I Have Rode.

I've rode a heap of horses, and a few of them were fools,
A few were rocky-gaited and another few were mules.
A few were fancy horseflesh that it cost a heap to own,
In colors all the way from black to Appaloosa roan.
A few were hammer-headed, and a few were hard to set,
But purt near all had special traits that I remember yet.
Ol' Prince was just a workhorse that I straddled as a kid,
Without no saddle half the time, but everything he did
Was with a willing spirit, whether tugging at a plow
Or busting over mountain trails to chouse a dodging cow.
Now Fanny was a little bay that throwed me once or twice,
Her step was light and airy, and she held her head up nice.

To ketch out in the pasture, ol' Spike was quite a scamp,
But he sure did savvy cow work, and he always stayed in camp.
Gray Frankie was a sweetie, sure-footed as a bear,
And Dixie was my brother's faithful lion-hunting mare.
Ol' Bill was built right beefy, yet he took a heap of pride
In stepping gay and frolicsome when saddled up to ride.
Smart Nick, our palomino, till he got cut on the wire,
Was gaited like a rockin' chair beside a cozy fire,
Yet still as tough a cowhorse as you'd ever want to straddle,
And prouder than a peacock of his looks beneath a saddle.
I've rode myself some horses, and I hope to ride some more
Before the Big Boss tallies off my final ridin' score.
Ol' Johnny, Dempsey, Trigger—I don't aim to name them all—
The build of some of them was short, the build of others tall.
In some the blood was mustang, and in some the breeding good,
But most of them most always seemed to do the best they could;
And that, my friends, is something that may not be quite so true
Of all the well-known human race—including me and you!

—S. Omar Barker (1894–1985),
Rawhide Rhythms (New York: Doubleday, 1968)

turnout of the team, is given for the combined freestyle and compulsory.

Vaulting is perhaps more widely practiced in Europe but is fast gaining popularity in the United States. Vaulting gained additional recognition as a demonstration sport at the 1996 Olympics in Atlanta, and enthusiasts of the sport hope to see it named an Olympic discipline in the future.

—MARY CONTI

Bibliography: Rieder, Ulrike. (1993) *Correct Vaulting* (U.S. ed.). Bainbridge Island, WA.: American Vaulting Association. Wiemers, Jutta. (1994) *Equestrian Vaulting.* London: J. A. Allen & Co.

Horseback Riding, Western

Western riding is so called because of the type of saddle used, which in turn influences riding style and practice. The style was significantly influenced by the traditions of the cattle rancher, as shown in the equipment, attire, and equine breeds associated with it.

History

Modern Western riding derives from early European horsemanship. The Spanish cavalry, needing security and comfort over long-distance journeys and precise control for perilous battles, used high-pommeled saddles with long stirrups, curb bits, and roweled spurs similar to today's Western tack. Settlers in North and South America adopted the Spanish traditions for riding and handling livestock, and equine breeds particularly suited for cattle work, such as the Spanish Barb, were imported.

Western horses and tack were pivotal in Western land exploration and management. The Western tradition of riding also played a major role in bringing law and order to the American frontier.

The Western, or Stock, saddle is larger and heavier, with a deep seat, long stirrups, and prominent horn on the pommel. These features increase security during tricky herding maneuvers, comfort for long hours spent sitting, and packing room for camping or roping gear. The horse is outfitted with a curb or snaffle bit on its bridle, but a Western rider relies more on a one-handed technique called reining, which along with seat and leg aids is used to control the animal, leaving the other hand free to manipulate roping implements.

Western attire is adapted to long days outdoors: sturdy denim pants, often worn under leather or suede chaps, long-sleeved cotton shirts for protection and coolness, wide-brimmed hats for shade, and thick-soled, heeled leather boots for walking on rough ground and keeping the foot in the stirrup.

Horse breeds common to Western riding are agile, calm, sure-footed, and hardy—important traits for cattle management. They include the American Quarter Horse, Appaloosa, Paint, Pinto, Palomino, Buckskin, Mustang, and Spanish Barb.

Rules and Play

Western horsemanship is still used, although less than in the past, in the modern ranching and livestock industry. The style and tradition thrive more in the show arenas, governed by the regulations of the American Horse Shows Association (AHSA).

Stock Seat equitation is the basic class in which riders are judged on the fundamentals of Western horsemanship. A Stock Seat competitor must display an erect upper body, lowered heels, quiet hands, and alert eyes. Judges look for the correct execution of these positions at the walk, jog (slow trot), and lope (slow canter) in both directions of the ring. Exhibitors are also asked to halt and back a straight line. Those who display the best position while conveying a sense of subtlety, control, balance, and athleticism generally succeed in the show arena.

In Western Pleasure classes, the horse, not the rider, is evaluated at the walk, jog, lope, and hand gallop.

Reining, a Western discipline unto itself, is similar to the sport of dressage. Reining horses are judged on their ability to perform various athletic moves and patterns, showing versatility, energy, and attunement to the rider while working on a slack rein. Reining competitors must perform specific patterns incorporating specified movements, except in the freestyle, which is designed by the rider and set to music. The four-minute exhibition may include costumes and props and sometimes relies upon an applause meter in addition to two or three judges to score competitors.

Exhibitors in the Working Cow Horse division must display traditional Western equitation skills and reining techniques and also show "cow sense"—savvy and intuition in controlling a cow. Cutting, another equestrian sport that requires the horse to manage cattle, gives the horse an entire herd to control and divide as opposed to the Working Cow Horse's single cow.

Trail Horse events test the horse's ability to negotiate obstacles designed to simulate trail conditions. Mounts must demonstrate smooth, comfortable gaits, and the agility, calm, and willingness to deal with obstacles of varying degrees of difficulty. Given the interest in this type of challenge, Western riding seems secure.

—MARY CONTI

Bibliography: Forget, J. P. (1995) *The Complete Guide to Western Horsemanship.* New York: Howell Book House. Strickland, Charles. (1995) *Western Riding.* Pownal, VT: Storey Communications.

Horseshoes

Horseshoe pitching and quoits involve tossing a horseshoe or metal ring over, or as close as possible to, a stake that has been driven into the ground. Both games have long been played recreationally, in informal settings; only horseshoe pitching has developed a routinized competitive tournament schedule.

History

The most common (also speculative) account of horseshoes' origin is that, during the early Roman occupation of Britain, Roman officers played quoits with specially crafted iron rings. Quoits, in turn, were claimed to be the descendant of the ancient Greek discus throw. Common Roman soldiers, unable to afford the fancier equipment, made do with cast-off horseshoes. Quoits itself is certainly an ancient game, played at least since the 2nd century C.E.

Horseshoe pitching in the United States was and is a social game; a 1932 authority called it "a standard informal picnic event." The first competition apparently took place in 1905, when a horseshoe pitching contest was held in Manhattan, Kansas. The genuine horseshoes tournament era began in 1909, in Bronson, Kansas, with the first "World Tournament." Such tournaments were frequent though irregular between 1909 and 1946. Since 1946, when President Harry S. Truman pitched horseshoes on the White House, national tournaments have been held annually.

Rules and Play

As it has been played in England since the 14th century, quoits requires players to toss a metal ring some 8 inches (20 centimeters) across with a 4-inch (10 centimeters) diameter opening—the "quoit"—over, or as near as possible to, a "hob," or stake. Two hobs, each driven flush to the ground or a bit above it, are situated in two clay beds some 18 feet (5.5 meters) apart. The game is won when one participant takes 21 points. Two points are earned for each "ringer," and 1 point for each quoit that lands nearer to the hob than the opponent's.

In the United States, throughout the 19th century, quoits was played in much the same way, though the "hob" might be called a "meg," the throwing distance longer, and the quoit itself either an iron ring or a flat stone.

Much of the art of horseshoe pitching lies in the way the shoe is held and how it is released. The ideal toss is often called the "one-and-a-quarter" and is attributed to one George May who, in 1920, achieved the previously unheard of 50 percent ringer percentage using the technique. The throw sounds easy enough, but takes a good while to perfect. The shoe must be held (if the player is right-handed) by one edge and turned so that both edges are parallel to the player's torso, closed portion to the right and opening to the left.

A "ringing" throw involves an underhand pitch, with a one-quarter turn to the right and, during its progress to the pit, one complete rotation, so that the shoe arrives at the other end of the court perfectly aligned to the stake. Top tournament players routinely score 80 percent ringers.

Horseshoe pitching, though it has achieved a fairly high degree of competitive organization, remains a friendly and inclusive game. It is still a recreation, and even cash prizes, though not negligible, are hardly enough to warrant professional status. There is nothing about the sport that will prevent it from developing an even higher competitive profile in the future, but for now, it manages to offer competitive recognition to its experts while preserving, for the great mass of enthusiasts, the attractions of a simple aiming and throwing game.

—Alan Trevithick

Hunters and Jumpers

See Horseback Riding, Hunters and Jumpers

Hunting

People hunt to get meat to eat, to get meat to sell to others, or for sport. Sport hunting resembles the other two forms only superficially. Typically, it is optional and informed by a profoundly personal relationship, often with a spiritual component, with nondomestic animals in the "wild" setting. Sport hunting is more a process than a goal-oriented behavior; the hunter's motivation and action are as important as the result. Contemporary hunts generally use firearms; historically, many weapons were used. Like subsistence or market hunters, sport hunters used snares, nets, and traps, and they supported efforts to develop new weapons as well and breed companion animals. Raptors, horses, and dogs, both scent and line-of-sight or courser, were all carefully bred for sport afield. Sport hunting motivated much of the development of hand-held firearms.

History

In antiquity, hunting that wasn't for the pot was usually considered as practice for war. For the ancients, the love

Safaris

A safari is a leisure or recreational activity that involves all forms of sport hunting combined with travel and lasting more than a day.

No doubt the many movies and novels involving safaris taking place at the end of the 19th century and through the first quarter of the 20th century helped create today's popular image. Some safaris were composed of many human bearers, a group of hunters, and a rich panoply of tents, outdoor gear, and associated accouterments. Others involved lumbering elephants slowly following the spoor of tiger or water buffalo. In India, sport-minded members of the officer corps enjoyed six or eight weeks of pig-sticking (racing down wild boar with lance and polo pony), setting up tents at a string of likely locations.

Later, with the ascendance of the internal combustion engine, the line of porters toting awkward bundles gave way to sedan cars and trucks bumping and bouncing along in this or that vast wilderness. In many ways the fictive representation, with its mob of support personnel, cluster of hunters, and mass of equipment, was quite accurate.

The concept of the safari matured and spread along with the European presence in colonized areas. Prime participants were employees of the government or colonial residents as well as wealthy sportsmen of all stripe. In the first two of these cases, the individuals were near but not near enough to desirable hunting areas.

Agricultural development may have altered the habitat or displaced existing wildlife. Officers in far-flung empire garrisons would be stationed at strategic sites, unlikely to be pristine wilderness. And of course representatives of chartered companies, governmental functionaries, colonial administrators of all sorts, would most likely be situated in urbanized areas. Yet, it was obvious, a great deal of exciting sport was comparatively easily accessible with the investment of a short journey.

Thus, sportsmen in the above situations quickly developed a tradition of travel linked to the express purpose of sport-hunting opportunities. Since it is quite typical for prey to exist in habitat some distance from the normal human habitation, much hunting automatically involves travel from home to the area of the hunt. A safari extends this basic environmental and cultural reality.

Moreover, since the same idea—travel plus hunting—fits other leisure opportunities, the term has broadened to usefully include the related activity of photo safaris, surf safaris, and so on. In these examples, participants try to "capture" the perfect photograph or the best possible wave. In order to do so, one travels from the normal human residence (now increasingly urbanized) to and through appropriate sites.

Traveling to the area of a hunt, particularly for the opportunity of taking part, is of course a very old phenomenon. The fully formed version, replete with expedition planning and specialized material, developed to coincide with the so-called Golden Age of Exploration in the early and mid-19th century.

Eventually, colonial expansion, as noted above, provided the opportunity for many hunters to enjoy safaris and to develop the concept somewhat differently from merely doing a bit of hunting while on a holiday or in the midst of other sorts of travel. In fact, "safari" was borrowed into English from Swahili, and in that language means literally trip or journey. For this reason, safari implies a bit more than simply traveling to the location of relevant game.

Historically, sport hunting has been strongly linked with socially powerful people and, by extension, their representatives. Throughout history, wardens, professional hunters, and others whose livelihoods devolve from working in the wilds have also occasionally worked to guide sporting hunters. With the development of colonies, a much wider (though still far from poor) segment of hunters was able to take to the field after exotic prey.

After all, local labor was cheap, game plentiful, and pursuit, to say nothing of bags, often unregulated, while the biggest chunk of travel expenses were often underwritten by virtue of traveling from home to abroad on other business. Quickly enough, professional hunters, for example, ivory harvesters in Africa, found commercial safaris, catering to nonresidents, to be a lucrative side line.

With destruction of habitat, diminution of wildlife herds, and increasing regulatory apparatus, commercial harvesting of game became less attractive, especially compared to the relatively low impact of sport safaris. Today's safari is likely quite expensive, geared toward the visitor much more than the resident, and fully regulated. Only the scofflaw poacher slaughters wildlife when the low-impact safari hunt guarantees sustaining a valuable renewable resource, helps fund preservation of habitat, and provides solid economic incentives to sustain the tradition in the wilds.

—*Jon Griffin Donlon*

of hunting was a gift of the goddess, bestowed on man and woman alike. Even then, sport hunters claimed special social probity. According to Xenophon, "not only have all the men who loved hunting been good people, but also the women to whom the goddess has given the love of the chase...." Xenophon gives several examples of important female hunters as if to explain that while less common, they were not rare.

Bows were apparently acceptable in the field (as would be crossbows later) because some prey was fleet of foot or wing. Probity in war and in sport demanded symmetrical weapons: fang to lance, toe to toe.

The reality, if not the idea, of sport as an analog of lethal conflict eroded over time. Eventually, the deeply fulfilling nature of the chase became the attraction. That the hunt was thought of as healthful for itself seems evident.

Rules and Play

Sport hunting is a widely varying practice that does not lend itself to general description of "rules." Hunting laws specify seasons for particular wildlife, weapons permitted, permitted take, and other variables; hunters must be licensed, as well. These laws vary by state. Local custom also influences what is hunted when, and only the naive would claim that all hunters adhere strictly to the rules.

Hunting and Society

Time brought fundamental changes to mankind's relationship with the wilderness and nonhuman animals. The traditional view of animal as consumable was joined by a much more complex appreciation of the place of other living things. The greatest impact was on harvest hunting (especially its industrialized version); the ancient moral relationship with prey was revisited.

As wasteful as some traditional hunting methods were, the technology to destroy entire populations of prey rarely existed. However the machine culture and the industrial-scale harvesting of varied prey by commercial agents in the 18th and 19th centuries brought wildlife destruction truly appalling in scale and magnitude. Whole communities of animals were nearly annihilated. Luckily, by the mid- and late–19th century an increasingly powerful objections were raised to that extreme predation.

Ironically, as senseless as the terrific waste of prey such as bison and pigeon certainly was, the bloodshed took place too far from most citizens for it to register well. Moreover, the marketed product, food, was much more acceptable. What was visible, and what did greatly help lead to widespread support for regulatory apparatus, was the ever expanding fashion industry.

Regulation of Hunting

Much animal law in the United States was initially designed to guarantee access to the outdoors and its bountiful harvest or tended to be "negative in tone, promoting destruction rather than protection." Legislatures were aware of Europe's oppressive game laws and were reluctant to re-create in the United States any of the Old World privileges of elite classes.

These Old World laws, which allowed "gentlemen" to flatten farmer's crops in pursuit of quarry that the yeoman couldn't even lawfully buy, were not made to prevent citizens from enjoying the hunt. Rather, as is often the vouchsafed reason for today's increased regulation, they were made in the yeoman's best interest. That is, they were designed "to prevent persons of inferior rank, from squandering that time, which their station in life requireth to be more profitably employed." With the 19th century's astronomical predation, how-

ever, pressure for conservation law increased in spite of these anachronistic associations.

Moreover, as cynics note, everyone is a conservationist once economic incentive has been removed by the near extermination of the target animal. If the harvest is no longer fruitful, the subject species is likely to be "protected."

Fur and Feathers

In the United States and perhaps elsewhere, restraint instilled by game shortages was attenuated by a growing economy that provided more people with more money. Such consumers liked to display their wealth, and ornaments derived from animals were one means of doing so.

Feather ornament had been popular in Europe since the time of the Crusades, an affectation quite likely picked up from the more sophisticated Islamic enemy, but the demand among 19th-century fashion-conscious women was much greater. This phenomenon nourished advanced environmental impact. What species were not being obliterated by the greedy meat hunters were likely victimized by plume, fur, or hide gatherers.

Negative public reaction ensued, partly in response to the enormous harvest of animals and also by a growing public awareness of the carnage exhibited by women's fashions. Fashion, although neither the cause nor the worst offender, helped fuel change.

The Rise of the Hunter-Naturalist

In 1887 the Boone and Crockett Club was founded, an organization representative of the philosophy of sport hunting that helped reshape traditional hunting beliefs—which valued efficient productivity and valorized food production—to be more practical in an industrial milieu.

Eventually, regulating and taxing sports hunters guaranteed support of vast habitat and wildlife populations, all available for future generations of hunters. Unfettered market gunning clearly would have resulted in a blighted wilderness. So influential and progressive was the code developed in the club that, eventually, much regional and national legislation reflected its philosophical input. The code covered such areas as restricted seasons, protected seasons for mating, gender-based and otherwise limited bags, and outlawing of unfair hunting methods and, of course, poaching. Poaching is an ongoing manifestation of the age-old resistance of some hunters to the control of the hunt by the elite—in contemporary terms, the lawmakers.

Conservation measures were so effective that game multiplied well beyond the requirements of a relatively small sport hunting community. A faux aristocracy (influential land owners, powerful politicians, and representatives of important lineages) went far to guarantee game availability for the public. Such people opted to examine closely the red tooth and talon of nature.

Much of the thrust of early conservation groups was to secure the future of game species; they wanted to regulate "today's" hunting to safeguard tomorrow's. In the meantime, the excesses of the fashion industry, evidence of which was visible on streets, in stores, and at entertainments and social events, helped convince the huge nonhunting public of the conservation law. The active conservation movement in the United States may be associated with four popular magazines that began publication in the late 19th century and formed a base for the quick, countrywide distribution of ideas. These four were, first, *American Sportsman* (1871), then *Forest and Stream* (1873), *Field and Stream* (1874), and finally, the *American Angler* (1881).

By 1900, this amalgam of science, philosophy, and sport yielded the sportsman-hunter (or, perhaps more clearly, the hunter-naturalist), supported by a general public anathema of the horrid squandering of animal and bird parts. This new philosophy incorporated not only the idea relatively well developed in Europe of the "fair hunt" but also a respect for outdoor scientific inquiry and sympathy for game animals. Rather than base the enjoyment of a hunt on quantitative results, the hunter-naturalists endeavored to create a qualitatively measured, rounded experience.

For these sport hunters (who provided the current model), what mattered most was the enjoyment of ritual, the salubrious effects of the outdoors, the heuristic aspects of the chase, and the generally wholesome components of a hunt episode. If they killed, they were to do so in the most sportsmanlike way.

Sport hunting at its best reflects "tradition of self-reliance, hardihood, woodcraft, and marksmanship." Qualities contributing to this alloy included, of course, ideas of gentlemanly conduct imported whole-cloth from the Old World, a vision of action established during the great Age of Adventure and the African safari, and the skills invented to break the American frontier.

—JON GRIFFIN DONLON

Bibliography: Altherr, Thomas L. (1978) "The American Hunter-Naturalist and the Development of the Code of Sportsmanship." *Journal of Sport History* 5, 7–22. Anderson, J. K. (1985) *Hunting in the Ancient World.* Berkeley: University of California Press. Doughty, Robin W. (1975)

Feather Fashions and Bird Preservation: A Study in Nature Protection. Los Angeles: University of California Press. Hobusch, Erich. (1980) *Fair Game: A History of Hunting, Shooting, and Animal Conservation.* New York: Arco Publishing. Schullery, Paul. (1988). *The Bear Hunters Century: Profiles from the Golden Age of Bear Hunting.* Harrisburg, PA: Stackpole Books.

Hurdling
See Track and Field, Hurdling and Running

Hurling
Hurling, considered perhaps the fiercest and fastest of all team games, is the national field game of Ireland. It is played by two teams of 15 players, who use sticks (hurleys or *camans*) made of ash to hit a small, hard ball (slitter or *sliothar*).

History
Hurling is first mentioned in the Irish Annals in a description of the Battle of Moytura (1272 B.C.E.). The invaders first defeated the residents in a game of hurling and then did the same in the battle for the lordship of Ireland. The oldest known Irish legal code, the Brehon Laws, mentions hurling, providing compensation for any player injured during a match.

Although today the game is played largely in the south, it has always been an All-Ireland sport. When England invaded Ireland in 1169, the game may have been imported to England, where traces of such a game survive in Cornwall and elsewhere. In the 14th century the game was so widespread in Ireland that a Kilkenny parliament banned hurling on common lands. By the mid-1800s, large wealthy landowners won and lost much money in bets on matches between teams picked from their tenantry.

Early on, two general forms of the game apparently existed. One was "hurling home," in which parish inhabitants aimed to move the ball across country from a common boundary between two parishes to a designated place. The second, known as "hurling at goals," was more organized, played within the lines of a pitch with a goal at each end and a specified number of players. The modern game probably emerged from two fairly distinct types of "hurling at goals." *Camánacht* (commons), more common in the north, resembled modern shinty and was played in winter, using a gorse stick to hit the ball, mainly along the ground. *Iomain*, common in the south, was played in summer using a much thicker stick (like the modern game) and the ball was frequently played in the air.

The Anglicization of Ireland seems to explain why the modern game of hurling developed most fully in the south, rather than the north. With the passing of the Act of Union in 1800, when many English and Lowland Scottish farmers moved to Ulster, a distinctively Gaelic culture was all but extinguished. But Irish resisted the pacification process, and outside Ulster (and particularly the southeast counties) hurling continued. Hurling declined during the famines of the 1840s, then was revived by the foundation of the Gaelic Athletic Association (GAA), part of the larger cultural resurgence. By then, hurling had vanished almost entirely to the north of Dublin and was suffering (desperately in the south) from famine and flagging nationalism.

This revival of Gaelic sports occurred as the British attempted to commandeer the high ground of popular culture in Ireland. Multiple groups, including the IRB and the Catholic Church, promoted Gaelic sport, particularly hurling, to counter English sporting and cultural influences. Fomenting such resistance, the GAA set up the All-Ireland championships, in which clubs played for the county title; the county winners met for provincial titles, and the provincial semifinalists meeting for All-Ireland honors. This format is followed today; in the All-Ireland hurling finals, teams from 2 of the 26 counties line up before 70,000 spectators and television cameras to engage in the "clash of the ash."

Rules and Play

The object of the game is hit the ball through "H"-shaped goalposts normally located 137 meters (150 yards) apart on a field 82 meters (90 yards) wide. The broad blade of the hurley allows the ball to be hit along the ground and overhead. The ball may be caught in the hand, kicked, and struck but not lifted with the hand. One of the chief skills of the game is to carry the ball on the blade of the hurley by bouncing it up and down while running at full speed. A team scores one point for hitting the sliothar over the cross-bar and between the posts and three points for driving it under the cross-bar into the goal. Since goal scoring in hurling difficult, scores tended to be low; results do not necessarily reflect the flow of the game or the differences between teams.

Fitness and skill are vital for success in hurling because of its pace and duration. Minimal substitutions are allowed, generally for injury. Games are typically 60 minutes (two 30-minute halves), although major provincial and All-Ireland games are 80 minutes (two 40-minute halves). Teams have a goalkeeper and 14 field players (down from the original 21-man teams). Appearances aside, statistics suggest that hurling is in fact less dangerous than any of the codes of football.

The All-Ireland hurling final at Croke Park, dominated by teams from Tipperary, Kilkenny, and Cork, is now a festival of nationalism and attendance for senior Irish politicians is almost mandatory. Increasing commercialization and sponsorship of the All-Ireland championship have raised the profile of the contest, and expatriate Irish now see the final of this unique and distinctly Irish game—on satellite television.

—TIMOTHY J. L. CHANDLER

Bibliography: Mandle, William. (1987) *The Gaelic Athletic Association and Irish Nationalist Politics, 1884–1924.* London: Helm. Smith, Raymond. (1969) *The Hurling Immortals.* Dublin: Spicer. Sugden, John, and Alan Bairner. (1993) *Sport, Sectarianism and Society in a Divided Ireland.* Leicester, UK: Leicester University Press.

Iaido

Iaido is the Japanese martial art of drawing and cutting in the same motion, or "attacking from the scabbard." Iaido is considered a method of self-development but is also practiced as a sport, with two competitors performing side by side, and a panel of judges declaring a winner.

History

The idea of cutting from the draw may have originated as early as the 11th century, but modern Iaido dates to about 1600. Iaido is practiced solo with real blades, in set routines called kata. Most styles trace their origin to Jinsuke Shigenobu (ca. 1546–1621), whose followers developed hundreds of different styles, dozens of which are still practiced. Today the two most popular are the Muso Jikiden Eishin Ryu and the Muso Shinden Ryu.

In the mid-20th century two major governing bodies for iaido were formed; the All Japan Iaido Federation, and the Iaido section of the All Japan Kendo Federation. Both organizations developed common sets of kata to allow students of different styles to practice and compete together. Although not overly common even in its country of origin, iaido has followed the Japanese martial arts around the world.

Rules and Play

The art has had many names over the years, but iaido was accepted about 1930. The "I" comes from the word *ite* (presence of mind) and the "ai" from an alternate pronunciation of the word *awasu* (harmonize) in the phrase *kyu ni awasu* (flexible response in an emergency).

The art is a Japanese *budo* and as such is intended mainly as a method of self-development and appeals to those looking for something deeper than a set of fighting skills. The concentration and focus needed to perfect the movements of drawing and sheathing a sharp sword while watching an (imaginary) enemy benefit the mind. The art also demands excellent posture and the ability to generate power from many positions. For many years iaido was considered esoteric, and it was often assumed one had to be Japanese to fully understand it. In the past decades that thinking has changed and iaido is now practiced around the world. Apart from its exotic look, iaido does not generally appeal to spectators, being restrained and quiet in its performance.

The main practice is done alone, and iaido kata contain four parts, the draw and initial cut (*nuki tsuke*), the finishing cut(s) (*kiri tsuke*), cleaning the blade (*chiburi*), and replacing the blade in the scabbard (*noto*). The swordsman learns many patterns of movement for dealing with enemies who may attack alone or in groups from various angles.

One of the simplest kata is as follows: From a kneeling position the sword is drawn from the left side and a horizontal cut is made from left to right while stepping forward. The sword is raised overhead and a two-handed downward cut is made. The blade is then circled to the right and the imaginary blood is flicked off while standing up. The feet are switched while checking the opponent, and the blade placed back into the scabbard while kneeling.

Various styles of iaido may practice with the long sword (over 60 centimeters [about 2 feet]), the short sword (30–60 centimeters [1–2 feet]), or the knife (under 30 centimeters [less than 1 foot]). Many styles also include partner practice in the form of stylized kata performed with wooden blades for safety.

The Japanese Sword

Iaido is practiced with the Japanese sword. This weapon has, for hundreds of years, been considered both a weapon and a work of art.

The first swords in Japan were straight double- and single-edged weapons called *ken*, likely created on the Asian mainland. Around 700 A.D. a native form called the *tachi* was created which was single-edged and curved. A relatively long, light blade useful for fighting on horseback, the *tachi* was worn on the left side, edge down, suspended from cord hangers. By the mid-1500s a shorter, more robust blade called a *katana* had became popular. This was worn edge up and with the scabbard through the belt rather than hung on a cord. The *katana* was mostly used two-handed but was otherwise similar to the *tachi*.

The Japanese blade was forged in a specialized manner. Pieces of smelted iron from a charcoal furnace were hammered and folded repeatedly using a charcoal fire. This created a mostly homogeneous piece of steel of a certain carbon content. Several pieces of steel were then placed together and forge welded so an inner core of low carbon was surrounded by a layer of high carbon steel. The blade was then hammered into shape.

The blade was coated with clay, thicker along the back and thinner at the edge, then heated and cooled in water. The edge cooled quickly and the back more slowly, thus creating a blade with small, hard crystals of metal on the edge and larger crystals on the back. The differing carbon contents and crystal type created a blade with a very hard (brittle) edge that would resist dulling, and a relatively more flexible back to prevent the blade from shattering on impact.

During many years of conflict, the sword was considered a secondary weapon on the battlefield, behind the bow or pole weapons such as the spear. If the primary weapon was lost, it was necessary to get the sword into play quickly and this is often seen as the beginning of Iaido techniques.

During the Tokugawa period (1603–1868) the Samurai class ruled the country and one of their symbols of rank was wearing two swords. The sword thus became the primary weapon of *budo* and hundreds of sword schools were developed, many surviving into the modern era. During this time an appreciation of the sword as an art object began, which continues today with thousands of sword collectors worldwide.

—*Kim Taylor*

Iaido has grading systems administered by two governing bodies. The All Japan Kendo Federation (and the International Kendo Federation) bases its curriculum mainly on a common set of 10 techniques, while the All Japan Iaido Federation has a set of 5. The swordsman must perform various techniques from these common sets. For the senior grades, techniques from an old style (*koryu*) must also be performed. A judging panel observes the performance and passes or fails the challenger. Both organizations use the *Kyu-Dan* system of ranking, with several student or *kyu* grades and 10 senior or *dan* grades.

Some older styles of iaido never joined a major organization. They argue that an organization containing several styles and a common set of techniques will lead to a modification or dilution of the pure movements of the individual style, and that all styles will eventually come to look alike.

Iaido competitions are becoming more common outside Japan. The usual format consists of two competitors performing several kata side by side, with a panel of judges deciding on the winner, who then moves on to the next round. The major organizations hold a number of competitions each year, and the International Kendo Federation is considering a world championship for iaido.

As in many martial arts, there is an ongoing discussion about whether competition is good in an activity intended to improve the practitioner. Those in favor of competition will point out that all sports benefit the players. Their opponents will suggest that the benefits of martial arts are quite different and incompatible with the benefits derived from competition. As is also true of other martial arts, the dispute is not likely to be resolved soon.

—KIM TAYLOR

Bibliography: Craig, Darrell. (1988) *Iai: The Art of Drawing the Sword.* Tokyo: Charles E. Tuttle. Taylor, Kim. (1992, 1994) *Kim's Big Book of Iaido.* Vols. 1–5. Guelph: Sei Do Kai. Warner, G., and Donn F. Draeger. (1982) *Japanese Swordsmanship.* New York: Weatherhill.

Ice Boating

Ice boating is a fast-paced winter sport that is also called ice yachting. An ice boat is propelled by the wind, and its basic design resembles a sailboat, with a hull, mast, and sails, plus runners, attached to its flat-bottomed hull, whose blades glide along the ice. Ice boats are sailed on frozen lakes, rivers, or bays, primarily in northern regions of Europe and North America, with specific weather conditions that freeze the water but also keep the ice clear of snow.

History

The birthplace of modern ice boating is often cited as 18th-century Holland, where people sailed wind-powered boats on the winter ice, but the sport was also practiced elsewhere in Europe. In America, regions of New York State and New Jersey were early centers for the sport in the 19th century. It subsequently became popular in the Upper Midwest United States and in Canada.

Early ice boats were very basic, with crude skate-like runners and simple sails and rigging. Some ice boats were merely conventional sailboats with runners attached to them. Starting in the mid-19th century, larger and more complex ice boats began to be built. In the United States these were often called Hudson River ice yachts, and they were usually owned by the very wealthy.

In the 20th century, ice boating's popularity spread with the development of small, inexpensive, portable boats. This trend began in 1931 in Milwaukee, Wisconsin, when an iceboater named Starke Meyer designed a boat that was steered by a pivoted runner in the bow (front) instead of the stern (rear), which had previously been more common. The Joys family, who were professional sailmakers in Milwaukee, devised a similar ice boat.

Ice boaters have formed many organizations over the years to sponsor races and other activities. The Poughkeepsie, New York, Ice Yacht Club, founded in 1869, was the first formal ice boating group in the United States.

Rules and Play

Like other sailors, ice boaters steer their craft, and pull in or let out their sails, to take best advantage of the direction and speed of the wind. An ice boat also has a pivoted runner and tiller in the bow or stern, which is turned to steer the boat (similar to the rudder on a sailboat). Iceboats also heel, or tip to one side, when running fast.

However, ice boating also involves unique skills and conditions. Ice boats do not experience the resistance that slows sailboats when moving through the water. The fast-moving ice boat also generates a separate wind, which increases its speed to three or four times the natural wind. Ice boats have unique steering characteristics, and the skipper must be careful to avoid spinning out of control on the slippery ice. Safety is a crucial consideration and helmets and other protective equipment are worn.

Modern ice boats have many designs and sizes. Boats are classified either by the size of their sail area or by the boat's design. Sail sizes are divided into classes, from sail areas of 23 square meters (250 square feet) or more to less than 7 square meters (75 square feet) of sail area. These are usually designated from Class A (large) to Class E (small). Design categories specify particular types of ice boats. The DN, for example, usually has a hull 3.7 meters (12 feet) long, 2.4-meter (8-foot) runners, and 5.5 square meters (60 square feet) of sail. The somewhat larger Skeeter has a hull about 6 meters (20 feet) long or longer and 7 square meters (75 square feet) of sail.

Courses for ice boat racing are determined by the direction of the wind and are marked by buoys some distance apart, commonly a mile. Judging is based on a combination of speed and the ability of the sailor to control the craft and follow the course as closely as possible.

—JOHN TOWNES

Bibliography: Roberts, Lloyd, and Warner St. Clair. (1989 [1980]) *Think Ice! The DN Ice Boating Book.* Burlington, VT: International DN Ice Yacht Racing Association.

Indy Auto Racing

The Indianapolis 500 is one of the world's premier auto races. It is the fastest long-distance event of its kind in the world, and its $8-million-plus purse is the largest offered for a racing event.

History

James A. Allison and Carl G. Fisher were the senior backers of the financial conglomerate that built the $2^1/_2$-mile oval macadam track in 1909. The race was first held on Memorial Day, 1911, and is still run annually on that holiday weekend. American-born Ray Harroun won the first Indianapolis 500 at an average speed of 74.59 miles per hour (mph). Critics of the sport cautioned that this was far too fast, and no one would be ever able to safely race faster than 100 mph.

In the early years, the cars were semitrack or road-racing vehicles with engines of 600-cubic-inch capacity. European automakers Peugeot, Mercedes, and Delage scored early successes during the 1910s. Over the years, cars evolved from the traditional cigar shape with upright cockpit set on four wheels to today's more compact, sleek, ground-hugging models.

Safety became a concern relatively early. In 1935, crash helmets were made mandatory for drivers, and a year later safety aprons were built so that a car could slide into the infield instead of being bounced back into the middle of the track and the path of a gaggle of speeding roadsters. In 1936, retaining walls were added and for the first time in years, no deaths or serious accidents occurred.

The early macadam surface proved to be treacherous, and was replaced with more than three million paving bricks. The resulting nickname, "The Brickyard," endures although the surface is now asphalt.

Up until the 1960s the Indianapolis 500 remained the greatest auto race in America. Then for two years in

Who's Who in the Pit Crew?

While a pit crew may be a 15-member team, only 6 are allowed to go over the wall at one time. Clearly, some do double duty. According to the *Marlboro Racing News,* these are the specific pit crew responsibilities that go on under the overall supervision of managers and advisers:

- Starter
- "Dead man"—controls the amount of fuel being delivered
- Fuel hose assistant
- Fire extinguisher—washes away fuel spillage as the car takes on the methanol
- Tire passer
- Inside front person—changes the inside front tire with an air gun and aims to do the job in 6–8 seconds
- Outside front person—changes the outside front tire;
- Fuel man—fits the fuel nozzle into the car's fuel tank (wears a three-layer fire suit)
- Jack and vent man—uses the air jack, which raises the car for tire changes
- Inside rear person—changes the left inside tire
- Outside rear person—changes the outside rear tire
- Lollipop man—has a special sign to show the driver his pit location and stopping point
- Board man—gives the driver critical information and instructions and vital information (increasingly, however, this information is relayed to the driver by car radio)
- Numerous expert engineers and mechanics

—Scott A. G. M. Crawford

a row, 1965 and 1966, Indy was won by a Formula 1 (Grand Prix racing) driver from overseas. With these victories (Scotsman Jim Clark and Englishman Graham Hill, respectively) the Indianapolis 500 became the world's most famous car chase. This trend continues with drivers such as Brazilian Emerson Fittipaldi (1989 and 1993 winner) and Canadian Jacques Villeneuve (1995 winner).

During the 1950s and early 1960s the Indy was dominated by the Offenhauser racer with its engine at the front end. However, under the influence of European-based Formula 1 racing, this shifted to rear-engine Grand Prix–type racers. In 1965, 27 of the 33 cars at Indianapolis used rear-mounted engines. Other innovations through the years have included turbine-powered cars and four-wheel-drive vehicles; subsequent rule changes have excluded some innovations.

The thrill of the race has long been tempered by tragedy. A total of 66 people, including 40 drivers, 14 mechanics, 2 track workers, 9 spectators, and 1 bystander outside the track, have been killed or fatally injured at the speedway (including pre-500 races of 1909 and 1910). On 16 May 1996, 37-year-old American Scott Brayton, the most experienced driver in the field for the Indianapolis 500 auto race, died during a trial run at the Indianapolis Motor Speedway when his car slammed into a wall at 230 mph after a tire deflated.

Rules and Play

The current track surface is asphalt. The long straights on the Indianapolis track measure 3,300 feet and the short straights 660 feet, the turns are 1,320 feet long, and there is a banked elevation of 9 feet, 6 inches.

The field is restricted to the 33 fastest contenders, who compete for starting position in qualifying runs in the weeks before the actual race. They travel counterclockwise around the track, which is banked at a 16-degree angle.

In the 1995 Indy car season the contests were being fought out by primarily Honda, Mercedes-Benz, and Ford Cosworth engines. In 1996, the same companies continue to battle for supremacy, joined by Toyota.

The Indy Cars

In 1990, Artie Luyendyk of the Netherlands triumphed at Indianapolis with an average speed of 185.984 mph; speeds at the 1995 race averaged 230 mph.

Technology exists today to produce Indy 500 racers capable of running as fast as 300 mph. Concerns about drivers' safety keep such vehicles out of the race.

Safety remains a primary concern of the race's organizers. Today, the racing vehicles are designed so that the driver is protected by a super-strong steel skeleton frame crafted into the chassis of the racer. In any accident, the front, sides, and end portion of these racers crumple easily to absorb high levels of the crash velocity. The inner pod, rather like an ejection seat in a jet plane, is designed to anchor, stabilize, and safeguard the driver.

The World of the Indy

Today the Indianapolis raceway complex is a city in itself, with amusement park, motels, recreational vehicle campground, and golf course, plus the Indianapolis Motor Speedway Hall of Fame Museum, which houses nearly 100 classic racing cars from all over the world. More than 30 Indianapolis 500 winning cars are on display, including vehicles whose names mean little today—such as Stutz, National, and Duesenberg.

The history of the Indianapolis 500 understandably is built around great drivers, great machines, and great races. Less visible, but equally important, is the key role of the pit crew. The margin of victory, especially in modern racing, clearly shows that this "team" effort is paramount. At the 1995 Indianapolis 500 the pit crew of winning driver Jacques Villeneuve changed all four tires and filled the racer with 23 gallons of methanol in 11 seconds.

The pit crew is directed by the team owner. In the history of the Indianapolis 500, one of the most successful team owners has been Roger Penske, who, up to 1994, raced cars in 26 Indianapolis 500 races and won 10. Penske also illustrates the radical shifts in fortune that occur in racing. In 1995, Penske's brand-new PC-24 cars did not adjust to the Indy course and their Mercedes engines did not challenge the Ford and Honda turbo V-85; as a result, his drivers, Emerson Fittipaldi and Al Unser Jr. (winners in 1993 and 1994 respectively), did not even start the race.

Modern Indy race drivers train and condition their bodies like other athletes. Emerson Fittipaldi, for example, regularly runs 5 miles (8 kilometers) a day and American driver Parker Johnstone revealed that he gets fit for driving through triathlon training. Drivers need to be superb athletes capable of enduring punishing conditions. At the Michigan 500 (an Indy 500 race on the 1995 PPG series), the air temperature was 95 degrees F (35 degrees C) and the surface track temperature reached 130 degrees F (54 degrees C). The eventual winner, Scott Pruett, defeated the runner-up, Al Unser Jr., by less than one car length after 500 miles (806 kilometers) of racing!

Prizes awarded since the first race in 1911 through 1996 total more than $100 million. Winner Buddy Lazier's $1,367,854 in 1996 raised the total for all winners to $19,743,169, more than half of that coming since 1983. The race draws the largest crowd of spectators—300,000 to 400,000—of any auto race.

Social analyst Lewis Mumford has criticized automobile racing as a sport that draws spectators mostly because of the possibility of a high-speed crash—perhaps valid in some cases. Yet this view overlooks the most lasting attraction of the sport: watching the skill and mental mastery of the drivers. It is the drivers who provide the "character" of the race.

—SCOTT A. G. M. CRAWFORD

Bibliography: Georgano, G. N., ed. (1971) *The Encyclopedia of Motor Sport.* New York: Viking Press. Rutherford, J. (1983) *Indianapolis Year Book.* Indianapolis, IN: Carl Hungess Publishing.

In-line Skating
See Skating, In-line

Intercollegiate Athletics

Intercollegiate athletics began and continue in Great Britain and in many other Commonwealth countries. But no other nation comes remotely close to duplicating the popular attention or the huge expenditures of money and effort that Americans lavish on college and university athletic programs.

Intercollegiate athletics in the United States includes football bowl games and championship basketball tournaments in which gifted and well-trained athletes under the supervision of expert coaches compete before national television audiences. The elite men's football and basketball programs generate huge revenues for their universities, although players are forbidden by anachronistic canons of amateurism from accepting anything more than free tuition, meals, and housing for their labors. Under intense pressure to win from alumni and fans and lured by the huge revenues generated by a successful program, universities and alumni boosters have staked inordinate amounts of institutional prestige on the athletic prowess of athletes in their late teens and early twenties. Their excesses have repeatedly created scandals that have tarnished the reputations of otherwise outstanding institutions.

The U.S. intercollegiate sporting universe also includes thousands of male and female athletes who compete in relative obscurity in non-revenue-producing sports at large universities and thousands more who are ordinary, nonscholarship students at smaller colleges and universities who devote themselves to sports they love.

History
Intercollegiate athletics began in the early 19th century at English universities and spread to the elite universities of the northeastern United States, the product of a complex interaction of social, cultural, and economic factors. The various sports embraced by collegians were themselves products of societal modernization, which brought uniform rules, quantifiable statistics, and rationalized training regimens to the sporting world, thus facilitating the evolution of folk games into modern sports. Efficient systems of transportation and communications made intercollegiate competition practical, and consumers with increasing levels of disposable income and an appetite for commercialized entertainment financed the creation and expansion of college athletic programs.

In the early 19th century, students at both U.S. and English colleges established informal clubs that sponsored intramural competition in crew, soccer, track and field, and bat and ball games. Intercollegiate competition emerged when these student athletic clubs began to schedule matches against their counterparts at other colleges. Crew was the first intercollegiate sport on both sides of the Atlantic. Oxford and Cambridge staged the first intercollegiate rowing competition at Henley in 1829, and these contests became an annual event a decade later. Students at the elite colleges of the U.S. Northeast expressed their strong cultural affinity for the English upper class by forming rowing clubs in the 1830s. The rowing clubs at Harvard and Yale staged the first intercollegiate athletic competition in the United States at New Hampshire's Lake Winnepesaukee in 1852. Ivy League schools sporadically held intercollegiate rowing competitions over the next several years. Although competition was interrupted by the Civil War, crew emerged as the most popular U.S. intercollegiate sport after the war. Like crew, intercollegiate baseball began before the Civil War and became increasingly popular in the postbellum years. Intercollegiate track and field matches also emerged in the United States after the Civil War.

The rise of intercollegiate athletics coincided with and was made possible by the reversal of the cultural antipathy toward sports shared by Calvinists and conservative evangelicals in both England and America. The muscular Christianity movement, which began in English private schools (called public schools in England) and universities in the 1850s, rejected the Pauline elevation of spirit over body and advanced physical exercise as a complementary component of spiritual development. The theologically liberal proponents of muscular Christianity rejected religious conservatives' belief that sports were "devilish pastimes" that encouraged idleness and glorified the inherently corrupt and sinful human body. Thomas Hughes's 1857 novel *Tom Brown's School Days* extolled the salutary moral effect of competitive sports on the students of England's Rugby School and strongly influenced the Anglo-American elite to view sports as a means of enhancing the spiritual and moral development of young men.

The theological liberalism that informed muscular Christianity was also linked to a fundamental transformation of U.S. higher education in the mid- to late 19th century. The traditional American pedagogical paradigm posited that young men should be trained in theology, moral philosophy, and the classics under rigid standards of discipline and piety. Intercollegiate sports were utterly out of place in this austere, theologically conservative environment. The progressive educational model adopted after the Civil War by elite northeastern colleges offered a professionally oriented curriculum, greater student autonomy, and a more secularized campus atmosphere. Intercollegiate sports were a manifestation of the new level of freedom enjoyed by students. Many progressive educators, eager to shed traditional canons of piety, embraced athletics as a healthful and morally beneficial extracurricular activity, and academics who opposed this trend found themselves powerless to quell the rising student mania for competitive sports.

The rise of American football in the latter decades of the 19th century transformed American intercollegiate athletics into a commercialized, professionalized form of mass entertainment that differed radically from the English model. The football teams of Princeton and Rutgers met in New Brunswick, New Jersey, on 6 November 1869, but this first intercollegiate football game in the United States was played under something approximating soccer rules. These schools played occasional soccer games against one another over the next several years, although teams negotiated the rules prior to each game. Harvard students, however, believed rugby to be superior to soccer (association football). Student representatives from Harvard, Yale, Princeton, and Columbia adopted the Harvard rules in 1876, and formed the Intercollegiate Football Association to regulate the sport. A series of rule changes adopted between 1876 and 1882 transformed rugby into the more complex American game of continuous possessions and set plays.

Football superseded crew as the most popular U.S. intercollegiate sport by the mid-1880s, in part because it fit well with the nascent movement to revitalize the competitive spirit of the northeastern elite. By the 1890s, many opinion leaders worried obsessively that young men raised in ease and affluence would never acquire the aggressiveness required to prosper in the cut-throat world of Gilded Age capitalism. They popularized the Cult of the Strenuous Life, a program of vigorous physical training and competitive sports for young men, as a means of countering the stultifying "overcivilization" of the bourgeois domestic sphere.

Competitive sports were believed to inculcate the masculine vigor and naked will to win that were essential to the social Darwinian worldview. The violence and martial overtones of football made it especially attractive to a generation of American men who despaired that they might never have the chance to test their manhood on the battlefield as their fathers had done in the Civil War. Yet football's advocates declared that it was no mere slugfest in which sheer brawn necessarily prevailed. The set plays, intricate teamwork, and division of labor by position created by the new rules were hailed as a reflection of the form and function of the modern industrial corporation. Football's proponents saw the gridiron as a training ground for the young men being groomed to fill top management positions in the increasingly complex world of American business. Elite opinion makers thus helped define football as both "scientific" and "manly," and this dualistic interpretation of the cultural text of football became widely accepted. Football's violence rendered it more "manly" than crew, baseball, or track, but its technical complexity allowed its proponents to define it as more "scientific" than the working-class sport of prizefighting.

The explicit linkage of competitive sports with the bourgeois construction of masculinity stunted the development of women's intercollegiate athletics. The Victorian medical establishment provided pseudoscientific legitimacy to the cultural construction of women as too physically and emotionally delicate to tolerate the stress of competitive sports. Despite these obstacles, students at elite women's colleges and some coeducational state universities began playing intramural and occasional intercollegiate games of baseball, croquet, tennis, and other sports in the 1870s and 1880s. Basketball became the most popular sport among college women soon after its invention in 1891, although female physical educators modified the rules to reduce the degree of competitiveness and physical exertion. Female players were restricted to specific zones on the court to prevent them from running the court, "overguarding" the ball handler was a foul, and defenders were not allowed to steal the ball. Yet the early development of women's intercollegiate athletics peaked around the turn of the century and did not resume its expansion until after World War II. Female physical educators led a movement to restrict female college athletic programs to intramural competition only. In 1923, the Women's Division of the National Amateur Athletic Federation formalized the opposition to competitive athletics that had hardened over the previous two decades by adopting a resolution opposing intercollegiate athletic competition for women.

Female physical educators were adamant that women's sports not become a spectator-centered form of commercial entertainment like football. Early football, like all other intercollegiate sports, had been run by and for students. Yet the explosive growth of football's popularity in the 1880s ended student control. The football team quickly became a locus of institutional pride and identity among students and alumni,

and games began to attract a fan base among the general population. Attracted by the prestige and lucrative gate receipts generated by a successful football team, private athletic associations dominated by alumni football boosters assumed control from the students and transformed football into an entertainment spectacle.

Yale Leads the Way

Under the direction of Walter Camp (1859–1925), Yale University established the prototypical big-time intercollegiate athletic program. Camp, popularly known as the Father of American Football, played football at Yale from 1876 until 1882 and dominated the rules committee that transformed rugby into American football. After graduation, Camp directed the Yale football program as the team's unpaid graduate adviser. While maintaining the fiction of student control, Camp instituted a rationalized and hierarchical system of selecting, training, and supervising the Yale team. He also created the Yale Athletic Association, an autonomous body over which Yale administrators had no direct control, to manage intercollegiate athletics at the university. These modern management techniques enabled Yale to dominate intercollegiate football during its formative decades. Between 1876 and 1900, Yale boasted a record of 231 wins, 10 losses, and 11 ties. The modern university athletic department evolved from the model established by Camp at Yale. Revenue maximization, the pursuit of victory at all costs, and resistance to faculty and administration oversight became the controlling principles of American intercollegiate athletics and supplanted the English athletic ideals of student control, gentlemanly competition, and elitist amateurism. Although baseball, crew, basketball, track and field, and other intercollegiate sports were less popular and generated smaller revenues, the athletic associations that controlled football assumed authority over them as well. Over the next several decades, university administrations gained administrative authority over these private associations, but the legacy of athletic autonomy has been a persistent source of conflict and scandal in American intercollegiate athletics.

Football became increasingly commercialized in the 1890s, and the money and prestige that accrued to winning football programs created a relentless pressure to win. Although football was clearly a profitable commercial venture, and Camp's professionalized management philosophy was adopted by other schools eager to emulate his success, American universities doggedly maintained a rhetorical allegiance to English-style canons of athletic amateurism. Yet the meritocratic ideal integral to modern sports and the democratic ideology that formed the core of the American national identity were incompatible with the elitism of amateur sportsmanship. Collegiate administrators and athletic authorities were unable to confront this fundamental contradiction that lay at the heart of their system of intercollegiate athletics, and the world of college football became increasingly chaotic. "Ringers" or "tramp athletes" moved from school to school, selling their athletic services to the highest bidder and making little pretense of being legitimate students. Many intercollegiate baseball players joined semiprofessional and minor league teams during the summer months, often playing under assumed names.

Southern, midwestern, and Pacific Coast universities started intercollegiate football and baseball programs in the late 1880s and early 1890s, and they were far less devoted to English-style notions of amateurism than the elite private colleges of the Northeast. Although providing any form of financial assistance to an athlete, including tuition scholarships, room, and board, violated the prevailing conception of amateurism, no regulatory body possessed the authority to establish and enforce a uniform set of standards. Charges and countercharges of unethical recruitment and payments to players reverberated through the collegiate sporting world and became fodder for the new cadre of muckraking journalists eager to expose corruption in American institutions.

These incessant scandals tarnished the image of intercollegiate sports in the 1890s and the first decade of the 20th century, but a crisis sparked by excessive football violence produced lasting institutional change. The rules of that era prohibited the forward pass and encouraged mass momentum plays such as the infamous flying wedge. Players who wore no helmets and little protective padding were extremely vulnerable to serious injury, and the increasing number of gridiron deaths inflamed public opinion. Universities throughout the Southeast canceled the final month of the 1897 football season following the death of a University of Georgia player during a game, and the Georgia legislature passed a bill that made playing football a felony punishable by a year on the chain gang. While the governor vetoed the legislation and most southern colleges resumed limited football schedules the following year, the outcry over both football violence and the ubiquitous allegations of professionalism intensified over the next several years. Even President Theodore Roosevelt, the leading apostle of the Cult of the Strenuous Life, publicly pressured Walter Camp, and the Intercollegiate Rules Committee, which he controlled, to reduce the level of football violence.

The Progressive Era

Eighteen gridiron fatalities during the 1905 season brought the football crisis to a head. Stanford and the University of California replaced football with rugby, and other schools threatened to ban football outright. A dissident faction of universities comprising mostly midwestern institutions forced Camp and his northeastern cohorts to acquiesce in the creation of the Intercollegiate Athletic Association (IAA) in January 1906. The IAA, which became the National Collegiate Athletic Association (NCAA) in 1910, was more broadly representative of institutions from outside the Northeast than Camp's Rules Committee. The NCAA carried out its mandate to open up college football. Its first significant action was to legalize the forward pass, which ended the massive pileups in which so many injuries had occurred. The more open, offense-oriented game spawned by the series of rules changes begun in 1906 made football more exciting and more marketable to a public increasingly interested in spectator sports.

The creation of the NCAA reflected the Progressive era impulse to establish institutionalized, bureaucratic control over an increasingly complex modern society. Although its power was initially limited to the establishment of standardized rules for all intercollegiate sports, over the succeeding decades it gradually assumed responsibility for the regulation of recruiting and player eligibility, the management of national championship tournaments, and most important, the negotiation of television contracts and distribution of television revenues. Regional athletic conferences such as the Western Conference, the forerunner of the Big Ten, were created during this period as part of this progressive search for order. These regional conferences retained the primary responsibility for the establishment and enforcement of recruiting and eligibility standards until after World War II, when the NCAA assumed this duty. Conference regulations eliminated some of the more flagrant abuses involving tramp athletes and the open bidding for the services of star athletes. University administrators, athletic authorities, and the general public tacitly redefined the definition of amateurism to include these highly professionalized college athletic programs.

Americans' appetite for sports made a quantum leap during the 1920s, an era popularly celebrated as the Golden Age of Sports. Increasingly sophisticated sports coverage in various media dramatized sports competition and popularized star players and coaches to a rapidly expanding national audience. Aided by this mutually profitable relationship with the media, college football became a multimillion-dollar entertainment industry in the 1920s. College football attendance doubled and ticket revenues tripled during the decade. The spectator-friendly game of dazzling forward passes and breakaway runs was uniquely positioned to benefit from the increased public demand for commercialized sports. Professional baseball was clearly the leading American sport, but no major league teams were located west of the Mississippi or south of St. Louis. College football, on the other hand, was a "major league" sport available to consumers in every section of the nation. College teams from the South, Midwest, and Pacific Coast became popular symbols of regional and local pride within the unifying framework of intersectional competition.

Midwestern universities supplanted elite northeastern schools as the leading football powers during the 1920s, a trend popularly hailed as a "democratization" of intercollegiate football. Large numbers of middle- and working-class fans who had never attended college nonetheless became passionate supporters of college teams, and game-day crowds of 50,000 or more filled massive new campus stadiums. Catholics across the nation formed a legion of "subway alumni" who cheered Notre Dame's successes in the formerly elitist bastion of intercollegiate football. Knute Rockne (1888–1931), the Norwegian immigrant who coached Notre Dame from 1918 until 1931, combined superior motivational skills, tactical innovations such as the Notre Dame shift, and a flair for manipulating the press to produce a phenomenal record of 105 victories, 12 defeats, and 5 ties. Columnist Grantland Rice (1880–1954), the most influential and widely syndicated of 1920s sports journalists, immortalized the 1924 Notre Dame backfield as the Four Horsemen. The death of Notre Dame halfback George Gipp (1895–1920) and Rockne's emotional admonition to "win one for the Gipper" in a 1928 locker room speech have become a cherished part of American folklore. Rockne himself died in a 1931 plane crash, and his own popular legend was embellished in the 1940 film *Knute Rockne—All American*. Ronald Reagan's portrayal of the already legendary Gipp boosted his career and earned him the enduring nickname of "the Gipper." University of Illinois halfback Red Grange became the most celebrated college football star of the 1920s, ranking behind only Babe Ruth and Jack Dempsey in his star-power and ability to attract fans to games. The increasingly powerful media of print, radio, and film during this Age of Ballyhoo transformed the best coaches and players into virtual mythic heroes and firmly embedded college football in the American cultural matrix.

Southern college football also came of age during the 1920s. The University of Alabama's dramatic come-from-behind upset victory over the Washington Huskies in the 1926 Rose Bowl was a dramatic demonstration that perennially inferior southern programs had achieved parity with those of other regions. The emotional reaction of southerners to their belated and hard-won football respectability reveals the symbolic potency of the cultural text of intercollegiate football. Progress-minded southerners viewed success in a sport that had for so long been the province of the Yankee elite as a vindication of their efforts to integrate the region into the national cultural and economic mainstream. Yet southerners simultaneously celebrated victories over teams from other regions as a vindication of the Lost Cause tradition that honored the ideals and values of the antebellum South. By the end of the 1920s, Americans of diverse regions, social classes, and ethnic backgrounds had imparted a richly layered and often contradictory set of cultural meanings to college football. Southerners would again demonstrate the symbolic malleability and emotional resonance of college football during the civil rights era. During the 1950s and 1960s, many white southerners proclaimed the successes of all-white college teams to be a vindication of white supremacy, but they hailed their racially integrated teams of the late 1960s and 1970s as evidence that a progressive, biracial society existed in the region.

The Rise of Basketball

College football maintained its popularity during the Great Depression, as attendance once again doubled between 1930 and 1937. The 1930s also witnessed the rise of basketball as a commercialized, spectator-centered intercollegiate sport. James Naismith (1861–1939) invented basketball in 1891 at the YMCA Training School in Springfield, Massachusetts, but college men were initially lukewarm to the sport. Male undergraduates with a passion for football were suspicious of a sport that prohibited physical contact and was popular among college women, and they collectively decided that basketball was insufficiently manly to warrant much attention. Between the 1890s and the early 1930s, amateur basketball was dominated by teams sponsored by the YMCA and the Amateur Athletic Union, and intercollegiate basketball lagged behind not only football but also baseball and track and field on college campuses. In the 1930s, however, the advent of the fast break and the one-handed shot (which later evolved into the jump shot), and rules changes such as the requirement that teams advance the ball past halfcourt within 10 seconds and the abolition of the center jump after each basket, did for college basketball what the forward pass had done for football a generation earlier. The plodding style of play that stifled offensive virtuosity was supplanted by a high-scoring and fast-paced game more attractive to both athletes and fans. By the end of the decade, fans eager for a sport to fill the void between the football and baseball seasons and collegiate athletic authorities alert for new sources of athletic revenue and prestige transformed intercollegiate basketball from a student-centered sport that attracted little attention prior to 1930 to a spectator-centered commercial product modeled on college football.

Although midwestern universities such as Indiana, Purdue, Kentucky, and Kansas excelled at the sport, the Northeast was the center of intercollegiate basketball throughout the 1930s and 1940s. Basketball generated lower overhead costs than football; thus many smaller colleges in eastern cities priced out of football competition established superior basketball programs. The quintessential city game was especially popular in urban ethnic communities, and large numbers of Jewish, Irish, and Italian athletes starred for these urban schools. A series of games held in the early 1930s in New York City's Madison Square Garden to benefit the city public welfare fund attracted sellout crowds, establishing the city as the center of intercollegiate basketball. In 1938, New York sportswriters established the National Invitational Tournament (NIT) to determine the national collegiate champion. Although the NCAA established its own championship tournament one year later, the press exposure and gate receipts generated in New York made the NIT the premier postseason tournament until the early 1950s. New York's position at the apex of the basketball world was diminished by the 1951 revelation that players from several New York–area teams had accepted payoffs from gamblers in exchange for keeping the margin of victory below the gamblers' point spread. Other instances of "point shaving" surfaced at midwestern universities, notably the University of Kentucky, and the scandals provoked a national examination of the decline of moral values in American life.

The NCAA Era

The basketball scandals and the advent of televised sports forced collegiate authorities to vest real regulatory authority in the NCAA in the early 1950s. At their 1952 convention, NCAA member colleges hired a full-time staff and charged it with overseeing the recruitment and remuneration of college athletes. NCAA members legalized the awarding of athletic scholarships regardless of financial need and removed prohibitions against the active recruitment of high school athletes by collegiate coaches, practices that had been allowed by several regional conferences since the late 1930s. The 1952 convention also voted to give the NCAA the power to impose penalties on institutions that violated the newly liberalized rules. The NCAA thus became a cartel empowered to limit the labor costs of its member athletic programs. The NCAA also acted as a cartel when it successfully limited live telecasts of college football games. Unrestricted broadcasts of college football in the late 1940s had caused a dramatic decrease in ticket sales. In 1951, the NCAA responded by severely limiting the number of televised games, and it apportioned the revenues generated by television contracts among member institutions.

College football attendance was stagnant throughout the 1950s, but the sport experienced another era of spectacular growth during the 1960s and 1970s. Sensational offensive displays delighted fans, and attendance soared from 20 million in the early 1960s to over 35 million in 1980. Television revenues from the NCAA regular season contracts grew from $3 million in 1964 to $75 million in 1983. The number of major postseason bowl games grew from 4 prior to World War II to over 20 by the late 1980s, and the largest of the bowls offered multimillion-dollar payouts to participating teams.

College basketball produced an even more impressive record of growth during this period. The growing predominance of African American athletes in college basketball created an electrifying style of play that featured crowd-pleasing aerial acrobatics and slam-dunks. The NCAA men's championship basketball tournament became a nationally televised extravaganza that commanded the rapt attention of sports fans every March. Prior to World War II, educators, administrators, and opinion leaders paid obligatory lip service to the chimerical notion that commercialism was both incidental and inimical to the true spirit of intercollegiate athletics. In the postwar period, and especially after the early 1960s, few people seriously proposed that big-time intercollegiate football or basketball should be anything other than commercial entertainment.

Financial woes have beset the intercollegiate sporting world in the 1980s and 1990s. The television revenues generated by the major football powers declined precipitously after a 1982 federal court decision declared the NCAA television monopoly to be a violation of antitrust laws. The television networks possessed increased leverage in the newly deregulated market, and revenues for regular season games fell by over 50 percent in 1984. Increased revenues from televised basketball have partially offset this decline, but over half of the money paid by CBS for the television rights to the NCAA men's basketball tournament is retained by the NCAA and not distributed to member institutions. The expansion of women's sports mandated by federal civil rights legislation has placed further financial pressure on many financially ailing athletic programs. Although reliable figures are notoriously difficult to obtain, as many as 90 percent of NCAA athletic programs consistently lose money, and some of these programs lose millions annually.

African American Participation

African American participation in big-time intercollegiate athletics reflects the larger black struggle for opportunity and racial justice. Institutional autonomy allowed colleges to field racially integrated teams, thus preventing a policy of total racial exclusion such as existed in organized baseball from taking root in intercollegiate athletics. A small but noteworthy number of blacks thus competed for a number of colleges in the Northeast, Midwest, and West between the late 1880s and the end of World War II. William Lewis (1868–1949) of Amherst became the first African American to compete in big-time intercollegiate football in 1889; Fritz Pollard (1894–1986) led Brown University to a Rose Bowl victory in 1916; Paul Robeson (1898–1976) starred at Rutgers University between 1915 and 1918 before embarking on his storied acting career; and Jackie Robinson (1919–1972) played football, basketball, and track for UCLA from 1939 to 1941. Still, segregated universities in the southern and border states totally excluded blacks, and integrated teams rarely included more than one or two black players. Black players also suffered the indignity of being excluded from games against southern teams under a so-called gentlemen's agreement. Intercollegiate athletics among historically black colleges began in the first decade of the 20th century, and those institutions formed the Colored Intercollegiate Athletic Conference in 1912. Black intercollegiate competition attracted a high level of popular attention among African Americans, although it remained at the margins of the dominant culture.

After World War II, this ad hoc racial policy that haphazardly combined tokenism, marginalization, and exclusion evolved into a model that more closely embodied the principle of meritocracy so fundamental to modern sports. Universities in the Northeast and Midwest and on the Pacific Coast recruited increasing numbers of black football and basketball players in the 1950s, and the trickle became a steady flow by the 1960s.

The victory of the Texas Western basketball team, which had five black starters, over an all-white Kentucky squad in the championship game of the 1966 NCAA tournament, was a powerful symbolic watershed. All major intercollegiate football and basketball powers, including those in the deep South, aggressively recruited black athletes by the 1970s. By the 1990s, the proportion of blacks in most major programs significantly exceeded their numbers in the population as a whole. Yet since the mid-1960s, many critics, most notably San Jose State University sociologist Harry Edwards, have charged that increased African American participation has failed to eliminate the historical pattern of racial discrimination in intercollegiate athletics. They argue that black athletes are exploited for the profit and prestige of predominantly white schools and that a pervasive atmosphere of racial discrimination suffuses the entire structure of intercollegiate athletics. Black athletes indeed have significantly lower graduation rates than their white counterparts, and very few major universities employ black head coaches. In 1983, the NCAA passed a measure known as Proposition 48, which mandated that athletes maintain a C average in 11 core high school courses and achieve a score of at least 700 on the Scholastic Aptitude Test in order to qualify for an athletic scholarship. Proposition 48 has disqualified a disproportionate number of black athletes, sparking allegations that this reform effort was in reality a covert attempt to reduce black participation in intercollegiate athletics. The meritocratic ethos of sports and the positive symbolism of multiracial athletic cooperation have since the end of World War II raised the optimistic expectation among many Americans that intercollegiate athletics could be an agent of racial progress. While achievements in this area have been substantial, they have often failed to meet these high expectations. The racial climate of American intercollegiate athletics has historically reflected the mixed record of cooperation, animosity, and uneasy coexistence that has characterized the history of American race relations.

Women

Like the African American civil rights movement, the feminist movement had a profound effect on intercollegiate athletics. After World War II, the female physical educators who controlled the athletic activities of college women gradually softened their opposition to intercollegiate competition, although they maintained their insistence that women's sports remain student-centered and uncommercialized. The feminist-inspired alteration of the cultural construction of American gender roles during the 1960s diminished the tautological equation of competitive sports with maleness and swelled the number of college women who sought the stimulation and rewards of athletic competition. Women's intercollegiate athletics received a major boost from the passage of Title IX of the Educational Amendments Act of 1972, which prohibited sex discrimination by any educational institution that accepted federal funding. Although Title IX guidelines did not take effect until 1978, and a series of legal and legislative challenges further delayed its full implementation, perennially cash-starved women's athletic programs received a steadily escalating revenue stream from the mid-1970s until the mid-1990s.

The rapid growth of women's intercollegiate athletics created an inexorable pressure to replace the traditional student-centered athletic model centered around the physical education curriculum with a commercialized, spectator-centered system. The administrative autonomy of women's collegiate athletic programs had long been a function of their poverty. Prior to the passage of Title IX, women's athletic programs received an average of only 2 percent of the revenue received by men's programs. Their newfound prosperity, however, led to their incorporation into male-dominated athletic departments. By the early 1980s, the NCAA had supplanted the Association for Intercollegiate Athletics for Women as the governing body for women's intercollegiate athletics. Women's athletic programs rapidly began to emphasize competitiveness, the relentless pursuit of championships, and the aggressive proselytizing of recruits. In short, they adopted the ethos of the male intercollegiate athletic model that female physical educators had successfully resisted since the late 19th century. Basketball maintained its status as the most popular women's intercollegiate sport. By the mid-1990s it attracted sizable attendance on scores of campuses, and the NCAA-sponsored women's national championship tournament attracted a large television audience. Other sports such as soccer, track and field, softball, and swimming benefited from expanded funding and

the increasing number of athletic scholarships available to women. By 1993, women comprised 34.8 percent of the nearly 300,000 varsity athletes at the 903 NCAA member institutions.

Athletic Programs Today

Only a relatively small number of schools generate enough revenue from their football and men's basketball programs to cover the expenses generated by sports that do not produce revenue and administrative overhead. The growth of women's sports programs due to increasing compliance with Title IX has added to the financial woes of many already debt-ridden university athletic departments. Yet these financial problems do not threaten the long-term survival of American intercollegiate athletics. Intercollegiate athletics have been a significant element of American popular culture for more than a century because they strike a responsive chord with the public. Millions of Americans see in them a reflection of such social ideals as competitiveness, meritocracy, social mobility, individual and group achievement, and communal pride. Universities eager to respond to the public will continue to reap profit and prestige by meeting the demand for intercollegiate sports.

—ANDREW DOYLE

Bibliography: Ashe, Arthur R., Jr. (1988) *A Hard Road to Glory: A History of the African-American Athlete,* 3 vols. New York: Warner Books. Chu, Donald. (1989) *The Character of American Higher Education and Intercollegiate Sport.* Albany: State University of New York Press. Costa, D. Margaret, and Sharon R. Guthrie, eds. (1994) *Women and Sport: An Interdisciplinary Perspective.* Champaign, IL: Human Kinetics. Mrozek, Donald. (1983) *Sport and American Mentality, 1880–1910.* Knoxville: University of Tennessee Press. Oriard, Michael. (1993) *Reading Football: How the Popular Press Created an American Spectacle.* Chapel Hill: University of North Carolina Press. Rader, Benjamin G. (1990) *American Sports: From the Age of Folk Games to the Age of Spectators.* Englewood Cliffs, NJ: Prentice-Hall. Smith, Ronald. (1988) *Sports and Freedom: The Rise of Big-Time College Athletics.* New York: Oxford University Press. Sperber, Murray. (1990) *College Sports Inc.: The Athletic Department vs. the University.* New York: Henry Holt. Thelin, John R. (1994) *Games Colleges Play: Scandal and Reform in Intercollegiate Athletics.* Baltimore: Johns Hopkins University Press. Veysey, Lawrence. (1965) *The Emergence of the American University.* Chicago: University of Chicago Press.

Jai Alai

Jai alai owes its unique development to the Basques, inhabitants of a small territory of southwestern France and northwestern Spain that borders the Bay of Biscay. Jai alai—*cesta punta* in Spanish—is the most exciting offspring of Basque pelota, the large family of games utilizing a hand or instrument to propel a ball. Jai alai is almost exclusively played professionally.

History

Jai alai means "merry festival" in Basque and was the original name of one of the greatest courts ever constructed for the game, Fronton Jai Alai, built in 1887 in San Sebastian, Guipuzcoa, Spain.

The novel element of jai alai, and what makes it uniquely Basque, is the basket, or *chistera,* used to toss the ball. This apparently replaced a long leather glove with a deep curve created in the 19th century that pelota players used. The size of the new gloves allowed players to hold the ball for an instant before hurling it back against the wall or to the opposing side. This stroke, known in Basque as *atchiki* (to hold) was a stronger and more accurate stroke. This made for faster, more spectacular games, but nevertheless led to a decline in playing; the games were more demanding and the new glove costly.

Numerous references point to a youngster named Juan Dithurbide, from the French Basque village of Saint-Pee-sur-Nivelle, as the first person to use a basket with which to play pelota. The *chistera* (French) or *cesta* (Spanish) was an oblong, shallow wicker fruit basket used by peasant farmers for gathering beans and fruit. According to the references, the boy, on impulse, picked up the fruit basket and struck a few balls against the

wall of a barn. Realizing the importance of his invention, Dithurbide began constructing *chisteras* in 1857 in order to sell them. His design was shorter and straighter than current *chisteras* and very similar in size and shape to the leather gloves. At first, the *chistera* was used mainly by the local children, but it soon caught on among adults. It was extremely similar in size and shape to the old leather glove, except that it was constructed from wicker. The use of the basket was enhanced by the simultaneous appearance of a rubber-cored ball.

The new games spread to Cuba, North and South America, and the Philippines. A Basque player in Argentina created a more advanced *chistera* in 1888 to compensate for residual weakness after he broke his wrist. This very long and curved *chistera* allowed players to propel the ball forward two-handed with a rhythmic upward and forward heave from the backhand side. This new way of swinging the *chistera* revolutionized the game.

Rules and Play

This new game, almost exclusively professional, came into being as *cesta punta.* The courts that jai alai is played on are known as "frontons." They may be open or enclosed, but all have a front wall, back wall, and left-side wall. The right side usually has a tiered terrace for spectators. The object of jai alai is to hurl the ball against the front wall with so much speed and spin that the opposing player can't return it. The ball can touch any wall, and it remains in play until it bounces on the floor twice. Traditional games in the Basque country are still played to 35 or 40 points.

The vogue of jai alai as a spectator sport and pretext for gambling affected the game adversely at the beginning of the 20th century. Popularity declined with increased professionalism and the rapid spread of soccer (association football). In 1921, the Fédéracion Française de Pelote Basque was formed, codified the various pelota games, wrote rules, classified players, and generally gave the game a responsible and coherent authority. Organizations in Spain and various South American countries followed suit. An international organization, the Fédéracion Internacionale de Pelota Vasca, in 1945 standardized an international code of rules for playing and umpiring. In 1952 the federation organized its first world championship in San Sebastian, Spain, with eight nations competing.

Professional jai alai entered the United States in 1904 as pelota. A fronton was built during the World's Fair held in St. Louis, Missouri. Although the fronton closed just two months later, professional pelota then moved on to Chicago and New Orleans, where it permanently assumed its new name of jai alai, mainly through the efforts of promoters who wanted to give it a more exotic sound.

The game declined in popularity due to the prohibition of alcohol, the illegality of gambling, and the economic hardship of the Depression. Miami, Florida, where pari-mutuel betting was legal, was an exception; in 1924, the organization World Jai Alai built a fronton and the game was an immediate success as a tourist attraction. Nevada followed Florida in legalizing betting, and a fronton opened at a hotel there in 1974. Other frontons opened later in Rhode Island and Connecticut.

Jai alai is now played everywhere in the world with a Basque population. While the method of scoring has been radically transformed to a round-robin type of play, the games still call for a great deal of strength and stamina, highly esteemed values in Basque society.

—TERESA BAKSH MCNEIL

Bibliography: Hollander, Zander, and David Schulz. (1978) *The Jai Alai Handbook.* Los Angeles: Pinnacle Books.

Jousting

Jousting is a single combat in which two knights on horseback meet with lances. Practiced for centuries for sport, exercise, and training, jousting today takes place only in exhibition, a spectacle rather than a sport.

History

Jousting and "the joust" belong to the general group *hastiludes,* translated literally as "play with lances." The term "jousting" probably derives from the Old French verb *joster,* meaning to come together and fight with lances. The joust became a sport in its own right as early as the 14th century.

Hastiludes, and thus jousting, were products of warfare. Knights on horseback as well as foot soldiers required training. Geoffrey of Preuilly is said to have invented tournaments for this purpose in Tours around 1066. Thus the tournament became a more or less peaceful mirror of an actual battle, involving horsed knights and armed squires, as well as "garçons" on foot, all in the courtyard at the same time. This format was known as a *mêlée,* in which two mixed sides skirmished in an enclosed field. The *behourd* emerged alongside the mêlée in 12th-century France. It, too, prepared the soldier for war and the young man for knighthood. By the end of the 14th century the mêlée was superseded by chivalric encounters with the lance, the sword, the battle ax, and the dagger

Two general versions of hastiludes existed: the tournament *à outrance* (with sharp weapons) and the tournament *à plaisance* (with blunted weapons). As early as 1223 another form had developed: the Round Table, in which Arthurian legends, the Holy Grail, and their heroes were imitated. Round Tables mostly ended with banqueting, singing, and dancing.

Partly originating from the judicial duel were two very serious versions of hastiludes fought with sharp weapons: the feat of arms and the chivalric combat. The feat of arms was used to settle hostilities between two conflicting parties and was always staged in the lists and by larger groups with standardized weapons supervised by an official judge. All sorts of sharp weapons could be used according to prior agreement and injury or and death were always the result. Chivalric combat was undertaken when one party had impugned the personal honor of the other and the matter could not be resolved in court. Sharp weapons agreed upon had to be of the same length (lance, sword) and caliber (mace). The combat lasted until defeat was signaled or until one of the parties incurred fatal wounds. As would have been the case had court proceedings been conclusive, the defeated was subsequently executed in public.

Both forms of the joust—with sharp weapons and with blunt weapons—flourished in England during the late 12th and early 13th centuries. During the reigns of Edward I (1272–1307) and Edward III (1327–1377), it started to outrun its counterparts, the various forms of hastiludes. By the 14th century, the joust overtook the mêlée. Single combats between knights in full armorial splendor charging with their lances won the day. Special armors for jousting were devised; heralds set up regulations, proclaimed the

The Judicial Duel

In the year 1127 a knight called Guy was accused by another knight by the name of Herrmann of taking part in the assassination of Charles the Benevolent of Flanders. When Guy denied the charge, Herrmann challenged him to decide the case in a judicial duel. The two fought for hours, using a variety of weapons, until at last neither of them had either lance or sword. The contest evolved into wrestling, and Herrmann proved the validity of his charge by seizing and tearing off Guy's vital parts. Thus the case was settled.

—*Joachim K. Rühl*

challenges, and organized the jousts; judges graded the individual performances and pageantry before and after the event. The joust came to be featured as the central event in nearly all chivalric meetings of the 14th century. Although jousters were experts in handling their horses and directing their lances, the joust itself had become absolutely removed from actual warfare.

Jousting had a special relationship to the chivalric romances of the day, which were also dominated by the French language. These romances perpetuated the French chivalric code of honor and extended French cultural influence—already well established through military exploits—all over Europe. Romances offered an idealized conception of partly idealized feats of arms, and the knights in turn tried to imitate the legendary heroes of the romances. English chevaliers customarily ride as Launcelot or even as Alexander of Macedon and adopted French allegorical names such as Coeur Loyal and Valiant Desire until late in the 16th century.

Rules and Play

Until the 1420s, the joust was customarily run in an open field. In 1430 a joust took place in Bruges, Flanders, that was staged in the "Portuguese fashion," in which they coursed on both sides of *"une seule liche à travers"* (along one single rope). This device was also used in France at that time.

In England and France a wooden barrier soon replaced the cord and cloth. But jousts continued to be run at large and along this partition during the same event for the next 150 years. In 1466, in an effort to harmonize divergent practices throughout the country as well as to score performance and rank competitors, King Edward IV had a kind of score system developed; this "Ordinances for Justes of Peace Royal," remained valid until 1596.

A "lance" was the unit for counting, and six courses each became the average number run. The herald would set up check lists with the challengers on one side and answerers on the other. After each name he would draw a score check in which he carefully entered hits and broken lances achieved as soon as the courses had begun. After the event, broken lances and hits were counted and challengers and answerers were ranked in their own groups. Ties were decided by further provisions to determine the best three jousters. This form of joust did not survive. What endured all over Europe was tilting at the ring, running at the quintain, and the newly developed form of the "carousel."

Jousting was done by men, although women formed the audience and distributed the prizes. Jousting was also extremely expensive for the participants. By the middle of the 14th century jousts had become international. Itinerant jousters from France answered challenges and knights from other parts of Europe showed up in London. Even Spaniards and Germans came to England.

The Eglinton Tournament in Ayrshire, Scotland, in 1839 was a last attempt to revive the tournament in Britain. In the 1980s and 1990s, the joust has become a prominent feature of nostalgic shows and pageantry. As in the Middle Ages, small groups of expert stuntmen offer their services to the owners of historic castles all over Europe, making quite a fortune for themselves.

—JOACHIM K. RÜHL

Bibliography: Barker, Juliet R. V. (1986) *The Tournament in England, 1100–1400.* Woodbridge, UK: Boydell Press. Keen, Maurice. (1984) *Chivalry.* New Haven, CT, and London: Yale University Press. Rühl, Joachim K. (1990b) "Sports Quantification in Tudor and Elizabethan Times." In *Ritual and Record. Sports Records and Quantification in Pre-Modern Societies,* edited by Marshall Carter and Arnd Krüger. New York: Greenwood, 65–86.

Judo

Judo, the "gentle way," is a martial art that emphasizes yielding to overcome one's opponent rather than matching strength against strength. Developed in Japan with a strong philosophical component, judo today is increasingly a competitive sport with a large international following.

History

The term *ju-do* appears first in the chronicles of the 1st century Chinese emperor Kuang Wu. The two Chinese characters that make up the word reflect the unique emphasis on softness and a compliant attitude that remains the hallmark of the discipline. The first, *ju,* connotes softness, pliancy, or gentleness and refers to the ideal use of power. The second, *do,* is an exceedingly rich term equivalent to the Chinese *tao,* meaning path, road, or way of life. Thus, *judo* can be translated as "gentle way," as opposed to *jujutsu,* which means "gentle technique."

The late 19th century saw the decline of the old Japanese feudal social order and the concomitant weakening of many of the jujutsu schools that were tied to samurai culture. In contrast, judo led the movement to rapidly modernize Japan. Judo was strongly influenced by Western rationality and attempts to make Japan internationally competitive by reinvigorating its people physically and spiritually. Judo emphasizes moral education, spiritual discipline, and aesthetic forms, rather than combat effectiveness. Although it retained many older empty-hand martial arts techniques, it systematized and initially emphasized spiritual development.

Kano Jigoro (1860–1938) codified and revived judo around 1900. Kano's judo stressed avoidance of force as an essential philosophical tenet. He eliminated especially dangerous jujutsu techniques. In 1882, Kano founded his school of Kodokan judo; his goal was to educate people physically, mentally, and spiritually. Kano believed that the ultimate aim of judo was the perfection of the individual so as to be of benefit to society and that the two principles of mutual welfare and utilitarian scientific rationality would "remodel the present society and bring greater happiness and satisfaction to this world." His school quickly grew after his students won a decisive competition against jujutsu practitioners in 1886; and by 1905, the majority of older jujutsu schools had merged with the Kodokan. By 1911, the Ministry of Education made Kodokan Judo a middle-school physical education requirement and after that, judo rapidly established itself throughout Japan and the world.

Rules and Play

Judo as systematized by Kano employs three major kinds of techniques: throwing (*nage waza*), groundwork (*katame waza* or *ne waza*), and striking (*atemi waza*). The set of throwing techniques, which is the most developed of these groups and comes from Kito school jujutsu, is subdivided into throws done from a standing position (*tachi waza*) and sacrifice throws (*sutemi waza*). The groundwork techniques, coming mostly from Tenshin-Shinyo school jujutsu, are subdivided into pinning holds (*osaekomi waza*), strangleholds (*shime waza*), and joint locks (*kansetsu waza*). Along with these, students learned resuscitation

---

"A Place to Study the Way"

In 1882, Kano Jigoro founded his school of Kodokan Judo. The name Kodokan is made up of three characters: *ko* (lecture, study, or method), *do* (way or path), and *kan* (hall or place). Thus it can be translated as "a place to study the way," and it designated the style of judo formulated by Kano. The first dojo (training hall) was at Eishoji temple in Tokyo and had only 12 mats (about 4 by 6 meters [13 by 20 feet]) and nine students in the first year. Yet the organization grew rapidly until the current Kodokan, the International Judo Center, was built. This modern, multistory building hosts over one million visitors each year and has several dojos (totaling over 500 mats), lodging, conference and exhibition facilities, administrative offices, a judo hall of fame, and a 500-seat viewing area. Today, the pupils of the Kodokan include men and women, young and old, of all races and nationalities, and are numbered in the millions.

—Kevin Grey Carr

(*kappa*) techniques as well. Lastly, judo's striking techniques involved all parts of the body, but are generally not as developed as in other martial arts and are downplayed today. The important unifying factor was that Kano based his judo on scientifically analyzed techniques that used one's opponent's force against him, so that a smaller person could throw a larger person through skillful application of physical principles.

Practically every aspect of competition (*shiai*) has been standardized. The playing space is a square of mats 14 to 16 meters (46 to 53 feet) on a side, but the actual contest area is a square 8 to 10 meters (26 to 33 feet) on a side, with a 1-meter (3-foot) red danger zone marking its limits. The two competitors (called *judoka*), dressed in heavy white cotton uniforms, face each other behind lines that are four meters (13 feet) apart. The winner is the first person to score one full point (*ippon*), which can be achieved in a variety of ways: executing a skillful throwing technique that results in one contestant being thrown largely on the back, maintaining a pin (*osaekomi*) for 30 seconds, applying an effective arm bar or an effective stranglehold (only in adult competition), one contestant being unable to continue and giving up, or one contestant being disqualified for violating the rules. One can also win by a combination of the four scoring levels: *ippon* (full point), *waza-ari* (half point), *yuko* (almost *waza-ari*), and *koka* (almost *yuko*).

Modern Judo

Judo was proscribed by the Occupation after the war, but revived by 1951, and the next year the International

Judo Federation was established with 17 participating countries. The first world judo championships were held in Tokyo in 1956, and in 1964 judo made its debut as an Olympic sport. Judo's international spread can be gauged by the number of countries that garnered medals at that competition—the Soviet Union, West Germany, South Korea, Austria, and the United States—and by the Dutchman Anton Geesink, who shocked the Japanese when he took the gold in the open category.

Ironically, it was with the realization of Kano's goal of making judo an Olympic sport that many of his initial formulations of the art fell by the wayside. The Olympic exposure gave the sport an enormous boost in the world, but since the 1960s the trend in judo has been toward increasing sportification: a marked emphasis on rationalization, quantification, standardization, and competition. In many judo schools, especially in the West, rituals such as bowing are hurried or ignored, and traditional elements are diminished or modified. For a significant number of practitioners, Dr. Kano is venerated less than successful tournament competitors, and his philosophical ideals like *jita kyoei, seiryoku zen'yo,* and well-roundedness are dismissed as "mumbo jumbo" that add nothing to the sport. The values on which judo was founded have substantially been replaced with a virtually exclusive emphasis on tournament competition.

The rules as they have developed also reflect the trend toward sportification. Since the 1960s, rules have been modified to cater to spectators who may not be trained enough to catch the subtleties of the lightning-fast techniques or the psychological intensity of the *judoka* in competition. One example of this is the "noncombativity" penalty that is given to a contestant who is not visibly aggressive. Other changes highlight the de-emphasis of philosophy and Japanese culture in the sport: the addition of multiple levels of scoring and penalties contrasts sharply with the original idea that the one point gave the contestant "no second chance" on the mat; weight classes undermine the idea that judo taught a skilled small person to overcome a larger one; and even though Japanese is used in the names of techniques and in tournament commands, the trend seems to be away from any identification with distinctively Japanese culture.

Commercialism is a related controversy. Judo remains a relatively small-scale sport and currently little money can be made in it. However, judo's increasing organizational scale and complexity, as well as international media exposure, bring more opportunity for its financial exploitation.

Modern judo, then, attracts two very different groups of people. One is attracted to its physical challenge and visual spectacle. Others are practitioners who see judo as perhaps an exotic, semimodern art that still uncorrupted by the aggressiveness and competition of Western team sports. Whether one of these views will prevail or judo will have to split apart remains to be seen.

—KEVIN GRAY CARR

Bibliography: Gleason, G. R. (1967) *Judo for the West.* South Brunswick, NJ: A. S. Barnes. Kano, Jigoro. (1986) *Kodokan Judo.* New York: Kodansha. Tegner, Bruce. (1967) *The Complete Book of Judo.* New York: Bantam Books.

Juggling

Juggling may be loosely defined as the sport of tossing and catching or manipulating objects (usually several, but not always), keeping them in constant motion, with many variations, in the number of items tossed, the number of tossers, and the techniques of tossing. Although organized competitions do exist, a consensus of rules and regulations defining juggling is difficult to obtain.

History

Juggling may have preceded both written language and oral histories. Perhaps because of its long and intimate association with magic (black and white) and itinerant performers, jugglers were long considered outcasts, and, as a result, little history survived.

The first known depiction of juggling appeared in Egyptian tombs around 2000 B.C.E. For the next 2,500 years, only sporadic references or drawings appeared, mainly in the Middle East. Then, until around 1000 C.E. jugglers were mentioned usually in association with traveling minstrels and cult-religions. After 1500, juggling slowly became more acceptable as recreation in Europe. At about this time, Mexicans were juggling, primarily as part of sacred ritual.

Not until the 19th century did juggling as we know it gain significant popularity. An infusion of Asian performance art in the West helped to spread interest and knowledge of juggling in European and U.S. theaters. By the 20th century, most jugglers worked in circuses and vaudeville-type settings, where their specializations were part of a larger venue.

During the 1950s and 1960s the decline of vaudeville left jugglers with fewer jobs. Since then, with the growth of television and the entertainment industry, there has been slow and steady growth of juggling in the United States and Europe. Currently, the scope of interest, diversity, technical mastery, and popular acceptance of juggling throughout the world far exceeds most previous standards.

Rules and Play

Nearly 1,000 jugglers, amateur and professional, pre-teens to founding members, attend each yearly festival of the International Juggling Association (IJA). Competitions include three stage events—juniors (open to IJA members under 18), individuals, and teams—for the presentation of juggling as both technique and art. Acts must qualify by passing a preliminary judging.

The more traditional styles, such as ball, club, ring, hat, and cigar box juggling are common. Slightly less well-known events include baton twirling, yo-yoing, top spinning, flag and scarf tossing, ball rolling, and hacky-sac juggling. In addition to performing on the ground, jugglers may also practice on stilts, unicycles, slack and tight ropes, pogo sticks, rolling globes, and free-standing ladders. Less frequently encountered are enthusiasts of Frisbee and boomerang tossing, Ping-Pong ball spitting, knife and playing card throwing, kite flying, ribbon waving, and revolver spinning.

Participants and teams compete in various categories. The principal goal is to juggle as many objects as possible; competitors must successfully juggle one number of objects before advancing to the next number.

Obtaining a consensus of juggling rules and regulations is not easy. One illustration of this occurred when a competitor at the International Jugglers Association used multiplexing. In multiplexing, objects are not thrown and caught one at a time but in combinations of two, three, or more, thus enabling the juggler to keep more objects in the air with fewer throws and catches (and so fewer chances for error). Objections were made; much discussion ensued, and the multiplexer, in the end, was disqualified.

Another form of juggling, contact juggling, obscures the boundaries of juggling, dance, and movement performance. In contact juggling, as the name implies, the juggler remains in contact (generally) with the juggled object. Not only are the elements of throwing and catching removed from the repertoire of the performer, but the number of objects employed is strikingly limited, sometimes to as few as one. The juggled (or manipulated) object(s) is moved in continuous contact with the juggler's body, on, around, over, or under.

Juggling around the World

Europeans, particularly the French, are more familiar with a style of foot-juggling (called antipodism) that is common in theater shows and circuses. In this style, the performer lies on his back with his legs toward the ceiling and manipulates, spins, rolls, tosses, and catches objects on the soles of the feet. When the juggled object is another human being, this skill is called risley.

In Japan, a very traditional juggle requires the performer to roll various objects around the rim of a delicate inflated parasol. Great skill lies in rolling the objects, which may not even be round, as slowly as possible on the very edge of the parasol. Also from Japan comes the art of ken dama. The ken dama at its simplest is a child's game, involving the catching of a ball with a hole in it on a pointed stick held in the hand. The ball and the stick are connected by a short piece of string. In the hands of an expert it is a fascinating choreograph of unexpected balances, tosses, and catches.

Chinese audiences enjoy vase tossing (also called jar manipulation), a difficult and dangerous feat involving the tossing and catching (usually on the forehead) of huge, heavy ceramic vases. Also traditional to China are devil stick and diabolo. The devil stick routine consists of spinning, tossing, and catching a stick (the devil stick) by hitting it with two other sticks held one in each hand. The devil stick is commonly never touched. Experts can manipulate a devil stick with each hand independently. The diabolo is cylindrical, skinny in the middle, and rolls along a string attached at each end to sticks held in the hands. By whipping the string from side to side, the juggler spins the diabolo very rapidly and can roll it, toss it, and catch it on the string. Accomplished performers can manipulate two or even three diabolos on one string simultaneously.

The International Jugglers Association was created in part out of concern that the sport and art of juggling, which, with the decline of vaudeville, was in danger of being lost. The IJA has more than 3,500 members in 50-plus countries. That danger now seems to have passed.

—RICHARD DINGMAN

Bibliography: Dingman, Richard A. (1996) *The Ultimate Juggling Book.* Philadelphia: Running Press Publishers.

Jujutsu

Jujutsu is a broad term that has been applied to a wide variety of different systems of both lightly armed and unarmed martial arts that differed markedly in style, appearance, and ideology. The word itself means "gentle technique." In theory, *ju* (gentleness) refers to the methods that enable a physically weaker man to overcome a stronger one; but each school interprets *ju* in a different way and some seem to completely ignore the term. Additionally, *jutsu* (technique) is in contrast to the spiritualized *do* (way or path) that is important to the philosophies of judo and other martial arts.

History

In Japan, the incidents of empty-hand combat that are recorded in the oldest chronicles are considered the earliest ancestors of present-day jujutsu. An ancient system of combat techniques called *sumai* (to struggle) is said to be a predecessor of all Japanese empty-hand martial arts. Court banquet wrestling called *sechie-zumo* was popular in the Nara (710–794) and Heian (794–1185) periods, but was primarily limited to ritual occasions. Only with the rise of the warrior class starting in the Kamakura period (1185–1333) did these techniques became important on a large scale. The almost constant civil war during the 16th century led to many different martial techniques (*bujutsu*). As strikes with an empty hand were ineffective against armor, warriors developed *yoroi kumi-uchi* (grappling in armor), which involved throwing, joint locks, and the use of a dagger at close quarters. Although no warrior was unskilled in *yoroi kumi-uchi,* the art was of minor importance, a last resort for samurai, for none but the most foolhardy would willingly face another in battle without a weapon. In the medieval period, empty-hand systems now placed under the rubric of jujutsu had many names, but all such styles were marked by their emphasis on practicality and their relative unimportance among the old martial practices. The real flowering of jujutsu schools occurred in the peacetime of the Edo period (1600–1868). Jujutsu came to refer primarily to the myriad schools of unarmed martial arts that proliferated among the samurai and later the merchant classes.

By 1615, with Japan unified, government needed to manage the potentially dangerous samurai population, made superfluous by peace and yet theoretically at the pinnacle of a rigid social order. To retain his power, the *shogun* used strong legislative and police control and restricted weapons severely. Yet at the same time, the government encouraged the samurai to bask in the martial glory of their past and engage in quasi-martial disciplines to release their energies, and samurai sought other ways to measure their abilities. The 17th and 18th centuries saw a significant rise in the number of schools specializing in empty-hand martial arts.

A Hazardous Sport

Despite the lessening importance of practical combat skills at the end of the Edo period, the competitions between jujutsu schools were quite dangerous. An old jujutsu instructor from the end of the era recalled:

> In those days the contests were extremely rough and not infrequently cost the participants their lives. Thus, whenever I sallied forth to take part in any of those affairs, I invariably bade farewell to my parents, since I had no assurance that I should ever return alive (Harrison 1955, 88).

Indeed, it was common practice for jujutsu practitioners to do *dojo arashi* (training hall storming) in which a wandering martial artist would provoke the head of some school to fight with him. In these challenges, an aspiring teacher could prove his skill by besting an established teacher, thus attracting followers and kudos. Stories of men who were crippled or died defending their honor in this way abound. Lafcadio Hearn (1852–1904), a famous early Japanologist, records his impressions of one jujutsu man's technique:

> By some terrible legerdemain he [a jujutsu expert] suddenly dislocates a shoulder, unhinges a joint, bursts a tendon, or snaps a bone—without any apparent effort. He is much more than an athlete: he is an anatomist (Smith 1966, 127).

Perhaps because of these bouts and the reckless use of jujutsu by its practitioners for illicit purposes, jujutsu fell out of favor with the general populace in the latter days of the Edo period. This bad reputation contributed in part to the decline of jujutsu schools in this century but has left us with some gripping tales of the use and misuse of the martial arts at the end of feudal times.

—*Kevin Grey Carr*

During the Edo period, over 700 jujutsu schools (*ryu*) are said to have been practiced. These jujutsu schools combined elements from earlier forms like *yoroi kumi-uchi,* but tended to specialize and exaggerate one or two major techniques (strikes, throws, chokes, etc.). Although emphasizing practicality, many schools began to prize beauty of motion as achieved by minimum use of strength rather than practical, combat-tested skills.

This era also brought the overlay of ethical and philosophical concepts on physical, technical practice. Thus, many schools began to put particular emphasis on mental and spiritual factors, and elaborate philosophical systems were designed around an idealized conception of the classical warrior arts as naturally promoting frugality and morality in all aspects of the trainee's life. These ideals heavily influenced the founders of modern *do* martial arts like aikido, judo, and karate-do.

One of the first schools to emphasize empty-hand techniques was Takenouchi-ryu, founded by Takenouchi Hisamori (1502–1595) in 1532. The *ryu* became widely known after a member of the school defeated a much larger opponent, and it is considered by some to form the core of later jujutsu. Takenouchi-ryu downplayed weapons but did not ban them. Only after the Edo period did pure empty-hand forms developed fully.

At least 179 other schools are mentioned in records of the Edo period. There was a lot of overlap in the techniques of these schools, but all laid claim to a "pure" tradition and a unique line of transmission.

The Edo period saw, too, the rise of the merchants. Although technically relegated to the bottom of the Edo social hierarchy and heavily taxed, the merchant class had far more freedom and money than many of the samurai, whose power was tightly controlled by the *shogun*. With weapons banned, commoners saw jujutsu as a natural choice if they wanted some of the trappings of their samurai "betters." Many samurai had little to support themselves financially and so grudgingly agreed to teach the rich merchants and other townspeople the martial arts. Later on, commoners who lacked martial experience and skill in weapons founded their own *ryu* and attracted all classes to their training halls. These schools hastened jujutsu's shift from a stress on combat effectiveness toward aesthetics and philosophy, entertainment, and commercialism.

The Meiji government (1868–1912) sought to re-establish imperial power and discredited many of the things associated with the samurai. Jujutsu was suppressed, and an imperial edict by Emperor Meiji declared it a criminal offence to practice the old-style combative martial arts. Some jujutsu masters practiced surreptitiously or traveled abroad to teach, but most schools were completely lost or subsumed into more "modern" martial arts like judo. In the war era, the government lifted the ban to promote jujutsu for nationalistic aims, thus further sullying the martial art's reputation. The jujutsu *ryu* had fallen into sharp decline from which they would never recover.

Rules and Play

Jujutsu is a relatively minor martial art both in Japan and abroad. As in the Edo period, modern "jujutsu" includes a confusing array of techniques and styles, with minimal organization of the diverse schools. Most *ryu* claim an unbroken line of descent from past masters, and thus set themselves firmly on the side of traditional martial arts. They tend to emphasize ritual, set formal exercises (*kata*), historical continuity, and philosophy. Although these schools call themselves a *jutsu* (practical technique), they more closely resemble the ideal of the *do* (a way of life that is supposed to spiritually transform a student's life). Especially in America, significant numbers of jujutsu schools emphasize the practical application of techniques and are opposed to spiritualization of martial arts practice. These factions of jujutsu are unified by their resistance to the aspects of sport and competition that have infiltrated many other martial arts.

Today's jujutsu schools mirror those of the Edo period in their diversity, and they must grapple with the same question for the future: is jujutsu an ossified cultural artifact of a glorified past or will it continue to grow and respond to the needs of the modern day?

—KEVIN GRAY CARR

Bibliography: Nelson, Randy F. (1989) *Martial Arts Reader.* New York: Overlook. Westbrook, Adele, and Oscar Ratti. (1974) *Secrets of the Samurai.* Rutland, VT: Charles E. Tuttle.

Karate

Karate is one of many "empty hands" martial arts practices. Its two basic techniques are blocking opponents' attacks and counterattacking. Contrary to popular image, karate practitioners spend very little time smashing bricks and boards. Karate is a competitive sport with a world championship, but does not have Olympic status.

History

The striking and kicking techniques of modern karate originate from a traditional fighting system, Okinawa-te, developed in Okinawa during the early 17th century. Modern karate was founded by Gichin Funakoshi (1868–1957). In 1906 he toured Okinawa giving the first public demonstration of Okinawa-te. The Japanese military quickly noticed the remarkable fitness and strength of its practitioners. Subsequently, a slightly refined version of the technique was included in the physical education curriculum of Okinawa. During these formative years, Okinawa-te became known as *karate-jutsu* (Chinese hand art). In 1916, Funakoshi introduced karate-jutsu to the Japanese public. But only after his 1922 karate demonstration at Japan's First National Athletic Exhibition in Tokyo did Funakoshi transform the originally lethal fighting techniques of Okinawa-te into a less violent fighting form of karate-do. He stayed in Japan, and was greatly influenced by the Budo code of Judo, and consequently embraced some of its main codes of discipline, etiquette, and dressing for karate. Both the uniform *(gi)* and the belt *(obi)* were taken over from judo, and the traditional Japanese bow was introduced as a new form of greeting for *karateka*.

Funakoshi continued to emphasize more acceptable and less violent styles. Soon karate-jutsu was taught in physical education classes at the University of Tokyo and other university towns. In 1936, Funakoshi established his first karate training hall *(dojo)* in Tokyo. New skills, techniques, and new restrictive rules were developed that allowed prearranged sparring *(kata)*. Initially, these fights were still extremely violent and real blows were delivered. Funakoshi's son then developed a new form of karate-do in which blows were no longer delivered but "pulled."

In 1937, Japan declared war on China, and Japan's traditional martial arts became integral to the military training of Japanese soldiers. In this anti-Chinese climate, Funakoshi tried to "Japanize" karate. In 1933, he changed the calligraphy and concept of its name. Eventually, he renamed karate-jutsu *karate-do,* which means "empty-hand way." Thus was a Chinese and Okinawan fighting style transformed into a modern Japanese martial art.

Paradoxically, karate was nevertheless perceived as a Chinese rather than Japanese Budo and was not permitted to be part of the so-called Budokukai, the government department responsible for the instruction of martial arts in the Japanese army. After Japan's defeat, the Western Allies banned all martial arts, although most continued to be practiced illegally. Since karate was not linked to the Budokukai governmental department, General Douglas MacArthur (1880–1964), the commander of the U.S. forces in the Far East, permitted karate clubs to reopen in 1947 and encouraged American and British servicemen to take part.

During the Korean War (1948–1951), many American soldiers were exposed to karate while stationed in Korea and Japan. On their return, they introduced

The Moral Dilemma of Karate.

One must keep in mind that it is not necessary to be a Buddhist, or belong to any religion for that matter, to be spiritually guided in an activity like karate. What is important to avoid unnecessary violence is to allow oneself to be guided by his love for others. Love is defined here as having a feeling of respect for others, treating others with compassion or at least with tolerance, and acting courteously and patiently toward them. Much of the spiritual neglect in karate can be placed at the feet of poorly qualified instructors. These people usually lack a thorough knowledge of the historical background of the art and understanding of the spiritual basis of karate. There can be little wonder then that they fail to instill the proper attitudes in their students. Instructors must stress that karate skills should never be used offensively or to "show off." If a student does not demonstrate desirable personality traits, the instructor is duty-bound to withhold advanced training until that student is socially and spiritually ready. Giving an immature person the capability of critically or fatally injuring another is akin to putting a loaded gun in the hands of a child. The child is less to blame, if damage is done, than the person who provided the gun. In a similar way, instructors should consider themselves responsible for their student's action.

—(1976) "Bill Wallace, Karate World-Champion." In Bill Wallace and Charles R. Schroeder, *Karate: Basic Concepts and Skills,* 9.

karate in the United States and Europe. More significant in the spread of karate was the series of demonstrations given by karate master Matsutatsu Oyama, who toured the United States in 1952.

Rules and Play

Karate as a modern sport consists of two major classes of techniques: blocking attacks by opponents and counterattacking. Certain conditions also permit throwing and joint-twisting techniques. Karate is based on the use of foot and hand techniques that implement blocking *(uke)*, punching *(tsuki)*, striking *(uchi)*, and kicking *(keri)*, ensuring, however, to pull all punches and kicks short of full contact. Powerful, fast, and accurate attacks are possible only if the body is kept in great balance and stability. The development of stance and posture, therefore, must be learned too.

Basic karate exercise takes place in training halls *(dojos)* and involves the training of single or a combination of techniques. In a more advanced class, *karateka* can practice these techniques in form of a simulated fight that enables them to carry out real fighting techniques.

Karate, like all martial arts, eventually took on the role of a modern sport. To become a competitive "sport," karate had to amalgamate its conflicting schools, traditions, and regulations and in 1957 the Nippon Karate Kyokai (Japanese Karate Association) was founded. During the same year, the association organized the first Shotokan karate championships in Tokyo.

However, traditionalists criticized its development as a competitive and commercialized modern sport. Shotokai karate broke from Shotokan in 1956, inaugurated a new organization, and called for a return to more traditional karate techniques. There are many other forms and organizations of karate, such as wadokai, kanshinryu, Chinese kung-ku, and kyokushiukai. Every karate style differs significantly from others, making contests between the rival karate practitioners impossible. In the wake of the Tokyo Olympic Games in 1964, attempts to unify the various Japanese karate associations led to the foundation of the Federation of All-Japan Karatedo Organisation (FAJKO). In 1969, the first All-Japan Karatedo championships were held. A year later the first World Karate Championships took place in Tokyo with the participation of 33 countries.

Karate, one of the toughest combat forms of the martial arts, has a considerable following of female participants. Over the last two decades, the number of championships for women has increased steadily, as have self-defense karate classes for women.

Since the 1970s, karate has become the most popular and widespread of the martial arts. It is estimated that there are some 15 million active practitioners of the various forms of karate worldwide.

The highly successful Kung-Fu films and the television show during the early 1970s caused a global proliferation of various karate and kung-fu fighting styles and led to a rapid popularization and spread of martial arts in general, particularly of karate, throughout America and Europe.

The negative side of this was a growing demand for full-contact fighting techniques, a distinct regression from the no-contact style of modern karate. Various karate organizations that do not belong to the World Union of Karatedo Organizations (WUKO) subsequently became critical regarding the no-contact rules. Increasing attempts to re-introduce some forms of full contact blows symbolize a worrying development among the fringe groups of karate. The first championships in Full Contact Karate began in 1980.

Karate organizations and individual karate clubs resist this, and try to control and enforce a strict code of practice that excludes lethal techniques. Since 1975,

WUKO has been campaigning to make karate an Olympic event.

—BENNY JOSEF PEISER

Bibliography: Draeger, Donn F. (1974) *Modern Bujutsu and Budo.* New York and Tokyo: Weatherhill. Frederic, Louis. (1991) *A Dictionary of the Martial Arts.* Rutland, VT, and Tokyo: Charles Tuttle. Funakoshi, Gichin. (1976) *Karate-Do Kyohan. The Master Text.* Trans. by T. Ohshima. London: Ward Loch. Mitchell, David. (1989) *The New Official Martial Arts Handbook.* London: Stanley Paul. Peiser, Benny J. (1996) "Western Theories about the Origins of Sport in Ancient China." *Sports Historian* 16: 136–162.

Karting

Karting is a motor sport that is also known as "go-karting." Karts are four-wheeled vehicles powered by internal-combustion engines. The frame is often uncovered, and karts seat only one person. While their size, power, and mechanical complexity do vary, karts are essentially small and simple.

History

Karting originated in southern California in 1956, when Art Ingels, a professional racing technician, constructed a tiny kart for his own amusement. Although karts have become larger and more sophisticated since then, Ingels's design has remained the basic prototype.

Ingels first ran his tiny kart as a hobby, then started a business named Caretta to manufacture karts commercially. The karts attracted public attention, and soon other companies began making them. The Go Kart Club of America was formed in 1957, and the first sanctioned kart race was held that year.

Interest in karting quickly spread in the United States and to Europe, Asia, and other parts of the world. Initially, it was a fad. The overall level of interest eventually subsided, but karting has remained a popular sport. Karting is especially competitive in Europe. In the 1990s there was a renewed level of interest in the United States.

Rules and Play

Most karts average in length from 1.5 meters (5 feet) to slightly over 1.8 meters (6 feet), and they are generally under 63 centimeters (25 inches) tall with a 100 centimeter (40 inches) wheelbase (width). The kart body is usually open, with railings for bumpers. Some karts, however, do have covered bodies that resemble larger race cars.

Karting vehicles and events are divided into several classes, including special classes for young drivers. Classifications are also based on the specifications of the karts.

Karts are classified by whether they have a direct-drive system (in which the engine is connected to the wheels by a chain) or use a gearbox. The basic kart has a single, rear-mounted engine. However, karts may also have side-mounted or twin engines. There are numerous sizes and categories of kart engines. Most karts have small two- or four-stroke motors that resemble lawnmower engines. Nevertheless the fastest karts are able to reach speeds of 140 miles per hour (225 kilometers per hour) or more.

The driver sits with legs extended or bent in front, and his feet operate the gas and brake pedals. In many karts, such as Sprint-type racers, the seat back is upright. In Enduro karts the seat is angled very low so the driver is reclining to reduce wind-resistance. Karts have extremely sensitive steering, so concentration and fast reflexes are important. In addition to the steering wheel, the driver shifts his weight to assist in turning. The sense of speed often seems more intense to the driver in karts than in larger vehicles.

Karting is an amateur sport. Young people who have access to suitable land often drive karts for fun or to practice their driving skills. More serious young karters and adults also participate in competitive events, including informal rallies and more formalized, sanctioned karting races. The guidelines for these are established by regional or national karting organizations. Among the largest such groups in North America are the World Karting Association and the International Kart Federation.

The specific rules and standards of karting differ from country to country. Most kart races are held on closed, round tracks, which are generally a mile or less. A popular form of racing includes short races with large fields of drivers running a series of laps for a designated distance or period of time. In longer, endurance contests, the drivers make many more laps.

Karting appeals to all ages and is accessible to large numbers of people. Its glory days as a fad have passed, but it seems likely to retain its loyal participants.

—JOHN TOWNES

Bibliography: Smith, Leroi ("Tex"). (1982) *Karting.* New York: Arco Publishing.

Kendo

Kendo, "way of the sword," is a traditional martial art of Japan. Like other Japanese martial arts such as judo, kendo was part of the training for the samurai class in

feudal times. In 1868, kendo acquired a special significance; it helped to preserve the feudal samurai code,
and with judo, shaped the character of the Japanese
people as they came under Western influences.

History

The origins of kendo as an art of sword fighting go
back more than 1,000 years (in feudal times it was
called Kenjutsu, Kenpo, Toujutsu, and Heiho). As a
sport it developed first in the middle of the 18th century, when protective equipment and bamboo sticks
were introduced by kendo master Chuzo Nakanishi between 1751 and 1763. This allowed fighting without
bloodshed. In those days kendo was usually practiced
by performing kata, formal attack, and parrying exercises with hard wooden or bladeless swords. For safety
reasons, practice duels were impossible.

Kendo's role in society has dramatically changed
since 1868, the start of the Meiji government, which
abolished feudalism, including the samurai class, and
promoted modernization and industrialization. Kendo
became old-fashioned and out of place. Then, in 1879 it
found a role in the police force, which mainly consisted
of former samurai warriors. Wars with China and Russia (1894–1895 and 1904–1905 respectively) promoted
kendo further. The army discovered kendo's value on
the battlefield through the hand-to-hand fighting during the Russo-Japanese War. The practice also became
a convenient medium for the Japanese to express their
desire for a continuity of the native culture, especially
the samurai code, in the face of Western influences. In
1895 the Dai Nippon Butokukai (DNB) (Great Japan
Military Virtue Association) was established to encourage kendo and other martial arts, and had a membership of 1,651,736 by 1910. Kendo was introduced into
the secondary school curriculum in 1914 and became
a compulsory subject in 1931.

Traditionalists saw kendo not as mere sport or
recreation but as a system of spiritual discipline linked
to nationalistic and militaristic ideologies. As a result,
DNB formally adopted the name kendo in 1919. Increasingly, devotees were fascinated with the depth and
complexity of kendo's technique. In 1927 the DNB formalized the 11 articles of the rules of competition
kendo. The sport began to take an organized, modern
form, a trend reinforced by the growing numbers of
student players, with the All Japan College Kendo Federation founded in 1928. As competitions developed in
the 1920s and 1930s, the number of rank holders increased from 9,179 in 1930 to 86,429 in 1940.

As militarism and fascism grew, especially after the

The Concept of Kendo.

The concept of Kendo is to discipline the human
  character
through the application of the principles of the
  Katana.
The purpose of practicing Kendo is:
To mold the mind and body,
To cultivate a vigorous spirit,
And through correct and rigid training,
To strive for improvement in the art of Kendo;
To hold in esteem human courtesy and honor,
To associate with others with sincerity,
And to forever pursue the cultivation of oneself.
Thus will one be able
To love his country and society,
To contribute to the development of culture,
And to promote peace and prosperity among all
  peoples.
—*Enacted by the All Japan Kendo Federation in 1975.*

---

start of the Sino-Japanese War in 1937, militarists and
nationalists again promoted kendo for its martial
virtues. Kendo became a compulsory subject in primary
schools in 1941. The use of real swords on the battlefield
affected the technique of kendo, and in 1943 its rules
were changed to revert to the art of real sword fighting.

With Japan's defeat in World War II and its occupation by the Allied Powers, kendo was banned and the
DNB dissolved. Unlike judo and kyudo (Japanese
archery), kendo was not permitted during the Occupation, because it had encouraged militant nationalism
and trained soldiers for sword fighting. Not until 1952
was the All Japan Kendo Federation (AJKF) established
and the All Japan College Kendo Federation revived.
All-Japan championships started in 1953. It was revived as a "new democratic sport" freed from ideological control, with efforts to devise more rational rules to
develop it as a modern sport. Kendo lost some practitioners who objected to kendo as mere sport. It was returned to the curriculum of high schools in 1953, and
junior high schools in 1957. The development of
women's kendo began after World War II, and its
growth has quickened since the 1970s. Since 1978, 40
percent of the membership of high school kendo clubs
has been female.

Rules and Play

Kendo players score a point by a blow or thrusting to
the designated protected target areas with the Shinai
(bamboo stick). Compared to other martial arts, the
target areas are very limited: the head above the temple,
either side of the trunk, and the right forearm at waist

level and both forearms when both hands are raised. The only thrust is made to the throat. Scoring is not decided merely by the power of the strike. When striking the targets, the blow must be made with the top third of the Shinai and on the side opposite the cord, its power must be controlled within limits, and it must be accompanied by the step and the designated call. Contests normally last five minutes. The first to score two out of three points wins. Older people are among the most skillful players; they excel at anticipating opponent's moves to create an open target. Since 1917 kendo has had a system of ranks from 1 to 10, with 10 the highest.

The International Kendo Federation (IKF) was established by 15 member nations in 1970. Since then, a world championship has been held every three years. The IKF increased its member nations to 30 by 1992; 8 were in Asia or Oceania, 5 in North and South America, and 17 in Europe.

Kendo was imported into Korea from Japan after 1876. It was introduced into the police force in 1895 and into the army in 1904 under the pro-Japanese government. After Korea became a colony of Japan in 1910, kendo was spread by colonial policemen and emigrating Japanese. When Korea regained independence in 1945, some Koreans continued to play kendo. The sport also grew in Taiwan, which had also been a Japanese colony. However, socialism eliminated kendo in North Korea and China.

In the United States, Brazil, and Canada, emigrating Japanese have spread kendo since before World War II, while in Europe, Southeast Asia, and Oceania, it started in earnest only after 1945.

Some nations, Korea in particular, are eager for kendo to become an Olympic sport, but much of the IKF has disagreed. The opponents, Japan in particular, believe international judo's adventurous spirit has been diminished by rule changes, they do not want to see kendo go the same way.

Although not well known elsewhere, kendo is one of the most popular sports in Japan, due partly to historical tradition, but more to its appeal as an enjoyable sport. Kendo had to take on the organized form of modern sport in order to survive and prosper.

—YASUHIRO SAKAUE

Kite Flying

Kite flying uses the power of wind to lift an object called a *kite,* which is named after a species of hawk. Most kites are attached to a long string or other line that is held by a person on the ground or tied to a stationary object. Kites are squares, diamonds, or other basic shapes; some are made up of complicated patterns of abstract forms or resemble birds, people, and other recognizable objects. Some kites are very small, while others have been as large as 9 meters (30 feet) long or more.

History
Kite flying was the first method humans devised to launch an object into controlled and sustained flight. Kites originated in China about 3,000 years ago and were adapted by other Asian cultures. In Asia, kites also had ornamental uses and symbolic connotations. They were often embellished with colorful designs, and they were used in rituals and pageants to bring good luck.

In ancient China, kites pulled carts. In the South Sea islands, canoes were attached to kites. In China, kites were flown to signal troops and to measure distances. Bells or pipes were attached to kites to make noises that would scare away enemies. Kites were also used for surveillance and other military purposes in later wars, including World War I and World War II, before they were replaced by airplanes, balloons, and other aircraft. At other times kites have been used to rescue people in shipwrecks and to move material in construction projects. Travelers later brought kites to the West. Between 1700 and the early 20th century, kites were used frequently in scientific research (recall Benjamin Franklin and electricity).

Interest in kites continued into the 20th century, but was largely overshadowed by motorized airplanes and other flying craft. The construction of electric and phone lines, tall buildings, and local ordinances also stymied kite flying.

The mid-1960s, however, saw a renewed interest in kites. Very sophisticated and creative kites were built with durable, lightweight modern materials like fiberglass and polyester. The contemplative nature of kite flying appealed to people in the "New Games" movement, which emphasized gentle forms of sport.

Rules and Play
Most kite flying is done with the kite flier standing on the ground. The method of launching and holding a kite depends on its size and design and on wind conditions.

Kites have a sturdy but lightweight underlying frame made of wood, fiberglass, or other material to hold it together, covered with cloth, paper, or other flexible material to catch the wind. Kites fly because the moving air and thermal currents (hot and cold air) that hit its surface are divided into areas of high and low pressure. These differences in pressure cause the kite to rise when they are stronger than inertia and gravity. The force that pushes a kite up and forward is known as "lift," while opposing forces that try to resist flight and movement are called "drag." Kites must maintain a balance between them. The variations among differently shaped kites cause them to fly somewhat differently. In some light kites, for example, a tail is added to intentionally increase drag, which increases stability. The flat kite has a straight, rigid framework in a designated shape, such as a square, diamond, or other form. The bow kite—also known as the Eddy or Malay kite—has cross-sticks that are slightly bent for added stability. It is named after William Eddy, a New Jersey photographer who invented it in the 1890s based on a design from Malaysia. The box kite has a three-dimensional framework, often a cube, with covering wrapped around it. Delta kites have wings and a perpendicular flap in a shape that resembles birds or airplanes. Soft kites have no framework, or a minimal, extremely flexible frame. Stunt kites have two or more lines, and their design gives the kite flier a maximum degree of control. Stunt kites can be made to rise, swoop down, and turn with great speed and precision.

Contemporary versions of the early experiments in aviation have again become popular as recreation. Parasailing is usually done over the water. While kite flying is not often considered a competitive sport, kites are sometimes used in contests. In India and other nations kite fighting has long been a popular sport. Players coat the strings and tails of their kites with glass and attempt to cut down their opponent's kite. Other competitive forms of kite flying have become popular, such as contests of prowess with stunt kites. Numerous organizations have been formed, such as the American Kitefliers Association. In the 1990s efforts were initiated to have kite flying included in the Olympic Games. Olympic or not, kite flying retains its lure.

—JOHN TOWNES

Bibliography: Morgan, Paul, and Helene Morgan. (1992) *The Ultimate Kite Book.* New York and London: Simon and Schuster and Dorling Kindersley.

Korfball

To watch a game of korfball is to see what look like portions of a netball, basketball, and handball game all fused into one. The sport is Dutch and, although traditionally played outdoors in the Netherlands, it is an ideal indoor sport. The primary objective is to score goals and prevent the opposition from doing likewise.

Much of its appeal is that it is coeducational. Korfball players catch, throw, and run, yet it is a very safe sport, a noncontact, no-collision activity. The premium is on skill, not power, brawn, and aggression.

History
Korfball was invented by Nico Broeukheuysen, a schoolteacher in Amsterdam in 1902. He had his pupils play the first game of korfball, with two teams of 12 players each (6 boys/6 girls), 3 playing zones, and 2 boys and 2 girls in each zone.

The game quickly became popular throughout the Netherlands. A Netherlands Korfball Association was founded in 1903, and in 1938 it was granted a royal charter. The Fédération Internationale de Korfball (FIK), the world organization for the control of korfball, was founded in 1923 with headquarters in Rotterdam.

Rules and Play
A korfball playing field is 40 meters (44 yards) by 90 meters (99 yards), marked by white tape pinned to the ground. The goal has a basket on top and stands 3.5 meters (11 feet, 6 inches) high. The goals are placed 10 meters (11 yards) from the end line. The ball is round with a pneumatic bladder inside a leather shell.

Players may not move from their zone (each team has four players in each of three zones), which requires players to be skillful in a relatively confined area. The ball is moved by hand movements only. Neither legs nor feet may be used and striking or fisting the ball is outlawed. A game lasts 90 minutes and scoring, as with basketball, is made by getting the ball into the basket.

Despite being an exhibition sport at the 1920 Antwerp Olympics, korfball has not developed into either a major or significant sport. A United States Korfball Federation was founded in 1978. At the first official world championships in 1984, eight countries took part. Korfball is officially played in 33 countries, including Armenia, the Czech Republic, Hungary, India, Papua New Guinea, Surinam, and Taiwan.

The high point of the Dutch korfball year is the annual indoor championship final, which attracts 7,000 to 10,000 spectators. Korfball may be a minor sport elsewhere, but in the Netherlands it has more than 100,000 players in 600 clubs.

—SCOTT A. G. M. CRAWFORD

See also Basketball; Handball, Team; Netball.

Kungfu
See Wushu

Lacrosse

Perhaps the "fastest game on two feet," lacrosse is a ball-and-stick team game that combines skills and strategies common to many sports. Lacrosse has developed into four dominant forms: box, men's field, women's field, and inter-crosse (recently declared the fastest-growing sport in the world). All versions involve running, scooping, passing, and shooting a ball, often at high speeds, into an opponent's goal with a leather-netted stick.

History

Steeped in culture and tradition, lacrosse is America's oldest sport. The earliest documented reference to lacrosse dates from the mid-1600s, but given its roots in the ancient religion of the Huron, Iroquois, Chippewa, and Sac, it probably began earlier. Under various names, including *tewaarathon,* the game was considered a gift from the Creator, believed to view tribes that played it favorably. Lacrosse was used to train warriors and resolve tribal conflicts. Legends describe inter-tribal contests among as many as 1,000 males. Referred to by the native people of North America as *Bagga-taway,* meaning "little brother of war," the matches lasted up to three days. Injury and death were fairly common—one illustration of its profound significance and physical nature. Native women were active spectators; some evidence suggests that they used branches to hit males deemed to be competing with less than full effort. Early equipment consisted of a wooden stick with a curved top, to which a net or pouch of deer or squirrel skin was attached. The earliest form of the game was played on a field from 1 to 15 miles long with a tree, rock, pole, or set of posts serving as goals.

The name of "lacrosse" apparently originated in 1636 when a Jesuit missionary named Jean de Brebeuf, while watching a Huron Indian contest, identified the similarities between the stick being used in the game and the *crosier* that bishops often carried during religious ceremonies. Through a process of translation the name *la crosse* emerged, eventually becoming *lacrosse.* By the 1790s, the sporting elements of the game had displaced most war themes, and rules established the number of players per team and field dimensions.

Geographically, Montreal is considered the cradle of modern lacrosse. Although the French likely engaged in informal competitions, and Anglo-Canadians had known game for some time, not until summer 1844 did settlers officially face Canada's first peoples in a match. The colonists lost. The game's appeal, however, attracted interest. In 1856, Montreal Lacrosse Club (MLC) was established, thus institutionalizing the game. The Canadian National Lacrosse Association was formed in 1867 (referred to by some as "the golden year of lacrosse"). The general view is that lacrosse became Canada's national sport on 1 July 1867, the day the Dominion of Canada itself was created.

Between the late 1860s and the early 1880s, lacrosse expanded in Canada and the United States, and first appeared in Australia and New Zealand. Within Canada, lacrosse developed predominantly in Montreal and Toronto. Unlike the United States, where the game was promoted largely through colleges and universities, in Canada it struggled for acceptance within the school system, where it faced the powerful traditions of British public school sports—rugby and cricket.

Female teachers introduced lacrosse to women in America. Significantly, women's lacrosse has had its own impact on the sport and must be given some credit for its emphasis on safety, which is a central feature of the newest form of the game, inter-crosse or inter-lacrosse.

The amateur game became an increasingly professionalized entertainment commodity characterized by franchises, sponsorships, and the need to attract paying spectators to compensate and retain star players who willingly sold their loyalty to the highest bidder.

Rules and Play

The four main forms of the game of lacrosse are: (1) box (indoor), (2) men's field, (3) women's field, and (4) inter-crosse (also known as inter-lacrosse, soft-crosse, or mod-crosse). The essence of the competitive team game is to run, pass, and shoot a ball into an opponent's goal. Each goal counts as one point, the winning team being decided by the most goals. Players use their sticks to move the ball and, while they are allowed to use their feet, the use of hands directly on the ball is strictly prohibited.

Lacrosse combines the characteristics of many sports—soccer (association football), field hockey, team handball, netball, and basketball. The basic equipment is a stick between 102 and 183 centimeters (40 and 72 inches) in length, traditionally wooden but increasingly being made of more technologically advanced and durable plastic and graphite materials. New leather and leather/string combination nets are contributing to greater accuracy and ball speed, at times over 160 kilometers (100 miles) per hour. A lacrosse ball is made of hard "indian" rubber.

Box lacrosse (also known as boxla or indoor lacrosse), which has gained professional status, is played in ice hockey rinks during the off-season when the floor is bare or covered with artificial turf. This version is probably the most popular form in Canada and is the most physical. Box lacrosse rules permit considerable body contact among the two six-player teams that compete within a fairly constrained playing area surrounded by boards.

The chief difference between men's and women's lacrosse is that body contact is not permitted in the women's game. Consequently, men require considerable protective equipment, as in box lacrosse, while women rely mostly on mouthguards and sometimes gloves. The field dimensions vary slightly, but are typically 100 meters (110 yards) in length and 55 meters (60 yards) in width. Men's field lacrosse allows for 10 players on the field per team, including a goalkeeper, 3 defensemen (who typically remain on the defensive

half of the field), 3 midfielders (who move between both offensive and defensive sides of the field), and 3 attackers (who tend to focus on offensive play and are primarily responsible for scoring directly or assisting in the scoring of goals). Women's field lacrosse shares the same basic objectives as the men's game, but teams have 12 players (11 field players and a goalkeeper), and the game is divided into two 25-minute halves.

Modified forms of lacrosse have existed for some time. The official version of inter-crosse, or inter-lacrosse, was initiated by the Fédération Quebecois de Crosse in the early 1980s. Recently touted as the fastest growing sport in the world, inter-crosse was inspired by pacifism and feminism as a response to the sometimes violent nature of the traditional game. This non-contact version of the game uses an aluminum and plastic stick and a soft rubber ball, emphasizes the principles of fair play, and is founded upon a specific set of four ideals, including respect, movement, communication, and adaptability. The appeal of inter-crosse can be attributed to its overall philosophy of enjoyment and participation, the inclusiveness in terms of age, physical size, gender, and disability, and its adaptability to different conditions. Even its premier event, the Inter-crosse World Games, requires each national team entry to be mixed by gender and is structured so that competition teams are picked through a random computer selection process of all participants. In effect, no nation can actually win the world title; instead an opportunity is offered for cultural exchange and understanding.

Formally, the game is played in Canada, Australia, England, the United States, Japan, Scotland, Wales, Belgium, Sweden, and Czechoslovakia. North America has recently seen a recent resurgence of the Iroquois Nationals team, which represents the Six Nations of the Iroquois (Seneca, Cayuga, Oneida, Onondaga, Mohawk, and Tuscarora) in Canada and the United States. The Lacrosse Foundation, which was originally founded in 1959, opened its new headquarters in 1991 in Baltimore, Maryland.

International competition has existed since 1876, when the Montreal Lacrosse Club played a series of matches against a combined Indian team from Caughnawaga and St. Regis during an exhibition tour that introduced the game to Great Britain, attended by Queen Victoria and the Prince of Wales (later King Edward IV). For men, the English Lacrosse Union emerged in 1892 and eventually led to a series of exchange visits with teams from the United States and Canada.

Lacrosse appeared only twice as an Olympic event,

in the 1904 (St. Louis) and 1908 (London) Games, but has often been a demonstration sport. Efforts continue to make lacrosse a permanent fixture of the Games. At the elite level, men's and women's world championships are held every four years. The men's competition was initiated by the International Lacrosse Federation in Toronto in 1967, while the International Federation of Women's Lacrosse Association was established in 1972. The largest single lacrosse organization is the United States Intercollegiate Lacrosse Association (USILA), which was formed in 1929. At present an estimated 364 colleges and universities have men's teams, 122 women's teams, and about 1,000 high school programs in the United States.

The Lacrosse Federation sums the game up thus: "Born of the North American Indian, christened by the French, adopted and raised by the Canadians, lacrosse has been wooed by athletes and enthusiasts of the United States and British Commonwealth for over 100 years. Practically all English-speaking nations have succumbed to the charm and challenge of lacrosse at one time or another."

—STEVEN J. JACKSON

Bibliography: Harvey, Jean, and Francois Houle. (1994) "Sport, World Economy, Global Culture, and New Social Movements." *Sociology of Sport Journal* 11: 337–355. Morrow, Don. (1989) *A Concise History of Sport in Canada,* edited by D. Morrow, M. Keyes, W. Simpson, F. Cosentino, and R. Lappage. Toronto: Oxford University Press, 45–68. Scott, Bob. (1976) *Lacrosse: Technique and Tradition.* Baltimore: Johns Hopkins University Press. Urick, Dave. (1988) *Lacrosse: Fundamentals for Winning.* New York: Sports Illustrated Winner's Circle Books.

Law, Sports

Sports law is the application of legal principles to all levels of competition of amateur and professional sport and to physical activity. It includes physical education, recreation, and exercise science and cuts across tort, contract, property (real estate and intellectual), constitutional, labor, and commercial law. Lawyers also act as consultants to sport and physical activity managers engaged in risk management.

History

Sports law is a 19th-century phenomenon whose growth parallels two trends. The first, the business of professional and amateur sport, saw amateur and professional athletes turning to lawyers for contract advice. Second, greater participation in organized recreational sport, fitness, physical education, and leisure has been accompanied by increases in injury. At the same time the American Federal Torts Claims Act (1946) permitted persons injured in sport and physical activity in a federal or state agency to bring suit against that agency.

Legal Concepts

Tort law, which concerns the breach of duty leading to liability for damages (negligence), is most often used in exercise science and physical education. Fighting among athletes, among spectators, and between athletes and spectators; horseplay; and sexual harassment raise issues of the deliberate commission of illegal acts. Equipment and facilities raise product liability questions. Contract principles are used with professional athletes, vendor agreements, and the employment of coaches.

Premise liability, which designates the roles of trespasser, guest, or worker on real estate, is significant in decisions in all areas of activity. Intellectual property affects professional, collegiate, and scholarship sport enterprises that seek to license team logos and apparel.

Constitutional law affects athletes chiefly through the First, Fourth, and Fourteenth Amendments. The First Amendment addresses search and seizure, including drug testing; the Fourth Amendment covers prayer on the playing field. The Fourteenth Amendment, or equal protection clause, in conjunction with various civil rights statutes, governs equity in race, sex, age, and national origin. Labor and commercial law affect how employer and employee interact and influence business practices.

Practice

Either player-employer relationships or accidents on the playing fields inspired early sports law practice. Certainly agents—lawyers and non-lawyers—played an important role in the early days of boxing and horse racing. Professional team sports may have been the first to employ lawyers; some team owners have been lawyers.

Legal Representation in Sport

Some lawyers actively representing athletes represent only team or individual sport players; others represent all athletes. In team sports contracts and contract negotiations, player organizations, and employment have common issues, which isn't the case within individual sports and between team and individual sports. Individual sport representation requires diverse skills and extensive knowledge of the sport. Most attorneys who represent plaintiffs and defendants in exercise and physical activity litigation do so as part of their personal injury law practice. Those who work in risk management must know law well, including court procedures, particularly evidence, as well as good understanding of the activity and its equipment and facilities.

Organizations in sports law are the American Bar Association (ABA), American Alliance for Health, Physical Education, Recreation and Dance (AAHPERD) and the National Recreation and Parks Association (NRPA). The Sports Lawyers Association and the Society for the Legal Aspects of Sport and Physical Activity work exclusively with sports law.

Unique Legal Decisions

Sport produces some unique legal decisions. A consumer, unhappy with the service or product of a business, can find a new service agency or product supplier. This is not the case with sport; few substitutes exist for scholastic, collegiate, and professional sport markets. Thus, courts find it hard to analyze the facts of sports business cases under typical business legal precedent.

Professional athletes' employment status, too, is unique. Only in sport does an employee join a collective bargaining unit and then negotiate individually for more. Athletes automatically become members of a player union, which negotiates basic contract elements, and accept the player union agreement. Highly skilled, outstanding athletes then bargain, usually through their agents, for additional economic and work-related privileges.

The exemption of baseball from antitrust law is, by far, the most unusual exclusion of sport from traditional business requirements. Antitrust law forbids an organization to create and maintain a monopoly. To determine that an organization has created a monopoly, the courts must identify the market, including the product and its geographic region. Three Supreme Court decisions, *Federal Baseball Club of Baltimore v. National League of Baseball* (1922), *Toolson v. New York Yankees* (1953), and *Flood v. Kuhn* (1972), have consistently exempted baseball from all antitrust laws.

—ANNIE CLEMENT

Bibliography: Appenzeller, Herbert. (1993) *Managing Sports and Risk Management Strategies.* Durham, NC: Carolina Academic Press. Barnes, John. (1988) *Sports and the Law in Canada.* Markham, Ontario: Butterworths. Carpenter, Linda Jean. (1995) *Legal Concepts in Sport: A Primer.* Reston, VA: AAHPERD. Clement, Annie. (1988) *Law in Sport and Physical Activity.* Dubuque, IA: Brown/Benchmark. Wong, Glenn M. (1994) *Essentials of Amateur Sports Law.* Westport, CT: Praeger.

Leadership

Sport leadership is an influential relationship through which the leader and followers, in a sport organization, pursue goals acceptable to both and to which both are individually committed. Sport leaders are found from club junior grades to international levels; they may hold official positions such as coach or captain, or may be unofficial, informal, or emergent leaders whose qualities influence others and engender commitment among followers.

Packianathan Chelladurai, perhaps the foremost writer and researcher in sport leadership and management, has helped to develop a model of sport leadership. The model suggests that the most effective player-coach achievement comes when the coach behaves the way the player prefers. Situations may influence coaches' behavior—level of competition, maturity, or personality—and team or group characteristics, which vary. Chelladurai was also key in developing the leadership scale for sports (LSS), which measures leader behavior, usually of the coach, and what behavior athletes prefer. This has five categories: training and instruction, democratic behavior, autocratic behavior, social support, and positive feedback.

The ethnic and cultural aspects of sport leadership remain relatively unexplored, yet matter if sport leaders are to respect participants' beliefs and cultural identities. Cultural factors that influence leadership include adaptation to differing norms, decision making, leadership styles and the language of sport leadership. The Maori of New Zealand have had their word *mana,* meaning "prestige" or "charisma," enter sport team leadership terminology of the national and international press to describe qualities of an inspirational leader. Sport leadership studies have considered U.S. wrestling, Japanese martial arts, Portuguese women's volleyball, Finnish youth sport, Australian field hockey, and Greek soccer.

Captaincy is a critical but rarely examined element in team leadership. Captains must effect the team game plan, adapt it through on-field decision making, and communicate. Off the field the coach-captain relationship is key. Research suggests that captains are team leaders who tend to be more experienced than other players and play in positions with a relatively high degree of interaction or decision making. At the elite level the ability of the captain to "lead from the front," with clear commitment, is valued, as is the leader's embodiment of the spirit of the game and personal courage, mental and physical.

Few investigators have observed sport leaders in all settings. One extended participant observation has provided an inside picture of an international team's leaders, from the national selection committee to test match changing rooms, including the full implementation of coach and captain roles. Studies have been carried out with an emphasis on observation of sport leaders, interviews to gather player perceptions, questionnaires to survey athletes, and research efforts to draw out leaders' perspectives.

Business theory and practice have drawn upon assumptions of sport leader roles and team development, and applied these to other settings. Sports leaders and achievers have contributed to, or been the subject of, writings on success in sport and business. International success has seen sport leaders recognized with promotion, awards, and large financial grants. In the Commonwealth, national sport leaders have been recipients of knighthoods and other British royal awards. Prominence as a sports leader has helped politicians and others toward success, and likely will continue to do so.

—ROBIN MCCONNELL AND C. D. (KIT) MCCONNELL

Bibliography: McConnell, R.C. (1995) *Sport Leadership— More Than Sport Management.* Albany, Auckland, New Zealand: Massey University. Walton, G. (1992) *Beyond Winning.* Champaign, IL: Leisure Press.

Legal Issues in Sport

Sports law has generally involved applying established legal principles to new problems generated by sport, including performance-enhancing drugs and the legal requirements imposed by changing international organizations. Generally, in most countries, sports law per se does not exist. Two exceptions: the United States still has an Amateur Sports Act (1978), and Australia has the Olympic Insignia Protection Act (1987), which enables the Australian Olympic Federation to regulate use of the Olympic rings and insignia in Australia.

Misuse of Drugs

Every sport in the world now contends with drug use, from snooker players who take beta blockers to weightlifters who take steroids. Young players, particularly, are vulnerable to the attractions of so-called social drugs like cocaine. Such drugs can enhance a player's performance; they can also lead to a life (and perhaps death) of abject misery. The International Amateur Athletic Federation (IAAF) has fought hard to eradicate the severe problem of drug misuse. This stance has itself caused major problems, which in some headline-grabbing cases has led to the involvement of both lawyers and courts.

The most serious case involved 400-meter sprinter Harry "Butch" Reynolds of the United States. Reynolds won the silver medal in the 1988 Olympics, but was banned from competition after a positive drug test in August 1990 in Monte Carlo. Reynolds challenged the ban by the IAAF, which decided not to defend the case; since it had no assets in the jurisdiction (Columbus, Ohio), no order could be enforced. The court found in favor of the plaintiff and awarded $27 million against the IAAF, which remained unalarmed because there were no assets in Ohio to which the award could be attached. However, Reynolds's lawyers obtained orders in other U.S. states where the IAAF did have assets. IAAF then decided to appeal the decision. The case eventually reached the Supreme Court of the United States, where the justices upheld the original decision of the IAAF to ban Reynolds.

The episode that perhaps best illustrates how closely intertwined sport has become with law and lawyers is that of British athlete Diane Modahl. Modahl was banned from sport for four years following a drug test she underwent under the auspices of the Portuguese Athlete Federation in June 1994 at a Lisbon meet. The test showed the presence of the prohibited substance testosterone in a ratio to epitestosterone of 42:1, a reading so high it was greeted with amazement and disbelief. Any reading above 6:1 indicates that an offense may have been committed.

Modahl was banned following a hearing of a disciplinary committee of the British Athletics Federation (BAF) in December 1994. She then appealed to an independent appeal panel constituted under the BAF constitution.

The hearing, deeply significant to the issue of doping control, centered on the testing protocol and process. The panel found that the evidence as a whole convinced them that the sample given by Modahl arrived at the laboratory duly signed and intact. It found, too, that although the laboratory had moved to a new site, the institution, not its address, was accredited. Although the panel found that in the procedures and the competence of its staff, the laboratory had departed from best practice, on the whole both were acceptable. The panel found that the samples tested were parts of the sample Modahl had given and that they had not been tampered with. Medical experts who gave evidence at the appeal hearing agreed that the pH of the B sample was remarkably high. This result, together with the odor of the sample, showed that bacterial degradation had occurred. Three experts agreed that they would not allow such a sample to be analyzed in their laboratories. The laboratory had, as requested, analyzed the samples; the question remained, however, how much reliance could be placed on the results? The panel was satisfied that the analysis of both A and B samples was properly carried out and that each showed an abnormal T/E ratio, greatly in excess of 6:1.

The hearing's key question was the possibility that degradation could have caused a false result. Two distinguished scientists testified that bacterial infection as found in Modahl's urine could affect the level of testosterone in a urine sample. More significant, however, was evidence produced of two experiments. These appeared to demonstrate that urine from two female athletes kept for 72 hours at 37 degrees Celsius (99 degrees Fahrenheit) showed markedly increased levels of testosterone.

The panel decided that it could not be sure, beyond a reasonable doubt, of Modahl's guilt. Possibly the high T/E ratio in the sample was due not to ingested testosterone but degradation of the samples caused by unrefrigerated conditions in which ensuing bacteriological action increased testosterone levels. The medical evidence, though inconclusive, had cast doubt on the original finding, and even the lawyers acting for BAF acknowledged that the panel decided correctly. The IAAF was not wholly convinced, however, and immediately announced that the panel's decision would go to an arbitration panel of the IAAF. In February 1995 Modahl launched a civil action for damages against the British Athletic Federation in respect of what she claimed were serious breaches of contract by BAF—the first time British sports administrators have been sued for alleged defective procedures. BAF announced that it would defend the action vigorously. The IAAF decided not to refer the case to an arbitration panel. Modahl was, therefore, able to resume her athletic career and to concentrate on her legal action against the British Athletics Federation.

Violence in Sport

Injury is endemic to many sports. In boxing, for example, opponents deliberately injure one another. Even if death results, the prospect for court proceedings anywhere is virtually nil. In England the immunity of boxers from legal liability rests on a case decided in 1882—*R. v. Coney.* This case involved a bare-knuckle prizefight that the court judged to be illegal. In actual fact it was not the fighters who were charged with a criminal offense but spectators, who were regarded as aiders and abettors.

Boxing, which was regulated by a proper system of rules, was regarded as an acceptable form of deliberately inflicted violence, but this exemption was questioned when the case of *R. v. Brown* (1994) was decided by the House of Lords, the highest court in England. The facts of Brown's case had nothing to do with sport. It involved the prosecution of a group of sado-masochistic men who were charged with inflicting criminal injuries on each other. By a 3-to-2 majority the court decided that the men were guilty although they had voluntarily consented to the injuries (and enjoyed the consequent pain). The decision provoked an outcry. Those convicted have taken their case to the European Court of Human Rights, which will decide whether the original decision was correct.

Changes to boxing-related law would require an act of Parliament, which is considered unlikely. In the case of some martial arts activities, the Law Commission proposed that protection from the criminal law not be extended to "unrecognised activities." Recognized (by the Sports Council) activities include tae kwon do, jujutsu, and karate, which have governing bodies in England. However, some kickboxing and Thai boxing groups applied for recognition; to date, it has not been granted.

Soccer (association football) and rugby generate examples of maliciously inflicted injury, and these can lead to criminal prosecutions. Indeed, in 1995 Scottish footballer Duncan Ferguson (who is now an Everton Football Club (F.C.) player in England) was convicted following a head butt against an opponent. He became the first professional soccer player to be imprisoned for an on-the-field assault.

One of the most prominent English cases was that of *Elliott v. Saunders* (1994). The plaintiff sued for damages caused in a tackle carried out by the defendant, who at the time was a Liverpool F.C. player. At the end of a long trial, the judge concluded that the action must fail. This was a sad outcome for Elliott, whose career had been ended by the tackle. One interesting feature, however, was that counsel for Liverpool F.C. announced that if the case went against his client, it would accept liability for the damage caused by the player. This represented the first time in a sports injury related case in England that a club had accepted that as an employer it was vicariously liable for its employee's wrongdoing, though it followed an Australian precedent.

Players' Rights

In Europe a new problem concerns the right of players to play the game. The game in question was soccer, and the player who forced the authorities to address the issue was Jean-Marc Bosman, a Belgian footballer.

Bosman wished to move from a Belgian club to a

French club at the end of his contract in 1990. His wish was frustrated because a transfer fee was demanded by the Belgian Club but not paid. Proceedings in a Belgian court were referred to the Court of Justice of the European Union. Also at issue was a restriction imposed by the Union of European Football Associations (UEFA), the governing body of European soccer, which only allowed three foreign players and two assimilated players to play in matches organized by UEFA for club sides. (Assimilated players are foreigners who have played for five years in another country, three of which must have been in youth football.)

In December 1995 the European Court ruled that no transfer fees could be demanded for out-of-contract players who are citizens of member states of the European Union who wish to move to another club in another member state. The court also declared illegal the restraints on the number of players from other member states in UEFA competitions. The abolition of transfer fees in cross-border transfers is understandable, since they restrict freedom of movement. Ironically, however, transfer fees can still be imposed within a member state.

Officials versus Players

The decision in the case of *Smolden v. Whitworth & another*, reported in the London *Times*, 23 April 1996, is one of the most controversial in the area of sport and the law. The court held a referee liable for crippling injuries suffered by a rugby union player. Ben Smolden suffered a severe spinal injury and paralysis when a scrum collapsed in a colts match (players below the age of 19) in 1991. The risk of severe neck or spinal injuries is well known to players, referees, coaches, and administrators. This case marks the first time in the United Kingdom that a referee has been held liable for failure to enforce the laws of the game.

In the match in question, the touch judge (an official who assists the referee) had warned the referee that serious injury could occur. Although the judge held the referee liable for breach of a duty of care (negligence), he stressed that his decision was based on the particular facts of the case, the vital fact that this had been a colts game, and none of it applied to international or senior rugby. The laws of the game were changed to permit fewer than eight players in a scrum and to ban contest scrimmaging (that is, the players are no longer allowed to push when trying to win the ball from the scrum). He also cleared the opposing hooker (Whitworth) of any liability. However, he saw nothing objectionable in the law of the land seeking to protect rugby players from unnecessary and poten-

tially highly dangerous, if not lethal, aspects of the game due to negligence.

Eventually, insurance coverage may protect referees from personal financial risk, but amateur referees may be reluctant to continue. Governing bodies of sport must treat this decision very seriously,. and ask how long will it be before referees at the highest professional level in sport are alleged to owe a duty of care to clubs in their application of the laws of the game?

—RAYMOND FARRELL

Bibliography: Grayson, Edward. (1994) *Sport and the Law.* 2d ed. London: Butterworths. Greenberg, Martin J. (1989) *Sports Biz—An Irreverent Look at Big Business in Pro Sports.* Champaign, IL: Leisure Press. Healey, Deborah. (1989) *Sport and the Law.* Kensington: New South Wales University Press. *Marquette Sports Law Journal. Newsletter* (Australia and New Zealand Sports Law Association [ANZSLA]). *Sport and the Law* (supplement to the official proceedings of the International Athletic Foundation Symposium on Sport and Law, Monte Carlo [1991]). (1995) Monaco. *Sport and the Law Journal* (British Association for Sport and Law).

Leisure

Many of us also think of leisure as the opposite of labor and of work time, which we understand as time obligated to one's occupation, to making a living. Sports are activities that we either engage in or watch during our leisure, which we view as "free" or discretionary time. We do have some difficulty fitting all of today's sport practices into this scheme, especially professional sports. For athletes, professional sports are forms of work rather than leisure practices. Still, this does not force us to abandon our belief in the differences between work and leisure. It just requires a little rationalizing: professional athletes produce the events that the rest of us enjoy in our leisure.

In historical terms this view of work and leisure as opposites and of sports as primarily forms of leisure— are relatively recent. In the West, they began during the 17th century and achieved their current form in the 19th century. Not coincidentally, this span of time also witnessed the development of market capitalism, large urban areas, and particular views of social class, race, and gender differences. All of these developments affected and were affected by the social definitions of work and leisure as separable categories of experience.

Before the 18th century, and since in some places, popular sports were integrated with ordinary life. The actual content of many sports drew from daily activities, as well as from legends and rituals. Many sports occurred on sites that people used regularly: roads, fields, forests, taverns, alleys, and rivers. Rare were pre-set times for sporting events, especially outside of the context of festivals and other celebrations. Instead, contests occurred in breaks from necessary tasks, as neighbors met and challenged one another to an im-promptu match, or as people gathered to drink and talk in alehouses and taverns.

Several examples from England and its North American mainland colonies before the middle of the 18th century illustrate this connection between sports and ordinary affairs. In both areas people participated in a wide variety of locally defined contests that today we would recognize as athletic events: foot races, dis-tance throwing matches, and even jumping contests. All incorporated physical skills that were both neces-sary and valued in everyday life. Hand-to-hand com-bats such as cudgeling (fighting with wooden bars or sticks), wrestling, and fist fighting were also common. Frequently, these matches, which pitted one individual against another, arose out of ordinary, face-to-face ex-changes—disputes, quarrels, or even challenges to one's reputation and community position. Among peo-ple who communicated physically, who talked with gestures and fists, and for whom physical characteris-tics such as strength and speed, skin color, hair, and sexual attributes were markers of identity and status, these displays of and challenges to one's physical prowess were important social acts.

Many other sports drew directly from necessary tasks and productive labor, or work. Pitching the bar, for instance, occurred on board ship among seamen who heaved an iron bar (used to weigh down the can-vas sails) for distance. Hammer throwing emerged among field hands and was similar to pitching the bar except for the implement, a hammer. Both matches, as well as the ubiquitous and multiform lifting contests, also occurred in natural breaks from laborers' tasks. They expressed and reinforced the physical strength required in seafaring and agricultural tasks.

Especially in England other sports derived from martial, or military, practices once critical to battlefield victories. Archery incorporated bow-and-arrow skills required of ordinary men who served as foot soldiers. Jousting, a contest of strength and agility in which two squires mounted and armed with lances rode pell-mell toward one another, each trying to unseat his opponent, emerged from the hand-to-hand combats of knights. Tilting arose out of the preparations for warfare, partic-ularly from the maneuvers undertaken to ensure accu-racy with the lance in battle. Tilting involved individual

competitors riding one at a time at full speed (at "full tilt"), lance in hand, toward a target—either an object (a quintain) or a ring that they attempted to spear. Fi-nally, horse racing emerged at least in part from the tasks and conditions of medieval warfare. A test of strength and stamina, horse racing had obvious martial implications, for a good, winning horse could mean the difference between life and death.

Field sports are particularly telling about the inte-grated nature of work and leisure. Hunting and fishing, for example, were not sports separable from the rest of life. Indeed, for many people hunting and fishing were at once necessary endeavors and contests that pitted hu-mans against animals, fish, fowl, and the environment.

What kind of society produced this approach in which our modern distinctions between work and leisure had little if any meaning? Before the 18th cen-tury, the society could have been just about any place on the globe where people lived primarily in hamlets and villages and provided for their needs and for local exchange by raising crops and animals, acquiring re-sources from forests and mines, fishing, and producing crafts. Cycles, seasons, and tasks dictated the sequence of events in any given year, much as one's lineage and land dictated one's place in a community, which usually had two social ranks—an upper, land-owning class and a relatively powerless lower segment. Many people held little stock in an afterlife; their interests lay in sur-viving this one, celebrating good times, and commem-orating their individual and collective pasts.

In England, an alternative to this traditional society began to emerge clearly by the 16th century, and two movements quickened the pace of its construction in the next century. One involved people who were con-cerned with England's external status, its place and power in the world, the enhancement of which, they be-lieved, required the expansion of markets and the ac-quisition of lands and raw material from abroad. The second movement involved people concerned with En-gland's internal directions. In their minds, England was not a sufficiently stable, productive, or moral country. Some of these critics, who were reformist Protestants, left England for North America, while others came to see that they shared a particular set of interests with the proponents of market expansion. Both groups wanted a more productive and efficient economy. To accomplish this end they had to extract more work out of more people, which required not only expanding productive labor but also regularizing and valuing it. Aided by clock technology, new schemes for invest-ment and capitalization, and structural changes in work relations and places (which included the institutionalization of work places separate from living places and specialized roles for workers and managers), these 17th-century reformists dramatically changed *what* people did as well as *when* they did it. In short, they constructed and valorized an emergent category of experience: work.

The construction of work and of work times and places also produced the recognition that some activities were not work and that there were nonwork times and places. To describe some of these activities, reformist Protestants relied on a traditional category: idleness. In their minds, these idle practices consumed time and often things of value but produced nothing of benefit, materially or morally. They included heavy drinking, gambling, and standing around, idle activities in which lower rank men and women engaged. The rank, or class, bias was always evident in the construction of social behavior categories.

What did these 17th-century reformers do with popular sports, which clearly predated a distinctive category of work and its eventual counterweight, leisure? Since the mid-16th century, some reformist Protestants had associated some sports with labor, partially because of their physical nature and close link to necessary tasks. They had argued that some sports improved one's ability to work; they either relaxed and refreshed people or they improved strength and physical conditioning. By the 1630s, one Anglican minister even claimed that sport "belongs not to rest, but to labour" (White 1635, 234).

Subsequent generations constructed another category of experience in which they placed many sports. This was leisure, which was neither idle time nor work time but the "hours which . . . Employment leaves Unengaged." It was also time that should not be spent in idleness but for "new Advantages, new Schemes of Utility" and for "Relaxation and Diversion" (*Virginia Gazette; Pennsylvania Gazette*). This notion of leisure, in short, afforded a marvelous time for some sports, productive sports, sports that were either worklike or considered beneficial to workers.

Many people justified these sports, which were among the first to be associated with a distinctive sphere of leisure, on the grounds of utility. They were useful, competitive recreations, beneficial either to work or to workers in the sense that 17th-century reformers intended. They were also traditional practices that had been formalized over a period of years. Conventions and rules had come to govern performances, which had been moved to specialized facilities like tracks and

rings and had become pre-arranged contests, some of them as stand-alone events. During the 18th century, races, spinning contests, and fights drew crowds in and of themselves; horse races even became festivals in which some communities realized themselves.

These traditional sports that were formalized and moved from their organic social and physical places in ordinary life to a separable sphere of leisure show some evidence of a movement that eventually produced modern sports. The popular sports of today, however, did not emerge until factories, manufacturing, and commercial financing replaced localized agriculture and natural resource extraction. When this occurred, as it did in Britain during the second half of the 18th century and in the United States by the mid-19th century, the transformation of sports entered yet another phase. Many traditional sports had scant lure for some urbanites, especially those with little need for horses, guns, or even fishing and who disliked what they considered the brutality of fighting, the waste of money at cards, and the indiscriminate social mingling at taverns.

They did, however, have leisure time, and they intended to fill it with games and displays of prowess that were entertaining, healthful, and morally and socially uplifting. So between 1750 and 1900, upper- and middle-class Britons and Americans, especially men, formalized and transformed a host of contests and games, including ball games, that they had played as youths. Importantly, few of the physical skills—running, jumping, catching, and throwing—had any direct connection with their work, but the structures of the resultant games and the on-field role specialization often drew from their work relations. Moreover, most games increasingly incorporated the specific time-discipline that was integral to urban, industrial societies. A specified number of innings in American baseball ensured that a contest would last the couple of hours between the end of work and dark, as fighting until one of two opponents could not continue never did. By the 1880s, games played for 1 hour or 90 minutes were even more precisely time-bound.

Sports were not always forms of leisure, nor were sports always what we would consider sports today. Work and leisure are distinctive and historically specific categories of experience, and they literally date only to the 17th and 18th centuries. Modern Western sports, in turn, date primarily to the 18th and 19th centuries, and they are by no means direct descendants of earlier forms. Societies that focused on agriculture and resource extraction and structured with villages and face-to-face relationships produced very different sports within the routines of ordinary life than do modern, urban, industrial, and commercial societies. Such sports were, however, as meaningful to people as our sports are today.

—NANCY L. STRUNA

Bibliography: Brailsford, Dennis. (1991) *Sport, Time, and Society: The British at Play.* London: Routledge. Holt, Richard. (1989) *Sport and the British: A Modern History.* Oxford: Oxford University Press. Struna, Nancy L. (1996) *People of Prowess: Sport, Leisure, and Labor in Early Anglo-America.* Urbana: University of Illinois Press.

Literature

This article contains two sections. The first covers writings about sports. The second covers the depiction of sports in imaginative literature.

THE LITERATURE OF SPORTS

In the United States, sports activities—from our Little Leagues to our jogging presidents—are reported in daily newspapers and on radio and television. The gymnasiums and fields of every school and the stadiums and coliseums in every major city are filled with spectators who buy programs and team guides. Americans are consumed by sports activities and events for fun, fitness, glory, and, in some cases, profit. The same can be said of many nations; every good-sized town in Great Britain has a soccer team and a book on its history, while the Germans have their *festschrift* for every *Turnfest*. In the industrialized world, where there is leisure time to pursue sport, there is also literature on it. But "sport" or "sporting" literature can be confusing because there are two distinctly different types.

Today, *sport literature* refers to athletic types of sport, such as wrestling, fencing, track and field, etc., while *sporting literature* refers to the older British pursuits of hunting, angling, falconry, and the like.

The most influential book ever written on sport is probably the nine-page book issued in 1618 by King James I, known as the *King's Book of Sports,* which declared certain sports and activities permissible on Sundays after church. The king's declaration caused a furor. Puritan influence was growing, and religious conflict was tearing England apart. When James died in 1625 his son, Charles I, became king. Charles reissued the declaration with minor changes, but the Parliament, which was increasingly hostile to the monarchy, rebelled. By 1643 the *King's Book of Sports* was ordered to be publicly burned by an angry Parliament. The Puritans were in power; Sunday sport was no longer allowed. In 1649

Charles I was beheaded. When, in 1660, his son, Charles II, regained the throne, many Puritans immigrated to the New World.

In Germany, Johann Christoph Friedrich Guts Muths (1759–1839) published *Gymnastik für die Jugend* (Gymnastics for Youth) in 1793. This manual on physical education promoted a variety of sports and skills at a crucial time, the period of the Napoleonic wars. By 1812 Napoleon was defeated soundly. The Germans defeated the French again in the Franco-Prussian War of 1870–1871. Following this defeat, Frenchman Pierre de Coubertin traveled the world to study sport and physical education in other nations. By the 1890s he had come up with a plan to promote fitness among French youth, as well as the rest of the world—a revival of the Olympic Games.

By the late 19th century sport had become an important cultural and educational influence in the United States and Europe. Thousands of books appeared in every subject: baseball, football, swimming, tennis, basketball, golf, and more. Newspapers gave more space to local sports heroes, and eventually whole sections of the newspaper were devoted to sport news and photos.

In the 20th century the popularity of certain sports has engendered an enormous amount of literature. There are more books on golf than any other sport, with baseball and American football close behind. A recent bibliography of American college football lists over 8,000 titles. The literature on soccer (association football) is popular everywhere but the United States. Great Britain has an enormous literature on cricket, eagerly sought after, that is virtually unknown in the United States.

Every sport subject has a core of important literature. While the majority of sport literature tends to be frivolous, every subject area has some scholarly material. Sport is a relatively new scholarly discipline, with an increasing amount of excellent work appearing since the 1950s. Baseball has developed a very strong following of historians and is probably the most well-documented sport. Yet misapprehensions persist: how many times have you read that Abner Doubleday invented baseball? (He didn't.)

Sport literature started in ancient times. The extensive (though piecemeal) literature of the ancient Greeks includes records of sports and athletics.

Bibliographies are available that catalog literature for virtually all popular sports, as well as the Olympic Games, and related topics such as sport in film. Reading the literature on sport can inform one about the sport. It is also one way to study the history and culture of a people or nation and to learn that in the end, it really is a small world.

—HARVEY ABRAMS

Bibliography: Burns, Grant. (1987) *The Sports Pages: A Critical Bibliography of Twentieth-Century American Novels and Stories Featuring Baseball, Basketball, Football, and Other Athletic Pursuits.* Metuchen, NJ.: Scarecrow Press. Cox, Richard William. (1991) *Sport in Britain: A Bibliography of Historical Publications, 1800–1988.* Manchester, UK, and New York: Manchester University Press. Henderson, Robert W. (1948) *The King's Book of Sports in England and America.* New York: New York Public Library. Jones, Donald G. (1992) *Sports Ethics in America; A Bibliography, 1970–1990.* New York: Greenwood Press. Lovesey, Peter, and Tom McNab. (1969) *The Guide to British Track and Field Literature 1275–1968.* London: Athletics Arena. McIntosh, Peter C. (1952, 1979) *Physical Education in England since 1800.* London: Bell & Hyman. Phillips, Dennis J. (1989) *Teaching, Coaching, and Learning Tennis: An Annotated Bibliography.* Metuchen, NJ.: Scarecrow Press. Scanlon, Thomas F. (1984) *Greek and Roman Athletics: A Bibliography.* Chicago: Ares Publishers. Smith, Myron J., Jr., compiler. (1994) *The College Football Bibliography.* Westport, CT.: Greenwood. Strutt, Joseph. (1969) *The Sports and Pastimes of the People of England.* First published in 1801. 1903 edition reissued with a preface by N. and R. McWhirter. London.

SPORT IN IMAGINATIVE LITERATURE

Homer and Virgil both included extended descriptions of games in their respective epics. In English literature references to sports abound in the works of Chaucer, Shakespeare, John Gay, and Alexander Pope, and they appear as well in such unexpected places as the novels of Anthony Trollope and Virginia Woolf.

The influence of sport on literature has never been as pervasive and substantial, however, as it has been in American literature of the 20th century. Obvious examples are the work of Ring Lardner, the Frank Merriwell novels, and the adolescent fiction of John R. Tunis. However, sport has had a subtler, but at the same time more profound influence on the fiction of F. Scott Fitzgerald (football and baseball in *The Great Gatsby*), Thomas Wolfe (football in the *Web and the Rock*), and Ernest Hemingway (bullfighting and fishing in *The Sun Also Rises,* baseball in *The Old Man and the Sea*). None of these works could be classified exclusively as sport fiction, but each has that quality that Michael Oriard has pointed out as essential to serious literature about sport: a work in which "no substitutes for sport would be possible without radically changing the book."

As sport has assumed more cultural and economic significance, it has also become more pervasive in our literature. Since the early 1950s sport has been a staple in some of the best fiction by some of North America's best-known authors. Bernard Malamud's *The Natural* (1952), which combines medieval mythology with baseball lore, provides a notable detonation point for an explosion of sport literature. Mark Harris's Henry Wiggen tetralogy began with *The Southpaw* the next year. Harris's *Bang the Drum Slowly* (1956) was also the source for the first of a string of "literate" sports films produced since the early 1970s, many about baseball.

Indeed, baseball dominates most American sport literature. Novels such as Robert Coover's *The Universal Baseball Association, J. Henry Waugh, Prop.* (1968), Philip Roth's *The Great American Novel* (1973), Jerome Charyn's *The Seventh Babe* (1979), Eric R. Greenberg's *The Celebrant* (1982), most of W. P. Kinsella's work, including *Shoeless Joe* (1982), and Donald Hay's *The Dixie Association* (1984) best represent that domination.

Shoeless Joe, with its titular hero's redemption, is somewhat anomalous in recent sport literature, which has tended to stress the darker side of sport. John Updike's Rabbit tetralogy illustrates the poignant truth first articulated by Homer's Nestor, that strength, beauty, and fame notwithstanding, all athletic heroes ultimately "yield to irksome old age." Football novels in particular have emphasized corporate corruption, injury and pain, and what Christian Messenger has referred to as the increasing commodification of the athlete. Frederick Exley's *A Fan's Notes* (1968), James Whitehead's *Joiner* (1971), Don DeLillo's *End Zone* (1972), Peter Gent's *North Dallas Forty* (1973), and Frank DeFord's *Everybody's All-American* (1981) are the best examples here.

No universally acclaimed basketball fiction has been written, but a considerable number of basketball novels have been published in recent years, and a great body of boxing fiction exists, best represented by Leonard Gardner's *Fat City* (1969). More recently, writers of sport literature have turned to field sports, especially fishing, with Norman Maclean's *A River Runs through It* (1976) as the standard-bearer, and while golf stories have existed as long as the sport.

A considerable body of good poetry and several widely acclaimed plays also use sport for raw material. Poets who have written about sport include James Dickey, John Updike, Dave Smith, Nancy Willard, James Tate, Gail Mazur, Fred Chappell, Tess Gallagher, Marianne Moore, Gary Gildner, and Robert Francis. Sports dramas that have been treated as serious literature include Rod Serling's *Requiem for a Heavyweight* (first

Literary Sport.

In Dorothy Sayers's classic whodunit *Murder Must Advertise* (1933), Lord Peter Wimsey, the detective operating under cover, unwittingly reveals himself at cricket:

"The nincompoop! The fat-headed, thick-witted booby!" yelled Mr. Brotherhood. He danced with fury. "Might have thrown the match away! Thrown it away! That man's a fool. I say he's a fool. He's a fool, I tell you."

"Well, it's all right, Mr. Brotherhood, " said Mr. Hankin, soothingly. " At least, it's all wrong for your side, I'm afraid."

"Our side be damned," ejaculated Mr. Brotherhood. "I'm here to see cricket played, not tiddlywinks. I don't care who wins or loses, sir, provided they play the game. Now, then!"

With five minutes to go, Wimsey watched the first ball of the over come skimming down towards him. It was beauty. It was jam. He smote it as Paul smote the Philistines. It soared away in a splendid parabola, struck the pavilion roof with a noise like the crack of doom, rattled down the galvanized iron roofing, bounced into the enclosure where the scorers were sitting and broke a bottle of lemonade. The match was won.

Mr. Bredon, lolloping back to the pavilion at 6.30 with 83 runs to his credit, found himself caught and cornered by the ancient Mr. Brotherhood.

"Beautifully played, sir, beautifully played indeed," said the old gentleman. "Pardon me—the name has just come to my recollection. Aren't you Wimsey of Balliol?"

Wimsey saw Tallboy, who was just ahead of them, falter in his stride and look round, with a face like death. He shook his head.

"My name's Bredon," he said.

"Bredon?" Mr. Brotherhood was plainly puzzled. "Bredon? I don't remember ever hearing the name. But didn't I see you play for Oxford in 1911? You have a late cut which is exceedingly characteristic, and I could have taken my oath that the last time I saw you play it was at Lords in 1911, when you made 112. But I thought the name was Wimsey—Peter Wimsey of Balliol—Lord Peter Wimsey—and, now I come to think of it—"

The mysteries of angling are central to the meaning of *The All of It* (1986), a novel by Jeanette Haien set in Ireland:

Yearning, he recalled the times in his life when he'd fished well through midge-ridden days in weather even meaner than this, and how, adroitly, Nature had put her claim on him and made him one with the very ground at his feet, and how, with every caste, past the gleaming green reeds of the shoreline shallows, he'd projected himself towards a specific spot in the rivers very heart, a different shading in the water that was like a quality of seriousness, or at a laze in the current's glide, some *felt* allurement of expectation which became (ah, fated fish) the focused haven of his energy.

—*Karen Christensen*

produced on television in 1956), Howard Sackler's *The Great White Hope* (1968), Jason Miller's *That Championship Season* (1972), and August Wilson's *Fences* (1986).

In short, all sports popular enough to attract a crowd have also attracted writers.

—DON JOHNSON

Bibliography: Bandy, Susan J., ed. (1988) *Coroebus Triumphs: The Alliance of Sports and the Arts.* San Diego, CA: San Diego State University Press. Johnson, Don, ed. (1991) *Hummers, Knucklers, and Slow Curves: Contemporary Baseball Poems.* Urbana: University of Illinois Press. Oriard, Michael. (1982) *Dreaming of Heroes: American Sports Fiction 1868–1980.* Chicago: Nelson-Hall. Umphlett, W. Lee, ed. (1991) *The Achievement of American Sport Literature: A Critical Appraisal.* Rutherford, NJ: Fairleigh Dickinson University Press.

Luge

The Olympic sport of luge involves one (singles) or two athletes (doubles), a sled, and an ice track of banked turns and straight-aways. This high-speed sport requires customized equipment and intense mental and physical skills.

History

Cave drawings of sleds dating back nearly 1,000 years in Scandinavia and elsewhere in Europe show sleds in use for both economic and recreational purposes. References to sled racing appear in chronicles of Norwegian history as early as 1480. Several centuries ago, in the mountains of Austria, Poland, Germany, northern Italy, and Russia, the luge was used for both travel and recreation. The word *luge* itself comes from a word meaning "sled" in the dialect of southern France.

The first tracks created specially for sledding appeared in the mid-1700s in the Russian capital of St. Petersburg and at Berlin's Bellevue Palace. Luge as a racing sport is traceable to British tourists who started sled racing on snowbound mountain roads in the Alps in the mid-19th century.

The first national luge competition was staged on a

course between Davos and Klosters in Switzerland in 1881 by European competitors. The first international race took place in 1883, with 21 competitors representing 7 nations, including the United States. The sport of luge racing soon spread to Germany and Austria.

The invention of the flexible sled in the 1930s, by an Austrian named Tietze, marked the beginning of the modern sport of luge. Unlike the bobsled, the luge has no mechanical parts; all maneuvering is done by the sledder's body. Until then, sledders had steered by touching the track with their gloved hands; the flexible sled allowed sledders to manipulate the independently mounted front runners with their feet.

The first world championships took place in 1955 in Oslo, Norway, where 8 nations participated, using the naturally iced artificial track at Holmenkollen. In 1964, lugers from 12 nations competed for the first time in the ninth Olympic Winter Games in Innsbruck, Austria. Germany has long dominated international luge competition.

Rules and Play

International luge racing takes place on a tubelike track of ice, supported by cement, stone, and/or lumber. On most tracks, artificial cooling agents and equipment maintain a coating of ice about 4.5 millimeters thick. International racing tracks, though classified as artificially refrigerated or naturally iced, are both considered artificial tracks. An average luge run is approximately 1.2 kilometers long for men and 1 kilometer for women, and can be completed in 38–50 seconds, depending on weather conditions and the course.

Weight, air resistance, friction, sled technology, and driving ability all affect speed. A racing sled is built and maintained within prescribed weights and dimensions. Natural steering requires only the slightest movement of the legs and shoulders together with split-second decision making. The best sliders steer the sled 80 percent of the time and can drive their sleds to precisely where they want them on the track. Subtle body motions change the flex of the sled's runners. While lying as flat as possible, the rider pushes in and down on the runners with the inside of his or her legs, and applies pressure to the back of the sled with the shoulders.

The racing sled consists of two runners, two blades, one sling or pod seat, and two undivided bridges. Luge sleds run on a pair of steel blades, which are attached to the sled's two runners. Before a race, athletes commonly spend three to four hours polishing their blades with varying degrees of abrasives. Since the smoothest blades will create the least amount of friction between the sled and the track, races are often won or lost on the basis of steel preparation.

The heavier the sled and driver, the faster they travel. In 1985, the International Luge Federation created a handicapping system still used today. The weight of a luge must not exceed 23 kilograms for singles and 27 kilograms for doubles. Lighter drivers are allowed to wear varying degrees of additional weight. All drivers may wear clothing weighing up to 4 kilograms (8.8 pounds).

The aerodynamic design of racing equipment and clothing is also crucial for success. Competitors wear skin-tight, cloth/Lycra speed-suits, impenetrable by wind, designed specifically for luge. Spikes may be worn on the gloves and can be a maximum of 4 millimeters long. The shoes (booties) are rounded on the bottom and narrow, so as to be aerodynamic when the athlete is in position, toes pointed.

During the race, the slider steers the sled along an imaginary line on the track, which he or she believes is the fastest way from the start to the finish. They steer by pressing their legs on the curved part of the runner, toward the direction desired, and pressing their shoulders on the seat of the sled.

International Competitions

International competition in luge includes the World Cup, World Championships, and the Winter Olympics. The three categories of competition are men's singles, women's singles, and doubles (which can be mixed). The World Cup circuit consists of up to 10 separate races held around the world. Top athletes receive points at each race according to finishing order. The points are added and an overall World Cup winner is decided at the end of the season.

The highly specialized nature and requirements of luge make it an unlikely candidate for widespread practice. As a spectator sport, it will remain one of the most exciting.

—HEATHER MCMORROW

Bibliography: Fédération Internationale de Luge. (1992) *International Luge Racing Regulations.* English version provided by the U.S. Luge Association. Lake Placid, NY.

Maccabiah Games

The Maccabiah Games, held in Israel every four years, is a sports competition with cultural and educational activities for Jewish athletes. While other all-Jewish games—gymnastic tournaments in Europe as early as 1903—preceded the Maccabiah Games, these games remain the only exclusively Jewish global sporting festival. Regional Maccabiah Games, organized by the MWU, are also held throughout the world.

History

The Maccabiah Games were proposed at the Maccabi World Congress of 1929 as an in-gathering, or *Aliyah,* of Jewish athletes every three years in what is now Israel (then the British Mandate of Palestine). The first Maccabiah Games, held in 1932, were founded by the Maccabi World Union (MWU). In the face of immense obstacles—no facilities or funding—money was found to build Israel's first sports stadium. Three hundred and ninety athletes from 14 countries took part in the games. The second Maccabiah, held in 1935, was also in Tel Aviv. One hundred and thirty-four German athletes defied the Nazi ban on sending a delegation, managed to obtain visas, then registered their protest against the Nazi government by refusing to hoist their country's flag in the opening ceremonies. The games took place when Jewish immigration was greatly restricted, causing many athletes to remain in the country. The worsening political situation in Europe prevented the third Maccabiah Games, scheduled for 1938, from taking place.

When the games resumed in 1950, they were the first major sporting event to be held in the sovereign state of Israel. The Holocaust had reduced the number of participants to 800 athletes from 19 countries. The fourth Maccabiah (1953) introduced the torch run from Modi'in, the burial place of Judah Maccabiah, to the stadium.

Subsequent games saw increased participation and expanded facilities. By the 14th Maccabiah of 1993, delegations from Eastern Europe took part for first time since the end of World War II. A South African delegation also participated for the first time in 20 years after an international boycott (prompted by apartheid racial policies) was lifted.

Events and Sports

The events at both the Maccabiah Games and the regional games are track and field, badminton, basketball, cricket, football, mini-football, gymnastics, rhythmic gymnastics, golf, handball, field hockey, ice hockey, judo, karate, half marathon, lawnbowls, netball, rowing, rugby, rugby 7, sailing, shooting, softball, sports aerobics, squash, swimming, tae kwon do, table tennis, tennis, triathlon, volleyball, beach volleyball, water polo, wrestling, and weightlifting. Also included in the games are chess, bridge, and backgammon.

The MWU has also sponsored many games throughout the world. The Maccabiah Winter Games were held in Banska Bystrica, Zakopane, in 1933 and the Baltic Maccabi Games in Lita in 1937. Permanent regional games are flourishing, including the European Maccabi Games and the Pan American Maccabi Games staged in Montevideo, Uruguay, both held in 1990; the North American Maccabi Youth Games in Detroit in 1990, the Maccabi Sports Carnivals in Australia and South Africa; and the Maccabi Games in Colombia.

—Rivka Rabinowitz

Bibliography: *The Maccabi: A Photographic History. On the Occasion of the 13th Maccabiah—A Photographic Exhibition of the 12 Maccabiot 1932–1985.* Ramat Gan, Israel: Pierre Gildesgame Maccabi Sports Museum. *A Sound Mind in a Sound Body—A History of Maccabi.* Ramat Gan, Israel: Pierre Gildesgame Maccabi Sports Museum. Wein, Chaim. *The Maccabiah Games in Eretz Israel.* Israel: Maccabi World Union and the Wingate Institute for Physical Education and Sport.

Management and Marketing

Sport management and marketing have been practiced since ancient Greek times. The first Olympic Games in 776 B.C.E. featured many of the same elaborate ceremonies and magnificent crowds that characterize today's Games, and must have needed managers, producers, promoters, and purveyors of food and drink.

Management

Sport management includes planning, organizing, leading, marketing, and evaluating within an organization that provides activities, products, or services related to sports or fitness. The two primary areas of sport management are the spectator sport industry, which focuses on consumer entertainment, and the fitness industry, which concentrates on consumer participation in sport activities.

Sport managers have increased in number and legitimacy in tandem with the phenomenal growth of the sport industry in the last 50 years. Sport is currently the 23rd-largest industry in the United States, accounting for over $180 billion of business per year.

The demand for qualified sport managers and marketers prompted the first university-sponsored sport management curriculum in 1966 at Ohio University. Currently, more than 100 sport management undergraduate and graduate degree programs operate across the United States. Programs are also rapidly developing in Canada, Europe, and Asia.

Sport management's strong physical-education orientation today is shifting toward business administration. Degree programs include courses on sport marketing, sport administration, sport law, and sport finance along with basic business courses. Two North American professional sport management associations have been formed: NASSM and the National Association for Sport and Physical Education (NASPE) Task Force on Sport Management.

Sport tourism, one rising subspecialty within the field, involves management and marketing of sport events and properties that draw tourists to a destination. Currently, the more than 150 city, state, or regional sport commissions have as their primary objective using sport to increase economic impact in an area through tourism and publicity.

Marketing

Sport marketing, a more established branch of the field, is variously defined: (1) the marketing of sport products and services (such as athletes, events, teams, equipment) and (2) the marketing of other consumer and industrial products or services through the use of sport (such as by event or team sponsorship and product endorsements by athletes). Sport events and teams are marketed to sell tickets and merchandise and to raise sponsorship and advertising dollars. Athletes are marketed to make them more familiar to the public, which increases their commercial value. Sport participation is marketed to increase demand for sport equipment, apparel, and services and to increase consumers' interest in watching, listening, and reading about sport. Marketing uses sport as a vehicle to promote the image of a company and sales of its products or services.

Sport marketing, although based on mainstream marketing, has distinctive limitations and issues. Unlike when selling soap or bread, when selling a sport, you are selling a memory, an illusion that differs with each consumer's past and present experiences. Did the team play well? Was the weather good? Did the consumers enjoy who they were with or nearby? With no control over the core product, the actual competition, sport marketers must adapt quickly to change and emphasize product extensions to stimulate consumer demand. Product extensions are features, such as halftime shows and game promotions, that add to the core product (e.g., the nine-inning baseball game). If the home team is not winning or lacks a star player, the marketing director frequently markets the players from the opposing team or emphasizes the entertainment value of the game.

Albert G. Spaulding initiated one now-common practice: athlete endorsements, "official" recognition status, and advertising sponsorships from companies associated with baseball support activities.

The most reliable method of attracting customers is to give them a winning team. But a winning team is not always possible and tickets must be sold during noncontending seasons as well. To sell tickets for a noncontending team, marketers use promotional stunts and events designed to create a festive entertaining atmosphere.

In 1984 Peter Ueberroth, a California businessman, became known as the man who saved the Olympic

Games from financial disaster. As executive director of the 1984 Los Angeles Olympic Organizing Committee, Ueberroth devised a model that made sponsorship much more sophisticated and demonstrated that the corporate sector was ready to embrace the Olympic Games. As a result of his marketing savvy, the 1984 Games netted $250 million. For the sport industry as a whole, Ueberroth set an example and opened the door to escalating corporate sponsorships. In 1984 corporations paid $4 million and in 1996 $40 million for the right to be an official Olympic sponsor.

At the international level Horst Dassler in 1956 began co-opting Olympic runners to endorse Adidas by handing out free shoes. Dassler subsequently created the structure of today's world of business-dominated international sport.

Career opportunities in sport management and marketing have increased dramatically. Today an estimated 4.5 million sport management–related jobs cover five major areas: marketing, entrepreneurship, administration, athlete representation, and media. Sport-related careers are found in not-for-profit charitable organizations; city or regional sport commissions; sport marketing and management agencies; corporations; intercollegiate athletics and professional sport; governing bodies, organizations, and leagues; sport manufacturing companies; media agencies; sport event organizing committees; travel agencies; and recreation, fitness, and sport facilities.

With more and more cable television stations and sports-related Internet, along with the creation of new sports events such as the Extreme Games, the future of sport management and marketing continues evolving and expanding, bringing a need for qualified sport management and marketing employees at all levels.

—LISA DELPY

Bibliography: Brooks, Christine. (1994) *Sports Marketing, Competitive Business Strategies for Sports.* Englewood Cliffs, NJ: Prentice-Hall. Graham, Stedman, Joe Goldblatt, and Lisa Delpy. (1995) *The Ultimate Guide to Sport Event Management and Marketing.* Burr Ridge, IL: Irwin Professional Publishing Company, 1995. Parkhouse, Bonny. (1991) *The Management of Sport.* St. Louis, MO: Mosby Year Book.

Marathon and Distance Running

Long-distance and marathon running are increasingly popular versions of a sport in which speed and endurance are the two standards. Long-distance running is done for recreation and in competition; marathon is exclusively competitive.

History

Long-distance races could be found in Britain as far back as the 17th century, when "running footmen," accustomed to traveling alongside horse-drawn carriages, participated in running competitions arranged by their employers. Working-class practitioners, cash prizes, spectator gambling, and distances from sprints to many miles characterized the sport, eventually known as pedestrianism.

In the 25 years leading up to the Civil War, professional long-distance running reached its height in the United Kingdom and the United States. Nationalism was important in attracting spectators to see representatives of both nations, including Native American and Irish runners, compete for the honor of their people. Gambling also attracted crowds.

After the Civil War, Edward Payson Weston (1839–1929) introduced the six-day "go as you please" races that combined walking and running, generally around an enclosed track where admission could be charged. Races of 24 hours, 48 hours, and 72 hours were also contested, as were races of 25, 50, and 100 miles (40, 80, and 160 kilometers). During the 1870s and into the 1880s, these races were popular throughout the United States at country fairs, indoor arenas, or roller-skating rinks. Rampant gambling and rumors of fixed races contributed to the decline of professional long-distance running and walking in the mid-1880s.

The middle and upper classes of Britain practiced long-distance running at least by the 1830s in the form of cross-country races held by the English public schools. By the late 1860s, nonschool amateur athletic clubs conducted such races. The first National Cross-Country Championship was presented in 1876; all the entrants got lost. The next event, a long-distance run of 12 miles (19 kilometers), produced a winner, P. H. Stenning. Among the participants, the teams from the south of England were mostly gentlemen, while those from the Midlands were working class. The standard of amateurism encompassed class distinction; it was considered unacceptable for amateur athletes to compete against tradespeople or laborers. The Amateur Athletic Association, formed in 1880, provided governance for cross country, while the creation of district associations and championships separated the factions geographically.

Rules and Play

A marathon race has been standardized at 42.5 kilometers (26.2 miles). The marathon footrace was created for the first modern Olympic Games as a ritual to connect them with the ancient Greek Olympic Games; this event commemorated the 490 B.C.E. Athenian victory at Marathon. Because no marathon footrace took place at the time, the race reflected the classical Games only through conveniently erroneous derivation.

As a quasi-ceremonial event, the marathon was not immediately standardized. The distance of the Olympic Marathon varied from 40 kilometers (24.8 miles) to 42.75 kilometers (26.5 miles) until 1924, when the present 42.195 kilometers (26.2 miles) was adopted. Repeated contests over courses intended to simulate the disputed 1908 Olympic Marathon popularized the 42.195 kilometers until it was accepted as the official marathon length.

The first marathon was a great victory for Greece. The winner, Spiridon Louys (1872–?), became a national hero.

In the United States, cross-country races covered from four to eight miles. The New York Athletic Club held individual cross-country championships yearly from 1883 to 1886. The events attracted a mix of top runners from elite and nonelite clubs. In 1887 the National Cross-Country Association was organized and held its first team championship race. Long-distance track footraces were also part of amateur sport in the United States and Canada during the 1880s.

The ideologically and politically motivated sport culture of Central Europe developed continental long-distance runners. In Sweden, Denmark, the Netherlands, Switzerland, and parts of the Austro-Hungarian empire, particularly Czechoslovakia, similar patriotic, scientifically based sports club systems emerged.

The first Olympic Marathon confirmed the validity of long-distance running to the world of amateur athletics, particularly within the member clubs of the Amateur Athletic Union of the United States (AAU). The first U.S. marathon, a 40-kilometer footrace from Stamford, Connecticut, to the Columbia Oval in the Bronx, New York, was held about six months after the Olympic Marathon. The Boston Athletic Association (BAA) Marathon began on 19 April 1897, and became an annual Patriots' Day event. By World War I the United States marathon was established as a nonuniversity sport with mostly working-class practitioners. In the years after the war, the Boston Marathon became an international event and remains one of the world's most important marathons, celebrating its hundredth running in 1996.

The Olympic Marathon, in the early years, continued to determine the international status of long-distance running, despite the poor staging of the first two

The New York City Marathon

The marathon boom of the late 20th century began with the New York City Marathon. The New York Road Runners Club planned the race in 1976 as part of the United States' bicentennial celebration; it was to be a citywide event that would accommodate many runners of all abilities. Heavily publicized, the New York City Marathon attracted over 2,000 starters. In 1977, there were almost 5,000 entrants; in 1978, nearly 10,000; by 1986, over 20,000.

Through the promotional efforts of New York Road Runners Club president Fred Lebow, the event acquired many important sponsors. Lebow also negotiated to ensure the support of various New York City agencies, particularly the services of the police and fire departments. Innovations, some the products of the New York Road Runners Club technical committee, enabled finish-line personnel to accurately record runners' times even when several runners crossed the finish line at once. As many of the marathon's thousands of participants had never raced such a distance before, the New York Road Runners Club recruited physicians, nurses, and emergency medical technicians to patrol the course and the finish line. As Kathleen Macomber of the New York City Marathon Committee said in a 1977 committee meeting, "If two or three people drop dead then we will be placed in a position of answering a lot of questions. We will have to be able to say that we acted like responsible citizens in allowing people to run twenty-six miles."
—Kathleen Macomber. "Minutes, 25 July 1977 Meeting, Marathon Committee,"
New York City Marathon for the Samuel Rudin Trophy, 3.

in 1900 and 1904. But the well-organized 1906 interim Athenian Games restored credibility to the Olympics and to the marathon footrace.

The Port Chester Marathon that ran from 1925 to 1941, the Yonkers Marathon that began in 1935 and is still contested, and the present-day New York City Marathon are all products of the New York City marathon culture.

The Olympics established Finnish athletes as the premier long-distance runners in the first half of the 20th century. In 1912, the 5- and 10-kilometer (8- and 16-mile) track races first appeared on the Olympic program. Hannes Kolehmainen (1889–1966), the "Flying Finn," won both. During the 1920s, Finnish athletes developed the first racing techniques specific to long distances. In the 1920s and early 1930s, Paavo Nurmi and Ville Ritola were almost unbeatable at the 5 and 10 kilometers. Finns remained a force in international events throughout the 20th century.

The Finns inspired other countries to encourage long-distance running. Twenty-five-mile races were held in conjunction with the Far Eastern Games in Tokyo in 1917 and in Shanghai in 1921; in 1923, these

Games adopted the 26 mile, 385 yard distance. The Commonwealth Games Marathon, held every four years, began in 1930; the European Championships Marathon, also held every four years, began in 1934. Footraces longer than marathons are still held, but on a very narrow scale.

Positive aspects of the working-class culture carried over to long-distance running. Workers had learned that getting and holding a job depended on friends, relatives, and connections in the field. Similarly, the marathon runner needed assistance to pursue his sport; in order to enter a race, an athlete often had to find transportation and a place to stay. Support usually came from a team. U.S. long-distance running teams increasingly included members of several minority groups, united by their working-class status as well as by their interest in long-distance running.

The Olympics reflected the emergence of new national powers in the marathon. Juan Carlos Zabala (1911–?), the 1932 winner, was a middle-distance track runner in Argentina who trained in Europe. The Japanese, a strong presence in the Olympic Marathon since 1928, took first and third places in 1936. After World War II, Japan, Argentina, and Finland would continue as significant contributors of great marathon runners; Japan began several prestigious marathons, most notably the Asahi in 1947. Emil Zatopek (1922–), Czechoslovakian winner of the 1952 Olympic Marathon, most influenced preparation for long-distance running with the development of "interval training," speed training for long-distance runners. But the most important newcomers were the marathoners from Ethiopia: Abebe Bikila (1932–1973), winner of the 1960 and 1964 Olympic Marathon, and Mamo Wolde (1931–), winner of the 1968 Olympic Marathon, whose Finnish coach used the latest European methods. Since then, Africa has continued to produce many of the world's finest marathoners.

New Zealand coach Arthur Lydiard had long advised relatively slow running—jogging—as part of training for long-distance runners, and as a suitable exercise for others, including middle-aged people and children. Bill Bowerman (1912–), professor of physical education and track coach at the University of Oregon, visited New Zealand in 1962, discovered Lydiard's methods, and later started jogging classes. The RRCA instituted the first "fun runs" in 1964;. many fitness runners graduated from these to official races.

The United States led the way in changing the marathon from an impoverished event practiced by only a few individuals to a generously sponsored sport open to thousands. Joe Henderson's 1969 publication, *Long Slow Distance: The Humane Way to Train,* bridged the gap between fitness joggers and competitive runners by suggesting a training program that emphasized mileage more than speed. Corporations perceived the enormous road racing participant fields as a market comprising middle-class, college-educated consumers. Further, the commemorative T-shirts given to the entrants were ideal for trademarks and other advertising. The idea of the participant marathon spread throughout the world.

Women and Distance Running

Middle-class, college-educated women formed a significant part of the jogging trend; their appeal to the corporate world as consumers was part of the acceptance of the women's marathon. The RRCA advocated long-distance competition for women through the 1960s. The increasing numbers of women who ran marathons, and their demands for AAU sanction, forced the organization to accept the women's marathon in 1972. Corporations sponsored long-distance running programs for women throughout the world, and the widespread participation of women in the marathon convinced the International Olympic Committee to institute a women's Olympic Marathon in 1984.

Long-distance running requires little except adequate footgear and enormous discipline and stamina. Its enduring popularity is likely to continue.

—PAMELA COOPER

See also Olympic Games, Ancient; Olympic Games, Modern; Pedestrianism.
Bibliography: Derderian, Tom. (1994) *Boston Marathon: The History of the World's Premier Running Event.* Champaign, IL: Human Kinetics. Martin, David E., and Roger W. H. Gynn. (1979) *The Marathon Footrace: Performers and Performances.* Springfield, IL: Charles C. Thomas. Shapiro, James E. (1980) *Ultramarathon.* New York: Bantam Books.

Martial Arts

The martial arts are self-defense, physical fitness, sport, and more. Fighting systems that originated in Asia represent a unique approach to the unity of mind and body. They are sources of individual and cultural identity, and offer us enriching symbols and rituals. The three principal categories are *Bugei,* meaning warrior arts intended for mortal combat; *Budo,* referring to arts focused on social, philosophical, and/or spiritual goals; and martially inspired sports, derivatives of the first two categories that are competitive in nature. These categories are flexible, essentially forming a continuum; any system could be practiced as a sport or as lethal combat. Some martial arts operate on multiple levels. Judo, can be practiced as self-defense, as a method of moral and social development, or as an Olympic sport. There are currently two Olympic sports: judo and tae kwon do. Judo first appeared at the Tokyo Olympic Games in 1964 and tae kwon do in 1988 at the Seoul Games.

Ultimate or Extreme Contests

During the 1990s a new kind of martial sport arrived: "no rules" tournaments. These contests are usually pay-per-view television extravaganzas open to all styles and touted as no-holds-barred fighting, generally with no rounds and no time-outs, but with referees and often time limits and rules such as no biting or eye-gouging. A contestant may signal submission at any time with either a verbal cry or by tapping the mat. Though condemned for their brutality, these contests have underlined the utility of jujutsu and other grappling systems.

Modern Trends

Contemporary martial sports focus on techniques and rules that appeal to television audiences—action and violence of full-contact competition. Olympic competition and national teams are also popular; Open tournaments have brought greater technical excellence, combination techniques, and speed, although perhaps undermining tradition. Synthesis promotes borrowing techniques from different styles that work under a particular set of rules. Many individuals have also created their own martial arts/sports.

The martial arts provide more than exercise; they can give a sense of belonging, order, and meaning to life and promote mind-body unification. The physical training builds strong, healthy bodies; the discipline promotes concentration and self-control. Spiritual training through meditation, breath control, and flowing movement builds internal power (*ki*), intuition, and the ability to see the world and ourselves as we really are.

—RONALD L. HOLT

See also Aggression; Aikido; Iaido; Judo; Jujutsu; Karate; Kendo; Tae Kwon Do; Tai Chi; Violence; Wushu.

Bibliography: Donohue, John. (1994) *Warrior Dreams: The Martial Arts and the American Imagination.* Westport,

---

Shoto Tanemura: A Living Master of the Ninja Warrior Ways

While he is not physically a big man, Grandmaster Shoto Tanemura seems to fill the entire *dojo* with his presence. One of two living authentic ninja masters, he is world-famous among the martial arts elite. Tanemura's knockdown power and weapons skills are awesome. His Genbukan Ninpo Bugei *dojo* is located just north of Tokyo, and the surrounding rice fields reverberate with the calls of cranes and the *kiai* of intense training. The school curriculum consists of Ninpo, Jujutsu, Goshinjutsu (self defense), weapons, Pa Kua, and Chi Kung.

Ninpo is the true ninja's martial art of stealth and perseverance. The historic ninja operated out of inaccessible mountain areas and specialized in intelligence gathering and commando operations. They were most prominent in Japanese history from the 13th to the 17th centuries.

Ninpo utilizes such principles as body shifting (*taisabaki*), relaxation, energy and breath-control, and body weight to defeat an attacker. Ninpo techniques must be natural, spontaneous, and appropriate to the intentions and motion of the attacker.

Master Tanemura began his martial arts training at the age of 9 and, after completing a degree in law and spending 14 years as a Tokyo policeman, is now teaching the 22 schools in which he holds masterships. He is not happy with the image of the ninja as an assassin or ruthless mercenary: "Movies and novels have contributed to the bad image. True Ninpo is the art of nobles and priests. Even today, few outsiders have seen true Ninpo martial arts," said the Grandmaster. He constantly stresses the importance of sincerity and etiquette in martial training as he travels around the world giving seminars on the ancient warrior arts.

Ninpo's origins (around C.E. 600) have not been clearly established, but it appears to be a synthetic art that has developed from Japanese and Chinese adepts. Their reputed mystic powers were based on knowledge from Taoist, esoteric Buddhist, and Shinto sources.

The ninja of old Japan achieved a ferocious reputation due to their unorthodox tactics, arduous training, and indomitable will to accomplish their mission. Training under Grandmaster Tanemura is rigorous and stoic, yet never harsh or oppressive.

Although the Grandmaster teaches openly to dedicated students, much of what he teaches is not to be filmed or printed in books. The oral teachings or *kuden* are transmitted from mind to mind. The Ninpo techniques are powerful, elegant, and deadly. "So I have to be careful and choose good persons for advanced training. The true ninja has a heart like a flower," said Tanemura.

—*Ronald L. Holt*

CT: Bergin & Garvey. Frederic, Louis. (1991) *A Dictionary of the Martial Arts.* Translated and edited by Paul Crompton. Rutland, VT and Tokyo: Charles Tuttle. Nelson, Randy F., ed. (1989) *Martial Arts Reader: Classic Writings on Philosophy and Technique.* Woodstock, NY: Overlook Press.

Martial Arts, Philippines

The Filipino martial arts of *kali, eskrima,* and *arnis* embrace a warrior ethic that once forged a deadly fighting spirit and still permeates the rules and regulations of sport competition. Significant in Asian culture and tradition, these martial arts only in the last 40 years became part of Western culture. Lacking a clear methodology of practice and instruction, they are not considered martial arts proper.

History

Filipino martial arts are commonly thought to have their roots in India, China, Indonesia, and Malaysia. With no indigenous system of combat, the Philippines preserved martial arts imported from other countries. Surviving throughout the archipelago's tribal and ethnic groups, however, are various local wrestling forms, such as *buno, gabbo,* and *dama.*

Legend places formal instruction in the martial arts as beginning the 13th century, when 10 chieftains fled North Borneo (Kalimantan) and resettled in the central Philippine island of Panay, where they established a school for future tribal leaders. In this *bothoan* (school), academic subjects and astrology were taught with martial arts. *Kali,* the martial art taught at the bothoan, was a systematized mixture of Chinese *kuntao,* Indonesian *pencak silat,* and Malaysian *langka silat.* Constant intertribal fighting and foreign wars changed kali in form and structure, spawning the "classical" martial art of eskrima and the "modern" martial art and sport of arnis.

Rarely seen in its pure form today, kali is structured around the related skills of hand-to-hand combat on three levels: weapon tactics, empty-hand tactics, and healing skills. Training in the use of arms *(pananandata)* consists of five weapon categories (slash and thrust, impact, projectile, flexible, and protectants). The five weapons categories are then subdivided into six different applications (solo or paired, long or short, heavy or light, curved or straight, single- or double-edged, and one- or two-handed). The empty-hand skills of kali are structured into four categories (striking, kicking, grappling, and pressure point striking).

During their colonization of the Philippines (1565–1898), the Spanish prohibited martial arts and the brandishing of sharp weapons and tools. Kali, however, was preserved through the *komedya* stage plays, socioreligious plays depicting Catholocism's superiority over pagan religions. The Spaniards, however, did not realize that the Filipinos used the battle scenes to preserve and practice their indigenous martial arts. Al-

---

The Death of Magellan

On 27 April 1521, Ferdinand Magellan engaged Raja (chief) Lapulapu and his warriors in a battle on the shores of Mactan Island. Magellan made the mistake of attacking at low tide and was thus forced into a hand-to-hand skirmish that cost him his life. An account of this battle was recorded by Magellan's chronicler, Antonio Pigafeta:

Our large pieces of artillery which were in the ships could not help us, because they were firing at too long a range, so that we continued to retreat for more than a good crossbow flight from the shore, still fighting, and in water up to our knees. And they followed us, hurling poisoned arrows four to six times; while, recognizing the captain, they turned toward him inasmuch as twice they hurled arrows very close to his head. But as a good captain and a knight he still stood fast with some others, fighting thus for more than an hour. And as he refused to retire further, an Indian threw a bamboo lance, leaving it in his body. Then, trying to lay hand on his sword, he could draw it out but halfway, because of a wound from a bamboo lance that he had in his arm. Which seeing, all those people threw themselves on him, and one of them with a large javelin thrust it into his left leg, whereby he fell face downward. On this all at once rushed upon him with lances of iron and bamboo and with these javelins, so that they slew our mirror, our light, our comfort, and our true guide (Pigafeta 1969, 88).

—*Mark Wiley*

---

though the use of swords (the primary weapon in kali) was prohibited, the Filipinos substituted rattan sticks. Kali retains its essence only in the Muslim areas of the southern Philippines.

In the latter part of the 19th century Spanish Filipinos (mestizos) were permitted to attend college in Europe, where many studied Western fencing. Upon returning to the Philippines they integrated this Occidental fencing form with ancestral kali forms. This integration evolved into a Filipino "classical" martial art of single stick *(solo baston),* double stick *(doble baston),* and stick and dagger *(espada y daga)* martial art that the Spanish termed *esgrima* (fencing), commonly known by Filipinos and spelled in Tagalog as eskrima.

With the influence of Western boxing during and after the Spanish-American War (1896–1898) and the Filipino-American War (1898–1942) and of Japanese martial arts during and after World War II (1942–1946), many of the classical eskrima systems evolved into the "modern" Filipino martial art known as arnis. In tandem with its Japanese and Korean counterparts, arnis has adopted structured, military-style group classes and a ranking system designated by colored belts. In the latter part of the 20th century, arnis has emerged as the national sport of the Philippines.

Rules and Play

Arnis tournaments were promoted in the 1920s, but few rules existed and no padding was worn. Only in 1975, with the founding of the National Arnis Federation of the Philippines (NARAPHIL), was the First National Invitational Arnis Tournament was held in Manila.

In the 1980s, tournaments were sponsored to further establish arnis as a national sport. In August 1989, WEKAF sponsored the First World Kali Eskrima Arnis Championships in Cebu City, Philippines, which brought together competitors from the Philippines, the United States, Europe, and Australia.

As a sport, arnis is played by two individuals in a court measuring 8.0 square meters (9.5 square yards). Players are paired and matched by standard weight divisions, much as in as wrestling. The game is played with rattan sticks measuring 76.20 cm (30 inches) in length and 2.54 cm (1 inch) in diameter. Players score by delivering clean strikes and thrusts to designated target areas on an opponent's body or by successfully disarming an opponent. To decrease the chances of injury, players wear a steel-padded helmet and protective body armor covering their thighs, upper body, and arms.

The current rules and regulations of sport arnis were drafted in 1991 by Arnis Philippines, the only official government-sanctioned martial arts organization. This organization brought arnis as a demonstration sport to the 1991 Southeast Asian Games (SEA Games). Arnis Philippines then formed the International Arnis Federation, which currently oversees operations in over 30 countries and is working to have arnis presented as a demonstration sport in the Olympics Games.

—MARK WILEY

Bibliography: Wiley, Mark V. (1997). *Martial Culture of the Philippines.* Tokyo: Charles E. Tuttle.

Martial Arts, South Asia

South Asian martial arts combine two ancient traditions, the Tamil and the Sanskrit Dhanur Veda. Still practiced today for health and recreation as well as in competition, these arts combine physical training with a strong psychological element intended to shape participants' approach to life.

History

Two traditions have informed the history, development, culture, and practice of extant South Asian martial arts—the Tamil (Dravidian) tradition and the Sanskrit Dhanur Veda tradition. The early Tamil Sangam "heroic" poetry informs us that between the 4th century B.C.E. and 600 C.E. a warlike, martial spirit predominated across southern India. Each warrior received "regular military training" in target practice, horse riding, and specialized in use of one or more weapons, such as lance or spear (*vel*), sword (*val*) and shield (*kedaham*), and bow (*vil*) and arrow. War was considered a sacrifice of honor.

The Sanskrit Dhanur Vedic tradition was one of 18 traditional branches of knowledge. Although the name "Dhanur Veda" indicates that the bow and arrow were considered the supreme weapons, the tradition included all fighting arts from empty-hand grappling techniques to many weapons. The two great Indian epics, the *Mahabharata* and *Ramayana,* record vivid scenes of princely use of these skills.

Practice of martial arts was a traditional way of life. Informed by assumptions about the body, mind, health, exercise, and diet implicit in indigenous Ayurvedic and Siddha system of medicine, rules of diet and behavior circumscribed training and shaped the personality, demeanor, behavior, and attitude of the long-term student so that he ideally used potentially deadly techniques only when appropriate. Expertise demanded knowledge of the most vulnerable "death" spots (*marman* in Sanskrit) of the body for attack, defense, or administration of health-giving massage therapies. Consequently, martial masters were also traditional healers.

Rules and Play

Historically each region of the subcontinent had its own martial techniques more or less informed by the Dhanur Vedic and Sangam traditions. Among those traditions extant today are Tamil Nadu's *varma adi* (striking the vital spots), and *silambam* (staff fighting, Kerala's *kalarippayattu*, North India's *mushti* (wrestling) and *dandi* (staff fighting), and Karnataka's *malkambh* (wrestler's post). Among these, Kerala's *kalarippayattu* (literally "exercises" practiced in a special earthen pit, *kalari*) is the most complete.

Kalarippayattu is unique to the southwestern coastal region known today as Kerala State. Dating from at least the 12th century and still practiced, *kalarippayattu* combines elements of the Sangam Tamil arts and the Dhanur Vedic system. Like their earlier counterparts, *kalarippayattu* practitioners traditionally sought to attain practical power(s) for combat use—powers attained through training and daily practice of its basic psychophysiological exercises and weapons work, mental powers attained through meditation in mantra as well as ritual practices and physical strength and power. The external body eventually should "flow like a river." Both boys and girls practiced the art for general health and well-being as well to prepare for martial practice.

Closely related to *kalarippayattu* in the southern Kerala region known as Travancore, which borders the present-day Tamil Nadu State, is the martial art known variously as *adi murai* (the law of hitting), *varma adi* (hitting the vital spots), or *chinna adi* (Chinese hitting). Some general features of the Tamil martial arts clearly distinguish them from *kalarippayattu*—they were traditionally practiced by Nadars, Kallars, and Thevars in the open air or in unroofed enclosures, and the forms begin with empty-hand combat rather than preliminary exercises. Students learn five main methods of self-defense, including *kuttacuvat* and *ottacuvat* (sequences of offensive and defensive moves in combinations), *kaipor* (empty-hand combat), *kuruvatippayattu* (stick fighting), *netuvatippayattu* (short-staff combat), and *kattivela* (knife against empty hand).

Beginning in 1958 with the founding of the Kerala Kalarippayattu Association as part of the Kerala State Sports Council, the Tamil forms become known as "southern-style *kalarippayattu*" in contrast to *kalarippayattu*, which became known as "northern" *kalarippayattu*. Students of northern and southern *kalarippayattu* practice a variety of form training, either solo or in pairs (with weapons), at the yearly district and statewide competitions and are judged by a panel of masters. Narrow but deep, these traditional arts persist.

—PHILLIP B. ZARILLI

Bibliography: Alter, Joseph S. (1992) *The Wrestler's Body: Identity and Ideology in North India*. Berkeley: University of California Press. Zarrilli, Phillip B. (in press) *"When the Body Becomes All Eyes": Paradigms and Discourses of Practice and Power in Kalarippayattu, a South Indian Martial Art*. New Delhi: Oxford University Press.

Masculinity

Masculinity and sport have a long but murky relationship. One view holds that sport gives males an arena to express underlying psychological and biological masculine traits, another that sport helps them become useful members of society by imbuing desirable skills, emotions, and personality traits. At the same time, modern sports are partially blamed for a masculinity that includes undesirable behaviors and ideals. Little

---

A Gay Athlete's Experience

Imagine walking into the crowded reception area of a major athletic facility at an international swimming competition. You have spent the last year training intensively, expecting that today you are going to swim faster than ever before. The foyer is packed with athletes, all of whom are at their peak of physical fitness, ready to race. The place is exciting.

On the deck just before the race the energy is amazing. So much power and speed in one place is awe inspiring. Everywhere you turn there are men stretching and shaking the tension out of their powerful muscles—lithe bodies being tuned for the last time before the final event. You, too, are ready to fly into action at the sound of the gun. Bang! In less than a minute the race is over. You swam your personal best—victory.

The last event in the meet is the relays, in some ways the most exciting part of any meet. Team spirit is at its height, and these guys are ready to tear up the water. As each swimmer flings himself into the pool there is a burst of energy, lane after lane. These are men pushing themselves to the limit; every fibre of every body feels itself to be the consummation of power and masculinity. The race is over. The mood is ecstatic.

Relief. You, with your teammates, hit the shower with the hundred or so other swimmers. Everyone is exhausted and delirious from the racing. This time in the showers, overwhelming with steam and muscle, marks the end of an athletic experience. These powerful men know what it means to be men and athletes.

You exchange an ironic glance and a knowing smile with the blond swimmer from Thunder Bay next to you. The two of you, in the midst of this concentrated masculinity, also know a great deal about what it means to be athletes and men. As gay men, you and your friend from Thunder Bay have experienced many things in common with the other men at the competition, most of whom are probably straight. Other experiences, however, have been and will be different.

—From B. Pronger, "Gay Jocks: A Phenomenology of Gay Men in Athletics," in *Sport, Men, and the Gender Order: Critical Feminist Perspectives*, edited by M. A. Messner and D. F. Sabo, Champaign, IL: Human Kinetics (1990), 394.

---

research has been done confirming or disproving any of this at the grassroots level.

Sport: An Expression of Male Biology?

Conventional wisdom often presents sports as satisfying male biological and psychological needs—a view is often reflected in sport physiology. Much evidence supports the idea that men are biologically more suited to sports than women; they run faster and jump farther. Many competitive sports require considerable strength; the sporting ideal that contenders begin a contest with an equal chance suggests that men should not play against women. Both male and female athletes take steroids containing male hormones to boost performance, which reinforces the link between male biology and sporting performance.

Feminists and sociologists both question evidence that sporting performance is linked to male biology. Feminists point out that outstanding performances, not average ones, are compared, and some women outperform most men in all sports. Studies of how social practices affect the body suggest that, in the short term, the practices men engage in from childhood result in "embodiment"—aggressive and space-occupying behavior—that is better suited to modern sports. Also, in the long term, modern sports may be selected to favor body types that men developed through involvement in particular social practices (e.g., work), thus enabling men to achieve better results than women, contributing to an overall societal of male physical superiority.

Sport as Preparation for Male Roles
Western cultures have long viewed sports as enhancing men's performance in work and family. Gary Fine's (1987) study of boys in the same country playing Little League baseball shows how boys are expected to learn not only how to play baseball, but also how and when to use particular moral codes; to value hard work, cooperation, and competition; and good citizenship. The premodern games of tribal societies supplied boys and men with the physical skills and social values required for their adult roles, as the Timbria may have learned their social values through the log-race.

Some sociologists argue that modern sport equips men for their role in capitalist societies. Thus, working-class men become an easily exploitable work force by learning to accept, for example, hierarchy and differential rewards, so benefiting capitalists. Sporting ideals, then, make inequitable economic relations appear just.

Sport: A Source of Masculine Empowerment?
Gender theorists agree that sport has negative effects on participants; it creates and reinforces gender-based hierarchies. Thus, sport restricts women and limits male alternatives to the white middle-class ideal. Evidence from interviews with athletes suggests all participants had to go along with the dominant ideals within sports. For example, they had to listen to, and often participate in, sexist and homophobic "locker room talk." In American football the ideal is that men should be physically big, show little reaction to physical pain, have a high level of emotional control, and be the dom-

inant partner in heterosexual relationships. Men live up to these ideals to different degrees and within this environment they are assessed and hierarchically arranged on this basis. Hence, small or gay men are likely to be judged as inferior. The negative masculine traits fostered through sporting practices include homophobia, an indifference to one's own and others' physical pain, a win-at-all-costs philosophy, and an inability to form intimate relationships with and a disrespect for women.

Both social reformers and feminist theorists accept that sport plays some role in shaping its participants, which raises the issue of the relationship between various sports and the dispositions they inspire. Judgments about whether certain characteristics are desirable are cultural and political ones. Competitiveness may be considered valuable or undesirable. What does seem clear is that if all are to enjoy and benefit from competitive sports, wider structural changes are necessary in gender relations.

—ANDREA ABBAS

Bibliography: Connell, R. W. (1995) *Masculinities.* Berkeley: University of California Press. Fine, G. A. (1987) *With the Boys.* Chicago: University of Chicago Press. Frankenberg, R. (1990) *Village on the Border.* Prospect Heights, IL: Waveland Press. Hargreaves, J. (1994) *Sporting Females: Critical Issues in the History and Sociology of Women's Sports.* London: Routledge. Messner, M. A. (1992) *Power at Play: Sports and the Problems of Masculinity.* Boston: Beacon Press. Messner, M. A., and D. F. Sabo, eds. (1990) *Sport, Men, and the Gender Order: Critical Feminist Perspectives.* Champaign, IL: Human Kinetics.

Media
The relationship between the media and sport has always been symbiotic. Newspapers developed sports pages to sell more papers; sports organizations welcomed publicity because it brought more spectators to the game. As radio and television gave national exposure to local teams, the amount of money available to club owners and players vastly increased, turning professionals from often ill-paid journeymen into media celebrities. As jet air travel globalized sport, the distinction between the best amateur and the professional players became impossible to maintain; even the Olympic movement abandoned founder Baron Pierre de Coubertin's original devotion to amateurism.

Still debatable is whether the quantitative change in the number of viewers of television has completely changed the quality of the sporting experience. Do children, for instance, deliberately emulate the petulant and violent player behavior they often see on television, ignoring the coaches who try to instill principles of fair play? Do most coaches, at all levels, put winning before the health and welfare of their players? Have international players become simply pawns in the hands of the media industry? Or has television simply opened up electronic seats for fans and made it impossible for sportswriters and commentators to glorify people and events those fans can now see for themselves? Has media money justified itself by providing training and competing opportunities for those who had previously been excluded from sports they could not afford to learn?

What is certain is that some sports have always been "more equal than others"; fans choose to what they will give their allegiance. The media can create or increase temporary interest in specific events, but unless what the media discuss or show is rooted in more than the event itself, interest evaporates.

Sportswriting

Media interest in sport began early in America's history. The first American newspapers were published weekly; in March 1733 the *Boston Gazette* reprinted from a London daily paper an account of a prizefight. The first American daily newspaper appeared on 30 May 1783. These newspapers published before the Civil War, many of them short-lived, concerned themselves chiefly with politics, wars, and murder, but sporadic reports on prizefights, horse racing, and cricket did appear. The first U.S. sports star created by the press was John Carmel Heenan. His 1860 prizefight with the English champion Tom Sayers was treated as a matter of international prestige.

Specialized sports magazines appeared remarkably early. John Skinner, a journalist, founded the first, *The American Turf Register and Sporting Magazine,* in September 1829. William Porter, founder of the weekly *The Spirit of the Times and Life in New York* in December 1831, which contained sporting news, bought Skinner's publication in 1839. The *Spirit's* sport reporting brought it a circulation of over 40,000 by 1840. Articles on sport also appeared in general interest magazines like *Harper's.*

Even before the Civil War, a few journalists did specialize in sport reporting for newspapers. Henry Chadwick reported on cricket for the *New York Times* and in 1862 became the baseball reporter for the *New York Herald.* After the Civil War, specialized sport reporting developed rapidly; in 1870, the *New York Times* even used a woman reporter to cover horse races. This early reporting, however, lacked focus, in part due to the sporadic nature of sports events.

It was Joseph Pulitzer who revolutionized newspaper coverage of sports (as he did of so much else) after buying the *New York Herald* in 1882. Pulitzer set up a special department for sports; while the sports section as we know it did not yet exist, by the 1890s most large city papers employed "sporting editors," and the work of their staffs occasionally occupied a full page in a daily newspaper. By then, professional baseball had been organized, college football teams were playing regularly, prizefighting had developed into boxing, and horse racing tracks had mushroomed.

Before the beginning of World War I, sportswriting had developed its own style; full pages, specially formatted, contained pictures and reports. New sports magazines appeared; *Sporting Life* was founded in 1883 and by 1886 had 40,000 readers. The *Sporting News,* founded in St. Louis in 1886 primarily to cover baseball in the west, soon began to cover other sports as well. All this reporting made the names and faces of star players known to thousands of fans who would never see their heroes in person, while some sporting events, such as baseball's World Series, began to capture the attention of casual readers. When the "white hope," James Jeffries, came out of retirement in 1910 to fight the black Jack Johnson for the heavyweight championship, the symbolic significance of the event led to a frenzy of reporting on the fight preparations.

Most sport reporting concerned local teams; colleges and universities were particularly avid for publicity. In 1893 Stanford University could not pay its professors, but $1,000 was found to hire a football coach, because a winning team was regarded as the college's best possible advertisement. Newspapers did their part by reporting team triumphs in mythic terms; football players became "heroes of the gridiron."

As separate sports departments were set up in daily newspapers, sportswriters started to get bylines; some became stars in their own right. Ring Lardner began covering South Bend's minor league baseball team for the *South Bend Times* in 1905; rather than simply reporting the game, he developed a story around a single play or personality. Hired by the *Chicago Examiner* in 1908, he covered the White Sox, traveling with the players on the train, and as was then customary, eating in the restaurant car with them, drinking with them, and staying at the same hotels. Lardner soon moved to the *Chicago Tribune* and traveled with the Cubs.

Editors allowed sportswriters to develop their own style; while the details of each game had to be accurately reported, the newspaper's aim was to attract readers. If, like Lardner, a sportswriter could be funny while making all the readers feel they'd been at the game, his future was assured. Early on, he started to use the "busher" language, modeled on the speech he'd heard from the semiliterate players he'd traveled with—and their fans, for Lardner often reported on a game from the bleachers. He wrote doggerel, and even began a serial poem called "A Epick"; he composed letters. Readers who had little or no interest in sport bought the *Tribune* to read his "Wake" column. In 1914, Lardner sold a baseball story to the *Saturday Evening Post;* his "Busher's Letters," allegedly written by an uneducated midwestern left-handed pitcher, turned into three volumes of *You Know Me Al.* Here, Lardner knocked the baseball hero off his pedestal, but without reducing his humanity.

Like most sportswriters of his time, Lardner covered far more than baseball. He often wrote about college football, but after the 1919 World Series' scandal, which deeply depressed him, he turned away from sportswriting altogether. While he was at work in Chicago, the so-called Class of 1911 was writing in New York. This group, which included Heywood Broun, Frederick Lieb, Grantland Rice, and Damon Runyon, concentrated not simply on a game's events, but on the players. Their writing was robust, vivid, and compelling. Well educated, these men often used sources far from sport to make their point.

In the sports pages, particularly in sports columns, Americans read about a world far removed from the grubby, daily grind. Not only did athletic heroes perform amazing feats; they did it with a superhuman grace and courage. The virtues of sportsmanship, teamwork, hard work, and coming back from adversity were reiterated. And sports apparently represented a democracy of talent. This sports world may have been a world of illusion, but it produced some powerful American writing. In 1956, Arthur Daley of the *New York Times* won a Pulitzer Prize for the "distinguished writing and commentary" of his sports columns, the first sportswriter to do so.

Radio

During the Depression sportswriters had to begin to compete for fans' attention with a new medium: radio. In 1920, a few thousand people owned radio receiving sets; by 1930, about 24 million did, and 44 million by 1940. Sportswriters were joined by sportscasters, as fans eagerly tuned in to live broadcasting of boxing, baseball, and college and some professional football.

These radio sportscasters were usually hired not for their knowledge of sport but for the quality of their voices; Graham McNamee was a professional baritone when he auditioned on a whim for the new St. Paul, Minnesota, radio station in 1923. That same year, he broadcast the New York Yankees vs. New York Giants World Series. Like Ted Husing, who began announcing for CBS in 1927, or Bill Stern who broadcast NBC's prominent sporting events between 1939 and 1952, McNamee brought his listeners excitement. Criticized later for their "gee whiz" style, these early radio announcers helped millions visualize and enjoy sporting events they could never hope to attend.

In the early days, all radio announcers, whether working for the emerging networks or for struggling local stations, had to possess glib tongues and vivid imaginations. Few teams were conscious of anyone but fans at the stadium, and play began when the teams were ready; radio sponsors, however, expected games to begin on time. Don Dunphy remembered sitting in a press box as a reporter for the *New York American* and hearing someone start to announce a completely imaginary hockey game because the players were still warming up when the broadcast had to begin.

Dunphy soon moved into radio himself; in 1935, he helped Earl Harper with a ticker broadcast, in which a Western Union telegrapher in the studio would give the studio announcers a distant game in Morse code. The studio supplied sound effects, including the national anthem, while the announcers broadcast a game they were not watching. Red Barber, the "Voice of Brooklyn," and Ronald Reagan, for the Cubs, both flourished in this nerve-racking situation.

Dunphy brought in guests to his regular evening WINS (New York) sports show, a novelty; he learned racetrack jargon to broadcast instant results sponsored by a new horse-racing sheet, the *Daily Pay Off.* He became "The Voice of Boxing," Gillette's announcer of Madison Square Garden bouts, only because of a network battle about how music broadcasting should be paid for. Sports organizations needed media publicity; the media regarded sports as only one of their concerns.

Television

As newspapers had faced radio reporting, after World War II both had to adapt to a new medium: television. Television was ready for marketing before World War II; on 17 May 1939, NBC's Bill Stern announced the Columbia-Princeton baseball game, the first live sporting event televised in the United States. The experiment was not successful, as the black-and-white reception was extremely poor, and the single camera could not track the ball properly. World War II delayed television's widespread use, but afterwards televisions quickly became commonplace. In 1950, about 9 percent of Americans had a television at home; by 1955, that figure had jumped to 65 percent and by 1965 to 93 percent. In 1970, 39 percent of homes contained color sets; by 1972, 64 percent did.

World War II ended the Depression; during the 1950s, disposable income was poured into sports. By 1958, jet travel enabled professional leagues to become truly national, as teams could now travel coast to coast in time to play the games of a normal season. Sports entrepreneurs and players had become used to radio; initially wary of loss of ticket sales, promoters began to see the monetary advantages of televising their product.

Anxious to televise sporting events of national significance, networks viewed regular games with some suspicion, for sports were not easily managed. They did not fit neatly into a schedule. They could be rained out. No one could guarantee an edge-of-the-seat contest (nor create one, as radio announcers often had done). While stadium fans might stay to watch a dull game, viewers would rapidly turn to a competing network.

These matters were important, because U.S. television networks made their profits, as radio had done, from advertisers. Roughly speaking, the difference between the costs of a particular show and the amount advertisers were willing to pay for slots during it represented the network's profit. Soap operas could be produced cheaply and could therefore play profitably to limited audiences; sports events needed multiple cameras, special electrical equipment, and numbers of skilled personnel, all at a specific site. Networks therefore aimed their regular sports programming at weekend fans, mostly males who had played particular sports. The aim was to make these men feel they were at the stadium itself. The high ratings were earned in prime time, on weekdays; that was reserved for shows expected to attract the whole family.

But as technology changed and cameras became less cumbersome, and producers learned their craft, the sports industry learned too. Professional football had struggled to compete with the college game during the Depression; radio had not helped much. It soon became clear, however, that while baseball is hard to televise effectively, football's larger ball and more varied but predictable plays made it riveting on television. In 1960, National Football League (NFL) owners agreed that all clubs should assign their individual television rights to the league, which would then negotiate with

the networks on their behalf. In 1961, Pete Rozelle, football's commissioner, secured antitrust exemption for these pooled agreements, and proceeded to use television to turn professional football into America's winter game.

Rozelle understood the commercial fact that stadium crowds were simply a backdrop for television viewers. NFL owners, assured of an equal share of growing television rights money, were prepared to accept rule and schedule changes to make football a more enthralling television spectacle. But when NBC and CBS seemed likely to balk at increased payments for the limited weekend schedule, Rozelle offered ABC a special schedule of games to be played during prime time.

In 1970, ABC was the poor relation of the big three networks; it was operating at a prime-time loss. Roone Arledge, president of ABC sports, was backed in his calculated gamble of attracting a family, rather than a male, football-fan audience, for *Monday Night Football*. Having produced and directed ABC's college football games, in 1961 he created the Emmy Award–winning sports anthology show the *Wide World of Sports*, that was soon copied by other networks, and led to such spinoffs as *The Superstars*.

Starting with college football, Arledge had been determined to make sports entertaining for viewers who weren't necessarily fans. He used every technological advance and every gimmick he could think of to make games come alive for those in the electronic seats. Commentators were to be teachers, not simply reporters; they were to draw in people who had never played the sport they were watching. For *Wide World of Sports*, Arledge hired Jim McKay, who had begun his career as a sportswriter for the *Baltimore Evening Sun* in 1946. In 1948, McKay moved into television and was hired by CBS in 1950, where he gained a wealth of experience in and out of sports. His broad background enabled him to pull together the varied events on *Wide World of Sports;* he focused on the people involved, not simply the events. He enjoyed the rapidly changing technology ABC provided and did exactly as Arledge had hoped; he made unfamiliar sports easy for Americans to watch and drew in new viewers while retaining the interest of the knowledgeable fan.

For *Monday Night Football*, Arledge drew on all his sports experience. The program was conceived of as entertainment, not simply as the translation of a stadium event to the TV screen. Rather than the weekend games' two announcers, three were employed; one of them, Howard Cosell, was chosen not for his football expertise but to make new viewers care about what they were seeing. Rapidly, he became a household name; excoriated by the knowledgeable, his nasal voice and erudite determination to "tell it like it is" undermined the jock culture of regular sports broadcasting, precisely as it was intended to do. The by-play between him and the irreverent "Dandy Don" Meredith, ex-Cowboys quarterback, increased the fun—and earned Meredith an Emmy.

Monday Night Football was the harbinger of things to come. If a television show is to garner high ratings, and thus to be attractive to high-paying advertisers, it must draw together viewers who share very few common interests. Advertisers have become increasingly sophisticated and want to be assured that a show is being watched not simply by large numbers of people, but by those whose age, income, and educational background will predispose them to buy certain products. Network television sporting events must therefore be presented in a format that is familiar to viewers, and that does not necessarily demand their full attention. The fragmentation of audiences cable television introduced put further pressure on networks to make their sports programming attractive to more than jocks—who would frequently tune in to ESPN.

Networks therefore make demands on sports organizations; publicity and dollars are exchanged for some control over scheduling, commercial breaks, and guaranteed levels of performance. Nowhere is this "take-and-give" clearer than in U.S. television networks' relationship with the International Olympic Committee (IOC).

In 1960, CBS paid $50,000 for the rights to the Winter Olympics in Squaw Valley, California, and $394,000 for the Summer Olympics in Rome. In contrast, NBC agreed to pay $705 million for the Sydney, Australia, Summer Games alone, to be held in 2000. What has made the Games worth so much more in 40 years?

Changes in technology have been one reason, but the Cold War and changes in television producers' axioms have had more to do with it. During the Cold War, the competition between the United States and communist countries, particularly the athletic powerhouses of East Germany and the Soviet Union, allowed television to capitalize on Americans' need to win. Medals become symbolic markers of national superiority. The abrupt collapse of the communist system took away that dimension of the Games, but the habit of thinking of the Games as important had been established. Now it had to be kept up.

Television sports programming was originally based on the proposition that U.S. audiences want to watch events while they are happening. Immense effort, therefore, went into trying to bring live Olympic coverage to the United States. But the different Olympic venues made this difficult, and very inconvenient when time zones abroad did not fit prime time in the United States. In 1964, NBC managed to broadcast the opening ceremonies from Tokyo live, although it was not until late summer that anyone knew whether pictures beamed via the satellite Syncam III would be of network quality. Film was flown in from Tokyo for the events themselves.

Live coverage presented other problems. In 1988, five goals were missed in two separate U.S. hockey games because no allowance was made at the site for the commercial breaks all U.S. networks required. Nothing could be substituted if bad weather caused postponement of events, as happened frequently at Albertville. Live coverage was also immensely costly.

Audience research conducted by CBS led to the discovery that "high profile" events were watched less for the result than for their intrinsic interest; so in 1984 ABC experimented with tape-delayed coverage from Sarajevo. In 1994, NBC decided that all events from Lillehammer would be taped.

Now the Olympics could be scripted like any other TV show. Skating, the event viewers liked best, was shown somehow each evening even when no competition was scheduled. Events such as the cross-country relay, dreary for most Americans, were cast in a format regular television viewers understood. Specific segments of the race, taken from different camera angles, were spliced seamlessly together. A commentary was fitted to the tape, drawing on such human interest stories (not relevant to the race the spectators were watching) as the heroism of one competitor whose brother had disappeared on the trail during training. The suspense techniques of soap opera were used to turn the event into a familiar living room drama. The whole was overlaid with a jazzy musical soundtrack. What was televised, in short, was not the cross-country relay, but a made-for-TV version quite different from what anyone at the site would have experienced.

Purists deplore such editing. But if the Olympics cannot be made familiar to, and comfortable for, most U.S. viewers, those viewers will simply change channels. Other countries televise the Games differently; the constraints on their programming are also different. For as U.S. interest in the Games has increased, so networks have each regarded televising them as a demonstration of technical expertise and communications superiority. Networks have been willing to lose money on the Games, as they compete with each other for public acclaim, which they believe will translate into regular programming ratings.

The Past and Present

Although the forms of sport reporting in the United States have changed over the years, continuities are evident. Television did not wholly replace radio commentary; many fans now turn off the sound and listen to radio announcing of the games they're watching. Sport talk shows have proliferated on radio; many encourage listeners to call in with questions and comments. Neither television nor radio displaced sportswriting; as any supermarket demonstrates, sports magazines have proliferated, especially those devoted to specific events. Sportswriters in daily newspapers still analyze games fans have watched or listened to; some sports columnists are still better known than many competitors. (In the late 1970s, Red Smith's column was syndicated in more than 500 newspapers, including many published overseas. When he died in 1982, the *New York Times* put his obituary on the front page.)

The patterns set by early sportswriters still, in many ways, persist. The media form that is dominant (now television) acts as a sport booster, for instance. Babe Ruth could not today be the hero contemporary writers made him, because fans could now see for themselves his immaturity, lack of self-discipline, and poor conditioning. But it is the print media that have brought the fundamental problems of modern sport to fans' attention; television does not dwell on gambling, drugs, exploitation of athletes, and other ugly facets of sport at all levels. This results partly from the changes in journalists' perception of their job; newspaper readers now expect to see the worst about every public figure and every public institution. But in the 1990s, television is the major beneficiary of sports' mythic hold on fans; television must therefore continue to help fans believe that what they are watching is "more than a game," so that they will repeat the experience. Whatever is said in print will now have little effect on stadium attendance or game ratings; sportswriters can therefore afford to attack as well as boost.

Other old patterns are still visible. Just as early sportswriters picked out and created stars, so does television. In the days before radio, few fans ever attended an event without having their perceptions shaped by what they had read beforehand about the contestants, coaches, and probable outcome. Television pre- and post-game shows, nightly news segments, and commentators similarly frame each event; fans perceive both what is on the screen, and what they expect and hope to see.

What television has done differently is to increase vastly the amount of money available to sports promoters. Some of that largesse trickles down to athletes, for scholarships, pay, training, and medical facilities, pensions, and, if they win, endorsements. Most of it, however, goes into the maw of those who run the enterprise, from school districts to colleges, to club owners, to national and international federations, and to the IOC. Like all human endeavors, sport has been corrupted on occasion; the stakes are now immeasurably higher.

But however much money television pours into sport, by itself it cannot ensure that viewers will watch. It is the fan who decides an event is worth time and energy; the fan who invests sport with transcendence. Delighted by "their" team's victory, or by a vision of extraordinary athletic prowess or grace, fans can just as easily be disgusted by greed, drug-enhanced performance, and lack of sportsmanship. For the media, sport is a marketable product; let any branch of it lose its commercial appeal, and the media will find a different, commercially successful product. The symbiotic relationship between media and sport can last only as long as people care. Sports and media management will therefore continue to make it their business to try to turn readers, listeners, and viewers into fans, and to ensure that sport retains its mythic embodiment of eternal verities. For fans agree with a British soccer (association football) manager who once said, "Football is not a matter of life and death. It's much more important."

—JOAN M. CHANDLER

Bibliography: Chandler, Joan. (1988) *Television and National Sport: The United States and Britain.* Urbana: University of Illinois Press. Dunphy, Don. (1988) *Don Dunphy at Ringside.* New York: Henry Holt. Elder, Donald. (1956) *Ring Lardner: A Biography.* New York: Doubleday. Husing, Ted. (1935) *Ten Years before the Mike.* New York: Farrar and Rinehart. Koppett, Leonard. (1981) *Sports Illusion, Sports Reality: A Reporter's View of Sports, Journalism, and Society.* Boston: Houghton Mifflin. Lardner, Ring. (1916) *You Know Me Al.* New York: George Doran. Newcomb, Horace, ed. (1994) *Television: The Critical View.* 5th ed. New York: Oxford University Press. Rader, Benjamin. (1984) *In Its Own Image: How Television Has Transformed Sports.* New York: Free Press. Whannel, Garry. (1992) *Fields in Vision: Television Sport and Cultural Transformation.* London: Routledge.

Medicine

The development of medical specialties began gradually in the 18th century and became formal only in the 20th century. Until then, lack of specific knowledge of the particular causes of illness and disability and the human body's reactions to them rendered all physicians generalists. Specialties developed primarily around the body organs or systems and in association with the various activities or occupations. Physical activities, including exercises and sports, present opportunities for illness and injury, as well as means to alleviate and cure deformity and disability. Working and studying in this area ultimately became the special field of practice we now call sports medicine.

History

The first surviving writing on the medical value of exercise and massage is found in the Ayurveda in India, traditional writings handed down from Dhan Vantari, the Hindu god of medicine, dating from between 1000 and 800 B.C.E. The Ayurveda recommends exercise and massage for the treatment of rheumatism. Herodicus (born in Thrace about 480 B.C.E.) and Hippocrates (born on the island of Cos about 460 B.C.E.) were gymnasts (one of the three classes of medical practitioners in ancient Greece; both recommended exercise for treatment of the sick even for mental diseases). Herophilus and Eristratus of the medical school of Alexandria in the 4th century B.C.E. also recommended moderate exercises. Asclepides, who was born in Bithynia in 126 B.C.E. and practiced in Rome, treated patients by massage and recommended walking, running, and diet measures. Rufus of Ephesus (60–120 C.E.) related the pulse to the apical heartbeat and described its characteristics in health and disease.

Galen of Pergamos (131–200 C.E.) was the first to develop systematic descriptions of the body, to recognize that the only action of muscle was contraction and that this took place in only one direction, that the stimulus for contraction came from the brain through the nerves. He also showed that the arteries contained blood from the right side of the heart and air from the lungs and described the formation of urine from blood serum. He was probably the first sport physician, since when he came to Rome he provided medical care of the gladiators who performed in public exhibitions in the arena. Aurelianus (5th century C.E.) used weights, pulleys, and hydrotherapy for rehabilitation following surgery. Paulus Aegineta (7th century C.E.) defined exercise as violent motion fitting body organs for their proper function.

Avicenna (Ibn Sina, born in Persia about 980 C.E.) followed Galen in prescribing health-furthering exercises, massage, and baths. The influence of these two men dominated medical practice in the West for 1,000 years.

Interest in medical gymnastics in Europe intensified during the Renaissance by the rediscovery of the original Greek contributions. Vergerius (1370–1444), professor of logic at the University of Padua, was one of the first Italian humanists to advocate regular physical exercise in the education of children.

Vittorino da Feltre (1373–1446) established under his patron, the Marquis Gonzaga of Mantua, a school for the children of his court. They entered at age four or five, were tested for their capabilities, and had exercise prescribed individually by age, body type, season, and time of day. The school practiced dietetics and employed a wide variety of sports. Gymnastics were conceived of as an integral and indispensable preliminary for educational success. This has influenced education in the Western world ever since.

The first printed book on exercise by a physician was *The Book of Bodily Exercise,* published in Spain by Dr. Christobal Mendez of Jaen in 1553. He advocated exercises for older as well as crippled persons, and wrote, "The easiest way of all to preserve and restore health without diverse peculiarities and with greater profit than all other measures put together is to exercise well." A landmark of this period was the 1569 publication of the six books on the art of gymnastics *(De arte gymnastica)* by Gerolamo Mercuriale, who classified gymnastics into preventive and therapeutic forms but warned against strenuous military exercises and athletics.

Joseph Duchesne (1546–1609) wrote in his *Ars Medica Hermetica* that "The essential purpose of gymnastics for the body is its deliverance from superfluous humors, the regulation of digestion, the strengthening of the heart and joints, the opening of the pores of the skin and the stronger circulation of blood in the lungs by strenuous breathing." He was the first to recommend swimming for strengthening the body as well as for lifesaving. Marsilius Cagmatis (1543–1612) of Verona in his *Preservation of Health* asked for specially educated physicians to introduce rowing into gymnastics and supervise games. Santorio Santorio (1561–1636) in Padua invented the weighing chair, which enabled him to measure insensible perspiration after gymnastics and to develop his basic theory of metabolic balance.

Laurent Joubert (1529–1583), professor of medicine at the University of Montpellier in France, a great

Medicina Gymnastica.

The Generality of Men, have for a long time had too Narrow Thoughts of Phyfick, as if it were in a manner Confined to little more than Internals, without allowing themselves the Liberty of common Reasoning, by which they easily might have found that the Human Body is liable to, and requires several Administrations of a very Different Nature, and that it is very unreasonable to suppose that since there are so many ways for Disease to enter upon us, there should be so few for Health to return by. Internals do indeed make up for the greatest part of the Means of Cure, but there are considerable Cases, where the very Nature of the thing requires other Methods; and this would appear very obvious, if it were not for our too Partial Consideration of the Body of Man, by attributing too much to the Fluids, and too little to the Solids, both which, though they have a Mutual Dependence upon one another, yet have each of them some Properties, and if our of Order, require something Particular in the Application to restore them again.

We see Contraries often prove Remedies to one another in the Juices, and Poisons become Beneficial when opposed to certain Humours why should we not allow of the same Rule in the Containing Parts of the Body? If by a Supine Course of Life, the Nervous parts are weakened and relaxed, why should we not suppose the contrary way of Living, the most likely to repair them? Since the Vigorous of those parts is acquired by use; they are the Active part of the Man, and not always liable to the Impressions of the Fluids, for though you invigorate the Blood ever so much by the most generous Medicine, the Nerves may remain Effete and Languid notwithstanding; but if the Nervous parts are extended and exercised, the Blood and the Humours must necessarily partake of the Benefit, and soon discover it by the Increase of their Heat and Motion.

Though some People have supposed a Warm Bath to be only a last Resort, yet it is quite otherwise, it being impossible to remove some Diseases of the Limbs without an universal equal Relaxation. Again, quite different from this is the equal Distribution of a greater Degree of Heat throughout the whole Body, which is procured by Habitual Exercise; in the former Method the Parts are relaxed, in this they are strengthened, and in every Respect the Effects are widely different, though in both ways there is a considerable Encrease of the Heat.

It is one thing to dispose Nature to collect her own Strength and throw off her Enemy; and it is another to assist her by the Corpuscula, the Minute parts of a Medicine given inwardly; the first way has Regard to the whole Animal Oeconomy; the second respects the Blood and Juices chiefly; the first may succeed, where the second cannot, because here the Laws of Motion, and the rules of the Oeconomy are enforced, and brought to be assisting to a Recovery of Health, which in some cases can't be effected by a private and simple attempt upon the Blood only.

As for the Exercise of the Body, which is the subject of this ensuing Discourse, if people would not think so superficially of it, if they would but abstract the Benefit got by it, from the Means by which it is got, they would set a great Value upon it; if some of the Advantages occurring from Exercise were to be procured by any one Medicine, nothing in the World would be in more Esteem than that Medicine would be; but as those advantages are to be obtained another way, and by taking some Pains, Men's Heads are turned to overlook and slight them. The habitual increase of the Natural Heat of the Body, as I took notice above is not to be despised.

If any Drug could cause such an effect as the Motion of the Body does, in this respect it would be of singular Use in some tender Cases upon this very Account; but then add to this the great Strength which the Muscular and Nervous parts acquire by Exercises, if that could be adequately obtained likewise by the same Internal Means, what a Value, what an Extravagant Esteem would Mankind have for that Remedy which could produce such wonderful Effects!

—From the preface to *Medicina Gymnastica or a Treatise Concerning the Power of Exercise. with Respect to the Annual Oeconomy; and the Great Necessity of it in the Cure of Several Distempers by Francis Fuller, M.A. The Third Edition.* London. Printed for Robert Knaplock at the Bishops-Head in St. Paul's Church-Yard, 1707.

---

advocate of daily exercise, considered physicians the only ones capable of prescribing gymnastics. He introduced therapeutic gymnastics into the medical course. With the development of physiology and the study of medicine in the 16th century came a new interest in all animal and human movement. Jean Canape became a leader in exercise physiology with the 1541 publication of his *The Anatomy of the Movement of Muscles.* Girolamo Cardano (1501–1576), the physician-mathematician, in 1551 conceived a theory of muscle movement from a mechanical standpoint that exerted a profound influence on physiology into the next century. The great iatromechanical physiologist G. A. Borelli (1608–1679)

described muscle tone and the antagonistic actions of muscles. He failed only when he identified the mechanism of muscle contraction as a rearrangement of existing structure in his great work, *On the Movement of Animals,* published posthumously in 1710.

In the early 18th century, Hoffmann in The Hague and Stahl at Halle wrote and lectured on the virtues of exercise in the prevention as well as the treatment of disease. Hoffmann, who classified occupational movements as exercises, following Bernardo Ramazzini (1633–1714), influenced C. J. Tissot, who in 1781 published *Medical and Surgical Gymnastics,* one of the most influential books of its day. As surgeon-in-chief of the French armies in 1808 he prescribed exercises for their general effects and strength development and essentially founded occupational and recreational therapy and adaptive sports.

Nicholas Andry (1658–1742) in the mid-18th century published his *L'orthopedie,* which gave the specialty of orthopedics its name. He prescribed a variety of exercises for the prevention and treatment of diseases in children. Pierre Jean Burette (1665–1747) was the first physician to write on the history of sports, especially ball games and discus throwing. In Russia, A. P. Protasov lectured in 1765 on "The Importance of Motion in the Maintenance of Health"; the physicians to the czar recommended that he walk, run, and ride horseback to correct his obesity; and N. M. Ambodik wrote, "A body without motion deteriorates and putrefies like still water" (Vinokurov 1961).

At the beginning of the 19th century, under the influence of Ling in Sweden, Clias in Berne, Jahn in Prussia, and Amoros in Paris, a true physical education was born, apart from therapeutic exercises and no longer under medical direction. Ling introduced system into exercise and George Taylor introduced Ling's system to America, where enthusiasm was so great that there was a shortage of trained gymnastic teachers. Zander supplied the demand with machines embodying levers, wheels, and weights for active, assisted, and resistive exercises that became popular all over the civilized world.

Progress in exercise physiology came in the 19th century with Claude Bernard's (1813–1878) demonstration of the body's physiological synthesis of chemicals, the demonstration by Guillaume Duchesne de Boulogne (1806–1875) of the complex interactions of striated muscle, the invention by William Einthoven (1860–1927) of the string galvanometer to study action potentials in the myocardium, and the development of the hierarchy of levels in the central nervous system by John Hughlings Jackson (1835–1911). R. Tait McKenzie (1867–1938) published his *Exercise and Education in Medicine* and effected his recommendations working with others in treating and rehabilitating the injured in World War I, thus beginning the modern concept of medical rehabilitation.

What was probably the first English publication in sports medicine was a section on first aid in *The Encyclopedia of Sport* (Byles and Osborn 1898). Credit for the first book on sports medicine in English must be shared by G. B. Heald of England, who in 1931 published *Injuries and Sport* (Heald 1931), and Dr. Walter E. Meanwell, team physician at the University of Wis-

consin, who that same year collaborated with Notre Dame football coach Knute Rockne to publish *Training, Conditioning and the Care of Injuries,* the first U.S. work on sports medicine.

Dr. Siegfried Weissbein of Berlin produced in 1910 *Hygiene des Sports* (Hygiene of Sport), probably the first book to deal comprehensively with what we now call sports medicine. In 1914, a one-volume contribution to the *Encyclopedia of Surgery* came from Dr. G. Van Saar under the title *Die Sportverletzungen* (Sports Injuries). Dr. Felix Mandel published *Chirurgie der Sportunfalle* (Surgery of Sports Accidents), a work on surgery of sports injuries in 1925. *Grundriss der Sportmedizin* (Foundations of Sports Medicine for Physicians and Students) (Herxheimer 1932), a study of exercise physiology by Professor Dr. H. Herxheimer of Berlin, was published in 1932.

The 1925 publication of Bancroft's *The Respiratory Function of the Blood* in 1925 was a landmark in the study of exercise physiology. Development continued with the 1927 publication of two monographs by A. V. Hill of London: *Muscular Movement in Man,* which introduced the concept of "the steady state of exercise," and *Living Machinery* (Hill 1927), which described the relationship of neuromuscular coordination and cardiorespiratory function to strength, speed, and endurance. The third edition of F. A. Bainbridge's *The Physiology of Muscular Exercise,* completely rewritten by A. V. Bock and D. B. Dill, and *Physiology of Muscular Activity* by E. C. Schneider helped lay firm foundations for future development in the field of exercise physiology. Basic contributions to strength training were provided in *Progressive Resistance Exercise* by Thomas De Lorme and A. L. Watkins in 1951, and the two publications by E. A. Muller and associates that defined and described isometric strength.

Modern Sports Medicine

Modern sports medicine has been defined and developed by the organization of clinical services to serve all people who are or wish to become involved in vigorous physical exercise in some part of their lives, and those who advise, assist, monitor, or care for them. This includes not only physicians and paramedical specialists but educators, exercise scientists, coaches, psychologists, and sociologists. Related developments include the organization of scientific societies; the formation of medical specialty groups; the proliferation of special conferences, seminars, and conventions; the establishment of journals, magazines, and newsletters; and the publication of monographs, books, and encyclopedias.

A special role has been played by the International Olympic Committee (IOC) because of its need to establish effective standards for athletic qualification and medical care of the athletes from the international sports federations who compete in the Olympic Games.

A group of 33 physicians attending the sports teams of 11 nations during the Winter Games of the IX Olympiad at St. Moritz, Switzerland, on 14 February 1928 established, under the leadership of doctors W. Knoll of Switzerland and F. Latarjet of France, a committee whose function was to plan for the First International Congress of Sports to take place during the Summer Games at Amsterdam in August of the same year. This was the first printed use of the term *sports medicine* to define the field. The resulting congress in Amsterdam attracted 281 physicians and specialists in physical education from 20 different countries. The first constitution of the Association Internationale Medico-Sportive (AIMS) was adopted, and Dr. F. J. Buytendijk was elected president. The constitution set out three principal purposes: (1) to inaugurate scientific research in biology, psychology, and sociology in relation to sports; (2) to promote the study of medical problems encountered in physical exercises and sports in collaboration with various international sports federations; and (3) to organize international congresses on sports medicine to be held during and at the site of the quadrennial Olympic Games.

The Second Congress of the Association Internationale Medico-Sportive (AIMS) was held in Turin, Italy, in 1933. Topics were grouped under nine headings: anthropology, evaluating physical fitness, medical control of sports, the kidney and sports, the heart in athletics, orthopedics and trauma in sports, respiratory physiology, fatigue, and women in sports. It was established that a general assembly of the new association, which became the Federation Internationale Medico-Sportive et Scientifique (FIMS), would be held at the time of the International Sports Medicine Congress in each Olympic year.

Eager to move ahead, French physicians organized a Third International Congress in Sports Medicine at Chamonix, France, in 1934. Physicians from eight European countries attended. New topics and proposals discussed were: performing sports at high altitudes, the teaching of physical education in all medical schools, the awarding of a special diploma to those passing examinations in these courses to enable the graduates to qualify for positions as school hygienists and physicians, the institution of a national and international system of medical licensing for athletes, and the standardization of medical charts for athletes.

A fourth international congress was held in Berlin in 1936, a fifth in Paris in 1937, and a sixth in Brussels in 1939. After World War II a general assembly was held in Brussels in 1947 among surviving members with new officers and a revised constitution. The seventh congress was held in Prague in 1948, the eighth in Florence in 1950, and the ninth in Paris in 1952. In that year the federation was given official recognition by the IOC. The tenth Congress met in Belgrade, Yugoslavia, in 1954; the eleventh in Luxembourg in 1956; the twelfth in Moscow in 1958; and thirteenth in Vienna in 1960; and the fourteenth in Santiago, Chile, in 1962.

The *Journal of Sports Medicine and Physical Fitness* was established under the auspices of the FIMS in 1961 and the International Bulletin transferred to the new *Journal,* which became the official publication of the FIMS. Congresses have been held every two to four years since, with the 23rd in Brisbane, Australia, in 1986.

The nature and structure of the FIMS has changed over the years, as membership categories varied. A Scientific Commission has been a constant. An Interfederal Medical Commission is made up of physicians appointed by the different international sports federations and it has generally functioned independently as an adviser to the IOC. The principal membership of the FIMS has come from the national sports medicine associations or authorities of countries, and this number has changed with the many changes in national identities since World War II. The member association from the United States is the American College of Sports Medicine (ACSM).

Other international organizations that have operated independently and/or cooperated with the FIMS include the International Council of Sport and Physical Education (ICSPE), a subdivision of UNESCO; the Conseil International du Sport Militaire (CISM), founded in 1948; the Federation Internationale Education Physique (FIEP); and the International Council on Health, Physical Education and Recreation (ICHPER).

The ACSM and its international membership has become the leading organization in this field and a principal purveyor of health promotion to the general public. Through its multidisciplinary membership it has translated scientific and technical knowledge into practical terminology and advice that can be understood and adopted at all levels of education. In 1974 it established certification for program directors (based on knowledge and performance in the field of health and fitness exercise) who took special seminars and passed examinations set by specialists. Certification as an exercise specialist followed in 1975, as an exercise test technician in 1976, as a health/fitness instructor in 1982, and as a health/fitness director and as an exercise leader in 1986. Clinical conferences directed to the interests and practices of physicians in sports medicine were instituted in 1987, and led in 1990 to the establishment of a team physician course in three parts leading to certification by examination.

The ACSM journal, established as the quarterly *Medicine and Science in Sports* in 1969, and reconstituted as the bimonthly *Medicine and Science in Sports and Exercise* in 1980 is the leading publication outlet and reference source in its field.

Medical and academic associations have also formed to serve physicians qualified in other specialties who are concerned about how sports and exercise affect their specialties. These groups include the American Orthopedic Society for Sports Medicine, the American Osteopathic Society for Sports Medicine, the American Academy for Sports Vision, and the Podiatric Academy for Sports Medicine.

The American Medical Society for Sports Medicine, established in 1991, grew from the desire to recognize or confer special qualifications in a field of medicine that lacks a recognized medical specialty. The American Academy of Sports Physicians, founded in 1987, requires prospective members to hold a medical license in their state of residency and certification by a primary specialty board and take a competency examination preceded by a special review course that is held annually. The American Board of Sports Medicine is a freestanding medical specialty board that appears to be a 1991 development from the American Academy of Sports Physicians.

Journalists and magazines dealing with sports medicine topics have been published in many countries and in different languages by medical and paramedical associations and organizations. Many are published in English since it has become the universal language of science.

Sports Medicine and the IOC

Medical supervision of athletes before and during the quadrennial Olympic Games extends back to the ancient Greek Games in their early years. A principal concern was the required 10 months of supervised training preceding each renewal and the regulation of the athlete's diet.

When the Olympic Games were revived in 1896

there was no provision for any medical element, although some teams were accompanied by physicians. The principal medical difficulty encountered in Athens in 1896 and the next four Olympic Games was heat exhaustion among marathon runners. They were subsequently required to have a physical examination—the first medical requirement for the Games. The first chief medical officer for the U.S. Olympic team was Graeme M. Hammond, M.D., at the Paris Games in 1924, assisted by two physicians, a nurse, nine athletic trainers, and two masseurs. The first Olympic Village to house the athletes, at the Los Angeles Games in 1932, included a small hospital staffed by three physicians.

Physicians have also been key in several areas of Olympic testing. Perceived difficulties about the sexual differentiation of some of the women competitors began with two competitors in the 1936 Berlin games. Both were revealed to be men dressed as women. As a result, examinations of the external genitalia were required for all women competitors before competition, a requirement changed in 1976 to the examination of a buccal smear to determine gender genetically.

The first testing of athletes for use of banned substances was carried out at the Mexico City Games in 1968.

Current Issues in Sports Medicine

The major issues in sports medicine today are the question of artificial aids to sports performance, the causes of sudden death in young, apparently healthy athletes, and the age at which young persons should enter competitive sports activities.

It is reliably demonstrated that the use of male testicular hormone and/or anabolic steroids may help some women improve performance in sports where strength is an important factor. It has not been reliably demonstrated that anabolic steroids can improve performance in men. Testosterone can help men improve performance if they are lacking its production to a measurable degree. The unrestricted use of anabolic steroids by men has led in some cases to serious physical damage and even death. The incessant testing for use of these steroids by young men has led them to believe they are being unjustly deprived of an advantage they might otherwise have. Women who have a high androgenic component naturally have tested positive for testosterone and have been banned from competition.

Sudden deaths of young athletes, amateur and professional, continue to occur from vascular accidents that involve cerebral coronary and other major arteries.

Hypertrophic cardiomyopathy may occur in boys and young men for reasons not yet fully understood. Since the appearance of this condition does not usually produce signs or symptoms that are characteristic, the question of prevention remains an enigma. How long and at what intensity apparently normal hearts can be trained and exercised before myocardial infarction and even cardiac arrest may occur is uncertain.

The financial lure of professional sports leads some parents of young children who show early interest and ability in competitive sports to encourage those children to participate in them. Questions are being raised by physicians and others as to the long-term physical and emotional consequences of adolescents competing in sports such as gymnastics, figure skating, and basketball at the international and professional levels. In response, some professional sports such as tennis now have age restrictions as to when competition can start, but there is no way to restrain the parents and children from hard training to reach that level before that age. Some children make the transition from play to competitive sport successfully, but many others do not.

These and other issues may someday be resolved, at least in part, through the efforts of sports medicine.

—ALLAN J. RYAN

See also Conditioning; Drugs and Drug Testing; Exercise.
Bibliography: Micheli, Lyle J., and Mark D. Jenkins (1995). *The Sports Medicine Bible.* New York: HarperCollins. Ryan, A. J. (1968) "Medical History of the Olympic Games." *Journal of the American Medical Association* 205, 11 (September): 715–720. Shahady, Edward J., and Michael J. Petrizzi. (1991) *Sports Medicine for Coaches and Trainers.* Chapel Hill: University of North Carolina Press. Sherry, Eugene, and Stephen Wilson. (1998) *Oxford Handbook of Sports Medicine.* New York: Oxford University Press.

Mesoamerican Ballgame

Mesoamerican ballgame is a nearly extinct sport played in ancient Mesoamerica. Its distinguishing features were use of a hard rubber ball and the practice of propelling the ball only with the hips. Once a ritual, divinitory, and symbolic game, the rubber ball game is now played for recreation only in simplified versions, in parts of Mexico.

History

In preconquest Mesoamerica, the rubber-ball game, known as *ullamaliztli* or *ollama liztli* in the Aztec language (Nahuatl), was played for some 2,000 years. The earliest evidence appears in the Mexican highlands in the form of early pre-Classic (circa 1500–1200 B.C.E.) clay figurines depicting ball players.

It was played with a solid natural rubber ball either by two individuals or by teams of 2 to 7 players, although some games were apparently played by teams of up to 11 or 12 players. Games were played on specially constructed courts known as *tlachtli.* Surviving monumental courts in ceremonial centers indicate the game's importance to elite classes who played it. Commoners played too, although probably on informal earthen courts, and nobles retained professional players. Beyond recreation, the game's most important aspects were ritual, divinitory, and symbolic. Gambling was common (of gold, clothing, slaves, and even children of the players); human sacrifice sometimes occurred. The game was played intensively in the Mexican highlands, the Mayan-speaking areas of southern Mesoamerica, and on both the east and west coasts. Archeological evidence suggests that it may have reached as far north as the Hohokam area of southern Arizona by about C.E. 700. Documents from the conquest period indicate that the game was played by nearly all adolescent and adult males, including both commoners and nobles (Santley, Berman, and Alexander 1991).

Despite expressions of admiration for the athleticism displayed in the game by native ball players, the Spanish missionaries soon ordered the ballcourts in Nahuatl-speaking areas of Mesoamerica destroyed because of the ritual and religious significance of the game to natives, deemed a barrier to their rapid conversion to Christianity and therefore unacceptable. The ballcourts in highland Mesoamerica were destroyed by 1585. The ballgame eventually disappeared in Mesoamerica, except for a few simplified survivals that linger in northwestern Mexico.

Rules and Play

Classic Mesoamerican ballgame was played on specially constructed courts with a solid ball of natural rubber that was heavy but bounced well. Generally, the ball could be struck by players with only their hips, buttocks, or knees. Systems of scoring varied but usually involved efforts to propel the ball into the opponent's "end zone" and to prevent the ball from coming to rest. In some cases, ballcourts were equipped with two stone rings mounted on tenons on either side of the central court area. If the ball was propelled through one of these rings, the game was won outright by the scoring team.

The most commonly known of the several types of courts is laid out in a capital "I" shape; others had open ends. Ballcourts are most often, but not always, oriented either north-south or east-west. Orientation may have represented seasonal, astronomical, and symbolic themes. The height and angle of walls probably also had symbolic aspects.

Ballcourts also differed substantially in size. The largest court in all of Mesoamerica is located at Chichén Itzá in the northern Yucatan and measures 70 by 168 meters (77 by 184 yards). This court is nearly 25 times larger than the next largest in the lowlands. Major urban centers sometimes had a main court, often located next to the square where the market was held, plus other, smaller courts. Spectators watched the games from the tops of the walls, which were accessed by means of external staircases.

Rules for play almost certainly varied as well. Unfortunately, early colonial chroniclers of the game generally failed to leave accounts of the rules of play. One exception mentioned only a few rules, including the scoring rules described above. He indicated that only "Great Lords" played in the primary ballcourts, two against two, three against three, or sometimes, two against three. They wore only a loincloth and hit the ball only with the hips and buttocks; striking the ball with another part of the body was regarded as an error.

The natural rubber balls varied in size, although most reports indicate that one was "somewhat smaller than a man's head." Injuries and even deaths due to blows received from the ball during play were common.

Ballplayers wore protective equipment that varied with time and place. This gear sometimes included cotton pads on the pelvis and waist as well as a U-shaped protective yoke around the waist or on one hip, cloth pads on the forearm, a pad on one knee, and a calf-length leather skirt worn over the loincloth.

The game was played for ritual purposes, to resolve disputes, to acquire social and political status, as a public sporting spectacle with heavy gambling, and purely for recreation. It was often accompanied by human sacrifice, sometimes of members of the losing team, but also of captives, and most often by decapitation.

Simplified versions of the ballgame still exist in northwestern Mexico. In one of these, played in the Mazatlán region of southern Sinaloa, the ball was propelled by the hips only. The other form, played in the north of Sinaloa, was described as "arm-ulama," meaning that the upper arms and shoulders could be used to propel the ball. Played for recreation on fields where court boundaries are marked by stones and lines drawn in the dirt, the present manifestation of the game no longer has the symbolic and cosmogonic con-

A First-Hand Account.

The Spanish friar Diego Durán claimed to have witnessed the game many times circa 1570 and described its play as follows:

It was a game of much recreation to them and enjoyment specially for those who took it as a pastime and entertainment, among which were some who played it with such dexterity and skill that they during one hour succeeded in not stopping the flight of the ball from one end to the other without missing a single hit with their buttocks, not being allowed to reach it with hands, nor feet, nor with the calf of their legs, nor with their arms.

. . . and at the ends of the court they had a quantity of players on guard and to defend against the ball entering there, with the principal players in the middle to face the ball and the opponents. The game was played just as they fought, i.e., they battled in distinct units. In the center of this enclosure were placed two stones in the wall one opposite the other; these two (stones) had a hole in the center, which was encircled by an idol representing the god of the game. . . . That we may understand the purpose which these stones served it should be known that the stone on one side served that those of one party could drive the ball through the hole which was in the stone; and the one on the other side served the other party and either of these who first drove his ball through (the hole in the stone) won the prize.

. . . All those who entered this game, played with leathers placed over their loin-clouts and they always wore some trousers of deerskin to protect the thighs which they all the time were scraping against the ground. They wore gloves in order not to hurt their hands, as they continuously were steadying and supporting themselves on the ground.

. . . They were so quick in that moment to hit with their knees or seats that they returned the ball with an extra ordinary velocity. With these thrusts they suffered great damage on the knees or on the thighs, with the result that those who for smartness often used them, got their haunches so mangled that they had those places cut with a small knife and extracted blood which the blows of the ball had gathered.

—*Durán 1971, quoted in Freidel, Schele, and Parker 1993, 341–342*

tent that was key to its existence in preconquest Mesoamerica. The positive side of this is that the low-scoring team loses only the game, not their heads.

—GARRY CHICK

Bibliography: Leyenaar, Ted J., and Lee A. Parsons. (1988) *Ulama: The Ballgame of the Mayas and Aztecs.* Leiden:

Spruyt, Van Mantgem & De Does. Scarborough, Vernon L., and David R. Wilcox, eds. (1991) *The Mesoamerican Ballgame.* Tucson: University of Arizona Press.

Modernization

Greek, Roman, medieval, or Renaissance anticipations of modern sports not withstanding, the formal, structural characteristics of our sports contrast sharply with those of earlier periods. Modern sports are secular rather than sacred; they are characterized by equality, specialization, rationalization, bureaucratization, quantification, and the quest for records. These abstract characteristics differ from but are related to the intense emotional experience of sports.

Primitive and ancient sports were frequently if not usually associated with religious ritual. The Mayans and the Aztecs played a ball game whose rules remain obscure despite considerable archeological evidence. We do know that the game was played within the sacred precincts of a temple, that it was a form of worship, and that it concluded with an act of human sacrifice. The Jicarilla Apache of the Southwest celebrated the return of spring and encouraged the earth's fertility by means of a relay race.

Although the ancient Greeks undoubtedly wrestled, threw the discus, and ran races simply for the excitement of the contest, their most important sports events were athletic festivals in honor of the gods. Since Zeus was the "father" of the gods, it was only natural that his festival at Olympia was even more important than those dedicated to lesser deities like Apollo (at Delphi), Athena (at Athens), and Poseidon (at Corinth). Legends traced the origin of the games, which were dated from 776 B.C.E., to the athletic accomplishments of heroes like Pelops and Herakles in the vicinity of the town of Elis in southwestern Greece. The time of the games was as sacred as the place. The games occurred during the second or third full moon after the summer solstice, and three heralds went forth to announce an Olympic truce for all men who wished to participate in the five-day festival. According to most accounts, the last day of the games was devoted entirely to religious ceremonies. There was a banquet. There were sacrifices to Zeus and the other gods, who were solemnly thanked for their sponsorship of the games, and the victors were awarded olive branches cut from the sacred grove of Zeus by a boy whose two parents were still alive. Christian disapproval of these pagan rituals brought them to an end—after more than 1,000 years of competition.

Modern sports are purely secular. Their participants can be personally devout, but there is a fundamental difference between obligatory pregame locker-room prayers and the worship of the gods by means of an athletic festival. For the Apache youths running between the circles of the sun and the moon or the Greek men racing in the stadium at Olympia, the contest was in itself a religious act.

The second distinguishing characteristic of modern sports is equality. In theory (but not always in practice), everyone has an opportunity to compete and the conditions of competition are the same for everyone. In layman's terms, it's what athletes can do and not who they are that counts.

Inequality in the opportunity to compete was typical of premodern sports whether they were sacred or secular. For the ritual race of the Jicarilla Apache and for the wrestling matches of the Diola of Gambia, whether or not a young man has reached puberty is what matters, not his swiftness of foot or strength of limb. Before the Romans conquered Greece and changed the Olympic rules, every participant in the Games had to be ethnically Greek, and women were excluded from the site even in the role of spectators.

The medieval tournament was a spectacular occasion at which the nobility demonstrated their skill with weapons (and implied their right to political power). The wealth required to arm, armor, mount, and train a knight was sufficient to keep peasants from the lists, and there were elaborate rules designed explicitly to bar participation by the increasingly affluent urban middle class. It was not sufficient for an ambitious knight to prove that his parents and grandparents were of noble blood. If he sullied his honor by marrying the daughter of a peasant or a merchant, he was disbarred from the tournament. If he was bold enough to appear despite his loss of status, he was beaten and his weapons were broken.

Social class continued formally to determine qualification as late as the 19th century. The infamous "amateur rule" in Britain was created to prevent the working class from competing against their "betters." In the regulations of the Henley Regatta (1879), we read, "No person shall be considered an amateur oarsman or sculler. . . . Who is or has been by trade or employment for wages, a mechanic, artisan, or laborer." Although amateurism has been redefined to the point where the stars of the National Basketball Association can now compete in the Olympic Games, amateurism survives in the rulebook of the National Collegiate Athletic Association (where its function is to protect the university's profits rather than to maintain the boundaries between social classes).

Exclusion on the basis of race or of sex have been obvious violations of the principle of equality. The segregation of American baseball and the system of apartheid in South Africa are two examples of the first kind of inequality. The reluctance of the International Olympic Committee to admit female athletes to the modern games was typical of turn-of-the-century attitudes. (Women's track and field became a part of the Olympic program in 1928; the women's marathon was introduced in 1984.)

More subtle is the dictate of equality in the conditions of competition. Royalty has long since surrendered the privileges it enjoyed in the medieval tournament. (When England's Henry VIII competed in a tournament, he broke more lances than his opponents did because he was allowed to joust more often than they were.) In modern times, inequalities have been diminished by dividing boxers, wrestlers, and weightlifters into weight classes. Performance-enhancing drugs have been banned not only because they can be dangerous but also because they unfairly advantage those who resort to them.

Specialization began in antiquity. Once it was determined that some rather than all should compete in a sport, the swift ran races and the slow became wrestlers, boxers, lifters, or throwers. By the Roman era, there was a class of professional athletes, that is, men who devoted themselves exclusively to chariot races and other sports contests. In the modern world, baseball, with its 9 defensive positions, is a good example of extreme specialization. American football is an even better example. Players are divided into 22 positions, not counting the "special teams," which are restricted to placekicks, kickoffs, and punts. A defensive lineman occasionally intercepts a forward pass and lumbers goalward in a moment of unaccustomed glory, but he quickly reverts to his specialized role.

Athletic specialization upon the field of play is paralleled by an intricate system of supportive personnel. Sociologists speak of primary, secondary, and tertiary involvement and discuss the roles of owners, managers, coaches, trainers, scouts, officials, publicists, vendors, spectators, journalists, and even sports sociologists.

Modern sports are rationalized in that there is a logical relationship between means and ends. In order to do this, we must first do that. To become a champion, one must do more than train long and hard. One must train scientifically. University-based specialists in sports physiology and sports psychology provide scientific information for the benefit of coaches and trainers. In the United States, where the relationship between theory and practice is relatively informal, the results of laboratory investigations, published in monographs and specialized journals, are often ignored. In the Soviet Union and the German Democratic Republic, however, special institutes were established to study sports and to administer an athletic system that compelled athletes to conform to whatever practices the experts deemed best.

Rationalization takes other forms as well. To facilitate competition, venues and equipment must be standardized. Ancient athletes raced the length of a stadium, but the stadium at Olympia was 192.27 meters and the stadium at Delphi was 177.5 meters; all modern 400-meter tracks are as nearly identical as modern ingenuity can make them. Standardization means that every modern sport has its specifications for sizes and shapes and allowable materials.

In premodern times, sports tended to occur seasonally, like the European folk football games that took place at Christmas and Easter, or episodically, like the baseball games played when the Brooklyn Eckfords challenged the New York Mutuals to a match. Modern sports are typically organized in the form of an elimination tournament or by leagues whose schedules allow every team to play every other team a fixed number of games.

Who runs the show? The games of preliterate societies were organized by priests or ritual adepts or elders who knew which sports most pleased the gods. Greek culture, for instance, included "gymnasiarchs" who—as their name indicates—were in charge of the gymnasiums. The Romans had a mania for order and developed administrative organizations that were imperial in scope, with elected leaders, detailed rules and regulations, entrance requirements, codes of conduct, and such "modern" niceties as membership certificates.

Modernity simply carries that tendency to an extreme. All modern sports are characterized by bureaucratic organization. The International Olympic Committee sits atop an organizational pyramid that includes not only the National Olympic Committees but also dozens of international sports federations, each of which controls scores of national federations. Except for the United States, which is an anomaly, every modern nation-state has a governmental ministry to promote elite and recreational sports.

One function of the sports bureaucracy is to record the statistics that are now an inevitable by-product of competition. The mania for quantification is, in fact, one of the most pronounced characteristics of modernity. Those who ask about the Gross National Product, the Consumer Price Index, and the Grade Point Average also want to know about the Earned Run Average and the Yards Gained Rushing. Heights are measured to the centimeter and times are calculated to the hundredth of a second. We live in a world of numbers.

The Greeks did not. They made no effort to time races, which would have been very difficult, and no effort to measure throws, which would have been quite simple. For the Greeks, man was still the measure of all things and not the object of endless measurements. The Romans did quantify their chariot races insofar as they counted the number of times a charioteer finished first, second, or third. Beyond that, they had no interest in the numbers. Medieval heralds recorded how many lances were broken at a tournament, but the quantified results seem to have been of less interest than descriptions of the pageantry that accompanied the jousting. In the Renaissance, scores were kept for fencing matches, but the focus of attention was on the pattern of geometrically prescribed positions taken by the contestants. To win awkwardly was little better than to lose.

Combine the modern impulse to quantify with the desire to win, to excel, to be the best—and the result is the concept of the record, the abstraction that permits competition not only among those present on the field but also between them and others spatially and temporally distant. The sports record is an unsurpassed but potentially surpassable quantified achievement. It is a number in the "record book" and in the corner of the television screen. It is a stimulus to unimagined heights of achievement and a psychic barrier that thwarts the athlete's best effort. It is a form of rationalized madness, a unique symbol of modern civilization. In a lyrical moment, a French athlete of the 1920s— André Obey—hoped that his daughter might "one day recite the litany not of our battles but of our records, more beautiful than the labors of Hercules."

The seven distinguishing characteristics of modern sports are not simply a random set of attributes. They interact systematically. The quest for records is unthinkable without quantification. After a certain point reached by the untrained body, records cannot be broken without specialization and rationalization, neither of which can develop very far without bureaucratic organization. The quest for records requires equality of opportunity to compete. What would be the point of a world's record for a hundred meters if 90 percent of the world's population were denied a chance to run? Finally, the fixation on quantified achievement can be explained as one result of the secularization of society. When we can no longer distinguish the sacred from the

profane or even the good from the bad, we are forced to content ourselves with modernity's deity: the Great God Number.

How did this happen? It was certainly not inevitable. Marxist scholars have, not surprisingly, emphasized economic factors. They have argued that modern sports are the result of capitalist development. This fails to explain why the Soviet Union and the German Democratic Republic developed the world's most advanced, and most modern, sports systems. A more plausible explanation takes us back to the scientific discoveries of the 17th century and to their popularization in the Age of the Enlightenment. The emergence of modern sports represents not the triumph of capitalism but rather the slow development of a mathematical, rational, empirical, experimental world-view. England's early leadership has less to do with capitalist development than with the intellectual revolution symbolized by the name of Isaac Newton and institutionalized in the Royal Society for the Advancement of Science. Rationality shapes the glass that passion fills to overflowing.

—ALLEN GUTTMANN

Bibliography: Adelman, Melvin. (1986) *A Sporting Time.* Urbana: University of Illinois Press. Carter, John Marshall, and Arnd Krüger, eds. (1990) *Ritual and Record.* Westport, CT: Greenwood Press. Guttmann, Allen. (1978) *From Ritual to Record: The Nature of Modern Sports.* New York: Columbia University Press. ———. *A Whole New Ball Game.* (1988) Chapel Hill: University of North Carolina Press. Mandell, Richard. (1988) *Sport.* New York: Columbia University Press.

Motocross

Motocross, a sporting competition similar to motorcycle racing, is particularly loved by younger people. The vehicle used has a different structure than a motorcycle, and the ride takes place across open country. Exciting for participants and spectators both, motocross is practiced for recreation and in competition.

History

Different sources have dated the first trial scramble race—as the sport was first known—to 1914, when the Scott manufacturing company in Yorkshire, England, organized it as recreation for their workers. Other historians reckon that the first off-road race was less formal, between police motorcyclists and a group of local motorcycle enthusiasts. One clear fact is that the origins of the sport are British, but the term *motocross* was first used in the Netherlands and Belgium.

The sport arrived in there 1920s and became popular in these countries because it could be adapted well to their geographical configuration.

By 1945, motocross boasted only a few loyal fans. It was still competing in popularity with the better-known, established sport of motorcycle racing. The motocross bike's unsuitability for daily use discouraged manufacturers from developing motorcycles that had to adapt to irregular tracks, with mud, stones, and uneven terrain. After the sport spread to the European continent, events remained sporadic.

The race through hills and on difficult tracks exalted the sense of exploration and the mastery of British sportsmen. If the motorcycle racer was perceived as the ideal continuation of a flat-race rider, the motocrossman might be considered similar to a hunting rider who tested his skill against the traps of the tracks. In Belgium the dunes, winding paths, and hillocks tempted motorcycle fans to explore their territory and test their skills in motocross. With the gradual asphalting of motorcycle tracks and the growing urbanization that followed World War II, the attractions of motocross to young motorcycle racers increased. A survey reported in *Il libro del motocross* revealed that motocross participants preferred their sport because it enabled them to escape oppressive urban roads and demonstrate their skill through an unorthodox drive on unwelcoming terrain.

In 1948, the Federation Internationale de Motocyclists (FIM) organized European championships, which were at first dominated by British manufacturers and racers. Despite the lack of proper tracks, young Russians used the bikes from state manufacturing companies along the notorious hills and arid grounds of their country to display their enormous potential for artistic expression. As in Belgium and Czechoslovakia (as early as the 1930s Czechoslovakia produced brilliant machines), the natural geographical conditions of Russia favored the development of this sport. Soviet and East German racers won seven world titles from 1965 to 1978. The World Cup for national teams began in 1947. Each country is represented by three riders, one for each power category. Competing countries have fought hard for the title and its accompanying prestige, which has led to interesting rivalries.

In the United States, motocross also developed after World War II, when it was imported by U.S. soldiers who had served in Europe. Motorcycle exhibitions that offered spectators the chance to observe the bikes in action favored the development of the sport and also ensured good earnings for promoters. In 1970, the U.S.

Enduro and Other Trials

One of the lesser-known off-road competitions is called *Enduro* (endurance). This sport has its origins in the early 20th century. Enduro is a long-distance competition in which the endurance of the motorcycles and the riders is sorely tested. In the United Kingdom, this event started in 1913 between British teams, and it expanded in 1914 to an international competition, where riders competed on bikes that were manufactured in their country of origin. This event lost its popularity in the 1960s. In 1968 FIM changed the rules and organized individual championships in which the racers had to complete a predetermined course in a fixed time.

The trial is also a current off-road competition with a long tradition. The first Six Days International Trial, started in 1909, took place in Scotland with several contests on very difficult courses of uneven terrain, such as river beds and rocky ground, where the racer must go through the difficult task of displaying his mastery. A trial world championship competition was organized in 1975.

The sidecarcross is a competition in which the sidecar is used on a motocross track. International contests were recognized by the FIM beginning in the 1970s, and a world championship was set up in 1980.

—*Gherardo Bonini*

national championship began, and in 1974 the U.S. Supercross circuit started touring the states. This tough circuit produced talented champions who began to participate in the European-staged world championships in the early 1980s. In 1981, the United States won the World Cup.

Rules and Play

Motocross participants are attracted by the aggressiveness and skill involved and excited by the crossing of situations, as well as by the typical unorthodoxy of the tracks and the drive. The structure of the motocross machine is different from the motorcycle; the two-stroke engine is largely used, the chassis is light yet sturdy, the suspension is essentially more flexible, the wheels are equipped with special hubs, and the tires have heightened sections. The leathers of the rider are made so as to protect him from irregular or muddy tracks. The world championships, supervised by the Fédération Internationale de Motocyclistes (FIM), were started in 1957.

Due to the reduced velocity (maximum 40 kilometers [25 miles] per hour), what was needed were machines that were not so much fast as strong and safe. They also had to manage obstacles and dangerous tracks; therefore, all the pieces—chassis, wheels, tires, drive—had to be maneuverable to lessen the counter-blows and the rebounds provoked by contact with the irregular track. Because the circuit is generally not over 5 kilometers (3 miles), races were easily facilitated in most countries; beaches were used, as well as indoor arenas and hillsides, where spectators could watch the entire feat.

In the 1960s, CZ replaced the four-stroke engine in favor of the more manageable two-stroke engine. The Japanese manufacturers that invaded the motorcycle racing market in the 1960s endeavored to use their exceptional technological abilities to produce the best vehicles; however, there has always been a noticeable lack of Japanese racers in both motorcycle racing and motocross. In Belgium, where motorcycles and bikes are in daily use, the figure of the motocrossman was used to nurture the Belgian sense of competition against the environment and landscape.

Today motocross is primarily a European sport. The grand prix events, which make up the world championship circuit, only occasionally schedule events in the United States and South America. In international world championship standard competitions, only 40 racers compete after a previous selection process. Once a racer enters into a motocross power category (125, 250, or 500 cc), they must finish the championship in the same category. From its humble origins as "scramble," the sport has become one of endurance, demanding serious athletic preparation plus a great capacity for concentration.

—GHERARDO BONINI

Bibliography: Vanhouse, Norman. (1986) *BSA Competition History.* Sparkford Foulis Haynes Publishing Group.

Motor Boating

Motor-boat racing is the basic term for competitions among drivers in engine-powered vessels used on the water. The sport is also referred to as power-boat racing or speed-boat racing. It combines elements of sailing and other traditional forms of boating with characteristics of modern motor sports such as automobile racing.

History

During the 19th and 20th centuries, motorized vessels replaced sailboats as the dominant means of water transportation, shipping, and military movement. The first generation of motorized boats were operated by steam engines, introduced in the late 18th century and becoming prominent in the 19th century. Steam-powered engines were also built into private yachts, whose (usually wealthy) owners occasionally raced one another in competitions.

The era of modern power boating is generally placed from the invention of the internal-combustion engine. One of the first motor boats of this type was built in France around 1865 by Jean Lenoir. In the 1880s, Gottlieb Daimler developed a gas-powered engine in Europe that became very influential. His engines were later installed on boats as well as on land-based vehicles.

Recreational and competitive motor boating grew quickly after 1900. As new power boats were developed, enthusiasts raced them informally or in organized competitions to test their capabilities against other boats. The sport of power-boat racing has continually served as a proving ground for new engines, hulls, and other technical advances that were later incorporated into products for the larger consumer and commercial boating markets.

The first power boats were rowboats or other traditional vessels with a basic motor and propeller attached. The first step toward specifically designed power boats came in 1907, when Ole Evinrude invented the outboard motor, which was portable and easy to attach to boats. Around the same time, the first hydroplanes appeared. These racing boats had bodies designed specifically for use with engines and high-speed operation. Their design included a shallow stepped hull that rose above the water as the boat moved faster. Another type of power-boat body, called the "V" hull because of its shape, was developed around 1910 and combined speed with stability. While later generations of power boats and engines became increasingly diverse and sophisticated, they continued to be based on the principles established by these early prototypes.

The earliest motor-boat races and events were often held under the auspices of existing motoring organizations or sponsored by yacht clubs. Soon, new organizations dedicated to power boating were established and sponsored an increasing number of organized power-boating meets. In the United States, representatives of yacht clubs in the northeast formed the American Power Boat Association (APBA) in 1903. Similar movements established an organized framework for power boating in other nations and on an international level. In 1922, the Union of International Motor Boating (UIM) was formed to foster and oversee the sport on a worldwide basis. The UIM, based in Europe, sanctions events and the international standings of racers, including world records. National and regional organizations, such as the APBA and its members, are affiliated with the UIM.

As the designs of motorized boats became more

varied it was increasingly difficult to compare their performance in races. This prompted efforts to define different categories of power boats, used in racing. Rules and guidelines also set the criteria for sanctioned events. These classifications became more numerous and specialized as new styles and technologies were introduced.

Speeds increased as the quality of boats and the skills of drivers improved. The top speed in the first Gold Cup race of 1904 was just under 39 kilometers (24 miles) per hour. The introduction of hydroplanes boosted speeds considerably to 160 kilometers (100 miles) per hour or more. In 1978, Kenneth Peter Warby achieved a world's water-speed record of 552.8 kilometers per hour (345.48 miles per hour or 300 knots) in New South Wales, Australia, in his hydroplane, the *Spirit of Australia.*

Rules and Play

Power boats are complex machines, and infinite variations are possible for body styles, engines, and other features. These features and their interaction determine the handling and performance of a particular boat. To bring consistency to the sport, power boats and racing events are divided into categories that are based on the specifications of the participating boats. A racing event may be entirely focused on one particular class of boat, or it may contain separate races for boats in several categories.

Major categories in the APBA, which are defined both by the type of boat and/or the form of race, include Inboard; Modified Outboard; Offshore; Outboard Performance Craft; Outboard Drag; Professional Racing Outboard; Stock Outboard; Unlimited Hydroplanes; RC (radio controlled) Model, Vintage, and Historic; American Performance Racing; and Personal Watercraft. Races may be individual; there are also regional tours and other series.

Races may be organized as heats or laps among groups of boats or in timed solo runs, overseen by officials of sanctioning organizations. The winners are frequently determined by average speed or top speed during a race. In endurance races, boaters try to cover as much distance as possible in a designated amount of time. Power boat races are often held on circular or oval courses of varying lengths. Races may also be based on laps.

Inland and offshore racing also differ. Inland races, held on lakes, rivers, and similar bodies of water, have long been a mainstay of power-boat racing. Offshore races take place in oceans and bays and other large

bodies of water connected to them; they cover various distances.

Cruising races, based on speed, for larger boats was an early form of competition. However, these boats could not compete for speed. Cruising was revived as a competition called the "predicted log," which relies on navigation and accuracy.

Drag racing, which emerged in the late 1950s, takes place on straight courses. It started in southern California, which remains its focal point.

In events for Stock (or Production in some instances) boats, the engine and body must remain true to the specifications they were manufactured with and may not be significantly altered. In Modified or Unlimited competitions, the owners and driver are allowed greater flexibility to customize the boat and engine more extensively to improve its performance.

The sport encompasses a wide range of boats, from large craft with ultra-high-performance jet engines of 1,000 horsepower or more to smaller vessels with outboard motors of 25 horsepower or less. The racing calendar includes thousands of regional, national, and international events held throughout the world.

Power-boat racing is also a popular spectator sport, often spectacular to watch, as when unlimited hydroplanes, or "thunderboats," race along the water at 160 kilometers (100 miles) per hour or more, shooting off large "roostertails" of water behind them.

Types of Boats

Body design is one basic method of classifying power boats; shape and construction affect how the craft handles in the water. Motor boat design involves trade-offs between speed and stability. The characteristics that allow a boat to move fast or turn quickly often make it less stable in the water; the features that increase its stability may also slow it down and make it less responsive to rapid turns. Boat designers and builders also consider many other factors, including whether the bow goes smoothly through waves on the uneven surface of the water or slaps the surface in an up-and-down motion.

The design of the hull, or lower portion of the boat, is especially important. At low speeds, the hull of a boat goes forward through the water, displacing it (pushing it aside) as the vessel moves ahead. However, as the speed and power increase, other forces also push the hull upward toward the water's surface and into the air, a principle known as planing. Boat designers and builders emphasize one or the other of these forces, depending on the priorities and use of the craft.

The "V" is a basic style of hull that combines the

stability of displacement and the speed of planing. These hulls become narrow at their bases. When traveling at low speeds they stay primarily in the water, but when they are moving faster they rise in the bow. V-boats are often used in offshore ocean racing because they are fast but also able to handle rough water. They are also known by specific styles, generic nicknames, or brand-names, such as Cigarette Boats, Open Vee's, Superboats, Fountains, and Scarabs.

The configuration and size of the passenger compartments and placement of the engine vary widely among different types of boats. Some racing boats have open spaces for drivers; others have enclosed cockpits. Some have an open deck and an enclosed compartment below.

Motor boats are commonly powered by internal combustion engines, similar to automobile engines. Boats are classified by the type and power of engines as determined by their piston displacement and other factors.

Another basic distinction is between inboard and outboard motors. Many modern outboards are so large that they are not removed, but still use basic outboard designs. Boat engines that combine features of these basic types are known as inboard/outboards. These are often mounted inside the boat like an inboard, but the drives that connect the engine to the propellers are similar to outboard designs so the propellers can be swiveled to turn the boat.

The style of propeller also affects performance. The propellers, which have several blades, are located either behind the stern or below or within the hull somewhat further forward. Boats may have one or more propellers and engines.

Turbine, or jet, engines are also used in power boats. These may be used to turn propellers or propel the boat directly by creating very strong currents of air or water through the hull. This type of motor ranges from very powerful aircraft or jet engines for high-performance racing craft to smaller versions used on recreational boats.

Some enthusiasts enjoy restoring and racing older power boats, a category known as vintage or historic racing. In addition to full-sized boats, power-boating organizations have also added special classes for other types of vessels, including miniature radio-controlled power boats.

Power Boating Issues

Motor-boat racing has attracted participants on many levels, including amateurs who build, maintain, and/or race their own boats. However, it also is an expensive sport, especially with the more advanced racing boats. While prize money became available for many events, drivers often had to rely on subsidies to cover the costs associated with racing. In the early 1950s, commercial sponsorships were allowed, which brought power boat racing to a new level.

Safety is a perennial concern in power boating—the same characteristics that make power boating exciting add danger. This is especially true for the fastest categories such as hydroplanes, which combine the dangers inherent with speeds of 100 miles per hour or more with volatile engines that occasionally explode or catch fire. Hydroplanes may sometimes lift too high and flip backward, an accident called a blowover. Another risk with many power boats is the possibility of injury or death when a driver or passenger accidentally comes into contact with the propeller.

Various safeguards have been instituted to reduce these risks; racers must wear helmets, lifejackets, and other protective gear. Other safety measures are the addition of closed cockpits on certain types of very fast racing boats, covers around propellers, and kill-switches that automatically cut the engine if the driver is dislodged from the boat.

Power boating has also raised environmental concerns, including its effect on the quality of life in areas where the boats are used and on marine animals and plants. Concerns include noise levels, the waves that these vessels can generate, and pollution, including fuel leaking into the water and the exhaust fumes that escape into the air and water. In response, manufacturers sought to develop cleaner, more efficient engines. In the 1990s in the United States the mandate of the Federal Clean Air Act was expanded to include control of boats and other recreational vehicles.

—JOHN TOWNES

Bibliography: Barrett, J. Lee. (1986) *Speed Boat Kings.* Ann Arbor: Historical Society of Michigan. Fostle, D. W. (1988) *Speedboat.* Mystic, CT: Mystic Seaport Museum Stores. "The Year in Review." (1994) *Propellor: Official Publication of the American Power Boat Association* (November).

Motorcycle Racing

Motorcycle racing, one of many kinds of vehicle racing, takes place on tracks. Motorcycling became popular toward the end of the 19th century, when industrial engineers in developed countries applied the newly invented engine to the velocipede structure.

History

Many countries lay claim to this sport: Italy, Germany, France, the United Kingdom, and the United States all submitted patents of rough motor velocipedes, but Gottlieb Daimler (1834–1900), developer of the Einspur machine (1885), is generally considered to be the father of the motorcycle.

Initially, motorcycle competition was combined with motor tricycles and automobiles; the first race exclusively for motorcycles was held in England in 1896. Within a few years, the internal combustion engine had surpassed the steam engine.

Experiments, crushing failures, successes, and hazardous attempts marked the early history of motorcycle racing. Early motorcycle competitions were organized over long distances, often linking the capitals of Europe. But events often failed, with only a handful of competitors finishing the course, because technical preparation and materials were not well enough developed to support the performances of the engine, whose capacity had reached 1,000 or 1,200 cc in some cases. The FIM tried to limit the power grades to 500 cc so as to avoid accidents, wasteful expenditures, and risks to the racers and spectators. These technical difficulties initiated improvements in motorcycles, and the search for record-breaking performances stimulated further progress.

Competitions in the United States also generally covered long distances, like the 200-mile (320-kilometer) Savannah (later Daytona) race. From the 1920s, courses on dirt and circular tracks excited the passions of U.S. spectators. The European circuits occurred in towns or villages or on artificial unasphalted tracks.

After World War II an irreversible distinction slowly emerged between heavier road and lighter racing motorcycles. The popularity of motorcycle racing diminished as the specialization of the competitions also divided the fans and, in the process, reduced their number—notwithstanding the attendance at a German circuit race of 400,000 spectators in 1951. The young generation watched Marlon Brando express his rebellion on a motorcycle in *The Wild One* (1954), and some years later Peter Fonda in *Easy Rider* (1969) turned in a performance, this one on a personalized Harley, that established the road motorcycle as symbol of youthful protest.

Britain, Germany, and Italy dominated the sport, with the best racers and the best motorcycles, until the 1960s, when the Japanese weighed in with Yamaha, Honda, Suzuki, and Kawasaki. Sponsors and high technology forced the established European firms Guzzi, Gilera, and BSA into retirement, for they could not afford to build high-powered racing motorcycles. From 1960 to 1995 Japan won 90 world titles for building motorcycles, but only 4 for racers. Perhaps as a result of delayed industrialization, the Japanese racers lacked the aggressive mentality and yearning to win necessary to compete in motorcycle racing.

Industrialization has opened new markets for motorcycles in South America, Asia, and other newly developed areas. Starting in 1949, FIM organized the world championship grand prix circuit. Racers had to compete in a number of competitions, each one hosted by a different country with a strong motorcycle racing tradition. Recently, the grand prix circuit has expanded to include Malaysia, Indonesia, and Venezuela in the consolidated and traditional grand prix of Italy, Belgium, France, Netherlands, Spain, Germany, and Sweden. In the 1970s, U.S. racers began to compete in the grand prix as well. Supported by Marlboro and other sponsors, the U.S. competitors won 13 of the last 18 titles from 1978 to 1995 in the 500 cc category. The daring of U.S. riders—who touched the asphalt with their knees on bends, reducing the distance in curves and facilitating passing—increased the popularity of the sport by reviving the old courageous style of Italian racer Tazio Nuvolari (1892–1953), who protected his elbow and his arm with cotton in order to reduce the danger involved in touching the walls.

Rules and Play

The Tourist Trophy race near Douglas on Britain's Isle of Man, first staged in 1907, became legendary. Continental racers tried in vain to conquer the contest, succeeding only in 1935. The Tourist Trophy set the standard for other races and fixed the power categories—250 cc, 350 cc, and 500 cc. In 1914 the wearing of helmets in the race became mandatory. In 1977 FIM removed the event from the World Championship program after 129 deaths from 1907 to 1976.

After upgrading from the 50 cc to the 80 cc power category in 1982, the FIM in 1989 eliminated contests for the 80 cc and 350 cc categories and inaugurated superbike competitions for 750 cc to reduce the organization's costs and better manage the grand prix circuit. The racer who achieves the best overall time during the grand prix gets 1 extra point. Until 1988 the winner got 15 points, the runner-up 12, and other competitors 10, 8, 6, 5, 4, 3, 2, or 1; in 1989 the winner earned 20 points, the runner-up 17, and the others 15, 13, 11, 9, 7, 5, 3, and 1. The 125 cc is strictly reserved for monocylindrical machines, 250 cc for bicylindrical units, and the 500 cc for four-cylinder bikes.

In the United States motorcycle racing was governed from 1903 by the Federation of American Motorcyclists and later by the Amateur Motorcycle Association (AMA).

Appeal of the Sport

Apart from the obvious fascination with speed and victory, aficionados were intrigued by the skill and danger involved in the races. Collapses, accidents, and deaths fed the myth of unlucky protagonists. The racer seemed a rough and lonesome hero, facing long courses that left him dusty, dirty, and tired. Nicknames such as "death angel" and "black devil" convey the popular conception of the motorcycle victor: custodian of dreams of freedom, always in near contact with death. Particularly curious is the Italian word for racer, *centauro*. Like the centaur, a mythological man-horse, the racer represents a union between man and motorcycle that is indissoluble.

The shift to asphalt tracks, which occurred gradually beginning in the 1950s, reflected growing concerns for safety; in fact, after the death of Leslie Graham (1911–1953) and other outstanding champions in 1953, racers forced manufacturers to boycott the German grand prix. A new sort of racer emerged: no longer heroic sacrificial victim, but professional racer and prime actor who demanded safety rules and standards. Not until the 1970s, however, when spectators were moved back from the track, allowing racers a larger area to slide in case of a fall and the space to avoid hitting spectators, did racers secure better conditions of safety. Progress included also improved equipment—Michelin introduced completely smooth tires in 1970—and other tools.

Women in Motorcycle Racing

Motorcycle racing is one of the last bastions of machismo: the actual image of the woman in this sport is that of a pin-up kissing the winner or the pom-pom girl parading among the racers before the start. In France and Italy during the early years of the sport, courageous women did actually challenge men in the field; in 1896 in France a championship was organized exclusively for women. In subsequent years, however, women participated only sporadically in this sporting arena. The Frenchwoman Violette Morriss (1835–?) world-record holder in shot put in the 1920s, caused a scandal by enrolling in motorcycle competitions and provoked admiration as well as condemnation for her aggressiveness and bravery. When Beryl Swain (1926–) finished the Tourist Trophy in 1962, the Tourist Trophy

Riders Association voted unanimously against allowing women into the competition in the future.

The lack of female competitors limits motorcycle racing; in noncompetitive motorcycle sports, however, women abound. Given people's fondness for inherently dangerous sports, motorcycle racing probably has a flourishing future.

—GHERARDO BONINI

Bibliography: Hawkes, Ken. (1962) "Their Place Is in the Stands." *World Sports* 28, 8. Sucher, Harry V. (1990) *Harley Davidson*. London: Bison Books.

Mountain Climbing

Mountain climbing is a unique sport. First, it is one of only a few completely new sports, those that are not adaptations and codifications of folk activities. Second, for the well over 100 years of history it has generally resisted the forces of institutionalization—it has no substantial governing bodies, no written rules, and no means of enforcing the socially constructed and socially accepted rules that do exist. Despite this, mountain climbing tends to work like most other sports. (See Rock Climbing for an explanation of the "rules" and techniques.)

History

People have been climbing mountains for all of human history. Precisely when humans began to climb mountains for sport is not clear. The late first generation of mountaineers selected a specific (and widely accepted, although clearly erroneous) date, thus creating a myth of the same order as Abner Doubleday and baseball. According to late first-generation mountaineers C. D. Cunningham and W. W. Abney, author and illustrator respectively of the first history of mountaineering, the sport began on 17 September 1854. Sir Alfred Wills inaugurated the sport by climbing the Wetterhorn. Rev. John Frederick Hardy's (1826–1888) ascent of Switzerland's Finsteraarhorn in 1857 was another contender for the first sporting ascent of a mountain. (Neither is correct.) Who climbed what mountain first matters because the first ascent of a mountain is the most obvious basis of competition in the sport of mountain climbing.

The end of the 18th century brought a new view of mountains. The Romantic movement redefined mountains as attractive, sublime places, and ascents of some well-known summits were included on the Grand Tour. By the late 18th century, the Age of Reason had motivated some Europeans to begin to climb mountains for the purposes of natural scientific research.

In the 1850s the practice of visiting the Alps to climb peaks and cross passes was recognized as a distinct form of activity. In Britain, these people, largely middle class, came together in 1857 to form the Alpine Club, an organization that resembled the new scientific and geographic societies that proliferated in the first half of the 19th century.

At this point, modern organized sports were beginning to be developed in English public (that is, elite private secondary) schools and universities, and the sense of athleticism, muscular Christianity, and rational recreation emerging in the mid-19th century also began to affect the new activity of mountain climbing. Romanticism, tourism, and science gave people a reason to be in the Alps and to climb mountains. Athleticism turned it into a sporting activity and established the whole language of conquest that came to characterize mountain climbing; it drove competition for first ascents; and mountain climbing was justified as moral, rational, and significant in the development of masculine character.

Thus, the origins of mountain climbing were caught up in notions of patriotism/Britishness, militarism, and Empire. The identification of Wills's ascent of the Wetterhorn as the first sporting ascent was important to the British because it was the first significant British ascent in the Alps (apart from tourist ascents of Mont Blanc). The date that the claim was made—1887—was in itself significant. This was at the height of Empire, and British claims to have initiated the "conquest" of mountains appeared natural after so much of Earth's territory had been claimed (the fact that the Alps were in the heart of Europe, in the territory of some of the competitors for empire, only added to the pleasure of the claim). By that time Britain also saw itself very clearly as a sporting nation and mountain climbing was by then identifiably a sport.

Wills's 1854 ascent of the Wetterhorn marked the start of a period of sustained mountain climbing in the Alps. During the next 10 years, culminating in the ascent of the Matterhorn by Englishman Edward Whymper (1840–1911), most of the major summits in the Alps were climbed for the first (recorded) time.

The real sporting motive for mountaineering did not appear until the period from 1865–1914. The first generation of British mountain climbers attempted to ensure that their form and style of mountaineering became the model for future generations. This included the following criteria: climbers must be accompanied by guides; the only equipment permitted were ropes and ice axes; whatever number was right for a climbing

Mountain Climbing and Martial Arts

In [budokan as in all of] the martial arts it is the basis of any practice to harmonize mind, body and spirit. Normally we tend to waste a lot of our energy, spilling it out in many directions from our bodies, like heat escaping from an uninsulated house. Learning to control and direct energy could benefit everyone in so many ways, but is something which is not considered even in sport. Just as we regrettably no longer use our basic senses to their fullest potential, so we ignore a capability that we all have and which could save so much effort and stress. This control, which has enabled me to be strong enough to cope with so many hardships in my mountaineering and continue when others have given up, I gained mainly through sitting absolutely still in meditation.

One of the easiest ways to explain about directing energy is to rest an extended arm on someone's shoulder and ask them to use all their strength to bend it. If you try to maintain a straight arm by muscular power you will soon tire. However, if you relax and concentrate on letting the energy flow smoothly out through the Centre (or *hara*) along the arm out through the tips of the fingers, like water from a hose, it is impossible for the arm to be bent. I demonstrated this to a group of medical students in Pakistan and they were so impressed they nicknamed me "Superwoman"! But after five minutes they could do it too.

Martial arts practice is like a bottomless pool; the deeper you look the more you want to see. That for me epitomizes mountaineering too. After I had been practicing for a few months I realized that my approach to many things in life, and especially my climbing, had changed. A lot of things I had learnt in the *dojo* could also be used to improve my climbing and, even more important, the way in which I taught climbing. I made myself and my students breathe out when making a strenuous move and to relax. I understood far more about how muscles and joints worked. Warming-up exercises were explained and done in a logical sequence. Much emphasis is placed on developing a supple spine, and ankles, wrists, fingers and toes, parts often neglected in normal keep-fit classes. Practicing slow controlled movements improved my balance and co-ordination. Moving from the Centre makes everything easier, and understanding that tiredness and pain do not mean one has to give up, the body can go on, has saved my life on several occasions. Best of all I was enjoying my climbing more than ever before. It was fascinating to find two activities which complemented each other so well.

—Julie Tullis, *Clouds from Both Sides*
(London: Grafton Books, 1985).

Julie Tullis (1939–1986) was the first British woman to climb an 8,000-meter peak (Broad Peak in 1984). She died after reaching the summit of the world's second highest mountain, K2, during the disastrous summer in which 13 climbers lost their lives on the mountain.

team, two was wrong and one was not even a consideration; taking risks was never acceptable and there was a clear sense of what was appropriate in terms of route, weather conditions, and so on; and climbers had to seek the easiest route to a summit, which subsequent ascents were expected to follow. (None of these any longer apply, an indication of major developments in the sport.) So, after 1865, the only way for the sport to develop was to climb the remaining major summits in the Alps, and to seek first ascents in other mountain ranges. Mountaineering spread to the Caucasus, New Zealand, Africa, the Himalayas, North and South America, and other mountain ranges such as in New Guinea and Japan. (Of course, the European climbers took their Alpine guides with them on their expeditions.) Alpine clubs were established in all of the European nations and in all of the developed nations where British/European forms of mountain climbing became the norm. Only on the West Coast of the United States (from approximately 1900 to 1930 in clubs such as the Seattle Mountaineers, the Mazamas, and the Sierra Club) and in the Soviet Union did a different style of mountain climbing develop—namely, the mass ascent of up to 50 and sometimes more climbers.

If this was all that constituted mountain climbing, there would be no sport. Thus, mountaineering split into two forms in the 1860s, one based on exploration, the other on sport. Exploration continues today, with first ascents of new mountains being made every year in the Himalayan range, in Greenland and Antarctica, and in northern Canada.

At the same time, the second generation of alpinists changed the forms and goals of mountain climbing to ensure its future as a sport. Some began climbing without guides and developing their own mountaineering skills (the norm today). They began to ascend minor peaks in the Alps and other regions and to attribute significance to these ascents, which were often technically more difficult and dangerous than the major summits. They sought new routes to the summits of already climbed mountains—almost always more difficult than the original route—and to attribute significance to these routes. They recorded such variations as the first winter ascent, first women's ascent, and speed of ascent, and they began to acknowledge that it was sometimes necessary to take risks in order to pioneer a new route.

Chomolungma/Mount Everest illustrate the two forms of mountain climbing. Attempts to make the first ascent (between 1921 and success in 1953) clearly fit into the exploration mode. As with the South Pole,

Everest became the site of a nationalist competition involving the British, and a British expedition was finally successful in placing a New Zealander—Sir Edmund Hillary (1919–)—and a Nepali Sherpa—Norgay Tenzing (1914–1986)—on the summit. By October 1992, 485 individuals from 38 countries had reached the summit of Everest (and there had been 115 verified deaths of climbers on the mountain). The sport of mountaineering has also been evident in various new routes established to the summit, among them the 1975 South-West Face expedition led by the first professional mountaineer, Sir Christian Bonington (1934–). While no others have the cachet of Chomolungma/Everest, the world's highest mountain (8,848 meters or 29,029 feet), most other peaks, especially the more accessible ones, have followed this pattern of development from exploration to sport.

Since the 1960s, mountaineering has become a popular sport. Economic growth in the developed nations and less expensive means of travel have resulted in a significant increase in the number of mountain climbers. Each generation of climbers tends to believe it has reached the ultimate in what is possible in the sport, and that no further developments are possible without taking suicidal risks or so flouting the informal rules of the sport as to be cheating. Each subsequent generation has proved its predecessors wrong by modifying the rules while still maintaining the sport's integrity, and deaths related to mountain climbing have stayed relatively low. However, the future of mountaineering seems set to continue with expeditions to increasingly isolated places and more difficult routes to the summits of previously climbed mountains.

—PETER DONNELLY

See also Rock Climbing.

Bibliography: Gillman, P., ed. (1993) *Everest*. Boston: Little, Brown. Unsworth, W. (1992) *Encyclopaedia of Mountaineering*. London: Hodder & Stoughton. ———. (1994) *Hold the Heights: The Foundations of Mountaineering*. Seattle: The Mountaineers.

Movies

It is now over 100 years since Edweard Muybridge carried out his celebrated series of "moving pictures" at the University of Pennsylvania. He was fascinated by the kinesiological examination of "beings" in motion. He studied and photographed runners, jumpers, walkers, race horses. While Muybridge was a scientist and a researcher, the early filmmakers at the end of the 19th century and into the 20th century capitalized upon a public who, in increasing numbers, enjoyed the spectacle of organized boxing.

Throughout the 20th century, British, European, and Australasian cinema makers have also realized that sporting scenarios make wonderful cinema.

Harvey Marc Zucker and Lawrence J. Babich edited *Sports Films* in 1987 and it continues to be the definitive source book for students of sports film. The book contains a list of 2,042 titles divided into 17 categories—baseball, basketball, boxing, football, golf, horses and other animals, Olympics, track and field, skates, soccer, rugby, cricket, hurling, tennis, handball, Ping-Pong, water sports, wheels, winter sports, wrestling, other sports, athletes in films, and actors' portrayals. The National Baseball Hall of Fame and Museum at Cooperstown, New York, chronicles 83 baseball movies dating back to *Little Sunset* and *Right Off the Bat*.

Sports movies, in recent years, have enjoyed a marked degree of Academy Award recognition. In 1976 the movie *Rocky,* a story about a mumbling, no-hope boxer called Rocky Balboa (Sylvester Stallone) won the Oscar for Best Picture. In 1980, another boxing movie, called *Raging Bull,* was a serious Oscar contender. Directed by Martin Scorsese, the film explored the turmoil that was the real life of boxer Jake LaMotta (Robert DeNiro). *Raging Bull* was nominated for Best Picture and DeNiro won the Oscar for Best Actor.

The following year *Chariots of Fire,* a fictionalized account of Scotland's Eric Liddell and England's Harold Abrahams running track at the 1924 Paris Olympics, earned three Oscars—for Best Picture, Costume Design, and Original Musical Score.

A close examination of the 1980s Oscar nomination for Best Picture reveals a succession of scenarios with significant, and often critical, sporting/athletic elements. For example, in *The Right Stuff* (1983) the physiological testing of the American astronauts highlights their athleticism; the 1984 nomination *A Soldier's Story* is a taut tale of murder, racism, and hatred set around the members of a black World War II U.S. Army baseball team; the 1987 film *Hope and Glory* is about childhood reminiscences of World War II in England, and cricket conversations neatly tie together a father and son; *Dangerous Liaisons* (1988) contains memorable, frenetic fencing action in a concluding duel to the death; and *Field of Dreams* (1989) remains the definitive philosophical baseball movie.

Today, the actual film location of *Field of Dreams,* outside of Dyersville, Iowa, has become a living museum. Baseball lovers come from all over the world to pay their respects to the ghosts of Shoeless Joe Jackson and Doc Graham, and play ball on a homemade diamond. The baseball field snuggles up to the surrounding cornfields, and yet the overwhelming sensation is of open plains, and the vast and dominating skyscape of the heartland of America.

—SCOTT A. G. M. CRAWFORD

See also Media.

Bibliography: Dickerson, G. (1991) *The Cinema of Baseball: Images of America, 1929–1989.* Westport, CT: Meckler. Sillitoe, A. (1968) *The Loneliness of the Long Distance Runner.* New York: Knopf. Zucker, H. M., and L. J. Babich. (1987) *Sports Films: A Complete Reference.* Jefferson, NC: McFarland.

Mythology

"Myth" is a term that is derived from the Greek *mythos,* meaning "word," "speech," "tale," or "story." A "story" is the essence of the term in the present context. But a "myth" can be more accurately defined as a traditional tale having collective importance for a society, often treating religious, cosmic, or heroic themes.

Mythical accounts of sports may be classified by their formal narrative contexts and rich variety of themes. Ultimately, their common significance lies in the theme of contest itself. In ancient Greek myth, sports episodes are found in essentially three different contexts, which have counterparts in many myths in other cultures. First, in the challenge contest, a divinity or hero is challenged by one of equal or lower status to a contest in a specific athletic discipline. Second in the festival contest, games are held to honor a god, a deceased hero, or a guest, or take place to mark a military victory. Finally, the bride contest is held, often by a father who is also the king, who gives to the victorious suitor both his daughter in marriage and succession to the throne. Aspects of the three forms can of course be combined in a single episode.

All three settings establish oppositions between individual gods or mortals, and in most cases the result is the conferral on the victor of an enhanced rank or honor. In the few cases in which the contest is a draw, both contestants are generally established as having equal honor. In its simplest form, the mythical sporting event pairs forces of "goodness," civilization, productivity, or order against those of "evil," barbarism, destruction, or chaos. In more complex forms, the antagonists each have positive and negative attributes, though usually the narrative is biased, on balance, to favor the more positive contestant. The presence of audience or referees guides the reader (or listener) in his or her sympathies toward the contestants.

Challenge Contests

In the challenge contest, typically an overly self-confident antagonist challenges a hero to competition in a specific event. The challenger is usually defeated, and often killed by the hero. The contest may closely resemble a duel, but the essential differences are that in duel, the overt object is killing or displacing an opponent from power, whereas in the contest, the quest for simple victory can escalate into a struggle for more serious stakes, often because of an overzealous attack by the challenger. The paired contestants often represent the civilized versus barbarian; the latter is characterized by *hybris* or "wanton violence" whose only motive is self-aggrandizement at the expense of the honor of another.

In the *Odyssey* (18.66–101), for example, Odysseus, himself disguised as an old beggar, is challenged to an impromptu boxing match by Iros, another beggar in the palace. Iros is not killed, but badly injured and evicted, much to the amusement of an audience of freeloading suitors. The episode serves as a relatively peaceful foreshadowing of Odysseus's slaughter of the suitors and further illustrates the violation of the code of guest-friendship by both the suitors and Iros. The civilized-barbarian opposition is frequent in Greek challenge contests, including some minor labors of Herakles.

Wrestling or some form of a weaponless combat sport is, along with the footrace, the most universal of contests found in myths, and is frequently found in the challenge myths. In the Old English epic, *Beowulf,* the hero defeats Grendel in wrestling. The Icelandic *Younger Edda* depicts Thor as victor over the female opponent Elli in wrestling. and the motif of a waylaying giant who wrestles passersby is found in the folktales of Scandinavians, Russians, and the Baltic peoples.

But good does not consistently defeat evil, as in the Greek pattern of wrestling contests. The oldest literary account of such a challenge is the wrestling match of Gilgamesh and Enkidu in the Mesopotamian *Epic of Gilgamesh* (Tablet 2), dated to the 13th century B.C.E. The gods create a savage man of nature, Enkidu, who challenges Gilgamesh, the king of Uruk and the builder of a great city, to a wrestling match. Gilgamesh prevails, again asserting through myth a higher valuation of civilization. The two immediately gain mutual respect through the ordeal and undertake several heroic adventures together.

Other great cultural leaders come to prominence after a wrestling match, including Jacob and Muhammad. Jacob, prior to meeting a hostile brother, Esau, wrestles until dawn a stranger who defeats him, but promises him a greater destiny with his new name, Israel (Genesis 32.25–29). The "stranger" is an agent of God, and the event is an obvious rite of passage, confirming Jacob's progress toward becoming patriarch of his namesake people. Muhammad's match also ends felicitously when the prophet persuades a skeptical strongman of the truth of his message by wrestling and defeating him twice. Contrary to the Greek pattern, the stories of both Jacob and Muhammad portray the challenger as victor. But like the Gilgamesh tale, these do not end in death and reinforce the physical and spiritual strength of a people's leader.

The challenge motif is also found in sports other than wrestling among non-Mediterranean cultures, for example in ball games, which are virtually absent from Mediterranean myths and cultures.

Challenge myths involving wrestling also frequently involve a hero who confronts awesome divine or natural forces. Again, Herakles is an archetype of such stories, notably taking on and defeating the divinity Thanatos (Death) on behalf of the doomed woman, Alcestis. In Sophocles' *Women of Trachis* (8–26), Herakles challenged and wrestled a shape-shifting bull-serpent-man, Acheloos, who tried to carry off Deianeira as bride. Herakles wins the match and the woman as his own bride.

Other cultures besides the Greeks describe challenges against divinities and beasts. In one struggle for control of the cosmos, the Phoenician Baal, a sky, weather, and fertility god, engages in freestyle combat with biting and kicking, against Mot, god of death, destruction, and drought. In another, Baal clubs and kills his opponent, Prince Sea (also called Judge River or Yam), god of the sea, rebellious waters, and anarchy. Quiche Maya myth collected in the 16th century C.E. in the *Popol Vuh* text tells of two ballplayers and gamblers, Hun-Hunahpu and Vucub-Hunahpu, who anger the underworld gods, are challenged to a competition by a messenger, accept, and are killed before the contest. The twin sons of Hun-Hunahpu, Hunahpu and Xbalanque, take up the challenge, compete, and survive several contests until Hunahpu is decapitated. His brother overpowers the underworld opponents and avenges his predecessors.

Festival Contests

In myth, such festivals may be held to honor a dead hero, a god, or a guest or celebrate a victory. The honor, glory, and fame of the victor is one fundamental motif, but the process of achieving victory also imparts lessons about the socially sanctioned behavior.

The association of athletic festivals with funeral games has been understood as a reflection of actual cults of the dead, a connection particularly evident in Greek myth and society from the 13th to the 5th century B.C.E. But the Slavs, Celts, Prussians, Maltese, East Asians, and Native Americans also had funeral games. Why they were held remains unclear, perhaps to honor the dead, assuage the consciences of the living, and honor the living ancestors of the hero.

The Greco-Roman tradition contains many one-time-only funeral games for heroes, including those for Abderos, Achilles, Aigialeos, Amarynceus, Anchises, Azan, Cyzicus, Eurygyes, Laius, Oedipus, Paris, Pelias, Patroclus, and Polydectes. Many local Greek festivals trace back to funeral games, including those for Adrastus, Aeacus, Alkanthoos, Amphitryon, Areithoos, and Herakles, as do the origins of the four major Panhellenic festivals.

Homer's 8th-century B.C.E. account of the games held by Achilles in honor of the hero Patroclus (*Iliad* 23) is the earliest and most influential treatment. Eight events are held: chariot racing, boxing, wrestling, a foot race, an armed duel, tossing a weight, archery, and javelin throwing. Aspects of this account are interestingly at odds with the practices of actual Greek sports known from later festivals, which may be a reflection either of archaic practices, or of poetic license.

Bride Contests

Contests in which the bride is the prize, perhaps based on actual customs, are widespread in world myth. Most frequent are races (foot or chariot), or archery, wrestling, and other tasks. Races may symbolize the goal-oriented aspect of marriage, particularly for females in traditional societies. The bride is usually the daughter of a king, and success implies succession to the throne. The premise for such myths is that physical prowess is the best measure of a suitable mate. Variations occur, including resistance of the father or the daughter to the marriage; rivalry between suitors, daughter, and father; use of trickery; murder of unsuccessful suitors or of the father.

The contest of Pelops and Oenomaus, mentioned above, is perhaps the most famous Greek myth of this sort. Apollodorus (Epitome 2.3–9) describes the father's anxiety over displacement: Oenomaus set the contest either because he himself loved Hippodameia or he had heard that he was fated to be killed by her husband. Pelops wins by bribing Oenomaus's charioteer with promise of half the kingdom or of one night

with the bride, then kills the driver before he can receive the reward.

In the *Mahabharata,* King Draupada sets a "bridegroom choice" archery contest for his daughter Draupadi. The festival is a wondrous spectacle with entertainers and wrestlers performing, and many elite guests. As in the *Odyssey,* the successful suitor must string a mighty bow and shoot an arrow through a hole into a target. Barons and kings fail, but Arjuna, posing as a holy brahmin, wins. Arjuna, like Odysseus, is recognized by his feat. Other bride contest myths include the *Nibelungenlied,* when Siegfried won a foot race in which he conceded handicaps to Gunther and Hagen. Then Gunther takes Brunhilde after Hagen treacherously kills Siegfried. In the Grimms' fairytale, "Six Came through the Whole World," a suitor for the king's daughter must fetch water from a disused well and defeat the girl in a race; he barely succeeds with the help of colleagues.

The inherent drama of a contest contains within it an antagonistic struggle seeking resolution. The antagonisms themselves reveal the categories that a culture holds in tension. The resolution often validates social hierarchies, practices, or ideals.

In the challenge contest, we have seen that a culture's positive and negative values can be put into conflict, sometimes mirroring the cosmic conflict seen in the creation myths. Great cultural figures, such as Gilgamesh, Jacob, and Muhammad, are put into challenge contests that underline their authority. In a few cases, women figures compete in a challenge, with or without a male companion, illustrating aspects of gender reversal to validate the powerful roles of women. Challenges faced by heroes against beasts or divinities show a human superiority to natural opponents like monsters and even death itself, overstated labors that are probably meant to encourage men in the lesser tasks of daily life.

Festival contests give social context a greater role, demonstrating how fame and glory may be won in peaceful competitions that parallel more serious activities. Here the prize-givers are like the rulers in society, setting and bending the rules to accommodate human circumstances. Societies that staged sports festivals in later times probably took inspiration from the courage and skill of their legendary ancestors, putting themselves in the place of those outsized heroes.

Mythical bride contests contradict most social practices of betrothal, but, through their symbolic structure, describe marriage to the right person literally as a goal worth pursuing. These mythical contests on the one hand highlight the tensions and anxieties of all betrothals, on the other validate the normative practice of not leaving the choice of bride to the vagaries of chance.

—THOMAS F. SCANLON

Bibliography: Kirk, Geoffrey S. (1970) *Myth, Its Meaning and Function in Ancient and Other Cultures.* Berkeley and Los Angeles: University of California Press. Poliakoff, Michael. (1987) *Combat Sports in the Ancient World. Competition, Violence, and Culture.* New Haven, CT: Yale University Press. Raschke, Wendy J., ed. (1988) *The Archaeology of the Olympics. The Olympics and Other Festivals in Antiquity.* Madison: University of Wisconsin Press.

Nationalism
See Patriotism

Native American Sporting Competitions

Many Native people participate daily in sporting events organized and run primarily by non-Natives. However, Native athletes also participate in a variety of competitions that are organized by Native people. This "Native" sport system includes both "traditional" sports competitions and "All-Native" competitions.

History

Canada and the United States enacted laws in the late 1800s that outlawed certain "traditional" cultural practices. For example, the Potlatch and the Sun Dance were banned, two ceremonies that were very important rituals in Native culture.

Native athletes were, at times, restricted from participating in "mainstream" sport as well. As an example, in 1880 the National Amateur Lacrosse Association in Canada categorized all Native athletes as "professionals," thus excluding them from participating in amateur lacrosse competitions. This occurred even though Native participants had been actively involved in lacrosse competitions with non-Native athletes up to that point, and it was Native Americans who had first introduced non-Natives to the game of lacrosse.

Native people continue to fight for their right to self-determination. This battle pertains to sport as well. Native-controlled sport competitions provide an opportunity for Native athletes to hone and demonstrate sporting skills. However, these competitions also provide a place where Native people can gather, visit with their relatives and friends, compare life experiences, recollect traditional sporting activities, avoid racist treatment from non-Natives, and foster pan-aboriginality—a united, proud awareness of being Native.

Traditional Sports Competitions

Several competitions involving traditional Native activities exist in North America. These events all help revive interest in traditional Native sports and promote community spirit and pride in being Native. Perhaps the oldest competition is the powwow, a summer gathering many centuries old. The contemporary powwow had its origins in warrior organizations on the Plains around the 1870s. Powwows almost died out by the 1930s, because of outside pressures on Natives to stop participating in "traditional" cultural practices. However, this trend started to reverse as Native organizers began to host powwows to honor the many Indian veterans who returned to their reservations from World War II. Powwows increased in number and became even more popular for Native people as cultural awareness and pride in being Native further increased during the 1960s civil rights movement.

Native organizers now offer over 100 powwows annually in North America, both on reservations and in urban areas, with large money prizes available at the major competitions. Some reserves hold "traditional" powwows, which encourage the audience to dance for fun and offer no competitive dancing for money. Native participants of all ages compete in powwows, and both Native and non-Native people attend as spectators. While dancing is the primary focus of powwows, organizers can also include rodeos, hand games, running

269

events, horse competitions, giveaways, parades, and traditional foods and crafts.

Native people in the northern parts of North America have also created "traditional" sport competitions. In Canada, the Northern Games and the Dene Games have been in existence since the 1970s. Native organizers created the Northern Games as a weekend festival of traditional Inuit (Eskimo) and Dene (Indian) games involving Native participants from the Northwest and Yukon Territories and Alaska.

Events planned by the organizers include primarily Inuit activities, such as one- and two-foot high kick, muskox push, blanket toss, one-hand reach, and mouth pull. These events were originally only done by males, although women now also compete. Female participants originally competed in the Good Woman contest, which includes various activities performed by women on the land, such as tea boiling, fire making, wood chopping, bannock (frybread) making, seal and muskrat skinning, and traditional sewing. Men now occasionally compete in this event. Judges award prizes for both speed and the quality of the work done. Athletes have also participated in Dene traditional activities on occasion, such as hand games, Indian blanket toss, pole push, stick pull, and the bow and arrow shoot.

The context of the Northern Games is in keeping with "bush consciousness." Organizers thus create a competition where participation rather than excellence is stressed, and where events begin and end according to "Native time"—that is, when enough people have gathered to make the event possible. Daily activities rarely begin before noon, and old-time dancing, as well as some of the events, often carry on well after midnight. Few spectators attend, as all individuals at the Northern Games are encouraged to participate. Organizers often choose judges just before the event, at which point the designated judges decide on the rules for that event and outline these guidelines to the participants.

The Dene Games were first held in 1977, when Native organizers in the community of Rae-Edzo (in the Northwest Territories) created a summer festival focusing on a softball tournament. Teams from many of the surrounding Native communities were invited to attend. By 1981, organizers began including a few traditional Dene games in this festival, along with stick gambling, a drum dance, and some water events. In 1984, a second Dene Games was begun by organizers for communities farther north.

Two regional Dene Games competitions now occur each summer, made up solely of traditional Dene games. This competition, like the Northern Games, is

Sport and Assimilation

Native organizers in sport have, over the years, continued to challenge government officials, arguing that Native physical activities, and Native ways of organizing sport, are as legitimate and important to fund as mainstream sport. For example, Canadian federal government employees decided to stop funding the Northern Games in the late 1970s because they felt the games did not fit within the department's "sport" mandate. The Northern Games Association, however, challenged the claim that their festival was merely cultural in nature:

> It seems that some outsiders view Northern Games only as a cultural organization. It is a cultural event of the best kind, but its focus is on games and sport. Sports in the south are also cultural events with a different purpose (i.e., a winning purpose in a win-oriented culture). Must we buy that ethic to be funded? (Northern Games Association, 1977, in Paraschak 1991, p. 82)

Native organizers also challenged the federal minister for fitness and amateur sport at a meeting in 1978. She was offering them the chance to establish an office in the National Sports Centre, which would serve as the governing body for Indian sport in Canada. Her opening comments included the following:

> ... if you think that what I am trying to do is assimilate you, you are right, because with sport there is no other way ... except to compete with other people. It does not mean cultural assimilation of the Indian people. It simply means that you get into the mainstream and compete like everyone else. (National Indian Brotherhood, 1978, in Paraschak 1995)

The Native leaders at the meeting turned down her offer precisely because it was assimilationist in nature:

> Politically, economically and socially we are alienated from power, but we still like to decide our own destiny despite the fact that we have no power.... [Assimilation] wip[es] out any idea that Indians may have of being Indians, wip[es] out our reserves, and our status. (National Indian Brotherhood, 1978, in Paraschak 1995)

Native people continue to fight for the right to define and organize sport in ways that fit within their culture, rather than be assimilated into mainstream sport.

—*Victoria Paraschak*

structured in keeping with "bush consciousness." Organizers include events such as the bow and arrow shoot, spear throw, ax throw, canoe races, hand games, and the Good Woman Contest. Winning athletes are often given medals, although traditional items such as mittens or a hand-painted paddle are also awarded on occasion.

A different group of Native people hosts competitions in a traditional winter activity—snow-snake. Snow-snake was historically played widely across North America; however, current competitions are held primarily among the Iroquois in Ontario, Canada, and in New York State. This competition involves sliding a spearlike stick, about 3 meters (10 feet) long, as far as possible along a flat, smooth surface (now an artificially created trough in the snow). Each team includes a shiner, a thrower, and a marker. The shiner, who often makes snow-snakes, is responsible for choosing the proper snow-snake and wax for the snow conditions. The thrower physically throws the snow-snake down the track. The marker serves as an umpire, determining the final landing place of his team's snow-snake. Through these snow-snake competitions, as well as through the powwows, the Northern Games, and the Dene Games, Native people are thus successfully keeping alive, and enjoying, many of their traditional cultural activities.

All-Native Sporting Competitions

The All-Native sport system has been created by organizers to provide mainstream sports opportunities specifically for Native athletes. Organizers of these events, which are usually invitational, enforce a Native participation base through race restrictions for competitors. For example, one All-Native bowling tournament required that participants be Indian or married to an Indian. More restrictive conditions were set for a 1980 Women's Fast Pitch National Championship, which required that players must be at least one-quarter Indian in order to compete. Organizers for the Little Native Hockey League were the most selective, insisting that participants must have a federal band number to compete.

These All-Native sports events tend to be annual tournaments held at the inter-reserve, provincial or state, national, or North American levels. Mainstream sports, such as golf, bowling, basketball, hockey, fastball, tennis, and lacrosse, are the focus of these tournaments. All-Native international sporting exchanges also occur with other countries, such as Australia and New Zealand. In such cases a Native team (from Canada, for example) goes to Australia to compete with aboriginal teams in that country.

A group of Native leaders from Alberta, Canada, organized the first North American Indigenous Games, which were held in Edmonton, Alberta, in 1990. These games, which are restricted to persons of Native heritage, involve athletes from both Canada and the United States. Teams from various provinces and states compete. Mainstream sports are the focus of this competition. Events at the 1993 games included archery, badminton, baseball, basketball, box lacrosse, boxing, canoeing, golfing, rifle shooting, soccer, softball, swimming, track and field, volleyball, and wrestling. Through these Indigenous Games, as well as the All-Native competitions and the international sporting exchanges, athletes can improve their skills in mainstream sports in a supportive context. Participants return home having "experienced the competition, learned about other Aboriginal cultures, made new friends and broadened their own horizons."

—Victoria Paraschak

Bibliography: Oxendine, Joseph. (1988) *American Indian Sports Heritage.* Champaign, IL: Human Kinetics. Roberts, Chris. (1992) *Powwow Country.* Helena, MT: American and World Geographic Publishing. "The North American Indigenous Games." (1993) *Native Journal* (August/September): 26.

Netball

Netball is one of many sports that developed its unique form and structure from another, transplanted sport—in this case, from the United States to Great Britain—and then, as a result of that move, evolving into a significantly different sport. Netball was introduced to England in 1895 as the indoor game of basketball, which it greatly resembles, although a staccato game and a sport of stop, start, catch, and shoot compared to the all-action fluidity of basketball.

History

The development of netball was much influenced by the Ling Association, an organization founded in England in 1899 to represent the professional and academic interests of physical educators. They saw the great education potential in the game, if only the motley assortment of rules could be compressed into one standard set of laws. With this in mind, a Ling Committee subcommittee drafted a set of rules that established a transatlantic compromise. Goals were to be replaced by points, and a shooting circle was introduced—these elements were part of the American game. Baskets were replaced by rings and nets; the name netball, rather than women's basketball, came into use.

In 1905 these English rules were introduced to Scotland, Wales, and Ireland, as well as the United States, Canada, France, and South Africa. The game was hailed for the sense of "control" it gave its players. This concept of "control" seems critical in understanding why a distinctly unmodern game received such vigorous support from athletic administrators and educational leaders: there is an absence of rhythm, speed, contact or collision, and all-out aggression, and points are *not* scored as a frantic climax to a sequence of strategies. It seemed to epitomize notions of rational recreation and a qualified acceptance of a liberation (of sorts) for women on the playing field. The game reaffirmed society's views of how women should behave. They could run and catch and be competitive, but the unrestrained athleticism of other ball games (for example, women's field hockey with a sprinting female capable of firing a shot at goal) was outlawed. Indeed, the set shot, when a netball player sets up and attempts a scoring shot, is a moment of "frozen" sports time with a virtual absence of offensive or defensive movement. Netball seems disciplined and orderly, a sport in which team tactics and an intelligent distribution of the ball takes precedence over individual flair and muscular exuberance.

The All-England Women's Netball Association was founded in 1926. During the 1930s many English county associations were formed.

From 1935 to 1956 netball experienced significant expansion and development despite the occurrence of World War II (1939–1945). There was the publicity and promotional momentum provided by the publication of *Netball Magazine* (1935) and *Netball* (1949). The British Broadcasting Corporation had its first radio broadcast of a game in 1947, the same year that a British netball team went abroad. That they visited Prague, Czechoslovakia, is noteworthy as the Iron Curtain was firmly in place and any type of cultural tour to communist satellite countries was rare.

Netball's shift from its school base to a broad platform of community, club, and university support largely explains its growth since World War II. The first world tournament in 1963 was attended by Australia, Ceylon, England, Jamaica, New Zealand, Northern Ireland, Scotland, South Africa, Trinidad and Tobago, Wales, and West Indies.

The game continues to adapt itself to the changing needs of different cultures and communities. In New Zealand a new form of the sport called "Kiwi Netball" is specially constructed for younger players. It can be played by females or males, or it can be a coeducational activity. The ball is smaller, the goalposts are lower, and different scoring systems provide many more scoring opportunities for participants. Nevertheless, this children's version of netball stays true to the basic essence of the senior game.

One of the most revealing statistical surveys on netball participation comes from the *Life in New Zealand Survey*. This 1991 national review indicates that 26 percent of New Zealand females aged 15 to 18 years participate regularly in netball. Among New Zealand Maori females, 25 percent played netball. This was the third most popular form of recreational activity after aerobics/jazzercise and swimming/diving/water polo. Netball, which has never threatened to enter the Olympic arena, does have its own world championship. In the 1980s and 1990s the most exciting teams have been from the West Indies and Australia. Although netball was a demonstration sport at the XIVth Commonwealth Games in Auckland in 1990, it remains essentially a low-key sport.

—SCOTT A. G. M. CRAWFORD

See also Basketball.
Bibliography: Nauright, J., and J. Broomhall. (1994) "A Woman's Game: The Development of Netball and a Female Sporting Culture in New Zealand, 1906–70." *International Journal of the History of Sport* 1, 3 (December): 387–407. Vamplew, W., K. Moore, J. O'Hara, R. Cashman, and I. F. Jobling, eds. (1992) *The Oxford Companion to Australian Sport*. Melbourne: Oxford University Press.

Olympic Games, Ancient

The ancient Olympic Games, known to us from ancient literature and art and from modern archaeology, were the oldest and most prestigious athletic competition of antiquity. The greatest writer of victory odes for athletes, Pindar (518–438 B.C.E.) wrote that Olympia is to other games as the sun is to the stars; there is no more glorious "place of festival" than Olympia. However they have inspired the modern Olympics, the ancient games must be seen in their own ancient Greek cultural context. Despite common misperceptions, the ancient Olympics differed from their modern counterpart in organization, events, and ideology. The ancient Olympics are important in their own right, not merely as an anachronistic model or moral touchstone for the modern Games.

With sacred rituals and wreaths of olive leaves as prizes, the ancient Olympic Games were part of a great religious festival (a regular gathering for worship and celebration) in honor of Zeus, the Greeks' chief god, held every four years in late summer at the same site, the sanctuary of Zeus at Olympia. The festival was crucial in providing a regular, hallowed context for games, helping the games last for well over a thousand years as the most enduring of Greek institutions. Until unified by Macedon in 338 B.C.E., ancient Greece was not a single nation politically but rather a host of small, fiercely independent city-states, but the Greeks recognized their language, their mythology, and their Panhellenic (all-Greek) Olympics as vital to their ethnicity, their Greekness. At the games of Zeus Greeks assembled to venerate their gods, to enjoy elite competition, and to appreciate their common culture. The Olympics even provided the classical Greeks with a shared chronology,

for happenings were dated by reference to years of the games. Each set of games was named after the winner in the men's sprint race, and an "Olympiad" was one set of games or the interval between the close of one games and the start of the next.

History

Earlier cultures had sports (physical rituals, recreations, competitions), but the Greeks remain distinctive for their institutionalization of athletics (public, intensely competitive physical contests) with regular festivals and prizes. The earliest Greeks, the militaristic Mycenaeans of the Bronze Age, seem to have held athletic contests, possibly with valuable prizes, as part of funeral practices in the second millennium B.C.E. Homer offers the earliest and greatest account of Greek athletics in the funeral games of Patroklos in Book 23 of the *Iliad*. Probably composed or compiled in the 8th century B.C.E., Homer's poems contain no clear reference to Olympic Games. This and a host of conflicting and suspect ancient traditions make the origins of the Olympics uncertain. The later grandeur of the Games understandably inflated notions of their antiquity and emergence. Literary and speculative sources say that Herakles founded the games to honor Zeus or that they were established by the legendary King Pelops from Asia Minor, who won a chariot race against the local king, Oinomaos of Pisa. Traditions also speak of a re-founding or reorganization of the Games during the Greek Dark Age (around the 9th century B.C.E.).

Archaeology suggests that major games were not an original part of early festivals at Olympia. By various interpretations the earliest contests at Olympia were held as sacred rituals, funeral games, offerings to gods, initiations, or reenactments of myths or heroic labors. Olympia was the site of a local and rustic Zeus cult by the 10th century B.C.E., and games may simply have emerged gradually and naturally. Historically, the traditional date of 776 refers not to the first Games but to the first attested Olympic victor, Koroibos of Elis, victor in the *stadion,* a sprint of around 200 meters (218 yards), the only event in the earliest Games. Although the reliability of the earliest entries in the Olympic Victor List compiled by later ancient authors has been challenged, the date of 776 is probably still acceptable if referring to a rather limited and localized contest. The growing number and expense of dedications (gifts to the gods) of metal objects (statuettes and vessels) suggest increased activity in the 8th century, especially around 725–700. Recent archaeology of the site and of wells dug near the stadium area suggests that major games developed around 700 and were expanded in 680 with the addition of equestrian events. In the Archaic Age (roughly 750–500 B.C.E.) patronage by city states and tyrants (autocratic leaders), such as Pheidon of Argos, enhanced the games. When colonization spread Greeks all over the Mediterranean basin, the colonies cherished the games as ties to the motherland.

The 6th century saw a great expansion and spread of Greek athletic festivals, and by the early 5th century Olympia emerged as the pinnacle of a circuit (the Periodos) of four great Panhellenic crown games. Modeled on Olympia, Pindar's "mother of contests," with wreath prizes and competitions open to all Greeks, the other games, at Delphi, Isthmia, and Nemea, were held in a set sequence, with at least one festival each year leading up to the Olympics as the finale. In the Classical Era (roughly 500–323 B.C.E.) the Greeks reveled in their athleticism and Olympia's facilities were expanded (see below). In the 4th century and the Hellenistic Era (323–31 B.C.E.) the Macedonian kings, beginning with Philip II and Alexander the Great, patronized but also politicized Olympia. The financial needs of the early Games had been modest, and, for religious reasons, the Games never had admission fees; but the later, more elaborate facilities and Games depended on benefactions and contributions. After the Roman general Sulla pillaged the site in 85 B.C.E., the Greeks honored Herod of Judea as president of the Games in 12 B.C.E. for his financial help. The Games adjusted to the wider imperial circumstances of the Roman Empire as some emperors were supportive, but Nero in 67 B.C.E. made a travesty of one inappropriately delayed set of Games by collecting fraudulent victories in irregular musical contests and a 10-horse chariot race held for his benefit. The Games were disrupted

by the invasion of the Germanic Herulians in 267 B.C.E. but continued into the Late Roman Empire. The Games endured and perished as part of a pagan festival: in 393 C.E. the Christian emperor Theodosius I ordered the closing of pagan cults and centers, and in 462 Theodosius II ordered the destruction of all pagan temples, but the Games continued until around 500 C.E.

Site and Facilities

The permanent home of the ancient Olympics was an isolated religious sanctuary on the Alpheios River in the territory of the state of Elis in southwestern Greece. Not a city, it lay about 58 kilometers (36 miles) from the city of Elis. Damaged by earthquakes, floods, and humans in antiquity and then abandoned and silted over for centuries, the site was discovered in the 18th century and later systematically excavated by German teams from 1875 on. Archaeology has revealed the history of the site, and the author Pausanias, who visited Olympia around 160–170 C.E., left a detailed and accurate account of what he saw. The area of the earliest constructions and the enduring center of the site was the Altis or sacred precinct of Zeus, marked by a low wall. Early simple cultic arrangements included open-air altars, notably the great altar of Zeus, shrines, and places for dedications among the sacred grove of trees. At Olympia the gods came first, then the athletes, and, last but not least, the spectators.

From the 7th century B.C.E. on, the sanctuary became embellished with architectural and artistic marvels. After the construction of the archaic Doric Temple of Hera, wife of Zeus, around 625, treasuries (small temples and storehouses) were built around 600 by city-states, especially colonies. The famous Doric Temple of Zeus (ca. 470–456) came to house a colossal statue of Zeus (ca. 430) by Phidias, hailed as one of the seven wonders of the ancient world. There were also facilities for priests and officials (Prytaneion, Bouleuterion), other shrines and temples (Metröon, Shrine of Pelops), and various stoas (covered colonnades). The Philippeion was added in the later 4th century B.C.E. as a shrine for heroized Macedonian kings. The arrangements of the Altis were largely set by the late 4th century, but the site acquired further benefactions, renovations, and political monuments. Over time the site became cluttered with dedications (even of weapons and war trophies) and statues—Pausanias mentions some 200.

Athletic facilities grew slowly around the periphery of the Altis. Except for equestrian events, contests took place in the stadium, but even in its later phases this most venerated venue of Greek sport was surprisingly modest to modern minds. One theory places one end of the early racecourse at an altar within the Altis, but the exact location of the earliest stadium remains uncertain. Nearby wells dug about 700 and a retaining wall (of around 550) for an low embankment on the south indicate an archaic stadium extending from the eastern edge of the Altis. A stadium built around 500, perhaps slightly further east, had a higher south embankment. Reflecting adjustments to the growth of the Games rather than a dramatic secularization of athletics, the next stadium was shifted 12 meters to the north and 75 meters further east around 475–450. This stadium had embankments on the south, north, and west, a capacity of around 40,000, and a track about 212 by 28.5 meters with start lines (in narrow slabs of stone) 192.28 meters apart. In the mid-4th century B.C.E. the stadium was further closed off from the sanctuary by the Stoa of Echo. The vaulted ceremonial entrance, the Krypte, formerly seen as a later addition of the 2nd century, may be from the later 4th century. The Olympic stadium was in use, with Hellenistic and Roman renovations, for several centuries but it had no assigned and no stone seating, except for a small area for officials, and water was provided only by small channels at the edge of the track. Similarly, there were no formal accommodations for spectators at Olympia; southwest of the Altis the Leonidaion of the 4th century B.C.E. was a guest house for dignitaries only.

Lying to the south of the stadium, the Hippodrome, the racecourse for horses and chariots, is unexcavated, but Pausanias says the track was 2 stades or 400 meters long with two turning posts and elaborate starting gates added in the mid-5th century. The earliest training areas at Olympia were so simple as to have left no remains except some bathing facilities of the 5th century to the northwest of the Altis. In this area the Palaestra, a small square colonnaded area specifically for practicing combat events, was built in the 3rd century B.C.E. Nearby was the Gymnasium, whose literal meaning is "a place where people are nude," but which functionally was a site for practicing track and field events. Added in the 2nd century B.C.E., this was a large rectangular facility with an open central court, running tracks, stoas on each side, and a monumental entrance.

Operation and Administration

Lacking our penchant for records and statistics, the administration of the ancient Games was, by our standards, very limited and authoritarian. The classical Games were supervised by highly revered officials (10

by the mid-4th century) called the "judges of the Greeks," the Hellanodikai, nobles chosen from the state of Elis who took an oath to be fair. Assisted by priests, whip-bearers, and crowd monitors, as referees and censors they controlled the preparations and decorum of athletes, decisions of victory, and prize giving. Their orders and judgments were absolute and irrevocable. Conspicuous for their purple robes and the forked sticks they carried, the judges could expel, fine, or scourge athletes for cheating or lying. Inscriptions show that even as early as the 6th century they had to enforce rules against foul play in wrestling. Bribery and fraud among athletes was forbidden, but it took place, for Greek athletes were as human as modern ones. Beginning in 388 B.C.E., several bronze statues of Zeus, the Zanes, paid for by fines imposed on athletes, flanked the route to the stadium and bore inscriptions warning against corruption.

Before each Games, heralds from Elis spread throughout Greece announcing the upcoming Games, inviting athletes, spectators, and missions of gift-bearing envoys from Greek states, and proclaiming a sacred truce. Initially of one and later three months' duration, the truce forbade the entry of armies into Elean territory and ordered safe passage through any state for all travelers to and from the Games, in effect as religious pilgrims. The orator Lysias said the Games were founded to promote Panhellenic friendship, but the truce has been romanticized. It did not stop wars: Sparta was fined for attacking Elean territory in 420, and Arcadians even invaded the sanctuary in 364.

Program of Events

For 50 years after 776 the earliest games had only the *stadion* but thereafter the program expanded before settling down to a fairly stable list of events by the late 6th century. Events were introduced as follows: 724, *diaulos* (double race of 400 meters down and back); 720, *dolichos* (long race of 20–24 lengths); 708, pentathlon and wrestling; 688, boxing; 680, *tethrippon* (four-horse chariot race of 12 laps); 648, *pankration* (all-in wrestling) and *keles* (horseback race of 6 laps); 632, boys' *stadion* and wrestling; 628, boys' pentathlon (discontinued thereafter); 616, boys' boxing; 520, *hoplitodromos* (race in armor, down and back); 500, *apene* (mule cart race); 496, *kalpe* or *anabates* (race for mares and dismounting riders; the *kalpe* and *apene* were dropped in 444); 408, *synoris* (two-horse chariot race of 8 laps); 396, contests for heralds and trumpeters; 384, four-colt chariot race; 268, two-colt chariot race; 256, races for colts; 200, boys' *pankration*.

The exact sequence of activities remains uncertain, but clearly by the 5th century athletic contests and religious rituals were intermingled over a five-day festival. Probably the first day saw the oath ceremony, boys' events, prayers and sacrifices; day two saw a procession of competitors and contests in the equestrian events, then the pentathlon; day three (that of the full moon) was central with a procession of judges, ambassadors, athletes, the main sacrifice (of 100 oxen) to Zeus, footraces, and a public feast; day four was wholly athletic with combat events and the race in armor (the *hoplitodromos*); day five saw the procession and crowning of victors, feasting, and celebrations. With related activities, including recitations, merchandising (for example, the selling of food and of artisanal wares such as votive figures) and personal and diplomatic partying and posturing, the festival took on the air of a medieval fair or a modern sporting spectacle, but it was never completely secularized.

Dramatically described by Homer and lavishly depicted in vase paintings, Greek athletic events demanded speed, strength, and stamina. The oldest and simplest contests, the footraces began with an auditory start as athletes stood upright with their toes in grooves in the stone starting sill. Judges assigned lanes by lot and flogged any false starters. On a straight track, longer races required that athletes run down and back, turning around wooden posts. Of events with military overtones, the hoplite race run with helmets and shields is the most obvious. The pentathlon consisted of five contests: a jump, the discus, the javelin, a run, and wrestling. The method of scoring remains debated but there was no complicated system of points.

Combat sports were called "heavy" contests because, without weight classes, rounds, or time limits, heavier athletes dominated. In these events in uneven fields an athlete might be allotted a bye and sit out as an *ephedros* (the term for those waiting for a turn to compete), gaining an advantage in the next round. Fouls or indications of lethargy were met with blows of the judge's stick. Wrestlers used an array of sophisticated holds and throws, and matches were decided by three of five falls (touching an opponent's back or shoulders to the ground, tying him up in a confining hold, or stretching him prone) or by submission. Boxers bound their hands with leather thongs, and victories were achieved when an opponent was knocked out or submitted. The *pankration* or "all powerful" combat was a brutal free-for-all combining boxing and wrestling. Sometimes wearing light boxing thongs, pankratiasts could punch, kick, and choke; only biting

and gouging were forbidden. Bouts continued until one athlete gave up or was incapacitated. A thrice-victorious mid-4th-century pankratiast, Sostratos of Sikyon, was famous for breaking the fingers of opponents. There are stories of deaths and even a posthumous victory: before expiring in a stranglehold, Arrhachion of Phigaleia is said to have dislocated his opponent's ankle, forcing him to submit to a dead but victorious man in 564 B.C.E. Athletes who unintentionally killed opponents had legal immunity.

The equestrian events were the most spectacular, for keeping horses in poor and rocky Greece was a proverbial sign of wealth. The owners, not the drivers, were declared the victors in these contests. Young jockeys rode horses bareback, and chariot races were even more hazardous as large fields of 40 or more entries of light, two-wheeled, wooden chariots raced over 12 laps and made sharp hairpin turns. Owners did not have to drive their own teams and usually hired drivers, a circumstance allowing Alkibiades of Athens to enter 7 teams in 416. Owners did not even need to be present, thus allowing even female victors. Kyniska, daughter of a Spartan king, won the *tethrippon* in 396 and 392 B.C.E.

Athletes

At their best, ancient Olympians showed dedication to their gods, families, and countries, performing magnificently while upholding ideals of endurance, humility, and moderation. Admittedly, Greek athletes were obsessed with individual first-place victory. Homer claimed there was "no greater glory" than that won by hands and feet, and Pindar said athletic victory was "the grandest height to which mortals can aspire," as close to immortality as a Greek could come. Participation was not enough: Pindar writes of embarrassed losers sneaking home. An uncontested victory when an athlete faced no challengers was rare, and most victories were hard ones, long sought and much celebrated.

Ancient Olympians represented many Greek states but only one Greek culture. Competitors had to be free (non-slave), male Greeks (non-"barbarians," although Romans were permitted later) not otherwise excluded by grave religious sin or Olympic sanctions. Early Games drew locally and Sparta dominated, but with the age of colonization athletes came from the Black Sea to North Africa. Southern Italy and Sicily became prominent, as did Alexandria later in the Hellenistic Era. Athletes usually represented their native states but they could declare themselves as representatives of other states. The runner Astylos won races for Kroton in southern Italy in 488 and again in 484, but in 480 he won for Syracuse in Sicily, supposedly to honor his friend, Hieron, tyrant of Syracuse. Athletes swore a solemn oath that they would abide by the rules and that they had been in continuous training for the previous 10 months. Subject to the judges' estimation of their physical maturity, athletes were eligible for boys' events from age 12 on but were excluded at 18 or perhaps 19. All athletes (and trainers) in the stadium, and jockeys but not charioteers in the hippodrome, competed nude. Ancient explanations about safety or advantages for speed aside, nudity was of cultic rather than practical origin. Except for one priestess of Demeter, women were barred from Olympia during the Games, ostensibly on pain of death, although one woman from a famous athletic family discovered on site was spared. At separate times, however, the site housed contests for females in the quadrennial Heraia, the Games of Hera.

Famous athletes were glorified even to the point of cultic hero worship, and ancient Olympians inspired many tall tales. The famous Milo of Kroton had six Olympic wins (boys' wrestling in 536, then 5 men's by 516) among his 31 in the Periodos, the circuit of Panhellenic crown games, over a career of at least 24 years. He is said to have eaten 18 kilograms (40 pounds) of meat and bread and 7.5 liters (8 quarts) of wine at one setting, and to have carried, killed, and then consumed a four-year-old bull. Supposedly he could hold a pomegranate in his fist and not bruise it even as others tried to pry it from his hand, and he could burst a cord tied about his forehead merely by the strength of his veins when he held his breath. Theagenes of Thasos, who won the *pankration* (476) and boxing (480) at Olympia, claimed some 1,400 wins in his long and much-traveled career.

Scholars debate the historical continuity or changes in the social origins of the ancient Olympians. Traditional views of an early golden age of pure, noble competitors have been challenged. Specialized training, professional coaching, excesses, and profit came early. Greeks had neither the concept nor a word for amateurism in the elitist 19th-century sense of banning material profit from sport. From the start, athletes of all classes accepted material as well as symbolic prizes and rewards. On site at Olympia victors won only a wreath of olive leaves, an intrinsically priceless gift picked from Zeus's sacred trees, along with ceremonial decorations and honors (fillets of wool, sprigs of vegetation, the herald's proclamation, and the right to establish a statue in the Altis). On his homecoming, however, a victor received extrinsic benefits, such as cash bonuses, free meals, and honorary seats at theaters and public gatherings for life. By the 6th century Athens gave its Olympic victors monetary rewards of 500 drachmas (about $340,000).

Beyond the Periodos many games with valuable material prizes (such as money, cloaks, olive oil) were available, and seeing prizes as gifts rather than wages, athletes competed wherever they wanted. The door was open for middle-class and even poor athletes, but those with family resources still had advantages for the required time, travel, and training under instruction. Financial subsidization of athletes is attested from around 300 B.C.E. on, but the dramatic record of archaic Kroton, whose runners won over 40 percent of the victories in the Olympic *stadion* from 588 to 484, may have involved civic intervention. By Hellenistic times at the latest, Greek athletics knew most aspects of modern professionalism; guilds of professional athletes existed from about 50 B.C.E. and were later subsidized by Roman emperors.

Like their modern counterparts, critics of ancient athletics found material for satire but had no effect. The 6th-century philosopher Xenophanes said that honors and rewards should go to intellectuals rather than athletes, and a fragment of Euripides' lost *Autolykos* from around 420 lampooned athletes, "the worst of the thousand ills of Greece," as musclebound gluttons, uncouth, useless, and parasitical members of the community. Although he wished otherwise, Plato admitted that most Greeks saw the life of Olympic victors as the happiest.

—DONALD G. KYLE

See also Pentathlon, Ancient; Olympic Games, Modern.

Bibliography: Kyle, Donald G. (1993) *Athletics in Ancient Athens*. Revised edition. Leiden: E. J. Brill.Matz, David. (1991) *Greek and Roman Sport. A Dictionary of Athletes and Events from the Eighth Century B.C. to the Third Century A.D.* Jefferson, NC: McFarland. Raschke, Wendy J., ed. (1988) *Archaeology of the Olympics*. Madison: University of Wisconsin Press. Swaddling, Judith. (1984) *The Ancient Olympic Games*. Austin: University of Texas Press. Sweet, Waldo E. (1987) *Sport and Recreation in Ancient Greece: A Sourcebook with Translations*. Oxford: Oxford University Press.

Olympic Games, Modern

Over their 100-year span, the Summer Olympic Games have grown from a quaint *fin de siècle* festival involving 13 countries and fewer than 300 athletes to a movement counting almost 200 of the world's countries as members of the Olympic family. The Summer Games now showcase the sporting exploits of over 10,000 athletes;

the Winter Games, over 2,000. The Olympic festival has evolved into the modern world's foremost sport spectacle and extravagant cultural ritual. Finally, the Games have become a phenomenon that energize nations the world over to mount elaborate financial and organizational efforts to be presented in a good light at the great quadrennial occasions. Political factions, ethnic groups, religious sects, economic cartels, media, artists, scholars, and "cause conscious" factions of almost every hue are both hypnotized and galvanized by what the Olympic Games can engender in the way of attention to cause, enhanced prestige, potentially huge profits, and opportunities for individual and group expression. No other regularly occurring world event casts such a penetrating global effervescence and, at the same time, such a tall shadow of frightening possibilities.

History

It took the modern world almost 2,000 years to become aware of the illustrious sporting legacy achieved by the cornerstone of Western civilization—the ancient Greeks. As 19th-century archaeologists began to discover remains of ancient stadiums, gymnasiums, statues, and vases by the thousands displaying painted scenes of athletic and sporting endeavor among Greeks, and as fragments of their preserved literature on sporting matters became known, the spirit of modern man was moved to attempt an emulation of such past glories. After all, health, fitness, physical education, competitive sporting prowess, and glorification of the body had served Greece supremely during its golden eras of antiquity; why could such things not serve similarly in modern times? One individual who thought they could was a French aristocrat named Pierre de Frédy, the Baron de Coubertin (1863–1937).

Concerned by the lack of a sporting ethic among his countrymen and an absence of physical education in the schools of France, Coubertin set about to initiate change. He traveled widely in England and the United States, impressed greatly by what he viewed in the way of sport and physical education in England's private "public schools" and American colleges and universities. Though Coubertin wrote and lectured vigorously on themes involving needed changes in French education, he was rebuffed by his country's education authorities. As a result, Coubertin's sport-education ideas turned toward international perspectives, one pet theme of which was the modern reincarnation of the epitome of ancient Greek athletic expressions, the Olympic Games.

In June 1894, Coubertin convened a conference at

the Sorbonne in Paris, the two points of business of which were to debate common eligibility standards for participation in international sporting competition and a possible revival of the Olympic Games. Although no meaningful conclusions were reached on the former, the latter was successfully endorsed by the assembly of over 200 delegates. An International Olympic Committee (IOC) was formed and the first Games were awarded to Athens in the spring of 1896. The choice of Athens was questioned by Europeans, many of whom felt that Greece was far removed from the mainstream of modern developments in athletics. In reality, however, the Greeks had staged two attempts to reestablish the ancient Games in modern context. Through the beneficence of millionaire Evangelos Zappas, successful festivals were held in 1859 and 1870. Further attempts were far less successful, but there is little doubt that Greeks of the latter 19th century had experienced modest episodes of modern sport organization and performance by 1896.

With the energetic organizational efforts of Greece's royal family, particularly Crown Prince Constantine, and the financial contributions of Georges Averoff, a millionaire benefactor reminiscent of Zappas, the 1896 Games were a huge success. Over 60,000 people attended the opening in the grand marble stadium restored specifically for the occasion. A small band of American athletes dominated the track and field events, but the Greeks themselves performed worthily. Spiridon Loues, a modest shepherd whose startling victory in the marathon event marked the only occasion in his lifetime that he competed in sport, became the toast of all Greece and an eternal memory in Greek sport history.

Growing Pains

The Games of the Second Olympiad were staged in France as part of the Paris World Exposition. Enveloped by the great fair, they failed miserably to capitalize on their auspicious opening four years earlier. The Paris Olympics were reported in the world's newspapers as anything but Olympic contests. Rather, they were mostly referred to as World University Championships or Exposition Contests.

The demeaning of the Olympic Games caused by organizing them as a sideshow to a World's Fair was a lesson ignored in 1904. The U.S. city of St. Louis made the Games of the Third Olympiad part of the Louisiana Exposition's physical culture exhibits and activities. Though athletic performance was superb, foreign participation was so scant that the events were largely

American championships. Nevertheless, the 1904 Games marked the modern Olympic movement's arrival in the United States and the Olympics became an indelible dimension of America's early–20th-century crusade for international sporting prominence.

Ensuing Olympic festivals were staged in London in 1908 and Stockholm in 1912 with the Stockholm festival marking the arrival of the Olympic Games as the world's premier international sporting event. National Olympic committees from 28 countries, located on all continents of the world, sent some 2,500 athletes to Sweden to compete in 102 events.

By 1914, the IOC had a new symbol, the now famous five-ring logo, and a motto, the Latin phrase, *citius, altius, fortius* (swifter, higher, stronger). For Coubertin, many of his expectations for the modern Olympic movement had begun to emerge. As expressed in 1908, Coubertin told the world that he had revived the Olympic Games in modern context with several motivations in mind:

1. as a cornerstone for health and cultural progress;
2. for education and character building;
3. for international understanding and peace;
4. for equal opportunity;
5. for fair and equal competition;
6. for cultural expression;
7. for beauty and excellence; and
8. for independence of sport as an instrument of social reform, rather than government legislation.

World War I prevented the holding of the Games in Berlin, but in 1920, with the world temporarily at peace, the Games unfolded in Antwerp. Prominent among members of the Belgium Organizing Committee was Count Henri Baillet-Latour, the IOC member who would succeed Coubertin as president.

When Coubertin and his original International Olympic Committee had convened in Paris in 1894 following the Sorbonne Conference, a number of sports had been considered for inclusion in the Olympic program. One of them, oddly enough, had been *patinage,* or ice skating. An indoor exhibition of figure skating had been presented by the London organizers in 1908. In Antwerp in 1920, Belgian officials organized figure-skating events once again, together with an exhibition ice hockey tournament. It would take the departure of Coubertin, an opponent of the concept of separate Winter Olympic Games, from the modern Olympic movement before such a phenomenon became reality. A modest winter sports festival was arranged in 1924

in Chamonix, France, separate and distinct from the Summer Games in Paris, but it did not become recorded as the first Winter Olympic Games until after the baron's retirement in 1925. Beginning in 1928, Winter Olympic Games were organized every four years.

The Games Reach Maturity

Cities the world over mount energetic and elaborately detailed plans to win the IOC's approval to host the Olympic Games. Such campaigns are underpinned by various motivations: civic and national pride and prestige, political gain, economic benefit. The quest by Los Angeles to host the Olympic Games provides an early example. A desire to promote the City of Angels as a tourist and vacation mecca, as a climatically healthful place in which to live, and as an area of great economic potential through the investment of capital for handsome dividends prompted Los Angeles to bid for the Games of 1920. Coubertin's intent to hold the 1920 (Antwerp), 1924 (Paris), and 1928 (Amsterdam) Games in Europe stalled the Los Angeles bid. But the persistence of William M. Garland and his Los Angeles colleagues finally paid off and the city received the Games for 1932. By the eve of the Games of the Tenth Olympiad, America, indeed much of the world, was in the midst of a devastating economic Depression. Despite this, the Games went on, and, it might be argued, in glorious fashion. Funding much of the festival from a $1 million state appropriation gained through a public referendum, the main events were held in the relatively new Los Angeles Memorial Coliseum. An Olympic Village was built for the first time, but only for men; the women were accommodated in the Chapman Hotel in downtown Los Angeles.

Largely a patriarchal expression in both organization and athletic participation during the first three decades of its history, the modern Olympic movement offered few opportunities for women. Through the pioneering efforts of an idealistic French woman, Alice Milliat, an international federation for women's sports (FSFI) was organized in 1921 and several successful editions of "Women's Olympic Games" occurred between 1921 and 1934. Though women had competed in Olympic demonstration events in 1900 in tennis and golf, in swimming and diving beginning in 1912, and even in track and field in 1928, it would require female Olympic stars comparable to Jim Thorpe, Paavo Nurmi, and Johnny Weissmuller before women's participation was taken seriously. In this regard, the startling performances of Sonja Henie, the youthful Norwegian skating beauty of the 1928, 1932, and 1936 Winter Games and the track and field accomplishments of the tomboyish American, Mildred "Babe" Didrikson, in the Los Angeles Games in 1932 initiated a trend that projected women into the limelight of the Olympic program.

Ominous signs of world discord permeated much of the 1930s, including the staging of the 1936 Summer Games in Berlin. When the Games of the Eleventh Olympiad had been awarded to Germany in 1931, the lingering vestiges of the Weimar Republic governed Germany. By the time that the Olympic flame was lit in Berlin's magnificent Olympic stadium in the summer of 1936, the National Socialists led by Adolf Hitler were in power. Under IOC rules, host cities, not national governments, are directed to organize and stage the Games. But Hitler's representatives were everywhere, controlling and shaping the Olympic festival to serve Nazi interests. Though much of the two-week celebration was an expression of German nationalism, Nazi propaganda, and Teutonic military culture, it was also an extravaganza featuring German organizational precision. Many countries, including the United States, feared sending a team to compete. Controversy arose in the United States: "to go or not to go," became the question debated at length by various factions allied with, as well as completely divorced from, the amateur sport movement in the country. Many viewed it as immoral to support an "evil" German regime by taking part. Nazi postures on religion and race defied Christian principles and ran counter to Olympic moral codes. In the end, a U.S. Olympic team sailed to Europe in the summer of 1936. Superb athletic performances abounded in Berlin, but none were more spectacular than those of Jesse Owens, the black American sprinter. Owens, at first a curiosity and then a celebrity in the eyes of most German spectators, won the 100- and 200-meter (109- and 218-yard) sprints, the long jump, and ran a leg on the winning 4 x 100 meter relay team, dispelling in graphic fashion the warped Nazi doctrine of Aryan supremacy.

By 1940 the world was at war once again. The 1940 Summer Games and Winter Games, which were awarded to Japan (Tokyo and Sapporo, respectively), were canceled, as were the 1944 Summer Games set for Helsinki.

Postwar Trials
With the conclusion of World War II in 1945, the IOC turned its attention to reestablishment of the Olympic Games. In the summer of 1948, the Games of the Fourteenth Olympiad were staged in war-ravaged London. Germany, Italy, and Japan were missing, banned as

perpetrators of the war, just as Germany had been disallowed from competing in the Games of 1920 and 1924 for identical reasons with regard to World War I. The Summer Games of 1948 were preceded by the Winter Olympics, held in St. Moritz. Both the 1948 Winter and Summer Games were a far cry from those in 1932 and 1936 in terms of organization, facilities, and pomp, but superb athletic endeavor more than compensated.

The results of World War II reshaped the map of the world and created vexing problems for leaders of the Olympic movement. The fracture of Europe into "East" and "West" spheres of political polarization, particularly the split of Germany into two countries, produced thorny consequences for the IOC. Germany returned to the Olympic Games in 1952 (Helsinki), represented by athletes from the West. For a series of four succeeding summer and winter Olympic festivals (Melbourne/ Cortina d'Ampezzo in 1956, Rome/Squaw Valley in 1960, Tokyo/Innsbruck in 1964, and Mexico City/ Grenoble in 1968), Germany was represented by a combined team of athletes from both East and West. The Soviet-controlled German Democratic Republic and the West-backed Federal Republic of Germany did not compete as individual nations until the Munich/Sapporo Games in 1972.

If the German problem was not enough to frustrate IOC leaders, then the emergence of the Soviet Union into Olympic matters, the place of South Africa in the Games, and ultimatums from the People's Republic of China promoted a constant state of turmoil. The Soviet Union's first appearance in the Olympic Games, in Helsinki in 1952, served notice that they were the Olympic power of the future. Their medal count in Finland was barely eclipsed by the United States. An elaborate scheme of early identification of young athletes, specialized sports schools, application of scientific research to sport performance, and elaborate financial support at all levels within the nation's sport mechanism ensured consistent representation on Olympic victory podiums. The Soviet approach prompted constant debate by IOC authorities, particularly on the question of "state professionals." But, the success of the Soviet model spurred many nations the world over to adopt various dimensions of the proven blueprint for athletic success.

South Africa had been a valued Olympic family member since its first participation in 1908. For almost half a century no one questioned South Africa's policy of apartheid, a policy in direct confrontation with the Olympic code's principle that participation in the

Games "shall not be denied for reasons of race." South Africa's Olympic teams had always been lily white. With the disintegration of European colonial empires on the continent of Africa following World War II, and the commensurate evolution of new nations reflecting black pride and political power, the racial policy of South Africa came under censure and severe challenge, internally and externally. One of the political measures exerted was a campaign aimed at forcing South African Olympic teams to be integrated, a first step in the dissolution of that nation's overall policy of discrimination toward people of color. With the backing of the Soviet Union, whose support on the measure was underscored by political and economic dividends to be gained in Africa, a steady campaign was waged. A boycott of the Games by a unified bloc of African countries was the trump card played. After having had its invitation withdrawn in 1964 and 1968, South Africa was finally expelled from the family of Olympic nations in 1972. Black Africa had won the battle, but not the war. South Africa's apartheid policies remained in effect for twenty years. In 1992 at Barcelona, black and white athletes finally marched together as members of a South African Olympic team reunited with the modern Olympic movement.

The triumph of Mao Zedong's Communists over the Nationalist followers of Chiang Kai-shek in China's drawn-out civil war of the 1930s and 1940s brought still another vexing problem. Which was the real China in the IOC's eye? Mainland Communists? Or Nationalists who had retreated to Formosa, an island off China's coast that eventually became known as Taiwan? Because the prewar national Chinese Olympic Committee had been in the hands of the Nationalists, the IOC recognized Taiwan, which in turn insisted upon being called the Republic of China. In a series of arguments and angry rebuffs, the People's Republic failed to move the IOC toward their point of view—the argument that with a population 50 times that of Taiwan, indeed a population figure that represented nearly one-third of the world's total numbers, it was the real China. Stubbornly, they remained aloof from the Olympics until 1984.

All this, and much more, caused the IOC presidency of Avery Brundage, who had succeeded Edstrom after the 1952 Summer Games, to be filled with controversy and crisis. Few could have been equal to the task of steering the Olympic schooner through such turbulent waters during the 1950s, 1960s, and early 1970s. But Brundage proved to be a capable captain. He remained consistent in proclaiming that sport should never be contaminated by politics; that the Olympic Games were for amateur athletes; that the Olympic movement should be insulated from the evils of commercialism; that women's competition should be reduced; that the Games should become smaller, not larger; indeed, that perhaps the Winter Olympics ought to be eliminated altogether. During his tenure as president (1952–1972), he fought tenaciously against South Africa's expulsion. As well, he constantly patrolled the halls of amateurism, protecting the hallowed Olympic precincts from encroachment by professionals. Sports conservatives lionized Brundage, liberals promoting change vilified him.

The 1968 Mexico Games will always be noted for the emergence of African athletes as track and field giants in distance racing. Between Kipchoge Keino, Naftali Temu, and Amos Biwott of Kenya, Mamo Wolde of Ethiopia, and Mohamed Gammoudi of Tunisia, Africans won every men's running event at distances over 800 meters. Sadly, a shocking episode that occurred shortly before the opening of the Games cast a pall on the gala festival and demonstrated how the Olympic Games can at times be used to draw national and international attention to sociopolitical causes. Throughout the 1960s, costs associated with staging the Olympics had spiraled to dizzying heights. In a relatively poor country like Mexico, where millions lived in poverty and squalor, huge expenditures for games in place of badly needed social welfare projects and programs proved a bone of contention to many, especially left-wing political radicals and idealistic university students. Protests and demonstrations on this point angered a Mexican government intent on ensuring a peaceful atmosphere during its appearance before the world. Confrontations between military police and university students boiled over into violent reaction, resulting in what has become known as the massacre of Tlatelolco Square. Depending on whose story is accepted, the Mexican government's or that of its antagonists, some 30 to 300 students were killed. There was another controversial episode. Almost a year before the Games began, U.S. civil rights activist Harry Edwards had attempted to rally black athletes to boycott the Games. This was an attempt to focus world attention on the pitiful socioeconomic and civil rights status of millions of black Americans. Black athletes were not unanimous in supporting the boycott. Few stayed home. But many left for Mexico City intent on making personal statements in order to focus attention on the issue. Tommy Smith and Jon Carlos, winners of gold and bronze medals in the 200 meters, mounted the victory podium, bowed their heads as the "Star-Spangled Banner" was played, and thrust black glove–clad fists aloft.

For all of Brundage's unyielding stance on most matters about which he felt strongly, one item succeeded in breaching his resolve. That item was television. One fundamental fact had always stood in the way of the IOC realizing its ambitions and endeavors. That stark reality was that it was usually poverty stricken. Though scorning any link to what he called "commercialism," Brundage recognized as early as the late 1940s the value of television in advertising the Olympic movement worldwide. But, as major sporting events in the United States increasingly penetrated television programming, he was led to consider the prospect of selling television rights for the Games. Stemming from a difference of opinion with television media in Melbourne at the 1956 Games, a confrontation prompted by arguments of whether the Olympics were *news* or *entertainment,* the IOC moved resolutely toward framing constitutional statutes in its charter for the protection of its product. Thus, the now famous Rule 49 came into being. Any television broadcasting of the Olympic Games longer than three-minute news briefs, aired three times per day, would have to be purchased. The Winter Games of 1960 in Squaw Valley were the first to be sold to U.S. television under the new rights-fee statute. They went to CBS for $50,000. CBS also won the exclusive U.S. rights for the Summer Games in Rome. The fee negotiated was $394,000. As the television giants ABC, CBS, and NBC competed vigorously for the right to air each succeeding edition of the Winter and Summer Games, the U.S. rights fees reached beyond the $2 million dollar mark in 1964, spiraled to over $100 million by 1980, and have reached $456 million from NBC for the centennial Games of 1996, with the European Broadcast Union paying an additional $250 million for European rights. The IOC in a very short span of years found itself rolling in dough.

Brundage's 20-year tenure as IOC president came to an end following a vote by the IOC at the 1972 Games in Munich. Never in Brundage's tenure was his power and authority under such severe challenge as it was by this time. At the Winter Games in Sapporo, Brundage had tried to deny entry to a host of alpine skiers, many of whom he felt to be violators of the Olympic amateur code. Their flagrant disregard for Olympic rules greatly angered him, especially their acceptance of "cash and kind" from ski equipment manufacturers in return for orchestrated display of the company's equipment on television, and their acceptance of money far beyond "reasonable expenses" for appearances at major ski meets on the world circuit. Brundage, his influence badly eroded by 1972, had to settle for a token expul-

sion. The scapegoat was Karl Schranz, the gold medal favorite in the alpine events, who was not permitted to compete.

The 1972 Munich Summer Games commenced in August in an atmosphere the reverse of that which existed the last time Germany had played host to the Olympics (1936). Instead of the red, black, and white colors identified with Nazis, soft pastels were the color theme. Instead of Nazi rank and file, cheery Bavarians greeted visitors. However, if there were doubts in the minds of some that sport and politics did not mix, the events of 5 and 6 September removed them. In Olympic history's most horrible incident, a group of Palestinian guerrilla-terrorists infiltrated the Olympic village, took members of the Israeli wrestling team hostage, and bargained for the release of 200 Palestinians incarcerated in Israeli jails. In a dramatic sequence of events at Munich's Fuerstenfeldbruck airbase, a shootout occurred between the guerrillas and German sharpshooters. Five of the eight Palestinians were killed, but not before all of the Israeli hostages were slain by the guerrillas. Brundage, in his last public act as IOC czar, arranged a huge memorial service in the Olympic stadium, and then dictated that "the Games must go on." The Olympics must never bow to "commercial, political and now criminal pressure," the 84-year-old Brundage exclaimed. With his exit from that forum, an Olympic career, the impact of which rivaled that of Coubertin's, came to an end. He was succeeded in office by Ireland's Michael Morris, the Lord Killanin.

Boycotts and Bucks

The horror of Munich dictated complex security mechanisms at all future Olympic festivals. At the Summer Games of 1976 in Montreal, about $1 million was spent on security, including support of a 16,000-man militia force. Montreal had struggled to meet preparation deadlines for the Games. In the end, labor disputes, construction problems, cost overruns, and a host of other problems burdened Mayor Jean Drapeau's city and *La Belle Provence* with millions of dollars of debt. To this day, the financial embarrassments incurred continue to be felt. At the same time, politics escalated as a major problem area for the IOC and its Olympic family members—the host city organizers, National Olympic Committees, and the International Sport Federations. Continuing their quest to end South Africa's racial policy, African countries argued that New Zealand should be barred from competing in the 1976 Games in Montreal because its national rugby team, the famous All-Blacks, had played matches against

South Africa, thus violating an IOC ban on participating against South African sports teams. In turn, the IOC argued that the rule applied only to Olympic sports, which rugby was not. The African complaint was dismissed. Thirty-two African countries and nations supporting their cause responded by returning home. The long-brandished African threat of boycott had finally been implemented.

The 1980 Summer Games had been awarded to Moscow. The Soviet state prepared diligently for its chance to showcase "the triumph of Communism" before the world. But, in December 1979 its military forces marched into neighboring Afghanistan to prop up a Communist-controlled government on the brink of being toppled by Islamic fundamentalist factions. In response to this act, U.S. President Jimmy Carter called for a world boycott of the Moscow Games. He didn't quite get "the world" to go along with him, but U.S. diplomatic pressures on the global community ultimately led 62 countries to boycott the Games. Eighty-one nations participated, the fewest number since the Melbourne Games 25 years earlier. The Moscow Games proceeded; Soviet and East German athletes dominated the sports contests. There was little doubt that the Soviet Union, which had poured millions of the state's precious rubles into preparing for the Games, was considerably angered by the boycott. It did not take them long to get revenge.

The historic city of Sarajevo in Yugoslavia hosted the Winter Games in 1984. Muslims, Serbs, and Croats combined efforts to produce a well-organized and orchestrated festival. Seven years later they were at war with each other and much of the beautiful city that had been host to a great world festival of sport, peace, and beauty lay in shambles, the bodies of thousands of its people buried in coffins made of wood torn from former Olympic sports buildings. After the financial debacle of Montreal in 1976, none but Los Angeles, California, presented a bid to host the 1984 Summer Games. In the end, the city tried to renege on its bid; secondary planning pointed towards a huge deficit, most of which would have to be paid by the taxpayer. Enter Peter Ueberroth and a group of associates, who laid a plan before the IOC to fund the Games with corporate sponsorships. But only cities are awarded Olympic Games, not private corporations; that was the rule. However, it was either Ueberroth's plan, or no Games. The IOC buckled. World television rights generated $260 million. Another $130 million was raised from 30 corporate sponsors pledged to pay at least $4 million each in return for rights to manufacture and market their products with the Olympic logo emblazoned on them. Further, 43 companies paid a premium to sell their products as the "official" Olympic drink (Coca-Cola), the official domestic beer (Schlitz), the official Olympic hamburger (McDonald's), and so on. By the time the Games were concluded, not only had they been carried off in solvent fashion, they made a profit for the organizers, in fact, of about $150 million. ABC television presented Olympic programming so blatantly nationalistic that even patriotic Americans cringed. The Soviets called the Games a farce; they weren't even there, having led a 17-nation Eastern bloc boycott for the embarrassment exacted on them in 1980.

The IOC was in an angry mood as it convened at meetings following the Los Angeles Games. Severe penalties were threatened to those who might pursue a boycott stance in the future. Large-scale boycotts ceased, but not because of IOC threats. In effect, boycotts just did not work: the Soviets had remained in Afghanistan for a sustained period, U.S. athletes won 174 medals in the absence of those from Eastern bloc countries, and a gathering storm of protest rose from athletes who had dedicated four years of their lives for a chance to become an Olympian only to see their chances obliterated by politicians. At the opening ceremonies of the 1988 Summer Games in Seoul, only Cuba and North Korea refused to attend. The Games of the Twenty-fourth Olympiad, bathed in Korean culture and charm, celebrated athlete and spectator harmony once again.

Confrontations between Olympian gods in antiquity formed the basis for Greek mythology. Showdowns between athletes of supreme Olympian-like status provide a modern similarity. The 100-meter sprint final in Seoul, featuring Carl Lewis of the United States against Canada's Ben Johnson, was akin to Herakles wrestling the Nemean lion. Johnson won in the extraordinary time of 9.73 seconds. Two days later it was determined that his post-race urine sample was saturated with residuals of performance-enhancing drugs. Johnson was disqualified; Lewis received the gold medal. The aftermath produced a national inquiry in Canada, revealing that drug-taking to improve athletic performance was not limited simply to those whose fame and fortune depended on the outcome of a less-than-ten-second run. The female star of the Seoul Games was U.S. sprinter Florence Griffith-Joyner, or "Flo Jo" as she was affectionately dubbed by the press. Griffith-Joyner ran the 100 meters less than one-half second slower than Ben Johnson's startling time. Her heavily muscled thighs and lightning reaction at the start raised questions in the minds of many as to what her pharmaceutical menu might have been in preparing for the Games. No charges were ever officially levied; Griffith-Joyner retired from competition immediately following the Korean Games.

In February 1988, Canada hosted its first Winter Games. Hoping to make a profit from them, Calgary pressed Ueberroth's 1984 financial model into place. An ABC television rights fee of $309 million and corporate sponsorship on the order of that seen in Los Angeles in 1984 ensured a profit and a lasting Calgary Olympic legacy in the form of sports facilities and a huge Olympic Trust Fund.

Albertville, France, was the scene of the last Winter Olympic Games to be celebrated in the same year that the Summer Games were held. Shortly before the Games opened, a failed coup by Communist "hard-liners" trying to stem a Soviet flirtation with democracy sponsored by Premier Mikhail Gorbachev sparked a series of events that disintegrated isolationist policies between East and West. Down came the Berlin Wall, symbol of separation between East and West Germany. Down came the doctrine of Communism that had ruled Soviet lives for the greater part of the century. Up rose new countries from the remnants of the old Union of Soviet Socialist Republics. Up rose the number of new nations in the Olympic family, many of them well-known former Soviet states, including Russia, the Ukraine, Estonia, and Belarus. The political events occurred so rapidly that most of the newly formed countries could not organize their independent National Olympic Committees in time for the Albertville Games. Rather than scuttle the hopes of prospective Olympic participants, the IOC allowed former Soviet state athletes to compete under a hastily contrived sobriquet, the Unified Team. Their flagbearer marched into the stadium for the opening ceremonies holding aloft the Olympic flag.

In 1980 an ailing Lord Killanin had been replaced as IOC president by a Catalan Spaniard, Juan Antonio Samaranch. Samaranch, once a roller hockey goalie and former Spanish ambassador to the Soviet Union, quickly asserted himself as an Olympic progressivist. Though Killanin had planted the seeds for reform, it was Samaranch who reaped the harvest. Under Samaranch's leadership, the IOC elected women to its ranks (currently there are 8). Samaranch also presided over new financial initiatives. Since the middle 1970s, the IOC had been restive about the fact that 97 percent of its operating revenue was derived from television income. By the middle 1980s, a new IOC revenue source took its place beside television. It was called TOP (The Olympic Program). Contracting with the Swiss licensing firm International Sport & Leisure (ISL), the IOC sold the rights to market the five-ring logo to a dozen multinational manufacturing firms. Coca-Cola, Kodak, and Federal Express were among the first TOP clients. The exclusive use of the logo was sold for a period of four years, an Olympic quadrennial. TOP I (1984–1988) produced $100 million, Top II (1988–1992) $170 million. The projected revenue from TOP III (1992–1996) will approach $400 million.

Under his presidency, too, Samaranch orchestrated the relaxation of eligibility rules that permitted a drift toward allowing the best athletes in the world to compete, irrespective of the fact that they might be professionals. Changes in Olympic eligibility rules prompted a sensational event to be orchestrated in Barcelona in 1992. With the concurrence of President Samaranch, the International Basketball Federation (FIBA) relaxed all rules against professionals competing. To many, the result was a travesty of sporting justice. The United States sent the foremost stars of the National Basketball Association to perform against the world. Long-established professionals, whose salaries in all cases were in the multimillion-dollar range, competed against relative neophytes from Angola, Lithuania, Croatia, and Puerto Rico. The results were predictable, lopsided wins in every contest on the way to the gold medal. Indeed, it often seemed that the aura of Magic Johnson, Larry Bird, Michael Jordan, Charles Barkley, and company was greater than that of the Games themselves, or of host Barcelona, one of the world's most beautiful cities.

The Future of the Olympic Games

As both the Winter and Summer Olympic festivals grew larger and larger in terms of new sports (and added events within sporting disciplines), competing countries, and athletes—and the administrative energy and resources needed to present them—the IOC debated the merits of alternating the Winter and Summer festivals, holding each four years apart in even-numbered years. Cynics said this plan was much ado about money. One fact was certain; with the intervals between Olympic years reduced to two instead of four, the world's Olympic psyche should be raised to a new level, creating all sorts of possibilities for those who benefit from selling or acquiring Olympic rights, whether in the form of television or Mars Bars.

Baron de Coubertin's original inspiration for what the Olympic Games might promote, that is, international peace, harmony, brotherhood, education, beauty, joy, and sportsmanship, never came as close to being realized as they did at the Lillehammer Winter Games in 1994. The Norwegians dedicated their Games to a war-torn sister Winter Olympic host city, Sarajevo. In his opening address, President Samaranch called for an "Olympic truce," pleading for the belligerent factions around the world to "put down your guns." The astounding Norwegian speedskater Johann Koss, winner of three gold medals, gave to the Olympic Relief Fund the entire amount of the money bestowed on him by his grateful country. Further, he donated the skates he wore in his events to an auction, the proceeds of which went to the same fund. And the Koss episode was but one of many that inspired those millions in the world who watched the events as they transpired.

As the Olympic Games face the future, the pathways they must negotiate are strewn with hazards. The IOC must grapple with problems relative to the immensity of the Games, to maintaining a fair playing field for competing athletes, to the effective distribution of its wealth for worthy initiatives. But, above all, it must remain especially sensitive to the understanding of what the modern Olympic movement is really all about: recognizing and encouraging cultural differences in the quest to develop a better world in which to live. It seeks to do this by presenting an Olympic philosophy it calls "Olympism," a belief that there is joy in the sporting effort, that there is educational value in the good example that sport most times portrays, and that a pursuit of ethical principles that know neither geographical nor cultural boundaries is a worthwhile endeavor.

—ROBERT KNIGHT BARNEY

Bibliography: Guttmann, Allen. (1992) *The Olympics: A History of the Modern Games.* Urbana: University of Illinois Press. Lucas, John A. (1992) *Future of the Olympic Games.* Urbana, IL: Human Kinetics. MacAloon, John A. (1981) *This Great Symbol: Pierre de Coubertin and the Origin of the Modern Olympic Games.* Chicago: University of Chicago Press. Simson, Vyv, and Andrew Jennings. (1992) *The Lords of the Rings: Power, Money and Drugs in the Modern Olympics.* Toronto: Stoddart Publishing Co.

Orienteering

The sport of orienteering, born in Scandinavia and fondly referred to by enthusiasts as "the thinking sport," has attributes that make it an ideal sport for our time. It requires minimal equipment, causes little harm to the environment, can be done for pleasure or competition, and can be enjoyed by people of all ages. Using a topographical map and a specially designed compass, the orienteer walks or runs a cross-country course through woods and fields, navigating streams and avoiding hills and rough terrain.

History

Orienteering was developed in 1895 in what was then the Kingdom of Norway and Sweden as a military exercise. The first nonmilitary orienteering event is believed to have taken place near Bergen, Norway, in June 1896. Subsequent events were held in southern Norway over the next few years. Orienteering was introduced to Sweden by Sigge Stenberg, a Swedish engineer who wrote about the sport after visiting Kristiania (now Oslo) in about 1900. The first Swedish national orienteering event was held in 1902.

Orienteering was soon adopted by the Swedish scouting movement as part of its outdoor training program. Ernst Killander (1882–1958), a Swedish scoutmaster and president of the Stockholm Sports Federation from 1917 to 1934, is considered the father of orienteering. Its popularity in Scandinavia during the 1930s is credited with helping the Finns resist the Soviet invasion in 1939 and enabling Norwegian resistance fighters to escape to Sweden following the 1940 German invasion.

The first international competition was held in Norway in 1932 between Norway and Sweden. Beginning in the 1930s, the sport—and competitions—spread elsewhere in Europe.

The word "orienteering" was coined in 1946 by Björn Kjellström (1910–1995), a former Swedish orienteering champion and lifelong promoter of the sport. The International Orienteering Federation (IOF) was formed in 1961 by Sweden, Norway, Finland, Denmark, Switzerland, Hungary, Czechoslovakia, Bulgaria, West Germany, and East Germany. Orienteering now has about 800,000 participants in 50 nations. Most participate in the traditional manner on foot; ski- and bicycle-orienteering are recent additions to the sport.

Rules and Play

The sport of orienteering consists of finding one's way to a designated point through unfamiliar terrain using a detailed topographical map and a special compass. Participants may walk or run, alone or in groups, purely for the pleasure of finding their way through the woods. In competition, orienteers may compete as individuals or on teams in various different events. Course lengths range from 1 to 15 kilometers (0.6 to 9.3 miles), and variations in terrain determine the degree of difficulty. Today's orienteering maps are five-color maps in the scale 1:15,000, or 1:10,000 in very detailed terrain. Even bigger scales are used for teaching and introductory purposes.

Top-Level Orienteering

The World Orienteering Championships (WOC) have been clearly dominated by the Nordic countries of Sweden, Norway, and Finland, where the sport got its start. Between 1966 and 1995, of a total of 220 medals won at the championships, these countries brought home 162. Only on very rare occasions were orienteers from other European countries able to win medals, with Sarolta Monspart from Hungary being the first non-Scandinavian gold medal winner ever in the women's individual in 1972. Likewise, of course, the most successful orienteers have been Scandinavian. Leading the list are Øyvin Thon of Norway, with seven gold and one silver medal, and Marita Skogum of Sweden, with six gold, three silver, and one bronze medal. Sweden's Annichen Kringstad was the only winner of three individual and three relay gold medals in a row between 1981 and 1985. Recently the situation has changed, however. In 1991 Hungary's Katalin Oláh won the individual event; two Czechs, Petr Kozac and Jana Cieslarova, won the newly established short-distance individual competitions; and Switzerland became the first non-Nordic country to be victorious in the men's relay. At the 1995 WOC in Germany, nine different countries were able to win at lest one medal in six different competitions. Katalin Oláh repeated her victory in the classic distance. Interestingly, no non-European countries have ever won medals in the WOC, although 16 of the IOF's member nations are non-European.

—*Roland Seiler*

The orienteering compass, developed in 1930, is actually a liquid-filled magnetic device that revolves on a transparent base. The base also serves as a protractor and contains various markings to assist with map reading and to help determine location, direction, and distance.

At competitive events, race officials set the course in advance, marking checkpoints with orange-and-white flags. Each competitor gets a map on which the control points have also been marked. Competitors are started at intervals of from two to five minutes. Using map and compass, they find their way sequentially from one checkpoint to the next in the shortest possible time.

Point-to-point orienteering is the sport's classic form and is used in regular competitions. The course setter selects control points in the field and participants find their own routes from one control point to the next. The goal is to find each of the control points in the predetermined sequence and in the shortest possible time. The numerous variations on point-to point

orienteering include "Score-O," in which competitors locate the control points in any order with the objective of finding as many as possible within a certain time; "ROGAINE" (Rugged Outdoor Group Activity Involving Navigation and Endurance), in which teams compete over a much larger area for anywhere from 6 to 24 hours using the Score-O format; and "Relay-O," which is designed for teams of three or four, each member of which uses a different course.

Preset courses are another major type of orienteering event, mainly for beginners and children. In this case, the course setter chooses the control points and presets the routes for competitors to follow.

People with physical disabilities may compete in "handicapped-O," in which competitors may receive help in moving along the preset course but must do their own plotting to find the control points.

Map reading is the fundamental skill required, but participants must also be able to compare features on a topographical map with actual terrain features. The compass is used to turn the map toward the north and sometimes to take a bearing in a certain direction.

Whereas beginners normally use most of their time for map interpretation and decision making, top-level competitive orienteers expend a great deal of physical effort. Their main challenge is to avoid making mistakes in map reading and compass use while running quickly in uneven terrain.

At present, the IOF has 41 full member nations and 6 associate member states. In 1966 the first World Orienteering Championships (WOC) were held in Finland. Orienteering has been a recognized Olympic sport since 1949, but has never been on the program at the Olympic Games.

Multiday events are becoming very popular. One of the biggest orienteering events is the annual Swedish five-*dagars* (five-day) event, which attracts up to 25,000 orienteers of all ages to participate in five competitions on consecutive days. Indeed, hundreds of orienteering events are organized around the world, most of them for all age groups, both sexes, and different levels of competitiveness.

—ROLAND SEILER

Bibliography: Braggins, Anne. (1993) *Trail Orienteering.* Doune, UK: Harveys. Palmer, Peter. (1994) *Pathways to Excellence—Orienteering.* Doune, UK: Harveys.

Paddleball

One-wall paddleball and four-wall paddleball are the names given to two related but different games. One-wall paddleball, played almost exclusively in the five boroughs of New York City, is much like handball, only played with a wooden paddle. Four-wall paddleball, invented in this century, differs significantly.

History

One-wall paddleball is essentially the Irish game of court handball in the United States. By 1940, some 95 percent of all New York City parks offered one-wall handball facilities. At some unknown point thereafter, innovative players began to use wooden paddles instead of bare hands.

By 1980, New York had an estimated 200,000 paddleball players, whose main difficulty was finding courts. None of the three "associations" in the city survived; one-wall paddleball's popularity is matched by its resistance to formal regulation—a principal charm for aficionados.

Four-wall paddleball, in contrast, was invented by Earl Riskey in 1930 at the University of Michigan, probably inspired by his observation of tennis players' off-season practice on indoor handball and squash courts. Some used regular tennis rackets, some made do with wooden table tennis paddles. Riskey envisioned a new game, which combined elements of tennis with a handball-style court and regulations.

When Riskey inaugurated the game, he found a regulation tennis ball too heavy and too sluggish. Experimentation revealed that he could remove the fuzzy covers of tennis balls by soaking them in gasoline, which yielded a core with the appropriate weight and action.

Piercing this core with a needle reduced the pressure to produce an appropriate action. A more sophisticated version of the ball was being commercially produced by 1950.

Four-wall paddleball was energetically promoted by its inventor and enthusiastically taken up by many at the University of Michigan. During World War II it was designated as one of the activities under the U.S. Armed Forces Conditioning Program. After the war, the game was taught at many sports and youth clubs that were either exclusively devoted to the sport or to a variety of the "lesser" racquet games. A National Paddleball Association was formed in 1952. That association, still extant, sponsored a national tournament in 1961, and by the 1970s tournament play was regularly scheduled.

Rules and Play

One-wall paddleball can be played against any available wall fronted by a hard and level area. The "regulation" court is 10.4 meters (34 feet) long by 6.1 meters (20 feet) wide. The wall against which the ball is hit runs (16 feet) high along one end of the court.

Custom is loose with regard to the paddle used in one-wall paddleball, though it is generally 20 centimeters (8 inches) wide by 40 centimeters (16 inches) long. Paddle surfaces may be taped; rough surfaces are discouraged. Any number and size of holes may be bored through the paddle. A player wins with 21 points unless his opponent has already scored 20, in which case the game continues until one player wins by a 2-point margin.

The four-wall paddleball court is identical to a racquetball court: 12.2 by 6.1 meters (40 by 20 feet), with front and side walls 6.1 meters high. The back wall is no less than 3.7 meters (12 feet) and the ceiling provides a fifth playable surface.

Four-wall paddleball may be played by two, three, or four players. A two-player game is a "single," a three-player game—with each player rotating against the other two—is called "cut throat," and a four-player game "doubles."

One-wall paddleball, like handball, has preserved its raffish, urban character. All of the city's ethnic groups play, though currently the best players are said to be Hispanics and African Americans. Facilities are available, though urban problems have taken their toll on upkeep, and few commercial indoor courts exist for winter use.

Four-wall paddleball has not thrived numerically;. probably fewer than 10,000 four-wall paddleball players practice in the United States, far below the 200,000 playing one-wall paddleball in New York City alone. The major obstacle to the flourishing of four-wall paddleball was most likely the rise in popularity of racquetball.

Yet the devotees of four-wall paddleball remain and, as with many of the "smaller" sports, its tournaments exhibit what one player calls a "family reunion" spirit, more dependent on sociability and shared history than on competitive or commercial aspiration.

—ALAN TREVITHICK

See also Handball, Court.
Bibliography: Nickerson, Elinor. (1982) *Racquet Sports, An Illustrated Guide*. Jefferson, NC: McFarland.

Pan American Games

The Pan American Games are the grandest sport festival of the Americas and the only one that brings together all countries of the hemisphere. Since 1951, when 21 countries and around 2,500 athletes participated in 19 events in Buenos Aires, the games have become an immense spectacle. The 1995 edition, returning to Argentina, involved more than 5,000 athletes (746 from the United States alone), 42 countries, and 37 sports. The games' slogan—"América: Espíritu, Sport, Fraternité"—uses the principal languages of the hemisphere: Spanish, Portuguese, English, and French. The games are governed by the Pan American Sports Organization (PASO; known as the Pan American Sports Committee during its early years).

The 1951 games featured an Olympic-type program of baseball, basketball, boxing, cycling, equestrian, fencing, gymnastics, modern pentathlon, polo, rowing, soccer, swimming and diving, shooting, tennis, track and field, water polo, weight lifting, wrestling, and

yachting. Women participated only in equestrian, fencing, swimming and diving, tennis, and track and field. Only a few U.S. athletes (including a seven-member basketball team and a single gymnast) made the long, costly trip to the initial Pan Ams, and host Argentina won the most gold and total medals. The Pan Ams have been characterized by frequent additions and deletions of various events.

Mexico hosted the 1955 games. The 1959 Pan Ams were planned originally for Cleveland, but financial problems intervened, and the games were held in Chicago. Fewer than 1,800 athletes, from 20 countries, attended the fourth games in São Paulo in 1963, the smallest participation in the games' history.

For the 1967 games in Winnipeg, 29 of the 33 eligible nations sent teams, but the United States was the only country with a complete contingent. Cuba's three victories (Rolando Garbey's gold medal to be repeated in the next two Pan Ams) set the pattern for their future dominance in boxing. In 1971 the games were held in Cali, Colombia. Cuba doubled the number of medals they won in 1967, to begin challenging U.S. supremacy. Brazil won men's basketball—the first time in Pan Am history the United States lost.

The 1975 games were originally awarded to Santiago de Chile, but after the brutal overthrow of President Salvador Allende in 1973, Chile's military government cancelled out. The first alternate, São Paulo, Brazil, also withdrew, and Mexico City stepped in with only 10 months to prepare. Thirty-three nations participated with over 4,000 athletes.

In 1979, Puerto Rico spent 60-million dollars on new facilities for the games. The detection of widespread drug use highlighted the 1983 Pan Ams in Caracas, Venezuela. Political conflict between the United States and both Cuba and Nicaragua was played up by the press during the 10th games in Indianapolis in 1987.

Cuba hosted the Pan American Games in 1991, which set new records in numbers of participating countries and athletes. The United States' economic embargo and travel restrictions made financing of the games difficult for the host. ABC had agreed on a figure of $9 million to pay for television rights, but initially the U.S. Treasury Department would not allow any payment to be made to Cuba. The dispute ended after legal wrangling, with three networks permitted to send crews and equipment, although ABC could spend only $1.2 million. Seventy-four new Pan Am records were set.

For the 1995 edition, the Pan American Games returned to Argentina, in Mar del Plata. Cuban women won volleyball for the seventh consecutive time. The United States sent a record 746 athletes and won an all-time high of 424 medals (169 gold). Second in number of medals was Cuba, with 238.

The 1999 games will be held in Winnipeg, Canada, with a shortened program that will probably eliminate non-Olympic events; team size may also be limited.

A few Winter Pan American Games have been planned but essentially without success.

—RICHARD V. MCGEHEE

Bibliography: Emery, C. R. (1972) *The Story of the Pan American Games.* Kansas City, MO: Ray-Gay. McGehee, R. V. (1994) "Los Juegos de las Américas: Four Inter-American Multisport Competitions." In *Sport in the Global Village,* edited by Ralph C. Wilcox. Morgantown, WV: Fitness Information Technology.

Parachuting

The sport of parachuting involves jumping from high places wearing a parachute, which is unfurled after jumping but well before approaching the ground. Parachuting is considered recreation, but remains an important safety practice for balloonists and pilots, and the military retains paratroopers. One of the major attractions of the sport is that it can be tried by almost anyone. The major deterrent besides fear is cost, as a total outfit for sport parachuting (main canopy, reserve canopy, pilot chute, carrier, and "risers") can run from $4,000 to $5,000.

History

Sport parachuting began as early as the 12th century, and, until manned flight began, served only to entertain and display inventiveness. The Chinese amused themselves by jumping from high places with early parachutes that were constructed more like umbrellas. Leonardo da Vinci attempted a parachute design in 1495; sketches show a wooden, pyramid-shaped device. In 1595, Fausto Veranzio created a wooden-framed, canvas parachute, then supposedly leaped from a tower in Venice. In the 1600s royal tumblers launched themselves from high places holding two large umbrellas.

In 1783, parachute use shifted from entertainment to safety. The Montgolfier brothers made their first balloon flight; the parachute was their escape route. A collapsible silk parachute was created by J. P. Blanchard (earlier parachutes had relied on rigid frames); that same year, Sebastian Lenormand jumped from a tower with a parachute 4.25 meters (14 feet) in diameter. In 1808 one Jodaki Kuparento became the first person to escape death by using a parachute when he jumped from a burning balloon over Warsaw, Poland.

Parachutists proliferated. Andre Jacques Garnerin was the first. In 1797 Garnerin jumped from 600 meters (2,000 feet) over Paris and then, in 1802, he leaped from more than 2,400 meters (8,000 feet) above London. Confidence in the parachute as a safety device grew, and in 1838 American John Wise intentionally exploded his balloon nearly 4,000 meters (13,000 feet) above ground and parachuted to safety.

An American, Captain Tom Baldwin, in 1887 created the harness that replaced the basket structure. The coatpack, or parachute worn on the back like modern parachutes, followed. A. Leo Stevens invented the ripcord in 1908. A female parachutist, "Tiny" Broadwick, made the first jump with a manually operated parachute when her parachute line caught on the tail of her airplane in 1914 and she cut the line.

Parachuting changed from a safety precaution to a useful military technique and a popular sport. In 1928, U.S. Army General Billy Mitchell demonstrated the military effectiveness of the parachute as he deployed airborne soldiers, or *paratroopers,* later used by both sides in World War II. Parachuting and sports were combined at a 1930 festival in what was then the Soviet Union where parachutists competed in a landing accuracy contest.

Sport parachuting began in the early 20th century and was a particular crowd-pleaser at air carnivals that featured aerobatics and assorted aerial stunts. In 1932, 40 parachutists participated in a contest at the U.S. National Air Races. Initially, the sport revolved around target jumping but, thanks to French experimentation in the late 1940s and early 1950s, free-falling was introduced, and brought "style" and "relative jumping" to sport parachuting.

In 1951, the First World Parachuting Championships were held in Yugoslavia. In 1955, the United States formed a team and competed in the World Championships the following year. The mid-1960s heralded a new technique: the creation of formations. A 6-man "star" was successfully done in 1964, an 8-man star a year later, and in 1970, a 20-person "star." By 1978, the sport was flourishing.

Rules and Play

Parachuting may be done solo or in groups. Either way, its allure lies in its excitement. After exiting a plane, the parachutist's body accelerates from 0 to 175 kilometers (110 miles) per hour in seconds. Technological advances make for safe parachuting, and modern lightweight sport parachutes make soft, stand-up landings reasonably easy to achieve.

Relative work—when two or more skydivers intentionally maneuver close to one another during free fall—is increasingly popular. Relative work began as 2 people parachuting together and now involves up to 150 people, yielding extraordinary results when successful, as in the 144-person formation over Quincy, Illinois, in 1988.

The equally thrilling freestyle competition is essentially a choreographed repertoire of creative movements by one or more skydivers, with more innovative and unusual movements every year. The 1995 Freestyle and Skysurfing World Championships were held in Ampfing, Germany. The competition offered medals in events such as men's and women's skysurfing, as well as men's and women's freestyle.

Sport parachuting lacks the popular appeal of major sports. Cost may be one factor—the total outfit for sport parachuting (main canopy, reserve canopy, pilot chute, carrier, and "risers") could run between $4,000 and $5,000. Also, the desire to jump out of airplanes, whatever the circumstances, is not universal. Nonetheless, it is fast growing and can be found in all corners of the globe.

—SIMON J. CRAWFORD

Bibliography: Poynter, Dan. (1992) *Parachuting: The Skydiver's Handbook.* Santa Barbara, CA: Para Publishing.

Parawing Sailing
See Sailing, Parawing

Patriotism
Systematic and competitive physical exercise has long been part of the vocabulary of the state. But only in the 19th century did different sports come to be seen as expressions of love and duty toward country. The rise of popular nationalism—based on the idea of mass democracy and modern communications and strengthened by Darwinist fears of racial decline—coincided with the growth of new kinds of sport suited a more urban industrial world, with tighter time and space constraints. Most great sportsmen have been men and were often role models for a new kind of patriotic masculinity that placed the trained body at the service of the state. But not until the rise of the fascist and communist regimes between the wars was sport conscripted as a whole for the national cause.

The Olympic Games provided a global forum for patriotic display, which was accentuated during the Cold War by ideological conflict. Massive commercialization of sport and media coverage may have shifted sport from a national to a global context, but apparently did not weaken sport as an expression of national feeling. Patriotism is alive and well and embedded in sports, taking a variety of forms according to prevailing traditions and circumstances.

The concept of patriotism itself was properly developed only with the French Revolution, but feelings of duty and affection to native land, expressed through physical training and combat, go back to the Greeks. Aristotle noted the patriotic role of sports in Sparta, but sports were not viewed as mass patriotic activity in classical times. In medieval society much of the population used their bodies to work rather than play, and it was the warrior nobility who gradually developed, through the tournament, a series of exercises that promoted the fighting skills required for the emergent dynastic states. Yet, for all the obvious military value of such activities to a state, premodern elites tended to think in terms of caste solidarity across territorial borders and display a correspondingly weak sense of national identity. With odd exceptions such as English archery in the later Middle Ages, common people were not expected to practice sports for patriotic purposes. Early modern games in Europe were for village amusement, not national defense. The fighting capacities of animals were regarded as more important than those of humans until the early 19th century, when the notion of a national champion, who might challenge foreigners, began to emerge through pugilism in Britain and the United States.

The concept of democratic citizenship expressed through the idea of the "nation in arms" defending the homeland arose with the proclamation of a democratic republic in 1792. Peasants or artisans were expected to put their bodies at the service of the state. The link with play or sports came from another source. It was a German reformer, Johann Christoph Friedrich Guts Muths (1759–1839), who pioneered modern physical culture. His ideas were not widely taken up until the French citizen army, which formed the basis of Napoleon's *grande armée,* had defeated Prussia in 1806 at Jena. Prussia initiated a series of reforms designed to strengthen the state, including the use of exercise in the national interest along lines developed by a young linguistic nationalist, Friedrich Ludwig Jahn (1778–1852). Jahn pioneered a new kind of patriotic gymnastics called *turnen,* based on group gymnastics, which, with over one million members by the end of the 19th century, proved key to the patriotic development of physical

Grieving for the Great One: Wayne Gretzky and the 1988 Crisis of Canadian National Identity

Tuesday, 9 August 1988. Canadian ice hockey legend Wayne Gretzky, "the Great One," "Number 99," sat before a crowded press conference announcing through his tears that he was being traded from the Edmonton Oilers to the Los Angeles Kings. This was no ordinary trade. Described as "Black Tuesday," it was the biggest headline in the *Edmonton Journal* since the end of World War II. The media characterized the event as leaving a "nation in mourning" with Canadians "Grieving for the Great One." Special telephone lines were established to provide an outlet for distraught fans seeking to vent their frustration, anguish, and disbelief. During subsequent days, several politicians attempted to block Gretzky's trade in parliament, arguing that he deserved protected status as a national treasure and resource.

The social significance of the Gretzky trade lies within the historical, political, economic, and cultural context of the year 1988 in Canada. Canadians have often been characterized as being overly fixated on their national identity. In part, this has been attributed to the close—some argue subordinate and vulnerable—position Canada has occupied with respect to its powerful southern neighbor, the United States. In 1988 the fear of Americanization peaked amidst Canadian Prime Minister Brian Mulroney's intent to sign the Canada-U.S. Free Trade Agreement (FTA) which, opponents argued, signaled the "end of Canada." Eventually, the FTA forced a Canadian federal election with Mulroney and his Progressive Conservative government successfully maintaining office.

Strikingly, two interrelated events in the life of Wayne Gretzky came to represent the popular cultural arm of the FTA and the impending threat of Americanization in 1988. First was his marriage to American actress Janet Jones in July 1988, which many described as the "second royal wedding"; second was Gretzky's trade to the Los Angeles Kings. Gretzky's marriage to the "Hollywood Princess" raised suspicions in Canada that she would eventually lure the King away from his Edmonton castle. The popular press was swift in noting the link between the marriage and the FTA and their symbolic threat of Americanization. Indeed, 24 days later Gretzky announced his trade, although he made it clear that the decision was a mutual one and it was quickly evident that there were many other factors involved, including his deteriorating relationship with Edmonton Oilers' owner Peter Pocklington. Nevertheless, there was a remarkable backlash against Janet Jones amidst the realization that Gretzky was truly leaving Edmonton and Canada and sparking public concern and debate at the highest levels. Opponents of the FTA, for example, used the Gretzky trade as a metaphor for Canada's eventual fate at the hands of the Americans. As one commentator stated, "If this is an indication of the free trade between Canada and the U.S., then Canada is in trouble." Of course Canada has survived, but it is clear that in 1988 Wayne Gretzky served as a symbolic representation of Canada as a nation, a nation in crisis, a nation left grieving for its Great One.

—*Steven J. Jackson*

culture (for the admirers of turnen, "sport" was considered British and unpatriotic).

Hence the association between popular exercise and patriotism began well before the educational reforms of the Victorian public schools from which many modern sports emerged. One of the main reasons for the systematic practice of team games like soccer (association football), rugby, and cricket in these elite schools of 19th-century Britain was to ensure the supply of healthy, competitive, and loyal young men to govern the fast-growing empire. British young men were brought up to believe that playing games was an arm of imperial defense while subscribing to the view that sport and politics should be kept apart. Politics here meant "party" politics; patriotism was not political, at least as far as elite educationalists were concerned. Sport was seen as part of a higher national duty.

Representative teams formalized the relationship between sport and patriotism through the new possibilities of international competition. This began with the emergence of competitive matches between England, Scotland, Wales, and Ireland in soccer (association football) and rugby in the 1870s. Cricket, however,

developed an imperial competitive structure, with teams selected on merit "testing" themselves against an Australian eleven.

It was an Irish patriot, Michael Cusack (1847–1906), who first explicitly recognized the role of sport in nationalist politics by denouncing "Anglo-Saxon" sports and setting up a rival patriotic body, the Gaelic Athletic Association (GAA), in 1884. The GAA has a special place in the history of the relationship between sport and patriotism and soon emerged as a formidable channel for popular cultural nationalism in Ireland, even imposing a ban, which lasted until 1971, on all those who played British sports. However, in other nations of the British Isles, sport galvanized national feeling differently, with Scottish soccer and Welsh rugby emerging as powerful expressions of national feeling within a shared sporting and constitutional framework. Similarly, elements of the British Empire, notably Australia, and later India and the West Indies, developed strong cultural bonds with Britain partly through cricket.

The mass nationalism of the late 19th century gave a special place to the patriotic display of physical superiority through sport. The French aristocrat, Baron

Pierre de Coubertin (1863–1937), originally founded the modern Olympic Games in 1896 partly to promote a healthy patriotism rather than a destructive nationalism through sport. These ideals were always a little naïve, and before long the frantic scramble for medals as a measure of national virility began. After the first faltering steps in 1896 in Athens and in 1900 in Paris, where it was still possible for gifted individuals to win events without much in the way of public backing, the Olympic Games became a serious exercise in national prestige. The British failure to win enough medals in 1908 in London, for example, fueled a debate about the alleged physical and moral degeneration of the population and the threat of German and U.S. competition. Similarly, the French, sensitive to the threat from the new German empire, came away from Stockholm in 1912 deeply concerned that the forthcoming Games in Berlin in 1916 would prove a national humiliation in the capital of their archenemy.

As it happened, World War I intervened. The Berlin Games were abandoned as the atmosphere of national hostility rose to a bloody crescendo. Sport and war were intertwined; mobilization made sports and athletics the central components of military life for new U.S. recruits. Troops played sports during the war to maintain morale and fitness, which along with new legislation for shorter working hours helped create a mass sports movement in Europe in the 1920s. The ethos of the newly democratized sports remained strongly patriotic. When the war was over, there was a strong feeling that Germany should be punished in athletics as well as in other ways, and the 1920 Olympic Games were given to Belgium. The Germans and their allies were excluded from these Games in Antwerp. The new Soviet Union set up a rival Red Sport International to remove the "bourgeois nationalist" dimension from sport, but predictably this turned out to be little more than a vehicle for Soviet foreign policy.

So it was Britain, France, and the United States that first formally introduced a patriotic qualification for participation in international sport. However, it was with the interwar fascist powers, especially Italy and later Germany, that the cult of sport for national purposes was most fully developed. Italian leader Benito Mussolini (1883–1945) saw sport as part of a physical revolution to make a new Roman Empire, inculcating a fierce competitiveness and collective masculinity in the service of the fascist state. Sports organizations were brought under corporate control and coordinated into a great "after work" movement (*Dopolavoro*). Yet, for all Mussolini's chauvinist excesses in sport, it was

the 1936 Berlin Olympic Games organized by Nazi leader Adolf Hitler (1889–1945) that became the centerpiece of interwar sport and the most striking example of its manipulation by nationalists. Ironically, the Games had been given to Germany in 1932 partly as a reward for its apparently successful disarmament and democratization. Within months Hitler came to power, and the Nazis soon saw the perfect opportunity to exploit sport for the greater glory of the Third Reich. A boycott movement arose in response that, although well supported in the United States, failed to develop strong roots elsewhere. The ideal of apolitical sport lingered on despite the brutal reality of the use of the Olympics by Hitler as a symbol of racial supremacy and political cohesion.

It was not just in Europe that sport became hopelessly entangled in the national project. Before the 1920s patriotic display was probably even more overt in the United States than elsewhere. This was especially true of the Army and Navy intercollegiate football games. Other nations responded. In Japan, baseball was taken up to assert national prowess through mastery of the sport of a rival power. Beating a dominant power at its own game had a special attraction in the colonial context. In India, soccer (association football) and cricket were seen as ways of showing the colonial power the strength of indigenous patriotic feeling. In Latin America, soccer, introduced by the British, spread quickly in Argentina and Brazil. The first World Cup for soccer was held in Uruguay in 1930 with intense nationalist feeling already evident when Uruguay took the title instead of their southern neighbors. Soccer has since grown into an extraordinary passion.

The complexity of this relationship was highlighted during the Algerian War, which broke out just as France was preparing for the 1958 World Cup Finals in Stockholm. The radical African states like Algeria were caught between denouncing the absurd nationalism of Western sport and wishing to assert their independence by participating in it, whether in the form of the great African runners of Kenya or Algeria or the new soccer powers like Cameroon, who have recently had a major impact on global sport through the World Cup. Sport offers unrivaled potential for rapid national recognition, with new nations of the Pacific Rim like South Korea hosting the Olympics. Meanwhile a sleeping giant of sport, the People's Republic of China, began to flex its muscles, especially in the emerging area of female sport.

Here China is following a path already well trodden by the totalitarian states of the former Soviet bloc, especially East Germany. With the impact of the Cold War on international sport after 1945, the communist bloc entered the sporting arena en masse, determined to show the superiority of the socialist system by breaking world records. This was most apparent in the case of the German Democratic Republic, which could not compete with the postwar economic miracle in the Federal Republic but could use sport as an arm of foreign policy to stress the health and patriotism of its youth. The Soviet Union took the largest haul of Olympic and other medals, mainly through superiority in field events and, like other communist states, exploiting the Western failure to develop women's sports. It was ideology that pushed women to the forefront as patriotic symbols, not just in events like swimming and running but also with performers like Romania's brilliant young gymnast Nadia Comaneci or the speedskater Karin Kania, who won eight medals for the German Democratic Republic from 1980 to 1988. Children with natural ability were taken very young to special schools and trained intensively, often with more systematic preparation and well-concealed use of drugs than was possible in the West. The goal of ideological superiority would become inextricably mixed up with the pursuit of national glory.

After a close relationship throughout this century, there are signs that sport and patriotism, though still strongly linked, are starting to unravel. The most extreme expressions of nationalist feeling in sport, notably the hooligan phenomenon, especially in soccer, have been strongly criticized and curbed somewhat. Of course, such behavior has largely been confined to expressions of local patriotism in sport, which has deep roots in traditions of youth culture. Ferocious rivalries of place based on club loyalties look set to remain a feature of the sporting landscape.

On the other hand, the increasing internationalization of sport has made foreign players far more familiar than before, turning them from hated symbols of a rival power to temporary local patriots. Eric Cantona (1966-), the brilliant, volatile French soccer player, has been adored by his own fans at Manchester United and loathed elsewhere. Soccer remains powerfully nationalistic, and the huge commercialization of late has done little to diminish this. In the United States, the Super Bowl is not just the most highly commercialized sporting event but also perhaps the most thoroughly drenched in patriotic ritual.

Comparable European phenomena like the Tour de France, the biggest single annual sporting event, may be less overtly patriotic, but in structural terms the Tour is the most patriotic of all sporting events. It was begun in 1903 by a French nationalist and is designed to display the variety and greatness of France. However, even if the tour is a kind of hymn to France, the range of nationalities involved these days ensures that it is France rather than the French who are venerated. The champion who dominated the early 1990s, Miguel Indurain (1965-), is Spanish and a national hero in his native country, where sporting patriotism has tended to be appropriated by the rival claims of Barcelona and Real Madrid, of Catalan autonomy and Castilian centralism.

Patriotism has historically been more closely associated with popular team sports than more elite individual ones, although the "Four Musketeers" in France between the wars were very popular for winning the Davis Cup, through which tennis was organized on a national basis. More recently, Germany has taken great pride in the achievements of Steffi Graf and Boris Becker, while enthusiasm in the United States for its heroes seems undiminished. Will this recent emergence of the sportsman or woman as media idol and sex symbol, vastly wealthy, with an international lifestyle and extensive commercial contracts, diminish the patriotic dimension of the performance? Will the adoption of new national identities by great players like Martina Navratilova or Monica Seles weaken the claim of sport as a vehicle for patriotism? Or, as seems more probable, will the patriotic force of sport be accentuated through new recruits only too willing to publicize the virtues of their adopted state and win a national following in the process?

Patriotism in the contemporary sporting world, therefore, is a rather more complex and ambiguous phenomenon. Golf has been one of the most successful sports in recent years, but until recently it was conspicuous by its relative lack of a patriotic dimension. This, however, has changed through television coverage of the Ryder Cup, with the incorporation of European players on the British side, and a nascent Europatriotism, which may be an important pointer for the future. On the one hand, golf has gone beyond the nation-state, reflecting the new realities of a more federal Europe; on the other, the new South Africa, freshly decked out in a more wholesome multiracial patriotism, presses the claims of its impressive sporting heritage under the formerly unthinkable leadership of Nelson Mandela, complete with Springbok cap. Nothing, perhaps, more dramatically illustrates the capacity of sport to adjust to changing forms of patriotism or underlines more emphatically its continued importance as a component of national identity.

—RICHARD HOLT

Bibliography: Holt, R. (1981) *Sport and Society in Modern France.* London: Macmillan. Holt, R., P. Lanfranchi, and J. A. Mangan, eds. (1996) *European Heroes: Myth, Identity, Sport.* London: Frank Cass. Mangan, J. A., ed. (1995) *Tribal Identities: Nationalism, Europe, Sport.* London: Frank Cass. Mason, Tony. (1995) *Passion of the People: Football in Latin America.* London: Verso.

Pedestrianism

Pedestrianism, a precursor to professional track and field, was a leading sport in Victorian England. Pedestrians either raced against one another or one contender tried to cover a given distance within a time. In either case, wagering was integral to the event.

History

Pedestrianism's first star was Foster Powell, whose best known feat was walking 100 miles in 23.25 hours. Captain Robert Barclay Allardice (1779–1854) then transformed the sport into spectacular entertainment. In 1808 he accepted a wager—1,000 guineas—to walk 1,000 miles in 1,000 hours. The wager, the walk, and Barclay himself caught the imagination of the public. As the days passed and Barclay walked steadily toward his goal, hundreds and then thousands of fans flocked to Newmarket to watch. Captain Barclay won his wager and became a folk hero.

By the middle of the 19th century pedestrianism was so well established in Great Britain that U.S. athletes found it profitable to travel to England to compete. The Americans won a good deal of money and broke earlier records in time and distance.

Rules and Play

The events were normally held on the great main roads, such as the Bath road out of London—a ready-made track conveniently provided with a milestone—or in parks, on race courses, or sometimes on commons. Certain standard distances soon became established—5, 10, 50, 100 miles (8, 16, 80, and 160 kilometers)—and performed repeatedly. The ultimate challenge was the 1,000-mile (1,613-kilometer) endurance event.

Pedestrian training and conditioning at the start of the 19th century was a hodgepodge of current scientific theory and medieval dogma, occasionally flavored with common sense. Captain Barclay recommended the following: To begin, athletes purged themselves of ill vapors and foul body poisons using regular doses of phosphate of soda. Daily exercise prescriptions called for 20 to 24 miles (32 to 38 kilometers), with a dawn warm-up

of a half-mile run followed by a 6-mile (10-kilometer) walk. Breakfast was rare beef or mutton chops with stale bread and old beer, followed by 6 more walking miles, no lunch, and a 30-minute nap in the supine position, then a 4-mile brisk walk with a four o'clock dinner repeating the breakfast menu. The cool-down for the day was a half-mile dash and then a final 6-mile walk, with bedtime at eight o'clock. Athletes were expected to keep mind as well as the body fully occupied. Free time was an opportunity for additional exercise, and cricket, bowls, and quoits were recommended.

Barclay also advocated "sweating." Once each week, the athlete, thickly muffled in a flannel shirt and long drawers, ran four miles at breakneck pace and immediately after consumed a pint of "sweating liquor," "composed of the following ingredients, viz. one ounce of caraway-seeds; half an ounce of coriander seed; one ounce of root licorice; and half an ounce of sugar candy; mixed with two bottles of cider, and boiled down to one half."

Pedestrians undoubtedly suffered from the training dictum of avoiding liquids. Indeed, the number of pedestrians reportedly experiencing frightful cramps may have been a result of the principle of minimum water consumption and the prohibition against salt intake. Nevertheless, pedestrians were allowed three pints of beer ("home-brewed beer, old, but not bottled") per day, and so complete dehydration was avoided.

As distances increased, the sport's credibility came under suspicion and athletes and trainers found themselves using a variety of stimulants to energize a human system struggling to cope with sleep deprivation, chronic muscular fatigue, and mental staleness. Perhaps the sport's demise was for the best.

—SCOTT A. G. M. CRAWFORD

Bibliography: Jamieson, D. A. (1943) *Powderhall and Pedestrianism.* Edinburgh: W. and A. K. Johnstone.

Pelota

Pelota is the generic name the Basques use for their numerous games that involve propelling a ball with a hand or instrument. Pelota's antecedent is the medieval game of *jeu de paume* (French for "palm game"), which has roots in the early Greek and Roman ball games. The extremely popular *jeu de paume* spread rapidly throughout the Continent in the 13th century. In the rural Basque provinces of northwestern Spain and southwestern France the game established a permanent stronghold, survived the passage of time, and acquired a unique identity.

History

The original form of pelota games are known as *jeux directs* or *juegos directos*. This form is descended from the simple, outdoor game of *jeu de paume* known as *longue paume*, which was played by two or more players facing each other who beat a ball back and forth across a net or line, using any convenient open space. *Rebot*, for example, was a five-per-side form of *jeux directs* played in the Basque country with leather gloves or *chisteras* (baskets) in an open courtyard (*place libre*). A ceremonious and traditional game, *rebot* is now played only rarely on Sundays after Mass in some Basque villages and towns.

Two distinct forms of pelota came to be played on three different types of courts: the *place libre*, an open outdoor court of variable dimensions with a single wall at one end; the *fronton*, which includes both covered and outdoor courts of varying dimensions with two or three walls; and the *trinquet* [or *tripot*] a small, rectangular covered court. In the small villages of the Basque country, it was most often the wall or arches of the church that were used for playing pelota.

Pasaka, a two-per-side version of *jeux directs*, is also played only rarely nowadays by the Basques. *Pasaka* is a descendant of the indoor version of *jeu de paume* known as *courte paume*. Bare hands or leather gloves are used to propel the ball over a net inside a *trinquet*. In both *rebot* and *pasaka*, scoring is similar to tennis, and a match consists of 13 games.

The games of *rebot* and *pasaka* were both played before the 18th-century introduction of rubber balls. Rubber-cored balls completely revolutionized the games of pelota, modifying existing games and sparking a whole range of new ones. The new group of handball games came to be known as *jeux indirects* or *juegos indirectos*, meaning that the ball was hit "indirectly" to the opposing player by the use of walls.

The new games were so popular they soon displaced the others almost completely. The games were much faster and were normally played with only one or two per side, whereas the older games required more players. The many variations of *jeux indirects* include *main nue, cesta punta, pala larga, yoko garbi, grand chistera, pala corta, raquette, remonte, sare*, and *palette*. As they are all within the same family, the games share similar tactics and strategies.

Main nue en place libre (bare hand in open court) is played either in singles or doubles against a single wall in an open court similar to that used for *rebot*. The ball must remain within the limits of the court and of the wall. *Main nue en trinquet* or *en fronton* (bare hand in

---

Clerical and Royal Patrons

During the 13th century, *jeu de paume* was the game most closely associated with the church. Clerici notes: "Church documents from the twelfth to the fourteenth centuries speak only of seminarians, priests, monks, parish priests, abbots and even bishops, all playing longue paume or courte paume, either indoors or out in the open, depending on the type of the game" (Clerici 1974, 21). In fact, Henderson believes that the cloister courtyard, where the clergy played handball, was the major contributor to the evolution of the indoor courts.

Until fairly recently, "cura-pelotaris" (priest-handball players) were quite common in Basque society, where playing pelota was considered a calling second only to the priesthood. The increasing professionalism led to the demise of the cura-pelotaris, but priests continued to be very much involved in the game, serving as judges of matches not only for their honesty but for their knowledge of the intricacies of the game.

Courte paume acquired royal favor and patronage. King Charles V of France (1337–1380) had courts built in his palace, the Louvre, and was reputed to be a good player. In 1530, a royal edict proclaimed the game illegal for all except the nobility. Louis XIII was supposedly an addict, but the game suddenly declined in popularity under Louis XIV, when billiards became the preferred royal pastime.

—*Teresa Baksh McNeil*

---

court or fronton) are more popular forms of handball for singles, doubles, or three-per-side because of the hazards of the walls. In the Basque countries, the champions at *main nue* are the elite of *pilotaris*, or ball players, for *main nue* is not only a physically demanding game but murderous to the bare hands.

Cesta punta, known as jai alai in other countries, is a two-per-side game played with a long *chistera* (basket) in a fronton (three-sided court). *Remonte* (Spanish for "to return") is similar, but the basket-glove used for *remonte* is narrower and much less curved than that used in other *chistera* games. *Remonte* and *cesta punta* are pelota's fastest and most difficult games.

Yoko garbi, meaning "pure game" or "clean game" in Basque, is a three-per-side form of pelota played with a small *chistera* in an open court with a single wall. *Yoko garbi* is played with two men near the wall and one in back. The game is very fast because of the shallow curve of the small basket glove. *Grand chistera* is a three-per-side variation played with even longer *chisteras*. These games are played most often by professionals in Spain, where gambling is popular and demands the consistently high standard of play that only professionals can provide.

Pala is a two-per-side form of pelota played with a long wooden bat in a fronton. The rules and distances are basically the same as for *cesta punta*. This hard-hitting game is one of pelota's fastest. Highly spectacular, difficult, and dangerous, *pala* is also played mostly by professionals in Spain and South America. *Pala larga* is played in the *place libre*, while *pala corta* is a two-per-side version played in a small fronton. *Raquette* (racquet) is a two-per-side form played with a loosely strung racket in a small fronton. The racket is shaped like a snowshoe. The game has basically the same rules as *pala corta* and employs the same tactics. *Sare* is a Basque word meaning net or basket and is a two-per-side game played with a loosely strung racket in a covered court. It is mainly played in Argentina. The tactics are basically the same as those used in most *trinquet* games. *Palette* (small shovel) is a two-per-side version played with a leather or rubber ball in a covered court or fronton.

The Basques venerate their best *pilotaris*. The first hero was Perkain, born in the French village of Les Aldudes around 1765. Perkain helped put pelota on the map. The games he played were forms of *longue paume* known as *bota luzea, mahi jokoa, lachoa,* and *rebot*. Of these, only *rebot* barely survives. The balls used by Perkain weighed as much as two pounds, and were hit back and forth.

Another star, the French Basque Jean Erratchun, born in 1817 and commonly known as El Gaskoina, the Gascon, changed the sport with his use of a longer glove with a deep curve in its end in which the ball could be held for an instant before being hurled back against the wall. This slice shot was known as *atchiki,* a Basque word meaning "to hold." The Spaniards took advantage of the new glove and began to dominate the sport. While the introduction of the new glove made pelota faster and more spectacular, its popularity declined for physical and economic reasons. When *chisteras* replaced gloves, and rubber balls were introduced almost simultaneously, the impact on pelota was revolutionary.

Chisteras of various forms are now standard equipment for at least four of pelota's most spectacular and popular games—*grand chistera, yoko garbi, remonte,* and *cesta punta.*

The 1890s saw pelota develop into a worldwide sport, with South America leading. Argentina became a mecca of the game. The new way of swinging the *chistera* led to its vogue as a spectator sport, which increased its professionalism and in turn, gambling.

The Fédéracion Française de Pelote Basque was formed in 1921. This body codified the various games, writing the rules, classifying the players, and generally giving the game a responsible authority. Spain and the South American countries followed suit. In 1924, pelota was included in the Olympic Games held in Paris, and five years later the Fédéracion Internacional de Pelota Vasca was founded, becoming fully operative in 1945. With difficulty, the organization wrote common rules for both play and umpiring from the dissimilar rules of the member nations, and the federation organized its first world championship in 1952 in San Sebastian, Spain. The federation also gave pelota a patron saint, the 16th-century Basque Jesuit missionary St. Francis Xavier, the cofounder of the Jesuit order. (St. Francis was a *pelotari:* a learned commission found on his skeletal right hand the telltale deformation of the phalanges that mark all handball players.)

Versions of pelota are now played in many countries throughout the world, wherever the Basques emigrated, including South America, Mexico, Cuba, and the United States. While its popularity is worldwide, nowhere does it remain more popular than where it evolved—in the rural Basque provinces of Spain and France.

—TERESA BAKSH McNEIL

See also Jai Alai.
Bibliography: Gallop, Rodney. (1970) *A Book of the Basques.* Reno: University of Nevada Press. Henderson, Robert W. (1947) *Ball, Bat and Bishop.* New York: Rockport Press.

Pentathlon, Ancient

The most famous of ancient Greek athletic contests, the pentathlon consisted of five subevents: a broad jump, the discus, the javelin, a run, and wrestling. Running and wrestling existed independently as events, but the jump, discus, and javelin were found in historical athletic programs only as part of the pentathlon. The ancient Olympic Games introduced and retained a pentathlon for men in 708 B.C.E. but immediately dropped a pentathlon for boys introduced in 628. The Pythian Games at Delphi introduced men's and boys' pentathlons in 586 and retained both, and Athens was unusual in offering three age classes (for men, youths, and boys) and second as well as first prizes for pentathletes.

Probably the pentathlon was established at Olympia and elsewhere to test excellence in three events (the discus, jump, and javelin) that were not independent events in the great games. Running and wrestling were perhaps added to fill out the contest or, when necessary, to help determine an overall victor.

The Greek pentathlon inspired masterpieces in vase painting, numismatics (for example, coins from the island of Cos), and sculpture, including the most famous athletic statue of all time, Myron's 5th-century-B.C.E.

Discobolos (discus-thrower). Often shown practicing to flute music to assist their rhythm and grace, pentathletes at advanced levels of competition were splendid athletes, but they were generally recognized as not as good in wrestling and running as specialists in those events. Aristotle (*Rhetoric* 1361b) said that those who excelled in everything were fit to be pentathletes, who had all-around beautiful bodies adapted for strength and speed, but other sources (such as Pseudo-Plato, *Lovers* 135e) called pentathletes second-raters who were defeated by specialists in their specialties. Certainly the events demanded versatility, skill, and stamina, since all were held, at Olympia at least, in one afternoon.

Rules and Play
Perhaps originating in ingots of iron, discuses in metal or stone varied in size and weight (17–35 centimeters [7–14 inches] and 1.5–6.5 kilograms [3–14 pounds], with 2.5 kg [5 pounds, 8 ounces) average]). Three were kept in the Treasury of the Sikyonians at Olympia for official competition. Although scholars disagree, vase paintings suggest that the Greeks threw the discus without making 360-degree turns.

Probably originating in practice for hunting or warfare, the javelin contest used light javelins of elderwood about 2 meters (5–6 feet) long with points sharpened in competition to mark distances. The throw was made, as in modern times, by running up with the javelin held horizontally, bringing it back, and then thrusting it forward.

Vase paintings of the jump illustrate the use of metal or stone jumping weights (*halteres*) shaped rather like dumbbells and varying in size and weight from 1.4 to 4.5 kilograms (3 to 10 pounds) to improve distances. After a short run-up, the athlete swung the weights forward at the take-off to aid his momentum, then thrust them backwards for added distance, and dropped them before they became a hindrance. Athletes had to take off from a starting board or sill and land under control with both feet making a clean mark in the pit. Distances were marked with small pegs. Ancient sources say that Chionis of Sparta jumped 16 meters (52 feet) in 664 B.C.E. and that Phayllos jumped 17 meters (55 feet), 1.5 meters (5 feet) beyond the *skamma*, a worked pit of soft soil some 15 meters [50 feet] long). This is about 8 meters (25 feet) beyond the modern record, so some scholars suggest a double or a triple jump, but, noting the scant evidence for multiple jumps in antiquity, others dismiss the accounts as folklore. The run, probably a sprint, and wrestling were probably held in the same fashion in the pentathlon as they were as independent events.

How ancient pentathlon was scored and victors decided remains unknown, although various theories exist. Some theories are simply too complicated or they allow the possibility of no winner. A persuasive theory by H. A. Harris (1972a, 34–35) argues that only first places counted. As soon as one athlete had three wins the contest ended, and the jump, discus, and javelin were held first.

More recent theories have disagreed about whether Philostratus's account can be vindicated by some system of relative placements with or without eliminations, about whether wrestling or the run or some event drawn by lot was used in the repêchage (the event used, when necessary, to narrow the field to two competitors for the wrestling match), and about whether eliminations took place after the third or the fourth event. These issues may remain unresolved because ancient evidence is weak and inconsistent.

The Greek-style pentathlon was revived in a modified form in the modern Olympics of 1912–1924 but the military pentathlon, with fencing and pistol shooting, is completely modern.

—DONALD G. KYLE

See also Olympic Games, Ancient; Pentathlon, Modern.
Bibliography: Harris, Harold A. (1972) *Sport in Greece and Rome.* London: Thames and Hudson. Kyle, Donald G. (1990) "Winning and Watching the Greek Pentathlon." *Journal of Sport History* 17: 291–305. Sweet, Waldo E. (1987) *Sport and Recreation in Ancient Greece.* New York and Oxford: Oxford University Press.

Pentathlon, Modern
Pentathlon is a modern sport based on a combination of traditional and modern military skills: riding, shooting, fencing, swimming, and running. Originally drawing the interest of soldiers, pentathlon now has participants from all walks of life.

History
The well-documented history of pentathlon began in the planning of the 1912 Olympic Games. Baron de Coubertin (1863–1937), the founder of the modern Olympic movement, suggested adding a multisport competition for soldiers. He referred to it as a military pentathlon, probably to distinguish it from the five-event contest that was already a part of the athletics schedule. Coubertin built this entirely new sport on the challenges a military courier or spy might have

encountered in the Napoleonic era. Alone behind enemy lines, a person might at any time need to ride a strange horse for a distance over broken country, fight a variety of opponents with a rapier and pistol, ford a deep river, and run cross country over unfamiliar terrain. By the 1920 Olympic Games at Antwerp, the competition was already known as the modern pentathlon, to complement the ancient or classic pentathlon. Until 1952, most pentathletes were military men.

Rules and Play
The modern pentathlon has always consisted of the same five disciplines, although the order has changed. The events are (1) riding cross country for a distance of between 2,500 and 5,000 meters (2,700 and 5,400 yards) over unfamiliar ground on a strange horse drawn by lot, against time and with penalties for faults; (2) fencing with an épée; a pool unique of one-touch bouts (i.e., a complete round-robin in which every pentathlete fences every other)—by far the longest phase of the competition, sometimes taking up to 14 hours; (3) shooting with a .22-caliber rapid-fire pistol; 20 shots at a silhouette target from a distance of 25 meters (27 yards); (4) swimming freestyle for 300 meters (328 yards) against time, conducted in heats; and (5) running cross country for a distance of about 4,000 meters (4,500 yards) over unfamiliar ground, against time.

Until 1984, one event was held per day for five days. That year, events were compressed into a four-day schedule; the fourth day began with shooting and concluded with running. Also, for a more dramatic finish, the run was conducted with a staggered start; the leader after four events started first, and each competitor followed at a handicapped lag reflecting his distance behind the leader. Thus, the order of finish in the run became the order of finish for the entire competition.

In 1988, the cross-country riding competition was changed to a stadium jumping competition. Moreover, the five events have been further compressed into a single day. All these changes reflect the continuing and pervasive pressure on the Olympic movement to emphasize elements that are more suitable for television.

Until 1952, modern pentathlon scoring was determined by adding the places a competitor earned in each event, with the lowest score winning; a perfect score would be five.

Since 1956, scoring for the pentathlon has resembled that of the decathlon: a set of charts assigns 1,000 points to a standard result, and a competitor receives more or fewer points depending on how the individual's result compares to the standard.

By nature, modern pentathlon is an individual competition. However, a team event is created by adding the aggregate individual scores of three competitors from each nation.

When Coubertin introduced his creation at Stockholm, it proved extremely popular with the host nation: Swedes took six of the first seven places. Sweden continued to dominate over the ensuing decades, producing eight of the first nine Olympic champions. Hungary and Russia have dominated since the 1950s, and Finland, Poland, Italy, and occasionally, the United States have been contenders.

A variation of modern pentathlon was featured as a demonstration event at the 1948 Olympic Winter Games at St. Moritz. The winter pentathlon consisted of Nordic skiing, alpine skiing, pistol shooting, riding, and épée fencing.

The outlook for modern pentathlon is cloudy, if not grim. It is an expensive activity for an individual to pursue. It is not "mediatique" (readily televisable), so commercial sponsorship is unlikely. The decision to discontinue team events has reduced the interest of national Olympic committees. Its public image has been repeatedly damaged by endemic cheating and other scandals. Finally, the advent of triathlon events (swimming, cycling, and running) threatens its continuation on the Olympic program after 1996.

—JEFFREY R. TISHMAN

Bibliography: Grombach, John V. (1956) *Olympic Cavalcade.* New York: Ballantine Books. *Olympic Sports: A Handbook of Recognized Olympic Sports.* (n.d.) New York: U.S. Olympic Committee.

Pesäpollo
See Baseball, Finnish

Pétanque
See Bowls and Bowling

Philosophy
Philosophers ask three basic questions, which correspond to the three major branches of philosophic inquiry: (1) what is reality? which is formally called metaphysics; (2) what is knowledge? which is formally called epistemology; and (3) what is value? which is called axiology.

The major question in the metaphysics of sport is what makes a given physical activity a sporting activity as opposed to some other related human movement activity (play, game, dance, recreation)? What are the basic features of sport that distinguish it from other forms of physical enterprise that ascribe value and significance to particular human movements? This question raises the related question: what distinctions and/or relations can be drawn between sport and phenomena such as play, game, and dance?

The primary question in epistemological study of sport is how one gains knowledge of forms of human movement like sport. Must one have an actual, lived experience of sport to claim knowledge of it, or can one gain such knowledge intellectually? The related question concerns the organization of knowledge appropriate to sport, not the psychological one of when is someone (psychologically) ready to learn certain sporting skills, but the logical one of how different forms of knowledge of sport can be fitted together into some coherent whole (for example, a coherent curriculum).

The ethical study of sport pivots on two questions: (1) how should human agents treat one another (and in the case of animal sports, sentient beings) in a sport setting? and (2) how should they behave, individually and collectively, in their pursuit of athletic excellence—that is, what forms of conduct and aids to performance are compatible with good (in the moral sense previously specified) athletic practice? This raises many issues about sportsmanship, winning, competition, and cheating; with gender issues that touch on the construction of feminine and masculine identities in sport and fair access to its resources and benefits; and, finally, with issues about animal use in athletics, particularly those that pit humans against animals that typically result in the death of animals (hunting). The second question has focused principally on the widespread use of performance-enhancing drugs in sport; specifically, it addresses the hidden and not so hidden technical imperatives and values of high-performance sport that impel athletes to take such drugs; questions the moral permissibility of such drug use and of efforts to deter and outlaw it; and explores the moral justification of mandatory drug testing programs designed to detect, mainly for punitive purposes, the presence of performance-enhancing drugs and, in some instances, recreational drugs.

Studies of the aesthetic features of sport essentially relate to two questions. The first concerns whether sports require a qualitative view of their forms of movement, grace, and style to adequately understand and fully appreciate what they are about. The second question asks whether forms of sport qualify as works of art. The issue here is not so much whether sports must be viewed mindful of their aesthetic properties,

but rather whether sports are intentionally conceived and crafted for aesthetic effect, and whether their context suits them for such a purpose.

Why submit a popular pastime like sport to a seemingly arcane and abstruse discipline like philosophy? My answer is simple; we cannot evade the questions philosophers raise, not, that is, without imperiling what we value most. Indeed, the choice here is not whether to consider such questions, but whether to consider them critically. Those of us who claim devotion to social practices like sport already hold views about their relative importance and value; that we do is part and parcel of our involvement in them. What philosophy asks of us is whether these views can pass critical muster, whether they can stand up to reflective scrutiny. This is no arcane or trifling question; on the contrary, it is the question by which we measure the all-important difference between an examined and an unexamined life.

—WILLIAM J. MORGAN

Bibliography: Metheny, Eleanor. (1968) *Movement and Meaning.* New York: McGraw-Hill. Morgan, William J., and Klaus V. Meier. (1995) *Philosophic Inquiry in Sport.* 2d ed. Champaign, IL: Human Kinetics. Slusher, Howard. (1967) *Man, Sport and Existence: A Critical Analysis.* Philadelphia: Lea & Febiger.

Physical Education

Physical education is defined as instruction in the development and care of the body ranging from simple calisthenic exercises to a course of study providing training in hygiene, gymnastics, and the performance and management of athletic games.

Hippocrates' *De Regimen,* probably composed around 400 B.C.E., endorsed exercise, or "therapeutic gymnastics," as a vital component of medicine. Concepts of hygiene and exercise set down by the Roman physician Claudius Galen (circa C.E. 130–200) profoundly influenced 19th-century Western medicine. During the mid-1800s, physical education rose to prominence following various social, ideological, and scientific developments. Amherst College established a Department of Physical Culture in 1860. Other institutions soon followed.

Following the Civil War, when athletics became integral to male collegiate life—Americans became interested in physical education and how physiological principles applied to health.

In 1885, the Association for the Advancement of Physical Education (AAAPE) was formed, now renamed the American Alliance for Health, Physical Education, Recreation, and Dance (AAHPERD; 1979–present). Similar societies—usually more limited in their scope and membership—were organized in several other countries. Women played important roles in these organizations and in the development of the field in general.

By 1889 educators, theologians, and physicians had come to view physical education as key to the moral, social, and physical development of youth, and promoted it in the schools. This burgeoning interest created an enormous need for teachers.

By 1903, more than a dozen normal schools (the teacher-training facilities of the time) of physical training existed. Historically black colleges too offered gymnastics and such sports as basketball as part of their physical education curricula.

Within physical education, attention was directed toward growth and development studies and collecting voluminous data on the effects of exercise upon the body. Female and male directors of college gymnasiums collected up to 56 measurements each from thousands of students. Such findings were published in numerous articles, reports, and monographs, including Arthur MacDonald's *Experimental Study of Children . . . Anthropometrical and Psycho-Physical Measurements of Washington School Children* (1899) and William Hastings's *Manual for Physical Measurements for Use in Normal Schools* (1902).

The field began producing journals to disseminate research findings and other developments. The first was the *American Physical Education Review,* established by the AAAPERD in 1896; many others followed. Research focused on child development and play.

The educational potential of play gained increasing attention during the early 1900s, resulting in more emphasis on psychosocial and pedagogical studies in training physical educators. During the early 1900s, as psychologists and others began to study the educational significance of play, games and sports became an increasing part of the physical education. Meanwhile, sports increasingly replaced gymnastics as the core of the school athletic curriculum.

World War I shaped physical education decisively. Reacting to criticism that large numbers of men drafted for military service were "unfit," both major parties made health and physical education legislation a plank in their 1920 platforms. By 1922, 28 states had enacted some type of requirement for physical education in public schools. Both interscholastic and intercollegiate programs for boys and men proliferated and

intramural programs (usually linked with men's physical education departments) grew rapidly.

The early 20th century also brought changes in the relationship between physical education and medicine. Medical education began to emphasize therapeutic over hygienic practices, and fewer physicians involved themselves in physical education. During the same period, four-year degree and graduate programs in physical education expanded. By 1942, 34 institutions offered the doctoral degree (either Ed.D. or Ph.D.)—the vast majority of which were closely linked with schools or colleges of education.

Leading female physical educators vigorously pursued efforts to maintain a distinct identity. Intercollegiate sports for girls and women continued, and most institutions adopted the "A Sport for Every Girl" philosophy promulgated by the Women's Division of the National Amateur Athletic Federation (organized in 1923). Playdays, later Sportsdays, became the typical form of women's "competition."

Recreation grew substantially between the wars. Massive unemployment during the depression (1929–1935) created immense amounts of free time. Parks, playgrounds, and sports facilities were constructed by the Works Progress Administration.

Demand for teachers continued and curricula shifted. At some institutions, faculty in cognate departments joined with physical education faculty and graduate students to investigate questions relevant to exercise and athletics. Scientific research in general, however, remained scanty. Before World War II, the most significant scientific advances came from other disciplines. British physiologist A. V. Hill (Nobel Prize, 1922) elucidated oxygen uptake and the production of lactic acid during exercise. American physiologist Francis G. Benedict and colleagues studied metabolism. Physical educators were familiar with—and frequently applied to their own work—the findings of leading scientists.

With the end of the war, research efforts increased in areas related to physical education. Investigations included longitudinal studies of the growth and motor performance of children and youth, development of new, influential concepts of motor learning, the motor abilities of children, kinesiological and exercise physiology analyses, and physiological performance.

By the 1960s, many more university and college departments had active research programs on the new subject. Six areas were identified as constituting the "academic discipline of physical education": biomechanics, exercise physiology, motor learning/sports psychology, sociology, history and philosophy, and administrative theory. As research and scholarship rapidly expanded, national and international journals reflecting these subject areas were founded in the 1970s—a decade during which many academic departments changed their names to such designations as Exercise and Sport Science, Kinesiology, and Human Performance.

The President's Council on Youth Fitness was established in 1956 in response to allegations that European and Japanese children had outperformed American children in a number of strength and flexibility tests. A decade of fitness testing ensued. The hope that this council would catalyze research was unfulfilled. Paradoxically, with mounting evidence that regular exercise improved health, public schools began relaxing their physical education graduation requirements.

The 1960s saw physical educators trying to define their field. Franklin Henry's often cited 1964 article "Physical Education—An Academic Discipline" argued that there is a "scholarly field of knowledge basic to physical education [that] . . . is constituted of certain portions of such diverse fields as anatomy, physics and physiology, cultural anthropology, history and sociology, as well as psychology." Henry characterized physical education as cross-disciplinary.

In 1972, Title IX of the Education Amendments Act profoundly influenced interscholastic and intercollegiate sports programs for females and set the stage for struggles for gender equality. One result was the rapid merger of formerly separate men's and women's college physical education departments. In the process, women were usually relegated to vice chair or some other ancillary position; hence, the number of women who headed professional/academic units declined sharply. At the same time, many younger women who might have become leaders in academic aspects of the field chose to devote their talents and energies to emerging athletic programs for the female student and to continuing battles over who would govern these.

During this period, too, some researchers argued for greater emphasis on research over service. Increasing numbers of researchers began to create new organizations and also to ally their work with the American College of Sports Medicine. Many institutions created stronger academic curricula, often differing with colleagues who saw the future of their field more in terms of "service" than "science." Nevertheless, research increased and multiple new journals appeared.

Increasing specialization led to disagreements regarding which areas were most important. Dissatisfac-

tion with the term "physical education" as the title by which departments would be known—whether emanating from within departments or prompted by wider campus concerns—led to such name changes as "Exercise Science and Physical Education"; "Exercise and Health Science"; "Exercise and Sport Sciences"; "Kinesiology"; "Human Movement Studies"; "Human Performance"; and "Human Biodynamics."

Recent decades have again seen more attention to physical activity in relation to health. A comprehensive *Surgeon General's Report on Physical Activity and Health* appeared in July 1996. The messages of these and other publications are strikingly similar to those that appeared 100 years ago.

The 1990s have found physical education grappling with the question of how to maintain unity within the field's diversity. The key question is whether the visions articulated a century ago by men and women about the field once universally known as "physical education" will finally be fulfilled.

—ROBERTA J. PARK

Bibliography: Massengale, John D., and Swanson, Richard A., eds. (1997). *History of Exercise Science and Sport.* Champaign, IL: Human Kinetics. Park, Roberta J., and Eckert, Helen M., eds. (1991). *New Possibilities, New Paradigms?* Academy Papers No. 24. Champaign, IL: Human Kinetics Books. Spears, Betty, and Swanson, Richard A. (1995). *History of Sport and Physical Activity in the United States.* 4th ed. Madison, WI: Brown & Benchmark.

Pigeon Racing

Pigeon racing is popular in Europe, Japan, and North America. The "athlete" is the pigeon who races against opponents—sometimes thousands—for titles and prize money. That the pigeons will reliably return to their homes when released hundreds of miles away is the basis of modern pigeon racing.

History

For centuries homing pigeons have been especially bred and trained to carry messages. The early Romans probably used pigeons as messengers, but Europeans may have forgotten this by the time of the Crusades, when the Muslim forces apparently had a monopoly on their use.

Pigeon racing as such began after 1800, popular in Belgium but also the Netherlands and France. Although all racing (and messenger) pigeons descend from the common rock dove that is seen in all city parks *(Calumba livid),* Belgian fanciers developed the modern racer from a variety of types, including Smierel, Camulet, Cropper, and Dragoon. Its earliest prototype was flown in Antwerp.

In England, racing developed later. In 1892, King George V gave the sport a considerable boost by setting up a racing loft with stock received from King Leopold of Belgium.

What assured the sport's popularity in continental Europe and the United Kingdom were the much-reported World War I exploits of certain birds, some of whom were actually credited with saving lives. One bird, Cher Ami, reached his destination in spite of grievous wounds, bearing information that helped to save almost 200 American lives. The spread of the sport to North America can be attributed not only to immigration from Europe, but also to this wartime romance of homing pigeons.

Rules and Play

Pigeon racers first need a loft in which to keep the pigeons—a small shelter, usually on a roof or on a raised platform, that the pigeons regard as "home," where they rest, feed, and raise their young. The home loft is also the pigeon's destination during a race. Owners must transport the birds to a "race site" from where they can be released.

Before the race, owners takes birds to a club headquarters, where special leg rings are checked and recorded by code number and the birds are cataloged by number, color, and sex. Each owner also brings a special timing clock, which is tested, wound, and sealed by club officials. The birds, in special crates, are then loaded onto the communal truck and taken off to the release site, anywhere from 100 to 1,000 kilometers (60 to 600 miles) away (a few races are even longer).

Speed is what is required of racing pigeons and, in good weather with favorable winds, 65 kilometers (40 miles) per hour is considered average. Bursts of speed up to 145 kilometers (90 miles) per hour have been reported.

Young birds, or rookies, usually begin training at less than a year old with races of fewer than 160 kilometers (100 miles), then work up to longer races. While in training, they are fed special diets of high-protein grain and various jealously guarded mixtures of vitamins and minerals. Often, pigeons are given extra carbohydrates prior to races, just as human athletes do. Also, it is rumored that some of the birds are on steroids.

Pigeon racing in Europe shows no signs of diminishing popularity. In North America, racing may be dwindling in the older eastern cities, but it is developing new centers in the West and Southwest. In Japan, where the sport is still relatively new, pigeon racing continues to develop, with some of the highest prices for famous European racing birds being paid by wealthy Japanese. The sport has always enjoyed some level of patronage by the wealthy; recently, some racing pigeons sold for more than $150,000.

The human owners of the pigeons derive their satisfaction from the breeding, training, and testing of their birds. Although the wealthy have interested themselves in pigeon racing, the basic requirements of the sport—the birds, the lofts in which to house them, and a time-keeping device—are well within the means of people with modest incomes.

—ALAN TREVITHICK

Pistol Shooting
See Shooting, Pistol

Politics

In both politics and sports, power, prestige, and profits are important motivators. Participation and victory motivate both individuals and organizations. Annual seasons and elections determine the winners and losers. The media report the results and market products or images for commercial and political purposes. Political establishments regulate sports to provide "equal" opportunities, economic "justice," legal "authority," and personal "attention."

The relationship between sports and politics has reflected a changing pattern of cultural practices and values. Cave drawings, classical statuary, medieval tapestries, Brueghel paintings, and videotaped highlights have recorded athletic activities over time. These lasting images usually reflect spectators' perceptions. Tribes, kingdoms, empires, and republics were bound by personal and group loyalties and functioned according to rules designed to stabilize and perpetuate the political body and maintain its economic status. Group living was a more effective way of providing food by hunting and agriculture, affording security against human and natural enemies, developing the specialization of individual talents, and making decisions affecting the welfare of the members. Loyalty to the family or tribal group heightened the spirit of rivalry with other groups.

As the science or art of government, politics was the basis for governance of the group. War was a traditional form of group rivalry and had a close relationship to sport. Ancient gladiatorial contests, medieval tournaments, and modern "war games" or "military exercises" combined competition with combat according to rules. The ritualistic aspects of sporting events from antiquity to the present have afforded opportunities for politicians and political demonstrations. As these practices were repeated, rules were established to govern sport contests. The Olympics attracted competitors from the Greek city-states who participated in athletic encounters undertaken as religious rituals. Formal rules governed the competitions, which were sponsored by politicians eager to offer popular entertainment.

In the Middle Ages, sports had a military character as the political formation of nation-states conferred great prestige on military leadership and valor. Early monarchs rode horses while traveling about their realms, hunting and conducting military campaigns. Migratory lifestyles gradually were replaced by increased urban populations with access to improved communications and transportation systems. Some sports involved animals and machines. Others, such as dice and cards, required minimal athletic activity. Bowling was an early competitive sport. Races—foot, swimming, and boat—were also popular. Renaissance society revived ancient traditions and advocated a way of life centered on human interests and values. Humanism opened new possibilities for participation in sporting events, especially in urban centers and among the leisured nobility. In 1532, Henry VIII had a tennis court built at Hampton Court Palace. By 1596, there were 250 tennis courts in Paris and 7,000 persons lived off the game.

By the 18th century, the upper classes had developed sporting events appropriate to their social status and occupations. The Enlightenment brought wealth and leisure for the rulers and created a middle class that sought to emulate their lifestyles. In Germany, Johann Christoph Friedrich Guts Muths (1759–1839) applied Enlightenment ideas to promote intensive, organized, disciplined physical activities in schools. Friedrich Ludwig Jahn (1778–1852) founded the patriotic Turnen gymnastics movement, which German politicians suppressed in 1819 as a liberal threat to the state. The lower classes copied and modified games and contests suitable for their resources, e.g., soccer (association football) and baseball. Emigrants and missionaries carried national sports overseas, and revolutionary and imperial armies took sports to new countries.

In the 19th century horse racing, cricket, boxing, and soccer took root in England and horse racing and baseball in the United States. Sports have played a major role in Americanizing successive waves of immigrants. In the closing decades of the century, American

football and basketball appeared, and track and field events became popular. Popularity brought the formation of governing organizations such as the American Amateur Athletic Union (AAU) in 1890 and the National Collegiate Athletic Association (NCAA) in 1905. At the local level, baseball's broad popularity in the United States meant profitability, which attracted politicians to the franchise, employment, gambling, land, and transit businesses associated with the game. Profitability also led to unsuccessful attempts to break the owners' legal monopoly.

The Olympics

The modern Olympics provided an international stage for the interplay of politics and sports. The Athens Games in 1896 were a tribute to the modern Greek state. Succeeding games at Paris, St. Louis, and London were held in connection with national celebrations at world's fairs. In 1912, the Swedes built a new stadium to host athletes from many countries. The political debacle of World War I eliminated the 1916 Games and affected participation in 1920 and 1924. In 1932, a California realtor with a federal tax exemption led the committee that organized the Los Angeles Games in a modern coliseum. In 1936, the Berlin Olympics were supported by Germany's Nazi party, which had come to power in 1933. Following the precedents of earlier organizing committees, the new rulers used state funds to stage games that showed the economic and social progress they had made. Leni Riefenstahl's *Triumph of the Will* and *Olympia* were cinematic celebrations of politics and sports. After another interruption for World War II, the Olympics were revived at London in 1948, Helsinki in 1952, and Melbourne in 1956. Three of the four host cities for the 1960 through 1972 Summer Olympiads were located in nations that were defeated in World War II—Rome, Tokyo, and Munich. The development of television and media coverage of impressive celebrations of international sports attracted political demonstrators. A boycott threat and civil riots at Mexico City in 1968 and boycott threats and the terrorist assassination of Israeli team members at Munich in 1972 threatened the continuation of the games. The 1976, 1980, and 1984 games were boycotted for political reasons by 28 African nations, the United States and its allies, and the Soviet Union and its allies, respectively. The Seoul Games in 1988 and the Barcelona Games of 1992 included spectacular tributes to political regimes in South Korea and Spain.

Paradoxically, the leaders of the Olympic movement have sought to avoid any political control, influence, or interference in the Games, while hailing them as a viable alternative to political conflicts and wars. They have sought to protect international athletic competition from the pervasive nationalism of the 20th century. At the same time, they have delegated vital responsibilities for the organization and administration of the Games to politically dominated national Olympic committees and local organizing committees.

National sports programs have reflected the mass appeal of a unifying subculture. Since 1930, soccer's World Cup competitions have become quadrennial spectacles for national politics as well as athletic contests. Emblematic of their supremacy in the sport, most of the World Cup finals have been won by three South American and two European nations: Brazil, Argentina, Uruguay, Germany, and Italy. Other sports are politically and economically popular regional events. Three-quarters of the World Cup Alpine skiing champions have come from Alpine countries. Particular sports have been dominated by countries with the facilities and broad public participation required for the events. Australia and the United States have won 69 percent of the Davis Cup tennis championships.

National policies often provided the incentives for government intrusion in sports. The British Physical Training and Recreation Act of 1937 recognized that sport was an "agent of political socialization." The American Amateur Sports Act of 1978 restructured amateur sports to control jurisdictional disputes between urban and academic sports organizations and strengthen the national Olympic team. The United States' 1980 decision to employ sport as an "appropriate tool for foreign policy objectives" by boycotting the Olympic Games was followed by a $10 million grant to the United States Olympic Committee and more than $50 million to support the 1984 Games held in Los Angeles.

Individual politicians have seldom missed opportunities to associate themselves with sports and winning teams. U.S. presidents hunted, boated, fished, walked, jogged, and played golf and tennis. Attempts of politicians and persons involved in sports to distance themselves from each other's domain have been unsuccessful. Politicians benefit from sports by receiving publicity that enhances the prestige of the government and political leaders, by using rituals and spectacles to gain public support and advantages over rivals, and by promoting physical fitness to produce healthy and competitive citizen warriors. Sportsmen benefit from politics by securing sponsorship or money, legal protection, performance facilities, and identification with national and local patriotic or institutional symbols and values. Moral influence and tradition do not fare well in competition with political and economic power. Sport maintains a degree of independence only when politicians endow it with a strong economic position. Nevertheless, the myth of sport autonomy and the idea that sport does not relate to politics is a "constantly recurring theme." The myth has its roots in the cultural reality of a common interest in participatory sports as recreational and fitness activities involving voluntary personal commitments of time and money. Typically, participants are amateurs. Politics and professionalism enter with the development of a desire to emulate successful competitive models, a decision to participate in organized, institutionalized team sports, and a commitment to sports that have governmental or commercial sponsorship.

Modern Societies

Sporting activities are based on the egalitarian concepts of modern societies. Modern societies have also been characterized by occupational specialization, sedentary occupations, and more leisure time. Americans assumed that "the pursuit of happiness" included the equality of opportunity to participate in sports as a fundamental political right. The elimination of racial discrimination was the subject of political pressure and legislation from 1946 to 1976. Title IX of the U.S. Education Act of 1972 made discrimination on the basis of gender illegal in all institutions receiving federal support.

Commercialization, institutionalization, and professional specialization in sports brought political involvement. Sports became profitable. The economic and political stakes resulted in the formation of cartels or voluntary associations to employ professional sports administrators, regulate competition, and pursue common political interests, such as International Olympic Committee, the National Collegiate Athletic Association, and major league baseball. The governance of sporting activities included allocating franchises and adopting rules governing the playing of the games and the employment of the players.

In a modern state, individuals vote in elections, participate in sports, and select forms of entertainment. Participation involves decisions based on physical fitness and personal satisfaction and investments in fees and equipment. Increased literacy stimulated newspaper coverage of sporting events. The popularity of sports brought commercialization, dividends, and wages. The advertising and marketing of consumer products in print, radio, and television focused public attention on sports and provided opportunities for political involvement and cultural propaganda. Commercial television depends on advertising, and advertisers prefer to invest their money in televised sports such as golf and tennis, which tend to attract affluent viewers. Television viewers and radio listeners provide a media market that exercises a major influence on the profitability and content of sporting events. In the United States, the National Broadcasting Company and the International Olympic Committee have announced contracts of $1.245 billion for the Summer 2000 and Winter 2002 Olympic Games. The $1.58 billion budget of the 1996 Atlanta Olympic Organizing Committee was threatened by the host city's plans to market sponsorships during the games.

The legalization or extension of legislative and juridical control over organized sport has characterized recent relationships between sports and politics. The sporting amateur's loyalty to the community, the school, or the club has been replaced by a system of legal rights and duties defined by contractual agreements. The economic importance of media sports has provided a basis for the legal control of sports and increased sports litigation. The control of profitable sports by private organizations is a frequent target of external legal intervention to protect public interests. Governmental agencies and sports cartels negotiate interpretations of legislative and judicial intent. Most legal actions concern the owners' monopolies in restraint of trade, players' rights as employees, and public safety. Governments provide legal support and power through sports councils and ministries and legislative sanction for the control and marketing of sport by jurisdictional bodies. These top sports officials are sometimes known by the telling term "czars."

—MAYNARD BRICHFORD

See also Law, Sports; Media; Patriotism.

Bibliography: Allison, Lincoln, ed. (1986) *The Politics of Sport.* Manchester: Manchester University Press. Espy, Richard. (1979) *The Politics of the Olympic Games.* Berkeley: University of California Press. Guttmann, Allen. (1992) *The Olympics, A History of the Modern Games.* Urbana: University of Illinois Press. Hoberman, John M. (1984) *Sport and Political Ideology.* Austin: University of Texas Press. Mandell, Richard D. (1984) *Sport, A Cultural History.* New York: Columbia University Press. Redmond, Gerald, ed. (1986) *Sport and Politics.* Champaign, IL: Human Kinetics Publishers.

Polo

Polo is a game played between two teams of four players each, mounted on horses and using mallets to hit a ball between goalposts. Polo is reputed to be the oldest mounted team game, apparently originating in the central plains of Asia and spreading to ancient Persia, China, and northern India. Played by mounted warriors, it likely resembled a battle more than a pastime. It enjoyed royal patronage and the support of the aristocracy and the ruling classes. Asian poets and authors refer to the game often.

History

Polo as it is now known was encountered in the Indian state of Manipur by English tea planters in the 1850s. Credit is given to Lieutenant John F. Sherer (1829–?), the so-called father of modern polo, for popularizing it with British planters and soldiers. It rapidly spread throughout India, where both the indigenous ruling classes and the British took up the game with a vengeance. However, polo vanished almost entirely from India after independence, in 1948.

In England military officers began playing in 1869; civilian clubs developed and eventually drafted the rules of the game. Polo has always been a game of the affluent. Although seriously challenged by the United States, Great Britain's preeminence lasted until 1914. Many of Britain's best players were lost in World War I, although the country still won the 1920 Olympics. With World War II came taxes that dealt a blow to polo by cutting the discretionary spending of the wealthy. But polo survived, and England currently ranks third in the world, after Argentina and the United States.

British ranchers took the sport to Argentina in about 1875, where it became immensely popular because ponies were easily and cheaply obtainable, and the flat pampas provided virtually ready-made grounds.

James Gordon Bennett, the proprietor of the *New York Herald,* brought polo to America in 1876. The game spread rapidly, with the main polo centers located in Buffalo, Philadelphia, Boston, San Diego, Chicago, St. Louis, and Aiken, South Carolina.

Polo was introduced to New Zealand by Royal Navy officers, in South Africa by army officers, and in Australia by pioneers and settlers. In France, Germany, and Spain it was the aristocrats and the titled who took the lead; in Brazil and Chile, the diplomats; in Uruguay, the ranchers. Polo is now played in about 40 nations.

Rules and Play

Played on a ground the size of nine football fields, polo requires horsemanship and the ability to strike a small wooden ball at speeds of over 48 kilometers (30 miles) per hour with a 127-centimeter (4 foot, 2 inch) stick. The basic pattern resembles soccer (association football), but on horseback. Fast and fluid, the game has almost no set plays. Forward strokes and backstrokes may be forward or backward, under the horse's neck or belly, and behind its tail. Players may be "bumped" by opponents—often the precursor of a fall. Each of the four players has a special function. Goal are scored by sending the ball across the back line between the goalposts. The team with the most goals wins.

What sets the game apart is the horses. If you cannot get to the ball, you cannot hit it. Most teams spend more in buying, training, and improving strings of polo ponies than on players' salaries. Most of the top mounts are Thoroughbreds since speed is essential. The horses, generally at least age three, are at times called ponies, a throwback to the early days of the game.

At the top are the international competitions, such as the World Championship, and the different cups between nations, followed by national championships, of which the Argentine, U.S., and British opens are the most prestigious. At a lower level are many and varied tournaments ranging from gold cups just below open level to interclub minor events.

The basic rule is "right of way," which extends ahead of the player and in the direction in which the player is riding. The right of way allows players to hit the ball on the offside (the right side) of the pony. Safety of both players and mounts is paramount in this rule.

Each period of play (called chukka in England and chukker in Argentina) lasts seven minutes, followed by a four-minute interval when players change ponies. Matches last from four to eight periods, depending on the importance of the tournament. If the score is tied at the end of regulation time, play continues until a goal is scored or the ball goes out of play.

To equalize games, every player has an official handicap, from 10 goals (the highest) to minus 2 (beginners). For example, a team whose total handicap adds up to 20 and is playing a 14-goal team must start the game giving 6 goals to the weaker team. Individual handicaps indicate quality of play, not the number of goals the player is expected to score.

Major Events

The primary inter-nation events are the Hurlingham Champion Cup in England, which ended in 1939; the Argentine Open, which began in 1893; the U.S. Open, which began in 1904; the Coronation Cup in England, which began in 1911, and the Cowdray Park Gold Cup in England, which began in 1956.

Internationally, there has been interest in both dual-nation and international matches. The Westchester Cup between the United States and Great Britain was first played in Newport, Rhode Island, in 1886, when Britain won. The United States ended British domination in 1921 and kept the cup until 1939; when play resumed in 1988, America again won, as it did in 1992. The Cup of the Americas began in 1928 and pits Argentina against the United States, with Argentina dominating. The Avila Camacho Cup began in 1941 and pits the United States against Mexico, with the series currently in the former's favor.

The only world polo championship took place in Argentina in 1949. The host country took first place, with the United States second and Mexico third. To promote competition, the International Polo Federation organized a world championship limited to a handicap of up to 14 goals, not a true measure of high skills. Since 1987, Argentina has won twice, the United States and Brazil once each.

In the Olympics, polo was awarded medals in the 1900 Paris Games, but the event was haphazard and some historians do not give it full Olympic status. The winning team, named Foxhunters, mixed American and British players. In 1908 in London, three British teams took part, representing clubs rather than countries; a foursome from the Roehampton Club took the gold. The first truly international competition was held in 1920 in Ostend, Belgium. Great Britain won the gold medal, followed by Spain and the United States. The last Olympic competition took place in Berlin in 1936; once more Argentina took the gold. Efforts continue to reinstate polo as an Olympic sport.

Outstanding Players

More than 60 players have attained the maximum ranking of 10 goals. However, no accurate yardstick can measure and compare highly different epochs and dissimilar styles of play, and polo lacks statistics and percentages that may give some objective indication of a player's prowess. Even today, with all due respect to the national handicap committees, there is an air of glorious uncertainty about handicaps and their true value. Generally, however, outstanding players have been characterized by strength in both leadership and skill. Today, polo players come from all walks of life. All top players are professionals.

—HORACIO A. LAFFAYE

Bibliography: Grace, Peter. (1991) *Polo.* New York: Howell. Hobson, Richard. (1993) *Riding—The Game of Polo.* London: J. A. Allen. Kendall, Paul G. (1933) *Polo Ponies*. New York: Derrydale Press. Meisels, Penina. (1992) *Polo*. San Francisco: Collins. Watson, J. N. P. (1986) *The World of Polo*. Topsfield, MA: Salem House.

Polo, Bicycle

Bicycle polo, derived from pony polo, is an exciting game in which riders on specially adapted bicycles use long-handled mallets to move a ball along a grass field, scoring goals through a defended goalpost.

History

The first reference to bicycle polo described a game played in the United States in the early 1880s by Kaufman and MacAnney, famous trick cyclists, who rode Star bicycles. In Ireland in the 1890s, R. J. Macredy, editor of *Cycling*, developed bicycle polo when he retired from active cycle racing. Soon bicycle polo was established in England and spread through Europe. England and Ireland played at the Crystal Palace, London, in 1901 (Ireland won 10 goals to 5).

European bicycle polo (Britain, Ireland, Belgium, France) modified the rules of pony polo to accommodate bicycles, whereas in the United Arab Republic, India, Pakistan, Ceylon, Malaysia, and Singapore the game was based strictly on pony polo. Skill and daring are required to move the ball down the field and to avoid collision; "a perfectly cool head, quick eye and almost instantaneous judgment are essential" ("Polo on Bicycles" 1896).

Bicycle polo was an exuberant and somewhat rowdy game in its early years. Player Len Baker, would ride straight through a group of players, flattening opponents right and left. He would then return, pick up a winded and muddied rival, and politely announce, "It's all in the game, ol' man."

Soon after the turn of the century, the sport declined, and little was heard of bicycle polo. Then, in 1929, Cyril S. Scott, a retired cycle racer, revived the game and formed a second Bicycle Polo Association. By 1930, formal rules were adopted, the same year the first public match was played. More clubs became involved. By 1931, the Bicycle Polo Association had become national. Interest revived again in 1966, and in 1968 the International Cycle Polo Federation was formed in Mexico City.

Rules and Play

Bicycle polo is played on a pitch, a rectangular grass field 100 meters (110 yards) long with upright bamboo goalposts 3.5 meters (4 yards) apart and 2.7 meters (3 yards) high. The pitch is divided by a center line and 23-meter (25-yard) lines between the center and goal lines. The mallet has an 81-centimeter (32-inch) or 86-centimeter (34-inch) leather-bound cane handle and a boxwood head 15 centimeters (6 inches) in length and 6.3 centimeters ($2^1/_2$ inches) in diameter. The mallet must be held in the right hand. The ball is made of bamboo root and is painted white; it must not exceed 8 centimeters ($3^1/_4$ inches) in diameter and 112 grams (4 ounces) in weight. In recent years, limited success has been experienced with a plastic ball that tends to last several games, as opposed to the bamboo ball that usually needs replacing every 15 minutes.

No more than eight players, both men and women, make a team; Six is ideal, with four taking the field. They are the full-back, half-back, two forwards, and one goal guard. The referee (on foot) is usually assisted by two judges and two linesmen—necessary because of the fast pace of the sport.

Periods of play are called "chukkers"—a game consists of six 15-minute chukkers separated by 1-minute breaks. The ball is driven up the field toward the goal. Players may use hands (but not to catch the ball) and feet, but only if the ball is airborne, and the front wheels of their bicycles to block the ball. Strict rules of play help to minimize collisions, and penalties are assessed for stealing ground before the whistle, dangerous play, and deliberate obstruction. Players need maneuverability and speed, so the bicycle used has a shortened wheelbase, fixed wheel, no brakes, and a very low gear ratio.

Bicycle polo seems likely to retain its steady but limited appeal.

—ANTHONY BUSH

Bibliography: Bartleett, H. W. *Bartleett's Bicycle Book*. ———. (1938) "The Story of Bicycle-Polo." *Cycling* (November 2). "Polo on Bicycles." (1896) *The Hub* (September 26).

Polo, Water

Of the several team water sports created in the late 1800s, water polo is the sole survivor. The sport today is played by teams of seven, each trying to throw an inflated ball into the opponents goal without touching the bottom of the pool. Water polo is a strenuous and exciting sport, and even though considered a minor sport, draws huge audiences when televised during the Olympics.

History

Water polo is called polo because, initially, players rode on floating barrels that resembled mock horses and swung at the ball with mallets. It began in 1869 when the Bournemouth Rowing Club set out to create aquatic soccer (association football). What they created was "football in water," which eventually came to be known as water polo. In 1870 the London Swimming Club agreed on a basic set of rules with the first official match supposedly occurring in 1874.

International water polo started in 1890 when England played Scotland, followed by the 1895 initiation of a biennial series between England and Ireland. From 1890 to 1895 the sport spread to Europe, becoming especially popular in Eastern European countries. The sport appeared at the 1900 Olympics. American rules were developed in 1897; in the United States, until after World War II, the sport was most popular in New York and Chicago. Beginning in 1906, the Amateur Athletic Union (AAU) supervised water polo. Today, the sport's controlling body in the United States is an organization called U.S. Water Polo.

Rules and Play

Water polo's strategy is simple. In a swimming pool, a seven-person team (one goalkeeper) attempts to throw an inflated ball into a small goal. Only the goalkeeper may touch the pool bottom. The game involves much physical contact and, for four periods of play, strong and speedy swimmers do nothing but swim while battling for control of the ball. The game has been described as brutal, with intense cardiorespiratory demands.

All water polo players are specialists, with dual roles on offense and defense. In the United States, "shooters" are the scoring specialists, "holemen" are key offensive players like a striker in soccer or a center in basketball, and "drivers" are the fastest swimmers. Teams are allowed six substitutions.

Water polo has a shot clock; a team cannot retain the ball for more than 35 seconds without attempting to score. Violations mean the opposition gets a free throw at the point of the foul.

Penalties fall into two categories—ordinary (standing on the bottom of the pool), or major (clubbing an opponent). Major penalties may earn a player 45 seconds in the penalty area, ejection from the game with substitution, or ejection from the game with no substitution for a "brutality" foul.

Players use an alternating breaststroke kick called the "eggbeater," which allows them to rise from the water and place their center of gravity several feet in the air. Such movement is of critical importance in receiving or intercepting the ball and especially in throwing the ball at the goal.

Teams use a round-robin tournament formation in which they play every other team once. For each game the winners earn 2 points, a draw gives 1 point, and losers earn 0 points. Total points determines the final standing.

Water polo embraces more than 1,000 teams, with 10,000 members of the United States Water Polo Association. The Pacific coastline dominates, with water polo enjoying growing popularity (at team and college levels) in California, Oregon, and Washington.

At the Olympics, water polo is exclusively male, although women's water polo has continued to develop. In 1993 the top five nations in women's water polo were Netherlands, Italy, Hungary, Australia, and the United States.

Water polo has tremendous potential for coeducational growth and promotion. Some hope that the sport might become the first NCAA intercollegiate sport that would allow men and women to compete together.

—SCOTT A. G. M. CRAWFORD

Bibliography: Brown, G., ed. (1979) *New York Times Encyclopedia of Water Sports*. Danbury, CT: Arno Press.

Pool
See Billiards

Powerlifting

Powerlifting is a sport that matches the strength of individuals of similar body weights in a competitive setting. It involves an athlete lifting as much weight as possible in three different events: the squat, the bench press, and the dead lift. The winner is the athlete with the greatest combined total weight using the highest weight lifted in each of the three events.

History

The Greeks and Romans used weights for strength development. In the early 18th century, weightlifting programs and strongman events became popular. During this time, odd lifts, which focused on repetitive lifting and included events such as the one- or two-finger lift; the squat; and the belly toss, were performed.

Early Olympic weightlifting competition included over 10 lifts, but by 1920 the number of lifts was reduced to 5. With the development of removable barbell plates, knurling texture on the bar to improve the hand grip, and thinner bar circumference, the dead lift became more popular and soon replaced the odd lifts. After World War II the bench press, as executed today, was developed. In 1928, when Olympic lifting was reduced to three events, many lifters began choosing between development of overall strength and agility or the higher level of skill needed for Olympic lifting. Powerlifting, which is a relatively young sport, evolved into its own when the sport of Olympic weightlifting became specialized with only two events: the snatch and the clean-and-jerk.

Powerlifting had greater appeal and application to athletics than weightlifting. The powerlifting events (the squat, the bench press, and the dead lift) require brief explosive efforts measuring coordination and agility.

The first Powerlifting World Championships was held in York, Pennsylvania, in 1965, with the first actual contests beginning in the early 1960s. Powerlifting has now grown in popularity worldwide with athletes from more than 12 countries involved in international competition. In 1973, the International Powerlifting Federation was formed and officially recognized. A year later the European Federation was organized.

During the 1970s, women became active in powerlifting. In the United States in 1978, the first women's National Powerlifting Championship was held. Prior to this, women participated in men's meets or meets sanctioned by the Amateur Athletic Union (AAU). Women competed directly against the men because no specific divisions were structured for females. Two years after the national meet in the United States, the first world championship was held for women.

Rules and Play

In competition, athletes have three attempts in each of the three events. After successfully completing a lift, the athlete increases the weight on the bar for the next attempt. The highest amount of weight in each event becomes a part of the total weight that determines the winner. An athlete will not be considered in the overall standings without completing a legal lift in all three events in order: the squat, the bench press, and the dead lift.

The squat primarily measures the lifter's leg and back strength. The lifter must position the bar horizontally across the back of the shoulders; when the signal is given, the body lowers via a squat motion until the front of the hip joint is lower than the top of the knee. The squat ends with the lifter in an upright balanced position with knees locked.

The bench press event tests upper body strength, specifically the chest and arms. The athlete lies on a flat bench, face up with feet flat on the floor or on a raised surface, then attempts to lower the barbell to the chest,

Powerlifting and Drugs

Use of performance-enhancement drugs, including steroids, has been a controversial issue within competitive powerlifting. The powerlifting world has primarily two types of governing bodies that are philosophically opposite concerning drug usage and drug testing. Drug-free organizations have been formed in an attempt to provide competition based on natural abilities and to prevent drug-using athletes from participating in the competition. These organizations have a list of banned substances, such as anabolic steroids and growth hormones, prescription diuretics, and psychomotor stimulants, that lifters are not permitted to use. Athletes competing in drug-free meets must be drug free for a minimum of three years, and all lifters are subject to drug testing at the discretion of the drug-testing committee and meet director. Polygraph, urinalysis, and/or blood testing are the drug-testing forms used. Lifters setting American and/or world records, and competing internationally can be expected to be drug tested, both in and out of competition situations.

At the international level, the World Drug Free Powerlifting Federation (WDFP) oversees competition in over 12 countries. It offers a greater number of competitive classifications than the International Powerlifting Federation (IPF), which does not require out-of-competition drug testing. Within North America, the largest of the drug-free organizations is the American Drug Free Powerlifting Association, Inc. (ADFPA), founded in 1981 by Brother Bennett Bishop (1931–1994). This organization sanctions all powerlifting competition in the United States.

The IPF, which has members from 20 countries, does not actively promote drug use for strength gains, but it does not subject athletes to as much drug testing as does the WDPF and it doesn't require out-of-competition drug testing. Within the North American continent, the largest organization that does not test for drugs is the American Powerlifting Federation (APF). The U.S. Powerlifting Federation (USPF) advocates a limited drug-testing program.

—*Darlene Young*

pause, then when the signal is given, press the bar to an extended arm position. The weight must be pressed so the arms extend evenly.

The dead lift is the last event and so most frequently determines the winner. The athlete uses the legs and back to lift the barbell from the platform floor. The lifter must raise into an upright position in one continuous motion until the knees are locked and the shoulders erect, then maintain this until signaled to lower the bar.

The nature of powerlifting requires that athletes weigh in within one and one-half hours of the competition so lifters can be classified by body weight. This guarantees that athletes match strength against lifters in similar weight categories. Winners are declared in each of the weight classes for both men and women. In some meets, a "best lifter" award may be determined using a formula to calculate the lifter who lifts the most weight in relation to actual body weight.

Powerlifting is an individual sport, but lifters often train with each other. Training partners encourage one another and assume the role of spotters. As a lifter extends beyond the current strength limits, spotters must help the lifter control the barbell.

Powerlifting attracts two kinds of athletes: those who specialize and compete solely in powerlifting, and those who compete in other sports using powerlifting as a form of strength conditioning. Because of the tremendous potential for developing strength with the squat, the bench press, and the dead lift, athletes whose sports require arm/shoulder and leg power frequently powerlift during the off-season. Much of the skill improvement seen in today's athletes can be attributed to increased involvement with strength programs.

—DARLENE YOUNG

See also Bodybuilding; Weightlifting.
Bibliography: Mentzer, M., and A. Friedberg. (1982) *Mike Mentzer's Complete Book of Weight Training.* New York: William Morrow. Todd, T. (1978) *Inside Powerlifting.* Chicago: Contemporary Books.

Psychology

Sport psychology focuses on the mental and behavioral processes of humans within the sociocultural context of competitive sport. Within this lies social behavior such as achievement or competition and associated thoughts and feelings: anxiety, self-esteem, and motivation. Sport psychology, the youngest of the sport sciences, became recognized as an academic field of study in the 1970s.

Sport psychology may be divided into four broad areas of study. First, the relationship between *personality* and sport participation has been widely studied. Second, the largest area of inquiry in sport psychology is attempting to understand *motivation* as the complex process that influences individuals to begin an activity and pursue it with vigor and persistence. Included in the broad category of motivation would be self-perceptions such as self-confidence, self-esteem, and stress that influence motivational behavior in sport. Third, *interpersonal and group processes* that influence individuals' behaviors in sport, such as the presence of spectators, group membership, and leadership, are studied in sport psychology. Included in this area are aggression and gender socialization, which are behaviors or characteristics that result from interpersonal

social processes. Fourth, the area of mental training or psychological-skills training encompasses the use of *intervention techniques* to learn cognitive skills and behavioral strategies that can enhance sport performance and personal development.

History

Around 1900, researchers first began to assess how the presence of others affected motor performance, an area that became known as social facilitation. However, the true beginning of sport psychology dawned with the work of Coleman Griffith, who as a professor at the University of Illinois engaged in the first systematic examination of the psychological aspects of sport between 1919 and 1938. He was also hired by Phillip Wrigley in 1938 as a sport psychology consultant for the Chicago Cubs baseball team, the first psychologist to consult with a professional sport team.

Psychological research with athletes began in Eastern European countries in the 1950s as part of the Soviet space program's exploration of mental techniques to enhance the performance of cosmonauts. The field grew through the 1980s in these countries under the control of central governments, which mandated research objectives targeted to improvements in self-regulation and performance. Clearly, these research objectives were politically motivated to promote excellence in international sports competition as an outgrowth of the socialist system.

In North America, sport psychology largely lay dormant after Coleman Griffith's time until the 1960s. This decade saw an upsurge of interest in personality and social facilitation research and the founding of several professional organizations. The 1970s saw the emergence of sport psychology as a legitimate scientific subdiscipline of psychology. Systematic research programs were established at several universities, graduate study became available, and the *Journal of Sport Psychology* began publication in 1979. Much of the research during this time was experimental laboratory study, testing theory from the parent discipline of psychology.

It was not until the 1980s that the field expanded with a growth in field research and increased interest in applied sport psychology or mental training with athletes. In 1985, the U.S. Olympic Committee hired the first full-time sport psychologist to oversee the research program and mental preparation of all Olympic sport programs in America. By the 1990s, sport psychology was studied and practiced throughout the world as respect for the young field grew with increasing awareness of the mind-body link that influences not only sport performance, but overall health and well-being.

Sport psychology, as the systematic scholarly study of human thought, emotion, and behavior in sport contexts, consists of four main areas: personality and sport participation, motivational processes, interpersonal and group processes, and intervention techniques to enhance sport performance and personal development.

Personality and Sport Participation

Personality is the unique blend of the psychological characteristics and behavioral tendencies that make individuals different from and similar to each other. Interestingly, the popular notion that distinct personality types exist in sport has not been supported by research. Also, no consistent personality differences between athletic subgroups (e.g., team versus individual sport athletes) have been shown to exist. Successful athletes have a more positive mood profile, more self-confidence, and more better strategies to focus attention and manage anxiety.

Sport psychology has also examined the effects of sport participation on personality development and change. Traditionally, Americans have believed the notion that "sport builds character" or that socially valued personality attributes may be developed through sport participation. However, research emphatically shows that competition serves to reduce prosocial behaviors such as helping and sharing, and this effect is magnified by losing. Sport participation has been shown to increase rivalrous, antisocial behavior, and aggression, and sport participation has also been linked to lower levels of moral reasoning. However, research in a variety of field settings has demonstrated that children's moral development and prosocial behaviors (cooperation, acceptance, sharing) can be enhanced in sport settings when adult leaders structure situations to foster these positive behaviors.

Motivational Processes

Motivation is a complex process that influences individuals to begin, pursue, and persist in an activity. Intrinsic motivation is self-fueling over the long term because it is based on controllable feelings of enjoyment and competence; extrinsic motivation relies on external reinforcers from the social environment.

Current theory views motivation as a cognitive process in which our behavior is a direct result of how we think and process information about ourselves and the world. The one common thread in the many theo-

Choking

Why do athletes "choke" in pressure situations? Choking is a popular term for performing poorly in stressful situations due to a lack of mental skill. Basically, choking occurs when attention is focused on the wrong things. Athletes choke because they lose control of their thought processes and their minds do not allow their bodies the freedom to perform effectively. Thus, choking begins with our thoughts, but it also affects our physical responses by creating tension in our muscles or excessive physiological arousal. Athletes need to understand their optimal arousal zone with regard to both mental as well as physical activation. Choking is the opposite of peak performance or flow. Peak performance and flow involve intrinsic motivation and total immersion in the activity itself, as opposed to focusing on the pressure of achieving the outcome. Thus, people that rely on extrinsic motivation are prime candidates to choke because they tend to focus all attention on extrinsic rewards such as winning or gaining approval from others.

To avoid choking, begin with thorough physical preparation. You must be able to relax and trust that your training and physical preparation has provided you with a sound automatic performance base. Set specific performance goals that allow you to focus on the process of performing that provides the attentional focus you need to perform optimally. You also need to know what your optimal zone is and have a competition focus plan that allows you to get centered into your optimal zone. This plan includes thoughts and feelings that you will program into your mind and body in the hours and minutes leading up to competition. You should mentally rehearse a refocusing technique that you can use at any time to rid yourself of distracting thoughts and feelings. You are now ready for the performance of your life!

Exercise and sport psychology is not infallible. It is unrealistic to think that athletes can totally avoid choking. John McEnroe, the great tennis champion, has said that choking is inevitable—that at some time every athlete falls victim to the mental pressure of the situation. Athletes should acknowledge that choking can occur and then be prepared in case it happens. Optimizing mental skills does not mean that athletes can control everything that happens to them, but it does means that they can learn to respond in productive ways when bad things do happen to them.

—Robin S. Vealey

ries of motivation is that *people are motivated to feel competent, worthy, and self-determining.* From birth, we all try to be competent in our environment. As our lives continue, our need to be competent is channeled in various areas through socialization. Thus, people differ in their motivation to achieve certain things.

Several important factors fuel this intrinsic motivation to be competent and self-determining. First, we all feel competent for different reasons. Research in exercise and sport psychology has shown that individuals have different goals for achievement and that to truly understand motivation we must understand how each person defines success or competence for him or herself. Another important factor that influences motivation is what psychologists call perceptions of control. Humans are motivated to be self-determining, which means we want to be in control of our own actions and behavior. Individuals with more internal perceptions of control are more motivated than individuals who feel others control them or that they are lucky.

Two important psychological constructs that affect motivation are self-esteem and self-confidence. Self-esteem is our perception of personal worthiness and the emotional feelings associated with that perception. Many psychologists view self-esteem as the most central core component of our identity, and thus it has a major influence on our motivation in sport and exercise. Self-worth or self-esteem is an important need for all individuals and it emanates from feeling competent and in control of our behavior in an achievement area that is important to us. The literature emphasizes that self-esteem is the direct result of social interactions, so social support and positive reinforcement for individual mastery attempts are crucial to the development of self-esteem. Self-confidence is also a critical factor in motivation and is similar to perceived competence. Athletes who feel more competent and self-confident are motivated to work harder to perform better in their sport. As with self-esteem, if we lack confidence in our ability, we need elaborate extrinsic incentives to motivate us.

Feedback and reinforcement can be used in a positive way to enhance peoples' feelings of competence, which then increases their intrinsic motivation. This area, called behavior modification, has been developed from animal research in psychology and deals with how the use of reinforcers influences human behavior. The fundamental assumption of behavior modification is that behaviors are strengthened when they are rewarded and weakened when they are punished or unrewarded. Extrinsic rewards are common in sport, such as trophies, scholarships, and even large salaries in professional sports. Research indicates that extrinsic rewards given in competition may serve to weaken or undermine existing intrinsic motivation. If the extrinsic rewards associated with competition are perceived as controlling by individuals, then intrinsic motivation decreases as individuals feel less self-determining.

Motivation involves intensity of behavior and the urge to be competent and successful. It is easy to see, then, that for some people this motivation, which was once positive and enjoyable, turns into anxiety and becomes stressful. The popular notion of "psyching up" by athletes refers to their levels of arousal, which is defined as physical and psychological readiness to perform. Think of arousal as a specific state of motivation in a particular situation. A popular misconception is that you can never be too motivated or highly aroused, but research has shown that high levels of arousal can hurt performance. Studies have shown that arousal is related to performance in a curvilinear or inverted-u model, which means that as arousal increases, performance increases to an optimal zone, after which further increases in arousal hurt performance. Optimal arousal is very personal—every individual has a unique optimal arousal zone. Another consideration in arousal is the type of task a person is performing. Complex and precise physical activities, such as putting in golf or shooting in archery, require lower levels of arousal for optimal performance as compared to those that use gross motor skills, such as football blocking or playing soccer.

When arousal passes the optimal zone, it usually becomes anxiety. Anxiety, then, is simply a negative response to a stressful situation in which athletes feel apprehension and threat to their self-esteem. Individual sport activities, such as wrestling and gymnastics, have been shown to elicit higher anxiety levels than competitive team sport activities, such as softball and basketball. This is because, with no teammates, athletes feel more personal pressure to perform well. This phenomenon carries over to competitive nonsport activities as well.

Stress and anxiety are not synonymous. Stress is defined as a perceived imbalance in what a person thinks he can do and what the situation demands, when the outcome matters. Much intervention in sport psychology focuses on reducing athletes' perceptions of stress, most of which, in sport, is based on fear of failure and fear of evaluation.

Interpersonal and Group Processes

Sport psychology also looks at interpersonal or group processes that influence individuals' behaviors, such as the presence of spectators, group membership, and leadership. Also, aggression and gender socialization result from interpersonal social processes.

Since the start of the 20th century, researchers have been fascinated with the effects of an audience on human performance or social facilitation. Findings suggest that the presence of other people increases our arousal, which then may hurt or help our performance.

Generally, spectators have a negative effect on someone who is learning a skill and a positive effect on someone who is very skilled. It is not the *mere* presence of others that causes this effect, but rather peoples' perceptions that they were being *evaluated* by others. Researchers have also documented the "home advantage," which shows that teams playing at home sites win a greater percentage of the time as compared to playing at away sites. However, the *reasons* for this home advantage are less clear and could even be attributed to expectancy, a self-fulfilling prophecy.

Group dynamics focuses on how being a part of a group influences performance as well as how psychosocial factors influence group behavior. Groups perform better, and group members are more satisfied, when they are cohesive, that is, they stick together and remain united in pursuing goals. Cohesion is facilitated by emphasizing uniqueness or a positive identity related to group membership and also when individual team members understand and accept their role within the group.

Also of interest in group dynamics is how group membership influences individual performance. Social loafing refers to a decrease in individual performance within groups. Individuals believe their performance is not identifiable and responsibility is diffused within the group. Social loafing, studies show, is easily reduced by monitoring performance and so making individuals more identifiable.

Effective leadership—influencing individuals and groups toward goals—influences sport participation enormously. Early research in this area sought a set of traits that defined effective leadership. This proved inconclusive; rather, leadership involves a process of interaction unique to a situation, depending on the characteristics of the athletes and those of the leader.

The social processes of competition in Western society are often seen as leading to aggression in sport—behavior directed toward inflicting harm or injury onto another person. In competitive situations, frustration inevitably fuels aggression. Frustration often results when a person's goals are blocked and, in competitive sport, the main objective is to block the goal achievement of the opponent. Social learning theory views aggression as a learned behavior. Thus, ice hockey players are glorified for fighting with opponents, and baseball players are encouraged and even expected to charge the mound and go after the pitcher if hit by a pitched ball. Research also links aggression to levels of moral reasoning. Athletes have lower levels of moral reasoning and so view aggression as more legitimate, compared to

nonathletes. It is popularly believed that competition reduces aggressive impulses in humans by providing a release or purging of aggression (called catharsis). However, studies suggest that aggressive tendencies *increase* after competing, engaging in vigorous physical activity, or watching a competitive event. Thus, competitive and physical activity participation and spectatorship do not serve as a catharsis for aggressive responses.

The social processes of gender formation and maintenance have been studied extensively, with important implications for sport behavior. A popular myth is that differences in the thoughts, feelings, behaviors, and physical performance capacities between males and females are biologically based. This explanation ignores the social complexity and variations in gender-related behavior and performance. However, males and females overlap substantially on *all* motor skills. This means that although the most highly trained male is stronger than the most highly trained female, some females are stronger than many males. Thus, although our society loves to assume that all females and males are stereotypically grouped according to popular beliefs about limits of sport and exercise performance, males and females actually are more similar than they are different. And most of the gender differences that *are* apparent in sport behavior are based not on biology, but rather on the differential socialization patterns of girls and boys, which typically advantage boys in terms of opportunity, support, and expectations for sport proficiency.

Gender differences are also assumed and have been found on various psychological characteristics such as self-confidence, aggression, and competitiveness. These differences, however, develop over time and are influenced by rigid gender socialization. Much gender research has not considered socialization and thus has reinforced existing and limiting gender stereotypes. Sport is a very sex-typed area; popular culture views it as more appropriate for males than females. This view exerts powerful socialization influences on young girls in deciding whether or not to participate. It is no coincidence that girls become less active in sports and physical activity at puberty, when society gives them the message that they now should focus on more "appropriate" activities in preparation for womanhood.

Intervention Techniques for Exercise and Sport
Often called mental training or psychological skills training, intervention techniques are used to learn behavioral strategies (e.g., goal setting) and cognitive skills (e.g., self-talk) that can enhance exercise and

sport behavior. Intervention techniques may be used to improve sport performance, develop important life skills for young people participating in physical activity, aid in rehabilitation from injury and disease, and enhance career transition and retirement from sport. Intervention strategies aim to maximize the chances of achieving "flow," or peak performance. Flow occurs when our abilities match the challenge of the situation, so effective goal setting allows individuals to plan and focus on specific challenges that push them to achieve based on personal ability levels.

Goal setting is used to focus on specific attainable behaviors presented as difficult yet reachable goals. Goals are most effective if they are difficult and systematically monitored and evaluated. Also effective in goal-setting is the use of short-term goals as progressive steps toward reaching a long-term goal and emphasizing on performance or controllable goals over outcome.

Self-talk, or personal statements that we all make to ourselves, also works as an intervention technique. There are many variations of this technique, but the basic premise is that what we say to ourselves drives our behaviors. The goal of effective self-talk is to engage in planned, intentional productive thinking that convinces your body that you are confident, motivated, and ready to perform. Athletes are taught to identify key situations or environmental stressors that cause them to "choke" and then plan and mentally practice a refocusing plan that can be used to focus attention appropriately in that situation.

Attention control and focusing is perhaps the most important cognitive skill at the point of sport competition. Athlete's performance depends on the cues they process from themselves and the social and physical environment. Self-talk strategies such as "centering" allow athletes and exercisers to select relevant cues and design physiological (e.g., deep breaths) and psychological (e.g., feeling strong, quick, and confident) triggers to best focus attention.

Imagery is using all the senses to create or re-create an experience in your mind or a mental technique that "programs" the mind to respond as desired. Imagery enhances motor performance, studies show, and although it cannot replace physical practice, it is better than no practice at all. Elite athletes regularly use imagery and is often cited as an important mental factor in their success. Novice athletes can use imagery to create positive mental blueprints of successful performances, while exercisers can use imagery to visualize their muscles firing and getting stronger during fitness training.

Physical relaxation techniques are used to teach individuals to control their autonomic functions, including muscular and hormonal changes that occur during sports and exercise. These techniques allow individuals to engage in physical activity with much greater mastery and control over how their bodies respond to competitive stimuli. Some physical relaxation techniques include breathing exercises, muscular tension-relaxation, and various types of meditation. For example, athletes can learn how to regulate physiological arousal by reducing their heart and breathing rates to induce a more relaxed state. Physical relaxation techniques can be used in conjunction with goal setting, imagery, and self-talk to optimize both physical and cognitive readiness to perform.

In summary, sport psychology, a young science, has only begun to scratch the surface of understanding the thoughts, feelings, and behaviors related to participation in physical activity. But the knowledge base that has developed over the last three decades is impressive as research continues to study personality, motivation, group processes, and intervention techniques related to sport.

—ROBIN S. VEALEY

Bibliography: Cox, R. H. (1994) *Sport Psychology: Concepts and Applications.* 3d ed. Madison, WI: Brown & Benchmark. Griffith, C. R. (1928) *Psychology and Athletics.* New York: Scribner's. Harris, D. V., and B. L. Harris. (1984) *The Athlete's Guide to Sports Psychology: Mental Skills for Physical People.* New York: Leisure Press. Horn, T. S., ed. (1992) *Advances in Sport Psychology.* Champaign, IL: Human Kinetics. LeUnes, A. D., and J. R. Nation. (1989) *Sport Psychology: An Introduction.* Chicago: Nelson-Hall. Martens, R. (1987) *Coaches Guide to Sport Psychology.* Champaign, IL: Human Kinetics. Martens, R., R. S. Vealey, and D. Burton. (1990) *Competitive Anxiety in Sport.* Champaign, IL: Human Kinetics. Murphy, S. M. (1995) *Sport Psychology Interventions.* Champaign, IL: Human Kinetics. Orlick, T. (1990) *In Pursuit of Excellence.* Champaign, IL: Human Kinetics. Orlick, T., and J. Partington. (1988) "Mental Links to Excellence." *Sport Psychologist* 2: 105–130. Salmela, J. H. (1992) *The World Sport Psychology Source Book.* 2d ed. Champaign, IL: Human Kinetics. Smoll, F. L., and R. E. Smith. (1996) *Children and Youth in Sport: A Biopsychosocial Perspective.* Madison, WI: Brown & Benchmark. Vealey, R. S. (1994) "Current Status and Prominent Issues in Sport Psychology Intervention." *Medicine and Science in Sport and Exercise* 26: 495–502. Weinberg, R. S., and D. Gould. (1995) *Foundations of Sport and Exercise Psychology.* Champaign, IL: Human Kinetics. Williams, J. M., ed. (1993) *Applied Sport Psychology: Personal Growth to Peak Performance.* 2d ed. Mountain View, CA: Mayfield.

Race Walking

Race walking is a sport in which some part of the foot must always be in contact with the ground. An Olympic sport since 1906, it is now practiced for fitness and recreation as well.

Race walking began in London in 1897. Since 1906, walking races have been a part of the Olympic track-and-field program and in 1919 the London-to-Brighton walking race (about 86.1 kilometers or 53.5 miles) had become an annual event, with women first participating in 1932. In the 1950s and 1960s a walking craze swept Great Britain, and hundreds of people, sometimes individually or in sponsored competitions, raced the length of the country.

The race walking world championship, the Lugano Trophy, was instituted in 1961. This biennial contest awards points to the first three walkers (from teams of four) in both the 20-kilometer (12.5-mile) and 50-kilometer (31-mile) races, and the point total determines team position. Race walking has long been plagued by the problem of "lifting," that is, the competitor's failure to keep at least one foot in contact with the ground throughout a race. Between 1956 and 1984, a series of controversies and disqualifications resulted.

Recently, race walkers have taken to ultramarathon distances. Malcolm Barnish's 1985 feat of walking 663.17 kilometers (412.08 miles) nonstop set a world record. It took him 6 days, 10 hours, and 32 minutes. From 10 June 1970 to 5 October 1974, American David Kunst walked and walked and walked. He became the first person to circumambulate the globe.

In the 1990s, the old-fashioned sport of race walking became part of the fitness fad because of its use in cardiorespiratory conditioning.

—Scott A. G. M. Crawford

Bibliography: Race Walking Association. (1962). *The Sport of Race Walking*. Ruislip, UK: Race Walking Association.

Racquetball

Once dubbed "high-speed tennis in a box," with heated rallies and diving retrievals, racquetball is one of the world's fastest racquet sports.

History

Racquetball was invented in 1949 in Connecticut by Joe Sobek, who designed the first short strung paddle, devised rules combining the basics of handball and squash, and named his modification "paddle rackets." The sport caught on quickly and by the early 1970s had spread across the nation.

Racquetball proved perfect when the fitness craze hit and Americans began searching for new and challenging athletic activities. The sport peaked in the mid-1980s, ebbed, then after 1987 regained its steady growth. Currently, some 9 million U.S. players enjoy the sport each year.

The first racquetball world championship was held in 1981 and one year later the United States Olympic Committee officially recognized the American Amateur Racquetball Association (AARA) as the national governing body for the sport. The International Amateur Racquetball Federation was founded in 1979; a decade later, the federation dropped the word "amateur" from its title and is now as the International Racquetball Federation (IRF).

Racquetball Is Fitness

Racquetball is fitness of the highest order. From the first serve, racquetball offers many of the benefits sought by today's fitness-conscious individuals in their exercise regimens, such as:

Caloric Consumption: A one-hour game of racquetball burns roughly 700 calories of energy (High Tech Fitness 1986). This equates to more calories per hour than aerobics, cycling at 29 kilometers per hour (18 miles per hour), circuit weight training, playing basketball, or playing tennis and as many as running an 8-minute, 30-second mile. The caloric consumption attributed to racquetball makes it an ideal sport for weight maintenance.

Total Body Muscle Tone: Since racquetball involves usage of all the major muscle groups (leg, trunk, arm, back, stomach) it is an excellent vehicle for developing and maintaining muscle tone.

Cardiovascular: During one hour of recreational play, the average player will run approximately two miles. During this time the player's heart rate increases and is maintained at 70–80 percent of its maximum. This provides a low-level cardiovascular fitness program, especially for lower-level players, and a cardiovascular maintenance program for more skilled and advanced players.

Balance and Coordination: Racquetball offers an excellent way to improve hand-eye coordination. In an aging society this is an important additional benefit of an exercise program not available in nonsport activities.

Flexibility: The tremendous range of motion required to participate in racquetball forces a certain amount of stretching, with resultant flexibility. Many participants also utilize a pre- and post-game stretching program.

—*Linda L. Mojer*

Rules and Play

Racquetball may be played by two or four players (doubles). The objective is to win each rally by serving or returning the ball so the opponent is unable to keep the ball in play. A rally is over when a player is unable to hit the ball before it touches the floor twice, return the ball so that it touches the front wall before it touches the floor, or when a hinder is called. Only the serving side may score. Losing the serve is called a sideout in singles. A match is won by the first side winning two games. The first two games of a match are played to 15 points. If each side wins one game, a tiebreaker game is played to 11 points.

Racquetball, a lifetime sport, is one of the best activities for aerobic development and used for conditioning in many Olympic sports. A tournament-level player burns more than 800 calories per hour.

Racquetball is now a full medal sport in the Pan American Games, the Central American Games, the Pacific Rim Championships, the South American Games, and the Bolivian Games. With increasing exposure to a previously untapped market of recreational players combined with the sport's track record of steady annual growth and the promise of becoming an Olympic event, racquetball is well positioned for the future.

—LINDA L. MOJER

Bibliography: Adams, L., and E. Goldbloom. (1991) *Racquetball Today*. St. Paul, MN: West Publishing. Mojer, Linda L., ed. (1990–). *Racquetball Magazine*. Colorado Springs, CO: Luke St. Onge/American Amateur Racquetball Association.

Rafting

Rafting races and competitions are generally either local or specialized events. Whitewater rafting was incorporated, for example, into Eco-Challenge, the multisport endurance marathon. Rafting has also been included and televised as part of "extreme sports" events. Rafting is a general term for the use of specific types of water craft. In general, rafts are broader and flatter than canoes and other vessels. Inflatable rafts are made of flexible chambers that become buoyant when filled with air.

Since the 1960s rafting has gained popularity as a recreational activity, particularly inflatable rafts that are used on calm lakes and streams or near beaches. Rafts are also used to navigate further out in oceans and bays. They are frequently used on fast-running rivers, a sport called white-water rafting or river running (see Canoeing and Kayaking).

Like canoes, rowboats, and other craft, most rafts have passenger compartments and are powered and steered by paddles, oars, or motors. Rafting differs from other types of boating primarily in the way the crafts handle. They create more drag in the water and require more power to propel. They are generally less responsive to turns than canoes or rowboats. However, they are stable and otherwise easy to control. Inflatable rafts can carry groups and are frequently used for commercial river tours and white-water expeditions.

The most inexpensive of the many inflatable rafts are simple in design and generally made of lightweight rubber and other material. Less responsive and more easily damaged, these are better suited to safe conditions.

Other rafts are designed and built for rigorous conditions. These are made of durable reinforced materials, such as nylon and neoprene. They also have more complex designs and features for added strength, safety, and handling. They often feature numerous individual air chambers. Rafts have also been developed that closely resemble canoes and other craft and have similar handling characteristics.

—JOHN TOWNES

See also Canoeing and Kayaking; Extreme Sports.
Bibliography: Armstead, Lloyd D. (1990) *Whitewater Rafting in Western North America.* Chester, CT: Globe Pequot Press.

Recreation
See Leisure

Religion

Today every major league baseball club and more than 100 minor league teams arrange nondenominational religious services each Sunday morning at the ballpark before the afternoon game. Approximately 50 percent of all major league players attend these sessions of prayer, Bible reading, and homily. As the Fellowship of Christian Athletes and other evangelical sports groups thrive, chaplains have become a fact of modern life for professional sports teams of all kinds.

Displays of piety abound at every level of sport and in every discipline, from amateur high schoolers to elite professionals, from the golf course to the boxing ring. Signs with biblical references sprout like mushrooms among the fans; coaches and athletes participate in highly visible pregame and postgame prayer, in pious gestures of supplication, and in televised nods to God for games won. Religion and sport march hand in hand, each reinforcing the other.

Old Gods and Games

Although now manifest in a uniquely modern form, this union of religion and sport is nothing new. Excepting rare moments of antagonism, sport has always been closely aligned with religious mythology and ritual. Through ceremonial dances and competitive games, the ancients sought to appease their deities in order to win fertile wombs, good crops, successful hunts, and victorious wars. Native Americans surrounded various kinds of ball games and foot races with religious ritual; Central American Mayans and Aztecs built elaborate stone courtyards adjacent to their religious temples.

Ancient religious myths often explained the origins with stories about competitive games. For example, some Central and South Americans accounted for the existence of the sun and moon with a tale about a ball game that took place at the dawn of civilization. Twin brothers challenged the gods to a game. The brothers lost the game, then their heads on the sacrificial altar. One of the heads was placed in a tree, and it began spurting a stream of sperm when a young virgin passed that way. Impregnated, the girl bore twins. Once they were grown to young manhood, the twins challenged the gods to yet another ball game. This time the gods lost the game, whereupon the severed heads of the two original twins ascended into the heavens and became the sun and the moon.

Ancestor worship joined fertility rites to produce funeral games in honor of deceased kinsmen and chieftains; commemorative festivals kept fame alive. In a portrayal of Greek life around 1000 B.C.E., Homer's *Iliad* gives a richly detailed account of some funeral games held in honor of a Greek soldier slain in battle at the gates of Troy. As young warrior-athletes engaged in chariot races, boxing and wrestling matches, and discus and javelin throws, they affirmed life in the face of death.

In Homer's rendition, the gods took active interest in the events. Like modern athletes who chalk up wins or losses to "the will of God," those ancient young Greeks blamed or praised the gods depending on the contest's outcome. An archer supposedly missed his target because he had failed to promise Apollo a sacrificial offering. Presumably, Apollo begrudged him victory. When a chariot driver dropped his whip in the midst of a race, he blamed Apollo for knocking it out of his hand but thanked the goddess Athena for helping him retrieve it. As early as 1000 B.C.E., athletes looked to the heavens for assistance. Eager to win the prize for a foot race, Odysseus charged down the stretch praying to Athena, "O goddess, hear me, and come put more speed in my feet!" Hundreds of local religious-athletic festivals thrived around the Greek-influenced rim of the Mediterranean, each one in honor of a Greek god. They appealed to Artemis to help them in the hunt, to Poseidon when they sailed the seas, to Aphrodite in matters of love. The Greeks firmly believed that all the gods, whatever their specialty, looked with favor on the male warrior virtues of physical strength, agility, and endurance, skills best taught and practiced in athletic contests. By the 5th century B.C.E., four major festivals dominated the Greek athletic circuit: (1) the Pythian Games at Delphi in homage to Apollo, (2) the Isthmian Games honoring Poseidon at Corinth, (3) the Nemean Games in Nemea, and (4) the Olympic Games at Olympia, the latter two in the name of the mighty Zeus.

Sport and Character.

The ball has just fallen again where the two sides are thickest, and they close rapidly around it in a scrummage: it must be driven through now by force or skill, till it flies out on one side or the other. Look how differently the boys face it. Here come two of the bull-dogs, bursting through the outsiders; in they go, straight to the heart of the scrummage, bent on driving that ball out on the opposite side. That is what they mean to do. My sons, my sons! you are too hot; you have gone past the ball, and must struggle now right through the scrummage, and get round and back again to your own side, before you can be of any further use. Here comes young Brooke; he goes in as straight as you, but keeps his head, and backs and bends, holding himself still behind the ball, and driving it furiously when he gets the chance. Take a leaf out of his book, you young chargers. Here comes Speedicut, and Flashman the School-house bully, with shouts and great action. Won't you two come up to young Brooke, after locking-up, by the School-house fire, with "Old fellow, wasn't that just a splendid scrummage by the three trees!" But he knows you, and so do we. You don't really want to drive that ball through that scrummage, chancing all hurt for the glory of the School-house - but to make us think that's what you want - a vastly different thing; and fellows of your kidney will never go through more than the skirts of a scrummage, where it's all push and no kicking. We respect boys who keep out of it, and don't sham going in; but you - we had rather not say what we think of you.

Then the boys who are bending and watching on the outside, mark them - they are most useful players, the dodgers; who seize on the ball the moment it rolls out from amongst the chargers, and away with it across to the opposite goal; they seldom go into the scrummage, but must have more coolness than the chargers; as endless as are boys' characters, so are their ways of facing or not facing a scrummage at football.

—Thomas Hughes, *Tom Brown's Schooldays*
(London: Macmillan, 1857).

Reckoned to be a vigorous warrior god who cast thunderbolts like javelins from the sky, Zeus bestrode the Greek Pantheon just as surely as the Olympic Games dominated the athletic circuit. Sometime around 1000 B.C.E., myth and ritual established him the patron deity at Olympia. The actual origins of the Games are unknown, but one legend depicts Zeus and a rival god, Cronus, engaged in a wrestling match in the hills above Olympia. Zeus won, inspiring religious ceremonies and quadrennial athletic contests as testimonies to his prowess. By the supposed authority of Zeus, athletes, trainers, and spectators were guaranteed safe passage every four years to Olympia, even in times of war.

Once they arrived at Olympia, athletes had to swear by Zeus that they had been in training for the past 10 months and that they would play fair and obey all the rules. If they broke their oaths, they were required to pay fines, which went toward the building of statues in honor of Zeus. During the 5th century B.C.E., a huge temple was erected of local limestone for the worship of Zeus. Shortly thereafter the most famous sculptor of the day, Phidias, constructed a magnificent statue seven times larger than life, encased in gold, silver, and ivory. It had Zeus sitting on a throne in the inner chamber of the temple. Admirers thought it one of the Seven Wonders of the World; critics complained about its outlandish size. If Zeus stood up, they noted, he would poke his head through the roof.

Of the five-day program of Olympic events fixed during the 5th century B.C.E., athletic contests consumed only two and a half days. The entire first day was devoted to religious rituals—a kind of prolonged opening ceremony when religion mattered more than patriotism or commercial glitz. Athletes and their trainers offered oaths, prayers, and sacrifices to Zeus. They presented gifts at the statues of past Olympic victors who had been deified, at the shrines of various lesser gods, and especially at the altars and statues of Zeus. Well into the first evening, Olympic participants marched in solemn processions and sang hymns of praise and devotion.

Then came a full day of athletic contests: chariot races and horse races in the morning, the pentathlon (discus and javelin throws, a broad jump, a sprint, and wrestling) in the afternoon. At sunset, however, attention shifted back to religious activities. By the light of a midsummer full moon, a ram was slain and offered as a burnt sacrifice to the accompaniment of prayers and hymns. The following morning, priests led Olympic judges, Greek city-state officials, athletes and their kinsmen, and trainers in a colorful procession to the altar of Zeus, where 100 oxen were ceremoniously slain. The oxen's legs were burned in homage to the gods; their carcasses were roasted for a big banquet on the last day of the festival.

However, long before the Greek Olympics ended in the 5th century C.E., faith in the old gods waned to such an extent that Olympia's religious trappings lost much of their original meaning. Other gods beckoned in the Greco-Roman world. The Romans largely took their gods from the Greeks, changing merely the names. In Roman hands, Zeus became Jupiter, but Jupiter was never associated with competitive sport. Although Rome's "bread and circus" days were also based on ancient religious festivals, religion and sport momentarily parted company in the brutality of the Colosseum and amid the gambling frenzy that surrounded the Circus Maximus.

Sport and Spire

Early Christians largely accepted Greek athletics. The apostle Paul frequently mentioned them to illustrate the spiritual race to be run and the incorruptible prize to be won by Christians. Roman sport was another matter. For well over two centuries, Christians were unwilling participants in Roman spectacles. Thrown into the arena as punishment for their unorthodox religious beliefs, they inevitably lost the Lions-versus-Christians game. Yet, even when the persecution ceased, Christians continued castigating Roman sport's "pagan" basis, its open association with gambling and prostitution, and its inhumane brutality.

With the collapse of the Roman Empire, the interaction of religion and sport shifted to northern Europe. Ancient games such as German *kegels* (bowling), French *soule* (association football), and the stick-and-ball games of Irish hurling and Scottish shinty all had religious associations akin to the competitive fertility rites of Native Americans. Light toyed with darkness, warmth with cold, and life with death in the pre-Christian mythologies of Europe. Muslims enlarged the pot in the 8th century when they brought old Egyptian fertility rituals across the narrow neck of the Mediterannean into Spain. For several centuries Muslim, Christian, and pre-Christian practices blended harmoniously, especially around the annual rites of spring renewal that Christians called Easter.

Various forms of ball play became integral to Easter season ceremonies all over Europe. Colorfully garbed French priests near Paris chanted a traditional liturgy and passed a ball back and forth as they danced down the church aisle celebrating springtime signs of Christ's resurrection. An archbishop near Lyon regularly led a ball game immediately after an Easter meal. As late as 1165, a theologian at the University of Paris protested church-sponsored ball play at Poitiers and Rheims. It derived from old pagan customs, he insisted. He was right, of course, but no one seemed to share his alarm.

The medieval church provided a time for parishioners to play. For six days of the week peasants and household servants worked. On Sunday they were expected to worship at the village church, yet no puritan pall hovered over Sunday. After the morning sermon and sacraments, villagers lounged or played in the afternoon. Since the church's holy days aligned with ancient seasonal holidays, villagers also played at festive occasions around Easter, during the harvest season, and at Christmastime. Italians regularly scheduled *palio* (horse races) on several of their many saints' days; each spring in England, peasant football thrived around the food, drink, music, and dance of Shrove Tuesday, just before the onset of Lenten austerity.

The church provided space as well as time for play. In those villages that had no commons, the churchyard or cloisters often served as the venue for mass recreation. Spires and stained-glass windows served as backdrops for wrestling matches, juggling exhibitions, and board games. A 14th-century English clergyman unintentionally admitted the popularity of these practices when he attempted to banish "dancing, playing at quoits [throwing iron rings onto a peg, similar to the American frontier game of horseshoes], bowling, tennis-playing, handball, football, stoolball, and all sorts of other games" on church property.

Medieval football, an ill-organized, uncodified game with no physical boundaries or limits on team size, required open countryside. That land was also owned by the church and rented out to wealthy landlords, who traditionally turned it over to peasant sport shortly before spring crop-planting and just after the autumn harvest. English and French clergymen frequently complained about property being damaged by hordes of drunken football players. A few critics pointed to the roughness of the game. In 1440, for example, a French bishop denounced football as a "dangerous and pernicious" activity that caused "ill feeling, rancor and enmities" under the guise of "a recreation pleasure." He forebade football games within his diocese. Medieval church leaders looked more benignly on upper-class sport. Like modern ministers who cater to early Sunday morning golfers, priests happily dispensed "quickie" communions at the break of dawn to aristocrats eager to get to the fields for hunting and hawking. Bishops sat jowl to jowl with the castle crowd at ceremonious jousting contests. Churchmen especially looked with favor on royal ("real") tennis, for the game apparently originated with French monks, abbots, and priests in monastic and church cloisters as *le jeu de paume* (literally, palm game). Players hit a small ball with their open hand over a rope stretched across the middle of the space available. They played the ball off walls and onto sloping roofs that efficiently kept the ball in play. According to legend, a French king visited a monastery, saw a game of tennis, and so admired that he had it copied in his royal palace. The term *tennis court* probably derives from the game's early location in the courts of European monarchs.

Renaissance churchmen enthusiastically linked tennis to the Renaissance ideal of well-balanced mental and physical skills. The Christian humanist, Desiderius Erasmus, a former monk, lauded tennis as an ideal game for exercising all parts of the body; England's Cardinal Thomas Wolsey arranged the construction of an indoor tennis court for King Henry VIII at Hampton Court. An Italian monk, Antonio Scaino da Salo, produced a treatise in 1555 that established the first simple set of written rules, a standard court size, and a scoring system. Tennis was "the most appropriate sport for the man of letters," Scaino insisted.

Puritans Make Their Mark

Protestant reformers gave a more mixed message about sport. Martin Luther encouraged his followers to participate in "honorable and useful modes of exercise" such as dancing, archery, fencing, and wrestling. For his own exercise, Luther engaged in the old German game of bowling. When the bowling ball banged against the pins, it reminded him of the Christian's duty to knock down the Devil. John Calvin, too, enjoyed bowling. He also played quoits, but he was critical of most other sports. Zealously devoted to the task of cleaning up the morals of the city of Geneva, he saw sport as a hindrance to holy living. Most games seemed too intimately associated with carnal pleasure on the one hand, idleness on the other. Competitive games also meant gambling and desecration of the Christian Sabbath, two of Calvin's great taboos. For Geneva's public policy as well as for private piety, Calvin was quite prepared to lump most sports with thievery and prostitution, and to ban them all.

Protestant exiles from England, Scotland, and Holland flocked to Geneva, where they imbibed Calvin's ethical mandates as well as his theological beliefs. Most of all, they partook of his supreme self-confidence derived from believing that each human being acts as an agent of divine redemption before acquiring eternal bliss. Returning home, they put their shoulders to the task of moral reform. English Calvinists led the way. Their zealous crusade to purify both church and society provoked people to call them Puritans.

This sect represented no monolithic bloc of opinion or practice. They often disagreed with each other over specific evils that needed to be eradicated, and ministers sometimes preached one thing, while their congregations did something else. When a puritanical preacher denounced "wakes or feasts, may-games, sports and plays, and shows, which trained up people to vanity and looseness, and led them from the fear of

Sunday Baseball.

The East Side Terrors were playing the Slashers,
Piling up hits, assists and errors.
Far from their stuffy tenement homes
That cluster thicker than honeycombs
They ran the bases 'neath shady trees
And were cooled by the Hudson's gentle breeze.

Mrs. Hamilton - Marshall- Gray,
Coming from church, chanced to drive that way.
She saw the frolicking urchins there,
Their shrill cries splitting the Sabbath air.
"Mercy!" she muttered, "this must stop!"
And promptly proceeded to call a cop,
And the cop swooped down on the luckless boys,
Stopping their frivolous Sunday joys.

Mrs. Hamilton - Marshall - Gray
Spoke to her coachman and drove away
Through beautiful parks and shady roads
Past splashing fountains and rich abodes.
Reaching home, she was heard to say
"How awful to break the Sabbath day!"

The Terrors and Slashers, side by side,
Started their stifling Subway ride
Down through the city, ever down
To the warping walls of Tenement Town.
Reaching their homes, the troublesome tots
Crept away to their shabby cots,
And thought of the far off West Side trees
And the cool green grass, and the gentle breeze,
And how they had played their baseball game
Till the beautiful Christian lady came.
—William Kirk, "Sunday Baseball,"
Baseball Magazine 6, 1 (May 1908): 29.

God," one could be sure that many people in England were still finding pleasure in these traditional pastimes.

Popular or not, folk games closely resembled old pre-Christian fertility rites and Roman Catholic holy days, inspiring the Puritans all the more to suppress them. They first tried moral preachments in the home, at church, and in the marketplace. When sermonizing met with negligible success, they went after the political means of reform. Much like the recent political moves of the radical right in the United States, English Puritans in the early 17th century put themselves forward as city councilors, mayors, and members of Parliament. They also seized positions of power in the army, and rode that horse to victory in a civil war that appropriately began while King Charles I was on the links of Leith, near Edinburgh, playing golf.

Briefly in power for a decade or so during the mid-17th century, the Puritans appointed army officers to serve as guardians of public morality. They struck at the heart of old church festivals and folk games by leveling fines and imprisonment against any display of public intoxication or gambling and against any desecration of the Sabbath. People, however, clung to their playful ways. Rigid prohibitions occasionally stirred hostile protests. According to a report from an Essex village, when the local Puritan vicar began the Sunday morning service in the parish church, "the people did usually go out of church to play at football, and to the alehouse and there continued till they were drunk, and it was no matter if they were hanged."

This rural resistance to Puritan reform finally triumphed. English villagers continued living out their lives in seasonal cycles with periodic festivals and games compensating for times of intense agricultural labor. Puritanism, largely confined to urban merchants and business classes for whom moral discipline and the work ethic made sense, did revive in Victorian England, but it was much too ethically rigorous for the more traditional, casual life of pre-industrial England. In the end, only the Puritan Sunday survived the Restoration of 1660. Until late in the 20th century, Sunday became sacrosanct in a fashion uniquely English, free of public amusements and sports as well as commercial activity.

Puritanism also met with mixed success in the English colonies of North America. Passions waxed and waned against activities reminiscent of old village pastimes. Moreover, in their prohibitions against gambling and Sunday amusements, New England divines were joined by Pennsylvania Quakers and New Netherlands Dutch Calvinists. Only those diversions that demonstrably led to the fulfillment of one's "call" to work found favor in earnest American eyes. Eighteenth-century Bostonian John Adams phrased it best: "I was not sent into this world to spend my days in sports, diversions, and pleasures." "I was born for business; for both activity and study." The Great Awakening, a religious revival in the mid-18th century, produced an even dimmer view of sports, as did the Second Great Awakening early in the 19th century.

Muscular Christianity

Rapid industrial and urban growth fostered a reassessment of the relation of religion and sport in Victorian England and the United States. Medical as well as moral concerns prompted liberal Anglicans Charles Kingsley and Thomas Hughes (author of *Tom Brown's Schooldays*) to articulate a "muscular Christianity" for Britain; Boston Unitarians Edward Everett Hale and

Thomas Wentworth Higginson did the same in the United States. All the while, a new international organization, the Young Men's Christian Association (YMCA), added health programs and competitive sport to its pietistic, evangelical purposes.

Sport and recreation programs became central to the social gospel espoused by turn-of-century liberal churches. Ministers as diverse as Washington Gladden, a Congregationalist pastor in Columbus, Ohio, and William S. Rainsford, rector of St. George's Episcopal Church on the Lower East Side of New York City, nudged their churches to sweeten the gospel with church gymnasiums and bowling, softball, and basketball teams sponsored by the church. The movement for urban parks and public playgrounds, too, stood high on the social gospel agenda.

In Chicago, social gospel was primarily associated with the Roman Catholic Church. By 1910, Chicago's Catholics boasted the largest church-sponsored baseball league in the United States; two decades later, Bishop Bernard J. Sheil founded the Catholic Youth Organization, to use boxing and basketball to prevent juvenile delinquency. During the 1920s, a nearby little Catholic college, Notre Dame, emerged as a national football power. Religious and sport mythology mingled freely in the virtual canonization of All-American halfback George Gipp and coach Knute Rockne.

For American Jews, too, religious traditions blended with the immigrant need to adopt sport as a means of Americanization. Jews especially took to the favorite immigrant sport of prizefighting, frequently with the Star of David emblazoned on a boxer's trunks. Less predictably, they also competed enthusiastically in the YMCA game of basketball, particularly around New York City. To become fully American, however, the "national pastime" of baseball was essential. Many Jewish authors feature baseball games and allusions to the game in their stories. Two Jewish baseball stars—Hank Greenberg in 1934 and Sandy Koufax in 1965—established themselves as ethnic heroes by refusing to play ball on the Jewish holy day of Yom Kippur.

Until shortly after World War II, Protestant evangelicals refrained from mixing religion and sport. Southern Baptists and Methodists especially had a long history of hostility toward competitive sports. They saw college athletic contests as occasions for raucous partying; they viewed professional sport as a Yankee invention for purposes of gambling, strong drink, and desecration of the Sabbath. After 1945, however, southerners took the lead in yoking sports to evangelical Protestantism. North Carolinian Billy Graham initiated the practice of having star athletes publicly "share" their conversion experience. Graham appropriately thought of his evangelistic organization as a "team" and frequently used sports stories and metaphors in his sermons. For purposes of association as well as mere space, he selected famous sports venues like Yankee Stadium and Madison Square Garden for his early crusades.

Mixed with Cold War rhetoric and a market mentality that hawked Jesus as if he were a breakfast cereal or bar of soap, this marriage of sport and born-again religion produced several new organizations. Sports Ambassadors (founded in 1952), the Fellowship of Christian Athletes (1954), and Athletes in Action (1966) are merely the top three of many booster groups that capitalized on athletics as a means of winning converts to Christ. These organizations catered primarily to high school and college athletes, but, by the 1960s, the evangelical spirit had also invaded professional locker rooms. It began with National Football League (NFL) teams, then moved to major league baseball. By 1975, every major professional football and baseball team employed a chaplain or at least scheduled religious services of worship prior to Sunday games.

A small but prominent group of athletes have turned from Judeo-Christian traditions to a Black Muslim allegiance to Allah. Heavyweight champion Cassius Clay led the way in the 1960s, changing his name to Muhammad Ali. College basketball giant Lew Alcindor similarly converted to Islam and took the name Kareem Abdul Jabbar. In 1995, boxer Mike Tyson emerged from prison wearing the garb and speaking the language of Islam. Racial pride apparently weighs heavily in the decision to become a Black Muslim.

Religion has certainly weighed heavily in the history of sport through the ages. Religious folk have frequently supported and even lauded sport as a cohort that supports social cohesion and moral principles. Sometimes they have protested sport's specific violations of current religious principles; occasionally they have lambasted sport in its entirety. Yet never have religion and sport been totally separate or indifferent to each other.

—WILLIAM J. BAKER

Bibliography: Baker, William J. (1988) Sports in the Western World. Urbana: University of Illinois Press. Higgs, Robert J. (1995) God in the Stadium: Sport and Religion in America. Lexington: University of Kentucky Press. Hoffman, Shirl J., ed. (1992) Sport and Religion. Champaign, IL: Human Kinetics. Levine, Peter. (1992) Ellis Island to Ebbets Field: Sport and the American Jewish Experience. New York: Oxford University Press. Novak, Michael. (1976) The Joy of Sports: End Zones, Bases, Baskets, Balls, and the Consecration of the American Spirit. New York: Basic Books. Oriard, Michael. (1993) Sporting with the Gods: The Rhetoric of Play and Game in American Culture. New York: Cambridge University Press. Prebish, Charles S. (1993) Religion and Sport: The Meeting of Sacred and Profane. Westport, CT: Greenwood.

Rifle Shooting
See Shooting, Rifle

Ritual
"All sports," wrote the German scholar Carl Diem on the very first page of his two-volume history of sports, "began in cult." This is an overstatement, but Diem was right to remind our more or less secular age that many sports began as religious ceremonies and many others have acquired ritualistic aspects. A ritual can be defined as any regularly repeated action that is felt by the actor to be significant beyond its material purpose. Sacrificing a heifer on the altar of the goddess Athena was a religious ritual, even if the meat was subsequently eaten; slaughtering a steer at the Chicago stockyard is a very different kind of action. Although the most important rituals are communal events of shared significance, like the inauguration of a president, people also have their private rituals, meaningful to them and to no one else, like the wearing of red socks. Within the realm of sports, a second distinction is useful. Sports events can be associated with rituals that are not, strictly speaking, necessary. If no one sang "The Star-Spangled Banner" before the first pitch of a baseball game, the players would nonetheless be playing baseball. Sports can also *be* rituals, which is very different. The ancient runners who raced the length of the stadium at Olympia performed a religious act in honor of Zeus. Without the presence of the god in the minds of the runners and the spectators, there might have been an athletic contest, but that contest would not have been a part of the Olympic Games. We can speak, in short, of sports *with* ritual and sports *as* ritual. We must acknowledge, however, that many sports events are both. In practice, it is often difficult to distinguish between the two.

There is no better example of sports *as* ritual than the pre-Columbian stickball game played by the tribes of the southeastern United States. The earliest reference to the game by a European was by Pierre François Charlevoix, who observed the Creek version of the game in 1721. In all probability, Charlevoix witnessed a ceremony that was centuries if not millennia old. Stickball changed very little between 1721 and the early 19th century, when the ethnographic painter George Catlin visited the area and recorded his impressions in his *Letters and Notes on the Manners, Customs, and Conditions of the North American Indians* (1844).

Resembling modern lacrosse, which grew from the Canadian version of stickball, the game played by the Creeks, Choctaws, and Cherokees was a contest between two teams, each using webbed sticks to hurl a small ball across their opponents' goal line. Villages were matched against one another and there were also intracommunal contests. Although women had their own very similar ball games, only men played ritual stickball. Each player submitted to strict dietary prohibitions based on religious considerations. "The Cherokee Ball Play," an essay published in 1890 in *American Anthropologist* by the ethnographer James Mooney, provides fascinating details.

Mooney reported that the Cherokee participants "must not eat the flesh of a rabbit . . . because the rabbit is a timid animal, easily alarmed and liable to lose its wits when pursued by the hunter. Hence the player must abstain from it, lest he too should become disconcerted and lose courage in the game. He must also avoid the meat of the frog . . . because the frog's bones are brittle and easily broken." The dietary taboo lasted for exactly twenty-eight days prior to the contest because four and seven were sacred numbers. As in many ritual sports, the most important taboo was against sexual intercourse. Thirty days of abstinence preceded the game, a good deal longer than the period stipulated for modern athletes by their superstitious coaches. Men whose wives were pregnant were thought to be endangered by pollution. They were not allowed to take part in the Cherokee stickball game.

The players spent the night before the game sequestered in a sacred precinct under the supervision of medicine men who carefully prepared them for the ritual encounter. Of the Choctaw medicine men, Catlin wrote that they were "seated at the point where the ball was to be started." While the players danced and "joined in chants to the Great Spirit," the medicine men smoked pipes as a form of prayer. Kendall Blanchard, whose *Mississippi Choctaws at Play* (1981) is our best modern source, notes that these "ritual experts . . . administered special medicine to the players, treated equipment, manipulated weather conditions for the day of the planned event, and appealed to the supernatural world for assistance." The night before the game, the bodies of the players were painted and appropriately adorned for appearance before the Great Spirit. In Catlin's words, "In every ball-play of these people, it is a rule . . . that no man shall wear moccasins on his feet, or any other dress than his breechcloth around his waist, with a beautiful bead belt, and a 'tail' made of white horsehair or quills, and a 'mane' on the neck, of horsehair dyed of various colors."

Mooney has a detailed account of the Cherokee ritual dance that was performed the night before the game.

The dancers are the players of the morrow, with seven women, representing the seven Cherokee clans. The men dance in a circle around the fire, chanting responses to the sound of a rattle carried by another performer, who circles around on the outside, while the women stand in line a few feet away and dance to and fro, now advancing a few steps toward the men, then wheeling and dancing away from them, but all the while keeping time to the sound of the drum and chanting the refrain to the ball songs sung by the drummer, who is seated on the ground on the side farthest from the fire. . . . The women are relieved at intervals by others who take their places, but the men dance in the same narrow circle the whole night.

At intervals, the players left the dance to accompany the medicine men to the river bank for elaborate ceremonies with sacred red and black beads representing the players and their opponents.

Among the other pregame rituals described by Mooney was scarification, performed by a medicine man with a seven-toothed comb made from the leg bone of a turkey. Twenty-eight scratches (four times seven) were made on each arm above the elbow and then below, on each leg above the knee and then below. More gashes were made on the breast and the back. When the medicine man was done, the player bled from nearly 300 wounds.

The game itself was played on a field without strict boundaries. The two goals, which consisted of two posts side by side or lashed together, might be 100 feet or several miles apart. There were no side lines. Teams varied from as few as 20 men to the 600 or so whom Catlin observed and painted. The game itself, in the Choctaw version, was accompanied by drums, by frenzied betting, and by female spectators who encouraged their men by lashing their legs with whips. During the game, rival medicine men rushed up and down the field and employed mirrors to cast reflected light, believed to be a source of strength, upon their respective teams (a tactic overlooked by modern coaches).

What significance was attributed by the players to their communal ritual? Stewart Culin, author of *The Games of the North American Indians* (1907), ventured an answer in an essay he contributed to Frederick W. Hodge's *Handbook of American Indians* (1907). "The ceremonies," wrote Culin, "appear to have been to cure sickness, to cause fertilization and reproduction of plants and animals, and . . . to produce rain. . . . The ball was a sacred object, not to be touched with the hand, and has been identified as symbolizing the earth, the sun, or the moon." About one thing we can be sure; the men who played the game and the women who watched it considered the pregame rituals to be an indispensable part of the entire ceremonial event. We can also be sure that the actual contest was thought to be just as infused with religious significance as the dances and the scarification that preceded it. Indeed, the convenient distinction between the "pregame" ceremonies and the "actual game" is a modern imposition. For the Cherokees, Choctaws, and Creeks the ritual actions of the medicine men were as much a part of the game as the attempt to fling the ball across the goal line.

Compared to the rituals of pre-Columbian stickball, those associated with modern sports are relatively simple. Football, for instance, has the raucous pregame pep rally, the solemn locker room prayer session, and the leggy antics of the cheerleaders; boxing has its portentous introductions and the ceremonial touch of the gloves that supposedly links pugilism with the medieval tournament. The Olympic Games are an exception to the rule. They were revived in 1896 by a man who was keenly aware of the importance of ritual.

In 1894, Pierre de Coubertin introduced his plan to revive the Games at a conference held at the Sorbonne in Paris. The ceremonies at the conference were not an instance of ritual (because they were a unique event), but they do demonstrate Coubertin's typical strategy. To persuade a skeptical audience that the ancient games had a modern relevance, he overwhelmed them with classical associations. The hall in which the conference took place was decorated with murals by the 19th-century neoclassical painter Puvis de Chavannes. Music was provided by the composer Gabriel Fauré, who orchestrated the ancient "Hymn to Apollo," and by Jeanne Remacle of the Opéra Française, who sang Fauré's composition. In his speech, which reminded the delegates of the glories of Greek civilization, Coubertin presented a vision of the Olympic Games as an instrument of international reconciliation. Coubertin's proposals were enthusiastically accepted, and he was authorized to form an International Olympic Committee.

The Olympic Games offered Coubertin ample opportunity to indulge his sense of ritual. He was personally responsible for many of the most striking ritual elements of the modern games. The opening ceremonies are a medley of these elements. Central to these ceremonies is the "parade of nations." The athletes might have been grouped by sports rather than by nations, but neither Coubertin nor his successors dared to make that symbolic gesture toward cosmopolitanism. Each team is preceded by its national flag, proudly carried by one of its athletic heroes. The Greek team is the first to enter the stadium because the modern games are a revival of the ancient games celebrated at Olympia (and because Athens hosted the first games of the modern era). The team representing the host nation marches last. Between the first and last teams come those of all the other participating nations.

Once the thousands of athletes are assembled on the grass within the 400-meter track, the Olympic flag, which Coubertin designed, can be hoisted. This flag, with its simple pattern of five linked rings, is among the world's most widely recognized symbols. The rings interlock because they are meant as an image of human interdependence. Their five colors and their white background were chosen by Coubertin to represent the many colors of the world's national flags.

The ritual of the Olympic torch was introduced in 1936 by Carl Diem, the German scholar quoted for his belief that all sports originated in religious cult. Diem was the mastermind of the organizing committee for the 1936 Games, which were held in Berlin. The torch is lit at Olympia, the site of the ancient games. (Although television commentators persist in placing the ancient games on Mount Olympus in northern Greece, Olympia was actually in the south.) From Olympia, the torch is passed from hand to hand until it reaches the site of the Games. The last runner, who is always a male or female athlete from the host nation, has the honor of lighting the Olympic torch. (The drama of this and other Olympic rituals is captured in Leni Riefenstahl's documentary film *Olympia* [1938].) An athlete from the host nation takes the Olympic oath, symbolic doves are released, the Olympic hymn is played, and the host nation's head of state solemnly declares the games to be open. (The single sentence of this declaration is undoubtedly the shortest speech Adolf Hitler ever made.) The spectators, having been suitably edified by a great deal of idealistic symbolism, are entertained by song and dance. By custom, many if not most of the songs and the dances are representative of the culture of the host nation. At Los Angeles in 1984, for instance,

George Gershwin's music and Native American dances were much in evidence.

During the Games, the most obvious ritual is the victory ceremony. Although the Olympic Charter claims that the Games are contests among individuals and not nations, nationalism pervades the ceremony. Some of the symbolism is so obvious that we are hardly conscious of it. The victor's medal is gold rather than silver or bronze because gold has always symbolized the most "noble" of metals. The victor's spot on the podium is elevated above those of the other medal winners because spatial positions are also metaphorical. Higher is higher. Some of the symbolism is obvious and controversial. While no one advocates that the victors receive a leaden medal or that they sit on the grass to receive it, many critics have lamented the playing of national anthems and the raising of national flags. Criticism has been ineffectual because the patriotic emotions unleashed by this ritual are greatly cherished. Although weeping is not really an Olympic ritual, it is nonetheless customary for even the hardiest athletes to have tears in their eyes as the anthem plays and the flag rises.

The closing ceremony has become almost as elaborate as the opening ceremony. One ritual was introduced by the athletes rather than by the Olympic officials. At Melbourne in 1956, the athletes, who were grouped into the traditional national teams, broke ranks, left their positions, and joined in a spontaneous festival of international fellowship. They sang and danced, embraced and hugged, and created a cherished event that actually does more to symbolize de Coubertin's dream of international reconciliation than any other Olympic ritual.

Private Rites

The premodern rituals of pre-Columbian stickball and the modern rituals of the Olympic Games are both communal. Sports have also had their share, and probably more than their share, of private rituals. These vary as widely as people do. There are athletes who cannot compete if they put on their right shoe before their left. Others are disconcerted and uncoordinated if they forget their bubble gum. Some kiss their spouse before they depart for the stadium (left cheek, right cheek, forehead, chin, lips—in that order and none other). Some close their eyes, dispel thoughts of marital bliss, and concentrate on the contest.

John Wooden, legendary basketball coach at the University of California, Los Angeles (UCLA), the man who led the university to seven successive National Collegiate Athletic Association (NCAA) championships, nicely exemplifies the pervasiveness and oddity of private ritual.

He performed an invariant pregame ritual. Before every contest, he won the favor of the gods by turning to wink at his wife (who always attended the game and always sat directly behind him), by patting the knee of his assistant coach, by tugging at his socks, and by leaning over to tap the floor. Only he knew the exact significance of these symbolic behaviors, but we can assume that Wooden believed them to be necessary adjuncts to his instructions in dribbling, passing, and shooting.

The more we look, the more we see. Unlike many premodern sports, modern sports are not rituals, but they are surrounded by them, embedded in them, and enriched by them.

—ALLEN GUTTMANN

Bibliography: Guttmann, Allen. (1978) *From Ritual to Record: The Nature of Modern Sports.* New York: Columbia University Press. MacAloon, John J. (1981) *This Great Symbol: Pierre de Coubertin and the Origins of the Modern Olympic Games.* Chicago: University of Chicago Press.

Rock Climbing

Rock climbing is a sport elusive of definition; different from mountain climbing, "scrambling," and hiking, rock climbing is generally distinguished by its structure, with climbs of recognized gradations of difficulty and danger.

History

Systematic rock climbing in Europe began in the late 18th and 19th centuries as naturalists ascended cliffs in search of specimens. Britain lays claim to the origins of both mountain and rock climbing. The first ascent in 1886 of Napes Needle in England's Lake District by W. P. Hasket Smith (1859–1946) is often designated the start of rock climbing. However, many climbs were completed and recorded before then, and a great deal of training for mountain climbing was occurring in Europe. Rock climbing became a sport in its own right toward the end of the 19th century.

In the mid-20th century, British climbers led an exponential leap in the difficulty of routes being climbed. This British dominance lasted through the 1960s, when an American style of big wall climbing (a mix of "free" and "aid") became the gold standard. By the 1970s climbers were developing a new style of French climbing in the Verdon Gorge and other areas. The French style of climbing is incredibly gymnastic in its difficulty but involves little danger because of the preplacement of closely spaced expansion bolts for protection.

Competitive speed climbing was developed in the Soviet Union and Eastern Europe, but never accepted in the West. However, the notion of competition and its commercial possibilities, combined with the new French style of climbing (in which climbers were beginning to find commercial sponsors), resulted in the development of "sport" climbing competitions. Competitions soon moved indoors onto artificial climbing walls with movable holds. Today, there is a fairly successful Grand Prix circuit and numerous local competitions.

Rules and Play

A normal, roped climb on rock or ice occurs with two climbers moving one at a time. The first climber sets off, reaches a point where he or she is able to secure him- or herself to the rock ("a belay"), and takes in the slack rope as the second person begins climbing. This ensures safety in case of a fall. The process continues as the second climber then belays, and pays out the rope to the first climber as he or she climbs the next "pitch" (roughly a rope length or the next convenient point for a belay). All such devices are known collectively as "protection." If protection does not damage the rock (as do pitons or expansion bolts) and is only used for safety, the technique is known as "free" or "clean" climbing. When protection is actually used by the climber to assist his or her progress, the technique is known as "aid" or "artificial" climbing.

Four factors determine the difficulty of a climb. The first is the actual difficulty of the moves the climb will require. Is the climb vertical or overhanging? Is there only one difficult move or many? "Exposure" refers to the danger of one's position on a climb. Third is the availability of places to put protection and the type of potential landing site. Moves that may result in a long fall onto sharp rocks are considered more difficult than if they could result in a relatively short fall onto sand. Length of a climb is fourth.

Various systems are then used to rate the climb. These include the Yosemite Decimal System, which uses a scale of difficulty from Class 1 (walking) to Class 5 (various levels of climbing); the Joshua Tree System, a simplified version of the National Climbing Classification System that runs from F1 to F15; the British system, which rates activity from "Easy" (scrambling) to "Exceptionally Severe"; and the Australian System, which puts difficulty at levels 1 through 29.

Although rock climbing has no institutionalized competitive structure, the sport functions much like others. The two specific types of competition are direct and indirect. Direct competition involves achieving the first ascent of mountains or of specific routes on mountains, cliffs, and frozen waterfalls. Direct competition also considers the first recorded ascent and such variations as first solo, first female, first all-female, or first winter ascent. Indirect competition is based on the style or quality of an ascent. It may refer to speed, but is usually considered in terms of how closely the ascent follows climbing's informal rule structure.

The system of rules and conventions that govern both direct and indirect competition is known to climbers as "ethics" and is socially constructed and sanctioned. Ethics are created and changed by consensus among climbers through face-to-face interaction and specialist magazines, transmitted by the same means, and enforced by both self-discipline and social pressure.

In the hierarchy of climbing, the most ethically difficult prohibits all equipment and tactics. Expeditions are the simplest in ethical terms because almost any equipment and tactics are allowed. A climber who follows the current rules of the game is climbing with "good style." Fast ascents are admired, particularly on the higher mountains since speed is related to safety.

The notion of competition and its commercial possibilities, combined with the new French style of climbing (where climbers were beginning to find commercial sponsors), brought "sport" climbing competitions in which climbers competed to see who could reach the greatest height on an increasingly difficult climb before falling off (to be held on the rope by a belayer).

The French style of climbing also came to be known as sport climbing. Together with top rope climbing at the rapidly expanding and popular climbing gymnasia, it has become the way in which many young people are introduced to the sport today.

The clash of sport climbing and "adventure" climbing, its more traditional and less technology-dependent predecessor, has produced rock climbing's most difficult ethical crisis. Sport climbing involves rapid institutionalization, commercialization, and many new climbers unaware of the traditions. It has also altered the risk-versus-difficulty equation that has characterized the sport for most of its history. Increasing technical difficulty in rock climbing was always tempered by climbers' willingness to increase their risks. The new styles eliminate much of the risk in the equation.

An uneasy truce now exists. Many climbers cross over between the sport and adventure styles. Certain locations have been mutually accepted as being for sport climbing only or adventure climbing only (others are in dispute); and many lifelong adventure climbers recognize the attraction of competitions. Blends of the two styles have produced an enormous variety of ethics, minutely debated by local climbers. This suggests that climbing is still in the hands of climbers and has not yet been taken over by bureaucrats or commercial interests.

—PETER DONNELLY

Bibliography: Tejada-Flores, L. (1967) "Games Climbers Play." *Ascent* 1: 23–25. Unsworth, W. (1992) *Encyclopaedia of Mountaineering*. London: Hodder & Stoughton. Wilson, K. (1981) *Hard Rock*. 2d ed. London: Granada Publishing.

Rodeo

Rodeo is an anglicized version of the Mexican *charreada* that developed in the western cattle country during the post–Civil War era. Rodeo events are timed events, in which athletes try to beat the clock, and rough stock events, in which athletes attempt to ride a bucking animal for a specified time.

History

All rodeo events except women's barrel racing have counterparts in the *charreada,* although American steer wrestling differs radically from the Mexican *cola* (bull tailing). *Charro* contests came to the United States with the cattle business and transmitted from Mexican *vaqueros* to Anglo and black cowboys along with the skills, terminology, and costumes of the range. Ranch-versus-ranch rodeos and informal contests among ranch hands helped spread the competition throughout the western United States and Canada.

Western fairs and holidays often featured rodeo and *charro* contests, in which individuals of diverse ethnicities competed for prizes. The closing of the frontier commercialized rodeo; western communities sought to perpetuate their heritage. Buffalo Bill Cody gets credit for staging both the first professional rodeo and the first Wild West show at North Platte, Nebraska, on 4 July 1882. Hoping to show spectators scenes from life in the "real West," Cody hired cowboys, Indians, and Mexican ropers and riders to reenact stagecoach robberies, war dances, a buffalo hunt, and Pony Express rides. Cody then became a Wild West show entrepreneur rather than a rodeo producer, while western communities followed his lead in developing contest rodeo into a viable sport. Rodeo and Wild West shows coexisted for the next 30 years, with most professionals active in both. The international popularity of the Wild West shows did much to create the audience for professional rodeo. The term *rodeo* did not become standard until after World War I; prior to that time the contests had various

names, including Frontier Days, Stampedes, Cowboy Contests, and Roundups.

Early rodeos were much more diverse than today's counterparts. Women, Hispanics from both the United States and Mexico, Native Americans, and African Americans participated. Native Americans competed in events reserved only for those who camped on the rodeo grounds and entertained the crowds, but were also free to enter the other contests. Bill Pickett (1870–1932), an African American cowboy from central Texas, gets credit for inventing bulldogging or steer wrestling. Rodeo and *charreada* were quite similar until after World War I, when the *charreada* was reorganized into an amateur team sport while rodeo remained an individual, professional sport.

Rodeo provided a hand-to-mouth living for most. Many early hands had unsavory reputations for drinking and carousing, which made rodeo unwelcome in some communities. The economic outlook improved with the introduction of the Madison Square Garden Rodeo in 1922. Its success spawned a series of lucrative eastern rodeos that capped off the season and provided top hands with large paydays, but also led to the gradual demise of races, novelties, and trick and fancy competitions because of space limitations.

Rodeo lacked structure, but fraud thrived. Unscrupulous promoters advertised staged events as legitimate contests, and "bloomers," who collected entry fees, gate receipts, and services for their rodeos, then fled during the final go-round, leaving local businesses and contestants unpaid. These problems led western producers in 1929 to form the Rodeo Association of America.

By the end of World War II, Gene Autry (1907–), the Hollywood singing cowboy, transformed rodeo. Autry purchased most of the major rodeo companies during the 1940s. Stressing pride, patriotism, and masculinity, he produced elaborate rodeos, with only six or seven contests.

In 1948, a group of Texas women founded the Girls' Rodeo Association (GRA), later renamed the Women's Professional Rodeo Association (WPRA), and began working with both local rodeo committees and the PRCA to ensure cowgirls a place in the sport. In 1955, WPRA President Jackie Worthington (1924–1987) and PRCA President Bill Linderman (1920–1965) signed the agreement ensuring that all women's contests at PRCA rodeos would have the WPRA sanction. Cowgirl barrel racing quickly became a standard contest at most PRCA-sanctioned rodeos. To provide women opportunities to compete in roping and rough stock

All-Girl Rodeos

An exciting new kind of rodeo, the all-girl rodeo, began in Texas in 1942. These were originally designed to entertain American troops while enabling cowgirls to compete in roping and rough stock riding events as they had in the 19th century. They also provided women opportunities to produce and officiate rodeos, which they had rarely done in the past. Fay Kirkwood (1900–?) organized the first all-girl rodeo at the Fannin County Fair Grounds in Bonham, Texas, from 26 to 29 June. Huge crowds and enthusiastic community support characterized the event. Locals compared Kirkwood's promotional efforts to those of nationally known producers and judged them superior. Kirkwood staged a second rodeo at Wichita Falls in July and August, while veteran cowgirl Vaughn Krieg (1904–1976) produced her own successful contest at Paris, Texas, in September. Both women intended to continue, with Krieg planning a nationwide tour, but World War II precluded this.

The contests resumed when two west Texas women, Thena Mae Farr (1927–1985) and Nancy Binford (1921–), produced their own all-girl rodeo at Amarillo, Texas, from September 23 to 26 September, 1947. Part of the annual Tri-State Fair, the rodeo enlisted 75 contestants from 25 states. Standing-room-only crowds set an arena attendance record, and reporters pronounced the producers ready for Madison Square Garden. Binford and Farr then incorporated Tri-State All-Girl Rodeo to produce additional contests. They maintained the practice of having all aspects of their rodeos handled by women, including the first female professional rodeo clown, Dixie Reger Mosley (1939–). Binford and Farr's effort also led to the formation of the WPRA in 1948.

Over 20 all-girl rodeos took place in 1950 alone, as the contests spread from Colorado to Mississippi. Soon men began producing all-girl rodeos. Although their publicity efforts paled in comparison to the women's, and they often employed males in a variety of capacities, they helped spread the sport. Regrettably, Binford and Farr left business at the end of the 1951. This was a major loss, as they alone produced contests for women organized exclusively by women with women's special needs in mind. Events like theirs have been quite rare in women's sport history and never again existed in professional rodeo. Subsequently these unique rodeos declined in popularity; often no more than three a year played to sparse crowds in remote arenas. Today the Women's Professional Rodeo Association sponsors only a few all-women rodeos, including their National Finals, in which cowgirls can rope and ride rough stock like their foremothers. A promising aspect of Americana has almost vanished, and few remember the record crowds and glorious publicity that characterized all-girl rodeos in their heyday.

—Mary Lou LeCompte

events, the WPRA sanctioned all-women rodeos. Extremely popular in the late 1940s and the 1950s, today these contests draw limited crowds, making prize money insufficient to meet expenses.

In 1959, the first National Finals Rodeo (NFR) took place at Dallas, Texas. The NFR, run by the PRCA itself, is now America's premier rodeo, and certainly the richest. Commercial sponsorship has become increasingly important since 1971 when the R. J. Reynolds Corporation contributed over $100,000 in cash prizes. Today, numerous sponsors and television contracts enrich successful contestants.

Rules and Play

Rodeo features timed events, in which the athletes try to beat the clock, and rough stock events, in which athletes attempt to ride a bucking animal for a specified time. The most popular timed events are steer wrestling, calf roping, steer roping, team roping, and barrel racing, or riding a circuitous path around barrels without toppling them. Steer and calf ropers try to rope the animals, jump from their horses, and tie the animals so they remain tied for a specified time. Team ropers work in pairs, the header roping the front of the animal, the heeler the rear. Steer wrestlers must jump from their horses, grab the steer's horns, and wrestle it to the ground. Animals get a head start, and contestants must stay behind a barrier until released or be penalized.

Rough stock events include bull riding, saddle bronc riding, and bareback bronc riding. In Professional Rodeo Cowboys Association (PRCA) rodeos, riders must stay on the animals for eight seconds. Those who succeed receive scores from the judges, who award scores of 0 to 50 points to both the animal and the rider, for a possible high score of 100 points.

The PRCA is the richest and most powerful of the multiple rodeo associations. It sanctions seven events, plus women's barrel races. Most organizations regulate attire; many conduct drug tests.

Local rodeo committees are the lifeblood of the sport. They pay sanctioning fees to the appropriate governing bodies and hire approved stock contractors, judges, announcers, clowns, and barrel men. For many small western communities, the annual rodeo is the biggest event of the year, and the Fourth of July is the biggest rodeo day in America. World champions are typically decided at a finals rodeo.

Animal rights is the biggest issue facing rodeo; activist groups have attempted to abolish the sport (humane societies have voiced objections since the late 19th century). Activists successfully lobbied state legislatures to outlaw certain contests, such as steer roping. The PRCA has responded with educational programs and legislation. They now have over 60 rules, endorsed by the American Veterinary Medical Association, to protect livestock. Rodeo, in fact, is much more dangerous to humans than animals.

Rodeo outside the United States

American rodeo is popular with international audiences. The 1887 European tour of Buffalo Bill's Wild West Show generated great enthusiasm, and the many Wild West shows and exhibition rodeos that followed left pockets of interest on every continent except Antarctica. Ultimately, many equestrian, cattle-raising cultures devised their own similar sports rather than copying the U.S. model. American-style rodeo is practiced primarily in the United States, Canada, Australia, and New Zealand.

While recalling a simpler time, major contests are sophisticated productions featuring computerized entry systems and electronic timing. Rodeos have long drawn big crowds in the major eastern cities. But rodeo's appeal to the eastern urban spectator is much the same as the appeal of western films: nostalgia for a mythical past and a chance to see "real cowboys" in action.

—Mary Lou LeCompte

Bibliography: Fredriksson, Kristine. (1985) *American Rodeo.* College Station: Texas A&M University Press. Johnson, Cecil. (1994) *Guts: Legendary Black Rodeo Cowboy Bill Pickett.* Fort Worth, TX: Summit Group. LeCompte, Mary Lou. (1993) *Cowgirls of the Rodeo: Pioneer Professional Athletes.* Urbana: University of Illinois Press. Pointer, Larry. (1985) *Rodeo Champions: Eight Memorable Moments of Riding, Wrestling, and Roping.* Albuquerque: University of New Mexico Press. Slatta, Richard W. (1990) *Cowboys of the Americas.* New Haven, CT, and London: Yale University Press.

Roller Skate Sailing
See Sailing, Icewing and Roller Skate

Roller Skating
See Skating, Roller

Rounders

Rounders was originally a nine-per-side bat-and-ball game from which the game of baseball evolved. It is thought to be a precursor to baseball because it combines elements of striking a ball and running around posts (bases) before scoring a rounder (run).

History

Rounders evolved from the early play of 18th-century participants into a game that accompanies most of the major ball games played in Britain. With some variations the Irish version of rounders is similar to softball. An early reference to rounders appeared in *A Little Pretty Pocket Book,* published in 1744, where it was called base-ball. Many of the rules for base-ball appeared in *The Boy's Own Book* by W. Clarke in 1829. The first official use of the term "rounders" appeared in 1856. It became sufficiently popular to have created the National Rounders Association in 1943.

Rules and Play

Rounders can be modified to accommodate various numbers of players, settings, areas, and conditions, but its official playing area is called a pitch. Four posts, each 1.2 meters (3 feet, 11 inches) high are placed at the corners of the running track. The bowling square is approximately 2.5 meters (8 feet, 2 inches) square and is 7 meters (23 feet) from the second post. The wooden bat, called a "stick," is round with a maximum length of 46 centimeters (1 foot, 6 inches) and a circumference of 17 centimeters ($6^3/_4$ inches) at its thickest. The hard-cored, leather-covered rounders ball should weigh approximately 70 to 85 grams ($2^1/_2$ to 3 ounces).

Rounders is a two-inning, nine-per-side game with the team hitting the ball called the "ins" and the other the "outs." Each side has two innings to score as many rounders (runs) as possible; the side with the most wins. An inning ends when all the batters are out. A team leading by 10 or more rounders during its first inning may invite the other team to "follow on" by taking its second inning immediately after the end of the first.

Customary player positions include a backstop who is directly behind the batsman, one fielder at each post, three deep fielders, and a bowler. The bowler, or pitcher, must deliver the ball from the bowler's square with a continuous and smooth underarm action, similar to a softball pitch. The ball is to be delivered to the hitting side and within reach of the batsman in the area between the player's head and knees.

A batsman scores a rounder if the ball is hit out of the fielders' reach, allowing him or her to run around the track and outside each of the first three posts and reaching the fourth post before being put out. A rounder can also be scored if the batsman takes a no ball and is not caught out while running around the track. A "half rounder" is scored if the player completes the circuit without hitting the ball or if the track is completed from the first post after the ball comes back into the forward area following a backward hit. A penalty "half rounder" is given to the batting team if the bowler pitches three consecutive no balls to the same batsman or if he or she is obstructed by a fielder.

A batsman has three chances to hit the ball; at the third failure the player is bound to run to the first post and take the chance of not being hit by the ball. After hitting a fair ball (i.e., one that stays in the play area) the batsman must run to the first post.

An "out" is accomplished if a fielder tags the batsman out while he or she remains in the batting square or is running around the track after hitting the ball, missing a good ball, or taking a no ball while both feet are outside the bowling square.

Quick-paced and physically demanding, rounders has remained popular with schoolchildren.

—DEAN A. ZOERINK

Bibliography: Gomme, Alice Betha, ed. (1964). *The Traditional Games of England, Scotland, and Ireland.* Vol. 2. New York: Dover Publications.

Rowing

The fluid strokes, high endurance, and mental discipline required for racing combined with the peaceful environment of rivers and lakes define the sport of rowing. Rowing is also known for its frail skinny "shells" that blend high technology with Old World craftsmanship.

History

Rowing followed the discovery that long oars moving against a fulcrum so that their blades could push ships through water were far more efficient than paddles. Its beginnings were harsh: more than 2,000 years ago the Greeks and Romans chained criminals and slaves to their mighty warships to power the heavy oars.

As rowing evolved, the social status of rowers rose. The Egyptians used ferrymen to transport nobility along the Nile, and the Vikings of Norway rowed the longboats they used for the their voyages of discovery. Gradually rowing became a trade, practiced by "watermen."

Competition followed as races became popular features of village celebrations, with fishermen, ferrymen, and even galley ships as the competitors. Meanwhile, the world began to expand beyond the Mediterranean, demanding longer voyages over open water, and sails first supplemented and then replaced oars.

By the 1700s the practice of rowing was almost entirely confined to ferrying goods or people along or across rivers and harbors. Nowhere was this more apparent than on the Thames River in England; there rowing began to take on the trappings of a sport.

Competion in England began in1716 when a grateful actor endowed a race for the apprentice watermen of the Thames who had ferried him back and forth for years. The race takes place each summer, a 7.8-kilometer (4 mile, 7 furlongs) course between the London and Chelsea Bridges. In the United States, racing began 50 years later among ferrymen in New York harbor. By 1850 racing in the United States had spread to Philadelphia, Detroit, and San Francisco.

Collegiate racing followed quickly. In England, the first Oxford and Cambridge race took place over a 3.2-kilometer (2-mile) course at Henley in 1829; in the United States, Harvard and Yale competed for the first time in 1852 on New Hampshire's Lake Winnepesaukee. It became known as "crew" because teams used four- and six-man shells.

Mid-19th-century rowers were primarily brawny ferrymen who in their spare time rowed for the pride of winning. Between 1850 and 1890 rowing competitions became particularly popular in the United States. Legions of professional rowers found racing to be far more lucrative and enjoyable than taxiing passengers or rowing cargo along rivers and across harbors, and competed for purses of up to $1,000.

The sliding seat spurred the growth of rowing. This major technological innovation enabled them to use their legs, the body's strongest muscle group, to provide most of the power. A few years later the swivel oarlock further refined rowing by allowing rowers to take much longer strokes than the thole pins used previously.

By 1900, beset by scandal, professional racing had all but disappeared. Collegiate rowing, faced with more accidents and higher costs, could not sustain its momentum in the early 1900s.

Yet rowing continued at such larger institutions as Yale, Harvard, the University of Washington, Pennsylvania, Navy, and Syracuse. These schools switched to the eight-oared shell with coxswain, thus minimizing the collisions. U.S. crews proved powerful in international competition. From 1920, American eights won eight successive Olympic gold medals. After 1960, West Germany and Eastern European countries dominated rowing.

In Europe, hundreds of rowing clubs provided the point of entry for participants. As a result, in spite of the interruption of World War II, the sport steadily attracted participants who were nurtured by the clubs. In contrast, rowing in the United States lost ground during the 1950s and 1960s. Although still a revered tradition at the larger institutions, it had become too exclusive to engage great numbers of people. By 1970, rowing had little new blood to keep it going.

Two developments in the early 1970s, both unexpected, ushered in a renaissance that is continuing through the 1990s. In the late 1960s, Arthur Martin (1917–1990), a naval architect from Maine, designed what came to be known as the Alden Ocean Shell. He was persuaded to manufacture 20 of the boats, which were introduced to the market in 1971. They sold. The Alden has elements of racing shell, canoe, and kayak, and became the shell for every rower. With little instruction, older women and older men could row it; it needed no boathouse, and initially cost under $1,000.

The Alden identified a market for so-called "recreational" shells, and several other shell manufacturers responded. Many rowers learned on Aldens, then gradually moved into racing shells.

Women had rowed in small numbers. After 1962, with the formation of the National Women's Rowing Association, the pace quickened, but with the passage of Title IX (mandating equal funding for women's sports) women's rowing took off. Today more women than ever are entering the sport and sticking with it. Women's rowing was introduced at the 1976 Olympics. Today estimates are that nearly half of all rowers are women.

Internationally, rowing has also experienced growth, particularly since 1984. Between 1984 and 1995, membership in the Fédération Internationale des Sociétés d'Aviron grew from 55 to 98 nations.

Rules and Play

Rowers pull their oars against a fulcrum, known as a rigger, to plant the blades in the water and send the shell through the water. The sliding seat differentiates rowing as a sport from rowing a rowboat as transportation. Good rowers are powerful but never rough, with no jerks in the stroke cycle. When they row as a crew they move their bodies in near perfect unison. Most power comes from the legs and the transition between the drive of the legs and the follow-through of the back should be smooth. Oar blades should enter the water at a 90-degree angle with little splash.

The "stroke rate" of a boat is the number of strokes per minute. Most eights sprint at the start of a race with a beat of 38 to 44 strokes per minute and then "settle" during the body of the race to 32 to 36. Watched most closely is the teamwork in rowing and how precisely the rowers' oar blades enter and exit the water together and how precisely they move their slides to the stern of the boat as they recover from the last stroke and prepare for the next. The coxswain faces forward, sitting opposite the first oarsman, who is called the "stroke." Together they orchestrate the performance, with the

---

The Legacy of Professional Rowing

Rowing historian Thomas C. Mendenhall observes that despite the scandals, the professional rowers in the late 19th century created a valuable legacy for the sport in America. He praises them for perfecting the skill of "watermanship" in small boats and for their contributions in teaching rowing to clubs and colleges in the early decades of the 20th century.

In the longer run, he wrote in 1980, "the fate of the professional sculler was one reason why rowing's history proved quite different from that of other sports in this country." His point was that rowing, unlike hockey, football, or basketball, never again became professional or big-time entertainment. Instead, it developed the reputation of being a sport purely for amateurs.

That reputation was underscored with the publication in 1985 of a book entitled *The Amateurs*, by David Halberstam, himself a rower. Describing the competition to represent the United States in rowing at the 1984 Olympics, Halberstam remarked that "in a nation where sports was big business, crew was apart." Rowing, he continued, had "in no way benefited from the extraordinary growth of sports, both amateur and professional, which had been caused by the coming of television. By the 1980s, the marriage between sports and television (and merchandising) was virtually complete. Sports that the electronic eye favored underwent booms of astonishing dimension and became opportunities for celebrity and affluence. Sports that the camera did not favor atrophied by comparison."

As a result, he concluded, rowing remained "an anomaly, an encapsulated nineteenth-century world in the hyped-up twentieth-century world of commercialized sports."

—Lewis C. Cuyler

---

cox not only steering, but also determining what the other competitors are doing and how to respond.

In the United States rowing is typically learned in secondary schools and colleges where the shell of choice is four- or eight-oared. In Europe, where clubs more frequently provide the point of access, many rowers begin in single sculls. The clubs also provide a cheaper means of entry to the sport and so attract the less affluent. Many excellent rowers do not begin until they are 40, 50, or even 60. Rowing remains popular in the former Soviet Union, and is gaining followings in Third World countries.

Equipment

The standard eight-oared shell is more than 18 meters (60 feet) long; even single racing sculls measure about 8 meters (27 feet) and less than 0.3 meters (1 foot) wide for a racing single, about 0.6 meters (2 feet) wide for an eight. All of the craft are called shells, but "sculls" and "shells" differ. The scull is the oar used for rowing when one rower uses two oars. The practice then is known as "sculling," and the name scull is used for the craft so propelled. A shell is rowed by two or more oarsmen or women, each using one oar.

The fastest boats are the eight-oared shells with a coxswain, who steers the craft and encourages the rowers. Their smaller siblings are the four-oared shells, some with coxswain and some without, and the pair, accommodating two rowers, each with one oar, again sometimes with a coxswain. Made of wood until about 1970, shells today are fiberglass, as are oars, now hatchet and triangle shaped for faster, easier rowing.

The single is by far the most common in the scull category. The racing singles weigh about 30 pounds (14 kilograms), seemingly too fragile to accommodate rowers weighing between 100 and 220 pounds (46 and 100 kilograms). The racing single's many cousins in the "recreational" category are all wider, shorter, more stable in the water and 30 to 40 pounds heavier.

Rowing workouts require at least a mile of open water, the more sheltered the better. Traditionally, rivers in urban settings, as well as lakes and reservoirs, have been the most popular. However, the development of the Alden Ocean Shell in the early 1970s has made ocean rowing increasingly popular.

In the rest of the world, rowing is popular on the Thames River in England and on the Nile in Egypt, as well as at Geneva, Switzerland; Ratzeburg, Germany; Vichy, France; Donaratico, Italy; Buenos Aires, Argentina; and Melbourne, Australia. In the words of one historian, rowing has become a "quiet phenomenon" of the 1990s.

—LEWIS C. CUYLER

Bibliography: Churbuck, D. C. (1988) *The Book of Rowing.* Woodstock, NY: Overlook Press. Ivry, Benjamin. (1988) *Regatta: A Celebration of Oarsmanship.* New York: Simon and Schuster. Mendenhall, Thomas C. (1986) *The History of Rowing.* U.S. Nationals Program.

Rugby Fives

The game of rugby fives is one of the simplest, and therefore probably one of the most ancient, of all games in which a ball is struck by alternate players against a wall or over some obstacle. Several other versions of "fives" also exist.

History

References to games of hand-tennis and hand-ball are widely found from the 16th century onward. While ac-

counts of why hand-ball is now called "fives" vary, the most likely explanation is that the name refers to the five fingers of the hand.

With the formation of the Rugby Fives Association (RFA) in 1927, attempts were made to standardize both the rules and the court. The latter was a slow and costly process spurred by the founding of competitive matches. However, many courts remain unregularized and are likely to remain so, given costs and the game's "minor" status.

Rules and Play

Rugby's form of the fives game is played by two (singles) or four players (doubles) in a four-walled court with a small hard white ball approximately the size of a golf ball. Teams consist of four players. A full match consists of four singles matches and two sets of doubles matches, each pair of one team playing each pair of the other team. The result is decided on the basis of points scored, not games won. Thus, a team can win more games than its opponents but still lose the match because it scored fewer points. The first side to score 15 points wins the game. However, if the score reaches 14–14 then the side that is "hand out" may select to play to either 15 or 16 points in order to win the game. Styles and techniques of play vary, but the essential requirement is the ability to hit the ball so that the opponent cannot return it. Players often "split" the court, back and front or left and right.

Fives has long been and still remains a "minor" sport in its two major strongholds, the public schools and Oxford and Cambridge. Viewing space is invariably limited and spectators few. Nevertheless, the Rugby Fives Association formed in 1947 continues to do all that it can to maintain and preserve this ancient court game.

—TIMOTHY J. L. CHANDLER

Bibliography: Rugby Fives Association. (1994) *Fives: Courts, Fixtures and Players.* Sutton Valence, UK: Rugby Fives Association.

Rugby League

Founded in 1895, rugby league football is a handling form of football played by two teams of 13 players, the object being to score the most number of points through the scoring of tries (four points), goals (two points), and drop goals (one point).

History

The sport originated with the foundation of the first rugby union football clubs in the north of England in the 1860s. Started by the upper middle classes, rugby rapidly spread to the working classes of Lancashire and Yorkshire. These new enthusiasts brought different cultural norms and expectations—especially demands for payment for play. By 1886, the influx of working-class players had become so great that the middle-class leadership of the Rugby Football Union (RFU) sought to curb their influence by outlawing payment.

But the popularity of the sport in northern England meant these regulations were ignored. Thus, in 1922, did rugby league develop apart from rugby union. The new organization won the support of most northern rugby clubs, professional and amateur, but failed to take hold in the rest of England and Wales. A series of rule changes effected up through 1907 made the sport faster and more open and made rugby league more than simply a variation on rugby union.

Rules and Play

Played with an oval ball on a field measuring no more than 112 meters (122 yards) by 68 meters (74 yards), a match comprises two halves of 40 minutes each, during which each side has sets of six tackles, or downs, in which to score before the ball is turned over to the other side. The ball is propelled by players running with it or passing it, although the forward pass is illegal.

In 1907 the sport spread to Australia and New Zealand. In 1908 an Australian side toured the British Isles and a British side reciprocated in 1910, beginning a series of "Test" matches for the "Ashes" between Britain and Australia that have traditionally been seen as the sport's ultimate challenge.

The rugby union authorities responded to the split of the Northern Union and its Southern Hemisphere supporters by forbidding rugby union players to have any contact with the rebel sport. Coupled with rugby league's roots in working-class communities in England and Australia, and its willingness to embrace the participation of minorities often excluded from other sports, these discriminatory sanctions helped to forge the sport's self-identity. "The workingman's game" and "the most democratic sport in the world" have been two of the most popular descriptions of the game by its supporters. The depression of the interwar years saw rugby league in England and Australia grow stronger. England was able to import rugby league players from Australia, New Zealand, and Wales. Welsh players still play a leading role in the English game.

French rugby league evolved along similar lines. Established in 1934, the sport was founded by players seeking open payment for playing. By the outbreak of World War II, rugby league was beginning to eclipse rugby union, but in 1941 the collaborationist wartime Vichy government, supported by the rugby union authorities, banned rugby league. Postwar, French rugby league flourished. The French initiated and hosted the inaugural world cup tournament in 1954. Britain won.

The immediate post–World War II decades saw the game increase in popularity. In 1950 Australia defeated Britain in a three-match Ashes series for the first time in 30 years. This signaled the start of a gradual shift in the balance of playing strength to Australia, which was to result in Britain winning only 2 out of the 16 series played between 1960 and 1994.

The game declined in the 1960s with excessive television coverage and the decline of the industries from which it drew its support. This led to a radical rule change in 1966. To make the game more unpredictable, the attacking team was restricted to possession of the ball for just four tackles, before the defending side were given the chance of winning the ball. Based on the four-down pattern of American football, the four-tackle rule proved too restrictive and was replaced in 1971 by the current system of a turnover every six tackles.

This heralded the beginning of the modern age of rugby league, which was to become dominated by the influence of the Australian game. Influenced strongly by the coaching methods of American professional football and marshaled by outstanding players, their national side swept all before them, their success helping the game to spread to the southern Pacific islands and threatening the traditional dominance of rugby union in New Zealand. But despite the relative stagnation of their domestic game, British clubs, led by Wigan, won all but one of the world club championship finals up to 1994.

—TONY COLLINS

See also Rugby Union.

Bibliography: Gate, Robert. (1989) *Rugby League, An Illustrated History.* London: Arthur Barker. Lester, Gary. (1988) *The Story of Australian Rugby League.* Sydney: Lester Townsend.

Rugby Union

The game of rugby union football, a nominally amateur 15-a-side ball game, is played on a rectangular field with an inflated oval ball that may be handled as well as kicked. The object of the game is to score more points than your opponents. Points are awarded for goals and also for tries.

History

At least in its early stages, rugby union's development is inseparable from that of related games: rugby league or association football (soccer). All three games are descended from the traditional folk games of pre-industrial Britain. The development of two of the major modern forms of football, rugby and soccer, can be divided into five main and over-lapping stages.

Between about 1750 to about 1840, rugby football began to emerge as a distinctive game; the following 20 years saw soccer doing likewise. The rules were first written down in 1845.

From about 1850 to about 1900, public school football spread into society and independent clubs were formed. National associations were set up: the Football Association (FA) in 1863 and the RFU in 1871. Soon afterward rugby and soccer began to attract paying spectators and the possibility emerged for men to "work" as full-time players. Accordingly, it was also at this stage that rugby split into the amateur game of rugby union and, in 1895, the professional game of northern union football, or what was to become, in 1922, Rugby League. In England in the early 1870s, rugby football was played by a relatively homogeneous upper-middle-class clientele and confined mainly to schools and clubs in the South. However, by the end of the 19th century, it had begun to percolate downward in the class hierarchy, particularly in the North. Gradually the game spread among and to men who had either not attended public school or, if they had, not the higher-status schools. This combination of socially exclusive clubs with more open clubs was a configuration full of potential axes of tension and conflict. These tensions emerged first in Yorkshire, and were given shape by the Yorkshire Challenge Cup established in 1876. This cup rapidly became a success. Many new clubs were formed as a result and the numerical strength of the Yorkshire Rugby Union increased. Rugby football began to be expressive of the values and social situation of the industrial classes—the bourgeoisie and the proletariat—a development that fueled the controversy over amateurism and professionalism, and hence the split between rugby union and rugby league mentioned earlier.

International Diffusion

By the end of the 19th century the rugby union game had spread to the British Empire's colonies and dominions, although this spread was uneven and in competition with other football games.

Despite this history, rugby union was to undergo its

The Webb Ellis Myth

It is widely believed that rugby acquired its distinctive form as the result of a single deviant act by an individual, William Webb Ellis. It was Ellis, according to the stone set in the wall at Rugby school, who, in 1823, "first took the ball in his arms and ran with it thus originating the distinctive feature of the rugby game." There is reason to believe that this story is a myth. It was first advanced in 1880 by Mathew Bloxam, a man who had left the school in 1820, three years before the supposed event. His account was based on hearsay recalled over fifty years later. It would probably have faded into obscurity had it not been for circumstances affecting the development of rugby football in the 1890s. By that time the game had spread to the North of England where it had begun to emerge as a commercial spectacle, with players and spectators drawn principally from the working class. This process of commercialization and "proletarianization" was conducive to conflict and led to the split of 1895. It cannot have been accidental that 1895 also witnessed the publication of the Old Rugbeian Society report that resurrected Bloxam's story. The same year the Old Rugbeians also had the commemorative stone erected.

The details of that report cannot be gone into here, other than to note that it was prompted by what Rugbeians perceived as the threat posed to their game by its spread to groups they considered "alien" and "inferior." They were increasingly being beaten "at their own game" by these groups. It was escaping from their control and changing in directions which ran counter to their values. Giving pride of place in their report to the Webb Ellis story, an origin myth which correctly located the beginnings of rugby football in their school, was an attempt to consolidate their ranks and reassert their proprietorship of the game.

However, there are further grounds for doubting the story. It is just not sociologically plausible that a deeply entrenched traditional game could have been changed fundamentally by a single act, particularly by a low-status individual such as Webb Ellis is reputed to have been. Furthermore, the story is incomplete. It fails to consider how the practice of "running in" became institutionalized over a period of thirty years. Neither does it explain why, also in the second quarter of the 19th century, rugby acquired such distinctive features as an oval ball, "H-shaped" goals, scoring above the cross-bar, and points for "tries" as well as "goals." Thus, in focusing on the development of carrying, the Webb Ellis story fails to explain all aspects of the emergent uniqueness of the game.

—*K. G. Sheard*

own process of professionalization, although this took place at different speeds and with varying degrees of resistance in the various countries that adopted the game.

The French Rugby Federation (Fédération Française de Rugby) was founded in 1920, but the game in France is believed to have been introduced by British students around 1870. By 1892 there were at least 20 clubs in existence, mostly in the Paris area. That year, a club championship was established; although not at that time a truly national championship, it was the world's first club championship. This, as with similar competitions elsewhere in the world, was to prove of great significance for the development of the game in France and, by 1895, under its influence, the game spread to other towns. Rugby quickly became a genuinely popular game, representative of towns and cities, particularly in the South, and received the monetary support of politicians, municipalities, and businesspeople. France had 575 clubs by 1955 with 38,168 players; 20 years later these figures had tripled to 1,485 clubs and 134,000 players.

By the late 1970s not only did France take part in the Five Nations Championship, the annual tournament between the teams of England, Scotland, Wales, Ireland, and France, but it had instituted a series of "B" international games so that by 1979 the French had met, at one level or another, 20 different countries. In 1978 France was at last admitted to the International Rugby Football Board (IRFB).

The increasing globalization of rugby inevitably intensified pressure upon the game's administrators not only to respond to commercial pressures and the demands of elite players for a share of the money flowing into the game, but somehow to reconcile this with the traditional commitments of some countries to amateurism. The establishment, in 1987, of the Rugby World Cup (RWC) made these demands and pressures difficult to resist. The developing commercial "revolution" in rugby was given focus by the cup, institutionalizing and formalizing previously ad hoc links with private capital and encouraging a further surge toward overt professionalism (Ryan 1994, 63). As the 1995 RWC approached a multiplicity of deals involving sponsorship, franchising, and television rights was worked out, with some countries' players again benefiting more than others (Ryan 1994, 64). "The profit from this RWC amounted to more than £22 million."

Rugby union became a professional sport when the IRFB declared in 1995 that the amateur principles upon which the game had been founded should no longer constitute the basis for its organization and that it should become an "open game." At the beginning of May 1996, the RFU was not only in dispute with the other home unions over how best to share the increased television money offered to the game, but also with the English Professional Rugby Union Clubs (EPRUC) over who was to control the game and how best to finance professionalism.

Rules and Play

Rugby goal-posts are H-shaped, similar to those used in American football, but not supported by a central pole. The game is played with an oval ball, also similar to that used in American football, but considerably larger. The rules of rugby union are called its "laws."

The aim of rugby union is to score "tries" by crossing the opponents goal-line and "grounding" the ball—placing it on the ground and exerting downward pressure. To secure a try, the ball may be either carried or kicked across the goal-line. A try is worth five points and may be "converted" into a "goal" by kicking the ball between the goal-posts—between the uprights (or the imaginary lines that extend above them) and over the cross-bar. If the conversion is successful, the goal becomes worth seven points (two for the kick).

Other forms of scoring are the "penalty kick" and the "dropped goal." Penalty kicks are taken from the point at which an offense against the laws has occurred, though some breaches of the laws, such as a "forward pass" and a "knock-on" (see below), are not penalty offenses. A "dropped goal"—again, any player may attempt such a kick, though, unlike the penalty, it occurs without any break in the continuity of play—is scored when a player drops the ball to the ground and kicks it at the moment of impact. If it passes between the posts and over the cross-bar it counts as three points.

The positions on a rugby team are based on the distinction between "forwards" and "backs" (these are the British terms). The forwards—there are eight in a side—are generally tall and/or heavy, and their main task is to supply the ball to the backs who, ideally, should be faster runners. However, all players, including the full-back, play defensive or offensive roles according to the state of play.

When a player is tackled and the ball or player touches the ground, the ball must be immediately released. It may be picked up by the first player on the scene, but usually the forwards on both sides struggle for possession. This is called a "ruck," and players must come in from their own side of the ball. Only the feet may be used to "hook" the ball back to the scrum-half in a ruck situation. If the tackled player stays on his feet and continues with the ball in his grasp, the forwards again struggle for possession, but the hands may now be used. This is called a "maul." But once the ball hits the ground, feet only may be used and the laws governing the ruck again come into effect.

If a player running with the ball inadvertently knocks it to the ground in a forward direction or passes it forward, a "set-scrum" is awarded.

Rugby players are people who remain undaunted by the broken noses, bruises, and other common side effects of the sport. As long as such people remain, so will rugby.

—K. G. SHEARD

Bibliography: Dunning, Eric, and Kenneth Sheard. (1979) *Barbarians, Gentlemen and Players: A Sociological Study of the Development of Rugby Football.* Oxford: Martin Robertson & Co. Godwin, T., and C. Rhys. (1981) *The Guinness Book of Rugby Facts and Feats.* Enfield, UK: Guinness Superlatives Ltd. Jones, J. R. (1960) *Encyclopaedia of Rugby Football.* London: Sportsmans Book Club.

Running

See Cross-Country Running; Marathon and Distance Running; Track and Field, Running and Hurdling

Sailboarding

Sailboarding, also called boardsailing and windsurfing, has grown from obscurity to full Olympic status within 20 years. It is a mix of surfing and sailing, and its appeal is that it is relatively inexpensive, easy to play, and flexible. Most sailboarders cartop their sailboards to wherever the wind best suits their level of skill, and in perhaps 30 minutes can assemble them and be in the water. Changing sail size keeps sails manageable over a wide range of wind strengths. Some people also like the social side of the sport.

History

The invention of sailboarding is a most controversial aspect of the sport, with claimants in the United States, England, and Australia. Wherever its origins, the sport grew slowly in California and very quickly in Europe in the 1970s. Because the sport was new, board designs changed swiftly to test the limits of the possible. In 1977, Larry Stanley developed footstraps while sailing Hawaii's big waves. Footstraps, along with shorter boards, made aerial maneuvers possible.

Unfortunately, stability and flotation decreased as board length and maneuverability increased, and expert-end boards became so small they sank when stationary. The 1980s brought funboards that tried to combine the best of both. This backfired in one sense; mass numbers of sailboarders began trying to perfect advanced techniques: water starting (using the wind to pull the sailor up and out of the water and into the sailing position), footsteering, and various turning maneuvers. High-performance boards have fully battened sails (sails with fiberglass strips inserted into pockets stretching from the leech, or back edge of the sail, to the mast); its semi-permanent curve makes it behave more like an airplane wing, and the airfoil shape increases speed. Harnesses, first designed to fit around the chest and later to support to the hips, compensate for limited arm strength.

A mast is attached to a board via a universal joint. This makes the rig (mast, sail, and boom) movable in any direction. The sailor stands and supports the rig by holding onto a wishbone-shaped boom and steers by adjusting sail position and shifting weight on the board.

Rules and Play

Sailboarders need board, sail, mast, and boom, plus a wetsuit in all but the warmest water.

Beginners first learn to balance on the board before adding the sail. For the easiest start, the board should be positioned across the wind with the mast pointing away from the wind. The sailor stands on the board and slowly pulls the rig up from the water (called uphauling) until the boom is reached. Steering is performed by raking the rig. Leaning it back pivots the boat more toward the wind, and leaning it forward turns the boat away from the wind. Carry either of these maneuvers on long enough, and the board will eventually turn completely around; the former is called coming about, the latter jibing. More advanced sailboarders let the wind pull them up, out of the water, and into sailing position (waterstarting) and steer by banking the board with their feet.

Sailboards are categorized by design. Some are designed for racing, in which competitors jockey for position at the starting gun (or start off the beach) and then sail around a series of buoys in a predetermined order and direction. Rules are based upon sailing rules. Division I boards are flat bottomed; division II boards have round bottoms. One-design classes feature identical boards. There are also slalom races and marathon events; the most notable marathon occurred in 1981–1982 when a Frenchman, Christian Marty, sailed across the Atlantic Ocean from Dakar, Senegal, to Cayenne, French Guiana, eating and sleeping on board.

Olympic sailboarding for men and women was first held at the 1984 Summer Games in Los Angeles, with 38 countries participating. Another major sailboarding competition is the Pan Am Cup sailed off the Hawaiian island of Oahu.

Speed sailing is another branch of the sport, and sailboards have held the world speed record for all forms of sailing craft.

Other sailboards are designed for freestyle sailing, in which performers attempt very intricate maneuvers. Sailboard jumping, both competitive and recreational, is a branch of freestyle. People now sail indoors, using jet engines to provide wind, and there is a professional indoor circuit. The sailboard principle is also used for both ice and land versions of the sport.

Tandem sailboards, with two sails and two sailors, as well as three-sailed tridems, also exist; for both, sailors must cooperate completely to steer.

The sport demands more balance and skill than pure strength, and men and women of all ages enjoy the sport in its many variations.

—SHIRLEY H. M. REEKIE

Bibliography: Evans, Jeremy. (1983) *Complete Guide to Windsurfing.* London: Bell & Hyman. Turner, Stephen. (1986) *Windsurfing.* New York: Gallery.

Sailing

Sailing is a mode of transportation across water that uses wind to power sails. Many enthusiasts sail purely for pleasure; others for pleasure and in competition.

History

Peoples of the Middle East sailed boats made of reeds circa 3500 B.C.E. and today still sail the very distinctive *dhows.* Greeks and Romans sailed galleys circa 1000 B.C.E. The Chinese developed the distinctive junk circa 300 C.E. The Vikings sailed longboats from 700 C.E. Each sailboat was designed to work well in the prevailing conditions of wind direction and strength, number of crew available, and available construction materials.

Sailing as sport rather than transportation possibly began in the Netherlands. Many words (including the word "yacht") are derived from Dutch words. In the 1660s, a race took place in London, England, between

King Charles II's boat and one owned by the Duke of York. The first regatta was organized in 1720 at the Water Club of Cork, Ireland. Sailing as a sport remained the province of the wealthy, and retains that association today. In the late 19th century, smaller, more affordale dinghies were built and raced. The oldest club in continuous existence was founded as simply the Yacht Club (the first to use such terminology) in London in 1815. It received royal patronage and became known as the Royal Yacht Club in 1820 and the Royal Yacht Squadron in 1830.

Rules and Play

Boats

Today virtually anyone can find a boat to suit them, whatever their age, physical condition (blindness, reliance on a wheelchair), and budget. Certain principles, however, apply to all sailing boats.

Early boats were probably only able to sail in the direction the wind was blowing. This direction, or point of sailing, relative to the wind is called running. Advances in rig design allowed sailors to sail perpendicularly across the wind. This point of sailing is called reaching.

Eventually, boats were designed that could advance in a direction 45 degrees to the wind. This is called beating, or sailing close hauled, because the most efficient sail position is hauled in close to the boat. No boat can sail directly into the wind; the sail would act like a flag, with wind on each side, and harness no power. Boats can, however, make indirect progress directly upwind by zigzagging.

Bernoulli's principle, which explains how planes get lift, can also explain how a sail works. If one imagines the sail to be like a wing, the curved surface makes air travel over it faster than over a flat surface, so that in front (or on top in a plane) of the curved surface is fast-moving air at low pressure, while the other surface has slower moving air and higher pressure. This gives a plane lift and a sail forward motion.

Sailors must know two, crucially different, ways to turn the boat around. The choice is to turn the bow (front) into the wind, or to turn the stern (back) into the wind. When turning the bow into the wind (called coming, or going, about), the sail flutters like a flag, and only momentum allows the boat to complete her turn. In turning away from the wind (called jibing, or gybing), the wind is always filling, thus propelling, the sail, first on one side and then after the sail is forced by the wind to swing across, on the other side.

Sailboats have no brake. As long as there is wind the

America's Cup

The America's Cup trophy began in England as the Hundred Guinea Cup because that is what it cost to make in 1851. It was given for a race around the Isle of Wight off England's south coast held that same year. The British organizers, the Royal Yacht Squadron, wrote to the newly founded New York Yacht Club, inviting American boats to sail over and race against them for the summer. The New York Yacht Club accepted and had a new boat purpose-built. The boat was a 101-foot (30.6-meter) schooner (sails in front and behind the mast, with two or more masts) named *America*. After seeing *America*'s speed, no British boat wanted to race her, but she was invited to race in the Hundred Guinea Cup race. Starting at anchor, as was the custom in those days, 14 British boats and the lone American boat began to race at 10 A.M. on the morning of 22 August. The course was printed in the program as being around the Nab Light, the most easterly point of the course, but the race card called only for the yachts to sail around the island. The distance was about 50 miles (80 kilometers), and no handicaps or time allowances were to be given.

In very light wind, *America* was the last to get underway but soon overtook all but four boats. These four went around the outside of the Nab Light rock, but *America* went inside and into the lead. *America* was never caught and won the race at 8:37 P.M. The first British boat was more than 10 minutes behind. A protest was made about the course sailed by *America* but was later withdrawn. Captain John Cox Stevens (1785–1857) was presented with the trophy later that evening. A story arose that Queen Victoria (1819–1901), on the Isle of Wight at the time of the race, was told that *America* was leading. When she asked which boat was second, she is supposed to have been told, "Your Majesty, there is no second." Had the then-current system of handicapping in place been used for the race, *America* would have probably won by about two minutes. As it was, *America*'s design influenced British boats for years to come.

Captain Stevens brought the cup home to New York, but sold *America* in Britain. In 1857, the New York Yacht Club offered the cup won by *America* as a trophy for a sailing match open to any country. (Match racing is one boat against one other.) The cup became known as the America's Cup and was one of the earliest international trophies in any sport. The next competition for it occurred in 1870 and it has continued to be contested at intervals ranging from 1 to 21 years ever since. The United States successfully defended the cup against all comers until 1983 when the longest winning stretch in any sport was ended by the Australians. Since then, Dennis Conner (1943–), sailing for the United States, regained the trophy he lost before, then lost it again, this time to New Zealand. The race is always hosted by the previous winners. The schooner *America* remained in England until the U.S. Civil War, when the boat was bought for the South. *America* ended up as a training ship at the U.S. Naval Academy but fell to pieces in 1945.

—*Shirley H. M. Reekie*

boat will move. To slow down, or stop, the sailor must angle the boat or sail so that it no longer catches the wind power. Restarting involves again trapping wind in the sail by angling the sail across the wind, either by using the tiller and rudder to turn the boat or by pushing the sail out by the boom (the pole along the foot of the sail) at an angle to the wind.

Sailing Categories

Sailing can be divided into several categories according to vessel type and use.

Cruising is a nonracing branch of sailing in which larger boats, usually with sleeping accommodation, are sailed on voyages ranging from overnight to around the world. Sailors who cruise must know navigation, anchoring, and meteorology—indeed, any skill that might be needed miles from help. Cruisers are usually equipped with instruments ranging from a compass and depth sounder to sophisticated Global Positioning System (GPS) navigation aids.

Cruisers carry different sails that are changed to suit the weather. As the wind rises, smaller sails are used to keep the boat from being overpowered. Sailors must know when they must avoid another boat. Generally, power yields to sail; many situations exist where the sailboat must give way.

Racing Competition

Ocean, or offshore, racing apparently began in October 1866, as the result of a wager. Three boats raced across the Atlantic, from New York to the Isle of Wight, England. *Henrietta* (32.6 meters [107 feet]) beat *Vesta* (32 meters [105 feet]) and *Fleetwing* (32.3 meters [106 feet]) in a very close race. Some people connected with the sailing world felt that racing in the open sea was too dangerous and, as a result, ocean racing grew up as a sport somewhat removed from dinghy and inshore keelboat racing.

A 630-mile (1,014-kilometer) race from Newport, Rhode Island, to Bermuda was first held in 1906 and since 1924 has been held every two years (except during World War II). On the other side of the Atlantic, and in the off year of the Bermuda Race, is the Fastnet Race, held since 1925, from the Isle of Wight up to the southwest coast of Ireland. The Fastnet Race is one of a series of races that make up the Admiral's Cup, one of the premier trophies in offshore racing. The 630-mile Sydney-Hobart, Australia, race, first held in 1945, is the third major offshore race.

Single-handed sailing around the world began in 1895 when Joshua Slocum (1844–1909), an American sea captain, started his voyage aboard *Spray*, a 36-foot (11.2-meter) boat. He sailed counterclockwise, making use of prevailing winds and currents, on a journey that took three years, with many stops. His book, *Sailing Alone around the World,* has become a classic in sailing literature.

Dinghies are the smallest, but most numerous, types of boats, and are distinguished by their retractable centerboards. Some dinghies have a very simple rig—one sail—but others can have a mainsail, a jibsail, a spinnaker (a balloonlike sail used in front of the mast on downwind legs, often brightly colored), and even a trapeze (a device that allows the crew to hook on to a wire, stand on the edge of the boat, and lever their weight way over the side to help keep the boat upright in windy conditions).

Racing Handicaps

Before boats were mass-produced, each was unique; consequently, various systems of handicapping were developed for more meaningful racing; the first was handicapping by rating.

In 1907, handicapping by meters replaced it and the handicap was determined by boat length, sail area, and other measurements. There were 6-, 8-, 12-, and 15-meter yachts. The 12-meter survived to become the prototype for much of the later 20th-century America's Cup racing and various meter classes became early Olympic classes. Sailing races vary. In one design, identical boats race together in fleet races. In handicap races, boats of different types race each other. Boats may start together, have their finish times recorded, and then work out who won on handicap. A visible handicap may be used in which the slower boats start first and the faster boats start last, at time intervals based on their handicap; the first boat over the finish line wins.

The rules for sailboat racing include the three basic right-of-way rules plus many others necessary for sailing at very close quarters. The London-based International Sailing Federation (ISAF) is trying to simplify the rules. Rules are always revised in the year following the Olympic Games.

Sailing races rarely have referees; no referee could see every situation on the course. Instead, all competitors are honor-bound to try to sail by the rules to the best of their knowledge and ability. If one sailor thinks another has wrongly interpreted a rule, the only remedy is to protest after the race, to get a ruling on a situation.

Sailboat construction has changed greatly in the last 50 years. Until then, most boats were built of wood,; today most are fiberglass; some are aluminum or cement, and a few are made of expensive new materials such as Kevlar. Many sailors still prefer the look of wood. Sails, traditionally made from flax or cotton, both of which had the tendency to rot if left wet, have also changed with technology and are now made from Dacron or sometimes Kevlar; the lighter spinnaker sails use nylon or Mylar.

As a sport, sailing is enjoyed around the world, and 108 countries are affiliated to the ISAF. Until recently, sailing has been a difficult sport to watch, because the boats cover a wide area, and sometimes take very different paths to the next buoy. Even experts find it hard to know which boat is leading. Television may remedy this. Use of microcameras mounted high in the rigging or at deck level may be part of the answer.

—SHIRLEY H. M. REEKIE

Bibliography: Knox-Johnston, Robin. (1990) *History of Yachting.* Oxford, UK: Phaidon. Reekie, Shirley H. M. (1986) *Sailing Made Simple.* Champaign, IL: Leisure Press.

Sailing, Ice Skate

Ice skate sailing is a northern European and North American winter recreation exclusively practiced outdoors in the daytime. The attractions are high speed combined with low cost; the portability of equipment, and the opportunity to brake. Few demands are made on newcomers; the ability to skate without extending one's arms is the only prerequisite skill.

History

Modern ice skate sailing began no earlier than the 17th century, when Dutch skaters began to use sharp-edged, iron blades. An assured grip on the slippery ice made it feasible to sail a round trip, which entails tacking upwind.

In the next century the Swedish botanist and explorer Carolus Linnaeus (1707–1778) sighted skaters "with sails like wings." Skate sails in the mid-19th century carried fowlers across the ice separating Denmark from Sweden, bearing the hunters to their prey. On the icy Muggelsee near Berlin, a three-person sail propelled German skaters at the turn of the century. Organized races began near Stockholm on Lilla Värtan Lake in 1887.

In 1896, an English skater named Adams sailed 48 kilometers (30 miles) within 60 minutes. Sail skaters raced weekly on the salty ice of Cove Pond in Stamford, Connecticut. Their speed reached 45 miles [72 kilometers] per hour. Skate sailors on Lake George, New York, hurtled at more than 110 kilometers (70 miles) per hour in the 1930s.

Rules and Play

Participants sail erect, wear ice skates on their feet, and hold sails measuring 3.3 to 8.8 square meters (35 to 95 square feet) with their hands and shoulders. Sheathed ice picks around the sailors' necks are indispensable for self-rescues. Life vests and helmets are advisable.

The best sailing skates unite long, flat blades to stiff, high, warm boots. Comparatively flat, they reduce sideslipping.

Often likened to simple kites, the shapes of many contemporary skate sails derive from parallel trapeziums. Balanced sails, which show no tendency to turn upwind or downwind, add triangular or circular jib and tail sections. The cloth of a traditional skate sail stretches tautly over a framework of spars, including a horizontal boom and a vertical mast.

In choosing a sail, sailors heed its area, the ratio of sail area to body weight, height, and the distance between the mast-boom crossing and the sail center-of-effort. Experienced sailors use smaller sails in stronger winds, and larger sails in lighter ones. Many skate sailors make their own sails.

A cruising sailor stands leeward of a skate sail, bending his knees to absorb any shocks caused by rough ice.

To steer upwind, the sailor slides the boom backward on his shoulder. This motion increases the sail area aft of the skater, who pivots like a weathervane. A 180-degree turn into the wind calls for sliding the boom far aft. The sail turns strongly into the wind, and slows and luffs when raising it overhead becomes necessary. This task demands both hands, first to lift the mast and afterwards to seize it on either side of the boom. When the sailor has transferred his grip, the sail plane parallels the ice surface, and the wind passes ineffectively over the craft. Now he completes the turn using only his skates, lowering the boom to his other shoulder as he begins sailing straight on the new course.

A sail skater can slow by changing his course angle or raising and turning the sail overhead. The sailor can use his skates to brake safely only with the sail plane parallel to the ice sheet. Releasing the sail, reducing its area, or heeling it also reduce speed. Lying on the wind is comfortable and safe when the breeze is steady and the blades sharp. If the wind dies momentarily, a proficient sailor recovers his balance by turning windward.

—RICHARD FRIARY

See also Sailing, Icewing and Roller Skate; Sandyachting.
Bibliography: Friary, Richard. (1996) *Skate Sailing*. Indianapolis: Masters Press. Goldberg, Daniel E. (1973) Skate Sail, U. S. Patent 3,768,823 (30 October).

Sailing, Icewing and Roller Skate

Icewing, roller skate, and ski sailing are closely related to ice skate sailing. Of the three sports, roller skate and ski sailing enjoy the greatest international popularity, although icewing sailing features the highest ratio of sailing speed to wind speed.

History

The icewing was invented by Anders Ansar (1942 –) in Stockholm, Sweden, in 1973. The semirigid craft resembles the detached tip of an airplane wing stood erect. By enclosing the sailor completely, it represents the greatest innovation in ice skate sailing during the 20th century. Its streamlining abolishes the air turbulence created by its sailor's body. Of all hand-held sails, only the icewing achieves this aerodynamic effect. Its wing-like shape thrusts it forward at nearly four times the wind speed, while standard ice skate sails reach a value of two to two and one-half.

Rules and Play

The icewing consists of two cloth sails, a solid top, and a rigid, curved leading edge. The two sails comprise the port and starboard sides of the craft, joining one another at the aft end and supported by a framework of aluminum tubing. The only opening is in the bottom.

Flat, sharp, and long skate blades minimize sideslipping and lend stability over rough ice or at high speeds and oppose the sideforce of the wind.

To enter an icewing, the sailor squats, facing the wind, and a helper places the icewing over the sailor. The sailor steers by maneuvering a waist-high horizontal control bar.

National icewing races take place annually, often near Stockholm on the Baltic Sea.

Roller Skate Sailing

Rollerskate sailing dates from the 1930s in the United States, but takes place internationally. It rewards a liking for speed: a roller skate sailor can reach 72 kilometers (45 miles) per hour. The sport is versatile because many kinds of hard surfaces are suitable.

Roller skates with plastic wheels, smooth bearings, and rigid boots are the preferred footgear, although side-by-side wheeled skates work, too. Wise roller skate sailors wear helmets as well as elbow, knee, and wrist guards. Roller skate sailors who sail heeled must beware stationary objects blocking the wind. Parked vehicles, for example, can create a low-pressure area on their leeward sides that fails to support a sail inclined from the vertical. Without support from the sail, the sailor may swoop or fall.

Ski Sailing

Skiers began to sail as early as 1917. The sport is practiced in North America and northern Europe. A variety of sail types are appropriate.

Ski sailing requires downhill skis and Alpine boots. The metal edges of these skis prevent side slipping and permit the sailor to hold a course.

The resistance of snow to skis exceeds that of ice to skates, so ski sailing requires a faster wind and a larger sail than ice skate sailing.

Wind-packed snow 5 centimeters (2 inches) thick offers an ideal surface for fast ski sailing. Loose, deep snow reduces speed, while a hard, icy surface affords too little traction, even to metal-edged skis. Wind and other physical processes like recrystallization convert loosely packed snow to dense snow, and this change increases sailing speed.

Ski sailing offers many advantages over ice skate sailing, regardless of the sail type employed: skis allow sailing during a greater part of the winter, with more places to practice the sport. Ski sailing at 80 kilometers (50 miles) per hour over a flat surface is not only feasible but thrilling.

—RICHARD FRIARY

See also Sailing, Ice Skate; Sailing, Parawing.
Bibliography: Friary, Richard. (1996) *Skate Sailing*. Indianapolis, IN: Masters Press.

Sailing, Parawing

Parawing sailing was invented in the early 1980s by a German, Wolf Beringer, and became a new, exciting, and highly maneuverable way to sail on land, all year, on many terrains. The parawing consists of a ram-air inflatable soft-fabric wing attached by multiple lines to a control bar held by the sailor and sometimes attached to the sailor by means of a quick release snap swivel and body harness.

Parawings are sailed over snow or ice with the sailor wearing skis or skates, over sand beaches or salt flats with the sailor wearing land or sand skis or foot steered "buggies," over paved surfaces with the sailor wearing in-line skates, or over turf with the sailor using grass skis, buggies, or various roller devices.

Parawing sailors take advantage of the same forces—particularly the phenomenon of "apparent wind." The unique control system allows changing the angle of attack of a parafoil wing.

In 1992, kite designer and builder Hans Schepker and skier George Theriault, inspired by Wolf Beringer, teamed up to design and produce parawings in America. Theriault became the first person in North America to sail with a parawing using snow and grass skis. He founded the North American Parawing Association, which publishes a newsletter and promotes the sport.

Parawing sailing appeals to many age groups. A nonathlete of any age can compensate by using the parawing's exceptional maneurverability and selecting suitable equipment.

—GEORGE THERIAULT

Sandyachting

Sandyachting is an exhilarating sport that uses the power of the wind to propel a wheeled craft along a sandy surface at speeds of up to 130 kilometers (80 miles) per hour.

History

The Chinese, in 550 C.E., developed the first wind-driven carriages and sail-powered chariots for battle. By 1600 Chinese royalty were participating in sandyachting races. Massive troop-carrying yachts were developed for use on Belgian beaches, and a 28-seater built in 1600 was used for 190 years for ferrying dignitaries and tourists between Scheveningen and Petten along the Belgian coast.

By the 1920s yachts appeared on British beaches, travelling 65 kilometers (40 miles) per hour. During the 1930s sandyachts became popular once more at French and Belgian beach resorts, and spoked motorcycle and car wheels replaced bicycle wheels, which could not withstand the considerable side-thrust forces.

The Americans were also sailing by the 1930s, but the single momentous event that shaped the future development of the sport occurred in the basement workshops of the *Detroit Evening News* in 1937, where employees built a little iceyacht and christened it *The Detroit News* (DN). Twenty-six years later, the Dutch mounted wheels on *The Detroit News* and revolutionized the sport by establishing the ideal configuration for a sandyacht, with one steerable wheel at the front, and two rear wheels with an axle between them.

The arrival of the DN on continental beaches in the early 1960s revolutionized the sport because the DN was tiny, simple in design, cheap to build, light, and extremely efficient with a sail of only 5.5 square meters.

Rules and Play

Sandyachting as a competitive sport goes back to the Dumont brothers of De Panne, Belgium, in 1898. World

War I abruptly stopped further development of the sport.

The International Federation of Sand and Land Yachts Clubs (FISLY) was formed in 1962 with representatives from France, Germany, Belgium, and Great Britain. The first official European championships were held in 1963, with all yachts racing together in an open class. As the DNs were racing with yachts two or three times their size, the fleet was subdivided in 1965 into three classes according to sail size.

By 1970 the massive Class 1 dinosaurs were almost extinct, but the DN concept had been quickly refined and developed within the increasingly popular Class 3, with the addition of an aerodynamic body shell and a powerful aerofoil section wing mast.

In 1975 the Windskate brought a second revolution. This tiny yacht of tubular construction was an instant success and became Class 4, but the lack of a formal specification meant that the yacht was quickly lengthened and widened in the quest for higher speeds. In 1980 Class 5 evolved to accommodate the simpler smaller tubular yachts with a basic pole mast and 5 square meters of sail. Generally, only Classes 3 and 5 remain today, equally popular.

Sandyachts can sail three or four times the speed of the wind and can sail upwind at an angle of 40 degrees to the eye of the wind. The latest competitive sandyacht with 5 square meters of sail can achieve 80 kilometers per hour in a wind of 24 kilometers per hour. Wheels have been refined to minimize rolling resistance, and the choice of ultrasmooth round profile tire is critical. A modern sandyacht can out-accelerate a sports car and out-perform the best rally driver on corners. Injuries are very rare, even at the international competitive level.

The excitement of racing lies in the cut and thrust of close competition. Yachts start from stationary positions on a two- or three-row grid, with pilots pushing their yachts initially to build up speed and find clean (unobstructed) wind before jumping in. Starts can be spectacularly chaotic, and minor collisions are common. A typical course involves two turning marks 3.2 kilometers (2 miles) apart, sailed in a clockwise direction. A normal race lasts 30 minutes, with the winner being shown the checkered flag after 30 minutes of sailing. As sandyachts have no brakes, gybe (with the wind) turns are often taken at full speed and on two wheels.

Sandyachting has only about 150 active participants in the United Kingdom due to its total dependence on weather conditions. In the United States there are about 1,000 participants. It is most popular in France, and yachts have priority on the beach. Other nations where it is popular are Germany, Belgium, the Netherlands, New Zealand, and Australia.

—A. R. PARR

Bibliography: Parr, Andrew. (1991) *Sandyachting—A History of the Sport and Its Development in Britain.* Pembrokeshire, UK: Gomer Press.

Senior Games

The U.S. National Senior Sports Classic, originally called the Senior Olympics, is a series of athletic competitions for people over the age of 50. It is part a larger network sometimes called the Senior Games movement that provides venues—state and local—for older people who want to continue participating in organized competitive sports. The Senior Games movement is fueled by three trends: increasing life expectancy, greater emphasis on fitness, and more awareness of the social, psychological, and physical benefits of sport for older people. As the baby boom generation ages, the movement will probably grow.

History

The concept of organized athletic competitions for older people became increasingly popular after 1960. Participants and supporters of Senior Games organized the first multisport National Senior Olympics in 1987 in St. Louis, Missouri. The U.S. National Senior Sports Organization was subsequently formed to coordinate the National Senior Sports Classic and related events on an ongoing basis.

The National Senior Sports Classic network grew rapidly in its first decade, as the number of athletes and events increased. The U.S. National Senior Sports Classic and the Senior Olympics have been held once every two years since 1987. The event is sponsored by the U.S. National Senior Sports Organization, its regional affiliates, and by residents of the city where the championship is held. Most competitors live in the United States, but people from other nations may participate. The 1995 National Senior Sports Classic had a field of almost 8,300 competitors. The regional events also grew, with as many as a quarter of a million participants.

Rules and Play

The National Senior Sports Classics and regional counterparts include traditional Olympic events and other challenging sports, plus less physically demanding activities. Swimming, track and field, softball, cycling, bowling, tennis, and volleyball lead in popularity. Competitions are also held in archery, badminton, basketball, golf, horseshoes, racquetball, shuffleboard, table tennis, and a triathlon.

Competitors become eligible to participate in the National Senior Sports Classic by placing in the top positions in state and regional meets. However, the goal is to provide incentive and opportunity for people of all ability levels. Many of the participating athletes focus more on the training process and on accomplishing their personal goals in a sport than on competition.

The events draw athletes of diverse backgrounds. At the 1995 National Senior Sports Classic championships, an estimated 66 percent of the competitors were male and 34 percent were female. Some compete in one event, others in several. Many have been lifelong athletes, including former competitors and medalists in the Olympics and other top athletic events and circuits, but others developed an interest in exercise or a particular sport in their later years. Some athletes compete despite physical disabilities, such as arthritis. Some have become active in competitive sports as a result of training programs they undertook to deal with heart disease, cancer, and other surgeries or illnesses.

Individual sports are organized into divisions based on age. Originally, the National Senior Sports Classic was limited to people age 55, lowered to 50 in 1997. (Some regional events retained the minimum age of 55.) The largest age group has traditionally been people in their sixties, but that limit may rise as more people view aging as a stage of life, not a pathological condition.

—JOHN TOWNES

Bibliography: Stathoplos, Demmie. (1995) "Silver Threads among the Gold." *Sports Illustrated* (3 July). Wilson, Lillie. (1991) "At the Senior Olympics." *American Demographics* (May).

Shinty

Shinty is a tough, essentially aerial game that involves flicking, passing, and tossing a ball with a curved stick. Players may not handle the ball. Nowhere is shinty anything but a minor sport.

History

Shinty (derived from the Gaelic word *sinteag* for "leap") may have come to Scotland by way of Ireland, and Hugh Dan Maclennan, a leading shinty expert, argues that shinty goes back thousands of years and was brought to northwest Scotland by Irish missionaries, along with Christianity and the Gaelic language.

The game can safely lay claim to being Scotland's national sport, although not its premier sport, which is soccer (association football). It is first mentioned in the Highlands and Inner and Outer Hebridean Islands of Scotland toward the end of the 18th century. The game was a sport of high physical contact and collision, carried out on a vast playing area with a minimum of rules, regulations, rest, or breaks.

Up to 1914 and the onset of World War I, shinty developed rapidly, and rules were drawn up and codified. Following World War I and up to the 1950s, however, shinty declined. Demographic shifts saw significant numbers of Scots move away from the Highlands and Islands and resettle in industrialized Glasgow and the North of England.

Rules and Play

Playing members number only in the low thousands, but there are currently 40 shinty clubs. The regional base continues to be in the Highlands and Islands; university clubs exist at Aberdeen, St. Andrews, and Edinburgh; there is a Lowland club at Tayforth; and émigré Scots can play for London Camanachd.

Shinty originally bore a close similarity to Ireland's premier sport, hurling. Today, while there are occasional mixed contests, the games as played at elite levels differ substantially. Shinty has 12 players per team and requires seven officials. The pitch size is not fixed and varies greatly from club to club. The crooked, broad-bladed shinty stick bears some resemblance to a field hockey stick.

The 12 players include a hail-keeper (goal-keeper), a full-back, three half-backs, a center back, a center-field, a center-forward, three half-forwards, and a full forward. A game lasts 90 minutes, with a half-time interval of 5 minutes. The game is essentially an aerial sport with the ball being tossed and flicked and passed. Only the goal-keeper may handle the ball. A goal is scored when the ball passes into the goal.

The game is tough. Fouls such as kicking, catching, or throwing the ball, obstruction, pushing, charging, hacking, and jumping at an opponent are severely penalized. Shinty, like hurling, is a game where the level of ball flow, spatial movement, and player fluidity create a special type of spectator exhilaration.

—SCOTT A. G. M. CRAWFORD

See also Hurling.
Bibliography: Maclennan, H. D. (1993) *Shinty: 100 Years of the Camanachd Association.* Nairn, UK: Balnain Books. Smout, T. C. (1986) *A Century of the Scottish People, 1830–1950.* New Haven, CT: Yale University Press.

Shooting, Clay Target

The three disciplines of clay target shooting are trapshooting, skeet shooting, and sporting clays. A shotgun is used in all three. Clay target shooting is practiced in most countries of the world, with practitioners of all ages, genders, and abilities. At least one of the clay target shooting disciplines is included in all the major international sporting events. As a sport that offers challenge without violence, its future seems secure.

History

With the development of the shotgun, shooting at flying birds became popular and developed into the sport of trapshooting, which was fairly well developed in England by 1750. At this stage, it was apparently confined to England. Trapshooting clubs began to form shortly after 1800, and the "Old Hats" public house located near London was the first place mentioned as a favorite resort for pigeon shooters. From England, trapshooting spread to other west European countries, to North America, and to the British colonies and dominions. The year 1831 has often been chosen as the beginning of organized trapshooting in North America.

The term *trapshooting* comes from the practice of imprisoning live birds in traps and then firing at them shortly after their release. Live pigeon shooting became a very popular sport, and competitions were held throughout Europe and North America. By the late 1860s, the supply of live birds dwindled as criticism increased, and trapshooters looked for a suitable inanimate substitute.

The first was the glass ball target and trap, developed in England around 1860 and introduced to North America in 1866. The glass ball did not satisfactorily simulate the bird in flight, hence the clay pigeon, invented in 1880 by George Ligowsky (1856–1891) of Cincinnati, Ohio. More challenging to shooters, its flight more closely resembled a live bird's flight. Annie Oakley (1860–1926), among others, helped to promote trapshooting throughout the United States and Europe. Her fame created an interest in trapshooting among the women of her time, and in the 1910s she taught hundreds of women to shoot.

The Interstate Trapshooting Association, organized in 1892, laid the groundwork for modern trapshooting and held what is regarded as the first Grand American Handicap Tournament. Today renamed the Amateur Trapshooting Association (ATA), ATA has 74,000 registered members.

At the end of the 19th century, trapshooting clubs and competitions were common throughout North America and Europe. Annual national championships were soon followed by international competitions. Trapshooting was introduced as a sanctioned international sport at the Second Olympiad in Paris, France, in 1900 and has been included at every subsequent Olympic Games except 1904, 1932, 1936, and 1948. La Fédération Internationale de Tir aux Armes Sportives de Chasse (FITASC), created in 1921, united international shooting sports bodies in 1929 to establish both the World Shooting Championships and the European Shooting Championships. The Union Internationale de Tir (UIT), in 1947, took over the responsibility for international trapshooting in the Olympics and the World Championships. Women began competing in the European Championships in 1954 and in the World Championships in 1962.

Skeet shooting was devised by three upland game hunters in 1910 as a way to practice hunting techniques. It was originally known as "Round the Clock Shooting" as the shooting arrangement was a complete circle of 25 yards with the circle marked off like the face of a clock. Changes were made to enhance its appeal: two traps were used to throw targets, double target shooting was added, shooting was done in a half circle, and a new set of rules was established. The sport was officially introduced to the United States in 1926. The first American Skeet Shooting Championship was held in 1935. Skeet was introduced in Britain and Europe in the 1930s, and both the British and the Europeans modified the sport. The National Skeet Shooting Association (NSSA), with 17,000 current registered shooters, was founded in the early 1930s and hosts the World American Skeet Shooting Championship annually. International skeet became an Olympic sport in the 1968 Olympics in Mexico City.

Sporting clays developed at the turn of the century when some shooters changed the location and number of trap machines to better simulate live bird shooting. In the last 20 years, sporting clays has become a serious competitive sport internationally. FITASC organized the first Sporting Clays World Championships for men and women in 1979. Popular in Europe, it did not become an organized sport in North America until the mid-1980s. Currently the National Sporting Clays Association (NSCA) has 14,000 registered members in North America and hosts the National Sporting Clays Championships.

Trapshooting

Early clay target shooting closely followed the rules of live pigeon shooting: five traps set in a straight line in front of the shooter. Modifications followed, until by the turn of the century, it was superseded in Canada and the United States by a single automatic trap that threw targets at a fixed elevation and random angles. Shooters, however, still used the same five positions.

The single automatic trap became the basis of American-style (ATA) trapshooting, found predominantly in Canada and the United States. Shooters use a 12-gauge shotgun to shoot at the clay targets. The trap squad (usually five people) shoots in rotation from five positions in a crescent-shaped formation 16 yards behind the trap, and only one shot is taken at each target.

While in the 1890s North American clubs were going to fewer traps, in Europe the first-class clubs went to 15 traps. They were fixed at ground level, with a trench behind that hid the traps from the shooters. This type of trapshooting developed into the current international-style trapshooting where 15 traps are arranged in a straight line in a traphouse (bunker/pit). Five shooting positions are in a straight line situated 15 meters to the rear and parallel to the traps, one position for each group of three traps. A squad consists of six shooters who move from one position to the next after each shot, eventually shooting five targets from each position. Competitors are allowed two shots at each clay target; one point is given for each clay target broken in the air. International-style trapshooting (also known as Olympic trap) is shot in most countries throughout the world.

In the mid-1980s, the UIT introduced a new International clay target event called Double Trap. In Double Trap two clay targets are thrown simultaneously from two of three traps situated in a traphouse. Three different settings using a combination of two of the three traps are used in competition. Double Trap became an Olympic sport for both men and women in 1996.

Skeet Shooting

Skeet began in the United States in 1926. The three types of skeet are: (1) American or Amateur Trapshooting Association (ATA), also known as the National Skeet Shooting Association (NSSA), (2) International, and (3) English. Skeet shooting uses the same clay targets and traps as trapshooting, but the field is set up differently. The skeet field consists of a high house and a low house and eight shooting stations arranged on a segment of a half circle. Each house contains a trap that throws a target in the direction of the other trap but over the center of the circle and always in the same line and at the same elevation.

In American NSSA skeet, shooters shoot a combi-

nation of single and double targets from eight stations. Shooters use four different gauges of shotguns: 12, 20, 28, and .410 and shoot at 100 targets with each gauge. In English skeet, shooters shoot from seven positions (there is no station eight), the targets are thrown 55 yards, and the event is shot with only a 12-gauge shotgun. In International skeet, shooters shoot singles and doubles from eight stations.

Sporting Clays

Sporting clays bears the closest resemblance to actual field shooting of any shotgun sport. Rather than using standardized distances and targets, sporting clays provides multiple target sizes, angles, speeds, and changes in terrain to add an element of surprise. The courses are designed so that the flight of the target simulates a species of game, such as ducks, pheasants, or rabbits. There are at least six types of targets: standard, mini, rocket, rabbit, battue, and midi. Each club specifies the number of stations and the number of targets that constitutes a round, typically 50 to 100 targets, with one or more shots from each station. The three popular styles of sporting clays are : (1) English, (2) FITASC, which is the abbreviation of the Fédération Internationale de Tir aux Armes Sportives de Chasse, and (3) Five Stand.

English sporting clays feature multiple "stands" or stations, which can be shot in any order.

In FITASC sporting clays (also known as International Sporting Parcours de Chasse) an event can consist of one parcours, a sequence of 25 targets, up to eight parcours for a 200-target event. The major difference between English sporting clays and FITASC is in the number of trap machines required, which varies considerably.

There are two ways to shoot FITASC—the traditional and the new. Traditional uses three or four shooting stations set in a horseshoe, line, or oval shape, depending on space and safety zones available. In the new way, each parcours still consists of 25 targets, but four shooting positions are the norm, and each of the four stations has a minimum of three dedicated machines. With the new system each parcours can accommodate a squad on each station and therefore takes less time to complete.

In Five Stand sporting clays, five different shooting stands are in a line. The shooter gets a presentation of five targets, usually a single and two pairs, from each stand.

—SUSAN NATTRASS

Bibliography: Campbell, Robert. (1969) *Trapshooting with*

D. Lee Braun and the Remington Pros. New York: Rutledge Books. Lugs, Jaroslav. (1968) *A History of Shooting*. Middlesex, UK: Spring Books.

Shooting, Pistol

The sport of pistol shooting involves shooting specifically designed pistols at targets that can be scored and ranked under carefully controlled conditions with strict safety standards and competition rules.

History

Pistols (whose origins remain unknown) came into common use in the 16th and 17th centuries but were not widely used in target shooting until the 18th century.

In the 18th century, the pistol gradually replaced the sword as the favorite weapon of duelists. The best way for a potential duelist to survive was to practice shooting at targets. Remnants of dueling remain in the modern sport: emphasis on protocol and fair play and gun features.

Nineteenth-century exhibition shooting with pistols encouraged the development of accuracy and skill by public performers. Pistol exhibitions at circuses or large public gatherings occurred in many countries, including Germany and the United States. In the United States, William F. "Buffalo Bill" Cody and Annie Oakley promoted an appreciation of pistol shooting skills through exhibitions.

At the end of the 19th century, clubs to promote pistol shooting were organized in France, Germany, the United States, and other countries. In 1896 three pistol events were included in the Olympic Games in Athens. The World Shooting Championship program in 1900 included a similar free pistol event. Both influenced the development of today's rules.

Events proliferated: A center-fire pistol event, for large-caliber pistols, was added to the world championship program in 1947, in 1970 a 25-meter standard pistol event for semiautomatic .22 caliber rimfire pistols and a 10-meter (33-foot) air pistol event. An experimental women's pistol event was on the world championship program in 1962, and a women's sport pistol event was added to the Olympics in 1984 and air pistol events for men and women in 1988.

Air pistol shooting made it possible for the sport to be practiced widely in many countries that did not have large ranges or widespread access to pistols that shoot powder-burning cartridges. Women participated in pistol shooting as early as the late 1800s, but their numbers were small until women's pistol shooting became an Olympic event.

Rules and Play

In pistol shooting governed by the UIT, the shooter must stand erect, holding and aiming the pistol toward the target with one hand only. Competitive pistol shooters must train several hours daily for 8 to 12 years before they are skilled enough to compete internationally.

Pistols used for target shooting differ from ordinary pistols in several aspects. Their longer barrels and greater weight enhance accuracy and the ability of the shooter to aim them precisely at targets. Target pistols must have larger sights that can be adjusted very precisely. The special orthopedic grips are carved to fit the hands of the shooter. Pistols used in some events are single-shot pistols, while even those used in multiple-shot events seldom utilize magazines holding more than five shots.

Pistol targets have black circular aiming areas printed in the center of a rectangular white background. Both the black bull's-eye and the area around the central black have scoring rings printed on the target.

The successful shooter must be able to hold a relatively heavy pistol steady for long periods while carefully aligning its sights with the target and releasing the trigger. In some events, the precision of the shooter is tested and shots can be fired quite slowly. In other events, the shooter must start with a loaded pistol at a ready position where the pistol is pointed down from the target at a 45-degree angle. At a ready signal, the shooter must raise the pistol and fire one or more shots in a very short period of time.

Today, target pistol shooting is a sport for the young and the old, for women and for men, and for people from many different countries.

—GARY ANDERSON

See also Shooting, Rifle.

Bibliography: Antal, Laslo. (1983) *Competitive Pistol Shooting*. East Ardsley, Wakefield, UK: EP Publishing. Blair, Wesley. (1984) *The Complete Book of Target Shooting*. Harrisburg, PA: Stackpole Books. Yur'yev, A. A. (1985) *Competitive Shooting*. Trans. by Gary L. Anderson. Washington, DC: National Rifle Association of America.

Shooting, Rifle

Rifle shooting is a discipline within the sport of shooting, with the objective of precisely aiming and releasing a projectile from a gun to strike a distant target as close to its center as possible.

History

Records of marksmanship sports were found in ancient Egypt and Assyria as early as 2000 B.C.E. Rifle shooting's history began with matchlock and wheel-lock muskets that were used in target contests as early as the 15th and 16th centuries in Europe and Japan. Firearms with more accurate rifled barrels began to appear in competitions in Central Europe by the 16th century. Rifled barrels with internal, spiral grooves to spin and stabilize projectiles made rifles accurate for shooters to control their impact precisely, which made them better for use in target training and competitions. Marksmanship training was intended to improve skills needed in battle.

Crossbow and rifle shooting contests were local events for six centuries or more before they were organized at national levels during the 19th century in Switzerland, England, Germany, the United States, and France. Diverse national rifle shooting traditions began to converge in 1896 when two rifle events were on the program of the first modern Olympic Games in Athens and in 1897 when five European nations held the first World Shooting Championship in Lyon, France. Those international contests led to the formation, in 1907, of the International Shooting Union, also known as the Union Internationale de Tir (UIT), the world governing body of shooting.

Rules and Play

All rifle shooting events use paper or electronic targets with scoring rings valued from 1 to 10 points. The size of the target and its scoring rings vary depending upon the shooting distance and type of shooting, but the central 10 rings of all modern rifle targets are small and difficult to hit.

Three different shooting distances are used in UIT and most national competitions. All rifle events in the first world championship were fired at a distance of 300 meters with center-fire target rifles. Small-bore events for .22 caliber rimfire target rifles shot at targets 50 meters away were added to the Olympic program in 1908 and the world championship program in 1929. Air rifle events for 4.5 millimeter caliber target air rifles shot at targets 10 meters away were added to the world championship program in 1970 and the Olympic program in 1984.

Modern shooting has experienced a decline in the use of center-fire rifles and a dramatic increase in the use of air rifles, which account for the growth of shooting in many countries.

Target rifles are heavier, with more precise sights, and special triggers that produce the highest degrees of accuracy. International competition use two basic rifle configurations. The traditional target rifle, called a free

rifle, derives from rifles used in the late 19th century that featured hook buttplates to assist in uniformly positioning the rifle on the shooter's shoulder and palm rests that extend below the rifle to help the shooter hold the rifle when standing. Free rifles are used in men\s 300-meter and 50-meter events.

The second rifle configuration, the standard rifle, has a lighter weight limit and cannot have hook buttplates, thumbhole stocks, or palm rests. Standard rifles represent an attempt to compete with a lighter, simpler, and less costly target rifle. This style of rifle is used by women in their 50-meter events, by men in a 300-meter standard rifle event, and by both men and women in 10-meter air rifle events.

Shooters assume three different positions to hold and aim the rifle. The most challenging is standing, followed by kneeling, and prone. National programs in the United States and a few other countries also require shooting in the sitting position. A fifth shooting position is used in benchrest shooting, which is practiced in some countries, most notably the United States.

The type of shooting done in competitions governed by the UIT is called slow-fire or precision shooting. Shooters are given suffcient time to aim carefully and control each shot. Competitions governed by the International Military Sport Council, and some national programs include rapid-fire shooting, where shooters are given a short period of time to fire a series of shots. Usually this requires shooting 10 shots in one or two minutes.

The most important contests today are the rifle events in the Olympic Games and World Shooting Championships. These events are practiced by the more than 135 member federations of the UIT and make rifle shooting one of the world's most popular competitive sports.

—GARY ANDERSON

See also Shooting, Pistol.

Bibliography: Blair, Wesley. (1984) *The Complete Book of Target Shooting.* Harrisburg, PA: Stackpole Books. Horneber, Ralf. (1993) *Olympic Target Rifle Shooting.* Trans. by Bill Murray. Munich: F. C. Meyer Verlag. Pullum, Bill, and Frank T. Hanenkrat. (1995) *The New Position Rifle Shooting.* Peachtree City, GA: Target Sports Education Center.

Shooting, Single-Shot

The single-shot rifle, as its name indicates, is able to fire only one shot at a time. The modern sport has four variations that differ in shooting position and distance.

History

The first contests for accuracy in the United States were usually backwoods affairs, with rifles fired over a log at an "X" inscribed on a distant board. Rifles were loaded with the powder and bullet pushed down from the muzzle. The military then was not interested in accurate fire, despite the significant achievements of the American colonists using rifled Pennsylvania arms in the Revolutionary War and on the frontier. That thinking was changed by the German-American *schuetzen* tradition and by American victories against the British using long-range rifles.

Competitive shooting did not begin in earnest until the immigration of many Germans who had failed to establish democracy in Germany's revolution of 1848. Among the customs they brought was shooting at targets from a standing position at 200 meters. They established *Schuetzenvereins,* or gun clubs, that became the basis for many U.S. shooting clubs. Members of the clubs were the core of the U.S. team in the Olympic international free rifle shooting tournaments after the turn of the century. These were popular until the anti-German sentiments of World War I brought about their demise.

The victory of the U.S. rifle team over the Irish in the 1874 long-range (1,000-yard) rifle competition on Long Island engendered a new interest in marksmanship in the U.S. military and sparked the popularity of shooting single-shot rifles from the prone position.

Rules and Play

The Schuetzen Tradition

After World War II, the specialized *schuetzen* rifles and shooting paraphernalia were still in former club members' attics, and in 1948 some members of the National Muzzle Loading Rifle Association decided to establish an organization that would allow competition with these rifles. They formed the American Single Shot Rifle Association (ASSRA). Since then, the ASSRA has grown to well over 2,000 members. The rifles used in ASSRA competition fired at 200 yards are limited to those that can load a single cartridge (brass case, powder, and bullet). The empty brass case must be removed before the next cartridge can be inserted and fired.

The Long-Range Tradition

Shooting with rifles at longer distances (sometimes over 1,000 yards) requires a different technique than that of *schuetzen* shooting. In long-range shooting, the bullet can be in flight for several seconds and can be affected by wind currents, for which compensation must

---

Colonists Triumph

After 12 years of competition the Irish team won the British long-range Elcho Shield trophy in 1873 and challenged the American "colonists" to a similar match at distances of up to 1,000 yards. The Americans accepted, although they had no previous experience of shooting at such long ranges. Thus, the international match began on 25 September 1874, at the newly constructed Creedmoor range on Long Island.

At 800 yards the Americans were ahead after one and one-half hours of shooting, with a score of 326–317. At 900 yards the Irish team closed that 9-point gap by scoring 312 against the American score of 310, even with a shot on the wrong target by J. K. Millner of the Irish team, which was a center shot that did not count. Thus, the 1,000-yard stage was to determine the outcome of this first international match.

The Irish closed the gap further at 1,000 yards, so that they were ahead by a point when it came time for Colonel John Bodine of the American team to fire the last shot of the match. If he missed the target, the Americans would lose by one point. If he made a center shot (bull's-eye), the Americans would win by three points. Clearly the pressure was on, and Bodine opened a ginger ale bottle beforehand to refresh himself. The bottle exploded and cut his hand. A cry of dismay rose from the crowd of some 8,000 spectators who were crowding the firing line down toward the targets. Bodine casually wrapped a handkerchief around his cut hand and got into position. A swath in the crowd of spectators was made so that he could have a sight of the target. Then he fired the final shot. All eyes were riveted on the target for the signal of what his score might be, and they saw the white bull's-eye scoring disc slowly rise over the target over a half mile away. A roar of jubilation rose from the spectators as the Americans won the match by 3 points and Colonel Bodine became the savior of America's national honor.

The illustrations of the teams from the account of the match in *Harper's Weekly* show the American team all of erect posture with top hats, turned toward the hero Bodine. The Irish team members, on the other hand, are hatless and slouched around Millner, who is beset with remorse for the crossfire that did not count, and he is given the hand of succor from Arthur Leech, the Irish team captain.

This American victory began a long history of U.S. interest in the accurate shooting sports.

—*Rudi Prusok*

---

be made when aiming. Shooters in this sport lie prone, facing the target with the rifle in front of them, or supine, with the rifle cradled between upraised knees. The rifles themselves usually are of larger caliber and have more recoil.

The Benchrest Tradition

The benchrest tradition allows the rifle to be fired from a shooting table and rested on a sandbag or other support near the muzzle. This stability permits testing of the various components that make a rifle shoot accurately (bullet, lubricant, powder charge) without the factor of human error and has helped to develop superaccurate rifles with heavy barrels. There was no formal benchrest competition until 1947, with the formation of the National Benchrest Shooters Association.

Silhouette Shooting
A recent development of single-shot rifle competition is shooting at steel targets that resemble game animals in silhouette. The sport originated in Mexico in the 1950s as *siluetas metalicas,* but that term applies now only to high-power rifle shooting at metal targets. The French-derived *silhouette* is used as a generic term for shooting with any weapon at animal-shaped targets.
—RUDI PRUSOK

See also Shooting, Rifle.
Bibliography: Trench, Charles C. (1980) *A History of Marksmanship.* New York: Exeter Books.

Shooting, Trap and Skeet
See Shooting, Clay Target

Shuffleboard
Shuffleboard is a popular court sliding game in which players use long poles to push flat disks onto designated scoring areas of marked courts. Play ranges from a casual cruise-ship pastime to intense competition.

History
The most direct ancestors of shuffleboard were games that originated in Britain during the Middle Ages and the Renaissance, notably lawn bowling and curling. Early games were associated with the aristocracy, and a playing area at home was a status symbol. However, the games also became popular among the lower classes, and playing tables were common in taverns. Some of the games were associated with gambling and were officially discouraged.

The basic elements of these old games were revived and given their contemporary identity as shuffleboard in the late 19th century. This revival coincided with the growth of the cruise-ship industry. The cruise-line owners needed to develop recreational activities for passengers. The companies devised new versions of these older sliding games to be played on large courts on the decks.

In 1913, the Ball family set up a land shuffleboard court at their hotel in Daytona Beach, Florida. The land-based game spread to other Florida resorts, and in the following decades became popular in other regions and

nations. Shuffleboard courts were often included in the public parks built in the early 20th century.

The early stages of this revival featured multiple versions of the basic game of shuffleboard, some with different names. In the 1920s, an effort began in Florida to establish a standard form of shuffleboard, and the National Shuffleboard Association was formed to coordinate the sport's development. Shuffleboard is widely played today, and numerous local, regional, and national leagues and tournaments are held in many locations.

Rules and Play
Shuffleboard courts can be located inside or outdoors. The playing surface must be smooth enough to allow the disc to slide down it, and is usually a hard surface such as wood, concrete, or terrazzo.

In the official version the standard shuffleboard court is 52 feet long and 6 feet wide. The two scoring areas are triangles located near the ends of the court that are farthest apart. At the two farthest ends of the court, behind the base of the triangles, are marked blocks that extend about 6 feet back where players stand to make their shots.

Each player has four discs, either red or black. In singles, the two players stand at the same end of the court and take turns making shots.

The disc must stop completely within the scoring area, without touching its lines, to count. A player may also make shots that deliberately lower the other player's score by using his disc to knock the opponent's disc out of a numbered zone or into the 10-off area. This is called *caroming.* Players can also use one disc to protect another disc from being struck by their opponent or to block the other player's access to a scoring area.

At its most basic level, shuffleboard can be played for light exercise and amusement by people who do not have the strength or endurance for more rigorous sports. At advanced levels, shuffleboard requires a great deal of concentration, strategy, and physical skill.
—JOHN TOWNES

Sidesaddle Riding
See Horseback Riding, Sidesaddle

Single-Shot Shooting
See Shooting, Single-shot

Skateboarding
Skateboarders ride four-wheeled boards that they propel with their feet and coast down inclined areas. Defying attempts at organization, skateboarding remains

recreational and popular with those who reject mainstream society.

History

The first skateboard was probably adapted from the fruit-crate skate-scooters of the 1930s. Californian surfers popularized skateboarding in the late 1950s as an activity for waveless days. Skateboarders, or "sidewalk surfers," formed part of the same subculture as surfers, and adopted the surfers' hedonistic, carefree lifestyle. The two activities shared technical similarities, and skateboarders often mimicked surfing maneuvers when riding the curves of swimming pools, sewer pipes, and street curbs. (Like many other activities with a high risk of injury, skateboarding is overwhelmingly a male pursuit.)

The sport has passed through several phases: "sidewalk surfing" in the 1960s, the punk and skatepark era in the 1970s, ramp skating in the late 1980s, and "grunge" in the 1990s.

The first phase ended in 1967, after disapproving authorities banned it as dangerous and the public condemned it as they did surfing—riders were depicted as selfish, irresponsible itinerants and louts. By 1967, skateboarding had gone underground.

In 1973 the urethane wheel resurrected skateboarding by giving skaters greater control of their boards and so increased their repertoire of tricks and moves. Skateboard parks consisting of specially designed pools, pipes, and obstacle courses became the rage.

In the late 1970s, punk, an antisocial subculture involving extremes of music, fashion, and attitude, adopted skateboarding much as surfers had. Punks, however, suffered the same image problems as had surfers. Medical authorities repeated their condemnation of the activity, city councils banned skateboarding or enforced existing ordinances, skate parks had trouble obtaining insurance, and many new parks closed down.

The National Skateboarding Association (NSA) was formed in 1981 with assistance from the Boy Scouts of America. The NSA attempted to give skateboarding a legitimate and positive image through competition and sponsorship from major companies. Many skateboarders resisted, preferring that the practice remain an unorganized activity, true to its original ideals.

The current phase of popularity is influenced by grunge, an underground youth style that rejects high consumption and yuppie competitiveness. Grunge youth repopularized such cooperative, individualistic activities as skateboarding. In the 1990s, skateboarders prefer street skating. Hip-hop, an urban style of music

and fashion, also has influenced skateboarding style and philosophy.

Skateboarding will undoubtedly maintain this decline-revive pattern. It is unlikely that it will ever be particularly respectable.

—DUNCAN HUMPHREYS

See also Extreme Sports.

Bibliography: Beal, Becky. (1995) "Disqualifying the Official: An Exploration of Social Resistance through the Subculture of Skateboarding." *Sociology of Sport Journal* 12: 252–267. Davidson, Judith A. (1985) "Sport and Modern Technology: The Rise of Skateboarding, 1963–1978." *Journal of Popular Culture* 18, 4: 145–157.

Skating, Figure

Once only a pleasant cold-weather diversion, gliding on ice wearing boots with metal runners has become figure skating, still practiced recreationally but also highly commercial and competitive and one of the most popular spectator sports.

History

Flint-shaped bone blades found all over northern Europe—one still thong-tied to the foot of a Neolithic skeleton found in a bog in Friesland (in what is now the northern Netherlands)—document skating's ancestry. The earliest literary mention of skating appears in the Scandinavian Eddas, tales collected in the 10th century that date back to 156 C.E., in which reference is made to the "beauty, arrows and skates" of Uller, god of winter, who "runs on bones of animals," as well as to runic heroes who count skating among their manly feats.

Skating was a necessity for the Dutch, who started building canals in the 12th century. By the 1500s it had become such an integral part of the Lowlands landscape that the Flemish artist Pieter Brueghel even painted skaters into his *Census at Bethlehem* (1556).

In England skating was an import, perhaps brought as early as the 5th and 6th centuries by invading Saxons and certainly no later than 1066 with the Norman invasion.

In 1660 the deposed Stuarts returned from exile at the Netherlands court, bringing with them the Dutch roll and more elegant iron skates, used by the Dutch since the 1400s. On 15 December 1662, diarist Samuel Pepys noted Charles II's son, the Duke of Monmouth, and his coterie skating in St. James's Park and remarked that "he slides very well."

By 1742, the first skating club had been founded in Edinburgh. Admission to the club was limited to men (women were not admitted until well over a century later) of eminent lineage who could skate a circle on each foot and jump over three hats. Those circles and the turns on them became the basis of modern figure skating, and triple and quad jumps of a different sort—no hats—the desideratum of elite competitors, male and female alike.

In the mid-1700s, skating spread across Europe and to North America as sophisticated recreation. American painter Benjamin West, later president of the Royal Academy, visiting London in 1760, was invited to show off his Philadelphia style in Kensington Gardens. His compatriot Gilbert Stuart, noted for his portrait of George Washington, immortalized the sport in *The Skater* (1782), which hangs in the National Gallery of Art, Washington, D.C. The sport's first textbook was British Artillery Lieutenant Robert Jones's 1772 *Treatise on Skating*.

Confined to frozen village ponds with no place to go but around, the Victorians soon began inventing elaborate geometric, filigree, and grapevine figures made possible by the extended heel and shorter radius curve of the blade developed by Henry Boswell in the 1830s. From these early figures were devised "combined figures" for two to eight skaters who traced patterns to and from an orange on the ice marking a center, rather like a minuet or sedate quadrille. The emphasis was on "doing it properly."

Across the Channel, the Parisians found skating was festive, and aesthetic form was as important as technical proficiency. These two impulses, precision and appearance, self-control and self-expression, interact to this day and are both present in competitive scoring in the marks for technical merit and presentation.

Skating continued to develop in the 19th century. The Philadelphia Skating Club and Humane Society (male members carried ropes to rescue people fallen through the ice) was founded in 1849. In 1863, the St. Petersburg club was founded in Russia; even the czar came to skate on the Neva River. Quebec City had the first covered rink—a roof over natural ice—in the late 1850s.

Private skating clubs and associations were sufficiently organized by 1892 for Austria, Germany, Great Britain, the Netherlands, Hungary, and Sweden to found the Internationale Eislauf Vereinigung, now the International Skating Union (ISU), which governs speed and figure skating. Canada joined in 1894, the U.S. Figure Skating Association in 1923. The World Figure Skating Championships have been held annually since 1896, except during the two world wars and in 1961, after a plane crash killed the entire U.S. team. As of 1996, there were 55 member nations, including a number of countries not commonly associated with ice skating, such as Israel, Mexico, and Thailand.

For most of its history, skating's face on the podium has been Caucasian, and Anglo-Saxon. This began changing in the late 1970s; since then, China's Chen Lu won the world championship in 1995 and the United States' Michelle Kwan in 1996 and 1998.

Rules and Play

Figures

The four edges combined with the three turns—bracket, loop, rocker—and counterturns placed on two- and three-lobed "eights" that the English developed became the ISU 42-figure compulsory syllabus. Figures, which had been two-thirds the cost and time of becoming a singles champion, were dropped from international competition in 1990.

Singles

The first world championship, for men only, was held in St. Petersburg in 1896. In 1902, because there was no specific rule barring women, the ISU had to let Britain's Mrs. Edgar (Madge) Syers (b. 1882) compete. When this unforeseen interloper placed second to defending champion Ulrich Salchow (b. 1877) of Sweden in a field of four, the ISU was so undone that it inaugurated a separate women's event in 1908, the same year pairs competition was instituted.

Skating was a male-dominated sport until Norway's Sonja Henie (b. 1912) burst on the skating scene in 1924 with ballet-trained vigor, invention, and speed to break all precedents. Henie went on to win 10 world and 3 Olympic titles, wearing colored costumes that rippled during spins and beige, then white, boots. Her corkscrew Axel had no lift or carry, and she had none of today's double or triple jumps, but Henie raised skating to a new plane.

If Henie gave the sport its glamour, its guts came from postwar North American men. Dick Button (b. 1929) of the United States challenged conventional style with a whole new concept of aggressive power skating. In 1948, 66 years after Norway's Axel Paulson (b. 1855) debuted his eponymous jump, Button doubled it—a forward take-off, two and a half revolutions, landing backward. The first triple was by Canada's Vern Taylor in 1978; the first by a woman was by Midori Ito in 1990. Now men do triple Axels in combination with other double and triple jumps without doing a turn or step in between.

Button invented the flying camel, and his flying sit-spin, split, and double jumps soared higher than the barrier at the edge of the rink. The idea was to be muscularly athletic; the artistry would be in making it look easy and natural.

In the 1970s, several developments revolutionized figure skating. The more challenging elements became essential. After Elaine Zayak (b. 1965) of the United States unleashed four triple toe loops and two triple Salchows to win the 1982 world championship, a breakthrough for women's athleticism, the ISU ruled that no triple could be repeated except in combination with another jump. Women are now landing triples, while men are throwing quads.

Two men, the aristocratic classicist John Curry (b. 1949) of Great Britain and the baroquely flamboyant Toller Cranston (b. 1949) of Canada, each with a uniquely personal idiom, gave permission for men to be more expressive and creative.

Pairs

Centuries of skating hand in hand led to a first tepid world pairs event in 1908. The development of modern pairs skating depended on improvements in women's skating (including liberation from long skirts) and the advent of Russian skaters.

Until the 1930s, a typical program consisted of shadow-skated footwork (where the two skaters move exactly in tandem in me-and-my-shadow fashion) between highlights such as spirals, one or two half-turn jumps, and tiny lifts, skated to march or ballroom dance music. The look was precise, safe, and genteel.

No Russian/Soviet had competed since Nicholas Panin won the Olympic special figures in 1908. Shrewdly, drawing on their rich ballet heritage, they concentrated first on pairs and later on dance, neither of which requires costly and time-consuming figures practice.

By 1969, the Protopopovs, then aged 32 and 35, considered old at that time—had won four world and two Olympic titles, and their fluid refinement was seen as the future for pairs. Instead, the pendulum swung to tiny Irina Rodnina (b. 1949) charging in with Alexei Ulanov (b. 1947) to her first world championship to usurp the throne with a routine of spectacular speed, daring, and difficulty. They were the first of the small-and-tall pairs, in which the size difference made it easy to move the woman around in the air.

Having gone way beyond hand-in-hand, pairs programs now include triple jumps, lifts, twists, and 7.6-meter (25-foot) triple throws, as well as increasingly complex footwork influenced by ice dancers.

Ice Dancing

Since the advent of Jayne Torvill (b. 1957) and Christopher Dean (b. 1958) of Great Britain in the 1980s, ice dancing, the last discipline to be developed, is often the first ticket to sell out at international meets.

In the 1930s, the English, by then a nation of ballroom dance adepts, saw the possibility of adapting other social dances to ice. New-dance contests produced foxtrots, tangos, a quickstep, blues, more waltzes, a paso doble and rumba, creating an enjoyable club activity and a set-pattern test and competition schedule. Still, a world championship, with an added free-dance worth 40 percent, was not held until 1952. Even with an original set-pattern dance event added in 1967, the International Olympic committee (IOC) did not consider dance athletic enough for the games until 1976, after the Soviets started steadily winning world dance in 1970 with their dramatic projection.

Skaters from western Europe and the United States were then better technicians, but what the Soviets may have lacked in technique, they more than made up for in facial and upper body expression. The "English style" was polite, the Russian, passionate, opening the possibility for ice dance to be a fully realized artistic medium.

Judging ice dance presents considerable difficulty, since the dance itself and the skating technique must be evaluated as a whole, unlike singles and pairs where it is easier to spot errors in individual elements. Dancing demands more sheer skating—blade to blade, never apart—than pairs. It also demands more subtle edge control, flow, complex footwork, holds, and positions. Seeing two compulsory dances that they already know helps judges winnow the field before they look at the original dance (to a preselected rhythm) and the free-dance (to music of the skater's own choosing.).

Team Skating

From a 1956 teenage marching drill team organized as a recreational outlet for club skaters in Ann Arbor, Michigan has come the highly competitive international sport of precision skating. Line, circle, block, wheel, and intersecting formations, edges incorporating intricate footwork and single jumps, but no lifts, are skated in unison to music. Teams have from 12 to 24 skaters, with juvenile through adult divisions. The fastest-growing skating discipline in the world, it received official recognition as an ISU world event in 1994 and has corporate sponsorship and television coverage.

Similarly, carnivals, which spawned the professional ice shows, have been a traditional club activity since the 1930s, but amateur show skating was not put into competition until 1980. From France the sport has spread across Europe. The first U.S. team, established in 1990 in Burlington, Vermont, hosted the 1996 international event.

The Business of Skating

After complaining for years that government support in communist countries made their skaters "paid professionals," in the early 1980s, it finally occurred to Western associations to seek capitalistic corporate sponsorship to augment existing income from sale of TV rights. Amateurs are now termed "eligibles," and skaters duly registered to do so with their national association may perform, compete, and teach for pay without penalty. The ISU itself sponsors open and grand prix events with money prizes.

Figure skating is now, unavoidably, big business. U.S. television networks, observing that its ratings were second only to those of football—sometimes even equaling Super Bowl figures—greatly increased coverage of skating in the 1990s. Accompanying skating's greater visibility has been a revolution in skating fashion, which formed part of the show-business spectacle of major skating events. Into the 1960s, the form was to carry the free leg—the one not bearing the skater's weight—bent. Today, this looks merely quaint. Flapping trousers and bent free legs were replaced, in the sixties, by aerodynamic lines of stretch ski cloth. In the 1980s, women's high-necked, minimally decorated dresses gave way to elaborately body-revealing and flashily decorated stretch fabrics. During the 1990s some longer skirts in chiffon appeared; but ironically, tights on men, which the Victorians had found inoffensive, were banned by the ISU in 1992.

—ASTRID HAGENGUTH

Bibliography: Copley-Graves, Lynn. (1992) *Figure Skating History: The Evolution of Dance on Ice.* Columbus, OH: Plataro Press. Smith, Beverly. (1994) *Figure Skating: A Celebration.* Toronto: McClelland & Stewart. Whedon, Julia. (1988) *The Fine Art of Ice Skating.* New York: Harry N. Abrams.

Skating, Ice Speed

Speed skating on ice is a purely competitive sport that is growing ever more popular, especially as a Winter Olympics sport that draws large crowds and television audiences.

History

By the middle of the 19th century, Holland's national sport was speed skating. The most successful speed skaters were workers who skated as part of their jobs. Thus, canal workers enjoyed great success in various competitions, some with sizable purses.

A key in the development and growth of speed skating was the advent of artificial "ice palaces," or rinks. As of 1900, New York, Paris, and London each had two rinks. Brighton, Brussels, Munich, Philadelphia, Brooklyn, and Baltimore had one each. In 1909, the world's first open-air artificial ice rink was opened in Vienna, Austria.

Ice speed skating eventually spread to Holland's neighbors, including Austria, Germany, and France. The Frieslanders of North Holland, helped by their close geographical proximity, introduced the sport to the Fens district of England.

The first international speed skating competition took place at Hamburg, Germany, in 1889. This was followed by the inaugural men's world championships in 1893. (Although men's speed skating was included on the program of the Chamonix Olympics in 1924, it was not until the Squaw Valley Olympics in 1960 that women's speed skating appeared.)

In the 20th century, speed skating has been closely bound up with the Olympics. As with skiing, the speed skating World Cup has created an annual circuit of events, and today the star speed skater travels the world from Cortina d' Ampezzo, Italy, to Sapporo, Japan.

Men's speed skating first appeared at the 1924 Chamonix Olympics. Nordic countries did exceptionally well, winning four of five gold medals. While no country has dominated men's speed skating, certain countries such as Norway, Finland, and Holland have always been highly successful.

In North America speed skating for many years was administered by an overall skating body. However, in 1960 the Canadian Amateur Speed Skating Association was founded. Four years later the United States followed suit by setting up the International Speed Skating Association.

Speed skating came of age in the United States at the 1980 Lake Placid Olympics when 22-year-old Eric Heiden, a native of Madison, Wisconsin, took five gold medals and inspired a generation of young American skaters. Until Heiden's sweep at the 1980 Olympics, the greatest Olympic speed skaters were either Norwegian or Dutch.

Most recently, speed skating has been transformed by the use of the clap skate, an old idea that was developed in the 1980s. Clap skates are equipped with a spring-loaded hinge in front that allows the boot's heel to rise and fall, thus keeping the blade in contact with the ice longer. The resulting economy of motion results in faster skating. On average, skaters wearing the skates go one second faster for each 400-meter round.

Rules and Play

International championship meets are normally two days long. Usually, the 500- and 5,000-meter events are staged on the first day and the 1,500- and 10,000-meter events on the following day. The best all-around performer over these four distances, as calculated on a points basis, becomes the overall individual champion.

The successful speed skater is a true all-around athlete, with the quickness of a sprinter and the staying power of a long-distance performer. This is comparable to a track runner training to perform well in both the 100-meter dash and the 10,000-meter race.

Modern speed skating is immediately recognizable by its competition format: two skaters going against one another and the clock. During the race the competitors alternate at preset intervals between the inside and outside lanes to prevent one skater from having an unfair advantage. This is known as "crossing over," and is difficult considering the skaters are moving at speeds sometimes in excess of 48 kilometers (30 miles) per hour.

A new type of speed skating, called "pack start" or short-track racing, was introduced at Calgary in 1988. Today, short-track racing is an integral part of Olympic and world speed skating. The tremendous attraction of short-track racing is that it revolves around groups of competitors in close contact. It is very similar to the "bunching up" of track runners in the final lap of the 800 or 1,500 meters. Short-track racing is much more exciting for spectators than traditional speed skating since there can be contact collisions, shadowing, drafting, and a cut-and-thrust atmosphere that makes it a civilized version of roller derby.

—Scott A. G. M. Crawford

Bibliography: Holum, D. (1984) *The Complete Handbook of Speed Skating.* Hillside, NJ: Enslow Publishing.

Skating, In-Line

In-line skating is a variant of roller skating employing a series of wheels, generally four or five, set in a straight line mimicking the ice skate. The modern in-line skate sacrifices the precise control of the dual-axle roller skate for greater speed, superior adaptability to a variety of surfaces, and easier mastery.

History

In-lines are actually the oldest type of roller skate. In-line skates were used in theatrical productions in the late 18th and early 19th centuries as substitutes for ice skates. Experimentation with different configurations eventually resulted in the superior maneuverability of the cushioned dual-axle roller skate. The in-line concept survived into the 1970s largely as an off-season training tool for skiers and ice skaters, benefiting from the introduction of plastic components and Polyurethane wheels. In 1979 Scott Olson, a 19-year-old American semi-professional hockey player, discovered the in-line skate as an off-season training aide. Olson modified the design for hockey use and sold the patent rights to a private investor in 1984. The resultant company, Rollerblade, launched a major marketing campaign that popularized in-line skating and made the company's name synonymous with in-line skates.

Early in-lines were wooden platforms mounting wooden wheels, attached to the foot with straps of leather or fabric. Modern skates employ space-age materials. The boot, or shell, encases the foot. Frames can incorporate a number of features depending upon their intended purpose, including "rocker" features to enhance maneuverability, brake pads, and even active braking systems. Wheels are chosen to suit the surface and activity of the skater, with variations in size and hardness.

Rules and Play

Sidewalk and rink skating serve as the introduction to organized in-line sports. The least regulated of these is "aggressive" skating—the performance of various acrobatic stunts, similar to stunt skateboarding in nature and its largely adolescent demographics. Aggressive skating also inherited some of skateboarding's bad reputation due to their close relationship and the damage each inflicted upon public property through both skating stunts and the often rebellious behavior of youthful subcultures. The in-line industry's formation in 1992 of the Skatesmart program, which promotes skating safety, attempted to adjust this image.

Organized competitive roller skating is governed internationally by the Fédération Internationale de Roller-Skating (FIRS), which accepts in-line skates in all categories and has established speed and hockey divisions reserved for in-line skaters. The codified and regimented nature of these activities stands in stark contrast to the more informal world of stunt skating, as does organized skating's appeal to a broader range of age groups.

One discipline of competitive skating, roller hockey, enjoyed a particularly substantial boost in popularity with the introduction of in-line skates. The 1992 Olympic Games in Barcelona featured an exhibition of roller hockey, the first roller sport in the Olympics. The game itself is based upon ice hockey with a few modifications relating to the different surfaces involved. In-line roller hockey has formed professional leagues and includes professional ice hockey players in its ranks.

In-lines quickly replaced traditional roller skates in speed competitions, both those sanctioned by FIRS and recognized national governing organizations and the less formal events, which increased in number as the popularity of in-line skating grew.

Only one discipline of internationally organized skating remains untouched by in-line skates. Artistic roller skating is still dominated by dual-axle skates due to their superior maneuverability and control. But artistic events are open to in-lines, and inventors continue to improve in-line designs.

In-line skating grew explosively in the later 1980s and early 1990s. In the United States alone an estimated 12 million people tried the sport at least once in 1993. In-line skates may now be found around the world, for both recreational and practical purposes. One reflection of this is their adoption by the American Amish community, renowned for its rejection of modern technology and recreational pursuits, as a means of transportation.

—JEFFERY CHARLSTON

Bibliography: Joyner, Stephen. (1993) *Complete Guide and Resource to In-line Skating.* Cincinnati, OH: Betterway. Rappelfeld, Joel. (1992) *The Complete Blader.* New York: St. Martin's.

Skating, Roller

Roller skating on four wheels, indoors or out, ranges from children skating in the park to speed skating and marathons.

History

The first roller skates were probably an adaptation of ice skates and used for transportation rather than sport. The first recognized inventor of roller skates was a Belgian manufacturer of musical instruments named Joseph Merlin, who produced the first roller skates with metal wheels in 1760. Roller skates debuted on stage in 1849, when Frenchman Louis Legrange wore them to simulate ice skates in the play *Le Prophete;* he mounted tiny rollers down the center of ice skates. By that time,

others had joined Merlin in producing skates; none had solved their major problem—skaters could neither control nor stop the skates.

A New Yorker, James Plimpton, solved the problem of controlling roller skates in 1863. Plimpton's skates used a rubber cushion to anchor the axles. This cushion compressed when the body was leaned, enabling the wheels of the skate to turn slightly when the skater shifted his or her weight. Plimpton's design is considered the basis for the modern roller skate.

The first world championship of roller hockey was held in Stuttgart, Germany, in 1936. The first world speed roller skating championships occurred just a year later in Monza, Italy. Competitive artistic roller skating existed at the same time, although the first artistic roller skating world championships were not held until 1947 in Washington, D.C.

World championships in all three recognized disciplines of competitive roller skating—artistic, speed, and hockey—have been held annually (for the most part) ever since.

Rules and Play

All three types of roller skating are governed in the United States by the United States Amateur Confederation of Roller Skating (USAC/RS). The sport is governed internationally by the Fédération Internationale de Roller Skating (FIRS).

Artistic skating is further broken down into dance, singles and pairs freestyle, and figures. Dance skating requires athletes to perform preannounced skating dance programs, a detailed series of steps at various points around the floor. Artistic skating—both singles and pairs—is very similar to ice figure skating, where athletes perform difficult routines set to music. Figures stresses skating fundamentals; competitors must trace painted circles on the floor.

Speed skating is one of the fastest sports in the world where speed is generated by human energy. It is a noncontact sport, requiring skaters to maneuver cleanly through the pack and into winning position.

Speed skating is divided into indoor and outdoor varieties, with indoor racing being an almost exclusively American pastime. Indoors, speed skaters take on a flat, 100-meter (110-yard) track in individual and relay events. Indoor speed skaters may wear either conventional four-wheeled skates or in-line skates.

Outdoor speed skating, the internationally accepted version of the sport, is competed on both banked tracks and road courses. The banked track is usually about 200 meters and has parabolic curves. A road competition is held on a flat course, either a closed course or an open stretch of road. Distances of 300, 500, 1,500, 3,000, 5,000, 10,000, and 20,000 meters are competed on the track, which also includes a relay. On the road, the same distances are run, with the relay being replaced by a marathon.

—ANDY SEELEY

Bibliography: Phillips, Ann-Victoria (1979). *The Complete Book of Roller Skating.* New York: Womman.

Ski Jumping

Building up speed as they ski down a real or constructed hill, ski jumpers then soar off the end, remain airborne as long as possible, and land as firmly and stylishly as they can. The attraction both to performers and to spectators is this prospect of humans flying in the air. The risks mean that a certain amount of psychological strength is necessary to perform a decent ski jump. Hence, ski jumping, even in the countries of origin, never has been a large participant sport. Still, as a spectator sport ski jumping holds a firm grip on people and draws large crowds, especially in Finland, Austria, Norway, and Japan.

History

Ski jumping as an activity first appeared in the Nordic region. Ski jumping as a sport seems to be a more specific Norwegian invention. The early sagas and legends of the Norse Viking era suggest similar challenges. Around the turn of the 18th century, military ski companies apparently started jumping.

The first formal jumping competitions were most often combined events, either downhill with a terminating jump, or cross-country with one or more jumps. A race in Trysil in 1862 was the first known pure jumping competition, a trend that continued. During this decade, also, attempts to formalize the activity into a sport began with races in the capital at Kristiania (present-day Oslo). The townspeople were undoubtedly impressed with what they saw—and wanted to control it: they made themselves referees and evaluators of how the sport was to develop into *ski-idrμt,* the concept of sport as a path to both physical and moral development. Ski jumping started to appear in other countries in the 1870s.

Ski jumping came to Sweden through Norwegian soldiers posted in Stockholm as part of the union military system. Here the alleged first "international ski jumping contest" took place in 1886. The spread continued to Finland, where skiers rather hesitantly took up the "Norwegian habit" around the turn of the cen-

tury, and the sport also spread into the Alps. Czechoslovakia, Poland, and Yugoslavia also embraced the sport after 1900. As early as the middle of the 19th century, Norwegian immigrants took jumping to North America. By the beginning of the 20th century ski jumps had been performed in such remote areas as Australia and South Africa as well.

In the final decades of the 19th century, Norwegians came to view ski jumping as the unrivaled national sport, part of Norway's need to define itself and its culture apart from Sweden. Skiing in general and ski jumping in particular stood out as characteristically Norwegian. Accordingly, one of the first official appearances by Norway's newly imported king and queen after they had arrived late in the autumn of 1905 was at the Holmenkollen ski-jumping festival.

Ski jumping has become central to the sports life of Finland and Austria. Other nations have also introduced changes; in North America, the height of the jump is also measured.

Constructed arenas became more common around the turn of the 19th century, and since the 1970s ski jumping has also been practiced in the summertime on artificial surfaces such as porcelain and plastic.

Rules and Play

Referees evaluate the style of the jumper in the air and while landing and award points accordingly. Generally, length of jump has counted more than style, although in 1996 landing style still counts as much as before.

A ski-jumping hill consists of four parts: (1) the inrun, (2) the jump itself (3) the landing *(unnarenn),* which is also the steepest part of the hill; and (4) the end of the run, or the halt.

Technique and Equipment

Jumping skis developed around the 1880s when the event was separated from racing, enabling the skiers to change from jumping to cross-country skis or the other way around. Jumping skis became heavier, thicker, and longer, and specialized imported hickory replaced homegrown wood. Bindings, boots, jumping-suits, and wax underwent similar changes, particularly with increased emphasis on length and winning. The fiberglass revolution was accompanied by a centralizing of the ski-manufacturing industry in the hands of a few Central European firms.

Modern equipment makes for longer, more aerodynamic jumps and larger hills. Still, the ideal jump should always seek to cover an optimal distance, but also harmonize the take-off, the flight, and the landing.

The original Telemark "drawn-up" style, with knees drawn up under the skier, was performed by legendary jumper Sondre Nordheim (1825–1897)—in which the jumper drew his skis up under himself (as in today's freestyle skiing). This was presumably an attempt to increase the length of the jump (or to impress the spectators). First, in the "upright style," the skiers stood up straight during the jump, arms along the side. As the hills grew larger, more aerodynamic styles forced their way in. A further development, the "Kongsberg bend," was notable for a marked bend in the hip, arms out, and controlled arm rotations.

After World War II the "Finn style" introduced a new marked step and increased emphasis on aerodynamics. Into the 1960s the dominant way of jumping was arms along the side, parallel skis, and an ever more aerodynamic posture in the air. The next new invention came with a shift of the sitting position in the in-run, promoted by the East Germans in the early 1970s, changing arms position from front to back. The last big innovation was the "V-style," introduced by the Swede Jan Bokløv (1966–) in 1986. His revolutionary idea was, instead of jumping with parallel skis, to jump with the skis spread in a V-shape (seen from behind). This style did not dominate the jumps immediately, but today it is the rule in competition. The immediate result of V-style jumps was longer jumps and fewer style points, since it broke the ideal of even parallel skis.

Style shifts have engendered controversy, chiefly between innovators and those favoring traditional methods. According to traditional Norwegian *idretts* (sport) ideology, ski jumping should not be artificially constructed acrobatics but a test of the skier's ability to meet and conquer natural obstructions in the terrain. This ideology has steadily eroded, but some elements have survived, barely, in that ski jumping remains an aesthetic sport: the skier who has the longest jumps does not necessarily win the competition.

Modern Competitive Jumping

Ski jumping has grown significantly as a modern competitive sport, as nations introduced their own events. Meanwhile, the Olympic Winter Games had grown from their inception in 1924 to rival the prestige of Holmenkollen, and in 1926 the FIS inaugurated a world championship in Nordic skiing (jumping, cross-country, and combination).

In the early years Norway dominated the international scene, but Finland, Austria, Germany—especially the former East Germany—and Czechoslovakia have outjumped the Norwegians for quite some time.

Today, world-class jumpers come from nations as varied as Japan, Italy, Sweden, France, Slovenia, Switzerland, Poland, and Russia, as well as from ski-jumping strongholds in Canada and the United States.

—MATTI GOKSØYR

Bibliography: Allen, E. John B. (1993) *From Skisport to Skiing.* Amherst: University of Massachusetts Press. Bø, Olav. (1993) *Skiing throughout History.* Oslo: Det Norske Samlaget.

Skiing, Alpine

Alpine skiing developed as a way to ski down the wooded mountain sides of the Alps, and has diversified into several styles. It is now practiced internationally for recreation and in competition and is a major recreational activity in North America and Europe.

History

The name alpine derives from the Alps, but long before skiing was introduced to the Alps, Norwegians had skied fast down their own hills (see Skiing, Nordic). Norwegians, though, were used to their open, sloping highlands. When they visited the Alps in the late 19th century, they told their hosts that these mountains with their wooded and steep sides were no place to ski. Even so, Germans, Austrians, Swiss, Italians, and later French skiers persevered and attracted a following of wealthy enthusiasts who crossed passes and even climbed mountains on skis.

Even before World War I, wealthy Europeans began to spend winter vacations in the mountains. People learned the *Arlberg crouch,* with a lift and swing of the body; Hannes Schneider's Arlberg technique became standard. The rich also traveled to Murren, where Arnold Lunn (1888–1974) headed the development of the new alpine disciplines of *downhill* and *slalom,* originally intended to help mountaineers descend from peaks safely. From Schneider's and Lunn's ski schools, students dispersed around the globe, spreading the techniques they had learned to Australia, the United States, Japan, and India.

During the 1920s, most of the mountainous countries of Europe realized that winter tourism offered vast new economic opportunities. Switzerland, with its stunning vistas, well-established health resorts, and summer tourist season, adapted easily. Germany popularized the Bavarian Alps successfully enough that the 1936 Olympic Games were staged at Garmisch-Partenkirchen. Only Austrians showed surprisingly little interest in accommodating the new sport.

Slalom Rules from 1924

Among the 18 rules for slalom were these:

1. A Slalom Race shall consist of a race in which Competitors are obliged to follow a course defined by flags or sticks.
2. A Slalom Race shall consist of two parts, the first part to be held on hard snow, the second part on soft snow.
3. Every Competitor shall be allowed one attempt at each part. No marks shall be given for style, but a Competitor's time shall be liable to be increased by penalties as follows:

    Ten seconds shall be added to a Competitor's time for a fall.

    Twenty seconds shall be added to a Competitor's time for a kick turn.

    A Competitor shall not be deemed to have fallen if he saves himself from falling with his hands, or if he stumbles. If a Competitor shuffles round to prevent his ski from sliding downhill by holding himself back with his sticks, he shall be deemed to have executed a kick turn.
4. A Competitor shall be disqualified:

    a) If he puts his two sticks together or if he puts both his hands on to a single stick.

    b) If neither of his skis passes between any pair of controlling flags.

    c) If he has a trial run round the course after the Judges have set the flags.

...

9. A Competitor is deeded to have finished when he breaks with his body, but not with his sticks or ski, the controlling tape which shall be affixed to the finishing post.

...

13. Two Timekeepers shall be appointed, to wit, an official Timekeeper and an assistant Timekeeper. The official Timekeeper shall announce audibly the time taken by each Competitor, and the times thus announced shall be checked by the assistant Timekeeper. No account shall be taken of minor discrepancies between the official Timekeeper's time and the times recorded by the assistant Timekeeper's watch.
14. Flag-keepers shall be appointed who shall stand by each pair of flags. It shall be the duty of each flag-keeper to direct competitors to his pair of flags and to ensure, as far as possible, that no Competitor shall be disqualified owing to failure to pass between the pair of flags for which he is responsible.
15. After the first Competitor has run down the Slalom course, no ski-runner shall be allowed on the course, and no attempts shall be made to improve the course by stamping out the snow or by filling up holes.

...

18. Competitors must use the same length of ski in both parts of the Slalom Race. No Competitor in a Slalom Race shall use skis that are not at least 10 per cent. longer than the height of the ski-runner.

—E. John B. Allen

As World War II approached, the military in several countries sought to take advantage of their skiers' skills. Mussolini and Hitler aimed for total control of skiing in their respective countries. The winners of the men's and women's alpine events in the 1936 Olympics were both Germans, seeming proof that the "new order" was fit enough to conquer the world. In Finland, skiers defended their homeland against the Soviets at the start of World War II, a deed that spurred the formation of the ski troops of the 10th Mountain Division of the U.S. Army. The Finnish ski defense was accomplished entirely by cross country skiers, though, and the men who joined the American 10th were virtually all alpine skiers. But it hardly mattered, since very little fighting was done on skis in World War II.

After the war, alpine skiing became more popular, and wartime experiments with over-the-snow vehicles, cable lift construction, and strong, light metals and alloys were adapted to the slopes. Wooden skis gave way to more durable and faster metal skis, now designed specially for either downhill or slalom. Nylon and other new synthetic materials replaced cotton and wool in winter clothing—and at the same time created new opportunities for fashion designers. Some of today's best-known destination resorts—Aspen, for example—were established during this period. With the rise of international air travel, once-elite alpine skiing was taken up by the middle classes as well.

Rules and Play

Downhill and slalom are the two principal alpine skiing events. Both originated in the idea that following the conquest of a mountain peak, an accomplished skier cut a track straight down the side of the mountain. These straight runs were possible above treeline, and up to the end of the 1920s, races were often called straight races. But once a skier reached the trees, straight running became impossible. Out of this problem grew the slalom, which Lunn named for the Norwegian *slalaam,* a race that required turning around natural obstacles. Lunn defined the downhill and slalom tracks with flags, put a premium on speed, and from 1922 on, rules were published for alpine events.

Downhill and slalom events for men and women became official in 1931, when they came under Fédération Internationale de Ski (FIS) jurisdiction, and have been part of the Olympic program both for men and women since 1936. Giant slalom, experimental as early as 1935, was sanctioned in 1972 and a Super-G in 1987. In giant slalom, the control gates for the course (the poles the skiers must go around in fast turns) are spaced farther apart than on a slalom course. Giant slalom and Super-G combine elements of both downhill and slalom. Downhill is essentially a race down a mountain with control gates used only to check unsafe speeds or to guide racers around dangerous obstacles.

Three other varieties of alpine skiing have developed: freestyle, speed skiing, and snowboarding. The FIS governs international skiing and now has committees working on these once marginal techniques. Freestyle skiing comprises two disciplines: mogul skiing and aerials. Speed skiing began as the *kilometre lance* in 1931 in Switzerland, when Leo Gasperl achieved 136.319 kilometers (84.723 miles) per hour. After the war, speed skiing excited a flurry of interest. In the interest of safety, the FIS has now established a maximum speed of 229.3 kilometers (142.5 miles). Speed skiing appeals to only a handful of athletes and attracts few spectators.

U.S. ski areas now vie with European alpine resorts in popularity. But the ease of global travel also had a negative effect on alpine skiing. The skier who skis three continents in one season will find the resorts everywhere much the same.

—E. JOHN B. ALLEN

See also Skiing, Freestyle; Skiing, Nordic; Snowboarding.

Bibliography: Allen, E. John B. (1993) *From Skisport to Skiing: One Hundred Years of an American Sport, 1840–1940.* Amherst: University of Massachusetts Press. Arnaud, Pierre, and Thierry Terret. (1993) *Le reve blanc, olympisme et sport d'hiver en France: Chamonix 1924 Grenoble 1968.* Bordeaux: Presses Universitaires de Bordeaux. Lloyd, Janis M. (1986) *Skiing into History 1924–1984.* Toorak, Victoria: Ski Club of Victoria.

Skiing, Freestyle

Freestyle skiing is a now standardized form of skiing acrobatics that consists of four subdisciplines: mogul, ballet, aerial, and the combined. Performance is evaluated for both technique and style.

History

The roots of freestyle skiing are in Scandinavia and the European Alps, but it developed in North America.

Among the skiers of last century's Telemark, Norway, the ideal was to master a series of techniques: turning, jumping, and going straight downhill at high speeds. *Ville låmir* (wild courses), located in steep terrain, included tough turns, moguls, and steep jumps. During the 1930s, Norwegian ski champions used skiing acrobatics in training. Their simultaneous somersault ski jumps were well-known exhibitions.

In Europe, acrobatics was considered an acceptable part of a skier's training program but not a "real" competitive sport. The less traditional American skiing culture was more open to alternative practices. In North America, skiing acrobatics had been part of professional ski shows since the turn of the century.

Freestyle skiing found its form as a standardized, competitive sport in the 1970s. The first competition is said to have taken place in Waterville Valley, New Hampshire, in 1966. The first professional competition was held in 1971, and the first World Cup freestyle tour was staged in 1978. During the 1970s, national championships were arranged in several European countries.

A decisive step in the sport's development was taken in 1979 when the International Skiing Federation (FIS) accepted freestyle skiing as an amateur sport. In 1986, the first official world championships took place in Tignes, France. At the Olympics it was a demonstration sport in 1988, mogul skiing was part of the official program in 1992, and both mogul and aerial competitions were contested in 1994 and 1998.

Rules and Play

Freestyle skiing consists of four subdisciplines: (1) aerial competition, (2) ballet, (3) mogul competition, and (4) the combined, which totals the scores of skiers who participated in the first three events.

The FIS defines an aerial competition as consisting of "two different acrobatic leaps from a prepared jump(s), stressing take-off, height and distance (referred to as 'air'), proper style, execution and precision of movement (referred to as 'form') and landing." Performances are evaluated by seven (or five) judges on three components. Five (or three) judges evaluate "air," which accounts for 20 percent of the score, and "form," which accounts for 50 percent, while the two remaining judges evaluate the landing, which accounts for 30 percent. The scores are added and multiplied with a degree-of-difficulty factor (DD) defined for each jump. For example, the DD factor for the most advanced triple somersaults with twists is about twice the DD factor for a single somersault.

A second subdiscipline is called ballet, but will, according to official FIS decisions, change its name to acroski in the future. Ballet is described by some as "figure skating on skis." A ballet competition includes one run, which according to the rules has to consist of "jumps, spins, inverted movements and linking steps blended together with artistic and athletic aspects into a well-balanced program, performed in harmony with music of the skiers choice."

In the third event, a run in a mogul competition is defined by the rules as "skiing on a steep, heavily moguled course, stressing technical turns, aerial maneuvers and speed."

The fourth subdiscipline is the combined, which is open to competitors who have started in all three events. A combined skier's score in each event is divided by the score of the highest scoring combined skier in that event, and the result is then divided by 10, which gives that skier's event scores. When adding the three events, the skier with the highest score is declared the winner. Aerial, ballet, and mogul disciplines require very different skills; good combination skiers are versatile athletes.

Cultural Aspects

Freestyle skiing occupies a middle position in the general trend toward differentiation in sport. Skiing acrobatics and demands on aesthetic qualities of performance have a long history. At the same time, freestyle skiing carries the distinctive marks of a modern, materialistic sport culture with a basis in the norms and values of Western youth. Up to the 1990s, almost all competitors came from the United States, Canada, Western Europe, and Scandinavia. Although requiring great skill, freestyle nevertheless emphasizes entertainment.

The terminology of the sport and the framework within which the events take place offer clues to its cultural background as well. Jumps are given popular names such as Mule Kick, Daffy, Spread Eagle, Helicopter, and Back Scratcher, while ballet maneuvers are called Gut Flip and Rock and Roll. The current change of name from ballet to acroski was initiative by the athletes themselves, who wanted to avoid the somewhat "feminine" image of ballet.

Freestyle skiing was viewed skeptically by the skiing establishment; it was also dangerously unregulated. Accepted by the FIS in 1979 and included in the Olympic Games in 1992, the sport has now become "clean." Today, safety precautions have decreased the risks. The main challenge today is to get a third subdiscipline, ballet, or acroski, on the Olympic agenda, considered unlikely given its limited commercial appeal.

Freestyle skiing is developing rapidly. With its high entertainment value and its appeal to sports fans with little or no roots in traditional skiing cultures, freestyle skiing no doubt will experience growth and increased popularity in the future.

—SIGMUND LOLAND

Bibliography International Skiing Federation. (1992) *FIS Freestyle. General Rules and Regulations. Rules for Specific Competitions.* Berne: International Skiing Federation.

Skiing, Nordic

Nordic skiing—which includes cross country skiing and ski jumping—reflects a tradition of practical, day-to-day skiing over 5,000 years old. Recreational Nordic skiing has maintained its low-key image; competitive skiing has now split into two events, each using a different style.

History

Written sources from China and Scandinavia tell of informal competition and the use of skis in war. In Scandinavia and northern Russia, skis found preserved in bogs date back four to five thousand years. From the Norse Sagas and Icelandic Eddas, we also know of early informal competition.

The first modern, organized competitions took place in the Norwegian military, probably in 1767. When the Norwegian ski troops disbanded in 1826, local civilian clubs took up the sport and organized races. The competition near Kristiania (which became the Holmenkollen) was first staged in 1879. By then, Norwegians had emigrated throughout the world and taken their skiing style with them. In Australia and the Americas, they introduced locals to the use of skis for traveling, visiting, and for winter enjoyment. Gold fever also infected immigrants who knew how to ski, and in the deep mountain snows of Kiandra (Australia) and California (United States), skis became common in the mining camps. Skiing mail carriers there were often hailed as heroes.

In 1888 Fridtjof Nansen (1861–1930) crossed southern Greenland at latitude 64 degrees on skis. When his book about the journey, *Paa Ski over Gronland,* was translated into German, it sparked an interest in skiing among the wealthy outdoorsmen of Europe. By 1900 Nordic skiing was "a rich man's passion" throughout Europe, and skiing clubs were formed.

With the formation of clubs worldwide, administrative organizations were founded on the local, regional, and national levels to organize meets and establish rules. To retain control of "their" sport, Norwegians called for an international ski congress in 1910 and held the secretaryship until the Fédération Internationale de Ski (FIS) was founded in 1924.

Cross Country Racing in 1907.

The first great cross country run ever pulled off in the United States took place starting from headquarters at 2 P.M. February 7.

It was a pretty sight to behold the uniformed members of Nor Ski Club, Chicago, starting from the headquarters with red, white and blue streamers to be posted along the nine mile course. A good natured and healthy looking lot of men, who would do honor to any regiment of infantry in Uncle Sam's army. The men were distributed along the course to watch at difficult passes, and report on any participant, who should in any way disobey the laws governing the contest. It is a very strict rule in Norway not to allow any participant in a cross country run to remove his skis during the contest, and this rule was adhered to in every detail. The skis could not be removed in jumping a fence or in clearing any other obstacle that might seem rather hard to overcome. The practical use of the ski is learned in runs of this nature, and it takes but a short time to get accustomed to handling the skis to advantage over obstacles of every description.

On a level surface, the Finns are the masters of the ski, while in a hilly and brushy country, the Norwegians cannot be beaten. The course of this run (the National Championship) was laid over a territory consisting of about four miles of hills and brush, three miles on the level and two miles on snow covered ice, thus giving the participating Finlanders a chance to gain on the level what their long skis naturally would lose through the brush, and the world famous Asarja Autio certainly knew how to avail himself of these level stretches as he practically flew over the snow as soon as the open availed itself, and he sustained his reputation by covering the distances two minutes ahead of the sturdy Norwegian runners, Elling Diesen and Gustav Bye, in the good time of 47 minutes and 30 seconds. The participants were in good condition, when they finished their hard run, and were well taken care of at headquarters. Warm milk was served as refreshments. It is of great importance, that the men posted along the course have a supply of bits of oranges or lemons to give the skiers as refreshments as they pass.

Ely Miner (22 February 1907): The ski race meet Sunday under the auspices of the Ely Finnish Athletic Club, was the best ever held in this city. There were twenty-three entries in the Men's race but out of that number only seven stayed to the finish. Asanias [*sic*] Autio won the first prize, covering the seven miles in 45 minutes and 45 seconds. Autio who resides in this city and claims to be the champion ski racer of the world, is anxious to meet anyone in the United States for a purse of $100 or over—the number of miles to be covered to be named by the party accepting the challenge.

—*National Ski Association Report*
(7 February 1907)

Recreational Cross Country Skiing

Recreational cross country skiing was the only form of skiing until the 1920s and 1930s. Early recreational skiers skied into the mountains in winter, and the more adventurous even attempted winter climbs on skis—both traditions that continue today. Most modern cross-country skiers, however, favor a run across meadows and through forests. Today the ski party is more likely to consist of families, or small, informal groups, not clubs.

Recreational Nordic skiing and ski equipment have been aggressively marketed in the United States since World War II, possibly because the beginning of the country's fitness cult coincided with Bill Koch's (1955–) unexpected Olympic silver medal for the 30-kilometer (18.6-mile) race at Innsbruck in 1976. Synthetic, no-wax skis have replaced wooden ones.

Competitive Cross Country Skiing

Cross country racing, first organized on national levels in Europe and America in the years before World War I, followed Norwegian rules. According to the Scandinavian *idraet* tradition, the purpose of outdoor sport was to produce an athlete who was not only fit but morally upright. The true hero was not the winner of these races, but the man whose combined points for cross country and jumping marked him as the best all-rounder.

After World War II, specialization became increasingly apparent as men and, from 1952 on, women trained for specific distances. By the 1960s, cross country racing had become such a specialized sport that club and recreational skiers no longer even considered entering any competitions. In China, however, and in other countries where skiing did not become so specialized, cross country events continued as club activities.

An offshoot of cross country skiing is the biathlon—a cross country race with target shooting at intervals—derived from the military ski patrol race. Biathlon became an Olympic event in 1960.

Before World War II, women participated only peripherally in Nordic ski competition. However, following World War II, women's cross country became part of the Olympic program at Oslo (Norway) in 1952 with a 10-kilometer event. At Lillehammer (Norway) in 1994 there were women's events of 5, 15, and 30 kilometers and a 4 x 5 kilometer relay, besides a 7.5 and 15 kilometer biathlon and a 4 x 7.5 kilometer relay. The 5-kilometer and 30-kilometer events were to be run in *classical stride,* the 15-kilometer event was to be run in the *free technique,* better described as the *skating step.*

Style Controversies

The arguments between proponents of the classic technique and those who favored the skating step are about 20 years old. The skating step—one ski in a track and the other used like a skate to push off—was first introduced at the Holmenkollen 50-kilometer race in 1971, and the Engadine (Switzerland) marathon in 1975 was won by a skier using the skating technique. The method proved faster over flatter terrain, but it also cut up the prepared track, was derived from another sport, and seemed to place more emphasis on winning by use of a modern technique than on honoring the classic cross country stride. By the late 1970s, the skating stride was used so effectively by the Finns that it was called the *Finnstep*, or *Siitonenschritt*, after Pauli Siitonen. Today the classical and free technique are separate cross country disciplines.

—E. JOHN B. ALLEN

See also Skiing, Alpine; Ski Jumping; Snowboarding.
Bibliography: Allen, E. John B. (1993) *From Skisport to Skiing: One Hundred Years of an American Sport, 1840–1940.* Amherst: University of Massachusetts Press.

Skiing, Water

Water skiing is a 20th-century sport, with origins in the ancient principle of using the power of one moving object to tow another. In water skiing the athlete is pulled along the surface of the water by a motorboat. In the basic style of the sport, the water skier wears a ski on each foot and holds a tow rope with both arms. Variations include the use of only one ski, barefoot skiing, and jumping off ramps, among others.

History

People probably attempted to water ski earlier, using sailboats, but its modern form began after 1900 with the development of the motorboat. As motorboats proliferated, boaters tried activities that evolved into the sport of water skiing, including towing sleds and other flat objects that people either sat or stood on. In the United States, Ralph Samuelson invented and demonstrated a pair of water skis in 1922 on Lake Pepin, Minnesota. At approximately the same time, near New York City, Fred Waller also invented and marketed a style of water ski, and he also invented the bridle at the end of the tow rope that water skiers hold.

By the 1930s efforts were being initiated to organize and promote the sport more widely. The American Water Ski Association (ASWA) was formed in 1939, and standardized rules and a structure of local clubs and competitions were established. Similar initiatives took place in other nations. In the late 1940s the World Water Ski Union (WWSU) was formed to coordinate the sport, sanction events and records, and formulate rules internationally.

Water skiing also captured the public's attention as a spectator sport. These shows featured spectacular stunts, beautiful women performing choreographed dance routines, and other crowd-pleasing activities on water skis.

After World War II water skiing grew steadily. It remained primarily an amateur sport, with trophies awarded more often than prize money. Professional competitive water skiing tours and events were eventually established, but the amateur emphasis remained. The distinction between amateur and professional aspects of the sport has been an ongoing debate.

Rules and Play

In the basic form of water skiing, the skier uses two skis and holds a horizontal bar connected to the end of the tow rope, which is attached to the motorboat. As the boat moves forward, the skis are pulled and lifted straight onto the water's surface. The skier rises to a standing position and is pulled along.

The minimum sustained speed for water skiing begins at around 24 kilometers per hour (15 miles per hour). As water skiers become more proficient and confident, they can be towed at increasing speeds. In 1983, Christopher Michael Massey, an Australian, established a water-ski speed record of more than 230 kilometers (144 miles) per hour.

The design of basic skis emphasize stability and ease of handling, with many variations and types of water skis for specific purposes. Advanced slalom skiers use single skis with two sets of bindings, one for each foot. Skis designed for stunts and other purposes may be shorter or more rounded. Other types of skis include the kneeboard, which is ridden in a kneeling position, and boards that are ridden without bindings (similar to a surfboard).

Many types of powerboats are used to tow water skiers. On a purely recreational level, a variety of general-purpose motorboats are suitable. Boats should have an appropriate size, body design, and engines powerful enough to tow a person without creating an excessive wake or otherwise overwhelming the skier. Certain powerboats are designed specifically for water skiing and are used by dedicated amateurs and in organized competitions and professional shows. The

AWSA has very stringent criteria for boats that can be used in sanctioned events to ensure consistency, performance, and safety.

Safety is an important concern, especially in the more advanced aspects of the sport, in which skiers travel at high speeds and perform flips and other potentially dangerous moves. Flotation vests are encouraged for all skiers, and helmets and other protective gear are often used.

Individual competitions and overall rankings of competitive water skiers are based on age and gender, in addition to categories for specific events. Traditionally, competitive water skiing tournaments feature three main competitions: slalom, tricks, and jumping.

In the slalom event, skiers maneuver back and forth on a course marked with buoys (usually six), while the boat follows a straight line down the middle. During the event the boat speed is increased and the tow rope shortened, which makes runs successively difficult.

In trick skiing, the competitors ski on a straight course and perform as many stunts as they can within their designated time (usually two 20-second passes). Trick skiing can include a wide variety of moves, such as twirling in the water, removing skis while in motion, and flipping out of the water.

In jumping, skiers go up an inclined ramp in the water, which launches them into the air. In addition to maintaining good form and control, skiers attempt to extend the length of the jump as far as possible before landing on the water. By the 1990s, skiers were achieving jumps of 60 meters (200 feet) and longer.

The sport also encompasses more specialized competitions. Freestyle jumping emerged in competition after the 1950s. In freestyle, jumpers add mid-air flips and other variations to the basic jump. Barefoot skiing was introduced publicly as a stunt at Cypress Gardens in 1947 and has since developed into a separate branch of the sport, with competitions and other events. Barefoot skiing and jumping were combined into an event known as barefoot jumping, and competitors have made jumps of over 26 meters (86 feet).

In the 1950s water skiing shows began to feature a stunt in which a water skier was connected to a large kite, which created air currents that carried him aloft as the boat gained speed. Referred to by several names—parasailing, paragliding, and kite skiing—the practice is popular among recreational skiers, although not done in competition.

Water skiing appeals to people on many levels. It offers the opportunity to experience being on the water in a more direct sense than is possible in a boat, combined with the excitement of skiing along its surface at high speeds.

—JOHN TOWNES

Bibliography: *A Profile of Water Skiing in the United States.* (1994) Winter Haven, FL: American Water Ski Association.

Skittles
See Bowls and Bowling

Sled Dog Racing
Sled dog racing is a sport in which harnessed dog teams compete. A team is controlled by a driver, otherwise known as a musher, and the primary goal is to maximize either the distance covered or speed.

History
European racing originated in Scandinavia, where competitions can be traced back to the 18th century. Although Eskimos used dog sleds for hunting, travel, and recreation in the precolonial period, the first North American races did not occur until the late 19th century. Possibly early competition grew out of rival groups of gold prospectors or fur trappers challenging one another to see who had the fastest sled and the best team of racing dogs.

The writer Jack London helped introduce these dogs, and indirectly their sleds, into the mainstream of American life. With his novels *The Call of the Wild* and *White Fang,* London described a wild dog (probably a composite of Siberian huskies or malamutes that he had seen) and explored notions of a dog being tamed and yet never escaping its savage origins.

The event that catapulted sled dog racing onto the front pages of newspapers around the world was a 1925 diphtheria outbreak in the Alaskan township of Nome. Hundreds of people were at risk and could not be reached by road or air because of ground conditions and severe weather, and the only way to get serum to them was by dogsled.

The sport was and is a minor one with limited international appeal, lending itself to polar and subpolar regions. The first organized race was the 1908 All-Alaskan Sweepstake, a round-trip race between the townships of Candle and Nome in Alaska. The distance was 656 kilometers (408 miles). In 1936 the Laconia Sled Dog Club of New Hampshire organized the first World Championship Derby. The International Sled Dog Racing Association was launched in 1966, which led to the development of a racing circuit. The most famous of these races is the Iditarod, inaugurated in 1973, which begins in Anchorage, Alaska, and crosses the Alaska Range, turns west along the Yukon River and continues up the Bering Sea coast to Nome. The race takes approximately 11 days.

Rules and Play

Sled dog teams—commonly seven or nine dogs—are traditionally composed of Siberian or Alaskan huskies. Racing sleds must be incredibly light and strong enough to carry equipment, provisions, or a sick or fatigued dog. Sled dogs must consume 800 calories daily when at rest in summer; during a long winter race, they may need up to 10,000 calories daily.

The Iditarod has become the most widely recognized sled dog race, but many more are held. In 1977–1978 200 sled dog races were held worldwide for a total prize money of $250,000. That year, the champion musher was a 44-year-old Athabascan Native American named George "Muhammad" Attla.

Sled dog racing may never be more than a minor sport, but its drama, romance, and challenge ensures a loyal core of fans.

—SCOTT A. G. M. CRAWFORD

Bibliography: *Living Dangerously.* (1989) Public Broadcasting System (documentary film).

Sledding
See Bobsledding; Luge; Sled Dog Racing; Tobogganing

Snooker
See Billiards

Snowboarding

Snowboarding, the art of standing upright on a board and maneuvering it across snow, is widespread in skiing regions throughout the world and even practiced in areas without mountains. Like surfers and skateboarders, snowboarders have imbued their sport with a philosophy of hedonism and pleasure seeking that has put them at odds with the skiing establishment—even as the sport itself becomes safer.

History

Snowboarding began in the 1960s and the first mass-produced snowboard came on the market in 1966. The snow surfer, or "Snurfer," was little more than a large skateboard. A hand-held rope provided steering and gave the rider some control over speed while the deck

was covered with staples to give the rider's feet traction. While the Snurfer was sold as a toy, the new leisure movement of the 1960s saw its potential as serious recreational equipment.

Snurfers were notoriously difficult to control and consequently banned by commercial ski fields. Snowboarding transferred to the backcountry, where it developed a cult following. In the mid-1970s, technological advances overcame the limitations of the Snurfer, but the ban remained in place.

In the late 1970s skateboarding began to affect snowboarding. At this time punk, an antisocial subculture involving extremes of fashion, music, and attitudes, adopted skateboarding. Punk "skaters" viewed ski slopes as the terrain of the yuppie. However, some professional skateboarders saw snowboarding as an appealing activity and promoted it to other skaters. Snowboarding simultaneously became "surfing on snow" and *the* winter activity for skaters.

In the mid-1980s, most ski areas had opened their slopes to snowboarders. Skiing had reached a growth plateau, and snowboarding offered ski areas a new youth market and economic potential, although this meant tolerating the countercultural and punk dimensions of snowboarders. It is from this point that snowboarding became popular.

By the 1990s skateboarding and snowboarding had developed a close relationship. Snowboarders adopted skaters' aggressive riding styles and their distinct fashions and attitudes; the latter were designed to shock. Skating also brought to snowboarding the styles and politics of "hip-hop," an urban black style of music and fashion. Skateboarding's influence dismayed many older snowboarders; they had worked hard to gain the public's—and particularly ski area operators'—acceptance and sought a more responsible image.

Complicating this tension was the fracturing of snowboarding into three distinct styles in the late 1980s: freestyling (influenced by skateboarding), alpine (largely influenced by skiing and surfing), and freeriding (a combination of both styles practiced on all slopes). Freeriders and freestylers view alpine snowboarders as skiers on boards. In North America, freeriders make up around 40 percent of snowboarders, freestylers nearly 50 percent, and alpine riders less than 10 percent. In Europe, however, alpine riders make up around 40 percent.

The debates within the snowboarding community spilled over into skiing. A small number of disruptive riders, exacerbated by a media frenzy, led several ski areas to re-ban snowboarding. However, the majority of ski area managers are trying to accommodate snow-boarders and reconcile both groups.

Snowboarding Today

Throughout the 1990s snowboarding has grown phenomenally, supported by the commercialization of an underground youth style called "grunge." Grunge youth oppose the high consumption and competitiveness of yuppie culture. Accordingly, they favor secondhand clothes and cooperative recreational games and activities such as snowboarding. This commercialization of grunge helps explain why snowboarding and skateboarding are so trendy.

Even conservative projections suggest that snowboarders will outnumber skiers by 2012. This dramatic growth prompted the governing bodies of skiing to reappraise the practice. The Fédération Internationale du Ski (FIS) formed a snowboarding committee largely, it seems, to take advantage of snowboarding's popularity and inclusion in the 1998 Winter Olympic Games. Battle lines were drawn when the International Olympic Committee recognized the FIS over snowboarding's own governing body—the International Snowboarding Federation (ISF).

Most competitive snowboarders and many recreational riders support the ISF in what they consider to be a hostile takeover by skiers. Snowboarders fear the loss of their identity and want to remain independent of skiers.

The winning of medals at the 1998 Olympics and the reality of lucrative commercial endorsements have further divided snowboarders over the issue of remaining an alternative sport or entering the mainstream. As in most sports, it seems likely that money will triumph.

—DUNCAN HUMPHREYS

Bibliography: Humphreys, Duncan. (1996) "Snowboarders: Bodies out of Control and in Conflict." *Sporting Tradition.* Werner, Doug. (1993) *Snowboarder's Start-Up.* Ventura, CA: Pathfinder.

Snowshoe Racing

Informal racing is probably as old as the snowshoe itself, serious racing has only emerged within the past 30 years. Races are held either on groomed trails, as for most Nordic ski events, or on unbroken snow.

History

The best evidence suggests that snowshoes have been used for the past 6,000 years, primarily by Amerindian peoples. Possibly also developed in Central Asia, the snowshoe never gained any real popularity there.

Snowshoe clubs popularized recreational snowshoeing in Canada. These clubs, some of them 200 years old, were popular among both French- and English-speaking populations, but more so among French Canadians. These and their counterparts in the United States never tried to formalize snowshoe racing.

Rules and Play

The traditional snowshoe was primarily a snow flotation device and, as such, not suited for high speed. In the 1970s, the snowshoe was drastically redesigned, which reduced size and weight and allowed for the use of a real racing stride. At the same time, athletes from other sports began to look for new ways to cross-train, keep fit, or enjoy themselves in winter. Snowshoeing was a natural option.

For racing, generally, a shoe can be no less than 20 centimeters (8 inches) wide and no shorter than 64 centimeters (25 inches) long. This size allows considerable flotation, yet it is small enough to accommodate a stride that is more like that of a modern runner than that of a heavily laden trapper.

The deck of the racing shoe is no longer webbed but solid, and generally made from rubberized or other treated nylon; it is no longer attached to the frame with rawhide lacing, but riveted or clipped to it. This preserves some of the flotation qualities of snowshoes while reducing overall size. Most modern shoes also feature a cleat at the toe or ball of the foot, and some are also cleated at the heel. The overall result is a much lighter and smaller shoe, with improved climbing ability, that still allows a certain amount of controlled downslope sliding.

The long tradition of "social snowshoeing" continues in Quebec and New England, and racing in the east has taken on a more competitive edge since 1988, when the first "North American Snowshoe Classic" was run. The newest centers of snowshoe racing, though, are in Wisconsin and Minnesota and in Colorado and the neighboring mountain states.

Several dozen races are held in Colorado every year, most sponsored by local running clubs or by snowshoe manufacturers. Course conditions are one of the key issues in racing today. Initially, many races were run on groomed tracks. This led to the feeling, and not only among "traditionalists," that snowshoe racing might lose all its distinctiveness and become merely a sort of handicapped running activity.

On the other hand, races through unbroken snow

were also problematic. When such races were staged, a typical strategy was simply to "hang back" while the leaders broke a more manageable path through the snow and then to capitalize on this in a sprint at the end. However, in an attempt to do away with this sort of "laggard's advantage," some recent races have featured a sequence of "primes," rather like in cycling races, to improve the ambitions of the pack.

At a recent conference held near Lake Saranac, New York, enthusiasts considered an Olympic future for their activity. Thus far, little progress has been made in bringing together any sort of international campaign to popularize this as yet minor form of winter racing. On the other hand, American snowshoe companies report that sales of new-style shoes are picking up, not only in North America but also in Scandinavia and Japan.

—ALAN TREVITHICK

See also Skiing, Nordic.
Bibliography: Bauer, Erwin A. (1975) *Cross-Country Skiing and Snowshoeing.* New York: Winchester Press.

Soaring

Soaring—also called "gliding" by some people—dates from the 1800s. The two terms, however, are quite different. Both are practiced by individuals who either fly for the sheer personal enjoyment of powerless flight (gliding), or who compete as either individuals or members of teams in local, regional, national, and international glider competition (soaring). Many pilots do both.

History

In 1848 Sir George Cayley, an eminent British scientist, is credited with having designed and built the first successful heavier-than-air device, a glider said to have carried a 10-year-old boy several yards after its launching from a hill. From the 1890s onward, research and development of gliders, flying techniques, and similar subjects were being notably pursued in Germany, England, and the United States.

World War I halted glider development, but when the Treaty of Versailles prohibited powered flight in Germany, one result was enormous progress in the development of soaring flight. The first world championships were held at Wasserkuppe, Germany, in 1937. Progress continued, but was slowed again during World War II when military applications of gliding forced sport flying into the background.

From then until now, the sport has flourished, and several countries boast aggressive, healthy soaring pro-

grams. At least 5,500 pilots throughout the world have earned diamond badges and over 150 have now flown flights farther than 1,000 kilometers (620 miles).

Rules and Play

Air flows over the wings of a glider in much the same way as it flows over the wings of a powered airplane, which is propelled through the air by the force of its engine. Glider flight can be achieved only by descending the glider, speeding it up, and causing air to flow around its wings and tail surfaces. In gliding flight, therefore, a glider (or sailplane, as it is often called) is always descending, usually at a rate of between 45 and 90 meters (150 and 300 feet) per minute in still air.

The acceleration of air over the wings of the glider produces a lifting force that counterbalances the weight of the glider and actually slows down its rate of descent. Were it not for the force of "lift," gliders would go straight down. Instead, they follow predictable "glide ratios." Glide ratio is a measure of how far a sailplane will travel forward (horizontal distance) for each foot of altitude it loses (vertical distance).

What makes soaring a sport is the challenge to the pilot of finding and using ascending air currents to keep the glider aloft—to cause it to climb faster than it is descending (which it always is)—and so achieve height, distance, or flight durations impossible in "still air." Updrafts are the fuel of gliders.

Pilots who excel at finding and using the invisible ascending currents are the champions and record holders, and the ones who reap the full enjoyment of solitary soaring flight.

Three classes of gliders are generally recognized in world competition: Open, 15-meter, and Standard. A fourth type of glider, the so-called "World Class" glider, has been internationally classified but it has yet to be built or compete on any widespread basis.

Except for motorgliders, which have engines that enable them to take off under their own power, other types of gliders require some outside force to create airflow over the wings. This gets the glider moving at sufficient speed so adequate airflow passes around the wings to overcome the force of gravity and cause it to fly.

Many different methods have been used to provide this speed: pushing gliders down the slopes of hills until airflow over the wings is sufficient to produce flight; dropping heavy weights on the ends of ropes to pull them into the air; pulling them with elastic-like ropes and "slingshotting" them to flying speed; pulling them into the air on long cables reeled in by engine-driven mechanical winches; pulling them into the air on ropes behind automobiles; and hooking them behind airplanes that take off and pull the glider to an altitude from which gliding flight can begin. Most gliding in the United States today starts with the glider being towed by a rope attached to a powered airplane. The technique is called "aerotow."

Types of Gliding

Glider pilots aim to soar, not glide. Soaring involves finding parcels of air going up at a greater rate than the glider is going down. The several methods of remaining aloft all involve pilot skill and knowledge in finding these air currents. They are generally categorized as thermaling, ridge flying, mountain wave flying, and land and sea breeze flying. An additional source of lift can be obtained by flying under or near newly developing cumulus clouds that owe their formation and sustenance to the updrafts found directly underneath them.

Soaring Competition

The International Gliding Commission (IGC) is the sport's governing body.

The first world championship of soaring was conducted in 1937 at Wasserkuppe, Germany. Recently, during every odd calendar year, the FAI sanctions a World Gliding Championship for each of the three classes of gliders (Open, 15-meter, and Standard). The world contest is usually held over a three-week period, with the first week devoted to official practice and the last two weeks to actual competition.

Individual phases of soaring competition are called "tasks." Each day at the world championship competition, pilots fly around a specifically assigned course composed of carefully selected and clearly defined turn points on the ground. These turn points are the ends of airfield runways, prominent road intersections, or other distinctly identifiable geographical landmarks over which competition pilots must precisely fly.

Win or lose, soaring pilots still score a victory: the triumph, however temporary, of a nonmechanized craft over the force of gravity.

—WALTER D. MILLER

Bibliography: Knauff, Thomas L. (1994) *Glider Basics from First Flight to Solo.* Iceland: Prentsmidja Arna Valdemarssonar hf. Piggott, Derek. (1977) *Understanding Gliding.* New York: Barnes & Noble. Stewart, Ken. (1994) *The Glider Pilot's Manual.* UK: Airlife Publishing. Wills, Philip. (1974) *Free as a Bird.* New York: Barnes & Noble.

Soccer

Soccer, or association football, has many names: bollfoer in Finland, calcio in Italy, fussball in Austria, fútbol in Argentina, futebol in Brazil, labdarugó in Hungary, podosfairiki in Greece, soccer in the United States, and voetbal in the Netherlands—but the game remains essentially the same. Today, more men and women play and watch association football than any other sport. The world governing body, the Fédération Internationale de Football Associations (FIFA) has occasionally claimed more members than the United Nations. Its membership has increased from 7 in its foundation year of 1904 to 73 by 1950 and 170 in 1990. The World Cup, as one of the world's most prestigious sporting events, is televised in every nation.

History

The modern game was invented by the British in the 19th century. There, the rules were codified, the first association football clubs were established, a regular calendar of fixtures was arranged, and competition was organized. The modern game was a by-product of the growth of the commercial, manufacturing, and professional middle class in Britain, especially that of the private secondary schools (known as public schools) set up for the education of their sons. Team games in particular had become a defining characteristic of public schools, and the pursuit of physical fitness had become something of a cult. Games were also supposed to teach certain qualities of character, curbing rampant individualism in the cause of one's house and later school and, after that, club, region, and country.

British public schools, however, tended to develop their own unique forms of football, so a single rule book was needed. In 1863, the Football Association (FA) was formed with the aim of producing a single game whose rules would be accepted by all. When participants could not agree about how far to allow the use of the hands and whether hacking (kicking an opponent who was running with the ball across the shins) should be permitted, adherents of those clubs that supported these "manly" features withdrew from the discussions and in 1871 formed the Rugby Football Union (RFU). The rest had formed the FA back in 1863. The FA and the RFU lie at the core of all modern football games.

The knock-out cup was copied from the house competition at Harrow School. In a knock-out cup, the names of the teams are put into a hat and drawn out in pairs. They play each other—that is a cup-tie—on the ground of the club whose name was drawn first. The winner goes through to the next round. Eventually only two will be left, and they will meet in the cup final. This competition both reflected and stimulated the growth of the game, especially in the provinces.

Cup-tie football changed the nature of the game in Britain. City, county, and national cup competitions built on the traditional rivalries between local communities and provided opportunities for excitement and gambling. Newspapers were quick to notice and promote the new sport, which large crowds were prepared to pay to see. Relatively high and regular wages, inexpensive transport both within and between cities, and the Saturday half-holiday all combined to make a fortnightly visit to a match well within the finances of working men. Many clubs began to pay their players, and there was a regular migration of young Scottish workers to English clubs. Professionalism in football was legalized in England in 1885 and in Scotland in 1893. In 1888, 12 leading clubs, all from towns in the Midlands or the North, banded together to play a regular schedule of home and away matches, at the end of which the club with the best record would be called champion. They called it the Football League (FL). At the other end of the spectrum, association football was introduced into the curriculum of the elementary schools by teachers in the 1880s.

Rules and Play

In its organized form association football is played between two teams of 11 players a side on a rectangular field not more than 110 meters (120 yards) long and usually 69–91 meters (75–100 yards) wide. The object of the game is to score a goal by kicking or heading (but not using the hands to propel) the ball over the opponent's goal line into a goal. The duration of the game is of two equal halves of 45 minutes. It is a simple game with only 17 rules, the most important of which deal with offside and the definition of and penalties for fouls and misconduct.

Although association football was a team game in 1870, the emphasis on the individual was strong. Once in possession of the ball, the player tried to keep it by running forward and dribbling it toward the opposing goal. The first specialist position mentioned in the laws of the game was that of goalkeeper, but only as that player on the defending side who, for the time being, was nearest to his own goal. The big change came with the adoption of the passing game with the ball deliberately and systematically being passed between members of the same side as they moved toward the goal. This new style underlined what seems obvious today:

that each team had a back, middle, and front section.

By the early 1880s, a forward had been withdrawn to make room for a third halfback, and a 2–3–5 formation was established. This formation was to dominate world association football until well into the interwar years.

Postwar changes in the patterns of play have also been largely connected with a determination to strengthen the defense. It is not clear who invented the 4–2–4 formation. It was the Brazilian team, which spectacularly won the World Cup in Sweden in 1958, who not only introduced Pelé but also played two center-halves, a double stopper of Bellini and Orlando, and two players in midfield. This strategy made conversion from defense to attack very quick, but it also made the two midfielders work very hard. England turned the 4–2–4 formation into the 4–3–3 in the mid-1960s by withdrawing an attacker to bolster the midfield. For the first time, the number of players whose primary duty was defense outnumbered those whose main role was attack.

Most leading teams now play variants of the formations 4–4–2 or 5–4–1, but association football has remained a game of fluid, flexible systems, a game where the individual can shine, a game of continuous movement of ball and players rather than one of prearranged set plays. An obsession with defense can produce tedious spectacles for the neutral observer, but, for those who identify with the teams, association football retains its ability to seize the emotions.

Soccer Spreads

Young Britons who went abroad to work or study took association football with them and taught the sport to local young men. European businessmen and students who traveled to Britain for education or training purposes were introduced to the sport, and they established their own clubs when they returned home. Swiss, Austrian, or German nationals who had traveled as engineers or merchants spread the game in Southern Europe.

The British community in South America started association football mainly in the large cities of Buenos Aires, Montevideo, Rio de Janeiro, and São Paulo, especially Buenos Aires. It was a popular spectator sport in the big cities and by the 1920s had shifted from a pastime for the elites to an opportunity for poor young men to win fame and fortune.

International matches beyond Britain began. Uruguay and Argentina met for the first time in 1901 and initiated what was to become the most often played international fixture. Austria met Hungary for the first time in 1902, and France and Belgium in 1904. The Fédération Internationale de Football Associations (FIFA) was formed in 1904. The first regional association football organization was in South America. The idea of an organization for the region bore fruit in 1916, when the Confederación Sudamericana de fútbol (CONMEBOL) was set up and the first official South American championship was held in Buenos Aires. Uruguay won that competition and, along with Argentina, has dominated a tournament known as the Copa America since 1975.

The first international tournament began in 1927, ended in 1930, and involved five countries—Austria, Czechoslovakia, Hungary, Italy, and Switzerland—playing each other at home and away.

With most association football remaining at the amateur level, the first tournament that might hope to produce a world's best national team was the Olympic Games. England won in 1908 and 1912, by which time 11 European countries had entered teams. After World War I, professionalism began to develop in places outside the British Isles. By the mid-1920s three of the strongest European footballing nations—Austria, Czechoslovakia, and Hungary—had professional leagues, which disqualified their best players from the Olympics. Britain's best were also professionals, and there was a good deal of suspicion that Uruguay, who had surprisingly but spectacularly won the Olympic football competition in 1924 and 1928, were also concealed professionals.

Brazil is the only country to appear in every championship between 1930 and 1994, winning a record four times. It has often been said that, after their own country, everyone supports the Brazilian team, mainly due to the skill and style that their players have, above all others, regularly brought to the sport. This extraordinary ability was particularly exemplified by the 1970 winning team including Pelé (Edson Arantes Do Nascimento, 1940–). In Brazil association football is a powerful source of national identity. Some Brazilians compared the third World Cup win in 1970 with Neil Armstrong's walk on the moon. France's jubilation in its victory over Brazil in the 1998 World Cup can have been matched only by the Brazilians' disappointment over their loss.

New Soccer Worlds

Association football had been introduced to Russia as a summer game by British, German, and other foreign workers in the 1890s. A national association was established in 1912 together with a short-lived national championship, in which the teams were allowed not more than three Englishmen.

After the Russian Revolution, association football, like other competitive sport, was criticized for its tendency toward commercialization and specialization and for turning the socialist masses into spectators rather than players. By the 1930s, however, competitive sport in general and association football particularly seemed ideal recreation for urban workers. A national league was set up in 1936 partly in the hope that it would reinforce a sense of cohesion in the huge, rambling country. The Russians did not participate in the Olympics until 1952 or the World Cup until 1958, but did join the Fédération Internationale de Football Associations (FIFA) in 1946. In 1949, the USSR launched a policy to achieve world supremacy in major sports, partly to show off Soviet athletes in a friendly environment but perhaps more to demonstrate the superiority of the Soviet system. Their insistence that their players were amateurs allowed these countries to dominate the Olympic Football Tournament between the Helsinki Games in 1952 and the Montreal Games in 1976. The Union of European Football Associations did not call the players of Czechoslovakia and Hungary professionals until 1988. Association football was the most popular game among the Eastern European workers and remains so in the unsettling period ushered in by the breakdown of the Soviet system. In the former Soviet Union there are 4.8 million registered players. Only the reunited Germany has more.

The United States was the land without association football. Yet the American Football Association (AFA) had been set up in 1884, the sport was played in several East Coast towns and cities, and the first international matches had been played with Canada in 1885 and 1886. Still, association football flourished largely among recent immigrants. It had no state support and was played in few schools or colleges.

In the 1960s, association football began to change from a working-class sport played by immigrants to a middle-class and suburban recreation played by the young in the better high schools and colleges. It also began to be developed as a game for girls and women. The year 1967 saw the creation of a national league resembling those in Europe and South America, except that foreign teams were imported to represent U.S. cities. The popularity of the National American Soccer League (NASL) was enormously boosted when Pelé came out of retirement to play for the New York Cosmos in 1975.

Ten years later the NASL had disbanded. Yet a sports-mad United States was awarded the 1994 World Cup by FIFA with the assurance that a national professional league would follow. It began its first season in the summer of 1996.

Association football has grown dramatically in Africa since World War II, but its development remains hampered by economic and political upheavals. The colonial powers, especially Britain and France, took the sport to Africa, but before independence only well-to-do Africans were likely to get the chance to play. Until the coming of free education, association football was only for the African elite.

In 1957, there were still only four independent football associations—Egypt, Ethiopia, South Africa, and the Sudan—but they set up the Confédération Africaine de Football and organized the first African Nations Cup in Khartoum. The top African players now head for Europe. Association football is one of the few paths to riches, social mobility, and status for young African men, and over 300 of them are currently playing in Europe.

Asia now has half the world's population and also half the world's registered association football players, but it has struggled to gain a commensurate place within the world game.

Association football is particularly popular in Bangkok, Hong Kong, Jakarta, and Kampala. Calcutta has the strongest league in India. South Korea has had an eight-team professional league since 1983 and has been a powerful force in the Asian Cup, played every four years since 1956, and in the Asian Games. In Japan, association football has always been a minority sport, but it was encouraged by the Olympic Games of 1964 and by Japan's bronze medal in the 1968 Mexico City Games. Association football even has a long history in China. Although it has inevitably been affected by the economic and ideological upheavals of the last half century, by 1994 it had a national professional league.

In Australia, where association football has never been the number one football sport in any state, it has nevertheless grown in importance as a result of postwar immigration, particularly from Greece, Italy, Turkey, and the former Yugoslavia. For many native Australians, however, these immigrant athletes gave the sport a distinctly un-Australian image, especially when crowd trouble reflected interethnic tensions. Association football is now the premier sport in the Middle East, particularly in the Gulf States where oil-rich conservative governments have promoted the game, importing Europeans and South Americans to teach and manage in modern stadiums, especially since the 1970s.

—TONY MASON

Bibliography: Mason, Tony. (1980) *Association Football and English Society, 1863–1915*. Brighton, UK: Harvester. ———. (1995) *Passion of the People? Football in South America*. London: Verso. Murray, Bill. (1994) *Football: A History of the World Game*. London: Scolar Press. Oliver, Guy. (1992) *The Guinness Record of World Soccer: The History of the Game in Over 150 Countries*. London: Guinness Publishing. Radnige, Keir. (1994) *Ultimate Encyclopaedia of Soccer*. London: Hodder and Stoughton.

Softball

Softball is the United States' number one team sport and favorite pastime, played at many levels by people from all walks of life—doctors, lawyers, insurance agents, accountants, and whoever else finds time to play. After playing comes time to discuss the game and why the team won or lost; plays become famous as they are retold the next day at work. For the millions who play softball, it's easy to play but hard to forget.

History

George Hancock, a reporter for the Chicago Board of Trade, invented "indoor baseball" on Thanksgiving Day 1887, as he and 20 or so young men gathered inside the Farragut Boat Club at the edge of Lake Michigan in Chicago, awaiting the results of the Harvard-Yale football game. Hancock made the pickup game a sport by drawing up a set of rules, creating a bat and a ball, painting permanent foul lines on the gymnasium floor, and calling his game "indoor baseball."

By midwinter the game was played in gymnasiums and lodge halls throughout Chicago, as a way to fill the void between football and baseball and ease the monotony of the exercise and calisthenics often held inside gymnasiums.

In the spring of 1888, Hancock moved his game outdoors. It was played on a smaller diamond and was called "indoor-outdoor." Hancock published the first set of indoor-outdoor rules in 1889. The popularity of the sport continued to rise.

In 1895 Lewis Rober Sr., a lieutenant in the Minneapolis Fire Department, augmented Hancock's game by inventing a game eventually known as kitten ball. Businesses and athletic associations favored the game because it could be played in a small amount of space with minimal equipment.

The basic game spread to the rest of the country, but

Not Quite Cricket

Softball came to London in 1962 when American film-makers Moe Frank and Norman Panama started an informal softball game, and in the opening scene of Frank's *A Touch of Class* an American character played by George Segal runs into Glenda Jackson while pursuing a fly ball in Hyde Park.

The Sunday game became known as the Hyde Park International Softball and Canoeing Organisation (HYPISCO), though team historians insist that no one ever went canoeing. Movie and athletic stars—including Tony Curtis, Charles Bronson, Eli Wallach, David Hemmings, director Martin Ritt, American football legend Jim Brown, and Australian cricketer Ian Cappell—were known to join in, but less-celebrated Americans complained that HYPISCO was as exclusive as some of the London clubs on Pall Mall a few miles to the east.

In 1972, Bob Fromer, a second baseman who had been snubbed once too often at HYPISCO, advertised in the weekly magazine *Time Out* and started a people's game on the edge of Regent's Park near the London Zoo—a game in which everyone, and anyone, would get to play.

The late 1970s was the golden age of Regent's Park Softball. There were often two or three games played at a time. Women were allowed, even encouraged, to play and Paul Gambaccini, an expatriate American and disc jockey on a popular London radio station, was the resident celebrity.

The first HYPISCO vs. Regent's Park match was played in June 1979 in Hyde Park, amidst the mud and drizzle that characterize British sport. The annual game became the high point of every season, and there was considerable hostility when Hyde Park consistently won by a single run. By the mid-1980s, however, HYPISCO, where only about 100 players participated since 1962, was aging. While a few Regent's Park die-hards clung to their bases, new blood and relative youth—the game had welcomed close to 1,000 players—gave them an advantage. By 1990, Regent's Park was winning most of the annual matches.

In 1983, an ad in *Time Out* drew 40 women, mostly British, to a sunny spot in Regent's Park where they started the first women's softball league in Britain. The league that first summer included the Artful Dodgers and a capable team from northeast London who referred to themselves as the Hackney Dykes. About the same time, representatives of the Hyde Park and Regent's Park teams, with some down-to-earth enthusiasts from the north of England and the women's teams, gathered to form the first British softball league, the South of England Softball Association (SESA).

A point of conflict between British and American players was always over the call to cancel a game. Americans saw rain pouring down at 7:00 A.M. and canceled the day's play. To the stalwart British, this was not cricket. And they, used to catching a cricket ball with bare hands, complained about wearing a large leather glove to catch the larger and softer softball. They liked the game, however: it was friendly, challenging but easy to pick up, and much shorter than a cricket match, leaving plenty of time for the pub.

Today, there are dozens of softball teams in London and elsewhere in the country, and the leagues have sponsorship from U.S. beer companies. While "softball" is not yet a household word in Great Britain, and most players are American, Canadian, or Japanese expatriates, softball in the park has become part of the London summer.

—Karen Christensen

---

with different rules, names, and ball sizes. In his 1940 book *Softball,* Arthur T. Noren best summarized softball in the 1920s and early 1930s: "Softball was being played all over the United States and in many foreign countries. The Great Depression, when thousands of the unemployed became involved in the game, brought more people to softball, who continued to play once the job market improved."

Leo Fischer, a sportswriter for *Chicago America,* and M. J. Pauley, a Chicago sporting goods salesman, promoted the game further with a softball tournament at the Century of Progress Exposition, or the Chicago World's Fair. They succeeded in getting 24 teams, 16 men's teams and 8 women's teams from 16 states. More than 70,000 people attended the first round of play, 350,000 during the entire event. Divisions included for fast pitch, slow pitch, and women. They then formed a national organization—the Amateur Softball Association (ASA)—of state and metropolitan organizations. The formation of the Joint Rules Committee on Softball (JRCOS) in 1934 brought a consistency as the game continued to grow in popularity. In the 1930s and 1940s, fast-pitch softball was the dominant game played, and pitchers of both teams would have double-digit strikeout totals. The JRCOS eventually changed the rules of the game to offset the balance between the batter and the pitcher by increasing the pitching distance from 37 feet, $8^1/_2$ inches to its present distance of 46 feet in 1950. The women's pitching distance also kept pace and was increased to 40 feet in 1965. In U.S. colleges women pitch from 43 feet.

Slow pitch had been part of the 1933 World's Fair, but did not develop further until it was added to the ASA's championship program in 1953. By 1960, it had surpassed fast pitch in popularity because more players were involved, older players could play, spectators got more action, and games could be played in less than one hour.

Today, games in the men's super slow-pitch division can take three to four hours. Recreational softball is still limited to one hour because so many teams play, and many localities prohibit playing past a certain hour. Many national tournaments are played.

Softball was first on the Olympic program in 1996.

Teams from eight countries—Australia, Canada, China, Chinese Taipei, Japan, the Netherlands, Puerto Rico, and the United States—entered the competition. Softball is now played in more than 90 countries.

—BILL PLUMMER III

Bibliography: Meyer, Robert G. (1984) *The Complete Book of Softball: The Loonies Guide to Playing and Enjoying the Game.* New York: Leisure Press. Zolna, Ed, and Mike Conklin. (1981) *Mastering Softball.* Chicago: Contemporary Books.

Spectators

Sports spectatorship has been a source of puzzlement and scorn for centuries. As early as the second century C.E., Lucian of Samosata constructed an imaginary dialogue between Solon and Anacharsis, a visitor to Athens whom Solon was conducting around the Lyceum, the famous gymnasium. Parts of the dialogue run as follows:

> Why do your young men behave like this, Solon? Some of them grappling and tripping each other, some throttling, struggling, inter-twining in the mud like so many pigs wallowing. . . . I don't know what comes over them. . . . I want to know what is the good of it all. To me it looks more like madness than anything else.

Anacharsis was probably referring here to the *pankration,* described by Finley and Pleket as " a combination of wrestling and judo with a bit of boxing thrown in." Solon justified it by reference to the popularity of the Games and the honor and glory brought by victory. Anarcharsis became even more bewildered:

> Why, Solon, that's where the humiliation comes in. They are treated like this not in something like privacy but with all these spectators to watch the affronts they endure, who, I am to believe, count them happy when they see them dripping with blood or being throttled. . . . However, though I can't help pitying the competitors, I'm still more astonished at the spectators. You tell me the chief people from all over Greece attend. How can they leave their serious concerns and waste time on such things? How they can like it passes my comprehension—to look on people being struck and knocked about, dashed to the ground and pounded by one another (quoted in Finley and Pleket 1976, 128–129).

His questions remain relevant. Why do some people apparently derive enjoyment from watching two men pummeling each other in a boxing ring? What sorts of satisfactions are obtained by the mainly male crowds who flock to see 22 people kicking a soccer ball about? Why should it be of interest to watch, either directly or on television, to see who can run fastest, jump highest or longest, or propel a hammer or javelin the farthest distance?

History

Many people view the "sports" of ancient Greece as a pinnacle of civilized sporting achievement. By contrast, the "sports" of ancient Rome are commonly viewed as a regression into barbarism, and certainly they were undoubtedly cruel. The brutality of the gladiatorial combats, the mock battles and the massacres, and the blood lust of the crowds who flocked to see them are well known.

Ancient Greek sport, however, would equally repel modern people, the surviving evidence suggests. The *hellanodikai,* the managers of the Olympics, employed two classes of assistants: the *mastigophoroi* or whip bearers, and the *rabdouchoi* or truncheon bearers. Their task was to keep both competitors and spectators under control, which suggests that the crowds were unruly.

Equally questionable is the assumption, perhaps especially common among adherents to the present-day ideology of "Olympism," of a direct line of descent between ancient and modern sports. The Dutch historian/philosopher, Huizinga, has shown that England in the 18th and 19th centuries, not Greece, formed "the cradle and focus of modern sporting life. In fact, many modern sports are descended from the folk games of medieval England. In England, as in the rest of medieval Europe, there were four main equivalents of modern sports: tournaments, hunts, archery contests, and folk games.

From the standpoint of spectator behavior, tournaments and folk games are the most interesting. Records of tournaments date from the 12th century and suggest a very violent type of "sport." "The typical tournament was a mêlée composed of parties of knights fighting simultaneously, capturing each other, seeking glory and ransoms. Significantly, between the 12th and 16th centuries, the tournaments were transformed increasingly into pageants involving "mock" rather than "real" violence. They became centrally concerned with spectacle and display, and as this process unfolded, the role of spectators, especially upper-class females, grew in importance. As a leading authority has expressed it: "The presence of upper-class women at tournaments plainly signals transformation in function. The perfection of military prowess became ancillary and the tournament became a theatrical production in which fitness to rule was associated with fineness of sensibility" (Guttmann 1986, 41).

Nevertheless, spectatorship continued to be a hazardous affair; stands reportedly collapsed in London in 1331 and 1581, resulting in numerous injuries and, on the latter occasion, loss of life—medieval precursors of events such as the Hillsborough tragedy in 1989, when 95 fans at a soccer match in Sheffield, England, were crushed to death.

Attendance at both tournaments and folk games was minuscule compared with the 200,000 who, we are told, regularly attended chariot races in the ancient world, and clearly was due to the smaller size of urban settlements in medieval Europe. The evidence also suggests a complete lack of the strict separation between players and spectators that we are accustomed to today. This was possible because these folk games were played across country and through the streets of towns rather than in a stadium on a specifically demarcated playing field or "pitch."

Folk games such as "knappan"—other local names included "hurling," "camp ball," "trap ball," "tip cat," and "dog and cat," and somewhat more generally various spellings of "football"—were the ancestors of such modern games as soccer, rugby, American football, hockey, baseball, and cricket.

The evidence suggests that they began to take on their modern forms in two main overlapping phases, one that began in the 18th century in which members of the landed aristocracy and gentry were predominant and another that began in the 19th century when the ascendant urban middle classes joined the landed classes. The first is principally interesting because the main actors were members of the aristocracy and gentry, and they seem to have had few objections to performing in front of large crowds or playing together with lower-status men—often their servants or retainers—who were paid for playing. The 18th century saw the emergence of more regularized and civilized and, in that sense, more "modern" forms of boxing, foxhunting, horse racing, and cricket.

The 19th century brought more regularized forms of track-and-field athletics and water sports and, above all, the development of more civilized ball games such as soccer, rugby, hockey, and tennis. The status of the middle-class groups who became increasingly dominant in sport and British society as the 19th century progressed was less secure, one consequence of which was the development of a socially exclusive amateur ideology in which sports should be for players only. Spectators came to be viewed as anathema.

These elite public-school amateurs evidently identified their own ethos with that of the English nation as a whole. According to them, sports participation is physically and morally beneficial—in building "character" and fostering "team spirit," for example—but spectatorship has no such desirable effects and can even be morally harmful. However, these elite amateurs' dislike of spectator sports was also due to the increase in spectatorship, mainly among the working classes, and involved the congregation of large crowds who behaved in an openly excited manner. This not only ran counter to their sports ethos, with its stress on the controlled expression of emotion, but was also perceived as a threat to public order.

In Britain, a long and unsuccessful rearguard action was fought by the devotees of amateurism against professional, spectator-oriented forms of sport. In the modern world, top-level sport has become increasingly commercialized, professional, and oriented toward the production of crowd-pleasing spectacles. It has become, that is, fundamentally capitalist in structure and orientation. To understand how that has come about, one must understand what it is that people get out of watching sport.

Fans

One of the main reasons that people watch sport is probably in search of excitement. Sports spectatorship appears to be about the playful and pleasurable arousal of emotion. Blended with emotion are the aesthetic pleasures derived from witnessing the skillful and graceful execution of a sports maneuver, and the satisfaction of discussing sports strategies.

Sports are also a form of nonscripted, largely nonverbal theater, and at the top level sports such as soccer, rugby, and American football can have a balletlike quality. Enhancing emotional arousal is spectacular presentation and the emotional "contagion" that derives from being part of a large, expectant crowd. However, to experience excitement at a sports event one has to *care*.

The people most committed to sport are commonly called "fans," an abbreviation of the term "fanatic." For the most committed fans, and perhaps for others besides, sport functions as a kind of surrogate religion; note the reverential attitudes of many fans toward their teams and their idolization of particular players. It may even be that sport has grown in social significance because it now performs some of the functions assigned to religion in earlier societies. That is, it may in part be catering to a type of need not being met elsewhere in our increasingly secular and scientific societies.

—ERIC DUNNING

See also Violence.
Bibliography: Dunning, Eric, ed. (1971) *The Sociology of Sport: A Selection of Readings.* London: Cass. Dunning, Eric, and Christopher Rojek, eds. *Sport and Leisure in the Civilizing Process: Critique and Counter-Critique.* London: Macmillan. Elias, Norbert, and Eric Dunning. (1986) *Quest for Excitement: Sport and Leisure in the Civilizing Process.* Oxford: Blackwell. Guttmann, Allen. (1986) *Sports Spectators.* New York: Columbia University Press.

Speed Skating
See Skating, Speed

Speedball

Speedball is a modern team game that combines soccer, basketball, and football skills, using the catching and passing skills of basketball, the kicking and punting tactics of soccer and football, and drop-kick skills. Speedball is safe and inexpensive and holds a large element of interest because of the different ways to score points. Soccer (association football), hockey, or football fields can be used, with goalposts added.

History
Speedball was originated in 1921 by E. D. Mitchell, the director of intramural sports at the University of Michigan, who sought a fall sport less dangerous than football and interesting to students of average athletic ability.

Speedball was successful and was adopted at colleges and universities nationwide, but primarily in the Midwest, as well as in secondary schools. In the 1930s, city recreation departments used it in their programs. However, by the end of the 1950s, speedball for men had died out at all levels; many schools started to play flag football or soccer, and speedball was a forgotten sport.

By this time, the game had proved particularly suitable for girls and probably had a larger following among women players than among men. By the 1950s it had become a very popular sport for girls and women in colleges and high schools throughout the Midwest. Speedball remained an important game for girls and women until the 1960s, when soccer took over.

Rules and Play
The game, played with 7 to 11 players, has incorporated the most desirable feature of soccer, the kicking element, and combined with it the passing aspects of basketball as well as allowing one dribble step. Touchdowns are scored by catching forward passes in the end zone. Players can't run with the ball. A player is not permitted to touch a ground ball with his or her hands and must play it as in soccer. A fly ball, defined as one that has risen into the air directly from the foot of a player, may be caught with the hands provided the catch is made before the ball strikes the ground again. In advancing the ball, the player may use one overhead dribble, that is, may throw the ball in the air ahead and run forward and catch it before it strikes the ground.

The rules vary for high school versus college and intramural versus varsity competitions, but the game is played in four periods of 10 minutes each (8 minutes at the high school level), with the object of scoring points by kicking the ball into the goal or though the goalposts, catching it in the end zone, or kicking out of the end zone. Play involves moving the ball toward the other team's end zone. Running with the ball is not permitted, nor is contact between the players, although they may guard each other and try to kick the ball away from the offensive player.

The three types of kicks allowed are punting (kicking the ball while it is in the air), drop kicking (kicking the ball after one bounce), and place kicking (kicking the ball while it is stationary).

Today speedball as a sport for women has largely disappeared, replaced by soccer, basketball, softball, hockey, and other formerly mostly or exclusively male sports.

—JOAN HULT

Squash Rackets
Squash rackets, generally known simply as squash, is a ball-and-racket court game with two players (singles) or four (doubles). Squash is now played by more than 10 million people in 120 countries and has become internationally known and accepted.

History
The first recorded reference to the game of squash rackets appeared in 1890 in the *Badminton Library of Sports and Pastimes.* As the story goes, schoolboys at England's Harrow School occupied themselves while waiting their turns for the rackets court by hitting a hard rackets ball around the courtyard, often breaking windows.

With increased popularity, various designs for squash's play area were introduced, eventually culminating in four walls of varying size. Courts were not standardized, but the early ones were constructed of wooden planks for both walls and floor, since wood was easier on the feet than asphalt.

Eustace Miles, a world champion rackets and tennis player, wrote the first book on the game of squash in 1901. Miles offered coaching tips in his book, although he felt that squash was generally a "selfish" game unless played as doubles in a larger court. Nevertheless, squash was considered good for the development of the body, health, mind, and character, and was regarded as a "grand game" for ladies, unlike many others of the period.

The first recognized squash championship was the American National in 1907. In 1920, the first Professional Championship of the British Isles was played between the only two entrants. The next championship, between the same two players, did not take place until 1928.

The English Squash Rackets Association was founded in 1928 to act as the game's central authority and to formulate, add to, and alter the rules. It was this body that decided to use the English spelling of "rackets" (as opposed to the French "racquets") and to reduce the number of squash balls to three varieties of hollow, black rubber.

The International Squash Rackets Federation (ISRF) was founded in 1967 as the game became a worldwide sport. The European Squash Rackets Federation was founded in 1973, followed by the Asian Squash Rackets Federation and others.

Rules and Play

Squash rackets is a ball game much like rackets, from which it was developed. The main differences are that squash rackets is played in a smaller court using a somewhat shorter racket and a hollow ball of black or colored rubber. The court has four walls and is 9.75 meters (32 feet) long and 6.40 meters (21 feet) wide. Most courts are indoors with wood floors, but countries with mainly sunny climates have outdoor courts with concrete floors.

The object of the game is to keep the ball in play, above this board. The two players ("singles") or four players ("doubles") take turns striking the ball. A rally (series of hits) continues until one player fails to return the ball above the board. Points are scored by the server on winning rallies, but on losing a rally, the receiver becomes the server. The player who first scores nine

points wins the game, unless both players reach eight points ("eight-all"). At this point, the player who first reached eight may choose to "set one" or "set two." Lively and relatively simple, squash rackets enjoys steady popularity.

—IAN D. W. WRIGHT

Bibliography: Miles, Eustace. (1901) *The Game of Squash.* New York: E.P. Dutton.

Steeplechase
See Horse Racing, Steeplechase

Stickball

Stickball is an urban form of baseball. The game developed in New York City immigrant communities in the late 1800s and flourished as a local sport until the end of the immigrant era in the 1920s. It was a small though continuing part of the assimilation process, and many young men from Eastern European nations took pride in playing their own street variety of American baseball.

The game was ideally suited to urban life. It required only two pieces of equipment: a bat made from a cut-off broom or mop handle and a ball—ideally a high-bouncing spaldeen, a pink, rubber ball manufactured by the Spalding sporting goods company and sold in local candy and five-and-dime stores. The playing field was a city street, with a "sewer" (actually a man-hole cover) serving as home plate and virtually anything else—other sewers, lamp posts, chairs, or boxes serving as the bases. Pitches were delivered on a single bounce (as in cricket), with only one strike per out. Pitching expertise was based on a combination of speed and curving, or putting spin on the ball to make it jump or move left or right as it crossed the plate. Balls hit over rooftops were also outs, to discourage losing balls, which were expensive.

A batter's reputation was based on the number of sewers he could reach, with two considered good and three legendary. Claims that some batters could reach four sewers seem to be more myth than fact.

The game began to decline in the 1920s, but has enjoyed a recent revival, particularly in retirement communities in Florida and southern California, where older men who played the game as young men are again playing and are encouraging local youths to play as well.

While this form of stickball has drawn the most attention, other forms of "baseball" stickball are also played in U.S. cities. The most popular is played in schoolyards or empty lots, and as with traditional stickball requires only a stick and a rubber ball. There is no home plate, but instead a rectangular batter's box drawn in paint or chalk on the building wall. There are no bases and instead hits are marked by distance—past the "pitcher's mound" on the fly a single, to the schoolyard fence a double, hit the fence a triple, over the fence a home run. Related to this version of stickball is stoopball, in which the "hitter" bounces the ball off the edge of a stoop or stairs on the front of a house. The fielder must then catch the ball before it hits the ground for an out. Again, there are no bases or base running, and the distance reached marks the number of bases.

—DAVID LEVINSON

See also Baseball, North American.

Stock Car Racing

Stock car racing events routinely are the largest professional spectator sports events each year in the United States in terms of attendance. Few of the cars that race are strictly "stock." Until recently stock car racing has been largely ignored by the traditional sources of sports news coverage.

History

The first automobile race in America was sponsored by the Chicago *Times Herald* in November 1893. The first track race was held in 1894 at the Rhode Island State Fair before 50,000 spectators. Early automobiles were so unreliable that most early contests focused upon time trials, achieving top speeds under ideal conditions, or were endurance contests to demonstrate automotive reliability.

The first paved automobile racing track was the Indianapolis Motor Speedway. The first race on the paved surface was in 1909, while the now famous 500-mile race on Memorial Day, now known as the Indianapolis 500, followed in 1911. Stock cars (all cars were "stock" when racing began) were banned from the Indianapolis 500 in 1919, but stock car racing continued in the Midwest.

Rules and Play

No American professional automobile race today is conducted strictly with stock vehicles, with the possible exception of the increasingly popular vintage automobile races. Those racing automobiles closest to showroom condition are not classed as stock cars at all, but are sports cars raced in the strictly showroom class of the Sports Car Club of America. Even these automobiles, however, may have altered tires, wheels, and suspensions. Among stock cars, the racing automobiles closest to original manufacturers' equipment specifications are the lowly hobby divisions of the various sanctioning organizations, the entry level in automobile racing.

Two distinct types of stock car racing coexist in the United States today. The highest level, in terms of prize money, quality of competition, and fame, are several sponsor-driven traveling circuits of competitors similar to golf and tennis circuits. Circuit races typically are held at the nation's largest paved tracks. The Winston Cup circuit is the most prestigious and well known of these race series. Some three dozen races are held during the year and the top ten finishers over the course of the year generally win at least one million dollars each.

Public knowledge of stock car racing has become increasingly focused upon the traveling race circuits, as these events are the most likely to be televised and receive newspaper coverage. Perceiving the value of these competitions, promoters have begun expanding the traveling series to other types of events. NASCAR, for example, now has pickup truck racing and several levels of circuit racing.

Most stock car racing takes place in weekly competitions at isolated short tracks featuring local part-time and semiprofessional drivers. Track promoters typically join sanctioning organizations such as NASCAR or IMCA (International Motor Contest Association) who define the classes of competitors, keep track of records, and make safety rules. Contesting vehicles are placed in classes based on size, body style, and engine displacement. The classes range from the entry-level "hobby division," which utilizes the smallest vehicles, to the super-modified division, which has the most powerful and most visually modified vehicles.

These race tracks typically range in length from $1/4$ to $5/8$ mile. Most tracks are banked dirt ovals with concrete grandstands on one or more sides and an interior pit area open to anyone willing to pay the higher admission price. Some promoters began paving their short tracks during the 1980s in an attempt to emulate the big leagues.

Short track racing continues to be highly regionalized with little interaction between competitors. NASCAR, founded in 1947, is the best-known and most nearly national of the stock car racing bodies and sanctions races at all levels of competition. The new racing organization created three classes of cars: strictly stock, modified stocks, and roadsters. NASCAR has eight regional short track circuits covering every region in the nation.

IMCA was the largest sanctioning organization in 1995, with races at 212 tracks. While sanctioning tracks in 28 states, most of its racing venues are in a band stretching from the northern Midwest southward to Texas.

Stock Car Culture

Stock car racing evokes strong feelings in the American public. These strong feelings probably stem from the common belief that its participants, and to a degree its spectators, come from the lowest levels of society. In some respects, the devotees of the sport themselves have encouraged this belief by creating "moonshining" and other mythologies of the early days of southern racing. Although these images of stock car racing are changing as a result of expanded television and journalistic coverage, many of the myths about the sport's beginnings continue.

Indeed, the demographics of the sport's typical spectator suggest that the most ardent followers tend to have less income and less education, and are less urban than the general population, but even a casual visit to a short track event would dispel the rumors of rowdy, inebriated crowds of troublemakers. The low ticket prices and rural nature of the sport tends to make most short track racing a family outing with little of the antisocial behavior often assumed to characterize these events.

Why this sport is so identified with the nation's rural underclass is unclear. Some suggest that this support stems from the alienation of these fans from traditional collegiate affiliations, a lack of experience with most team sports, and a rural/small town association that makes "big city" professional athletics anathema to their lives. Others suggest that its fans can identify with the Chevrolets, Pontiacs, and Fords on the major league circuits.

Like other sports, the deluge of television contract money increased prize money and incentives for advertisers to sponsor cars and races. This exposure has put stock car racing at the brink of great change. Superspeedway racing has become a major sport with traditional mainstream sponsors. The best drivers are millionaires; team owners and car builders now operate complex business empires that typically extend into automobile dealerships and other related automotive activities. The costs of short track racing have increased and so have the potential rewards.

At the same time, in competitions, one rarely sees cars driven off the used car lots with duct tape numbers on their sides. Even the audiences have changed with the sport's growing respectability. Simultaneously, part of the traditional appeal of the sport, its "outlaw" image, is rapidly fading.

—RICHARD PILLSBURY

Sumo

Sumo is a traditional Japanese wrestling sport that has always included a strong element of religion and ritual. With its complex hierarchies and systems of play, sumo is an exclusively Japanese practice, even when practised by non-Japanese athletes.

History

Some historians have used archaeological evidence, such as the terra-cotta figures known as *haniwa,* to claim prehistoric origins for sumo. Others have seen the beginnings of sumo in the mythic hand-to-hand unarmed combats recorded in the 8th-century *Kojiki* ("Record of Ancient Matters"). In fact, sumo can be reliably traced no farther back than 821, when sumo matches constituted one of the three great annual tournaments of the imperial court, recently moved from Nara to Kyoto.

The sumo tournament was held on the grounds of the imperial palace. An area behind the *Shishinden* ("Hall for State Ceremonies") was strewn with white sand for the ceremonial occasion. Thirty-four wrestlers, drawn from the "right" and "left" imperial bodyguards, entered the garden to the accompaniment of two drums and two gongs. They were followed by officials, musicians, and dancers. Then came the emperor and his courtiers. The "left" team wore paper hollyhocks in their hair, the "right" wore calabash blossoms. Matches were decided by falls or when a helpless wrestler was dragged by his opponent to the tent that housed his team. (In today's matches, winning and losing are determined in almost the same way: the winner is the wrestler who throws his opponent to the ground or forces him out of the ring.) After each match, the musicians beat their drums, struck their gongs, and performed a ritual dance. The results were recorded by arrows thrust into the sand.

These annual tournaments were suspended from 1120 to 1156, sporadically revived until 1185, and then discontinued. Sumo, however, persisted in other forms—as *no sumo* (field wrestling) and *kusa sumo* (grass wrestling) or as *shinji-zumo* (wrestling in the service of the gods). The most famous version of the last was *karasu-zumo* (crow wrestling). It took place at the Kamo Shrine in Kyoto, where boys who represented the god Takemikazuchi wrestled against other boys who represented the secular world. There was also *onna-zumo* (women's wrestling), which seems to have been arranged for men's titillation.

Modern sumo can be traced to the early 18th century, when Yoshida Oikaze and other *toshiyori* (elders) codified the sport and introduced some of the rituals that make sumo a distinctively Japanese form of wrestling. Matches were staged for the pleasure of the shoguns who, until the Meiji Restoration of 1868, wielded far greater political power than the emperors. According to P. L. Cuyler's *Sumo: From Rite to Sport* (1979), "Shogunal sumo lifted the sport out of the vulgar world of entertainment and imparted to it a sense of ritual that later became its major characteristic."

Rules and Play

The administration of the sport, even today, is a complex mixture of traditional and modern elements. All sumo wrestlers are members of a *heya* (room), the equivalent of a stable in horse racing. The most famous of these *heya* were established in Edo (modern Tokyo) between 1751 and 1781. The elders who ran them received official recognition by the shogun in 1773 and by the emperor in 1885. At that time, there were 105 elders. The organization was restructured in 1926 when *heya* from Tokyo joined those from Osaka to form a more nearly national organization. In 1958, this organization, frequently reformed and renamed, became the *Nihon Sumo Kaikyo* (Japanese Sumo Association). In 1989, there were 41 *heya* informally organized into five great families. The Yoshida family, which claims to have been involved with sumo since the 13th century, was so dominant in the administration of the sport that it was not until 1951, after a 17-year-old became the official head of the family, that they finally agreed to let the official sumo organization decide which wrestlers should be elevated to the top rank.

The pyramid of ranks is extremely complicated. Beginners enter the system as *maezumo* (before sumo). They receive room, board, and a small allowance. They are also given new names, which are invariably written in *kanji* (Chinese characters). If the *maezumo* are successful in the six annual 15-day tournaments, they rise to become *jonokuchi*, who are given individual rankings. Further successes mean promotion to the *jonidan, sandamme, makushita,* and *juryo* ranks. Only about 1 in 60 wrestlers rises to *juryo* status. If they reach this rank, they are classified as *sekitori* and al-

lowed to change from black or dark blue loincloths to white ones and to participate in the ring-entering ceremony. They wrestle daily during the tournaments, receive a regular salary in addition to their winnings, and have apprentice wrestlers to assist them. When they are not actively engaged in the sport, they are also allowed to wear kimono and *haori* (a man's light coat).

The five ranks above *juryo*—the *maegashira, komusubi, sekiwake, ozeki,* and *yokozuna*—comprise the *makuuchi* division. Wrestlers of this elevated status are allowed four minutes for *shikiri*, the crouching, stamping, and glaring that precedes the actual combat (which usually lasts only a few seconds).

Election to the 11th and highest rank—that of the *yokozuna*—is a great honor that is bestowed on very few wrestlers. From all other ranks, one can be demoted after a number of losses. A *yokozuna* cannot be thus humiliated. (If his powers begin to wane, he is expected to retire.) A series of successful tournaments will raise a gifted wrestler to the *ozeki* rank, but promotion to *yokozuna* is granted only to wrestlers who are deemed by the elders to have *seishin* (spirit). Although a few foreigners have become *ozeki*, it is all but impossible for them to become *yokozuna*. When Hawaii-born Jesse Kuhaulua retired in 1976, the elders ruled that foreign-born wrestlers not be allowed to achieve elder status. The elevation of the American Chad Rowan ("Akebono"), however, may signal a shift in Japanese attitudes.

Westerners who attend a sumo tournament are struck not only by the huge size of the wrestlers, some of whom weigh over 182 kilograms (400 pounds), but also by the many rituals that characterize the sport. Among the ritual elements is the design of the *doyo* (the ring), which consists of a circle inscribed in a square. The *doyo*, which dates from the middle of the 17th century, is flanked by four pillars that stand at the four corners of the rectangular "ring." These pillars are painted blue for the god of spring, red for the god of summer, white for the god of autumn, and black for the god of winter. At some moment in the 18th century, it became customary for four elders to lean against these four pillars in order to assist the referee in his decisions. They were known as the *naka aratame* (middle determiners). The circle within which the wrestlers grapple is formed by 20 bags of rice straw stuffed with earth. Before each bout, the *doyo* is purified by handfuls of salt. The *shimenawa*, or ropes that the *yokozuna* wear wound about their waists, represent the ropes that adorn Shinto shrines. These ropes date from the 16th century.

Some of sumo's many traditions are very old, but others can be traced back only to the 18th century. Yoshida Oikaze, for instance, introduced the ring-entering ceremony in 1791 when sumo was staged for the Shogun Ienari and something suitably ceremonial was in order. Today, all *sekitori* participate in the ceremony, which includes an entrance by means of the *hanamichi* (path of flowers). The wrestlers circle the ring, face inward, clap their hands, raise their arms, lift their aprons slightly, and file out. For the *yokozuna*, the ceremony is slightly different. He appears with a *tsuyu harai* (dew sweeper) and a *tachi mochi* (sword-bearer). He wears a thick white rope over his apron. After his hand movements, he goes to the center of the ring, stamps his feet, lies down, rises, stamps again, and repeats his hand movements. The stamping is intended to drive away demons. (The salt that the wrestlers strew upon the *doyo* has the same function.) The *yumitorishiki* (bow dance) first occurred at this time, when the shogun expressed his pleasure by handing one of the wrestlers, the great Tanikaze Kajinosuke, a bow. Tanikaze's dance was an expression of his gratitude.

Unlike most sports, sumo has not undergone a steady process of secularization to rid it of its religious elements. On the contrary, sumo has been characterized less by modernization than by "traditionalization," by a conscious effort to introduce religious elements into a previously secular institution and to link the sport more closely to the culture of medieval Japan. The referee's hat, which looks like the headgear of a Shinto priest from the Heian period (794–1185), was adopted in 1909. His colorful kimono, which mimics Heian courtly attire, also dates from this period of nationalistic fervor. The roof that is suspended above the *doyo,* for indoor matches as well as outdoor ones, was originally shaped like the roof of a traditional Japanese farmhouse. In 1931, in the midst of another highly nationalistic period, the roof was redesigned to resemble the roof of the Ise Shrine, the most sacred of all Japanese religious sites.

The elders who "traditionalized" 20th-century sumo were quite successful. Sumo flourishes today as baseball's only serious rival among spectator sports. Together, the two sports aptly symbolize Japan's desire to be, simultaneously, a traditional and a modern society.

—ALLEN GUTTMANN

Bibliography: Cuyler, P. L. (1979) *Sumo: From Rite to Sport.* New York: Weatherhill.

Surfing

Surfing, the art of standing upright on a board and guiding it across the face of a breaking wave, exists today as both a hedonistic pastime or subculture and a highly disciplined professional sport. Two sets of conditions frame the social history of modern surfing: (1) the cultural contexts in which surfing developed as a hedonistic pursuit and a competitive sport and the various attempts to reconcile the respective philosophies of these two forms and (2) the development of surfboard technology and its influence on riding styles and the codification of surfing.

History

Polynesians surfed in premodern times. Early European explorers and travelers in the Pacific wrote highly of their skills, especially those of the Hawaiians. U.S. missionaries in Hawaii, however, took a different view. They considered surfing an "evil and immoral activity," allowing as it did unrestrained intermingling of the sexes. They banned surfing, and by the end of the 19th century only a few dozen Hawaiians surfed. Young *haole* (European-American) Hawaiians "rediscovered" surfing early in the 20th century. Surfing's reemergence coincided with a new culture of pleasure sweeping the Western world, which cast it as a healthy, thrilling, and acceptably hedonistic pastime. Surfing diffused to the Pacific Rim following its "rediscovery."

Distinctive beach cultures in Hawaii, Australia, and California shaped the growth of surfing. The Hawaiian beach, especially Waikiki, symbolized early 20th-century hedonism. It was the archetypal paradise with grass skirts, *leis* (flower necklaces), the *hula* (a "suggestive" dance), and surfing. In Waikiki beach boys and *wahines* (beach girls) preserved Hawaii's relaxed, casual, and hedonistic culture.

In contrast, Australian surfing developed within the SLSA's peculiar cultural milieu of militaristic athleticism. In return for safety and rescue services for beachgoers, local councils and shires ceded control of beaches to SLSA clubs, which cast a shadow of discipline over local beaches. The typical Australian surfer was a duty-bound lifesaver with little time to ride waves for pleasure.

California was the early center of technical and cultural developments. Traditional Hawaiian *alaia* (long) boards were long, heavy, flat-bottomed, and hence extremely difficult to maneuver. The cumbersome boards slid down the face of waves, and surfers changed direction by dragging one foot in the water. In the 1920s, Californian Tom Blake (1900–?) developed lighter "hollow boards" and added a fin. Although Blake's hollow boards were long, they were relatively light, stable, and maneuverable. Surfers could now "trim" (set their boards to run at the same speed as the wave) and change direction by leaning and shifting their weight and by bending their knees and pushing. More stylistic body movements—bent knees, arched backs, outstretched arms—accompanied finned hollow boards; grace and deportment replaced the rigid, upright statue-like stances associated with the *alaia* boards.

In the late 1940s and early 1950s, Californians Bob Simmons (?–1954) and Joe Quigg ushered in a second revolution in board technology. Simmons placed Styrofoam between plywood and balsa wood and experimented with resin-soaked fiberglass cloth to seal his "sandwich boards." Quigg developed the short and highly maneuverable malibu boards, named after the California beach where they first became popular. Wooden boards "died" in 1958 when polyurethane and improved catalysts (used to harden the fiberglass resin) became commercially available.

Unlike surfers in Hawaii and Australia, where limited transport and a more formal club environment confined devotees to local beaches, more affluent California surfers traveled in search of better waves. Cheap air travel in the late 1940s took many Californians back to Hawaii where they had observed idyllic conditions on Oahu's North Shore during wartime postings. "The search," or "surfari," became synonymous with escapism; combined with "the warm *aloha* of Hawaii," which pioneer California surfers took back to the mainland, it became the foundation of a distinctly hedonistic lifestyle and subculture. Surfers adopted their own argot, humor, rituals, and dress.

Surfing subculture burgeoned in California in the late 1950s. It spread internationally through Hollywood-produced surf films, notably *Gidget*, "pure" surf films made by devotees, including *Slippery When Wet*, *The Big Surf*, and *Surf Trek to Hawaii*, and specialist surfing magazines such as *Surfer* and *Surfing*. Surfing subculture challenged accepted limits of social tolerance. The "brown eye" (exposing the anus to public view from a passing vehicle) was a popular antisocial act among surfers in California. Such behavior, as well as concerns about the utility of "the search," which conjured up images of subversive "itinerants," "nomads," and "wanderers," fueled a social backlash against allegedly undisciplined surfers. Some local authorities closed beaches; others banned surfboards.

In 1954, the Waikiki Surf Club organized the first International Surfing Championships at Makaha, Hawaii. Judges awarded points for length of ride, number of waves caught, skill, sportsmanship, grace, and deportment. The Makaha championships founded a new sport. Surfers were divided on the issue of competition. Renowned big wave rider, Australian Bob Pike, articulated the sentiments then held, and still held, by many surfers when he said that "competitions are against the spirit of surfing, which is supposed to be a communion with nature rather than a hectic chase for points." The development of competitions sparked an internal debate over the meaning of surfing. Some surfers defined themselves as pleasure seekers, others as disciplined athletes.

Social antagonism toward hedonistic surfers provided the impetus for them to organize regional and national associations around the world in the early 1960s. At the first World Surfing Championships (1964) in Manly, Australia, representatives of national associations formed the International Surfing Federation. Surfers recognized that organized competition was essential for public acceptance.

Codification of the sport proved difficult. In the late 1950s, surfing styles reflected regional variations. Californian and Australian surfers introduced creative maneuvers such as "cut backs" and "nose riding," trying to preserve the poise that had characterized surfing since the introduction of the hollow board. The malibu ushered in "hot-dog" surfing, a style based on maximum turns and tricks (stalling, walking the nose, dipping the head into the wall of the wave). The Hawaiians resisted the new style. But the most intense debate over style was between Californians and Australians.

Debate over style had major ramifications for the development of competitive surfing. It fueled dissension over judging methods and scoring and led to accusations of corruption, cronyism, nepotism, and bias. Competitive surfing declined in the late 1960s under these conditions, and codification stalled as debate raged over style.

Style, however, was not the sole cause of the decline in competition. The counterculture, an amalgam of alternate lifestyles (typically utopian) and political activism, also penetrated surfing. Soul-surfing (surfing for "the good of one's soul") became an oppositional cultural practice symbolizing the counterculture's idealism. Soul-surfers applied increasingly esoteric interpretations to surfing: waves became dreams, playgrounds, podiums, and even asylums, and the search for perfect waves became an endless pursuit. Surfing signified escape, freedom, and self-expression. Most importantly, soul-surfers scorned competitions.

The counterculture's anticompetition ideals delayed professional surfing by perhaps a decade. It only developed apace after the counterculture, unable to reconcile alternative independence in an interdependent society, waned in the early 1970s. As pervasive as the counterculture was, it never totally subsumed the sport. Not all surfers embraced its alternate philosophies; its disjointed tenets made absolute subscription impossible anyway. For example, neither *kamaaina haoles* (nonindigenous Hawaiians born on the islands or residents there for a lengthy period) nor indigenous Hawaiians welcomed soul-surfers. They viewed them as a threat to paradise. Nonetheless, the counterculture also had a positive impact on professionalism. Its work-is-play philosophy enabled a group of perspicacious Australian surfers to reevaluate competition. They recognized that professionalism could offer competitors, administrators, and a host of small business people an avenue to eternal hedonism.

The 1968 Duke Kahanamoku contest in Hawaii marked a turning point in the development of professional surfing. The objective was to establish a professional circuit and a surfers' association to govern the sport and give it credibility. What followed was years of wrangling about interests, philosophies, competition, commercialization, and virtually all other issues related to surfing.

The early 1970s witnessed the beginning of a third revolution in board technology. Tom Hoye and other Californians developed "twin-fin" boards, which allowed radical maneuvers anywhere on the face of the wave. Twin-fins, however, were slower than single fins and tended to "slip." In 1980, Australian professional surfer Simon Anderson introduced the "thruster"—a design utilizing three fins, one set on the midline and one on each side. Three fins gave surfboards more "thrust" (power and speed) when turning and solved the instability problem associated with twin-fins. Although polyurethane and fiberglass still remain the principal materials of construction, surfboard shapers continue to experiment with thinner, lighter, faster, and more maneuverable boards. These boards, combined with the intense competition of professionalism, have progressively transformed surfing into a more "gymnastic" activity.

Rules and Play

Competitions on the Men's World Championship Tour consist of three preliminary rounds and three finals. Surfers can catch a maximum of 10 waves but only the best 4 waves count toward the surfer's total score. Five international judges adjudicate all heats and finals.

Judges look for "the most radical controlled maneuvers" performed with "speed and power in the most critical section of a wave."

Professional surfing has grown remarkably since the first year of the circuit when men contested 14 events for less than $78,000 prize money, and women competed in 5 events for under $20,000. In 1990, men met in 21 events for nearly $2 million, while in 1992 women competed in 15 events for $320,000. The ASP restructured its grand prix circuit in 1992 and introduced a two-tier structure—a World Championship Tour and a "feeder" World Qualifying Tour. In 1995, the former comprised 10 events for men worth $1.15 million, while the latter included 60 men's events worth $1.5 million. There is only one professional surfing circuit for women. The 1996 Women's World Tour comprises 15 events worth $320,000.

Despite growth and restructuring of the circuit, several factors constrain professional surfing. First, unlike stadium sports, corporate advertisers have free access to ocean, wave, and surfing imagery, allowing them to create images at little cost to themselves. Second, official associations cannot manufacture the conditions that make surfing a dramatic spectator sport. Lastly, most surfers still aspire to a peculiar hedonistic lifestyle rather than a competitive sport.

—DOUGLAS BOOTH

Bibliography: "Australia's Fifty Most Influential Surfers." (1992) *Australia's Surfing Life* 50: 88. Booth, Douglas. (1995) "Ambiguities in Pleasure and Discipline: The Development of Competitive Surfing," *Journal of Sport History* 22, 3: 189–206. Carroll, Nick, ed. (1991) *The Next Wave: A Survey of World Surfing.* Sydney: Angus and Robertson. Finney, Ben, and John Houston. (1966) *Surfing: The Sport of Hawaiian Kings.* Johannesburg: Hugh Keartland Publishers. Lueras, Leonard. (1984) *Surfing the Ultimate Pleasure.* New York: Workman Publishing. McGregor, Craig. (1968) *Profile of Australia.* Chicago: Henry Regnery. Noll, Greg, and Andrea Gabbard. (1989) *Da Bull: Life over the Edge.* South Laguna, CA: Bangtail Press. Timmons, Grady. (1989) *Waikiki Beachboy.* Honolulu: Editions Limited. Young, Nat. (1983) *The History of Surfing.* Sydney: Palm Beach Press.

Swimming, Distance

Long-distance swimming demands all of the physiological and psychological attributes needed for speed swimming. The colossal difference is that in long-distance swimming, good technique must be maintained for many hours, over many miles, and in the face of awesome levels of pain and exhaustion.

History

The classical chronicle of distance swimming has Leander swimming the Hellespont to meet Hero, a distance of two and one-half miles round-trip. In the 19th century, Lord Byron popularized long-distance swimming with a series of distance swims in the Mediterranean Sea.

The English Channel was and is the goal of many distance swimmers. That fewer than 7 percent of the swimmers who try the swim complete the trip testifies to the difficulty of the task. The traditional route (the one taken by Gertrude Ederle in her 1926 swim) is from Cape Gris Nez, France, to Dover, England. While the distance is only 32 kilometers (20 miles), currents, tides, drift, and weather conditions can add several miles to the actual distance swum.

The first claimed English Channel crossing took place in 1815 when Jean-Marie Saletti, a French soldier, escaped from an English prison hulk in Dover and swam to Boulogne. While he certainly escaped by sea, it is more than possible that he used a raft or small boat.

Captain Matthew Webb achieved the first authenticated swimming of the English Channel on 24–25 August 1875. Webb covered the distance in a 21-hour, 45-minute swim. As freestyle was not yet invented, Webb used alternating cycles of breaststroke and sidestroke. To this day he reigns supreme as the greatest showman in the history of the sport. Captain Webb transformed long-distance swimming venues into a three-ring circus, one part carnival, one part festival, and one part rip-roaring recreational vacation sport.

The next successful Channel crossing took place in 1911. Edward Temme was the first swimmer to cross the Channel in both directions—but not consecutively. He swam from France to England in 1927 and seven years later swam from England to France.

Two-way English Channel swims originated in 1961, when an Argentinian, Abertondo, swam the Channel in both directions in a combined time of 43 hours, 5 minutes. In such swims a 5-minute intermission is allowed at the changeover point. The fastest crossing of the English Channel was completed by an American woman, Penny Dean, on 29 July 1978. Her time was 7 hours, 40 minutes.

Today the crossing of the Cook Strait from the South Island to the North Island of New Zealand is considered a more severe challenge than the English Channel. The fastest swim around Manhattan Island in New York City was 5 hours, 53 minutes, by American Kris Rutford on 29 August 1992.

Long-distance swimming is now recognized by the American Athletic Union, and a one-hour swim championship measures how far one can travel in one hour. At the 1978 championships in the men's 25–29 and 75–79 divisions, the leading distances were 5,240 yards (4,793 meters) and 3,260 yards (2,982 meters), respectively. In the women's 25–29 and 75–79 divisions, the leading distances were 4,235 yards (3,873 meters) and 1,575 yards (1,441 meters), respectively.

The golden era of long-distance swimming as a major spectator sport was relatively short but, as Judith Jenkins George, has observed:

> Thousands of spectators were drawn to the oceans, lakes and pools to observe the swimming marathons of the 1920s and 1930s. The fad of endurance swimming lasted less than a decade yet during this time, it captivated the public's interest and the athlete's imagination as a test of courage and stamina.

—SCOTT A. G. M. CRAWFORD

Bibliography: George, J. J. (1995) "The Fad of North American Women's Endurance Swimming during the Post–World War I Era." *Canadian Journal of History of Sport* 26, 1 (May): 52–72. Willoughby, D. P. (1970) *The Super Athletes.* New York: A. S. Barnes.

Swimming, Speed

Speed swimming is defined as sprints and middle distances, up to 1,500 meters, which is currently the longest distance in international competitions in pools. It includes freestyle, backstroke, breaststroke, and butterfly and is one of the major amateur sports around the world.

History

Speed swimming was practiced throughout the ancient world for utilitarian and health reasons. The Egyptian hieroglyph for swimming depicted a man's head and one arm forward and the other back, and in Greek the phrase for the fundamentals of education was "the alphabet and swimming." The recurrence of the Latin words *iactare* and *alterna,* which indicate raising the arms alternately above the surface of the water, and other pictorial and literary sources provide evidence that some form of crawl was a common stroke. Greek historians Herodotus (485–425 B.C.E.) and Thucydides (484–425 B.C.E.) wrote about the significance of swimming, but it was Pausanias (2nd century C.E.) who recorded that swimming races were held in honor of the Greek god, Dionysus. In the Middle Ages, books on the art of swimming were published throughout Europe. In Japan in 1603, an imperial edict made swimming an integral part of the curriculum, thereby promoting interschool competition, which led to nationally organized swimming races.

Not until the 19th century did regular, organized speed swimming events begin to develop. Swimming baths were opened in Liverpool, England, in 1828 and other cities soon followed. Sydney, Australia, saw similar developments in competitive swimming. The first "world championship" is also believed to have been held in Australia; on 9 February 1858, Joseph Bennet from Sydney beat an Englishman, Charles Steedman (1830–?), in a 100-yard event. The first major race in the United States, billed as the national championship, was held by the New York Athletic Club in 1883.

In continental Europe, European championships were conducted in 1889 by the Erste Wiener Amateur Swim Club in Vienna; the only two events were over 60 and 500 meters (65.62 and 546.81 yards). The success of swimming races in Britain from the mid-19th century led to a proportional increase in the prizes, which were usually won by "professional swimmers," who were swimming teachers involved in giving lessons in return for money. Interclub swimming competition soon led to the formation of associations. In 1837 the National Swimming Society (NSS) was formed to define and organize races that were promoted by the weekly sporting periodical *Bell's Life*.

After the formation in 1886 of the Amateur Swimming Association, teachers of swimming in Great Britain were excluded from racing. Since that time speed swimming has developed mostly through the efforts of amateur swimming organizations.

Swimming events were held in Athens at the inaugural Olympic Games of 1896. Three events, the 100, 500, and 1,200 meters were conducted in the Bay of Zeas near Piraeus. Immediately after the London Olympics in 1908 Belgium, Denmark, Finland, France, Germany, Great Britain, Hungary, and Sweden formed the Fédération Internationale de Natation Amateur. FINA's main roles were to establish rules for swimming events and international competitions, to verify and monitor world records, and to organize the swimming programs of the Olympic Games. FINA was also instrumental in the International Olympic Committee's (IOC) decision to introduce swimming for women at the 1912 Olympic Games in Stockholm.

The keeping of world-record times has been a significant aspect of speed swimming, and a race against the clock is an important element of the "spirit of sport." Other factors, though, must be considered when comparing times. Social acceptability and regulations, not swimming efficiency, governed both the style and materials of men's and women. The neck-to-knee costumes worn into the 1930s were made of a wool or heavy cotton, which retained much more water than nylon, which was introduced in the 1950s, or the brief Lycra costumes of the 1980s. It was not until the 1924 Olympics in Paris that events were held in a stadium constructed especially for swimming and divided into lanes separated by floating markers.

Rules and Play

The basic rule in speed swimming is that the swimmer who touches the wall first wins. Rules cover strokes and set standard race distances and events (relays, medleys). Strokes have evolved as swimmers discovered more efficient ways to move through the water.

One of the major developments was the American kick. Duke Kahanomoku (1890–1968) from the Hawaiian Islands, and later Johnny Weissmuller, epitomized this style by swimming in the hydroplane position, which enabled the kick to start at the hip and thereby obtain maximum efficiency from the legs, as only the flat of the foot broke the surface. Since that time there have been many variations of leg kick in the crawl, many of them cyclical.

Breaststroke, forms of which are very old, began as a slow and jerky stroke. In 1928 Olympic gold medalist Yashiyuki Tsuruta (1903–1986) of Japan introduced another modification that produced a fast, nonjerky stroke that basically remained until 1956.

Since the beginning of the 1950s, surface breaststroke improved remarkably as focus shifted to the power from the arm movement, thereby modifying the traditional belief that the legs provided primary propulsion.

Swimming breaststroke under the water was faster than the surface style, which was why many successful breaststrokers swam longer underwater on starts and turns, but underwater breaststroke was banned after 1957 because it gave a distinct advantage and detracted from the spirit of the stroke.

The rules of butterfly stipulate that it is a double-crawl with simultaneous movements of the arms and legs. The best butterfly swimmers have used the dolphin kick, which was banned in breaststroke events because it did not comply with the strict rules of the stroke that required a symmetrical sideways and backwards movement.

Backstroke speed swimming is a relatively recent

phenomenon, not recorded until the beginning of the 20th century. The 1900, 1904, and 1908 Olympic champions all used an arm-over-arm technique, but the back-crawl method used at the 1912 Olympic Games by Harry Hebner (1989–1968) has dominated since.

Western nations have dominated speed swimming. At the Olympic Games from 1896 through 1992, U.S. male and female swimmers have dominated in all strokes, winning 266 gold, silver, and bronze medals. The 1996 Olympics showed signs of change. China won 6 medals, Ireland 4, Brazil and South Africa 3, and Cuba 2. The U.S. total of 26 medals did not exceed the combined total of the three top scorers: Australia (13), Germany (12), and Russia (8).

—IAN JOBLING

Bibliography: Colwin, Cecil. (1992) *Swimming into the Twenty-first Century.* West Point, NY: Leisure Press. Counsilman, James, and Brian Counsilman. (1994) *The New Science of Swimming.* Englewood Cliffs, NJ: Prentice-Hall.

Swimming, Synchronized

Competitive synchronized swimming, often called "synchro," involves routines performed to "synchronize" with and interpret music in the performance of a variety of swimming strokes and complex body actions. Routines may be performed as solo, duet, or team (up to eight members).

History

The elements of synchro—swimming strokes, figures, sculling, and floating—are as old as swimming itself. A bas relief from the Assyrian palace of Nimroud, about 880 B.C.E., portrays underwater swimmers, and old Japanese wood-block prints show men performing figures such as somersaults and demonstrating a position much like modern synchro's "ballet leg." "Scientific and Ornamental Swimming" for men was found in 1892 in England, with Canada beginning, in 1898, a similar men's competition, "Stunts and Strokes." At the turn of the century, women had floating pattern groups in Germany, Belgium, the Netherlands, and France.

Water show activities did underlie the development and popularization of synchro, beginning in 1907 with exhibitions by Annette Kellerman (?–1975), who performed in a glass tank in countries around the world. Katharine Curtis (?–1980) developed synchronized swimming in the United States, experimented, in 1915, with water figures, and added music. She extended this, in 1923 for her University of Chicago classes, to combinations of various "tricks," strokes, and floats that were

Sport or Theater?

While a complex, rapidly developing sport may be expected to generate many internal problems, synchro's main controversy, "sport or theater," is generated externally, by media that are unwilling to consider as "sport" anything not meeting the "swifter, higher, stronger" standard. But even *Sports Illustrated,* despite normally less than flattering reviews, admitted in its report on the 1984 Los Angeles Olympics, "Synchronized swimmers may look like cupcakes, but they're tough cookies, half the routine is performed upside down in a pool." Its water-show beginnings still haunt it. The idea that water ballet is show, while synchronized swimming is sport, has been hard to sell to swimming officials, the public, and the media. Its acceptance into the Olympic Games came only after Lord Killanin, then chair of the International Olympic Committee, saw it for himself at the third World Water Aquatic Championships. "I am very impressed. I saw synchronized swimming for the first time today. It is a very elegant sport."

Synchro enjoys more popularity and acceptance as a sport in parts of the world outside the United States. In every Olympic competition, 1984 through 1996, it has been one of the first sports to sell out all audience tickets.

Another issue is male participation. Interestingly, at the turn of the century competitions in the equivalent of figures were for males. Then the beautiful spectaculars of aquacades and films accented the female attraction. Early U.S. competitions included male championships, but they were never popular. Neither U.S. nor international rules prohibit male participation except for the Olympic Games and the World Aquatic Championships. Presently, male participation is greater in Europe than in the United States and Canada. Indeed, in 1991, the French national champion duet was a mixed pair and a junior male qualified, in 1996, to be part of the U.S. National Junior Team and will compete in competitions that allow males. Men are included in the U.S. masters program.

—*Dawn Bean*

finally "synchronized" to musical beats and measures, "just as in dancing." Her students appeared, as the "Kay Curtis Modern Mermaids," in the 1933–1934 Chicago "Century of Progress" Fair, performing three times daily for audiences of up to 10,000. The term "synchronized swimming" was coined by announcer Norman Ross to describe those shows.

Competitive development was spurred by Frank Havlicek, a student in Curtis's class at Chicago's Wright Junior College, who suggested in 1939 that the collegiate routines could form the basis for competitions between colleges. Rules were drawn up, leading to the first known competition. The AAU sanctioned it as a sport in 1940. The first national championship was delayed until 1946. In 1978, United States Synchronized Swimming, Inc., was formed to govern the sport.

Canada concurrently developed competitive forms of synchro, beginning in 1951. Both Canada and the United States helped spread the sport worldwide through international exhibitions during the 1950s. Synchronized swimming became an official world sport in 1954 when the Fédération Internationale de Natation Amateur (FINA) accepted it as a swimming "discipline."

The first truly international competition, held under FINA auspices, was the Pan American Games of 1955 in Mexico City. Synchro was included in the World Aquatic Championships in 1973 in Belgrade, Yugoslavia. Its Olympic debut came in Los Angeles, California, in 1984.

Rules and Play

Internationally, competition is held in senior class, junior class (ages 14–17), and by age groups (12 and under, 13–14, and 15–17), as well as in masters programs for adults 25 and over.

Competition includes three events: figure competition, technical program, and free routine. The figure competition is similar to a diving competition, where each competitor performs a set of closely prescribed movements for one judging award. The technical routine is set to music and contains compulsory actions, similar to the technical program in ice dance competitions. The free routine is longer, and the athlete has complete freedom in choosing actions to perform. A competition must include at least two of the three events.

In each routine event, two scores—for technical merit and artistic impression—are awarded by panels of five to seven judges. Technical merit includes execution, synchronization, and difficulty and counts for 60 percent of the routine's score. Artistic impression, which counts for 40 percent, includes choreography, music interpretation, and manner of presentation.

In figure competition, each athlete is judged individually on four separate figures. Each consists of complex body movements in a specified sequence and design. Actions include spins, twists, somersaults, and many other special movements that are named for identification. Rules may vary by nation.

Synchronized swimming is now practiced on every continent in the world, with more than 60 nations conducting national programs.

The top international competitions, each held every four years, are the Olympic Games (restricted in 1996 to team events only), the World Aquatic Championships (including solo, duet, and team events), and the Goodwill Games (solo and duet only). The FINA World Cup and Junior World Championships are held every two years.

—DAWN BEAN

Bibliography: Bean, Dawn, ed. (1979–1992) *Synchro.* Santa Ana, CA. Gundling, Beulah, and Jill White. (1988) *Creative Synchronized Swimming.* Champaign, IL: Leisure Press. Swan, Margaret, Donald Kane, and Dawn Bean. (1984, 1989) *Coaching Synchronized Swimming Effectively.* Champaign,. IL: Human Kinetics.

Table Tennis
See Tennis, Table

Tae Kwon Do

Tae kwon do ("the way of kicking and striking") is a Korean martial art practiced by more than 20 million students in over 140 countries. Like other martial arts, tae kwon do emphasizes physical and mental discipline, obedience, and respect as a path to self-mastery. Tae kwon do's distinctiveness arises from its emphasis on kicking, especially powerful flying kicks, as its main weapon.

History

Most commentators suggest three possibilities for the early development of tae kwon do. One account traces tae kwon do to Korea's three-kingdom era (50 B.C.E.), when Silla Dynasty warriors, the Hwarang, spread a traditional martial art, tae kyon ("foot-hand"), throughout Korea. A second idea is that tae kwon do began as a form of Chinese boxing established at Shaolin Temple in 520 C.E. by Bodhidharma, the legendary Indian monk and founder of Zen Buddhism. A third suggestion is that tae kwon do is an offshoot of Japanese or Okinawan karate, which it resembles. It is probable that tae kwon do represents an overlay of other Asian martial arts on a native Korean form of punching and kicking.

For practical purposes, modern tae kwon do history begins in the 20th century: when the Japanese prohibited the local practice of martial arts ("Subak") when they occupied Korea in 1909. Present-day Korean martial artists argue that the Japanese interdiction inspired a conscious struggle to establish a Korean martial arts culture.

The international police action of the early 1950s seems to have increased the visibility and prestige of Korean martial arts. In 1955, a conclave of the leaders of Korean martial arts schools attempted to identify an authoritative style of martial art that could be promoted both nationally and internationally. Tae kwon do was ultimately chosen as the name of this style and Korean general Hong Hi Choi, was designated the official founder of tae kwon do.

By 1973 the Korean government had recognized the World Tae Kwon Do Federation (WTF) as the sole legitimate organization that sets international standards and awards world titles for tae kwon do performance, as well as national titles through its affiliates.

The International Olympic Committee admitted the WTF as a member organization in 1980, and named tae kwon do a demonstration sport in the 1988 Seoul Olympics, ensuring worldwide media attention.

Rules and Play

Tae kwon do teaches an immediate physical reaction, unmediated by mental response, that directly meets the opponent's force. It uses both quick linear movements, like karate, and circular flowing movements, like tai chi chuan. Tae kwon do distinguishes itself from other Asian martial arts by its emphasis on powerful kicking techniques. This feature makes tae kwon do more accessible to children and women, whose flexibility and lower body strength give them an advantage in this martial art.

The techniques of tae kwon do teach rhythm, timing, balance, agility, and breath control. Tae kwon do students learn to defend against attacks from all directions, using both sides of their body and all arms and

Children's Home Rules

1. Children must show respect to their parents and family members at all times.
2. Children shall greet their parents when they enter the home and tell them goodbye when they leave.
3. Children will be truthful at all times.
4. Children will maintain a good relationship with their brothers and sisters.
5. Children must help with household chores.
6. Children will keep their own room neat and clean.
7. Children must keep their body, hair and teeth clean at all times (every day).
8. Children will not interrupt adult conversations.
9. Children will study their school work at school and at home.
10. Children must show respect for teachers and peers at all times.

Children who do not obey their parents may be reduced in rank.

legs. Self-mastery is achieved through regular, frequent repetition of physical techniques.

All movements fall into four elementary categories: kicks, strikes, stances, and blocks. Forms, sparring, and breaking, the three main categories of training and competition, require coordinated combinations of these basic movements. Breaking of boards and bricks demonstrates the focus and power of a student.

The introduction of tae kwon do as an Olympic event has widened a division between schools that focus on physical performance, competition, and winning (sport tae kwon do) and schools that combine the study of physical technique with a philosophical orientation (traditional tae kwon do). This division seems likely to grow.

Philosophy

Tae kwon do, like many other Asian martial arts, probably spread as part of the ascetic training practices of monks and warriors. Indeed, the common Asian term for life force (qi) is used in tae kwon do, as is the term for path or way (do). Its philosophy is usually expressed more often in routine training exercises or etiquette than in an extended study of specific beliefs. Students employ respectful forms of address to their masters; and groups recite the tae kwon do oath and tenets at each session.

The emphasis on different aspects of tae kwon do philosophy differs from one part of the world to another, as masters change it to suit new circumstances. Traditionally, for instance, Korean men learned tae kwon do in military and public educational contexts,

and accepted the strict obedience and discipline associated with such institutions. In the United States, by contrast, most students purchase lessons from a private school ("do jang"), and many pursue tae kwon do training for individual self-improvement and personal fitness.

The very diversity of tae kwon do continues to be controversial, since the styles and organizations that are officially approved are vastly outnumbered by the new ones that appear continually. The standardization of tae kwon do performance in the Olympics is likely to promote further the dominance of "authorized" styles and associations.

—MARGARET CARLISLE DUNCAN

Bibliography: Choi, Hong Hi. (1993) *Taekwon-do: The Korean Art of Self-Defence.* 3d ed. 15 vols. Mississauga, Ontario: International Taekwon-Do Federation. *Journal of Asian Martial Arts* (1992–). Erie, PA: Via Media. Park, Yeon Hee, and Jeff Liebowitz. (1993) *Taekwondo for Children: The Ultimate Reference Guide for Children Interested in the World's Most Popular Martial Art.* East Meadow, NY: Y. H. Park. ———. (1993) *Fighting Back: Taekwondo for Women.* East Meadow, NY: Y. H. Park. Park, Yeon Hee, Yeon Hwan Park, and Jon Gerrard. (1989) *tae kwon do: The Ultimate Reference Guide to the World's Most Popular Martial Art.* New York: Facts on File.

Tai Chi

Taijiquan or Grand Ultimate Boxing, often simply called *taiji,* or tai chi in the anglicized version, is a Chinese martial art of the *Neijia* or soft/internal school that uses soft, slow movements, but is a premier martial art as well. Taijiquan is intrinsically linked to the Daoist (Taoist) philosophical, meditative, and medical tradition.

History

Chinese legendary history attributes taijiquan's origin to Zhang Sanfeng, a Daoist adept who was canonized in 1459, but taijiquan enters recorded history centuries later as a tremendously effective martial art practiced esoterically by the people of Chenjiagou (Chen village) in Henan Province. A form of the art was first demonstrated and taught in public in Beijing by Yang Luchan (1799–1872), who had learned it in Chenjiagou. Yang is said to have accepted all challenges from the many Beijing martial arts masters, never to have been bested, and never to have injured an opponent seriously. He became known as "Yang the Invincible" and was appointed martial arts instructor to the Imperial Court. The form publicly taught by Yang and his successors is the source of popular conceptions of taijiquan as an only vaguely martial, though particularly beneficial, health and longevity exercise. However, the more obviously martial and physically very strenuous Chen style continues to be practiced, as do the derivative Wu, Hao and Sun styles.

Rules and Play

As a martial art taijiquan employs a cultivated subtlety of touch to sense an opponent's strength in order to instantly redirect his or her motion so that one's defensive movement effectively neutralizes it and becomes a counterattack as well. Descriptions of this capacity use such phrases as "when the opponent is still, be still; when the opponent moves, move first," and "use four ounces to deflect a thousand pounds." The technique depends upon the ability to maintain gentle physical contact with the opponent without resisting, i.e., to "never meet force with force." The taijiquan player's counter to the aggressive move, once the instant has been seized and the movement's force captured, can be any of a number of techniques. Most simply and most benignly, the taijiquan player can accelerate or redirect the opponent's motion, sending him or her many feet away. Alternatively, any of a variety of in-fighting techniques ranging from low kicks to punches to open-hand strikes and grappling techniques can be employed singly or in combination, practically simultaneously with the blending with the opponent's force. The initial contact is said to be as soft as cotton, the counter that it becomes, as springy as steel.

The sensitivity, skill, strength, and mental attitude necessary to perform such feats spontaneously and without effort are cultivated partly through the practice of solo forms, or sequences of patterns, and partly by other means. Form practice is a form of meditation in motion and requires great concentration without tension. Paired practice routines in which one works with a partner to simulate martial encounters exist in varying degrees of formality, ranging from duo form sequences to freestyle sparring. The full range of taijiquan skills includes the use of weapons as well; the sword, broadsword, spear, and staff are used according to the principles of the art. The expectation is that the player will gradually learn to direct and augment the flow of vital energy within the body with his or her mind in harmony with the breath and that bodily functions will be enhanced as the body is renewed by the improved circulation of the *qi*.

The mechanical principles of taijiquan involve natural erect stances that combine great stability with nimbleness of foot. Movement begins at the *dantian,* an anatomical point at the body's center of gravity, just below the navel. With no tensing of muscles and with remarkable mechanical efficiency and relaxed precision, the weight is shifted and energy transmitted via the waist to the hands. In effect the legs, spine, and arms become like five bows, resulting in springy whole-body strength to be applied at the optimum instant.

From a Chinese cultural perspective the medical and psychological value of the art as well as its martial potential are quite reasonable expectations.

During the Cultural Revolution taijiquan was under political attack in the People's Republic of China, but now it has been reinstated as a national treasure and a uniquely Chinese form of art and sport. Basic Taijiquan is now taught there publicly in parks and other suitable places, as it is in other parts of the Chinese world. Advanced instruction is available, and form competitions are held frequently.

The soft, slow movements of the popular Yang style of taijiquan are often performed by the disabled and the elderly in the Chinese world to strengthen the constitution generally and to promote longevity. Disciplined daily practice of the art is said to enhance the quality and circulation of *qi* (ch'i) or vital energy within the body, tone all the muscles, improve all bodily functions, and engender a calm and relaxed mental attitude. Taijiquan is a premier martial art as well, and one that can be utilized effectively even very late in life.

—MICHAEL G. DAVIS

Bibliography: Jou, Tsung Hwa. (1983) *The Tao of Tai-Chi Chuan: Way to Rejuvenation.* Edited by Shoshana Shapiro. Warwick: Tai-Chi Foundation. Sutton, Nigel. (1991) *Applied Tai Chi Chuan.* London: A. & C. Black.

Taijiquan
See Tai Chi

Takraw

Takraw, "the international ball game of Southeast Asia," is a team sport played with a rattan or plastic ball in which players may not touch the ball with their hands.

History

A takraw-like game, kemari, was played in Japan from perhaps the 7th century, and a similar sport was in evidence in south-central China, in what is now Yunnan province. However, it is in Southeast Asia that the game truly came into its own. All of the Southeast Asian countries where the game is currently played offer some "national origin" myths for the creation of the sport, but none offers incontrovertible proof that takraw has one and only one specific birthplace.

In Southeast Asia, where takraw-like games have achieved their most distinctive forms, evidence of the sport dates from the 11th century, particularly what are now modern Malaysia and Sumatra. These games were apparently very much like the game now called sepak raga (which in Malay translates as kickball) and were played frequently in royal courts.

In the Philippines, a takraw-like game called kasipa or sipa was being played prior to 1380. Before the Spanish colonization, it was apparently an important activity during coronation celebrations and remained, throughout the Spanish and American periods, a popular pastime at wedding celebrations and village fiestas.

Rules and Play

The ball is traditionally woven of rattan (*rottan* in Malay)—a tough vegetable material from the climbing palm creeper of the genus *Calamus*.

Sepak raga, the traditional Malay game, is played by a six- or seven-man team. The men form a circle and kick or head the ball to one another in a continuous round, the goal being simply to keep the ball from touching ground. As in all forms of takraw, feet, knees, shoulder, elbows, and head—everything but the hand and the forearm—can be used. The winning team is the team that keeps the ball aloft for the required period of time—usually about 30 minutes—with the most kicks. A similar game is played in Thailand.

In hoop takraw, which is very popular in Thailand, three large hoops are suspended over a circular court, and the players must put the ball through them as often as possible. The team, usually of seven, is cooperative, attempting to keep the ball "alive"—off the ground—and flying through the hoop as often as possible during a 30-minute period. Style counts in hoop takraw: simple shots score lowest and more difficult ones higher.

Another Thai form of the game is called "flag takraw." This requires the player to move as quickly as possible along a narrow track, all the while keeping the ball aloft through kicks of the foot and jerks of the head and elbows.

Yet another Thai takraw game, sometimes called "in-carrying takraw" requires a single player to catch and carry as many balls as possible without using his hands. He may hold them with his teeth or under an arm. The standard goal is 12 balls, but experts have caught and held as many 17.

Sepak takraw, one form of which is sometimes called "net takraw," is the game that has achieved the most "international" status, being played by amateur and semiprofessional teams throughout the region. Sepak takraw is played on a rectangular court 13.4 by 6.1 meters (44 by 20 feet). Across the centerline is stretched a net 1.52 meters (5 feet) from the ground. A "service circle" is drawn in each half-court.

The game is played between two squads—called regus—of three players each. A regu wins the set with 15 points. As in volleyball, each team is entitled to hit the ball three times before sending it across the net, but the three hits can come from the same player. Points are won or lost when the ball touches the ground in or out of the court, or does not cross the net after being played three times by the offensive regu.

The net used in modern sepak takraw was introduced only in the 1920s, and in general the game was played according to various local rules for many years. However, in Singapore before World War II, the main Malay form of the game was included in high school variety programs, and after the war an association called the Singapore National Body of Sepak Takraw (PARSES) was formed.

PARSES, together with the emerging takraw organizations in Malaysia and Thailand agreed, in 1965, on a uniform set of regulations and on the name sepak takraw. The final outcome of regional negotiations was the formation of the Southeast Asian Games Federation, which sponsors competitive events such as the games in Bangkok in 1965, the first to feature what could be called "world-class" takraw. Since the mid-1960s, takraw has been a major competitive international sport in the Southeast Asian region.

Wider acceptance for the sport outside of Southeast Asia has been slow but steady. In 1990, after vigorous campaigning, sepak takraw was included in the 11th Asian Games in Beijing.

With internationalization comes standardization, and, if sepak takraw continues to grow, the hand-woven rattan ball—one of the game's most distinctive features—may become a thing of the past. A company in Singapore now manufactures absolutely standard takraw balls, woven in the traditional pattern to be sure, but of precisely milled plastic strips, not rattan. The Thais are already playing competitively with such balls, and the acceptance of plastic seems all but inevitable.

With the traditional rattan ball on its way to the museum, with agreed-upon international rules and recognized venues, sepak takraw seems securely established on the international sports scene. Longtime popularity in Southeast Asia and more recent Chinese patronage of the game ensure its survival as a major competitive sport.

—ALAN TREVITHICK

See also Footbag.

Bibliography: Wagner, Eric A. (1989) *Sport in Asia and Africa: A Comparative Handbook.* New York: Greenwood Press.

Technology

Sport and technology have been interconnected throughout human history. Hunting and gathering peoples created athletic games that employed the technological kits with which they wrested a living from the environment and engaged in warfare. Those cultures used *atl-atls,* spears, bows and arrows, and other such implements in some of their games and sports. Many of the original human athletic games employed familiar tools as basic ingredients in competitions. (Technologies are not merely inanimate objects; they are also organizations of human energy designed to solve problems.)

The technological developments that sparked the agricultural revolutions that gave rise to the first urban civilizations also generated new sporting technologies. Ancient civilizations around the globe constructed monumental architectural sites for sports. Ancient Greeks built stadiums, hippodromes, gymnasiums, and palestras. Greek sports and Greek athletic architecture spread around the Mediterranean world. In the centuries that followed, Roman coliseums sprouted in the vast lands that fell under the sway of their empire.

At least 1,500 years ago, Native peoples in the Americas built massive courts with stone walls that served as the locations for ball games.

In the Dark Ages, monumental architecture devoted to sports declined markedly in Europe and the Middle East. However, in medieval and early modern times Western cultures frequently organized sports around military technologies. Native American, Asian, and African cultures also cultivated martial skill through sports that used weaponry. Skilled artisans produced "tools" for other elite and folk recreations such as tennis, golf, and early forms of cricket, baseball, and football.

The Industrial Revolution

The technological dynamism of the Industrial Revolution radically changed the nature of society and sports. A wide variety of technological advances amplified athletic games and pastimes. The 19th century brought such innovations as the process for "vulcanizing" rubber, which altered golf, tennis, and other athletic balls and their games. New machines such as the bicycle created new sports and recreations. Athletes in industrialized nations became enamored of new and specialized devices that allowed for greater achievements and higher standards of play. That dynamic and evolutionary process produced the later "hi-tech" athletic shoe industry, a multibillion-dollar business selling the notion that technology does indeed enhance sporting performance.

During the 19th and 20th centuries modern sport became a central feature in the mass cultures created by the new technological civilizations. Giant stadiums sprang up in industrial cities. The selling of sports and sporting equipment became a big business in which technological innovations often produced significantly larger market shares.

The transportation and communication revolutions that underpinned the Industrial Revolution also transformed the sporting cultures of first European and North American nations and then those of much of the rest of the globe. The railroad facilitated the rise of professional baseball and college football in the United States, engendering rivalries between cities and colleges. Technologies were instrumental in transforming folk recreations into national pastimes.

The development of national presses in industrialized nations made reading the sports pages a daily habit for millions of newspaper subscribers. New international media promoted sporting rivalries between nations. The re-creation of the Olympic Games in 1896, facilitated by communication and transportation technologies that allowed athletes from around the world to compete and spectators from around the world to witness the results, created one of the most important spectacles for modern global technological civilization.

In the 20th century, technological innovations led to new games, superior performances, and enhanced access by spectators to the burgeoning global sporting culture. From airplane races to Ultimate Frisbee, new gadgets spawned new sports. Innovations such as artificial turf, synthetic tracks, artificial climbing walls, and fiberglass vaulting poles radically changed the ways in which some games were played and certain sports were performed.

Modern technological developments also raised aesthetic and ethical dilemmas for sport. Did aluminum baseball bats produce pleasing sounds? Did they confer unfair advantages on batters? Did graphite tennis rackets with larger string surfaces distort the fundamental nature of tennis? Should biomedical advances, from the development of anabolic steroids to blood-doping techniques designed to enhance the oxygen-carrying capacity of distance runners, be applied to athletic performances? If better athletes could be made, should they be made?

In modern industrialized cultures, and particularly in the United States since the late 19th century, sport itself has been understood as a social technology, one that can teach cooperation, bring assimilation and unity, and instill humanity. Whether or not they overestimate the power of sport to change society, many of the late 19th- and 20th-century promoters of athletics consider sport the single most significant social technology for shaping modern cultures.

Thus sport itself was transformed into a technological system by the inventors of modern athletic ideas and institutions. Technology shapes not only the kinds of athletic games that modern peoples play, not only the way they play those games, not only the level of their achievement in those games, but the very meanings and purposes of sport. Sports themselves have become accepted as technologies designed for making social changes.

—MARK DYRESON

See also Modernization.
Bibliography: Baker, William. (1982) *Sports in the Western World.* Totowa, NJ: Rowman and Littlefield. Guttmann, Allen. (1978) *From Ritual to Record: The Nature of Modern Sports.* New York: Columbia University Press. Katz, Donald. (1994) *Just Do It: The Nike Spirit in the Corporate World.* New York: Random House. Rader, Benjamin. (1984) *In Its Own Image: How Television Has Transformed Sports.* New York: Free Press.

Tennis

Tennis is among the most thoroughly international of competitive sports. Played on a hard court by two or four players, this sport is played in situations that range from the most casual to the most intense—no stakes to very high stakes indeed.

History

The origins of the modern game of tennis are usually traced back to 23 February 1874, when the British patent office issued a provisional license to Major Walter Wingfield for "A Portable Court of Playing Tennis." Wingfield's game of lawn tennis was a descendant of the much older game of court tennis, as well as other racket games, but Wingfield was the first to codify the outdoor game and market it commercially. The game immediately achieved considerable success game, became popular at English country houses, and also soon came to be played at London's sports clubs.

In the spring of 1877 the All England Croquet Club, in the London suburb of Wimbledon, decided to hold a tennis tournament and drew up new revised rules for the game. These rules became the basis for the modern game. Over time Wimbledon became the most important tennis tournament in the world, and its innovations often led the way for other competitions. Wimbledon added a women's singles competition to the championships in 1884, as well as a men's doubles event; the other two major events of the tournament, women's doubles and mixed doubles, were added in 1913.

Seeding, the deliberate placing of designated strong players so they would not meet in the early rounds of a tournament, was introduced into competitive tennis at Wimbledon in 1924, and soon became standard in all tournaments.

Power diffused, however, in 1884 with the founding of the Lawn Tennis Association, which would share the profits produced by the championships. The sport's spread to other countries was also a factor.

Tennis arrived in the United States within months of Major Wingfield's patent. A first tournament was held in Nahant, Massachusetts, in 1876, and in 1880 a national tournament was played at the Staten Island Cricket and Baseball Club. Disputes over proper procedures led to the formation in 1881 of the U.S. National Lawn Tennis Association (USLTA, later simply the USTA), which became the country's governing tennis body. The first official national championship tournament for men was held at the elegant Casino in Newport, Rhode Island, in 1881; a women's tournament was added in 1887. As in England, private clubs became the major venues for tennis in the United States.

Lawn tennis also spread quickly to many other countries. Clubs were founded in Scotland, Brazil, and India in 1875, and in 1877 the first clubs were founded in Ireland and France. The first tournament in Australia was played in 1879, and South Africa had a championship in 1891. The game was also played in Denmark, Switzerland, the Netherlands, Greece, Turkey, Lebanon, Egypt, and Finland by 1890.

Despite its international spread, tennis was dominated by a few countries, notably England, the United States, France, Australia, and New Zealand. The early domination of tennis by several countries is also apparent in the history of the Davis Cup, the sport's major international team competition. From the first competition in 1900 through 1973, only four entrants won the cup: the United States, England, France, and Australia/New Zealand (the latter two competed as one team to 1923). Remarkably, for one stretch from 1937 through 1973, only Australia and the United States won the cup.

Rules and Play

Tennis is a game played by two people (singles) or by two teams of two people (doubles), outdoors on surfaces of grass, clay, or asphalt, and indoors on a variety of surfaces, including asphalt and carpet.

The player's goal is to hit the ball into the prescribed area of the court in such a way that it cannot be returned. A player serves an entire game and is allowed two service attempts for each point. The point is lost by the first player who hits the ball into the net, out of bounds, or who allows the ball to bounce more than once in his own court. A set is won by the first player to win six games while leading by at least two games; if neither player gains a winning margin, today a tie-breaker is normally played at 6–6. The tie-breaker (and the set) is won by the first player to win 7 points while leading by at least 2. In championship play, women's matches are normally won by taking two of three sets, and men's either two of three or three of five sets.

The competitive game has never been restricted to a single type of surface. Grass was originally the most important surface. The French championships have always been played on clay, as have most tournaments in continental Europe and South America. Grass has declined sharply in popularity over time: although it remains in use at Wimbledon, it was abandoned in the United States for championships in 1975, and in Australia in 1988. The U.S. nationals briefly switched to clay, but since 1978 the tournament has been held on asphalt courts, as are the Australian championships. The great majority of professional tournaments, indoor as well as outdoor, are now held on hard courts.

Perhaps the most important recent change in the basic rules of tennis competition came with the adoption of the tie-breaker. First used in a major tournament at the U.S. national championships in 1970, and soon thereafter throughout competitive tennis, the tie-breaker was invented by Jimmy Van Alen, founder of the Tennis Hall of Fame. Played when the score reached 6 games all, in its original version the tie-breaker was won by the first player to win 5 points, who thereby won the set by a score of 7–6. Many players objected to the sudden death nature of this version, in which a single point could determine the outcome of a set in favor of whichever player won it when the tie-breaker score

Tilden on Centre Court

To Tilden the Centre Court [at Wimbledon] was a real and a true inspiration. When he first trod its velvet sward and hurled the ball to the place his strategic brain saw to be the right one, he was no mere earthbound mortal playing a match as he had played hundreds before. The untoward features of the classic rectangle irked him not; to him they were almost non-existent. He was not aware of the gloominess, the cramped, cribbed and confined nature of his supreme battles; nor did it trouble him that the magnificent distances of the Forest Hills and Newport courts, and their freedom of movement and ideal conditions of light and air, were lacking. What he said to himself was something like this:

"Here am I, America's representative, given the opportunity, the fates being kind, to do what no other American has yet done. Under my feet is the turf which the giants of all lawn tennis time have trod. Looking on are the shades of the Renshaws, the Baddelys, the Dohertys, and scores of others almost equally great, watching my strokes, noting my strategy and tactics, nodding, approvingly or the reverse, as they envision my bearing and take cognizance of my every action. Around me, filling every available bit of space, are the men and women who compose the most distinguished and critical gallery in all the lawn tennis world; even royalty has come to view the scene and add luster and éclat to it. 'Twould ill become me to do aught but acquit myself well, to justify my selection as one of the representatives of my country. I must act worthily, as beseems the game and its followers. And may the best man win."

— "A Little Story" in *ALT*, 1921, reprinted in Wm. T. Tilden II and Stephen Wallis Merrihew, *Match Play and the Spin of the Ball* (New York, 1925).

stood at 4–4, and it was subsequently changed. The version in use today awards the set to the first player to win 7 points, while leading by at least two.

The Spread of Tennis

Prominence in competitive tennis has become much more widely diffused geographically, and the once-dominant countries are dominant no more. Wimbledon has had men's singles champions from seven different countries since 1950, and men from nine different countries have won the U.S. title in the same period. Similar trends are visible in the French men's championship and the Davis Cup. Of the early tennis powers, only the United States has remained an important source of champions throughout the sport's history with Czechoslovakia, Sweden, Russia, the former Yugoslavia, and Spain now major sources of top players.

One important factor in this geographical diffusion

has been fundamental changes in the organization of the sport. From the origins of tennis through the 1960s, the sport's major competitions were organized by national associations, as well as by the International Lawn Tennis Federation, which included the national associations as its members. Very early in the history of tennis, the sport's governing associations decided that their competitions would be open exclusively to amateurs. Players won no money for playing or any other activities related to the game. This amateur regime was challenged periodically by professional promoters and by players who wished to earn money from the game. As early as 1926 a small group of players left amateur tennis to tour as professionals, and over the next four decades many of the sport's greatest champions followed their lead, turning professional and traveling in small groups. Some of these players earned respectable incomes for their efforts, but their matches were often regarded as exhibitions rather than genuine competitions, and they did not generate sustained public interest comparable to that produced by Wimbledon, the U.S. championships, the Davis Cup, and the other major amateur competitions.

The Open Era

This situation changed dramatically during the 1960s. Faced by a new challenge from World Championship Tennis, a venture funded by Texas oil millionaire Lamar Hunt, that threatened to lure more and more of the top amateurs into professional competition, English tennis officials announced that in 1968 Wimbledon would be open to all players regardless of their status. The other national associations quickly followed, and 1968 initiated the era of Open tennis. Men began to compete for prize money at Wimbledon and elsewhere in that year. In 1970, under the leadership of Gladys Heldman, founder and editor of *World Tennis* magazine, and of former Wimbledon and U.S. champion Billie Jean King, the women organized their own professional tour. Once Open tennis was established, the prize money grew rapidly. And prize money is of course only part of the earnings of today's professional tennis players.

The rising earnings of players have produced considerable changes in the balance of power in the control of the game. In 1972 the Association of Tennis Professionals (ATP) was founded as a union for male professionals, and the Women's Tennis Association (WTA) was founded in 1973 as a union for women pros. By 1990, the ATP had succeeded in bringing all men's professional tournaments (except the Davis Cup and the national championships of England, the United States, France, and Australia) under their control, and the WTA had done the same for women's professional tournaments. Professionals have joined the ranks of the highest-paid professional athletes in the world and have a substantial voice in governing their sport.

The economic rewards of the Open era have clearly been an important factor in the spread of competitive tennis around the world, for tennis is one of the few sports played professionally in virtually every country.

Tennis in the United States

The general outlines of the sport's evolution are broadly reflected in the its history in the United States. From early in the game's history, the United States has not only been the largest single producer of world-class players, but it has also been the largest commercial market for the sport and has had many more recreational players than any other country.

From its precious New England origins, American tennis gradually spread more widely, both geographically and socially. The geographic shift has been the more thorough, as the temperate parts of the country—most notably Florida, Texas, and California—have become the centers of the sport. The same trend is visible in intercollegiate tennis.

The social shifts are reflected in the national championships' move from Newport to the public National Tennis Center in New York. The social shift in tennis's orientation has been more limited. Although tennis is no longer dominated by the wealthy, and public courts have gained importance relative to private clubs as training grounds for young players, tennis remains an expensive game to learn and play, and most competitive players come from middle-class families. Some social barriers that existed in the past have disappeared. Jewish players, for example, rarely played competitive tennis before the 1960s. Such discrimination has greatly diminished, and there have been a number of successful Jewish players in the United States since the 1960s. Yet other barriers have been more persistent. Poverty is a clear example. Occasional champions from poor families have appeared in American tennis, including several cases in which children from impoverished immigrant backgrounds became outstanding players. The number of competitive U.S. players from poor or lower-class families has never been great, however, and has not clearly increased over time.

A persistent feature of American tennis has been the small number of blacks who have become competitive players. For many years this was clearly due in part to the actions of tennis officials. Racism was a hallmark of the exclusive private clubs that served as the breeding grounds for tennis officials, and the officials carried this policy of exclusion over to their associations. In 1950, Althea Gibson became the first black allowed to play in the U.S. championships, but the color line did not simply fall thereafter. Arthur Ashe, who grew up in Richmond, Virginia, and played there as a junior until 1960, was never allowed to enter junior tournaments sanctioned by the Mid-Atlantic Tennis Association, the local subdivision of the USTA. But even later, in an era of diminishing official racial discrimination, blacks have not been attracted to tennis in large numbers. The triumphs of Gibson (U.S. and Wimbledon champion in 1957 and 1958) and Ashe (U.S. champion in 1968 and Wimbledon champion in 1975), and the success of the Williams sisters in the 1990s have not served as inspirational examples that would result in the systematic entry of large numbers of young blacks into competitive tennis. In 1993, for example, there were 5 blacks among the 45 women nationally ranked by the USTA, and only 2 blacks among the 75 nationally ranked men.

The Effect of Technology

Perhaps the most systematic change in the way competitive tennis is played has been the recent trend toward the use of greater power. This has been due in large part to technological change in the design and construction of tennis rackets. Until the 1960s, the best rackets were made of wood. This changed with the introduction of the steel racket in 1967, followed by aluminum, graphite, fiberglass, and then composites made of graphite, fiberglass, and such new materials as boron and Kevlar. These composites are considerably stronger than wood or metal, and the rackets can consequently be lighter than traditional rackets.

Another major change in racket design occurred in 1976, when Prince Manufacturing introduced a racket with a wider and longer face that had a surface area more than 50 percent larger than conventional designs. The inventor, Howard Head, had intended only to increase the racket's effective hitting area, but he discovered that enlarging the head also had the unanticipated benefit of increasing the power generated by the racket. By the 1990s, conventional head sizes had disappeared in favor of oversized and new intermediate, mid-sized heads; today's rackets have heads 25 to 60 percent larger than those of conventional rackets.

The most recent significant innovation in racket design appeared during the late 1980s. Called the "widebody" because of the extreme thickness of the racket head, the new design is stiffer and generates even greater power than earlier designs. The widebody, which quickly became popular among recreational players, has not yet gained wide acceptance among professional men players, but is almost universally used by professional women players.

These changes in racket design and have systematically rewarded the use of greater power. The two-handed backhand, used sporadically in earlier times, but popularized during the 1970s by Bjorn Borg, Jimmy Connors, and Chris Evert, proved to be ideally suited to the new, larger racket heads. The two-handed backhand has become a staple of the competitive game. The serve has also been affected by the new rackets, as today's game places an even greater emphasis on power serving than was the case in the past. Although opinions differ enormously on the desirability of recent changes in competitive tennis, there is virtually unanimous agreement among both defenders and critics of today's game that the new racket technology is responsible for a much greater reliance on power in all areas of the game than ever before.

These technological changes are also viewed by some to be related to the success of younger players. The more powerful rackets available today can compensate for young players' lack of size and strength, while the increasing speed of the game rewards the faster reflexes and greater foot speed of these players. The increasing popularity of tennis during the 1970s produced larger numbers of junior competitions and training programs. The greater financial rewards available in professional tennis have also spurred the establishment of tennis academies, where children can live and train year-round.

A succession of women players has become successful at very young ages: Tracy Austin reached the world's top 10 in 1978 at 16, Andrea Jaeger in 1980 at 15, Steffi Graf in 1985 at 16, Gabriela Sabatini in 1986 at 16, Monica Seles in 1989 at 16, and Jennifer Capriati in 1990 at 14. In addition, between 1985 and 1990, the three most important tournaments in men's tennis, each more than a century old, all had their youngest singles champions, as Boris Becker won Wimbledon in 1985 at 17, Michael Chang the French Open in 1989 at 17, and Pete Sampras the U.S. Open in 1990 at 19. Many observers have concluded that competitive tennis players are now maturing earlier, and retiring earlier, than in the past. However, although this may be true for the top players, it is not the case for professionals in general. Prior to Open tennis, competitive players were typically young, because they were amateurs and had to earn a living. With the advent of Open tennis, the mean age of competitive players rose sharply, as many found they could earn more money playing tennis than in other careers. As these trends imply, the length of competitive players' careers has increased substantially in the Open era. For both men and women, the most important long-run demographic change during recent decades has been an increase in the mean ages of competitive players, with lengthening careers that have clearly been produced by the prize money of Open tennis.

—DAVID W. GALENSON

Bibliography: Baltzell, E. Digby. (1995) *Sporting Gentlemen: Men's Tennis from the Age of Honor to the Cult of the Superstar.* New York: Free Press. Collins, Bud, and Zander Hollander, eds. (1994) *Bud Collins' Modern Encyclopedia of Tennis.* Detroit: Visible Ink Press. Mewshaw, Michael. (1993) *Ladies of the Court: Grace and Disgrace on the Women's Tennis Tour.* New York: Crown Publishers.

Tennis, Paddle

Paddle tennis is a version of tennis that is played on a smaller court. Players use solid light paddles and balls that are less pressurized than tennis balls. In paddle tennis (as in standard court tennis), players may not hit shots bounced off screens.

Paddle tennis was invented in Michigan in 1898 by Frank P. Beal, a minister who developed it to train young people for standard court tennis. To make the adult version more manageable for children, he established a smaller court.

Beal moved to New York City in the 1920s, and the game became a popular playground game there. It also spread to other parts of the United States, especially California. Adults also had begun to play paddle tennis, and in 1923 the American Paddle Tennis Association was formed.

Different versions of the game and courts developed, which made it difficult to organize tournaments on a national basis.

In 1959, the courts were enlarged to a standard size of 50 feet by 20 feet, divided into two service areas on each side, and a net in the center of the court 31 inches (0.7 meters) high. The methods of service were also changed, including the addition of a one-serve-only rule. Also adopted were rules requiring that the ball bounce once on the other side before a volley. These changes resolved some differences, and in the early 1980s, regional organizations merged and adopted more standardized rules.

—JOHN TOWNES

See also Tennis; Tennis, Platform.

Tennis, Platform

Platform tennis is a form of tennis that was originally designed to be played outdoors in winter on courts built on raised platforms that could be cleared of snow and ice. The game combines elements of court or lawn tennis with several other sports, including squash, racquetball, and paddle tennis.

History
Platform tennis originated in Scarsdale, New York, in 1928 when two tennis players, Fessenden S. Blanchard and James K. Cogswell, wanted to develop an outside court they could use for racket in the colder weather and wound up developing a new sport and court to go with it. They used the wooden paddles and rubber balls that were already being used in paddle tennis and devised rules that were based on tennis but that accommodated the smaller size of the court.

The game became popular among their friends, and in 1931 the nearby Fox Meadow Tennis Club installed a platform tennis court. Other tennis clubs adopted the sport, and in 1934 the American Paddle Tennis Association was formed. The name was changed to the American Platform Tennis Association in the early 1950s to avoid confusion with the original form of paddle tennis and its related organizations.

Platform tennis, originally a sport primarily for the affluent, became more widely popular in the 1960s and 1970s. Courts were built in parks, resorts, and on other sites, and it was played in warmer seasons and climates.

Rules and Play
Platform tennis is played on a court surrounded by a wire-mesh fence. The layout is similar to tennis courts but with smaller proportions. Paddles are made of wood, plastic, aluminum, and other materials.

The basic rules of platform tennis are based on court tennis. Although platform tennis can be played by two opponents as a singles game, it is more often played by four people as doubles. Competitive matches and tournaments are doubles matches.

Games are scored in the same way as tennis. The rules for platform tennis differ from court tennis in two basic ways: (1) platform tennis allows only one serve per point; (2) the ball remains in play if it lands within the area of play, but then bounces up and hits the side or back screens.

These differences give platform tennis its unique characteristics. Although play can be fast and strong, it is less oriented to rapid, powerful shots than tennis.

Strategy in placing shots and the use of the screens to carom the ball at appropriate angles are especially important. Many young people play platform tennis, but the game is also popular among older players because although it is demanding it does not necessarily require the same amount of running, speed, and exertion as tennis.

—JOHN TOWNES

See also Tennis; Tennis, Paddle.

Bibliography: Sullivan, George. (1975) *Paddle. The Beginner's Guide to Platform Tennis.* New York: Coward, McCann & Geoghegan.

Tennis, Real

Real tennis, the ancestor of modern (lawn) tennis, is the descendant of a ball game that presumably originated in the north of medieval France in the early 13th century.

History

Good reasons support the assumption that tennis was initially a goal game, a variety of medieval football played by clerics in the cloisters of their monasteries. This explains the architecture of the real tennis court, which features three penthouses with slanting roof and a hazard called the grille. Penthouse and grille were apparently adapted from the arcaded walks of the cloisters and the lattice window of the locutorium, respectively. The oldest courts in existence are those of Hampton Court, erected in 1532–1533 (rebuilt in 1625), and Falkland Castle in Scotland, in 1539.

The name *real tennis* was coined in the latter part of the 19th century when adepts of the game, filled with deep misgivings about the apparent success of the newfangled lawn tennis, stubbornly called their brand the *real* tennis. In the United States, real tennis is referred to as court tennis; in Australia it is royal tennis. In France, it has preserved one of its many medieval names, *jeu de la paume,* literally "game of the palm [of the hand]"; in French, this term must be distinguished from *jeu de paume,* which denotes the facility or court. Today, the distinction between *jeu de la paume* (the game) and *jeu de paume* (the facility) is not always made; that is why the sport is now officially known as *jeu de courte paume.*

Originally a pastime of the medieval clergy, real tennis was early on adopted by the young noblemen receiving their education from them. It continued as the favorite exercise of the aristocracy for many centuries and was known as the "Game of Kings" accordingly. From the late 16th century on, tennis increasingly became a prerogative of university students. In addition, commercial courts existed in almost every important town of Europe. However, tennis was also soon appropriated by townspeople and the medieval peasantry. The former appended smaller roofs to the gables of their houses, and the latter resorted to makeshifts such as stone slabs or corn sieves in order to execute the service properly.

Women have been notably absent from real tennis courts until very recently. As late as 1903, J. M. Heathcote could write: "We may not wish to encourage our wives and daughters to emulate . . . Margot . . . and to compete with us in an exercise fatiguing to all, and to them possibly dangerous, but we accord to them a hearty welcome when they honour the 'dedans' (as spectators) with their presence."

Rules and Play

Played with the palm of the hand (and the feet) by its inventors, real tennis has made use of the sheepgut-strung racket since about 1500 C.E. Stuffed with animal hair originally, the still solid balls now consist of strips of heavy cloth tape wound into a ball, tied with twine, and covered with white felt. They are still sewn by hand by the club professional.

The courts vary in size, standardized playing fields being a feature of modern sports since the 19th century only. Real tennis courts are about half the length of a lawn tennis court and slightly wider.

Real tennis is played in much the same way as lawn tennis: the ball must be struck after its first bounce or on the volley. The distinctive features of the game are due to the fact that the medieval player put to good use the peculiarities of the original court. One of the game's chief attractions is balls ricocheting off the walls. The rule deviating most from lawn tennis is the so-called chase rule. Whereas in lawn tennis the ball is dead if it bounces a second time, in real tennis the spot of the second impact (known as "the chase") is marked. Whenever the score is within a point of winning the game (the scoring method is the same as in lawn tennis) or whenever two chases have occurred, the players change ends to contend the chase or chases. In order to do this, the player who made a chase in his opponent's court has to "defend" it, by preventing the ball of his opponent from landing, if it bounces a second time, closer to the rear wall than in the case of his own chase.

The sport has six national governing bodies and recent years have seen a revival of real tennis, especially in Australia.

—HEINER GILLMEISTER

Bibliography: Butler, L. St.J., and P. J. Wordie, eds. (1989) *The Royal Game.* Fordhead, Kippen, Stirling, UK: Falkland Palace Real Tennis Club. de Bondt, Cees. (1993) *"Heeft ye-man lust met bal, of met reket te spelen . . . ?" Tennis in Nederland 1500–1800.* Hilversum: Uitgeverij Verloren. Garnett, Michael. (1991) *Royal Tennis for the Record.* Romsey, Victoria: Historical Publications.

Tennis, Table

Table tennis is a modified and miniaturized version of other kinds of tennis; it is played with extremely light, hollow plastic balls and rubber-faced wooden paddles. The sport is played in homes and recreation centers worldwide; it is also credited with improving relations with the Peoples Republic of China during the Nixon administration. Table tennis became part of the Olympic Games in 1988.

History

Table tennis—often known by the English Jaques and the U.S. Parker Brothers trade name of "Ping-Pong"—is generally considered to be of English origin. Miniature "tennis" was played indoors in England in the 1880s and 1890s, largely among the formally dressed gentlefolk as a mixed-company after-dinner diversion.

Table tennis began to find mass acceptance at the turn of the century, and quickly spread to every continent. The game was inexpensive and athletic and provided wholesome family entertainment. Ping-Pong postcards, party invitations, and even musical pieces were the order of the day. Strangely, as incredibly fashionable as table tennis had become in England and the United States for those few years at the beginning of the century, it just as incredibly became unfashionable.

In 1922, however, a Cambridge University student, Ivor Montagu (1904–1984), began to interest himself in codifying the laws of the game, including the retention of the double-bounce serve. In January 1926, England's Montagu, along with representatives from four other countries—Austria, Germany, Hungary, and Sweden—founded the International Table Tennis Federation (ITTF). World championships began in 1926. On its formation in 1933, the U.S. association (in 1993 renamed at its Colorado Springs Olympic Headquarters as USA Table Tennis or USATT) immediately affiliated with the ITTF.

Rules and Play

Though table tennis carried over much from lawn tennis (even perpetuating for a time lawn tennis scoring or variations in court-dividing line-markings), it was im-

---

How Sponge Technology Has Changed Play

Before 1952 serious players used the uncovered wooden blade, then preferred a sandpaper, or cork, or hard-pimpled rubber covering. When Japan's Hiroji Satoh won the 1952 world championships with a thick sponge rubber racket, the sport was forced to absorb a great controversy. Should the new "soundless" racket be banned, or not? After much debate it was not—but the thick sponge of the 1950s has been replaced by a plethora of thinner, far more sophisticated sponge coverings. Today's rackets, after some standardization in 1959, have easily removable sheets of sponge-based pips-out or inverted pips-in rubber with varying properties that greatly increase the speed and spin a player can put on the ball and that in some cases allow him to be quite strategically deceptive.

Because some players began using combination rackets that, to judge by the color, appeared to have the same kind of sponge sheet on both sides but really didn't—that is, one side may have had an antispin sheet that provided a dead return and the other, just the opposite, an inverted sheet that gave off a lively return—opponents were confused, their timing thrown hopelessly off, when the user twirled the racket in play to deceive them. So to combat this bit of trickery, deemed unfair, the ITTF passed a rule that one side of the racket had to be colored black, the other red, whether both sheets of sponge rubber were identical or not.

Another matter of concern to the ITTF is the length of the pimples on a racket, for how they bend or don't, and how the ball comes off such a covering, is of great importance to competitors. Even the glue that a champion player uses to repeatedly affix a new sheet of sponge rubber to the blade (likely after every match) is important, for its fresh application likewise helps to increase his powerful play.

As a result of this technological advance, there are few defenders left in the sport, for neither by chopping nor by lobbing can one repel the force of the topspin attack. Instead, beginning with the serve, and the return of serve, both of which over the years have become of primary importance, each player seeks as best he can to quickly get ball control over his opponent and to end the point immediately or as soon as possible.

—*Tim Boggan*

---

mediately apparent that some modification had to be made to the "single-bounce" tennis serve (where the server's ball could not bounce until it was on his opponent's side). Obviously, since serving overhand would be viciously absurd, a quite early rule that had been popularized demanded an underhand one-bounce serve.

During the seven decades of serious tournament play, controversy has inevitably emerged—over, for example, the use of various illegal serves (still a bone of contention today) or over nonattacking, interminably slow play—and consequently have brought necessary rule changes.

One major controversy has been over the use of sponge rubber jackets, initiated by Japanese players in the 1950s. It is fair to say that there is table tennis before sponge, and table tennis after sponge. They are almost two different games. Players may use the shake-hands or penholder grip down through the years (and which is a seemingly never-ending controversy itself), but with regard to the sport's essential characteristics of speed and spin, and the new athleticism that serious play requires, the technological changes in the racket coverings in the last 40 years have brought about profound changes.

Today the standardized "Expedite Rule" stresses a 15-minute time period for any one game. Then, if the game isn't finished, players must alternate services for the rest of the match, with the stipulation that if the server's opponent successfully returns a thirteenth ball he automatically wins the point.

Table Tennis around the World

The multiethnic, multicultural appeal of table tennis remains strong today as can be seen from the 80 ITTF member-countries that sent players to the 1995 Tianjin, China, world championships. In 1995, of the top 10 men and top 10 women players in the USATT, half were from China, another 5 were from Vietnam, Yugoslavia, Nigeria, South Korea, and Romania, and only 5 were native-born (Dunn 1995).

Meanwhile, the best table tennis players—most recently, the Chinese and Swedish men and the Chinese and South Korean women—continue to thrive, as do their lesser counterparts, in professional leagues and increasingly larger prize money tournaments in both the East and West.

In the begining, Hungarians dominated table tennis, particularly Victor Barna, perhaps the most famous name in table tennis. The 1940s saw the emergence of Asian players and by the mid-1970s Chinese players were at the top. From 1956 through 1969, Japanese women won six out of seven world women's singles titles, and Japanese men were also successful. For the last 25 years, however, the Japanese women and for the last 15 years the Japanese men have been unable to match the achievements of their Chinese and Korean neighbors.

In 1971, after emerging from their Cultural Revolution, the Chinese coined the diplomacy phrase, "Friendship first, competition second," and proceeded to reacquaint the world, especially the so-called "Third World" of Asian, African, and Latin American countries, with their table tennis expertise . . . and their friendly propaganda. China's diplomacy went so far as to some-

times allow Chinese players to take it easy on their opponents, even, it was thought, in major championships.

In the 1980s and early 1990s, a new wave of Swedish athletes wrested away championships that had seemed second nature to the Chinese. These victories illustrated what a country—with a total population less than any one of China's three major cities—could do, at least for a generation or two, with a superb table tennis development program, a unifying team spirit, and a will to win.

Today, however, the Chinese have come back to capture men's, women's, doubles, and team titles. There are good reasons for this. The Chinese have strong veteran players and also exceptional young players who are just out of their teens.

—TIM BOGGAN

Bibliography: Barna, Victor. (1962) *Table Tennis Today.* London: Arthur Barker. Boggan, Tim. (1976) *Winning Table Tennis.* Chicago: Henry Regnery. Clark, Coleman. (1933) *Modern Ping-Pong.* New York: John Day. Craydon, Ron. (1995) *The Story of Table Tennis—The First 100 Years.* Hastings, UK: English TTA.

Thoroughbred Racing
See Horse Racing, Thoroughbred

Tobogganing
Tobogganing involves sliding down an ice- or snow-covered slope on a small sled. Three primary types of toboggans are used in competition: the skeleton or Cresta Run toboggan, the luge toboggan, and the bobsleigh or bobsled. This entry focuses on skeleton or Cresta Run tobogganing, in which the rider assumes a head first, prone position upon the toboggan.

History
The term "toboggan" has been traced back to the French-Canadian word *tabaganne,* which was originally derived from an Algonquian word *odabaggan,* meaning sled.

Native American people in eastern Canada are credited with creating the toboggan. They fashioned a simple, highly functional sledge or sled from long thin strips of birchwood poles or slats with turned-up ends, fastened together with deer leather thongs. These toboggan sleds were first used to transport items across the frozen northern terrain of various lake and river systems. The narrow design of the toboggan permitted it to "float" easily on the trail packed down by a snowshoer who pulled it along behind. On downhill

Hesta of the Cresta.

This poem illuminates the legendary female tobogganing pioneer, Hesta, who as the poem attests, rode down the Cresta Valley three years before the run was officially constructed:

Now Hesta rode the Cresta
Midst the snows of '82
Tho' her mother had impressed her
It was *not* the thing to do.
She said "It's nice,
I like the ice,
It thrills me thru' and thru'."
In defiance of her mummy
She slid upon her tummy.

Unfortunately, folk heroine Hesta lost control at what is known as the Shuttlecock curve and wound up in a hospital, like many of her real-life male and female contemporaries.

Early women tobogganists rode the course in the requisite attire of their day: skirts. In spite of this hindrance, some women riders turned in very respectable performances. Women riders were also resourceful and developed techniques such as wrapping a band of elastic around their skirts above the knees to keep them from flapping on a run. Women toboggan pioneers such as Mrs. J. M. Baguley drew attention in 1919 as she placed in the last eight competitors of the Curzon Cup. She finished ahead of her husband by one-eighth of a second aggregate time in the first half of a race over three heats. Some women participants risked the label "fast" when they chose to wear breeches on the runs during this era. Mrs. J. M. Baguley set a course record on 14 February 1921, when she rode from junction to finish in 48.9 seconds. This time would have put her in the top 10 finishes at the 1948 Olympics. Due to some bad spills on the course among women tobogganists, a heated debate arose in the 1920s concerning their participation in the sport. Ultimately, women were banned from, or granted only limited access to, the course, due to several incidences of female mishaps on the course run. Women associate club members may ride the course only on the last day of the Cresta season from junction to finish.

—*Katharine A. Pawelko*

stretches, the rider sat on the sled and steered it with sticks.

Tobogganing as a sport began on the slopes of Mount Royal near Montreal, Canada, during the 19th century. In Europe, recreational tobogganing was described in documents as far back as the 16th century.

Visitors from Great Britain and the United States introduced tobogganing at the Alpine recuperative centers in Davos and St. Moritz, Switzerland, and the sport soon became popular among tourists in the snowclad Swiss Alps region. Tobogganing was considered to be an excellent form of recreation for people with disabilities, since it could be done while sitting in an upright position.

Much experimentation in the design of both toboggans and runs took place during this period. In 1879 two toboggan runs were designed and constructed at Davos, Switzerland. Shortly thereafter, in 1881, national toboggan competition began on a course located between the hamlets of Davos and Klosters in Switzerland. The Davos Tobogganing Club was formed in 1883 and began to sponsor races among teams from different local luxury hotels-cum-sanitariums. By March 1883 international competitions were being held in Switzerland on the Davos-Klosters toboggan run, which was over 3,000 meters in length. In the later part of that decade, tobogganing became popular in Canada, Switzerland, Germany, Austria, the United States, and Russia.

Toboggan runs were designed and engineered to provide a directed curving, downhill course (or chute), which increased the speed, skill requirements, and competitive appeal of the activity for participants and spectators, while minimizing hazards and mishaps.

During the period of rising participation and popularity as a winter sport (1880s), tobogganing evolved and branched into the three main forms of skeleton or Cresta tobogganing, lugeing (which developed from the one-person toboggan), and bobsledding (dubbed the "bob-sleigh" because the early riders leaned back and then "bobbed" forward to increase speed on the straightaway sections). In 1964 luge became an Olympic event and replaced skeleton or Cresta tobogganing as a competitive sport. At this juncture, luge tobogganing emerged from the shadow of bobsledding events, which had already attained Olympic status in 1924.

The Fédération Internationale de Bobsleigh et Tobogganing (FIBT) was originally founded in 1923 and governed bobsledding, tobogganing, and luge international rules and events. The Fédération Internationale de Bobsleigh et Tobogganing was reorganized in 1957 as the official international governing body for bobsledding and skeleton tobogganing.

Several U.S. communities have begun to sponsor winter carnivals or snow bowls. One example of these occurs at Ragged Mountain at Camden, Maine. This is where the U.S. National Tobogganing Championships are held on New England's newly restored and longest toboggan slide (134 meters). Participants ride the ice-coated wooden chute on traditional ash or maple sleds.

Rules and Play

The term "skeleton" refers to the simple, skeleton-like outline of the toboggan frame, originally crafted from steel, wood, and canvas or leather. Today, the skeleton toboggan is constructed of steel or fiberglass.

Design changes further improved the toboggan. In 1901 the sliding seat was developed. By 1903 a snub-nosed toboggan was introduced. Ball-bearings were later used to improve the sliding seat apparatus. Since this period, the design of the skeleton toboggan has remained essentially the same.

The Cresta run is an extremely winding and challenging course with steep banks rebuilt each year by the St. Moritz Toboggan Club in Switzerland. Races typically begin from either the top or from junction to the finish. Top to finish represents the full length of the course.

The prime Cresta toboggan competition occurs during the subzero temperature season between January and February, when 50 events are often scheduled. Cresta course races are composed of three heats; the winner is the person with the shortest cumulative time from the three runs. The runners on the toboggan may not be heated. Toboggans used in the Cresta run may be any size, shape, or weight, with speed and stability being the guiding design factors. A critical selection factor for competitors is that the toboggan dimensions must be a "good fit" for the user in terms of length, width, height, and weight. Mechanical brakes and steering components, however, are not allowed on the toboggan.

The type of toboggan preferred on the Cresta course is known as the "steel skeleton." One person rides upon the skeleton toboggan. "Raking" equipment, composed of steel spiked toe pieces screwed into the boots worn by tobogganists, is applied to the run for steering and braking purposes.

Good judgment gained through experience is necessary for both selection of the most appropriate toboggan and appropriate strategies and techniques for the course. Tobogganists wear spiked shoes to help them gather initial momentum during a 50-meter sprint start, which is accomplished in a bent-over position by pushing the skeleton toboggan along the track. Once they achieve the desired momentum, riders lunge smoothly onto the sled. To negotiate corners or prevent slipping on iced banks, sledders use a technique called head steering: the rider shifts position so the body weight is primarily to the rear of the toboggan, which has deeply grooved runners. This arrangement permits the front of the toboggan to be steered by swinging or jerking it from side to side. Changes in direction may be initiated by slightly tilting the head. While the feet are seldom used, they may be sparingly and judiciously applied to help steady, steer, and control the pace on banks or corners.

—KATHARINE A. PAWELKO

Bibliography: Conover, Garrett, and Alexandra Conover. (1995) *A Snow Walker's Companion: Winter Skills from the Far North.* Camden, ME: Ragged Mountain Press. Cross, Gary. (1990) *A Social History of Leisure since 1600.* State College, PA: Venture.

Track and Field, Decathlon

The decathlon is a 10-event, standard men's track and field event contested over two days. The 100-meter dash, long jump, shot put, high jump, and 400-meter dash are held on the first day. The 110-meter hurdles, discus throw, pole vault, javelin throw, and 1,500-meter run make up the second day's schedule. A scoring table awards points for individual performances and the athlete with the highest score after ten events is the winner. The women's counterpart is the seven-event heptathlon.

History

The modern decathlon has an ancient Greek heritage and was added to the modern Olympic program in 1912. Native American Jim Thorpe of the Carlisle Indian School won the initial Olympic title but was subsequently stripped of the honor.

The term decathlon comes from the Greek—*deka* for "ten" and *athlos* for "contest." At the turn of the century, Scandinavian nations (Sweden, Denmark, Finland) experimented with multievent competition. The Danes called theirs a "decathlon" and offered a national decathlon championship as early as 1900.

Various multi-event contests were held early in the century, but it was the Swedes who proposed a pair of such contests for men, a pentathlon (substituting the 1,500-meter run for wrestling) and a decathlon. In Stockholm in 1912, Sauk Indian Jim Thorpe (1888–1953) gave the event mythology and lore when he won the pentathlon and decathlon by huge margins. During the awards ceremony Sweden's King Gustav declared him the "world's greatest athlete"—the title accorded Olympic decathlon champions and world-record holders ever since. (In 1913, as a scapegoat for amateur AAU rules, Thorpe lost the medals after he played a few games of minor league baseball while on summer break. They were restored in 1982, almost 30 years after his death.)

The first official multi-event scoring tables, using 1908 Olympic records as a basis, were provided in the

Lost Opportunities

The decathlon has an official history. It is the account of those exceptional athletes who answered to the title of World's Greatest Athlete. Icons such as Jim Thorpe, Bob Mathias, Rafer Johnson, and Daley Thompson deserved the billing. All were Olympic champions. But the sport also has a counter-history, the saga of the forgotten, lost, and ignored. Sometimes talented athletes who would have been decathlon favorites or cofavorites never made it to the Olympic starting line. Wars, boycotts, political chicanery, injuries, and amateur policy all intervened to relegate them to historical footnotes.

Two such athletes were World War II victims. Big Bill Watson, an all-around talent from the University of Michigan, won the USA Amateur Athletic Union title in 1940 with 7,523 points, 400 points higher than anyone else in the world that season. Watson was a world-class shot-putter and long-jumper and a very adequate sprinter, hurdler, and vaulter. His place in decathlon history was virtually assured until the 1940 Games, originally awarded to Tokyo, were canceled.

Watson won a pair of national titles and some observers believe he would have won the 1944 Olympic crown as well. Yet those Olympic Games were also canceled by the war. By the time the 1948 London Games were contested, Bill, who became a Detroit policeman, had retired. He suffered from severe depression in later years because of his lost Olympic opportunity. His melancholy life ended in 1973 when he was gunned down on a Detroit street.

Heino Lipp's parable has a happier ending. A giant at 1.93 meters and 100 kilograms (6 feet, 4 inches and 220 pounds), the Estonian Lipp grew up while Adolph Hitler and Joseph Stalin bitterly fought over his Baltic homeland. Estonia passed to the Soviet sphere and the USSR declined an invitation to compete at the 1948 London Olympic Games. Several days after 17-year-old Bob Mathias astonished the track world, Lipp topped his winning London score by 445 points. *Track and Field News* ranked Lipp first in the decathlon world for the 1948 season.

The Lipp family was noted for wartime activities promoting Estonian sovereignty. Heino was periodically captured and jailed as a political prisoner by Soviet authorities. For several seasons after the war, in spite of being the world's top decathlete and Europe's best shot-putter, Lipp was never allowed to leave the Soviet Union. On several occasions he just missed breaking Glen Morris's world decathlon standard. When the Soviets did join the Olympic family for the 1952 Olympic Games, Lipp was denied an opportunity to compete. The Games were held in Helsinki, just across the Bay of Finland from Lipp's home in Estonia.

Forty years later Heino Lipp did have an Olympic moment. A year after Estonia gained its autonomy from the Soviets, he became its flag-bearer at the 1992 Barcelona Olympic Games. Natives wept as their greatest hero—with the blue, black, and white flag in his clutch—led his country back into the Olympic arena during opening ceremonies.

—*Frank Zarnowski*

spring of 1912 by the Swedes. Since 1912, world decathlon records have been set on the different tables on 37 occasions, 8 of them at Olympic Games.

Rules and Play

Decathlon events have retained their order since the first contest in 1911, except for the 1912 Olympics. The decathlon itself is a specialty whose constituent athletes are fascinated by versatility; decathletes *prefer* doing well at 10 sports rather than superbly at 1. They are the Renaissance men of sport. The event requires ample training. Few decathletes, for example, ever trained harder than Bruce Jenner, who was known to devote seven hours per day to workouts. Training routines must attempt to enhance speed, strength, agility, and endurance.

Decathlon world records have been held by someone from each major race (white, African American, American Indian, and Asian). Nevertheless, acceptance and success in the decathlon has been largely confined to North America and Europe, leading some to conclude that the Olympic decathlon is an Europe versus North America contest.

No decathlete can rely on a few competent individual performances to win. The scoring tables reward balance and consistency, and no contest is won with a single great mark. Yet a decathlon is easily lost with a single weak event. This forces the decathlete into a physical cost/benefit analysis. The athlete must decide, for example, whether to put more emphasis on the shot put at the expense of running training.

Mental factors play a bigger role in the decathlon than they do in other events. The main challenge is maintaining concentration and focus throughout the ten events. Frantic struggles against antagonistic opponents are rare; contestants compete against themselves and the scoring table. The adversaries are time, distance, fatigue, and the fear of failure. Other competitors are fellow competitors, helpful motivators, and often good friends.

Today the decathlon is truly popular only in Germany. In 1995 approximately 1,100 U.S. athletes and 5,000 worldwide participated in at least two decathlons per year. The Soviet Union systematically promoted the event before 1991 but the change in economic/political systems has relegated it to a "developing" world decathlon power. The United States has recently regained the world decathlon lead, mostly as a result of corporate endorsements.

—FRANK ZARNOWSKI

Bibliography: Kamper, Eric, and Bill Mallon. (1992) *The Golden Book of the Olympic Games.* Milan: Vallardi and

Asociates. Wallechinsky, David. (1984, 1988, 1992) *The Complete Book of the Olympics.* New York: Viking; Boston: Little, Brown. Zarnowski, Frank. (1996) *Olympic Glory Denied.* Glendale, CA: Griffin Publishing.

Track and Field, Jumps and Throws

Various forms of competitive and achievement-oriented jumping and throwing activities are part of the overall menu of track and field events. They take place on the "field" inside or around the running track, though they have, over time, gradually assumed particular sites within the arena. The jumping events are made up of the high jump, the long jump, the triple jump (formerly called the hop, step, and jump) and the pole vault. The throwing events involve the propulsion of the following implements: the shot, javelin, discus, and hammer.

Jumps

A high jump test was the requirement of the king's warriors in Celtic Ireland about the time of Jesus Christ. At Dessau, in Germany, around 1776, Johann Friedrich Simion introduced high jump stands with holes and pegs to support a bar, the first of its type known. The first great amateur jumper was the Englishman Marshall Brooks, who in 1876 jumped 1.89 meters (6.20 feet). The next 25 years saw some great jumpers in Ireland and the United States, most of whom did a roll over the bar from a straight-on approach. Dick Fosbury and Debbie Brill of Canada revolutionized the event with their backward arch, called the Fosbury Flop and the Brill Bend, both used to set record heights.

Pole vaulting apparently began around 1791, when a pole vault stand was known to exist at Schnepfenthal School in Germany, but early impetus for competitive pole vaulting developed in England. The event was featured in the Lake District (northwest England) sports events.

By the 1890s, sand landing pits had superseded earth in the United States. The early 1900s saw the ascendancy of U.S. vaulters, who were the first seriously to use the slightly flexible bamboo pole in about 1906. U.S. vaulters also had a hole with a backboard into which they planted their pole instead of thrusting a spiked pole into the ground.

In the late 1930s, a Russian vaulter experimented with a flexible green bamboo pole to achieve a world-class vault. Raised sand and sawdust landing pits were being used at this time. Flexible Swedish steel poles were popular in the 1940s. However, experiments from as early as 1948 had taken place with hollow fiberglass poles, and from 1961 they ruled supreme. From a mod-est height of 4.83 meters (15.85 feet) with a heavy slow reactive pole, the record had shot up to 6.14 meters (20.14 feet) with longer, lighter, more reactive poles.

Evidence of broad jumping appears in Germany around 1776. There was a graduated jumping ditch wider at one end than the other. Jumping pits appear to have been introduced in the 1860s with broken earth into which to land. At a later date, sawdust was mixed with the sod and by 1900 sand pits were fairly common.

In the 1920s top jumpers began to cycle their legs while jumping, a technique known as the hitch-kick, which helped them achieve a better leg shoot on landing and hence longer distances. At the Mexico City Olympics Bob Beamon of the United States achieved a phenomenal jump of 8.90 meters (29.19 feet), hailed as a jump of the 21st century.

The triple jump was added to the program at the 1896 Olympics, given that it may have been an ancient Olympic event. Dreisprungen ("three jumps") took place in Bavaria from at least the 15th century. Triple jumping has had a long history in Scotland with mention of the event, hop, step, and jump, during the 18th century.

Throws

Putting a stone of about 7.3 kilograms (16 pounds) or heavier, a shot putt, has been a sport in Europe since at least the 12th century, especially in Scotland, Bavaria, and Switzerland. Regular competition with measured throws began in the Scottish Border Games of the 1820s.

From 1880 to the early 1900s, the Irish were the best shot putters in the world. The usual practice was to throw from a 7-foot (2.13-meter) square with stop-board until 1908 when a 7-foot circle became standard.

Parry O'Brien introduced the style of starting his movement across the circle from a backward position, culminating with a strong rotational drive of the arm prior to release. He advanced the record 16 times between 1953 and 1959 to 19.30 meters (63.30 feet). During this time, the concrete circle superseded the cinder circle.

Women began putting the 8-pound (3.6-kilogram) shot in the United States in 1907, and in Europe a 5-kilogram (11-pound) shot was used between 1918 and 1924, after which 4 kilograms (8 pounds, 13 ounces) became the international standard. In the 1920s and 1930s, the Germans were the best, and from 1945 onward the former Soviet Union has dominated the event, although East Germans and Czechs have also been prominent.

The Greek poet Homer speaks of the discus being

thrown by the Myceaneans at Troy, which is considered to have taken place around 1200 B.C.E. The modern Greeks included the event in their Olympic revival games of 1859, 1870, 1875, and 1889. Discus throwing was revived in 19th-century Sweden and included in the Olympic Games of 1896 in Athens.

The actual discus has hardly changed from 1896, when it weighed 2 kilograms (4 pounds, 6 ounces) and was made of wood with a metal rim. The Swedes produced a heavy-rim discus of regulation size and weight in the 1970s, which allowed more pulling power to be generated for those throwers with strong fingers.

Improvement in throwing was slow between the years 1920 and 1941 with Americans advancing the record year by year. In 1934, Swede Harald Andersson threw 52.42 meters (171.98 feet), and the next year Willi Schroder of Germany, 53.10 meters (174.21 feet). Generally, throwers in the 1930s appreciated the fact that their discus went further if thrown into the wind. American Al Oerter won Olympic golds at the four games between 1956 and 1968.

Women in Europe were throwing the men's or junior men's (1.5 kilograms [3 pounds, 5 ounces]) discus in 1917 and 1921. The following year the 1-kilogram (2 pound, 3 ounce) implement came into general use. Germany and Poland had the top throwers in the 1920s and 1930s and the Soviet Union from the 1940s onward with Romania, Czech Republic, Bulgaria, and East and West Germany also having prominent throwers.

The hammer throw was known among the Vikings 800 C.E. They threw a hammer to lay claim to land, of which the best throwers claimed the largest share. An 11th century English legend mentions a hammer-throwing champion in England. In the 16th and 17th centuries throwing the hammer and other similar implements was popular. Measured hammer throwing emerges as a regular sport in Scotland and Ireland from 1828.

In 1878 the Amateur Athletic Club of London introduced a 7-foot throwing circle, which was increased to 9 feet (2.7 meters) in 1887 probably to accommodate the turn, but it is uncertain who developed the turning technique. Soon after this, particularly in the United States, flexible malacca cane shafts were used to help improve distance.

Changing techniques in turning before throwing led to improved distances. In the late 1940s and early 1950s, a small tungsten-head hammer was marketed, and the record was advanced even further. Then the Soviet school of throwers emerged and with the benefit of weight training improved the record year by year. Other contributing factors were the concrete circle, which re-

placed cinder in 1955, providing athletes with a smoother and "quicker" surface from which to throw, and the likelihood of throwers taking steroids after 1965. Since the stricter clamp-down on drugs, the standard has dropped a few meters. Women's hammer throwing stems from 1988 with the countries of the old Soviet Union to the fore.

Homer described javelin throwing for distance, and the Mycenaeans practiced it around 1200 B.C.E. The javelins thrown by the Greeks of 500 B.C.E. were thin and made of wood, with a string wound around the center of gravity. When thrown, the thrower would hold onto the end of the string. This pulling caused rotation of the javelin, giving greater stability and hence further distance. The Celts in Ireland, about the time of Jesus Christ, describe a distance-throwing javelin as having a flaxen string. Javelin throwing in warfare was comparatively common in many parts of the world through into modern times, and competitive throwing is known in Africa and South America within living memory with distances of 120 and 130 meters (394 and 427 feet) respectively having been claimed.

Both the Swedes and the Finns were holding competitions from 1883. The javelin first became an international event at the unofficial 1906 Olympic Games held at Athens.

Until 1953, top-class javelins were made in Scandinavia of selected and cured wood. Aluminum and Swedish steel javelins had appeared in the late 1940s, but the revolution in aerodynamic design was pioneered by Dick Held in the United States. His new javelin was of greater circumference and gave a 27 percent increase in surface area; he got away with it because there was no rule against it at the time (one was introduced in 1957 after his experiment).

The big strong men, of whom some probably took steroids, steadily improved the record until Uwe Hohn of East Germany threw the amazing distance of 104.80 meters (343.83 feet) in 1984, which exceeded the safe throwing area within a stadium. The IAAF took swift action in 1985 and decreed the center of gravity of the javelin be moved forward 4 centimeters (1.6 inches). This had the effect of making the javelin nose-dive earlier in its flight, thus shortening the distance thrown. Women have a record of javelin throwing from 1912 through 1921 with the 800-gram (28.5-ounce) men's model and the regulation 600-gram (21.4-ounce) one from 1922. The Americans and Germans produced the best throwers in the 1920s and 1930s, the Soviet Union in the 1950s and 1960s and in the 1970s.

—David Terry

Bibliography: Matthews, P. (1996) *Athletics 1995: The International Track and Field Annual.* Surbiton, UK. Quercetani, R. L. (1990) *Athletics: A History of Modern Track and Field Athletics 1860–1900 Men and Women.* Milan: Vallardi & Associati. Zur Megede, E., and R. Hymans. (1995) *Progression of World Best Performances and Official I.A.A.F World Records.* Monaco: IAAF.

Track and Field, Running and Hurdling

Track races tend to take center stage in the repertoire of events making up track and field competitions. In outdoor competitions these events generally range from 100 meters to 10,000 meters. Flat races (i.e., without hurdles), which lie between these extremes, are the 200 meter, 400 meter, 800 meter, 1,500 meter, and 5,000 meter. Indoors, the shortest distance is usually 60 meters and the longest 3,000 meters. Track running is usually categorized on the basis of the distance run; hence, sprints are up to 400 meters, middle distances from 800 meters to 3,000 meters, and long distances from 5,000 meters up.

The number of events the International Amateur Athletics Federation (IAAF, the international governing body) recognizes for world record purposes has diminished considerably over the last half century. With a growing societal emphasis on *speed,* there has been a decline in running for distance—the furthest distance that can be run in a given time. Events such as the one-hour run are rarely run today. Apart from the 1 mile, events measured in imperial units are no longer widely practiced.

History

The Greeks and Romans engaged in track racing, using the *stade,* a distance of about 190 meters (210 yards)—the length of the straight sprint track. Other races were multiples of this distance, ranging from about 7 to 24 *stades.* In practice, however, the standard of measurement differed from place to place and courses, therefore, differed considerably in distance.

Other premodern track racing is associated with certain Native American nations. The Jicarilla, for example, had modest "running tracks" that were subject to modest amounts of preparation. In the Osage nation a 4-kilometer (2.5-mile) running track was constructed to keep warriors fit. A Crow running track is recorded as being 5 kilometers (3.1 miles) long and horseshoe-shaped.

The first running track in England was built at Lord's Cricket Ground in London in 1837—a narrow path for two-man races, but faced with gravel and measured by surveyors. More typical, however, were races held on manicured grass surfaces. In mainland Europe and North America, most running tracks were made of various combinations of cinders, clay, or shale. Certain tracks developed the reputation of being faster than others.

The first synthetic running track was built in the United States in 1950. Today, in the wealthier countries of the world, it is estimated that over 90 percent of all official track meets take place on such surfaces, which have improved performance in all track events.

Before the invention of starting blocks, sprinters used to dig small holes in the track in order to assist them in getting a good start. The crouch start had existed in the late 19th century. Invented in 1927, starting blocks were used in Chicago in 1929 and further improved performance.

Rules and Play

Track racing differs from other forms of racing (for example, cross country) in that it takes place on a specially prepared circuit.

Today's championship races must take place on a track of a particular synthetic composition that must be 400 meters in circumference. To equalize the distances athletes run, races up to 400 meters are run in lanes, and races 200 meters and 400 meters have staggered starts. In 800-meter races, the athletes usually run the first turn in lanes to avoid the congestion that might occur. Tracks for major competitions usually have eight lanes marked out.

Despite these technological innovations, track athletics has not been able to fully neutralize the natural environment. Hence, 100-meter and 200-meter races accompanied by a following wind of more than 2.00 meters per second are regarded as invalid for record purposes.

Other innovations in track racing have been the refinement in timekeeping and the use of drugs. Stopwatches have given way to electronic timing, events being timed to hundredths of a second. Photo-finish electrical timekeeping has become the norm and today often determines the result and the timing of track races.

Legends and Landmarks

Track running has tended to be the most glamorous group of events in the overall track-and-field menu. At different periods of time, particular events and individuals have dominated the world running stage. In the 1920s and 1930s, long-distance runners from Finland, notably Paavo Nurmi, dominated the running scene. He increased the amount of training beyond the conven-

3 Minutes 59.4 Seconds— The 4-Minute Mile.

I barely noticed the half mile, passed in 1 min. 58 sec., nor when round the next bend, Chataway went into the lead. At three-quarters of a mile the effort was still barely perceptible; the time was 3 min. 0.7 secs., and by now the crowd were roaring. Somehow I had to run that last lap in 59 seconds. Chataway led round the next bend and then I pounced past him at the beginning of the back straight, three hundred yards from the finish.

I had a moment of mixed joy and anguish, when my mind took over. It raced well ahead of my body and drew my body compellingly forward. I felt that the moment of a lifetime had come. There was no pain, only a great utility of movement and aim. The world seemed to stand still or did not exist, the only reality was the next two hundred yards of track under my feet. The tape meant finality—extinction perhaps.

My body had long since exhausted all its energy, but it went on running just the same. The physical overdraft came only from greater will power. This was the crucial moment when my legs were strong enough to carry me over the last few yards as they could never have done in previous years. With five yards to go the tape seemed almost to recede.

My effort was all over and I collapsed almost unconscious.... The stop-watches held the answer, the announcement came—"Result of the one mile ... time, 3 minutes"—the rest was lost in the roar of excitement.

—Roger Bannister, *First Four Minutes*

tional norm and ran with stopwatch in hand so that his pace might be regulated in the most rational way.

During the 1940s the Swedes dominated middle-distance running with the presence of Gunder Hägg and Arne Andersson. Hägg came close to breaking one of the legendary barriers of track athletics, the four-minute mile. However, it was not until 1954 that the Englishman, Roger Bannister, achieved the performance that people had dreamed of with his historic time of 3 minutes 59.4 seconds at the Oxford University running track at Iffley Road. In the 1960s the middle distances were dominated by athletes from Australia and New Zealand.

During the late 1980s and early 1990s, African runners have led in middle- and long-distance running. The Kenyans and Ethiopians have been most prominent, but Morocco and Algeria are also contenders. That Kenya and Ethiopia have been able to produce such a long line of world-class distance runners has shattered the myth that black athletes were "natural sprinters" and could not achieve world-class performances over long distances.

The United States has traditionally dominated the sprint events. Jesse Owens in the 1930s and Carl Lewis in the 1980s caught the imagination of the world's media. Jesse Owens is widely regarded as the world's greatest sprinter ever. Owens is most renowned for winning gold medals for the 100 meters, 200 meters, 4 × 100 meters, and a long jump event at the Olympic Games in Berlin in 1936, all with Olympic records, at a time when Adolf Hitler was preaching Aryan supremacy.

The Europeans have traditionally dominated women's sprint running, although in recent years the balance of power has shifted somewhat to the United States and Caribbean. In the postwar years, the power of the eastern Europeans was displayed in many events; in the early 1990s, the Chinese astounded the world with a number of staggering performances, including the astonishing performance of Wang Junxia, who became the first woman to break the half-hour for 10,000 meters with a time of 29 minutes 31.78 seconds. The first man to break this barrier had been Taisto Mäki of Finland in 1939.

That women might match men's performances was traditionally thought impossible, but the curves showing improved performances of men and women are inexorably converging. However, relatively few women compete in track racing. The more women who compete, the greater the stimulus for better competition—and hence improved performance.

Drug use is felt to be widespread, and the IAAF imposes bans on athletes who have been found to have used certain "banned substances." Among the best known are anabolic steroids. The most famous drug-taker in track annals was probably Ben Johnson from Canada who, having broken the 100-meter world record in winning the Seoul Olympics with a time of 9.79 seconds, was found to have taken a banned drug, stripped of his medal, and temporarily banned from competition. When re-admitted to the sport he was again found guilty of drug abuse.

Athletes are variously motivated to take part in track. Some wish to demonstrate something about themselves or to improve their personal best time. They may run against the clock to break records or significant barriers such as the 4-minute mile or the 10-second 100 meters, to beat a particular rival or win a medal. Finally, and increasingly, athletes may race to make money.

—JOHN BALE

Bibliography: Baker, William J. (1986) *Jesse Owens: An American Life.* New York: Free Press. Bale, John, and Joe

Sang. (1996) *Kenyan Running: Movement Culture, Geography and Global Change.* London: Frank Cass. Nabokov, Paul. (1981) *Indian Running.* Santa Fe, NM: Ancient City Press. Quercetani, Roberto L. (1990) *Athletics: A History of Modern Track and Field Athletics.* Milan: Vallardi and Associates.

Tractor Pulling
See Truck and Tractor Pulling

Traditional Sports, Africa

African names dot the landscape of modern sport. Senegal's Louis Phal, Nigeria's Dick Tiger, and Ghana's David Kotey head a substantial list of African boxers who have won world championships. Without Tunisian Alain Mimoun, Ethiopian Abebe Bikila, Kenyan Kipchoge Keino, and Tanzanian Filbert Bayi, recent Olympic track history would be much poorer. For several years Nigeria's Akeem Abdul Olajuwon and Sudan's Manute Bol have performed successfully (in Olajuwon's case, brilliantly) in a U.S. professional National Basketball Association that is dominated by African American athletes.

This modern prowess is built on a broad foundation of premodern, or "traditional," African experience. In the Nile River valley and on the grassy veldt of South Africa no less than in the tropical rain forests of the Congo River basin and at the edges of the massive Sahara Desert to the north, Africans played, devised local rules for various games, and competed athletically for centuries before Europeans intruded. To be sure, much traditional "sport" in Africa, as elsewhere, derived from impulses to win the favor of ancestors and the unseen deities or to promote fertility. Competitive, highly ritualized games supposedly ensured productive crops and hunts as well as a fruitful marriage bed.

Sticks and Stones

Little first-hand evidence survives of traditional sub-Saharan activities. We learn most about traditional patterns of African play behavior from the diaries, letters, and treatises of explorers and missionaries, many of whom were unsympathetic, and from early-20th-century anthropologists.

In Africa, Egypt is unique in its documentation of ancient sport. Miniature sculptures, papyrus fragments, and inscriptions and paintings on the walls of temples and tombs depict a lively sporting culture in ancient Egypt. Even pieces of equipment have survived, ranging from chariots and fish hooks to balls and board games. All bear witness to pharaohs and aristocrats eager to prove their superiority as huntsmen, chariot drivers, archers, and runners. As elsewhere, these activities originated in the requirements for hunting and war.

For most of traditional Africa, no clear line separated hunters and warriors from the sporting impulse. Africans hunted and fought with sticks, if not spears, in hand, and in similar fashion they competed athletically. The Zulu and Mpondo of southern Africa frequently promoted stick fights within tribes and occasionally between neighboring tribes. They carried a stick in one hand (holding it in the middle) for parrying the opponent's blow, and a stick in the other hand for clouting the opponent's head. Egyptian sources suggest that this type of competitive activity was common in the land of the Nile as well as the Congo.

Some Africans threw sticks for distance and accuracy. Akin to the Greek javelin, this form of competition obviously originated with the spear. Among the Baganda of the present state of Uganda, the standard stick measured only about 46 centimeters (18 inches) in length. Sometimes the Baganda threw for distance, other times to hit a foe's stick. Rolling target games provided variations on the accuracy theme. In a way similar to the hoop-and-pole games enjoyed by western Native Americans, Africans everywhere rolled ball-shaped stones or roots down hills, and sometimes along level ground, while tribesmen competed with one another to hit them with spears, arrows, or stones.

Competitive stone-tossing took another form among the Kamba of Kenya and the Zulu of South Africa. They piled stones in front of several competitors and required each one to toss a stone in the air, pick up another with the same hand, and catch the airborne stone before it hit the ground. This simple game rewarded and enhanced agile hands and mental concentration.

Little evidence of competitive ball play can be found in traditional Africa. Among the San people of South Africa, women formed lines and excitedly passed a round object (about the size of an orange, cut from a root) back and forth, more on the order of a cooperative children's exercise than a competitive game. San men devised a competitive game using a ball made from the thickest portion of a hippopotamus's hide, the neck, a chunk of which they hammered into a round, elastic object that would bounce when thrown upon a hard surface. Then they placed a flat stone in the ground, and threw the ball hard onto the stone. When it bounced high in the sky, they pushed and shoved for an advantageous position to catch it before it hit the ground. This game is noteworthy because ball games were so rare.

Some African tribes, like the Boloki of the Upper Congo River and the Bachiga of western Uganda, rowed competitively on nearby waterways; Kenya's Luo people traditionally tested their new boats by means of a race on Lake Victoria. In the mountains of East Africa, where Olympic runners have trained so effectively in recent years, the Maasai of Kenya competed and excelled in the footrace.

Another Olympic event, the high jump, also had antecedents in traditional Africa. In a rite of passage, the tall, aristocratic Tutsi of Rwanda and Burundi catapulted off a hardened anthill and soared at remarkable heights over a stick or rope suspended between two upright poles. Watussi male youths were regarded as men when they could clear their own height.

Wrestling Traditions

Wrestling was the most omnipresent of all sport in traditional Africa. Ancient Egypt again leads the way in preserving visual representations. If one were to judge solely from the famous wall paintings in royal tombs at Beni Hasan dating from 2000 to 1500 B.C.E., one would conclude that wrestling was the national pastime in ancient Egypt. Wrestling prepared soldiers for combat and provided a ceremonial exhibition at festive events. Egyptian wrestlers evidently grappled in a no-holds-barred style, trying to trip or throw each other to the ground.

Several Egyptian etchings and paintings feature Nuba wrestlers from the Sudan (to the south) competing with Egyptians. In the hilly central section of the Sudan, the larger Nuba villages held wrestling matches periodically through the harvest season from November to March. Heralds went out from a host village to its neighbors, announcing by horn and drum the forthcoming event and issuing challenges to would-be competitors. Entire villages, adorned in colorful headdresses and beads, and fortified with beer newly brewed for the occasion, descended on the central marketplace of the sponsoring village. Ceremonial dances and chants preceded the wrestling matches, which began in the early afternoon. The competitors, covered with white ashes (symbolic of sacred power), finally engaged in a catch-as-catch-can tussle, each one attempting to throw the other on his back. Victory brought a rousing cheer from village partisans, and when the matches ended shortly before nightfall, a festive party of dance, food, and strong drink followed.

In Nigeria, too, wrestling was a prominent feature of village life. With colorful rituals strikingly similar to the Nuba, the Igbo of southern Nigeria promoted wrestling contests every eighth day for three months or so during the rainy yam-growing season, then finished with a day of matches in honor of the corn deity. Igbo wrestlers were not allowed to become fatigued or angry with each other, for either condition would displease the gods and cause the crops to go bad.

For young Igbo males, wrestling meant initiation into adulthood. The Bachama of northeast Nigeria not only embraced ceremonial wrestling, but also welcomed neighboring Jen, Bwaza, Mbula, and Bata peoples to send teams to compete with Bachama's best. A Bachama myth explains the origins of wrestling. According to one version, a one-legged man came from the east leading a ram on a tether, bringing the idea of a harvest festival. He wandered from village to village, challenging all comers. He proceeded without defeat until he came to the villagers telling the yarn. One of their forefathers beat him, and from that day forward they held festivals of celebration and wrestling matches. Another version has the one-legged man losing and dying immediately, but that night his spirit appeared to the man who defeated him. The spirit denied being dead. He vowed not only to protect the village but also to return visibly to life at the next wrestling festival. Thus, for the Bachama, wrestling represented resurrection and life.

Wrestling styles varied from place to place. Unlike the intense but controlled Igbo, the Khoikhoi of southwest Africa engaged in bloody, no-holds-barred fights. Bambara wrestlers, in Mali, wore razor-sharp bracelets to intimidate and debilitate their opponents. Competitors in southeast Africa reportedly wrestled with only one arm, and from a kneeling position at that. Boys in the same region grappled from a sitting position.

Although wrestling was customarily reserved for boys and young men, women occasionally wrestled. Nuba and Ibo women did so once a year, soon after the harvest. Wrestling prowess won the females respect and attention from male youths. Anthropologists have also found evidence of young women wrestling in Senegal and Cameroon. In Benin and Gabon, girls sometimes wrestled males to whom they were betrothed. Those contests frequently turned into lightly disguised forms of sexual intimacy. In Gambia, the dominant female wrestler often married the male champion.

Waning and Waxing

Within the past century or so, several factors have coalesced to cause the waning of traditional African sport, especially wrestling. First, a revived, more aggressive Islam swept across northern Africa in the 19th century in opposition to the "pagan" rituals, gambling, and consumption of alcohol that usually accompanied festive sport of old.

British missionary schools, too, had a negative effect on native patterns of play and athletic competition. Anglican schoolmasters taught discipline and teamwork through games like soccer (association football) and cricket.

The emergence of a capitalist mentality also worked to the detriment of native games. Particularly in the cities, new labor demands cut into old concepts of abundant free time. Wed to the seasons and time-consuming rituals, traditional sport could scarcely make the transition to urban settings. Soccer, boxing, and track especially lent themselves to the urban need for orderly recreation and spectatorship.

Traditional sport is not dead, however. Albeit stripped of many of its ritualistic and mythological trappings, wrestling still thrives in Nigeria. School schedules rather than agricultural cycles now determine the time of competitive meets.

Traditional sport appeals to African nationalists. An old Igbo wrestler, Okonkwo, is the central character in Nigerian novelist Chinua Achebe's famous tale, *Things Fall Apart* (1959). Appearing in print just one year before Nigerian independence, *Things Fall Apart* depicts the texture of traditional life and its brutal downfall. Having beaten the previous wrestling champion, Okonkwo proudly lives off his reputation as "the greatest wrestler and warrior alive" until he lashes out at the newly arrived guardians of English law and order. The novel begins with village drums beating and flutes playing in celebration of Okonkwo's athletic prowess; it ends some 30 years later with his body hanging from a tree, a victim of modern, alien ways.

—WILLIAM J. BAKER

Bibliography: *Sport in Africa: Essays in Social History*, edited by William J. Baker and James A. Mangan. (1987) New York: Africana. Decker, Wolfgang. (1992) *Sports and Games of Ancient Egypt*, trans. Allen Guttmann. New Haven, CT: Yale University Press. In *Sport in Asia and Africa: A Comparative Handbook*, edited by Eric C. Wagner. Westport, CT: Greenwood. 1989.

Traditional Sports, Asia

Traditional Asian sports are a diverse group. Some sports are—or were—linked to local royal cults, some are explicitly connected with forms of religious worship, and some seem clearly to be linked to traditional ways of getting food. Some seem less purely competitive than sports tend to be in a contemporary Western sense.

Martial Arts

Every region of Asia has produced some form of martial arts. Even India, not commonly thought to be a center for martial arts, boasts an ancient tradition of wrestling. However, most Asian forms of martial arts are found in China, Central Asia, and Southeast Asia.

Mongol-Buh, for instance, is a Mongolian form of wrestling that attracts up to 30,000 participants at some events, in a country with barely more than two million inhabitants. Mongol-Buh resembles, to some extent, Japanese sumo, but competitors do not wrestle within a bounded ring, and the palms of the hands, unlike in sumo, may touch the ground. Aside from its formal sporting characteristics, the sport appeals to Mongolian patriarchal tradition, being considered one of the three "manly" sports—the other two are archery and horseback riding. In Inner Mongolia, in July and August, the three sports are demonstrated during the course of Nadams: tribal meetings, of ancient origin, that were traditionally designed to promote negotiations over the disposition of pasturelands.

Nu-shooting, a form of archery, is popular in the southwestern provinces of China. Modern competition in the sport is organized by the Chinese authorities at officially sanctioned "minority peoples" events. Both bow and arrow are wooden, and the arrowhead is bamboo: at least as currently practiced, "modernization" would violate the spirit of Nu-shooting.

Krabi-Krabong is a Thai martial art, less well known than Thai boxing, that involves the skillful wielding of swords, spears, and axes. Competitors may use a combination of weapons, and it takes much practice to master the variety of requisite techniques. Here is a "sport" that, as now presented, may more accurately be characterized as a ritual performance: a traditional music (*De-Ligua*) is played at "matches," and the action builds up to a climax according to a prearranged composition.

Silat, an Indonesian activity, is also highly ritualized and often performed at explicitly religious events. Accompanied by gong music, Silat performers, either empty-handed or swinging a long axlike weapon, dance out a choreographed sequence of movements. A related form, Penac Silat, is performed in neighboring Malaya, usually with two swords, not an ax.

Animal Sports

Animal racing—with horse, camel, buffalo, yak, and dog—is well known in Asia, particularly among the formerly nomadic inner-Asian peoples. Polo is often claimed to be Asian in origin, and forms of it are still played in Afghanistan and northeastern Pakistan. Many traditional Central Asian animal races involve either shooting from horseback (with bow or gun) or directly competing for possession of an animal. These obviously derive from formerly subsistence-oriented activities of nomadic, pastoral peoples.

Nonracing animal sports—pitting animals against humans as in bullfighting, or one animal against another as in cockfighting, have been popular in many parts of Asia. Manifestly cruel to animals and usually associated with betting, animal sports receive little support from the sports authorities. Nevertheless, such pastimes continue to thrive throughout Asia.

Thailand, in particular, offers a great variety of animal sports featuring not just cocks or bulls but also crickets, beetles, and fish.

The most famous of the fish-fighting games involves the species *Betta splendens,* which, following the guppy and the goldfish, has become the world's most popular aquarium fish. The luxurious fins of the male betta, which make it attractive to aquarists, also make it provocative to other males, which constitutes the basis for the contest. Two males are placed in the same small bowl, bets are placed, and the fish rush and bite at one another until one is exhausted—or dead. The winner, usually injured during the fight, is carefully nursed back to health to fight another day, and proven champions are sold, for large sums, for breeding.

A less physical form of animal competition is the "dove-cooing contest" in which specially bred doves are judged on the quality, pitch, and duration of their calls. This sport, which has become most popular in Thailand—one fancier is said to have recently paid more than $40,000 for a prize cooer—is also popular in Malaysia, Singapore, Indonesia, India, and elsewhere. Doves were greatly prized by the Indian Mughal kings prior to the 16th century, and it seems that doves have long been admired, for their physical form, their calling, and their flight.

Aerial Activities

Asia is home to several pastimes that might be called "aerial sports." In Korea, during festivities celebrating the arrival of spring, women, in a standing position, compete to see how high they can swing. They manage, in some cases, to fly almost 20 meters (22 yards) off the ground.

However, of all the various Asian "aerial" activities, it is no doubt Thai kite-fighting, forms of which are also seen in Korea and China, that is the best known and most popular. The Thai form involves the use of two types of kite, one a five-pointed star, the male

chula, the other a diamond-shaped female *pakpao.* Male kites can be as long as 2.3 meters ($7^1/_2$ feet) and, when aloft, require the attentions of a team of from 8 to 10 young boys, commanded by a captain, who sits in a sort of "fighting-chair" equipped with a pulley and levers. The male kite, which is fitted with bamboo claws and other weapons, is deliberately flown into a female kite's territory, in an attempt to capture "her." The female kite, on the other hand, is not allowed to cross into "male" territory, but, in true "double-standard" fashion, relies on smaller size and maneuverability to flit and dodge out of range, so that the male kite eventually loses control and falls to the ground.

Though "male" and "female" kites are the most popular, not all Thai kite-flying involves a "courtship" battle. A northern Thai kite, called the *sanu,* is as tall as 1.8 meters (6 feet) and emits a singing vibration when in the air; it is judged according to both the height it attains and the quality of the melody it produces. Other Thai kites are shaped like famous figures in Thai puppetry, and are flown in events that take on the quality of scripted theater.

Water Sports

Throughout China and Southeast Asia, boat races are popular, and have been for hundreds of years. In most cases, the boat is carved to resemble a ceremonial dragon, and the races originally formed essential parts of royal and religious rituals designed to display the naval power of kings. Today, in some regions, such races are still given religious significance, but elsewhere they are purely competitive.

In southern China, boat races are intimately connected to rituals that focus on the importance of the rains, essential to good rice yields. Chinese "dragon-boat" races are thought to be very old, perhaps from the 5th century B.C.E. They are still popular today, primarily in southwestern parts of China.

The Future

Most of these sports are not highly organized, at least beyond the local level, and most are also noncommercial. Some—Nu-shooting, for instance—survive as an approved showcase activity for an ethnic minority, while others, like fish-fighting, hardly seem to be sports in any contemporary sense. Nevertheless, it should be borne in mind that takraw, for instance, while once a simple village pastime played according to many local sets of rules throughout Southeast Asia, has become a professional and internationally followed team sport. That is to say, not only are "traditional" sports interesting in their own right, they also constitute a reservoir of activities out of which the next pan-regional or even "global" pursuit may develop.

—ALAN TREVITHICK

See also Animal Baiting; Buzkashi; Cockfighting; Cudgels; Kite Flying; Martial Arts; Takraw.
Bibliography: Knuttgen, Howard G., Qiwei Ma, and Zhonguan Wu, eds. (1990) Sport in China. Champaign, IL: Human Kinetics. Wagner, Eric A. (1989) Sport in Asia and Africa: A Comparative Handbook. New York: Greenwood Press.

Traditional Sports, Europe

Traditional sports of Europe are those that had their roots in physical activities that existed before the spread of modern, internationally organized sport. A large range of activities, only some of which survive, were widely enjoyed in the towns and villages of Europe in the Middle Ages and the early modern period. Despite much local variation, many of the most popular activities share broad similarities. What we do know of traditional games tends to come from visual material, such as Pieter Brueghel's paintings of children's games of the 1560s, or from literary sources, such as the inventory provided by Rabelais in 1534 in The Life of Gargantua and His Son Pantagruel. Charles Cotton's The Compleat Gamester (1674) offers the first detailed account of the varied activities that were to be found in England after the Restoration of the monarchy in 1660 and the return of the full range of traditional sports, some of which had been banned during Cromwell's Commonwealth (1649–1660). During the later 17th and throughout the 18th centuries some handbooks of play appeared, culminating in detailed descriptions of popular games and pastimes in Diderot's famous Encyclopaedia (1751–1780) and Joseph Strutt's The Sports and Pastimes of the People of England (1801). In addition, there were reformers like Guts Muths, whose Games for the Young (1796) tried to reform existing activities for new educational purposes.

As the forces of modernization broke up old communities and established a new urban industrial way of life in much of Europe, the loss of the old ways of playing was noticed by ethnographers from the later 19th century onward, who began to record the survival of traditional games as part of a vanishing folk culture. The search for "völkisch" cultural roots—a feature of the new racial nationalism of the late 19th and early 20th centuries, as well as of interwar fascism—accentuated the fascination for what was seen as "gesunkenes Kulturgut" (submerged cultural tradition). Children's games survived better than many others; thus, traditional games as a whole ran the risk of seeming puerile and trivial compared to the new sports that were enjoying enormous success throughout Europe after World War I. Interest in traditional games has revived in recent years and has received official encouragement from the Council of Europe.

Ball Games

The rich variety of traditional ball games can either be played by hand or foot or with a batting device. Traditional European team-handball games include parkspel on the Swedish island of Gottland, kaatsen in the Dutch province of Frisia, balle pelote in Belgium and France, pallone elastico in Italy, and pelota in Spanish Valencia or in the Basque country. Most of the ancient and violent football forms have disappeared and have been replaced by modern soccer (association football), except for the traditional calcio fiorentino in Florence (Italy).

Some ball games, such as Gaelic football in Ireland, are played with both hands and feet. Gaelic football and hurling were reintroduced in the 1880s in Ireland, with great success, by cultural nationalists alarmed at the spread of new British sport. All kinds of batting devices are used, from racquets, as in real tennis and in France's longue paume game, to the sticks that are used to play crosse, a variant of golf played in northern France and Belgium, or in the rather rough team games of shinty in Scotland and hurling in Ireland.

Other ball games use a tambourine (France and Italy), a forearm cover or "bracchiale," as in the Italian pallone, or a "chistera," as in the spectacular jai alai of the Basques.

Bowl and Pin Games

Bowl games are played with a solid spherical object that is either rolled or thrown at a target. In pin games, targets are knocked down. Italian bocce and the French jeu de boules are now played far from their original home countries. A special case is the game of closh, which was popular in the 15th and 16th centuries. In this game a shovel-shaped bat is used to roll a heavy round bowl through an iron ring fixed in the ground. Nowadays the game is still frequently played in the Belgian and Dutch Provinces of Limburg, where it is known as beugelen, and in the adjacent region in Germany. The same type of game has a variant in Portugal (jogo do aro) and on the Lipari Islands near Sicily (pallaporta). Apart from the well-known flat green bowls, which spread from England to the former British colonies, a variety of bowling games are found in Britain and in the central and southern European countries.

The modern game of 10-pin bowling as played in the United States has several historical variants, some of which are highly standardized and mechanized, such as *kegeln* in Germany and bordering countries. Other pin games range from Karelian pins, in which a stick is thrown instead of a bowl, to *pendelkegeln* (Germany and Hungary), in which the bowl swung at the pins hangs on a wire.

Throwing Games

Throwing a stick or a stone as far as possible or to hit a target is a basic human movement pattern. In Sweden's traditional *varpa* game the projectiles are heavy discs. Smaller discs or coins, or sometimes stones, are used in both children's and adults' throwing games. *Barrà*, a particular type of javelin throwing, is practiced in northern Spain. This iron bar weighs 3.5 kilograms (7 pounds, 11 ounces) and measures 1.5 meters (1.6 yards); it is launched after several body rotations.

Hammer throwing and tossing the caber are typical events of the well-known Scottish Highland Games. A log-throwing event virtually identical to caber-tossing is found in Portugal, where it is known as *jogo do panco*, and in Sweden, where it goes by the name of *stang-störtning*. The latter game was demonstrated at the 1912 Olympic Games in Stockholm, together with *pärkspel, varpa,* and *glima*. Stone-putting is practiced in the traditional festivals of Swiss farmers in the Alps.

The game known as road bowls in Ireland, *klootch-ieten* in the Netherlands, and *bosseln* or *klootschiessen* in East Frisia (Germany), is an interesting example both of the expression of regional ethnic identity and of the growing international awareness of traditional games. In 1969 these three independent groups of bowling enthusiasts joined together to form the International Bowl Playing Association.

Toad in the hole is the name of an English pub game, which has several continental variants such as *jeu de grenouille* in France, which in turn is called *la rana* in Spain, *jogo do sapo* in Portugal, and *pudebak* in Flanders. The toad is a thick, heavy, brass disc. The hole is enshrined within a specially made wooden box on four legs.

Shooting Games

Shooting games have flourished in all cultures and have evolved into modern high-tech sports. Popinjay shooting, in which the target is a "jay" or set of "jays" attached to a tall mast is still a very popular traditional sport in Flanders (Belgium). It was even featured in the 1900 Paris Olympic Games and the 1920 Antwerp Olympic Games.

The Play Forms of Our Forefathers and the Sport of Our Children

The Olympic Games, which stem from a modern invention, occupy the place of honor in our popular recreations. They are controlled by an official international regulation.

Although we fully approve of this, we want to point at the disdain which is shown—unjustifiedly—towards the games of strength and agility, which have contributed so much to the physical development of our forefathers and which were for them such a pleasant delight.

Here we have to safeguard a respectable tradition, as these games are deeply rooted in the inner life of our peasantry and cannot be extracted from it without grieve.

Our soccer players should not forget the game of handball or the longbow or any other games, too many to enumerate, because they all require the exercise of the eye and the hand and because they all develop dexterity, precision, nervous strengthening and body flexibility.

We call upon all our readers to inform us as completely as possible on the local forms of play and amusements which are still in use in their region, and especially those which are typical for a specific province or which are linked with the natural characteristics of the area.

We will offer a price to the fifty correspondents who will provide the best information by sending in photographic pictures and short descriptions. These results will then be published in "Ons Land" in order to contribute in this way to the revival of traditional folk games (1919, *Ons Land* 1[1]: 11).

This sad call to readers appeared in the very first issue of the first volume of the Flemish weekly *Ons Land* (Our Country) of 1919. This newspaper report illustrates the problematic relationship between traditional games and modern sport at the crucial turning point in the history of physical culture in Europe, namely the end of World War I. These traditional games were described as at risk of being ousted by the introduction of modern sports. The next issues of the magazine included six reader responses describing a number of traditional games, especially local bowl games. There was no trace, however, of the prize that was promised.

—*Roland Renson*

Some present-day crossbow guilds in Flanders originated in the 14th and 15th centuries and can thus be considered as the first sports clubs in Europe. The impressive crossbow-shooting festivals of the Italian *balestrieri* (crossbow), such as are held in the magnificent city of Gubbio in the Umbrian hills and elsewhere, also have a long historical pedigree. Witnessing the pageantry of such competitions of crossbowmen competing to win a *palio* (flag) is like stepping back into the living past.

When firearms were introduced, many archery and crossbow societies replaced their traditional weapons with culverins or carbines. These associations of riflemen, especially in Germany and Austria, but also in Denmark, are highly organized and have preserved to a notable extent their character as patriarchal men's clubs, especially in rural areas.

Fighting Games

Wrestling is probably the oldest and the most universal traditional sport of humankind. So-called Greco-Roman wrestling, which has acquired official Olympic status, has no connection with the wrestling styles of Greek and Roman antiquity, and the type of wrestling practiced during the ancient Olympic Games has much more in common with present-day *pelivan* (Turkish wrestling) or even with modern judo.

In Europe, international competitions have already been staged, in which *glima* (game of gladness) wrestlers from Iceland were matched with adepts of the *lucha canaria* (Canary wrestling) style practiced in the Canary Islands. Moreover, an International Federation of Celtic Wrestling was founded in 1985, bringing together Icelandic *glima,* Scottish *backhold,* and Breton *gouren.*

In *savate,* also called *French boxing,* both fists and feet are employed to hit the opponent; this traditional sport is structurally related to Thai kickboxing. *La canne* (stick fighting) was also once popular in France. *Jogo do pau* is a Portuguese version of stick fighting with some similarities to Japanese kendo.

Tilting, the favorite sport of the knights of medieval Europe, was officially abolished in France in 1559 when King Henry II was mortally wounded in a confrontation with his captain of the guard. However, some of its variants have survived. They include ring tilting and quintain, which can be practiced either on land or water. Ring tilting is still very popular in the Dutch province of Zealand; quintain is practiced at the yearly festival of Foligno in Italy, and similar jousts are held on water, as in the case of the *joutes girondines* (jousts from the Gironde area) in France and the *fischerstechen* (fishermen-tilting) in Germany.

Forms of sword play have been practiced throughout Europe for centuries. Many of these sports have been highly ritualized and stylized to make them less lethal. Special protective gear is worn by practitioners of sports such as fencing, which has had Olympic status since the first modern Olympic Games in 1896. Tug

of war was practiced for the last time as an Olympic event during the Antwerp Games in 1920, but it is still organized in international competition by the Tug of War International Federation (TWIF).

Animal Games

Several animal games have gained a reputation as "blood sports" in the course of history and have been officially banned in many countries. Such cruel sports as bull-baiting and bear-baiting were popular in medieval and 16th- and 17th-century England, but these baitings, in which specially trained bulldogs were used, have not survived the so-called civilizing process. Cockfighting, however, is still very popular in the north of France. In Belgium and other countries where cockfights are illegal, these games still have clandestine but loyal supporters. Animals are also matched in fair competitions, as in pigeon racing and dog racing. In most of these animal competitions, people train and coach the animals. In other cases, people engage in direct and hazardous confrontation with animals, as in bull-running in France and Spain, and bullfighting in France, Portugal, and Spain. Goose-riding and other "games" in which animals such as geese, ducks, or cocks are decapitated, survive in most of the Catholic regions of Europe.

Locomotion Games

Some traditional hill races are part of the Scottish Highland Games and the Grasmere sports festivals in the English Lake District. *Fierljeppen* (jumping for distance—with a fen-pole) has survived in the Dutch province of Frisia as a spectacular form of pole vaulting over smaller rivers. Even more spectacular, however, is the *salto del pastor* (shepherd's jump) practiced on the Canary Islands, in which a leaping pole is used to jump off cliffs and hill slopes. Among the Saami people of Norway, Sweden, and Finland, who depended almost entirely for their subsistence on their reindeer, traditional sports tend to highlight riding skills during reindeer-sledge races. The famous *Palio* of Siena, a traditional annual horse race in the very heart of the old Italian town, attracts so many visitors that it is now an internationally known tourist attraction. Traditional rowing contests (for men and women) are yearly held during the *regata storica* (ancient regatta) of Venice in Italy and during the *regatas de traineras* (whaling boats) in the bay of San Sebastian in the Spanish Basque country. In Cornwall the Falmouth Working Boat Association was formed some years ago to regulate the old-style regattas for the Truro River oyster dredgers.

Acrobatics

In all cultures, people try to keep in good physical shape by performing coded sets of physical exercises. Because of the limitations of the human neuromuscular system, which has hardly changed since the emergence of *Homo sapiens*, acrobatic performances are strikingly similar regardless of historical period or culture. The acrobatics that we see in the modern circus are, for example, very similar to those performed in the arenas of ancient Rome. Nor are the vaults and somersaults of modern gymnastics very different from the tumbling exercises described in 1599 by the Italian professional acrobat Tuccaro (1536–1604).

The *Cong-Fou* gymnastic exercises of the Chinese Taoist monks described by the French Jesuit Amiot (1779) had so much in common with the Swedish gymnastics system of Per Henrik Ling (1776–1839) that the French physician Nicolas Dally (1857) was tempted to believe that Ling had simply copied them.

Turnen, the typical German apparatus gymnastics created by Friedrich Ludwig Jahn (1778–1852), has evolved into the internationally established discipline of Olympic gymnastics. The early Turnen movement nevertheless cherished so-called *volkstumliche Spiele* (ethnic games) as a part of its nationalist philosophy. A striking example of traditional acrobatics are the *castells* or human pyramids formed by amateur gymnasts in Barcelona (Spain) as towering symbols of their Catalan identity.

The extraordinary range of traditional sports shows the great richness of the European games heritage. Modern sport faces the major danger of losing diversity as the global market and mass communications provide an ever narrower range of activities for the young. Similarly, traditional sports may be lost forever or they are preserved here and there merely as examples of quaint old customs. Yet, apart from their intrinsic worth, traditional sports are valuable as a kind of alternative model of sport, showing how earlier generations did things differently and providing the basis for a critique of some of the more absurd competitive excesses of modern sport.

Whereas earlier generations tended to see sport as part of a distinctive folk tradition, the recent tendency is to import sports that have deep roots in the traditions of other cultures, notably Asian. Yet judo, for all that it may be carried out under the same rules in the Netherlands as in Japan, has very different cultural associations in the two countries. Similarly, the sumo contests that from time to time are presented in Europe risk appearing to be freak shows or exotic spectacles. As to the survival of existing traditional games, the enormous increase in traffic in the latter half of the 20th century has had a strikingly destructive effect on the street as a place for play. Children, who until recently have been the most effective agency for the transmission of a living culture, increasingly live indoors, watching television and "playing" computer games, some of which bear marked similarities to older games, rolling balls and throwing objects around a screen. Pouring old wine into new bottles is always happening in cultural history, and it may be that the traditional games will live on in new forms.

—ROLAND RENSON

See also Animal Baiting; Archery; Bowls and Bowling; Cudgels; Highland Games; Pelota; Trapball.

Bibliography: Endrei, W., and L. Zolnay. (1986) *Fun and Games in Old Europe,* Budapest: Corvina. Taylor, A. R. (1992) *The Guinness Book of Traditional Pub Games.* Enfield, UK: Guinness. Webster, D. (1973) *Scottish Highland Games.* Edinburgh: Reprographia Edinburgh.

Traditional Sports, North and South America

The sport of the Americas is as varied and complex as its kaleidoscope of cultures and histories. Nonetheless, common threads run through traditional sport in the native Western Hemisphere. These commonalities include the ball game as one major unifying theme in Native American history and prehistory and the nature of sport in Native America as part of a playful worldview that gives a particular flavor to Native American life and culture.

In the late 1400s, in North and South America, 13 distinct language families existed, with hundreds of languages and distinct cultural groups. Each group had its own recreational activities, which included physical skill games or sports. The themes that run through all of these activities can be subdivided into sports of physical skill, sports of mechanical skills, sports involving animals, and ball games.

Sports of Physical Skills

These activities involve competition that stretches the limits of physical strength, endurance, and speed. Generally individual sports, they do in some cases pit teams against each other. These sports include racing, swimming, wrestling, boxing, pulling, and shoving.

Foot racing is probably universal among the peoples of North and South America. The most noteworthy of these racing events are the distance events that feature endurance more than speed. Among the New

World's best-known racers are the Tamahumara Indians of northern Mexico. These people have been known to run over 240 kilometers (150 miles) at a stretch and play games that involve kicking a ball or carrying a log over a course of more than 120 kilometers (75 miles). The Zuñi and other Pueblo Indians of the southwestern United States engage in marathon running. A form of ball racing is also common among the Pueblo peoples, as well as the Pima, Papago, and certain Indians of the North American Plains (e.g., Mandan). Among the Ge in South America, relay races are run in which contestants carried heavy logs said to be about one meter (three feet) in length and weigh 90 kilograms (200 pounds). Log races are also common among the tribes of eastern Brazil.

Wrestling is equally common to Native America, though reported more frequently among the South American than North American groups. Among the Navajo, two men compete amidst great ceremony, each attempting to seize the other and throw him on his back to the ground. Similar practices are common among South American tribes. Among the Yahgan and several Guiana tribes, group wrestling is common.

Competitive swimming is likewise common among Native Americans, who were noted for their expertise. Although probably not the first to use the "crawl" stroke, American Indian swimmers, in particular among groups like the Mandan, have developed the technique to its full effectiveness.

Other such traditional sport activities include various forms of tug-of-war, a contest in which teams pull on opposite ends of a large rope in an effort to drag the opposition across a line or through a wet, muddy, or otherwise uninviting neutral zone. Among the Ona, teams of men compete against each other in an analogous activity in which they line up in two rows and strain to shove the opposition backward in what might be called a "push-of-war." Boxing, though not widespread, does occur among Native Americans.

Mock fights and battles are also common to Native American traditional sport. Some involve hurling stones, small clubs, or burning sticks. For example, among the Quimbaya of South America, a line of women face a line of men and boys, and both rows assault each other with weapons or projectiles, with several participants usually wounded or even killed. Of the various competitive tests of strength involving lifting or pulling skills, one of the most interesting is a competition among the Cozarini of South America to demonstrate strength by pulling a heavy wooden bar through two perpendicular poles.

Sports of Mechanical Skills

The sports of mechanical skills also involve physical skills and place a premium on hand-eye coordination, but their focus is the mastery of a piece of equipment or technique. These include competitive archery, spear-throwing, snow snake, hoop-and-pole, chunkey, and other sports using a particular device. Though most focus on individual performance, some can be played as team sports.

Archery is of the most common forms of sporting entertainment among the Indian populations of the New World. The bow and arrow was a highly developed and widely used technology across both the North and South American continents long before European intervention. In sport, Indians shot for distance, speed, and at moving targets. The Mandan practice a game of arrows in which the object was for a single archer to keep as many arrows as possible in the air at a time. The Goajiro of South America competed by shooting at pieces of fruit or skin balls tossed into the air.

Snow snake is one of the most popular traditional sports among the Indians of Canada and the northern United States. This sport involves tossing a stick ("the snake") approximately two meters (six feet) in length across the ice. The object is to sling the stick further than the opposition. Though reserved largely for men, the sport is also played by women, but generally with smaller sticks. Variations of snow snake are adapted to certain regions of the southwestern United States, and similar games have been reported among Indian groups in South America.

Hoop-and-pole is also traditional among Native Americans. The game's several variations all involve throwing a pole, a spear, or a dart at a rolling hoop, aiming to have it come to rest close to the inert hoop, ideally underneath it. Although more commonly reported in North America, the game and variations of the game appear in certain areas of the South American continent.

Chunkey, played largely by Indian groups in the southeastern United States, is a variant whose the object is to toss a long stick or spear beside a rolling chunkey stone in such a way that the two come to rest at the identical spot.

Animal Sports

A few of the traditional animal sports may pre-date European influence, but most involve the horse and thus are dated only within the past 500 years. (Hunting and fishing are, for these populations, subsistence skills, not sports.)

Horse racing and other forms of competitive horseback riding are popular; Competitive horse racing is also reported among several South American groups.

Dog-sled racing is a popular event among Alaskans today, and some Eskimos participate, from the many regional races to the major annual event, the Iditarod. Some dog racing is reported in the modern Eskimo community, but early ethnographic literature does not mention it, suggesting that it has developed only since European colonization of Alaska.

Another interesting, perhaps unique, sport involving animals has been called the "turtle game," played by the Cashinawa of South America. This activity involves a group of men immobilizing a land turtle by binding it with cord and then attempting to repel efforts by a team of women to release the turtle.

The Ball Game

The ball game is the cornerstone of traditional sports among Native Americans. All variations involved two competing teams with equal numbers of players, the movement of a ball by a team of players up and down a field, scoring points by striking or penetrating the goal of the opponent, and winning by being first to accumulate an agreed-upon total number of points.

The earliest records of the ball game come from Mesoamerica and suggest this sport may have been played by the Olmecs over 3,000 years ago. In the classic ball games of prehistoric middle America, teams representing whole communities used their hips to drive a large rubber ball up and down a well-defined ball court; thus the frequent use of the term "hip-ball game" to describe the event. The object was to strike the goal of the opponent or knock the ball through small rings that protruded from the walls on the side boundaries of the court. Players were not allowed to touch the ball with their hands in this fast-moving game, and sometimes the ball play resulted in injury, even death.

Later the Mayans would play the game (*pok-ta-pok*); then the Aztecs (*tlachi*). The great ball games of the Aztecs were of economic, social, political, and religious significance. They were the setting for heavy gambling, they drew large crowds of spectators, their outcomes frequently had political consequences, and always there were elaborate ritual trappings.

Archaeological evidence suggests that the Mesoamerican ball game was exported to areas far from the valley of Mexico. Ball courts have been found as far north as the southwestern United States, where it appears that as recently as 1,500 years ago the Hohokam peoples were playing the classic ball game. The game, or some variation, has found its way into many areas of South America as well.

In many ways the various types of ball games that ultimately emerged in both South and North America descend from the Mesoamerican ball game. Equipment varies; the ball is driven by various means of kicks, butts, or sticks; and the rules are different from one setting to another. But underneath its outwardly diverse manifestations, the American ball game is essentially still the American ball game.

Perhaps the most widespread North American ball game was shinny. Similar to modern field hockey, shinny is played with a curved stick that is used to propel the ball. The object of the game is to drive the ball through the opponent's goal. Among many groups, shinny is played largely by women. A similar game is played in South America.

Other ball games include double ball, football, hand-and-ball, tossed ball, and fire ball. The latter is played by members of the Iroquois tribe and involves kicking a burning ball down a field and through an opponent's goal. Among South American tribes, the Chake and several other Andean groups play a type of basketball in which the object is to pitch a small ball or round object into a basket affixed to the end of a pole. The Tucuna and several other Amazonian groups are said to play a type of badminton, standing in a circle, trying to keep a shuttlecock made of maize husk in the air by striking it with the palms of their hands. The Yahagan play a similar game using a ball of "seal gut stuffed with feathers or grass." Among the Ge of South America, a paddle ball game is played in which participants hit a small rubber ball back and forth with paddles attempting to keep it from hitting the ground.

One of the most interesting American ball games is one known as the racket game, battattaway, match game, or stickball. This game, known to the Choctaws as *toli,* is the parent of lacrosse and remains popular today among several tribes in the southeastern United States. The game involves two teams who compete by moving a small ball toward the goal of the opposition by using only rackets. In most cases, the contests are accompanied by extensive ritual and celebratory behavior, surrounded by heavy gambling, and marked by violence and frequently bloodshed.

The racket game was played and is still played by several North American Indian groups, in addition to the Choctaw, Cherokee, Chickasaw, Creek, Catawba, and Seminole, for example. Though largely limited to the Eastern Woodlands of the United States in its distribution, stickball illustrates the major characteristics of traditional sport among the native populations of North and South America. These sports involve entire communities, heavy gambling, represent alternatives to armed conflict, had minimal rules and routine violence, and were infused with ritual (including sorcery).

Also, despite the apparent focus on competition, winning was not the principal goal in the classic stickball match. It was as though there were an unstated assumption that ultimately fate determines the outcome of a ball game. The individual player could only do his or her best, and this became the real purpose of the game. And, absent supernatural foul play, the best team won. So, discipline, quality of performance, seriousness of commitment, and those other elements that make a team the best were the goals of the individual combatants.

Native American Traditional Sport and Worldview

The significance of traditional sport among Native Americans goes beyond the playing fields, the courts, and the tracks. From the Eskimos in the Alaskan north to the Yahgan of Tierra del Fuego, sport has its roots in the very essence of Native American life, what I have referred to in another context as a "playful worldview." That all-encompassing playfulness in Native American life sets it apart from the more serious, less playful style of industrial Europe, a contrast perhaps at the heart of the clash between the native cultures of the New World and the invaders from the Old. Europeans saw it as an indication of indolence and sloth when in fact it was simply another way of dealing with the day-to-day realities of human life. Native American traditional sport and the seeming preoccupation of Native Americans with that sport are simply illustrations of this approach or style. Traditional sport is critical to understanding.

Traditional Sport Today

Currently, traditional sport in the Americas is limited largely to rural and out-of-the-way areas and the back streets of large cities. In many cases, sports that once were an important part of community life have disappeared.

In some cases, there are deliberate efforts to revive these activities in some formal way. Among the Indians of the U.S. Southeast, the racket game has in the past two decades made a significant comeback. But generally, there is no concerted effort to feature and preserve the traditional sports of America.

Traditional sport is woven deeply into the fabric of folk life across the North and South American conti-

nents, both past and present. It is a statement about culture, about meaning, and about life. It assumes a special significance as an element in the intranational relations between ethnic and racial groups in the complex, pluralistic world of today's Americas. Traditional sport in North America and in South America is thus an institution that deserves greater attention than it now commands from scholars, academic organizations, special interest groups, and governments.

—KENDALL BLANCHARD

See also Mesoamerican Ball Game.

Bibliography: Armstrong, John M., and Alfred Metraux. (1963) "The Goajiro." *Bureau of American Ethnology Bulletin* 143, 4: 369–383. Blanchard, Kendall. (1981) *Mississippi Choctaws at Play: The Serious Side of Leisure.* Urbana: University of Illinois Press. Culin, Stewart. (1907) "Games of the North American Indians." *Annual Report of the Bureau of American Ethnology* 24. Washington, DC: Government Printing Office. Oxendine, Joseph B. (1988) *American Indian Sports Heritage.* Champaign, IL: Human Kinetics.

Traditional Sports, Oceania

The term Oceania usually refers to the Pacific Basin, Micronesia, Melanesia, Polynesia, and Australia; here Indonesia is also included. With so a wide expanse of space and so many different cultures, it is not surprising that the traditional sports of the region are quite varied as well.

Australian Aboriginals

Although the indigenous peoples of Australia lived by hunting and gathering, they also engaged in sports, many of which were tied to their subsistence skills. The major ones were:

1. Tree climbing.
2. Spear the Disc.
3. Pit Throwing. A heavy stick or bone attached to a piece of twine was thrown over an emu net into a hole dug specifically for the game.
4. Returning Boomerang throwing.
5. Target and Distance Throwing: Competitions involving the throwing of sticks, boomerangs, spears, or any other object at a specific target.
6. Kangaroo Rat, or Weet Weet: In this group game, the kangaroo "rat," which was made out of a single piece of wood, was thrown so that it slid or bounced along the ground; the aim was to achieve the furthest distance and/or the greatest number of hops.
7. Wrestling.

8. Mungan-Mungan: In the center of the designated playing areas a *wormar* (a white painted stick representing a young girl) was placed, and the object of the game was for the young boys to keep the *wormar* away from the older men. Passing and tackling were essential features of the game, which continued until one team was too exhausted to play.

9. Catchball: Catchball was the favorite and most widespread ball game and was played by both sexes. The game involved players tossing the ball back and forth while other players attempted to intercept it in the air.

10. Football: The most common mode of play was to kick the ball high into the air higher and farther than anyone else.

11. Hockey: A ball-and-stick game, resembling the European game of shinny, was played by both sexes.

Through "play" and "friendly contests," Aboriginal males maintained and improved their fighting prowess. Young boys imitated their elders in sham fights in which they used weapons such as toy spears, woomeras, and boomerangs. Adults participated in intertribal tournaments, called "pruns" by the Mallanpara Aborigines of Central Queensland. Although basically entertainment, such meetings followed the rules of fair play and were used to settle personal scores and tribal disagreements such as territorial disputes or theft of women.

With the exception of intertribal tournaments, the rules were few, easily understood, and often temporary, and officials or referees were almost nonexistent. Victory was generally of minor significance, and winners were rarely honored, for the emphasis was maximum participation and enjoyment. Games and sports in Aboriginal culture served to solidify internal relationships and promote good will and social intercourse.

Effect of European Colonization

Within 50 years of the arrival of the alien culture the Aboriginal population had decreased by over 80 percent. Economic, political, and educational policies were enacted to ensure that the primitive natives were "civilized." Sport was critical to this process and served as a vehicle of acculturation. Games such as cricket were effective agents of "Anglicization" and inculcated European values and norms. As traditional culture was destroyed, so too were the indigenous games and sports.

The assimilation of Aborigines into European games and sports has been relatively effective and complete. In the schools and on the reserves and missions the "normal" games are now cricket, rugby, and netball. Beginning only in the mid-1980s has an appreciation of Aboriginal heritage evolved and some traditional activities revived.

National competitions restricted to Aborigines have been organized, such as the National Aboriginal Australian Rules Carnivals and interstate Aborigine Rugby League Carnivals. Occasionally, at these gatherings or other special Aborigine Sports Days, activities such as boomerang and spear throwing and fire-making contests are held for the men. Inexplicably, females are invited to compete in sack races and races whereby flour drums are balanced on their heads, which was never part of the tradition. In 1969 the Aboriginal Sports Foundation was formed, and it has received financial assistance from the federal government. The foundation is active in fostering sports competition among Aborigines but has never made any serious attempt to promote traditional sports and games.

Melanesia

The geographical area known as Melanesia consists of a group of southeastern Pacific islands located northeast of Australia between the Equator and the Tropic of Capricorn. Twelve traditional sports are known and two other activities based on physical skill were practiced, but not competitively.

1. Canoe Racing.
2. Spear Throwing.
3. Land Diving: A unique sport and a forerunner to the modern bungee jumping, land diving was reported among the natives of Maleka in the New Hebrides. A tower some 80 feet in height was constructed and the base around it cleared of debris and rocks. Vines were attached at various heights on the tower, and young men, after binding the vine around their ankles, dived head first into the prepared pit. The winner was the one diving from the highest point.
4. Racing.
5. Foot Fighting: The game involved ferocious kicking, with the object being to knock down all members of the opposing team.
6. Wrestling.
7. Tug of War.
8. Batting the Ball: The ball, made of the hard fruit of the *kaui kents* tree, was thrown to the opposing team, who attempted to bat the ball

back with a piece of wood. The game was played for hours for enjoyment.

9. Football: Various team games involving kicking the ball were played in Aoba, New Hebrides, Wogeo, New Guinea, Central New Guinea, Manus, and the Admiralty Islands. Balls ranged from native oranges, coconuts, breadfruit, or hard *konts* fruit. Few rules existed; the object was, simply, to kick the ball though a goal that was usually a couple of pieces of sticks.

10. Handball: The most popular type of ball was a pig's bladder, although the fruit from the *kai* tree and balls made from pandanus and coconut palm leaves were also used. One player attempted to punch the ball for at least 10 consecutive hits, while members of the opposing team tried to disrupt his juggling.

11. Shinty: A team game resembling the modern sport of field hockey was played in the Torres Strait Islands, the New Hebrides, and Fly River in New Guinea. The game involved hitting a wooden ball with a stick, often of bamboo, and was played on the beach. Few rules existed and the object appears to have been ball possession rather than scoring goals.

12. Surfboard Riding.

13. Cat's Cradle.

Effect of European Colonization

In certain instances assimilation has not been complete, and the old culture has managed to survive the dominance of the new. The game of cricket on the Trobriand Islands furnishes a fascinating example. Introduced by the British missionaries as a substitute for intertribal combats, cricket has been modified by the Trobrianders from the traditional English game, and aspects of their traditional culture have been incorporated into the game so that the sport as it is now played is distinctly "Trobriand." Full of ritual significance, the restructured game is an essential component of Trobriand culture.

Micronesia

Micronesia consists of a myriad of small coral islets, reefs, and volcanic islands located in the western Pacific, north of the Equator.

Only a few of the various Micronesian societies have games. The Palauans and Truckese played games of physical skill and chance. The Majuro on the Marshall Islands and Makin on the Gilbert Islands played games of physical skill only. The Ifaluk on the Central Caroline Islands engaged in games of physical skill and strategy, but none of chance. Other Micronesian societies, according to anthropologists, did not have competitive sports of any type.

Polynesia

The name Polynesia comes from the Greek, and means "many islands." The sports and games of these societies are more complex, more abundant, and more competitive than in other regions. Some 16 traditional Polynesian sports have been identified:

1. Running Races.
2. Swimming Races.
3. Canoe Races.
4. Cockfighting.
5. Boxing.
6. Wrestling.
7. Fencing: Various forms of fencing, or fighting with wooden sticks, were reported among the Hawaiians, Samoans, and Maoris. Samoans also indulged in club-fights where stalks of coconut leaf were used as a substitute for clubs.
8. Tug of War.
9. Ball Games: A variety of games involving a spherical object were recorded, with balls made from *kapa* being the most prevalent. Tough stalks of plantain leaves twisted closely and firmly together were also used, as were pandanus leaves stuffed with grass. The most common ball game was a kicking form where the ball was struck with the foot in an attempt to kick it beyond the goal line.
10. Bandy: A ball-and-stick game similar to hockey was reported in Tahiti.
11. Bowling Disks (Maika): An extremely popular competitive game in Hawaii to roll spherical disks along the ground in a prescribed area. The game, which involved intense gambling, resembled modern versions of lawn bowling, where often the disks are given a bias by the thrower to round a corner.
12. Pitching Disks.
13. Darts.
14. Spear Throwing.
15. Tree Climbing.
16. Sledding *(holua)*: The Hawaiians raised this unique sport to an elaborate level of organization and status. Sledding head first down steep hillsides on special sleds at breakneck speeds, the holua was one of the most dangerous but

exciting Hawaiian sports. Boards were made from breadfruit wood.

The Makahiki Games (often compared to the ancient Greek Olympics) of the ancient Hawaiians was an annual multisport festival that lasted for four lunar months from mid-October to mid-February. All work ceased, and war was *kapu* (forbidden), while all Hawaiians relaxed and enjoyed sports, dancing, and feasting. Top athletes came together to compete in sports such as surfing, the *holua*, spear-throwing, wrestling, and bowling disks.

The Hawaiians and the New Zealand Maori have made the most dedicated and comprehensive attempts to preserve and maintain their traditional games and sports.

The Americanization of the Sandwich or Hawaiian Islands has been complete, and it is nowhere more obvious than in Waikiki. By 1830 most of the traditional culture had disappeared, and the new American-European culture emerged. The over 100 ancient Hawaiian games and sports disappeared with the enthusiastic reception of European culture. In 1934 President Franklin D. Roosevelt became one of the first Americans to call for a revival of the traditional sports, and a once-only *Makahiki Festival* was reenacted in 1935. A more successful venture was Aloha Week. It continues today, and its most popular event is the Moloka'i-to-O'ahu canoe race. In 1977, at Waimea Falls Park, the first permanent Hawaiian games site was constructed, and the *Makahiki Festival* is now organized annually in October.

Indonesia

Indonesia, the largest archipelago in the world, lies at the crossroads of the continents of Asia and Australia. There are 13,700 scattered islands, of which the largest are Sumatra, Java, Kalimantan, Borneo, and Sulawesi. Irian Jaya, which is part of the island of New Guinea, is also part of Indonesia.

The thousands of islands and disparate cultural groupings contained a rich diversity of traditional sports, although only a few have been identified.

1. Boat racing.
2. Bull races.
3. Sepak Takraw: This is an aggressive, competitive team game that appears to be a cross between volleyball and football.
4. Cockfighting.

The term "sport" has really quite limited application to these preindustrialized societies of Oceania. Only the Polynesians, particularly the Hawaiians, displayed complex social organizations and technologies that enabled highly organized, institutionalized competitive sports to emerge.

Competition, and the determining of winners and losers, was generally accepted in the various societies as being the essential characteristic of a sport. However, the simpler the society, the less concern with the outcome, and the more emphasis on collaborative play, turn taking, and participation.

—REET HOWELL

See also Bandy; Boomerang Throwing; Boxing; Cockfighting; Darts; Hockey, Field; Shinty; Surfing; Takraw; Tug of War.

Bibliography: Armstrong, Alan. (1964) *Maori Games and Haka.* Wellington, NZ: A. H. and A. W. Reid. Blanchard, Kendall, and Alyce Cheska. (1985) *The Anthropology of Sport: An Introduction.* South Hadley, MA: Bergin and Garvey. "Notes on the Ethnology of the Wheelman Tribe of South-Western Australia." *Anthropos* 31: 679–711. Holmes, J. H. (1908) "Introductory Notes on the Toys and Games of Elema, Papuan Gulf." *Journal of Royal Anthropological Institute* 37: 280–288. Howell, Reet A., and Maxwell L. Howell. (1987) *A History of Australian Sport.* Sydney: Shakespeare Head Press. Huizinga, Johan. (1950) *Homo Ludens: A Study of the Play Element in Culture.* Boston: Beacon Press. Mitchell, D. (1967) *Ancient Sports of Hawaii.* Honolulu, HI: Bishop Museum.

Trampolining

Trampolining is a 20th-century manifestation of people's desire to escape gravity. To enthusiasts and serious athletes alike, trampolining offers an exhilarating form of exercise that develops balance, timing, muscular control, and coordination.

History

Circus legend has it that a 19th-century professional tumbler named Du Trampoline came up with the idea of adapting the safety nets used by aerialists for use as part of tumblers' routines. However apocryphal that legend (and since *trampolín* means "springboard" in Spanish, suspicion is in order) professional acrobats and tumblers used something like a trampoline for many years before the modern apparatus was invented. In 1936, an American diving and tumbling champion, George Nissen, built the prototype of the modern apparatus and the sport of trampolining, at first called "rebound tumbling," was born.

With the outbreak of World War II, the sport attracted

the interest of the U.S. military, who incorporated it into the exercise program for airmen. The sport was viewed as an ideal exercise for promoting physical conditioning and mental confidence while simultaneously releasing the tensions produced by an intensive training schedule. After the war, enthusiasm for the sport spread rapidly among physical educators and gymnasts. Competitive trampolining was introduced in the United States as a special event at the 1947 Amateur Athletic Union (AAU) meet in Dallas, Texas, and was included in the Pan-American Games in 1954. Interest soon spread to Great Britain, Europe, South Africa, and Japan. The first world championships were held in Great Britain in 1964 and, beginning in 1969, have been held every two years.

Rules and Play

The modern trampoline consists of a resilient "bed," made of canvas, nylon, or woven webbing, attached by springs to a metal frame that suspends the bouncing surface well above the ground.

When the trampolinist lands on the bed after a bounce, the springs and elasticity of the bed absorb the impact of the body, converting the force of the impact into a recoil that propels the gymnast into the air again. Trampolinists learn to use the energy of the recoil to attain optimum heights for the performance of various routines. The heights achievable on a trampoline allow for the execution of some acrobatic maneuvers that could not even be attempted by a floor-bound gymnast. Advanced trampolinists need about 25 feet of headroom to carry out their routines.

With experience, the trampolinist learns to perform backward and forward somersaults and twists, as well as multiples and combinations of these maneuvers. Two, even three, people can perform on a trampoline using either alternating or simultaneous bouncing techniques, but this demands teamwork, close coordination, and precise timing since the athletes must share the rather limited area of the trampoline bed for their takeoffs and landings.

In trampoline competition, competitors are judged on their performance of compulsory and voluntary routines. In each case, a competitor performs a 10-bounce routine in which a different maneuver is completed on each of the consecutive bounces, with no extra bounces in between, and the trampolinist must land on his or her feet after the tenth maneuver of the routine. The elements of the routine are rated by degree of difficulty, and competitors gain or lose points according to their skill at performing them.

—BONNIE DYER-BENNET

See also Gymnastics.
Bibliography: Griswold, Larry. (1966) *Trampoline Tumbling*. New York and South Brunswick, NJ: A. S. Barnes.

Trap and Skeet Shooting
See Shooting, Clay Target

Trapball

Trapball was once played widely in England, Scotland, Wales, Ireland, and France. What distinguished trapball and its variants from other batting games is that the ball was not pitched by a player, but was propelled into the air either by a mechanical device—the "trap"—or by some other special procedure. The ball was then batted into play. Some versions of the game were scored and competitive, with team players taking turns batting and fielding.

Trapball was played in the British Isles during the 14th century. However, since records of it refer to one of the most involved mechanical versions of the game, less sophisticated forms were probably played at an earlier time. Games were often associated with Christian fairs and festivals that were held around Easter, especially Shrove Tuesday, Easter Monday, and Whitsuntide. The specific origins of trapball remain unknown.

Trapball required a "trap," a wooden device, mounted on a stand, shaped somewhat like a shoe with the "heel" portion hollowed out and a lever fixed into it on which the ball rested. One end of the lever extended out of and slightly above the "shoe" itself. When smartly struck by the bat, the level catapulted the ball—usually a hard wooden knot an inch or two in diameter—out of the trap where it could then be batted out into the field by the same player. The bat itself was often a broad and flat, almost like a racket, but it was sometimes round and only an inch and one-half in diameter.

Trapball's only possible modern equivalents are devices that lob tennis balls or baseballs at players for practice in returning or batting, and these are intended for solo, not team, play. The game has otherwise not survived.

—ALAN TREVITHICK

See also Bandy; Hockey, Field; Hockey, Ice; Hurling; Rounders; Shinty.
Bibliography: Dunning, Eric, and Kenneth Sheard. (1979) *Barbarians, Gentlemen and Players*. Oxford: Martin Robinson.

Triathlon

Triathlon is an endurance race that combines competition in three distinct disciplines. The most typical form of triathlon involves swimming, biking, and running (usually in that order) for specified distances. Participants win by being the fastest over the entire racecourse.

History

The sport of triathlon emerged in California in the early 1970s; precisely how and why remain uncertain. It may be that the sport emerged as an offshoot of a typical beach situation. One boy in the water says to another, "I'll race you to the refreshment stand." Quickly, they're off, first swimming to the shore and then running to the food vendor, perhaps eventually even racing home on their bikes. Slight formalization produced an informal multisport event. In those early days, the sport has been described as much more "happy go lucky." Those participants might be amused at the current high-tech sport that has focused on every aspect of triathlon with a single overarching concern—to increase the speed at which triathletes can complete an event.

Rules and Play

The best-known triathlon is the Hawaii Ironman Triathlon (HIT). It is an ultradistance event that involves a 2.4-mile swim followed by 112 miles of cycling and a 26.2-mile marathon run. As is true in virtually all triathlons, a participant completes the events sequentially with only brief stoppages or slowdowns (known as transitions) to change equipment and clothes. These transitions count against the triathlete's total race time. Because brief seconds or minutes can separate competitors, many triathletes train for the transitions as well as the three sports.

Most competition among triathletes occurs at shorter distances than those in ironman contests (of which the HIT is only one). Still, all triathlons are clearly endurance events taking nearly an hour to complete for the best athletes in even the shortest races. Several "levels" of distance can be specified. Approximately 75 percent of triathlons in recent years have occurred at the popular international distance. These races involve 1.5-kilometer (0.93-mile) swims, 40-kilometer (24.86-mile) bike stages, and 10-kilometer (6.2-mile) run courses. A triathlon at this distance will appear in the Olympic Games scheduled for 2000 in Sydney. Finally, the grossly misnamed *sprint-distance* triathlons range around 0.25 miles (400 meters) for the swim, 10 to 20 miles (15–32 kilometers) on the bike, and a 2–5-mile (3.2-kilometer) run.

The sport's governing body, the International Triathlon Union (ITU) has a membership that includes nearly 120 national governing boards for triathlon, representing two million or more affiliated triathletes worldwide. There is a viable professional tour for both men and women competing in triathlons at various distances throughout the world.

Triathlon Culture

Residual components of the earlier, less formal, sport culture are visible in several aspects. One is resistance by many triathletes to joining national governing boards; instead they pay a one-day licensing fee to participate in events. Another is that triathlon is a somewhat expensive and time-consuming pursuit and thus, it is primarily an activity of the middle class (and probably upper-middle class at that). In addition, triathlon still has a strong commitment to its amateurs, with the national amateur age-group championships televised each year.

There is something primal about triathalon. Fit, healthy, and vigorous individuals striving alone yet as comrades against their personal demons, a grueling course, and even possible (although rare) death. Unsurprisingly, sublime feelings may result from such self-tests. More than just a "runner's high," the rapture that some triathletes report is probably due to both physical and psychological factors.

Despite the relative youth of this sport form, the emergence of mountain bike and ultra-endurance (e.g., double-ironman) triathlons may reflect a nostalgic search for authenticity in the sport. Many triathletes believe strongly that the *raison d'être* of triathlon is the intensely personal struggle to overcome the myriad sources of self-doubt. It involves dedication and fortitude that places the greatest premium on individual effort. The increasing technological orientation, bureaucratization, and commercialization of the sport detract from that focus.

Commercialization also underscores the major current controversy in the sport, drafting. Drafting occurs when one triathlete follows another too closely. The trailing athlete obtains an advantage in that the lead individual bears the brunt of the physical impact of the fluids (air/wind and water/current) around them. In the running and swimming phases, drafting's impact is not an issue. During the bike phase, however, the practice has been highly regulated by the national governing boards. Much of the effort of triathlon officials (triathlon's referees) is devoted to the prevention and elimination of bike drafting.

Currently the ITU is battling to make drafting legal, arguing primarily on the basis of commercial appeal.

For the triathletes who practice the primal struggle, the ITU's victory would be, for them, another loss.

—B. JAMES STARR

Bibliography Cook, Jeff S. (1992) *The Triathletes: A Season in the Life of Four Women in the Toughest Sport of All.* New York: St. Martin's Press. Jonas, Steven. (1986) *Triathloning for Ordinary Mortals.* New York: W. W. Norton. Plant, Mike. (1987) *Iron Will: The Heart and Soul of Triathlon's Ultimate Challenge.* Chicago: Contemporary Books. Tinley, Scott, with Mike Plant. (1986) *Winning Triathlon.* Chicago: Contemporary Books.

Trotting
See Horse Racing, Harness

Truck and Tractor Pulling

The sport of truck and tractor pulling has its roots in the midwestern United States. Over a period of 40 years, it has grown into a popular motor sport as it has branched out to other regions of America. In so doing, it has cultivated a wide appeal among many diverse groups. Still, it has not abandoned its rich rural heritage, which has helped it translate to other regions of the world with common rural cultures. Truck and tractor pulling, but specifically tractor pulling, is rural America's contribution to motor sports.

History

The sport can trace its roots to America's farmland. Farmers had long met to test the pulling prowess of their horse teams, so it was only a matter of time before they met to do the same for their tractors. Those origins explain why its rural image is so persistent and why its core audience has stayed so fiercely loyal. A contest involving vehicles that many spectators grew up with can forge deep bonds and create intense loyalty.

In 1969 representatives from eight Midwest pulling states met in Indianapolis to establish uniform rules and to give the activity structure. Their action turned pulling into a bona fide sport and led to the formation of the National Tractor Pullers Association (NTPA), which has since grown into America's premier sanctioning body for the sport. The organization has approximately 1,500 members and sanctions more than 325 events annually.

Rules and Play

The basic premise of the sport is the classic contest between an irresistible force (the pulling vehicle) and an immovable object (the sled). The goal is for the pulling vehicle to go a specified distance—most commonly 100 yards—while it is the sled's job to stop the vehicle. He who goes the farthest wins the contest.

Early on, sleds were simple, deadweight pulling platforms, loaded with concrete blocks, a tractor, or a truck. Another early type was the step-on sled. These early sleds were replaced by the mechanical weight transfer sled. The credit for this introduction goes to Billy K. Watkins (1929–) of Illinois, who in 1970 was granted a patent for his sled, which has evolved into the sophisticated pulling sleds used today.

The sport has changed considerably, and now has weight classes in which the vehicles compete and new kinds of vehicles, such as pickups and semis. But by far the most significant changes have been in horsepower. In the sport's earliest years, participants competed with the same vehicle they used on the farm. The phrase "pull-on-Sunday, plow-on-Monday" with the same vehicle succinctly describes early practices.

From the mid-1950s to the mid-1970s, pulling vehicles were restricted to a speed of 8 miles per hour. When this rule was abolished in 1974, the nature of the sport, with regard to both vehicle performance and fan appeal, changed dramatically. Speed entered the game and brute pulling force took a back seat.

In the beginning, organized pulling was the province of only two kinds of vehicles. One was the stock tractor, a vehicle just as it came from the factory. But as changes were made to the drive train and the engine, the all-purpose tractor that was used for competition one day, for farm chores the next, slipped into history. What emerged was a vehicle used strictly for pulling competition. Eventually, the stock tractor went through a series of technological changes until it became today's Super Stock tractor.

The other kind of vehicle also started out as a stock tractor, but there the similarity ends. Participants took a stock tractor and replaced its engine. Examples of the engines used in this "modified" tractor came from automobiles, airplanes, even tanks. This type of vehicle is known as Modified. The Modified vehicle took another path change when two Ohio brothers, Carl Bosse (1943–) and Paul Bosse (1945–), adapted some engineering they saw used in other applications to the sport of pulling. What they devised was a way to hook up more than one engine and send that combined power on a single driveshaft. Their "invention" was called the crossbox and it changed the face of pulling forever.

Following the Bosse brothers, Modified competitors took stock tractors and gutted them, leaving only the frame, and then piling on engines. It led eventually to the multi-engined vehicle that is today the sport's most significant pulling vehicle from the standpoint of power.

Yankee Ingenuity and Pulling

If there is any characteristic that is typically American, it is "Yankee ingenuity." No group of individuals is more reflective of this characteristic than American farmers, who are the most avid participants in pulling. Farmers, a self-employed lot, have always had by virtue of necessity to "do it themselves." Why should pulling be any different? The Bosse brothers, who adopted the crossbox to pulling, are only the most well-known examples. They loved to tinker and build things.

Part of this "can-do" spirit may be explained by the "homegrown" nature of the sport. Early participants were forced to do all their own "manufacturing" because what they wanted to do to their vehicles wasn't commercially available. They couldn't buy parts to "soup-up" their tractor because what they were doing to their tractors went beyond its stock nature. As a result, everything had to be home-made. And look at the Modified vehicle. Before participants invented it, that vehicle did not exist. This vehicle had to be "invented" from the ground up.

This need spawned in time a cottage industry, peopled by folks who were mechanical geniuses and had a great reservoir of Yankee ingenuity. Yet as with any skill over time, some folks became better at it than others, specialization set in, and eventually businesses were born and thrived. Some ended up building chassis, some cut tires, and others transmissions and rear ends, while still others became experts at building turbochargers, the devices that make it possible for today's Super Stock tractors to attain 1800 horsepower, compared to today's stock tractor off the assembly line that produces in the range of 125–150 horsepower.

Whereas participants in other motor sports most likely got parts "off-the-shelf," each participant in pulling was forced to be his own factory, using his lathe and other specialized equipment to custom-make parts. The Allison engine offers the best example of this phenomenon.

They stopped factory production of the Allison engine at the end of World War II, yet they play a big role today powering Modified vehicles. Some participants have gone so far as to build specialized tools just to work on these antiquated engines. That is perhaps carrying "can do" to an extreme. Still, this "do-it-yourself" attitude is a source of intense pride as participants almost get more of a thrill out of building the vehicle and the parts than what the vehicle does on the track.

As time goes on, this "do-it-yourself" trend is changing, but it is still the rule rather than the exception.

—*Michael B. Camillo*

Tractor Pulling Today

A majority of the pulling events are held at state and county fairs, and tractors are still the sport's most recognizable vehicles. Pulling has not flourished in other regions of the United States as it has in the Midwest. This may be because of cultural attitudes. The rural South would seem to be ideal tractor pulling territory, but so far it has met with limited success, perhaps because the South already has a strong stock-car racing tradition.

However, the South has a strong following with regard to truck pulling. In fact, trucks as pulling vehicles is the South's contribution to pulling. Although the sport is basically a rural American phenomenon, its adoption outside America has been relatively easy, since all it takes to play is a vehicle. As more and more Europeans became interested in pulling, more vehicles were sold overseas. In 1978, pulling was launched in Europe, where the audience also is largely rural in ten nations. Their sanctioning body is the European Tractor Pulling Committee.

—MICHAEL B. CAMILLO

Bibliography: *Puller*. (1971–) Worthington, OH: National Tractor Pullers Association.

Truck Racing

Trucks have become widely accepted as racing vehicles since 1970. While most truck racing is focused on pickups and other small vehicles, large tractor-trailer cabs are also raced. Both track and off-road races are held.

History

For many years, interest in four-wheel-drive vehicles and pickup trucks was limited to small groups of enthusiasts, and competitions were often very informal. That began to change around 1960, as light pickup trucks and other utility vehicles started to became more popular among general consumers. Manufacturers developed a wide variety of hybrids that combined characteristics of passenger cars with utility vehicles, such as the International Harvester Scout, which resembled a very large station wagon.

In the 1970s and 1980s consumer utility and recreational vehicles became major segments of the automotive market. By 1995, they were outselling conventional sedans in many regions. This prompted a parallel surge of interest in the use of these vehicles in sports. Television also made events like remote off-road races more accessible to general viewers.

Rules and Play

Pickups and other recreational and utility vehicles compete in a variety of off-road sports, from shorter timed races to longer endurance events. Among them are the Baja series of desert races, the Pikes Peak Hillclimb, and the Camel Trophy Mundo Maya '95, a grueling 20-day race through Central America. Certain types of contemporary truck racing are very similar to their automotive counterparts, or are divisions of auto-oriented racetrack sports, such as National Association of Stock Car Auto Racing (NASCAR) Super Truck racing.

Prominent racer and promoter Mickey Thompson (who died in 1988) developed stadium truck racing, a sport that combined off-road with closed-track racing. Dirt tracks were set up in outdoor racetracks and later in indoor stadiums. Other truck sports also take place in these venues, including truck-pulling competitions.

Trucks gained an important foothold in the world of traditional closed-track stock-car racing in 1994, NASCAR established a new Super Truck division. Super Trucks are modified pickups that adhere to rules and guidelines for engines and body construction similar to those for NASCAR stock cars. Super Truck races are much like NASCAR's Winston Cup series and other stock car events. Trucks also became more widely used in drag-racing, and the National Hot Rod Association established a category for modified trucks used as dragsters.

The truck-racing scene went through much flux in the 1980s and early 1990s. New sports were developed, and major racing associations added events or divisions for trucks and sport-utility vehicles. Although not all of the new truck-racing circuits or events succeeded or survived, utility vehicles were well established in competitive motor sports by the mid-1990s. Given the growing interest in stock car racing, the subcategory of truck racing has a promising future.

—JOHN TOWNES

Bibliography: Geist, Bill. (1994) *Monster Trucks & Hair-in-a-Can: Who Says America Doesn't Make Anything Anymore?* New York: Putnam. Excerpted as "Really Big Trucks." *New York Times Sunday Magazine* (23 October 1994).

Tug of War

Tug of war is a contest of strength and skill that pits two teams of grunting, groaning, and grimacing competitors against each other as they pull on opposite ends of a thick rope. To the uninitiated, the spectacle seems to involve only brute strength. In actual fact there are significant elements of skill and technique and, during the event, there is a remarkable level of team cohesion as members pull together and maintain a high degree of tension on the rope.

Tug of war is said to have originated in the harvest-gathering of ancient China; to have been used to train slaves to haul stones up the Sphinx; to have developed from the routines used by sailors in hoisting sails and by soldiers in hauling guns up the mountains of India's northwest frontier.

According to the Rev. Dr. Gregor of Rossshire the tug of war game was orchestrated to the following rhythmic tempo where the emphasis seems more on a romantic pairing off than athletic competition.

Apples and oranges, two for a penny,
Come all ye good scholars, buy ever so many.
Come choose the east, come choose the west,
Come choose the one you like the best.
(Gomme 1898)

As early as the 1840s, tug of war appeared on the programs of various Scottish Highland Games. By 1880, the Amateur Athletic Association recognized tug of war and it became (albeit more as a more sinewy sideshow than as team sport) at track and field meetings. In 1900, the event was first featured at the Olympics and continued to be an event through 1920.

In 1958 a Tug-of-War Association was formed in Great Britain and there have been national outdoor championships since then with European championships inaugurated in 1965.

In the United States, tug of war retains a niche in agricultural and county fairs, circuses, carnivals, celebrations, and picnics. Tug of war also continues to be a popular recreational pastime of fraternities and sororities on U.S. college campuses. It has also found a regular place in what has come to be known as corporate challenge "character building" workshops that strive to develop teamwork. Its simple organization, with group rather than individual focus, convinces many management executives that it may be a key to forging strategies for creating optimum team goals and objectives—a theory remote only in time from using tug of war to train sailors or slaves to pull together.

—SCOTT A. G. M. CRAWFORD

Bibliography: Gomme, G. L., ed. (1898). *A Dictionary of British Folk-Lore. Part 1: Traditional Games.* Vol. II. London: David Nutt. Hoffman, F. W., and W. G. Bailey. (1991) *Sports and Recreations.* New York: Harrington Park Press.

Umpires and Umpiring

What's the difference between a playground basketball game and the NBA finals? A key distinction is the men in striped shirts, running up and down the NBA court, blowing their whistles—the referees. Whatever they are called—referee, official, umpire, linesman—they are a vital element of modern sports. Umpires and the authority vested in them is one critical feature that distinguishes modern sports from traditional and informal sports and games.

History

In the ancient Olympic Games, the event that is closest to the modern notion of sport, the judge was seen as an individual under the gods' direct control. In Imperial Rome, the "arbiter" was unknown in competitions. In sport or, more accurately, in games there was, however, a nonparticipant, a neutral figure who might be called a "master" rather than a referee or umpire. But there were no codified rules for the games to govern his decisions. In Asian societies, the situation was quite similar. In China nearly 4,500 years ago, football was controlled by the emperor, while in Imperial Japan, local contests were judged by the aristocracy, whose decisions were believed to reflect the rules established by the emperor.

The modern concept of umpiring and the modern role of the umpire emerged in Florence in the 14th and 15th centuries when Florence football spread so fast that the Senatus of Pisa issued a statement of rules and, in 1415, the Mondovi Statement was issued by the Piedmontese town of Mondov. These rules mark the start of modern umpiring because they were imposed by a neutral party, were not based on supernatural or royal authority, and required the presence of a neutral person—the umpire—whose word was expected to be accepted by all competitors.

It was not until the 19th century, however, that rules and umpiring became firmly established as an element of organized sport. In the 18th-century British colleges' "dribbling game" we get the first complete set of rules, including penalties for fouls. The first written soccer (association football) rules were codified at Cambridge in 1846. On 26 October 1863, in London's Freemason's Tavern, the Football Association was founded. Football was subsequently spread throughout the British Empire, as were its rules, which were followed everywhere the game was played and enforced on the field by the neutral referee.

Today, it is impossible to think of any sport without at least one on-the-field judge. A few sports, such as Japanese sumo, have only one on-field umpire, while many others require multiple umpires, usually with one in overall command and the others providing specialized functions. Many competitions also have off-field officials who rule on various matters such as drug use, meeting deadlines, using legal equipment, and wearing appropriate attire. Beyond these on- and off-field officials, official bodies may rule after the fact on matters that cannot be decided on the field. In addition, technology now influences umpiring and in some sports is beginning to replace some tasks traditionally performed by humans. Professional American football for a few years experimented with television replays to make decisions about on-field play. Electronic timing devices are used to identify false starts in sports such as track and swimming and to identify the winners in many sports, and the "Cyclops" electronic eye is used to

426

detect serving faults in many major tennis tournaments. Thus, like sport in general, umpiring has become more specialized and scientific.

The Varieties of Umpiring

The following brief survey of umpiring in a few major sports indicates umpiring's various forms.

In American football a game is supervised by seven officials in the National Football League (NFL), four to seven at the college level. All officiating crews have a referee with general oversight and control of the game; the referee is assisted by umpires, linesmen, field judges, back judges, line judges, and side judges. In NFL matches they communicate with radios. The referee is the sole authority for the score, and his decisions on rules and other matters pertaining to the game are final. All officials have a joint responsibility for calling fouls.

In North American baseball umpires control the game. One behind home plate calls balls and strikes on the batter, determines whether a batter has been hit by a pitch or has interfered with the catcher, or vice versa, and calls runners safe or out at home plate. He and the other three umpires, stationed near first, second, and third base, may call hit balls foul or fair; the other three call runners safe or out at the first three bases. An umpire may ask for help from his fellows if he was out of position to see a play. In the playoffs, two extra umpires are added for the left and right field foul lines.

Basketball referees follow detailed rules based on founder James Naismith's five principles. The officials include two or three referees, two timers, and two scorekeepers.

In boxing the referee is stationed inside the ring with the boxers and regulates the bout. In some jurisdictions, the referee scores the contest along with two judges outside the ring. In most jurisdictions, however, the referee does not participate in the judging, and ringside officials score the bout.

All National Hockey League and international games and many collegiate ice hockey games are under the control of one referee, two linesmen, and various off-ice officials. Referees are responsible for calling penalties and are the final arbiters of whether a goal has been scored. Linesmen call offsides and icing infractions; they may also stop play in order to inform a referee that a team has too many players on the ice.

Soccer (association football) is under control of the referee, who is assisted by two linesmen. The sole judge is the referee. He can reverse the linesmen's calls (especially an offside play). In international games (and advanced national leagues as well) there is the so-called fourth man, who sits in the stands to check the referee's actions. In Europe there are plans to link the referee, linesmen, and the fourth man with a microradio system.

Tennis requires the most officials—11 at major events. These are the chair umpire, net-cord judge, center linespersons (2), service-line persons, baseline judges (2), and sidelines persons (4). The chair umpire controls the match, keeps score, and may overrule the other officials. The 10 other officials have highly specialized functions; the net-cord, center line, and service line persons function only until a serve is in play.

Umpiring Issues

Umpiring is a profession, and in all major sports umpires undergo careful training and testing, belong to professional umpiring organizations, and are paid for their services. Very few umpires are former athletes. In some sports, such as American baseball, umpiring is a full-time occupation; in other sports, such as American football, umpiring is a part-time occupation, and most umpires make their living from other occupations. Once an exclusively male occupation, umpiring now includes female umpires, although their work continues to be limited mainly to competitions involving women athletes. There is strong resistance to women officiating at male competitions, although the National Basketball Association hired two female officials for the 1997–1998 season with little fanfare. Being a successful umpire requires a full knowledge of the rules, good eyesight, quick reflexes, the ability to make decisions, physical stamina, a steady disposition, and leadership skills.

From the viewpoint of the athletes whose performance is influenced by the umpiring decisions, it is equally important that the umpire be fair. Fair does not necessarily mean that the umpire adheres rigidly to the rules, but rather that he or she is consistent from event to event and from player to player. For example, in American baseball it is well known that different umpires have different "strike zones." That is, some umpires have a "high" strike zone, others a "low" strike zone, and still others a "wide" strike zone. This means that umpires will vary in the pitches they call a strike or a ball. This variation does not bother players so long as each umpire is consistent from inning to inning and game to game. Similarly, in many major sports, umpires may be consistently inconsistent in applying certain rules from player to player. In American basketball, for example, certain star players are rarely called for certain violations such as traveling, while other players are penalized. Players accept this inconsistency on the grounds that the star players have "paid their dues."

Umpire organizations, which generally represent umpires in particular sports, are involved in recruiting, teaching, and training umpires, negotiating their salary and labor demands, and assisting in the revision of rules of play. They are also becoming involved in a new problem facing umpires in some sports—player abuse in the forms of taunting, physical threats, and physical assault, and the possibility of legal liability if an umpire's decision results in injury. In addition, the willingness of courts to become involved in decisions made by umpires or off-field officials raises questions about the "ultimate" authority of umpires.

—MARCO GALDI

See also Law, Sports.

Bibliography: Brinkman, Joe, and Charlie Euchner. (1987) *The Umpire's Handbook.* New York: S. Greene. Guttmann, Allen. (1978) *From Ritual to Record: The Nature of Modern Sports.* New York: Columbia University Press. Rader, Benjamin G. (1983) *American Sports: From the Age of Folk Games to the Age of Spectators.* Englewood Cliffs, NJ: Prentice-Hall. Thompson, William A. (1985) *Modern Sports Officiating: A Practical Guide.* 3d ed. Dubuque, IA: William C. Brown.

Values

The value of sport and values in sport have been controversial at least since the time of the ancient Greeks. How can it be true that sport is at the same time the developer of moral and immoral character? The French existentialist writer Albert Camus contended that everything he knew about ethics he had learned from sport, while the social historian Wray Vamplew has asserted that the qualities instilled in sport were precisely those thought desirable in Nazi train drivers to Dachau. To unravel this apparent paradox requires the drawing of some distinctions.

Values and Valuing

Sport experts suggest that sports have all or some of the following types of values: contributive, extrinsic, inherent, instrumental, intrinsic, and relational.

It might be said that there are only two sources of value in sport; sports persons (subjects) and sporting practices (objects). The subject poses two types of valuing: the value lies in the activity itself, or is intrinsic. A golfer may value her activity precisely because it represents a particular type of activity in which certain powers of concentration and skills are required. Another person may value the very same game because it is a way of making money, achieving social status, or displaying her prowess. These factors are related to the activity but not part of it; this is extrinsic value.

The nature of motivation and the nature of valuing are also closely associated. Many coaches lament that their athletes are motivated by external factors. What is deeply problematic here is the contingency of the valuing and hence motivation. If what motivates the child to engage in sports is the social status, or the medals, or the glory, or the coach's praise, or simply the winning, what happens when the sport no longer achieves these ends?

At the other end of the continuum, one can consider not the sportsperson's own dispositions, but the nature of sports themselves; whether and in what ways they are valuable. Many claims of the value of sport are "instrumental." Sports are not necessarily valuable in their own right but instrumental in achieving things that are in themselves valuable. Similarly, to say that sports are of contributive value is to say that they may contribute to the achievement of an end external to themselves.

Many different values are cited in the notion of virtue, with sports seen as the means to this end. Politicians talk about the role of sports in group and national identity and the recognition of responsibility; physicians praise sports for their health-related value. Educators praise sports for their ability to achieve group solidarity; physiologists note how sports can elevate basic functions, such as lung power and cardiac output. Psychologists say that sports can be a useful means for people to blow off steam in relatively harmless ways; militarists praise them for their capacity to instill loyalty and obedience to authority. Religious leaders praise sports that metaphorically engender the will to fight the good fight and run the race to the finish; economists note how they can reduce lost work days; marketing moguls praise them for the success in promoting products; and so on. The sheer diversity of ends that sports can achieve is almost bewildering. One could be forgiven for thinking them to be a universal panacea.

Yet at the same time, some of these same types of people argue against sports—physicians because of injuries, educators because they detract from academic pursuits, and so on. Their counterassertions may lead us to believe that the instrumental value of sport is canceled out by the negatives it is instrumental in bringing about.

The Inherent Value of Sports

To look only to these types of values ignores what is valuable in sports in and of themselves. Inherent value is most easily described negatively; it is easier to say what it is not than what it is. In describing the instrumental value of sports, it is the external ends that are really valued. If this is the case, then if another means is more successful, effective, efficient, or simply more economic in achieving those ends, then there is every reason to engage in that activity and not sports. So if sports are found to be poor at developing self-esteem, then the psychologist may deny their value. If militarists find that brave footballers can be craven cowards in war, they cease to value sports. When politicians decide that other curricular subjects are better at developing national identity, they no longer value them.

When people say they value sports for their own sake, or in their own right, they say that the value is part of the practices themselves. These characteristics may vary from sport to sport according to their nature but some common features are qualities such as skillful action, powers of anticipation, tactical imagination, speed, strength, emotional intensity, and competitiveness.

Many academics in sport have tended to move without qualification between the subject and object and therefore ignore the distinction between intrinsic and extrinsic valuing and instrumental and inherent. However, a third, mediating category is conceivable. Many theorists of sport have failed to recognize the sometimes particular relationship between means and ends in sport.

In arguing that sports are often seen as means to external ends they fail to recognize that the relationship is not necessarily neutral. There is a strong tendency to isolate a particular end and to say that sport is merely a means to achieve that end. Yet for complex activities at least, the means-end distinction is too crude. Setting out the value of such activities in terms of means and ends often involves focusing upon certain aspects of an activity while losing the broader picture that gives them sense. Sporting activities are better conceived of as complex wholes of which the components are essentially inseparable. The satisfactions involved in activities like athletics, lacrosse, table tennis, and surfing are commonly spread over a lifetime and often involve dedication, commitment, imagination, tolerance, self-sacrifice, the endurance of hardship, and other factors. They are not merely neutral routes to the securing of pleasure. When you wish to enjoy a game of baseball you do not go to play a game of tennis. This is because, again, of the differing nature of the sports and the particular motivations to play this sport rather than that. The pleasure derived in and through the performance is wedded uniquely to the form of action and the participant. Sports under this description, both inherently and instrumentally, are valuable in that they achieve the aims of the participant who values them relationally. This takes into account the sportsperson's relationship to the activity and, secondly, it takes into account the inherent and instrumental value of the activity that the athlete secures in his or her participation. Viewed in this light, sports become mixed goods; they are valuable in their own right and as particular means to potentially valuable ends.

Values, Sports, and Society

In further examining value in sports, new issues arise: "What is the relationship between values in sport and values in society?" And "which values ought to predominate in sports?" There can be no doubt that sports can be played, taught, coached, refereed, and administered badly or well.

What is clear is that an exclusive concern with sport as an instrumentally valuable means to external ends constitutes a form of abuse. It is not clear how long they would survive, let alone flourish, under such alien forces. It is equally clear that, in elite sports at least, the pressure of one external end, wealth accumulation, is greatly undermining the integrity of sports as mutual quests for excellent performances within the letter and spirit of agreed rules. Capitalist and communist societies, for very similar reasons, have often reduced the values of sport to one: winning. To do so is often to undermine the logic that gives sport both its sense and its magic. Yet in contrast to this win-at-all-costs ethic, is perhaps another less pernicious logic and lobby. The noncompetitive sports movement, if not a contradiction in terms, also seeks to undermine the contesting nature of sports by exalting the process over and above the logical end. If everyone wins, no one wins, it can be said.

Sports, perhaps, are best thought to be valuable as rituals. They derive their meaning from basic actions that were once necessary for survival but are now largely obsolete. We now throw, run, jump, and catch just because we can, and moreover strive to do them as excellently as they can be done. Sports are felt to be obligatory to those who come to love them; they can be played well and badly; they have consequences though they are not to be done merely for them. The value they have is perhaps best thought of as their capacity to give value to the life of people who are committed to them. To paraphrase Chesterton, "if a thing is worth doing at all, it is worth doing badly." The vast majority of sportsmen and women enjoy the value sports have and give despite their won-lost record, not because of it.

—M. J. MCNAMEE

Bibliography: Coakley, J. J. (1994) *Sports in Society.* St. Louis: Mosby. Shields, D., and B. J. Bredemier. (1995) *Character Development and Physical Activity.* Champaign, IL: Human Kinetics. Simon, R. L. (1991) *Fair Play; Sports, Values, and Society.* Boulder, CO: Westview Press.

Vintage Auto Racing

Vintage automobile racing is a sport that combines collecting and competition. Enthusiasts restore and maintain historic old high-performance cars and drive them in organized races. The sport emphasizes the faithful preservation of the cars' original appearance, performance characteristics, and mechanical construction.

History

The history of vintage auto racing extends back to the early 20th century, when new generations of cars began to replace the original pioneer vehicles. People who cherished the older cars started to collect and preserve them and eventually formed clubs to sponsor rallies and other events. After World War II, the interest in collecting and displaying vintage cars gained new momentum, along with an overall growth of automotive racing sports.

Vintage auto racing began to evolve into a distinct sport because a growing number of collectors wanted to run their cars in actual races. Many vintage racing groups and events were subsequently organized beginning in the 1960s, and by the 1990s more than 100 annual vintage automobile racing events took place in North America. The sport is also popular internationally.

Rules and Play

Vintage racing is distinct from hot-rodding and other automotive sports that use modified older cars. Vintage auto racers, in contrast, do not alter their cars' basic design and construction. Instead, they strive to maintain it in peak condition, exactly as it was originally built.

Most vintage auto racing associations are based on either geography or specific types of automobiles. The sport's overall scope is illustrated by the divisions within the Sportscar Vintage Racing Association (SVRA), a large organization in the United States that sponsors events in many categories. In SVRA, Group 1 includes small-bore production-based cars from 1955 through 1967, such as Alfa Romeos, Lotus Elites, and Mini-Coopers. Group 2 is for high-performance professional racing cars, such as the Formula 1 and the F-Libre. Group 3 includes Corvettes, Austin Healeys, Triumphs, and other production-based sports cars built from 1955 through 1962. Group 4 is composed of classic racing cars built through 1959, including Ferraris, Elvas, and Lotuses. Group 5 includes sports racing cars built from 1960 through 1965 and FIA championship coupes built through 1972, including such specialized sports racers as the Elva MK-7, Cooper Monaco, and the Ferrari 512. Group 6 covers production sports cars and high-powered V-8s from 1963 through 1972, such as Jaguars, Cobras, and Sunbeam Tigers. Group 7 is for racing cars from 1966 through 1972, such as the Gulf Mirage and the Lola. Other rare and very old classic cars that are driven at high speeds, but not actually raced, are included in a special category.

Vintage racing events range from local, informal gatherings to large races that attract drivers and spectators from around the world. Major vintage races are held at historic and prominent racetracks like Watkins Glen in New York, Lime Rock in Connecticut, and Sebring in Florida. They also take place at smaller tracks, or as touring races on open roads and other sites.

Some events loosely recapture the general spirit of older racing. Others re-create the actual routes and conditions of particular races as faithfully as possible. For example, the Mille Maglia was a historic 1,609 kilometer (1,000 mile) Italian road race that was discontinued in 1956 and has since been revived in the same location as a prominent event for vintage race cars. A separate re-creation of the Mille Maglia has also been held along similar mountainous roads in California.

Vintage cars are often expensive to buy, restore, and maintain, so owners tend to be affluent or extremely dedicated. Some owners contract with professional teams to maintain the vehicles. In the 1990s a branch of the sport using retired stock cars emerged as a less expensive alternative.

—JOHN TOWNES

Bibliography: Egan, Peter. (1993) "Vintage Racing vs. 'Real' Racing." *Road & Track Magazine* (July). Yates, Brock. (1995) "A Strange Thing Is Happening: Old Stuff Is In." *Car and Driver Magazine* (November).

Violence

All sports are inherently competitive and hence conducive to aggression and violence; however, in some (such as boxing, rugby, soccer [association football], and American football) violence and intimidation in the form of a "play fight" or "mock battle" between two individuals or groups are central ingredients. Such sports involve the socially acceptable, ritualized expression of violence, but just as real battles that take place in war can involve a ritual component, so these mock battles that take place on a sports field can involve elements of, or be transformed into, nonritual violence.

Ideally, modern sport resolves the contradiction between friendship and hostility. When people play too seriously, however, the tension level may rise to a point where the balance between friendly and hostile rivalry is tilted in favor of the latter. In such circumstances, the rules and conventions designed to limit violence and steer it into socially acceptable channels may be suspended, and the people involved may start to fight in earnest. In soccer (association football), rugby, or American football, for example, they may play with the aim of inflicting physical damage and pain. The standards governing the expression and control of violence are not the same in all societies, and in Western societies they differ between groups and sports and have not been the same in all historical periods. In fact, a "civilizing process" regarding the expression and control of violence has been central to the development of modern sports.

Western Europe has experienced a decrease in people's desire and capacity for obtaining pleasure from attacking others. One result of this complex phenomenon is an increase in socially generated competitive pressure, which encourages people to use violence in a calculated manner. This complex process can be illustrated by the development of rugby.

Rugby descended from medieval folk games in which matches were played between unrestricted numbers of people, sometimes in excess of 1,000. The boundaries of the playing area were loosely defined, and games were played over open countryside as well as through the streets of towns. The rules were oral and locally specific rather than written and instituted by a central controlling body. All the folk antecedents of modern rugby shared at least one common feature: they were all play struggles involving toleration of physical violence far more severe than would be permitted or regarded as desirable in today's rugby.

The medieval Welsh folk game of knappan is one of those antecedents that demonstrates the levels of violence that most would find unacceptable in modern sport. With as many as 2,000 participants, perhaps on horseback, knappan was a wild affair, which is what one would expect in a type of game characterized by unrestricted numbers of players; loosely defined oral rules; the use of sticks to hit other players as well as the ball; the players themselves, not a referee, controlling the matches; and the absence of an outside body to establish the rules and act as a court of appeal in cases of dispute.

Such games were closer to "real" fighting than modern sports. Modern sports are more abstract, more removed from serious combat. After all, the people of preindustrial Europe enjoyed all sorts of pastimes—cock fighting, dog fighting, bull and bear baiting, watching public executions—that reflected "the violent tenor of life" in Europe during the "autumn" of the Middle Ages.

By contrast with its folk antecedents, modern rugby exemplifies a game that is more civilized in at least four senses. It involves

1. Written rules that demand strict control over physical force and that prohibit it in certain forms.
2. Penalties that can be brought to bear on offenders.
3. The role of referee, who, standing "outside" and "above," attempts to control the game.
4. Centralized rule-making and rule-enforcing bodies.

Although the game was not entirely nonrational and highly emotional in the past, the balance has shifted to favor rationality. Because of the structure of modern rugby and the relatively civilized personalities of its players, pleasure in playing is now derived more from the expression of skill and muted forms of force than from the overt physical intimidation and infliction of pain that was characteristic of its antecedents.

Nevertheless, rugby remains a very rough game. The limitations of the civilizing process are evident from the aggressive features that still exist in the game, such as the "ruck," which provides the opportunity for kicking and stamping on players who are lying on the ground, and the tactic of "raking" one's boot studs across their faces.

Rugby has probably grown more violent in recent years. It has certainly grown more competitive, as is shown by the introduction at all levels of cups and leagues and by its acquisition of openly professional status in 1995. Growing competitiveness has increased the importance of victory, which, in turn, has increased the tendency of players to play roughly (within the rules) as well as to use illegitimate violence in the pursuit of success. They do not gain pleasurable satisfaction from such violence per se but come under pressure to use it as a means of achieving goals.

The civilizing development of rugby reflects the development of modern sports in general, particularly those that involve more or less explicit forms of combat. However, the growing competitive pressure that leads to more *covert* use of rational violence in sport is simultaneously conducive to *overt* violence, which occurs when competitors momentarily lose their self-control and strike an opponent in retaliation.

Violence and Spectators

Violence at sports events often involves the spectators in some fashion. Players may attack spectators, spectators may commit violent acts against athletes, or spectators may fight amongst themselves. Soccer (association football) has proven to be exceptionally problematic.

One reason that hooliganism occurs more frequently in conjunction with soccer may be soccer's relative lack of overt violence, allowing spectators to release their aggressive feelings vicariously. However, spectator violence is a regular accompaniment of rugby in the south of France and occurs frequently in conjunction with American football in the United States.

The popular conception that soccer hooliganism is more frequent than spectator violence in other sports may be due to the social composition of soccer crowds. Worldwide, most soccer spectators come from those lower-class segments of society in which aggressive behavior is the norm. In most societies, groups lower down the social scale are more likely to form intense "we group" bonds that involve an equally intense hostility toward "outsiders"—the opposing team and its supporters.

The association between hooliganism and soccer is also partly a function of the greater worldwide media exposure that the game receives. The media also tend to generate myth, which contributes to the public perception. For example, in the years up to the mid-1960s, the occurrence of soccer hooliganism in Central and South America, continental Europe, Scotland, Wales, and Ireland was regularly reported in the English press, together with statements to the effect that such behavior "couldn't happen in England." Spectator violence, however, had indeed been rife at English soccer matches before World War I and never died out completely. Similarly, following the 1985 Heysel tragedy, in which 39 fans died at the European Cup Final in Brussels, it came to be believed globally that soccer hooliganism was a uniquely English "disease"; yet, the worst recorded hooligan-related soccer tragedy in modern times occurred at the match between Peru and Argentina in Lima in 1964, when more than 300 people were reported to have died. Although its incidence varies between countries and within countries over time, no soccer-playing country has been spared hooliganism.

Powerful groups with a commercial interest in spectator sports (e.g., sports organizations and breweries) may contribute to masking or distorting what is, in fact, a more serious incidence of sports spectator violence in North America than is generally acknowledged. Comparable interest groups in Europe, however, have not succeeded in similarly masking or distorting the problem of soccer hooliganism.

What is certain is that player and spectator violence in sport constitutes a worldwide problem and that, in its various manifestations, it represents a serious and threatening breach of the ethos of fair play.

—ERIC DUNNING

See also Rugby Union; Soccer; Spectators.
Bibliography: Dunning, Eric, Patrick Murphy, and John Williams. (1988) *The Roots of Football Hooliganism.* London: Routledge. Elias, Norbert, and Eric Dunning. (1986) *Quest for Excitement: Sport and Leisure in the Civilizing Process.* Oxford: Blackwell. Giulianotti, Richard, Norman Bonney, and Mitch Hepworth. (1994) *Football, Violence, and Social Identity.* London: Routledge. Williams, John, Eric Dunning, and Patrick Murphy. (1989) *Hooligans Abroad.* 2d ed. London: Routledge. Yiannakis, Andrew, Thomas McIntyre, Merrill J. Melnick, and Dale P. Hart, eds. (1991) *Sport Sociology: Contemporary Themes.* Dubuque, IA: Kendall Hunt.

Volkssport

Volkssport, popular sport, is neither one single sport nor a well-defined group of sports. It is as distinct in different countries as the words *volk* (Flemish, German), *narod* (Russian), *folk* (Danish), *népi* (Hungarian), and people (English) are in different languages. "Popular sport" can denote traditional, ethnic, or indigenous games as well as new games; regional sports as well as premodern folk sports; spontaneous sports of the lower classes as well as artificial folkloristic display; sport under right-wing ideologies (*völkisch*) as well as under left-wing concepts (*sport popolare*).

History

There was no volkssport before the establishment of modern industrial society. In earlier times, sport denoted pastimes—hunting, falcony, and fishing—of social classes that clearly distinguished themselves from "folk," mainly the nobility and gentry. The aristocratic tournaments and the later noble exercises were exclusive, too. Meanwhile, the common people had a game culture of their own.

In early modern Europe, peasants and city dwellers held their own festivities, which often centered around dances, games, and competitions of strength and agility. These games were connected with ritual festivities—often Christianized forms of pagan celebrations—like *Jul* or Christmas, erecting the May tree, Shrovetide, Midsummer dance of *Valborg* or St. John, harvest festivities, marriage, or *kermis* or wake.

Stand wrestling—like Breton *gouren* and Swiss *Schwingen*—was popular, with many regional variations. Races with grotesque impediments made people stumble (children's sack races are a descendant of this form). Violent ball fights through the open landscape—like Irish hurling and Breton *soule*—pitted village against village and expressed local and social identity. Mock tournaments made fun of aristocratic competitions. Aim-casting games with balls (*boule*) and plates (*palet*), sword dances and round dances, bird shooting, acrobatic shows, and animal fights were put together with theater display, music, masquerade, meals, and intoxication to form a whole festival.

The ruling classes tried persistently to restrict, control, or prohibit folk-game culture. The Protestant Reformation, the Catholic Counter-Reformation, and, especially, Puritanism and Pietism banned folk games because they were pagan.

Modern Rise and Differentiation of Volkssport

With the rise of industrial society during the 19th century, gymnastics and sport were developed and promoted by schools and the military. In the process, elements of the earlier folk culture were transformed and integrated into the new "rational" body culture. This led, however, in different directions.

Certain elements of folk activity—from, for example, soccer, hurling, and wrestling—were transferred to new patterns of producing results and records and were thus sportified. Other elements from acrobatics and "harmless," so-called minor games were integrated into the systems of gymnastics (*volkstümliches Turnen*) and thus institutionalized for health and education. Further elements, especially from folk dance,

---

Swiss Folk Wrestling as Superstition and Disorder.

We have heard that the common people (*das gemeine Volk*), as peasants and farm-servants, here in Schwarzenburg for a long time have been meeting on Christmas night at the place where the religious and secular justice is administered, and hold there a wrestling match (*Schwinget*) until midnight. They challenge and try their strength against each other, and who throws the other on the ground becomes famous hereby. They also believe that who trains that night will be vigorous and healthy the coming year. They do not only put faith into this superstition, but they also, as it has often happened, damage their limbs, shed their blood, and this leads to loud crying, cursing, swearing and other frivolous manners. Some come even from Freiburg to participate. Some have already been punished and this event has been forbidden and condemned by our decree.

—Letter of a Swiss court to the government in 1611. (Schaufelberger 1972, vol. 1, pp. 22–23)

---

but also from such athletic exercises as Bavarian *Fingerhakeln* and Swiss *Schwingen*, were discovered as displays of regionality and nationality or as touristic attractions and thus folklorized. Controversies about the national origin of these games and dances arose, and attempts were made to reconstruct their "authentic" forms and to keep them "pure" in the form of invented traditions. In this context, the modern concept of volkssport took form.

Under the title of volkssport a quite new framework was created for something that was valued as ancient and traditional. Certain games were now removed from their original context and specialized in clubs and associations, where they were subjected to special rules.

The rise of volkssport also marked a new fascination with and significance of "folk" and the "popular" for modern culture, contrasting sharply the former derogatory attitudes toward these activities. Volkssport broke the patterns of distinction between high and low in society.

The reference to "folk" was, however, more than a shift of attitudes about how to approach physical culture. In social reality, volkssport could become subversive, a trend especially evident in regions of ethnic and national minorities. In Ireland in 1884, for example, the Gaelic Athletic Association first promoted hurling as a sport of liberation from the British rule and was closely connected with Republican nationalism. In Brittany a committee for *gouren* wrestling was begun in 1928, regulating classes of weight, record listing, dress, and ceremonies; like the later Federation for Breton Traditional Sport, it reflected aspirations to Breton autonomy and nationalism inside France.

The demarcation of class cultures in industrial society added another dimension to volkssport. In 1938, Danish Social Democratic workers' culture started *Fagenes Fest*, a festival of popular competitions such as witty races and tug-of-war between different professions. In Portugal, meanwhile, a communist-oriented practice of "popular games" still competes with a conservative tendency in the framework of *jogos tradicionais*.

The taming and standardization of folk activities by modern disciplinary sport had, thus, its limits. Volkssport has always had two faces: one disciplined, one subversive. Witness the struggle to include tug-of-war in the early modern Olympic Games; after 1920 it was excluded again because of its persistent image as non-serious folk competition. Meanwhile, however, the modernization of tug-of-war continued with the addition of championships, federations, and standardization.

Decolonization, Festivity, and Identity

Since the 1980s, volkssport has received new attention. In 1985 the first "Eurolympics of the Small Peoples and Minorities" were hosted by Friesland in the Netherlands and included competitions in Celtic wrestling, Frisian *Streifvogelen*, and singing. In 1990 the first *Journée Internationale de Jeux et Sports Traditionnels* took place in Carhaix (Brittany). The festival included Breton folk games, Basque trunk hacking, Gaelic football, Icelandic *glima*, Scottish backhold wrestling, children's games, and tug-of-war. In 1992, even as it welcomed the Olympic Games, the city of Barcelona hosted a "Festival of the Particular Sports of Spain" with competitions of force, regional forms of wrestling, and Catalonian *pelota*.

That the Council of Europe sponsors these types of activities and that organizations of Olympic sport try to occupy this field—as by the festival "Traditional Sports and Games of the World" in Bonn 1992—underscores the new significance of volkssport. In 1995 representatives from 24 countries set up in Copenhagen an "International Sport and Culture Association" with a plan to promote meetings of popular sport (*folkelig idræt*) and cultural festivities as a challenge to the standardization imposed by Olympic sport.

The new attraction of volkssport also illuminates a change in the relation of the Western culture to the rest of the world. During the 19th and 20th centuries, sport

Inuit Festivity—Jump and Shamanism

At the end of December or the beginning of January, the Eskimo of the Chukotsky National District organize the rite known as *sayak*. The inviting family cleans their house, preparing wooden ducks and painted ceremonial paddles, blubber lamps, and a ceremonial pole in the middle of the room. The guests, all women, arrive in the twilight with reindeer meat, sugar, and other food. While the celebrant father beats the drum and sings a ritual song, they dance around the pole with free-flowing gestures and afterwards they exchange food. The next morning, the celebrant goes from house to house striking the drum and invites the women once more. This time, the dance takes on a different character, as the women stamp rhythmically; it lasts a long time and requires great physical strength and endurance. Some dancers collapse in ecstasy while the singer cries "Ogo-go-go-go-go" to "scare away" the evil spirit of death from the fallen person. In the evening there is a joint meal. The last day, young boys do the same type of dance, and in the evening girls and boys join in songs. At night, the family members paint their faces with black lines and join with the guests in meal and rituals, including a ritual healing of every member of the family, dance, and common songs. In competition everybody jumps after small paddles, which are tied high up on a thong, and tries to pull down as large a paddle as possible. Gifts are exchanged, and the evil spirits are "thrown out" with shouts and noise. Finally the shaman depicts in songs the future life of the celebrant.

During the years of Soviet power, the Eskimo economy and way of life changed with the advent of electricity, modern industrial techniques, European clothing, uniform education, and party membership. "Soviet medical institutions have driven out the shaman with his charlatan methods of 'treatment'." The victory of socialism finally brought the "breaking up and liquidation of primitive customs and beliefs" (I. K. Voblov, *Anthropological Papers of the University of Alaska* 7, 1959, pp. 71–90).

—Henning Eichberg

history had consisted of the diffusion of Western sports to Africa, Asia, and Latin America and the disappearance of regional popular games and activities. This long-term colonization process has been recently counteracted by the revival—especially since the 1970s—of volkssport. The martial art *pencak silat* and the ball game sepak takraw, for example, found new support in Indonesia and Malaysia

The break with the long-term colonization in sports assumed dramatic forms in Eastern Europe and Middle Asia around 1989. The Soviet state had established a monopoly in standard sport as a way to achieve internal uniformity and high achievement in international competition. Folk sports among the Soviet nationalities were—with few exceptions—repressed as "nationalist," "separatist," and "religious." The resurgence of folk activities was part of the revolution that made the Soviet empire break down. The Kasakh New Year's festivity *nauryz* reappeared with its dances and games. Mongolians return—in the sign of Jingis Khan—to ancient festivities with nomad equestrianism, belt wrestling, and bow and arrow. Thus have festivity and volkssport long marked identity and revolution.

Volkssport shows premodern, modern, and transmodern traits, while contrasting with the mainstream of sport in the following respects:
The framework of volkssport is not discipline but festival.
Volkssport is connected with cultural activities of different kinds—music, joint song, dance, theater—and therefore never a "pure" discipline.
Volkssport does not aim to produce results but to foster togetherness.
Volkssport resists standardization and, instead, celebrates difference. In contrast to the display of sameness and hierarchy, it makes otherness visible.
Volkssport is linked to regional, ethnic, social, or national identities and opposes tendencies of uniformity. It opposes a "folk" view from below to colonization from above.

—HENNING EICHBERG

Bibliography: Burke, Peter. (1978) *Popular Culture in Early Modern Europe*. London: Temple Smith. Eichberg, Henning, and Jørn Hansen, eds. (1989) *Körperkulturen und Identität*. Münster: Lit. Guttmann, Allen. (1994) *Games and Empires. Modern Sports and Cultural Imperialism*. New York: Columbia University Press. Vroede, Erik de, and Roland Renson, eds. (1991) *Proceedings of the Second European Seminar on Traditional Games. Actes du Deuxième Séminaire Européen sur les Jeux Traditionnels*. Leuven: Vlaamse Volkssport Centrale.

Volleyball

Volleyball, invented at the beginning of the 20th century, is on one level a simple recreational game and on another level an intensely competitive sport.

History

William G. Morgan invented volleyball in 1895 to be a pleasant and diverting indoor winter game that could augment the rather austere regimen of gymnastic exercises of late 19th century physical education in America.

Morgan specifically created volleyball for his clients at the YMCA in Holyoke, Massachusetts, most of whom were businessmen, middle-aged, frankly stout and unathletic, and in general not up to the challenges of basketball. The original volleyball was played by two teams who pushed a slow, oversized ball back and forth over a net that was only a few inches higher than some of the players. Originally calling his game "mintonette" because he used a badminton net, he subsequently changed it to volleyball, as better suited to the game's nature.

Volleyball, like basketball, spread very quickly and for similar reasons. Moreover, both games were enthusiastically promoted by the YMCA and the Young Women's Christian Association (YWCA), both of which had chapters throughout the world. Thus volleyball, like basketball, initially moved across the globe in support of a pragmatic and "muscular" Christianity.

In the United States itself, the first national championship was played in 1922 in New York City. The Pittsburgh team carried away the trophy. In 1928, the United States Volleyball Association (USVBA) was formed.

Volleyball was introduced into Japan in 1913 by F. H. Brown, yet another YMCA organizer. Very quickly thereafter, "bareboru" became a regular feature of the Japanese sports scene. The YMCA was active in other parts of Asia as well, notably China, India, and the Philippines.

During and after World War I, American soldiers played the game in Europe, not least of all because many YMCA instructors had been inducted into the army as physical education instructors. Many YMCA and YWCA organizers stayed on after the war, and the game grew in popularity through the 1920s, particularly in France where many local volleyball clubs were established. The Russians too became interested in the game, and the Soviets and their client states were to become, with Japan, major competitive players of the game.

The first international volleyball tournament in Europe was held in Paris in 1931.

By 1920, volleyball had become popular in Central and South America, particularly in Peru and Brazil. Both countries would eventually become top volleyball competitors.

In 1946, the International Volleyball Federation was formed. The federation's most active original members were France, on the one hand, and the Soviet Union, Poland, Yugoslavia, and Czechoslovakia—all communist nations—on the other. The United States showed no interest at the time in top-level volleyball, and the predominance of communist nations in top-level play ensured that the game would be played in a specific and highly politicized atmosphere for the next two decades.

The only international volleyball played by the United States during this period was a "match" between the U.S. and Soviet embassy staffs in The Hague in 1955. According to the *New York Times,* the Soviets—who had proposed the friendly game—"beat the United States on the volleyball court this afternoon in a setting redolent of the spirit of coexistence, cooperation and goodwill."

In 1961, the Olympic Organizing Committee voted to allow volleyball into the Games. The Soviets and their clients, and the Japanese, were naturally great advocates of the change, and, at the 1964 Games in Tokyo, the Japanese, Soviet, Czech, and Polish teams were the main players. The Japanese women's team was formed in 1953 and sponsored by the Nichibo Spinning Mills near Osaka. Hirofumi, who worked as the company's manager in charge of office supplies procurement, drove his team very hard: practice, after work, was 6 hours a day 7 days a week, all year. Though such methods were criticized by some, it has to be said that Hirofumi's 1964 team performed splendidly. Significantly, the first U.S. national training center for the game, near Houston, Texas, was dedicated to women's volleyball: a rare case of a sport being led, in development and top-level participation, by women. However that may be, the U.S. men's team took the gold medal at the 1984 Olympics, the women took the silver, and the United States has since been a world power in the sport.

Rules and Play

Volleyball was originally played over a net that was just 6 feet, 6 inches, but that height has been raised several times, and is now 7 feet, $11^5/_8$ inches for men and 7 feet, $7^1/_2$ inches for women.

Standard play is between two teams of six players. On each side of the net the teams are arrayed in two rows of three: left, center, and right forwards and left, center, and right backs. The goal of the receiving team is to return the ball to the opposite side. They may handle the ball three times before the ball is returned and, indeed, the strategy of the game depends crucially on just such ball handling. In the basic volleying process there are a number of essential skills to be mastered.

Blocking is handled by the front line. All body contact with the net must also be avoided, which adds another level of challenge to mastering the block.

The "spike," one of the more dramatic offensive maneuvers in volleyball, can be sent into the opposing court at speeds above 60 miles per hour, leaving very little reaction time for opponents.

The serving team wins a point if the other side is unable to return the ball; if it loses, there is a "side-out" and the other team takes the serve. The players on the team that scores a side-out rotate clockwise so that each player begins the new set playing from a new position. Players must be in their appropriate positions at the moment the ball is served. After the serve, however, players may move to any position on the court and it is this feature that introduces the possibility of functional specialization into a game that was designed to be "universal" in terms of the skills required by all of its players. The post-serve movement of players is also, of course, a key matter of overall strategy in the game.

A game is won when a side has taken 15 points, so long as the other team trails by 2 points or more.

Beach volleyball—though played by many purely as a recreation, and by top-level players as a form of training—has developed its own competitive rules, teams, and a professional tour with corporate sponsorship. It became an Olympic sport in 1996 in Atlanta.

—ALAN TREVITHICK

Bibliography: Beal, Doug. (1985) *Spike! The Story of the Victorious U.S. Volleyball Team.* San Diego, CA: Avant Publishers. MacGregor, Barrie. (1977) *Volleyball.* Brighton, Sussex: EP Publishing. United States Volleyball Association. (1992) *The World of Volleyball* (video). North Palm Beach, FL: The Athletic Institute.

War and Sports

At the nadir of Western civilization's history, in a "no man's land" between the trenches that marked the killing fields of World War I, British and German soldiers emerged from their fortifications during a Christmas cease-fire to bury their dead, plant a tree, and play a game of soccer (association football). That match represented something crucial about the nature of sport. Sport and war have been inextricably linked throughout human history.

Early History

In hunting and gathering cultures sports such as foot races and contests of strength represented a form of war game. Others, such as archery, spear and javelin throwing, sling-shot competitions, and other sports using war implements, familiarized people with weapons. Both types were important social institutions and means of transmitting warrior craft from generation to generation.

War games adapted with the development of agricultural civilizations (ca. 15,000–10,000 B.C.E.) to match newer cultural patterns of warfare. Most war games still served to create the physical and psychological stamina necessary for combat and to train people to use the increasingly sophisticated weaponry. The agricultural civilizations also used war games to build the communal solidarity and to create the complex social organizations necessary for ancient warfare. These civilizations created ball games, foot and horse races, and a variety of other sports that celebrated warrior prowess.

While ancient sports certainly had religious, political, and social components not immediately related to combat, most of them *were* related to war either directly or indirectly. In ancient Mesoamerica and in ancient Egypt, elaborate ball games served both as simulations of war situations and as contests to curry favor with the gods. In the Mesoamerican contests the losers, as in actual combat, sometimes faced death. Athletic champions and military conquerors were accorded similar forms of hero-worship. Indeed, the classical Greek term for an athletic contest, *agon,* also described military battles.

The classical Greeks organized a sophisticated system of sports, which had important religious, political, and military significance. Greek athletic festivals featured games with direct military applications—chariot races, foot races, wrestling and boxing matches, duels with spears, javelin throws, and archery contests. These festivals and the Olympic Games they spawned beginning in 776 B.C.E. served as important religious ceremonies as well as celebrations of warrior prowess. The Olympics included military-related events such as foot races featuring armored runners and the violent *pankration*—a brutal fight between athletes in which almost any tactic was permitted and which sometimes led to deaths of not only the vanquished but also the victors. The Olympic Games continued until at least 390 C.E.

Roman sports were more committed to training soldiers than Greek games. They built coliseums throughout the empire in which they staged particularly warlike contests such as chariot races, animal combats, artificial naval battles, and, most popular of all, gladiator contests. Such brutal spectacles lasted for several centuries, although opposed by many Greek critics, some Roman intellectuals, and early Christians who were frequently martyred in the circuses. In the

5th century c.e., after the triumph of Christianity in the Roman Empire, the pagan spectacles were effectively banned. Even the Olympic Games, which the Christians associated with paganism, slowly faded into extinction.

Following the collapse of the Roman Empire, elite warrior classes of the medieval period—the feudal knights—engaged in games that were directly related to the dominant form of warfare—armored troops fighting on horseback. Horse racing, organized hunts, and mock combats at tournaments trained the aristocracy for battle. They marked their social position in the war games organized by feudal rulers. Knights competed in melees—hand-to-hand combats on foot between varying numbers of combatants. They also competed in jousts—competitions in which two mounted horsemen equipped with lances charged one another in an effort to knock their opponent from his steed. The medieval games were organized to reinforce chivalric notions of honor, class, and duty. Knights fought for the honor of ladies or regions. No one below the rank of knight was permitted to compete, and chivalric conceptions of duty obliged knights to participate in these sometimes fatal war games.

Modern Times

In early modern Europe (ca. 1400–1750) the monarchs of emerging nation-states continued to patronize warlike sports, but melees and jousts were replaced with more technologically up-to-date competitions such as fencing and shooting contests. In Great Britain the "manly art" of boxing was revived and organized for the first time since the collapse of the Roman Empire.

As Europeans conquered and colonized the American continents, they encountered with indigenous peoples who also played sports related to their native styles of warfare. Various forms of ball games, wrestling, foot races, and spear-throwing and archery contests trained Native American warriors in combat arts.

Contact with Europeans often transformed or destroyed indigenous cultures and their unique sports. In Japan an elaborate feudal Samurai culture with sports that trained the warrior classes—similar in many respects to medieval European chivalric sports—disappeared in the 19th century as Japan decided to modernize and Westernize. First played by the Japanese in 1873, "modern" baseball quickly replaced "traditional" Samurai games.

The industrial revolutions and rise of nationalism, which transformed world civilizations from the late 18th century through the late 20th century, altered the nature of both war and sport. The new technological

patterns of warfare made combat less of a contest of physical prowess and more of a struggle of psychological stamina, social morale, and efficient machinery. Although modern armies and navies still needed physical vigor and stamina, they also began to rely more on patriotic energy, mental endurance, and teamwork. The new modern sports (which militarists around the world insisted were essential for creating modern armed forces) stressed social and psychological recreations of warfare rather than the practice of the actual physical skills required by modern combat.

The mass gymnastics movement that swept through the early 19th-century German and Scandinavian states characterized one form of modern war games. Instructors led groups through a series of exercises that were designed as athletic versions of military drills; this led to the creation of *Turnen* societies (as the German clubs devoted to gymnastics were called) throughout much of Germany and Scandinavia. The *Turnen* movement was quickly incorporated into military drills for the new conscript armies that sought to repel Napoleon Bonaparte's (1769–1821) French legions.

In Great Britain and its colonies the modernizing versions of traditional folk games were linked to the production of national military might. The English proclaimed that "the battle of Waterloo was won on the playing fields of Eton." The idea that modern Anglo-American sports manufactured military might became a powerful ideology in the industrializing world by the mid-19th century. The colonial powers, including the United States, also used sports in efforts to impose Western styles of civilization on the peoples of Asia, Africa, and the Pacific.

As national militaries adopted sporting war games to prepare troops for the rigors of combat and to teach martial skills through simulated war, debates developed as to which system of athletics produced better warriors. France's defeat in the 1870–1871 Franco-Prussian War convinced many French nationalists and militarists that they would have to adopt Germanic or Anglo-American sporting practices to revive their nation's martial talents and restore French prestige. Although some observers, especially Anglo-American critics, sarcastically claimed the French failed to adopt any athletic style, France adapted Anglo-American games into a uniquely French sporting culture. In the 1890s France's Baron Pierre de Coubertin (1863–1937) revived the Olympic Games. Anglo-American sports provided the foundation for most of the Olympic contests. Paradoxically, Coubertin resurrected the Olympics to lessen the chance of war between nations and to build a strenuous French nationalism in case the Olympics failed to secure international peace. By encouraging nationalism the modern Olympics have always been, at least in part, a form of war game.

During the Meiji Restoration (1868) in the midst of Japan's late-19th-century race to modernize, Japanese elites borrowed Western sports in order to reorganize their educational and military systems. Inspired by American ideas that linked the skills developed by baseball to the execution of tasks required by modern warfare, Japanese leaders thought that baseball would teach the mass public the discipline, talent, and technological knowledge needed to fight modern wars.

In the United States modern American football served as the war game for American martial culture. Promoted by nationalistic militarists such as Theodore Roosevelt (1858–1919), American football's ethos and structure simulated military organization. The annual football match contested between the nation's two oldest military academies, the Army and the Navy, has become an important ritual in American popular culture. In the Commonwealth and in former colonies of Great Britain rugby represents the same military organization and ethos exhibited in American football. In demilitarized modern Japan baseball still serves as a substitute war game.

For much of the world, militaristic ideologies find expression through soccer (association football). African, Asian, European, and Latin American nations consider the World Cup a test of national vigor and an indication of military prowess. In 1936, an Olympic match between Peru and Austria created a firestorm of South American ill will against Germany and Austria. In 1970, El Salvador and Honduras engaged in a military conflict (the "Soccer War") over a disputed World Cup qualifying match.

In 1912 Olympic Games officials created the modern pentathlon, a war game that supposedly mimicked a soldier's duties in combat. It combined equestrian, swimming, and running races; fencing combat; and shooting contests. This contest is still part of today's Olympic Games and continues to be dominated by military competitors. Not until 1952 at the Helsinki Olympics did a nonmilitary competitor, Sweden's Lars Hall (1927–), capture a gold medal.

The biathlon, a combination of cross-country skiing and rifle shooting, originated during the early 20th century in Scandinavia as a military ski patrol contest. International championships began in the 1950s, and, in 1960, the Olympic Games included the event on the winter program.

As the 21st century approaches, modern sports continue to be used throughout the world in military preparedness programs. International sporting events, particularly soccer matches and the Olympic Games, continue to create an intense nationalism that sometimes breaks out into armed conflict. Perhaps international sport will eventually contribute to global harmony. Perhaps the effort to make sports into games for peace fails to recognize the ancient historical links between sport and war. Certainly, as long as sport continues to nurture nationalism, it will have a difficult time lessening the potential for national conflict.

—MARK DYRESON

See also Aggression; Biathlon; Jousting; Olympic Games, Ancient; Olympic Games, Modern; Patriotism; Pentathlon; Politics; Violence.

Bibliography: Baker, William. (1982) *Sports in the Western World.* Totowa, NJ: Rowman and Littlefield. Carter, John Marshall. (1988) *Sports and Pastimes of the Middle Ages.* New York: University Press of America. Guttmann, Allen. (1994) *Games and Empires: Modern Sports and Cultural Imperialism.* New York: Columbia University Press. Hoberman, John. (1984) *Sport and Political Ideology.* Austin: University of Texas Press. Holt, Richard. (1989) *Sport and the British: A Modern History.* Oxford: Clarendon. Keegan, John. (1993) *A History of Warfare.* New York: Alfred A. Knopf.

Weightlifting

Competitive weightlifting goes beyond the general conditioning and development of strength of weight conditioning and requires total body strength, power, speed, flexibility, and balance. The snatch and the clean-and-jerk are the two events in competitive weightlifting.

History

The tomb of Beni Hasan revealed wall paintings showing men and women exercising with stone weights as early as 3500 C.E. Illustrations from the 2040 B.C.E. tomb records of Prince Baghti depicted movements that are strikingly similar to the one-hand snatch or swing. Ancient Greeks and Romans used different shaped and weighted stones called *halteres* for exercising. In China, weighted objects of various kinds were used for heavy exercise to prepare troops for battle.

The Greeks were the first to develop organized approaches to weight training and had weight activities that were practical and usually related to warfare. They used lifting stones, which later were replaced by a bar with a bell on each end for added resistance. (The bell clapper was removed to silence the bell, thus the term "dumbbell.") Legend has it that a Crotonan man called Milo was the first to use progressive-resistance exercise. Milo's progressive resistance exercise consisted of daily lifting and carrying a baby calf throughout its maturation into a full-grown bull. The Romans also shared this appreciation of weight training, but with the decline and fall of the empire, the value and direction of physical exercise diminished.

During the Dark Ages, weight training became the tool of the warrior; shows of strength became popular entertainment. Such competitions have remained relatively unchanged in Switzerland, Spain, and Scotland as well as in the Swedish island of Gotland.

In the 18th century, interest in physical strength and well-being reappeared. Physical education was reintroduced to the university curriculum. Exercise apparatus developed along with programs using free-weights and simple machines. Training emphasized musculature strength and endurance rather than physical development.

Professional strongmen became popular. Bending bars of iron, lifting every object from people to animals, and breaking chains were common. Felice Napoli of Italy, a circus and a fairground performer, is credited with starting the strongman boom. He influenced Professor Louis Attila, who had the foresight and vision to see weightlifting and bodybuilding as an activity in its own right. He trained many of the best-known performers of the time and crowned heads of state. He popularized the use of hollow shot leaded weights and developed the bent press or screw press.

In the mid-1800s, lifting as we know it today developed in parallel in several countries throughout Central Europe and in the United States. Early weightlifting contests had programs consisting of "odd lifts" focusing on repetitive lifting. These included using everything from one or two finger lifts and lifting with the teeth, to the more standard snatch, press, and clean-and-jerk.

From the bar with the "dumbbells" evolved the solid globeweight introduced by Triat of France. Later, Louis Attila developed the hollow globes that could be weighted with everything from sand to quicksilver. The French developed the first disc-loading set, which was produced by M. M. Pelletier Monnier and used ideas of Professor Desbonnet. In the late 1920s Charles Rigoulot (1903–1962) used an 8-foot bar to exceed the world record for executing the clean-and-jerk; thus the advantage of a long springy bar was discovered. In 1905 the Milo Barbell Company produced the first barbell

set with interchangeable plates. Rotating collars were later added.

In 1896 the first modern Olympic Games were held. Weightlifting was included but subsequently excluded in the 1900 games. Weightlifting returned to the Olympic program in St. Louis in 1904. No weightlifting was included in the 1908 (London) or 1913 (Stockholm) Games.

Father Bill Curtis was one of the first to develop and use a system of weight training for overall strength and health rather than striving for higher poundage in a specific lift. W. A. Pullum, known as the "the Wizard of Weight-lifting," was the first man to concentrate on technique rather than strength. He established the first scientific weightlifters' school in 1906, and in 1912 became the first Britain to lift double his body weight. Henry Steinbon (1893–1989), a German strength expert and professional wrestler, became the chief advocate of the "quick lifts," the one-hand snatch and the clean-and-jerk.

The International Weightlifting Federation, formed in 1920, brought official status to the sport. Weightlifting returned to the Olympics with a new set of rules and regulations. From 1920 on, most of the interest would be on international lifts of the one- and two-hand snatch, one- and two-hand clean-and-jerk, and military press. The press, snatch, and jerk would become the standard lifts until the press was removed in 1972.

In 1929 the AAU assumed leadership of weightlifting and began to sanction meets. For the first time, in 1932 an AAU-sanctioned team performed at the Los Angeles Olympics. Initially lackluster, lifting in the United States improved such that Americans began placing at the top of world competition.

Women entered the weightlifting scene in the 1940s, with the first recorded weightlifting meet for women held in the United States in 1947. Women have competed internationally in Olympic-style weightlifting since that time but have not yet been included in the Olympic Games. From the start, Chinese women have consistently dominated weightlifting competition.

In the early 1960s Eastern bloc countries considered Olympic lifting a major sport and began to dominate. In 1972, the press was dropped, leaving only the snatch and jerk.

Olympic lifting standards have risen significantly with increased numbers of competition opportunities, improved scientific training, and use of strength-enhancing drugs. The countries that have taken a moral and ethical stand against drug usage are now at a distinct disadvantage. Other countries prepared medical research to pursue new drug designs and to create methods of successfully avoiding drug detection. During the 1972 Munich Olympics, the first two positive cases of doping in weightlifting were found. In the 1976 Olympics eight disqualifications for anabolic steroid use were made. The controversy over the use of performance-enhancement drugs in lifting continues.

Rules and Play

In a weightlifting competition today, males compete in 10 weight classes from Fly (54 kilograms [119 pounds]) to Superheavyweight (108-plus kilograms [238-plus pounds]). Women compete in 9 weight classes starting at 46 kilograms (101.5 pounds) and going up to 83-plus kilograms (183-plus pounds). Age divisions include: junior (12 through 17 years), junior (18 through 20 years), senior (21-plus), and master (35-plus). The two-hand snatch and two-hand clean-and-jerk are the only lifts included in competitive Olympic lifting.

Each lifter has three opportunities to complete a successful or legal lift for the snatch and then for the clean-and-jerk. The athlete must record one legal lift in both events to be considered in the final placing. The heaviest weight lifted for each event is used for the total of the combined lifts. The grip used for both lifts is very specific to weightlifting and is called the hook technique. The hook grip is established by first wrapping the thumb around the bar and then overlapping the thumb with the first and second finger; thus the thumb becomes a hook on the bar.

The snatch is an explosive movement when the barbell is lifted from the platform to an overhead position in one continuous motion. The intricate snatch technique makes this lift the more difficult of the two weightlifting movements. The lifter must pull the bar from the platform to chest level and then overhead with arms fully extended in one fluid motion. The body must be positioned under the bar in this movement just before the bar is extended overhead evenly. To complete this the athlete uses the squat style.

The clean-and-jerk technique allows for the greatest amount of weight to be lifted. Two distinct movements are involved in this lift: the clean, which is the lifting of the weight from the platform to shoulder height, and the jerk, which is the thrusting of the weight from the chest and shoulders to an overhead position. In the clean, the weight is lifted first to waist level using the legs, hips, and back muscles. The lifter must then pull the body under the bar using a squat or a split technique. From here, the lifter stands, resting the weight on shoulders and chest. An explosive jump is used to propel the weight upward, splitting the legs to help lower the body under the bar. After the weight is overhead, the lift is completed by bringing the legs together using a series of small steps to achieve an erect stance. The lift is complete when the body becomes motionless.

—DARLENE S. YOUNG

See also Bodybuilding; Powerlifting.
Bibliography: Kirkley, G., and J. Goodbody, eds. (1986) *The Manual of Weight-Training*. London: Stanley Paul. Mentzer, M., and A. Friedberg. (1982) *Mike Mentzer's Complete Book of Weight Training*. New York: William Morrow. Todd, T. (1978) *Inside Powerlifting*. Chicago: Contemporary Books. Webster, D. (1976) *The Iron Game*. Irvine, UK: John Geddes Printer.

Women's Sports

This article contains two entries. The first, by Gertrud Pfister, discusses the development of women's sports in Europe; the second, by Joan Hult, concentrates on women's sports in North America. These are the regions of the world in which women's sports developed most quickly and thus influenced women's participation in sports elsewhere in the world. Women's participation in sport is also discussed throughout the encyclopedia in articles on individual sports as well as in general articles.

WOMEN'S SPORTS, EUROPE

Since most societies have been and still are dominated by men, men have tended to take the leading role in body and movement culture. Nonetheless, women have usually been able to develop and practice their own specifically female culture alongside the men's, and some women have always successfully demanded the opportunity to participate in men's sports. Questions remain, however. Have today's women, at least those in the industrialized world, really overcome the obstacles that once kept them from sports participation? Do sports now answer the social and cultural needs of girls' and women's lives?

Pre-Industrial Society

The body and movement cultures of pre-industrial societies were associated with religion and magic, economic processes, and warfare, a paucity of rules, a low level of administrative organization, and an absence of abstract records. Women participated in many if not most pre-industrial physical activities, but their participation varied according to the division of labor be-

Women on Wheels before WWI.

My friend Miss Clara Beyer and I were probably the first ladies to exhibit themselves to a scandalized public on a cycle (a three-wheeler, actually). That was in 1890. At first we had our cycles brought to the outskirts of town and rode on the deserted forest roads, the occasional passer-by hailing us with righteous indignation or with sneers and innuendo. Later we dared to ride through the town itself at dawn. Finally, one splendid afternoon, we set out bravely from the Berlin town square. Hundreds of people gathered on the instant, and a swarm of ragamuffins kept pace with us, chanting remarks of the most charming sort. In short, we ran the gauntlet which caused us to ask ourselves whether the game was worth the candle.

We were fighting a positively fanatical hatred. Pointless to compare ourselves with equestriennes: cycling remained unfeminine, though why remained unanswered. It was enough to bring us to tears. But when, once outside the town, we would speed along under the green canopy of trees, chest expanded and heart racing, we would reaffirm our eternal loyalty to cycling.

The first ladies bicycle race in September 1893 was a breakthrough. For the first time, a numerous and largely sports-minded public saw a phalanx of able female cyclists, tastefully clothed, mastering the machine. How different from seeing a lone woman cycling amidst a hooting mob! Thus the ice was broken, and now only the occasional old fogy dared describe a female bicyclist as an unfeminine creature.

And that is as it should be. Quite apart from the pleasure of the thing the rapid movement, comparable only to flying, in God's fresh air the beneficial influence of bicycling on a woman's body and spirit is utterly unmistakable.

No more missed trains, no more crowded horse-trolley, no more dearth of hackney-carriages! Free to decide to the minute when and where one wants to be! Those are the spiritual pleasures of cycling. Physically, too, we feel its benign influence. Can any migraine withstand a splendid bicycle ride? And how delectable is the modest meal in a humble country inn when we have put a goodly distance behind us!

Now, as to dress: the first thing to consign to the attic is the corset. An experienced female cyclist can only be amused by the question, "skirt or trousers?" A woman has exactly the same number of legs as a man; she uses them, especially in bicycling, in exactly the same way as a man, and should clothe them just as sensibly, giving each leg its own covering rather than placing both into one. (Has it ever occurred to anyone to put both arms into one sleeve?) The most practical garment for bicycle touring is a pair of trousers, only slightly fuller than a modern gentleman's plus-fours. Of course, one does not parade around in these upon arrival, but draws over them the skirt one has prudently brought along on the handlebars.

One piece of advice to new female disciples: in matters of cycling, seek medical advice only from a doctor who is himself a cyclist. It is quite incredible what opinions a noncycling doctor (probably a dying breed, by the way) can voice. Of course, only she whose state of health permits it should bicycle. But that is the only limitation; I admit no other.

For an older lady, the decision to clamber onto a bicycle is more difficult than for a young one. I believe that in the future, old ladies will not need to learn to ride a bicycle; they will grow old as bicycle riders. And the children who are growing up with this machine will consider it an indispensable tool, a part of their very lives.

—Condensed from Amalie Rother, *Women's Bicycling* (Munich, 1897), translated by Rodelinde Albrecht.

---

tween the sexes as well as with norms, values, conceptions, and relations of power.

In ancient Greece, gymnastic exercises and sports contests evolved from the structures, values, and ideals of a bellicose culture of aristocratic men. Women, whose roles were generally restricted to those of wives and mothers, were neither politically nor legally equal to men. They were prevented from exercising in public gymnasia and from witnessing—much less participating in—the Olympic Games that took place quadrennially in honor of Zeus.

At Olympia girls did run races in honor of Hera, the consort of Zeus, but this event, known as the Heraia, was a local fertility rite that lacked the prestige of the great panhellenic sports festivals. In Sparta's militaristic society, girls underwent systematic physical training designed to make them into healthy mothers of future warriors. Some form of physical education for girls may have taken place outside of Sparta, but gymnastics and sports contests were basically a theater for the demonstration of masculine physical prowess and beauty.

Little evidence points to Roman women's participation in sports. Respectable Roman women apparently avoided sports except as spectators at chariot races and gladiatorial games.

In the Middle Ages, European sports often occurred in close conjunction with religious festivals, but the regional differences and class divisions prevented the emergence of a single, universally accepted system of physical activities.

The predominance of male power notwithstanding, some women achieved privileged status at court or in a nunnery. Some of them rode horseback and enjoyed the sport of falconry; some played simple ball games. Aristocratic women also played an ancillary role at the medieval tournaments that were an important aspect of the life of a medieval knight. Tournaments not only hardened the warrior's body and prepared it for battle; they were also vivid symbolic demonstrations of social order. Women's presence was important to admire and encourage the combatants and to acknowledge men's right to rule.

In medieval towns, the most popular sports—archery, wrestling, fencing—were also related to warfare, a relationship that generally excluded women from the archery guilds that were a prominent part of urban life. Middle-class women were occasionally allowed to compete among themselves in an archery contest, especially in Flanders and in Holland. Archery matches throughout Europe were also important social events that would have been painfully incomplete without admiring female spectators.

Among the peasantry, women were so essential in the struggle for mere survival that it seemed only natural for them to share in many of the sports of their fathers, husbands, and sons. They appear in medieval art not only as dancers but also as participants in the widely popular (and wildly chaotic) game of folk football. In England, France, Germany, Switzerland, and Italy, girls and women ran races for smocks and similar prizes.

However, our picture of preindustrial body and movement culture is incomplete. If women appear far less frequently than men, one reason is that men have written the histories and interpreted the documents (which, in turn, were produced mostly by men).

The Eighteenth and Nineteenth Centuries

In the late 18th and early 19th centuries, Western political, economic, and social institutions were decisively altered by new forms of technology and production, by the French Revolution and similar political upheavals, and by the philosophical currents of the "Age of Reason." Work began to move from fields and households to factories and offices, changing the nature of the family, which had traditionally combined economic and domestic functions. Faith in scientific rationality, especially in the form of medicine and biology, began to replace religion as the basis of society's conception of the gender order. All these changes tended to increase rather than decrease the perceived differences between men and women. Although a few voices called for greater equality between the sexes, most Europeans believed that men and women are by nature complementary opposites. The myth of manly strength and womanly weakness generally prevailed, as did the doctrine of "separate spheres" that sent men into the political and economic realms while women, especially those of the middle classes, were expected to devote themselves to the home and the church.

Turnen, Gymnastics, and Sports

Modern sports are the result of the confluence of several developments in the late 18th and early 19th centuries in Europe (and, to a lesser extent, in the United States). One such development was German gymnastics (*Turnen*), which evolved from the ideas and practices of pedagogues like Johann Christian Friedrich Guts Muths and from the political program of Friedrich Ludwig Jahn. For Jahn, *Turnen* was an expression of nationalism, a means to overcome the feudal order that had cut Germany into a patchwork of antagonistic states. His movement was also aimed at the expulsion of the French, whom Napoleon had led to a series of military victories over divided Germany.

Given his patriotic goals and emphasis on military preparedness, Jahn saw no reason to include women in his program. Besides, clambering up poles and swinging from ropes were "unseemly" activities for "the weaker sex." The exclusion of women from the ranks of the *Turnen* seemed so "self-evident" that Jahn and his followers never bothered to explain or justify it.

Like Jahn, the Swedish physical educator Per Henrik Ling (1776–1839) was influenced by Guts Muths. Ling combined the anatomical and physiological knowledge of his era with the ideas of "natural philosophy" to create an allegedly scientific system of simple exercises intended to promote balance, harmony, and health. The core of his system, however, included military as well as hygienic exercises. The institute that he established in Stockholm in 1813 spread his ideas throughout northern and western Europe. Although Ling envisioned his program as solely for men and boys, Swedish gymnastics eventually become the seedbed of women's physical education.

In France, the evolution of gymnastics took a militaristic turn under the guidance of Francisco Amoros (1770–1848), a Spanish officer who emigrated to France and established a training school at which exercises were conducted by military command. One result of his influence, which remained dominant for most of the century, was that the French, like the Germans and the Italians, associated gymnastics with bellicose nationalism. The predictable result of this military emphasis was the nearly total neglect of girls' and women's gymnastics in France as in every other European country.

The 19th century, however, brought increasing concern about the effects of industrialization and urbanization on girls' and women's health. Patriotism seemed to require that something be done. There was soon a lively debate over female physical education.

Among the first to champion physical exercise for girls was Phokion Heinrich Clias (1782–1854), a propagandist active in Switzerland, France, and England. His *Kalisthenie* (1829), from which we derive the term "calisthenics," was a landmark in the history of women's physical education. Its influence can be attributed in large part to the emphasis Clias placed on gentle exercises that enhanced female grace and beauty. German pedagogues like Johann Adolf Ludwig Werner also published books advocating gymnastics for young women. By 1850 a number of gymnastic clubs offered courses intended to make girls healthier and more attractive. It is unlikely that many girls benefited from these opportunities, and most who did came from affluent middle-class homes.

In the latter half of the 19th century, governments the length and breadth of Europe legislated one or another form of compulsory physical education for girls, but many of these laws remained inactive until early in the 20th century. Only late in the 19th century did significant numbers of girls schools began to include gymnastics in their curriculum. When they did, the teachers were usually careful to limit their pupils' movements to regimented drill, which instilled obedience. To preserve "decency," German girls, for example, were not allowed to perform exercises that required them to spread their legs or to lift them above the waist.

While German girls marched and executed the standardized movements prescribed by Adolf Spiess (1810–1858) and other schoolmasters, English girls took slow walks and suffered the boredom of calisthenics. In an effort to improve the situation, the London School Board looked abroad. In 1881 Martina Bergmann (later Bergmann-Österberg; 1849–1915) was summoned from Stockholm's school of Lingian gymnastics to take charge of girls' physical education. It was hoped that "Swedish gymnastics" would provide inexpensive rational discipline without militaristic associations. The ideal was noncompetitive physical development without sacrificing femininity.

During these years, the British transformed their traditional physical pastimes into what we now recognize as modern sports, with rules, organizations, and standardized contests. In the course of the 19th century, schoolmasters at Eton, Rugby, and other public schools made a cult of cricket, crew, and football. Sports were an essential part of "muscular Christianity." They were thought to be the basis of moral manhood.

Girls and women were not entirely excluded from the nascent sports culture of the 18th and 19th centuries.

"The Pursuit of Beauty."

I saw an aged, aged man
One morning near the Row,
Who sat, dejected and forlorn,
Till it was time to go.
It made me quite depressed and bad
To see a man so wholly sad—
I went and told him so.
I asked him why he sat and stared
At all the passers-by,
And why on ladies young and fair
He turned his watery eye.
He looked at me without a word,
And then—it really was absurd—
The man began to cry.
But when his rugged sobs were stayed—
It made my heart rejoice—
He said that of the young and fair
He sought to make a choice.
He was an artist, it appeared—
I might have guessed it by his beard,
Or by his gurgling voice.
His aim in life was to procure
A model fit to paint
As "Beauty on a Pedestal,"
Or "Figure of a Saint,"
But every woman seemed to be
As crooked as a willow tree—
His metaphors were quaint.
"And have you not observed," he asked
"That all the girls you meet
Have either 'Hockey elbows' or
Ungainly 'Cycling feet'?
Their backs are bent, their faces red,
From 'Cricket stoop,' or 'Football head.'"
He spoke to me with heat.
"But have you never found," I said,
"Some girl without a fault?
Are all the women in the world
Misshapen, lame or halt?"
He gazed at me with eyes aglow,
And, though the tears had ceased to flow,
His beard was fringed with salt.

"There was a day, I mind it well,
A lady passed me by
In whose physique my searching glance
no blemish could descry.
I followed her at headlong pace,
But when I saw her, face to face,
She had the 'Billiard eye'!"
—From *Mr. Punch's Book of Sports*

Some participated in rural cricket matches. Aristocratic women competed in archery contests. Lower-class women in London often engaged in boxing matches, to the delight of the mostly male spectators. On the whole, however, modern sports were considered a masculine preserve.

The Turn-of-the-Century Triumph of Modern Sports

Women's roles changed rapidly with the industrialization and modernization of society at the end of the 19th century. Feminism became a powerful force. Universities opened their doors to female students, and educated women began to enter the professions. Men discovered that more and more women were ready and willing to participate in "manly" sports. Participation was, of course, influenced by such factors as national culture and social class. In Spain, where the economy remained agrarian and where the Roman Catholic Church exercised great authority, only aristocratic or upper-middle-class women indulged in such daring pastimes as golf, tennis, and skiing. Gymnastic exercises for girls were virtually unknown and were certainly not a part of public education. In the liberal democracies of northern and western Europe, female athletes found much readier acceptance. In France, as well as in other European countries, technological improvements in the bicycle progressed to the point where large numbers of women caught "cycling fever" and a few of them actually defied convention and competed in bicycle races (which were discontinued when conservative opinion expressed outrage at such "unwomanly" forms of amusement).

There was, in fact, still widespread opposition to women's sports even in northern and western Europe. Critics relied on an arsenal of medical, moral, and aesthetic arguments. Track and field contests were condemned with special fervor because they were thought not only to encourage an unwomanly competitiveness but also to threaten a woman's health.

Despite opposition, most European countries had at least the beginnings of women's sports before the outbreak of World War I. Germany had women's sections of men's gymnastics clubs, independent clubs for women, and even a number of women's sports clubs, as did England and France and—to a lesser extent—Italy. Although the costs of tennis, golf, and rowing tended to restrict participation in these sports to the affluent, there was also a movement for workers' sports. The German federation for workers' sports, founded in 1893, attracted a number of female members. The

Czechs were also active in the field of workers' sports. In these federations, and in those of France, Belgium, and Scandinavia, female members generally had the same rights as male members, at least on paper, which was usually not the case in middle-class clubs and federations.

Track and field is an excellent place to describe more closely the barriers faced (and eventually overcome) by female athletes. In Germany, the first track and field contests for women met with strong opposition. When the Berlin sports club Comet staged a Damensportfest in 1904, the club hoped to lure a large number of sensation-hungry spectators. The 400-meter race did, indeed, generate revenue and publicity, but it also raised a number of questions about the appropriateness of the race. When repeated, with the added attraction of some French participants, the race provoked less public interest than expected. The official journal of the German Track and Field Federation took the "ladies race" as an occasion to condemn women's races. The runners' style was satirized as a "duck waddle," and their efforts were written off as a misunderstanding of female emancipation. In truth, these Damensportfeste had less to do with emancipation than with voyeurism and sensationalism. Despite the failures of the first attempts to inaugurate women's track and field, interest in such events was growing.

In France as well as in Germany, athletic meets were men's affairs. Pierre de Coubertin criticized such meets, along with football games, as "unworthy spectacles." Despite such efforts at "guardianship" and despite the turmoil of World War I, French women did stage such events in the years 1914–1918. After the war, Alice Milliat (1884–1957) organized international competitions for women and an international federation to administer them.

In England, the beginnings of women's participation in modern sports goes back to the women's colleges of Oxford and Cambridge, founded in the 1870s, and to London's polytechnical schools, where many clubs were created for female students to do gymnastics and other sports.

With the increasing acceptance of women's gymnastics and sports came striking changes in dress. In the 19th century, as a rule, sports were done in everyday clothing, but the popularity of the bicycle forced a change in costume for safety's sake. (One solution was a long dress that could be divided and rebuttoned into a pair of makeshift trousers.) The early decades of the 20th century brought gradual acceptance of knee-length shorts. The controversy over sports dress was not merely a debate about clothing; at issue were symbols of male power.

Twentieth-Century Society and the Gender Order
In most European nations, women moved a step forward in the direction of legal equality, but even where they achieved the right to vote and hold office, they were still regarded as "the second sex." A woman who chose to embark on a professional career suffered from discrimination; she who chose domesticity was expected to acknowledge her husband as the head of the household. Clothing reform was also less than complete. There was more freedom of movement as ankle-length dresses and tight corsets were discarded. Nudists discarded even more articles of clothing and proclaimed a new, more athletic ideal of femininity. Short hair, a tanned body, and narrow hips were thought to be fashionably "modern." The liberation of the body was purchased, however, at a cost. Women internalized aesthetic ideals, like slenderness and a youthful look, that required considerable effort.

Progress in Gymnastics and Women's Sports
In the postwar years, sports, which were increasingly subjected to the processes of modernization, achieved a new zenith of popularity. The globe was spanned by a network of international sports federations such as the Fédération Internationale de Football Association (1904), which administered soccer (association football), and the International Amateur Athletic Federation (1912), which oversaw track and field. Women were by no means immune from the fascination of sports, and large numbers of them engaged in increasingly strenuous contests.

Although few people doubted that girls and women should be physically active for the sake of their health, their participation in highly competitive sports led to fierce controversies. At their core was the debate over the compatibility of competition and motherhood. The weightiest arguments against strenuous sports came from medical experts, especially gynecologists, who inveighed against competition and against participation in "manly" sports such as soccer. (The danger was that a female might be "masculinized.") Again and again, the Cassandras of the medical profession complained about the female athlete's diminished fertility and her disinclination to bear children.

The Olympic Games were a highly visible arena for these controversies over the appropriateness and desirability of women's sports. Although Coubertin had revived the Games in 1896 as a purely male enterprise and continued to oppose women's participation to the day of his death in 1937, a dozen female golfers and tennis players competed in Paris in 1900 in the Olympic Games that were held in rather confused conjunction with a world's fair. Subsequently, the number of female athletes rose slowly but continuously. Prior to World War I, women were limited to sports that the men of the International Olympic Committee deemed appropriately feminine. (Swimming and diving were introduced at Stockholm in 1912.) In the 1920s, the struggle centered on track and field. While the International Amateur Athletic Federation and the International Olympic Committee wanted to keep the "core" of the games free from the contamination of female runners, jumpers, and throwers, the Fédération Sportive Féminine Internationale (FSFI), which Alice Milliat had founded in 1921, agitated for their inclusion in the Olympic program. The FSFI held its own Jeux Olympiques in 1922 (Paris), 1926 (Göteburg), 1930 (Prague), and 1934 (London). In response to this challenge from the FSFI, the IOC reluctantly inaugurated women's track and field at the 1928 Games in Amsterdam. Once the dike of discrimination was breached, no amount of argument was able to hold back the tide of women's sports at the Olympic Games. The number of sports contested by women and the number of female contestants have both grown steadily.

In Olympic sports as in others, the opportunities for women varied from country to country. In Germany, women were encouraged to participate in sports contests, including those in track and field, that had earlier been considered "unwomanly," but women's soccer remained taboo. In France, however, where a variety of female sports federations had been founded, women not only competed in track and field, they also formed soccer teams and played in national tournaments. The rougher game of *barette,* similar to rugby, also had its French enthusiasts. In other parts of the continent, including Scandinavia, women's sports were less widely accepted.

The national differences in opportunity can be clearly observed in the figures for between-the-wars Olympic participation. Except for the Games in distant Los Angeles (1932), female athletes representing Germany constituted generally about 7 percent of their nation's Olympic team, while their Norwegian counterparts were not only far fewer in number but also much more likely to limit their participation to "feminine" sports. Only after World War II did Spain send a single female athlete to the Olympics.

Women involved in sports held differing opinions

on the question of participation in the Olympic Games. With few exceptions, German sports organizations were sexually integrated., while French and British women tended to form their own organizations. The French, who were the dominant force in the international federation for women's sports, favored Olympic participation; the British, organized in the Women's Amateur Athletic Federation, wanted to continue the tradition of separate "Women's Olympics" (which, ironically, the French had inaugurated).

Toward the end of the 1920s, the mass media began to celebrate the achievements of female athletes. Among the early idols were the temperamental, flamboyant, unconventionally dressed French tennis player Suzanne Lenglen, the German airplane pilot Elli Beinhorn, who made headlines not only with her round-the-world flights but also by her marriage to a famed automobile racer, and Sonja Henie, the beautiful Norwegian "Ice Princess" who skated her way from the Olympic Games to a career in Hollywood. The headlines that announced Gertrude Ederle's successful swim across the English Channel were comparable to those that celebrated Charles Lindbergh's solo flight across the Atlantic.

While the achievements of female athletes continued to be met with a mix of fascination and disgust, gymnastics were gradually transformed into an almost entirely female domain. Throughout Europe, a variety of systems and schools were propagated, some emphasizing health and hygiene, some more intent on the aesthetics of human movement. Strongly criticizing modern sports and their obsession with quantified achievement, the proponents of gymnastics were concerned principally with the quality of the movement experience, the form and shape of the body, and the harmonious development of the whole person. Common also was a tendency to cultural criticism; gymnastics were affirmed as a "natural" contrast to the mad pace and artificiality of modern civilization. Although the gymnastics movement propagated a rather traditional image of womanhood, it spoke to many who believed that it offered an essentially feminine movement culture that was free from men's interference and control. For such thinkers, gymnastics meant movement without competitiveness and without role conflict.

Women's Sports and Fascism

In the fascist ideologies espoused by the dictatorial regimes of Mussolini's Italy, Hitler's Germany, and Franco's Spain, biological and racist ideas were revived to restructure the gender order and to recast masculinity and femininity as the polar opposites they were

thought to be in the 19th century. These regimes sought to reduce women, once again, to their wifely and maternal roles.

The fecund female body and the hardened male body were central to Hitler's "racial hygiene" and to his dreams of dictatorial expansionist power. In addition to health and "racial purity," Nazi physical education was intended to inculcate an ideology of racial superiority, community, military preparedness, and strong leadership. As the term "political physical education" indicates, gymnastics and sports were subordinated to politics. Physical education was a central pillar in the structure of the Nazi state. It was supposed to prepare men for their predetermined biological role as fighters and women for theirs as mothers. In Nazi discourse and in the medical literature influenced by it, discussions of women's sport centered on two questions: What enhances and what diminishes a woman's reproductive function? By providing "healthy" and "appropriate" exercises, organizations like the Bund Deutscher Mädel (Federation of German Maidens) tried to institutionalize the goals of motherhood and the health of the community. Although Nazi ideology had originally been opposed to sports competition for women, Hitler realized the propaganda advantages that were sure to accompany demonstrations of physical superiority. His regime supported female athletes in a number of ways, and the 1936 Olympic Games in Berlin seemed to prove him right. Although the Games were staged to demonstrate—to the point of absurdity—the cult of masculinity, Germany fielded the most successful team of female athletes.

Developments after World War II

After the devastation and deprivation of World War II, the peoples of Europe turned eagerly to sports that, even in occupied Germany, represented a more attractive world than the ubiquitous ruins of the postwar world. With the gradual return of ordinary life came a call for women to resume the domestic roles they had been forced to abandon by the exigencies of war. The 1950s were a decade that emphasized traditional ideals of home and hearth.

Simultaneous with the renewed debate about the appropriateness of women's participation in strenuous competition came the ideological struggles of the Cold War. The confrontation of communism with liberal-democratic capitalism left its mark on sports. Signs were observable everywhere in Europe, but especially obvious in Germany, divided down the middle by the ideological line that separated East and West. Whether they sought the role or not, the female athletes of the Federal Republic of Germany and those of the German Democratic Republic bore the banners of two embattled political-economic-cultural regimes.

Women's Sport under Communism

The performance of the Soviet Union's female athletes at the 1952 Olympics held in Helsinki astonished the world. For nearly 40 years, athletes from the communist regimes of Eastern Europe continued to dominate the women's events at the Olympic Games (except of course, in 1984, when Romania was the only communist nation to send a team to Los Angeles). When observers marveled at the "big red sports machine," they tended to think of the women, especially those from East Germany.

Olympic success was the result of a number of interrelated factors: the centralized search for athletic talent, which began with the systematic recruitment of children; scientific research designed to maximize performance; the concentration of economic resources on sports; the high prestige and social security granted to successful athletes; material rewards (such as trips abroad); and medical manipulation through drugs. As a result of the communist sports bureaucrats' ruthless pursuit of gold medals and world championships, women and girls were trained to the point where, in Western eyes, they no longer seemed female. In an attempt to make their female athletes culturally acceptable, communist regimes propagated new ideals of women's roles and female physiques. "Muscular femininity" might have been their unspoken motto.

The concentration on elite athletes came at the expense of recreational sports. Facilities available to ordinary citizens were poor and teachers of physical education had far lower status than coaches of national teams. Eastern European women were triply burdened; their vocational, domestic, and political obligations left them little time or energy for sports participation. Although propagandists proclaimed the contrary, the women of the communist world were far less likely than those of the West to be involved in recreational sports.

In the West, the debate over femininity and sports was resumed. When athletes from the communist bloc introduced new acrobatic movements into women's gymnastics, many Western Europeans found the contortions ugly and unfeminine. The first reaction of the German Gymnastics Federation was to defend its ideal of femininity; since the simple, graceful, rather static movements the federation favored were unlikely to earn high scores, the federation decided in 1954 to withdraw from international competition. In time, however, the logic of modern sports forced Western women to do as the communists did or to abandon their sporting ambitions.

In other sports, there were attempts to halt the trend toward "masculinization." In many European countries, women were discouraged from playing soccer. It was not until the 1970s that the Fédération Internationale de Football reversed itself and began to sponsor world championships for women. The International Olympic Committee (IOC) waited another 20 years before bringing women's soccer into its program. It was so difficult to disprove the myth of woman's weakness that the IOC resisted the woman's marathon race until 1984.

Despite the laudable effort to end sexual discrimination at the Olympic Games, the program remains unequally divided between men's and women's events. In 1988, for instance, only 26 percent of the athletes at Seoul were female; only a third of the events were for them. Even then, a woman's chances to compete in the Olympics depended on her nationality. Women were 35 percent of the British team, 18 percent of the Spanish team—and they were entirely absent from many teams representing Islamic nations; in order to win the 1,500-meter race at Barcelona in 1992, Algeria's Hassiba Boulmerka had not only to outrun her rivals but also to surmount the psychological barrier of fundamentalist death threats.

Women's Sports Today

The inequalities observable at the Olympics are paralleled by those in the lives of ordinary women interested in recreational sports. Despite the dramatic changes of recent decades, women are by no means as likely as men to be involved in sports. This is clear both from surveys and from the membership rolls of European sports federations. In England, Germany, and Norway, approximately 40 percent of adult women say that they participate in sports, but one must be attentive to the definitions employed by the researchers. In England, walking is considered a sport; in Finland, elderly berry-pickers are counted as athletes. German data are more complete and more reliable. Nearly 30 percent of all Germans are members of a sports club; 37 percent of the members are female. In Norway, girls and women are 38 percent of all club members. In Spain, however, the situation is quite different. Only 26 percent of the women claim to be athletically active (as opposed to 48 percent of the men).

To a greater degree than is the case for men, age and

social class are important influences on women's sports participation. In German clubs, for instance, girls begin to cease participating in sports from their 14th year while boys continue to be quite active until they are at least 18. In every European nation, men and women of higher social status are more likely than the less affluent to be athletically active, but the effect of this variable is greater for women than for men. The result is that only a minuscule number of middle-aged and elderly working-class women participate in sports of any sort.

For those women who do participate, the spectrum of available options is far greater than in the past. Young women now participate in sports once thought to be exclusively male: marathon running, soccer and rugby, water polo, even boxing and weightlifting. Of course, there continues to be a gender difference in rates of participation in various sports. Men are still more likely than women to engage in sports that require aggressive body contact. Gymnastics, aerobics, and dance continue to attract far more women than men. It must also be said that the financial support for women's sports is still less than offered to men. Except in tennis and golf, opportunities for women to earn their living as openly professional athletes remain almost nonexistent. Women are radically underrepresented in sports administration at every level, from the International Olympic Committee to the local sports club. They are rarely to be found in the press box or as commentators on televised sports. There is, however, one area where women have made major gains. Although women are still a minority of the scholars engaged in the academic study of sports (about 7 percent in Germany), their voices can now be heard.

—GERTRUD PFISTER

Bibliography: Blue, Adrianne. (1987) *Grace under Pressure: The Emergence of Women in Sport.* London: Sidgwick and Jackson. Guttmann, Allen. (1991) *Women's Sports: A History.* New York: Columbia University Press. Hargreaves, Jennifer. (1994) *Sporting Females: Critical Issues in the History and Sociology of Women's Sports.* London: Routledge. Pfister, Gertrud, and Christine Peyton, eds. (1989) *Frauensport in Europa.* Ahrensburg: Czwalina.

WOMEN'S SPORTS, NORTH AMERICA

North American sports were once an almost exclusively male domain; today girls and women are easily visible as spectators and participants at all levels of sport.

1820–1880—Agrarianism to Marketplace

The foundations of women's sport and recreation in the United States were set down in the period from the Revolutionary War to the 1820s, when most men's and women's lives were interdependent and revolved around rural living and shared tasks. Typical pastimes and recreational activities for girls and women included walking, sledding, skating, horseback riding, swimming (more like bathing in the sea), and simple games. Outdoor sporting activities included hunting and fishing parties, fox hunting, and boating (canoeing and river boat races). For the wealthy few, there were sailing and yachting. Occasional competition could be found in horse races, foot races, spinning and corn husking contests, and similar folk games. Shuttlecock and 10-pin bowling moved toward more highly structured competition.

In the decades from 1820 to 1880, the United States transformed from an agrarian to an industrialized nation. In the process, women's lives changed significantly. Women no longer shared work with men in the same way. Consequently, for certain segments of the population—notably the middle class—the polarization of gender roles increased. The social responsibilities and behavior patterns reflected in these separate roles form the basis for conceptions of "masculinity" and "femininity" that found powerful expression in U.S. sporting traditions.

The separation of men's and women's worlds into two separate "spheres" or cultures during the 19th century was reflected in a dominant pattern of men moving toward competitive sport and women toward recreation and sport for health's sake. Whereas working-class females still labored long hours, increasing leisure time allowed some women to develop club sports, engage in healthful activities, or participate in popular mass sport fads. A few bold women engaged in what were considered masculine activities. Which women's sports developed and which did not, as well as the type and intensity of competition, depended upon culturally ingrained traditions based on gender perceptions controlled by men. Sports were seen as a way to train young males for adulthood and enable them to develop and maintain manly characteristics of physical strength and prowess, plus leadership. Sport for girls and women was intended to foster health, pleasant social interactions, and democratic ideals; and only incidentally character building or competition.

Exercise had been a significant aspect of pre–Civil War "health-reform" movements—several of which benefited women. Early "women's rights" advocates such as Elizabeth Cady Stanton spoke out in favor of physical education for females, and books such as Catharine Beecher's *Physiology and Calisthenics for*

Schools and Families (1856) provided educators with examples of exercises to be used by girls as well as boys. Many aspects of the earlier health-reform movement were incorporated into the physical education programs that began to appear at women's colleges during the last third of the 19th century.

1880–1920—The Growth of Gender-Based and Class-Based Sport

The so-called "new woman" of the 1890s and early 1900s was characterized by an independent spirit and athletic zeal. Some women began to enjoy wider professional and personal choices. Only with economic independence could patterns of social behavior change. This freedom permitted the rise of the female educational establishment with its abundance of new role models and commitment to professional achievement and social goals for women. These women heralded the dawn of the feminist movement, which culminated in the passage of the Nineteenth Amendment (1920) to the United States Constitution, giving voting rights to women.

Political changes and economic changes were accompanied by reforms of sport attire, including "bloomers" and other trouserlike garments. Perhaps the most significant of these changes accompanied the growth of bicycling, which became ever more popular in the 1890s. Safety dictated a more "rational" form of dress, and many younger women commented on the increased sense of freedom they obtained from cycling through the countryside.

Sex-appropriate team sports were ones in which men didn't compete, such as field hockey, and ones whose rules were severely modified by women for female participation, such as basketball and volleyball. Softball was tolerated because it did differ from baseball and arose from indoor baseball. Track and field, including long-distance running, was marginally acceptable in a recreational setting, but competition was discouraged.

With the invention of basketball in 1891, competitive sport became available to women. By 1892, the game was played at Smith College and had even reached California. It soon crossed class boundaries. By the 1920s, it was played as a team game both in interscholastic competition and in the developing industrial leagues. Although field hockey attracted fewer players, it spread through many women's colleges and universities. The initiator of the modern Olympics, Pierre de Coubertin, steadfastly objected to women's participation in the Games, but women did engage in demonstrations of tennis and golf at the 1900 Paris Games. At

London in 1908, archery, figure skating, and tennis were on the program. Not until Amsterdam in 1928, however, was some track and field included; exaggerated reporting of the results of the 800-meter run, however, led to the elimination of that event from the women's program until Rome in 1960.

During this epoch, the divide widened between upper-class and working-class female athletes. Wealthy women played tennis, golf, fencing, and water sports, and they participated in the winter sports of skiing, figure, and speed skating; working-class women engaged in the less feminine team sports of softball and track and field. The only truly competitive team sport other than basketball (and the mild team sport of volleyball) was field hockey, an anomaly in the history of sport for women because it was international in the scope of competition, it was vigorous, and it was played by upper-class rather than working-class women. In the late 1800s, sports like roller skating and pedestrianism enjoyed brief popularity among females.

As women moved from recreational activities to sport, club facilities and competitions became necessary. The first women's club, the Ladies' Club of the Staten Island Cricket and Baseball Club, connected itself to the men's club in 1877 as an avenue to competitive tennis. Immediately accepted as a sex-appropriate sport for affluent women, tennis was taught in the colleges, and by 1900 it had appeared in public parks, playgrounds, and recreation centers throughout the country. Local and college tennis tournaments originated in 1881, and the first national tournament was organized for women in 1887.

Upper-class women participated in sex-segregated activity, but during the 1880s they also joined their husbands at country and athletic clubs and conducted local, regional, and even a few national championships through the clubs. The sports included croquet, archery, fencing, bowling, swimming, and tennis. The older, more established skating and riding clubs also gained momentum as manuals were published for both sports. Clubs were formed for the winter sports of snowshoeing, skiing, and skating. Outdoorswomen, particularly in the West, continued to enjoy fishing, hunting, hiking, riflery, camping, and mountain climbing.

Sport Crazes and Exhibitions

When the croquet (1866) and later the archery (1870s) crazes swept the country, women donned fashionable attire to compete with and then socialize with men. Both sports had national championships for women. The popularity of both sports, however, was short-lived, and more active, exciting sports like tennis gained the support of affluent women. Albeit encumbered by tight corsets, heavy petticoats, and long full skirts, women persisted in sport participation.

A large group of bold women (mostly from the laboring or immigrant class) moved outside the security of their gender roles to participate in competitive events such as horse racing, cycle races, novelty cycle/horse races, distance swimming, and riflery shooting. Less acceptable but nonetheless present on the fringes of sport were the "antifeminine" exhibitions of strong women, weightlifters and body builders, wrestlers, and even a fair number of women boxers.

Three Sports: A Snapshot

A quick glance at three major women's recreational and competitive sports in the 1880–1920 period reveals the special circumstances and development of women's sport in this era.

(1) Bicycling Mania. Two independently occurring phenomena—clothing reform and bicycling mania—interacted with and influenced each other. The happy result was that by the end of the 1890s women were able to shed the costumes of the past and feel a new independence of movement and spirit. The bloomer gave the average woman a sporting chance, first in cycling and then in basketball, tennis, and other sports.

The cycling rage was the most popular activity in the decades of the 1880s and 1890s for women of leisure, college women, and for professional women. The activity caused a mass exodus to the out-of-doors, for any woman who could afford the price of a bicycle.

(2) Field Hockey. Field hockey and, later, lacrosse were a legacy from the women of Great Britain to the women's colleges and secondary private schools of the East, making this team sport gender-acceptable. Enthusiasm for field hockey led the way to various types of international and high-level competition in the educational domain as well as the public sector, starting with a U.S. field hockey team that traveled to England in 1920.

As an elite sport, field hockey provided vigorous competition, and by the end of this era field hockey players had moved into sectional national and international competition. By this time a large number of the players in these competitions were physical educators, some of whom also sponsored collegiate teams to compete against the clubs and against each other. The varsity competition was often conducted by the very women who were anti-varsity in all other sports.

(3) Basketball. The real love affair in women's sport was embodied in basketball everywhere in this country, surpassing all other team sports on all levels and across all socioeconomic boundaries. In education it was the most popular sport. In popular culture, it was the favorite team sport for competition and recreational play. Basketball was the only team sport for which women completely modified men's rules to make the game more appropriate for female athletes.

By 1920 basketball was played with six players, the court divided into three equal courts with one permitted dribble, no physical contact or horizontal guarding, and no loud talking or coaching from the bench. The next 85 years were spent in discussion and debate about modifications of the basketball rules, and after each such discussion the women's rules more nearly resembled the men's. Finally in the fall of 1971, the five-player, full-court unlimited dribble won the approval of women physical educators and the Amateur Athletics Union. Throughout the next era basketball will be the major concern in relation to varsity playing and the public sector competition. Women, however, have played varsity basketball since Berkeley played Stanford in 1896. So, too, elite basketball has been played from the AAU National Championship in 1926 forward to the Olympics of the present era.

1920–1950—The Democratic Ideal

Urbanization, greater employment for women, an increasingly mobile population with more leisure time, and relaxation of many restrictive social standards all contributed to a climate favoring greater opportunities for women in many spheres in life. Sport was one of these. The period is sometimes referred to as "the golden age of sport" because of the rapid expansion of both professional and college sport for men; growth was more limited in women's sport. During the 1920s, Helen Wills (Moody) emerged as a dominating figure in women's tennis, winning numerous U.S. championships. Two years later, Mildred "Babe" Didrickson (Zaharias) broke three world records in the Amateur Athletics Union (AAU) national track and field championships at the 1932 Los Angeles Olympics.

Softball might well be labeled a sport of the Depression years. Although women in elite women's colleges played men's baseball in the era of the 1880s–1890s (and even a few in the 1860s), indoor baseball, which became the team sport of softball, was the truly popular sport of working-class men and all classes of women. The federal government supported recreation programs that sponsored softball leagues. The industrial leagues (in both sports) featured teams sponsored by small businesses whose company names were proudly emblazoned as advertising on the uniforms. Often, however, individuals developed their own teams.

The decade of the 1940s further altered the sporting attitudes and behavior patterns of women, for they had experienced success as respected contributors to the nation through their work in the war plants, the armed services, and in other important positions.

Public Domain Industrial Leagues, Olympics, and AAU
The decades from 1920 to 1950 witnessed a significant growth in recreational and competitive sport for women. Women joined company teams, industrial leagues, YWCA teams, company-sponsored basketball competition, track and field teams, bowling leagues, and summer softball leagues. Upper- and middle-class women moved in greater numbers to the recreational and competitive organizations of such diverse sports as tennis, golf, swimming, badminton, alpine skiing, skating, canoeing, and kayaking. At the grass-roots level, high schools, churches, clubs, industry, YWCA, Catholic Youth Organizations (CYO), and the Amateur Athletic Union (AAU), and National Sport Governing Bodies (NGBs) of the Olympics sponsored athletic programs, particularly in track, basketball, softball, and swimming.

Another recurring theme in the saga of women's competitive athletics in United States in this era is the struggle between leaders of the governing bodies of women's and men's athletics for control of organized amateur competition for women.

By the 1920s, for the first time, female athletic heroes from the United States emerged from the Olympic Games and national championships, especially in the sports of tennis, golf, and figure skating. Americans of all social classes thrilled to their success, now heralded by national women's magazines and covered in the press and motion pictures. In addition, local heroes were found in abundance, even when national ones were limited. Media coverage even included women from track and field and other nonfeminine sporting traditions. Track and field was still considered "too masculine" for women, unless a track athlete was beautiful, in which case she became the sweetheart of the press and magazines. Individuals like Babe Didrikson (1911–1956), for example, who was voted the finest female athlete of the first half of the 20th century, was really not a role model or media fixture in her magnificent 1932 Olympic performance because she was not "feminine" enough and competed in "male" sports. Only after Didrikson became a professional golfer and

later as the second wave of feminist values took hold was she accepted as a role model.

Sport in the Educational Domain
In the decades between World War I and World War II, high school and college sports programs for girls and women were widely—but not exclusively—controlled by female physical educators whose aim was to foster a lifetime of participation. The primary emphasis was the health and social well-being of the participant. For the most part, intensely competitive sporting activities were shunned, for a variety of reasons. "A sport for every girl/Every girl in a sport"—the motto of the National Amateur Athletic Federation—exemplified such attitudes. In high schools and colleges the teachers were offering instructional programs in all the popular individual, team, and intramural sports, and they sponsored interest clubs in a variety of sports. Varsity competition flourished in rural high schools and in other pockets of the country.

Apprehensions about the male model of athletics and a desire for larger participation led high school teachers and many college leaders of physical education to endorse competitive restraints and to mandate female self-determination in athletic governance.

Educators characterized varsity teams as overemphasizing the "winning syndrome, corruption and commercialism rampant in men's athletics." This concept resulted in this alternative model of athletics for females, developed by women, involving play days and sports days, which was a natural outgrowth of conformity and accommodation of gender roles for women.

This vision of separate competition for girls and women led to conflicts, controversy, and gender relation struggles. Competitive athletics persisted throughout the period in the public domain and often in varsity sport.

During World War II, the necessity for physical fitness was emphasized for all citizens, and intense competition was suggested by the federal government for all high school girls, the armed forces, and the public domain. Women physical educators, therefore, helped develop federally suggested programs of fitness, and many young service women (and officers) participated themselves in such programs.

1950 and After—Revolution in Women's Sports
During the second half of the 20th century, profound changes have occurred in U.S. society. Among the more significant changes have been civil rights and equal rights legislation.

For women's sport, no federal legislation was more important than Title IX of the Education Amendments Act of 1972, which mandated parity between the genders in educational opportunities. These regulations together ushered in an age of reform and liberation—nothing short of a metamorphosis in women's lives in employment, education, and other sectors of society.

These new conceptions of equal rights and privileges for all citizens regardless of race or gender, changing cultural values regarding women, and developments fostered by the women's liberation movement, joined with the enactment of federal regulations, created a social climate conducive to the rapid rise of interest in sports of all kinds—interscholastic, intercollegiate, amateur, professional, and recreational. In the 1970s, and even more so in the 1980s, vast numbers of girls and women began to participate in sports, and, whereas formerly, dominant cultural values dictated that sports exemplifying grace and agility were most appropriate for females, sports that required strength, speed, and power now became increasingly acceptable.

Interscholastic and Intercollegiate Athletics after 1950

During World War II, many women had gained organizational and administrative experience in the armed services, Red Cross, and industry. Many female physical educators counted among those who served, and a number of them increasingly recognized the need for higher standards of competition for girls and women. By the 1960s, some state high school associations had expanded opportunities for girls, and more recreational leagues and clubs opened their doors to girls (including those economically disadvantaged). By 1969, the Division for Girls and Women's Sports of the American Association for Health, Physical Education, and Recreation had begun to schedule national intercollegiate championships for college women. In 1971, the Association for Intercollegiate Athletics for Women (AIAW), which traced its organizational roots to the National Women's Basketball Committee (1989), was formed. By 1981–1982, AIAW offered national championships in 19 collegiate sports. The following year, these were jointly sponsored by AIAW and the National Collegiate Athletic Association (NCAA); and, by 1983, the AIAW had collapsed, a victim of internal disagreements and external pressures—not the least of which were fears that rapidly growing women's sports would siphon off funding that traditionally had been directed to men's intercollegiate programs.

Title IX

In the years immediately following the passage of Title IX, considerable disagreement existed concerning the shape emerging women's programs should take. Some individuals favored emulating the model of the NCAA; others objected to recruiting, "athletic scholarships," and what they perceived as an unwholesome commercialization of school-based sports. Following the demise of the AIAW, collegiate sport for females has been governed by the regulations of the NCAA or, for smaller institutions, the National Association of Intercollegiate Athletics (NAIA). At the same time there has been a dramatic increase in the numbers of females engaged in college (and even high school) competitive programs, accompanied by a massive decline in the percentage of women who administer such programs. A sharp decline is also evident in the percentage of women who serve as the head coaches of women's sport teams.

Title IX has changed the configuration of college and university physical education and athletics. With the mergers of men's and women's physical education departments in the 1970s came the separation of athletics, intramurals, and instruction. Instructional programs were conducted with coeducational classes that favored teaching sports that were acceptable for both genders. Such sports include volleyball and softball, lifetime sports, and fitness activities. In addition, with the mergers, the women physical educators and their national organization, the National Association for Girls and Women in Sport (NAGWS) lost authority over rules, officiating, and governance of athletics and sports.

Fitness and Recreation

Since the 1960s, millions of new converts have been made to such recreational, noncompetitive pursuits as aerobics, jogging, and aquacalisthenics. Backpacking, mountain climbing, bicycling, cross-country skiing, and other outdoor pursuits grew rapidly after the mid-1960s—each attracting increasing numbers of female participants. Women have become the primary focus of the burgeoning "fitness" industry, and many women have achieved a greater sense of freedom and self-motivation as a result of their experiences in physical activity and sport. Others have become proficient at weightlifting and other forms of physical activity that once were deemed inappropriate.

Triathlon, marathon running, distance swimming, rugby teams, soccer teams, and flag football teams now attract a sizable number of girls and women. The fast growth of these sports demonstrate that for the first time women see fitness as a personal need and sports as offering a new freedom to create personal well-being. Furthermore, women are increasingly willing and able to move into the male domain of sport without apology and with little criticism from the public. What were once "elite" sports have become less so, now offering grass-roots opportunities to a multitude of children and teenagers regardless of their economic status. Even in athletic and sport clubs where the cost is greater (figure skating, gymnastics, golf, and skiing), clubs and recreation centers attempt to provide opportunities to compete for those who could not otherwise participate.

The Olympics
The entry of the United States into the modern Olympic Games occurred for men in 1896. Women made their first appearance almost by chance in the next two Olympic Games in golf and tennis (1900) and archery (1904). The AAU and all the national sport governing bodies were an important positive voice on behalf of female athletes for competitive athletics. As early as 1914 and 1916, the AAU maintained the records in swimming and track and by 1923 accepted women to register for other sports. In the early 1920s, basketball, track and field, and, a bit later, gymnastics, came under AAU jurisdiction. It was the beginning of the largest public programs for women in high-level competition in the country.

Women physical educators were silent regarding the gender-appropriate sports in the Olympics; that is, golf, archery, swimming, gymnastics, tennis, and figure skating, but they later (1928, 1932, and 1936) protested the entry of women into the "unladylike" sport of track and male domination of competitive sport through the AAU.

The greatest boon to Olympic sport for women was Title IX, which provided a feeder system, and the Federal Amateur Sport Act (ASA) of 1978. The act expanded the powers of the U.S. Olympic Committee to control international competition and the growth and expansion of Olympic sports in the United States. This law resulted in all sport governance groups working in harmony toward a single goal: the enactment of programs for U.S. amateur athletes at all ages and levels of abilities.

Women benefited from new funding for "underdeveloped sports," because all collegiate and other women's sports were classified as underdeveloped. The act is instrumental in assisting previously denied populations to achieve opportunity; women are just such a target population. With the new regulations of ASA, national festivals are sponsored each summer by the USOC. These events and tours for younger elite athletes assist young athletes as never before. Each sport (NGB) is devoting more time, energy, and money to grass-root programs as well as spending more on building a pool of young athletes. This new emphasis on grass roots has permitted team sports like soccer, handball, and volleyball to increase their numbers, not only for Olympic hopefuls but for an entire generation of young players.

Achievements of African American Women in Athletics
During the late 1800s and early 1900s, calisthenics and sports programs developed at many historically black colleges. Atlanta University's monthly student newspaper, the *Scroll*, announced that basketball was first introduced for women in 1899. By the 1920s and 1930s, students were engaged in track meets and basketball games with Tuskegee Institute and other institutions. Organizations such as the Phyllis Wheatley Y.W.C.A. of Washington, D.C., promoted basketball, tennis, and other sports for local girls. In the early 1920s, Lucy Slowe challenged the assertion that tennis was "too sophisticated" for black women while capturing the national championships of the All-Black American Tennis Association.

A particularly striking success of the 1950–1990 era has been the achievements of African American women in Olympic and other high-performance sports. Indeed, there had been numerous excellent athletes in earlier decades. However, such achievements as that of Tuskegee's Alice Coachman (who won the 1948 Olympic women's high jump) and other female African American athletes rarely received the attention they merited. The remarkable performances of triple gold medalist Wilma Rudolph at Rome in 1960 did not go unnoticed, however, and she was subsequently named recipient of the Sullivan Award as the year's outstanding female athlete. At recent Olympics, Florence Griffith-Joyner and Jackie Joyner-Kersee have gained considerable media attention as well as athletic laurels.

Although they had been very successful in the 1920–1940 period at AAU National Championships in basketball and track, African American women were not found in elite sports, except tennis. During the present and past era African American women participated in all the sports of the working-class women including softball, basketball, and bowling. In addition, middle-class African Americans competed in tennis.

This participation was due, in part, to the American Tennis Association (ATA), which encouraged female participation and provided the tournament outlet. Althea Gibson (1927–) came out of the ATA, winning its National Singles Championship in 1949. She moved on to win the French Open, Wimbledon, and the U.S. Open Championships, all in the 1950s. She paved the way for black men's and women's participation in previously all-white championships.

By midcentury African American athletes occupied a central position in the sport of track and field. Beginning in the 1930s black women stepped in the field abandoned by middle-class white women who deemed the sport "unfeminine." Black runners appeared on the U.S. team in the 1932 and 1936 Olympics. They won their first medals in the 1948 Games.

Perhaps the greatest contribution in sport by African American athletes is their supremacy and medal counts in the Olympics of 1952–1972. Nineteen Olympians coming from Tuskegee Institute and Tennessee State won over 20 medals. Best known was Wilma Rudolph (1940–1994), whose performance in the 1960 Olympics was the first widely televised track event. With her three gold medals, she almost single-handedly rekindled U.S. interest in women doing better in the Olympic competition.

African American women competed in track and field in the Olympics from 1932 forward, but only in 1964 did they begin to compete in other sports (volleyball). Now over half of the Olympic basketball team is African American, as are most of the track athletes and a few individuals in other sports. Just a decade and a half ago only a few black basketball players were on the collegiate scene, but appearing on behalf of Delta State in the Final Four of the NCAA championships was one of them, Lucia Harris (1955–), the first woman basketball player inducted into the men's (and now men's and women's) National Basketball Hall of Fame.

Professional Sports

Professional sports during the period 1950–1990 reflected the exceptional gutsiness of athletes on exhibition teams; the heart and drive of those in the many team sports that failed; the love of sport reflected in participation on poorly paying teams; and the joy of spectacular commercial success and influence in the popular culture. For example, from 1936 to the 1970s, the All-American Red Heads basketball team toured the country in a manner similar to the Harlem Globetrotters. The All-American Baseball League lasted through the early years of the 1950s. A professional basketball league in the 1970s and 1980s, however, failed for lack of a large pool of talent and audience appeal. Professional bowling, golf, and tennis fared very well, with tennis becoming the most popular women's professional sport, due primarily to Billie Jean King (1944–), who burst into national prominence at the right moment in history. In 1973, she won a great public tennis match with another professional, Bobby Riggs, in "the Battle of the Sexes," started a women's sport magazine, and almost single-handedly started the professional circuit for tennis. In the late 1990s, though, professional golf in general is growing while tennis is declining.

Other short-lived and long-lived professional teams include track and field, swimming, and, of course, the highly successful figure-skating shows. The newest professional team is a baseball team, the Silver Bullets, which competes against men's teams. The difficulty here is not having a pool of women baseball players, so softball players are attempting to turn their skills to baseball. The future looks bright, however, for basketball, for the men's National Basketball Association (NBA) formed a women's league in 1997 that has drawn large crowds in some cities, and the American Basketball League (ABL) began play in 1996. The basketball feeder system is now excellent, with collegiate basketball and Olympians and an educated audience near at hand. There are also now professional women boxers, although they are few in number and do not draw a large following. The most popular new professional sport is beach volleyball, with its doubles teams and brief "feminine" clothing. In 1998, the international success of the U.S. and Canadian women's hockey teams had led to plans to start a professional league.

The influx of girls and women into the sports arena is forcing changes and redefinitions of the role and function of sport in U.S. culture. These new role definitions will fuel the expansion of gender-role expectations. As the perceived female attributes of beauty and form interplay with the masculine attributes of strength and power and they merge into sporting experiences without gender, the acceptance of the female role in sport has the potential to free male and female athletes to have human experience, not sex identified or defined, leading toward a less rigidly defined sport culture.

Sport much resembles U.S. society itself in its heterogeneity and capacity for individuals to participate in diverse sports at different levels once the organized sport structure is in place. The previously divided stream of female and male athletics has become a mighty river that finally enjoys equal contributions and

support from the educational domain and popular culture. With all kinds of new sports promotions and parity in athletics on the horizon, the opportunities for girls and women in the United States appear limitless.
—JOAN HULT

Bibliography: Cahn, Susan K. (1994) *Coming on Strong: Gender and Sexuality in 20th Century Women's Sport.* New York: Free Press. Costa, Margaret, and Sharon Guthrie, eds. (1994) *Women and Sports: Interdisciplinary Perspectives.* Champaign, IL: Human Kinetics. Cohen, Greta L., ed. (1993) *Women in Sport: Issues and Controversies.* Newbury Park, CA: Sage Publications. Gai, Ingham Berlage. (1994) *Women in Baseball: The Forgotten History.* Westport, CT: Praeger. Guttmann, Allen. (1991) *Women's Sports: A History.* New York: Columbia University Press. Hargreaves, Jennifer. (1994) *Sporting Females: Critical Issues in the History and Sociology of Women's Sports.* New York: Routledge. Hult, Joan S., and Mariana Trekell, eds. (1991) *A Century of Women's Basketball: From Frailty to Final Four.* Reston, VA: National Association for Girls and Women in Sport. Verbrugge, Martha. (1988) *Able-Bodied Womanhood.* New York: Oxford University Press. Vertinsky, Patricia. (1990) *The Eternally Wounded Woman.* Manchester: Manchester University Press.

Worker Sport

The growth in regular wage earners created the mass labor movement in the late 19th century; the labor movement brought improved conditions, such as the Saturday half-holiday and shorter working hours. These two conditions—worker solidarity and more leisure—framed the rise of worker sport.

History

Germany became the hub and catalyst of the worker sports movement, with over 350,000 worker athletes in various worker clubs even before World War I. A worker sports movement began to take shape there in the 1890s with the foundation of the Worker Gymnastics Association, in conscious opposition to the nationalistic German Gymnastics Society (Turnen). Its influence spread to North America with the migration of entire German communities. This was followed in Germany by the Solidarity Worker Cycling Club and the Friends of Nature Rambling Association in 1895, the Worker Swimming Association in 1897, the Free Sailing Association in 1901, the Worker Track and Field Association in 1906, the Worker Chess Association in 1912, and the Free Shooting Association in 1926.

Austrian, British, and French workers set up analogous associations. By 1913 there were enough members internationally for the worker sports federations of five European nations, Belgium, Britain, France, Germany, and Italy, to come together at Ghent on the initiative of the Belgian socialist Gaston Bridoux to establish the Socialist Physical Culture International.

By the time the various worker federations regrouped after World War I, two new tendencies, both divisive and controversial, were emerging.

The first was the growing movement away from noncompetitive recreation (physical culture) to competitive organized sport. This shift toward team sports and competitions was a response to popular pressure within the working class.

Also generating controversy was the growing division between social democrats or socialists, on the one hand, and communists, on the other, over leadership and aims of the worker sports movement. A number of worker sports organizations broke away from the Lucerne Sports International (LSI), a branch of the Bureau of the Socialist International, after the formation of the International Association of Red Sports and Gymnastics Associations, better known as Red Sport International (RSI), in Moscow in 1921 as a branch of the Communist International or Comintern.

Relations between the two worker sports internationals were hostile right from the start, the RSI accusing its "reformist" rival of diverting workers from the class struggle through its policy of political neutrality in sport. True, the socialists were not trying to make the sports movement into an active revolutionary force; instead, it was to be a strong, independent movement within capitalist society that would be ready, after the revolution, to implement a fully developed system of physical culture. The RSI, on the other hand, wished to build a sports international that would be a political vehicle of the class struggle; it did not want merely to produce a better sports system for workers in a capitalist world.

By the time they eventually came together, in 1936, it was too late to save the worker sports movement from fascist repression.

The Worker Olympics

While the worker sports movement did not take issue with much of the Coubertin idealism concerning the modern Olympic Games, it did oppose the Games themselves and developed its own Olympiads on the following grounds.

First, the bourgeois Olympics encouraged competition along national lines, whereas the Worker Olympics stressed internationalism, worker solidarity, and peace.

Second, while the Olympics restricted entry on the grounds of sporting ability, the worker games invited all.

Third, the IOC Games were criticized for being confined chiefly to the sons of the rich and privileged (through the amateur code and the domination of national Olympic committees by the upper classes). By contrast, the Worker Olympics were explicitly against all chauvinism, racism, sexism, and social exclusivity; they were truly amateur, organized for the edification and enjoyment of working women and men, and illustrated the fundamental unity of all working people irrespective of color, creed, sex, or national origin.

Finally, the labor movement did not believe that the Olympic spirit of true amateurism and international understanding could be attained in a movement dominated by an aristocratic-bourgeois leadership.

The first of such international Olympic festivals was hosted by the Czechoslovak Worker Gymnastics Association in Prague, 26–29 June 1921, and advertised as the first unofficial Worker Olympics. It attracted worker athletes from 13 countries: Austria, Belgium, Britain, Bulgaria, Czechoslovakia, Finland, France, Germany, Poland, Switzerland, the USA, USSR, and Yugoslavia.

The first official Worker Olympics were arranged by the 1.3-million-member Lucerne Sport International in Germany, seven years after the end of World War I. They were billed by the organizers as a festival of peace. As a British representative put it, if wars are won on the playing fields of Eton, peace can be won on the democratic sports fields of the Workers International Olympiads.

The Winter Games, held in Schreiberhau (now Riesengebirge), attracted contestants from 12 countries, while the summer Frankfurt Games had representatives from 19 countries and over 150,000 spectators. Although wins were recorded, the accent was on mass participation and socialist fellowship.

As a counter to both the socialist games of Frankfurt and the "bourgeois" Olympics of Amsterdam in 1928, the communist sports movement put on the First Workers Spartakiad in Moscow. Despite the boycott by both socialist and bourgeois sport groups, some 600 worker athletes from 14 countries (15 percent of the total entry of 4,000) were said to have taken part. The winter counterpart to the Spartakiad took place in late 1928 in Moscow with 636 participants in skiing, speed skating (women and men), biathlon, and a special skiing contest for postal workers, rural dwellers, and border guards.

The LSI, as sponsor, now had over 2 million members, including 350,000 women (over one-sixth of the total), and arranged a festival in winter at Mürzzuschalg and in summer at Vienna that far outdid in spectators, participants, and pageantry the 1932 "bourgeois" Olympics at Lake Placid and Los Angeles.

By design the Vienna Olympiad coincided with the opening of the Fourth Congress of the Socialist International and it was pointedly noted that, whereas the political International assembled no more than a few hundred delegates, the sports International brought together the masses themselves.

Alarmed at the popularity and growing strength of the worker sports movement, governments stepped up their repressive actions. When communist workers tried to organize a Second Spartakiad in Berlin in 1932, they first ran into visa problems and then, when several hundred worker athletes had managed to reach Berlin, the games were banned.

Under attack from fascism, the socialists and communists at last came together in a popular front and jointly organized a third Worker Olympics, scheduled for Barcelona in Republican Spain from 19 to 26 July 1936. They were to be in opposition to the "Nazi Olympics" held in Berlin a week later. But the third Worker Olympics never took place. On the morning of the scheduled opening ceremony, the Spanish fascists staged their military putsch. Some worker athletes remained in Spain to fight in the International Brigade during the Spanish Civil War, and many who returned home (like the Canadians, who included the national high jump champion Eva Dawes) were banned from sport by their national federations—while those athletes who had given the Nazi salute to Hitler in the Berlin Olympic opening ceremony returned as national heroes.

After the abortive Barcelona Games, the communist and socialist coalition rescheduled the third Worker Olympics for Antwerp in 1937. Although more modest, the Antwerp Games did present an imposing display of worker solidarity. Following this success, a fourth Worker Olympics was planned for Helsinki in 1943, but war brought down the curtain on the period of worker Olympic festivals.

The Post–World War II Era

The worker sports movement survived World War II bowed but undefeated; the radically changed circumstance of the postwar world inevitably brought a transformation of the movement. Basically, the new role was one of selective cooperation and amalgamation with the national sports federations and clubs, by contrast with the prewar separate development.

The new situation was brought about by several factors. First, the Soviet Union had broken its isolation: it emerged from World War II a victor, its military and political power having penetrated into Central and Eastern Europe. In the conditions of international friction, or Cold War, that ensued, with two rival blocs facing each other in a divided Europe, sport became a relatively harmless arena for international competition, for "defeating" one's ideological opponent. Second, with the process of decolonialization and mounting democratization of both the Olympic movement and bourgeois sport generally, the belief grew that international sport, particularly the Olympic Games, could be opened up to working people, women, and ethnic groups and used for peace, democracy, and the isolation of racist systems. Third, the emphasis within worker sport switched to campaigning inside "bourgeois" organizations for funds, playgrounds, open spaces, and facilities for working people, and for women's sport, against commercialism and chauvinism.

All the same, a separate worker sports movement did manage to survive. Immediately after the war, the socialists in Western Europe set up the International Worker Sports Committee (IWSC) in London in 1946. Despite a peak of 2.2 million members in 14 countries in the late 1940s, however, the IWSC never attained the importance that the prewar movement had. The most influential worker sports organization today is that in Israel: Hapoel (The Worker) is Israel's largest and strongest sports organization; it is the only instance (outside remaining communist states) where a worker sports organization controls its country's sport.

The worker sports movement did try to provide an alternative experience based on workers' own culture and inspired by visions of a new socialist culture. To this end it organized the best sporting program it could, regardless of the level, whether a Sunday bike ride or a Worker Olympic festival, founded on genuinely socialist values. Its story is as much a part of the history of sport and of the labor movement as is Coubertin's Olympics or trade unionism.

—JAMES RIORDAN

Bibliography: Hoberman, John. (1984) *Sport and Political Ideology.* London: Routledge and Kegan Paul. Krüger, Arnd, and James Riordan, eds. (1996) *The Story of Worker Sport.* Champaign, IL: Human Kinetics. Riordan, James. (1991) *Sport, Politics and Communism.* Manchester: Manchester University Press.

Wrestling, Freestyle

In freestyle wrestling, competitors may take a wide variety of holds on both the upper body and legs but they may not grasp the opponent's clothing to secure a hold. A freestyle wrestler can win the bout either by pinning the opponent or by scoring points for successful tactics. Wrestling is virtually alone among combat sports in allowing the opportunity for full physical confrontation with limited possibility of serious injury.

History

Depictions of wrestling appear as early as 3000 B.C.E. in the ancient Near East. Essentially all the tactics seen in modern freestyle wrestling, including the most sophisticated throws, can be found among the 406 wrestling pairs depicted on the walls of the Middle Kingdom tombs at Beni Hasan in the Nile valley, and both sculpture and literature from Mesopotamia show that the sport was popular there in antiquity. References to wrestling festivals are frequent in epics and hymns of ancient and medieval India, and in a story remarkably akin to the Greek legend of the female warrior and athlete Atalanta, Marco Polo tells of a Tartar princess who challenged her hapless suitors to a wrestling contest. Wrestling was part of the Olympics of ancient Greece since the Eighteenth Olympiad in 704 B.C.E. The Greeks appear to have been the first to structure their competitions as a formal elimination tournament. The earliest surviving work in Western literature, the *Epic of Gilgamesh,* describes wrestling, as does the earliest surviving work of Greek literature, Homer's *Iliad.*

The Nuba of the lower Sudan have held wrestling festivals for centuries, if not millennia, and there appears to be remarkable continuity between the costumes of the Nubian wrestlers seen in Egyptian sculpture and the gourd-strung skirts that the Nuba wrestlers still wear. A highly popular folk wrestling of India performed on the mud surface of the *akhara* also continues an ancient tradition. Freestyle wrestling has been popular in the British Isles for many centuries, and the Lancashire style in particular has had a profound influence on modern wrestling. In this tradition, often called "catch as catch can," contestants begin standing and continue the contest on the ground if neither contestant scores a fall from standing. In the Irish collar-and-elbow style, wrestlers begin the bout by grasping the collar with one hand and the elbow with the other; if neither man achieves a fall from this position, open wrestling continues, both standing and on the ground, until a fall is scored. Irish immigrants brought this style to the United States, where its tactics were widely adopted.

Amateur freestyle wrestling developed slowly in Europe. Freestyle did not appear until the St. Louis Olympics of 1904, where there was competition in seven weight categories. Since 1921, the Fédération Internationale des Luttes Amateurs (FILA), with headquarters in Lausanne, Switzerland, has set the rules, scoring, and procedures that govern wrestling competition at the World Games and the Olympics, and these were adopted by the Amateur Athletic Union (AAU) in the United States for its freestyle competitions.

Freestyle wrestling spread rapidly in the United States after the Civil War, and by the 1880s its tournaments drew hundreds of participants. Urbanization, increased industrialization, and the disappearance of the frontier formed the context in which this highly individual combat sport—along with boxing—found new and heightened popularity. A professional circuit, by no means corrupted into the staged theatrics of its later years, emerged in this era, as did amateur organizations. 1900 saw the first intercollegiate wrestling match. Professional wrestlers formed the National Wrestling Alliance in 1904. With the first Eastern Intercollegiate Wrestling Association tournament in 1905 a rapidly expanding roster of tournaments for college and secondary school wrestlers began. In 1927, rules were formulated for intercollegiate wrestling and in the following year, the first NCAA wrestling tournament took place.

Time limits for bouts and a system for determining a victor when neither wrestler has gained a fall are developments of the 20th century. By 1911, rudimentary guidelines for determining victory by the referee's decision in intercollegiate matches emerged, also keeping those bouts to a maximum of 15 minutes. This time length has decreased steadily over the century; in 1996, FILA bouts consist of two periods of three minutes each with a 60-second rest period between the periods, and intercollegiate bouts consist of one three-minute period, followed by two periods of two minutes each. Intercollegiate rules do not allow a rest period.

Rules and Play

Under modern international rules, a wrestler scores a fall on his opponent and immediately wins the bout by holding his shoulders motionless on the mat long enough to allow the referee to ascertain the total control needed for a fall. U.S. intercollegiate rules specify that the shoulders must be *pinned:* motionless for one full second for college competition and two seconds for secondary school contests. Under earlier FILA rules, rolling an opponent across his shoulders

> # Wrestling Theory and Practice
>
> ## *Akhara*
>
> What is an *akhara?* It is a place of recreation for youth. It is a shrine of strength where earth is turned into gold. It is a sign of masculinity and the assembly hall of invigorated youth. Strength is measured against strength and moves and counter moves are born and develop.... An *akhara* is where one prays and where offerings are given and distributed. Its earth is saluted and taken up to anoint one's shoulders and head. And then one wrestles and the sound of slapping thighs and pounding chests fills the air. Grunts and groans of exertion echo ominously. One trounces and in turn is trounced. Exercise is done. Laziness and procrastination are drowned in sweat.
>
> —Ratan Patodi, *The Art of Indian Wrestling*
> (translated by Joseph S. Alter)

counted for a fall; under current rules, this tactic counts for two points.

Under current FILA rules, if neither wrestler scores a fall, victory is determined by the number of points scored for successful tactics. These include taking the opponent to the mat or exposing his shoulders to the mat. Up to five points are awarded for "grand technique," in which one wrestler lifts his opponent in an arc of great amplitude or height and returns him to the mat with his shoulders exposed in danger of a fall. NCAA rules allow up to three points for a "near fall" but do not award extra points for "grand technique." In both FILA and NCAA rules, when one wrestler scores 15 points more than his opponent, the judges will stop the bout and declare him the winner by technical superiority. "Time advantage"—the time each contestant has had his opponent under his control on the mat—counts for one point at most today. Modern FILA and intercollegiate rules divide contestants into 10 weight categories.

Reflecting contemporary values of sporting ethics and recreational hygiene, FILA and intercollegiate rules from their earliest years stressed the safety of the competitors. Holds and tactics that jeopardized life or limb or whose object was punishment of the opponent, rather than leverage, have been consistently illegal. These include the full nelson, strangleholds, twisting hammerlocks, the flying mare with the opponent's arm locked, and slamming the opponent to the mat. Modern rules have gone farther in banning virtually any hold that pressures a joint in a direction contrary to its normal movement. (These refinements stand in stark contrast to the roughness of ancient Greek wrestling, which allowed strangleholds and granted Olympic titles in 456 and 452 B.C.E. to a wrestler named Leontiskos, whose principal tactic was breaking his opponent's fingers.)

The intensely individualistic nature of the sport makes it an excellent touchstone for a society's posture toward the polarities of competition and cooperation. Whereas the ancient Greek poet Pindar twice spoke of the disgrace that accompanied the defeated wrestler, anthropologists report that despite the importance of wrestling to the Nuba of present-day Sudan, defeat is borne gracefully. Among the nomadic Mongolians, the wrestler who lost in the festivals had to give his clothing to his opponent and hold a banquet for him and all his kin; in contrast, a Muslim chant sung at Turkish popular tournaments reminded victors and defeated that on the last day, all stood equal in the Prophet's band.

Wrestling was regularly a rite of passage for gods, heroes, and kings. Perhaps the best-known wrestler in Western civilization is the biblical Jacob from the book of Genesis, who can become the patriarch Israel only after wrestling all night with a mysterious being identified in the biblical text merely as "a man" (*'iysh*). The Sumerian hero Gilgamesh, whose epic antedates Genesis, only emerges as a serious and determined leader after wrestling the formidable Enkidu. The 8th century C.E. Byzantine king Basil I, according to court historians, defeated a boastful Bulgarian wrestler, and at the Field of the Cloth of Gold pageant in 1520, Francis I of France threw Henry VIII of England in a wrestling bout. Although the stories of George Washington as a wrestler are of dubious provenance, contemporary sources tell of Abraham Lincoln's wrestling prowess.

In modern international wrestling, wrestlers from the former Soviet Union have had remarkable success, with strong showings also from Japan, Turkey, Iran, Sweden, Finland, and the United States. Given its long history and broad significance beyond simple sport, wrestling remains well postitioned for a strong future.

—MICHAEL B. POLIAKOFF

See also Arm Wrestling; Sumo; Traditional Sports, Africa; Traditional Sports, North and South America; Traditional Sports, Oceania; Wrestling, Greco-Roman.

Bibliography: Alter, Joseph S. (1992) *The Wrestler's Body.* Berkeley: University of California Press. Morton, Gerald W. (1985) *Wrestling to Rasslin: Ancient Sport to American Spectacle.* Bowling Green, OH: Bowling Green State University Press. Poliakoff, Michael B. (1987) *Combat Sports in the Ancient World: Competition, Violence, and Culture.* New Haven, CT: Yale University Press.

Wrestling, Greco-Roman

Greco-Roman wrestling is actually a development of 19th-century Europe, where it became popular as both an amateur and professional sport and appeared in the first modern Olympics. It has maintained its popularity, especially among wrestlers in Europe.

History

Various indigenous forms of wrestling in Europe that restrict holds to the upper body may have contributed to the development of the Greco-Roman style. The British style of Cumberland and Westmoreland wrestling, for example, allows a variety of trips that are not permitted in Greco-Roman, but its restriction of arm holds to the upper torso is similar.

The continental name, Greco-Roman, reflected the classicizing tendency of European athletic movements of the 18th and 19th centuries. It was widely, though mistakenly, believed that the Greeks had a separate wrestling competition called upright wrestling in which only upper body holds were permitted. By the late 19th century, Greco-Roman wrestling enjoyed great prestige and popularity in continental Europe.

The sport never achieved lasting popularity in the English-speaking world, yielding place to the more natural and unstructured freestyle forms. Its popularity in Europe, on the other hand, was such that virtually all 19th-century capital cities hosted international tournaments, often with enormous prizes.

Greco-Roman wrestling appeared at the first modern Olympics in 1896 in Athens, where three contestants competed in the heavyweight class. Freestyle, by comparison, did not appear in the Olympics until the 1904 games in St. Louis. During this century, the former Soviet Union, Bulgaria, Romania, Japan, Sweden, and Finland have shown remarkable success in Olympic competition.

Rules and Play

In the Greco-Roman style, wrestlers may not take holds below the waist or even use their legs actively in holds; thus the leg takedowns and trips fundamental to freestyle wrestling are barred. The arm drags, bear hugs, and headlocks of freestyle wrestling, on the other hand, are a central part of the Greco-Roman wrestler's repertoire and are carefully refined. Far from creating a dull contest, the restriction of holds to the upper body has encouraged the use of a spectacular series of throws called souples, in which the offensive wrestler lifts his opponent in a high arch while falling backward to a bridge on his own neck and bringing his opponent's shoulders into contact with the mat. Even in wrestling on the mat (*par terre*), the Greco-Roman wrestler must seek ambitious body-lock and gut-wrench holds to attempt to turn his opponent for a fall. The ability to arch backward from a standing position onto one's own neck confidently and safely while lifting and turning the opponent to the mat is crucial for success. The rules of the International Amateur Wrestling Federation (Fédération Internationale des Luttes Amateurs) strictly prohibit stalling, and after 15 seconds of inconclusive action on the ground, the bout must resume with both wrestlers in a neutral standing position and working toward a throw.

Until the formalization of the federation's rules in 1921, Greco-Roman bouts were notorious for their length. On the professional circuit, bouts of two or three hours were not uncommon. Even the early Olympic bouts were prolonged: in 1912, Anders Ahlgren of Sweden and Ivar Boehling of Finland battled for nine hours in the finals before the officials declared the match a draw and awarded both men a silver medal.

Under modern rules, a bout consists of two periods of three minutes each, and a point system identical to that of international freestyle determines the victor in the absence of a fall. As in freestyle, a fall is scored when one wrestler holds his opponent's shoulders motionless on the mat long enough for the referee to ascertain total control. The age categories, weight classes, and dress follow the same rules as freestyle.

The Greco-Roman bouts of the professional circuit were characterized by a high level of brutality: body slams, choke-holds, head-butting, and even the introduction of caustic substances to weaken an opponent were known. Today, all tactics that jeopardize the life or limb of an opponent are strictly forbidden, and notwithstanding spectacular back arches, bridges, and throws, Greco-Roman matches proceed with a very high level of safety.

—Michael B. Poliakoff

See also Wrestling, Freestyle.
Bibliography: Martell, William A. (1973) *Greco-Roman Wrestling*. Champaign, IL: Human Kinetics. Petrov, Rajko. (1986) *Freestyle and Greco-Roman Wrestling*. Lausanne, Switzerland: Fédération Internationale des Luttes Amateurs.

Wushu

Composed of two characters, wushu is the Chinese term usually translated as "martial arts." "Wu" is associated with military and warfare; "shu" with the skill,

---

Martial Arts and the American Imagination

The significant place the martial arts have found in the American imagination is a product of the ease with which the characteristics of these arts and their practitioners have been merged with mythic patterns concerning warriors in American culture. The martial arts have such a resonance in the popular imagination due to the fact that their outward appearance is so different, but their symbolic structure is flexible enough to be melded into a new, syncretic cultural entity.

The American fascination with the martial arts is equally a product of the split between what we wish we were and what we are. Our affinity for these arts is the complex result of individual needs and cultural conditioning. Despite our convictions that we are engaging in something very new, we are in reality recreating and perpetuating a mythic pattern that has great resonance within us.

In seeking skill, we deal with lack of control.

In the celebration of the individual, we find social definition.

In an activity of iconoclasts, we find boundary and structure.

In the new and strange, we unconsciously re-create an old and familiar mythic pattern.

—John Donohue, "Wave People: The Martial Arts and the American Imagination." *Journal of Asian Martial Arts* 3, 1 (1994): 22.

---

way, or methods of doing an activity. As a classifying term, wushu covers the Chinese martial traditions from their origins in early Stone Age cultures to a wide variety of martially inspired practices seen today.

Although primarily composed of fighting arts, wushu has long been associated with physical conditioning, dance, drama, meditative exercise, and competitive exhibition. Wushu developed as a vital aspect of China's culture and came to influence the martial traditions of neighboring countries and eventually the rest of the world.

Rudimentary forms of Chinese martial arts took root in the early Neolithic times, used to protect individuals, families, and clans. They also provided entertainment, as in games of "head butting" in which contestants donned animal horns. By the Zhou Dynasty (1122?–256 B.C.E.), wushu had already reached a highly advanced level. In the 5th century C.E., the crossbow and iron weapons came into use, ushering in new modes of fighting arts.

Long years of turmoil from internal or external threats have taught the Chinese to rely on martial arts as a security measure. Those who possessed the most advanced systems felt that they had an advantage in protecting their empire, clan, or family. Therefore, the fighting systems that evolved were highly secretive and taught only to select individuals or groups.

Martial art styles were usually named for the people, places, or philosophic ideas associated with them. There are a few hundred known Chinese styles, but many more styles and substyles remain to be categorized. For simplicity, martial art styles are sometimes placed into general categories, such as Northern/Southern, Internal/External, or Daoist/Buddhist, and sometimes they are categorized according to their place of origin.

Of special importance in the evolution of some Chinese martial arts is their association with temples. During times of turmoil, temples were often places of refuge. Some temples, such as the Shaolin, became "universities" where leading experts contributed to the preservation and evolution of the martial arts.

Some martial traditions have become extinct due to the rise of modern weaponry. Nonetheless, in China many martial arts remain intact. The continued popularity of these arts is due, in part, to their pervasive presence in Chinese culture. As moving art forms, the martial arts are valued living expressions of their developers' creativity and genius. Martial art forms are also cherished for their therapeutic benefits, and in China the majority of people practicing a martial art do so primarily for this reason. However, the martial arts can be found in theatrical productions, self-defense classes, military training programs, entertainment industries, meditative practices, and sporting events.

In China today, where entertainment and health care are in short supply, wushu, as a form of exercise and sport, offers an attractive alternative. Martial art exhibitions have a long-standing tradition in China. Local competitions have been augmented by national ones, and international teams have been formed.

Competitive martial art exhibitions have transformed traditional solo routines by incorporating gymnastic elements for greater visual effects.

More than ever, individuals are attracted to the study of wushu not simply as a physical activity, but as a way of self-discovery. Therefore, despite its organizational disarray as a sport, wushu will certainly increase in popularity.

—MICHAEL A. DEMARCO

See also Martial Arts.

Bibliography Dreager, Donn, and Robert Smith. (1969) *Comprehensive Asian Martial Arts.* Tokyo: Kodansha International. Kauz, Herman. (1992) *A Path to Liberation: A Spiritual and Philosophical Approach to the Martial Arts.* New York: Overlook Press. Reid, Howard, and Michael Croucher. (1983) *The Way of the Warrior: The Paradox of the Martial Arts.* Woodstock, NY: Overlook Press.

Yachting

Yachting has been an Olympic sport since 1900, although with a name change to Olympic sailing in 2000. All Olympic races are held by class in which competitors race each other in identical boats in a fleet race. Generally, the smaller and simpler boats are the least expensive, and so have the larger world following, leading to larger Olympic fleets. Sailboard fleets have had over 50 countries competing.

The first Olympic yachting races held were in 1900, in France, at Meulan and Le Havre, when seven classes ($^1/_2$, $^1/_2$–1, 1–2, 2–3, 3–10, 10–20 tons, and open) were raced. Only six nations (France, Germany, Great Britain, Netherlands, Switzerland, and the United States) competed, perhaps because the events had been announced only four months before the Games. No yachting events were held at the 1904 St. Louis Games, but the sport was back on the program in 1908 and has remained an Olympic sport ever since.

In 1908, most Olympic events were held in London, but sailing venues were Ryde, on the Isle of Wight, for most classes, and on the Clyde in Scotland, for the 12-meter event. Five classes were used (6, 7, 8, 12, and 15 meters) and five nations took part. There were no entries for the 15-meter class; only one 7-meter entry, which had among the crew Frances Rivett-Carnac, who thus became the first Olympic yachtswoman; and both 12 meters had British crews. In 1912, races were held for 6-, 8-, 10-, and 12-meter boats, with a total of 21 boats from five nations.

In 1920, Olympic yachting began to have small boat (dinghy) racing, which has continued in some form ever since. An astonishing 14 classes raced. Seven classes had only one entrant, and this created a major move toward the use of one-design classes (where all boats in the fleet are of the same type and exactly alike) from 1924 on. In 1924, a 12-foot Voetsjol class became the first Olympic single-hander, and 6- and 8-meter boats were also raced.

In 1932, in Los Angeles, the Star class was raced for the first time. It remained an Olympic class until 1996. Other classes were the Snowbird (a single-hander, each of which was provided by the organizing committee, and exchanged after each race among the 11 competitors), and the 6 and 8 meter. In 1936, in Kiel, the Olympia-Jolle replaced the Snowbird as the single-hander. A total of 26 nations raced 59 boats.

Following the canceled Olympics of 1940 and 1944, the 1948 Games began to look more like modern racing. The classes were Firefly, Dragon, Star, Swallow, and 6 meter. The courses were, for the first time, started into the wind. Seventy-five boats competed.

In 1952, the Finn made its first appearance as the single-hander, replacing the Firefly. Finns remain an Olympic class to this day. The same classes (Finn, Flying Dutchman, Star, Dragon, and 5.5 meter) were used in 1960, 1964, and 1968.

Communication with onshore coaches (whether by shouting or over radio) was banned in 1964, and semi-professional sailors—people who made their living as sail makers—began to dominate events. In 1972, the Soling and Tempest joined the competition classes, and the 5.5 meter was dropped.

The lack of correlation between Olympic classes and classes most popular with the general public showed some correction in 1976 when the classes raced at Kingston on Lake Ontario, Canada, were Finn, Flying Dutchman, 470, Soling, Tempest, and Tornado (the first catamaran raced in the Olympics). The Star came back in 1980 to replace the Tempest, but yachting was more seriously affected than most sports in the boycott of that year because the events were held at Tallinn, in Estonia, which several countries refused to recognize as being part of the Soviet Union. The number of boats, 53, was the lowest since 1956.

In Los Angeles in 1984, an entirely new type of sailing was added: sailboarding. Other classes remained the same. This idea was extended to a women-only class of sailboarders in 1992 and a women's single-hander, the Europe, was added to the men's Finn. For 1996, the classes were Europe (women), Finn (men), Laser, 470 (men), 470 (women), sailboard (men), sailboard (women), Soling (men and women), Star (men and women), and Tornado (men and women). Of the eight different classes, two are keelboats, one is a catamaran, one is a sailboard, and four are centerboard dinghies, which closely approximates to world popularity of the various types of racing boats.

The large number of recreational boaters suggests that yachting, as an Olympic event or other race, will remain popular.

—Shirley H. M. Reekie

See also Sailing.

Bibliography: Knox-Johnston, Robin. (1990) *History of Yachting.* Oxford, UK: Phaidon. Richey, Michael W., ed. (1980) *The Sailing Encyclopedia.* New York: Lippincott & Crowell.

Index